Auditing

FOURTEENTH CANADIAN EDITION

THE ART AND SCIENCE OF ASSURANCE ENGAGEMENTS

Auditing

FOURTEENTH CANADIAN EDITION

THE ART AND SCIENCE OF ASSURANCE ENGAGEMENTS

ALVIN A. ARENS
Former PricewaterhouseCoopers Emeritus Professor
Michigan State University

RANDAL J. ELDER
Syracuse University

MARK S. BEASLEY
North Carolina State University
Deloitte Professor of Enterprise Risk Management

CHRIS E. HOGAN
Michigan State University

JOANNE C. JONES
York University

With contributions by
BARTOSZ M. AMERSKI
York University

VICE PRESIDENT EDITORIAL: Anne Williams
ACQUISITIONS EDITOR: Keara Emmett
MARKETING MANAGER: Spencer Snell
CONTENT MANAGER: Emily Dill
PROJECT MANAGER: Sarah Gallagher
CONTENT DEVELOPER: Anita Smale
MEDIA DEVELOPER: Olga Avdyeyeva

PRODUCTION SERVICES: Cenveo® Publisher Services
PERMISSIONS PROJECT MANAGER: Joanne Tang
TEXT PERMISSIONS RESEARCH: Integra Publishing Services
INTERIOR DESIGNER: Anthony Leung
COVER DESIGNER: Anthony Leung
COVER IMAGE: © PonyWang/iStock/Getty Images
Plus/Getty Images

Pearson Canada Inc., 26 Prince Andrew Place, North York, Ontario M3C 2H4.

9780134613116

2 18

Library and Archives Canada Cataloguing in Publication
Arens, Alvin A., author
    Auditing : the art and science of assurance engagements / Alvin
A. Arens, PricewaterhouseCoopers, Emeritus Professor, Michigan State
University ; Randal J. Elder, Syracuse University ; Mark S. Beasley,
North Carolina State University, Deloitte Professor of Enterprise
Management ; Chris E. Hogan, Michigan State University ; Joanne C. Jones,
York University. – Fourteenth Canadian edition.

Includes index.
ISBN 978-0-13-461311-6 (hardcover)

    1. Auditing—Textbooks. 2. Textbooks. I. Elder, Randal J., author II. Beasley, Mark S.,
author III. Hogan, Chris E. (Chris Elizabeth), 1964-, author IV. Jones, Joanne C.
(Joanne Cavell), 1961-, author V. Title.

HF5667.A69 2018   657'.45   C2018-900538-6

Contents

Preface

Auditing: The Art and Science of Assurance Engagements is an introduction to auditing and assurance services. It is intended for use in an introductory auditing course, for one-semester or two-semester instruction at the undergraduate or graduate level. The book's primary emphasis is on the auditor's decision-making process in a financial statement audit and, to a lesser degree, other types of assurance engagements. As the title of the book reflects, auditing is an art, as it requires considerable use of professional judgment and skepticism, but it is also a science, resting upon a solid frame of technical skills and knowledge of multiple disciplines associated with auditing, such as accounting, tax, and information systems.

One of the most fundamental concepts in auditing concerns the nature and amount of evidence the auditor should gather after considering the unique circumstances of each engagement. If students of auditing understand the risks to be addressed in a given audit area, the circumstances of the engagement, and the decisions to be made, they should be able to determine the appropriate evidence to gather and how to evaluate the evidence obtained. In order to help students develop these skills, we provide a professional judgment framework to help students reflect upon common judgment traps and to develop their own judgment and professional skepticism.

Our objective is to provide up-to-date coverage of globally recognized auditing concepts with practical examples of the implementation of those concepts in real-life settings. We integrate the most important concepts in auditing in a logical manner to assist students in understanding decision-making and evidence accumulation in today's complex auditing environment. Throughout the book, we emphasize international and Canadian developments affecting auditing in a global and economically volatile context. Key concepts related to professional judgment and risk assessment are integrated into all the planning chapters, as well as each chapter dealing with particular transaction cycles and related accounts. We provide numerous real-life vignettes and examples from actual audit planning documents to enhance students' understanding of the concepts. We also provide numerous diagrams, decision frameworks, and visual depictions to help clarify concepts such as independence, control activities, materiality, and the various substantive tests in the key transaction cycles.

What's New to This Edition?

Despite its practical nature, many students often view auditing as an abstract subject. To address this, we continue to work on revising the book so that the material is more accessible and understandable to students. We highlight the more substantive changes below.

Current Coverage of Auditing Standards

New auditing standards are released without regard to textbook revision cycles. As auditing instructors, we appreciate how critical it is to have the most current content available. This edition includes coverage of the most recent standards released (the most significant being the changes to the auditor's report) and highlights impending changes that have been announced by Canada's Auditing and Assurance Board. As with the previous edition, we continue to revise the book so that the concepts and terminology are closely aligned with Canadian Audit Standards.

In addition to ensuring current coverage, we provide several vignettes to illustrate that, despite the constraining effect of standards, there is considerable variation in audit practices within the profession. Unlike accounting standards, which define how to consistently measure and report economic events, audit standards outline the process of verifying the accounting. This means that there is no one "right" answer and there may be many acceptable ways in which to reach the goal of providing reasonable assurance that the information is fairly presented.

New Audit Reporting Standards

The new and revised audit reporting standards are perhaps one of the most significant changes in audit standards in the last 40 years. We introduce the new audit report in Chapter 4, providing a sample audit report of a private company. Throughout the textbook, we provide excerpts from audit reports from jurisdictions that have already adopted the new international standards to illustrate key audit matters. We revisit the new and revised audit reporting standards in Chapter 19 and use a consolidated public company to illustrate the different elements of the audit report. Given the significant changes, Chapter 19 has been significantly revised, with new vignettes and homework problems.

Professional Ethics and the *CPA Code of Professional Conduct*

We introduce new material in Chapter 3 to help clarify the role of the professional in society and to define professional ethics. We also include some simple tests that professionals use to decide the "right" thing to do. Chapter 3 has also been revised to provide an overview of the key elements of the *CPA Code of Professional Conduct* and to include a decision tree to assess independence threats. We introduce several new vignettes to illustrate the high cost of an auditor's lack of independence.

New Coverage of Auditor's Responsibilities

To reflect recent changes in auditing standards, Chapter 4 has been revised to include the auditor's responsibilities to assess going concern. We revisit this important responsibility in Chapter 18, on completing the audit, and again in Chapter 19, which discusses audit reports. Chapter 18 also discusses the revised standards concerning the auditors' responsibility for other information.

Emphasis on Professional Judgment and Skepticism

The essence of being a competent auditor is the ability to exercise professional judgment and to apply the appropriate level of professional skepticism. While an understanding of the appropriate level of skepticism is achieved through experience, we believe that introducing this concept early in students' professional journey will assist in their development. We discuss the importance of a questioning mindset and the need to critically evaluate audit evidence to strengthen student awareness of the elements of effective professional skepticism. We have introduced several new vignettes and homework problems that help students think further about challenges and threats to applying professional skepticism in the context of an audit.

The Logic of the Audit Process— Risk Identification and Risk Response

We continue to refine the textbook material to promote deeper learning and to enable students to better understand the underlying logic of the audit process. To assist with these goals, we start with simplifying the visualization of the audit process, which is first introduced in Chapter 4. To further reinforce this, we start each relevant chapter with the audit process diagram and highlight which objectives and activities are covered in that chapter.

We start our examination of the audit process with Chapter 5, on audit evidence. Given that evidence is the foundation of the audit, in this edition we have placed the chapter on audit evidence earlier in the book. The chapter has been revised to help clarify concepts and focuses on how to determine whether the audit evidence is persuasive. To help students develop this important skill, we have developed several task-based simulations and professional judgment questions. We have also reorganized Chapters 6 to 10 to follow the logical sequence of the audit process. We have expanded our coverage of the auditor's performance of risk assessment procedures, including identification of significant risks, and have clarified the distinction between pervasive risks and risks that are specific to particular accounts and assertions. Chapter 6 covers client acceptance and continuance, planning, and materiality. Chapter 7 highlights audit risk and the risk of material misstatement. Chapters 8 and 9 emphasize the importance of internal control as part of the risk assessment process, and Chapter 10 brings the discussion together in its focus on audit strategy. Subsequent chapters that address the transaction cycles include extensive coverage of fraud risk, inherent risk, and internal control risk. We continue to provide up-to-date, real-life examples drawn from actual audit plans and audit reports to illustrate the different types of audit strategies employed in the various transaction cycles.

Expanded Coverage of Control Risk and the Role of Information Technology

Our coverage in Chapters 8 and 9 of internal controls has been restructured to first introduce the COSO's *Internal Control—Framework* in Chapter 8, followed by the auditor's assessment of control risk in Chapter 9, which has been revised to better integrate the auditor's consideration of entity-level controls and transaction cycle controls. We have also added new material to help students understand the different types of controls and how to apply professional judgment in evaluating control effectiveness. Building upon the 13th edition, we continue to emphasize IT controls and integrate them into the audit process. We provide new material and vignettes to illustrate the challenges of auditing in complex IT environments.

Other Assurance Services

Our coverage of other assurance services in Chapters 1 and 20 highlights emerging opportunities for public accountants to provide assurance about corporate social responsibility and sustainability reports. Chapter 20, which focuses on other services outside of the financial statement audit provided by public accountants, covers the new standards for review engagements and the attestation standards for engagements other than audits or reviews of historical financial information (CSAE 3000) and direct reporting engagements (CSAE 3001). New material has been added to help clarify the difference between an attestation and a direct reporting engagement. Sample reports based upon the new standards are provided, and new vignettes (including the recent Oscars™ snafu) and homework questions are provided to help students appreciate the various issues related to providing assurance for non-financial information.

A New Approach to Hillsburg Hardware Limited

Those of you who are familiar with Hillsburg Hardware Limited, which has been a feature of this book for a very long time, will note some significant changes. To increase realism and more accurately reflect the Canadian business environment, we have revised the nature of the organization. We have also reframed the presentation of the financial information and company background as a simulation, which now includes excerpts of interviews with client personnel. New questions are included in Chapter 10 that require students to consider the changes that have occurred since the preliminary planning and the impact of those changes on the current year's audit.

New and Revised Problems and Cases

All chapters include multiple choice questions as well as research activities that require students to use the Internet to research relevant auditing issues. All chapters include several new and revised professional judgment problems and cases. Many of the problems are based upon actual companies. Additionally, each chapter identifies new or revised Discussion Questions and Problems that instructors can use in class to generate discussion about important topics. These problems are highlight by an "in-class" discussion icon in the margin next to the related question. Each chapter also identifies questions that may require students to research standards as well other material using the Internet. While many of these research problems expose students to the *CPA Canada Handbook—Assurance*, other questions require students to examine recently issued financial statements or other corporate filings, or they expose students to best practices thought papers as part of the assignment.

Organization

This text is divided into four parts. The chapters are relatively brief and designed to be easily read and comprehended by students.

Part 1: The Auditing Profession (Chapters 1–3)

The book begins with an opening vignette that provides as an example the Corporate Sustainability Report issued by United Parcel Services (UPS) to help students see the increasingly important role of auditors in providing assurance on a broad range of information important to key stakeholders. Chapter 1 aims to answer the question, "Who are the auditors and why are they important?" The chapter explains the different types of auditors and assurance services. Chapter 2 covers the public accounting profession, with a particular emphasis on the standard setting responsibilities of the International Auditing and Assurance Standards Board (IAASB) and the Canadian Auditing and Assurance Standards Board (AASB). Chapter 2 provides an overview of the *CPA Canada Handbook—Assurance*, Canadian auditing standards, and auditors' responsibilities. It also provides a discussion of audit quality. Chapter 3 starts with a discussion of professional ethics, the rules of professional conduct, and the importance of independence and how to assess independence threats. The chapter concludes with an investigation of the expectations gap and auditors' legal liability, with a discussion of some recent Canadian cases.

Part 2: The Audit Process (Chapters 4–10)

Part 2 presents the audit process. The concepts in this part of the book represent the foundation of the book. The first chapter describes the overall objectives of the audit, auditor and management responsibilities, professional skepticism, a professional judgment framework, audit objectives, and management assertions. The chapter concludes with an overview of the audit process and introduces Hillsburg Hardware Limited, which is used to illustrate planning and development of an audit strategy as well as many other concepts throughout the book.

Chapter 5 discusses the general concepts of evidence quality, the development of audit procedures, and audit documentation. Chapter 6 deals with client acceptance and continuance, and the preliminary planning of the engagement, including understanding the client's business and environment as part of the auditor's risk assessment procedures, using analytical procedures as an audit tool and making preliminary judgments about materiality. Chapter 7 provides expanded coverage of the auditor's performance of risk assessment procedures used to assess the risk of material misstatement due to fraud or error, and how the auditor responds to risks of significant misstatement with further audit procedures. Chapter 8 outlines the key components of an effective system of internal controls over financial reporting consistent with the 2013 revision of COSO's *Internal Control—Integrated Framework*. Because most internal control systems are heavily dependent on information technologies, this chapter integrates coverage of IT general controls and application controls. Chapter 9 shows how effective internal controls can reduce planned audit evidence in the audit of financial statements, and it outlines procedures auditors perform as tests of those controls to support a low or moderate control risk assessment. Chapter 10 provides an overall strategic risk-based audit strategy, linking planning to assertion-based audit programs.

Part 3: Application of the Audit Process (Chapters 11–17)

These chapters apply the concepts from Part 2 to planning a sample and to the specific transaction cycles. We begin in Chapter 11 with a general discussion of audit sampling for tests of controls, substantive tests of transactions, and tests of details of balances. The chapter, which uses the revenue cycle as the basis for its examples, covers both nonstatistical and statistical sampling. The remaining chapters deal with a specific transaction cycle or part of a transaction cycle. We start with the most significant cycle for most organizations—revenue. We provide an overview of the cycle and then consider the inherent and fraud risks associated with revenue, and discuss how to design and conduct internal control and substantive tests in response to the significant risks, as well as specific fraud procedures. We conclude the chapter by providing an illustration of applying professional judgment in the development of the audit strategy for the revenue cycle of two actual organizations. Throughout the chapter, we provide numerous real-life examples to illustrate key concepts. The remaining chapters follow a similar format. Cash is studied late in the text to demonstrate how the audit of cash is related to most other audit areas.

Part 4: Completing the Audit, Reporting, and Other Assurance Engagements (Chapters 18–20)

This part begins with two chapters on the final two phases of the audit process—completion and reporting. The first chapter deals with performing additional tests to address presentation and disclosure objectives, summarizing and evaluating the results of audit tests, reviewing audit documentation, communicating with those charged with governance, and all other aspects of completing an audit. Chapter 19 provides a detailed discussion of the new and revised audit reporting standards. The chapter covers all the potential elements of the new audit report, which has changed dramatically. The chapter emphasizes conditions affecting the type of report the auditor must issue and the type of audit report applicable to each condition under varying levels of materiality. The last chapter, on other assurance services, deals with various types of engagements and reports, other than the audit of financial statements. Topics covered include review and compilation services, agreed-upon procedures engagements, and assurance engagements dealing with nonfinancial information. We conclude by discussing the future of assurance services and the continued evolution of assurance standards in the face of changing assurance needs.

MyLab Accounting

MyLab Accounting delivers proven results in helping individual students succeed. It provides engaging experiences that personalize, stimulate, and measure learning for each student, including a personalized study plan.

MyLab Accounting for the Fourteenth Canadian Edition of *Auditing: The Art and Science of Assurance Engagements* includes many valuable assessments and study tools to help students practise and understand key concepts from the text. Students can practise an expanded number of select end-of-chapter questions, review key terms with glossary flashcards, and explore integrated case content.

MyLab Accounting can be used by itself or linked to any learning management system. To learn more about how MyLab Accounting combines proven learning applications with powerful assessment, visit **www.pearson.com/mylab**

Instructional Support Materials

INSTRUCTOR'S RESOURCE MANUAL The Instructor's Resource Manual assists the instructor in teaching the course more efficiently. The features include instructions for assignments, practical examples to help the students understand the material, and helpful suggestions on how to teach each chapter effectively. It also includes a sample course outline and mapping the chapters' topics to the CPA Competency Map.

INSTRUCTOR'S SOLUTIONS MANUAL This comprehensive resource provides detailed solutions to all the end-of-chapter review questions, multiple-choice questions, problems, and cases.

COMPUTERIZED TESTBANK Pearson's computerized test banks allow instructors to filter and select questions to create quizzes, tests, or homework. Instructors can revise questions or add their own, and may be able to choose print or online options. These questions are also available in Microsoft Word format.

POWERPOINT SLIDES Electronic colour slides are available in Microsoft PowerPoint. The slides illuminate and build on key concepts in the text.

IMAGE LIBRARY The Image Library is an impressive resource that helps instructors create vibrant lecture presentations. Almost all figures and tables in the text are included and organized by chapter for convenience. These images can easily be imported into Microsoft PowerPoint to create new presentations or to add to existing ones.

PEARSON ɛTEXT Pearson eText gives students access to their textbook anytime, anywhere. In addition to note taking, highlighting, and bookmarking, the Pearson eText offers interactive and sharing features. Instructors can share their comments or highlights, and students can add their own, creating a tight community of learners within the class.

LEARNING SOLUTIONS MANAGERS Pearson's learning solutions managers work with faculty and campus course designers to ensure that Pearson technology products, assessment tools, and online course materials are tailored to meet your specific needs. This highly qualified team is dedicated to helping schools take full advantage of a wide range of educational resources, by assisting in the integration of a variety of instructional materials and media formats. Your local Pearson Canada sales representative can provide you with more details on this service program.

Acknowledgments

I would like to thank the following individuals who contributed their time and energy in sharing their opinions and best practices, and helped to make this book representative not only of sound theory but of the actual work done in the field of audit and assurance:

> Bailey Church
> *Telfer School of Management, University of Ottawa*
> Tammy Crowell
> *Rowe School of Business, Dalhousie University*
> Craig Emby
> *Beedie School of Business, Simon Fraser University*
> Camillo Lento
> *Lakehead University*
> Wendy Popowich
> *JR Shaw School of Business, Northern Alberta Institute of Technology*
> Larry Yarmolinsky
> *York University*

In addition, I thank all the editorial and production staff at Pearson Canada for putting together a high-quality product, including Megan Farrell and Keara Emmett (Acquisitions Editors), Emily Dill and Nicole Mellow (Content Managers), Anita Smale (Developmental Editor), Sarah Gallagher (Project Manager), Spencer Snell (Marketing Manager), and Jyotsna Ojha (Senior Project Manager at Cenveo Publisher Services).

Joanne C. Jones

We thank our families, who encourage and support us through the many hours of writing, researching, and rewriting; our students, who push us to think "out of the box"; our colleagues, particularly Sandra Iacobelli, Peter Rumyee, and Larry Yarmolinsky; and the numerous practitioners who continue to keep us up to date with the ever-changing audit environment.

Joanne C. Jones
Bartosz Amerski

About the New Canadian Authors

Joanne C. Jones, PhD, CPA, CA

This is the second Canadian edition to be authored by Joanne C. Jones, who is an associate professor of auditing at York University. Joanne teaches auditing and her research focuses on issues such as professionalism and ethics in accounting, the impact of regulation on audit practice, and the globalization of the accounting profession. She also investigates academic ethics and accounting education, and has published several instructional audit cases in academic peer-reviewed journals. Joanne is an active reviewer for several academic journals and currently serves as the associate editor at *Accounting Perspectives*. Prior to earning her PhD, she worked for several years as an external auditor with KPMG and as the associate director of education with the Institute of Chartered Accountants of Ontario (now CPA Ontario).

Bartosz Amerski, CPA, CA

We are again pleased to have Bartosz Amerski as contributing author for the Fourteenth Canadian Edition.

Bartosz teaches auditing and accounting at York University, where he has received recognition and awards for his excellence in teaching and creating a positive learning environment for his students. Bartosz also teaches in the new CPA Ontario's Professional Educational Program (PEP) and the Prerequisite Educational Program (PREP). He has completed a Masters of Laws (LL.M.) at Osgoode Hall Law School and is an audit director with the office of the Auditor General of Ontario. Prior to that, Bartosz worked at Ernst & Young as an external auditor.

The Auditing Profession

Who are auditors, and why are they important? These first three chapters provide background for performing financial statement audits, which is our primary focus. This background will help you understand why auditors perform audits the way they do.

Our book begins with a who's who of assurance services and describes the role of accountants, public accounting firms, and other organizations in doing audits. The chapters in Part 1 emphasize the regulation and control of public accounting through auditing and ethical standards, and discuss the legal responsibilities of auditors.

THE DEMAND FOR AUDIT AND OTHER ASSURANCE SERVICES

LEARNING OBJECTIVES

After studying this chapter, you should be able to:

1 Describe auditing and its purpose.

2 Distinguish between auditing and accounting.

3 Explain how auditing reduces information risk.

4 Determine the causes of information risk.

5 Explain how information risk can be reduced.

6 Identify major types of audits and auditors.

7 Explain the general characteristics of an assurance engagement.

8 Describe assurance and nonassurance services provided by public accountants and distinguish the audit of financial statements from other assurance services.

Brown Goes Green

United Parcel Service (UPS) is one of the largest shipment and logistics companies in the world, delivering more than 15 million packages a day in more than 220 countries. At the peak of the holiday season, UPS delivers 34 million packages daily. That's a lot of packages moved by planes and delivery trucks, and it obviously comes with a large carbon footprint. The UPS company nickname is "Brown" because of the company's brown delivery trucks and uniforms, but that does not capture the company's commitment to sustainability.

Recently, the company reduced its annual carbon emissions by 1.5 percent, even though delivery volume increased by 3.9 percent. One way the company reduces carbon emissions is through its proprietary On-Road Integrated Optimization and Navigation (ORION) IT system, which uses an advanced algorithm and customized map data to provide optimal route advice to drivers. The system reduced fuel usage by 5.7 million litres in 2014, resulting in a reduction in annual CO_2 emissions of 14 000 metric tons. ORION is not only good for the environment, but it helps the bottom line. UPS estimates that a reduction of 1.6 kilometers driven per delivery driver per day will save the company up to $50 million per year.

The UPS Corporate Sustainability Report is prepared in accordance with the G4 framework established by the Global Reporting Initiative (GRI). The company received the "Materiality Matters" check from the GRI, indicating that it had fulfilled the necessary general standards of disclosures. The increase in sustainability reporting by companies such as UPS has also resulted in increased interest in the accuracy of the reported information, and the GRI recommends external assurance by accountants or other qualified experts to provide users with increased confidence in the accuracy of the information. The UPS Corporate Sustainability Report includes a limited assurance report along

continued >

with a reasonable assurance report on the company's global statement of greenhouse gas emissions from a Big 4 public accounting firm. Many predict this form of assurance will be a frequent service performed by tomorrow's Chartered Professional Accountants (CPAs).

Sources: UPS, *The Road Ahead: UPS 2016 Corporate Sustainability Report*, accessed June 27, 2017, at **https://sustainability. ups.com/media/ups-pdf-interactive-2016/index.html**. Global Reporting Initiative, *The External Assurance of Sustainability Reporting*, Amsterdam, 2013, accessed June 27, 2017, at **https://www.globalreporting.org/resourcelibrary/GRI-Assurance.pdf**.

This opening vignette involving the UPS *Corporate Sustainability Report* illustrates the increasingly important role of auditors in providing assurance on sustainability and other information of interest to a broad range of stakeholders. Of course, reporting on financial statements of public companies, as well as private companies, government agencies, and non-profit entities, remains the primary role of auditors in public accounting.

This chapter introduces the purpose of auditing and other assurance services, as well as the auditor's role in society. The chapter also explains why there is a demand for auditing and other assurance services, the many different kinds of auditors, and the variety of skills needed to be a good auditor.

NATURE AND RELEVANCE OF AUDITING

LO 1 Describe auditing and its purpose.

Auditing is both an art and a science. It takes a combination of the auditor's professional judgment and skepticism (the art) and knowledge of the relevant subject matter, rules, and procedures (the science) to perform a high-quality audit. We will now examine auditing more specifically using the following definition.

Auditing is the accumulation and evaluation of evidence regarding assertions about information to determine the degree of correspondence between the assertions and established criteria and to report the results to interested users. Auditing should be done by a competent, independent person.

Auditing—the accumulation and evaluation of evidence regarding assertions about information to determine and report on the degree of correspondence between the assertions and established criteria.

The definition includes several key words and phrases. For ease of understanding, we'll discuss the terms in different order than they occur in the description.

Assertions, Information, and Established Criteria

The objective of an audit is to provide a conclusion (or assurance) by assessing the assertions made and the information provided by the preparer. This is performed by considering the established criteria, gathering evidence, and reaching conclusions on the fair presentation of the information. In order to do this, the information must be in a verifiable form.

Information can and does take many forms. Auditors routinely perform audits of quantifiable information, including companies' financial statements and individuals' federal income tax returns. Auditors also perform audits of more subjective information, such as the effectiveness of computer systems and the efficiency of manufacturing operations. The focus of this text is the financial statement audit.

The criteria used to evaluate the assertions made and the information provided varies depending on the information being audited. For example, in the audit of historical financial statements conducted by public accounting firms, the criteria is the relevant accounting framework such as International Financial Reporting Standards (IFRS), Accounting Standards for Private Enterprises (ASPE), or Accounting Standards for Not-for-Profit Organizations (ASNPO). This means in the case of Canadian Tire, for instance, that management asserts that the financial statements are prepared in accordance with the IFRS accounting standards. It is the job of the auditors to determine whether the financial statements have been prepared in accordance with IFRS and to provide reasonable assurance to the users that the financial statements accurately reflect the management's assertions.

In our opening vignette, the management of UPS asserted that the Corporate Sustainability Report (the information) was prepared in accordance to the G4 framework (the criteria) established by the Global Reporting Initiative (GRI) (the standard setter). In this case, the auditors evaluated this assertion by considering the criteria and gathering evidence, and then reporting their conclusion on the fair presentation of the information.

For more subjective information, or when there are no generally accepted standards, it is more difficult to establish criteria. Typically, auditors and the entities being audited agree on the criteria well before the audit starts. For example, in an audit of the effectiveness of specific aspects of computer operations, the criteria might include the allowable level of input or output errors as defined by the organization.

Accumulation and Evaluation of Evidence

Evidence—any information used by the auditor to assess whether the information being audited is stated in accordance with established criteria.

Evidence is any information used by the auditor to assess whether the information being audited is stated in accordance with the established criteria. Evidence takes many different forms, including:

- Electronic and documentary evidence about transactions
- Written and electronic communication from outsiders
- Observations by the auditor
- Oral testimony of the auditee (client)

To satisfy the purpose of the audit, auditors must obtain sufficient quality and quantity of evidence. In order to determine what types and amount of evidence is necessary, auditors must assess the risk of material misstatement. Based upon the evidence gathered, the auditor will then determine the degree of correspondence between the information and established criteria. Deciding what evidence to gather and evaluating the evidence are critical aspects of every audit and the primary focus of this text.

Competent, Independent Person

Professional judgment—analytical, systematic, and objective judgment carried out with integrity and recognition of responsibility to those affected by its consequences.

Integrity—the quality of being honest and courageous.

Professional skepticism—an attitude that includes a questioning mind, a critical assessment of audit evidence, and the willingness to challenge the auditee's assertions.

Independence in mind—the auditor's ability to exercise objectivity.

The auditor must be qualified to understand the engagement risks and the criteria used, and be competent to know the types and amount of evidence to accumulate in order to reach the proper conclusion after examining the evidence. While having the appropriate technical knowledge and skills are key to being competent, in order to reach the proper conclusion (which means exercising **professional judgment**), an auditor must act with **integrity** and with **professional skepticism**, be independent, and recognize responsibility to the users of the audit report.

Professional skepticism underlies auditors' professional judgment. It is an attitude that includes a questioning mind, a critical assessment of audit evidence, and a willingness to challenge the auditee's assertions. Sound professional judgment requires the auditor to exercise objectivity (be free of biases, conflicts of interest, or undue influence). This is referred to as having **independence in mind**. The competence of the individual performing the audit is of little value if he or she is biased in the accumulation and evaluation of evidence. It is likely that a biased auditor will not use the appropriate level of professional skepticism, which can result in inadequate evidence and insufficiently critical evaluation of the evidence.

Auditors strive to maintain a high level of independence in order to keep the confidence of users relying on their reports. Auditors reporting on company financial statements are **independent auditors**. Even though such auditors are paid a fee by a company, they are normally sufficiently independent to conduct audits that can be relied on by users. Even **internal auditors**—those employed by the companies they audit—usually report directly to top management and the board of directors, keeping auditors independent of the operating units they audit.

Independent auditors—public accountants or accounting firms that perform audits of commercial and noncommercial entities.

Internal auditors—auditors employed by a company to audit for the company's board of directors and management.

Independent auditor's report—the communication of audit findings to users.

Report

The final stage in the audit process is preparing the **independent auditor's report**, which communicates the outcome of the auditors' evaluation to interested users. Reports differ in nature, but all inform readers of the degree of confidence that the auditor has that the assertions made and the information provided by management corresponds to the established criteria. Reports also differ in form and can follow a standardized format, as in the case of the financial statements auditor's report, or can be highly customized report, as in the case of an audit of effectiveness of computer systems or an audit of the efficiency of manufacturing operations.

An Illustration of the Definition of Auditing

The key parts in the description of auditing are illustrated in Figure 1-1 using the audit of a large corporate tax return by a team of Canada Revenue Agency auditors.

The audit team would likely include auditors who are competent in auditing and corporate taxes, as well as knowledgeable about the particular industry and the related complex tax issues. The auditors first perform a risk assessment based upon several factors, such as past tax audit history, industry sector issues, unusual or complex transactions, corporate structure, participation in aggressive tax planning, and openness and transparency. The auditors next accumulate and examine the relevant evidence, such as the organization's financial statements, books, and records, as well as information from third parties that do business with the organization. The procedures selected would depend upon the auditors' professional judgment. After completing the audit, the audit team will issue an audit report that provides their conclusion, based upon evidence gathered and their interpretation of tax law, as to whether the tax return is in compliance with the Income Tax Act. The taxpayer receives a notice of reassessment that reflects the audit report's findings.

Figure 1-1	Audit of a Corporate Tax Return

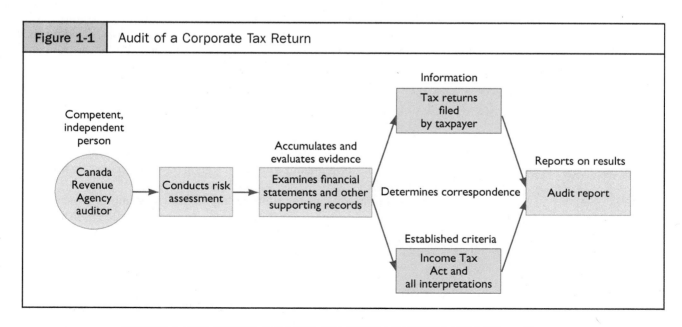

DISTINCTION BETWEEN AUDITING AND ACCOUNTING

Many financial statement users and members of the general public confuse auditing and accounting. The confusion occurs because most auditing is concerned with accounting information, and many auditors have considerable expertise in accounting matters. The confusion is increased by giving the title "public accountant" to individuals who are qualified to provide assurance on the financial statements. However, financial statement auditors do not account for anything.

Accounting—the recording, classifying, and summarizing of economic events in a logical manner for the purpose of providing financial information for decision making.

Accounting is the recording, classifying, and summarizing of economic events in a logical manner for the purpose of providing financial information for decision making. The function of accounting is to provide certain types of quantitative and qualitative (notes to the financial statements) information that management and others can use to make decisions. Accountants must have a thorough understanding of the principles and rules that provide the basis for preparing the accounting information. Accountants also help to develop the systems used to record an entity's economic events in a timely way and at a reasonable cost.

As we are all aware, financial statements are prepared using many judgmental evaluations or estimates. Therefore, it is not possible to produce financial statements that are absolutely precise. For instance, when management provides an allowance for doubtful accounts, it represents management's best estimate of the likelihood of collectability. When auditing accounting data, the concern lies in evaluating whether recorded information reasonably reflects the economic events that occurred during the accounting period within specified dollar ranges (called **materiality**). Misstatements or omissions are considered to be material if, individually or in the aggregate, they would likely influence the economic decisions of users who rely upon the financial statements. In simple terms, if the users would have reached a different opinion of the financial statements if they had received a set of financial statements with the corrected misstatement or omission, then that misstatement or omission is material. As one can imagine, establishing materiality requires considerable professional judgment.

Materiality—amount of misstatements, individually or in the aggregate, that would likely influence the economic decisions of users.

Since accounting standards are the criteria for evaluating whether the accounting information is properly recorded, auditors must understand the relevant accounting standards. These standards are constantly evolving as business practices and standards change—there are different accounting standards for public companies, private enterprises, not-for-profit organizations, and public sector entities.

In addition to understanding accounting, the auditor must also possess expertise in internal controls, risk assessment processes, and the accumulation and interpretation of audit evidence. It is this expertise that distinguishes financial statement auditors from accountants. Determining the proper audit procedures that mitigate risks, deciding on the number and types of items to test, and evaluating the results are tasks that are unique to the auditor.

ECONOMIC DEMAND FOR AUDITING

Businesses, governments, and not-for-profit organizations use auditing services extensively. Publicly accountable organizations, such as businesses listed on securities exchanges or large not-for-profit organizations, are legally required to have an annual financial statement audit.

A look at the economic reasons for auditing highlights why auditing is valuable. Consider a bank manager's decision to make a loan to a business. The decision will be based on such factors as previous financial relations with the business and the financial condition of the business as reflected by its financial statements. Assuming the bank makes the loan, it will charge a rate of interest determined primarily by three factors:

1. *Risk-free interest rate.* This is approximately the rate the bank could earn by investing in Canada Treasury bills for the same length of time as the business loan.

2. *Business risk for the customer.* This risk reflects the possibility that the business will not be able to repay its loan because of economic or business conditions such as a recession, poor management decisions, or unexpected competition in the industry.
3. *Information risk.* **Information risk** reflects the possibility that the information upon which the decision to make the loan was made was inaccurate. A likely cause of the information risk is inaccurate financial statements.

Information risk—the risk that information upon which a business decision is made is inaccurate.

Auditing has no effect on either the risk-free interest rate or business risk, but it can have a significant effect on information risk. If the bank manager is satisfied that there is minimal information risk because a borrower's financial statements are audited, the bank's risk is substantially reduced and the overall interest rate to the borrower can be reduced. For example, assume that a large company has total interest-bearing debt of approximately $1 billion. If the interest rate on that debt is reduced by only 1 percent, the annual savings in interest is $10 million. Many lenders such as banks require annual audits for companies with large bank loans outstanding.

CAUSES OF INFORMATION RISK

LO **4** Determine the causes of information risk.

As society becomes more complex, there is an increased likelihood that unreliable information will be provided to decision makers. There are several reasons for this, including the remoteness of information, bias and motives of the provider, voluminous data, and complex exchange transactions.

Remoteness of Information

In a global economy, it is nearly impossible for a decision maker to have much first-hand knowledge about the organization with which it does business. Information provided by others must be relied upon. When information is obtained from others, its likelihood of being intentionally or unintentionally misstated increases.

Biases and Motives of the Provider

If information is provided by someone whose goals are inconsistent with those of the decision maker, the information may be biased in favour of the provider. The reason can be honest optimism about future events or an intentional omission or emphasis designed to influence users. In either case, the result is a misstatement of information. For example, when a borrower provides financial statements to a lender, there is considerable likelihood that the borrower will bias the statements to increase the chance of obtaining a loan. The misstatement could be incorrect dollar amounts or inadequate or incomplete disclosures of information.

Voluminous Data

As organizations become larger, so does the volume of their exchange transactions. This increases the likelihood that improperly recorded information is included in the records—perhaps buried in a large amount of other information. For example, if a large government agency overpays a vendor's invoice by $2000, the overpayment is unlikely to be uncovered unless the agency has instituted reasonably complex procedures to find this type of misstatement. If many minor misstatements remain undiscovered, the combined total can be significant or even material.

Complex Exchange Transactions

In the past few decades, exchange transactions between organizations have become increasingly complex and therefore more difficult to record properly. The increasing complexity in transactions has also resulted in increasingly complex accounting standards.

For example, the correct accounting treatment of the acquisition of one entity by another poses relatively difficult accounting problems, especially as it relates to fair value estimations. Other examples include properly combining and disclosing the results of operations of subsidiaries in different industries and properly valuing and disclosing derivative financial instruments.

LO **5** Explain how information risk can be reduced.

REDUCING INFORMATION RISK

As mentioned previously, material misstatements can have serious implications for users' economic decisions. Managers of businesses and the users of their financial statements may conclude that the best way to deal with information risk is simply to have the risk remain reasonably high. A small company may find it less expensive to pay higher interest costs than to increase the costs of reducing information risk (e.g., by having an audit). Similarly, the bank is willing to accept more information risk because of the higher interest it is receiving from the small business.

For larger businesses, it is usually practical to incur such costs to reduce information risk. There are three main ways to do so:

Canada Revenue Agency (CRA) auditors—auditors who work for the Canada Revenue Agency and conduct examinations of taxpayers' returns.

1. *User verifies information.* The user may go to the business premises to examine records and obtain information about the reliability of the statements. Normally, this is impractical because of cost. However, some users perform their own verification. For example, the **Canada Revenue Agency (CRA)** does considerable verification of business and individual tax returns. Similarly, if a business intends to purchase another business, it is common for the purchaser to use a special audit team to independently verify and evaluate key information of the prospective business.
2. *User shares information risk with management.* There is considerable legal precedent indicating that management is responsible for providing reliable information to users. If users rely on inaccurate financial statements and as a result incur a loss, they may have the basis for a lawsuit against management. A difficulty with sharing information risk with management is that users may not be able to collect on losses (as in the case of bankruptcy).
3. *Audited financial statements are provided.* The most common way for users to obtain reliable information is to have an independent audit. Typically, management of a private company or the audit committee for a public company engages the external auditor to provide assurances to users that the financial statements are reliable.

CONCEPT CHECK

C1-1   What is meant by determining the degree of correspondence between information and established criteria? What are the criteria for the audit of a company's financial statements?

C1-2   What are the major causes of information risk? How can information risk be reduced?

C1-3   Explain how and why the auditor makes information trustworthy and credible.

External users (such as shareholders and lenders) rely on financial statements to make business decisions. They look to the independent auditor's report as an indication of the statements' reliability. Decision makers can then use the audited information on the assumption that it is reasonably complete, accurate, and unbiased. They value the auditor's assurance because of the auditor's integrity, independence, expertise, and knowledge of financial statement reporting matters. As a result, in order for the audit to be effective, the interests of external users must be protected throughout the engagement. Figure 1-2 illustrates the accountability relationships among the auditor, client, and financial statement users.

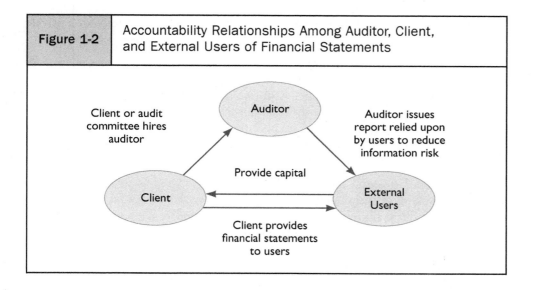

| Figure 1-2 | Accountability Relationships Among Auditor, Client, and External Users of Financial Statements |

COMMON TYPES OF AUDITS

LO **6** Identify major types of audits and auditors.

There are many different types of audits depending upon the subject matter under consideration. Table 1-1 summarizes the type of information, criteria, and evidence used in three common types of audits—the financial statement audit, the compliance audit, and the operational audit.

A **financial statement audit** is conducted to determine whether the financial statements (the information verified) are stated in accordance with specified criteria (the applicable accounting framework).

A **compliance audit** requires expert knowledge of the relevant legislation, regulations, or policies (the criteria), as well as knowledge of controls-related processes. A compliance audit is conducted to determine whether the auditee is following specific procedures, rules, or regulations set by some higher authority. Auditors perform compliance audits for private businesses and various government

Financial statement audit—an audit conducted to determine whether the financial statements of an entity are presented fairly, in all material respects, in conformity with an applicable financial reporting framework.

Compliance audit—an audit performed to determine whether an entity complied with specific laws, regulations, rules, or provisions of contracts or grant agreements.

| Table 1-1 | Examples of Three Types of Audits |

Type of Audit and Description	Example	Information	Established Criteria	Available Evidence
Financial statement audit: an audit conducted to determine whether the overall financial statements of an entity are stated in conformity with an applicable reporting framework.	Perform the annual audit to determine if Canadian Tire Corporation's financial statements are in conformity with IFRS.	Canadian Tire's financial statements	The reporting framework is IFRS	Documents, records, inquiries, and outside sources of evidence
Compliance audit: an audit performed to determine whether an entity has complied with external criteria (i.e., specific laws, regulations, rules, or provisions of contracts or grant agreements) or internal criteria (i.e., organizational policies and procedures).	Determine if bank covenants for loan continuation have been met.	Company records	Loan agreement provisions	Financial statements and calculations by the auditor
Operational audit: a review of any part of an organization's operating procedures and methods for the purpose of evaluating economy, efficiency, and effectiveness.	Evaluate whether the computerized payroll processing for subsidiary H is operating economically, efficiently, and effectively.	Number of payroll records processed in a month, costs of the department, and error rate	Company standards for economy, efficiency, and effectiveness in payroll department	Error reports, payroll records, and payroll processing costs

divisions and units. The following are examples of compliance audits for a private business:

- Determine whether accounting personnel are following the procedures prescribed by the company controller.
- Review wage rates for compliance with minimum wage laws.
- Examine contractual agreements with bankers and other lenders to be sure the company is complying with legal requirements.
- Determine whether a supplier is in compliance with the organization's supplier code of conduct or child labour laws.

Governmental agencies and departments are subject to considerable compliance auditing because of extensive regulation, while many private and not-for-profit organizations have prescribed policies, contractual arrangements, and legal requirements that may require compliance auditing. Compliance audits for government-funded programs are often done by public accounting firms and are discussed in more detail in Chapter 20.

Results of compliance audits performed for private companies are typically reported to management, rather than outside users, because management is the primary group concerned with prescribed procedures and regulations. As a result, internal auditors, who are employed by the organization, often perform compliance audits. When an organization such as the CRA wants to determine whether individuals or organizations are complying with its requirements, the auditor is also employed by the organization (the CRA) issuing the requirements.

Operational audit—a review of any part of an organization's operating procedures and methods for the purpose of evaluating economy, efficiency, and effectiveness.

An **operational audit** or a performance audit evaluates the efficiency, effectiveness, and economy of any part of an organization's operating procedures and methods. At the completion of an operational audit, management normally expects recommendations for improving operations.

In operational auditing, the reviews are not limited to accounting, but can include evaluation of the organizational structure, computer operations, production methods, marketing, or any other area in which the audit team is qualified. As a result, many operational audits require a multidisciplinary specialist team that clearly understands the organizational and operational facets under audit. Operational and compliance audits are the main types of audits conducted by governmental and internal auditors; however, public accountants can also do these types of engagements.

TYPES OF AUDITORS

Throughout our previous discussion, we have highlighted which auditors typically perform various types of audits. Here, we provide an overview of five types of auditors—internal auditors, government auditors, Canada Revenue Agency auditors, forensic accountants and fraud auditors, and public accountants. There are other specialist auditors, which we will refer to throughout the text, who play an important role in the financial statement audit, such as the tax expert who audits the tax provision, and the information systems specialist who assesses the information systems controls.

Internal Auditors

Internal auditors work for individual companies, banks, hospitals, universities, and governments. The Institute of Internal Auditors (IIA) defines internal auditing as "an independent, objective assurance and consulting activity designed to add value and improve an organization's operations. It helps an organization accomplish its objectives by bringing a systematic, disciplined approach to evaluate and improve the effectiveness of risk management, control, and governance processes."[1]

---

[1] Institute of Internal Auditors, "About internal auditing," accessed August 15, 2017, at **https:// global.theiia.org/about/about-internal-auditing/pages/about-internal-auditing.aspx**.

As the IIA definition highlights, internal auditors provide a variety of assurance services, such as financial and internal control audits, operational audits, compliance audits, system security audits, and forensic and fraud investigations. These types of audits add value and can improve organizational operations, as well as help reduce fraud, waste, and abuse in organizations. Internal auditors also perform consulting activities such as assistance in evaluating new systems prior to implementation and in assessing risks within the organization.

Many internal auditors of public companies provide assurance to management or boards of directors that internal controls are designed adequately and operating effectively. These engagements are in response to the regulatory requirements. National Instrument 52–109 (Certification of Disclosure in Issuers' Annual and Interim Filings) in Canada and Section 404 of the Sarbanes-Oxley Act (usually referred to as SOX) in the United States (which applies to Canadian subsidiaries of U.S. companies and Canadian companies listed in the United States) require public companies to report management's assessment of the effectiveness of internal control over financial reporting.

To effectively perform assurance engagements, an internal auditor must be independent of the line functions in an organization but will not be completely independent of the entity as long as an employer–employee relationship exists. In order to maintain independence, internal auditors typically report directly to the **audit committee** of the board of directors and senior management. While internal auditors provide management with valuable information for making decisions, it is unlikely that users from outside the entity will want to rely on information verified by internal auditors because of their lack of independence (explained further in Chapter 3). This lack of independence is the major difference between internal auditors and external auditors.

Audit committee—a committee of the board of directors that is responsible for auditor oversight. It is an objective and independent liaison between auditors, management, and the board of directors.

Internal auditors' responsibilities vary considerably, depending upon the employer. For example, management of one company may decide that internal auditors should be extensively involved in systems development, whereas others may decide that their work should focus primarily on financial controls and fraud audits. Internal audit staff size can range from one or two to hundreds of employees, each of whom has diverse responsibilities, including many outside the accounting area.

Many internal auditors are members of the Institute of Internal Auditors (IIA), which has more than 185 000 members worldwide and establishes standards for ethics and for the practice of internal auditing. The IIA issues a highly regarded designation, Certified Internal Auditor (CIA), to auditors who have completed the necessary examination and experience requirements.

Government Auditors

The Government of Canada, various provincial governments, and several large Canadian municipalities (i.e., Calgary, Edmonton, Winnipeg, Toronto, Ottawa, Halifax, and Montreal) all have an auditor general who is responsible for auditing the ministries, departments, and agencies that report to that government. These government auditors may be appointed by a bipartisan legislative committee or by the government in that jurisdiction. They report to their respective legislatures and are responsible to the body appointing them.

The primary responsibility of the government audit staff employed at the offices of auditors general is to perform the audit function for government. The extent and scope of these audits are determined by legislation in the various jurisdictions. For example, the Auditor General of Canada is required to perform the following audits:

1. Internal audits into financial matters or compliance with regulations, and whether or not the operations are conducted in an efficient, effective, and economic manner.
2. External audits of the financial statements.
3. Special examinations of efficiency, effectiveness, and economy (every five years).

In some ways, these government auditors are much like external auditors. They are organizationally independent of the government entities they audit, and the Auditor General reports directly to the legislature. Further, most of the financial information prepared by government agencies and, in some cases, by Crown corporations is audited by these government auditors before the information is submitted to the various legislatures. Since the authority for expenditures and receipts of government agencies is defined by legislation, there is considerable emphasis on compliance in these audits. In many provinces, experience as a government auditor fulfills the experience requirement for the CPA designation.

Performance audits—public sector audits, also referred to as value-for-money audits, that encompass economy, efficiency, and effectiveness.

In Canada, auditors general often conduct **performance audits**, sometimes called value-for-money audits, because they help determine whether value is received for the money spent. The purpose of these audits is to determine whether the organization or program being audited is achieving its objectives effectively, economically, and efficiently. The professional standards for these audits are published in the *CPA Canada Assurance Handbook*. The audit reports are publicly available and, each year, when the Auditor General's annual report is released, the findings generate considerable media attention as well as political controversy.

Canada Revenue Agency Auditors

The Canada Revenue Agency is responsible for the enforcement of the federal tax laws as they have been defined by Parliament and interpreted by the courts. A major responsibility of this agency is to audit the returns of taxpayers to determine whether they have complied with the tax laws. These audits are solely compliance audits, and the auditors who perform them are referred to as Canada Revenue Agency auditors.

It might seem that the audit of returns for compliance with the federal tax laws would be a simple and straightforward problem. However, tax laws are highly complicated, and there are hundreds of volumes of court interpretations. The tax returns being audited vary from the simple returns of individuals who work for only one employer and take the standard tax deductions to the highly complex returns of multinational corporations. Taxation problems could involve individual taxpayers, sales tax, goods and services tax, corporate taxes, or trusts, and an auditor involved in any of these areas must have applicable expertise to conduct the audit.

AUDITING IN ACTION 1-1
Canada's Provincial Auditors General: Patrolling Effectiveness and Protecting the Public Interest

The types of audits conducted by Canada's provincial auditors general cover a broad range of subjects. For instance, the 2013 Nova Scotia Auditor General's report concluded that the province's welfare system was failing to adequately monitor foster children and other kids in care and that investigations into alleged abuse were taking too long. In Ontario, the Auditor General concluded that the Ministry of Education had inadequate oversight of private schools and, as a result, there were several significant deficiencies in the system. For instance, 30 private schools issued 1500 more diplomas than the number of Grade 12 students enrolled in those schools, raising the possibility of diploma fraud. Many of the significant findings in the British Columbia Auditor General's 2013 report were related to serious security flaws in the province's computerized criminal justice database. The auditors found that attackers could gain access to sensitive information related to criminal cases, such as details on sealed court records, youth cases, and pardoned people. Perhaps even more disturbing, the Department of Justice would never know that unauthorized access had occurred.

As these examples highlight, while the auditors general help to identify inefficiencies within government, they also help to fortify public institutions, even if their findings shake things up!

Sources: Dirk Meissner, "Auditor-general flags security flaws in justice database," *Globe and Mail*, January 13, 2013. Allison Auld, "Nova Scotia auditor general finds deficiencies in oversight of foster kids," *Huffington Post Politics*, December 2, 2013. Karen Howlett, "Ontario schools handed out 1,500 fraudulent diplomas in one year," *Globe and Mail*, December 13, 2013. Office of the Auditor General, "Minimal ministry oversight means parents need to be vigilant in selecting their children's private school, auditor general finds," News Release, December 10, 2013.

Forensic Accountants and Fraud Auditors

Forensic accounting and fraud auditing are one of the fastest growing areas within the audit world, mainly because of the huge growth in white-collar and occupational fraud. Public accounting firms, companies, police forces, regulators, and law firms often hire these auditors to investigate financial statement fraud, asset misappropriations, money laundering, bribery, theft of information via computer hacking, and a long list of other fraudulent activities. Fraud auditors and forensic accountants may also assist in the financial statement audit. Canadian assurance and auditing standards require a fraud risk assessment as part of the financial statement audit, which is often performed by a fraud auditor or forensic accountant.

Forensic accountants combine their accounting knowledge with investigative skills in various litigation support and investigative accounting settings. The day-to-day work of forensic accountants and fraud auditors involves interviewing key people, studying accounts, and, increasingly, examining electronic documents, writing investigation reports, testifying at trials, and understanding factors that motivate individuals to commit fraud. A characteristic that distinguishes fraud auditors and forensic accountants from other auditors is their persistence and doggedness in following up suspicions—what is referred to as an "investigative mindset."

Forensic and fraud auditors may be specialists in external auditing, internal auditing, information systems, private investigation, tax accounting, or other disciplines. They may also have specialist designations such as the CPA-CFF (Certified in Financial Forensics) or the CFE (Certified Fraud Examiner) offered by the Association of Certified Fraud Examiners.

Public Accountants

Public accountants provide accounting services to the public. Of those services, which include assurance services as well as accounting and tax advice, the most well-known service is the financial statement audit. As we have highlighted, there are various auditors and types of audits; however, in the case of public accountants, when the term "audit" is used, it is usually in reference to the financial statement audit. Only public accounting firms can conduct financial statement audits or reviews, and only Canadian CPAs with a public accountant's licence can sign an assurance report related to financial statements.

AUDITING IN ACTION 1-2
Fraud Examiners Use Big Data and Other Tools to Fight Financial Fraud

Annual global fraud losses are projected to be more than $3.5 trillion (U.S.), based on average fraud loss per organization of 5 percent of revenues. As a result, demand for forensic accountants and fraud examiners continues to increase. Worldwide, there are nearly 75 000 members of the Association of Certified Fraud Examiners (ACFE), the world's largest anti-fraud organization, who perform a variety of forensic investigations. Fraud examiners and forensic accountants use rigorous accounting skills and a flair for investigation to sniff out fraud, uncover money laundering, and trace missing assets.

Because fraud is increasingly digital, data analytics is one of the best weapons in fraud detection. Cloud computing allows companies to consolidate data across locations and search for and detect unusual patterns in real time. For example, using Benford's Law (a formula for the expected frequency of digits in a list of numbers), one forensic team detected that several call centre operators had issue fraudulent refunds to themselves, friends, and family members that totalled several thousand dollars.

"Forensic accountants are really financial detectives," says Alex Brown of the Institute of Chartered Accountants of England and Wales' forensic group. Brown has worked on cases involving Caribbean money laundering, Eastern European smuggling, and major commercial disputes. "I was attracted to forensic accountancy because, like science, you need to have investigative skills," says forensic trainee Amy Hawkins. "I really like the sleuthing side of the job, where you're finding out whodunit and where the money went." Forensic accountant Simon Bevan adds, "When you find that killer document, it's a real reward for all your hard work."

Sources: Association of Certified Fraud Examiners, home page, accessed June 27, 2017, at **www.acfe.com**. Sarah Diamond, "How to use big data to fight financial fraud," *Forbes*, September 2014. Amy McClellan, "Forensic accountancy: Hot on the trail of the fraudsters," *The Independent*, April 26, 2006.

An audit required by law, as in the case of public companies and not-for-profit organizations that meet certain revenue thresholds, is referred to as a statutory audit.

Because of the widespread use of audited financial statements in the Canadian economy, as well as businesses' and other users' familiarity with these statements, it is common to use the terms "external auditor," "independent auditor," "public accountant," and "licensed public accountant" synonymously. We will refer to these auditors as public accountants, or PAs. In order to be able to practise public accounting, a PA must be a member of good standing in one of the provincial CPA institutes, meet the qualifications per the provincial public accounting act for performing an audit or review engagement, and be independent. Public accountants are required to perform their work in accordance with their professional standards, which are set out in the *CPA Canada Assurance Handbook*.

CONCEPT CHECK

C1-4 Describe and explain the differences and similarities between financial statement, compliance, and operational audits.

C1-5 Describe and explain the differences and similarities among the various types of auditors.

ASSURANCE AND NONASSURANCE SERVICES OFFERED BY PUBLIC ACCOUNTING FIRMS

Assurance services are usually associated with the work performed by public accountants under their professional standards. Regardless of the subject matter or criteria, companies often seek out public accountants to provide independent assurance on various types of information, due to their independence, competence, and rigorous professional standards. While assurance over historical financial statement information is the sole domain of public accountants, in the case of other types of assurance services, PAs often compete with a variety of other professionals.

The General Characteristics of an Assurance Engagement

LO **7** Explain the general characteristics of an assurance engagement.

Assurance engagement—an engagement in which the assurance professional obtains sufficient evidence to express a conclusion to users about the outcome of the measurement or evaluation of an underlying subject matter against criteria.

An **assurance engagement** is an independent professional service in which the assurance provider expresses a conclusion on the outcome of an evaluation or measurement of a subject matter against criteria. Such services are valued because the assurance provider is independent and perceived to be unbiased with respect to the information being examined. For individuals making business decisions, such services improve the reliability and the relevance of the information used as the basis for their decisions.

Any engagement that fulfills the following criteria is an assurance engagement:

- Existence of a three-party relationship
- Subject matter
- Criteria
- Gathering of sufficient appropriate evidence
- Expression of opinion or conclusion

Although Figure 1-2 illustrates the three-party accountability relationship with respect to a financial statement audit, this relationship applies to all assurance engagements. The client is accountable to the users and, because the users rely upon the auditor's report, the auditors are also accountable to the users. The subject matter and the criteria for assurance engagements can vary widely. The criteria for some information may be well-established standards, such as IFRS or the G4 reporting framework for sustainability reporting, or, as in the case of organic foods, there may not be one agreed-upon standard. The criteria may be specific to a particular agreement, or it may be agreed upon between the auditor and the users.

Assurance engagements can be either moderate or high assurance, which directly impacts what is judged to be sufficient and appropriate evidence. To help understand what this means, think about assurance in terms of the degree of confidence that the auditors have in the correspondence between the subject matter and the criteria. For instance, the UPS Corporate Sustainability Report referred to in the opening vignette was a limited (moderate) assurance engagement, and the PA's report provided a conclusion that the report was prepared, in all material respects, in accordance with the applicable criteria and stated, "nothing has come to our attention." In order to reach that conclusion, or to provide that limited degree of confidence to the users, the PA would rely primarily upon analytics and inquiry. In contrast, for the reasonable (high) assurance report on the company's global statement of greenhouse gas emissions, the PA provided an opinion that the statement was prepared, in all material respects, in accordance with the applicable criteria. In order to provide that opinion, or to be reasonably confident that the statements are free of material errors, the report would have to involve much more persuasive evidence.

Public accountants may issue either an attest assurance report or a direct report. For instance, a financial statement audit is an **attestation engagement**. In this type of engagement, management (usually referred to as "the client") measures or evaluates the subject (in other words, prepares the financial statements) and provides the auditor with a written assertion that the financial statements are in accordance with the applicable accounting framework. The auditor evaluates the assertions regarding the information, using suitable criteria, and issues an assurance report that attests to the reliability of the assertions.

In some assurance engagements, the auditee does not make a public assertion or prepare a report such as a set of financial statements, statement of greenhouse emissions, or a tax return. In these types of engagements, the assertion is implied. The auditor directly measures or evaluates the underlying subject matter against the suitable criteria, and issues a report that includes the auditors' findings and a conclusion as to whether the subject matter conforms to the applicable criteria. This type of engagement is called a **direct engagement**. Many of the audits conducted by auditors general are direct reporting engagements. For instance, in the case of a performance audit, the auditor would directly measure or evaluate a particular activity, such as hospital wait times, and report on the economy, effectiveness, and efficiency of that activity. Similarly, in the case of a compliance audit, the auditor would directly evaluate an entity's compliance with some requirement, which could be internal (i.e., human resource policies) or external (i.e., health and safety regulations) as measured by a suitable criteria and express a conclusion. Although the most common engagement for public accountants is an attestation engagement, direct reporting engagements are common in the public sector. As a result, public accountants do perform direct reporting engagements for their public sector clients.

Assurance Engagements Related to Historical Financial Statements

As previously mentioned, PAs can provide a variety of assurance engagements, with different levels of assurance, and for a wide variety of information. Audits, reviews, and audits of financial information other than financial statements are common attestation engagements related to financial information.

Audit of Historical Financial Statements The most well-known example of assurance services is the financial statement audit. As already highlighted, in the case of public accounting the term "audit" usually refers to the financial statement audit. The public accountant provides reasonable assurance that the financial statements are in accordance with the applicable accounting framework.

Publicly traded companies in Canada are required to have audits of their financial statements. Auditor reports can be found in the public company's annual report, and many companies' audited financial statements can be accessed via the internet from the System for Electronic Document Analysis and Retrieval (SEDAR) at **www.sedar.com**. Public companies also post copies of financial statements to their corporate websites (check the investor relations tab for any public company). Although not required by the Canada Business Corporations Act, many privately held companies also have annual

Attestation engagement—a special form of assurance engagement, such as a financial statement audit, in which the auditor evaluates the information provided by one party, using suitable criteria, and issues a report that attests to the reliability of this information to another party.

Direct engagement—a special form of assurance engagement, such as the Report of the Auditor General of Canada, in which the auditor directly measures and evaluates the underlying subject matter against the criteria and issues a report that includes the subject matter information and a conclusion as to whether the subject matter conforms to the applicable criteria.

LO **8** Describe assurance and nonassurance services provided by public accountants and distinguish the audit of financial statements from other assurance services.

financial statement audits. While the most popular reason for the annual audit is to obtain financing from banks and other institutions, private companies who have plans to go public or ones with an inactive minority shareholder often decide to have an audit as well. Government and not-for-profit organizations often have financial statement audits due to regulatory requirements, as well as to meet the requirements of lenders or funding sources.

Review of Historical Financial Statements

In the case of smaller, nonpublic companies, users are often satisfied with a review engagement, which has a lower level of assurance and lower cost than an audit. As in the case of an audit, management asserts that the financial statements are fairly stated in conformity with an applicable financial reporting framework. However, a review engagement provides only limited (moderate) assurance, rather than high assurance, as in the case of an audit engagement. Although cost saving is a major consideration, the underlying reason why a user would be amenable to limited assurance is based upon the level of information risk (usually referred to as their assurance needs). Review engagements are discussed in more detail in Chapter 20.

Audit of Financial Information Other Than Financial Statements These engagements are audits of specific income statement or balance sheet accounts (e.g., sales, receivables, inventory) or audits of a single financial statement (e.g., balance sheet or operating statement). For example, an auditor might provide an opinion on the sales at a Shoppers Drug Mart in a Saskatoon shopping mall because the store's rent is based on sales and the owner of the mall requires an audit opinion.

Assurance Engagements for Other Information Assurance engagements for other information include both attestation and direct reporting engagements. The *CPA Canada Assurance Handbook* provides specific standards for the following attestation engagements: effectiveness of internal control over financial reporting, attestation services on service organizations, reports of compliance with agreements and regulations, and greenhouse gas emissions. For all other nonfinancial information, such as Irving Tissue Corporation's "MAJESTA Tree Planting Promise," there are two umbrella standards, one for attest engagements and one for direct engagements.

Audit of Effectiveness of Internal Control Over Financial Reporting As mentioned in the description of internal audits, managers of public companies are required to report on the effectiveness of internal controls. In addition to this requirement, the Sarbanes-Oxley Act also compels auditors to evaluate management's assessment of internal controls, which is an attestation to the effectiveness of internal control over financial reporting (there is no similar audit requirement under Canadian legislation). This evaluation, which is integrated with the audit of the financial statements, increases user confidence about future financial reporting because effective internal controls reduce the likelihood of future misstatements in the financial statements. This type of report is discussed further in Chapters 8 and 20.

Audit of Controls of Service Organizations Many companies outsource some or all of their information technology (IT) needs to an independent computer service organization rather than maintain an internal IT function. As part of the financial statement audit, the PA is required to obtain an understanding of the client's internal controls over financial reporting. However, this is difficult to do if the client is using a service organization. In those instances, the service centre engages a public accounting firm to obtain an understanding and test internal controls at the service organization and to issue an attestation report for the use of all customers and their independent auditors.

Compliance With an Agreement or Regulations Another popular attestation service provided by public accountants is commonly referred to as a "special report." These types of engagements are opinions on compliance with an agreement or regulations. For example, an auditor may provide an opinion on the company's compliance with specific terms of its bank loan agreement, such as the current ratio as defined in the agreement.

Assurance Engagements on Greenhouse Gas Statements Many companies are required to provide information on greenhouse gas (GHG) emissions in their financial statements, as well as to provide separate reports to various provincial and federal regulators. As we have already seen in the opening vignette, companies such as UPS engage public accountants to attest that their statement of GHG emissions is in accordance with the relevant criteria, Greenhouse Gas Protocol Corporate Accounting and Reporting Standard. Given the complexity of the subject matter, multidisciplinary teams, which would include subject matter experts (such as engineers and scientists) and assurance experts (the PAs), would perform these engagements.

Assurance Engagements for Other Nonfinancial Information There are almost no limits on what other nonfinancial information a public accountant can provide assurance services for. For instance, in Auditing in Action 1-3, we refer to PricewaterhouseCoopers, which since 1935 has attested to the ballot accuracy, secrecy, and integrity of the voting process of the Academy Awards, now called The Oscars. And, as highlighted in the opening vignette and Auditing in Action 1-3, a growing area of other assurance services for large public accounting firms is assurance over sustainability statements and reports. And there are many more types of assurance services being currently provided—one recent survey of large American CPA firms identified more than 200 assurance services being performed.

Assurance services related to other nonfinancial information are not the sole domain of public accounting firms. For instance, companies such as Loblaw and Apple regularly use assurance providers such as Bureau Veritas to get assurance that their suppliers comply with health and safety regulations, child labour guidelines, and many other employee welfare issues. Among the variety of service providers that offer

AUDITING IN ACTION 1-3
And the Oscar Goes To... La, La, Oops! Wrong Envelope!

PricewaterhouseCoopers (PwC) has been responsible for providing assurance over the integrity of the voting process for the Academy Awards since the 1935 awards ceremony. It would seem PwC performed its role well until the 2017 Academy Awards, when the firm was suddenly at the centre of one of the most sensational stories in Oscars' history. So what went wrong?

To ensure that no errors are made in announcing the awards, PwC uses two complete sets of the envelopes entrusted with two PwC partners who are on each side of the stage. Up until the last award of the evening, for best picture, everything was running smoothly. At that point, a PwC partner handed Warren Beatty, the award presenter, the wrong envelope. Instead of the envelope containing the winner for best picture, the partner accidentally handed Mr. Beatty a duplicate of the envelope for best actress—an award Emma Stone had accepted for her role in *La La Land* just moments before. Faye Dunaway, presenting the award with Mr. Beatty, erroneously announced that *La La Land* had won the Oscar for best picture. Moments later, the two PwC partners came onstage and the *La La Land* producers announced that *Moonlight* was, in fact, the winner.

Many are now questioning why is it necessary to have an accounting firm at the Oscars. In fact, for the first six Academy Award ceremonies, there were no accountants involved. However, people continually questioned the integrity of the voting process and the legitimacy of the outcomes. For instance, in the first few years, a disproportionate number of winners were among the Academy's

36 founders. In 1934, the new Academy president announced that he had retained the services of PwC to oversee the voting for the 1935 Oscars. As the Academy president noted in 2010, trust and integrity have been the foundation of their relationship with PwC.

Yet after the snafu in 2017, some speculate that the relationship has soured. PwC released a statement early the next day apologizing and taking responsibility for the mistake. Immediately after the mistake, the president of the Academy announced that the two PwC partners responsible for the snafu had been permanently removed from all Academy activities and that AMPAS's relationship with PwC was under review. However, despite the negative publicity, AMPAS decided to continue its longstanding relationship with PwC. AMPAS and PwC have developed new controls, including a ban of cellphones (apparently the partner who had handed out the wrong envelope was tweeting a picture of Emma Stone at the time) and the addition of a third balloting partner.

Sources: Francine McKenna, "Why Oscars may not fire PwC, even as Academy president says two partners are now banned," *Marketwatch*, March 1, 2017, accessed June 27, 2017, at **www.marketwatch.com/story/the-reasons-pwc-may-keep-its-lock-on-the-oscars-audit-2017-02-28**. Scott Feinberg and Gregg Kilday, "Oscars: The Academy's long, cozy relationship with its accountants," *Hollywood Reporter*, March 3, 2017, accessed June 17, 2017, at **www.hollywoodreporter.com/race/oscars-academys-longstanding-relationship-accountants-question-981547**. Sandy Cohen, "Academy bans cellphones for PwC accountants after Oscars fiasco," *Toronto Sun*, March 29, 2017, accessed June 17, 2017 at **www.torontosun.com/2017/03/29/cellphones-banned-backstage-for-accountants-after-oscar-flub**.

assurance services for various types of nonfinancial information, some adhere to strict accreditation standards that translate into common practices among their peers, while others are not required to do so. As we see in Auditing in Action 1-4, public accounting firms can have the competitive advantage due to their reputation for competence and independence, as well as the profession's rigorous standards. An assurance opinion from a public accountant is seen as credible in the marketplace.

Nonassurance Services Offered by Public Accounting Firms

Public accounting firms perform numerous other services that generally fall outside the scope of assurance services. Some of these are related to financial statements, while others would be considered financial planning or management advisory services.

Compilations A compilation involves the accountant preparing financial statements from a client's records or from other information provided. A compilation is much less extensive than a review, and the cost is much less. No assurance is provided by a compilation, and readers are cautioned that the financial statements may not be appropriate for their purposes.

Tax Services Accounting firms prepare corporate and individual tax returns for both audit and non-audit clients. In addition, sales tax remittance, tax planning, and other aspects of tax services are provided by most firms.

Management Advisory Services Management advisory includes services such as retirement planning and personal financial planning. Most accounting firms also provide services that enable businesses to operate more effectively, including simple suggestions for improving accounting systems, help with marketing strategies, computer installation, and pension benefit consulting. The firm offering these types of services needs to be aware of independence rules that prohibit the provision of some of these services to assurance clients, as is discussed in Chapter 3.

Accounting and Bookkeeping Services Some small clients lack the personnel or expertise to prepare their own subsidiary records. Many small accounting firms work with accounting software packages to help clients record their transactions. Often, such clients proceed with a compilation engagement.

AUDITING IN ACTION 1-4
Corporate Responsibility Reporting Expands Globally

Corporate responsibility and sustainability reporting is now a mainstream practice and no longer the sole domain of early pioneers such as The Body Shop International and Canada's Vancity Savings Credit Union. Corporate responsibility reporting continues its tremendous growth, with rapid increases in emerging economies, and is now standard practice for many companies around the globe. Over half of companies reporting globally include corporate social responsibility information in their public financial reports. In contrast, only 20 percent of companies reported this information in 2011, and less than 10 percent in 2008. The debate has changed from whether corporate responsibility is worth the cost, to what information should be reported and how it should be presented.

Reporting using the Global Reporting Initiative (GRI) guidelines is increasingly standard, with 78 percent of reports issued by companies around the world prepared based on GRI guidelines.

Although only two countries (France and South Africa) require assurance on corporate responsibility reports, many companies seek out assurance in order to demonstrate credibility with external stakeholders. Over half (59 percent) of the Global *Fortune* 250 now opt for assurance, up from 46 percent in the 2011 survey. As KPMG notes, "The question is no longer 'Should we assure on our CR data?' but rather 'Why would we not?'" Major accounting firms were the choice of assurance provider for two-thirds of the G250 firms that issued responsibility reports with external assurance. Other assurance providers included certification bodies and technical expert firms. These trends suggest that providing assurance on corporate responsibility reporting will continue to be an area of significant growth for public accounting firms.

Source: KPMG International, *The KPMG International Survey of Corporate Responsibility Reporting 2013*, Amsterdam, 2013.

SUMMARY

This chapter defined auditing and distinguished auditing from accounting. Audits are valuable because they reduce information risk, which, in the case of a financial statement audit, lowers the cost of capital. The chapter outlined the common types of audits and different types of auditors. The final part of the chapter explained the general characteristics of an assurance engagement and described assurance and nonassurance services which public accountants can provide.

MyLab Accounting
Make the grade with MyLab Accounting: The questions, exercises, and problems marked with a ⊕ can be found on MyLab Accounting. You can practise them as often as you want, and most feature step-by-step guided instructions to help you find the right answer.

Review Questions

1-1 **1** Your local veterinarian is complaining about all of the "accountants" he has had to work with—the government has been in to look at his income taxes, the bookkeeper has been sick so he has had to hire someone else, and now you are coming in to do an audit. Using the definition of an audit, explain to the veterinarian what you will be doing with the financial statements.

1-2 **2** In conducting audits of financial statements, it would be a serious breach of responsibility if the auditor did not thoroughly understand accounting. However, many competent accountants do not have a thorough understanding of the auditing process. What causes these differences?

1-3 **1** **3** Explain why auditor independence is so important in conducting a financial statement audit.

1-4 **1** Explain why an auditor who is not independent may not exercise the appropriate degree of professional skepticism.

1-5 **1** What are the information and established criteria for the audit of Glickle Ltd.'s tax return by a Canada Revenue Agency (CRA) auditor? What are they for the audit of Glickle Ltd.'s financial statements by a public accounting firm?

1-6 **1** Explain why the auditor needs to know how to conduct a risk assessment.

1-7 **1** What is the relationship between the risk assessment process and the collection of audit evidence?

1-8 **3** **4** **5** Distinguish among the following three risks: risk-free interest rate, business risk, and information risk. Which one or more of these does the auditor reduce by performing an audit?

1-9 **3** **4** **5** Explain how fair value accounting may increase information risk. How does fair value accounting increase risk for a financial statement auditor?

1-10 **6** What are the major differences in the scope of the audit responsibilities for public accountants, auditors from offices of auditors general, Canada Revenue Agency (CRA) auditors, and internal auditors?

1-11 **6** Describe the different types of assurance engagements that an internal auditor, government auditor, forensic auditor, and public accountant could provide for a hospital.

1-12 **6** What are the differences and similarities among audits of financial statements, compliance audits, and operational audits?

1-13 **6** List five examples of specific operational audits that could be conducted by an internal auditor at a manufacturing company.

1-14 **7** Explain the difference between limited assurance and reasonable assurance.

1-15 **7** **8** What knowledge does the auditor need about the client's business in an audit of historical financial statements? Explain how this knowledge may be useful in performing other assurance or consulting services for the client.

1-16 **6** **8** Which audit professionals could conduct the audit of a company that manufactures automobiles? Provide examples of the types of assurance or nonassurance engagements they could perform.

Multiple Choice Questions

1-17 〔1〕〔5〕〔6〕 The following questions deal with audits by public accounting firms. Choose the best response.

a. Which of the following best describes why an independent auditor is asked to express an opinion on the fair presentation of financial statements?
   (1) It is difficult to prepare financial statements that fairly present a company's financial position, operations, and cash flows without the expertise of an independent auditor.
   (2) It is management's responsibility to seek available independent aid in the appraisal of the financial information shown in its financial statements.
   (3) The opinion of an independent party is needed because a company may not be objective with respect to its own financial statements.
   (4) It is a customary courtesy that all shareholders of a company receive an independent report on management's stewardship of the affairs of the business.

b. Independent auditing can best be described as:
   (1) A branch of accounting.
   (2) A discipline that attests to the results of accounting and other functional operations and data.
   (3) A professional activity that measures and communicates financial and business data.
   (4) A regulatory function that prevents the issuance of improper financial information.

c. Which of the following professional services is an attestation engagement?
   (1) A consulting service engagement to provide computer-processing advice to a client.
   (2) An engagement to report on compliance with statutory requirements.
   (3) An income tax engagement to prepare federal and provincial tax returns.
   (4) The preparation of financial statements from a client's financial records.

d. Which of the following attributes is likely to be unique to the audit work of public accountants as compared to the work performed by practitioners of other professions?
   (1) Independence.
   (2) Competence.
   (3) Due professional care.
   (4) Complex body of knowledge.

1-18 〔5〕〔6〕 The following questions deal with types of audits and auditors. Choose the best response.

a. Which of the following best describes the operational audit?
   (1) It requires the constant review by internal auditors of the administrative controls as they relate to the operations of the company.
   (2) It concentrates on implementing financial and accounting control in a newly organized company.
   (3) It attempts and is designed to verify the fair presentation of a company's results of operations.
   (4) It concentrates on seeking aspects of operations in which waste could be reduced by the introduction of controls.

b. Compliance auditing often extends beyond audits, leading to the expression of opinions on the fairness of financial presentation and includes audits of efficiency, economy, effectiveness, and:
   (1) Accuracy.
   (2) Adherence to specific rules or procedures.
   (3) Evaluation.
   (4) Internal control.

Discussion Questions and Problems

1-19 〔1〕 Daniel Charon is the loan officer of the Georgian Bay Bank, which has a loan of $540 000 outstanding from Regional Delivery Service Ltd., a company specializing in the delivery of products of all types on behalf of smaller companies. Georgian Bay's collateral on the loan consists of 20 small delivery trucks with an average original cost of $45 000.

Charon is concerned about the collectability of the outstanding loan and whether the trucks still exist. He therefore engages public accountant Susan Virms to count the trucks, using registration information held by Charon. Virms is engaged because she spends most of her time auditing used automobile and truck dealerships and has extensive specialized knowledge about used trucks. Charon requests that Virms issue a report stating:

- Which of the 20 trucks are parked in Regional's parking lot on the night of June 30.
- The condition of each truck, using the categories "poor," "good," and "excellent."
- The fair market value of each truck using the current "blue book" for trucks, which states the approximate wholesale prices of all used truck models based on the "poor," "good," and "excellent" categories.

REQUIRED

a. Identify which aspects of this narrative fit each of the following parts of the definition of auditing:
  (1) Information.
  (2) Established criteria.
  (3) Accumulates and evaluates evidence.
  (4) Competent, independent person.
  (5) Report of results.
b. Identify the greatest difficulties Virms is likely to face doing this assurance engagement.

1-20 1 3 4 Consumers Union is a non-profit organization that provides information and counsel on consumer goods and services. A major part of its function is the testing of different brands of consumer products that are purchased on the open market and then the reporting of the results of the tests in *Consumer Reports*, a monthly publication. Examples of the types of products it tests are middle-sized automobiles, residential dehumidifiers, flat-screen TVs, and boys' jeans.

REQUIRED

a. In what ways are the services provided by Consumers Union similar to assurance services provided by public accounting firms?
b. What characteristics do you think a reliable consumer evaluation service would have? How do those characteristics compare to those of a reliable auditor?
c. What incentives or pressures might cause Consumers Union not to perform its responsibilities?
d. What incentives and pressures might cause an auditor not to perform his or her responsibilities?
e. Compare the concept of information risk faced by a shareholder of Toyota when using the financial statements with the information risk problem faced by a buyer of a Toyota automobile.
f. Compare the four causes of information risk faced by users of financial statements as discussed in this chapter with those faced by a buyer of an automobile.
g. Compare the three ways users of financial statements can reduce information risk with those available to a buyer of an automobile.

1-21 1 2 6 Vial-tek has an existing loan in the amount of $1.5 million with an annual interest rate of 9.5 percent. The company provides an internal company-prepared financial statement to the bank under the loan agreement. Two competing banks have offered to replace Vial-tek's existing loan agreement with a new one. First National Bank has offered to lend Vial-tek $1.5 million at a rate of 8.5 percent, but requires Vial-tek to provide financial statements that have been reviewed by a public accounting firm. Second National Bank has offered to lend Vial-tek $1.5 million at a rate of 7.5 percent, but requires Vial-tek to provide financial statements that have been audited. The controller of Vial-tek approached a public accounting firm and was given an estimated cost of $12 000 to perform a review and $20 000 to perform an audit.

REQUIRED

a. Explain why the interest rate for the loan that requires a review report is lower than that for the loan that does not require a review. Explain why the interest rate for the loan that requires an audit report is lower than the interest rate for the other two loans.
b. Calculate Vial-tek's annual costs under each loan agreement, including interest and costs for the public accounting firm's services. Indicate whether Vial-tek should keep its existing loan, accept the offer from First National Bank, or accept the offer from Second National Bank.

c. Assume that First National Bank has offered the loan at a rate of 8 percent with a review, and the cost of the audit has increased to $25 000 due to new auditing standards requirements. Indicate whether Vial-tek should keep its existing loan, accept the offer from First National Bank, or accept the offer from Second National Bank.

d. Explain why Vial-tek may desire to have an audit, ignoring the potential reduction in interest costs.

e. Explain why the public accounting firm estimated that the audit engagement would cost significantly more than the review engagement.

f. Explain how knowledge of ecommerce technologies and a strategic understanding of the client's business may increase the value of the audit service.

1-22 **1 2 3 6** Dave Czarnecki is the managing partner of Czarnecki and Hogan, a medium-sized local PA firm located outside of Kamloops. Over lunch, he is surprised when his friend James Foley asks him, "Doesn't it bother you that your clients don't look forward to seeing their auditors each year?" Dave responds, "Actually, many of my clients look forward to discussing their business with me. Auditing is only one of several services we provide. Most of our work for clients does not involve financial statement audits, and our audit clients seem to like interacting with us."

REQUIRED

a. Identify ways in which a financial statement audit adds value for clients.

b. List services other than audits that Czarnecki and Hogan likely provide.

c. Assume Czarnecki and Hogan have hired you as a consultant to identify ways in which they can expand their practice. Identify at least one additional service that you believe the firm should provide, and explain why you believe this represents a growth opportunity for PA firms.

1-23 **5** Five university students majoring in accounting are discussing alternative career plans. Abdullah plans to become a Canada Revenue Agency (CRA) auditor because his primary interest is income taxes. He believes the background in tax auditing will provide him with better exposure to income taxes than will any other available career choice. Portia has decided to go to work for a large public accounting firm for at least five years, possibly as a permanent career. She believes the variety of experience in auditing and related fields offers a better alternative than any other available choice. Kimberleigh has decided on a career in internal auditing with a large industrial company because of the many different aspects of the organization with which internal auditors become involved. Sara plans to become an auditor for the office of the provincial auditor general because she believes that this career will provide excellent experience in computer risk assessment techniques. William would ultimately like to become a certified fraud examiner but is not sure where the best place is to begin his career so that he can achieve this long-term goal.

REQUIRED

a. Discuss the major advantages and disadvantages of each of the five types of auditing careers.

b. What do you think is the best early career choice for William, the student interested in ultimately becoming a certified fraud examiner?

c. What other types of auditing careers are available to those who are qualified?

1-24 **7 8** As discussed in the chapter-opening vignette and on page 3, companies are increasingly issuing reports on corporate social responsibility. Visit the Global Reporting Initiative website (**www.globalreporting.org**) and answer the following questions.

REQUIRED

a. What is the vision and mission of the Global Reporting Initiative?

b. What is a sustainability report? Explain the use of sustainability reports in integrated reporting.

c. Explain the two "in accordance" GRI guideline reporting options. What is the GRI guidance on assurance for "in accordance" reports?

1-25 **6** An individual who wishes to practise public accounting must be a member of one of the relevant provincial accounting bodies and meet the qualifications for performing an audit or review engagement. Access your relevant provincial accounting body and answer the following questions.

REQUIRED

a. Identify the education requirements for the CPA Certification Program.

b. List the work experience requirements for the CPA designation.

c. What are the educational and work experience requirements for becoming a public accountant?

d. What are the requirements to remain a CPA member in good standing?

Professional Judgment Problems and Cases

1-26 **1** **3** **6** **8** A small, but expanding, specialty home-products retailer recently implemented an internet portal that allows customers to order merchandise online. In the first few months of operation, its website attracted a large number of visitors; however, very few placed orders online. The retailer conducted several focus-group sessions with potential shoppers to identify reasons why shoppers were visiting the website without placing orders. Shoppers in the focus group made these comments:

1. "I am nervous about doing business with this retailer because it is relatively unknown in the marketplace. How do I know the product descriptions on the website are accurate and that the stated return policies are followed?"
2. "I am reluctant to provide my credit card information online. How do I know that the transmission of my personal credit card information to the retailer's website is protected?"
3. "Retailers are notorious for selling information about customers to others. The last thing I want to do is enter personal information online, such as my name, address, telephone number, and email address. I am afraid this retailer will sell that information to third parties and then I'll be bombarded with a bunch of junk email messages!"
4. "Websites go down all the time due to system failures. How do I know that the retailer's website will be operating when I need it?"

REQUIRED
Discuss whether this situation provides an opportunity for PAs to address these customer concerns. How could a PA provide assistance?

1-27 **1** **6** A large conglomerate is considering acquiring a medium-sized manufacturing company in a closely related industry. A major consideration by the management of the conglomerate in deciding whether to pursue the merger is the operational efficiency of the company. Management has decided to obtain a detailed report based on the intensive investigation of the operational efficiency of the sales department, production department, and research and development department.

REQUIRED
a. What professionals could the conglomerate hire to conduct the operational audit? What skills should be present in the audit team?
b. What major problems are the auditors likely to encounter in conducting the investigation and writing the report?

1-28 **1** **3** **7** **8** The Oscars snafu described in Auditing in Action 1-3 is not the first time that there has been a major mix-up at an awards ceremony. Denise Garrido was 2013 Miss Universe Canada for only 24 hours. She was dethroned after an independent audit of the judges' scores discovered a typo in the top five entries. It turned out that Riza Santos was the actual winner and Garrido was the third runner-up. In 2007, a similar situation occurred in the Miss California pageant and, in 2013, an NBC reality show, *The Voice*, had to toss out votes cast online and by text because of "inconsistencies" observed.

REQUIRED
a. Pageants and awards shows—such as the Oscars, Junos, and Canadian Screen Awards—all use external auditors to enhance their reputation. Explain how an external auditor improves the reputation of pageants and awards shows.
b. When the incorrect result was announced, there was a breakdown in the process. What do you think went wrong with the process? How do you think the 2013 *The Voice* audit contributed to this breakdown?
c. John Simcoe is the partner in charge of PwC Canada's practice for technology, information communication, and entertainment and media audit and assurance. John provides assurance services for the Junos, and Canadian Screen Awards and explains that these assurance engagements are much more than "counting ballots." He states that they are "actually quite complex." What are some of the key factors that PwC considers when involved in these types of assurance engagements?
d. The Miss Universe Canada pageant announced that it will be implementing additional safeguards to prevent a similar situation from happening again. Explain what types of assurance and nonassurance services a public accounting firm can offer that would reduce the risk of similar errors occurring in the future.

1-29 **1** **2** **3** **8** Joy Wu, a PA, is planning her first audit of a closely held small business. In prior years, Wu compiled the financial statements of the company. She also helped to set up its accounting system and supervised the work of the company's bookkeeper, who has limited knowledge of accounting. This year, management wants Wu to perform an audit because a local bank has requested audited financial statements as a condition for granting the company a large loan needed to expand operations. During her discussions with management, Wu agreed to conduct the audit and to continue to supervise the company's day-to-day accounting. This will facilitate the audit work by giving her a good knowledge of the company's business transactions. The company would like Wu to continue to closely advise and support management with the bank loan negotiations to secure the best possible loan terms.

REQUIRED
a. Describe the different types of work that Wu is considering and the stakeholders involved in or affected by this work.
b. Is it possible for Wu to do all of this work and still be independent? Why or why not? (*Hint:* How do you think the various engagements will affect her professional skepticism when performing the audit?)

(Extract from AU2 CGA-Canada Examinations developed by the Certified General Accountants Association of Canada © 2010 CGA-Canada. Reproduced with permission. All rights reserved.)

THE PUBLIC ACCOUNTING PROFESSION AND AUDIT QUALITY

STANDARDS REFERENCED IN THIS CHAPTER

CSQC 1 – Quality control for firms that perform audits and reviews of financial statements and other assurance engagements

CAS 200 – Overall objectives of the independent auditor and the conduct of an audit in accordance with Canadian Auditing Standards

CAS 220 – Quality control for an audit of financial statements

CSOA 5000 – Use of the practitioner's communication or name

LEARNING OBJECTIVES

After studying this chapter, you should be able to:

1 Describe the public accounting industry.

2 Identify the organizations that affect the public accounting profession and their role.

3 Describe how the *CPA Canada Handbook—Assurance* is organized.

4 Use Canadian Auditing Standards to explain the purpose of and the principles underlying the financial audit.

5 Understand the drivers of audit quality and explain the competing pressures auditors face that threaten audit quality.

6 Identify quality control standards and practices within the auditing profession and apply those standards and practices to enhance audit quality.

A Focus on Audit Quality

The 2008–09 financial crisis, as well as several high-profile corporate collapses, have kept alive the debate over improving financial statement audit quality. Around the globe, professional accounting bodies, regulators, and other stakeholders are considering how to enhance audit quality. For instance, on the international front, the International Audit Assurance Standards Board (IAASB) has made audit quality central to its work plan and has developed a *Framework for Audit Quality*. As a follow-up, it recently issued *Enhancing Audit Quality in the Public Interest: A Focus on Professional Skepticism, Quality Control and Group Audits*, and the board plans to examine how the standards can improve around these three areas and, hopefully, improve audit quality.

One of the difficulties of assessing audit quality is that there is no agreed-upon definition or measurement of audit quality. The auditing profession's standards describe quality as a function of many factors, including firm leadership ("tone at the top"), independence, integrity, objectivity, personnel management, client acceptance and continuation procedures, engagement performance, and monitoring. The American Public Company Accountability Oversight Board (PCAOB)

continued >

has developed a set of potential Audit Quality Indicators, or AQIs. Canada and several jurisdictions are pilot testing or have tested the use of AQIs. Regulators and professionals are optimistic about the potential benefits of AQIs—they focus the attention of the audit partner on important factors such as staff workloads and partner–staff ratios, which is likely to have an additional positive impact on audit quality.

Based upon its recent inspections, the Canadian Public Accountability Board (CPAB) concludes that the quality of public company audits is improving. However, the CPAB asserts that there is room for improvement. One key area that remains a challenge is auditing in emerging markets— especially in identifying and responding to risks that are specific to that particular country. As Jeremy Jagt, national assurance line leader at Grant Thornton, noted, "The reality is that different countries are in different places—the maturity of the audit profession in a jurisdiction can be an issue; the number of years the audit regulator has been active; even business culture issues can weigh in on results." Despite the observed improvements, regulators have recently expressed concern over the significant growth in firms' advisory services and that the potential conflicts of interests could erode audit quality.

Sources: Canadian Public Accountability Board (CPAB), Center for Audit Quality, CAQ Approach to Audit Quality Indicators. Gundi Jeffrey, "Audit quality improving, CPAB says," *The Bottom Line,* May 2014, p. 17. Gundi Jeffrey, "Firms prosper amid economic challenges," *The Bottom Line*, April 2016, pp. 13, 20. Ken Tysiac, "CAQ proposes an approach to communicating audit quality indicators," *Journal of Accountancy*, April 24, 2014.

We learned in the first chapter that public accountants play an important role in society by adding value to financial reporting through providing assurance. As the opening vignette illustrates, high-quality audits are of interest to many stakeholders, including investors, the **Canadian Public Accountability Board (CPAB),** securities regulators, analysts, and the audit profession itself. In this chapter, we will consider the role of these parties in the conduct of the financial statement audit. We will also consider the purpose of the financial statement audit, the auditor's responsibilities and expectations, and how auditors ensure that they perform high-quality audits.

Canadian Public Accountability Board (CPAB)—an independent oversight body whose mandate is to promote high-quality external audits of publicly listed companies. One of its core responsibilities is conducting regular inspections of participating audit firms.

AN OVERVIEW OF THE CANADIAN PUBLIC ACCOUNTING INDUSTRY

LO **1** Describe the public accounting industry.

Public Accounting Firms

There are currently more than 5000 public accounting firms in Canada. These firms range in size from a sole practitioner to the more than 5600 professional staff employed by Canada's largest public accounting firm, Deloitte LLP (Table 2-1). Four size categories are used to describe public accounting firms: "Big Four" international firms, national network firms, large local and regional firms, and small local firms.

Big Four International Firms The four largest public accounting firms in Canada are called the "Big Four" and are the first four firms listed in Table 2-1. These international firms have offices throughout Canada and the world and audit nearly all of the largest companies in Canada and worldwide, and many smaller companies as well.

National Network Firms Four firms in Canada are called national network firms because they have offices in most major cities. These firms are large but considerably smaller than the Big Four. The national network firms perform the same services as the Big Four firms and compete directly with them for clients. Each national firm is affiliated with firms in other countries and therefore has international capability.

Table 2-1	Revenue and Other Data for the Largest Public Accounting Firms in Canada				
2015 Size by Revenue	**Firm**	**Revenue (000)**	**Partners**	**Professionals**	**Canadian Offices**
Big Four					
1	Deloitte LLP	2 088 000	886	5 626	56
2	KPMG LLP	1 324 162	669	3 902	37
3	Pricewaterhouse Coopers LLP	1 290 000	533	4 381	27
4	Ernst & Young LLP	1 111 000	356	3 283	17
National Network					
5	Grant Thornton Canada	597 000	378	2 702	143
6	MNP LLP	597 000	412	1 256	60
7	BDO Canada LLP	534 000	442	2 382	118
8	Collins Barrow	213 500	238	858	50
Regional and Large Local[1]					
9	Richter	101 900	61	417	3
10	Mallette	71 781	75	650	28
11	Crowe Soberman LLP	40 360	26	108	1
11	Crowe MacKay LLP	38 400	34	165	8
12	HLB/Schwartz Levitsky Feldman	38 000	49	182	6

[1] Only the five largest firms in this category are listed.

Source: Based on Gundi Jeffrey, "Canada's accounting Top 30," *The Bottom Line*, April 2016, pp. 13–21.

Regional and Large Local Firms Regional and large local firms are firms with professional staffs of more than 50 people that service a specific geographic market. There are fewer than 50 public accounting firms in this category. Some have only one office and serve clients primarily within commuting distance. Others have several offices in a province or region and serve clients within a larger radius. These firms compete with other public accounting firms, including international Big Four firms, for clients. Many of the regional and local firms are affiliated with associations of public accounting firms to share resources for such matters as technical information and continuing education.

Small Local Firms Most of these public accounting firms have fewer than 25 professionals in a single office. Many small local firms do not perform audits and primarily perform reviews and compilations along with accounting and tax services. Those that do perform audits are primarily for smaller businesses, municipalities, and not-for-profit organizations, although some do have one or two clients with public ownership.

Structure of Public Accounting Firms

The organizational form used by many public accounting firms is either a sole proprietorship or a partnership, although most provinces allow special-purpose limited liability partnerships or professional corporations. In a typical firm, several professionals join together to practise as partners, offering auditing and other services. The partners normally hire professional staff to assist them in their work.

The organizational hierarchy in a typical public accounting firm includes partners, managers, supervisors, seniors or in-charge auditors, and staff accountants, with a new

Table 2-2	Staff Levels and Responsibilities	
Staff Level	**Average Experience**	**Typical Responsibilities**
Staff accountant	0–2 years	Performs most of the detailed audit work.
Senior or in-charge auditor	2–5 years	Coordinates and is responsible for the audit field work, including supervising and reviewing staff work.
Manager	5–7 years	Helps the in-charge plan and manage the audit, reviews the in-charge's work, and manages relations with the client. A manager may be responsible for more than one engagement at the same time.
Senior manager	7–10 years	Leads the engagement and reviews the team's work. Works directly with the partner and assists in client relationship.
Partner	10+ years	Leads the engagement, reviews the overall audit work, and is involved in significant audit decisions. A partner has the ultimate responsibility for conducting the audit and maintaining client relations.

employee usually starting as a staff accountant and spending two or three years in each classification before achieving partner status. The titles of the positions vary from firm to firm, but the basic structure is the same in all of them. When we refer to "the auditor," we mean the particular person performing some aspect of a financial statement audit. It is common to have one or more auditors from each level on larger engagements.

Table 2-2 summarizes the experience and responsibility of each classification. The hierarchical nature of public accounting firms helps promote competence and high-quality audits, as individuals at each level of the audit supervise and review the work of others at the level just below them in the organizational structure. A new staff accountant is supervised directly by the senior or in-charge auditor. The in-charge, as well as the manager and partner, will review the staff accountant's work. It is important to note that not only the staff accountant's work is reviewed, but also that of the in-charge, the manager, the senior manager, and the partner. This is all part of ensuring audit quality.

Requirements to be a Public Accountant

The requirements to become a public accountant are quite rigorous, involving obtaining an undergraduate degree and the Chartered Professional Accountant (CPA) designation, which requires completion of graduate level education, professional exams, and practical experience. The CPA must also have a public accountant's licence.

CONCEPT CHECK

C2-1 How are public accounting firms organized?

Students enrolled in the CPA program are expected to develop two kinds of competencies during their period of practical experience: pervasive qualities and skills, and six technical competencies (financial reporting, strategy and governance, management accounting, audit and assurance, finance, and taxation). Those students who plan to be public accountants must complete the assurance and taxation electives in the professional education program and meet specific chargeable hour requirements at an authorized CPA training office.

What type of public accounting firm would you prefer to work for—a large or a small firm? You might consider the types of clients and the services offered by the firm. The large public accounting firms tend to offer a full range of assurance and nonassurance services, and have a wide variety of clients, in terms of both size and industry. They also perform the majority of public company audits. Small firms tend to have small and medium-sized clients in a variety of industries. However, some small firms do specialize in particular industries. For instance, a major focus of the Toronto firm of Cowperthwaite Metha is small, not-for-profit organizations (which includes about 120 childcare centres). New staff accountants in small firms are given a variety of clients and tasks and start handling clients very quickly. In contrast, given their breadth of services and clients, large firms often assign new staff accountants to a few clients with specific tasks.

Apart from the types of clients, the work environments of large firms can be very different from small firms. One recent graduate interviewed in *Career Incubator*, an online career magazine for Canadian students and graduates, described the different work environments: "If you want a relaxed, friendlier environment, it's better to work for a smaller firm. But if you are a very outgoing, competitive person, then you may like a bigger firm better." Other things to consider when deciding on large versus small firms include the following:

- Large firms often hire in big groups with 40 or more new accountants starting at once. This can create a lot of pressure to compete and work overtime. But it also means new accountants have several peers to share experiences with, whereas those in small firms may not.

- Large firms tend to invest a lot of money in formal training and mentoring, whereas small firms cannot do that and promote more "learning as you go." One new accountant explains, "I really had to learn on the job. It's good for my career, but it's tough at the beginning." Also, you need to depend upon your supervisors to train you. This can be challenging at small firms "when the people that are supposed to be training you are very busy handling their own workloads."

- For those new accountants who want to see other parts of Canada or the world, large international firms offer many opportunities for relocation or short-term assignments in other countries.

Sources: Vicky Tobianah, "What size accounting firm should you work for—small or large?" *Career Incubator,* September 13, 2011, accessed June 22, 2017, at **http://talentegg.ca/incubator/2011/09/13/what-size-accounting-firm-should-you-work-at-small-or-large/**. Cowperthwaite Metha, *About Us*, accessed June 22, 2017, at **http://187gerrard.com/about/**.

While public accountants all share the same skill set and work in the same industry, the work environments of larger firms and smaller firms do differ. Auditing in Action 2-1 provides insights from recent accounting graduates on their experiences at different public accounting firms.

LO **2** Identify the organizations that affect the public accounting profession and their role.

ORGANIZATIONS AFFECTING THE CANADIAN PUBLIC ACCOUNTING PROFESSION

Financial statement users trust auditors to attest to the integrity of financial statements. In order to maintain that trust, auditors must consistently perform high-quality audits. There are several organizations, which we discuss in this section, that provide oversight, develop standards and professional guidance, and institute educational programs to increase the likelihood of high audit quality and professional conduct.

CPA Canada

CPA Canada, which represents the CPA profession nationally and internationally, is the umbrella organization for the CPA designation and provincial accounting bodies. CPA Canada plays a key role in audit quality. It supports the setting of accounting, auditing, and assurance standards for business, not-for-profit organizations, and government. It also enhances audit quality through several collaborative efforts with regulators, such as the Canadian Public Accountability Board (CPAB).

Another important role of CPA Canada is its assistance to the provincial accounting bodies in developing uniform standards of qualification for admission of CPAs and maintaining appropriate standards of professional conduct. It is responsible for developing the CPA Professional Education Program (CPA PEP) and the CPA Common Final Examination (CFE).

CPA Canada also provides a range of member services and professional literature; undertakes research and develops guidance on current issues in accounting, assurance, financial reporting, risk management, and governance; and fosters relationships with key stakeholders nationally and internationally. It plays an important role in promoting the accounting profession through organizing national conferences and advertising campaigns, encouraging new assurance services, and developing specialist certifications to help market and ensure the quality of services in specialized practice areas.

Provincial CPA Organizations

Individual CPAs are not members of CPA Canada, but rather members of their provincial CPA organizations. These provincial accounting bodies are responsible for maintaining admission, licensing, and mandatory continuing education requirements; conducting reviews of public accounting firms; investigating complaints; and disciplining members, firms, and students.

Auditing and Assurance Standards Board (AASB)

Canada's **Auditing and Assurance Standards Board (AASB)** has the authority, through federal and provincial business corporations acts and securities legislation, to set generally accepted auditing standards (GAAS) for financial statement audits. The AASB also sets the standards for other services offered by public accountants, such as **assurance standards** for nonfinancial information and review engagements, as well as standards for nonassurance services such as compilations and agreed-upon procedures engagements. While the AASB is committed to adopting International Standards on Auditing (ISAs) as Canadian Auditing Standards (CASs), it plays an important role in ensuring that the Canadian point of view is presented to the International Auditing and Assurance Standards Board (IAASB). The AASB is funded by CPA Canada and its board members are volunteers appointed by the Auditing and Assurance Standards Oversight Board (AASOB).

Auditing and Assurance Standards Board (AASB)— an independent board of CPA Canada that has the responsibility for issuing auditing and assurance standards for financial statement audits and other types of assurance and related services engagements.

Assurance standards—standards for assurance engagements other than historical financial statements. The requirements are included in "Other Canadian Standards" in the *CPA Canada Handbook—Assurance*. Assurance standards are issued by the Auditing and Assurance Standards Board.

International Auditing and Assurance Standards Board

The International Auditing and Assurance Standards Board (IAASB) is an independent standard-setting body that sets international standards for auditing and assurance, and other related standards. It is also responsible for facilitating the convergence of international and national auditing and assurance standards. As of the time of writing, over 113 jurisdictions are using or are in the process of adopting International Standards on Auditing (ISAs). The IAASB consists of a full-time chair and 17 volunteer members, who are appointed by the International Federation of Accountants (IFAC).

Canadian Public Accountability Board (CPAB)

After the Sarbanes-Oxley Act of 2002 was passed in the United States creating the Public Company Accounting Oversight Board (PCAOB), a similar body was implemented in Canada called the Canadian Public Accountability Board (CPAB) (**www.cpab-ccrc.ca**). The CPAB's mission is to contribute to the public's confidence in the integrity of financial reporting in reporting issuers in Canada by promoting effective regulation and high-quality, independent auditing. (The term "reporting issuers" is used to describe publicly held companies and mutual funds listed on a Canadian stock exchange that are required to file annual audited financial statements with their listing exchange.)

In order to achieve its mission, the CPAB focuses on four priorities: effective inspections, risk management, thought leadership, and stakeholder engagement. A key role of the CPAB is its practice inspection program. Public accounting firms are required to register with CPAB and are subject to quality control inspections by CPAB if they audit "reporting issuers." At the time of writing, there were 284 registered firms on the CPAB website.[1] Of that total, there were 153 Canadian, 58 American, 13 Australian, 11 British, and 6 Hong Kong firms, with the remainder from various countries around the world.

In addition to its practice inspection program, the CPAB plays an important role in enhancing audit quality through its thought leadership and stakeholder engagement activities. For instance, the CPAB has hosted several Audit Quality Symposiums, where international regulators, CPA Canada, auditors, and various other stakeholders shared their views on ways to enhance audit quality.

Public Company Accounting Oversight Board (PCAOB)

Triggered by the bankruptcies and alleged audit failures involving such companies as Enron and WorldCom, the Sarbanes–Oxley Act is considered by many to be the most important legislation affecting the American auditing profession since the 1933 and 1934 Securities Acts. The provisions of the Act dramatically changed the relationship between publicly held companies and their audit firms.

The Sarbanes–Oxley Act established the Public Company Accounting Oversight Board (PCAOB), appointed and overseen by the U.S. Securities and Exchange Commission (SEC). Like the CPAB, the PCAOB provides oversight for auditors of public companies and performs inspections of the audit firms. However, unlike the CPAB, it also establishes auditing and quality control standards for public company audits. This is a key difference between the Canadian and American approaches. In Canada, although the CPAB will provide feedback on the standard-setting process, standard setting is the AASB's responsibility. Another difference is that auditing standards for private company audits are issued by the American Institute of Certified Public Accountants (**www.aicpa.org**). The AICPA, which is similar to CPA Canada, is the umbrella organization for the U.S. Certified Public Accountant designation and the state Certified Public Accountant associations. In Canada, there is only one set of auditing standards and one standard setter (the AASB).

In the United States, the PCAOB conducts inspections of registered accounting firms to assess their compliance with the rules of the PCAOB and SEC, professional

---

AUDITING IN ACTION 2-2
Canada's Role in the Global Standards Arena

Despite being a relatively small country, Canada plays a prominent role in developing International Assurance Standards. Since its first meeting in 1978, several Canadians have served on the International Audit and Assurance Standards Board (IAASB), acted as technical advisors, and chaired several task forces to develop or clarify various standards. In 1985–87, Canadian Justin Fryer was the chair of the IAASB.

Darrell Jensen, the current chair of the Canadian Auditing and Assurance Standards Board (AASB), explains what this means for Canada's reputation and its influence in the international standards arena: "Our participation is very strong with the International Auditing and Assurance Standards Board's activities, and Canada's voice there is respected. I'm impressed with the influence we've had on the development of ISAs. I also think that the perspective we gain by actively participating at the international level gives us a broader perspective and has benefits when we develop Canadian-made standards."

Jensen's comments also highlight that Canada does not automatically adopt ISAs, as he elaborates: "I would also note that we have the ability to make amendments to ISAs for Canadian-specific circumstances when we feel that it is in the public interest for Canadians." A key part of the AASB's standard-setting process, which ensures that the standards are of high quality, is research and consultation with all stakeholders—not just the audit profession.

Sources: IAASB, *International Auditing and Assurance Board: A Brief History of its Development and Progress*, 2007. Daniella Girgenti & Glenn Rioux, in "She said, he said: Q&A with auditing standards board leaders," *CPA Magazine*, April 2014. Excerpt reprinted with permission of the Chartered Professional Accountants of Canada, Toronto, Canada. Any changes to the original material are the sole responsibility of the author (and/or publisher) and have not been reviewed or endorsed by the Chartered Professional Accountants of Canada.

---

[1] Based on Canadian Public Accountability Board, "Participating firms," accessed August 11, 2017, at **http://www.cpab-ccrc.ca/en/firms/Pages/default.aspx**.

standards, and each firm's own quality control policies. The PCAOB requires annual inspections of accounting firms that audit more than 100 issuers and inspections of other registered firms at least once every three years. Similar to CPAB, violations could result in disciplinary action by the PCAOB and be reported to the SEC. In 2016, 40 Canadian audit firms were registered with the PCAOB; 31 of them are subject to inspection because they regularly issue audit reports on U.S. issuers.[2] Between 2005 and 2015, the PCAOB conducted 137 inspections of Canadian audit firms; the vast majority of these inspections were conducted jointly with the CPAB.

Provincial Securities Commissions

Securities regulation in Canada is a provincial matter; therefore, companies that issue securities in Canada must abide by rules promulgated by the **provincial securities commissions**. The national umbrella organization, the Canadian Securities Administrators (www.csa-acvm.ca), sets policies to which the member commissions agree to adhere. The provincial securities commissions are responsible for administering the purchase and sale of securities within their jurisdictions.

Provincial securities commissions—provincial organizations with quasi-legal status that administer securities regulations within their jurisdictions.

Actions of the securities commissions have important implications for public company auditors. For instance, the CSA was responsible for the requirement that listed companies' auditors must register with and be inspected by the CPAB. Similarly, when the Canadian audit profession proposed that auditors issue audit opinions on internal controls, as is the requirement in the United States, the British Columbia Securities Commission successfully stopped this proposal on the basis of the unnecessary costs for its reporting issuers (the majority of whom are small).

The provincial securities commissions also have the ability to prosecute public accountants and the companies they audit. Recently, the Ontario Securities Commission (OSC), the largest securities commission, fined the CEO and the board chair of Zungui Haixi Corporation for several breaches of Ontario securities law, which included imposing limitations on the scope of the audit procedures of Zungui's auditor during its audit. Although the OSC rarely makes allegations against auditors, it did in this case. In fact, it was the fourth time such allegations have been levelled against an auditor by the OSC over the past 23 years. However, in that same year, the OSC also made allegations regarding another audit and many observers consider this to be an indication that Canadian auditors are under greater scrutiny than in the past.[3]

Securities and Exchange Commission (SEC)

Many large Canadian companies are listed on American stock exchanges, and therefore must meet the requirements of the **Securities and Exchange Commission (SEC)**. The SEC assists in providing investors in public corporations with reliable information upon which to make investment decisions. Although the SEC has taken the position that accounting principles and auditing standards should be set by the PCAOB or the profession, it still has considerable influence in setting generally accepted accounting principles and disclosure requirements for financial statements.

Securities and Exchange Commission (SEC)—a U.S. federal agency that oversees the orderly conduct of the securities markets. The SEC assists in providing investors in public corporations with reliable information upon which to make investment decisions.

As is the case for Canada's securities regulators, the SEC plays an important role for those public accountants who audit public companies. The SEC has the power to establish rules regarding public accountants as well as to prosecute them (and the companies that they audit) for violating SEC regulations. While the majority of these enforcement actions are against American auditors, the SEC has the authority to prosecute any auditor, irrespective of location, in connection with an audit of a company listed on a U.S. stock exchange. For instance, in the past few years, the SEC has brought enforcement actions against two Canadian audit partners that had violated the SEC's

---

[2] Public Company Accountability Oversight Board, accessed October 20, 2016, at **https://pcaobus. org/Registration/Firms/pages/registeredfirms.aspx**.

[3] Based on Jeff Buckstein, "New audit allegations against E&Y," *The Bottom Line*, September 2013.

auditor independence rules, two U.K. audit partners for deficient audits of a British subsidiary that had committed accounting fraud, twelve Brazilian partners for issuing materially false audit reports and altering working papers to conceal audit deficiencies, and four Chinese Big Four affiliate firms for refusing to produce audit work papers and other documents related to China-based companies under investigation by the SEC.

Legal Liability

The ability of individuals as well as clients to sue public accounting firms exerts considerable influence on the way in which public accountants conduct themselves and audits. As the recent case of Sino-Forest Corp. highlights, it can be a costly process. In that case, an Ontario judge approved a $117 million deal to settle allegations made by investors that Ernst & Young failed to conduct an appropriate audit.

CONCEPT CHECK

C2-2 What external factors ensure that audit and assurance engagements are completed at a high standard of quality?

C2-3 Which organizations develop and maintain the standards that public accountants use? Identify three organizations involved in standard setting for the PA profession.

LO **3** Describe how the *CPA Canada Handbook—Assurance* is organized.

AN OVERVIEW OF CPA CANADA ASSURANCE STANDARDS

The *CPA Canada Handbook—Assurance* represents the authoritative requirements underlying the financial statement audits, other types of assurance engagements, and related services activities carried out by public accountants. Table 2-3 provides an overview of how the handbook is organized.

Table 2-3	Overview of the *CPA Canada Handbook—Assurance*
Section	**Explanation**
Preface	This section explains how the Handbook is organized. It also explains the authority of the various sections. The practitioner must comply with all of the Canadian standards relevant to the engagement.
Canadian Standards on Quality Control	The standards for public accounting firms' systems of quality control.
Canadian Auditing Standards (CAS)	The standards for the financial statement audit.
Other Canadian Standards (OCS)	The standards for (1) audits of information other than the financial statements, (2) reviews of financial statements and other information, and (3) other related services engagements.
Assurance and Related Services Guidelines (AuG)	From time to time, the AASB issues guidelines for an urgent issue or a unique Canadian circumstance. Guidelines have the same status and authority as application and other explanatory material in the standards. However, guidelines do not impose requirements; rather, they are meant to assist the practitioner.
Canadian Standard on Association Standard (CSOA 5000)	This standard deals with engagements that are within the scope of the Handbook. The purpose of this section is to explain the public accountant's professional responsibilities when: • the entity requests consent to use the PA's report or name in connection with accompanying information; • the entity requests to use the PA's report in another language; and • the PA becomes aware of inappropriate use of report or name.

Table 2-4	An Overview of Canadian Auditing Standards

Sections	Topic
200–299	General Principles and Responsibilities
300–499	Risk Assessment and Response
500–599	Audit Evidence
600–699	Using Work of Others
700–799	Audit Conclusions and Reporting
800–899	Specialized Areas

Based on Chartered Professional Accountants of Canada (CPA Canada)

Canadian Auditing Standards

LO 4 Use Canadian Auditing Standards to explain the purpose of and the principles underlying the financial audit.

The Canadian Auditing Standards (CAS), which are the standards for the financial statement audit, are based upon ISAs originally developed and released by the IAASB of the International Federation of Accountants (IFAC). The CASs are organized as shown in Table 2-4.

These standards are organized around the following principles:

- Purpose of an audit (Purpose)
- Personal responsibilities of the auditor (Responsibilities)
- Auditor actions in performing the audit (Performance)
- Reporting (Reporting)

These principles, which are discussed in CAS 200, are summarized in Figure 2-1. The principles are not specific enough to provide any meaningful guide to practitioners;

CAS

Figure 2-1	Principles Underlying the Financial Statement Audit

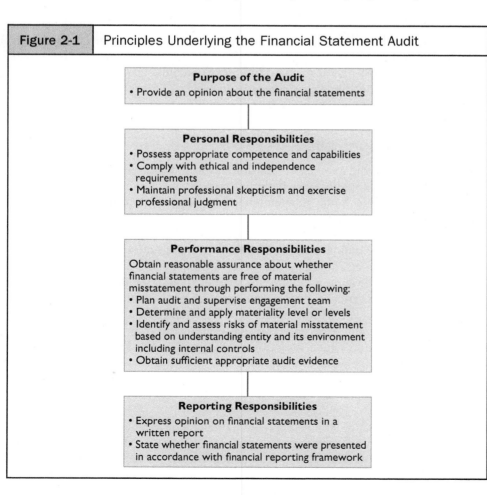

Purpose of the Audit
- Provide an opinion about the financial statements

Personal Responsibilities
- Possess appropriate competence and capabilities
- Comply with ethical and independence requirements
- Maintain professional skepticism and exercise professional judgment

Performance Responsibilities
Obtain reasonable assurance about whether financial statements are free of material misstatement through performing the following:
- Plan audit and supervise engagement team
- Determine and apply materiality level or levels
- Identify and assess risks of material misstatement based on understanding entity and its environment including internal controls
- Obtain sufficient appropriate audit evidence

Reporting Responsibilities
- Express opinion on financial statements in a written report
- State whether financial statements were presented in accordance with financial reporting framework

however, they provide a framework that defines the purpose of the financial statement audit as well as the auditor's ethical and professional responsibilities. This framework helps auditors to fulfill the following overall objectives of financial statement audit (CAS 200.11):

- Providing reasonable assurance that the financial statements are not materially misstated;
- Considering both potential fraud and error;
- Communicating whether the financial statements comply with an applicable financial reporting framework using the expression of an opinion;
- Reporting on the financial statements; and
- Communicating auditor findings in accordance with the CASs.

PURPOSE OF THE FINANCIAL STATEMENT AUDIT

The purpose of an audit is to provide financial statement users with an opinion issued by the auditor on whether the financial statements are presented fairly, in all material respects, in accordance with the applicable financial reporting framework. That opinion enhances the users' confidence in the information presented in the financial statements.

An audit is conducted based on the premise that management is responsible for the preparation of the financial statements in accordance with the applicable financial reporting framework selected by management, and that management has designed, implemented, and maintained internal controls relevant to the preparation and presentation of financial statements that are free of material misstatements.

An auditor also presumes that management will provide the auditor with access to all information relevant to the preparation and presentation of financial statements, including unrestricted access to persons within the entity from whom the auditor may obtain audit evidence. Canadian Auditing Standards state that the auditor can conduct the audit only if management agrees to provide this supporting evidence and both acknowledges and understands its responsibilities.

Personal Responsibilities

Principles related to the auditor's responsibilities in the audit stress important qualities that the auditor should possess, including professional competence and due care, compliance with ethical and independence requirements, and professional skepticism and professional judgment.

Exercise Professional Competence and Due Care Auditors are responsible for having appropriate competence and capabilities to perform the audit. This is normally interpreted as requiring the auditor to have formal education in auditing and accounting, adequate practical experience for the work being performed, and continuing professional education. Recent CPAB reports clearly demonstrate that auditors must be technically qualified and experienced in those industries in which their clients are engaged. In any case in which the public accountant or the PA's assistants are not qualified to perform the work, a professional obligation exists to acquire the requisite knowledge and skills, suggest someone else who is qualified to perform the work, or decline the engagement.

CAS **Comply With Ethical and Independence Requirements** CAS 200 states that auditors must comply with ethical requirements and independence. The relevant independence and ethical requirements—which include integrity, objectivity, confidentiality, and professional behaviour—are outlined in rules of professional conduct applicable to the practice of public accounting and issued by various professional accounting bodies. The provincial CPA bodies have harmonized their rules of professional conduct so that, generally, the same set of rules applies to all PAs in Canada. The rules of professional conduct and auditing standards stress the need for independence in an audit engagement. Of particular importance are requirements for public accounting firms to follow several practices to increase the likelihood of independence of all personnel. For example, there are established procedures on larger audits when there is a dispute between management and the auditors. Specific methods to ensure that auditors maintain their independence and comply with other relevant ethical requirements are studied in Chapter 3.

Maintain Professional Skepticism and Exercise Professional Judgment Auditors are responsible for maintaining professional skepticism and exercising professional judgment throughout the planning and performance of the audit. Auditing standards describe professional skepticism as an attitude that includes a questioning mind, being alert to conditions that might indicate possible misstatements due to fraud or error, and critically assessing audit evidence. Simply stated, auditors are to remain alert for the presence of material misstatements, whether due to fraud or error, throughout the planning and performance of an audit.

In making judgments about the presence of material misstatements, auditors are responsible for applying relevant training, knowledge, and experience in making informed decisions about the courses of action that are appropriate in the circumstances of the audit engagement. Auditors are responsible for fulfilling their duties diligently and carefully.

Performance Responsibilities

Responsibilities related to the performance of the audit relate to auditor actions concerning evidence accumulation and other activities during the actual conduct of the audit. CASs require that the financial statement audit be conducted using a risk-based approach, which is explained in detail in Part 2 of this text. To express an opinion on the financial statements, the auditor obtains reasonable assurance about whether the financial statements as a whole are free from material misstatement, whether due to fraud or error. To obtain reasonable assurance, the auditor fulfills several performance responsibilities.

Adequate Planning and Supervision Adequate planning should set out the engagement team responsibilities, the nature of the entity's business, risk-related issues, problems that may arise, and a detailed approach to perform the engagement. Supervision is essential in auditing because less experienced staff members often perform a considerable portion of the audit. Supervision includes tracking the progress of the audit engagement, and considering the competence and capabilities of individual team members (including whether they have sufficient time to carry out their work and understand their instructions). It also includes addressing significant matters that arise and modifying the planned approach accordingly, as well as identifying matters that require consultation with or consideration by more experienced team members.

Determine and Apply Materiality Levels Because the auditor's opinion is about whether the financial statements contain material misstatements, the auditor is responsible for determining and applying an appropriate materiality level or levels throughout the audit. A misstatement is considered material if knowledge of the misstatement will affect a decision of a reasonable user of the financial statements. Chapters 7 and 19 discuss how auditors determine and apply materiality levels.

Identify and Assess Risks of Material Misstatement To adequately perform the audit, the auditor is responsible for identifying and assessing the risks that the financial statements contain material misstatements and then performing further audit procedures in response to those risks to determine if material misstatements exist. To adequately assess the risk of material misstatements, the auditor must have an understanding of the client's business and industry, which helps the auditor to identify significant client business risks and the risk of significant misstatements in the financial statements. For example, to audit a bank, an auditor must understand the nature of the bank's operations, the regulations applicable to banks, and the risks affecting significant accounts such as loan loss reserves.

One of the most widely accepted concepts in the theory and practice of auditing is the importance of the client's system of internal control for mitigating client business risks, safeguarding assets and records, and generating reliable financial information. If the auditor is convinced that the client has an excellent system that includes adequate internal controls for providing reliable data, the amount of audit evidence to be accumulated can be significantly less than when controls are not adequate. In some instances, internal control may be so inadequate that it is not possible to conduct an audit.

Sufficient Appropriate Evidence The auditor is responsible for obtaining sufficient appropriate audit evidence about whether material misstatements exist through designing and implementing appropriate responses to the assessed risks. Decisions about how much and what types of evidence to accumulate for a given set of circumstances require professional judgment. A major portion of this book is concerned with the study of evidence accumulation and the circumstances affecting the amount and types needed.

Reporting

The requirements related to reporting note that the auditor is responsible for expressing an opinion in the form of a written report about whether the financial statements are presented fairly, in all material respects, in accordance with the applicable financial reporting framework. This opinion is based on the evaluation of audit evidence obtained and the auditor's findings. If the auditor has no reservations, then an audit report with an unmodified audit opinion is issued. Figure 2-2 shows the specific wording for an auditor's report, with an unmodified audit opinion, of a private company, Hillsburg Hardware, which we will be referring to throughout the text. The report describes the financial statements being audited, the auditor's unmodified opinion, and the basis for the opinion; it also describes the responsibilities of management, those charged with governance of the entity being audited, and the auditor.

CONCEPT CHECK

C2-4 Describe the principles underlying Canadian Auditing Standards and explain their purpose.

If the auditor has reservations, the opinion must be modified (referred to as "qualified") to explain the nature of the reservations (to be explained in Chapter 19). If the auditor is unable to modify the audit opinion, then the auditor should withdraw or resign from the engagement. The audit report and the purpose of the individual sections are discussed in Chapter 19. We will also highlight in that chapter that the audit report, which has been basically unchanged for over 40 years, has recently undergone a significant facelift.

Figure 2-2 | The Auditor's Report Explained

INDEPENDENT AUDITOR'S REPORT

The report is addressed to the members or shareholders of the organization.	To the Shareholders of Hillsburg Hardware Limited:

This section sets out the basic details of the engagement—the applicable reporting period, name of company, and what was audited.

Opinion

We have audited the accompanying financial statements of Hillsburg Hardware Limited, which comprise the balance sheet as at December 31, 2018, the statements of earning and surplus and cash flows for the year ended, and notes, comprising a summary of significant accounting policies and other explanatory information.

The auditor sets out his or her overall finding in an opinion and the applicable accounting framework (ASPE). This is an example of an unmodified or "clean" audit opinion.

In our opinion, the accompanying financial statements present fairly, in all material respects, the financial position of Hillsburg Hardware Limited as at December 31, 2018, and the results of operations and its cash flows for the year then ended in accordance with Canadian accounting standards for private enterprises.

The auditor explains the basis of conclusion—have conducted audit in accordance with Canadian GAAS and obtained sufficient and appropriate audit evidence. Also informs readers that auditor is independent and in compliance with ethical requirements.

Basis for opinion

We conducted our audit in accordance with Canadian generally accepted auditing standards. Our responsibilities under those standards are further described in the Auditor's Responsibilities for the Audit of the Financial Statements section of our report. We are independent of the Company in accordance with the ethical requirements that are relevant to our audit of the financial statements in Canada, and we have fulfilled our other ethical responsibilities in accordance with these requirements. We believe that the audit evidence we have obtained is sufficient and appropriate to provide a basis for our opinion.

Responsibilities of Management and Those Charged with Governance for the Financial Statements

Management is responsible for preparing the financial statements according to applicable accounting framework (in this case ASPE), for internal controls in the company, and for assessing the going concern assumption.

Management is responsible for the preparation and fair presentation of these financial statements in accordance with Canadian accounting standards for private enterprises, and for such internal control as management determines is necessary to enable the preparation of financial statements that are free from material misstatements, whether due to fraud or error.

In preparing the financial statements, management is responsible for assessing the Company's ability to continue as a going concern, disclosing, as applicable, matters related to the going concern using the going concern basis of accounting unless management either intends to liquidate the Company or to cease operations, or has no realistic alternative but to do so.

Highlights those charged with governance responsibility.

Those charged with governance are responsible for overseeing the Company's financial reporting process.

(continued)

| Figure 2-2 | (Continued) |

Responsibilities for the Audit of Financial Statements

Our objectives are to obtain reasonable assurance about whether the financial statements as a whole are free from material misstatement, whether due to fraud or error, and to issue the auditor's report that includes our opinion. Reasonable assurance is a high level of assurance, but not a guarantee that an audit conducted in accordance with Canadian generally accepted auditing standards will always detect a material misstatement when it exists. Misstatements can arise from fraud or error and are considered material if, individually or in aggregate, they could reasonably be expected to influence the economic decisions of users taken on the basis of these financial statements.

As part of an audit in accordance with Canadian generally accepted audit standards, we exercise professional judgment and maintain professional skepticism throughout the audit. We also:

> This section provides an overview of the objective of the audit, explains the concepts of reasonable assurance and materiality, and provides details of the auditor's responsibilities. The last paragraph highlights the auditor's reporting responsibilities to those charged with governance (the audit committee or the board of directors) of Hillsburg.

- Identify and assess the risks of material misstatement of the financial statements, whether due to fraud or error; design and perform audit procedures responsive to those risks; and obtain audit evidence that is sufficient and appropriate to provide a basis for our opinion. The risk of not detecting a material misstatement resulting from fraud is higher than one resulting from error, as fraud may involve collusion, forgery, intentional omissions, misrepresentations, or the override of internal control.
- Obtain an understanding of internal control relevant to the audit in order to design audit procedures that are appropriate in the circumstances, but not for the purpose of expressing an opinion on the effectiveness of the Company's internal control.
- Evaluate the appropriateness of accounting policies used and the reasonableness of accounting estimates and related disclosures made by management.
- Conclude on the appropriateness of management's use of the going concern basis of accounting and, based on the audit evidence obtained, whether a material uncertainty exists related to events and conditions that may cast significant doubt on the Entity's ability to continue as a going concern. If we conclude that a material uncertainty exists, we are required to draw attention in our auditor's report to the related disclosures in the financial statements, or if such disclosures are inadequate, to modify our opinion. Our conclusions are based on the audit evidence obtained up to the date of our auditor's report. However, future events or conditions may cause the Entity to cease to continue as a going concern.
- Evaluate the overall presentation, structure, and content of the financial statements, including the disclosures, and whether the financial statements represent the underlying transaction and events in a manner that achieves fair presentations.

We communicate with those charged with governance regarding, among other matters, the planned scope and timing of the audit and significant audit findings, including any deficiencies in internal control that we identify during the audit.

[signature of]

Boritz, Kao, Kadous & Co., Ltd.

March 1, 2019

Halifax, Nova Scotia

LO **5** Understand the drivers of audit quality and explain the competing pressures auditors face that threaten audit quality.

THE DRIVERS OF AUDIT QUALITY

Many people think of the financial statement audit as a black box. When one considers that the only piece of information that stakeholders receive from auditors is the audit report, a highly standardized report that essentially provides a pass/fail judgment (see Figure 2-2), there is certainly merit to this claim. Recently, there has been a growing consensus that more transparency into the audit process is a good thing for all stakeholders involved. As mentioned in this chapter's opening vignette, around the globe, several initiatives are underway to increase the transparency of the audit and to enhance audit quality. Later in the textbook, we will discuss one such initiative, the new and revised audit reporting standards, which clarify and expand auditors' reporting responsibilities.

One problem with providing more insight into the audit process is that there is no clear consensus over the definition of audit quality. Despite the difficulty in defining audit quality, there is much agreement that a quality audit would include a rigorous audit process and quality control procedures, with an appropriate level of professional skepticism, and that complies with professional standards. Another essential element would be that the audit team was sufficiently knowledgeable, skilled, and experienced, and had sufficient time to perform the audit work.

In its report *Building Sustainable Audit Quality*, the CPAB emphasized that the key to providing high-quality audits is the audit firm culture, which maintains the appropriate balance between commercialism (managing the economic business of the firm) and professionalism (sustainable high-quality audits). Based upon its inspections, the CPAB recommends that firms can improve audit quality if they focus on four key areas: build the right teams; provide the right support; conduct in-process reviews; and assign accountability for audit quality, as illustrated in Figure 2-3.

Build the Right Teams The people conducting the audit have the greatest impact on audit quality. As highlighted in the standards, audit teams need to have the right technical competence and industry experience. In addition, teams need to have sufficient time to perform a high-quality audit. The CPAB recommends that firms perform periodic reviews of all engagements to assess the teams' strengths and weaknesses and their workloads.

Provide the Right Support An open consultation environment within the firm can improve audit quality. Partners and staff should feel comfortable to consult with the appropriate technical leaders when they do not have the necessary specialized knowledge. Reviews by technical experts outside of the engagement team can also improve audit quality.

Figure 2-3	Key Areas of Audit Quality

Source: Reproduced with permission of Canadian Public Accountability Board, *Building Sustainable Audit Quality*, June 2014.

Conduct In-Process Reviews Rather than conducting the reviews when the audit is complete, conduct reviews during the audit engagement to have a greater impact on audit quality. For instance, the reviews may lead teams to reconsider their audit approach and perform different or additional procedures before the audit is complete. These reviews can also serve as important teaching and learning opportunities.

Assign Accountability for Audit Quality When audits fail, the engagement partner is often blamed. However, several functions of the firm contribute to audit quality; therefore, the responsibility for audit quality should be assigned to those specific individuals and included in their job descriptions. Perhaps the most important factor is firm leadership, or what is referred to as "tone at the top." Ultimately, it is the firm's managing board of partners who are responsible for quality assurance.

Audit quality indicators—metrics for measuring audit quality.

In addition, audit quality should be part of performance evaluations and, as discussed in the opening vignette, firms and other stakeholders are developing metrics for measuring audit quality (what is referred to as **audit quality indicators** or AQIs). Some potential metrics are ratio of partners to staff, average years of experience and staff composition, training hours, chargeable hours by staff level, and percentage of high-risk clients. This list is by no means exhaustive, but provides some examples of how to measure audit quality.

CONCEPT CHECK

C2-5 What factors affect audit quality?

The Role of Other Parties in Audit Quality

While the audit team and firms' quality control practices are key drivers of audit quality, there are several organizations that play an important role. In addition, there are other key parties directly involved in the audit process that affect audit quality—management, the audit committee, and (possibly) an internal audit. We will discuss each of these in later chapters.

LO 6 Identify quality control standards and practices within the auditing profession and apply those standards and practices to enhance audit quality.

QUALITY CONTROL

For a public accounting firm, **quality control** comprises the methods used to make sure that the firm meets its professional responsibilities to clients and others. These methods include the organizational structure of the public accounting firm and the procedures the firm establishes. For example, a public accounting firm might have an organizational structure that assures the technical review of every engagement by a partner who has expertise in the client's industry. Auditing standards require each public accounting firm to establish quality control policies and procedures. The standards recognize that a quality control system can provide only reasonable assurance, not a guarantee, that auditing standards are followed.

Quality control—policies and procedures used by a public accounting firm to make sure that the firm meets its professional responsibilities.

Elements of Quality Control

Many elements work together in the quality control process for financial statement audits and review engagements.

Canadian Auditing Standards *CPA Canada Handbook* Section CSQC 1 describes general standards of quality control for firms performing financial statement audits and review engagements. The Canadian Standards on Quality Control (CSQC) are closely related to but distinct from Canadian Auditing Standards. To ensure that the requirements of the auditing standards are met on every audit, a public accounting firm must follow specific quality control procedures consistently on every engagement.

Quality controls are therefore established for the entire public accounting firm, whereas CASs are applicable to individual engagements (and there is a specific standard, CAS 220, which provides quality control standards for individual engagements).

Each firm should document its quality control policies and procedures. Procedures that a public accounting firm employs will depend on the size of the firm, the number of practice offices, and the nature of the practice. The quality control procedures of a 150-office international firm with many complex multinational clients would vary considerably from those of a five-person firm specializing in small audits in one or two industries.

The system of quality control should include policies and procedures that address the six elements. They are listed in Table 2-5 with brief descriptions and procedural examples that firms might use to satisfy the requirement.

External Inspections The provincial CPA organizations conduct practice inspections for two reasons: (1) to protect the public interest by ensuring that public accountants are adhering to professional standards set out in the *CPA Canada Handbook—Assurance*; and (2) to help public accountants improve their professional standards. These inspections, which are mandatory for CPAs in public practice, involve reviewing quality control

Table 2-5	Elements of Quality Control	
Element	**Summary of Requirements**	**Example of a Procedure**
Leadership responsibilities for quality within the firm ("tone at the top")	The firm should promote a culture that quality is essential in performing engagements and should establish policies and procedures that support that culture.	The firm's training programs emphasize the importance of quality work, and this is reinforced in performance evaluation and compensation decisions.
Relevant ethical requirements	All personnel on engagements should maintain independence in fact and in appearance, perform all professional responsibilities with integrity, and maintain objectivity in performing their professional responsibilities.	Each partner and employee must answer an "independence questionnaire" annually, dealing with such things as share ownership and membership on boards of directors.
Acceptance and continuation of clients and engagements	Policies and procedures should be established for deciding whether to accept or continue a client relationship. These policies and procedures should minimize the risk of associating with a client whose management lacks integrity. The firm should also only undertake engagements that can be completed with professional competence.	A client evaluation form, dealing with such matters as predecessor auditor comments and evaluation of management must be prepared for every new client before acceptance.
Human resources	Policies and procedures should be established to provide the firm with reasonable assurance that: • All new personnel are qualified to perform their work competently. • Work is assigned to personnel who have adequate technical training and proficiency. • All personnel participate in continuing professional education and professional development activities that enable them to fulfill their assigned responsibilities. • Personnel selected for advancement have the qualifications necessary for the fulfillment of their assigned responsibilities.	Each professional must be evaluated on every engagement using the firm's individual engagement evaluation report.
Engagement performance	Policies and procedures should exist to ensure that the work performed by engagement personnel meets applicable professional standards, regulatory requirements, and the firm's standards of quality.	The firm's director of accounting and auditing is available for consultation and must approve all engagements before their completion.
Monitoring	Policies and procedures should exist to ensure that the other quality control elements are being effectively applied.	The quality control partner must test the quality control procedures at least annually to ensure that the firm is in compliance.

processes as well as individual audit and/or review engagement files. While inspections are normally completed every three years, they can be done annually if the inspectors conclude that the practice unit does not maintain adequate practice standards.

The provincial practice inspection committee can impose sanctions. These include reinspection the following year and referral to the provincial association's professional conduct committee, which can require the member to take courses, remove the practice unit's right to train students, expel the member from the professional body, and withdraw the member's right to use the appellation "chartered professional accountant."

In addition to the practice inspections, the CPAB conducts annual inspections for audit firms that have 100 or more reporting issuers. There are 14 firms that fall into this category—all of the Big Four plus 10 other firms. CPAB also inspects, at least every two years, firms with between 50 and 99 reporting issuer audits. Over three years, the majority of the 163 Canadian audit firms registered with CPAB are inspected. Many of the foreign firms are subject to oversight by other audit regulators. These firms are inspected periodically based on CPAB's risk analysis.

The CPAB publishes an annual report summarizing its findings, organized by size of firm. From time to time, it may issue a special report regarding specific concerns over audit quality. With regard to its individual firm inspections, it can choose to impose restrictions, such as limiting the right to audit reporting issuers. It can also report the deficiencies to the relevant provincial securities commission (which can also impose sanctions and restrictions). If the member firm does not appropriately address the recommendations for improvement, CPAB could make the individual firm's inspection report public. To date, this has not happened.

External inspections can be beneficial to the profession and individual firms. The profession gains if reviews result in practitioners doing higher quality audits. A firm can also gain if the inspection improves the firm's practices, thereby enhancing its reputation and effectiveness and reducing the likelihood of lawsuits. However, as highlighted in Auditing in Action 2-3, improving audit quality is a trade-off between costs and benefits.

Audit Quality Initiatives Since the global financial crisis in 2008–09, regulators, standard setters, and other key stakeholders have developed several audit quality initiatives that will result in changes to the audit process both in North America and internationally. Recognizing that Canada will be affected by these global initiatives, the CPAB and CPA Canada instituted a research and consultation process, Enhancing Audit Quality (EAQ), to gain stakeholder input on key issues emerging with respect to

AUDITING IN ACTION 2-3
Practice Inspection and Audit Quality

A key objective of practice inspections is to assess whether assurance practitioners and their firms comply with professional standards. Inspections are conducted by qualified PAs licensed by the same provincial association as the practitioner. If the inspectors find any files or quality control procedures unsatisfactory, the PA may be required to revise processes, attend training courses, or have more frequent practice inspections (that the PA would have to pay for).

Similar to the CPAB, the various provincial accounting bodies issue a summary report, *Focus on Inspection Reportable Deficiencies*, to all their practising offices. This report, which is publicly available, summarizes key common deficiencies. For instance, the 2016–17 summary issued by CPA Ontario reported that, of the 580 assurance-based practices inspected, 12 percent needed reinspection and only 1 percent were referred to the Professional Conduct Committee. An area which continues to be of concern is the implementation of quality controls; the report noted that "there were still issues with respect to the cyclical monitoring of completed assurance files." For smaller firms, the lack of resources for monitoring processes can be a challenge, but it is a necessary component of high-quality assurance engagements. With regards to improving audit quality, the report recommended that audit firms should focus on identifying root causes of audit deficiencies and implement action plans.

Source: Based on CPA Ontario, "Focus on practice inspection reportable deficiencies, 2016–17," accessed August 11, 2017, at **https://media. cpaontario.ca/cpa-members/public-practice/practice-inspection/ pdfs/1012page4081.pdf**.

enhancing audit quality globally. The EAQ's steering group, led by the former chair of the Ontario Securities Commission, developed a report of what it considered to be the three top priorities for the Canadian audit profession: auditor independence, auditor reporting, and the role of the audit committee.[4] We will discuss some of the report's recommendations throughout the textbook.

With the publication of the report, the EAQ had fulfilled its mandate. However, audit quality is still very much in the spotlight. For instance, the AASB's strategic plan has identified audit quality as the top priority. Further, the CPAB's focus on leadership and stakeholder engagement has led to several resources and publications on audit quality, including projects concerning consistency of audit execution, auditing in foreign jurisdictions, and professionalism versus commercialism. Similarly, CPA Canada has developed its own publications as well as an electronic communications tool, *Audit Quality Blog*, designed to provide updates on audit quality and to engage various stakeholders in the discussion.

CONCEPT CHECK

C2-6 What is quality control and how is it monitored?

---

[4] See CPA Canada, "Enhancing audit quality (EAQ) initiative: FAQs," accessed June 26, 2017, at **https://www.cpacanada.ca/en/business-and-accounting-resources/audit-and-assurance/ Enhancing-Audit-Quality/Enhancing-audit-quality-EAQ-initiative-FAQs**.

SUMMARY

This chapter discussed the nature of the public accounting profession and the activities of public accounting firms. Because public accounting firms play an important social role, several Canadian organizations provide oversight to increase the likelihood of appropriate audit quality and professional conduct. These are summarized in Figure 2-4. Shaded circles indicate items discussed in Chapter 1 or 2. The two remaining topics, legal liability and rules of professional conduct, will be discussed in more depth in Chapter 3.

MyLab Accounting
Make the grade with MyLab Accounting: The questions, exercises, and problems marked with a 🌐 can be found on MyLab Accounting. You can practise them as often as you want, and most feature step-by-step guided instructions to help you find the right answer.

Figure 2-4	Ways the Profession and Society Encourage Public Accountants to Conduct Themselves at a High Level

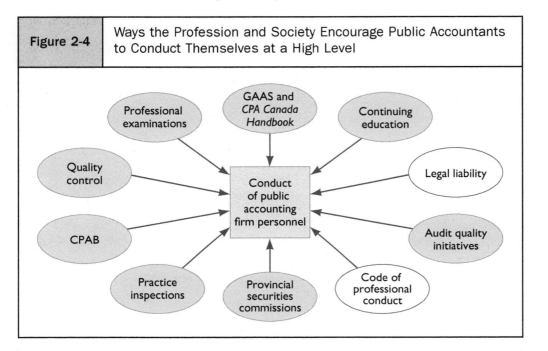

Review Questions

2-1 〔1〕 What are the advantages and disadvantages of practising as a large public accounting firm rather than as a small one?

2-2 〔1〕 What major characteristics of the organization and conduct of public accounting firms permit them to fulfill their social functions competently and independently?

2-3 〔1〕 Research the rules in your province with respect to accounting firm structure. Are limited liability partnerships (LLPs) permitted? What is the primary difference between a public accounting firm organized as a partnership and one organized as an LLP? Why would a public accounting firm choose to organize as an LLP?

2-4 〔2〕 Auditing standards have been criticized by different sources for failure to provide useful guidelines for conducting an audit. Critics believe the standards should be more specific to enable practitioners to improve the quality of their performance. As the standards are now stated, some critics believe that they provide little more than an excuse to conduct inadequate audits. Evaluate this criticism of auditing standards.

2-5 〔2〕〔3〕 What role does the CPA *Canada Handbook—Assurance* have in the professional activities of public accountants in Canada?

2-6 〔2〕 Who is responsible for establishing auditing standards for Canadian companies?

2-7 〔2〕 What is the difference between the American and Canadian standard-setting processes?

2-8 〔2〕 What is the role of the CPAB?

2-9 〔2〕 Describe the role of International Standards on Auditing. Discuss whether a PA who conducts an audit in accordance with generally accepted auditing standards simultaneously complies with international standards on auditing.

2-10 〔3〕〔4〕 Distinguish between generally accepted auditing standards and generally accepted accounting principles, and give two examples of each.

2-11 〔4〕 Explain how appropriate competence and capabilities contribute to a PA's qualifications to conduct a financial statement audit. What are the various ways in which PAs fulfill these responsibilities?

2-12 〔4〕 What are the objectives and purpose of the financial statement audit?

2-13 〔5〕 What is meant by "audit quality," and what factors influence it?

2-14 〔6〕 What is meant by "quality control" as it relates to a public accounting firm?

2-15 〔6〕 The following is an example of a public accounting firm's quality control procedure requirement: "Any person being considered for employment by the firm must have completed a basic auditing course and have been interviewed and approved by an audit partner of the firm before he or she can be hired for the audit staff." Which element of quality control does this procedure affect and what is the purpose of this requirement?

2-16 〔6〕 State what is meant by "practice inspection." What are the implications of the term for the public accounting profession?

Multiple Choice Questions

2-17 〔1〕〔2〕 You have been engaged to audit the financial statements of a Canadian public company. Which of the following statements is correct?
(1) Your firm must be registered with the CPAB.
(2) Your firm will be subject to auditing and quality control standards issued by the provincial securities commission.
(3) Your firm must be either a national or Big Four CPA firm.
(4) You will be engaged to audit both the quarterly and annual financial statements of your client.

2-18 〔4〕 The following questions deal with auditing standards. Choose the best response.
a. Which of the following best describes what is meant by "Canadian Auditing Standards"?
(1) Acts to be performed by the auditor.
(2) Measures of the quality of the auditor's performance.
(3) Procedures to be used to gather evidence to support financial statements.
(4) Audit objectives generally determined on audit engagements.

b. The Responsibilities principle underlying Canadian Auditing Standards includes a requirement that:
(1) The audit be adequately planned and supervised.
(2) The auditor's report states whether or not the financial statements conform to generally accepted accounting standards.
(3) Professional judgment be exercised by the auditor.
(4) Informative disclosures in the financial statements be reasonable adequate.

c. What is the general character of the responsibilities characterized by the Performance principles?
(1) The competence, independence, and professional care of persons performing the audit.
(2) Criteria for the content of the auditor's report on financial statements and related footnote disclosures.
(3) The criteria of audit planning and evidence gathering.
(4) The need to maintain independence in mental attitude in all matters pertaining to the audit.

2-19 **6** The following questions concern quality control standards. Choose the best response.

a. The nature and extent of a public accounting firm's quality control policies and procedures depend on:

	The PA Firm's Size	The Nature of the PA Firm's Practice	Cost–Benefit Considerations
(1)	Yes	Yes	Yes
(2)	Yes	Yes	No
(3)	Yes	No	Yes
(4)	No	Yes	Yes

b. Which of the following are elements of a PA firm's quality control that should be considered in establishing its quality control policies and procedures?

	Human Resources	Monitoring	Engagement Performance
(1)	Yes	Yes	No
(2)	Yes	Yes	Yes
(3)	No	Yes	Yes
(4)	Yes	No	Yes

c. One purpose of establishing quality control policies and procedures for deciding whether to accept a new client is to:
(1) Enable the PA firm to attest to the reliability of the client.
(2) Satisfy the PA firm's duty to the public concerning the acceptance of new clients.
(3) Provide reasonable assurance that the integrity of the client is considered.
(4) Anticipate before performing any field work whether an unqualified opinion can be issued.

Discussion Questions and Problems

2-20 **4** Sarah O'Hann enjoyed taking her first auditing course as part of her undergraduate accounting program. At home during her semester break, she and her father discussed the class and it was clear that he didn't really understand the nature of the audit process, as he asked the following questions:
a. What is the main objective of the audit of an entity's financial statements?
b. The audit represents the CPA firm's guarantee about the accuracy of the financial statements, right?
c. Isn't the auditor's primary responsibility to detect all kinds of fraud at the client?
d. Given that the CPA firm is auditing financial statements, why would it need to understand anything about the client's business?
e. What does the auditor do in an audit other than verify the mathematical accuracy of the numbers in the financial statements?

REQUIRED

If you were Sarah, how would you respond to each question?

⊕ **2-21** [6] For each of the following procedures that are taken from the quality control manual of a public accounting firm, identify the applicable element of quality control from Table 2-5 and explain why the procedure is important for the audit engagement.

a. Appropriate accounting and auditing research requires adequate technical reference materials. Each firm professional has online password access through the firm's website to electronic reference materials on accounting, auditing, tax, and other technical information including industry data.

b. The partners accept responsibility for leading and promoting a quality assurance culture within the firm and for providing and maintaining a quality assurance manual and all other necessary practical aids and guidance to support engagement quality.

c. Audit engagement team members enter their electronic signatures in the firm's engagement management software to indicate the completion of specific audit program steps. At the end of the audit engagement, the engagement management software will not allow archiving of the engagement file until all audit program steps have been electronically signed.

d. At all stages of any engagement, an effort is made to involve professional staff at appropriate levels in the accounting and auditing decisions. Various approvals of the manager or senior accountant are obtained throughout the audit.

e. No employee will have any direct or indirect financial interest, association, or relationship (for example, a close relative serving a client in a decision-making capacity) not otherwise disclosed that might be adverse to the firm's best interest.

f. Each office of the firm shall be visited at least annually by review persons selected by the director of accounting and auditing. Procedures to be undertaken by the reviewers are illustrated by the office review program.

g. Existing clients of the firm are reviewed on a continuing basis by the engagement partner. Termination may result if circumstances indicate that there is reason to question the integrity of management or its independence, or if accounting and auditing differences of opinion cannot be reconciled. Doubts concerning whether the client–auditor relationship should be continued must be promptly discussed with the director of accounting and auditing.

h. Individual partners submit the nominations of those persons whom they wish to be considered for partner. To become a partner, an individual must have exhibited a high degree of technical competence; must possess integrity, motivation, and good judgment; and must have a desire to help the firm progress through the efficient dispatch of the job responsibilities to which he or she is assigned.

i. Through the continuing employee evaluation and counselling program and through the quality control review procedures as established by the firm, educational needs are reviewed and formal staff training programs are modified to accommodate changing needs. At the conclusion of practice office reviews, apparent accounting and auditing deficiencies are summarized and reported to the firm's director of human resources.

j. All potential new clients are reviewed before acceptance. The review includes consultation with predecessor auditors and background checks. All new clients are approved by the firm management committee, including assessing whether the firm has the technical competence to complete the engagement.

k. Each audit engagement must include a concurring partner review of critical audit decisions.

2-22 [5] [6] The following comments summarize the beliefs of some practitioners about quality control and practice inspection.

The Canadian quality control and practice inspection authorities are quasi-governmental regulators of the profession. There are two effects of such regulation:

• It gives a competitive advantage to national public accounting firms because they already need formal structures to administer their complex organizations. Quality control requirements do not significantly affect their structure. Smaller firms now need a more costly organizational structure, which has proven unnecessary because of existing partner involvement on engagements. The major advantage smaller public accounting firms have traditionally had is a simple and efficient organizational structure. Now, that advantage has been eliminated because of quality control requirements.

• Quality control and practice inspection are not needed to regulate the profession. Elements of quality control have always existed, at least informally, for quality firms. Three things already provide sufficient assurance that informal quality control elements are followed without practice inspection. They are competitive pressures to do quality work, legal liability for inadequate performance, and a code of professional ethics requiring that PAs follow generally accepted auditing standards.

REQUIRED

a. State the pros and cons of these comments.

b. Evaluate whether control requirements are worth their cost.

Professional Judgment Problems and Cases

2-23 **2** **4** **6** Mobile Home Manufacturing Company is audited by the public accounting firm Rossi and Montgomery. Mobile Home Manufacturing has decided to issue shares to the public and wants Rossi and Montgomery to perform all the audit work necessary to satisfy the requirements for filing with the Ontario Securities Commission (OSC). The public accounting firm has never had a client go public before.

REQUIRED

a. What are the implications of Rossi and Montgomery accepting the engagement?

b. List the additional issues confronting the auditors when they file with the OSC, as compared with dealing with a private company audit engagement.

c. Using the auditors' personal and performance responsibilities and performance requirements as outlined by Canadian Auditing Standards, explain how these issues will impact the audit engagement of Mobile Home Manufacturing.

d. What important quality controls would ensure that Rossi and Montgomery perform a high-quality audit of Mobile Home Manufacturing Company?

2-24 **5** **6** According to the CPAB, an audit firm culture that maintains the appropriate balance between commercialism (managing the economic business of the firm) and professionalism (sustainable high-quality audits) is the key to maintaining high-quality audits.

REQUIRED

a. Why do you think the relationship between commercialism and professionalism has a large impact on audit quality?

b. What type of quality controls can audit firms put into place to ensure that partners and staff maintain that appropriate balance?

2-25 **5** **6** In the opening vignette, the concept of audit quality indicators (AQIs) was discussed. These AQIs are quantitative measures that provide insight into audit quality. The intent is to have firms publish these AQIs in an audit quality report and have it publicly available.

REQUIRED

a. How useful do you think AQIs are to potential clients and financial statement users?

b. Do you think Canada's regulators should require that firms provide an Audit Quality Report and publish their AQIs? Why or why not?

c. Below is an example of some common factors associated with audit quality. Propose a quantitative measure that would provide insight into that indicator.

Element	Audit Quality Indicator	Example Calculation
Leadership and Tone at Top	How top leadership is being viewed by audit staff.	
Human Resources	All personnel participate in continuing professional education and professional development training.	
Engagement Performance	Adequate partner involvement in all phases of audit.	
	Adequate allocation of audit hours to phases in the audit.	
Monitoring	Quality Review Results.	

2-26 **4** Daiyu Cheng, a recently qualified PA, has been assigned by her firm, Liu & Liu LLP, to serve as the senior auditor in charge of the fieldwork on a new audit engagement. The client is Demonte Credit Union (Demonte), a medium-sized credit union that is heavily involved as a mortgage lender in the local real estate market. This is the first credit union that Liu & Liu will be auditing. Cheng has not previously been involved in audits of financial institutions. The credit union's predecessor auditors resigned unexpectedly during the current fiscal year, and they have not responded to Liu & Liu's request for information for over one month. Liu & Liu has agreed to perform the engagement since the financial statement audit needs to be completed and submitted to the credit union's provincial regulator within 10 days of the annual meeting. The regulator uses the financial statements to assess whether Demonte meets the conditions of its deposit insurance and to determine the annual deposit insurance premium for Demonte.

The client has provided Liu & Liu with the predecessor audit firm's unqualified audit report on last year's financial statements. The engagement partner tells Cheng to concentrate her efforts on understanding Demonte's business and internal control environment, including Demonte's internal control systems, but not to rely upon internal controls. The partner instructs Cheng to perform extensive tests on the key balance sheet asset and liability accounts, such as mortgage loans receivable.

Cheng performs the audit as instructed and finds no material misstatements, but is not always certain if she has collected sufficient evidence regarding mortgage loans receivable. She is glad that Demonte's CFO was able to spend time with her and explain what all his schedules meant, especially since so many of the mortgage holders did not confirm the details of their mortgages. The engagement partner has several client deadlines and is unable to spend much time at Demonte, but spends a few hours reviewing Cheng's work. Since Cheng is the firm's best senior auditor and she did not find any material misstatements, the partner issues an unqualified opinion on the financial statements.

When Demonte's CFO meets with the partner, he expresses pleasure that Liu & Liu was able to meet the deadline for the annual meeting and that the audit had gone much better than past audits had. The previous audit firm always spent more time and had more staff assigned to the engagement. This year's audit had been much less disruptive for Demonte's accounting staff.

REQUIRED

Briefly describe each of the principles underlying Canadian Auditing Standards and indicate how the actions of Cheng and the partner resulted in a failure to comply with each principle. Organize your answer as follows:

Brief Description of Principle	Actions of Cheng and the Partner Resulting in Failure to Comply With the Principle

(Adapted from AU2 CGA- Canada Examinations developed by the Certified General Accountants Association of Canada © 2010 CGA-Canada with permission Chartered Professional Accountants of Canada, Toronto, Canada. Any changes to the original material are the sole responsibility of the author (and/or publisher) and have not been reviewed or endorsed by the Chartered Professional Accountants of Canada.)

2-27 **5** **6** Access the CPA Canada's Audit Quality Blog at **https://www.cpacanada.ca/en/connecting-and-news/blogs/audit-quality-blog**.

REQUIRED

a. Explain the purpose of the Audit Quality Blog.

b. Choose one of the blog posts that you think is interesting and/or controversial. Summarize the key points in the post and discuss your views on the issue.

PROFESSIONAL ETHICS AND LEGAL LIABILITY

CHAPTER

3

LEARNING OBJECTIVES

After studying this chapter, you should be able to:

1 Explain the fundamental principles that guide public accountants' professional ethics.

2 Recognize ethical dilemmas that public accountants typically encounter and recommend acceptable courses of action.

3 Explain the impact of ethical blind spots on auditors' ethical reasoning.

4 Understand the rules of professional conduct and apply that knowledge to resolve ethical conflicts.

5 Identify and evaluate threats to independence and recommend appropriate safeguards to eliminate or reduce the threats to an acceptable level.

6 Describe the CPA (Chartered Professional Accountant) profession's enforcement mechanisms for public accountants' conduct.

7 Explain the relationship between the expectations gap and lawsuits.

8 Understand and analyze auditor legal liability.

9 Explain how the profession and individual public accountants can reduce the threat of litigation.

Big 4 Partner Convicted of Insider Trading for Disclosing Confidential Information

Auditors frequently receive access to confidential client information, such as earnings information before the earnings announcement or information about planned mergers and acquisitions. It is a fundamental ethical principle of the Canadian *CPA Code of Professional Conduct* that CPAs cannot exploit such information to their personal advantage or the advantage of a third party. Also, like the American Institute of Certified Public Accountants' (AICPA) *Code of Professional Conduct*, the Canadian code prohibits members in public practice from disclosing any confidential information without the consent of the client. Trading in publicly traded companies on such inside information before it becomes public is also often a violation of securities laws on insider trading.

As a senior partner in the Los Angeles office of KPMG, Scott London had access to client information such as company earnings reports and planned acquisitions. Although he did not personally trade using this information, he passed the information on to Bryan Shaw, a friend who was in the jewellery business. Over the course of several years, Shaw used the tips to make trades that resulted in profits of over $1 million. In exchange for the information, Shaw would arrange to meet

continued >

49

continued London on a street near his business and give him bags containing $100 bills wrapped in $10 000 bundles. In court documents, Shaw also stated he gave London a $12 000 Rolex watch, jewellery, and concert tickets.

London's defense team argued that London began providing the tips because he wanted to help Mr. Shaw, whose jewellery business was struggling, and that he went down a "slippery slope." Although the judge noted that the $70 000 that London received was a "drop in the bucket" compared to his annual salary of over $900 000, he also noted that by the 14th time London engaged in this activity, "it wasn't inadvertent." London was sentenced to 14 months in prison and fined $100 000. Although KPMG was unaware of London's actions, the company was forced to resign from clients Herbalife and Skechers because London was the lead partner on these audit engagements.

Sources: Stuart Pfeifer, "Former KPMG partner Scott London pleads guilty to insider trading," *The Los Angeles Times*, July 1, 2013, accessed June 25, 2017, at **http://articles.latimes.com/2013/jul/01/business/la-fi-mo-kpmg-scott-london-insider-trading-20130627**. Tamara Audi, "Former KPMG partner Scott London gets 14 months for insider trading," *The Wall Street Journal*, April 24, 2014, accessed June 25, 2017, at **https://www.wsj.com/articles/former-kpmg-partner-scott-london-gets-14-months-in-prison-for-insider-trading-1398367240**.

In the preceding chapters, we highlighted that the value of the audit report and the demand for audit services depends on public confidence in the independence and integrity of public accountants. This chapter discusses ways in which the profession and society encourage public accountants to conduct themselves at a high level of ethics. We first focus on the profession's role and discuss professional ethics, independence, and the *CPA Code of Professional Conduct*. We will then move to society's role and how, through the legal system, it holds auditors accountable for their professional conduct.

LO 1 Explain the fundamental principles that guide public accountants' professional ethics.

PROFESSIONAL ETHICS AND PUBLIC ACCOUNTANTS

Throughout Chapters 1 and 2, we were introduced to the public accounting profession and touched upon the key defining characteristics of public accountants: integrity, competence, professional skepticism, and independence. Each of these helps define the professional ethics that guide public accountants' professional conduct. Before we discuss ethics in more depth, let's consider the definition of a professional. According to the Center for Study of Professional Ethics at the Illinois Institute of Technology (**http://ethics.iit.edu/teaching/professional-ethics**), a professional is a member of an occupational group, who:

1. Sees other members, including those employed elsewhere, as peers/colleagues.
2. Exercises judgment when performing specialized tasks and follows relevant professional standards.
3. Accepts the profession's agreement to work in a morally permissible way (usually as set out in the profession's code of ethics) as an obligation of his or her role.

As the definition highlights, exercising judgment in the application of specialized knowledge is a key characteristic of a professional. However, that judgment is expected to be in keeping with professional standards, the profession's code of ethics, and the public's expectations of the professional's role.

Ethics—a set of moral principles or values.

Ethics can be broadly defined as a set of moral principles or values. We use these values to guide us in how we should act in various situations. Each of us has such a set of values, although we may or may not have considered them explicitly. **Professional ethics** are the morally permissible standards of conduct that apply to the members of a particular profession. Given their position of trust, professionals are expected to conduct themselves at a higher level than most other members of society. Although

Professional ethics—the morally permissible standards of conduct that apply to the members of a profession.

Table 3-1	Fundamental Ethical Principles—CPA Ontario *Code of Professional Conduct*

The following list of ethical principles incorporates characteristics and values that are associated with CPAs' ethical behaviour.

Professional behaviour	CPAs conduct themselves at all times in a manner that maintains the good reputation of the profession and its ability to serve the public interest.
Integrity and due care	CPAs are expected to be straightforward, honest, and fair in all professional relationships. They are also expected to act diligently and in accordance with applicable technical and professional standards when providing professional services.
Objectivity	CPAs do not allow their professional or business judgment to be compromised by bias, conflict of interest, or the undue influence of others.
Professional competence	The public expects the accounting profession to maintain a high level of competence. This underscores the need for maintaining individual professional skill and competence by keeping abreast of and complying with developments in the professional standards.
Confidentiality	CPAs have a duty of confidentiality in respect to information acquired as a result of professional, employment, and business relationships, and they will not disclose to any third party, without proper cause and specific authority, any information, nor will they exploit such information to their personal advantage or the advantage of a third party.

Based on the CPA Ontario Code of Professional Conduct

professions often share similar ethical standards, each profession has its own unique responsibilities and professional ethics.

In the case of public accountants, the overriding responsibility is the protection of the public interest. Auditor independence and integrity is also paramount. This is because the structure of the auditor–client relationship has an inherent conflict of interest in that the company that issues the financial statements pays the public accountant (PA) yet the primary beneficiaries of the PA's services (the audit opinion) are the financial statement users. The auditor often does not know or have contact with those users but has frequent meetings and ongoing relationships with client personnel. If users were to believe that PAs lacked integrity and/or independence, then the opinions (their services) they delivered would be worthless.

The five fundamental principles (summarized in Table 3-1) that guide the ethical behaviours of PAs are professional behaviour, integrity and due care, professional competence, confidentiality, and objectivity. According to the *CPA Code of Professional Conduct*, these ethical principles are aimed first and foremost at serving the public interest and, second, at achieving orderly and courteous conduct within the profession.

A FRAMEWORK FOR ETHICAL REASONING

LO **2** Recognize ethical dilemmas that public accountants typically encounter and recommend acceptable courses of action.

The fundamental ethical principles are an important part of the PA's ethical decision process. Choosing the right principles requires knowledge of professional standards, responsibilities, and expectations of ethical conduct, an understanding of the consequences, and the ability to recognize an ethical dilemma. Further, public accountants must not only be able to recognize and resolve an ethical dilemma but they must take the appropriate ethical action. Some refer to this as "what you *should* do versus what you *would* do." Let's consider Qin's situation.

Qin is the senior auditor in charge of the September 30, 2017, financial statement audit of Paquette Forest Products Inc., a forest products company that produces lumber and paper products in northern Manitoba. The company employs 375 people and is the main employer in the remote town of Duck Lake, Manitoba; the other businesses in Duck Lake provide goods and services to Paquette Forest Products and its employees. In the course of the audit, Qin discovers that the company has had a number of failures of the equipment that removes the sulphuric acid from the paper production process and, as a result, thousands of litres of untreated water have been dumped into the Loon River and Duck Lake. Qin learns that the cost of replacing the equipment so that no further spills are likely would strain cash reserves. If ordered to replace the equipment by the environment ministry, the company would be forced to raise additional capital or cease operations. What should Qin do?

Qin is facing an **ethical dilemma.** He is aware that the situation or dilemma may affect the welfare of others, such as the employees and shareholders of Paquette Products, the citizens of Duck Lake, the audit firm and its professionals, and the profession itself. In addition to identifying the dilemma, he will need to evaluate the outcomes and determine what is right and wrong, and then fulfill the obligations of his professional role. In order to resolve the dilemma, he has to make a value assessment of the "right" choice versus other decision alternatives and decide upon the best course of action. Hopefully, he will carry out the most ethical course of action.[1]

While most auditors will not face a dilemma as extreme as Qin's, all auditors will face many ethical dilemmas over the course of their careers. Dealing with a client who threatens to seek a new auditor unless an unqualified opinion is issued presents a serious ethical dilemma. Deciding to confront a client who materially overstated departmental revenues in order to receive a larger bonus is tough to do. Deciding whether or not to report a supervisor's negligence to a partner is a problem you may face as a staff accountant.

Figure 3-1 presents the **framework for ethical decision making.** It is a common framework that has been adapted to incorporate the context of an audit professional. The Institute of Chartered Accountants of England and Wales (ICAEW, see **http://www.icaew.com**) developed the guiding questions to encourage reflection beyond the rules of professional conduct and to consider the broader implications of the issue. The ethical reasoning framework encompasses personal interests and consequences, the auditor's responsibilities, and societal values.

Figure 3-1	A Framework for Ethical Decision Making
Obtain relevant facts and identify the issues	• Do you have all the relevant facts? • Are you making assumptions? If so, can facts be identified to replace those assumptions? • Is it really your problem? Can someone else help?
Identify the ethical issues	• What are the professional, organizational, and personal ethical issues? • What fundamental ethical principles are affected? • Are there threats to independence? If so, are there any safeguards? • Would those ethical issues affect the reputation of the profession? • Would those issues affect the public interest?
Identify who is affected and how each is affected	• Who are the individuals, the organizations, and other stakeholders? • In which way are they affected? • Are there conflicts between stakeholders?
Consider and evaluate courses of action	• Consider organizational policies, applicable laws and regulations, universal values and principles, consequences, and potential rationalizations. • Test your proposed course of action. • Would a similar course of action be used in a similar situation? • Would the course of action stand up to the scrutiny of peers?
Implement the course of action	• When faced with an ethical issue, it may be in your best interests to document your thought processes, discussions, and other decisions taken.

---

[1] This reasoning process is based upon James Rest's Model of Ethical Action. Rest was an American psychologist well known for his research on cognition and morality.

Ethical decisions are challenging. The first challenge, which we will discuss later, is recognizing that you are faced with an ethical issue. The second challenge is deciding which values matter most. The third challenge is putting the ethical decision into action, which some refer to as moral courage. Let's consider Bryan Longview's ethical dilemma and apply the framework for ethical reasoning presented in Figure 3-1.

Bryan Longview has been working for six months as a staff assistant for De Souza & Shah, public accountants. Currently he is assigned to the audit of Reyon Manufacturing Corp. under the supervision of Karen Van Staveren, an experienced audit senior. There are three auditors assigned to the audit, including Karen, Bryan, and a more experienced assistant, Martha Mills.

During lunch on the first day, Karen says, "It will be necessary for us to work a few extra hours on our own time to make sure we come in on budget. This audit isn't very profitable anyway, and we don't want to hurt our firm by going over budget. We can accomplish this easily by coming in a half hour early, taking a short lunch break, and working an hour or so after normal quitting time. We just won't write that time down on our time report."

Bryan recalls reading in the firm's policy manual that working extra hours and not charging for them on the time report is a violation of De Souza & Shah's employment policy. He also knows that seniors are paid bonuses instead of overtime, whereas staff are paid for overtime but get no bonuses.

Later, when Bryan discusses the issue with Martha, she says, "Karen does this on all of her jobs. She is likely to be our firm's next audit manager. The partners think she's great because her jobs always come in under budget. She rewards us by giving us good engagement evaluations, especially under the cooperative attitude category. Several of the other audit seniors follow the same practice."

We will now apply the ethical judgment decision making framework to Bryan's ethical dilemma.

Obtain Relevant Facts and Identify the Ethical Issues

In order to identify the ethical issue, it is necessary to think about "what" the issue is. At first, this seems to be a fairly straightforward issue. Bryan recognizes that Karen's request violates firm policies. However, he is aware that this is common practice in the firm and that supervisors like Karen use this practice to meet the expected budget. He is also aware that Karen places high value on career advancement. If he reports, he is at risk of having a poor engagement evaluation.

But Karen's request has broader implications. Bryan also knows that these practices affect the firm's quality control, since budgeting and time management will not be accurate. By violating one firm policy, he and his other team members could be on the slippery slope to violating other practices, such as signing off on incomplete work. It may also affect professional skepticism and the quality of work done by Bryan and his peers.

Given the facts, the ethical issue in this situation is not difficult to identify: *Is it ethical for Bryan to work hours and not record them as hours worked?*

Identify Who Is Affected and How Each Is Each Affected

Typically, more people are affected than might be expected in situations in which ethical dilemmas occur. The following are the key persons involved in this situation:

Who	How Affected
Bryan	Being asked to violate firm policy.
	Hours of work will be affected.
	Pay will be affected.
	Quality of work may be affected.
	Performance evaluations may be affected.
	Attitude about firm may be affected.

(continued)

(Continued)

Who	How Affected
Martha	Same as Bryan.
Karen	Success on engagement (in terms of meeting budget) and in firm may be affected. Hours of work will be affected. Quality of audit engagement may be affected. Stated DeSouza & Shah firm policy is being violated. May result in underbilling clients in the current and future engagements. May affect firm's ability to realistically budget engagements and bill clients. May affect firm's ability to perform quality audit engagements. May affect firm's ability to motivate and retain employees. May result in unrealistic time budgets.
Staff assigned Reyon Manufacturing in the future	May result in unfavourable time performance evaluations. May result in poor quality audit work. May result in pressures to continue practice of not charging for hours worked.
Other staff in firm	Following the practice on this engagement may motivate others to follow the same practice on other engagements. Following such practices may send the message that making the budget is more important than performing thoughtful and careful work.

In addition to the effects on staff, there are also ramifications for the public accounting firm and the audit profession itself. We will consider them when we evaluate our alternatives.

Consider and Evaluate Courses of Action

Now we will consider and evaluate the alternatives. Bryan's available alternatives are as follows:

- Refuse to work the additional hours.
- Perform in the manner requested.
- Inform Karen that he will not work the additional hours or will charge the additional hours to the engagement.
- Talk to Karen about his concerns about her request.
- Talk to a manager or partner about Karen's request.
- Refuse to work on the engagement.
- Quit working for the firm.

When evaluating each alternative, it is necessary to consider what is morally permissable in the particular context. As highlighted in Figure 3-1, that would involve consideration of organizational policies, applicable laws and regulations, rules of professional conduct, and universal values and principles.

What Are the Consequences? In deciding the consequences of each alternative, it is essential to evaluate both the short- and long-term effects. Long-term effects are often difficult for people to visualize when making a decision. However, consequences should be considered in a broad context—both from a time perspective and from the various stakeholder perspectives. Bryan must think not only about himself, Karen, his peers, and the firm, but also about the profession and society at large.

There is a natural tendency to emphasize the short term because those consequences will occur quickly and it is often difficult to envision the long-term consequences. For example, consider the potential consequences if Bryan decides to work the additional hours and not report them. In the short term, he will likely get good evaluations for cooperation and perhaps a salary increase. In the longer term, what will be the effect of not reporting the hours this time when other ethical conflicts arise? Consider the following similar ethical dilemmas Bryan might face in his career as he advances:

- A supervisor asks Bryan to work 3 unreported hours daily and 15 unreported hours each weekend.
- A supervisor asks Bryan to initial certain audit procedures as having been performed when they were not.
- Bryan concludes that he cannot be promoted to manager unless he persuades assistants to work hours that they do not record.
- Client management informs Bryan, who is now a partner, that either the company gets an unqualified opinion for a $40 000 audit fee or the company will change auditors.
- Management informs Bryan that the audit fee will be increased $25 000 if Bryan can find a plausible way to increase earnings by $1 million.

Potential Rationalizations There are alternative ways to resolve ethical dilemmas, but care must be taken to avoid rationalizations for unethical behaviour. In Bryan's case, a rationalization that inhibits his ability to evaluate alternatives effectively is that "everyone is doing it"—Karen is following an accepted practice among her peers. Rationalizations, such as "If it's legal, it's ethical," "No one will know," "It's not hurting anyone," and "It's not my responsibility" act as justifications to rationalize questionable alternatives or to ignore the ethical dimension of the issue.

Test Course of Action Figure 3-1 highlights two types of tests, the universal test (would a similar action be taken in a similar situation?) and the peer test (would the action stand up to the scrutiny of peers?), to help assess the appropriateness of the course of action. Below is a list of tests that a CPA could use to consider the appropriateness of the course of action:[2]

- *Harm test*—Would this option do less harm than any alternative?
- *Rights test*—Would this option violate anyone's rights, especially a human right?
- *Publicity test*—Would I want my choice published in the newspaper?
- *Defensibility test*—Could I defend my choice of this option before a judge, a committee of my peers, or my parents?
- *Virtue test*—What does this say about my character if I choose this option often?
- *Professional test*—What would my provincial accounting body's disciplinary committee say about this option?
- *Colleague test*—What would my colleagues say when I describe my problem and suggest this option as my solution?
- *Firm test*—What would the firm's quality control partner or legal counsel say about this?

Implement the Course of Action

Only Brian can decide the appropriate option to select in the circumstances after considering his ethical values and the likely consequences of each option. At one extreme, Bryan can decide the only relevant consequence is the potential impact on his career. Most of us would believe that Bryan is unethical if he follows that course of action. At the other extreme, Byran can decide to refuse to work for a firm that permits even one supervisor to violate firm policies. Many people would consider such an extreme reaction naïve. Most public accounting firms have policies such as an anonymous hotline to report unethical behavior and provide employees with mentors.

---

[2] This list is adapted from Michael Davis, "Professional ethics without moral theory: A practical guide for the perplexed non-philosopher," *Journal of Applied Ethics and Philosophy*, no. 6, 2014, pp. 1–9, accessed August 10, 2017, at **http://doi.org/10.14943/jaep.6.1**.

Members (which include students who are enrolled in the professional education program) of the provincial accounting bodies can also consult with the peer support program and obtain advice on how to proceed.

LO **3** Explain the impact of ethical blind spots on auditors' ethical reasoning.

Ethical blind spots—unconscious judgmental tendencies that can hinder the ethical decision making process or cause the decision maker to fail to recognize the ethical dimension of a choice.

ETHICAL BLIND SPOTS

While an ethical reasoning framework can guide an auditor through an ethical dilemma, it may not be sufficient in helping to identify ethical issues. That is because decision makers are often susceptible to judgment traps or what is referred to as **ethical blind spots.** We have already highlighted how rationalizations deter effective evaluation of alternatives. Ethical blind spots are perhaps worse than rationalizations since the decision maker is unaware of the blind spot and it can inhibit the auditor from even recognizing an ethical dilemma in the first place.

In their book, *Ethical Blindspots: Why We Fail to Do What's Right and What to Do About It,*[3] Max Bazerman and Ann Tenbrunsel argue that unethical behaviour often occurs "because people are unconsciously fooling themselves." They explain this "unconscious fooling" in terms of what they refer to as ethical blind spots. One blind spot, which they label ethical fading, tends to eliminate ethics from the decision. For instance, when we frame the situation as doing what is required by the law or simply considering financial costs, we have elevated various stakeholders and consequences. In essence, we no longer frame it as an ethical dilemma. In the case of another blind spot, motivated blindness, we fail to see the ethical issue because it is in our self-interest not to notice. Some argue that the WorldCom and Enron audit failures can be attributed to auditors' strong bias toward their clients' interests, which lead to the inability to see the ethical dilemma.

CONCEPT CHECK

C3-1 Suppose that you share a ride to a client with another audit staff member. Your colleague proposes that you both submit mileage reimbursement requests for each day of the audit even though you share rides. Explain the ethical decision framework and apply to this situation.

C3-2 Why are ethical decisions so difficult? Consider the role of rationalizations and ethical blind spots.

LO **4** Understand rules of professional conduct and apply that knowledge to resolve ethical conflicts.

PROFESSIONAL GUIDANCE ON ETHICAL CONDUCT

The ethical reasoning framework highlights the fact that auditors' decisions are made with consideration of the rules of professional conduct. The provincial accounting bodies determine the rules of professional conduct for members and students, and have harmonized their rules of professional conduct so that the same set of rules applies to all PAs in Canada and serves both members and the public. The CPA code applies to all members and firms irrespective of the type of services being provided and is not restricted only to those in public practice.

The professional code of conduct in Canada is both principles-based and compliance-based. In our discussion of ethics, we highlighted the fundamental ethical principles that guide auditors' professional conduct. These fundamental principles emphasize the shared values of the profession and encourage doing the right thing.

---

[3] M. Bazerman and A. Tenbrunsel, *Ethical Blindspots: Why We Fail to Do What's Right and What to Do About It,* Princeton: Princeton University Press, 2012.

However, many critics of a principles-based code emphasize that principles are difficult to enforce because there are no minimum standards of behaviour. Therefore, in some instances, the code includes carefully defined rules.

The advantage of this compliance-based approach is that the accounting body is able to enforce minimum behaviour and performance standards. However, a disadvantage is the tendency of some practitioners to define the rules as maximum rather than minimum standards. A second disadvantage is that some practitioners may view the code as the law and conclude that if some action is not prohibited, it must be ethical. In other words, practitioners will say, "Show me where it says I can't do it." As the ethical reasoning framework emphasizes, a PA must consider the broader principles and values of the profession when deciding whether a particular action is acceptable or not.

We will restrict the remainder of our discussion to the CPA Ontario *Code of Professional Conduct* (as an example of provincial rules of conduct) and focus our discussion on relevant rules from Section 200 (Public Protection) and Section 300 (Professional Colleagues). We then revisit independence and discuss the independence standard for assurance engagements.

Public Protection

Section 200 of the *Code of Professional Conduct* represents the standards of conduct that ensure the protection of the public interest and the maintenance of the profession's reputation.

Rule 201—Maintenance of good reputation of the profession The rules of accounting bodies in Canada require their members to behave in the best interests of their profession and the public interest. This means accountants should not take advantage of the trust placed in them. An accountant should not be publicly critical of a colleague (i.e., by making a complaint about the colleague's behaviour to their professional body or by being critical, as a successor auditor, to the new client) without giving the colleague a chance to explain his or her actions first. Similarly, an auditor should not voluntarily resign from an audit engagement that is underway without good and sufficient reason. Reasons may include:

- The auditor loses trust in the client.
- The auditor is in a situation where the auditor's independence or objectivity could be reasonably questioned.
- The client pressures the auditor to perform illegal, unjust, or fraudulent acts.

Rule 202—Integrity, due care, and objectivity Clients, employers, and the public expect that an auditor or firm will bring the qualities of objectivity, integrity, and due care to all professional services. It is therefore essential that members not compromise their professional judgment to the will of others.

Integrity is one of the hallmarks of the profession. One of a professional accountant's most important assets is his or her reputation for honesty and fair dealing; if users of financial statements audited by or prepared by an accountant do not believe in the practitioner's honesty or fairness, the value of the financial statements or the audit is diminished.

Members must always remain objective, act with integrity, and continually assess and manage the risks to objectivity and integrity. The Code states that the requirement to be objective is not the same as independence. Objectivity is a state of mind. Independence is not only a state of mind; it also includes the appearance of independence, in the view of a reasonable observer. We will discuss independence in more depth later in the chapter.

Rule 203—Professional competence The rules of conduct require practitioners to maintain competence; similarly, GAAS state the necessity of "adequate technical training and proficiency in auditing." The public expects that all professionals will strive to keep abreast of the latest techniques and methodologies. Professional accountants are required to attend a certain number of continuing professional education courses a year.

An auditor should not undertake an audit of a client unless that auditor has knowledge both of that client's business and industry, and of the technical aspects of the audit. For example, the audit of an insurance company requires knowledge of auditing the policy reserves that form a significant part of the insurance company's liabilities. Many larger accounting firms form industry specialization groups within the firm that are responsible for all audits within their specialty.

Rule 204—Independence The value of auditing depends heavily on the public's perception of the **independence** of auditors. The reason that many diverse users are willing to rely upon the PA's audit opinion as to the fairness of financial statements is that users expect the PA to have an unbiased viewpoint. The rules of professional conduct require members who are engaged in the practice of public accounting to be independent when they perform assurance services and specified auditing procedures engagements (we will discuss this type of engagement in Chapter 20). PAs must be free of any influence, interest, or relationship that impairs professional judgment or objectivity.

Independence is considered to encompass two dimensions: "independence in fact" and "independence in appearance." **Independence in fact** exists when the auditor is actually able to maintain an unbiased attitude throughout the audit. **Independence in appearance** is the result of others' interpretation of this independence. If auditors are independent in fact but users believe them to be advocates for the client, most of the benefit of the audit function will be lost. We will discuss the conceptual framework of the independence standard later in the chapter.

Rule 205—False and misleading documents and oral representations No members, whether in public accounting or industry, can sign or associate with false or misleading information (this includes letters, reports, and written or oral statements) or fail to reveal material omissions from financial statements. PAs can lose faith in management when information is withheld. Users of financial statements prepared by or audited by professional accountants are entitled to believe that the financial statements are complete and fairly present the financial position of the company, to believe that the financial statements are not false and misleading, and to rely on the integrity of the accountants involved.

Rule 206—Compliance with professional standards PAs are required to comply with professional standards when preparing and auditing financial statements. These standards include the standards of the professional body but, more importantly, accounting standards and GAAS as set out in the *CPA Canada Handbook—Assurance*.

Rule 208—Confidentiality of information The rules of conduct for PAs state that members shall not disclose any confidential client information or employer information without the specific consent of the client or employer. The rules also prohibit using **confidential or inside information** to earn profits or benefits. The confidentiality requirement applies to all services provided by public accounting firms, including tax and management services.

During an audit or other type of engagement, practitioners obtain a considerable amount of information of a confidential nature, including officers' salaries, product pricing and advertising plans, and product cost data. If auditors divulged this information to outsiders or to client employees who had been denied access to the information, their relationship with management would become strained and, in extreme cases, would cause the client harm. As we have seen in the opening vignette involving

Independence—impartiality in performing professional services.

Independence in fact—the auditor's ability to take an unbiased viewpoint in the performance of professional services.

Independence in appearance—the auditor's appearance of maintaining an unbiased viewpoint in the eyes of others.

Confidential or inside information—client information that may not be disclosed without the specific consent of the client except under authoritative professional or legal investigation.

an American certified public accountant, this type of violation can damage the PA's career, as well as the reputation of the firm and the profession.

Ordinarily, the public accounting firm's working papers can be provided to someone else only with the express permission of the client. This is the case even if a PA sells his or her practice to another public accounting firm or is willing to permit a successor auditor to examine the working papers prepared for a former client. Permission is not required from the client, however, if the working papers are subpoenaed by a court, or are used as part of practice inspection or in connection with a disciplinary hearing. If the working papers are subpoenaed, the client should be informed immediately, as the client and the client's lawyer may wish to challenge the subpoena.

While the rules of professional conduct with respect to confidentiality are quite clear, the auditor may be confronted with a situation where he or she must choose between confidentiality and other rules of conduct or another course of action. For instance, in Qin's situation regarding Paquette Forest Products, he is faced with a conflict between his duty to maintain confidentiality and his duty to protect the public interest.

Rule 210—Conflicts of interest If an auditor is asked to provide assurance services for two or more clients who are competitors, then the auditor needs to obtain consent from each client and must also use procedures to protect confidential information. As we have already discussed, the auditor's access to confidential information can create conflicts of interest. Auditors may obtain information from one assurance client that may be important to another. For instance, the auditor discovers that a client is in serious financial information and is also the auditor of a major supplier of that client. If the supplier is unaware of this information, the auditor cannot use this information and advise the supplier to write down the receivable. However, the auditor has a conflict of interest that must be resolved.

Rule 211—Duty to report breaches of the CPA Code The CPA Code of Conduct of the professional accounting bodies requires members who are aware of another member's breach of the rules to report to the profession's discipline committee after first advising the member of the intent to make a report. The bodies are self-regulating. It is important that the member be notified of the intent to report the breach in case there are mitigating circumstances of which the reporting member is not aware.

Rule 214—Fee quotations and billings Members must obtain adequate information before providing a fee quotation. For example, in order to conduct an audit engagement, it is necessary to understand the client's accounting policies and internal controls. It therefore follows that in order to estimate a fee, the auditor would need to conduct an appropriate assessment of the client's accounting policies and internal controls.

Rule 215—Contingent fees The charging of a fee based on the outcome of an audit, such as the granting of a loan by a bank, could easily impair the auditor's independence. Contingent fees are prohibited for audits, reviews, compilation engagements, and any other engagements that require the auditor to be objective.

Rule 217—Advertising, solicitation, and endorsements A profession's reputation is not enhanced if the members openly solicit one another's clients or engage in advertising that is overly aggressive, self-laudatory, or critical of other members of the profession or that makes claims that cannot be substantiated. As a consequence, the professional accounting bodies in Canada prohibit solicitation of another PA's client and advertising that is not in keeping with the profession's high standards. Also, when endorsing a product or service, the PA must take care that it does not create a conflict of interest or impair objectivity.

Rule 218—Retention of documentation and working papers The PA has an obligation to retain documents for a reasonable period of time. This is necessary to properly carry out professional services as well as in case of litigation, practice inspections, or disciplinary hearings. Some documentation may need to be retained indefinitely (this is usually included in what is referred to as the Permanent File). This documentation could include financial statements; agreements, contracts, and leases; minutes; investment/share capital information; tax returns and assessment notices; and detailed continuity schedules for items such as capital assets and future taxes.

CONCEPT CHECK

C3-3 Explain the need for a code of professional ethics for PAs.

C3-4 Explain the rule of contingent fees. Why is this rule necessary?

Professional Colleagues

The preamble of the CPA Code of Conduct emphasizes that the following fundamental principles should guide collegial relations: that client interests are placed ahead of the interest of the member or firm and that professional courtesy and cooperation are expected at all times. The two rules that we discuss demonstrate how collegiality is a necessary requirement for audit quality.

Rule 302—Communication with predecessor The CPA Code of Conduct requires that a (potential) successor auditor, prior to accepting an appointment as auditor, communicate with the incumbent auditor to inquire if the incumbent is aware of any circumstances that might preclude the successor from accepting the appointment. The successor would ask the potential client to authorize the incumbent to provide the information requested. If the client refuses to do so, the successor should be reluctant to accept the appointment because it is likely that the client is hiding something.

The rules also require that the incumbent respond promptly to the successor's request and be candid in responding. The communication between the incumbent and the successor is important because it prevents a successor from unknowingly accepting an appointment that might, if all the facts were known, be rejected. For example, if the incumbent resigned after finding that management of the client was dishonest and was engaged in fraud, it is unlikely that any public accounting firm would accept the client if the incumbent revealed that knowledge. In short, the required communication protects prospective successors, and thus the profession, from getting involved with undesirable clients.

Rule 303—Provision of client information A predecessor should supply reasonable information to the successor about the client. Ordinarily, the predecessor is not expected to supply copies of more than the information related to the prior year's financial statements and tax returns. Professional courtesy dictates that the predecessor cooperate and allow the successor to review the working papers, and answer the successor's questions. This not only ensures a smooth transition, but it also enables the PA to meet the *CPA Canada Handbook—Assurance*'s requirement that the auditor obtain information related to opening balances.

CONCEPT CHECK

C3-5 Identify the circumstances under which a PA can disclose confidential information without client permission.

C3-6 How does communication with the predecessor auditor improve audit quality?

THE INDEPENDENCE STANDARD FOR ASSURANCE ENGAGEMENTS

LO 5 Identify and evaluate threats to independence and recommend appropriate safeguards to eliminate or reduce the threats to an acceptable level.

Rules 204.1 to 204.10 provide a systematic principles-based framework to assess independence for assurance engagements. Since it is impossible not to have relationships with others, the intent of the framework is to provide PAs the means by which "to evaluate the significance of economic, financial, and other relationships in light of what a reasonable observer would conclude to be acceptable in maintaining independence."[4] In Auditing in Action 3-1, the SEC referred to the same criteria in assessing the partners' actions.

Figure 3-2 provides an overview of the standard, which requires the auditor to: (1) identify the threats; (2) evaluate the significance of the threat and determine if any safeguards can be applied to eliminate the threat; and (3) for each insignificant threat, document the rationale. Figure 3-2 highlights the fact that that it is also necessary to consider whether there are any prohibitions that would preclude undertaking or completing the proposed engagement.

Identify Threats

When deciding to accept a new assurance client or to continue providing assurance services to an existing client, the PA will evaluate whether the service creates a threat to independence. The five threats to independence are self-interest, self-review,

---

AUDITING IN ACTION 3-1
When Successful Client Relationships Cross the Line

Like all professionals, developing successful client relationships is necessary for public accountants. It enables PAs to provide quality assurance engagements and, through their in-depth knowledge of their client's operations, PAs are able to provide valuable insights to the client. However, unlike most professionals, PAs are required to be independent, and there is often a fine line between what is an appropriate versus inappropriate auditor–client relationship. When does a PA cross that line and become too "familiar" with a client? Consider the two recent cases involving partners with Ernst & Young U.S.

The first case involved a romantic relationship between an audit partner and the CFO at the client. According to the SEC, "Their relationship was marked by a high level of personal intimacy, affection and friendship, near daily communications about personal and romantic matters (as well as work-related matters), and the occasional exchange of gifts of minimal value on holidays such as Valentine's Day and birthdays."

In the second case, the audit partner was given the responsibility to "develop" and "mend" the relationship with a client who had informed Ernst & Young that it was considering changing firms. In his role as relationship partner, the partner spent $109 000 in travel and entertainment between 2012 to 2015, while socializing with the company's CFO and his family. During that period, the partner and CFO shared hundreds of personal texts, emails, and voicemails. The CFO and partner frequently referred to each other as friend and shared personal information not typical of a professional relationship.

In both cases, the SEC asserted that a "reasonable investor with knowledge of all relevant facts and circumstances" of the partners' personal relationships would conclude that they were not capable of being objective in their roles as audit partners. The SEC noted that it was the first time it had enforced actions against auditors for failing to remain independent "due to close personal relationships between auditors and client personnel." Given the size of the fines, $9.3 million, it would seem that the SEC takes such violations quite seriously. Apart from the fines, Ernst & Young was dismissed as auditors for both of the clients and in one case, Ernst & Young withdrew its audit reports for the past two years and those years had to be re-audited.

Sources: Madeline Faber, "Ernst & Young was just fined $9.3 million for inappropriate client relationships," *Fortune*, September 20, 2016, accessed June 27, 2017, at **http://fortune.com/2016/09/20/ernst-and-young-fine-relationships/**. Matt Levine, "Love, friendship and public accounting don't mix," *Bloomberg View*, September 19, 2016, accessed June 27, 2017, at **https://www.bloomberg.com/view/articles/2016-09-19/love-friendship-and-public-accounting-don-t-mix**. Cydney Posner, "Auditor independence follow-up (updated)," *PubCo@ Cooley* (blog), accessed on June 27, 2017, at **https://cooleypubco.com/2016/09/23/auditor-independence-follow-up/**.

---

[4] Chartered Professional Accountants of Ontario, *CPA Code of Professional Conduct*, 2016, p. 15.

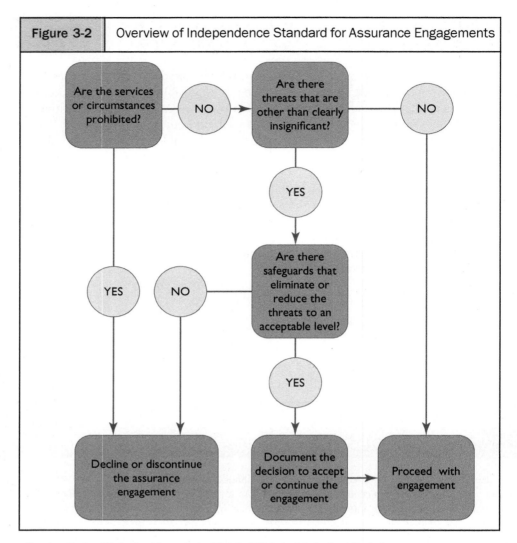

| Figure 3-2 | Overview of Independence Standard for Assurance Engagements |

Based on Chartered Professional Accountants of Ontario, CPA Code of Professional Conduct

advocacy, familiarity, and intimidation. Table 3-2 defines these threats to independence and provides examples.

Some of these threats affect overall independence. If you own shares in your client's business (**self-interest threat**) or are trying to help the client obtain financing (**advocacy threat**), you stand to gain from the result of the financial statement audit. A self-interest threat can also exist when a significant portion of the firm's revenue comes from a single assurance client. A more subtle threat may exist if the audit fees are unpaid for a long time. This can create a threat similar to a loan to a client.

The **self-review threat** means that you are auditing your own work. Imagine that you have assisted the client in designing an information system that calculates the costs for an inventory system. The new system seems to be working well, and there are excellent reports that track inventory movement and out-of-stock situations. However, during the design phase, you neglected to put in controls to highlight when the system creates a negative inventory situation, either due to clerical or programming error. What would you do during the audit? Perhaps you would be less likely to point out this error to the client in a management letter because it would imply that you did not properly perform your work during the system design. Alternatively, you might not detect the system inadequacy during your analysis of internal controls; you believe that it is such an excellent system that you do not need to complete a detailed analysis of internal controls. This example shows how a self-review threat can be very dangerous to the completion of a quality audit engagement.

Self-interest threat—a threat to independence where the member has a financial interest in the client or in the financial results of the client.

Advocacy threat—a threat to independence where the firm or member is perceived to promote (or actually does promote) the client's position.

Self-review threat—a threat to independence where the PA is in the position of having to audit his or her own work during the period.

Table 3-2	Threats to Auditors' Independence

Threat to Independence (defined)	Examples
Self-interest threat—when the member could receive a benefit because of a financial interest in the client or in the financial results of the client or due to a conflict of interest.	The firm or member owns shares in or has made a loan to the client. The client fees are significant in relation to the total fee base of the PA or of the firm.
Self-review threat—when the PA has made judgments in previous engagements that need to be evaluated in making conclusions on the assurance engagement (in other words, the PA is placed in the position of having to audit his or her own work or systems during the audit).	The PA might have prepared original data or records for the client as part of a bookkeeping engagement, or was an employee or officer of the organization. The PA could also have designed and implemented an accounting information system used to process client records.
Advocacy threat—when the firm or member is perceived to promote (or actually does promote) the client's position; that is, the client's judgment is perceived to direct the actions of the PA.	The PA is acting as an advocate in resolving a dispute with a major creditor of the client. The firm or PA is promoting the sale of shares or other securities for the client or is receiving a commission for such sales.
Familiarity threat—occurs when it is difficult to behave with professional skepticism during the engagement due to a belief that one knows the client well.	There is a long association between senior staff and the client (e.g., being on the engagement for 10 years). A former partner of the firm is now the chief financial officer of the client.
Intimidation threat—the client personnel intimidate the firm or its staff with respect to the content of the financial statements or with respect to the conduct of the audit, preventing objective completion of field work.	The client threatens to replace the audit firm over a disclosure disagreement. The client places a maximum upon the audit fee that is unrealistic with respect to the amount of work that needs to be completed.

Auditing in Action 3-1 provides two examples of the **familiarity threat.** In both cases, the partners had close personal relationships with their clients that could threaten their ability to objectively evaluate evidence or to be sensitive to "red flags" that may suggest a high fraud risk. What if those partners had realized that the senior executives of the company had intentionally overstated revenue in order to meet the ratios required by the covenants of a bank loan? As one might imagine, it can be very difficult to come forward and report one's friends or romantic partners.

Familiarity threat—a threat to independence that occurs when it is difficult to behave with professional skepticism during the engagement.

The **intimidation threat** is the possibility that the auditor may be intimidated by threat, by a dominating personality, or by other pressures, actual or feared, from the client. A frequent example is the threat that the audit firm may lose the audit engagement if the auditors do not agree with a particular accounting policy. However, many intimidation threats are much more subtle. Imagine you are an audit junior and the CFO is questioning why you are wasting her time with your constant questions. This could certainly influence the conduct of the audit.

Intimidation threat—a threat to independence that occurs when the client intimidates the public accounting firm or its staff with respect to the content of the financial statements or with respect to the conduct of the audit.

Evaluate the Significance of the Threat

When the PA assesses the significance of the threat, she considers whether there are any safeguards that will eliminate or reduce the threat to an acceptable level. The Rules of Professional Conduct define an acceptable level as the level where a reasonable observer would likely conclude that independence is not compromised.

Identify and Apply Safeguards

Required or prohibited actions and internal controls can serve as safeguards to eliminate or reduce threats to independence. When identifying safeguards, the PA should consider: (1) professional, legislative, or regulatory safeguards; (2) safeguards within

Table 3-3	Safeguards to Independence

Safeguard Category	Examples
Created by the profession, legislation, or securities regulation	Education and training provided by the professional accounting body Practice review conducted by the professional accounting body or by the CPAB (Canadian Public Accountability Board) Periodic rotation of senior members on the engagement
Provided by the client	A qualified, independent audit committee Corporate governance policies that restrict certain services with the external auditor Corporate polices or ethical codes that stress ethical behaviour and provide channels to discuss ethical issues
Available within the firm's systems and procedures	Tone at the top encouraging high-quality auditing and professional skepticism Firm policies and procedures that promote awareness and ensure compliance for independence Rotation of senior personnel on client engagements Required consultation

the client; and (3) safeguards within the firm. Table 3-3 lists these safeguards with examples. Safeguards that the firm can identify and apply must either eliminate the threats or reduce them to an acceptable level.

Safeguards by the Profession and Legislation Safeguards by the profession and legislation include rules regarding partner rotation, partner compensation, limits on the percentage of a firm's revenue from one client, and specific prohibited services. Other safeguards are independence reviews performed by the provincial practice inspectors and by CPAB inspectors. These reviews involve reviewing the quality control processes that the firms have in place as well as reviewing independence at the engagement level.

Safeguards at the Client Safeguards at clients can include policies that prohibit certain services and/or that encourage ethical conduct as well as a variety of controls. Some of the key safeguards are related to the audit committee.

An **audit committee** is a subcommittee of a company's board of directors that is independent of management and is responsible for oversight of both external and internal auditors. Incorporating acts generally require that the audit committee must be independent outside directors (i.e., not part of company management). Access to an active audit committee by internal and external auditors is one of the indicators of a healthy corporate governance structure.

Organizations listed on a Canadian or American stock exchange (regardless of size) are required to have an audit committee consisting of at least three independent directors who are financially literate. Publicly accountable enterprises (e.g., universities, large hospitals) are required to have an audit committee. Although not required to, many large private companies have audit committees. A typical audit committee decides such things as which public accounting firm to retain and the scope of services the public accounting firm is to perform. The audit committee also meets with the public accounting firm to discuss the progress and findings of the audit, and helps resolve conflicts between the public accounting firm and management.

The external auditor has the right to attend meetings of the audit committee. At least annually, the auditor should inform the audit committee of the following items: the level of the auditor's independence; all relationships between the auditor and his

Audit committee—selected members of a client's board of directors, who liaise with and provide a forum for the auditors to remain independent of management.

or her related business or practice and the entity and its related entities; and the total fees charged (separating out audit and non-audit services).

Safeguards at the Firm Public accounting firms have in place a range of safeguards to ensure independence. These include employee training programs, peer reviews, client acceptance, and continuance policies that help to identify threats, and engagement quality reviews. To ensure their effectiveness, as mentioned in Chapter 2, firms have monitoring mechanisms in place.

For Each Identified Independence Threat, Document How It Was Resolved

For each new and ongoing assurance engagement, audit engagement management, such as the partner and the manager, are required to evaluate, in writing, the independence of the firm and the staff assigned to the engagement. This formal **independence threat analysis** forms part of the documentation for the engagement. The documentation should include the threat, a description of the safeguard to eliminate or reduce the threat to an acceptable level, and how that safeguard eliminates or reduces that threat to an acceptable level. If the conclusion is that there are no safeguards to adequately reduce the threats, then the only alternatives are to decline or discontinue the assurance engagement (or, if applicable, the noninsurance services that are creating the threat).

Independence threat analysis— assessment of independence threats for a particular engagement.

Specific Prohibition

Prohibitions serve as an effective means to prevent independence threats. In some cases, the prohibition does not mean that the firm cannot take on the engagement; rather, it means that the individual affected cannot take part in the engagement. The following are prohibitions applicable to all assurance engagements:

- Members of the engagement team (and immediate family members) may not have a direct or material indirect financial interest in the entity.
- The firm or members of the engagement team may not have a loan from or a loan guaranteed by the entity (except in normal course of business, e.g., a bank).
- The firm and members of the engagement team cannot have a close business relationship with the entity, a related entity, or management (unless the financial interest is immaterial).
- Members of the engagement team may not have an immediate family member who is an officer or director of the client, who is in a position to exert significant influence over the subject matter, or who has an accounting role or financial reporting oversight role.
- A member of the engagement team must not serve as a director or officer during the period covered by the assurance report.
- Members and firms are prohibited from performing management functions (unless the entity's management directs and supervises their work).
- Members of the engagement team must obtain client approval for making journal entries and accounting classifications. The creation of original or source documents such as cheques and invoices is prohibited.
- Members and students on the engagement team and the firm may not accept other than insignificant gifts or hospitality from the assurance client.
- Key audit partners cannot be evaluated or compensated based on selling non-assurance services. (Key audit partners include the lead engagement partner, the engagement quality control reviewer, and other partners who make key decisions or judgments with respect to the audit.)

- A member or firm cannot charge a fee that is significantly lower than market (referred to as "low balling") unless it can be demonstrated that the engagement will follow all applicable standards.
- In general, firms cannot provide the following services to their assurance clients:
  - Accounting and bookkeeping.
  - Valuation services that involve a high level of subjectivity and will have a material effect on the financial statements.
  - Internal audit services.
  - Financial information systems design or implementation.
  - Litigation support services.
  - Legal services.
  - Corporate finance services.
  - Tax planning and related advisory services that have material effect on financial statements.

Prohibitions Specific to Listed Entities **Listed entities** are generally what we think of as public companies. The specific definition is those entities whose debts or shares are listed on a recognized stock exchange (in Canada and elsewhere) and that have market capitalization and total assets greater than $10 million.

The following prohibitions are only applicable to listed entities:

- A member or a firm cannot perform an audit if a person who would participate in the audit is an officer or director, or is in a financial reporting oversight role of the entity (unless a year has elapsed since the date the financial statements were filed with the relevant securities regulator).
- The firm cannot perform an audit if the chief executive officer (CEO) of the audit firm is an officer or director or is in a financial reporting oversight role of the entity, unless a year has elapsed since the person was the CEO of the firm.
- Key audit partners must leave the audit team after seven years. Lead partners cannot participate in the engagement for that particular company until five years have elapsed, and other key partners must wait until two years have elapsed.
- Unless specific measures are taken, firms are prohibited from performing the financial statement audit if 15 percent of the firm's total revenue comes from a listed entity for two consecutive years.
- Firms cannot provide actuarial or human resources services, and cannot provide tax calculations for purposes of preparing audit entries. In the case of valuation services, if they will be subject to audit procedures, they are prohibited regardless of materiality.

> **Listed entities**—entities whose debts or shares are listed on a recognized stock exchange (in Canada and elsewhere) and that have market capitalization and total assets greater than $10 million.

CONCEPT CHECK

C3-7 Distinguish between independence of mind and independence in appearance. Identify an activity that may not affect independence of mind but is likely to affect independence in appearance.

C3-8 Explain the role of the audit committee in enhancing auditor independence.

> **LO 6** Describe the CPA profession's enforcement mechanisms for public accountants' conduct.

ENFORCEMENT OF THE CODE OF PROFESSIONAL CONDUCT

The rules of conduct for CPAs are established and administered provincially. As described in Table 3-4, the various professional bodies have the power to impose penalties ranging from public censure in the body's newsletter or requiring that courses be taken to upgrade skills, to levying fines or expulsion. In some cases, the fines can be quite substantial.

Table 3-4	For Whom the Bell Tolls

Examples of Sanctions That Can Be Imposed Against PAs or Firms When Standards Are Violated
Publication of the name(s) of the violator(s) and the nature of the convicted offence
Sanctions from regulatory bodies such as the CPAB, OSC, or the SEC (e.g., refusal to accept new publicly listed clients for a period of time)
Refusal to renew PA licences for individuals or firms (with the CPAB)
Increased frequency of peer review
Appointment of an external monitor
Fines and/or payment of costs such as legal fees
Requirements to change quality control procedures
Mandatory education
Suspension of designation or expulsion from the professional accounting body

Since the professional accounting bodies are self-regulating, there is a danger that the public will perceive the disciplinary process as not being as stringent as it should be. This issue is dealt with by including laypersons on disciplinary committees and being transparent regarding disciplinary committee proceedings. (All information pertaining to disciplinary proceedings are available to the public.)

THE EXPECTIONS GAP AND AUDITOR LITIGATION

LO **7** Explain the relationship between the expectations gap and lawsuits.

As highlighted in the previous section, the professional accounting body can impose a variety of sanctions when public accountants fail to fulfill their professional responsibilities. However, these sanctions do not provide compensation for losses or damages that stakeholders may have incurred. In those instances, as illustrated in Auditing in Action 3-2, stakeholders may turn to the legal system to seek remedy.

Accounting professionals tend to agree that in most cases when an auditor has failed to uncover material misstatements and the wrong type of audit opinion is issued, it is appropriate to question whether the auditor exercised due care in performing the audit. **Audit failure** occurs when the auditor issues an inappropriate audit opinion as the result of an underlying failure to comply with the requirements of generally accepted auditing standards (GAAS). An example is a firm assigning unqualified assistants to perform certain audit tasks where they failed to notice material misstatements in the client's records that a qualified auditor would have found.

Audit failure—a situation in which the auditor issues an erroneous audit opinion as the result of an underlying failure to comply with the requirements of generally accepted auditing standards (GAAS).

In the case of audit failure, the law often allows parties who suffered losses to recover some or all of the losses caused by the audit failure. In practice, because of the complexity of auditing, it is difficult to determine when the auditor has failed to use **due care.** Also, legal precedent makes it difficult to determine who has the right to expect the benefit of an audit and recover losses in the event of an audit failure. Nevertheless, when an auditor fails to exercise due care, it often results in liability and, when appropriate, damages against the public accounting firm. However, the connection between audit failure and audit liability is not straightforward.

Due care—completing the audit with care, diligence, and skill.

The difficulty arises when there has been a business failure but not an audit failure. A **business failure** occurs when a business is unable to repay its lenders or meet the expectations of its investors because of economic or business conditions, such as a recession, poor management decisions, or unexpected competition in the industry. When a company goes bankrupt or cannot pay its debts, it is common for financial statement users to claim there was an audit failure, particularly when the most recently issued auditor's opinion indicates that the financial

Business failure—the situation when a business is unable to repay its lenders or meet the expectations of its investors because of economic or business conditions.

In June 2011, Carson Black, an analyst with Muddy Waters LLC, alleged forestry giant Sino-Forest Corp. was a "Ponzi scheme," charging that the company's $3 billion worth of timber assets were inflated. At that time, the Mississauga-based Sino-Forest, with timber holdings in China, was wildly popular with investors, and was the most valuable forestry company on the Toronto Stock Exchange (TSX), valued at more than $6 billion. By May 2012, it was a very different story. Sino-Forest had collapsed into bankruptcy, the auditors Ernst & Young (EY) had resigned, and the TSX had delisted the shares.

Following those catastrophic events, a $9.18 billion class action lawsuit was launched on behalf of Sino-Forest's investors against the company, its former executives, its auditors, and its underwriters. In addition, the Ontario Securities Commission (OSC) alleged that the company and some of its former executives were involved in a complex fraudulent scheme to inflate assets and revenue, made materially misleading statements, and falsified evidence of ownership for a vast majority of its timber holding. The regulator stated that it would seek up to $84 million in monetary penalties. In a separate statement of allegations, the OSC claimed that EY failed to perform sufficient audit work to verify the existence and ownership of Sino-Forest's timber assets and failed to perform the audit with an appropriate level of professional skepticism.

In late 2012, EY agreed to a $117 million settlement with respect to the class action lawsuit launched on behalf of the investors. It is the largest Canadian settlement ever with an auditor in this type of case. In the fall of 2014, EY and the OSC reached an $8 million settlement for its audits of Sino-Forest and another Chinese company, Zungui Haixi Corp., under the OSC no-contest rules, allowing the firm not to admit any wrongdoing. While this means that EY has neither denied nor admitted wrongdoing, the OSC lawyer, Yvonne Chisholm, noted that the auditor did not show enough "professional skepticism," it overlooked flaws in its clients' accounting records, and it did not conduct proper reviews. EY's lawyer, Linda Fuerst, told the hearing that the "honesty and integrity of Ernst & Young and its people were never in question." She said the settlement avoids the time, expense, and uncertainty of what would have been lengthy hearings. As EY's lawyer noted, auditor litigation is quite costly. In the case of the Big Four firms, 10–20 percent of the audit revenues are set aside for litigation costs.

Sources: Andy Hoffman and Jeffrey Gray, "EY settlement sets record for auditors," *Globe and Mail,* December 3, 2012, accessed June 27, 2017, at **http://www.theglobeandmail.com/globe-investor/ey-settlement-sets-record-for-auditors/article5945226/**. Ontario Securities Commission, Statement of Allegations in the Matter of Ernst & Young LLP. Richard Blackwell, "Ernst & Young reaches $8 million settlement over Sino-Forest audit," *Globe and Mail,* September 30, 2014, accessed June 27, 2017, at **http://www.theglobeandmail.com/report-on-business/ernst-young-reaches-8million-settlement-over-sino-forest-audit/article 20854668/**.

statements were fairly stated. Even worse, if there is a business failure and the financial statements were misstated, users may claim that the auditor was negligent, or lacked competence or independence, even if the audit was conducted in accordance with GAAS.

So how can an auditor issue an inappropriate opinion when the audit was conducted appropriately (in other words, according to GAAS)? In every audit, there is a possibility that the auditor will conclude after conducting an appropriate audit that the financial statements were fairly stated when, in fact they were materially misstated. This is what is called **audit risk.** Audit risk is unavoidable, because auditors gather evidence on a test basis and because well-concealed frauds are extremely difficult to detect. Therefore, as the legal counsel for E&Y claimed in the Sino-Forest case, the fact that the auditors did not detect the fraud does not mean that there was audit failure.

Audit risk—the risk that the auditor will conclude that the financial statements are fairly stated and an unqualified opinion can therefore be issued when, in fact, they are materially misstated.

Expectations gap—the gap between public expectations of the auditor's role and responsibilities and the auditor's responsibilities per GAAS.

The underlying cause of conflict between statement users and auditors is often attributed to the **expectations gap.** Most auditors believe that the conduct of the audit in accordance with auditing standards is all that can be expected of auditors. However, as highlighted in Table 3-5, many users have different expectations of the auditor's role and responsibilities. This expectations gap often results in unwarranted lawsuits, which ultimately result in millions of dollars spent in defence.

In the next part of this chapter, we will consider the major sources of legal liability, focusing on the two parties who bring claims against auditors—clients and third parties.

Table 3-5	The Expectations Gap—Common Issues

Financial Users' Expectations	Auditors' Responsibilities per Canadian Audit Standards
Auditors should accept the primary responsibility for the financial statements.	Management is responsible for the preparation and fair presentation of the financial statement in accordance with applicable accounting framework.
Auditors certify financial statements.	Auditors express an opinion on the financial statements based on their audit work.
A clean opinion guarantees the accuracy of financial statements.	The auditor obtains reasonable assurance that the financial statements are free from material misstatement.
Auditors perform a 100 percent verification.	The auditor gathers evidence on a test basis. The procedures selected vary according to the auditor's professional judgment.
Auditors should give early warning about the possibility of business failure.	It is management's responsibility to assess and disclose details regarding entity's ability to continue on a going concern. When the auditor has significant doubt regarding going concern, the auditor is required to assess management's plans and to highlight in the audit report the going concern note included in the financial statements.
Auditors are supposed to detect fraud.	The auditor is required to identify the risks that exist due to error and fraud (that could give rise to the risk of material misstatement) and to adjust the audit strategy accordingly.

MAJOR SOURCES OF AUDITOR LIABILITY

LO 8 Understand and analyze auditor legal liability.

Auditors have a responsibility under common law to fulfill implied or expressed contracts with clients. They have **legal liability** to their clients for negligence and/ or breach of contract should they fail to provide the services or should they fail to exercise due care in their performance. Auditors may also be held liable under the common law tort of negligence or provincial securities acts to parties other than their clients in certain circumstances.

Legal liability—the professional's obligation under the law to provide a reasonable level of care while performing work for those he or she serves.

The four main sources of auditors' legal liability, with examples, are summarized in Table 3-6.

The principal issue in cases involving alleged negligence is usually the standard of care required. Although it is generally agreed that nobody is perfect—not even a professional—any significant misstatement will create a doubt regarding competence. In the auditing environment, failure to meet GAAS is often strong evidence

Table 3-6	Major Sources of Auditors' Legal Liability

Source of Legal Liability in Assurance Engagements	Example of Potential Claim or Charge
Common law liability to client	Client sues auditor for not discovering a defalcation during the audit.
Common law liability to third parties	Bank sues auditor for not discovering materially misstated financial statements.
Liability under provincial securities acts	Purchaser of shares issued by a company sues auditor for not discovering materially misstated financial statements in a prospectus (this is called the "primary market"). Purchaser of shares on the secondary market sues auditor for not alerting the purchaser of material misstatement.
Criminal liability	Court prosecutes auditor under the Criminal Code of Canada for knowingly issuing an incorrect auditor's report.

of negligence. Under tort law, if an auditor is considered negligent, clients and third parties may sue the auditor. In order to prove negligence, the plaintiffs (the clients or third parties) must satisfy the following tests:

1. The auditor owed a duty of care to the plaintiff.
2. The auditor breached the duty of care.
3. The plaintiff suffered a loss.
4. The plaintiff's loss resulted, in part or wholly, from the auditor's breach of duty.

Liability to Clients

The most common source of lawsuits against CPAs is clients. Given that the auditor and client have a contractual relationship, unless there is a dispute over what services the auditor was engaged to perform, duty of care is usually not an issue. However, duty of care suits can happen in cases when accountants have performed a review engagement but the client was under the impression that the accountant would be performing audit procedures.

Client suits vary widely, including such claims as failure to complete a non-audit engagement on the agreed-upon date, inappropriate withdrawal from an audit, failure to discover an embezzlement (theft of assets), and breach of the confidentiality requirements of CPAs. Typically, the monetary amount of these lawsuits is relatively small, and they do not receive the publicity often given to suits involving third parties and public companies.

A typical lawsuit brought by a client involves a claim that, as a result of negligence in the conduct of the audit, the auditor did not discover an employee theft. The lawsuit can be for breach of contract, a tort action for negligence, or both. Tort actions are more common because the amounts recoverable under them are normally larger than under breach of contract.

Liability to Third Parties Under Common Law

In certain circumstances, a public accounting firm may be liable to third parties including actual and potential shareholders, vendors, bankers and other creditors or investors, employees, and customers. Since there is no contract, third parties must rely upon tort law. A significant legal hurdle for these claims is establishing that the auditor owed a duty of care.

Below is a brief summary of some key cases that have established auditor liability in Canada.

Ultramares Corporation v. Touche (1931) This American case is considered to be precedent setting for auditor liability. This case resulted in the *Ultramares* doctrine—auditors are not liable for ordinary negligence to parties with whom they do not have a privity (contractual) relationship. The judge concluded it would be inappropriate to hold the auditors liable to third parties, since this would open the doors to indeterminate liability of an indeterminate amount to an indeterminate number of people. Given that the auditors' audit report can be widely distributed and used for a variety of purposes, this doctrine is important in limiting auditors' liability.

Hedley Byrne & Co Ltd v. Heller and Partners Ltd (1964) A.C. 465 This British case had a large impact on auditors in commonwealth countries. It introduced the concept of foreseeable third parties. The court ruled that auditors are liable to third parties in situations where the auditors knew beforehand that the third parties would be relying upon their audit report. As a result, it expanded auditor liability beyond privity of contract.

Gordon T. Haig v. Ralph L. Bamford et al. (1977) This Canadian case confirmed that privity of contract is not necessarily a valid defence. In this case, the use of the audit report by the investors was foreseeable—the auditors knew the financial statements were to be used in a specific transaction. Further, auditors had knowledge of an identifiable class of limited third parties who would rely upon the financial statements.

The court held that the auditors owed a duty of care to the investors even though the auditor did not know their individual identities.

Hercules Management v. Ernst & Young (1997) This important Canadian case limits the scope of auditors' duty of care and was considered the answer to the profession's concerns over indeterminate liability. The shareholders of Hercules had claimed the auditors had negligently prepared the audit report upon which they relied for their investment decisions, causing them damages.

The court concluded that the shareholders were foreseeable users; however, it also took into account indeterminate liability. The case established that auditors would only owe a duty of care when:

- The auditor had knowledge of the specific third party or a narrow class of third parties; and
- The specific third party or limited class of third parties relied upon the financial statements for the specific purpose of the transaction for which they were prepared.

In this case, the judge concluded that the auditors did not prepare the audit reports in order to assist the shareholders in making personal investment decisions or for any purpose other than the standard statutory purpose (which is to evaluate management stewardship). On that basis, the judge ruled the auditor did not owe a duty of care to the shareholders, and dismissed the negligence claim. This case has had long-lasting impact on limiting auditor liability to shareholders.

The Estate of the Late Peter N. Widdrington v. Elliot C. Wightman et al. (2011) The judgment passed in this long-running case, known as *Castor Holdings*, is expected to have wide reaching impact for the audit industry. (See Auditing in Action 3-3 for details on the case.) The court ruled that the auditors (Coopers and Lybrand)

AUDITING IN ACTION 3-3
The Story of Castor Holdings' Litigation—A Long, Arduous Journey

Castor Holdings Limited was an unregulated financial intermediary that made its money by raising capital for commercial real estate projects. Despite its 1990 audited financial statements reporting assets of $1.8 billion, Castor declared bankruptcy in early 1992. Investors, lenders, and creditors soon learned from the bankruptcy trustee that the reported assets were virtually worthless. A multitude of lawsuits against the company's executives and the auditors, Coopers and Lybrand (C&L), ensued. In 1998, the Widdrington claim was selected as a test case that would go to trial first. In September 1998, just two months after C&L merged with accounting firm Price Waterhouse to form PricewaterhouseCoopers (PwC), the Widdrington trial (referred to as "the Castor case") began.

The long-running trial finally concluded on April 14, 2011, when Quebec Superior Court judge Marie St-Pierre issued her 753-page trial judgment. The Quebec judge concluded that the audited financial statements of Castor Holdings were materially misstated and misleading. She also concluded that C&L failed to perform the audit in accordance with generally accepted auditing standards. In her judgment, she noted that "superficiality and brevity characterized the audits" and that the audit planning "was performed in an automatic, thoughtless manner without professional judgment or serious consideration of anything other than going through the motions of mindlessly filling out forms." The Quebec Court of Appeal, which upheld the trial judgment, noted that the audit work performed by Coopers was "botched" and that it was "easy to see why the result was a fiasco." A final appeal was heard at the Supreme Court of Canada, which upheld the Quebec Court of Appeal's judgment.

On July 15, 2015, the 23-year legal saga came to an end when creditors voted to approve a settlement of $240 million. The former partners had to personally pay $74.5 million and the remainder came from money remaining in the company and from insurers and other parties.

Sources: Fishman Flanz Meland Paquin LLP, News Release, "The end of the Castor saga: Coopers' negligence and liability are confirmed as the Supreme Court of Canada denies leave to appeal," January 9, 2014, accessed July 15, 2017, at http://www.newswire.ca/en/story/1287557/the-end-of-the-castor-saga-coopers-negligence-and-liability-are-confirmed-as-the-supreme-court-of-canada-denies-leave-to-appeal. Janet McFarland, "Settlement approved for Castor Holdings in two-decade legal battle," *Globe and Mail*, July 22, 2015, accessed July 15, 2017, at http://www.theglobeandmail.com/report-on-business/industry-news/the-law-page/settlements-approved-for-castor-holdings-in-two-decade-legal-battle/article25635207/. Norton Rose Fulbright LLP, "The autopsy on the Castor saga," July 7, 2011, Lexology, accessed August 11, 2017, at http://www.lexology.com/library/detail.aspx?g=c2413c50-e1c3-494d-b92d-c4dd2d380af1.

owed a duty of care to the investors and that the auditor had breached that duty of care. Although the judge's interpretation of duty of care was consistent with *Hercules*, the ruling has important implications for indeterminate liability. The judge noted that, as a result of the decision, there were more than $1 billion of potential claims, yet she did not attempt to limit Coopers' liability based upon the concept of indeterminate liability. Rather, she noted that the auditors could have taken steps to protect themselves when they saw the broad purposes for which their work product was being used.

Liability to Third Parties Under Securities Law

Until recently, class action suits, such as Sino-Forest, were rare in Canada. However, amendments to provincial securities legislation have made it easier for shareholders to pursue securities class action suits. Securities legislation gives investors the right to sue auditors (in their role as expert) for misrepresentation in their audit report. Because the investors do not have to prove that they relied upon the representation, the duty of care restrictions from *Hercules* do not apply. In cases such as Sino-Forest, where the company is no longer solvent, auditors often become a target for class action suits. This is what is referred to as the "deep pockets" theory.

Criminal Liability

Most of us are familiar with some of the high profile U.S. cases, such as the Madoff scandal, in which the auditor was convicted of criminal charges related to fraud. In Canada, auditors can also face potential criminal liability related to fraudulent financial statements and possible civil action, if found guilty. However, these types of cases are extremely rare.

CONCEPT CHECK

C3-9 Who can sue auditors besides clients?

Auditors can also face criminal and quasi-criminal liability for breaches of securities legislation, in which the securities regulator makes the allegations. For instance, it is an offence under the Securities Act of Ontario to make a materially misleading or untrue statement or omission in any document required to be filed or submitted to the regulator. A violation of this provision could lead to a fine of as much as $5 million and/or imprisonment for a term of up to five years less a day.

LO 9 Explain how the profession and individual public accountants can reduce the threat of litigation.

THE PROFESSION'S RESPONSE TO LEGAL LIABILITY

The profession as a whole can do a number of things to reduce practitioners' exposure to lawsuits. Below are some specific activities:

- *Standard setting:* The IAASB and CPA Canada must constantly set standards and revise them to meet the changing needs of auditing. For example, changes to the auditing standards on auditor's responsibility to detect fraud were issued to address users' needs and expectations as to auditor performance.
- *Oppose lawsuits:* Public accounting firms must continue to oppose unwarranted lawsuits even if, in the short run, the costs of winning are greater than the costs of settling.

- *Educate users.* As we have learned, there is a large expectations gap regarding auditor's responsibilities. In order to reduce this gap, CPA Canada, leaders of public accounting firms, and educators should educate investors and others who read financial statements as to the meaning of an auditor's opinion and the extent and nature of auditors' work. In addition, users need to understand that auditors do not guarantee the accuracy of the financial records or the future prosperity of an audited company. People outside the profession need to understand that accounting and auditing are arts, not sciences. Perfection and precision are simply not achievable.
- *Sanction members for improper conduct and performance.* As highlighted in our discussion of professional ethics, the profession has an obligation to police its own membership.

Public accountants may also take specific action to minimize their liability. Below are some of the key actions:

- *Deal only with clients possessing integrity.* There is an increased likelihood of having legal problems when a client lacks integrity in dealing with customers, employees, units of government, and others. A PA firm needs procedures to evaluate the integrity of clients and should dissociate itself from clients found to be lacking integrity.
- *Maintain independence.* Independence is more than merely financial. Independence requires an attitude of responsibility separate from the client's interest. Much litigation has arisen from auditors' too-willing acceptance of client representations or from client pressure. The auditor must maintain an attitude of *healthy professional skepticism.*
- *Understand the client's business.* In several high profile litigation cases, the lack of knowledge of industry practices and client operations has been a major factor in auditors failing to uncover misstatements. As highlighted in Chapter 2's opening vignette, the CPAB has noted that a major cause of audit failure in audits of a company with foreign operations is the lack of understanding of the client's business and its practices.
- *Perform quality audits.* Quality audits require that auditors obtain appropriate evidence and make appropriate judgments about the evidence. It is essential, for example, that the auditor understand the client's internal controls and modify the evidence to reflect the findings. Improved auditing reduces the likelihood of failing to detect misstatements and the likelihood of lawsuits.
- *Document the work properly.* The preparation of good audit documentation helps the auditor perform quality audits. If an auditor has to defend an audit in court, quality audit documentation is essential, and should include *an engagement letter and a representation letter* that define the respective obligations of the client and the auditor.
- *Exercise and maintain professional skepticism.* Auditors are often liable when they are presented with information indicating a problem that they fail to recognize. Auditors need to strive to maintain a healthy level of skepticism, one that keeps them alert to potential misstatements, so that they can recognize misstatements when they exist.

CONCEPT CHECK

C3-10 Explain why some experts argue that the best defence against legal liability is careful client acceptance and continuance processes.

SUMMARY

The demand for audit and other assurance services provided by public accountants depends upon public confidence in the profession. This chapter discussed the unique ethical responsibilities of PAs and the *CPA Code of Professional Conduct*, which are enforced by the provincial accounting bodies, in providing guidance on what is morally permissible. Foremost of all ethical responsibilities for all PAs is the need for independence. The independence standard provides a framework to help guide PAs in identifying threats to independence and recommending appropriate safeguards. Other rules of conduct are designed to maintain public confidence in the profession.

The chapter also highlighted the role of the legal system in holding PAs accountable for their professional conduct. It provided insight into the legal environment in which PAs operate and the significant costs associated with litigation. No reasonable PA wants to eliminate the profession's legal responsibility for fraudulent or incompetent performance. It is certainly in the profession's best interest to maintain public trust in the competent performance of the auditing profession, while avoiding liability for cases involving strictly business failure and not audit failure. Aside from the profession and individual auditors taking steps to reduce litigation risk, the profession and society need to narrow the expectations gap. This involves a reasonable trade-off between the degree of responsibility the auditor should take for the financial statements and the audit cost to society.

Review Questions

3-1 **1** **2** What are the fundamental ethical principles for professional accountants? How can those principles aid in analyzing an ethical dilemma?

3-2 **1** **5** Why is an auditor's independence so essential?

3-3 **4** What consulting or non-audit services are prohibited for auditors of public companies? Explain why it is generally agreed that prohibitions on consulting and non-audit services will improve auditors' professional judgment and professional skepticism.

3-4 **5** Many people believe that a professional accountant cannot be truly independent when payment of fees are dependent on the management of the client. Explain two approaches that could reduce this appearance of lack of independence.

3-5 **4** Assume that an auditor makes an agreement with a client that the audit fee will be contingent upon the number of days required to complete the engagement. Is this a violation of the *CPA Code of Professional Conduct*? What is the essence of the rule of professional conduct dealing with contingent fees, and what are the reasons for the rule.

3-6 **4** **6** The rules of conduct of professional accountants require them to report a breach of the rules of conduct by a member to their profession's disciplinary body. What should they do before making such a report?

3-7 **4** After accepting an engagement, a PA discovers that the client's industry is more technical than at first realized and that the PA is not competent in certain areas of the operation. What should the PA do in this situation?

3-8 **4** Why is it so important that a successor auditor communicate with the incumbent before accepting an appointment as auditor? What should the successor do if the incumbent does not reply?

3-9 **7** Distinguish between business risk and audit risk. Why is business risk a concern to auditors?

3-10 **8** A common type of lawsuit against public accountants is for the failure to detect a defalcation. Should the auditor be responsible for failure to detect a defalcation? Explain why. Give authoritative support for your answer.

3-11 **7** Discuss why a number of Chartered Professional Accountant (CPA) firms have willingly chosen to settle lawsuits out of court. What are the implications to the profession from such actions?

3-12 [8] Distinguish among the auditor's potential liability to the client, liability to third parties under common law, and criminal liability. Describe one situation for each type of liability in which the auditor could be held legally responsible.

3-13 [9] In what ways can an individual public accountant positively respond to and reduce liability in auditing?

Multiple Choice Questions

3-14 [4] [5] An auditor strives to achieve independence in appearance to:
(1) Comply with the auditing standards of fieldwork.
(2) Become independent in fact.
(3) Maintain public confidence in the profession.
(4) Maintain an unbiased mental attitude.

3-15 [4] In which one of the following situations would a Chartered Professional Accountant be in violation of the *Code of Professional Conduct* in determining the audit fee?
(1) A fee is based on whether the CPA's report on the client's financial statements results in the approval of a bank loan.
(2) A fee is based on the outcome of a bankruptcy proceeding.
(3) A fee is based on the nature of the service rendered and the Chartered Professional Accountant's expertise instead of the actual time spent on the engagement.
(4) A fee is based on the fee charged by the prior auditor.

3-16 [4] A single-partner Chartered Professional Accountant firm took on a new client in the uranium mining industry. Most of the firm's clients operate in the retail service sector and the firm had until then never dealt with any business operating in the uranium sector. The audit fees for the new client are significant and the partner has indicated that "the staff assigned to the audit should be quickly able to learn the ins and outs of uranium and be able to perform a quality audit."
Which Rule of Professional Conduct has most likely been violated in the following situation?
(1) Association with false and misleading information.
(2) Contingent fees.
(3) Advertising and solicitation.
(4) Competence.

3-17 [5] Which of the following is not a safeguard to independence?
(1) A qualified, independent audit committee.
(2) Firm policies that limit direct communication between junior staff and the client's senior executives.
(3) Tone at the top encouraging high-quality auditing and professional skepticism.
(4) Periodic rotation of senior members on the engagement.

3-18 [7] Which of the following best defines the "expectations gap"?
(1) The difference between auditors and shareholders in their understanding of the financial statements of a specific company.
(2) The difference between what the company's directors know about the current affairs and future plans of the company and what information is shared with the auditors.
(3) The difference between what the company reports to the public and what the auditors state in their report.
(4) The difference between what the public believes the auditors performed as part of the audit and what actual work was conducted following the auditing standards.

3-19 [5] Zaspa Inc. is a public company that manufactures and sells tennis racquets. The company has expanded internationally and its auditors have resigned due to the fact that they have insufficient staff to meet the needs of the expanding business. In light of this fact, Zaspa has approached your firm, EA LLP, to take on the audit going forward. As part of client acceptance procedures, EA LLP must conduct an independence threat analysis. Below is a list of relationships.

For each EA LLP staff member below, explain the type of potential threat(s) to independence, determine whether or not the threat is significant (and explain why) and recommend a possible safeguard (if any) that can minimize the threat.

EA LLP Staff Member	Potential threat(s) to Independence (leave blank if none)	Is Threat Significant?	If Significant, Recommended Safeguard
Toni Kowalsky, partner. Toni and Zaspa's CEO, Roger, run a local summer tennis camp together. Toni and Roger became friends when they both worked at Zaspa. Toni left her role as finance VP at Zaspa 18 months ago.			
Patrick Sholer, senior manager. Patrick is a big tennis enthusiast and bought Zaspa tennis racquets for himself and his family.			
Chris Washolc, manager. Chris worked in Zaspa's internal audit department on review of payroll system controls, but left Zaspa two years ago.			
Sam Rivers, audit senior. Sam owns 1000 shares in Zaspa, inherited from his father's estate.			
Yolanda Ladna, audit senior. Yolanda plays on a semi-competitive volleyball team with four of Zaspa employees.			
Anna Madras, audit junior. Anne's father is a finance VP at Zaspa's parent company, which is listed on the TSX.			

Discussion Questions and Problems

3-20 **2 3** Tom Holton has a far too busy personal life to work overtime. To make certain that work does not interfere with his other plans, he tests only part of the assigned sample. For example, if he is asked to test 25 cash disbursement transactions, he tests the first 15 but indicates that he has tested all 25. Tom never comes across any problems and due to his ability to beat the time budget he has been given several recognition rewards. One partner has told him that employees like him are highly valued—ensuring that audit engagements are profitable is very important to the firm.

A supervisor, curious about Tom's amazing ability to beat the time budget, decides to carefully redo Tom's work. The supervisor concludes that Tom is signing off procedures without completing them. She immediately reports this to the partner in charge of the audit engagement.

REQUIRED
a. Using the ethical decision framework, analyze the situation and recommend what the partner should do.
b. Explain how rationalizations and ethical blindspots may have played a role in Tom's decision to test only part of the assigned sample.
c. Assume the partner discovers that Tom has a child who is extremely ill and Tom is the primary caregiver. Would this change your previous recommendation in Part a? Why or why not?

3-21 **4** Diane Harris, a PA, is the auditor of Fine Deal Furniture, Inc. In the course of her audit for the year ended December 31, 2015, she discovered that Fine Deal had serious going-concern problems. Henri Fine, the owner of Fine Deal, asked Diane to delay completing her audit.

Diane is also the auditor of Master Furniture Builders Ltd., whose year-end is January 31. The largest receivable on Master Furniture's list of receivables is Fine Deal Furniture; the amount owing represents about 45 percent of Master Furniture's total receivables, which, in turn, are 60 percent of Master Furniture's net assets. The management of Master Furniture is not aware of Fine Deal's problems and is certain the amount will be collected in full.

Master Furniture is in a hurry to get the January 31, 2016, audit finished because the company has made an application for a sizable loan from its bank to expand its operations. The bank has informally agreed to advance the funds based on draft financial statements submitted by Master Furniture just after the year-end.

REQUIRED

What action should Diane take and why?

3-22 **5** The following situations involve the provision of non-audit services.
a. Providing bookkeeping services to a listed entity. The services were preapproved by the audit committee of the company.
b. Providing internal audit services to a listed entity that is not an audit client.
c. Designing and implementing a financial information system for a private company.
d. Recommending a tax shelter to a client that is a publicly held listed entity. The services were preapproved by the audit committee.
e. Providing internal audit services to a listed entity audit client with the preapproval of the audit committee.
f. Providing bookkeeping services to an audit client that is a private company.

REQUIRED

For each situation, indicate whether providing the service is a violation of the rules of professional conduct for PAs. Explain your answer.

3-23 **4** Each of the following scenarios involves a possible violation of the rules of conduct.
a. John Brown is a PA, but not a partner, with three years of professional experience with Lyle and Lyle, Public Accountants, a one-office public accounting firm. He owns 25 shares of stock in an audit client of the firm, but he does not take part in the audit of the client and the amount of stock is not material in relation to his total wealth.
b. In preparing the corporate tax returns for a client, Phyllis Allen, PA, observed that the deductions for contributions and interest were unusually large. When she asked the client for backup information to support the deductions, she was told, "Ask me no questions, and I will tell you no lies." Phyllis completed the return on the basis of the information acquired from the client.
c. A private entity audit client requested assistance of Kim Tanabe, PA, in the installation of a computer system for maintaining production records. Kim had no experience in this type of work and no knowledge of the client's production records, so she obtained assistance from a computer consultant. The consultant is not in the practice of public accounting, but Kim is confident in her professional skills. Because of the highly technical nature of the work, Kim is not able to review the consultant's work.
d. Five small Moncton public accounting firms have become involved with an information project by taking part in an inter-firm working paper review program. Under the program, each firm designates two partners to review the working papers, including the tax returns and the financial statements, of another public accounting firm taking part in the program. At the end of each review, the auditors who prepared the working papers and the reviewers have a conference to discuss the strengths and weaknesses of the audit. They do not obtain the authorization from the audit client before the review takes place.
e. Roberta Hernandez, PA, serves as controller of a Canadian company that has a significant portion of its operations in several South American countries. Certain government provisions in selected countries require the company to file financial statements based on international standards. Roberta oversees the issuance of the company's financial statements and asserts that the statements are based on international financial accounting standards; however, the standards she uses are not those issued by the International Accounting Standards Board.
f. Bill Wendal, PA, set up a casualty and fire insurance agency to complement his auditing and tax services. He does not use his own name on anything pertaining to the insurance agency and has a highly competent manager, Renate Jones, who runs it. Bill frequently requests Renate to review with the management of an audit client the adequacy of the client's insurance if it seems underinsured. He feels that he provides a valuable service to clients by informing them when they are underinsured.
g. Michelle Rankin, PA, provides tax services, management advisory services, and bookkeeping services, and conducts audits for the same private company client. She requires management to approve, in writing, transactions and journal entries. Since her firm is small, the same person frequently provides all the services.

Indicate whether each is a violation and explain why you think it is or is not.

🌐 **3-24** 〔4〕 Each of the following situations involves possible violations of the rules of conduct that apply to professional accountants.

a. Martha Painter, PA, was appointed as the trustee of the So family trust. The So family trust owned the shares of the So Manufacturing Company, which is audited by another partner in Martha's office. Martha owns 15 percent of the shares of the So Manufacturing Company and is also a director of the company, in the position of treasurer.

b. Marie Godette, LLB, has a law practice. Marie has recommended one of her clients to Sean O'Doyle, a PA. Sean has agreed to pay Marie 10 percent of the fee Sean receives from Marie's client.

c. Theresa Barnes, PA, has an audit client, Choi Inc., which uses another public accounting firm for management services work. Unsolicited, Theresa sends her firm's literature covering its management services capabilities to Choi on a monthly basis.

d. Alan Goldenberg leased several vehicles from his friend Norm. Norm said that he would give Alan a $200 commission for each referral. Alan referred to Norm several clients who were interested in leasing vehicles. After a few months, Alan was pleased to receive a cheque for $3000 in the mail. Several of his clients had decided to change automobile leasing companies.

e. Edward Golikowski completed for his client financial projections that covered a period of three years. Edward was in a hurry and inadvertently stated that they covered five years; so he redid the client's calculations, rather than checking assumptions and doing field work, even though he attached an assurance report.

f. Marcel Poust, a PA, has sold his public accounting practice, which includes bookkeeping, tax services, and auditing, to Sheila Lyons, a PA. Marcel obtained permission from all audit clients for audit-related working papers before making them available to Sheila. He did not get permission before releasing tax- and management-services-related working papers.

For each situation, state whether it is a violation. Where there is a violation, explain the nature of the violation and the rationale for the existing rule.

🌐 **3-25** 〔5〕 Ann Archer serves on the audit committee of JKB Communications Inc., a telecommunications start-up company. The company is currently a private company. One of the audit committee's responsibilities is to evaluate the external auditor's independence in performing the audit of the company's financial statements. In conducting this year's evaluation, Ann learned that JKB Communications' external auditor also performed the following IT and e-commerce services for the company:

a. Installed JKB Communications' information system hardware and software selected by JKB management.

b. Supervised JKB Communications' personnel in the daily operation of the newly installed information system.

c. Customized a prepackaged payroll software application, based on options and specifications selected by management.

d. Trained JKB Communications' employees on the use of the newly installed system.

e. Determined which of JKB Communications' products would be offered for sale on the company's website.

f. Operated JKB Communications' local area network for several months while the company searched for a replacement after the previous network manager left the company.

Consider each of the preceding services separately. Evaluate whether the performance of each service is a violation of the rules of professional conduct.

3-26 〔4〕 The following are situations that may violate the general rules of conduct of professional accountants. Assume in each case that the public accountant is a partner.

a. Simone Able, a public accountant, owns a substantial limited partnership interest in an apartment building. Juan Rodriquez is a 100 percent owner in Rodriquez Marine Ltd. Juan also owns a substantial interest in the same limited partnership as Simone. Simone does the audit of Rodriquez Marine Ltd.

b. Horst Baker, a public accountant, approaches a new audit client and tells the president that he has an idea that could result in a substantial tax refund in the prior year's tax return by application of a technical provision in a tax law that the client has overlooked. Horst adds that the fee will be 50 percent of the tax refund after it has been resolved by Canada Revenue Agency. The client agrees to the proposal.

c. Chantal Contel, a public accountant, advertises in the local paper that her firm does the audit of 14 of the 36 largest drugstores in the city. The advertisement also states that the average audit fee, as a percentage of total assets for the drugstores she audits, is lower than that of any other public accounting firm in the city.

d. Olaf Gustafson, a public accountant, sets up a small loan company specializing in loans to business executives and small companies. Olaf does not spend much time in the business because he works full time in his public accounting practice. No employees of Olaf's public accounting firm are involved in the small loan company.

e. Louise Elbert, a public accountant, owns a material amount of stock in a mutual fund investment company, which, in turn, owns shares in Louise's largest audit client. Reading the investment company's most recent financial report, Louise is surprised to learn that the company's ownership in her client has increased dramatically.

REQUIRED

Discuss whether the facts in any of the situations indicate violations of the rules of conduct for professional accountants. If so, identify the nature of the violation(s).

3-27 **8** Helmut & Co., a public accounting firm, was the new auditor of Mountain Ltd., a private company in the farm equipment and supply business.

In early February 2015, Helmut & Co. began the audit for the year ended December 31, 2014. The audit was to be run by Frost, a senior who had just joined Helmut from another firm. Frost was to be assisted by two juniors.

Mountain, the president of Mountain Ltd., approached Frost and said that the Bank of Trail was prepared to increase its loan to Mountain upon receipt of the 2014 financial statements.

The juniors were assigned the accounts receivable and inventory sections, both of which were significant in relation to total assets, while Frost concentrated on the income statement and the remaining balance sheet accounts. The audit was finished quickly, and after a cursory review of the file and statements by Helmut, senior partner of Helmut & Co., the signed auditor's report was appended to the financial statements, which were delivered to Mountain, which, in turn, sent them to the bank.

The bank increased the loan significantly, principally on the basis of the very successful year the company had enjoyed despite the fact that the farm supply business was depressed. Several months later, Mountain Ltd. made an assignment in bankruptcy. The trustee found that many accounts receivable were still outstanding from the balance sheet date and that inventory on hand included substantial quantities of obsolete and damaged goods that had been included in the year-end inventory at cost. In addition, the year-end inventory amount included inventory that had been sold prior to the year-end.

Bank of Trail sued Helmut & Co. for negligence.

REQUIRED

Discuss Helmut & Co.'s defence. Is lack of privity a defence in this case? Was Helmut & Co. negligent? Explain your answer fully.

Professional Judgment Problems and Cases

3-28 **5** Marie encounters the following situations in doing the audit of a large auto dealership. Marie is not a partner.

1. The sales manager tells her that there is a sale (at a substantial discount) on new cars that is limited to long-established customers of the dealership. Because her firm has been doing the audit for several years, the sales manager has decided that Marie should also be eligible for the discount.

2. The auto dealership has an executive lunchroom that is available free to employees above a certain level. The controller informs Marie that she can also eat there any time.

3. Marie is invited to and attends the company's annual holiday party. When presents are handed out, she is surprised to find her name included. The present has a value of approximately $200.

Use the three-step process in the independence conceptual framework to assess whether Maria's independence has been impaired.

a. Describe how each of the situations might threaten Marie's independence from the auto dealership.
b. Identify a safeguard that Marie's firm could impose that would eliminate or mitigate the threat of each situation to Marie's independence.
c. Assuming no safeguards are in place and Marie accepts the offer or gift in each situation, discuss whether she has violated the rules of conduct.
d. Discuss what Marie should do in each situation.

3-29 **4** Donna, a public accountant, is approached by the owner of one of her clients, for whom she normally compiles monthly and annual financial statements, to perform an audit of the company's inventories. The client, Fantastic Fashions Ltd., is a chain of retail clothing stores that operates in several local shopping malls.

The owner explains that he is seeking new bank financing that will be secured by the inventories as collateral for the loan, and that the bank has requested an audit of the recorded inventories as a condition of granting the loan. The bank insists that it will lend no more than 75 percent of the amount of inventories as shown on an audited schedule of inventories that the owner has been asked to submit.

Because the owner is in urgent need of cash, he offers to pay Donna an audit fee equal to 10 percent of the loan amount, and Donna agrees to these terms. She then performs an audit of the inventories in accordance with generally accepted auditing standards, and issues a standard unqualified audit opinion, except that the opinion paragraph reads as follows: "In my opinion, this schedule presents fairly, in all material respects, the inventories of Fantastic Fashions Ltd. as at March 31, 2016, in accordance with generally accepted accounting standards for private enterprises."

REQUIRED

a. Prepare an independence analysis of the owner's request. Should Donna have accepted the engagement? Why or why not?
b. Did Donna violate any rules of professional conduct? If so, identify which rules and explain.

(Extract from AU2 CGA-Canada Examinations developed by the Certified General Accountants Association of Canada © 2010 CGA-Canada. Reproduced with permission. All rights reserved.)

3-30 **4** **5** In the aftermath of the Oscars envelope mix-up, the president of the Academy of Motion Picture Arts and Sciences (AMPAS) announced that was re-evaluating its long-running relationship with PwC. AMPAS and its affiliates is a not-for-profit organization.

PwC, which was hired by the AMPAS in 1934, is the Acadamy's financial statement auditor and provides tax services as well the services related to the Oscar balloting process. The AMPAS reported in its tax return that the total cost of its accounting services was $145 000.

Smaller organizations like the Hollywood Foreign Press Association, which produces the Golden Globes, pay more for their tax return preparation alone. Further, according to a Los Angeles area professional accountant who specializes in not-for-profits, the 1 700 hours that PwC stated it spent in the ballot process would cost more than $500 000.

Some commentators wonder if the AMPAS and PwC relationship is perhaps too cozy. In addition to the length of the relationship, the CFO, who joined the Academy in 2001, previously worked for PwC and his wife is a partner at PwC.

Source: Francine McKenna, "Why Oscars may not fire PwC, even as Academy president says two partners now banned," *Market-Watch*, March 1, 2017, accessed on June 9, 2017 at **http://www.marketwatch.com/story/the-reasons-pwc-may-keep-its-lock-on-the-oscars-audit-2017-02-28**.

REQUIRED

a. Prepare an independence analysis of the relationship between AMPAS and PwC. Do you think that threats to PwC's independence are such that it affects the conduct of the audit?
b. Did PwC violate any rules of professional conduct? If so, identify which rules and explain.

3-31 **4** **5** Robert Lewandowski, the owner of iEat Inc., a private company that designs and installs interactive computer display terminals in coffee shops and restaurants, recently switched auditors and hired his friend Chris Persson to perform the company's annual financial statement audit. iEat needs the audit as part of its financing arrangement with a private lender. Chris recently received his Chartered Professional Accountant (CPA) designation and was eager to make some money to pay off his student loans. So he offered Robert a discount and promised to perform the audit for 15 percent less than any other accounting firm.

To appease the private lender, Robert told Chris that iEat must have a clean audit opinion. Chris told Robert that it should not be a problem as he recently wrote the Certified Fraud Examiner exam, and because of that his work would be superior to that of other "older" auditors who may not be as up-to-date on the most recent auditing and accounting standards. Chris also felt obligated to help his friend, as two years ago Robert co-signed on a mortgage for Chris's condo. Since Chris trusted Robert he did not bother to communicate with the previous auditor of iEat.

By discounting his audit fee and promising to perform audits better and faster than other accounting firms, over a short period of time, Chris was able to add a few other clients. When the iEat audit was scheduled to start in March 2018, Chris was so busy with other audits and the preparation of corporate tax returns for his audit clients that he had no time to conduct the iEat audit. Instead, he hired Adam and Ewa, two recent university accounting graduates to do the work.

Chris told Adam and Ewa to quickly review their university audit textbook and begin the iEat audit immediately. He instructed them to first draft a clean audit opinion and email it to him and in three weeks return back with an audit file that would support the drafted clean opinion. Burdened with their student loans and facing a tough job market, Adam and Ewa accepted this new challenge. They also felt that it would help them in their preparations for the CPA PEP Assurance module.

To get Adam and Ewa started on the iEat audit Chris provided them the audit plan for another audit client he was working on. This audit program did not always match up with what had to be done at iEat, so Chris instructed Adam and Ewa to delete whatever was not relevant, but not to add anything, as that would only make things more complicated and could delay the completion of the audit.

Chris was also glad when he found out that Adam was related to the controller of iEat. He thought that this relationship would make the audit go more smoothly and quickly. Alexandra, the controller, was Adam's aunt and he lived with her when he attended his last year of university. Alexandra had also promised to hire Adam once he received his CPA designation.

Chris came to iEat only once over the course of the three-week audit to discuss iEat's corporate tax return with Chris and Alexandra. He did, however, like to Snapchat with Ewa and at least once a day sent her a goofy Live Story.

From his audit class, Adam remembered that it was important for auditors to attend and observe the year-end inventory count, so he became concerned when he found out that Ewa failed to show up and observe the year-end count at two warehouses that were assigned to her. Instead, Ewa went out clubbing to celebrate her friend's birthday. The iEat audit program stated that inventory should be observed at three warehouse locations, but Adam had only observed the inventory at one warehouse. When Adam told Chris about what happened, he told him to get inventory listing sheets from Alexandra for the two warehouses assigned to Ewa and make sure that the inventory balance in iEats's general ledger agreed with the total for all their inventory sheets. At the end of the audit Adam and Ewa brought their working papers to Chris, who had little time to review them, as he was still busy with completing iEat's tax return. Chris recorded his conclusion that "the financial statements are fairly stated" and asked Adam to print the audit opinion they drafted for him at the start of the audit.

REQUIRED

Identify and discuss the *Rules of Professional Conduct* violated and the nature of the violations. In addition, identify and discuss any actions taken during the audit that have resulted in the failure to comply with generally accepted auditing standards.

3-32 **2** Barbara Whitley had great expectations about her future as she sat at her graduation ceremony in May 2015. She was about to receive her Master of Accountancy degree, and the following week she would begin her career on the audit staff of Green, Thresher & Co., a public accounting firm. Things looked a little different to Barbara in February 2016. She was working on the audit of Delancey Fabrics Ltd., a textile manufacturer with a calendar year-end. The pressure was enormous. Everyone on the audit team was putting in 70-hour weeks, and it still looked as if the audit would not be done on time. Barbara was doing work in the property

area, vouching additions for the year. The audit program indicated that a sample of all items over $10 000 should be selected, plus a non-statistical sample of smaller items. When Barbara went to take the sample, Jack Bean, the senior, had left the client's office and could not answer her questions about the appropriate size of the judgmental sample. Barbara forged ahead and selected 50 smaller items on her own judgment. Her basis for doing this was that there were about 250 such items, so 50 was a reasonably good proportion of such additions. Barbara audited the additions with the following results: The items over $10 000 contained no errors; however, the 50 small items contained a large number of errors. In fact, when Barbara projected them to all such additions, the amount seemed quite significant.

A couple of days later, Jack Bean returned to the client's office. Barbara brought her work to Jack in order to inform him of the problems she found, and got the following response, "Barbara, why did you do this? You were supposed to look only at the items over $10 000, plus 5 or 10 little ones. You've wasted a whole day on that work, and we can't afford to spend any more time on it. I want you to throw away the schedules where you tested the last 40 small items and forget you ever did them."

When Barbara asked about the possible audit adjustment regarding the small items, none of which arose from the first 10 items, Jack responded, "Don't worry, it's not material anyway. You just forget it; it's my concern, not yours."

REQUIRED

a. In what way is this an ethical dilemma for Barbara?
b. Using the ethical decision making framework, analyze Barbara's ethical dilemma.
c. What should Barbara do to resolve the dilemma?

3-33 **8** The public accounting firm of André, Mathieu, & Paquette (AMP) was expanding very rapidly. Consequently, it hired several junior accountants, including Sam Small. The partners of the firm eventually became dissatisfied with Small's production and warned him that they would be forced to terminate him unless his output increased significantly.

At that time, Small was engaged in audits of several clients. He decided that to avoid being fired, he would reduce or omit entirely some of the standard auditing procedures listed in audit programs prepared by the partners. One of the public accounting firm's clients, Newell Corporation, was in serious financial difficulty and had adjusted several of the accounts being examined by Small to appear financially sound. Jim prepared fictitious working papers in his home at night to support the supposed completion of auditing procedures assigned to him, although he did not in fact examine the adjusting entries. The public accounting firm rendered an unqualified opinion on Newell's financial statements, which were grossly misstated. Several creditors, relying on the audited financial statements, subsequently extended large sums of money to Newell Corporation.

REQUIRED

Would the public accounting firm be liable to the creditors who extended the money because of their reliance on the erroneous financial statements if Newell Corporation should fail to pay them? Explain.

Source: Adapted from AICPA. Used with permission of AICPA.

3-34 8 Jan Sharpe recently joined the public accounting firm of Spark, Watts, and Wilcox. On her third audit for the firm, Sharpe examined the underlying documentation of 200 disbursements as a test of purchasing, receiving, vouchers payable, and cash disbursement procedures. In the process, she found 12 disbursements for the purchase of materials with no receiving reports in the documentation. She noted the exceptions in her working papers and called them to the attention of the audit supervisor. Relying on prior experience with the client, the audit supervisor disregarded Sharpe's comments, and nothing further was done about the exceptions.

Subsequently, it was learned that one of the client's purchasing agents and a member of its accounting department were engaged in a fraudulent scheme whereby they diverted the receipt of materials to a public warehouse while sending the invoices to the client. When the client discovered the fraud, the conspirators had obtained approximately $70 000, of which $50 000 was recovered after the completion of the audit.

REQUIRED

Discuss the legal implications and liabilities of Spark, Watts, and Wilcox as a result of the facts just described.

3-35 7 8 As mentioned in Auditing in Action 3-2, Ernst & Young recently paid the largest settlement in a Canadian class action suit related to its audits of Sino-Forest. It subsequently paid an $8 million penalty to the OSC in relation to its audits of Sino-Forest and the athletic shoe manufacturer, Zungui Haixi Corp. In its press releases regarding both of the settlements, Ernst & Young did not admit to any wrongdoing.

REQUIRED

a. Using appropriate sources, research the case and decide whether or not you agree with the OSC's allegations that Ernst & Young failed to perform sufficient audit work to verify the existence and ownership of Sino-Forest's timber assets and failed to perform the audit with an appropriate level of professional skepticism.

b. Discuss your views on Ernst & Young's agreement to settle the class action suit and the OSC case despite claiming its audit work met all professional standards.

The Audit Process and Risk Assessment

Part 2 introduces the audit process and focuses on the activities related to planning—in particular risk assessment. Because the planning concepts covered in these chapters will be used extensively throughout the rest of the book, it is essential for you to master this material and fully understand the importance of planning and risk assessment.

- Chapter 4 explains auditors' and management responsibilities, assertions, and audit objectives, and provides a brief overview of the audit process.

- Chapter 5 deals with general audit evidence concepts.

- Chapters 6 and 7 explain the activities related to identifying and assessing the risk of material misstatement by understanding the entity and its environment.

- Chapters 8 and 9 explain the application of the COSO (Committee of Sponsoring Organizations of the Treadway Commission) framework to understand internal control and the assessment control risk at the financial statement level and assertion level.

- Chapter 10 summarizes and integrates risk assessment and audit evidence, and explains the development of an overall risk response.

Many of the concepts throughout the remainder of the book are illustrated with examples based on Hillsburg Hardware Limited. The trial balance, financial statements, and other background information are included in the Appendix at the end of the textbook.

AUDIT RESPONSIBILITIES AND OBJECTIVES

Now that you have an understanding of the environment within which an auditor functions, we can begin to look at the specifics of the financial statement audit.

LEARNING OBJECTIVES

After studying this chapter, you should be able to:

1 Explain the objective of conducting an audit of financial statements.

2 Explain management's responsibility for the financial statements and internal controls.

3 Explain the responsibilities of those in charge of governance for financial statements and internal controls.

4 Explain the auditor's responsibility for discovering material misstatements due to fraud or error.

5 Explain and apply the key elements of an effective professional judgment process.

6 Describe the need to maintain professional skepticism when conducting the audit.

7 Identify the benefits of a cycle approach to segmenting the audit.

8 Explain how the auditor obtains assurance by auditing classes of transactions and ending balances in accounts, including presentation and disclosure.

9 Distinguish among the management assertions about financial information.

10 Link management assertions with audit objectives.

11 Explain how the audit process ensures that audit objectives are met and evidence is sufficient and appropriate.

Riding the Tiger: Indian Computer Company Engages in Billion Dollar Fraud

During the period 2003 to 2008, Satyam Computer Services Limited, an information technology services company based in Hyderabad, India, that serviced more than a third of the Fortune 500 companies, roiled Indian stock markets when it announced it had deceived investors by engaging in a massive fraud. Company chairman Ramalinga Raju resigned after announcing that 50.4 billion rupees (US$1.04 billion) of the 53.6 billion rupees the company listed as assets in its financial statements for the second quarter ending in September 2008 did not exist.

continued >

During the period of the fraud, senior management manufactured over 6000 fictitious invoices representing over $1 billion in revenue for services that were never provided, in some cases for customers that did not exist. Management also created false bank statements to reflect payments on the false invoices and support the fictitious cash balances. Satyam provided certain employees with an administrative "super user" login identification and password that allowed them to access the invoice management system to record the false invoices. This process allowed those invoices to be included in revenue, but concealed their existence from the heads of Satyam's business units, who would recognize that the services had not been provided.

Satyam's auditors sent confirmations to verify the existence of the bank balances. However, they did not maintain control over the confirmations as required by auditing standards. The audit engagement team relied on Satyam management to mail out the confirmation requests to the banks, and to return the confirmation responses to the engagement team, instead of directly contacting the banks as required by auditing standards.

Raju admitted that he intentionally maintained the inflated revenues and profits because public knowledge of the company's poor performance would likely lead to a takeover of the company, thereby exposing the fraud. Raju indicated, "It was like riding a tiger, not knowing how to get off without being eaten." On January 7, 2009, the New York Stock Exchange suspended trading of the company's American Depository Shares (ADS). When trading resumed on January 12, 2009, Satyam's ADS price declined nearly 85 percent to close at US$1.46. The Government of India assumed control of the company by dissolving Satyam's board of directors and then selected a strategic investor to run the company.

Sources: Securities and Exchange Commission, "SEC charges Satyam Computer Services with financial fraud," News Release 2011-81, April 5, 2011, accessed June 24, 2017, at **www.sec.gov/news/press/2011/2011-81.htm**. SEC Litigation Release 21915, April 5, 2011, Securities and Exchange Commission, accessed June 24, 2017, at **www.sec.gov/litigation/complaints/2011/comp21915.pdf**. Public Company Accounting Oversight Board, PCAOB Release No. 105-2011-002, April 5, 2011, accessed June 24, 2017, at **pcaobus.org/Enforcement/Decisions/Documents/PW_India.pdf**.

The Satyam story illustrates failure by the auditors to achieve the objectives of the audit of the company's financial statements. This chapter describes the overall objectives of the audit, the auditor's responsibilities in conducting the audit, and the specific objectives the auditor tries to accomplish. Without an understanding of these topics, planning and accumulating audit evidence during the audit has no relevance.

THE OBJECTIVE OF CONDUCTING AN AUDIT OF FINANCIAL STATEMENTS

LO 1 Explain the objective of conducting an audit of financial statements.

CAS 200 of the *CPA Canada Handbook* explains that the purpose of the financial statement audit is to express an opinion on the financial statements. This opinion represents the auditors' assurance to the users. It is an assessment of whether the financial statements are presented fairly, in the context of materiality, in conformity with an applicable financial reporting framework as the criteria for the assessment.

If the auditor believes that the statements are not fairly presented or is unable to reach a conclusion because of insufficient evidence or prevailing conditions, the auditor has the responsibility to notify the users through the auditor's report. Subsequent to their issuance, if facts indicate that the statements were not fairly presented, as in the Satyam case, the auditor will probably have to demonstrate to the courts or regulatory agencies that the audit was conducted in a proper manner and the auditor reached reasonable conclusions.

CAS 200 also highlights that in addition to the auditor, two other parties—management and, where appropriate, those charged with governance—have certain responsibilities that are fundamental to the conduct of the audit.

STATEMENT OF MANAGEMENT'S RESPONSIBILITY FOR FINANCIAL REPORTING

The consolidated financial statements have been prepared by management. Management is responsible for the fair presentation of the consolidated financial statements in conformity with generally accepted accounting principles in Canada which incorporates International Financial Reporting Standards. Management is responsible for the selection of accounting policies and making significant accounting judgements and estimates. Management is also responsible for all other financial information included in management's discussion and analysis and for ensuring that this information is consistent, where appropriate, with the information contained in the consolidated financial statements.

Management is responsible for establishing and maintaining adequate internal control over financial reporting which includes those policies and procedures that provide reasonable assurance over the safeguarding of assets and over the completeness, fairness and accuracy of the consolidated financial statements and other financial information.

The Audit, Finance and Risk Committee, which is comprised entirely of independent directors, reviews the quality and integrity of the Corporation's financial reporting and provides its recommendations, in respect of the approval of the financial statements, to the Board of Directors; oversees management's responsibilities as to the adequacy of the supporting systems of internal controls; provides oversight of the independence, qualifications and appointment of the external auditor; and, pre-approves audit, audit-related, and non-audit fees and expenses. The Board of Directors approves the Corporation's consolidated financial statements and management's discussion and analysis disclosures prior to their release. The Audit, Finance and Risk Committee meets with management, the internal auditors and external auditors at least four times each year to review and discuss financial reporting, disclosures, auditing and other matters.

The external auditors, PricewaterhouseCoopers LLP, conduct an independent audit of the consolidated financial statements in accordance with Canadian generally accepted auditing standards and express their opinion thereon. Those standards require that the audit is planned and performed to obtain reasonable assurance about whether the consolidated financial statements are free of material misstatement. The external auditors have unlimited access to the Audit, Finance and Risk Committee and meet with the Committee on a regular basis.

(signed) Calin Rovinescu
Calin Rovinescu
President and Chief Executive Officer
February 16, 2017

(signed) Michael Rousseau
Michael Rousseau
Executive Vice President and Chief Financial Officer

Source: Air Canada. (2016). Consolidated Financial Statements and Notes. Used with permission.

MANAGEMENT'S RESPONSIBILITIES

LO 2 Explain management's responsibility for the financial statements and internal controls.

The auditor's report, which was introduced in Chapter 2 (see Figure 2-2), outlines management's responsibilities. The responsibility for adopting a sound and appropriate financial reporting framework and corresponding accounting policies (including assessing the appropriateness of the going-concern basis of accounting), maintaining adequate internal control, and making fair representations in the financial statements *rests with management* rather than with the auditor. Because it operates the business daily, a company's management knows more about the company's transactions and related assets, liabilities, and equity than the auditor. In contrast, the auditor's knowledge of these matters and internal controls is limited to that acquired during the audit.

The annual reports of many public companies include a statement about management's responsibilities and relationship with the public accounting firm. Figure 4-1 presents Air Canada's Statement of Management Responsibility for Financial Reporting, which was included in its 2016 annual report. Read the report carefully to determine what management states about its responsibilities.

Management's responsibility for the fairness of the representations (assertions) in the financial statements carries with it the privilege of determining which disclosures it considers necessary. Although management has the responsibility for the preparation

In preparing the consolidated financial statements for 2015–16, the Government of Ontario and the Auditor General of Ontario had a dispute over the appropriate accounting treatment of pension assets for Ontario Public Service Employees Union Pension Plan and the Ontario Teachers' Pension Plan. This dispute became public when the government decided to release its consolidated financial statements without an audit opinion from the Auditor General.

Bonnie Lysyk, the Auditor General, argued that the two pension plans did not meet the definition of an asset because the government did not have ready access to the funds. Lysyk stated that she "no longer believes the government should include on its bottom line its share of assets from the teachers' and public servants' pension funds." As a result, Lysyk concluded that financial statements were materially misstated—the net debt and accumulated deficit being understated by $10.7 billion and the bottom line being understated by $1.5 billion. For the first time in 23 years, the Auditor General issued a qualified audit opinion.

Needless to say, the Ontario government was not happy. It had promised to eliminate its fiscal deficit before the next scheduled election in 2018, and if it restated its financial statements this would not be possible. The government stood by its accounting policy and chose not to include the qualified audit opinion. It argued, "recognizing the asset will provide an accurate representation of the province's financial position. This means that the province will continue to represent pension assets on its financial statements as it has since 2001."

Given that from 2001 to 2016, three auditors general, including Lysyk, did not raise any concerns regarding the pension assets, one wonders what had changed? When asked, Lysyk said that during the 2015–16 audit, her office took a closer look at the government's claim to the pension assets and found that the government's interpretation of the accounting standards was wrong. As at time of writing, this is something that the government continues to dispute.

Sources: Robert Benzie, "Government rejects auditor's claim, concludes $10.7B pension surplus an asset," *Toronto Star*, February 16, 2017, accessed June 14, 2017, at **https://www.thestar.com/news/queenspark/2017/02/16/auditor-refuses-to-back-down-in-107b-pension-feud.html**. Robert Benzie, "Accounting spat leads to differing Ontario deficit figures," *Toronto Star*, October 3, 2016, accessed June 14, 2017, at **https://www.thestar.com/news/queenspark/2016/10/03/accounting-spat-leads-to-differing-ontario-deficit-figures.html**. Treasury Board Secretariat, "Release of Ontario's 2015–16 financial statements," News Release, October 3, 2016, accessed June 14, 2017, at **https://news.ontario.ca/tbs/en/2016/10/release-of-ontarios-2015-16-financial-statements.html**. Treasury Board Secretariat, "Pension asset expert advisory panel submits report," News Release, February 13, 2017, accessed June 14, 2017, at **https://news.ontario.ca/tbs/en/2017/02/pension-asset-expert-advisory-panel-submits-report.html**.

of the financial statements and the accompanying footnotes, it is acceptable for an auditor to draft this material for the client or to offer suggestions for clarification as long as management understands and approves to mitigate self-review threats as discussed in Chapter 3.

In the event that management insists on financial statement disclosure that the auditor finds unacceptable, the auditor can either issue a qualified or an adverse opinion or, as a last resort, withdraw from the engagement. Auditing in Action 4-1 provides an interesting insight into what can happen when those responsible for the financial statements (in this case the Ontario government) and the auditor do not agree on a particular accounting issue. Reporting is discussed further in Chapter 19.

In the case of public companies, the chief executive officer (CEO) and chief financial officer (CFO) must certify that: (1) the financial statements fully comply with the requirements of the stock exchange; (2) the statements do not contain any misrepresentations or material omissions and present fairly the financial condition of the company; and (3) disclosure controls and procedures or internal controls over financial reporting have been designed, evaluated, and disclosed. The various provincial securities acts provide for fines and possible criminal penalties for anyone who knowingly falsely certifies those statements.

In addition to responsibility for preparation of the financial statements and internal controls, CAS 200 also highlights that it is management's responsibility to provide the auditor with the following:

- Access to all information that is relevant to the preparation of the financial statements such as records, documentation, and other matters;
- Any additional information that the auditor may request; and
- Unrestricted access to persons within the entity from whom the auditor determines it necessary to obtain audit evidence.

RESPONSIBILITIES OF THOSE CHARGED WITH GOVERNANCE

Corporate governance "is a set of relationships between the company's management, its board, its shareholders, and other stakeholders. Corporate governance also provides the structure through which the objectives of the company are set, and the means of attaining those objectives and monitoring performance are determined."[1] In most entities, those charged with governance usually form some sort of governing body, such as a board of directors. In some smaller entities, however, one person may be charged with governance: for example, the owner–manager, where there are no other owners, or a sole trustee.

How management and those charged with governance divide up their responsibilities regarding financial reporting and the audit will depend on the organization's governance structure and relevant laws and regulations. As highlighted in the auditor's report in Chapter 2 (Figure 2-2), management is responsible for financial statement preparation and internal controls, while those charged with governance are responsible for oversight of the financial reporting process (which would include oversight of management and the financial statement audit). As part of those oversight responsibilities, those in charge of governance approve the audited financial statements. You will note in Figure 4-1 that Air Canada's board of directors and the audit committee approved the financial statements.

If the organization has an audit committee (we discussed its role in relation to auditor independence in Chapter 3), that board subcommittee is responsible for oversight of management in relation to financial statement preparation and internal controls and the external auditor. Publicly accountable entities—which include public companies, cooperative business enterprises, regulated financial institutions, rate-regulated enterprises (such as utility companies), government business enterprises, and government business-type organizations—are required by legislation to have an audit committee. Although there is no legislative requirement, many large private companies and not-for-profit organizations also have audit committees.

You will note that in the Air Canada financial statement excerpt there is reference to the responsibilities of the Audit, Finance, and Risk Committee (that company's equivalent to the audit committee). In addition, the chair of the board and the chair of the audit committee signed the first page of the financial statements (the balance sheet) to indicate that they have approved the financial statements. In the case of Air Canada, the audit committee reviews the quality and integrity of the corporation's financial reporting; oversees management's responsibilities as to the adequacy of internal controls; oversees the independence, qualifications, and appointment of the external auditor; and, preapproves audit and audit-related fees and expenses.

LO **4** Explain the auditor's responsibility for discovering material misstatements due to fraud or error.

CAS

AUDITOR'S RESPONSIBILITIES

CAS 200 of the *CPA Canada Handbook* states that the overall objectives of the audit of the financial statements are:

1. To obtain reasonable assurance about whether the financial statements as a whole are free from material misstatement, whether due to fraud or error, thereby enabling the auditor to express an opinion on whether the financial statements are prepared, in all material respects, in accordance with an applicable financial reporting framework; and

---

[1] Organisation for Economic Co-operation and Development, *OECD Principles of Corporate Governance*, revised in April 2004, accessed March 16, 2015, at **www.oecd.org/corporate/ca/ corporategovernanceprinciples/31557724.pdf**.

2. To report on the financial statements, and communicate as required by the CASs, in accordance with the auditor's findings.

This paragraph and the related discussion in the standards about the auditor's responsibility to detect material misstatements include several important terms and phrases.

Material Versus Immaterial Misstatements

Auditors are responsible for detecting material misstatements. Misstatements are usually considered material if the combined uncorrected errors and fraud in the financial statements would likely have changed or influenced the decisions of a reasonable person using the statements. Although it is difficult to quantify a measure of materiality, auditors are responsible for obtaining reasonable assurance that this materiality threshold has been satisfied. It would be extremely costly (and probably impossible) for auditors to have responsibility for finding all immaterial errors and fraud.

Reasonable Assurance

Assurance is a measure of the level of certainty that the auditor has obtained at the completion of the audit. Auditing standards indicate that reasonable assurance is a high, but not absolute, level of assurance that the financial statements are free of material misstatements. The concept of reasonable, but not absolute, assurance indicates that the auditor is not an insurer or guarantor of the correctness of the financial statements. Thus, an audit that is conducted in accordance with auditing standards may fail to detect a material misstatement.

The auditor is responsible for reasonable, but not absolute, assurance for several reasons:

1. Most audit evidence results from testing a sample of a population such as accounts receivable or inventory. Sampling inevitably includes some risk of not uncovering a material misstatement. Other factors that require significant auditor judgment include: the areas to be tested; the type, extent, and timing of those tests; and the evaluation of test results. Even with good faith and integrity, auditors can make mistakes and errors in judgment.
2. Accounting presentations contain complex estimates, which inherently involve uncertainty and can be affected by future events. As a result, the auditor has to rely on evidence that is persuasive, but not convincing.
3. Fraudulently prepared financial statements are often extremely difficult, if not impossible, for the auditor to detect, especially when there is collusion among management.

If auditors were responsible for making certain that all the assertions in the statements were correct, the types and amounts of evidence required and the resulting cost of the audit function would increase to such an extent that audits would not be economically practical. Even then, auditors would be unlikely to uncover all material misstatements in every audit.

Errors Versus Fraud

Auditing standards distinguish between two types of misstatements: errors and fraud. Either type of misstatement can be material or immaterial. An **error** is an ***unintentional*** misstatement of the financial statements, whereas **fraud** is ***intentional***. Two examples of errors are: (1) a mistake in extending price times quantity on a sales invoice, and (2) overlooking older raw materials in determining the lower of cost and market for inventory.

An auditor is concerned with any fraud that may cause a material misstatement in the financial statements. Two types of intentional misstatements are particularly

Error—an unintentional misstatement of the financial statements.

Fraud—an intentional misstatement of the financial statements.

CAS

relevant for consideration of fraud risks: **misappropriation of assets**, sometimes called employee fraud, and **fraudulent financial reporting**, sometimes referred to as management fraud. An example of misappropriation of assets is a clerk taking cash at the time a sale is made and not entering the sale in the cash register. An example of fraudulent financial reporting is the intentional overstatement of sales near the balance sheet date to increase reported earnings.

Auditor's Responsibilities for Detecting Material Errors

Auditors spend a great portion of their time planning and performing audits to detect unintentional mistakes made by management and employees. Auditors find a variety of errors resulting from such things as mistakes in calculations, omissions, misunderstanding and misapplication of accounting standards, and incorrect summarizations and descriptions.

CAS 200 highlights that there are certain assertions where there are potential limitations on the auditor's ability to detect material misstatements:

- Fraud, particularly fraud involving senior management or collusion;
- The existence and completeness of related parties and transactions;
- Non-compliance with laws and regulations; and
- Future events or conditions that may cause the entity to cease as a going concern.

Auditor's Responsibilities for Detecting Material Fraud

Auditing standards make no distinction between the auditor's responsibilities for searching for errors and searching for fraud. In either case, the auditor must obtain reasonable assurance about whether the statements are free of material misstatements. The standards recognize that fraud is often more difficult to detect because management or the employees perpetrating the fraud *attempt to conceal the fraud*, similar to the Satyam case. Still, the difficulty of detection does not change the auditor's responsibility to properly plan and perform the audit to detect material misstatements, whether caused by error or fraud.

Fraudulent Financial Reporting Versus Misappropriation of Assets

Both fraudulent financial reporting and misappropriation of assets are potentially harmful to financial statement users, but there is an important difference between them. Fraudulent financial reporting harms users by providing them with incorrect financial statement information for their decision-making. When assets are misappropriated, stockholders, creditors, and others are harmed because assets are no longer available to their rightful owners.

Typically, fraudulent financial reporting is committed by management, sometimes without the knowledge of employees. Management is in a position to make accounting and reporting decisions without employees' knowledge. Further as illustrated in the opening vignette regarding the Satyam fraud and the "super user" login identification, management is in the position to override controls and conceal detection.

Usually, but not always, theft of assets is perpetrated by employees and not by management, and the amounts are often immaterial. However, there are well known examples of extremely material misappropriation of assets by employees and management, similar to the Cinar fraud described in Auditing in Action 4-2.

There is an important distinction between the theft of assets and misstatements arising from the theft of assets. Consider the following three situations:

1. Assets were taken and the theft was covered by misstating assets. For example, cash collected from a customer was stolen before it was recorded as a cash receipt, and the account receivable for the customer's account was not credited. The misstatement has not been discovered.

Sometimes, misappropriation of assets involves significant amounts and occurs at the very top of the organization. During the 1990s, Ronald Weinberg and Micheline Charest—the husband and wife team that founded the animation company Cinar Corporation—were at the top of their game. The company—considered the leader in nonviolent, prosocial, and educational children's programming—had won two Emmy awards for *Arthur* and produced various other popular children's programs. They had it all—a magnificent mansion in an exclusive area of Montreal, membership in exclusive clubs, and vacation homes in Canada and the Caribbean. Charest was even listed as one of the most powerful women in show biz, ahead of Madonna and Barbra Streisand.

However, by 2000, that had all changed. Cinar's board had accused the power couple, along with the CFO, Hasanain Paju, of funnelling $122 million into Bahamian bank accounts. The board fired the power couple along with the CFO, alleging that they used the company as a "private bank" to fund home renovations, personal investments, and other inappropriate transactions. In addition, a group of Canadian writers claimed that Cinar was using U.S. writers instead of Canadian writers, thus making it ineligible for special tax credits from the Canadian government. The tax authorities and the RCMP had launched fraud investigations. The auditors, Ernst & Young, had resigned because management could not provide "reasonable assurances" regarding the impact on the financials from possible illegal or fraudulent acts or related-party transactions.

On March 15, 2002, without admitting guilt, Charest and Weinberg each agreed to pay an unprecedented $1 000 000 fine to the Quebec Securities Commission. The couple also reached a settlement regarding the special tax credits. In 2004, tragedy struck and Charest died after complications from plastic surgery. And in 2008, Weinberg reached an undisclosed settlement with Cinar over the misappropriated funds. However, the tale does not end there.

In 2011, the Quebec provincial police, Sûreté du Québec (SC), arrested Weinberg, Panju, and two other associates (in an investment scam related to the misappropriated funds) on charges of fraud and forgery. On January 17, 2014, Panju pleaded guilty to undisclosed crimes. The judge noted these crimes were "reprehensible" and placed a publication ban on details surrounding the trial. Panju was sentenced to four years in prison.

After much legal wrangling, on May 12, 2014, Weinberg and his two co-defendants were on trial for fraud and laundering money in the Caribbean. In June 2016, Weinberg was sentenced to 8 years and 11 months for his leading role in the massive fraud. His co-defendants each received 7 years and 11 months for their participation.

Sources: Julian Sher, "Cinar fraud arrest caps tale that rocked film industry," *Globe and Mail*, March 2, 2011, accessed June 14, 2017, at **http://www.theglobeandmail.com/news/national/cinar-fraud-arrest-caps-tale-that-rocked-film-industry/article570787/**. Bertrand Marotte, "Cinar CFO asked to take the fall, court filing says," *Globe and Mail*, March 21, 2009, accessed June 14, 2017, at **http://www.theglobeandmail.com/report-on-business/cinar-cfo-asked-to-take-the-fall-court-filing-says/article1033533/**. "Police allege $120M fraud involving Cinar founder," *Canadian Press*, March 2, 2011, accessed June 14, 2017, at **http://www.ctvnews.ca/police-allege-120m-fraud-involving-cinar-founder-1.613668**. "Former CA sentenced to four years in jail," *Montreal Gazette*, January 24, 2014. Michael Nguyen, "Ex animation exec goes on trial for $126M fraud," *Calgary Sun*, May 12, 2014, accessed June 14, 2017, at **http://www.calgarysun.com/2014/05/12/ex-animation-exec-goes-on-trial-for-126m-fraud**. Paul Delean, "Fraud trial of Cinar founder Ronald Weinberg and investment execs begins in Quebec superior court," *Montreal Gazette*, May 12, 2014, accessed June 14, 2017, at **http://montrealgazette.com/business/fraud-trial-of-cinar-founder-ronald-weinberg-and-investment-execs-begins-in-quebec-superior-court**. Bertrand Marotte, "Cinar founder Weinberg given nearly nine years in fraud case," *Globe and Mail*, June 22, 2016, accessed June 17, 2017, at **http://www.theglobeandmail.com/report-on-business/industry-news/the-law-page/cinar-founder-ronald-weinberg-two-others-sentenced/article30557421/**.

2. Assets were taken and the theft was covered by understating revenues or overstating expenses. For example, cash from a cash sale was stolen, and the transaction was not recorded. Or, an unauthorized disbursement to an employee was recorded as a miscellaneous expense. The misstatement has not been discovered.
3. Assets were taken, but the misappropriation was discovered. The income statement and related footnotes clearly describe the misappropriation.

In all three situations, there has been a misappropriation of assets, but the financial statements are misstated only in situations 1 and 2. In situation 1, the balance sheet is misstated; whereas in situation 2, revenues or expenses are misstated.

Auditor's Responsibility for Related Party Relationships and Transactions

Because related parties are not independent of each other, both ASPE (Accounting Standards for Private Enterprises) and IFRS (International Financial Reporting Standards) have specific accounting and disclosure requirements for related party relationships, transactions, and balances. However, as highlighted in CAS 550, *Auditors'*

Responsibilities Regarding Related Parties, given the nature of related parties, there is an increased risk of misstatement, due either to fraud or to error.

CAS

CAS 200 and CAS 550 highlight the inherent limitations on auditors' ability to detect misstatements that involve related parties. For instance, management may be unaware of the existence of all related party transactions or relationships. Also, related party transactions create a greater chance for collusion, concealment, or manipulation by management. Despite this, auditors are responsible to perform audit procedures to identify, assess, and respond to the risks of material misstatement arising from the entity's failure to appropriately account for or disclose related party relationships, transactions, or balances.

Auditor's Responsibility to Consider Laws and Regulations

In obtaining reasonable assurance that the financial statements are free of material misstatement, the auditor takes into account applicable legal and regulatory frameworks relevant to the client. For example, when auditing the financial statements of a bank, the auditor would need to consider requirements of banking regulators.

CAS

CAS 250, *Consideration of Laws and Regulations in an Audit of Financial Statements*, acknowledges that the auditor's ability to detect material misstatements arising from failure to comply with laws and regulations is impacted by the following factors:

- There are many laws and regulations, relating principally to the operating aspects of an entity, that typically do not affect the financial statements and are not captured by the entity's information systems relevant to financial reporting.
- Non-compliance may involve conduct designed to conceal it, such as collusion, forgery, deliberate failure to record transactions, management override of controls, or intentional misrepresentations being made to the auditor.
- Whether an act constitutes non-compliance is ultimately a matter to be determined by a court or other appropriate adjudicative body.

Noncompliance—Acts of omission or commission intentional or unintentional, that are contrary to prevailing laws or regulations. These acts may have been committed by the entity, or by those charged with governance, by management, or by other individuals working for or under the direction of the entity.

One of the difficulties for the auditor is determining how laws and regulations impact financial statements. The auditor's responsibilities regarding **noncompliance** with laws and regulations (frequently referred to as illegal acts) depend upon whether the laws and regulations have a direct or indirect impact on the amounts and disclosures in the financial statements.

Laws and Regulation with a Direct Effect Laws and regulations that fall within the direct effect category are those that are generally recognized to have a direct effect on the amounts and disclosures in the financial statements. For example, the Cinar case (in Auditing in Action 4-2) highlighted a violation of federal tax laws. This type of violation directly affects income tax expense and income taxes payable.

When laws and regulations have a direct effect on the financial statements, the auditor is responsible to obtain sufficient and appropriate audit evidence about the organization's compliance with the provisions of those particular laws and regulations. As an example, in order to assess whether there is a material misstatement of income tax expense or income taxes payable, the auditor may perform a variety of procedures, including discussions with client personnel, examination of Canada Revenue Agency assessment notices, and performance of analytical procedures to assess whether the recorded amounts are reasonable.

If the auditor finds that the organization is in non-compliance, he or she is required to obtain an understanding of the nature of the act and how it occurred, and obtain information to evaluate its possible impact on the financial statements.

Laws and Regulations with an Indirect Effect Laws and regulations that are considered to have an indirect effect on the financial statements are those where compliance is fundamental to the operating aspects of the organization, to its ability to continue its business, or to avoid material penalties. For example, the payment of a bribe by a subsidiary in a foreign country could lead to expulsion of the company and/or expropriation of the company's assets; both the balance sheet and income statement could be affected.

Failing to properly dispose of untreated waste products could make the company liable for fines and penalties; the income statement could be affected. Even if the magnitude of the illegal act itself is not material, the consequences could be.

In contrast to laws and regulations with a direct effect, the auditor is only responsible to perform specified audit procedures to help identify non-compliance with the indirect laws and procedures. These procedures would include:

- Inquiring of management and those charged with governance about whether the entity is in compliance with such laws and regulations.
- Inspecting correspondence, if any, with the relevant licensing or regulatory authorities.

During the audit, other audit procedures may bring instances of suspected non-compliance to the auditor's attention. However, CAS 250 states that, other than inquiry of management, the auditor should not search for such illegal acts unless there is reason to believe they may exist. As highlighted in Auditing in Action 4-3, if the auditor is unable to determine the impact of noncompliance, it may be necessary to resign from the engagement. We will discuss further audit procedures when non-compliance is identified and auditor reporting responsibilities in cases of noncompliance later in the book.

`CAS`

Auditors' Responsibility to Evaluate Going Concern

Under the going-concern basis of accounting, the financial statements are prepared on the assumption that the entity is a going concern and does not have the intention,

AUDITING IN ACTION 4-3
It's a Matter of Professional Judgment—The Livent Audits

"It's a matter of professional judgment" was the Deloitte partners' response to the Institute of Chartered Accountants of Ontario (the ICAO, now CPA Ontario) during a disciplinary committee hearing regarding charges of professional misconduct in relation to their performance of the Livent audits, which involved fraudulent financial reporting. However, the disciplinary committee disagreed and concluded that three of the four Deloitte partners were guilty of professional misconduct.

At its peak, Livent was the largest live theatre company in North America, producing hits such as *The Phantom of the Opera*. In 1998, after the 1997 audit was completed and filed with the OSC, new owners took over and soon discovered that the financial statements were a fraud. The misstatements involved improper recognition of revenue and the improper deferral and capitalization of expenses. Later that year, Livent filed for bankruptcy. Several senior members of Livent management were found guilty of fraud and the two founders, Garth Drabinsky and Myron Gottlieb, served time in prison. Both were paroled in 2012. It's estimated that investors lost $500 million when Livent collapsed in 1998.

When commenting on the disciplinary case, Bruce Jenkins, the deputy chief of Deloitte at the time, asked, "What constitutes professional misconduct? Is the fact that you did not get it right professional misconduct? We do not believe so. We don't believe there is a right or wrong answer regarding accounting."

He further explained: "The fraud involved the manipulation of Livent's accounting and computer records.... But such manipulation had nothing to do with the way we handled the four accounting transactions we audited."

Jenkins contended that Deloitte followed GAAS: "We considered this engagement as high risk," says Jenkins, "We had a number of partners involved and had a lot of consultation."

However, the ICAO disciplinary committee noted in its decision, "It is not sufficient for auditors to identify the risks and make appropriate plans to deal with them. The audit must be properly executed." The disciplinary committee noted that the auditors were aware senior management was deceptive in its explanations of certain accounting transactions; however, the auditors failed to consider the broader implications of that deception and failed to exercise appropriate professional judgment and skepticism.

The committee further explained, "The proper exercise of professional judgment requires the auditor to reach a correct conclusion. It is not enough for the auditor to have an appropriate process, to identify the issues, and to correctly set out what should be done."

Sources: Ken Mark, "Deloitte will appeal ICAO ruling," *The Bottom Line*, 2008. "What was Livent Inc.?" *Globe and Mail*, March 24, 2009, accessed June 14, 2017, at **http://www.theglobeandmail.com/report-on-business/what-was-livent-inc/article4281112/**. Institute of Chartered Accountants of Ontario Disciplinary Committee, "In the matter of Douglas Barrington, FCA, Peter Chant, FCA, Anthony Power, FCA, and Claudio Russo, CA, members of the Institute under Rule 206 of Rules of Professional Conduct, Decision and Reasons for Decision, February 11, 2007."

or the need, to liquidate or curtail materially the scale of its operations in the forseeable future (which is usually one year). It is not the auditor's responsibility to determine whether or not an entity can prepare its financial statements under the going-concern assumption; this is the responsibility of management. As highlighted in the auditor's report (Figure 2-2), as part of preparing the financial statements, management is responsible for assessing the entity's ability to continue as a going concern and disclosing, if applicable, matters related to going concern using the going-concern basis of accounting. However, if management intends to either liquidate the entity or cease operations, or has no realistic alternative, then the financial statements should be presented on a liquidation basis of accounting.

CAS

CAS 570, *Going Concern*, explains that it is the auditor's responsibility to obtain sufficient appropriate audit evidence regarding, and to conclude on, the appropriateness of management's use of the going-concern basis of accounting in the preparation of the financial statements. In addition, based upon the evidence obtained, the auditor is responsible for concluding whether there is a material uncertainty about the entity's ability to continue as a going concern. However, given that the assessment is based upon future events, there are inherent limitations on the auditor's ability to detect material misstatements. CAS 570.7 cautions that the auditor cannot predict future events and that the absence of any reference to going-concern uncertainty in the auditor's report is not a guarantee of the entity's ability to continue as a going concern. We will revisit going concern in various stages of the audit process: client acceptance and planning (Chapter 6), conclusion (Chapter 18), and reporting requirements (Chapter 19).

CONCEPT CHECK

C4-1 Is it possible for the auditor to conduct the audit without reliance on management? Why or why not?

C4-2 Which is harder to detect: financial reporting fraud or misappropriation of assets? Why?

C4-3 Explain the difference in the auditor's responsibility towards direct-effect versus indirect-effect laws and regulations.

LO 5 Explain and apply the key elements of an effective professional judgment process.

A FRAMEWORK FOR PROFESSIONAL JUDGMENT

Professional judgment is the essence of auditing. In order to perform a quality audit, auditors must make quality judgments about evidence (e.g., Does the evidence support the existence of timber assets?), probabilities, and options (e.g., Which audit procedures are to be performed?). In its research report *Professional Judgment and the Auditor*, the Canadian Institute of Chartered Accountants (now CPA Canada) said:

> Professional judgment in auditing is the application of relevant knowledge and experience, within the context provided by auditing and accounting standards and Rules of Professional Conduct, in reaching decisions where a choice must be made between alternative possible courses of action.[2]

Professional judgment—an analytical and systematic decision process that involves the application of relevant knowledge and experience with the context of auditing and accounting standards and Rules of Professional Conduct. It is objective, prudent, and carried out with integrity and recognition of responsibility to those affected by its consequences.

The report further explained that **professional judgment** is analytical and systematic, objective, prudent, and carried out with integrity and recognition of responsibility to those affected by its consequences. This means that auditors must be able to justify a decision on the basis that it:

- Is well thought out;
- Is objective;

---

[2] Canadian Institute of Chartered Accountants, *Research Report: Professional Judgment and the Auditor,* Toronto: CICA, 1995, p. 5.

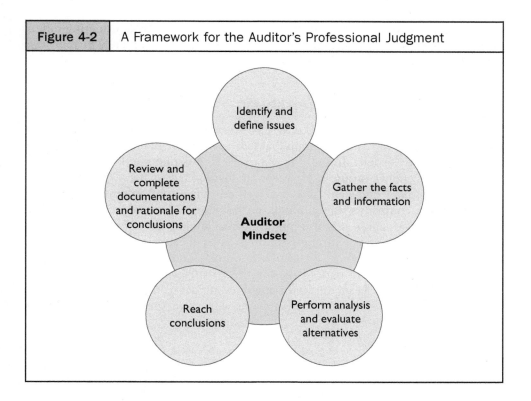

Figure 4-2	A Framework for the Auditor's Professional Judgment

- Meets the underlying principles of GAAP and GAAS;
- Has evidence to support the decision;
- Maximizes the likelihood of "good" consequences;
- Is carried out with truthfulness and forthrightness; and
- Considers the impact on the financial statement users.

The professional judgment process depicted in Figure 4-2 is based upon various frameworks developed by several national professional accounting bodies (CPA Canada, the Institute of Chartered Accountants of Australia, and the Institute of Chartered Accountants of Scotland, as well as the American Center for Audit Quality). Although the framework may seem simple, such frameworks are considered to be effective tools in guiding thinking and encouraging auditors to be aware of their own judgment biases and traps and what can go wrong.

Identify and Define the Issue

Although it seems to be rather straightforward, this is an important step. In simple terms, we must be clear about "what" we want to solve, or we may solve the wrong problem. This is often referred to as "framing the problem." A famous quotation attributed to Albert Einstein explains why this is so important:

> If I had an hour to solve a problem and my life depended on the solution, I would spend the first 55 minutes determining the proper question to ask, for once I know the proper question, I could solve the problem in less than five minutes.

To identify and define the issue, it is helpful to consider different perspectives (e.g., investors, lenders, management, regulators, other auditors, analysts, customers, or other parties affected by the transaction). This can help the auditor to focus on the real issue (or the "what"). By considering different viewpoints, the auditor can also consider the "why" of the issue. For example, when evaluating a management estimate, is the issue really the reasonableness of the estimate, or the implications of that issue on the client meeting its bank loan requirements? By considering different perspectives and thinking about the "why," auditors are more likely to apply the appropriate professional skepticism.

Gather the Facts and Information

This is a crucial step in auditing. It often involves evaluating the information that is readily available, as well as information that may need to be obtained from others (for example, a forestry expert). In order to obtain facts, it is important that the auditor understand the client's business. However, as highlighted in the Center for Audit Quality's *Professional Judgment Resource*,[3] gathering facts and information is more than getting the company's story through discussion only. It involves being alert for disconfirming information. It is also important that auditors do not overly rely upon information solely from accounting personnel, but rather include the right people who may be in sales, shipping, or human resources. Auditors also need to investigate potential management biases (e.g., are there management bonuses?) and how they impact the "facts." Related to gathering relevant facts is the need to identify the relevant accounting and auditing standards. As with all judgments, auditors should consult with other auditors.

Perform Analysis and Evaluate Alternatives

The auditor's ability to analyze the relevant facts and evaluate the alternatives is directly related to how well the issue was defined in the first place. In this step, the auditor should identify and evaluate all alternatives. However, the auditor must be careful in selecting the first available alternative. At this stage, the auditor should be mindful of potential judgment tendencies, traps, and biases that can limit that auditor's ability to effectively evaluate alternatives. The auditor can avoid many of these judgment traps through consultation with others.

Reach and Document Conclusions

An important part of this step is the auditor's ability to take a "stand back" point of view and consider the issue within the broader context—How does it relate to other evidence in the file? What is its impact on the financial statements? Another key part is documentation. While documentation is often considered in light of the review process, documentation can drive quality decisions. Documentation of the auditor's thought process—why the auditor believes the conclusion is correct, why other options were considered, and why they were discarded—can be very useful in ensuring the auditor maintains objectivity. It can also safeguard against what is referred to as the confirmation bias (unconsciously giving an inordinate weight to evidence that supports the auditor's conclusion).

LO **6** Describe the need to maintain professional skepticism when conducting the audit.

PROFESSIONAL SKEPTICISM

At the centre of the professional judgment framework is the auditor's mindset. In Chapter 1, we learned that integrity, objectivity, and skepticism represent the art of auditing. These essential skills and qualities, which are the essence of the auditor's mindset, are necessary for each step of the judgment process.

---

[3] Center for Audit Quality, *Professional Judgment Resource*, 2014, accessed June 13, 2017, at **www.thecaq.org/reports-and-publications/professional-judgment-resource**.

Auditing standards require that an audit be designed to provide reasonable assurance of detecting *both* material errors and fraud in the financial statements. To accomplish this, the audit must be planned and performed with an *attitude of professional skepticism* in all aspects of the engagement. Sound professional judgment also requires the auditor to exercise objectivity. Objectivity and professional skepticism are closely related. It is likely that a biased auditor will not use the appropriate level of professional skepticism.

Aspects of Professional Skepticism

Professional skepticism consists of two primary components: a questioning mind and a critical assessment of the audit evidence. While auditors would like to believe that the organizations they accept as clients have integrity and are honest, maintaining a questioning mind helps auditors offset the natural bias to want to trust the client. A questioning mindset means the auditor approaches the audit with a "trust but verify" mental outlook. Similarly, as the auditor obtains and evaluates evidence supporting financial statement amounts and disclosures, professional skepticism also involves a critical assessment of the evidence that includes asking probing questions and paying attention to inconsistencies. When auditors embrace the responsibility to maintain a questioning mind and to critically evaluate evidence, they significantly reduce the likelihood of audit failure.

Professional skepticism—a questioning mind and a critical examination of audit evidence. The appropriate level of professional skepticism varies depending upon the risks of the particular situation.

Key Traits of Professional Skepticism Like good art, appropriate professional skepticism is often difficult to define and recognize; however, it is easy to criticize. Table 4-1 summarizes some key traits or qualities that are associated with auditors' professional skepticism.

Potential Judgment Traps and Biases

While auditors need to be skeptical of audit evidence, auditors also need to be skeptical of their own judgment process.[4] In addition to using a judgment framework, awareness of **judgment traps** and biases (often referred to as judgment tendencies) can assist auditors and auditing students in making better judgments. Table 4-2 summarizes some of the common judgment tendencies.

Judgment traps—common systematic judgment tendencies and biases that can impede the quality of the professional judgment process.

Table 4-1	What Are Qualities of Professional Skepticism?
Questioning mind	The tendency to inquiry, with some sense of doubt
Suspension of judgment	Withholding judgment until you have appropriate evidence (i.e., not jumping to conclusions)
Search for knowledge	A desire to investigate beyond the obvious
Interpersonal understanding	Recognition that people's motivations and perceptions can lead to biased decisions
Autonomy	The conviction to decide on your own rather than being influenced by others
Self-esteem	The self-confidence to resist persuasion and to challenge assumptions

Source: Republished with permission of American Accounting Association, from A Development of a Scale to Measure Professional Skepticism." Auditing: A Journal of Practice and Theory: 29(1): 149–171, Kathy Hurtt, © 2010; permission conveyed through Copyright Clearance Center, Inc

---

[4] Kathy Hurtt, Helen Brown-Liburd, Christine Early, and Ganesh Krishnamoorthy, "Research on auditor professional skepticism: Literature synthesis and opportunities for future research," *Auditing: A Journal of Practice and Theory*, vol. 32, no. 1, 2013, pp. 45–97.

Table 4-2	Judgment Traps and How to Avoid Them

Common Judgment Traps	Strategies to Avoid Them
Confirmation	• Make opposing case and consider alternative explanations • Consider potentially disconfirming or conflicting information
Overconfidence	• Challenge opinions and experts • Challenge underlying assumptions
Anchoring	• Solicit input from others • Consider management bias, including potential for fraud or material misstatement
Availability	• Consider why something comes to mind • Obtain and consider objective data • Consult with others and make the opposing case

Source: Center for Audit Quality, *Professional Judgment Resource*, 2014.

Confirmation Bias This judgment tendency refers to the auditor's potential to put more weight on information that is consistent with their initial beliefs or preferences. The end result may be that the auditor does not adequately consider contradictory evidence. This bias is a common. Think about when you are analyzing an accounting case in one of your courses. After reading the case, you come up with a preliminary recommendation and your analysis is focused on supporting that recommendation. You have fallen into the trap of confirmation bias.

Overconfidence Bias This judgment tendency is the potential for the auditor to overestimate his or her own ability to perform tasks or to make accurate risk assessments. This type of bias can lead to the inability to see different points of view or contradictory evidence. The auditor may also be reluctant or see no need to involve others in the analysis. Several past CPAB reports have noted that auditors often do not involve specialists at times when it seems they should or, if they do, they tend not to question their findings. It is possible that these auditors were susceptible to the overconfidence bias.

Anchoring This judgment tendency refers to when the auditor is "anchored" by the initial numerical number and not adjusting sufficiently when forming a final judgment. Auditors can be particularly susceptible to this since management provides them with preliminary figures and supporting documentation. It also occurs in the choice of auditing procedures. Auditors refer to the prior year's working papers, which increases the likelihood of using the same procedures as last year without reflecting on whether the procedures are appropriate.

Availability This judgment tendency can cause auditors to estimate or forecast the likelihood of an event based on how easily they can recall an example or instance of that event. This bias can dampen professional skepticism, particularly when the auditor is faced with a rare event. For example, although there is much discussion of fraudulent financial statements, for most auditors this is a rare event. This means that auditors do not have a vivid fraud client experience to draw upon and can potentially miss fraud when they come across it, or they do not consider fraud when accepting potential clients.

CONCEPT CHECK

C4-4 What are the four steps of the professional judgment framework and how is it a useful tool? What are some common judgment traps?

C4-5 Why is professional skepticism considered essential to the proper exercise of professional judgment?

The Work Environment In addition to individual biases, the general characteristics of the work environment, such as time pressures, can contribute to applying less than ideal professional skepticism. Engagement teams' and individual auditors' performance often include performance measures based upon time budgets. However, this type of pressure can lead auditors to fail to put in the increased effort that is required. Also, junior auditors may struggle with all the overwhelming technical details (firm policies, GAAS, terminology, audit methodology) and are focusing on simply trying to understand the issues. As one can imagine, it is difficult to apply the appropriate level of professional skepticism in such a situation.

FINANCIAL STATEMENT CYCLES

LO **7** Identify the benefits of a cycle approach to segmenting the audit.

Now that we know what an auditor's responsibilities are, we provide an overview of how auditors organize the audit's financial statements. Audits are performed by dividing financial statements into smaller segments or components. The division makes the audit more manageable and aids in the assignment of tasks to different members of the audit team. For example, most auditors treat capital assets and notes payable as different segments. Each segment is audited separately but not on a completely independent basis (e.g., the audit of capital assets may reveal an unrecorded note payable). After the audit of each segment is completed, including interrelationships with other segments, the audit results are combined and evaluated. A conclusion can then be reached about the financial statements taken as a whole.

There are different ways of segmenting an audit. One approach is to treat every account balance on the statements as a separate segment. Segmenting that way is usually inefficient, however, as it could result in the independent audit of such closely related accounts as inventory and cost of goods sold.

Cycle Approach to Segmenting an Audit

A common way to divide an audit is to keep closely related types (or classes) of transactions and account balances in the same segment. This is called the **cycle approach**. For example, sales, sales returns, cash receipts, and charge-offs of uncollectable accounts are four classes of transactions that cause accounts receivable to increase and decrease. Therefore, they are all parts of the sales and collection cycle. Similarly, payroll transactions and accrued payroll are parts of the human resources and payroll cycle.

Cycle approach—a method of dividing an audit by keeping closely related types of transactions and account balances in the same segment.

To understand the logic of using the cycle approach, think about the way in which transactions are reported in journals and summarized in the general ledger, trial balance, and financial statements. Transactions (normally from computer files) are organized into journals, with the totals being posted to the general ledger and other records (such as master files or databases). The general ledger is reported as a trial balance and summarized as financial statements. Figure 4-3 shows that flow.

The cycles used in this text are listed below and are then explained in detail. Note that each of these cycles is so important that one or more later chapters addresses the audit of each cycle:

- Revenue and collections cycle.
- Acquisition and payment cycle.
- Human resources and payroll cycle.
- Inventory and distribution cycle.
- Capital acquisition and repayment cycle.

The accounts for Hillsburg Hardware Limited are summarized in Table 4-3 by cycle, and include the related journals and financial statements in which the accounts appear. (Hillsburg Hardware Limited is a fictional company that we use to

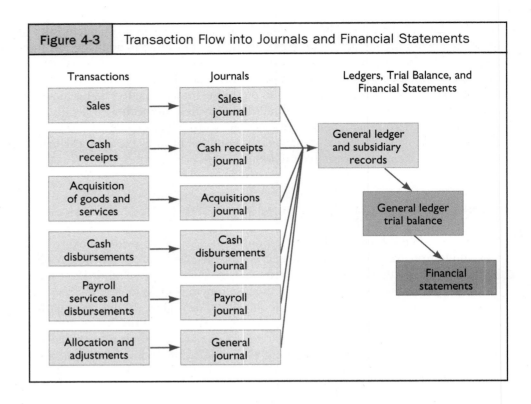

| Figure 4-3 | Transaction Flow into Journals and Financial Statements |

Transactions

- Sales
- Cash receipts
- Acquisition of goods and services
- Cash disbursements
- Payroll services and disbursements
- Allocation and adjustments

Journals

- Sales journal
- Cash receipts journal
- Acquisitions journal
- Cash disbursements journal
- Payroll journal
- General journal

Ledgers, Trial Balance, and Financial Statements

- General ledger and subsidiary records
- General ledger trial balance
- Financial statements

help explain various concepts throughout this book. For further details on the company and its background, as well as the relevant financial information, refer to the Appendix at the end of this book.)

The following observations expand upon the information contained in Table 4-3:

- All general ledger accounts and transaction types for Hillsburg Hardware are included at least once. For a different company, the number and types of transactions and general ledger accounts would differ, but all would be included.
- Some journals and general ledger accounts are included in more than one cycle. When that occurs, it means the journal is used to record transactions from more than one cycle and indicates a tie-in between the cycles. The most important general ledger account included in and affecting several cycles is the general cash account (cash in bank). General cash connects most cycles.
- The capital acquisition and repayment cycle is closely related to the acquisition and payment cycle. The acquisition of goods and services includes the purchase of inventory, supplies, and general services in performing the main business operations. Transactions in the capital acquisition cycle are related to financing the business, such as issuing stock or debt, paying dividends, and repaying debt.
- Although the same journals are used to record transactions for both cycles, and the transactions are similar, there are two reasons for treating capital acquisition and repayment separately from the acquisition of goods and services. First, the transactions are related to financing a company rather than to its operations. Second, most capital acquisition and repayment cycle accounts involve few transactions, but each is often highly material and therefore should be audited extensively. For both reasons, it is more convenient to separate the two cycles.
- The inventory and distribution cycle is closely related to all other cycles, especially for a manufacturing company. The cost of inventory includes raw materials (acquisition and payment cycle), direct labour (human resources and payroll cycle), and manufacturing overhead (acquisition and payment and human resources and payroll cycles). The sale of finished goods involves the sales and collection cycle. Because inventory is material for most manufacturing or distribution companies, it is common to borrow money using inventory

| Table 4-3 | Cycles Applied to Hillsburg Hardware Limited | | |

| | | General Ledger Account Included in the Cycle | |
Cycle	Journals Included in Cycle (Figure 4-3)	Balance Sheet	Income Statement
Revenue and collections	Sales journal Cash receipts journal General journal	Cash in bank Trade accounts receivable Allowance for uncollectable accounts Other accounts receivable	Sales Sales returns and allowances Bad-debt expense
Acquisition and payment	Acquisitions journal Cash disbursements journal General journal	Cash in bank Inventories Prepaid expenses Land and buildings Computer and delivery equipment Furniture and fixtures Accumulated amortization Trade accounts payable Goods and services tax payable Accrued income tax Deferred tax Other accrued payables	Advertising[S] Amortization Auditing [A] and related services Computer maintenance and supplies Gain on sale of assets Income taxes Insurance [A] Legal fees and retainers [A] Miscellaneous general expense [A] Miscellaneous office expense [A] Miscellaneous sales expense [S] Office repairs and maintenance Postage [A] Rent [A] Sales and promotional literature [S] Sales meetings and training [S] Stationery and supplies [A] Taxes [A] Telephone and fax [A] Travel and entertainment—selling [S] Travel and entertainment—administrative [A]
Human resources and payroll	Payroll journal General journal	Cash in bank Accrued payroll Accrued payroll benefits	Salaries and commissions [S] Sales payroll benefits [S] Executive and office salaries [A] Administrative payroll benefits [A]
Inventory and distribution	Acquisitions journal Sales journal General journal	Inventories	Cost of goods sold
Capital acquisition and repayment	Acquisitions journal Cash disbursements journal General journal	Cash in bank Notes payable Accrued interest Long-term notes payable Accrued interest Capital stock Retained earnings Dividends Dividends payable	Interest expense

Note: S = Selling expense; A = General and administrative expense

as security. In those cases, the capital acquisition and repayment cycle is also related to inventory and distribution.

Relationships Among Cycles

Figure 4-4 illustrates the relationship of the cycles to one another. In addition to the five cycles, general cash is also shown. Each cycle is studied in detail in later chapters. Figure 4-4 shows that cycles have no beginning or end except at the origin and final disposition of a company.

A company begins by obtaining capital, usually in the form of cash. In a manufacturing company, cash is used to acquire raw materials, capital assets, and related goods and services to produce inventory (acquisition and payment cycle). Cash is also used

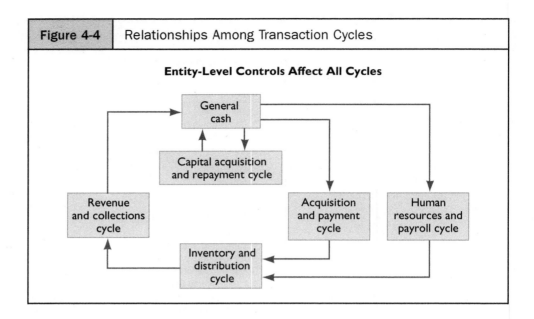

Figure 4-4 | Relationships Among Transaction Cycles

Entity-Level Controls Affect All Cycles

to acquire labour for the same reason (human resources and payroll cycle). Acquisition and payment and human resources and payroll are similar in nature, but the functions are different enough to justify separate cycles. The combined result of these two cycles is inventory (inventory and distribution cycle). At a subsequent point, the inventory is sold and billings and collections result (revenue and collections cycle). The cash generated is used to pay dividends and interest and to start the cycles again. The cycles interrelate in much the same way in a service company, where there will be no inventory but there may be unbilled receivables and work-in-progress of unbilled services.

Entity-Level Controls

The cycle approach helps the auditor to focus on the flow of transactions and to identify at which points the risk of misstatement could occur and what transaction controls (also referred to as application controls) mitigate those risks. In addition to the individual transaction cycles and their related controls, the auditor evaluates the effectiveness of **entity-level controls**. As Figure 4-4 highlights, there are also entity-level controls that address pervasive risks. These controls affect multiple processes, transactions, accounts, and assertions. For instance, if the CFO is able to override controls and record fictitious transactions, misstatements could occur in multiple transaction cycles. Policies and procedures related to corporate governance (e.g., audit committee oversight of internal controls), and to information technology (e.g., program changes or, in the case of Satyam, user access controls) would have a pervasive effect on multiple processes.

Entity-level controls—controls that have a pervasive effect on multiple processes, transactions, accounts, and assertions.

CONCEPT CHECK

C4-6 Describe what is meant by the cycle approach to auditing. Why does the audit process use cycles?

C4-7 What are entity-level controls and what is their significance to the audit process?

LO 8 Explain how the auditor obtains assurance by auditing classes of transactions and ending balances in accounts, including presentation and disclosure.

SETTING AUDIT OBJECTIVES

Understanding the risks and controls within each cycle helps auditors to develop audit objectives that guide them in determining what audit procedures to use and what audit evidence to obtain. Auditors conduct financial statement audits using the cycle approach by performing audit procedures for the transactions making up the ending

Figure 4-5	Balances and Transactions Affecting Those Balances for Accounts Receivable

Accounts Receivable (in thousands)

Beginning balance	$ 17 521		
Sales	$144 328	$137 087	Cash receipts
		$ 1 242	Sales returns and allowances
		$ 3 323	Charge-off of uncollectable accounts
Ending balance	$ 20 197		

balances, the account balances, and related disclosures. Figure 4-5 illustrates this concept by showing the four classes of transactions that determine the ending balance in accounts receivable for Hillsburg Hardware Limited. Assume that the beginning balance of $17 521 was audited in the prior year and is therefore considered reliable. If the auditor could be completely sure that each of the four classes of transactions (sales, cash receipts, sales returns and allowances, and charge-offs) was correctly stated, then the auditor could also be sure that the ending balance of $20 197 was correctly stated. However, it is almost always impractical to obtain complete assurance about the correctness of each class of transaction. This results in less than complete assurance about the ending balance in accounts receivable. In almost all audits, overall assurance can be increased by also auditing the ending balance of accounts receivable. Auditors have found that, generally, the most efficient way to conduct audits is to *obtain some combination of assurance for each class of transactions and for the ending balance in the related accounts.*

Using our example in Figure 4-5, the auditor will develop transaction-related audit objectives for each of the four classes of transactions. Similarly, the auditor will develop balance-related audit objectives for the accounts receivable ending balance, as well as presentation and disclosure-related audit objectives for the relevant financial statement disclosures for the sales and collection cycle. How these audit objectives are set is based upon more specific factors, which is the auditors' risk assessment of assertions. We discuss assertions in the next section.

MANAGEMENT ASSERTIONS AND AUDIT OBJECTIVES

LO **9** Distinguish among the management assertions about financial information.

Accounting paints a picture of past financial transactions and communicates this to the reader through the financial statements. As you can imagine, financial statements represent very complex and interrelated sets of assertions. At the most aggregate level, the financial statements include broad assertions such as "total liabilities as at December 31 are $50 million," "total revenue for the year is $9 million," and "net income for the year is $3 million." As highlighted previously, in order to prove those assertions, a more refined analysis is needed.

Management assertions are implied or expressed representations by management about: (1) classes of transactions or events: (2) related account balances in the financial statements; and (3) the classification, presentation, or disclosure of information in the financial statements. Consider Hillsburg Hardware Limited, whose management asserts that cash of $827 568 was present in the company's bank accounts or on the premises as of the balance sheet date. Unless otherwise disclosed in the financial statements, management also asserts that the cash was unrestricted and available for normal use. Similar assertions exist for each asset, liability, equity, revenue, and expense item in the financial statements. These assertions apply to classes of transactions, account balances, and all of the material in the financial statements, including the note disclosures.

Management assertions are directly related to accounting standards in the financial accounting framework used by the company (such as ASPE or IFRS), as they are part of the *criteria that management uses to record and disclose accounting information in financial statements*. Return to the definition of auditing in Chapter 1. It states, in part, that auditing is a comparison of information (financial statements) to established criteria (assertions according to the financial reporting framework). Auditors must therefore understand and evaluate the assertions to do adequate audits.

CAS International and Canadian auditing standards (CAS 315.A111) classify assertions into three categories:

1. Assertions about classes of transactions and events for the period under audit.
2. Assertions about account balances at period end.
3. Assertions about financial statement presentation and disclosure.

The specific assertions included in each category are listed in Table 4-4. The assertions are grouped so that assertions related across categories of assertions are included on the same table row. We will use these groupings to first discuss the management assertions, and then discuss the audit objectives. For all assertions, the audit objective is to prove with sufficient and appropriate evidence that the assertion is true.

Management assertions help the auditor to focus his or her attention on all the various aspects of the transactions, account balances, and required disclosures that need to be considered. In other words, they help the auditor to assess risk or "what can go wrong" and to ensure that enough attention has been placed on the most

Table 4-4	Management Assertions for Each Category of Assertions	
Assertions About Classes of Transactions and Events	**Assertions About Account Balances**	**Assertions About Presentation and Disclosure**
Occurrence—Transactions and events that have been recorded have occurred and pertain to the entity.	*Existence*—Assets, liabilities, and equity interests exist.	*Occurrence and rights and obligations*—Disclosed events and transactions have occurred and pertain to the entity.
Completeness—All transactions and events that should have been recorded have been recorded.	*Completeness*—All assets, liabilities, and equity interests that should have been recorded have been recorded.	*Completeness*—All disclosures that should have been included in the financial statements have been included.
Accuracy—Amounts and other data relating to recorded transactions and events have been recorded appropriately.	*Valuation and allocation*—Assets, liabilities, and equity interests are included in the financial statements at appropriate amounts and any resulting valuation adjustments are appropriately recorded.	*Accuracy and valuation*—Financial and other information is disclosed appropriately and at appropriate amounts.
Cutoff—Transactions and events have been recorded in the correct accounting period.		
Classification—Transactions and events have been recorded in the proper accounts.		*Classification and understandability*—Financial and other information is appropriately presented and described and disclosures are clearly expressed.
	Rights and obligations—The entity holds or controls the rights to assets, and liabilities are the obligation of the entity.	

relevant assertions. While all the assertions are relevant to each class of transactions, balances, or disclosures, some assertions are more relevant than others. To determine which assertion is more relevant, the auditor should consider:

- Management bias, incentives, and pressure.
- The complexity or nature of the assertion. (Is it subjective, such as inventory obsolescence?)
- The risk of fraud and error.

For instance, in the case of cash, existence and cut-off are two relevant assertions, whereas valuation is not usually as important. That is because there is not much judgment into valuing cash. However, since cash can be susceptible to fraud and error (as highlighted in both the Satyam and Cinar frauds), existence is generally a relevant assertion. Similarly, cut-off is a relevant assertion for cash because timing errors often occur at the end of a period On the other hand, valuation is likely to be a relevant assertion for inventory due to the considerable judgment involved with determining if inventory is appropriately recorded at its net realizable value.

Auditors use the risk assessment of assertions to develop audit objectives. An audit objective is the object of the auditor's investigation: it is what the auditor is trying to find out. Recall that the auditors' primary responsibility is to determine whether management assertions about financial statements are justified. In order to answer that question, the auditor develops audit objectives that provide a framework to help the auditor accumulate sufficient appropriate evidence and decide on the proper evidence to accumulate given the identified risks.

Relevant assertions—assertions that have a meaningful bearing on whether an account is fairly stated and are used to assess the risk of material misstatement and the design and performance of audit procedures.

LINKING ASSERTIONS WITH AUDIT OBJECTIVES

LO **10** Link management assertions with audit objectives.

Management makes several assertions about transactions. These assertions also apply to other events that are reflected in the accounting records, such as recording depreciation and recognizing pension obligations.

Assertions and Transaction-Related Audit Objectives

For each assertion about a certain class of transaction, the auditor develops corresponding **transaction-related audit objectives**. In this discussion, we use the examples of transaction-related audit objectives and relevant assertions for sales transactions. We focus on sales because it is the key class of transactions for most organizations. Figure 4-6 illustrates the assertions and transaction-related audit objectives for Hillsburg's sales.

Occurrence Management's assertion is that all recorded transactions included in the financial statements have actually occurred during the accounting period. For example, management asserts that recorded sales transactions represent exchanges of goods or services that actually took place.

When developing transaction-related audit objectives for occurrence, the auditor asks: *Have the recorded transactions really occurred?* For this objective, the auditor requires evidence that proves the recorded transactions actually occurred. Occurrence is usually a relevant assertion for sales because revenue recognition fraud is the most common type of financial reporting fraud. An occurrence error would result in an overstatement of the transactions. For instance, the inclusion of a sale in the sales files or journal when no sale occurred violates the occurrence objective.

Completeness Management's assertion is that all transactions that should be included in the financial statements are in fact included. For example, management asserts that all sales of goods and services are recorded and included in the financial statements. The completeness assertion is opposite from the occurrence assertion. The

Transaction-related audit objectives—five audit objectives that must be met before the auditor can conclude that the total for any given class of transactions is fairly stated. The transaction-related audit objectives are occurrence, completeness, accuracy, cutoff, and classification.

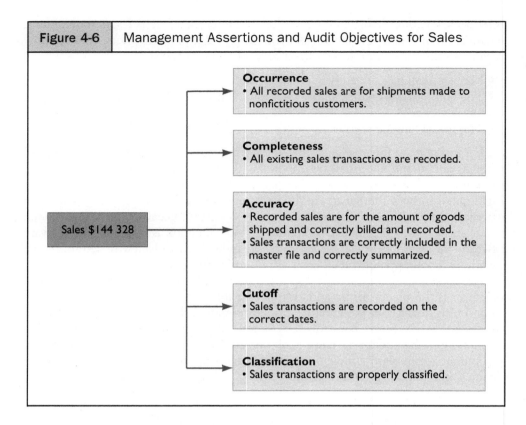

Figure 4-6	Management Assertions and Audit Objectives for Sales

Sales $144 328

Occurrence
• All recorded sales are for shipments made to nonfictitious customers.

Completeness
• All existing sales transactions are recorded.

Accuracy
• Recorded sales are for the amount of goods shipped and correctly billed and recorded.
• Sales transactions are correctly included in the master file and correctly summarized.

Cutoff
• Sales transactions are recorded on the correct dates.

Classification
• Sales transactions are properly classified.

completeness assertion claims that no transactions that should have been recorded have been omitted, whereas the occurrence assertion claims that no transactions that should not have been recorded are included. Thus, violations of the occurrence assertion relate to account overstatements, whereas violations of the completeness assertion relate to account understatements.

When developing transaction-related audit objectives for completeness, the auditor asks: *Are all transactions included and recorded?* For this objective, the auditor requires evidence that all transactions that should be included in the files or journals have actually been included. A completeness error would result in the understatement of the transaction. For instance, the failure to record a sale when a sale has occurred violates the completeness objective. Auditing this assertion means auditing what has not been recorded, which creates difficulty for the auditor, especially if management has some sort of incentive to understate the particular account. Generally, completeness of sales is not the most relevant assertion; however, there are situations where this may not hold true. For instance, in small businesses where tax minimization is a key goal, management may be motivated to understate sales.

Accuracy Management's assertion is that all transactions have been recorded at correct amounts. Using the wrong price to record a sales transaction, and a calculation error in the extensions of price times quantity, are examples of violations of the accuracy assertion.

When developing transaction-related audit objectives for accuracy, the auditor asks: *Are transactions recorded correctly?* For this objective, the auditor requires evidence that proves the accuracy of information for accounting transactions. Depending upon the way that records or information systems are organized, the auditor may develop accuracy objectives for any or all of the following components: (1) initial data entry, (2) summarization, and (3) posting.

Accuracy of data entry for sales transactions would be violated if the quantity of goods shipped were different from the quantity billed, the wrong selling price were used for billing, or there were extension or adding errors (perhaps due to program errors) during billing.

Summarization is the process of grouping or totalling some transactions for the purpose of posting. For example, the sales account may have only a daily total of the transactions from the sales subsystem. A summarization error occurs in sales if the daily total is added incorrectly or the total of internet sales is not added correctly.

Posting is the process of recording transactions to the general ledger account. Many systems post every single transaction to the general ledger, while others record only a daily, weekly, or monthly total. A posting error occurs if the wrong sales amount was updated to the customer master file, or the wrong total for internet sales was transferred to the general ledger. Since the posting of transactions to subsidiary records, the general ledger, and other related master files is typically accomplished automatically by computerized accounting systems, the risk of random human error in posting is minimal. Once the auditor has established that the automated information systems are functioning properly, there is a reduced concern about the accuracy of summarization and posting.

Cutoff Management's assertion is that all transactions are recorded in the proper accounting period. An example of a cutoff error in sales is recording sales transactions in December when the goods were not shipped until January. As this example highlights, cut-off errors result in accounts being either overstated or understated, and they are therefore closely related to the occurrence and existence assertions. For instance, the previous cut-off error would result in accounts receivable being overstated and inventory being understated.

When developing transaction-related audit objectives for cut-off, the auditor asks: *Are transactions recorded on the correct dates?* For this objective, the auditor requires evidence that cutoff transactions, those that occur close to period end, are correctly accounted for. For example, in the case of a wholesale company such as Hillsburg, the auditor would perform procedures to verify that sales transactions are recorded on the date of shipment or when risks of ownership are transferred (based upon whatever is the relevant policy for the client).

Classification Management's assertion is that all transactions are recorded in the appropriate accounts. Recording long-term receivables in current accounts receivable is one example of a violation of the classification assertion.

When developing the transaction-related assertions for the classification assertion, the auditor asks: *Are the transactions included in the client's journals properly classified?* For this objective, the auditor requires evidence that the transactions are properly classified. Some examples of misclassifications of sales are: including cash sales as credit sales, recording a sale of operating capital assets as revenue, and misclassifying sales according to category (e.g., misclassifying commercial sales as residential sales).

Assertions and Balance-Related Audit Objectives

Assertions about account balances at year-end are about amounts shown in the balance sheet (called the statement of financial position under IFRS). Because of the way audits are done, **balance-related audit objectives** are almost always developed for the ending balance in balance sheet accounts, such as accounts receivable, inventory, and notes payable. However, balance-related objectives are also developed for certain income statement accounts. These usually involve nonroutine transactions and unpredictable expenses, such as legal expenses or repairs and maintenance. Many income statement accounts that are closely related to balance sheet accounts are tested simultaneously with the corresponding balance sheet account (e.g., amortization expense with accumulated amortization, or interest expense with notes payable).

When developing balance-related audit objectives, the objectives guide the auditor to accumulate evidence that verifies details of the account balance, rather than verifying the account balance itself. For example, in auditing inventory, the auditor obtains the inventory listing from the client and applies the balance-related audit objectives to the inventory items in the listing. In this discussion, we use the examples of balance-related audit objectives and relevant assertions for the inventory account, which is often the

Balance-related audit objectives—five audit objectives that must be met before the auditor can conclude that any given account balance is fairly stated. The balance-related audit objectives are existence, rights and obligations, completeness, valuation, and allocation.

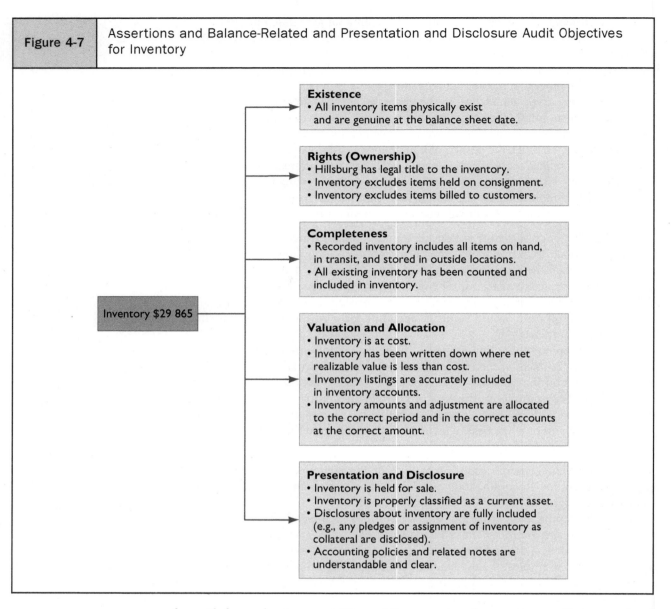

Figure 4-7 Assertions and Balance-Related and Presentation and Disclosure Audit Objectives for Inventory

Inventory $29 865

Existence
• All inventory items physically exist and are genuine at the balance sheet date.

Rights (Ownership)
• Hillsburg has legal title to the inventory.
• Inventory excludes items held on consignment.
• Inventory excludes items billed to customers.

Completeness
• Recorded inventory includes all items on hand, in transit, and stored in outside locations.
• All existing inventory has been counted and included in inventory.

Valuation and Allocation
• Inventory is at cost.
• Inventory has been written down where net realizable value is less than cost.
• Inventory listings are accurately included in inventory accounts.
• Inventory amounts and adjustment are allocated to the correct period and in the correct accounts at the correct amount.

Presentation and Disclosure
• Inventory is held for sale.
• Inventory is properly classified as a current asset.
• Disclosures about inventory are fully included (e.g., any pledges or assignment of inventory as collateral are disclosed).
• Accounting policies and related notes are understandable and clear.

largest balance sheet account. Figure 4-7 summarizes the assertions and balance-related and presentation and disclosure audit objectives for Hillsburg's inventory.

Existence Management asserts that all assets, liabilities, and equity interests included in the balance sheet are genuine and actually existed on the balance sheet date. For example, management asserts that the merchandise inventory included in the balance sheet physically exists and is available for sale at the balance sheet date.

When developing the balance-related audit objectives for this assertion, the auditor asks: *Do all amounts included exist?* For this objective, the auditor requires evidence that proves the inventory actually physically exists. Although the auditor has obtained the inventory listing and the total agrees with the amount recorded in the trial balance, the auditor has not obtained audit evidence to prove the existence assertion. An important procedure to prove the existence assertion is the physical inventory observation. For instance, if the same inventory is accidentally counted twice, the auditor will determine this through the physical observation. If inventory were counted twice, it would be inflated or overstated, which is an existence error.

Rights and Obligations Management asserts that the entity has proper rights to all assets and proper obligation to pay liabilities that are the obligations at a given date. For example, management asserts that the organization has legal title to the inventory.

When developing these audit objectives, the auditor asks: *Are the assets owned? Do the liabilities belong to the entity?* For these audit objectives, the auditor requires evidence that proves ownership and the obligation. For example, audit objectives for rights and obligations of the inventory of Hillsburg Hardware Limited could include that (1) the company has title to all inventory items listed, and (2) inventories are not pledged as collateral unless it is disclosed. To assess those objectives, the auditor will review contracts with suppliers and customers and inquire of management for the possibility that consigned goods are included in the inventory balance.

Completeness Management asserts that all accounts and amounts that should be presented in the financial statements are in fact included. For example, management asserts that all inventory items are recorded.

When developing the completeness balance-related audit objectives, the auditor asks: *Are all amounts recorded?* For these audit objectives, the auditor needs evidence that no items have been omitted from recorded inventory balance—including items in transit and items stored at outside locations.

Valuation Management asserts that assets, liabilities, and equity interests have been included in the financial statements at appropriate amounts, including any valuation adjustments to reflect asset amounts at net realizable value.

In developing the valuation balance-related audit objectives, the auditor asks: *Are the assets recorded at the amounts estimated to be realized?* This objective concerns whether an account balance has been reduced for declines from historical cost to net realizable value, or properly valued if fair value accounting is being used (such as for marketable securities). In the case of inventory, this objective considers whether or not appropriate write-downs for obsolescence have been made.

Allocation In developing the allocation balance-related audit objectives, the auditor asks: *Are all amounts included appropriate?* Allocation includes several concepts: (1) accuracy of adjustment or recorded amount, (2) timing of the adjustment, and (3) adjustment to the correct accounts.

Accuracy of adjustment requires that the correct adjustment or allocation be calculated. For example, the write-down of inventory must be correctly determined, and the amortization of fixed assets should be for an appropriate amount that reflects the useful life (and fair value if fair value accounting is used).

Timing of adjustment refers to the allocation of the adjustment to the correct financial periods. For example, a write-down of inventory should pertain to the current fiscal period, while amortization of fixed assets needs to be allocated to the periods when the asset was in productive use.

Adjustment to correct accounts requires that the adjustment be posted to the correct general ledger accounts. Changes in inventory values would be posted to cost of goods sold for the current period, while changes to the fair value of assets could be posted to equity accounts. If the useful life of an asset has changed, this could result in postings to both the current year's amortization costs and to equity accounts.

The allocation balance-related objective is closely linked to the transaction-related audit objective of classification. If the transactions are posted correctly, then the balances will also be recorded in the correct accounts. For example, on the inventory listing, the inventory should be correctly classified by type. An adequate chart of accounts that differentiates among the different types of assets and liabilities is an important enabler of correct transaction classification and of general ledger account allocation.

Assertions and Presentation- and Disclosure-Related Audit Objectives

With the increasing complexity of transactions and the need for expanded disclosures about these transactions, **presentation and disclosure audit objectives** have increased in importance. The assertions for presentation and disclosure address

Presentation and disclosure audit objectives—four audit objectives that must be met before the auditor can conclude that presentation and disclosures are fairly stated. The presentation and disclosure audit objectives are occurrence and rights and obligations, completeness, accuracy and valuation, and classification and understandability.

whether components of the financial statements are properly classified, described, and disclosed. Refer to Figure 4-7 for examples of presentation and disclosure-related objectives for Hillsburg's inventory. The assertions are described below.

Occurrence and Rights and Obligations Management asserts that disclosed events have occurred and are the rights and obligations of the entity. For example, if the client discloses that it has acquired another company, it asserts that the transaction has been finalized.

Completeness Management asserts that all required disclosures have been included in the financial statements. As an example, management asserts that all material transactions with related parties have been disclosed in the financial statements.

Accuracy and Valuation Management asserts that financial information is disclosed fairly and at appropriate amounts. Management's disclosure of the amount of unfunded pension obligations and the assumptions underlying these amounts is an example of this assertion.

Classification and Understandability Management asserts that the amounts are appropriately classified in the financial statements and footnotes, and the balance descriptions and related disclosures are understandable. For example, management asserts that the classification of inventories as finished goods, work-in-process, and raw materials is appropriate, and the disclosures of the methods used to value inventories are understandable. As one can imagine, the evaluation of understandability requires considerable professional judgment. We discuss this in more detail in our discussion of developing presentation- and disclosure-related audit objectives.

Developing Presentation and Disclosure-Related Audit Objectives

When developing presentation- and disclosure-related audit objectives, the auditor will look at each amount and/or note in the financial statements, and then develop specific presentation- and disclosure-related audit objectives linked to the type of account and the nature of the communication issue. The auditor will then determine what type of audit procedures and evidence will prove the relevant audit objective.

However, the audit objectives for the general presentation of the financial statements and for understandability are somewhat unique. The overall purpose of all presentation- and disclosure-related audit objectives is to assess whether the financial statements portray (through the transactions, accounts, and notes) the economic reality of what actually occurred as well as any significant judgments management made. For instance, accounting standards, such as IAS (International Accounting Standards) 1, require disclosure of the judgments management made in applying significant accounting policies. If the judgments related to a complex investment are described in a confusing or incomplete manner, despite the amount being recorded per the relevant accounting framework, the reader cannot understand how management made those judgments. Similarly, readers expect a clear description of accounting policies.

When developing audit objectives for understandability, the auditor will ask: *Are classes of transactions, account balances, and related disclosure requirements clearly presented in the financial statements?* The auditor will need to assess the financial statements and notes from the perspective of a reasonably informed business user to determine whether the information is presented in a clear way, portraying the events and actions of the organization.

CONCEPT CHECK

C4-8 What are management assertions about financial information?

C4-9 How does the auditor use management assertions during the financial statement audit?

THE AUDIT PROCESS: HOW AUDIT OBJECTIVES ARE MET

LO **11** Explain how the audit process ensures that audit objectives are met and evidence is sufficient and appropriate.

The auditor must obtain sufficient appropriate audit evidence to support all management assertions in the financial statements. As stated earlier, this is done by accumulating evidence in support of an appropriate combination of transaction-related, balance-related, and presentation and disclosure-related audit objectives.

The auditor must decide on the appropriate combination of audit objectives and the evidence to meet those objectives on every audit. To do this, auditors follow an audit process, which is a well-defined methodology for conducting the audit to ensure that the evidence is sufficient and appropriate and that all required audit objectives are both specified and met. The audit process, based upon the Canadian Audit Standards, is shown in Figure 4-8. The rest of this chapter provides a brief overview of the audit process.

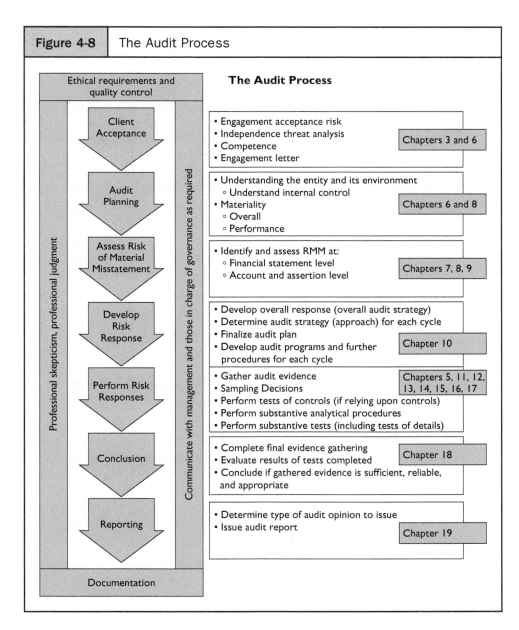

Figure 4-8 | The Audit Process

The green boxes surrounding the blue downward pointing arrows contain factors that are continuous and relevant to the entire audit process:

- Ethical requirements and quality control.
- Professional skepticism and professional judgment.
- Communication with management and those in charge of governance.
- Documentation.

Each of these factors is important for a high quality audit. As we discussed in Chapters 2 and 3, the relevant ethical requirements (integrity, objectivity, confidentiality, and professional behaviour) and quality control processes (such as in-process reviews and appropriate supervision) ensure that a quality audit is performed. Further, as highlighted in this chapter, both professional skepticism and professional judgment are key to a critical evaluation of audit evidence. We have also touched on the importance of documentation in ensuring quality decisions are supportable and drive the review process. We will revisit documentation throughout the book. Finally, ongoing communication with management and those in charge of governance is essential for conducting a quality audit as it's management that is responsible for preparing the financial statements. Later in the book, we will discuss further the auditor's responsibilities with regards to communicating internal control weaknesses, misstatements, fraud, and other issues that arise during the audit.

Client Acceptance

At the beginning of each audit engagement, the audit firm will perform a risk assessment to determine whether the engagement should be accepted or continued in the upcoming year. Key factors that are taken into consideration in this assessment include whether or not the firm has the competence, capabilities, and resources to take on the engagement. The firm will also assess the integrity of the client, as well as any threats to independence and possible risks to the audit firm associated with accepting the specific client. Only if the decision is to proceed with the engagement does the auditor provide an engagement letter and continue with the audit process.

Audit Planning

For any given audit, there are many ways an auditor can accumulate evidence to meet the overall audit objectives, but two overriding considerations affect the approach the auditor selects:

1. Sufficient, high-quality audit evidence must be accumulated to meet the auditor's professional responsibility.
2. The cost of accumulating the evidence should be balanced against the quality of the evidence.

Concern for sufficient appropriate evidence and cost control necessitates planning the engagement. The plan should result in an effective audit approach at a reasonable cost. The auditor performs procedures to assess the risk that material misstatements in the financial statements may be present. This enables the auditors to focus their efforts on those areas that are most susceptible to material misstatements and avoid over-auditing low risk areas (i.e., to avoid being inefficient). Two risk assessment procedures critical to planning and designing an efficient and effective audit process are introduced here and discussed in subsequent chapters.

Understand the Entity and Its Environment To adequately assess the risk of misstatements in financial statements and to interpret information obtained throughout the audit, the auditor must have a thorough understanding of the client's business and related environment, including knowledge of management incentives, strategies, and processes. The auditor should study the client's business model perform

analytical procedures, and make comparisons to competitors. The auditor must understand any unique accounting requirements of the client's industry. For example, in an audit of a life insurance company, the auditor must understand how loss reserves are calculated.

Analytical procedures— evaluations of financial information through analysis of plausible relationships among financial and nonfinancial information.

Understand Internal Control As part of understanding the entity, the auditor obtains an understanding of the client's internal control—both the entity-level controls (the control environment) and transaction-level controls (control activities). As we discussed earlier in this chapter, entity-level controls address pervasive risks. This means they have a pervasive impact at the financial statement level. For instance, if the client's accounting area was understaffed, this could lead to many errors in the preparation of the financial statements. When auditors understand transaction-level controls, they are assessing risk at the assertion level and focusing on the processes that initiate, authorize, and record transactions in a specific cycle.

Materiality One of the key decisions made in the planning of the audit is assessing materiality. CAS 320 states that materiality is based upon the common financial information needs of the users as a group and is the amount by which errors or omissions could reasonably affect the economic decisions of those users. The auditor uses materiality to determine the nature, timing, and extent of audit procedures and to evaluate the effect of misstatements on the financial statements.

Assess Risk of Material Misstatement

The purpose of the auditor's assessment of risks of material misstatement at the financial statement and assertion levels is to identify where misstatements may occur and the depth of audit work required for the individual accounts and transaction streams. For example, if the client is expanding sales by taking on new customers with poor credit ratings, the auditor will assess a higher risk for net realizable value of the accounts receivable and plan to expand testing in that area.

The auditor uses the knowledge of the entity and its environment to assess the likelihood of material misstatement at both the financial statement level and the assertion level. Risks at the financial statement level pervade the financial statements as a whole. This means that these risks could potentially affect many assertions related to classes of transactions, account balances, and/or presentation and disclosures. Some of these risks—financial reporting fraud, laws and regulations, related parties, and going concern—we have discussed in this chapter.

When considering risks at the assertion level, the auditor considers both inherent and control risks. Inherent risk refers to the susceptibility of a class of transactions, account balance, or disclosure to the risk of material misstatement before consideration of internal controls. The auditor then identifies the relevant controls that will mitigate the inherent risk and assesses control risk. Control risk refers to the risk that a material misstatement could occur in an assertion or class of transactions, account balance, or disclosure, and that it will not be prevented (or detected and corrected) on a timely basis. If internal controls are considered effective, planned control risk can be reduced and the amount of audit evidence to be accumulated can be significantly less than when internal controls are not adequate.

Develop Risk Response

The outcome of the planning and assessment of risk of material misstatement is the overall audit plan, which represents the auditor's risk response. This plan, which is communicated to management and those in charge of governance, includes the audit strategy for the overall audit and for the components of the audit (accounts with potential for material error, or material transaction streams). On an ongoing basis, these risks and the audit plan are discussed with the audit team, and audit plans are modified as required.

Overall Audit Strategy (Risk Response) CAS 330 lists the following overall responses to address the assessed risks of material misstatement at the financial statement level:

- Emphasize to the audit team the need to maintain professional scepticism.
- Assign more experienced staff, those with special skills, or use experts.
- Provide more supervision.
- Incorporate an element of unpredictability into the further audit procedures to be performed. This is necessary if the auditor has determined there is a high fraud risk.
- Make general changes to the nature, timing, or extent of audit procedures.

How these responses are carried out depends upon the nature of the audit engagement and the auditor's risk assessment.

Audit Strategy (Approach) for Accounts and Assertions Depending upon the control risk assessment, the auditor determines the appropriate audit strategy or approach for the particular accounts and assertions. The auditor may use a combined strategy (or approach), where the auditor plans to rely upon controls, or a substantive strategy, when the auditor does not plan to rely upon controls. The auditor then develops audit programs, which list the procedures to be performed.

Perform Risk Responses

The further audit procedures (or audit tests) are designed to respond to the risks of material misstatement, at the assertion level, which were identified in the risk assessment phases. The auditor considers the mix of different types of tests and the type of sampling to be used to actually conduct the tests, and adds unpredictability (or randomness) to the testing process. The tests are designed based upon materiality, specific risks such as the potential for management bias or override, fraud risks, or complex transactions identified.

Tests of control—audit procedures to test the effectiveness of control policies and procedures in support of a reduced assessed control risk.

Perform Tests of Control Before auditors can justify reducing planned assessed control risk when internal controls are believed to be effective, they must first perform **tests of control**. For example, assume a client's internal controls require computer matching of all relevant terms on the customer sales order, shipping document, and sales invoice before sales invoices are transmitted to customers. This control is directly related to the occurrence and accuracy transaction assertions for sales. The auditor might test the effectiveness of this control by comparing a sample of sales invoices to related shipping documents and customer sales orders, or by performing tests of the computerized controls related to this process.

As the tests are completed, the results are evaluated to determine if there should be any changes in assessed risks or in the design of the audit procedures.

Substantive tests of details—audit procedures testing for monetary misstatements (due either to error or to fraud) in the details of the classes of transactions, balances, and disclosures in order to determine whether the transaction-related, balance-related, and presentation and disclosure-related audit objectives have been satisfied.

Perform Substantive Tests Substantive tests are procedures performed to obtain direct evidence about dollar amounts and disclosures in the financial statements. There are three general categories of substantive tests: substantive tests of details (of classes of transactions, account balances, and disclosures), substantive analytical procedures, and substantive tests of key items. The nature and extent of the types of tests performed depends upon the risk of material misstatement.

Substantive tests of details are specific procedures intended to detect monetary misstatements in classes of transactions, balances, and disclosures. An example of a test of details for the accuracy of transaction-related objective for sales is that the auditor uses computer software to compare the unit selling price on duplicate sales invoices with an electronic file of approved prices. An example of a test of details to test the balance-related audit objective for the accuracy of accounts receivable is direct written communication with the client's customers.

Substantive analytical procedures—analytical procedures that evaluate classes of transactions, balances, and disclosures through analysis of plausible relationships among both financial and nonfinancial data at the assertion level.

Substantive analytical procedures are analytical procedures performed at the assertion level that assess the overall reasonableness of transactions, balances, and disclosures using plausible relationships among financial and nonfinancial information.

CAS 520, *Analytical Procedures*, highlights that different types of analytical procedures provide different levels of assurance. Analytical procedures involving, for example, the prediction of total rental income on a building divided into apartments (taking the rental rates, number of apartments, and vacancy rates into consideration) can provide persuasive evidence on the occurrence of revenue. In contrast, calculation and comparison of gross margin percentages as a means of confirming a revenue figure may provide less persuasive evidence on the occurrence of revenue.

CAS

There is a close relationship among understanding the entity and its environment, understanding internal control and assessing control risk, analytical procedures, and the substantive tests of the financial statement account balances. If the auditor has obtained a reasonable level of assurance for any given audit objective by performing tests of controls and substantive analytical procedures (which provide persuasive evidence), the substantive tests of details for that objective can be significantly reduced. In most instances, however, some substantive tests of details of significant financial statement accounts are necessary.

Conclusion

After the auditor has completed all the procedures for each audit objective and for each financial statement account, it is necessary to combine the information obtained into an audit summary memorandum to reach an *overall conclusion* as to whether the financial statements are fairly presented. This is a highly subjective process that relies heavily on the auditor's professional judgment. In practice, the auditor continuously combines the information obtained as he or she proceeds through the audit.

Reporting

When the audit is completed and those in charge of governance have approved the financial statements, the PA will issue an auditor's report to accompany the client's published financial statements. The report must meet well-defined technical requirements that are affected by the scope of the audit and the nature of the findings. These reports are studied in Chapter 19. Like all other phases, the audit report decision involves considerable professional judgment.

CONCEPT CHECK

C4-10 What is the relationship between assessing risk of material misstatement and developing risk response during the financial statement audit?

C4-11 When is quality control conducted during the audit? How does this affect risk assessment?

SUMMARY

This chapter described the responsibility of both management and those charged with governance for the financial statements and internal control, and the auditor's responsibility to audit the financial statements. This chapter emphasized the critical importance of maintaining an attitude of professional skepticism and highlighted a professional judgment process to help auditor decision-making. The chapter also discussed management assertions and the related objectives of the audit and the way the auditor subdivides the audit to result in specific audit objectives. The auditor then accumulates evidence to obtain assurance that each audit objective is satisfied. The illustration for sales transactions and accounts receivable shows that the auditor can obtain assurance by accumulating evidence using tests of controls, substantive tests, and substantive analytical procedures. In some audits there is more emphasis on certain tests such as substantive analytical procedures and tests of controls (referred to as the combined audit strategy), whereas other audits emphasize substantive tests (referred to as the substantive audit strategy).

MyLab Accounting
Make the grade with MyLab Accounting: The questions, exercises, and problems marked with a ⊕ can be found on MyLab Accounting. You can practise them as often as you want, and most feature step-by-step guided instructions to help you find the right answer.

Review Questions

🌐 **4-1** ① State the objective of the audit of financial statements. In general terms, how do auditors meet that objective?

🌐 **4-2** ② ③ Distinguish between the responsibilities of management, of those in charge of governance, and of the auditor for the financial statements being audited.

🌐 **4-3** ④ Distinguish between the terms "errors" and "fraud and other irregularities." What is the auditor's responsibility for finding each?

🌐 **4-4** ④ Distinguish between financial reporting fraud and misappropriation of assets. Discuss the likely difference between these two types of fraud on the fair presentation of financial statements.

🌐 **4-5** ④ List two major characteristics that are useful in predicting the likelihood of fraudulent financial reporting in an audit. For each of the characteristics, state two things that the auditor can do to evaluate its significance in the engagement.

🌐 **4-6** ④ What is the auditor's responsibility when noncompliance with laws and regulations is identified or suspected?

🌐 **4-7** ⑤ What are the elements of an effective professional judgment process?

4-8 ⑤ Consulting with others is an important step in making professional judgments. Explain how consultation can overcome judgment traps and biases.

4-9 ⑤ Explain how "framing the problem" can help overcome judgment traps when auditing subjective areas such as fair value estimates.

🌐 **4-10** ⑦ Describe what is meant by "the cycle approach to auditing." What are the advantages of dividing the audit into different cycles?

🌐 **4-11** ⑦ Why are sales, sales returns and allowances, bad debts, cash discounts, accounts receivable, and allowance for uncollectable accounts all included in the same cycle?

🌐 **4-12** ⑨ ⑩ Distinguish between audit objectives and management assertions. Why are the audit objectives more useful to auditors?

🌐 **4-13** ⑦ ⑧ An acquisition of equipment repairs by a construction company is recorded in the incorrect accounting period. Which transaction-related audit objective has been violated? Which transaction-related objective has been violated if the acquisition has been capitalized as a capital asset rather than expensed?

🌐 **4-14** ⑧ A banker found a set of financial statements difficult to read, and the disclosures seemed to be incomplete. Which presentation and disclosure-related objectives have been violated? Why?

4-15 ⑨ Distinguish between the existence and completeness balance-related audit objectives. State the effect on the financial statements (overstatement or understatement) of a violation of each in the audit of accounts payable.

🌐 **4-16** ⑨ ⑩ Identify the management assertion and balance-related audit objective for this audit objective: All recorded fixed assets exist at the balance sheet date.

🌐 **4-17** ⑨ ⑩ Explain why existence is a relevant assertion for fixed assets. How does identifying relevant assertions affect audit objectives and evidence accumulation?

🌐 **4-18** ⑩ Identify the management assertion and presentation and disclosure-related audit objective for the specific presentation and disclosure-related audit objective: Read the fixed asset footnote disclosure to determine that the types of fixed assets, depreciation methods, and useful lives are clearly disclosed.

🌐 **4-19** ⑪ Describe the various phases of the audit process. What is the relationship of the phases to the objective of the audit of financial statements?

Multiple Choice Questions

🌐 **4-20** ① The following questions concern the reasons auditors do audits. Choose the best response.
   a. Which of the following best describes the reason why an independent auditor reports on financial statements?
   (1) A misappropriation of assets may exist, and it is more likely to be detected by independent auditors.
   (2) Different interests may exist between the company preparing the statements and the persons using the statements.

(3) A misstatement of account balances may exist and is generally corrected as the result of the independent auditor's work.

(4) Poorly designed internal controls may be in existence.

b. Because of the risk of material misstatement, an audit should be planned and performed with an attitude of:

(1) Objective judgment.

(2) Independent integrity.

(3) Professional skepticism.

(4) Impartial conservatism.

4-21 〔4〕 What assurance does the auditor provide that errors and fraud that are material to the financial statements will be detected?

Errors	Fraud
(1) Limited	Negative
(2) Reasonable	Reasonable
(3) Limited	Limited
(4) Reasonable	Limited

4-22 〔9〕 〔10〕 The following questions deal with management assertions. Choose the best response.

a. An auditor will most likely review an entity's periodic accounting for the numerical sequence of shipping documents to ensure all documents are included to support management's assertion about classes of transactions of:

(1) Occurrence.

(2) Completeness.

(3) Accuracy.

(4) Classification.

b. In the audit of accounts payable, an auditor's procedures will most likely focus primarily on management's assertion about account balances of:

(1) Existence.

(2) Completeness.

(3) Valuation and allocation.

(4) Classification and understandability.

Discussion Questions and Problems

4-23 〔1〕 〔2〕 〔4〕 Frequently, questions have been raised regarding the responsibility of the independent auditor for the discovery of fraud (including defalcations and other similar irregularities) and concerning the proper course of conduct of the independent auditor when his or her examination discloses specific circumstances that arouse suspicion about the existence of fraud.

REQUIRED

a. What are (1) the function and (2) the responsibilities of the independent auditor in the examination of financial statements? Discuss fully, but do not include fraud in this discussion.

b. What are the responsibilities of the independent auditor for the detection of fraud and other irregularities? Discuss fully.

c. What is the independent auditor's proper course of conduct when his or her examination discloses specific circumstances that arouse his or her suspicion as to the existence of fraud and other irregularities?

(Adapted from AICPA.)

4-24 〔1〕 〔2〕 〔4〕 It is well accepted that, throughout the conduct of the ordinary audit, it is essential to obtain large amounts of information from management and to rely heavily on management's judgments. After all, the financial statements are management's representations, and the primary responsibility for their fair presentation rests with management, not the auditor. For example, it is extremely difficult, if not impossible, for the auditor to evaluate the obsolescence of inventory as accurately as management can in a highly complex business. Similarly, the collectability of accounts receivable and the continued usefulness of machinery and equipment are heavily dependent on management's willingness to provide truthful responses to questions.

REQUIRED

Reconcile the auditor's responsibility for discovering material misrepresentations by management with these comments.

4-25 **1** **2** **4** Recently, there have been a significant number of highly publicized cases of management fraud involving the misstatement of financial statements. Although most clients possess unquestioned integrity, a very small number, given sufficient incentive and opportunity, may be predisposed to fraudulently misstate reported financial conditions and operating results.

REQUIRED

a. What distinguishes financial reporting fraud from other types of fraud?
b. What are an auditor's responsibilities, under generally accepted auditing standards, to detect financial reporting fraud?
c. What are the characteristics of financial reporting fraud that an auditor should consider in order to fulfill the auditor's responsibilities for detecting management fraud under generally accepted auditing standards?
d. Three factors that heighten an auditor's concern about the existence of financial reporting fraud include: (1) an intended public placement of securities in the near future; (2) management compensation dependent on operating results; and (3) a weak internal control environment evidenced by lack of concern for basic controls and disregard of the auditor's recommendations. What other factors should heighten an auditor's concern about the existence of financial reporting fraud?

(Adapted from AICPA.)

4-26 **11** Following are seven audit activities:
1. Examine invoices supporting recorded fixed-asset additions.
2. Review industry databases to assess the risk of material misstatement in the financial statements.
3. Summarize misstatements identified during testing to assess whether the overall financial statements are fairly stated.
4. Test computerized controls over credit approval for sales transactions.
5. Send letters to customers confirming outstanding accounts receivable balances.
6. Perform analytical procedures comparing the client with similar companies in the industry to gain an understanding of the client's business and strategies.
7. Compare information on purchase invoices recorded in the acquisitions journal with information on receiving reports.

REQUIRED

For each activity listed above, use Figure 4-8 to indicate in which phase of the audit the procedure was likely performed (client acceptance, audit planning, assess risk of material misstatement, develop risk response, perform risk responses, conclusion, or reporting).

4-27 **5** The following independent scenarios describe auditor decisions made during an audit engagement.
1. Chen Li worked on the audit of Diagnostic Imaging Services (DSI), which provides diagnostic imaging services to hospitals in Ontario. Chen was assigned responsibility to audit the allowance for hospital receivables. For the past several years, DSI's accounting policy required that the recorded allowance for hospital receivables be set to equal the total amount of receivables over 180 days past due. Prior audit testing of the allowance in previous years has found that the subsequent write-offs of hospital receivables has closely approximated the amount included in the allowance. During the current year audit, Chen examined the amount recorded in the general ledger allowance account and reconciled that amount to the amount shown in DSI's consolidated aged trial balance in the 180 days past due amount. Given that the dollar amounts agreed, Chen concluded that the allowance was in accordance with DSI accounting policy and fairly stated. While media reports and other industry publications suggested that recent regulatory changes in hospital funding were affecting hospitals' ability to pay, Chen concluded that DSI's allowance was fairly stated given the amounts complied with DSI's policy.
2. Sherry Zipersky was assigned responsibility for evaluating the goodwill impairment testing process at Yukon Metals, Inc. Because Yukon Metals' growth strategy was based mostly on acquisitions, the company had experience in performing annual impairment tests of goodwill.

The client provided Sherry extensive information along with detailed schedules that documented management's testing approaches, and it provided her support for key assumptions made by management. Sherry reviewed the schedules in detail and tested the key calculations. While Sherry's firm has a number of valuation specialists as part of its staff, Sherry decided not to request their assistance in making an independent assessment of goodwill impairment given that the client's documentation was extensive and it would take too much time to have the firm's valuation specialists complete an independent assessment.

3. Jason Jackson was responsible for auditing the occurrence of sales transactions in the audit of Asheville Manufacturing. As part of his testing, he reviewed the contracts signed between Asheville Manufacturing and its customers to determine that the transaction terms justified the recording of sales for the year under audit. In addition, he examined documentation related to the sales transactions, including the customers' purchase orders, shipping documents, and invoices generated by Asheville. The evidence examined supported the correct recording of sales in the current year. However, Jason also noticed in the customer files copies of email exchanges between Asheville Manufacturing sales agents and the customers suggesting that some of the terms of the sales agreements could be waived at the customers' discretion. Jason decided to rely on the contracts and sales transactions documentation to conclude that the sales were properly stated, given that the other information was only included in emails.

4. Allison Garrett works on a number of audits of technology equipment manufacturers and has developed extensive knowledge and experience in the industry. On the recent audit engagement of financial statements for Zurich Technologies, Allison was responsible for auditing the valuation of inventories, including the reserve for obsolescence. Given her familiarity with the industry, Allison decided to conduct a quick substantive analytical procedure regarding the days in inventory and determined that the reserve was fairly stated, given that it was in line with reserves established by some of her other clients. She determined that additional evidence was not necessary to be obtained because of her experience with other clients.

REQUIRED

For each of the scenarios listed above, describe the most likely judgment trap that ultimately biased the auditor's decision-making in the audit.

4-28 [7] The following general ledger accounts are included in the trial balance for an audit client, Jones Wholesale Stationery Store.

Accounts receivable	Depreciation expense –	Prepaid interest expense
Accrued sales salaries	furniture and equipment	Property tax expense
Accumulated amortization of	Furniture and equipment	Property tax payable
furniture and equipment	Income tax expense	Purchases
Advertising expense	Income tax payable	Rent expense
Allowance for doubtful	Insurance expense	Retained earnings
accounts	Interest expense	Salaries-office and general
Amortization expense—	Interest income	Sales
furniture and equipment	Interest receivable	Sales salaries expense
Bad-debt expense	Inventory	Telephone and fax expense
Bonds payable	Notes payable	Travel expense
Cash	Notes receivable	Unexpired insurance
Common stock		

REQUIRED

a. Identify the accounts in the trial balance that are likely to be included in each transaction cycle. Some accounts will be included in more than one cycle. Use the format that follows.

Cycle	Balance Sheet Accounts	Income Statement Accounts
Revenue and collections		
Acquisition and payment		
Human resources and payroll		
Inventory and distribution		
Capital acquisition and repayment		

b. How would the general ledger accounts in the trial balance most likely differ if the company were a retail store rather than a wholesale company? How would they differ for a hospital or a government unit?

4-29 **9** The following are two balance-related audit objectives in the audit of accounts payable.
1. All accounts payable included on the list represent amounts due to valid vendors.
2. There are no unrecorded accounts payable.

The list referred to in the objectives is the aged accounts payable trial balance produced using the supplier master file. The total of the list equals the accounts payable balance on the general ledger.

REQUIRED
a. Explain the difference between these two balance-related audit objectives.
b. For the audit of accounts payable, which of these two balance-related audit objectives would usually be more important? Explain.

4-30 **8** The following (1 through 17) are the balance-related, transaction-related, and presentation- and disclosure-related audit objectives.

Assertions About Classes of Transactions and Events	Assertions About Account Balances	Assertions About Presentation and Disclosure
1. Occurrence	6. Existence	11. Occurrence and
	7. Rights and obligations	12. Rights and obligations
2. Completeness	8. Completeness	13. Completeness
3. Accuracy		14. Accuracy and
	9. Valuation and	15. Valuation
	10. Allocation	
4. Cutoff		
5. Classification		16. Classification and
		17. Understandability

REQUIRED

Identify the audit objective (1–17) of each of the following audit procedures for the audit of sales accounts receivable, and cash receipts for the current fiscal year.
a. Examine a sample of duplicate sales invoices to determine whether each one has a shipping document attached.
b. Add all customer balances in the accounts receivable trial balance and agree the amount to the general ledger.
c. For a sample of sales transactions selected from the sales journal, verify that the amount of the transaction has been recorded in the correct customer account in the accounts receivable total field of the customer master file.
d. Inquire of the client whether any accounts receivable balances have been pledged as collateral on long-term debt and determine whether all required information is included in the footnote description for long-term debt.
e. For a sample of shipping documents selected from shipping records, trace each shipping document to a transaction recorded in the sales journal.
f. Discuss with credit department personnel the likelihood of collection of all accounts with a balance greater than $100 000 and greater than 90 days old as of the year-end.
g. Examine sales invoices for the last five sales transactions recorded in the sales journal in the current year and examine shipping documents to determine that they are recorded in the correct period.
h. For a sample of customer accounts receivable balances at the year-end, examine subsequent cash receipts in the following month to determine whether the customer paid the balance due.
i. Determine whether all risks related to accounts receivable are adequately disclosed.
j. Foot the sales journal for the month of July (halfway through the fiscal year) and trace postings to the general ledger.
k. Send letters to a sample of accounts receivable customers to verify whether they have an outstanding balance at the fiscal year-end.
l. Determine whether long-term receivables and related party receivables are reported separately in the financial statements.

Professional Judgment Problems and Cases

4-31 [4] [11] Jane was the audit supervisor in charge of the audit of an advertising agency. Unfortunately, two other audit supervisors in the office resigned and moved on to other positions. Rather than hiring or promoting another supervisor, the firm reallocated clients. Jane was asked to take on some of the other audit clients and spend less time reviewing files and supervising staff. The audit managers and partners were expected to do a more thorough audit review to help compensate for the fewer than usual supervisors.

Jane felt harried, and her audit staff at the advertising agency were upset that she had not been present there for several days. The tax provision looked complex, and Jane decided to leave the tax section for the tax manager to review.

To Jane's horror, she discovered six months later that the tax provision had been incorrect by over $100 000. The client was upset that the financial statements were materially misstated and decided to seek other auditors.

REQUIRED

Using your knowledge of audit standards and the audit process, explain which audit phases were poorly executed in the audit of the advertising agency. Provide suggestions for improvement to help prevent this type of error in the future.

4-32 [1] [4] [11] Renée Ritter opened a small grocery and related products convenience store in 1993 with the money she had saved working as a Loblaws store manager. She named it Ritter Dairy and Fruits. Because of the excellent location and her fine management skills, Ritter Dairy and Fruits grew to three locations by 1998. By that time, she needed additional capital. She obtained financing through a local bank at 2 percent above prime, under the condition that she submit quarterly financial statements reviewed by a public accounting firm approved by the bank. After interviewing several firms, she decided to use the firm of Gonzalez and Fineberg, PAs, after obtaining approval from the bank.

By 2002, the company had grown to six stores, and Ritter developed a business plan to add another 10 stores in the next several years. Ritter's capital needs had also grown, so she decided to add two business partners who both had considerable capital and some expertise in convenience stores. After further discussions with the bank and continued conversations with the future business partners, she decided to have an annual audit and quarterly reviews done by Gonzalez and Fineberg, even though the additional cost was almost $15 000 annually. The bank agreed to reduce the interest rate on the $5 000 000 loan to 1 percent above prime.

By 2007, things were going smoothly, with the two business partners heavily involved in the day-to-day operations and the company adding two new stores per year. The company was growing steadily and was more profitable than they had expected. By the end of 2008, one of the business partners, Fred Warnest, had taken over responsibility for accounting and finance operations, as well as some marketing. Annually, Gonzalez and Fineberg did an in-depth review of the accounting system, including internal controls, and reported their conclusions and recommendations to the board of directors.

Specialists in the firm provided tax and other advice. The other business partner in the dairy, Ben Gold, managed most of the stores and was primarily responsible for building new stores. Ritter was president and managed four stores.

In 2012, the three business partners (now the executive management of the company) decided to go public to enable them to add more stores and modernize the existing ones. The public offering was a major success, resulting in $25 million in new capital and nearly 1000 shareholders. Ritter Dairy and Fruits added stores rapidly, and the company remained highly profitable under the leadership of Ritter, Warnest, and Gold.

Ritter retired in 2015 after a highly successful career. During the retirement celebration, she thanked her business partners, employees, and customers. She also added a special thanks to the bank management for their outstanding service and to Gonzalez and Fineberg for being partners in the best and most professional sense of the word. She mentioned their integrity, commitment, high-quality service in performing their audits and reviews, and considerable tax and business advice for more than two decades.

REQUIRED

a. Explain why the bank imposed a requirement of a quarterly review of the financial statements as a condition of obtaining the loan at 2 percent above prime. Also, explain why the bank did not require an audit and why the bank demanded the right to approve which public accounting firm was engaged.

b. Explain why Ritter Dairy and Fruits agreed to have an audit performed rather than a review, considering the additional cost of $15 000.

c. What did Ritter mean when she referred to Gonzalez and Fineberg as "partners"? Does the PA firm have an independence problem?

d. What benefit does Gonzalez and Fineberg provide to shareholders, creditors, and management in performing the audit and related services?

e. What are the responsibilities of the PA firm to shareholders, creditors, management, and others?

4-33 [4] [6] [11] The following information was obtained from several accounting and auditing enforcement releases issued by the Securities and Exchange Commission (SEC) after its investigation of fraudulent financial reporting involving Just for Feet, Inc.:

- Just for Feet, Inc., was a national retailer of athletic and outdoor footwear and apparel based in Birmingham, AL. The company incurred large amounts of advertising expenses and most vendors offered financial assistance through unwritten agreements with Just for Feet to help pay for these advertising expenses. If Just for Feet promoted a particular vendor's products in one of its advertisements, that vendor typically would consider agreeing to provide an "advertising co-op credit" to the company to share the costs of the advertisement. Just for Feet offset this co-op revenue against advertising expenses on its income statement, thereby increasing its net earnings.

- Although every vendor agreement was somewhat different, Just for Feet's receipt of advertising co-op revenue was contingent upon subsequent approval by the vendor. If the vendor approved the advertisement, it would usually issue the co-op payment to Just for Feet in the form of a credit memo offsetting expenses on Just for Feet's merchandise purchases from that vendor.
- In the last few weeks of fiscal year 1998, the company's CFO, controller, and VP of operations directed the company's accounting department to book $14.4 million in co-op receivables and related revenues that they knew were not owed by certain vendors, including Adidas, Asics, New Balance, Nike, and Reebok. The entry represented one-half of the total accounts receivable balance at year-end. The auditors requested supporting documentation regarding the journal entry; however, client management never provided any. The auditors had mailed out confirmations to 13 vendors (representing 76 percent of the total accounts receivable balance). Five of the returned confirmations confirmed the amount owing, eight had ambiguous information regarding the amount owing, and one clearly stated that "no additional funds" were due to Just for Feet. The auditors completed their fieldwork three months after year-end and, as of that date, Just for Feet had not received any payments for the undocumented vendor allowances.
- Subsequently, it was revealed that the vendor allowances were fictitious and that the VP of operations had convinced the five vendors to sign and return the confirmations. These fraudulent practices, along with others, resulted in over $19 million in fictitious pretax earnings being reported, out of total pretax income of approximately $43 million. The SEC ultimately brought charges against a number of senior executives at Just for Feet, some vendor representatives, and the auditors. Ultimately, the auditors were fined and sanctioned by the SEC. In response to the sanctions, the auditors issued a press release stating: "Among our most significant challenges is the early detection of fraud, particularly when the client, its management and others collude specifically to deceive a company's auditors."[5]

REQUIRED

a. What does it mean to approach an audit with an attitude of professional skepticism?

b. Refer to the professional judgment framework and answer the next three questions:

   i What circumstances related to the accounting treatment of the vendor allowances should have increased an auditor's professional skepticism? Why?

   ii What factors might have caused the auditor to inappropriately accept the assertions by management that the vendor allowances should be reflected in the financial statements?

   iii Develop three probing questions related to the vendor allowances that the auditor should have asked in the audit of Just for Feet's financial statements.

---

[5] Stephen Taub, "Deloitte statement irks SEC," *CFO*, April 28, 2005, accessed June 19, 2017, at **http://ww2.cfo.com/accounting-tax/2005/04/deloitte-statement-irks-sec/**.

c. Based upon the case facts, do you agree with the auditors' statement regarding their inability to detect frauds involving collusion between client management and outsider parties?

4-34 **5** Refer to Auditing in Action 4-3 regarding the Livent audits.

a. Explain how this case illustrates the importance of framing.

b. The ICAO disciplinary committee argues that professional judgment requires a correct conclusion. How do you reconcile this with the common view that audit and accounting are very subjective?

4-35 **5** **6** This problem requires you to access a copy of the Canadian Public Accountability Board's 2013 Annual Inspection Report at **http://www.cpab-ccrc.ca/Documents/ Topics/Public%20Reports/2013_Public_Report_EN .pdf**. Refer to Appendix D of the report, which summarizes the most common inspections findings and groups them by category.

REQUIRED

1. Read the examples provided for risk assessment. Which judgment *bias* would most likely lead auditors not to appropriately link risk assessment to risk response?

2. Read the examples provided for the audit of estimates and explain which phase of the audit process each example relates to.

3. Explain why the CPAB recommended that the auditors needed to apply a heightened sense of professional skepticism. Why do you think professional skepticism is so important in assessing management estimates?

4-36 **8** **9** The Canadian Securities Administrators (CSA) regularly perform reviews of the quality of interim and annual information filed with the provincial securities regulators. Part of this review includes the quality of financial statements presentation and disclosure. In their July 2014 review, the CSA highlighted that there were many deficiencies related to financial statement note disclosure. Access the CSA Staff Notice 51-341 at **http://www.osc.gov.on.ca/documents/en/ Securities-Category5/csa_20140717_51-341_cdr-activi-ties-fiscal-end.pdf**.

REQUIRED

1. Refer to Appendix A of the Staff Notice, read the example on impairment of assets, and explain what presentation and disclosure assertions were violated.

2. How do you think the audit evidence for presentation and disclosure-audit objectives is similar to the transaction-related and balance-related audit objectives? How do you think it differs?

3. Regulators such as the CSA are putting greater emphasis on presentation and disclosure. The international accounting standard setter, IASB (International Accounting Standards Board), and its American counterpart, FASB (Financial Accounting Standards Board), are working on a joint Financial Statement Presentation Project that plans to address fundamental issues related to presentation and display of financial information. Why do you think regulators and standard setters are so concerned about the presentation and disclosure assertions?

AUDIT EVIDENCE

Audit evidence was defined in Chapter 1 as any information used by the auditor to determine whether the financial statement being audited is stated in accordance with the established criteria. The information is a decision tool—it varies widely in the extent to which it persuades the auditor whether financial statements are stated in conformity with an acceptable financial reporting framework.

STANDARDS REFERENCED IN THIS CHAPTER

CAS 230 – Audit documentation

CAS 500 – Audit evidence

CAS 520 – Analytical procedures

LEARNING OBJECTIVES

After studying this chapter, you should be able to:

1 Understand the purpose and types of audit evidence used throughout the audit process.

2 Explain the three audit evidence decisions to determine what evidence to gather and how much to accumulate.

3 Use professional judgment to determine the degree of persuasiveness of audit evidence.

4 Describe the types of audit procedures for gathering audit evidence.

5 Design analytical procedures for the various phases of the audit process.

6 Understand the purposes of audit documentation.

7 Prepare organized audit documentation.

8 Explain how technology affects audit evidence and audit documentation.

9 Understand and apply professional skepticism to evidence and documentation decisions.

CEO Confesses to Falsifying Documents to Hide Fraud for Over 20 Years

Nine days after his surprise Las Vegas wedding, Russell Wasendorf, chief executive officer of Peregrine Financial Group (PFG), was found unconscious in his car with a tube running from the exhaust pipe into the vehicle. (At the time, Peregrine was the second largest US nonbank, nonclearing Futures Commission Merchant [FCM].) By week's end, regulators had discovered about $215 million in missing customer money, the futures trading firm had filed for Chapter 7 liquidating bankruptcy, and its fancy offices were closed. A suicide note was found inside the car admitting that the CEO had committed fraud for over 20 years.

continued >

continued

The fraud was exposed when the National Futures Association (NFA)—the futures/options industry's self-regulatory group—decided to switch from hard copies to electronic statements for regulatory filings. The NFA had sent an audit team to review Peregrine's books and to pressure Peregrine into participating in a new online system for verifying accounts, which would have likely made it impossible for Wasendorf to continue the fraud. Wasendorf had fooled the NFA a year earlier after the regulator received a report on a Friday that Peregrine's account for customer balances had less than $10 million. The following Monday, the NFA received a fax purportedly from the bank indicating that the account held more than $200 million; investigation revealed that the fax had been sent by Wasendorf.

In the signed note found in his car, Wasendorf admitted to using a computer, scanner, and Photoshop to make "very convincing forgeries" of bank statements and official correspondence from the bank. To prevent other Peregrine employees from learning about the real bank balances, Wasendorf insisted that only he could open mail from the bank. Auditors typically confirm bank balances directly with the bank. However, Wasendorf supplied the auditor as well as the NFA with the address for a post office box that he controlled for the mailing of the confirmations. Wasendorf also had exclusive control over the customer segregated account and its financial reporting. From June 2008 through July 2012, Wasendorf withdrew and transferred approximately $36 million from the customer segregated funds account to persons and entities that were not Peregrine customers.

Although Wasendorf's son was Peregrine's president, Wasendorf claimed that he was the sole perpetrator of the fraud. He indicated that the scheme began out of financial desperation, as he was unable to obtain capital. In a plea agreement, Wasendorf admitted that, from about the early 1990s through about July of 2012, he stole millions of dollars from PFG's customers. Wasendorf was sentenced to 50 years for fraud, embezzlement, and lying to regulators—the maximum sentence allowed by law for his offences of conviction. "By lying to investors and regulators, Wasendorf defrauded thousands of innocent investors out of a staggering $215 000 000," said Acting United States Attorney Sean R. Berry. "The lengthy prison sentence imposed today is just punishment for a con man who built a business on smoke and mirrors."

Sources: Jacob Bunge, Scott Patterson, and Julie Steinberg, "Peregrine CEO's dramatic confession," *The Wall Street Journal*, July 14–15, 2012. Jacob Bunge, "Peregrine CEO arrested," *The Wall Street Journal*, July 13, 2012. Azam Ahmed and Peter Lattman, "At Peregrine Financial, signs of trouble seemingly missed for years," *The New York Times*, July 13, 2012. Federal Bureau of Investigation Omaha Division, press release, "Peregrine Financial Group CEO sentenced to 50 years for fraud, embezzlement, and lying to regulators," January 13, 2013, accessed July 20, 2017.

The foundation of any audit is the evidence obtained and evaluated by the auditor. The auditor must have the knowledge and skill to accumulate sufficient appropriate evidence on every audit to meet the standards of the profession. As described in the opening vignette, new technologies can improve the quality of audit evidence, but can also create new opportunities for evidence to be compromised. This chapter deals with the types of evidence decisions auditors make, the evidence available to auditors, and the use of that evidence in performing audits and documenting the results.

LO 1 Understand the purpose and type of audit evidence used throughout the audit process.

CAS

NATURE OF AUDIT EVIDENCE

Most of the auditor's work in forming an audit opinion consists of obtaining and evaluating audit evidence. CAS 500 explains that audit evidence is information used by the auditor in arriving at conclusions upon which the audit opinion is based. Evidence includes information generated by the auditor, third parties, and the client. Some evidence is persuasive information, such as the auditor's count of marketable securities, and some is less persuasive, such as client employee responses to auditors' questions.

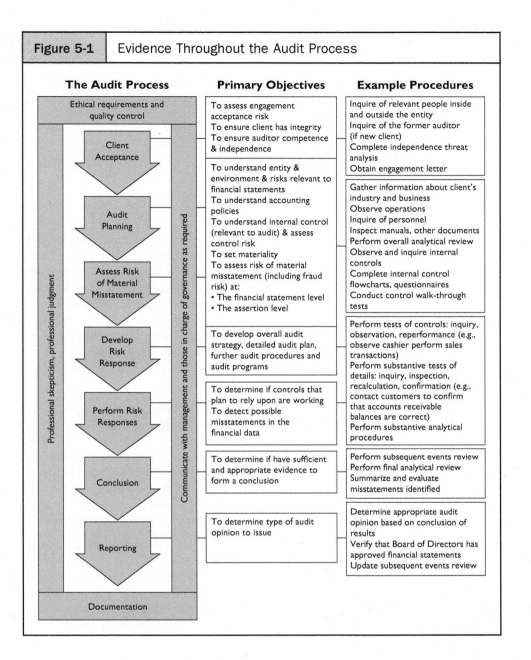

Figure 5-1 | Evidence Throughout the Audit Process

The Audit Process	Primary Objectives	Example Procedures
Client Acceptance	To assess engagement acceptance risk To ensure client has integrity To ensure auditor competence & independence	Inquire of relevant people inside and outside the entity Inquire of the former auditor (if new client) Complete independence threat analysis Obtain engagement letter
Audit Planning / **Assess Risk of Material Misstatement**	To understand entity & environment & risks relevant to financial statements To understand accounting policies To understand internal control (relevant to audit) & assess control risk To set materiality To assess risk of material misstatement (including fraud risk) at: • The financial statement level • The assertion level	Gather information about client's industry and business Observe operations Inquire of personnel Inspect manuals, other documents Perform overall analytical review Observe and inquire internal controls Complete internal control flowcharts, questionnaires Conduct control walk-through tests
Develop Risk Response	To develop overall audit strategy, detailed audit plan, further audit procedures and audit programs	Perform tests of controls: inquiry, observation, reperformance (e.g., observe cashier perform sales transactions) Perform substantive tests of details: inquiry, inspection, recalculation, confirmation (e.g., contact customers to confirm that accounts receivable balances are correct) Perform substantive analytical procedures
Perform Risk Responses	To determine if controls that plan to rely upon are working To detect possible misstatements in the financial data	
Conclusion	To determine if have sufficient and appropriate evidence to form a conclusion	Perform subsequent events review Perform final analytical review Summarize and evaluate misstatements identified
Reporting	To determine type of audit opinion to issue	Determine appropriate audit opinion based on conclusion of results Verify that Board of Directors has approved financial statements Update subsequent events review

Ethical requirements and quality control

Professional skepticism, professional judgment

Communicate with management and those in charge of governance as required

Documentation

Evidence is both information that supports and corroborates management's assertions, and any information that contradicts those assertions. In some cases, it can be the absence of information (for example, management refuses to provide a requested document). By taking into account this different information, the auditor has performed a critical evaluation of audit evidence—which is the essence of professional skepticism.

As illustrated in Figure 5-1, evidence is gathered in all phases of the audit process and is used to help the auditor make a variety of judgments and conclusions—to accept (or continue with) the client, to plan the audit, to decide where there could be a risk of material misstatement in the financial statements, to develop an appropriate risk response, and to conclude as to the type of audit report. Most of the evidence is gathered and evaluated through the use of audit procedures, which we will discuss in the next section.

AUDIT EVIDENCE DECISIONS

A major decision facing every auditor is determining the appropriate types and amounts of evidence needed to conclude that the client's financial statements are fairly stated. There are three key decisions about what evidence to gather and how much to accumulate:

1. Which audit procedures to use (the "nature").
2. Which items to select for testing (the "extent").
3. When to perform the procedures (the "timing").

Audit Procedures

Audit procedure—detailed instruction for the collection of a type of audit evidence.

An **audit procedure** is the detailed instruction that explains the audit evidence to be obtained at some time during the audit. Audit procedures collect evidence from a wide variety of sources, such as physical inventory counts, comparison of cancelled cheques with cash disbursements, journal entries, and shipping document details.

As Figure 5-1 illustrates, the nature of audit procedures varies according to the objective(s) of the phase in the audit process. The nature of audit procedures refers to their purpose (risk assessment, test of controls, or substantive procedure) *and* type (inspection, observation, inquiry, confirmation, recalculation, reperformance, or analytical procedure). We will discuss types of techniques for gathering evidence later in the chapter.

Risk Assessment Procedures During the early phases of the audit process, the auditor performs a variety of risk assessment procedures, which include inquiries, analytical procedures, and inspection and observation. The purpose of risk assessment procedures is to obtain an understanding of the entity and the environment, including internal controls, and to identify and assess the risk of material misstatement in the financial statements. Risk assessment procedures do not provide sufficient appropriate evidence on which to base an audit opinion but are used for planning the audit, assessing risk of material misstatement, and developing an appropriate risk response.

Tests of Controls Auditors use their understanding of internal controls to assess control risk at the assertion level (this is part of the Assessment of Risk of Material Misstatement—see Figure 5-1). If, through the risk assessment, the auditor understands that internal control policies and procedures are effective, the auditor may assess control risk at a moderate or low level. However, the evidence collected through risk assessment procedures is not sufficient to have reasonable assurance that the controls are operating effectively. Or put another way, the auditor does not have sufficient evidence to conclude that controls are operating effectively. Therefore, the auditor must perform further audit procedures, specifically tests of control.

To test controls, the auditor selects some processes or procedures (i.e., controls) carried out by client staff and makes sure they have operated effectively. For example, a test of control would be the auditor observing cashiers performing sales transactions and noting that the cash registers will not open unless a sale has occurred. Auditors collect evidence regarding internal controls through inquiry, observation, and reperformance.

Substantive Procedures Unlike control tests, which focus on processes, substantive procedures focus on transactions or accounts and are designed to detect monetary misstatements. Substantive procedures include tests of details and analytical procedures. Test of details are what they sound like: tests that look at the details of transactions and accounts. Analytical procedures are broader and look at relationships.

When auditors perform substantive tests, they are looking for evidence that supports the figures and disclosures in the financial statements. The focus of the substantive testing is the assertions, a concept introduced in Chapter 4. For instance, assume the auditor is testing the existence of accounts receivable. The auditor can perform an analytical procedure that looks at the relationship between accounts receivable and revenue. However, analytical procedures are generally not sufficient evidence to conclude that the accounts receivable account is fairly stated. Therefore, the auditor will need to perform tests of details as well. For instance, the auditor may decide to select a sample of customer balances and confirm the amounts recorded in the client's accounts receivable subledger (i.e., the details) with the client's customers. In addition to analytical procedures and confirmations, auditors gather evidence for substantive procedures through inquiry, inspection, and recalculation.

The Why, What, How, and When of Audit Procedures

Audit procedures need to be detailed and specific—why the procedure is being done, what is being done, how it is being done, and when it is to be done. For example, the following is a substantive audit procedure for the verification of cash disbursements:

- To test occurrence (the why), during the interim audit (when), obtain the cash disbursements report (how), and for the outstanding cheques, compare the payee name, amount, and date on the cancelled cheque with the cash disbursement report (what).

Which Items to Select Once an audit procedure is determined, the auditor may (1) select all items in the population, (2) select specific items in the population, (3) use audit sampling, or (4) use some combination of first three. The choice depends upon the purpose of the test and the particular circumstances, such as the extent of automated controls and the risk of material misstatement, as well as the practicality and/or efficiency of the procedure.

Referring back to our example audit procedure related to cash disbursements, if there are few items, the auditor may decide it is both efficient and effective to select all items. In most situations, the auditor will decide which items to select based upon the purpose of the test and the assessed risks. Assume the population is 6600 cheques and the auditor has determined that it is necessary to select 40 cancelled cheques. The auditor could select specific items, such as the 40 cheques with the largest amounts (also known as "key items") or those cheques most likely to be in error; or the auditor could use sampling and select the 40 cheques randomly; or some combination of these methods could be used.

Timing An audit of financial statements usually covers a period such as a year, and an audit is often not completed until several weeks or months after the end of the fiscal period. The timing of audit procedures can vary from early in the accounting period to long after it has ended. Normally, the financial statement audit is completed one to three months after year-end. In part, the timing decision is affected by client deadlines. For instance, public companies are required to file audited financial statements with in 90 days. However, timing is also influenced by when the audit evidence will be most effective. For instance, if the client has a periodic inventory system, the auditor should observe the inventory count that occurs at year-end since it is the most effective way to identify errors. Another factor the auditor will take into consideration when deciding on timing is the availability of audit staff.

Audit procedures often incorporate which items to select (including the size of the sample) and timing. The following is a more complete version of the audit procedure previously used. (Italics identify the assertion or objective of the test (the why), timing (the when), the steps to perform the procedure (the how), and which items to select (the what).

- *Occurrence* (why): During the *interim audit* (when), *obtain* (how) the *October* bank reconciliation and cash disbursements report, and *compare* (how) the payee name, amount, and date on the cancelled cheque with the cash disbursements report for a *randomly selected sample* (how) *of 40* (what) outstanding cheque numbers.

Audit Program

Audit program—detailed instructions for the entire collection of evidence for an audit area or an entire audit; always includes audit procedures and may also include sample sizes, items to select, and timing of the tests.

The set of detailed instructions for the entire collection of evidence for an audit area is called an **audit program**. Normally, there is an audit program for each component of the audit (e.g., accounts receivable and sales). An excerpt of an audit program that includes audit procedures (the how), sample size, items to select (the what), timing (the when) and the relevant assertion (the why) is given in Table 5-3 on page 137.

LO 3 Use professional judgment to determine the degree of persuasiveness of audit evidence.

PERSUASIVENESS OF EVIDENCE

Persuasiveness of evidence—the degree to which the auditor is convinced that the evidence supports the audit opinion; the three determinants of persuasiveness are the sufficiency, appropriateness, and timeliness of the evidence.

Generally accepted auditing standards (GAAS) require the auditor to obtain *sufficient appropriate audit evidence* to be able to draw reasonable conclusions on which to base the audit opinion. Because of the nature of audit evidence and the cost of doing an audit, it is unlikely that the auditor will be completely convinced that the opinion is correct. However, the auditor must be persuaded that his or her opinion is correct with a high level of assurance. By combining all evidence from the entire audit, the auditor is able to decide when he or she is sufficiently persuaded to issue an auditor's report. The determinants of **persuasiveness of evidence** are appropriateness (relevance and reliability), sufficiency (enough evidence), and timeliness (covering the appropriate period).

Appropriateness

Appropriateness—the degree to which evidence can be considered relevant and reliable.

Appropriateness refers to the quality of evidence, that is, the degree to which the evidence can be considered relevant and reliable in meeting audit objectives. If evidence is considered to be highly appropriate, it is a great help in persuading the auditor that the financial statements are fairly stated. Note that appropriateness of evidence deals only with the audit procedures selected. Appropriateness cannot be improved by selecting a larger sample size or different population items. It can be improved by selecting audit procedures that are more relevant or that provide more reliable evidence.

Relevance

Relevance of evidence—the pertinence of the evidence to the assertion or control being tested.

Relevance of evidence deals with the logical connection with the design of the audit procedure and the assertion or control that is being tested. The relevance of information used as audit evidence may be affected by the direction of the testing. For example, assume the auditor is concerned that a client is failing to bill customers for shipments (completeness assertion). If the auditor selected a sample of duplicate sales invoices and traced each to related shipping documents, the evidence is *not relevant* for the completeness objective because it tests for occurrence instead. A relevant procedure would be to compare a sample of shipping documents with related duplicate sales invoices to determine if each shipment had been billed. The second audit procedure is relevant because shipment of goods is a normal criterion used for determining whether a sale has occurred and should have been billed.

Reliability

Reliability of evidence—the reliability of evidence depends upon its source and nature. In general, the reliability of evidence is increased when it is obtained (1) directly by the auditor, (2) from an independent provider, (3) from qualified providers such as law firms and banks, or (4) from consistent and multiple sources.

Reliability of evidence refers to the degree to which evidence can be believable or worthy of trust. Reliability is influenced by its source and nature as well as the specific circumstances under which it is obtained, such as the client's internal controls. While exceptions do exist, in general, the reliability of audit evidence increases when it is obtained (1) directly by the auditor, (2) from an independent source, (3) from a qualified source, such as law firms and banks, or (4) from consistent or multiple sources. In the case of evidence obtained from the client, it is considered to be more reliable (5) if the client's internal controls are effective. Audit evidence that is (6) objective is more reliable than subjective audit evidence.

(1) Evidence Obtained Directly by Auditor Evidence obtained directly by the auditor through observation, reperformance, and inspection is more appropriate than information obtained indirectly or by inference. For example, if the auditor observed recent additions to property, plant, and equipment, noted serial numbers, and traced the historical cost from original invoices, the evidence would be more reliable than if the auditor relied on documents and calculations provided by the client's controller.

(2) Independence of Source Evidence obtained from a source outside the entity is more reliable than that obtained from within, assuming that the external party is at arm's length from the organization. For example, external evidence such as communications from banks, lawyers, or customers is generally regarded as more reliable than answers obtained by asking the client. Similarly, documents that originate from outside the client's organization are considered more reliable than those that originate within the company and have never left the client's organization. An example of external evidence is an insurance policy, whereas a purchase requisition is internal evidence.

(3) Qualifications of Source Although the source of information is independent, the evidence will not be reliable unless the individual providing it is qualified to do so. Therefore, communications from law firms and bank confirmations are typically more highly regarded than accounts receivable confirmations from persons not familiar with the business world. Also, evidence obtained directly by the auditor may not be reliable if he or she lacks the qualifications to evaluate the evidence. For example, examination of an inventory of diamonds by an auditor who is not trained to distinguish between diamonds and glass would not provide reliable evidence of the existence of diamonds.

(4) Consistency From Multiple Sources With respect to a particular assertion, the auditor could use multiple sources of evidence. Consider, for example, obsolescence of inventory at Hillsburg Hardware. The auditor could calculate inventory turnover, review recent purchasing invoices, talk to shipping personnel, and observe physical inventory in the warehouse. If shipping personnel stated that no old stock existed, but the auditor observed old inventory (perhaps dusty or dirty boxes of products), then the auditor would need to investigate further to clarify the inconsistency. Evidence consistent with all sources is more reliable than inconsistent evidence.

(5) Effectiveness of Client's Internal Controls When a client's internal controls are effective, evidence generated by the client is more reliable than when controls are weak. For example, if internal controls over sales and billing are effective, the auditor can obtain more accurate and complete evidence from sales invoices and shipping documents than if the controls are inadequate. When considering internal controls, the auditor also considers the likelihood of management override and the pervasive impact of management integrity.

(6) Degree of Objectivity Objective evidence is more reliable than evidence that requires considerable judgment to determine whether it is correct. Examples of objective evidence include confirmation of accounts receivable and bank balances, the physical count of securities and cash, and the adding (footing) of a list of accounts payable to determine if it is the same as the balance in the general ledger. Examples of subjective evidence include communication from a client's lawyers as to the likely outcome of outstanding lawsuits against the client, observation of obsolescence of inventory during physical examination, and inquiries of the credit manager about the collectability of noncurrent accounts receivable. In evaluating the reliability of subjective evidence, the qualifications of the person providing the evidence are important.

Sufficiency

The quantity of evidence obtained determines its **sufficiency** (CAS 500, par. 5[e]). For some audit objectives, quantity is measured primarily by the sample size the auditor selects. For a given audit procedure, the evidence obtained from a sample

Sufficiency—the quantity of evidence; appropriate sample size; degree of precision.

CAS

of 100 would ordinarily be more sufficient than that from a sample of 50. For other objectives, sufficiency is determined primarily by the number and quality of procedures performed to meet the audit objective. In the case of analytical procedures, sufficiency is determined by the degree of precision.

Several factors determine the appropriate sample size in audits. The two most important are the auditor's expectation of errors and the effectiveness of the client's internal controls. To illustrate, assume that, during the audit of Lau Computer Parts Inc., the auditor concludes that there is a high likelihood of obsolete inventory due to the nature of the client's industry. The auditor would sample more inventory items for obsolescence in this audit than in one where the likelihood of obsolescence was low. Similarly, if the auditor concludes that a client has effective rather than ineffective internal controls over recording capital assets, a smaller sample size in the audit of purchases of capital assets is required.

In addition to sample size, the individual items tested also affect the sufficiency of evidence. Samples containing population items with large dollar values, items with a high likelihood of error, and items that are representative of the population are usually considered sufficient. In contrast, most auditors consider samples insufficient that contain only the largest dollar items from the population, unless these items make up a large portion of the total population amount.

Timeliness

The **timeliness** of audit evidence can refer either to when it was accumulated or to the period covered by the audit. Evidence is usually more persuasive for balance sheet accounts when it is obtained as close to the balance sheet date as possible. For example, the auditor's count of marketable securities on the balance sheet date would be more persuasive than a count two months earlier. That is because errors may have occurred in the two-month period and the auditor would not be aware. For income statement accounts, because the ending balance reflects the cumulative transactions for the year, the evidence is more persuasive if there is a sample from the entire period under audit rather than from only a part of the period. For example, a random sample of sales transactions for the entire year would be more persuasive than a sample from only the first six months.

Combined Effect

The persuasiveness of evidence can be evaluated only after considering the combination of sufficiency, appropriateness, and timeliness in the context of the risk of material misstatement for that audit objective. A large sample of evidence is not persuasive unless it is relevant to the audit objective or assertion being tested. A large sample of evidence that is neither appropriate nor timely is also not persuasive. Similarly, a small sample of only one or two pieces of appropriate and timely evidence also lacks persuasiveness. The auditor must evaluate the degree to which all three qualities have been met in deciding persuasiveness.

The relationship between the three audit evidence decisions and qualities that determine persuasiveness of evidence is shown in Table 5-1.

Persuasiveness and Cost

In making decisions about evidence for a given audit, both persuasiveness and cost must be considered. It is rare that only one type of evidence is available for verifying information. The persuasiveness and cost of all alternatives should be considered before selecting the best type or types. The auditor's goal is to obtain a sufficient amount of timely, reliable evidence that is relevant to the information being verified, and to do so at reasonable cost. Automated audit procedures can often allow high volumes of testing at a lower cost than manual testing.

Table 5-1	Relationships Among Evidence Decisions and Persuasiveness

Audit Evidence Decisions	Quality Affecting Persuasiveness of Evidence
Nature of audit procedures	Appropriateness
	Relevance
	Reliability
	• Obtained directly by the auditor
	• Independence of source
	• Qualifications of source
	• Consistency of evidence
	• Effectiveness of internal controls
	• Objectivity of evidence
Extent of Testing	Sufficiency
	• Adequate sample size
	• Selection of proper population items
Timing	Timeliness
	• When procedures are performed
	• Portion of period being audited

CONCEPT CHECK

C5-1 Explain why the auditor's count of marketable securities is more persuasive evidence than responses to questions by the client's employees.

SPECIFIC TYPES OF AUDIT PROCEDURES

LO **4** Describe the types of audit procedures for gathering audit evidence.

The *CPA Canada Handbook* specifies that audit evidence may be obtained by the following types of audit procedures: inspection, observation, external confirmation, recalculation, reperformance, analytical procedures, and inquiry. These terms are defined and explained in CAS 500, par. A10 to A25.

CAS

The order in which these procedures are listed and discussed should not be interpreted as implying the relative strengths of the types or categories of evidence. In other words, the fact that "inspection" appears at the top of the list does not mean that any evidence belonging to that category is automatically stronger than evidence belonging to another category. The quality of each type of evidence, regardless of type, must be evaluated carefully.

Inspection

Inspection encompasses two types of evidence: (1) inspection or count of a tangible asset or (2) inspection of the client's documents and records. The first type of evidence is most often associated with inventory and cash but is also applicable to the verification of securities, notes receivable, and property, plant, and equipment. The distinction between the inspection of assets (such as marketable securities and cash) and the inspection of documents (such as cancelled cheques and sales documents) is important for auditing purposes. If the object being examined (such as a sales invoice) has no inherent value, the source is called documentation. For example, before a cheque is signed, it is a document; after it is signed, it becomes an asset; and when it is cancelled, it becomes a document again.

Inspection—the auditor's physical examination or count of a tangible asset, or inspection of a document.

Inspection or Physical Examination of Tangible Assets Inspection is a direct means of verifying that an asset actually exists (existence assertion), and is regarded as one of the most reliable and useful types of audit evidence. Generally, inspection is an objective means of determining both the quantity and the description of the asset. In some cases, it is also a useful method for evaluating an asset's condition or quality. However, proper valuation for financial statement purposes usually cannot be determined by inspection, since the auditor is not typically qualified to judge such qualitative factors as obsolescence or authenticity (net realizable value for the valuation objective). Note that inspection is not sufficient evidence to verify that existing assets are owned by the client (rights and obligations objective), since assets could be in the client's possession but on consignment.

Inspection of Documents The documents examined by the auditor are the records used by the client to provide information for conducting its business in an organized manner. Since each transaction in the client's organization is normally supported by at least one document or computer file, there is a large volume of this type of evidence available. For example, the client often retains a customer order, a shipping document, and a duplicate sales invoice for each sales transaction. These same documents, whether in paper or electronic form, are useful evidence for verification by the auditor of the accuracy of the client's records for sales transactions. Documentation is a form of evidence widely used in every audit because it is usually readily available to the auditor at a relatively low cost. Sometimes it is the only reasonable type of evidence available.

Documents can be internal or external. An **internal document** is one that has been prepared and used within the client's organization and is retained without ever going to an outside party such as a customer or a vendor. Examples of internal documents include duplicate sales invoices, employees' time reports, exception reports, and inventory receiving reports. An **external document** is one that has been in the hands of someone outside the client's organization who is a party to the transaction being documented, but is either currently in the hands of the client or readily accessible. In some cases, external documents originate outside the client's organization and end up in the hands of the client. Examples of this type of external document are vendors' invoices, cancelled notes payable, and insurance policies. Other documents, such as cancelled cheques, originate with the client, go to an outsider, and are finally returned to the client.

Whether an auditor will accept a document as reliable evidence depends on whether it is internal or external, and when internal, whether it was created and processed under conditions of good internal control. Internal documents created and processed under conditions of weak internal control may not be reliable evidence, because there could be errors or deliberate changes.

Since external documents have been in the hands of both the client and another party to the transaction, there is some indication that both members are in agreement about the information and the conditions stated on the document. This explains why external documents are regarded as more reliable evidence than internal ones. Some external documents have exceptional reliability because they are prepared with considerable care and have been reviewed by lawyers or other qualified experts. Examples include title papers to property such as land, insurance policies, indenture agreements, and contracts.

When auditors use documentation to support recorded transactions or amounts, it is often referred to as **vouching**. To vouch recorded acquisition transactions, the auditor might, for example, verify entries in the acquisition journal by examining vendors' invoices and receiving reports and thereby satisfy the occurrence objective. If the auditor traces from the receiving reports to the acquisitions journal to satisfy the completeness objective, however, it is not appropriate to call it vouching; this latter process is called **tracing**.

Many documents are available only in electronic form. For example, many companies use electronic data interchange (EDI) of standardized business transactions. Purchase, shipping, billing, cash receipt, and cash disbursement transactions may be available only in electronic form. Financial statement assertions most affected by EDI are completeness and accuracy. The auditor would also need to assess authorization of transactions, resulting in a need to test automated controls for these objectives.

Internal document—a document, such as an employee time report, that is prepared and used within the client's organization.

External document—a document, such as a vendor's invoice, that has been used by an outside party to the transaction being documented and that the client now has or can easily obtain.

Vouching—the use of documentation to support recorded transactions or amounts.

Tracing—the use of documentation to determine if transactions or amounts are included in the accounting records.

Other forms of automation, such as image processing systems (whereby documents are scanned and converted into electronic images rather than being stored in paper format), also require auditors to assess the strength of such electronic evidence based upon controls in place over changes to the documents.

Observation

Observation consists of looking at a process or procedure being performed by others. The auditor may tour a plant to obtain a general impression of a client's facilities or watch individuals perform accounting tasks to determine whether the persons assigned responsibilities are performing them. Observation provides evidence about performance of a process is rarely enough by itself because there is the risk that the client's personnel involved in accounting activities are aware of the auditor's presence. They may do their work to a higher standard when the auditor is present. Other kinds of corroborative evidence will also be used.

Observation—looking at a process or procedure performed by others.

External Confirmation

External confirmation describes the receipt of a written or oral response from an independent third party verifying the accuracy of information that was requested by the auditor. The request is made to the client, and the client asks the independent third party to respond directly to the auditor in writing. Since confirmations come from sources that are independent of the client, they are a highly regarded and often-used type of evidence. External confirmations are relatively costly to obtain and may cause some inconvenience to those asked to supply them. If oral confirmations are used, they must be followed up with a written summary to provide adequate documentation for the audit file.

External confirmation—the auditor's receipt of a written or oral response from an independent third party verifying the accuracy of information requested.

Whether or not confirmations should be used depends on the reliability needs of the situation as well as the alternative evidence available. For instance, confirmations are seldom used in the audit of capital-asset additions because these can be verified adequately by inspection of documentation and physical examination of the asset. While external confirmations are generally a very reliable form of evidence, the auditor must be aware that the third party providing the confirmation may be careless or not competent, may not have the correct information, or may be a related party. Or, as highlighted in the opening vignette and Auditing in Action 5-1, the confirmation itself may be false.

AUDITING IN ACTION 5-1
Secure Electronic Audit Confirmations: A Way to Enhance Audit Efficiency and Reduce Confirmation Fraud

Although confirmations are considered high-quality evidence, traditional paper confirmations can be quite costly and perhaps, even a bigger concern, the confirmation may be false. As well as the fraud highlighted in our opening vignette, several high profile frauds have involved fraudulent confirmations. Here are three of the largest: the Italian dairy company Parmalat (US$4.9 billion in fake confirmations), Indian technology firm Satyam (US$1 billion), and Dutch supermarket giant Royal Ahold (US$5.1 billion).

In the United States, all the major banks, the top 100 certified public accountant firms (including the Big Four firms), and 10 000 small practitioners participate in the secure third-party confirmation clearing house, **Confirmation.com**. Confirmation.com, with over 80 000 auditors participating worldwide, is the leader in electronic confirmations. It provides a secure environment for transmitting the confirmation to authenticated confirmation respondents, and it handles accounts receivable and accounts payable confirmations as well as bank confirmations. Some of the key benefits of participating in the clearing house are that it validates identity and it reduces errors as well as the risk of interception and response time. Auditors who use the service can even access audit confirmations through their smartphones.

Sources: Confirmation.com: The World's Leading Provider of Secure Electronic Confirmations, accessed July 20, 2017, at **http://www.cftc.gov/ucm/groups/public/@newsroom/documents/file/tac072612_confirmation2.pdf**.

Table 5-2	Information Frequently Confirmed	
Information		**Source**
Assets		
Cash in bank		Bank
Accounts receivable		Customer
Notes receivable		Maker
Owned inventory out on consignment		Consignee
Inventory held in public warehouses		Public warehouse
Cash surrender value of life insurance		Insurance company
Liabilities		
Accounts payable		Creditor
Notes payable		Lender
Advances from customers		Customer
Mortgages payable		Mortgagor
Bonds payable		Bondholder
Owners' Equity		
Shares outstanding		Registrar and transfer agent
Other Information		
Insurance coverage		Insurance company
Contingent liabilities		Company law firm(s), bank, and others
Bond indenture agreements		Bondholder
Collateral held by creditors		Creditor

CAS

External evidence is considered more reliable than evidence obtained from within the organization (CAS 500). Confirmations should be tailored to the auditor's risk assessment. Practically, this means that confirmations should be used unless the auditor has alternative high-quality evidence or believes for some reason that the confirmations received would be unreliable. The major types of information that are frequently confirmed, along with the source of the confirmation, are indicated in Table 5-2.

To be considered reliable evidence, confirmations must be controlled by the auditor from the time they are prepared until they are returned. If the client controls the preparation of the confirmation, performs the mailing, or receives the responses, the auditor has lost control and, with it, independence; thus, the reliability of the evidence is reduced.

Recalculation

Recalculation—repeating or checking the mathematical accuracy of calculations completed by the client.

Recalculation involves rechecking the computations and mathematical work completed by the client during the period under audit. Rechecking of computations consists of testing the client's arithmetical accuracy and includes such procedures as extending sales invoices and inventory; adding data files, reports, and subsidiary ledgers; and checking the calculation of amortization expense and prepaid expenses. A considerable portion of auditors' recalculation is done using spreadsheet or audit software.

Reperformance

Reperformance—the redoing of procedures and internal controls (other than mathematical calculations) of the client by the auditor.

Reperformance comprises the auditor's independent tests of client accounting procedures or controls that were done as part of the entity's accounting and internal control system. Whereas recalculation involves rechecking a computation, reperformance involves checking other procedures. For example, the auditor may compare the price on an invoice to an approved price list, or reperform the aging of accounts receivable. Another type of reperformance is for the auditor to recheck transfers of information, which consists of tracing amounts to verify that when the same information is included in more than one place, it is recorded at the same amount each time. For example, the auditor normally completes limited tests to verify that the information in the sales history files has been included for the proper customer and at the correct amount in the subsidiary accounts receivable files and is accurately summarized in the general ledger.

Reperformance, particularly the process of checking posting and summarization, relies heavily upon the use of **computer-assisted audit tests (CAATs)**—tests that the auditor conducts using computer software or using the data or systems of the client. The two most common forms of CAATs are the use of test data and generalized audit software.

Test data involves the use of fictitious transactions to determine whether client programs are functioning as described. Test data are most commonly used to determine whether the system rejects transactions that it should reject, such as invalid customer numbers, unapproved prices, unapproved credit terms, or invalid dates. This is because the client data files need not be disrupted and the testing can be performed quickly and efficiently.

Generalized audit software consists of a software package that is used by the auditor to run routines against client data. Two common packages in Canada are Audit Command Language for Personal Computers (ACL-PC) and Interactive Data Extraction and Analysis (IDEA). The auditor obtains a copy of the client data files and runs one or more of the following types of activities against the data file. The examples shown are typical tests that would be run against the customer master file together with open item accounts:

- *Mathematical calculations*: addition of debit and credit amounts, extensions.
- *Aging functions*: aging of the accounts to recreate figures in the aged accounts receivable trial balance.
- *Comparisons*: between the outstanding balance and the credit limit.
- *Sampling*: using random, dollar-unit, interval, or stratification.

Analytical Procedures

Analytical procedures consist of evaluation of financial information through plausible relationships among financial and nonfinancial data. For example, an auditor may compare the gross margin percent in the current year with that of the preceding year. As illustrated in Figure 5-1, analytical procedures are used extensively throughout the audit process—as part of planning and assessing risk of material misstatement, in performing risk response, and in the completion phase of the audit. We first introduce the purpose of analytical procedures and then discuss the different types of analytical procedures more extensively.

Understand the Client's Industry and Business Auditors must obtain knowledge about a client's industry and business as a part of planning an audit. By conducting analytical procedures in which the current year's unaudited information is compared with prior years' audited information or industry data, changes are highlighted (see Figure 5-1: this is referred to as *overall analytical review*). These changes can represent important trends or specific events, all of which will influence audit planning. For example, a decline in gross margin percentages over time may indicate increasing competition in the company's market area and the need to consider inventory pricing more carefully during the audit. Similarly, an increase in the balance in property, plant, and equipment may indicate a significant acquisition that must be reviewed.

Assess the Entity's Ability to Continue as a Going Concern Analytical procedures are often a useful indicator for determining whether the client company has financial problems. Certain analytical procedures can help the auditor assess the likelihood

Computer-assisted audit tests (CAATs)—tests that the auditor conducts using computer software or using the data or systems of the client.

Test data—the use of fictitious transactions to determine whether client programs are functioning as described.

Generalized audit software—a software package that is used by the auditor to run routines against client data.

Analytical procedures—use of comparisons and relationships to determine whether account balances or other data appear reasonable.

of failure. For example, if a higher-than-normal ratio of long-term debt to net worth is combined with a lower-than-average ratio of profits to total assets, a relatively high risk of financial failure may be indicated. Not only will such conditions affect the audit plan, but they may indicate that substantial doubt exists about the entity's ability to continue as a going concern, which requires an explanatory paragraph in the audit report.

Indicate the Presence of Possible Misstatements in the Financial Statements Significant unexpected differences between the current year's unaudited financial data and other data used in comparisons are commonly called **unusual fluctuations**. Unusual fluctuations occur when significant differences are not expected but do exist, or when significant differences are expected but do not exist. In either case, the presence of an accounting misstatement is one possible reason for the unusual fluctuation. If the unusual fluctuation is large, the auditor must determine the reason and be satisfied that the cause is a valid economic event and not a misstatement. For example, in comparing the ratio of the allowance for uncollectible accounts receivable to gross accounts receivable with that of the previous year, suppose that the ratio has decreased while, at the same time, accounts receivable turnover also decreased. The combination of these two pieces of information indicates a possible understatement of the allowance. This aspect of analytical procedures is often called "attention directing" – this helps the auditor identify areas that have a risk of material misstatement and develop an appropriate risk response in the form of more detailed procedures in the specific audit areas where misstatements might be found.

Provide Evidence Supporting an Account Balance In many cases, an analytical procedure can be used to provide evidence supporting recorded account balances. When a predictable relationship exists and the analytical procedure is based on reliable inputs, **substantive analytical procedures** may be performed as part of the risk response stage, although they are not required. In such cases, the analytical procedure constitutes substantive evidence in support of the related account balances. Depending on the significance of the account, the predictability of the relationship, and the reliability of the underlying data, the substantive analytical procedure may eliminate the need to perform detailed tests of the account balance. In other cases, detailed tests will still be performed, but sample sizes can be reduced, or the timing of the procedures can be moved farther away from the balance sheet date.

Inquiry

Inquiry is obtaining *written* or *oral* information from the client in response to questions from the auditor. Although considerable evidence is obtained from the client through inquiry, it usually cannot be regarded as conclusive because it is not from an independent source and may be biased in the client's favour. Therefore, when the auditor obtains evidence through inquiry, it is normally necessary to obtain corroborating evidence through other procedures. Corroborating evidence is additional evidence to support the original evidence. As an illustration, when the auditor wants to obtain information about the client's method of recording and controlling accounting transactions, he or she usually begins by asking the client how internal controls operate. In order to corroborate this, the auditor performs a walk-through and tests of controls to determine if the controls function as described.

Unusual fluctuations—significant unexpected differences indicated by analytical procedures between the current year's unaudited financial data and other data used for comparisons.

Substantive analytical procedures—an analytical procedure in which the auditor develops an expectation of recorded amounts or ratios to provide evidence supporting an account balance.

Inquiry—obtaining written or oral information from the client in response to questions during the audit.

CONCEPT CHECK

C5-2 How does the quality of internal controls affect evidence?

C5-3 Describe two audit procedures that the auditor should use to reduce the risk of financial statement misstatement during the financial statement closing process.

C5-4 Why are CAATs important for recalculation and reperformance?

Table 5-3	Nature, Extent, and Timing Types of Audit Procedures for the Completeness of Inventory

| | Nature of Audit Procedures | | Extent of Testing | Timeliness |
Type of Test	Type of Procedure	Detailed Audit Procedure	Sample Size and Items to Select	Timing and Period Covered
Control Test	Observation	Observe client's personnel counting inventory to determine whether they are properly following instructions.	100%—Observe all count teams	Balance sheet date
Substantive Test of Detail	Inspection	Count a sample of inventory and compare quantity and description to client's counts.	120 items—40 items with large dollar value, plus 80 randomly selected	Balance sheet date— entire year
Control Test and Substantive Test of Detail	Reperformance	Compare quantity on client's perpetual records to quantity on client's counts.	70 items—30 items with large dollar value, plus 40 randomly selected	Balance sheet date— entire year
Substantive Analytical Procedure	Analytical procedure	Calculate inventory turnover for each quarter and compare to previous year.	N/A	Balance sheet date— entire year

Appropriateness of Types of Procedures

As illustrated in Table 5-3, auditors decide the nature, extent, and timing of audit procedures, which results in a variety of procedures that will provide reasonable assurance for each particular assertion—in this case the completeness of inventory. As discussed earlier in the chapter, in order to determine if the evidence is appropriate the auditor needs to consider whether it is relevant and reliable.

Table 5-4 includes the seven types of audit procedures related to five of the six criteria that determine the reliability of evidence. Note that two of the characteristics that determine appropriateness of evidence—relevance and timeliness—are not included in Table 5-4.

Several observations are apparent from a study of this table:

- First, the effectiveness of the client's internal controls has a significant effect on the reliability of most types of evidence. Obviously, internal documentation from a company with effective internal controls is more reliable because the

Table 5-4	Reliability of Types of Audit Procedures

Criteria to Determine Reliability

Type of Audit Procedure	Independence of Provider	Effectiveness of Client's Internal Control	Auditor's Direct Knowledge	Qualifications of Provider	Objectivity of Evidence
Inspection—Physical Examination	High (auditor does procedure)	Varies	High	Normally high (auditor does procedure)	High
Inspection—Documents and Records	Varies—external documents more independent than internal documents	Varies	Low	Varies	High
Observation	High (auditor does)	Varies	High	Normally high (auditor does)	Medium
Inquiries of the client	Low (client provides)	Not applicable	Low	Varies	Varies—low to high
External confirmation	High	Not applicable	Low	Varies—usually high	High
Recalculation	High (auditor does)	Varies	High	High (auditor does)	High
Reperformance	High (auditor does)	Varies	High	High (auditor does)	High
Analytical procedures	High/low (auditor does/ client responds)	Varies	Low	Normally high (auditor does/client responds)	Varies—depends on the reliability of the data

documents are more likely to be accurate. Conversely, analytical procedures will not be appropriate evidence if the internal controls that produced the data provide inaccurate information.

- Second, both inspection—physical examination and reperformance—are likely to be highly reliable if internal controls are effective, but their use differs considerably. This effectively illustrates that two completely different types of evidence can be equally reliable.
- Third, inquiry alone is usually not sufficient to provide appropriate evidence to satisfy any audit objective.

Cost of Types of Evidence

The two most expensive types of evidence are physical examination and external confirmation. Physical examination is costly because it normally requires the auditor's presence when the client is counting the asset, often on the balance sheet date. For example, inspection of inventory can result in several auditors travelling to widely separated geographical locations. External confirmation is costly because the auditor must follow careful procedures in the confirmation preparation, mailing, receipt, and follow-up of nonresponses and exceptions.

Inspection of documents, reperformance, and analytical procedures are moderately costly. If client personnel provide documents and electronic files for the auditor and organize them for convenient use, inspection usually has a fairly low cost. When auditors must find those documents themselves, however, inspection can be extremely costly. Even under ideal circumstances, information and data on documents are sometimes complex and require interpretation and analysis. It is usually time-consuming for an auditor to read and evaluate a client's contracts, lease agreements, and minutes of the board of directors meetings.

Because analytical procedures are considerably less expensive than confirmations and physical examinations, most auditors prefer to replace substantive tests of details with analytical procedures when possible. For example, it may be far less expensive to calculate and review sales and accounts receivable ratios than to confirm accounts receivable. If it is possible to reduce the use of confirmations by performing analytical procedures, considerable cost savings can be achieved; but analytical procedures require the auditor to decide which analytical procedures to use, make the calculations, and evaluate the results. Doing so often takes considerable time. The cost of reperformance tests depends on the nature of the procedure being tested. Comparatively simple tests such as reperforming the comparison of invoices to price lists are likely to take minimal time. However, reperforming procedures such as the client's bank reconciliation are likely to take considerable time.

The three least expensive types of evidence are observation, inquiries of the client, and recalculation. Observation is normally done together with other audit procedures. An auditor can easily observe whether client personnel are following appropriate inventory counting procedures at the same time as he or she counts a sample of inventory (physical examination). Inquiries of clients are done extensively on every audit and normally have a low cost. Certain inquiries may be costly, such as obtaining written statements from the client documenting discussions throughout the audit. Recalculation can vary in cost. It can be low when it involves simple calculations and tracing that can be done at the auditor's convenience. Costs per transaction are reduced when the auditor's computer software is used to perform these tests after obtaining a copy of the client data files.

Terms Used in Audit Procedures

Audit procedures are the detailed steps, usually written in the form of instructions, for the accumulation of the seven types of audit evidence. They should be sufficiently clear to explain to members of the audit team what is to be done, why, and how.

While auditors appreciate the importance of applying the appropriate level of professional skepticism, it is often difficult to actually answer the question, "Did you use the appropriate level of professional skepticism?" This is particularly true for inexperienced auditors. In recognition of this, the Auditing and Assurance Standards Board and the Institute of Chartered Accountants Australia have developed a paper, *Practical Ways to Improve the Exercise and Documentation of Professional Skepticism in an ISA Audit,* to provide guidance in this area.

Here are some questions to consider for auditors who are performing procedures and evaluating the evidence that they have collected:

1. What reasonable alternatives other than those put forward by management have I considered?

2. What evidence have I obtained that supports management's assertions and what evidence does not support those assertions?

3. Does the evidence I have obtained integrate with that obtained in other areas of the audit?

4. How have I responded to identified discrepancies or inconsistencies?

5. How do I know that the audit evidence I have obtained is reliable?

6. What were the results of my stand-back review before concluding on the procedures performed and the evidence obtained?

7. What is my basis for drawing conclusions about the sufficiency and appropriateness of the evidence I have obtained?

Source: Adapted from Auditing and Assurance Standards Board and the Institute of Chartered Accountants Australia, *Practical Ways to Improve the Exercise and Documentation of Professional Skepticism in an ISA Audit,* May 2013, accessed July 20, 2017, at **http://www.frascanada.ca/canadian-auditing-standards/resources/reference-material/item74244.pdf**.

Several different terms commonly used to describe audit procedures are presented and defined in Table 5-5. To help you understand the terms, an illustrative audit procedure and the type of evidence are shown in the table.

Table 5-5	Terms, Audit Procedures, and Types of Evidence	
Term and Definition	**Illustrative Audit Procedure**	**Type of Audit Procedure**
Examine—A reasonably detailed study of a document or record to determine specific facts about it.	Examine a sample of vendors' invoices or data to determine whether the goods or services received are reasonable and of the type normally used by the client's business.	Inspection
Scan—A less detailed examination of a document or record to determine if there is something unusual warranting further investigation.	Scan the sales report, looking for large and unusual transactions. For large sales history files, use audit software to run an exception report for large amounts.	Analytical procedures
Read—An examination of written information to determine facts pertinent to the audit and the recording of those facts in a working paper.	Read the minutes of a board of directors' meeting, and summarize all information that is pertinent to the financial statements in a working paper.	Inspection
Compute—A calculation done by the auditor independent of the client.	Compute the inventory turnover ratios, and compare to previous years as a test of inventory.	Analytical procedures
Recompute—A calculation done to determine whether a client's calculation is correct.	Recompute the unit sales price times the number of units for a sample of duplicate sales invoices, and compare the totals to the client's calculations.	Recalculation
Foot—An addition of a column of numbers to determine if the total is the same as the client's.	Foot the sales history files using audit software, and compare all totals to the general ledger.	Recalculation
Trace—An instruction normally associated with documentation or reperformance. The instruction should state what the auditor is tracing and where it is being traced from and to. Frequently, an audit procedure that includes the term "trace" will also include a second instruction, such as "compare" or "recompute."	Trace a sample of sales transactions from the sales reports to sales invoices, and compare customer name, date, and the total dollar value of the sale. Trace postings from the sales reports to the general ledger accounts.	Recalculation Reperformance

(continued)

Table 5-5	Terms, Audit Procedures, and Types of Evidence (*Continued*)	
Term and Definition	**Illustrative Audit Procedure**	**Type of Audit Procedure**
Compare—A comparison of information in two different locations. The instruction should state which information is being compared in as much detail as is practical.	Select a sample of sales invoices and compare the unit selling price as stated on the invoice to the master files of unit selling prices authorized by management.	Reperformance
Count—A determination of assets on hand at a given time. This term should only be associated with the type of evidence defined as physical examination.	Count petty cash on hand at the balance sheet date.	Inspection
Observe—The act of observation should be associated with the type of evidence defined as observation.	Observe whether the two inventory count teams independently count and record inventory quantities.	Observation
Inquire—The act of inquiry should be associated with the type of evidence defined as inquiry.	Inquire of management whether there is any obsolete inventory on hand at the balance sheet date.	Inquiries of client

Source: Based on Glover, Steven M., and Douglas F. Prawitt. "Enhancing Auditor Professional Skepticism: The Professional Skepticism Continuum." Current Issues in Auditing 8.2 (2014): p1-p10.

LO **5** Design analytical procedures for the various phases of the audit process.

 CAS

DESIGN ANALYTICAL PROCEDURES

CAS 520.4 defines analytical procedures as *evaluations of financial information through analysis of plausible relationships among financial and nonfinancial data.* Analytical procedures use comparisons and relationships to assess whether account balances or other data appear reasonable relative to the auditor's expectations.

When performing analytical procedures, the auditor's investigation of unusual fluctuations is triggered by relationships among financial and nonfinancial data that differ from expectations developed by the auditor. For example, as a test of the overall reasonableness of recorded commissions, the auditor might compare current-year recorded commission expense to an expectation of commission expense based on total recorded sales multiplied by the average commission rate. For this analytical procedure to be relevant and reliable, the auditor has likely concluded that recorded sales are correctly stated, verified that all sales earn a commission, and established that the average actual commission rate is readily determinable (and able to be verified).

Analytical procedures may be performed at any of three times during an engagement:

1. *In audit planning*, preliminary analytical review is *required* to assist in determining the nature, extent, and timing of audit procedures. This helps the auditor identify significant matters requiring special consideration later in the engagement. For example, the calculation of inventory turnover before inventory price tests are done may indicate the need for special care during those tests. Analytical procedures done in the planning phase typically use data aggregated at a high level, and the sophistication, extent, and timing of the procedures vary among clients. For some clients, the comparison of prior-year and current-year account balances using the unaudited trial balance may be sufficient. For other clients, the procedures may involve extensive analysis of quarterly financial statements based on the auditor's judgment.

2. *During the risk response*, analytical procedures are often done as a substantive test in support of account balances. These tests are frequently done in conjunction with other audit procedures. For example, the prepaid portion of each insurance policy might be compared with the same policy for the previous year as part of doing tests of prepaid insurance. The assurance provided by analytical procedures depends on the predictability of the relationship, as well as the precision of the expectation and the reliability of the data used to develop the expectation. When analytical procedures are used as substantive tests in the risk response stage, auditing standards require the auditor to document in the working papers the expectation and factors considered in its development. The auditor is also required to evaluate the reliability of the data used to develop the expectation, including the source of the data and controls over the data's preparation.

3. *During the completion of the audit*, analytical procedures are also *required*. Such tests serve as a final analytical review for material misstatements or financial problems and help the auditor take a final "objective look" at the audited financial statements. Typically, a senior partner with extensive knowledge of the client's business conducts the analytical procedures during the final review of the audit files and financial statements to identify possible oversights in an audit.

The usefulness of analytical procedures as audit evidence depends significantly on the auditor developing an *expectation* of what a recorded account balance or ratio *should be*, regardless of the types of analytical procedures used. Note in Table 5-5 that scan is also a type of analytical procedure. Scanning analytics are different from the other types of analytical procedures in that scanning analytics search within accounts or other entity data to identify anomalous individual items, while the other types use aggregated financial information.

Auditors develop an expectation of an account balance or ratio by considering information from prior periods, industry trends, client-prepared budgeted expectations, and nonfinancial information. The auditor typically compares the client's balances and ratios with expected balances and ratios using one or more of the following types of analytical procedures. In each case, auditors compare client data with the following:

1. Industry data.
2. Similar prior-period data.
3. Client-determined expected results.
4. Auditor-determined expected results.

Compare Client and Industry Data

Suppose you are doing an audit and obtain information about the client and the averages in the client's industry (see Table 5-6).

If we look only at client information for the two ratios shown, the company appears to be stable with no apparent indication of difficulties. However, compared with the industry, the client's position has worsened. In 2017, the client did slightly better than the industry in both ratios. In 2018, it was a half percent worse. Although these two ratios by themselves may not indicate significant problems, the example illustrates how comparison of client data with industry data may provide useful information about the client's performance. For example, the company may have lost market share, its pricing may not be competitive, it may have incurred abnormal costs, or it may have obsolete items in inventory.

The Financial Post Company (**www.financialpost.com**) and Dun & Bradstreet Canada Limited (**www.dnb.ca**) accumulate financial information for thousands of larger companies and compile the data for different lines of business; local credit bureaus compile data for companies in their community. Many public accounting firms purchase these publications for use as a basis for industry comparisons in their audits.

The most important benefits of industry comparisons are that they are an aid to understanding the client's business and are an indication of the likelihood of financial failure. The ratios in Dun & Bradstreet Canada, for example, are primarily of a type

Table 5-6	Example of Comparison of Client and Industry Data			
	Client		**Industry**	
	2018	2017	2018	2017
Inventory turnover	3.4%	3.5%	3.9%	3.4%
Gross margin percent	26.3%	26.4%	27.3%	26.2%

that bankers and other credit executives use in evaluating whether a company will be able to repay a loan. The same information is useful to auditors in assessing the relative strength of the client's capital structure, its borrowing capacity, and its likelihood of financial failure.

A major weakness of using industry ratios for auditing is the difference between the nature of the client's financial information and that of the firms making up the industry totals. Since the industry data are broad averages, the comparisons may not be meaningful unless the auditor takes into account the unique characteristics of the client.

Compare Client Data with Similar Prior-Period Data

Suppose the gross margin for a company has been 26 to 27 percent for each of the past four years but is 23 percent in the current year. This decline in gross margin should be a concern to the auditor. The cause of the decline could be a change in economic conditions. However, it could also be caused by misstatements in the financial statements, such as sales or purchase cut-off errors, unrecorded sales, overstated accounts payable, or inventory costing errors. The auditor should determine the cause of the decline in gross margin and consider the effect, if any, on evidence accumulation.

A wide variety of analytical procedures allows auditors to compare client data with similar data from one or more prior periods. Here are some common examples.

Compare the Current Year's Balance With That for the Preceding Year One of the easiest ways to make this test is to include the preceding year's adjusted trial balance results in a separate column of the current year's trial balance spreadsheet. The auditor can easily compare the current year's and previous year's balances to decide early in the audit whether a particular account should receive more than the normal amount of attention because of a significant change in the balance. For example, if the auditor observes a substantial increase in supplies expense, the auditor should determine whether the cause was an increased use of supplies, a misstatement in the account due to a misclassification, a misstatement in supplies inventory, or a combination of both.

Compare the Detail of a Total Balance With Similar Detail for the Preceding Year If there have been no significant changes in the client's operations in the current year, much of the detail making up the totals in the financial statements should also remain unchanged. By comparing the detail of the current period with a similar detail of the preceding period, it is often possible to isolate information that needs further examination. Comparison of details may take the form of details over time or details at a point in time. A common example of the former is comparing the monthly totals for the current and preceding years for sales, repairs, and other accounts. An example of the latter is comparing the details of loans payable at the end of the current year with those at the end of the preceding year.

The comparison of totals or details with previous years has two shortcomings. First, it fails to consider growth or decline in business activity. Second, relationships of data to other data, such as sales to cost of goods sold, are ignored. Ratios, which we discuss next, help overcome those shortcomings.

Compute Ratios and Percentage Relationships for Comparison With Those of Previous Years Table 5-7 describes five ratios and the possible misstatements they could detect to show the usefulness of ratio analysis. In all cases, the comparisons should be with calculations made in previous years for the same client. There are many potential ratios and comparisons available for use by an auditor. Appendix 5A describes other examples. Normally, the auditor will arrange to have trial balance information entered annually into audit software that calculates a range of ratios and comparisons automatically.

Table 5-7	Internal Comparisons and Relationships
Ratio or Comparison	**Possible Misstatement**
Raw material turnover for a manufacturing company.	Misstatement of inventory or cost of goods sold or obsolescence of raw material inventory.
Sales commissions divided by net sales.	Misstatement of sales commissions.
Sales returns and allowances divided by gross sales.	Misclassified sales returns and allowances or unrecorded returns or allowances subsequent to year-end.
Sales taxes payable (current year) divided by sales taxes payable (preceding year).	Failure to properly accrue sales taxes owing at year-end.
Each of the individual manufacturing expenses as a percentage of total manufacturing expense.	Significant misstatement of individual expenses within a total.

Many of the ratios and percentages used for comparison with previous years are the same ones used for comparison with industry data. For example, it is useful to compare current year gross margin with industry averages and those of previous years. The same can be said for most of the ratios described in Appendix 5A.

There are also numerous potential comparisons of current and prior-period data beyond those normally available from industry data. For example, the ratio of each expense category to total sales can be compared with those of previous years. Similarly, in a multi-unit operation (e.g., a retail chain), internal comparisons for each unit can be made with previous periods (e.g., the revenue and expenses of individual retail outlets in a chain of stores can be compared).

Compare Client Data With Client-Determined Expected Results

Since **budgets** represent the client's expectations for the period, an investigation of the most significant areas in which differences exist between budgeted and actual results may indicate potential misstatements. The absence of differences may also indicate that misstatements are unlikely. It is common, for example, in the audit of local, provincial, and federal governmental units, to use this type of analytical procedure.

Whenever client data are compared with budgets, there are two special concerns. First, the auditor must evaluate whether the budgets were realistic plans. In some organizations, budgets are prepared with little thought or care and therefore are not realistic expectations. Such information has little value as audit evidence. Second, there is a possibility that current financial information in the budget was changed by client personnel to conform to the actual results. If that has occurred, the auditor will find no differences in comparing actual data with the budget, even if there are misstatements in the financial statements. Discussing budget procedures with client personnel is done to satisfy the first concern. Assessment of control risk and detailed audit tests of actual data are usually done to minimize the likelihood of the latter concern.

Budgets—written records of the client's expectations for the period; a comparison of budgets with actual results may indicate whether or not misstatements are likely.

Compare Client Data With Auditor-Determined Expected Results

Another common type of comparison of client data with expected results occurs when the auditor calculates *the expected balance for comparison with the actual balance.* In this type of substantive analytical procedure, the auditor develops an expectation of what an account balance should be by (1) relating it to some other balance sheet

In its 2013 report, the CPAB (Canadian Public Accountability Board) noted that substantive analytical procedures (SAP) in the auditing of revenue were inadequately performed for the following reasons:

- Not appropriately setting the precision for the procedure.
- Not adequately assessing factors used to set expectations, including the underlying assumptions and data relied upon.
- Not appropriately corroborating variances between the expectations and actual results. Specifically, variances were usually discussed with management with little or no verification to independent sources.

Why would this happen? In an experimental study conducted by Steve Glover and his colleagues, biases appeared to play a role. In their study, they found that auditors have "favourable outcome biases" when evaluating the results of aggregate analytical procedures (recall that aggregate analytical procedures tend to produce weak evidence). This means that when there was no significant difference between the expectation and the unaudited numbers, the auditors tended to attribute more strength to the analytical procedure than warranted. When experienced auditors were cued to evaluate the weakness of the aggregate procedure, it helped to counteract this bias. However, this did not aid inexperienced auditors since it appeared they did not have the necessary knowledge base.

In the 2013 report, CPAB recommended that substantive analytical procedures can be improved by providing more guidance around when they can/should be used as the primary source of audit evidence and, due to the high degree of professional judgment involved, the procedures should be conducted by audit staff with significant experience (manager level or above). The second recommendation is consistent with Glover and his colleagues' findings that experienced auditors do have the knowledge that can enable them to question the results.

Sources: *CPAB 2013 Public Report*. Steven M. Glover, Douglas F. Prawitt, and T. Jeffrey Wilks, "Why do auditors over-rely on weak analytical procedures? The role of outcome and precision," *Auditing: A Journal of Practice and Theory*, vol. 24, no. s-1, 2005, pp. 197–220.

CAS or income statement account or accounts, or (2) making a projection based on some historical trend. CAS 520 describes the process of developing substantive analytical procedures:

- *Develop an independent expectation.* The auditor develops independent expectations by identifying plausible relationships based upon his or her own knowledge of the business, industry trends, or other accounts. It can be based upon either financial or nonfinancial data.
- *Define a significant difference.* When designing substantive analytical procedures, the auditor must decide on the amount of difference from the expectation that can be expected without further investigation.
- *Compute the difference.* In this step, the auditor compares the expected amount to the recorded amount.
- *Investigate significant differences.* As highlighted in Auditing in Action 9-3, inquiry does not constitute adequate evidence when investigating differences. The auditor will need to consider what evidence and further audit procedures are needed in order to corroborate management's explanations.

Suppose that, in auditing a hotel, you can determine the number of rooms, room rate for each room, and occupancy rate. Using those data, it is relatively easy to estimate total revenue (rooms × occupancy rate × room rate) from rooms to compare with recorded revenue. The same approach can sometimes be used to estimate such accounts as tuition revenue at universities (average tuition × enrollment), factory payroll (total hours worked × wage rate), and cost of materials sold (units × materials cost per unit).

Figure 5-2 illustrates how the auditor may make an independent calculation of interest expense on notes payable by multiplying the average ending balances and interest rates for both short-term and long-term notes payable as a substantive test of the reasonableness of recorded interest expense. Notice how the auditor's substantive analytical procedure begins with the development of the auditor's expectation of

Hillsburg Hardware Limited
Overall Test of Interest Expense
12/31/18

Schedule __N-3__ Date
Prepared by __TM__ 3/06/19
Approved by __JW__ 3/12/19

Interest expense per general ledger .... 2 408 642 ①

Computation of estimate:

Short-term loans:

Balance outstanding at month-end: ②

Jan.	2 950 000
Feb.	3 184 000
Mar.	3 412 000
Apr.	3 768 000
May	2 604 000
June	1 874 000
July	1 400 000
Aug.	1 245 000
Sept.	1 046 000
Oct.	854 000
Nov.	2 526 000
Dec.	4 180 000
Total	29 043 000

Average (÷ 12) 2 420 250 @ 10.5% ③ 254 126

Long-term loans:

Beginning balance 26 520 000 ②
Ending balance   24 120 000 ②
                   50 640 000

Average (÷ 2) 25 320 000 @ 8.5% ④ 2 152 200

Estimated total interest expense 2 406 326

Difference .... 2 316 ⑤

Legend and Comments
① Agrees with general ledger and working trial balance.
② Obtained from general ledger.
③ Estimated based on examination of several notes throughout the
   year with rates ranging from 10% to 11%.
④ Agrees with permanent file schedule of long-term debt.
⑤ Difference not significant. Indicates that interest expense per books is reasonable.

interest expense for short-term notes payable and combines that with the auditor's calculation of an estimated interest expense for long-term notes payable to arrive at the expected amount of total interest expense of $2 408 326. Because of the fluctuating nature of the short-term notes payable balance from month to month, the auditor's calculation of a 12-month average balance and average interest rate generates a more precise estimate of expected interest expense. Less precision is needed for long-term notes payable given the constant rate of interest across the year and the stable nature of the balance outstanding. This working paper also effectively documents the auditor's expectation that is required by auditing standards for substantive analytical procedures.

Precision of the Analytical Procedures

The degree of precision of analytical procedures depends upon the following factors:

- *Disaggregation of data.* The more detailed the level at which the analytical procedure is performed, the greater the potential precision. For example, analytical procedures performed on the overall revenue amount recorded in the financial statements are not very effective at highlighting significant offsetting differences that are more likely to be noticed if the auditor performed the analysis by product line or geographic region.
- *Data reliability.* The more reliable the data, the more precise the expectation. As we discussed previously, the source of the information, the quality of controls in producing the information, and the independence of the source all determine reliability of the data.
- *Plausibility and predictability of relationship.* The more plausible and predictable the relationship, the more precise the expectation. Plausibility refers to whether the relationship to test the assertion makes sense. Predictability depends upon the factors used, the underlying assumptions, and data. Some audit areas (for instance, interest income based upon interest rates) are very predictable, whereas other types of revenue may have too many variables to be predictable.
- *The type of analytical procedure.* We discussed the types of analytical procedures previously. If the auditor needs a high level of assurance from substantive analytical procedures, then he or she should develop a relatively precise expectation by selecting the appropriate procedures (those involving the auditor developing expectations) rather than a simple trend analysis (e.g., compare the change in an account from year to year).

LO **6** Understand the purposes of audit documentation.

CAS

Audit documentation—the written or electronic audit documentation kept by the auditor to support audit conclusions; this includes risk assessments, procedures or tests performed, information obtained, and conclusions reached.

CAS

DOCUMENTATION

As explained in CAS 230, **audit documentation** is the written or electronic record of risk assessments, procedures or tests performed, information obtained, and conclusions reached. Audit documentation should include all the information the auditor considers necessary to conduct the examination adequately and to provide support for the auditor's report.

Purposes of Audit Documentation

The overall objective of audit documentation is to aid the auditor in providing reasonable assurance that an adequate audit was conducted in accordance with GAAS. More specifically, the documentation (often referred to as working papers), as it pertains to the current year's audit, provides a basis for planning and documenting all phases of the audit, a record of the evidence accumulated, the results of the tests, support for determining the proper type of auditor's report, and a basis for review by supervisors and partners. Proper controls need to be in place to ensure that the working papers are completed on time (within 60 days of the audit report date according to CAS 230 par. A21) and that the file is archived at that time. Increasingly, working papers are maintained as computerized files using specialized software, with the only paper component being documentation provided by the client or external parties.

Basis for Planning the Audit If the auditor is to plan the current year's audit adequately, the necessary reference information must be available in the working papers. The papers include such diverse planning information as conclusions on client risk analysis, descriptive information about internal control, a time budget for individual audit areas, the audit program, and the results of the preceding year's audit.

Record of the Evidence Accumulated and the Results of the Tests The working papers are the primary means of documenting that an adequate audit was conducted in accordance with Canadian GAAS. If the need arises, the auditor must be able to demonstrate to regulatory agencies such as the provincial securities commissions and to the courts that the audit was well planned and adequately supervised; the evidence accumulated was appropriate, sufficient, and timely; and the auditor's report was proper considering the results of the examination.

Support for Determining the Proper Type of Auditor's Report The working papers provide an important source of information to assist the auditor in choosing the appropriate auditor's report to issue in a given set of circumstances. The data in the papers are useful for evaluating the adequacy of audit scope and the fairness of the financial statements.

Basis for Review The working papers are the primary frame of reference used by supervisory personnel to evaluate whether sufficient appropriate evidence was accumulated to justify the auditor's report.

In addition to the purposes directly related to the auditor's report, the working papers can also serve as the basis for preparing tax returns, filings with the provincial securities commissions, and other reports. They are a source of information for issuing communications to the audit committee and management concerning various matters such as internal control weaknesses or operations recommendations. Working papers also provide a frame of reference for training personnel and aid in planning and coordinating subsequent audits.

File Archive

CAS 230 explains that the final version of the audit file should be assembled within 60 days after the date of the audit report. At that time, firms initiate a "file freeze," also called a file archive. This means that if any additional information is added after that date, it needs to be separately identified and added at the front of the file, rather than throughout the working papers. Such additional information would need to be carefully assessed to ensure that it does not affect any of the audit conclusions. This method of archiving the file helps maintain the integrity of the audit conclusions.

Contents and Organization Each public accounting firm establishes its own approach to preparing and organizing working papers, and the beginning auditor must adopt his or her firm's approach. The emphasis in this text is on the general concepts common to all working papers.

Figure 5-3 illustrates the organization of a typical set of working papers. They contain virtually everything involved in the financial statement audit. There is a definite logic to the type of working papers prepared for an audit and the way they are arranged in the files, even though different firms may follow somewhat different approaches. Firms organize their working papers using electronic folders that correspond to the phases of the audit. Table 5-8 lists common categories of working papers, the typical contents of those working papers, and examples. Many firms have most of the documents in electronic form, including scanned documents from the client. The current electronic working paper file includes all documents pertaining to the current audit, including the client working trial balance and financial statements.

Figure 5-3	Working Paper Contents and Organization

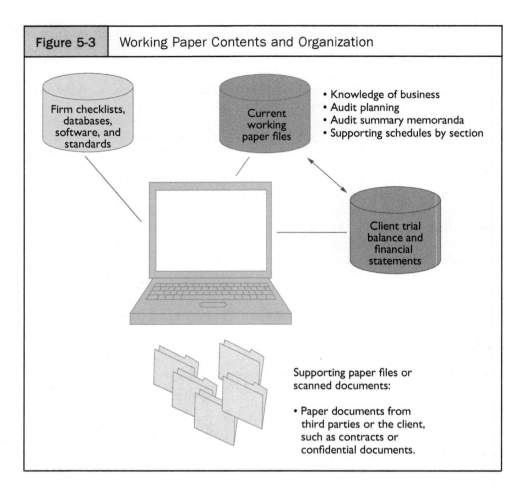

- Knowledge of business
- Audit planning
- Audit summary memoranda
- Supporting schedules by section

Firm checklists, databases, software, and standards

Current working paper files

Client trial balance and financial statements

Supporting paper files or scanned documents:

- Paper documents from third parties or the client, such as contracts or confidential documents.

Table 5-8	Typical Electronic Working Papers and Their Purpose

Category of Working Paper and Typical Content	Examples of Working Papers Included
Knowledge of business: historical and continuing information about the business	Articles of incorporation, bylaws, bond indentures, significant contracts such as executive remuneration and long-term debt agreements, documentation of corporate governance processes
Audit planning: risk analysis documents, calculation of materiality, staff scheduling, completed planning checklists, audit programs, flowcharts, and documentation supporting internal controls (which could also be filed in the supporting schedule section)	Analytical procedures from the prior and current audit, analysis and conclusions for control risk overall
Audit Summary Memoranda	
Supporting schedules by section: Analytical procedures, completed checklists by section, audit programs by section, copies of scanned documents, multi-year working papers, contracts that are specific to a particular account, documentation of controls that pertain to particular accounts or transaction flows (which could also be filed in the supporting schedule section)	*Current year:* analysis of control risk by assertion by cycle and account, audit programs for tests of control and tests of detail by account, copies of insurance policies or large fixed-asset addition invoices that were examined *Multi-year:* long-term debt; shareholders' equity accounts; property, plant, and equipment and amortization; notes payable (which include prior year and current year analyses)

The current file is built from a roll-forward of the prior year file, use of firm databases and standards, and addition of current field work such as tests of controls included as supporting schedules. Use of electronic documents permits flexibility in organization. For example, the internal control documentation for the sales cycle could be included in the audit planning section or in the supporting schedule section for sales, with cross-referencing so that it can be rapidly located.

Working papers are password protected so that only the audit team members can access the client file, and once a staff member has completed a document, he or she can make no further changes. The documents are archived and logged to track which changes were made by staff, supervisors, managers, or partners.

Since the basis for preparing the financial statements is the general ledger, the amounts included in the general ledger are the focal point of the examination. As early as possible after the balance sheet date, the auditor obtains the client financial statements and a copy of the general ledger accounts and their year-end balances (usually in electronic form, called the trial balance). Working papers are typically organized by groups of accounts that correspond to a line or segment of financial statement accounts. For example, one supporting schedule section would be cash, while another would be accounts receivable.

PREPARATION OF WORKING PAPERS

LO 7 Prepare organized audit documentation.

Read Auditing in Action 5-4, and imagine yourself in Rhonda's position several years after completing an audit. The proper preparation of supporting schedules to document the audit evidence accumulated, the results found, and the conclusions reached is an important part of the audit. The auditor must recognize the circumstances requiring the need for a schedule and the appropriate design of schedules to be included in the files. Although the design depends on the objectives involved, working papers should possess certain characteristics:

- Each working paper should be properly identified with such information as the client's name, the period covered, a description of the contents, the name of the preparer, the date of preparation, and an index code. Where automated working-paper software is used, defaults can be set up in the software, simplifying this process.
- Working papers should be indexed and cross-referenced to aid in organizing and filing. One type of indexing uses alphabetic characters. The primary or "lead" schedule for cash would be indexed as A-1, the individual supporting working papers for details about general ledger accounts making up the total cash on the financial statements indexed as A-2 through A-4, and so on, as additional working papers are required.
- Completed working papers must clearly indicate the audit work performed. This is accomplished in three ways: by a written statement in the form of a memorandum, by initials or name beside the audit procedures in the audit program, and by notations directly on the working paper schedules. Notations on working papers are accomplished by the use of tick marks or symbols written adjacent to the detail on the body of the schedule. These notations must be clearly explained at the bottom of the working paper.
- Each working paper should include enough information to fulfill the objectives for which it was designed. If the auditor is to prepare working papers properly, the auditor must be aware of his or her goals. For example, if a working paper is designed to list the detail and show the verification of support of a balance sheet account, such as prepaid insurance, it is essential that the detail on the working paper reconciles with the trial balance general ledger insurance account.
- The conclusions that were reached about the segment of the audit under consideration should be plainly stated.

Rhonda McMillan had been the in-charge auditor on the audit of Blaine Construction Company in 2012. Now she is sitting here, in 2018, in a room full of lawyers who are asking her questions about the 2012 audit. Blaine was sold to another company in 2013 at a purchase price that was based primarily on the 2012 audited financial statements. Several of the large construction contracts showed a profit in 2012 using the percentage of completion method, but they ultimately resulted in large losses for the buyer. Because Rhonda's firm audited the 2012 financial statements, the buyer is trying to make the case that Rhonda's firm failed in its audit of contract costs and revenues.

The buyer's attorney is taking Rhonda's deposition and is asking her about the audit work she did on contracts. Referring to the audit files, his examination goes something like this:

Attorney: Do you recognize this exhibit, and if you do, would you please identify it for us?

Rhonda: Yes, this is the summary of contracts in progress at the end of 2012.

Attorney: Did you prepare this schedule?

Rhonda: I believe the client prepared it, but I audited it. My initials are right here in the upper right-hand corner.

Attorney: When did you do this audit work?

Rhonda: I'm not sure, I forgot to date this one. But it must have been about the second week in March, because that's when we did the field work.

Attorney: Now I'd like to turn your attention to this tick mark next to the Baldwin contract. You see where it shows Baldwin, and then the red sort of cross-like mark?

Rhonda: Yes.

Attorney: In the explanation for that tick mark it says: "Discussed status of job with Elton Burgess. Job is going according to schedule and he believes that the expected profit will be earned." Now my question is, Ms. McMillan, what exactly was the nature and content of your discussion with Mr. Burgess?

Rhonda: Other than what is in the explanation to this tick mark, I have no idea. I mean, this all took place over five years ago. I only worked on the engagement that one year, and I can hardly even remember that.

Rhonda's work was not adequately documented, and what was there indicated that her testing relied almost exclusively on management inquiry without any required corroboration. The evidence collected was not sufficient and not relevant. Her audit firm was required to pay a significant settlement for damages to the buyer.

The common characteristics of well-designed working papers are indicated in Figure 5-4.

Ownership of Working Papers

The working papers prepared during the engagement, including those prepared by the client for the auditor, are the property of the auditor. The only time anyone else, including the client, has a legal right to examine the working papers is when they are subpoenaed by a court as legal evidence or when they are required by the public accountants' (PAs') professional organization in connection with disciplinary proceedings or practice inspection. At the completion of the engagement, working papers are retained on the public accounting firm's premises for future reference or sent offsite for secure archiving.

Confidentiality of Working Papers

As discussed in Chapter 3, auditors need to maintain a confidential relationship with the client. The rules of conduct of the professional accounting bodies require their members not to disclose any confidential information obtained in the course of a professional engagement except with out the consent of the client or, as was noted above, when required by the courts or by the professional accounting associations.

During the course of the examination, auditors obtain a considerable amount of information of a confidential nature, including officer salaries, product pricing and advertising plans, and product cost data. If auditors divulged this information to outsiders or to client employees who have been denied access, their relationship with management would be seriously strained. Furthermore, having access to the working papers would give employees an opportunity to alter information on them. For these reasons, care must be taken to protect the working papers at all times.

Figure 5-4 | Common Characteristics of Well-Designed Working Papers

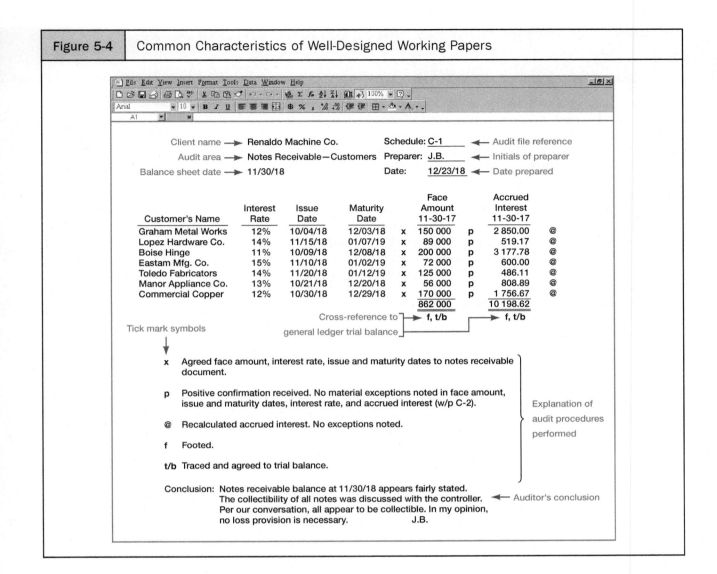

Ordinarily, the working papers can be provided to someone else only with the express written permission of the client, since the client owns the data on the working papers. This is the case even if a PA sells his or her practice to another public accounting firm. Permission is not required from the client, however, if the working papers are subpoenaed by a court or are used in connection with disciplinary hearings or practice inspection conducted by the auditor's professional body. The auditor would normally consult with a lawyer and inform the client in these cases.

EFFECT OF TECHNOLOGY ON AUDIT EVIDENCE AND AUDIT DOCUMENTATION

LO 8 Explain how technology affects audit evidence and audit documentation.

When evidence can be examined only in machine-readable form, auditors use computers to read and examine evidence. Generalized audit software programs, such as ACL and Interactive Data Extraction and Analysis (IDEA) software, are designed specifically for use by auditors. These programs are typically Windows-based and can

Auditors have long embraced technology to improve audit efficiency. For instance, most working papers are prepared using software, such as firm software for risk analysis and materiality decisions, databases containing industry-based audit programs, and templates for calculating information such as interest expense and prepaids. For every type of working paper that you can think of, it is likely that software or a spreadsheet template is available. In addition, software is used for audit time budgets, time recording, and the management of the audit firm, such as software for billing, payroll, general ledger, and financial statements. Information systems specialists use a variety of software to conduct computer-assisted audit tests geared to the risks and needs of the audit team.

However, a recent American Institute of Certified Public Accountants (AICPA) white paper discusses how technology will transform the way the audit is performed. For instance, it talks about how audit procedures can be deconstructed into tasks that can be performed wherever it is most effective. The local onsite audit team can focus on tasks that only they can perform, such as observing performance of internal controls or meeting with the client, while back-end tasks, such as confirmations, can be performed remotely by third-party service providers. In the case of Big Four firms, some audit tasks have begun to be outsourced as well. For instance, there may be a team of specialists in the Bangalore office that specializes in journal entry testing.

Sources: Diane Janvrin, James Bierstaker, and D. Jordan Lowe, "An examination of audit information technology use and perceived importance," *Accounting Horizons*, vol. 22, no. 1, 2008, pp. 1–21. Linda Stroude, "No rest for the auditor," *CAmagazine,* August 2008, pp. 33–34. Paul Byrnes, Tom Cristie, Trevor Stewart, and Miklos Vasarhelyi, "Re-imagining auditing in a rewired world," *AICPA White Paper,* August 2014.

easily be operated on the auditor's desktop or notebook computer. The auditor obtains copies of client databases or master files and uses the software to perform a variety of tests of the client's electronic data. These audit software packages are relatively easy to use, even by auditors with little IT training, and can be applied to a wide variety of clients with minimal customization. Auditors may also use spreadsheet software to perform audit tests.

As highlighted in Auditing in Action 5-5, Auditors often use engagement management software to organize and analyze audit documentation. Using audit management software, an auditor can prepare a trial balance, lead schedules, supporting audit documentation, and financial statements, as well as perform ratio analysis. A major benefit of computerized analytical procedures is the ease of updating the calculations when entries to the client's statements are adjusted. If there are several adjusting entries to the client's records, the analytical procedures calculations can be quickly revised. For example, a change in inventory and cost of goods sold affects a large number of ratios. All affected ratios can be recalculated immediately.

The software also facilitates tracking audit progress by indicating the performance and review status of each audit area. Tick marks and other explanations, such as reviewer notes, can be entered directly into computerized files. In addition, data can be imported and exported to other applications, so auditors may download a client's general ledger or export tax information to a commercial tax preparation package. Auditors also use local area networks and groupshare software programs to access audit documentation simultaneously from remote locations.

LO 9 Understand and apply professional skepticism to evidence and documentation decisions.

PROFESSIONAL SKEPTICISM, EVIDENCE, AND DOCUMENTATION

In Chapter 3, we discussed the skepticism continuum and in Auditing in Action 5-2, we highlighted questions to consider when evaluating whether the appropriate level of professional skepticism was applied. Figure 5-5 summarizes the relationship between professional skepticism, evidence, and documentation.

As Figure 5-5 highlights, the auditor adjusts the level of both evidence and documentation according to the amount of skepticism necessary, based upon the risk

Figure 5-5	Applying Professional Skepticism to Evidence and Documentation Decisions

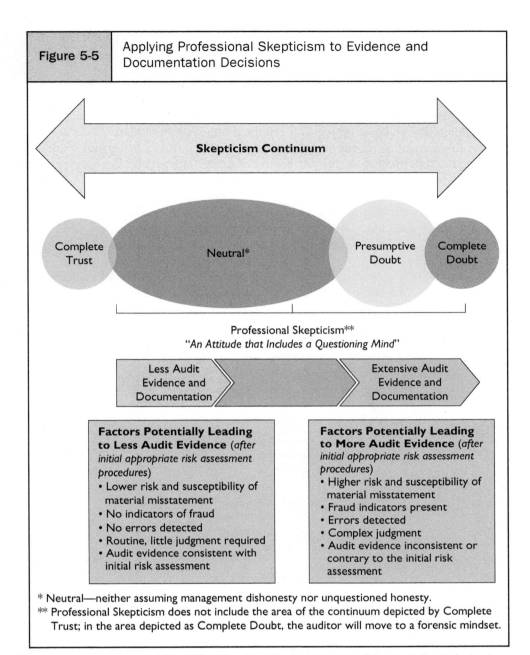

* Neutral—neither assuming management dishonesty nor unquestioned honesty.
** Professional Skepticism does not include the area of the continuum depicted by Complete Trust; in the area depicted as Complete Doubt, the auditor will move to a forensic mindset.

Source: Republished with permission of American Accounting Association, from Enhancing Auditor Professional Skepticism: The Professional Skepticism continuum. current issues in auditing 8.2 (2014): P1-P10, Steven M. Glover, Douglas F. Prawitt, © 2014; permission conveyed through Copyright Clearance Center, Inc.

of material misstatement and whether the evidence collected is consistent with the original risk assessment. By conceptualizing professional skepticism in this manner, rather than applying the same attitude of skepticism throughout the audit, the auditor will match the amount of evidence and documentation to the circumstances applicable to each audit area and assertion. For instance, if a particular account is immaterial, it would not require evidence beyond what was gathered in the risk assessment stage. In contrast, high-risk material accounts that have fraud indicators present, have had errors detected, or involve complex judgment and/or inconsistent audit evidence would require a higher degree of professional skepticism. This would result in extensive evidence and documentation.

CONCEPT CHECK

C5-8 Explain why the level of professional skepticism can vary among audit procedures.

Appendix 5A:
Common Financial Ratios

Auditors' analytical procedures often include the use of general financial ratios during planning and final review of the audited financial statements. These are useful for understanding recent events and the financial status of the business and for viewing the statements from the perspective of a user. The general financial analysis may be effective for identifying possible problem areas, where the auditor may do additional analysis and audit testing, as well as business problem areas in which the auditor can provide other assistance. When using these ratios, auditors must be sure to make appropriate comparisons. The most important comparisons are to those of previous years for the company and to industry averages or similar companies for the same year.

Ratios and other analytical procedures are normally calculated using spreadsheets and other types of audit software, in which several years of client and industry data can be maintained for comparative purposes. Ratios can be linked to the trial balance so that calculations are automatically updated as adjusting entries are made to the client's statements. For example, an adjustment to inventory and cost of goods sold affects a large number of ratios, including inventory turnover, the current ratio, gross margin, and other profitability measures.

We next examine some widely used financial ratios.

Short-Term Debt-Paying Ability

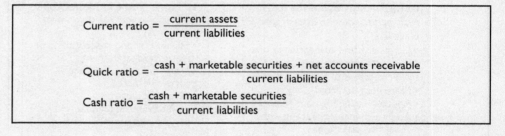

$$\text{Current ratio} = \frac{\text{current assets}}{\text{current liabilities}}$$

$$\text{Quick ratio} = \frac{\text{cash} + \text{marketable securities} + \text{net accounts receivable}}{\text{current liabilities}}$$

$$\text{Cash ratio} = \frac{\text{cash} + \text{marketable securities}}{\text{current liabilities}}$$

Companies need a reasonable level of liquidity to pay their debts as they come due, and these three ratios measure liquidity. It is apparent by examining the three ratios that the cash ratio may be useful to evaluate the ability to pay debts immediately, whereas the current ratio requires the conversion of assets such as inventory and accounts receivable to cash before debts can be paid. The most important difference between the quick and current ratios is the inclusion of inventory in current assets for the current ratio.

Liquidity Activity Ratios

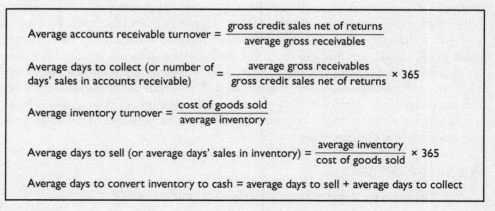

$$\text{Average accounts receivable turnover} = \frac{\text{gross credit sales net of returns}}{\text{average gross receivables}}$$

$$\text{Average days to collect (or number of days' sales in accounts receivable)} = \frac{\text{average gross receivables}}{\text{gross credit sales net of returns}} \times 365$$

$$\text{Average inventory turnover} = \frac{\text{cost of goods sold}}{\text{average inventory}}$$

$$\text{Average days to sell (or average days' sales in inventory)} = \frac{\text{average inventory}}{\text{cost of goods sold}} \times 365$$

$$\text{Average days to convert inventory to cash} = \text{average days to sell} + \text{average days to collect}$$

If a company does not have sufficient cash and cash-like items to meet its obligations, the key to its debt-paying ability is the time it takes the company to convert less-liquid current assets into cash. This is measured by the liquidity activity ratios.

The activity ratios for accounts receivable and inventory are especially useful to auditors, who often use trends in the accounts receivable turnover ratio to assess the reasonableness of the allowance for uncollectible accounts. Auditors use trends in the inventory turnover ratio to identify potential inventory obsolescence. Average days to collect is a different way of looking at the average accounts receivable turnover data. The same is true of average days to sell compared to average inventory turnover.

Ability to Meet Long-Term Debt Obligations

$$\text{Debt-to-equity ratio} = \frac{\text{total liabilities}}{\text{total equity}}$$

$$\text{Tangible net assets-to-equity ratio} = \frac{\text{total equity} - \text{intangible assets}}{\text{total equity}}$$

$$\text{Times interest earned} = \frac{\text{operating income}}{\text{interest expense}}$$

$$\text{Times interest and preferred dividends earned} = \frac{\text{operating income}}{\text{interest expense} + [\text{preferred dividends}/(1 - \text{tax rate})]}$$

A company's long-run solvency depends on the success of its operations and on its ability to raise capital for expansion, as well as its ability to make principal and interest payments. Two ratios are key measures creditors and investors use to assess a company's ability to pay its debts.

The debt-to-equity ratio shows the extent of the use of debt in financing a company. If the debt-to-equity ratio is too high, it may indicate that the company has used up its borrowing capacity and has no cushion for additional debt. If it is too low, it may mean that available leverage is not being used to the owners' benefit.

The ability to make interest payments depends on the company's ability to generate positive cash flow from operations. The times interest earned ratio shows whether the company can comfortably make its interest payments, assuming that earnings trends are stable.

Profitability Ratios

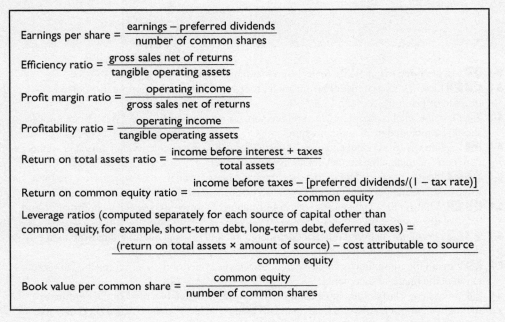

$$\text{Earnings per share} = \frac{\text{earnings} - \text{preferred dividends}}{\text{number of common shares}}$$

$$\text{Efficiency ratio} = \frac{\text{gross sales net of returns}}{\text{tangible operating assets}}$$

$$\text{Profit margin ratio} = \frac{\text{operating income}}{\text{gross sales net of returns}}$$

$$\text{Profitability ratio} = \frac{\text{operating income}}{\text{tangible operating assets}}$$

$$\text{Return on total assets ratio} = \frac{\text{income before interest} + \text{taxes}}{\text{total assets}}$$

$$\text{Return on common equity ratio} = \frac{\text{income before taxes} - [\text{preferred dividends}/(1 - \text{tax rate})]}{\text{common equity}}$$

Leverage ratios (computed separately for each source of capital other than common equity, for example, short-term debt, long-term debt, deferred taxes) =

$$\frac{(\text{return on total assets} \times \text{amount of source}) - \text{cost attributable to source}}{\text{common equity}}$$

$$\text{Book value per common share} = \frac{\text{common equity}}{\text{number of common shares}}$$

A company's ability to generate cash for payment of obligations, expansion, and dividends is heavily dependent on profitability. The most widely used profitability ratio is earnings per share. Auditors calculate additional ratios to provide further insights into operations.

Gross profit percent shows the portion of sales available to cover all expenses and profit after deducting the cost of the product. Auditors find this ratio especially useful for assessing misstatements in sales, cost of goods sold, accounts receivable, and inventory.

Profit margin is similar to gross profit margin but subtracts both cost of goods sold and operating expenses in making the calculations. This ratio enables auditors to assess potential misstatements in operating expenses and related balance sheet accounts.

Return on assets and return on common equity are measures of overall profitability of a company. These ratios show a company's ability to generate profit for each dollar of assets and equity.

SUMMARY

An important part of every audit is determining the proper types and amounts of audit evidence to gather. The persuasiveness of the evidence depends on both its appropriateness and sufficiency. The appropriateness of audit evidence is determined by its relevance in testing the relevant assertion or control and its reliability.

Analytical procedures are the evaluation of recorded accounting information by computing ratios and developing other plausible relationships for comparison to expectations developed by the auditor. These analytical procedures are used in planning to understand the client's business and industry, and are also used throughout the audit to identify possible misstatements, reduce detailed tests, and assess going-concern issues. The use of analytical procedures has increased because of their effectiveness at identifying possible misstatements at a low cost, and they are required in the planning and completion phases of the audit.

Audit documentation is an essential part of every audit for effectively planning the audit, providing a record of the evidence accumulated and the results of the tests, deciding the proper type of audit report, and reviewing the work of assistants. High-quality CPA (Chartered Professional Accountant) firms make sure that audit documentation is properly prepared and is sufficient for the circumstances in the audit. Professional skepticism plays an important role in determining the level of evidence and documentation necessary—as professional skepticism is increased so is the level of audit evidence and documentation.

Review Questions

⊕ **5-1** **2** List the three major evidence decisions that must be made on every audit.

⊕ **5-2** **1** **2** Describe what is meant by "an audit procedure." Why is it important for audit procedures to be carefully worded?

⊕ **5-3** **2** Describe what is meant by "an audit program for accounts receivable." What three things should be included in an audit program?

⊕ **5-4** **2** Explain why the auditor can only be persuaded with a reasonable level of assurance, rather than convinced, that the financial statements are correct.

⊕ **5-5** **2** **3** Identify the three factors that determine the persuasiveness of evidence. How are these three factors related to audit procedures, items to select, and timing?

⊕ **5-6** **3** **4** What are the characteristics of a confirmation? Distinguish between a confirmation and external documentation.

⊕ **5-7** **3** **4** Distinguish between internal documentation and external documentation as audit evidence, and give three examples of each.

⊕ **5-8** **5** Explain the importance of analytical procedures as evidence in determining the fair presentation of the financial statements.

⊕ **5-9** **5** Your client, Harper Ltd., has a contractual commitment as a part of a bond indenture to maintain a current ratio of 2.0. If the ratio falls below that level on the balance sheet date, the entire bond becomes payable immediately. In the current year, the client's financial statements show that the ratio has dropped from 2.6:1 (or 2.6) to 2.05:1 (or 2.05) over the past year. How would this situation affect your audit plan?

5-10 **5** Distinguish between attention-directing analytical procedures and those intended to reduce detailed substantive procedures.

5-11 **5** Gail Gordon, public accountant, has found ratio and trend analysis relatively useless as a tool in conducting audits. For several engagements, she computed the industry ratios included in publications by The Financial Post Company and compared them with client ratios. For most engagements, the client's business was significantly different from the industry data in the publication, and the client would automatically explain away any discrepancies by attributing them to the unique nature of its operations. In cases in which the client had more than one branch in different industries, Gail found the ratio analysis no help at all. How could Gail improve the quality of her analytical procedures?

5-12 **5** Describe the liquidity activity ratios and explain why ratios are useful to auditors.

5-13 **5** It is imperative that the auditor follow up on all material differences discovered through analytical procedures. What factors affect such investigations?

5-14 **7** Define what is meant by "a tick mark." What is its purpose?

5-15 **6** **7** Why is it essential that the auditor not leave questions or exceptions in the working papers without an adequate explanation?

5-16 **6** **7** What types of working papers can be prepared by the client and used by the auditor as a part of the working paper file? When client assistance is obtained in preparing working papers, describe the proper precautions the auditor should take.

5-17 **6** **7** Who owns the working papers? Under what circumstances can they be used by other people?

Multiple Choice Questions and Task-Based Simulations

5-18 **3** Which of the following types of documentary evidence should the auditor consider to be the most reliable?
(1) A sales invoice issued by the client and supported by a delivery receipt from an outside trucker.
(2) Confirmation of an account payable balance mailed by and returned directly to the auditor.
(3) A cheque, issued by the company and bearing the payee's endorsement, that is included with the bank statements mailed directly to the auditor.
(4) An audit schedule prepared by the client's controller and reviewed by the client's treasurer.

5-19 **3** Audit evidence can come in different forms with different degrees of persuasiveness. Which of the following is the least persuasive type of evidence?
(1) Vendor's invoice.
(2) Bank statement obtained from the client.
(3) Computations made by the auditor.
(4) Pre-numbered sales invoices.

5-20 **3** Which of the following presumptions is correct about the reliability of audit evidence?
(1) Information obtained indirectly from outside sources is the most reliable audit evidence.
(2) To be reliable, audit evidence should be convincing rather than merely persuasive.
(3) Reliability of audit evidence refers to the amount of corroborative evidence obtained.
(4) Effective internal control provides more assurance about the reliability of audit evidence.

5-21 **1** **2** **3** Which of the following statements concerning audit evidence is true?
(1) To be appropriate, audit evidence should be either persuasive or relevant, but need not be reliable.
(2) The measure of the quantity and quality of audit evidence lies in the auditor's judgment.
(3) The difficulty and expense of obtaining audit evidence concerning an account balance is a valid basis for omitting the test.
(4) A client's accounting records can be sufficient audit evidence to support the financial statements.

5-22 **6** **7** The following questions concern audit documentation. Choose the best response.
a. Which of the following is *not* a primary purpose of audit documentation?
(1) To coordinate the audit.
(2) To assist in preparation of the audit report.

(3) To support the financial statements.

(4) To provide evidence of the audit work performed.

b. During an audit engagement, pertinent data are compiled and included in the audit files. The audit files primarily are considered to be:

(1) A client-owned record of conclusions reached by the auditors who performed the engagement.

(2) Evidence supporting financial statements.

(3) Support for the auditor's representations as to compliance with auditing standards.

(4) A record to be used as a basis for the following year's engagement.

5-23 **4** Classify each of the presented audit procedures according to the types of evidence collection procedures: (1) inspection or physical examination, (2) confirmation, (3) inspection of documents, (4) analytical procedures, (5) inquiries of the client, (6) recalculation, (7) reperformance, and (8) observation.

Audit Procedure	Type of Audit Evidence
Review the accounts receivable with the credit manager to evaluate their collectibility.	
Compare a duplicate sales invoice with the sales journal for customer name and amount	
Count inventory items and record the amount in the audit files.	
Obtain a letter from the client's attorney addressed to the CPA (Chartered Professional Accountant) firm stating that the attorney is not aware of any existing lawsuits.	
Extend the cost of inventory times the quantity on an inventory listing to test whether it is accurate.	
Obtain a letter from an insurance company to the CPA firm stating the amount of the fire insurance coverage on buildings and equipment.	
Examine an insurance policy stating the amount of the fire insurance coverage on buildings and equipment.	
Calculate the ratio of cost of goods sold to sales as a test of overall reasonableness of gross margin relative to the preceding year.	
Obtain information about internal control by requesting that the client fill out a questionnaire.	
Trace the total in the cash disbursements journal to the general ledger.	
Watch employees count inventory to determine whether company procedures are being followed.	
Examine a piece of equipment to make sure that a major acquisition was actually received and is in operation.	
Calculate the ratio of sales commission expense to sales as a test of sales commissions.	
Examine corporate minutes to determine the authorization of the issue of bonds.	
Review the total of repairs and maintenance for each month to determine whether any month's total was unusually large.	
Obtain a written statement from a bank stating that the client has $15 671 on deposit and liabilities of $500 000 on a demand note.	
Obtain a letter from management stating that there are no unrecorded liabilities.	

5-24 **3** For each of the audit procedures presented, identify the management assertion(s) the procedure covers (A–G), and indicate the quality of audit evidence (low, moderate, high) obtained through the procedure.

Assertions:

A. Cut-off

B. Accuracy

C. Completeness

D. Existence

E. Valuation

F. Occurrence

G. Rights & Obligations

Audit Procedures	Assertion(s) (A,B,C,D,E,F,G)	Quality of Audit Evidence (Low, Moderate, High)
Discuss with management any payroll liabilities that appeared in the prior year's financial statements that have not been accrued for in the current year.		
Discuss with management its estimate for allowance for doubtful accounts.		
Obtain and review shipping documents for a sample of sales transactions.		
Send letters to company's lawyers to confirm the number of outstanding legal claims and estimated dollar amounts to resolve each claim.		
Review title documents related to a company's recently purchased parcel of land.		
Review and recalculate the company's amortization schedule.		
Recount a sample of inventory items on the warehouse floor and trace count results to accounting records.		
Recalculate management's provision for damaged inventory.		

5-25 **3** According to the Canadian Organic Food Standards, the "organic" label can only be placed on apples that are grown without the use of chemical pesticides. You recently decided to start eating only organic apples. However, you heard that an undercover investigation by CBC's *Marketplace* has revealed that the organic farm where you want to buy the apples uses chemical pesticides to grow all of their apples. You are now worried that the more expensive "organic" labeled apples that you want to buy might not really be organic.

Based on what *Marketplace* has uncovered, what assertion did the organic farm violate?

A. Existence

B. Completeness

C. Accuracy

D. Rights & Obligations

E. Valuation

F. Occurrence

For each procedure indicate the reliability level of evidence (low, medium, high) obtained.

Procedures	Quality of Evidence
Call the organic farm and ask if they use chemical pesticides.	Low
Buy apples grown at the organic farm and taste them to see if you can sense any chemical pesticide.	
Send a letter to the organic farm asking them to confirm in writing that they did not use chemical pesticides to grow their apples.	
Contact *Marketplace* and confirm with them that their story relates to the organic farm where you want to buy the apples.	
Buy apples grown at the organic farm, take them to a laboratory, and have them tested to see if they contain any traces of chemical pesticides.	

Discussion Questions and Problems

5-26 **3** The following are eight situations, each containing two means of accumulating evidence:

1. Confirm accounts receivable with business organizations versus confirming receivables with consumers.

2. Physically examine 8 cm steel plates versus examining electronic parts.

3. Examine duplicate sales invoices when several competent people are checking one another's work versus examining documents prepared by a competent person in a one-person staff.
4. Physically examine inventory of parts for the number of units on hand versus examining them for the likelihood of inventory being obsolete.
5. Confirm a bank balance versus confirming the oil and gas reserves with a geologist specializing in oil and gas.
6. Confirm a bank balance versus examining the client's bank statements.
7. Physically count the client's inventory held by an independent party versus confirming the count with an independent party.
8. Physically count the client's inventory versus obtaining a count from the company president.

REQUIRED

a. For each of the eight situations, state whether the first or second type of evidence is more reliable.
b. For each situation, state which of the factors discussed in the chapter affect the appropriateness of the evidence.

5-27 5 In the audit of Worldwide Wholesale Inc., you performed extensive ratio and trend analyses. No material exceptions were discovered except for the following:
1. Commission expense as a percentage of sales had stayed constant for several years but has increased significantly in the current year. Commission rates have not changed.
2. The rate of inventory turnover has steadily decreased for four years.
3. Inventory as a percentage of current assets has steadily increased for four years.
4. The number of days' sales in accounts receivable has steadily increased for three years.
5. Allowance for uncollectable accounts as a percentage of accounts receivable has steadily decreased for three years.
6. The absolute amounts of amortization expense and amortization expense as a percentage of gross property, plant, and equipment are significantly smaller than in the preceding year.

REQUIRED

a. Evaluate the potential significance of each of the exceptions above for the fair presentation of financial statements.
b. State the follow-up procedures you would use to determine the possibility of material misstatements.
c. What do these changes indicate about the overall financial position of Worldwide Wholesale Inc.?

5-28 5 As part of the analytical procedures of Mahogany Products Inc., you perform calculations of the following ratios.

Ratio	Industry Averages		Mahogany Products Inc.	
	2018	2017	2018	2017
1. Current ratio	3.30	3.80	2.20	2.60
2. Days to collect receivables	87.00	93.00	67.00	60.00
3. Days to sell inventory	126.00	121.00	93.00	89.00
4. Purchases divided by accounts payable	11.70	11.60	8.50	8.60
5. Inventory divided by current assets	0.56	0.51	0.49	0.48
6. Operating earnings divided by tangible assets	0.08	0.06	0.14	0.12
7. Operating earnings divided by net sales	0.06	0.06	0.04	0.04
8. Gross margin percentage	0.21	0.27	0.21	0.19
9. Earnings per share	$14.27	$13.91	$2.09	$1.93

REQUIRED

For each of the preceding ratios:
a. State whether there is a need to investigate the results further and, if so, the reason for further investigation.
b. State the approach you would use in the investigation.
c. Explain how the operations of Mahogany Products Inc. appear to differ from those of the industry.

5-29 **1** **2** **3** Parts Inc. sells electrical components to large department stores and also has a few cash sales to electricians. Sales invoices are prepared for all sales. Cash sales are recorded to the cash receipts journal and cash is deposited to the bank each day. All sales to large stores are credit sales and are handled by sales clerks by telephone or facsimile. The sales clerk takes the customer's request, checks the authorized customer list for credit limits (if it is a credit sale), prepares the sales invoice, and sends one copy to the inventory control department, which sends the ordered goods to the shipping department. For cash sales, the inventory control clerk brings the items sold to the sales counter and the goods are given to the purchaser at the time of sale. For credit sales, the shipping clerk signs the inventory control copy of the sales invoice and then prepares a shipping invoice. A third copy of the sales invoice is forwarded to the accounting department so that a clerk can enter the sale into the sales journal. The shipping invoices are maintained in the shipping department in case a shipment needs to be checked. All goods are shipped FOB shipping point.

REQUIRED

a. Design two audit procedures that will provide evidence of the existence of sales. Identify the nature of the procedure and the documents you are using, and explain why these procedures will show whether recorded sales are valid.

b. Design two audit procedures that will provide evidence of the completeness of sales. Identify the nature of the procedure and the documents you are using, and explain why these procedures will show whether recorded sales are complete.

(Reprinted from AU1 CGA-Canada Examinations developed by the Certified General Accountants Association of Canada © 2011 CGA-Canada, with permission Chartered Professional Accountants of Canada, Toronto, Canada. Any changes to the original material are the sole responsibility of the author (and/or publisher) and have not been reviewed or endorsed by the Chartered Professional Accountants of Canada.)

5-30 **4** List two examples of audit evidence that the auditor can use in support of each of the following:

a. Recorded amount of entries in the purchase journal.

b. Physical existence of inventory.

c. Accuracy of accounts receivable.

d. Ownership of capital assets.

e. Liability for accounts payable.

f. Obsolescence of inventory.

g. Existence of petty cash.

5-31 **3** The following questions concern the reliability of the evidence in question 5-30.

REQUIRED

a. Explain why confirmations are normally more reliable evidence than inquiries of the client.

b. Describe a situation in which confirmation will be considered highly reliable and another in which it will not be reliable.

c. Under what circumstances is the physical observation of inventory considered relatively unreliable evidence?

d. Explain why recalculation tests are highly reliable but of relatively limited use.

e. Give three examples of relatively reliable documentation and three examples of less reliable documentation. What characteristics distinguish the two?

f. Give several examples in which the qualifications of the respondent or the qualifications of the auditor affect the reliability of the evidence.

g. Explain why analytical procedures are important evidence even though they are relatively unreliable by themselves.

5-32 **2** **3** The following audit procedures were performed in the audit of inventory. The audit procedures assume the auditor has obtained the inventory count records that list the client's inventory. The balance-related assertions are also included.

AUDIT PROCEDURES

1. Using audit software, extend unit prices times quantity, foot the extensions, and compare the total with the general ledger.

2. Trace selected quantities from the inventory listing to the physical inventory to make sure the items exist and the quantities are the same.

3. Question operating personnel about the possibility of obsolete or slow-moving inventory.

4. Select a sample of quantities of inventory in the factory warehouse, and trace each item to the inventory count sheets to determine if it has been included and if the quantity and description are correct.
5. Using both this year's and last year's inventory data files, compare quantities on hand and unit prices, printing any with greater than a 30 percent or $15 000 variation from one year to the next.
6. Examine sales invoices and contracts with customers to determine if any goods are out on consignment with customers. Similarly, examine vendors' invoices and contracts with vendors to determine if any goods on the inventory listing are owned by vendors.
7. Send letters directly to third parties who hold the client's inventory and request that they respond directly to us.

Balance-Related Assertions	
Existence	Valuation
Rights and obligations	Allocation
Completeness	

REQUIRED
a. Identify the type of audit evidence used for each audit procedure.
b. Identify the balance-related assertion(s) satisfied by each audit procedure.

5-33 **2** **3** *Mythbusters* is a popular science program on the Discovery Channel. The show's hosts—experts in special effects, art, robotics, electricity, and building—use the scientific method to test the validity of popular "myths" associated with movies, news stories, and adages (such as "You can't teach an old dog new tricks").
1. How does the role of the hosts of *Mythbusters* compare to the financial statement auditor? (Think about what they are examining and how they examine it.)
2. Some common myths about financial statement auditors are:
   a. They examine every transaction.
   b. They ensure the financial statements are accurate.
   c. They prepare the financial statements.
   d. They detect fraud.
   e. They must be accountants.
   What kinds of evidence can you use to dispel these myths?
3. How would you determine whether the evidence you would use is reliable and/or accurate? Rate the evidence that you would use based upon reliability and accuracy, then explain your ratings.
4. How does your evidence compare to the types of evidence that auditors use?

Professional Judgment Problems and Cases

5-34 **3** **4** You are an audit manager on the year-end audit of Nicolas Manufacturing. Your team was assigned a new junior audit staff member, Michelle, who recently graduated from university. Michelle performed the following two audit procedures and provided you with a written explanation about the reliability of audit evidence that she obtained as part of each procedure.

Procedure # 1
To verify the valuation of accounts receivable, I obtained from the A/R manager the Excel schedule where he calculated the year-end adjustment posted to the allowance for doubtful accounts. I reviewed the formulas used in the calculation and recalculated all the totals. Since the recalculation was done directly by me (auditor), the reliability of this audit evidence is high and I confirm that the accounts receivable balance at year end is valued correctly; no further work required.

Procedure # 2
To verify the existence of inventory, I attended the year-end inventory count. While walking around the warehouse, I inquired of employees who were taking the count about any possible inventory that could have been missed during the count, such as items located on top shelves. The employees told me that they haven't missed any items. The reliability of this evidence is high as the inquiry was done directly by me (auditor). I confirm that the inventory balance exists; no further work is required.

REQUIRED
1. Discuss Michelle's comments about the reliability of her audit evidence. In your discussion consider if the evidence that Michelle obtained is sufficient to support her conclusions.
2. Review the assertions covered by each procedure. Does Michelle's work cover the stated assertion? If not, what assertion did Michelle's work cover?

3. Recommend more reliable evidence that Michelle could obtain to support her conclusions.

5-35 `5` Lesley Stopps, a public accountant, is the auditor for Great Western Lumber Company Ltd., a wholesale wood milling company. Lesley calculated the gross margin for three product lines and compared it to industry information (summarized in the table below).

c. Whether you think a sole practitioner would have the competence to perform a quality audit of an organization such as Peregrine Financial Group. (Keep in mind that although it is not a public company, it has a regulator, the U.S. Commodity Futures Trading Commission, which is similar to a securities regulator.)

Great Western and Industry Gross Margins					
2018 Gross Margin %		**2017 Gross Margin %**		**2016 Gross Margin %**	
Great Western	**Industry**	**Great Western**	**Industry**	**Great Western**	**Industry**
Hardwood	36.3	32.4	36.4	32.5	36.0	32.3
Softwood	23.9	22.0	20.3	22.1	20.5	22.3
Plywood	40.3	50.1	44.2	54.3	45.4	55.6

In discussing the results, the controller told Lesley that Great Western has always had a higher gross margin on hardwood products than the industry because it focuses on the markets where it is able to sell at higher prices instead of emphasizing volume. The opposite is true of plywood where it has a reasonably small number of customers, each of which demands lower prices because of high volume. The controller also told Lesley that competitive forces have caused reductions in plywood gross margin for both the industry and Great Western in 2018 and 2017. Great Western has traditionally had a somewhat lower gross margin for softwood than the industry until 2017, when the gross margin went up significantly due to aggressive selling.

Lesley had researched the industry and found that hardwood gross margin was stable and approximately 3.5–4 percent lower than Great Western's every year. Industry gross margin for plywood has declined annually but is about 10 percentage points higher than Great Western's. Industry gross margin for softwood has been stable for the three years, but Great Western's has increased by a fairly large amount.

REQUIRED

a. Based upon the changes in gross margins, which product sales could be potentially misstated? What calculation helps to quantify the risk of material misstatement?

b. Identify the potential causes of the change in gross margin.

c. How would potential over- or understatements discussed in part (b) affect the audit process?

d. What additional steps or procedures should Lesley perform to corroborate what the controller has told her (aside from researching the industry)?

5-36 `1` `2` `3` Refer to the opening vignette regarding Peregrine Financial Group. In 2013, the U.S. Commodity Futures Trading Commission (CFTC) charged Jeannie Veraja-Snelling, a U.S. certified public accountant and sole practitioner, with failing to perform an audit in accordance with GAAS. Based upon the case facts, explain:

a. What significant control deficiencies the auditor appeared to miss.

b. The deficiencies in the auditor's confirmation process.

5-37 `1` `2` `3` Grande Stores is a large department store chain with catalogue operations. The company has recently expanded from 6 to 43 stores by borrowing from several large financial institutions and from a public offering of common shares. A recent investigation has disclosed that Grande materially overstated net income. This was accomplished by understating accounts payable and recording fictitious supplier credits that further reduced accounts payable. An OSC investigation was critical of the evidence gathered by Grande's audit firm, Montgomery & Ross, in testing accounts payable and the supplier credits.

The following is a description of some of the fictitious supplier credits and unrecorded amounts in accounts payable, as well as the audit procedures.

1. *McClure Advertising credits.* Grande had arrangements with some vendors to share the cost of advertising the vendor's product. The arrangements were usually agreed to in advance by the vendor and supported by evidence of the placing of the ad. Grande created a 114-page list of approximately 1100 vendors, supporting advertising credits of $300 000. Grande's auditors selected a sample of 4 of the 1100 items for direct confirmation. One item was confirmed by telephone, one traced to cash receipts, one to a vendor credit memo for part of the amount and cash receipts for the rest, and one to a vendor credit memo. Two of the amounts confirmed differed from the amount on the list, but the auditors did not seek an explanation for the differences because the amounts were not material.

The rest of the credits were tested by selecting 20 items (one or two from each page of the list). Twelve of the items were supported by examining the ads placed, and eight were supported by Grande debit memos charging the vendors for the promotional allowances.

2. *Springbrook Distributors credits.* Grande created 28 fictitious credit memos totalling $257 000 from Springbrook Distributors, the main supplier of health and beauty aids to Grande. Grande's controller initially told the auditor that the credits were for returned goods, then said they were a volume discount, and finally stated they were a payment so that Grande would continue to use Springbrook as a supplier. One of the Montgomery & Ross staff auditors concluded that a $257 000 payment to retain Grande's business was too large to make financial sense.

The credit memos indicated that the credits were for damaged merchandise, volume rebates, and advertising allowances. The audit firm requested a confirmation of the credits. In response, Jon Steiner, the president of Grande Stores, placed a call to Mort Seagal, the president of Springbrook, and handed the phone to the staff auditor. In fact, the call had been placed to an officer of Grande. The Grande officer, posing as Seagal, orally confirmed the credits. Grande refused to allow Montgomery & Ross to obtain written confirmations supporting the credits. Although the staff auditor doubted the validity of the credits, the audit partner, Mark Franklin, accepted the credits based on the credit memoranda, telephone confirmation of the credits, and oral representations of Grande officers.

3. *Ridolfi Inc. credits.* Credits of $130 000 based on 35 credit memoranda from Ridolfi Inc. were purportedly for the return of overstocked goods from several Grande stores. A Montgomery & Ross staff auditor noted the size of the credit and that the credit memos were dated subsequent to year-end. He further noticed that a sentence on the credit memos from Ridolfi had been obliterated by a felt-tip marker. When held to the light, the accountant could read that the marked-out sentence read, "Do not post until merchandise received." The staff auditor thereafter called Harold Ridolfi, treasurer of Ridolfi Inc., and was informed that the $130 000 in goods had not been returned and the money was not owed to Grande by Ridolfi. Steiner advised Franklin, the audit partner, that he had talked to Harold Ridolfi, who claimed he had been misunderstood by the staff auditor. Steiner told Franklin not to have anyone call Ridolfi to verify the amount because of pending litigation between Grande and Ridolfi Inc.

4. *Accounts payable accrual.* Montgomery & Ross assigned a senior auditor with experience in the retail area to audit accounts payable. Although Grande had poor internal control, Montgomery & Ross selected a sample of 50 for confirmation of the several thousand vendors who did business with Grande. Twenty-seven responses were received, and 21 were reconciled to Grande's records. These tests indicated an unrecorded liability of approximately $290 000 when projected to the population of accounts payable. However, the investigation disclosed that Grande's president made telephone calls to some suppliers who had received confirmation requests from Montgomery & Ross and told them how to respond to the request.

Montgomery & Ross also performed a purchases cut-off test by vouching accounts payable invoices received for nine weeks after year-end. The purpose of this test was to identify invoices received after year-end that should have been recorded in accounts payable. Thirty percent of the sample ($160 000) was found to relate to the prior year, indicating a potential unrecorded liability of approximately $500 000. The audit firm and Grande eventually agreed on an adjustment to increase accounts payable by $260 000.

REQUIRED

Identify deficiencies in the sufficiency and appropriateness of the evidence gathered in the audit of accounts payable of Grande Stores.

5-38 5 9 Refer to Auditing in Action 5-3. The CPAB (Canadian Public Accountability Board) report highlights the common deficiencies in applying substantive analytical procedures (SAP) to the analysis of revenue.

a. Explain what the first two points mean in terms of the degree of precision in developing the SAP.

b. Explain what the third point means for professional skepticism.

c. Explain why professional skepticism is so important when developing SAP and evaluating the results for the revenue stream.

d. In both its 2012 and 2013 reports, CPAB concluded that substantive analytical procedures are only appropriate in relatively limited circumstances. Explain why you think that CPAB came to this conclusion.

5-39 6 Ann Donnelly is a senior audit manager in a Toronto office of a public accounting firm. Her prospects for promotion to partner are excellent if she continues to perform at the same high-quality level as in the past. Ann was recently married, and she and her husband bought a large home in a prestigious neighbourhood.

Ann just returned from a vacation and was immediately called into an audit partner's office for a discussion related to one of her publicly traded audit clients. This audit engagement, which had been completed with an audit report issued several months prior, had been selected for a CPAB inspection and the partner is concerned. CPAB inspections can be stressful for the primary engagement partner and often result in the identification of audit deficiencies by the CPAB, which are then discussed with the audit firm. The partner is concerned he will look bad and may even face penalties from the firm if there are serious deficiencies identified.

In the current meeting between Ann and the partner on the audit engagement, they feel they need to provide further support for one of the judgmental audit areas on the audit engagement in order to avoid scrutiny from the CPAB, and that they also need to go through the working papers and ensure that all work was appropriately signed off by the manager and partner. The partner suggests to Ann that she include an additional memo to support their conclusion on the judgmental audit area in question, that she date this memo as if she had completed it at the time she and the staff originally did the work, and that she ensure all required signatures are in the working papers. Ann reminds the partner this is in violation of CAS 230 and the firm's quality control standards; however, the partner assures Ann that no one will know and they can avoid possible penalties that would result if they do not ensure that their audit engagement will pass inspection. "After all," the engagement partner reminds Ann, "you will soon be considered for promotion to partner and you would not want a negative inspection outcome on a prior engagement to stand in your way of making partner."

REQUIRED

a. Refer to CAS 230 A.1, A.21, and A.22 and explain what the standard says about the requirement to complete a file. What does the standard say about whether documentation can be added after the documentation completion date?

b. Refer to the ethical decision making framework in Chapter 4 and recommend what Anne should do.

CLIENT ACCEPTANCE, PLANNING, AND MATERIALITY

Chapter 4 introduced the audit process and provided a broad overview. In this chapter, we begin to examine the process in more depth, starting with two critical stages of the audit process—client acceptance and audit planning.

LEARNING OBJECTIVES

After studying this chapter, you should be able to:

1 Understand why adequate audit planning is essential.

2 Use professional judgment to make client acceptance/continuance decisions.

3 Gain an understanding of the client's business and environment.

4 Perform and evaluate preliminary analytical procedures.

5 Evaluate preliminary audit planning activities and develop preliminary overall audit strategy.

6 Understand and apply the concept of materiality to the audit.

7 Use professional judgment to determine overall (or planning) materiality.

8 Use professional judgment to determine performance materiality.

9 Use professional judgment to determine specific materiality.

10 Apply materiality to evaluate misstatements and to complete the audit.

STANDARDS REFERENCED IN THIS CHAPTER

CAS 210 – Agreeing the terms of audit engagements

CAS 300 – Planning an audit of financial statements

CAS 315 – Identifying and assessing the risks of material misstatement through understanding the entity and its environment

CAS 320 – Materiality in planning and performing an audit

CAS 450 – Evaluation of misstatements identified during the audit

CAS 600 – Special considerations: audits of group financial statements

CAS 610 – Using the work of internal auditors

CAS 620 – Using the work of an auditor's expert

The Fall Of Enron: Did Anyone Understand Its Business?

The bankruptcy of Enron Corporation represents one of the biggest corporate collapses in American history. Despite being listed as number seven on the Fortune 500 list with a market capitalization of $75 billion before its collapse, Enron's meltdown was rapid. The fall began in October 2001 when Enron officials reported a shocking $618 million quarterly loss related to allegedly mysterious and hidden related party partnerships with company insiders. Then, in early November 2001, company officials were forced to admit that they had falsely claimed almost $600 million in earnings dating back to 1997, requiring the restatement of four years of audited financial statements. By the end of 2001, the company was in bankruptcy. *continued >*

continued Enron was created in 1985 out of a merger of two gas pipelines, and was a pioneer in trading natural gas and electricity in the newly deregulated utilities markets. In its earlier years, Enron made its money from hard assets like pipelines. However, by the end of the 1990s, 80 percent of Enron's earnings came from a more vague business known as "wholesale energy operations and services." Enron had built new markets, such as in the trading of weather securities. In early 2001, speculation about Enron's business dealings began to surface. One highly regarded investment banker publicly stated that no one could explain how Enron actually made money.

In the wake of the collapse, many wondered how these issues could have gone undetected for so long. Many point to Enron's incredibly complicated business structure and related vague and confusing financial statements. "What we are looking at here is an example of superbly complex financial reports. They didn't have to lie. All they had to do was to obfuscate it with sheer complexity," noted John Dingell, U.S. Congressman from Michigan. Others even allege that the men running the company never understood their business concept because it was too complicated.

Apparently, the complexity and uncertainty surrounding Enron's business and financial statements fooled its auditors, too. Enron's auditor faced a flurry of attacks, class action lawsuits, and a criminal indictment that ultimately led to the firm's demise. In December 2001 congressional testimony, the audit firm's CEO admitted that the firm's professional judgment "turned out to be wrong" and that they mistakenly let Enron keep the related entities separate when they should have been consolidated.

The Enron disaster continues to provide many lessons for the auditing profession. One to be underscored for auditors is the paramount importance of understanding the company's business and industry to identify significant business risks that increase the risk of material misstatements in the financial statements. Without that understanding, it will be almost impossible to identify the next Enron.

Source: Based on Bethany McLean, "Why Enron Went Bust," *Fortune*, December 24, 2001, pp. 58–68.

As the chapter's opening vignette illustrates, Enron's complex and confusing business structure helped disguise material misstatements in Enron's financial statements for several years. Gaining an understanding of the client's business and industry is one of the most important steps in audit planning. This chapter explains audit planning in detail, including gaining an understanding of the client's business and industry, performing preliminary analytical procedures, developing an overall audit strategy, and making a preliminary judgment about materiality.

LO **1** Understand why adequate audit planning is essential.

THE IMPORTANCE OF AUDIT PLANNING

The purpose of planning is to provide for effective conduct of the audit (CAS 300, par. 04), and there are three main reasons why the auditor should plan engagements properly:

1. To enable the auditor to obtain sufficient appropriate audit evidence;
2. To help keep audit costs reasonable; and
3. To avoid misunderstandings with the client.

Obtaining sufficient appropriate audit evidence is essential if the public accounting firm is to minimize legal liability and maintain a good reputation in the professional community. Keeping costs reasonable helps the firm remain competitive and retain its clients. Avoiding misunderstandings with the client is important for good client relations and for facilitating quality work at a reasonable cost. For example, suppose the auditor informs the client that the audit will be completed before June 30 but is unable to finish it until August because of inadequate staff. The client is likely to be upset with the public accounting firm and may even sue for breach of contract.

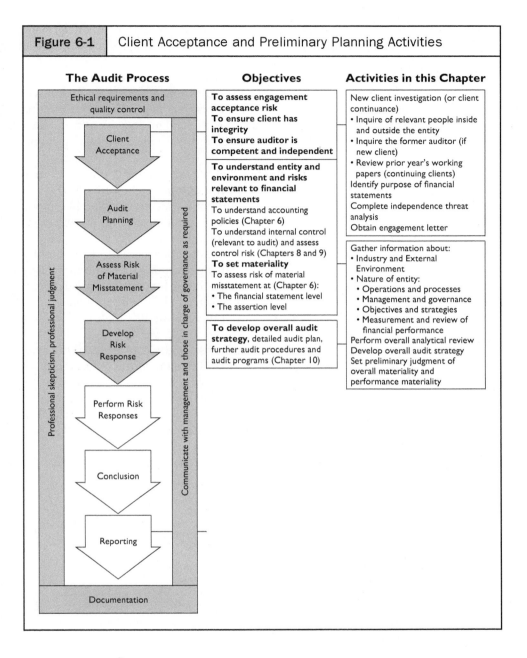

Figure 6-1 | Client Acceptance and Preliminary Planning Activities

The Audit Process	Objectives	Activities in this Chapter

The shaded arrows of Figure 6-1 highlight the four phases associated with audit planning. In this chapter we cover the preliminary engagement objectives (client continuance, assessment of auditor independence and competence, and establishing understanding of the terms of engagement) that must be completed prior to actually planning the audit. We also cover the preliminary planning activities that assist the auditor in developing a preliminary audit strategy—understanding the entity and the environment, performing the preliminary analytical review, and establishing overall and performance materiality. We cover the remaining objectives of the planning phase in the subsequent chapters.

Before beginning our discussion, we briefly introduce three risk terms: *acceptable audit risk, client business risk,* and *risk of material misstatement.* These three risks significantly influence the conduct and cost of audits, and therefore much of the early planning of audits deals with obtaining information to help auditors assess these risks.

Acceptable audit risk is a measure of how willing the auditor is to accept that the financial statements may be materially misstated after the audit is completed and an unqualified opinion has been issued. When the auditor decides on a lower acceptable

Acceptable audit risk—a measure of how willing the auditor is to accept that the financial statements may be materially misstated after the audit is completed and an unqualified opinion has been issued.

audit risk, it means that the auditor wants to be more certain that the financial statements are *not* materially misstated. Zero risk is certainty, and a 100 percent risk is complete uncertainty.

Client business risk is the risk that the entity will fail to achieve its objectives or execute its strategies. Business risk can arise from a variety of factors, including significant changes in industry conditions, events such as regulatory changes, or setting inappropriate objectives or strategies. For example, the auditor may identify declines in economic conditions that adversely affect sales and the collectability of accounts receivable.

Risk of material misstatement is the risk that the financial statements are materially misstated prior to audit. This consists of two components, inherent risk and control risk. Inherent risk is a measure of the auditor's assessment of the likelihood of material misstatement in an account balance before considering the effectiveness of controls. Control risk is the risk that material misstatement will not be prevented, or detected and corrected, on a timely basis. For example, if the auditor finds that changing economic conditions are causing declining sales and increasing credit risk, the auditor would conclude that inherent risk for accounts receivable is high. Further, if the auditor finds that this risk is beyond the client's control, the auditor would conclude that the risk of material misstatement is high for accounts receivable.

Assessing acceptable audit risk, client business risk, and risk of material misstatement is an important part of audit planning because it helps determine the amount of evidence that will need to be accumulated and the experience level of staff assigned to the engagement. For example, if risk of material misstatement for inventory valuation is high because of complex valuation issues, more evidence will be accumulated in the audit of inventory valuation and more experienced staff will be assigned to perform testing in this area.

CAS 300.9 states that the auditor must develop an audit plan that includes the following components:

- The nature, timing, and extent of audit procedures for the purpose of risk assessment.
- The nature, timing, and extent of additional audit procedures, linked to the individual audit assertions.
- Any other audit procedures that are needed for the audit to be conducted in accordance with GAAS.

In order for auditors to develop a detailed plan of action, they must have a clear understanding of the risks of material misstatement in the financial statements—the "what could go wrong" picture.

CLIENT ACCEPTANCE AND CONTINUANCE

Before actually planning the audit, the auditor performs the following *preliminary engagement activities*:

1. Perform procedures to assist the auditor in deciding whether to accept or continue doing the audit for the client. An experienced auditor (usually a partner) typically makes this decision.
2. Consider ethical requirements, including independence.
3. Identify the purpose of the financial statements.
4. Obtain an understanding with the client about the terms of the engagement. The purpose of this is to avoid misunderstandings.

CAS 300 A.5 explains that these preliminary engagement activities assist the auditor in identifying and evaluating events or circumstances that may adversely affect the auditor's ability to plan and perform the audit.

Client business risk—the risk that the client will fail to achieve its objectives related to (1) reliability of financial reporting, (2) effectiveness and efficiency of operations, and (3) compliance with laws and regulations.

Risk of material misstatement—the risk that the financial statements are materially misstated prior to audit. It represents auditor's expectation of misstatements after considering the effect of internal controls on inherent risk.

CAS

LO 2 Use professional judgment to make client acceptance/continuance decisions.

CAS

Decide to Accept or Continue the Audit Engagement

Even though obtaining and retaining clients is not easy in a competitive profession such as public accounting, a public accounting firm must use care in deciding which clients are acceptable. The firm's legal and professional responsibilities are such that clients who lack integrity or argue constantly about the proper conduct of the audit and fees can cause more problems than they are worth.

Quality Control As we learned in Chapter 2, one of the key elements of quality control is the firm's policies and procedures regarding client acceptance or continuance. These policies should provide the firm with assurance that it will only undertake engagements where the firm:

- Is competent to perform the engagement—this includes capabilities as well as time and resources;
- Can comply with relevant ethical requirements; and
- Has considered the integrity of the client.

Based upon the broad criteria above, each public accounting firm develops its specific client acceptance and continuance policies. For example, some firms may refuse clients in what they perceive to be high-risk industries (either because of the nature of the industry or the competence of the firm) and may even discontinue auditing existing clients in those industries. Some smaller public accounting firms will not do audits of publicly held clients because of the complexity of regulatory filings and the potential litigation risk. If we relate this to overall audit risk, an auditor is unlikely to accept a new client or continue serving an existing client if overall acceptable audit risk is below the threshold the firm is willing to accept.

New Client Investigation Before accepting a new client, most public accounting firms investigate the company to determine its acceptability. To the extent possible, the prospective client's standing in the business community, financial stability, and relations with its previous public accounting firm should be evaluated. For example, many public accounting firms use considerable caution in accepting new clients from newly formed, rapidly growing businesses. Many of these businesses fail financially and expose the public accounting firm to significant potential liability.

For prospective clients that have previously been audited by another public accounting firm, as we learned in Chapter 3, the new (successor) public accountant (PA) is required to communicate with the predecessor auditor. The purpose of the requirement is to help the successor auditor evaluate whether to accept the engagement. The communication may, for example, inform the successor auditor that the client lacks integrity or that there have been disputes over accounting principles, audit procedures, or fees.

The burden of initiating the communication rests with the successor auditor. In keeping with the auditors' confidentiality responsibilities, permission must be obtained from the client before the communication can be made. The predecessor auditor is required to respond to the request for information. In the event that there are legal problems or disputes between the client and the predecessor, the latter's response can be limited to stating that no information will be provided. The successor should seriously consider declining a prospective engagement, without considerable investigation, if a client will not allow contact with the predecessor auditor or the predecessor will not provide a comprehensive response.

Even when a prospective client has been audited by another public accounting firm, other investigations are needed. Sources of information include local lawyers, other public accountants, banks, and other businesses. Many practitioners take advantage of the internet as a search tool to learn more about the potential new client and its key operations. In addition, they use database search tools or customized search engines to examine financial data or recent publications about the client.

Continuing Clients Considering whether or not to continue doing the audit of an existing client is as important a decision as deciding whether or not to accept a new

Table 6-1	Indicators that Raise Doubt about Management's Integrity
History of non-compliance with laws and regulations, such as bribery or tax evasion.	
Poor reputation for honesty or ethics in the business community.	
Suspicions that management might be involved in criminal activities, such as money laundering.	
Highly complex transactions or activities that do not appear to be necessary.	
Poor tone at the top (refer to entity-level controls in Chapter 4).	
Management reluctant to provide requested information.	
History of not disclosing important information in past engagements.	

client. For that reason, public accounting firms evaluate existing clients annually to determine whether there are reasons for not continuing to do the audit. Previous conflicts over such things as the appropriate scope of the audit, the type of opinion to issue, or fees may cause the auditor to discontinue association. The auditor may also determine that the client lacks basic integrity and therefore should no longer be a client. If there is a lawsuit against a public accounting firm by a client or a suit against the client by the public accounting firm, the firm should not do the audit because its independence could be questioned. Table 6-1 provides a summary of some key indicators that could raise doubt about management's integrity.

Even if none of these conditions exist (i.e., previous conflicts, concerns over management intergrity, or lawsuits), the public accounting firm may decide not to continue doing audits for a client because of excessive risk. For example, a public accounting firm might decide that there is considerable risk of a regulatory conflict between a governmental agency and a client, which could result in financial failure of the client. Even if the engagement is profitable, the risk may exceed the immediate benefits of doing the audit. In other high-risk clients, the public accounting firm may conclude that the client is acceptable. However, the fee proposed to the client is likely to be higher due to the higher audit costs.

Consider Relevant Ethical Requirements

CAS CAS 300 requires that the auditor comply with ethical requirements, which were discussed in Chapters 2 and 4, including competence and independence. Depending upon the specific client, there may be other ethical matters to evaluate such as confidentiality issues that could arise.

Assess Competence As mentioned above, the auditor must consider whether there is staff with the capabilities to perform the audit, as well as the time and resources to perform the audit. If the auditor does not have the expertise or available staff to audit the client, then the engagement should be declined.

Assess Independence As we learned in Chapter 3, in order to assess independence, the auditor conducts an independence threat analysis. The five threats to independence (i.e., self-interest, self-review, advocacy, familiarity, and intimidation) must be explicitly assessed, and any potential threats described. The auditor then determines whether it is possible to implement safeguards to mitigate the threat (e.g., changing the partner in charge of an engagement to deal with the familiarity threat). If safeguards can be put into place, or there are no threats, the engagement can be accepted or continued. If there are threats without compensating safeguards available, or the safeguards do not adequately mitigate the threat, the engagement must be declined or, in the case of a continuing client, the auditor would resign.

Identify the Purpose of the Financial Statements

CAS CAS 210, *Agreeing the Terms of the Audit Engagement*, specifies two pre-conditions for an audit—the use by management of an acceptable financial reporting framework

and the agreement with management and those in charge of governance on the terms of the engagement. To assess the first precondition, the auditor would confirm with the client that the financial statements would be prepared under the relevant financial reporting framework, such as IFRS or ASPE, and would also consider the purpose of the financial statements, and the nature of the reporting entity.

Understanding the purpose of the financial statements requires the auditor to consider the likely financial statement users and their intended uses of the financial statements. The most likely uses of the financial statements can be determined from previous experience in the engagement and discussion with management. However, the auditor would inquire about plans for additional capital (such as issuance of shares or procurement of a bank loan) to determine if there are additional users. The auditor is likely to accumulate more evidence when the financial statements are to be used extensively or for a specific purpose (for instance, investors deciding to invest in a particular company, prospective lenders evaluating whether to grant a loan, or a current lender evaluating whether the company meets the specific lending covenants).

Obtain an Understanding of the Terms of the Engagement

The second pre-condition of an audit is that a clear understanding of the terms of the engagement should exist between the client and the public accounting firm. CAS 210 requires that auditors obtain an understanding with the client in an **engagement letter**, including engagement objectives, the responsibilities of the auditor and management, identification of the financial reporting framework used by management, reference to the expected form and content of the audit report, and the engagement's limitations. For a private company, like Hillsburg Hardware, the engagement letter is typically signed by management. Figure 6-2 is the engagement letter for Hillsburg Hardware Limited.

The engagement letter should also state any restrictions to be imposed on the auditor's work, deadlines for completing the audit, assistance to be provided by the client's personnel in obtaining records and documents or, if the client has an internal audit department, any assistance with the actual audit work, and schedules to be prepared for the auditor. The letter often includes an agreement on fees. The letter is important for planning the timing of the audit. For example, if the deadline is soon after the balance sheet date, a significant portion of the audit must be done before year-end. If unexpected circumstances arise or if client assistance is not available, arrangements must be made to extend the amount of time for the engagement.

The auditor must carefully assess client-imposed restrictions on the audit as they could affect the procedures performed, auditor independence, and possibly even the type of audit opinion issued. If the client's management imposes a limitation on the scope of the auditor's work, such as denying access to certain information, the auditor should decline the audit engagement if the limitation could result in the auditor having to disclaim the opinion on the financial statements. Table 6-2 provides some

> **CAS**
>
> **Engagement letter**—a written agreement between the public accounting firm and the client as to the terms of the engagement for the conduct of the audit and related services.

Table 6-2	Possible Scope Limitations That Would Cause the Auditor to Decline an Engagement
Unrealistic deadlines are imposed by management.	
The auditor doubts that the records and/or documents provided by the client will be available or reliable.	
Management imposes restricted access to certain persons within or outside the entity who may have relevant information or evidence.	
The auditor has restricted access to certain premises (such as warehouse or operating locations).	
The auditor has doubts about management integrity.	
Management will not accept certain staff members chosen by the firm to perform the audit.	
Management has indicated its intention to not sign requested written representations at the end of the audit.	

Source: Based on CPA Canada, *Guide to Review Engagements*, Toronto, 2016.

| Figure 6-2 | Engagement Letter |

June 14, 2018

Boritz, Kao, Kadous & Co., LLP
Halifax, Nova Scotia
B3M 3JP

Mr. Rick Chulick, President
Hillsburg Hardware Limited
2146 Willow Street
Halifax, Nova Scotia
B3H 3F9

Dear Mr. Chulick:

The purpose of this letter is to outline the terms of our engagement to audit the financial statements of Hillsburg Hardware Limited for the year ending December 31, 2018.

Objective, scope, and limitations

Our statutory function as auditor of Hillsburg Hardware Limited is to report to the shareholders by expressing an opinion on Hillsburg Hardware Limited's financial statements. We will conduct our audit in accordance with Canadian generally accepted auditing standards and will issue an audit report.

It is important to recognize that there are limitations inherent in the auditing process. Since audits are based on the concept of selective testing of the data underlying the financial statements, they are subject to the limitation that material misstatements, if they exist, may not be detected. Because of the nature of fraud, including attempts at concealment through collusion and forgery, an audit designed and executed in accordance with Canadian generally accepted auditing standards may not detect a material fraud. Further, while effective internal control reduces the likelihood that misstatements will occur and remain undetected, it does not eliminate the possibility. For these reasons, we cannot guarantee that misstatements or other illegal acts, if present, will be detected.

Our responsibilities

We will be responsible for performing the audit in accordance with Canadian generally accepted auditing standards. These standards require that we plan and perform the audit to obtain reasonable assurance about whether the financial statements present fairly, in all material respects, the financial position results of operations, and cash flows in accordance with Accounting Standards for Private Enterprises. Accordingly, we will design our audit to provide reasonable, but not absolute, assurance of detecting fraud, errors, and other irregularities that have a material effect on the financial statements taken as a whole, including illegal acts the consequences of which have a material effect on the financial statements.

One of the underlying principles of the profession is a duty of confidentiality with respect to client affairs. Accordingly, except for information that is in or enters the public domain, we will not provide any third party with information related to Hillsburg Hardware Limited without Hillsburg Hardware Limited's permission, unless required to do so by legal authority, or by the rules of professional conduct/code of ethics.

We will communicate in writing to the those charged with governance the relationships between us and Hillsburg Hardware Limited that, in our professional judgment, may reasonably be thought to bear on our independence. Further, we will confirm our independence with respect to Hillsburg Hardware Limited.

The objective of our audit is to obtain reasonable assurance that the financial statements are free of material misstatement. However, if we identify any of the following matters, they will be communicated to the appropriate level of management, including the those charged with governance:

(a) misstatements, other than trivial errors;

(b) fraud;

(c) misstatements that may cause future financial statements to be materially misstated;

(d) illegal or possibly illegal acts, other than those considered inconsequential;

(e) significant weakness in internal control; and

(f) certain related-party transactions.

The matters communicated will be those that we identify during the course of our audit. Audits do not usually identify all matters that may be of interest to management in discharging its responsibilities. The type and significance of the matter to be communicated will determine the level of management to which the communication is directed.

We will consider Hillsburg Hardware Limited's internal control over financial reporting solely for the purpose of determining the nature, timing, and extent of auditing procedures necessary for expressing our opinion on the financial statements. This consideration will not be sufficient for us to render an opinion on the effectiveness of internal control over financial reporting.

Management's responsibilities

Management is responsible for:

(a) The fair presentation of Hillsburg Hardware Limited's financial statements in accordance with Accounting Standards for Private Enterprises;

continued >

Completeness of information:

(b) providing us with and making available complete financial records and related data and copies of all minutes of meetings of shareholders, directors, and committees of directors;

(c) providing us with information relating to any known or probable instances of non-compliance with legislative or regulatory requirements, including financial reporting requirements;

(d) providing us with information relating to any illegal or possibly illegal acts, and all facts related thereto;

(e) providing us with information regarding all related parties and related-party transactions;

Fraud and error:

(f) the design and implementation of internal controls to prevent and detect fraud and error;

(g) an assessment of the risk that the financial statements may be materially misstated as a result of fraud;

(h) providing us with information relating to fraud or suspected fraud affecting the entity involving
(i) management, (ii) employees who have significant roles in internal control, or (iii) others, where the fraud could have a material effect on the financial statements;

(i) providing us with information relating to any allegations of fraud or suspected fraud affecting the entity's financial statements communicated by employees, former employees, analysts, regulators, or others;

(j) communicating its belief that the effects of any uncorrected financial statement misstatements aggregated during the audit are immaterial, both individually and in the aggregate, to the financial statements taken as a whole;

Recognition, measurement, and disclosure:

(k) providing us with an assessment of the reasonableness of significant assumptions underlying fair value measurements and disclosures in the financial statements;

(l) providing us with any plans or intentions that may affect the carrying value or classification of assets or liabilities;

(m) providing us with the measurement and disclosure of transactions with related parties;

(n) providing us with an assessment of significant estimates and all known areas of measurement uncertainty;

(o) providing us with claims and possible claims, whether or not they have been discussed with Hillsburg Hardware Limited legal counsel;

(p) providing us with information relating to other liabilities and gain or loss contingencies, including those associated with guarantees, whether written or oral, under which Hillsburg Hardware Limited is contingently liable;

(q) providing us with information on whether or not Hillsburg Hardware Limited has satisfactory title to assets, liens or encumbrances on assets, and assets pledged as collateral;

(r) providing us with information relating to compliance with aspects of contractual agreements that may affect the financial statements;

(s) providing us with information concerning subsequent events; and

(t) providing us with written confirmation of significant representations provided to us during the engagement on matters that are
(i) directly related to items that are material, either individually or in the aggregate, to the financial statements;
(ii) not directly related to items that are material to the financial statements but are significant, either individually or in the aggregate, to the engagement; and
(iii) relevant to your judgments or estimates that are material, either individually or in the aggregate, to the financial statements.

Coordination of the Audit

Assistance is to be supplied by your personnel, including preparation of schedules and analysis of accounts, as described in a separate attachment.

Fees

Our fees are based on the amount of time required at various levels of responsibility, plus out-of-pocket expenses (i.e., travel, printing, telephone, and communications) payable upon presentation of billing. We will notify you immediately of any circumstances we encounter that could significantly affect our estimate of total fees.

We appreciate the opportunity to be of service to Hillsburg Hardware Limited. The above terms of our engagement shall remain operative until amended, terminated, or superseded in writing.

If you have any questions about the contents of this letter, please raise them. If the services as outlined are in accordance with your requirements and if the above terms are acceptable, please sign the copy of this letter in the space provided and return it to us.

Yours very truly,
J.E. Boritz
Boritz, Kao, Kadous & Co., LLP
Accepted by:
Title: President
Date: June 14, 2018

Arthur Andersen partner Michael Jones, in his documentation of the critical meeting attended by key Andersen partners to discuss their client continuance decision, recorded the following:

> We discussed Enron's dependence on transaction execution to meet financial objectives, the fact that Enron often is creating industries and markets and transactions for which there are no specific rules, which requires significant judgment and that Enron is aggressive in its transaction structuring. We discussed consultation among the engagement team, with Houston management, practice management, and the PSG (Professional Services Group) to ensure that we are not making decisions in isolation.

> Ultimately, the conclusion was reached to retain Enron as a client citing that it appeared that we had the appropriate people and processes in place to serve Enron and manage our engagement risks. We discussed whether there would be a perceived independence issue solely considering our level of fees. We discussed that the concerns should not be the magnitude of fees but on the nature of fees.

As you can see, the partners addressed several of the key issues in the client acceptance decision—the nature of the client, whether the firm had the competencies to perform the engagement, and auditor independence. Unfortunately, the partners' conclusion, that Arthur Andersen had the appropriate processes in place to keep audit risk at an acceptable level, was incorrect.

Source: Based on Linda Thorne, Dawn Massey, and Joanne Jones, "An investigation of social influence: Explaining the effect of group discussion on consensus in auditors' ethical decision making," *Business Ethics Quarterly*, vol. 14, no. 3, 2004, 525–551.

examples of potential scope limitations that would likely cause the auditor to conclude that it will be unlikely to collect sufficient and appropriate evidence and therefore decline or discontinue the engagement.

CONCEPT CHECK

C6-1 Why does the auditor assess clients for acceptability prior to conducting the audit engagement?

C6-2 What are some of the typical reasons that a client wants a financial statement audit?

LO 3 Gain an understanding of the client's business and environment.

CAS

UNDERSTAND THE NATURE OF CLIENT'S BUSINESS AND ENVIRONMENT

CAS 315, *Identifying and assessing the risks of material misstatement through understanding the entity and its environment*, requires the auditor to obtain knowledge of the entity's business and environment in order to assess the risk of material misstatement. This is a key way in which the auditor reduces audit risk to an acceptably low level. A thorough understanding of the client's business and industry, and knowledge about the company's operations, enable the auditor to identify those business risks that might result in material misstatements. The auditor then evaluates whether the entity has adequate processes in place to address those business risks.

Figure 6-3 provides an overview of the approach to understanding the client's business and environment. In this chapter, we focus on the industry, the regulatory and external environment, and the various factors that help us understand the nature of the entity's business.

Industry, Regulatory, and External Environment

To develop effective audit plans, auditors of all companies must have the expertise to assess the client's environment—including its industry, as well as the regulatory and the broader external environment. There are three primary reasons for

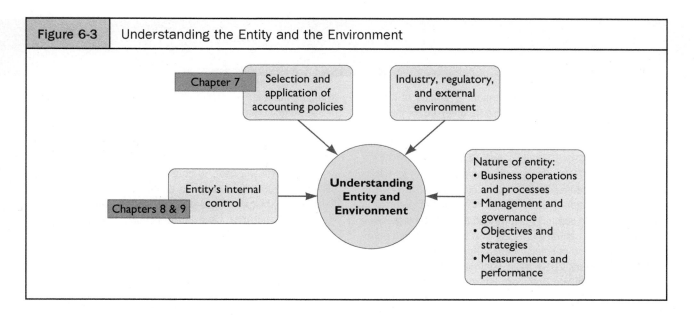

Figure 6-3 | Understanding the Entity and the Environment

Chapter 7 — Selection and application of accounting policies

Industry, regulatory, and external environment

Chapters 8 & 9 — Entity's internal control

Understanding Entity and Environment

Nature of entity:
• Business operations and processes
• Management and governance
• Objectives and strategies
• Measurement and performance

obtaining a good understanding of the client's industry, regulatory, and external environment:

1. Risks associated with specific industries may affect the auditor's assessment of client business risk and acceptable audit risk—and may even influence auditors against accepting engagements in riskier industries, such as mining, high technology, biochemical, or small financial service organizations.
2. Many risks are common to all clients in certain industries. Familiarity with those risks aids the auditor in assessing their relevance to the client. Examples include potential inventory obsolescence in the fashion clothing industry, potential accounts receivable collection risks in the consumer loan industry, and risks of inadequate reserves for losses in the casualty insurance industry.
3. Many industries have unique accounting requirements that the auditor must understand to evaluate whether the client's financial statements are in accordance with the applicable financial reporting framework. For example, if the auditor is doing an audit of a city government, the auditor must understand governmental accounting and auditing requirements. Unique accounting requirements exist for not-for-profit organizations, financial institutions, and many other organizations.

As highlighted in the Enron case discussed in the opening vignette of this chapter, audit failure is often the result of the auditor's lack of understanding of the client's industry. Relevant factors that auditors take into consideration include industry conditions such as the competitive environment, supplier and customer relationships, and technological developments. For instance, an auditor of a utility company would want to know how recent deregulation in this industry has increased competition and pricing.

The regulatory environment includes the applicable financial reporting framework (for instance, public companies are required to use IFRS), and the legal and political environment. To assess the legal and political environment, the auditor would consider factors such as legislation and regulation that significantly affect the client's operations, taxation, and environmental requirements. As highlighted in Chapter 4, the auditor has a responsibility to consider both direct and indirect laws and regulations. Auditing in Action 6-2 illustrates two examples of non-compliance with indirect laws and regulations that have a significant impact on the financial statements as liabilities and, potentially, in relation to the client's ability to continue as a going concern.

The following two cases provide graphic examples of lack of compliance with regulations and illustrate the need for the auditor to understand the client's regulatory environment.

Niko Resources Ltd. (Calgary, Alberta), an oil and gas company, was fined $9.499 million and placed on three years' probation in June 2011. The cause? Providing access to a vehicle and travel expenses (estimated at close to $200 000) to a government official of Bangladesh. The apparent purpose of these bribes was to suppress government action after explosions occurred at Niko's natural gas fields. Niko was prosecuted under Canada's Corruption of Foreign Public Officials Act.

In early January 2012, Valle Foam Industries (Brampton, Ontario) and its affiliate Domfoam International Inc. (Montreal, Quebec) were fined $12.5 million by the Competition Bureau. After a two-year investigation, the two companies admitted that they had worked with their competitors to fix the prices of their foam products for more than 11 years.

As a result of these events, the auditors of these companies would need to be alert to the fact that the weak controls increase the risk of material misstatement, and they will have to adjust the audit strategy to take into account the possibility of additional control violations or illegal acts. An important consideration for the auditor is to determine what processes these companies have put in place to avoid similar events from happening in the future.

The auditor will need to consider the impact of the illegal act on the company's ability to continue as a going concern. For instance, being charged under Canada's Corruption of Foreign Officials Act may result in the company being barred (for up to 10 years) from bidding on federal government projects or those financed by the World Bank. This can significantly impact an organization's ability to earn revenue and continue as a going concern.

Sources: Based on Emily Jackson, "Brampton firm fined $12.5 million for price fixing," *Toronto Star*, January 6, 2012, p. B2, accessed July 22, 2017, at **http://www.thestar.com/business/2012/01/06/brampton_firm_fined_125_million_for_price_fixing.html**. Lauren Krugel, "Niko fined $9.5M for Bangladeshi bribe," *Toronto Star*, June 25, 2011, p. B3. Jonathon Ratner, "SNC-Lavalin Group could face ban from government contract bidding," *Financial Post*, February 23, 2015, accessed July 22, 2017.

The auditor must also understand other external factors, such as general economic conditions, interest rates and availability of financing, and inflation or currency revaluation. For instance, in the case of a utility company, the auditor would want to consider how fluctuations in energy prices impact firm operations.

Nature of Entity's Business

CAS CAS 315 explains that understanding of the nature of an entity is necessary so that the auditor can understand the organization's structure (such as whether it has subsidiaries or other components in multiple locations), as well as its ownership structure.

Business Operations and Processes

The auditor should understand factors such as major sources of revenue, key customers and suppliers, sources of financing, and information about related parties that may indicate areas of increased client business risk. For example, many technology firms are dependent on one or a few products that may become obsolete due to new technologies or stronger competitors. Dependence on a few major customers may result in material losses from bad debts or obsolete inventory.

Tour Client Facilities and Operations A tour of the client's facilities is helpful in obtaining a better understanding of the client's business operations because it provides an opportunity to observe operations firsthand and to meet key personnel. By viewing physical facilities, the auditor can assess physical safeguards over assets and interpret accounting data related to assets, such as inventory in process and factory equipment. With such first-hand knowledge, the auditor is better able to identify risks from factors such as unused equipment or potentially unsalable inventory. Discussions with non-accounting employees during the tour and throughout the audit also help the auditor learn more about the client's business to aid in assessing risk.

Identify Related Parties Transactions with related parties are important to auditors because they must be properly recorded and disclosed in the financial statements if they are material or if information about them could affect decision making. Generally accepted accounting standards for IFRS, ASPE, and ASNPO require disclosure of the nature of the related-party relationship; a description of transactions, including dollar amounts; and amounts due from and to related parties. Transactions with related parties are not arm's-length transactions. There is a risk that they were not valued at the same amount as they would have been if the transactions had been with an independent party. Most auditors assess inherent risk as high for related parties and related-party transactions, because of both the accounting disclosure requirements and the lack of independence between the parties involved in the transactions.

The auditor should identify all related parties and related-party transactions, as both quantitative and qualitative considerations are used to decide whether related-party transactions should be disclosed. A party is considered to be a related party if it has the ability to influence decisions, either directly or indirectly. A **related-party transaction** is any transaction between the client and a related party. Common examples include sales or purchase transactions between a parent company and its subsidiary, exchanges of equipment between two companies owned by the same person, and loans to officers. A less common example, called economic dependence, is the potential for exercise of significant influence on an audit client by, for example, its most important supplier or customer, lender, or borrower.

Related-party transaction—any transaction between the client and a related party.

Because material related party transactions must be properly recorded in accordance with accounting standards and disclosed, all related parties need to be identified and included in audit documentation early in the engagement. Having all related parties included in the audit files, as well as making sure all auditors on the team know who the related parties are, helps auditors identify undisclosed related-party transactions as they do the audit. Common ways of identifying related parties include inquiry of management, review of shareholder and board minutes, review of Ontario Securities Commission (OSC) or Securities and Exchange Commission (SEC) filings, and examining shareholder listings to identify principal shareholders.

For publicly listed entities that have shares traded on the SEC, the auditor needs to be aware of regulatory restrictions. The Sarbanes–Oxley Act prohibits related-party transactions that involve personal loans to any director or executive officer of a public company. Banks and other financial institutions in the United States, as in Canada, however, are permitted to make normal loans, such as residential mortgages, to their directors and officers using market rates.

Management and Governance

Since management establishes a company's strategies and business processes, an auditor should assess management's philosophy and operating style, and its ability to identify and respond to risk, as these significantly influence the risk of material misstatements in the financial statements. A study of 340 financial reporting fraud cases found that, in 90 percent of the cases, either the chief executive officer (CEO) or the chief financial officer (CFO) was involved in perpetuating the fraud.

A firm's governance includes its organizational structure, as well as the activities of the board of directors and the audit committee. An effective board of directors helps ensure that the company takes only appropriate risks, while the audit committee, through oversight of financial reporting, can reduce the likelihood of overly aggressive accounting. (will be discussed further in Chapter 8.) To gain an understanding of the client's governance system, the auditor should consider the company's code of ethics and evaluate the corporate minutes.

Code of Ethics For any organization, a code of ethics and the processes to ensure adherence are a powerful signal of corporate conduct. Auditors should become knowledgeable about the company's code of ethics, and examine any changes and waivers of the code of conduct that have implications for the governance system and related integrity and ethical values of senior management.

Minutes of Meetings The corporate minutes are the official record of the meetings of the board of directors and shareholders. They include summaries of the most important topics discussed at these meetings and the decisions made by the directors and shareholders. Information relevant to the audit included in minutes includes authorizations and discussions by the board of directors affecting inherent risk.

Common authorizations in the minutes include compensation of officers, new contracts and agreements, acquisitions of property, loans, and dividend payments. While reading the minutes, the auditor should identify relevant authorizations and include the information in the working papers by making an abstract of the minutes or by obtaining a copy and underlining significant portions. Before the audit is completed, there must be a follow-up of this information to ensure that management has complied with decisions made by the shareholders and the board of directors. As an illustration, the authorized compensation of officers should be traced to each individual officer's payroll record as a test of whether the correct total compensation was paid. Similarly, the auditor should compare the authorizations of loans with notes payable to make certain that these liabilities are recorded.

Information included in the minutes affecting the auditor's assessment of inherent risk is likely to involve more general discussions. To illustrate, assume that the minutes state that the board of directors discussed two topics: changes in the company's industry that affect the usefulness of existing machinery and equipment, and a possible lawsuit by Environment Canada for chemical see page at a plant in Ontario. The first discussion is likely to affect the inherent risk of obsolete equipment and the second one the inherent risk of an illegal act; both could affect the financial statements (the valuation of property, plant, and equipment, and the disclosure of a contingent liability).

Client Objectives and Strategies

Strategies are approaches followed by the entity to achieve organizational objectives. Auditors should understand client objectives related to:

1. Reliability of financial reporting.
2. Effectiveness and efficiency of operations.
3. Compliance with laws and regulations.

Despite management's best efforts, business risks arise that threaten management's ability to achieve its objectives. For example, product quality can have a significant impact on the financial statements through lost sales and through warranty and product liability claims. Toyota, Inc., suffered significant losses arising from business risks when production problems involving gas pedals and brakes in several of its most popular vehicles triggered significant declines in sales and shareholder value.

As part of understanding the client's objectives in relation to compliance with laws and regulations, the auditor should be familiar with the terms of client contracts and other legal obligations. These can include such diverse items as long-term notes and bonds payable, stock options, pension plans, contracts with vendors for future delivery of supplies, software usage and maintenance contracts, government contracts for completion and delivery of manufactured products, royalty agreements, union contracts, and leases.

Most contracts are of primary interest in individual parts of the audit and, in practice, receive special attention during the different phases of the detailed tests. For example, the provisions of a pension plan would receive substantial emphasis as a part of the audit of the unfunded liability for pensions. The auditor should review and abstract the documents early in the engagement to gain a better perspective of the organization and to better assess risk. Later, these documents can be examined carefully as a part of tests of individual audit areas.

Measurement and Performance

A client's performance measurement system includes key performance indicators that management uses to measure progress toward its objectives. These indicators go beyond financial statement figures, such as sales and net income, to include measures tailored to the client and its objectives. Such key performance indicators may include market share, sales per employee, unit sales growth, unique visitors to a website, same-store sales, and sales per square foot for a retailer.

Risk of material misstatement may be increased if the client has unreasonable objectives or if the performance measurement system encourages aggressive accounting. For example, a company's objective may be to have the leading market share of industry sales. If management and salespeople are compensated on the basis of achieving this goal, there is increased incentive to record sales before they have been earned or record sales for nonexistent transactions. In this case, if there are inadequate controls, the occurrence and cut-off assertions have a high risk of material misstatement.

Performance measurement includes ratio analysis and benchmarking against key competitors. As part of understanding the client's business, the auditor should perform ratio analysis or review the client's calculations of key performance ratios. Performing preliminary analytical procedures will be discussed next.

PERFORM PRELIMINARY ANALYTICAL REVIEW

LO **4** Perform and evaluate preliminary analytical procedures.

As first introduced in Chapter 5, auditors are required to perform preliminary analytical procedures as part of the risk assessment procedures to better understand the client's business and industry and to assess the client's business risk. One such procedure compares client ratios to industry or competitor benchmarks to provide indication of the company's performance. Such preliminary tests can reveal unusual changes in ratios compared to previous years, or compared to industry averages, and help the auditor to identify areas with increased risk of material misstatements that require further attention during the audit. Table 6-3 provides some examples of analytical procedures that the auditor could use.

The Hillsburg Hardware Limited example is used to illustrate the use of preliminary analytical procedures as part of audit planning. Table 6-4 presents key financial ratios for Hillsburg Hardware Limited, along with comparative industry information that auditors might consider during audit planning.

Table 6-3	Examples of Analytical Procedures Used During Audit Planning
Analytical Procedure	**Purpose**
Calculate key ratios for the client's business and compare them with industry averages.	To understand the client's industry and business.
Calculate the debt-to-equity ratio and compare it with those of previous years and successful companies in the industry.	To assess going concern.
Compare the gross margin with those of prior years, looking for large fluctuations.	To identify possible misstatements. To plan nature, timing, and extent of further audit procedures.
Prepare common-sized financial statements.	To identify high-risk audit areas. To aid in assessment of fraud risk.
Compare prepaid expenses and related expense accounts with those of prior years.	To identify possible misstatements. To plan nature, timing, and extent of further audit procedures.

	Table 6-4	Examples of Planning Analytical Procedures for Hillsburg Hardware Limited		

Selected Ratios	Hillsburg 12/31/18	Industry 12/31/18	Hillsburg 12/31/17	Industry 12/31/17
Short-Term Debt-Paying Ability				
Cash ratio	0.06	0.22	0.06	0.20
Quick ratio	1.50	3.10	1.45	3.00
Current ratio	3.86	5.20	4.04	5.10
Liquidity Activity Ratios				
Accounts receivable turnover	7.59	12.15	7.61	12.25
Days to collect accounts receivable	48.11	30.04	47.96	29.80
Inventory turnover	3.36	5.20	3.02	4.90
Days to sell inventory	108.65	70.19	120.86	74.49
Ability to Meet Long-Term Obligations				
Debt to equity	1.73	2.51	1.98	2.53
Times interest earned	3.06	5.50	3.29	5.60
Profitability Ratios				
Gross profit percent	27.85	31.00	27.70	32.00
Profit margin ratio	0.05	0.07	0.05	0.08
Return on assets	0.13	0.09	0.12	0.09
Return on common equity	0.25	0.37	0.24	0.35

These ratios are based on the Hillsburg Hardware Limited draft financial statements (see the Appendix at the end of the book). Hillsburg is a wholesale distributor of hardware equipment to independent, high-quality hardware stores in eastern Canada. The company is a niche provider in the overall hardware industry, which is dominated by national chains such as Home Depot and Lowes. Hillsburg's auditors identified potential increased competition from national chains as a specific client business risk. Hillsburg's market consists of smaller, independent hardware stores and the large dealer-owned cooperative, Home Hardware. Increased competition could affect the sales and profitability of these customers, likely affecting Hillsburg's sales and the value of assets such as accounts receivable and inventory. An auditor might use ratio information to identify areas where Hillsburg faces increased risk of material misstatements.

The profitability measures indicate that Hillsburg is performing fairly well despite the increased competition from larger national chains. Although lower than the industry averages, the liquidity measures indicate that the company is in good financial condition, and the leverage ratios indicate additional borrowing capacity. Because Hillsburg's market consists of smaller, independent hardware stores, the company holds more inventory and takes longer to collect receivables than the industry average.

In identifying areas of specific risk, the auditor is likely to focus on the liquidity activity ratios. Inventory turnover has improved but is still lower than the industry average. Accounts receivable turnover has declined slightly and is lower than the industry average. The collectability of accounts receivable and inventory obsolescence are likely to be assessed as high inherent risks and will therefore likely warrant additional attention in the current year's audit. These areas likely received additional attention during the prior year's audit as well.

In addition to ratio analysis, auditors also perform a horizontal and vertical analysis of the financial statements (this is referred to as common-sized financial statements). In a **horizontal analysis**, the account balance is compared to the previous period and the percentage change in the account balance is evaluated. In **vertical analysis**, financial statement items are converted to a percentage of a common base, such as sales.

Horizontal analysis—analysis of percentage changes in financial statement numbers compared to the previous period.

Vertical analysis—analysis in which financial statement numbers are converted to percentages of a base, also called common-size financial statements.

Vertical common-size financial statements allow comparison between companies or for the same company over different periods, revealing trends and providing insight into how different companies compare. Vertical common-size income statement data for the past three years for Hillsburg Hardware are included in Figure 6-4. Hillsburg's sales have increased significantly over the prior year. Note that accounts such as cost of goods sold, sales salaries, and commissions have also increased significantly but are fairly consistent as a percentage of sales, which we expect for these accounts.

Figure 6-4	Hillsburg Hardware Vertical Common-Size Income Statement

HILLSBURG HARDWARE LIMITED
VERTICAL COMMON-SIZE INCOME STATEMENT
Three Years Ending December 31, 2018

	2018		2017		2016	
	(000) Preliminary	% of Net Sales	(000) Audited	% of Net Sales	(000) Audited	% of Net Sales
Sales	$144 328	100.87	$132 421	100.91	$123 737	100.86
Less: Returns and allowances	1 242	0.87	1 195	0.91	1 052	0.86
Net sales	143 086	100.00	131 226	100.00	122 685	100.00
Cost of sales	103 241	72.15	94 876	72.30	88 724	72.32
Gross profit	39 845	27.85	36 350	27.70	33 961	27.68
Selling expense						
Salaries and commissions	7 739	5.41	7 044	5.37	6 598	5.38
Sales payroll benefits	1 422	0.99	1 298	0.99	1 198	0.98
Travel and entertainment	1 110	0.78	925	0.70	797	0.65
Advertising	2 611	1.82	1 920	1.46	1 790	1.46
Sales and promotional literature	322	0.22	425	0.32	488	0.40
Sales meetings and training	925	0.65	781	0.60	767	0.62
Miscellaneous sales expense	681	0.48	506	0.39	456	0.37
Total selling expense	14 810	10.35	12 899	9.83	12 094	9.86
Administration expense						
Executive and office salaries	5 524	3.86	5 221	3.98	5 103	4.16
Administrative payroll benefits	682	0.48	655	0.50	633	0.52
Travel and entertainment	562	0.39	595	0.45	542	0.44
Computer maintenance and supplies	860	0.60	832	0.63	799	0.65
Stationery and supplies	763	0.53	658	0.50	695	0.57
Postage	244	0.17	251	0.19	236	0.19
Telephone and fax	722	0.51	626	0.48	637	0.52
Rent	312	0.22	312	0.24	312	0.25
Legal fees and retainers	383	0.27	321	0.25	283	0.23
Auditing and related services	303	0.21	288	0.22	265	0.22
Amortization	1 452	1.01	1 443	1.10	1 505	1.23
Bad debt expense	3 323	2.32	3 394	2.59	3 162	2.58
Insurance	723	0.51	760	0.58	785	0.64
Office repairs and maintenance	844	0.59	538	0.41	458	0.37
Miscellaneous office expense	644	0.45	621	0.47	653	0.53
Miscellaneous general expense	324	0.23	242	0.18	275	0.22
Total administrative expenses	17 665	12.35	16 757	12.77	16 343	13.32
Total selling and administrative expenses	32 475	22.70	29 656	22.60	28 437	23.18
Operating income	7 370	5.15	6 694	5.10	5 524	4.50
Other income and expense						
Interest expense	2 409	1.68	2,035	1.55	2 173	1.77
Gain on sale of assets	(720)	(0.50)	0	0.00	0	0.00
Earnings before income taxes	5 681	3.97	4 659	3.55	3 351	2.73
Provision for income taxes	1 747	1.22	1 465	1.12	1 072	0.87
Net income	$ 3 934	2.75	$ 3 194	2.43	$ 2 279	1.86

The auditor is likely to require further explanation and corroborating evidence for the changes in advertising, bad debt expense, and office repairs and maintenance:

- Note that advertising expense has increased as a percent of sales. One possible explanation is the development of a new advertising campaign.
- The dollar amount of bad debt expense has not changed significantly but has decreased as a percent of sales. The auditor needs to gather additional evidence to determine whether bad debt expense and the allowance for doubtful account are understated. (The auditor is concerned about the valuation assertion.)
- Repairs and maintenance expense has also increased. Fluctuations in this account are not unusual if the client has incurred unexpected repairs. The auditor should investigate major expenditures in this account to determine whether they include amounts that should be capitalized as a fixed asset. (The auditor is concerned about the allocation assertion.)

CONCEPT CHECK

C6-3 Provide an example of two types of analytical review that are used to assess client business risk.

LO 5 Evaluate preliminary audit planning activities and develop preliminary overall audit strategy.

DEVELOP OVERALL AUDIT STRATEGY

After performing preliminary planning activities, the auditor will develop and document an overall audit strategy that establishes the scope, timing, and direction of the audit and that guides the development of the audit plan. As we cover more of the planning activities, we will revisit overall strategy in subsequent chapters. The overall audit strategy sets out:

- Types and allocation of resources to be deployed for specific audit areas;
- Timing of audit procedures; and
- Materiality.

This strategy considers the nature of the client's business and industry, including areas where there is greater risk of significant misstatements. The auditor also considers other factors such as the number of client locations and the past effectiveness of client controls in developing a preliminary approach to the audit.

Resources Required for Engagement

The planned strategy helps the auditor determine the resources required for the engagement, including engagement staffing.

Select Staff for Engagement Assigning the appropriate staff (with the necessary competence and level of experience) to the engagement is key to ensuring audit effectiveness and efficiency and to meeting quality control standards in GAAS. On larger engagements, there are likely to be one or more partners and staff at several experience levels doing the audit. On smaller audits, there may be only one or two staff members. Specialists may also be assigned. For example, when there are complex information systems and controls, significant changes in existing systems, and/or evidence is only available in electronic form, the audit team should include an IT specialist.

A major consideration is the need for continuity from year to year. An inexperienced staff assistant is likely to become the most experienced nonpartner on the engagement within a few years. Continuity helps the public accounting firm maintain familiarity with technical requirements and close interpersonal relations with the client's personnel. The extent of assistance provided by the client, including work done by the internal audit department, also affects staffing. Throughout the planning and conduct of the audit, the entire team meets to share information and to ensure awareness of risks.

Evaluate Need for Outside Specialists As the story involving the gold claim at Bre-X illustrates, if the audit requires specialized knowledge, it may be necessary to consult a specialist. CAS 620 establishes the requirements for selecting specialists and reviewing their work. Examples include using a diamond expert in evaluating the replacement cost of diamonds and an actuary for determining the appropriateness of the recorded value of insurance loss reserves. Another common use of specialists is consulting with lawyers on the legal interpretation of contracts and titles or business valuation experts on fair value accounting treatments.

The auditor must have sufficient understanding of the client's business to recognize whether a specialist is needed, and to evaluate the specialist's professional qualifications and understand the objectives and scope of the specialist's work. The auditor should also consider the specialist's relationship to the client, including circumstances that might impair the specialist's objectivity. The use of a specialist does not affect the auditor's responsibility for the audit and the audit report should not refer to the specialist unless the specialist's report results in a modification of the audit opinion.

Evaluate Whether Internal Audit Work Can Contribute Many organizations establish internal audit departments as part of their internal control and governance structures. For those clients that have an internal audit department, the internal auditors may be able to contribute to audit efficiency in two ways—either the auditor uses the internal auditors' work (such as internal audit reports) or the internal audit provides direct assistance to the external auditor.[1] CAS 610 explains that if the auditor determines that the internal audit has the necessary competence, integrity, and objectivity, it is possible that the auditor can rely upon the internal auditor's work in certain circumstances. The general guideline is that the higher the assessed risk of material misstatement is, the more restricted the nature and extent of work that should be assigned to internal auditors. If the external auditor decides that the internal auditors can provide direct assistance, the external auditor must directly supervise and review the internal auditor's work. The external auditor will also obtain written agreement from an authorized representative that internal auditors are allowed to follow the external auditors' instructions, as well as written agreement from the internal auditors that they

---

[1] Companies listed on the New York Stock Exchange are required to have an internal audit function. Canadian stock exchanges do not have a similar requirement.

will keep specific matters confidential as instructed by the external auditors and will inform the external auditors of any threats to their objectivity.

> **CONCEPT CHECK**
>
> **C6-4** Under what types of circumstances does the auditor need an internal specialist and/or external specialist?

Evaluate Reliance on Other Auditors If a client has multiple locations or subsidiaries, the audit firm may need to engage other auditors. Prior to engaging the component auditor (the auditor of a component of the reporting entity, such as a subsidiary or division), the group auditor (the auditor responsible for the consolidated financial statements) will ensure that the component auditor is competent and independent, and that the component auditor operates in a regulatory environment that actively oversees auditors.

CAS A critical element of a multi-location audit (which the CAS 600 refers to as a group audit) is to determine the amount of work to be performed at each component. The audit team in charge of the audit will need to clearly communicate to the component auditors the engagement team's requirements. The group auditor will need to obtain an understanding with the component auditor regarding the extent of work to be performed as well as clear guidance on performance materiality (which we will discuss later in the chapter).

Timing of Engagement

As highlighted in our discussion of understanding the terms of the engagement, the timing of the engagement depends upon client reporting deadlines. It also depends upon practical matters such as when the client conducts the inventory count, which the auditor plans to observe. In Chapter 5, we learned that the timing of procedures is also dependent upon the effectiveness of client's internal controls and the risk of material misstatement in specific accounts. We will discuss these factors in subsequent chapters.

The final part of the overall audit strategy is materiality, which will discuss in the next section.

LO 6 Understand and apply the concept of materiality to the audit.

CAS

MATERIALITY

After performing preliminary planning activities, the auditor will make a preliminary judgment of materiality for the financial statements. CAS 320, *Materiality in planning and performing an audit*, explains materiality:

> Misstatements, including omissions, are considered to be material if they, individually or in the aggregate, could reasonably be expected to influence the economic decisions of users taken on the basis of the financial statements.

One of the biggest misunderstandings around materiality is the belief that determining materiality is simply a matter of following the audit firm's guidelines or a general rule of thumb. However, consider the explanation in Ernst & Young's audit report for InterContinental Hotel Group (Note: UK regulations require that the auditors include materiality in the audit report). In this case, materiality is "based upon 5 percent of adjusted profit before tax, excluding exceptional items." While 5 percent of net income is a common rule of thumb, and Ernst & Young would certainly have materiality guidelines that would constrain the audit team's choices, the decision would still require considerable professional judgment. For instance, how did those auditors decide that 5 percent was appropriate, and that net income was an appropriate base? As CAS 320.2 highlights, in determining overall materiality:

- Judgments are made in light of the circumstances surrounding the entity and are affected by the size and nature of the misstatement, or a combination of both.

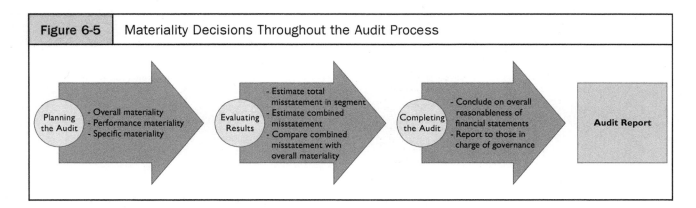

| Figure 6-5 | Materiality Decisions Throughout the Audit Process |

- Judgments about what is material to users of the financial statements are based on a consideration of the common financial information needs of users as a group, not each user individually (such as a bank, bondholder, or shareholder).

It is important to remember that **materiality** is a relative rather than an absolute concept. A misstatement of a given magnitude might be material for a small company, whereas the same dollar error could be immaterial for a large one. For example, a total error of $1 million would be extremely material for Hillsburg Hardware Limited because net income before tax is about $5.7 million. It would be immaterial for a company such as InterContinental Hotels and Resorts, which has total assets and net income of several billion dollars. In other words, it is impossible to establish any dollar-value guidelines for materiality applicable to all audit clients.

Materiality is a driver of the entire audit process—from planning, to evaluating the results and completing the audit. Figure 6-5 summarizes the various materiality-related decisions that occur during the audit process. The first three decisions are made in the planning stage and form the benchmarks to evaluate the results of the audit testing, to make conclusions (on the financial statements as a whole, as well as the various accounts and disclosures), and to complete the audit (which includes issuing the audit report and reporting to those in charge of governance). If the auditor determines that there is a material misstatement, he or she will bring it to the client's attention so that a correction can be made. If the client refuses to correct the statements, a modified opinion must be issued. (We discuss the types of opinions in Chapter 19.)

Materiality—the magnitude of an omission or misstatement of accounting information that, in the light of surrounding circumstances, makes it probable that the judgment of a reasonable person relying on the information would have been changed or influenced by the omission or misstatement.

DETERMINE OVERALL MATERIALITY

CAS 320 states, "When establishing the overall audit strategy, the auditor shall determine materiality for the financial statements as a whole." This is what is referred to as **overall materiality**.

Figure 6-6 provides an overview of the concept of overall (or planning) materiality. As the figure highlights, determining overall materiality starts with identifying the financial statement users and considering what information in the financial statements would be of most interest to them. It is important to note that overall materiality is based upon users' needs and expectations, not those of the auditor based upon audit risk. Figure 6-6 provides some of the key external users and their economic decisions. Others could be employees, tax authorities, regulators, members, contributors, unions, and government agencies. It's important to remember that management is also a key user and, as we discuss throughout the chapter, the potential impact of performance incentives is an important consideration in determining overall materiality.

There are three steps involved in determining overall materiality:

1. Select an appropriate benchmark.
2. Determine the percentage to be applied to the selected benchmark.
3. Justify the choice (explain the judgment).

LO **7** Use professional judgment to determine overall (or planning) materiality.

Overall materiality—materiality for the financial statements as a whole.

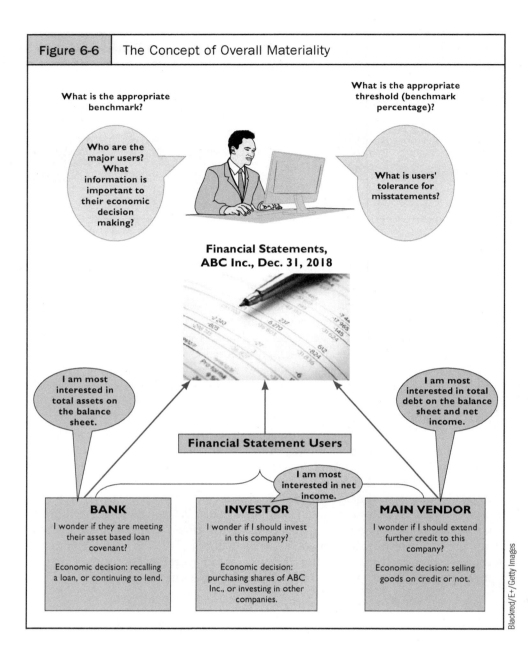

Figure 6-6	The Concept of Overall Materiality

Blackred/E+/Getty Images

Select the Benchmark

As highlighted in Figure 6-6, in order to select the appropriate benchmark, auditors develop an understanding of the users of the financial statements. Examples of benchmarks include revenue, profit before taxes, total assets, and expenses. The auditor makes a judgment about which benchmark to use by understanding what the users of the financial statements are most likely concerned about. For example, if the entity is mainly financed by equity investors who are concerned with financial performance, then the auditor will likely use net income before taxes as a benchmark.

CAS

CAS 320 identifies a number of factors that affect the selection of an appropriate benchmark. These include:

- Elements of the financial statements (assets, liabilities, equity, income, expenses).
- Whether there are items on which the users tend to focus (for example, the users may tend to focus on net income).
- Past history with audits (numerous adjustments required? any restatements?).
- The nature of the entity and the industry.

Table 6-5	Common Materiality Benchmarks	
Entity Description	**User Decision**	**Common Benchmark**
Mature entity that is financed by equity (public company with shares widely held)	Evaluate entity performance	Net income before taxes
Start-up entity that is financed by equity and has not yet generated net income (public company with shares widely held)	Evaluate entity viability	Revenue, assets, or net assets
Mature entity that is financed by one private equity investor whose net income is consistently low because the owner/manager takes much of the income by way of bonus; the entity has some debt financing which requires an audit	Evaluate entity ability to repay debt	Net income adjusted for the owner/ manager bonus, or total assets
Entity that is financed mainly by debt	Evaluate entity ability to repay debt	Total assets
Not-for-profit organization	Evaluate whether organization spending is consistent with objectives of the organization	Total revenue or total expenses

- The entity's ownership structure and the way it is financed (for example, if the company is solely financed by debt, then the users may put more emphasis on assets than earnings [as in the case of shareholders]).
- The relative volatility of the benchmark (for example, if net income changes dramatically from year to year, it may not be an appropriate benchmark).

Table 6-5 provides examples of different types of organizations, the associated user needs, and the most common benchmark used by auditors.

Identify the Financial Data Identifying the financial data to use for the benchmark is not as straightforward as it appears. Usually, when the auditor is planning the audit, the current year-end results are not available (since the planning is done prior to year-end). The auditor usually uses the prior period's financial results, the period-to-date results, and budgets/forecasts for the current period, adjusted for significant changes (e.g., acquisitions) and changes in the industry/environment. Some auditors will use an average of two or three prior years to avoid the potential for benchmarks to be influenced by unusual or one-off results.

Determine the Benchmark Percentage

Auditors are expected to set overall materiality at the highest amount of misstatement that would not influence the economic decisions of financial statement users. Some common rules of thumb that can be used as a starting point for calculating materiality are summarized in Table 6-6 below:

As highlighted in Figure 6-6, in order to determine an appropriate benchmark percentage (what is often referred to as the materiality threshold), the auditor will

Table 6-6	Common Rules of Thumb for Calculating Materiality	
For-Profit Entities	**Not-for Profit Entities**	
- 3 to 7 percent of income from continuing operations before taxes (this may need to be normalized)	- 1 to 3 percent of revenue	
- 1 to 3 percent of total assets	- 1 to 3 percent of expenses	
- 3 to 5 percent of shareholders' equity	- 1 to 3 percent of total assets	
- 1 to 3 percent of revenue		

So what benchmarks and percentages are used in practice? The UK's Financial Reporting Council (FRC, the UK equivalent to the CPAB, conducted a detailed analysis of 153 extended audit reports. (Audit reports of UK public companies disclose key audit matters and materiality. This is not a requirement of international or Canadian auditing standards.) The analysis encompassed a wide range of industries (retail, construction, real estate, industrial products, support services, banking, software, and mining), and found that the majority of the auditors (76 percent) used a benchmark based upon net income (either adjusted net income or net income before tax), with a few using revenue, assets, equity, and a variety of other benchmarks. This should not be surprising, since net income is a key performance measure for many public companies. However, it is not the universal benchmark.

Below is a sample of some benchmarks and percentages that are being used by a variety of public companies listed on the London Stock Exchange, by Canada's largest municipality (Toronto), and by the Toronto Transit Commission:

Entity	Industry	Benchmark	Percentage
Diploma plc	Specialized technical products (such as hydraulic seals and specialized wiring)	Net income before taxes	5%
British Sky Broadcasting Group	Home entertainment, communications, and pay TV	Adjusted net income before taxes	4%
New World Resources	Mining	Revenue	1%
City of Toronto	Municipality	Budgeted expenditures	1.25%
Toronto Transit Commission	Public transportation	Total operating expenses	1.5%

Sources: Based on Diploma PLC, *Annual Report & Accounts 2014*, London, 2014. British Sky Broadcasting Group, Annual Report, 2014. New World Resources, *Annual Report and Accounts, 2013*, Amsterdam, 2014. PricewaterhouseCoopers, *City of Toronto Audit Plan for the Year ending December 31, 2014*, Toronto, 2015. Toronto Transit Commission audit committee report, PricewaterhouseCoopers, *Consolidated Financial Statements audit plan for the year ended December 31, 2013*, Toronto, 2014.

consider the users' sensitivity or tolerance for misstatements. Users' sensitivity or tolerance to misstatements depends upon the purpose of the financial statements (which we discussed earlier in the chapter). For instance, although a common percentage for for-profit organizations is 5 percent of net income, it may be increased or decreased depending upon the relevant circumstances. Consider a small private company with two owners. Imagine that the owners intend to sell the company and the purchase price is based on the financial statements. In this situation, it is most likely that the users (the current owners and the perspective buyers) would have a low tolerance (or high sensitivity) to small errors. Based upon this, the auditor would use the lower end of the percentage threshold. However, in the previous year, the higher end of the range would be acceptable since the purpose of the financial statements was to assess the company's performance and not to determine a purchase price. In other words, at that point in time, the owners were less sensitive to errors in the financial statements.

Given that the benchmark and the threshold are based upon the users' needs and the specific circumstances, it is not surprising, as illustrated in Auditing in Action 6-4, that there can be considerable variation in the percentages as well as the appropriate bases.

Justifying the Materiality Decisions

CAS

Given that CAS 320 expects auditors to use professional judgment in materiality, there are no specific guidelines as to what the percentages and benchmarks should be. While firms do develop their own guidelines to both guide and constrain auditors' choices, auditors must provide adequate justification for their materiality decisions. The key to this is to document the auditor's decisions and rationale in the working paper files.

Documenting Materiality Decisions for Hillsburg Figure 6-7 is the working paper completed by the audit senior, documenting the decisions regarding materiality.

Figure 6-7	Determining Materiality for Hillsburg Hardware

Materiality

Entity: Hillsburg Hardware Limited

Period Ended: December 31, 2018

Objective: To determine:
Overall materiality based upon users of the financial statements.
Performance materiality to reduce the probability that the aggregate of uncorrected and undetected misstatements exceeds overall materiality.
Specific materiality and specific performance materiality where required.

Identify Principal Users of Financial Statements

Users	Factors that would influence users' decision making
Investment company	The investment company will be evaluating management performance and be interested in return on investment. Key benchmarks that would influence its decisions are profitability and future revenue growth.
Bank	The bank is most concerned with loan repayment and compliance with the bank covenants, which are to maintain positive cash flow—measured as EBITA (earnings before interest, taxes, depreciation, and amortization) and a minimum quick ratio of 1.25. The key benchmarks that would influence the bank's decision are adjusted net income (EBITA) as a proxy for cash flows and for the bank covenant requirements.
Hillsburg Family	The Hillsburg family will be evaluating management performance and interest on their return on investment, as well as their annual income from dividends (it is a key source of their personal income). Key benchmarks that would influence the family's decision are profitability, adjusted net income (EBITA), and future revenue growth.

A. Overall Materiality
Use professional judgment as to the highest amount of misstatement(s) that could be included in the financial statements without affecting the economic decisions taken by the financial statement users listed above.

Type of Entity	Basis for Calculation	This Period Anticipated	Prior Period	Benchmark Percentage Applied	Possible Materiality	Comments
Profit-oriented	Operating income (adjusted for depreciation)	$8822 ($7370 + 1452)	$8137	3 to 7% Users' sensitivity for misstatements is considered to be low (Hillsburg family) to medium (investment company and bank).	$265 000 to $618 000	Income is small in relation to revenue but still the most important yardstick for users of financial statements.
	Gross Revenues	$143 086	$131 226	1 to 3%		
	Other (describe such as assets)					
Not-for-Profit	Total revenues or expenses			N/A	N/A	
	Other (describe)			N/A	N/A	
		Amount	Reasoning			
	Previous period	$407 000	EBITA was determined the most meaningful measure based upon needs of the users of the financial statements. Given the users' sensitivity (low to moderate), 5% was chosen as the benchmark percentage.			
	Preliminary	$441 000				

(continued)

Figure 6-7 *(Continued)*

B. Performance Materiality

Set performance materiality at an amount based upon, but lower than, overall materiality (such as between 60 percent and 75 percent of overall materiality). Use professional judgment about expectations of misstatements that could arise in the current period. Consider the business and fraud risks identified, the results of performing risk assessment procedures, and the nature/extent of misstatement in prior audits.

	Amount	Rationale
Previous period	$305 000	Based on 75% of overall materiality.
Preliminary	$331 000	Based on 75% of overall materiality as we have not found many misstatements in prior years (other than revenues and inventories) where we plan to reduce our performance materiality (see below).

Adjusted performance materiality levels (where considered necessary to address particular risk of misstatement in a class of transactions, account balances, or financial statement disclosures).

Financial Statement Area or Disclosure(s)	Amount	Rationale
Revenue		
Previous period	$24 000	Some cutoff errors were found in prior periods.
Preliminary	$265 000	Current year's preliminary analytical review indicates potential for misstatement.
Inventory		
Previous period	$244 000	Errors in inventory counts noted in the past.
Preliminary	$265 000	Current year's preliminary analytical review indicates potential for misstatement.

C. Specific Materiality

This would apply for certain (uncommon) situations where the users of the financial statements have specific expectations with regard to one or more particular financial statement area.

Describe the user(s) expectation/sensitivity and the specific transactions, balances, or disclosures affected.		None (overall materiality is sufficiently small to address quick ratio for loan covenants).
	Materiality	
Previous period	N/A	
Preliminary		

D. Performance materiality for specific circumstances in C

Financial Statement Area or Disclosure(s)	Amount	Rationale
Previous period	N/A	
Preliminary		

E. Trivial misstatements

This is an amount below which misstatements would be clearly trivial and not recorded on the summary of audit differences $4 400 (1 percent of overall materiality).

Prepared by: ___LN___   Date _10/15/18_   Reviewed by: ___JA___   Date _10/31/18_

Source: Based on CPA Canada, "PEG Forms—Audit Form 420," *Professional Engagement Guide*, Toronto: CPA Canada, 2017.

Determining Trivial Amounts

You will note that, in Figure 6-7, as part of planning, the auditor also determined the quantitative threshold for **trivial amounts**, which, according to CAS 450, "will be matters that are clearly inconsequential, whether taken individually or in aggregate and whether judged by any criteria of size, nature or circumstances." In practice, as part of the audit plan that the auditor presents to the audit committee, the auditor and the audit committee agree upon the appropriate quantitative threshold based upon overall materiality (although some audit committees may wish to be advised of all misstatements). For instance, in the case of the City of Toronto, the auditor reports all adjusted and unadjusted differences in excess of 1 percent of overall materiality to the audit committee.

Trivial amounts—matters that are clearly inconsequential, whether taken individually or in aggregate and whether judged by any criteria of size, nature, or circumstances.

Revising Overall Materiality

Since overall materiality is set early in the planning stage, events may occur subsequently that may change the original calculation. CAS 320 provides some examples that would cause the auditor to revise materiality, for example, if the company decides to dispose of a major part of the business, or if the actual results are substantially different from the anticipated period-end results.

CAS

DETERMINE PERFORMANCE MATERIALITY

LO 8 Use professional judgment to determine performance materiality.

As well as overall materiality, CAS 320 requires that auditors determine **performance materiality**. This is set at an amount less than the overall materiality, and it serves two functions:

Performance materiality—an amount less than materiality that the auditor uses to plan and conduct the financial statement audit engagement, to reduce the likelihood that uncorrected errors exceed materiality.

- To reduce **aggregation risk** (the risk that aggregate uncorrected and undetected misstatements individually below materiality will exceed overall materiality for the financial statements.
- To provide a "safety buffer" against the risk of undetected misstatements.

Performance materiality is all about risk. How much lower it is than overall materiality will depend upon the assessed level of the risk of material misstatement. As you will note in the materiality working paper for Hillsburg Hardware (Figure 6-7), the auditor takes into consideration the business and fraud risks, the results of performing risk assessment procedures, and the nature/extent of misstatement in prior audits.

Aggregation risk—the risk that aggregate uncorrected and undetected misstatements individually below materiality will exceed overall materiality for the financial statements.

In practice, auditors set performance materiality as a percentage of overall materiality. It is generally recommended to be between 50 percent (high risk) and 75 percent (low risk).[2] (However, as illustrated in Auditing in Action 6-5, the top of the range for some firms is higher.) Performance materiality guides the level of work performed. If it is set too high, the auditor might not perform sufficient procedures to detect material misstatements. Conversely, if performance materiality is too low, the auditor may perform more audit procedures than necessary.

A study of the American Big Eight firms' materiality guidelines[3] found that the following factors are taken into consideration when setting performance materiality:

- Overall engagement risk is considered high (e.g., high-risk industries, unusually high market pressures, first-year audit engagement, and special purpose financial statements);
- Fraud risks (e.g., tone at the top, internal or external pressures, ineffective governance controls, incompetent accounting personnel, contentious behaviour with auditors, evasive responses to audit inquiries);
- A history of identified misstatements in prior period audits;

---

[2] Based upon CPA Canada, *Professional Engagement Guide* (PEG), Toronto, 2017.

[3] Aasmund Eilifsen and Mark Messier, "Materiality guidance of major public accounting firms," *Auditing: A Journal of Practice and Theory,* vol. 34, no. 2, 2015, pp. 3–26, **http://dx.doi.org/10.2308/ajpt-50882**.

In a recent review of materiality at the region's Big Six firms, the United Kingdom's Financial Reporting Council (FRC) found that firms have widely different policies on both overall materiality and performance materiality. The recommended performance materiality ranged from a low of 50-75 percent to a maximum allowable high of 90 percent. This firm emphasized a judgmental approach, which emphasized a focus on historical errors; the firm is considering lowering its guidelines. The FRC also found that the firms defaulted to the highest rate in the allowable range and it concluded that there was "no evidence that any judgment had been exercised. Auditors should ensure that the consideration of risk is a key factor in setting performance materiality."

The FRC found that, although the firms had specific performance materiality guidelines, the FRC did not identify any instances where these were enforced in practice. However, the FRC did note that all the firms require more detailed work to be performed for sensitive areas such as executive remuneration and related party transactions, irrespective of the overall materiality level set.

Source: Based on Financial Reporting Council, *Audit quality thematic review: Materiality*, London: Financial Reporting Council, 2013, accessed July 19, 2017, at **https://www.frc.org.uk/Our-Work/Publications/ Audit-Quality-Review/Audit-Quality-Thematic-Review-Materiality.pdf**.

- Increased number of accounting issues that require significant judgment and/or more estimates with high estimation uncertainty;
- Identified misstatements during the course of the current year audit that indicate that the remaining margin for possible undetected misstatements is insufficient;
- A deficient control environment;
- A history of material weaknesses, significant deficiencies, and/or a high number of deficiencies in internal control;
- High turnover of senior management or key financial reporting personnel; and
- The entity operates in a number of locations.

In the planning stage, performance materiality (not overall materiality) is used to identify what areas need to be audited, how much and what type of work is needed, and to calculate sample sizes. For instance, if an account has a low risk of material misstatement and is below performance materiality, then the auditor may choose to do nothing. However, if the account is above performance materiality, the auditor will need to some testing. The nature and extent of testing will depend upon how large the account balance is in relation to performance materiality and the risk of material misstatement. Later in the audit, performance materiality is used to evaluate results of substantive tests and conclude whether or not an account is materially misstated.

Adjusting Performance Materiality

You will note in Figure 6-7 that the auditor adjusted performance materiality for two accounts, revenue and inventory, which the auditor determined had a higher risk of material misstatement based upon previous years' results and the current year's analytical procedures. Both are factors that auditors would consider when deciding to lower performance materiality for particular account balances, classes of transactions, or disclosures.

LO 9 Use professional judgment to determine specific materiality.

Specific materiality—a materiality level based upon a specific group of users' needs and determined for a particular class of transactions, account balance or disclosure.

DETERMINE SPECIFIC MATERIALITY

There are some situations where the economic decisions of a specific group of users would be influenced by misstatements in particular classes of transactions, account balances, or disclosures. This is referred to as **specific materiality**. (You will note that, in Figure 6-7, Section C refers to materiality for specific circumstances.) When auditors develop specific materiality, they take into consideration the specific user requirements (say, a particular regulator) and the user's sensitivity to small changes in relation to a specific class of transactions, balance, or a particular disclosure on the financial statements. For example, auditors often set a specific materiality for executive compensation and related party transactions. That is because shareholders (or members) and regulators (such as the securities commission and the Canada Revenue Agency) are very sensitive to small changes with regards to those two classes of transactions. Or it may be that users are particularly sensitive to the consequences of the misstatement in a particular class of transactions, an account balance, or note disclosure. For example, if failure to make adequate patent payments could result in loss of a key technology, the auditor may use a lower level of materiality for those transactions. If the auditor determines a specific materiality, then it is necessary to set a specific performance materiality for that specific circumstance.

APPLYING MATERIALITY—EVALUATING RESULTS AND COMPLETING THE AUDIT

 LO 10 Apply materiality to evaluate misstatements and to complete the audit.

So far, we have discussed the role of materiality in planning the audit. In this section, we will briefly discuss the role of applying materiality to the decisions related to evaluating the results, completing the audit, and reporting. We will discuss this in more detail when we consider determining audit sample sizes (Chapter 11), developing and performing substantive and control audit tests (Chapter 12 to Chapter 17), and evaluating audit results (Chapter 18).

Accumulating Misstatements During the Audit

CAS 450 requires the auditor to accumulate misstatements during the audit other than those that are below the clearly trivial threshold, which the auditor will determine in the planning stage. As CAS 450 highlights, "clearly trivial" is not another expression for "not material." This is important to note since CAS 450 requires the auditor to request that **uncorrected misstatements** be corrected; clearly trivial amounts can be ignored when proposing adjustments to the client management.

CAS 450 explains that it may be useful for the auditor to categorize misstatements as follows: (1) **factual misstatements**, those about which there is no doubt; (2) **judgmental misstatements**, differences in management's judgment concerning recognition, measurement, presentation, and disclosure in the financial statements and the auditor's judgment; and (3) **projected misstatements**, the auditor's best estimate based upon a sample. Auditors would request management to correct any factual misstatements and have discussions with management in order to reach agreement about whether adjustments for judgmental differences are necessary. However, it may be difficult to persuade management to post projected misstatements. We will discuss this in more depth in Chapter 18.

Assessing the Materiality of Misstatements

Having accumulated and categorized the misstatements, the auditor will determine if the remaining uncorrected misstatements are material, individually or in aggregate. In assessing the materiality of misstatements, the auditor will consider both the quantitative and qualitative nature of the misstatements.

Certain types of misstatements are likely to be more important to users than others, even if the dollar amounts are the same. There may be instances where management will try to argue that an amount is quantitatively immaterial and therefore does not need to be corrected in the audited financial statements. However, as highlighted in Table 6-7, qualitative factors are important in determining whether a misstatement is material or not.

CAS

Uncorrected misstatements—misstatements that the auditor has accumulated during the audit and that have not been corrected by the client.

Factual misstatements—misstatements identified by the auditor about which there is no doubt.

Judgmental misstatements—misstatements identified by the auditor that represent differences arising from management's judgment, including those concerning recognition, measurement, presentation, and disclosure in the financial statements (including the selection or application of accounting policies) that the auditor considers unreasonable or inappropriate.

Projected misstatements—the auditor's best estimate of misstatements in populations, involving the projection of misstatements identified in audit samples to the entire populations from which the samples were drawn.

Table 6-7	Qualitative Reasons Why the Misstatement Is Material

Materiality may be a threshold; however, it is more than a simple decision about whether the misstatement is over or under the numerical threshold of quantitative materiality. CAS 450 provides a list of qualitative factors that may cause the auditor to reconsider whether a quantitatively "immaterial" misstatement is actually material:

- The potential effect of the material misstatement on trends, especially trends in profitability;
- A misstatement that changes a loss into income or vice versa;
- The potential effect of the misstatement on the entity's compliance with debt covenants, other contractual agreements, and regulatory provisions;
- The existence of statutory reporting requirements that affect materiality thresholds;
- A misstatement that has the effect of increasing management's compensation;
- The significance of the misstatement or disclosures relative to performance measures such as earnings per share or net income relative to expectations; and
- Management's motivation with respect to the misstatement, such as managing earnings or smoothing earnings trends.

CONCEPT CHECK

C6-5 What is the difference between overall materiality and performance materiality? How does the use of performance materiality affect the audit process?

C6-6 Why do auditors use specific materiality?

Forming an Overall Opinion and Reporting

When issuing the audit report, the auditor will conclude on the overall reasonableness of the financial statement using the benchmark of overall materiality. Again, qualitative factors must be considered. In the rare circumstance that there is an uncorrected material misstatement, the auditor must determine if the misstatement is materially pervasive or if it can be isolated to specific accounts or disclosures. This will determine which type of audit report is issued. We will discuss these reporting decisions in more depth in Chapter 19.

Communicating with Management and Those in Charge of Governance Throughout the audit, the auditor has numerous communications with management and those charged with governance regarding overall materiality, the trivial misstatement threshold, and identified misstatements. CAS 450 requires auditors to communicate all misstatements to management on a timely basis. Further, the auditors must communicate with "those in charge of governance uncorrected misstatements and the effect that they, individually or in aggregate, may have on the opinion in the auditor's report."

SUMMARY

MyLab Accounting
Make the grade with MyLab Accounting: The questions, exercises, and problems marked with a can be found on MyLab Accounting. You can practise them as often as you want, and most feature step-by-step guided instructions to help you find the right answer.

A major purpose of audit planning is to gain an understanding of the client's business and industry, which is used to assess acceptable audit risk, client business risk, and the risk of material misstatements in the financial statements, as well as to determine materiality. Figure 6-8 summarizes the major parts of audit planning discussed in this chapter and the key components of each part, with a brief illustration of how a public accounting firm applied each component to a continuing client, Hillsburg Hardware Limited.

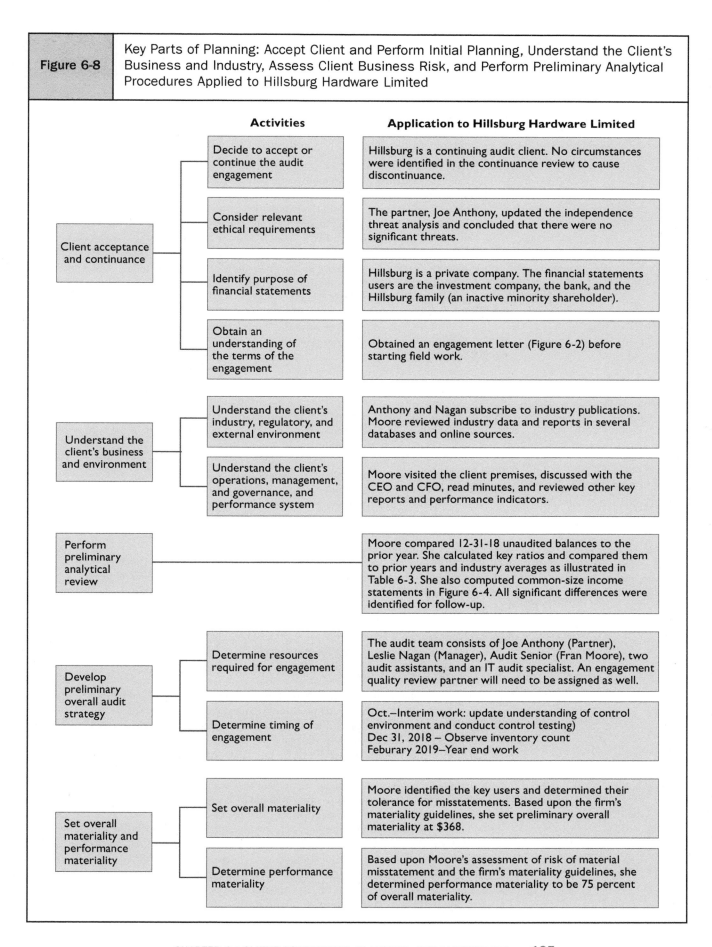

Figure 6-8 Key Parts of Planning: Accept Client and Perform Initial Planning, Understand the Client's Business and Industry, Assess Client Business Risk, and Perform Preliminary Analytical Procedures Applied to Hillsburg Hardware Limited

	Activities	Application to Hillsburg Hardware Limited
Client acceptance and continuance	Decide to accept or continue the audit engagement	Hillsburg is a continuing audit client. No circumstances were identified in the continuance review to cause discontinuance.
	Consider relevant ethical requirements	The partner, Joe Anthony, updated the independence threat analysis and concluded that there were no significant threats.
	Identify purpose of financial statements	Hillsburg is a private company. The financial statements users are the investment company, the bank, and the Hillsburg family (an inactive minority shareholder).
	Obtain an understanding of the terms of the engagement	Obtained an engagement letter (Figure 6-2) before starting field work.
Understand the client's business and environment	Understand the client's industry, regulatory, and external environment	Anthony and Nagan subscribe to industry publications. Moore reviewed industry data and reports in several databases and online sources.
	Understand the client's operations, management, and governance, and performance system	Moore visited the client premises, discussed with the CEO and CFO, read minutes, and reviewed other key reports and performance indicators.
Perform preliminary analytical review		Moore compared 12-31-18 unaudited balances to the prior year. She calculated key ratios and compared them to prior years and industry averages as illustrated in Table 6-3. She also computed common-size income statements in Figure 6-4. All significant differences were identified for follow-up.
Develop preliminary overall audit strategy	Determine resources required for engagement	The audit team consists of Joe Anthony (Partner), Leslie Nagan (Manager), Audit Senior (Fran Moore), two audit assistants, and an IT audit specialist. An engagement quality review partner will need to be assigned as well.
	Determine timing of engagement	Oct.–Interim work: update understanding of control environment and conduct control testing) Dec 31, 2018 – Observe inventory count Feburary 2019–Year end work
Set overall materiality and performance materiality	Set overall materiality	Moore identified the key users and determined their tolerance for misstatements. Based upon the firm's materiality guidelines, she set preliminary overall materiality at $368.
	Determine performance materiality	Based upon Moore's assessment of risk of material misstatement and the firm's materiality guidelines, she determined performance materiality to be 75 percent of overall materiality.

Review Questions

6-1 [2] What factors should an auditor consider prior to accepting an engagement? Explain.

6-2 [1] What benefits does the auditor derive from planning audits?

6-3 [2] What are the responsibilities of the successor and predecessor auditors when a company is changing auditors?

6-4 [3] Explain why auditors need an understanding of the client's industry. What information sources are commonly used by auditors to learn about the client's industry?

6-5 [3] In recent years, the global economy has experienced recession levels unprecedented since the Great Depression, and the instability of the euro continues to cause volatility in stock and bond markets. Why might it be important for you to consider current economic events as part of planning an audit?

6-6 [3] When a PA (public accountant) has accepted an engagement from a new client that is a manufacturer, it is customary for the PA to tour the client's plant facilities. Discuss the ways in which the PA's observations during the course of the plant tour will be of help as he or she plans and conducts the audit.

6-7 [3] An auditor acquires background knowledge of the client's industry as an aid to his or her audit work. How does the acquisition of this knowledge aid the auditor in distinguishing between obsolete and current inventory?

6-8 [3] Jennifer Bailey has many clients in the manufacturing business. She has worked in this sector for many years and believes that she knows the industry well. Explain why, despite her considerable knowledge, it is important for Jennifer to assess client business risk. List the benefits to the inclusion of this task as part of the client risk analysis process.

6-9 [3] Identify the three categories of client objectives that the auditor should understand. Indicate how each objective may affect the auditor's assessment risk of material misstatement and evidence accumulation.

6-10 [3] Define client business risk, and describe several sources of client business risk. What is the auditor's primary concern when evaluating client business risk?

6-11 [3] Describe top management controls and their relationship to client business risk. Give two examples of effective management and governance controls.

6-12 [3] Identify four types of information in the client's minutes of the board of directors' meetings that are likely to be relevant to the auditor. Explain why it is important to read the minutes early in the engagement.

6-13 [3] For the audit of Radline Manufacturing Company, the audit partner asks you to carefully read the new mortgage documents from Green Bank and extract all pertinent information. List the information in a mortgage that is likely to be relevant to the auditor.

6-14 [3] Define what is meant by a "related party." What are the auditor's responsibilities for related parties and related-party transactions?

6-15 [3] Charles Ngu is assessing the management and governance structure of Major Appliance Manufacturing Co. Describe three types of evidence that Charles would gather, and state the relevance of the evidence to the assessment of the management and governance structure of the company.

6-16 [4] What are the purposes of preliminary analytical procedures? What types of comparisons are useful when performing preliminary analytical procedures?

6-17 [4] When are analytical procedures required on an audit? What is the primary purpose of analytical procedures during the planning phase of the audit?

6-18 [4] During the planning phase of every audit, Roger Morris, CPA (Chartered Professional Accountant), calculates a large number of ratios and trends for comparison with industry averages and prior-year calculations. He believes the calculations are worth the relatively small cost of doing them because they provide him with an excellent overview of the client's operations. If the ratios are out of line, Morris discusses the reasons with the client and often makes suggestions for how to bring the ratio back in line in the future. In some cases, these discussions with management have been the basis for management consulting engagements. Discuss the major strengths and shortcomings in Morris's use of ratio and trend analysis. (Consider in light of professional judgment and professional skepticism.)

6-19 [6] Define *materiality* as it is used in accounting and auditing. What is the relationship between materiality and the phrase "obtain reasonable assurance" used in the auditor's report?

6-20 **6** **7** Explain why materiality is important but difficult to apply in practice.

6-21 **7** What is meant by *planning materiality*? Identify the most important factors affecting its development.

6-22 **7** **10** Assume Rosanne Madden, a CPA, is using 5 percent of net income before taxes as her major guideline for evaluating materiality. What qualitative factors should she also consider in deciding whether misstatements may be material?

6-23 **1** **2** Assume materiality for the financial statements as a whole is $100 000, and performance materiality for accounts receivable is set at $40 000. If the auditor finds one receivable that is overstated by $55 000, what should the auditor do?

6-24 **5** How would the conduct of an audit of a medium-sized company be affected by the company's being a small part of a large conglomerate as compared with its being a separate entity?

6-25 **7** What is meant by using benchmarks for setting a preliminary judgment about materiality? How will those benchmarks differ for the audit of a manufacturing company and a government unit such as a school district?

Multiple Choice Questions and Task-Based Simulations

6-26 **2** The following questions pertain to client acceptance. Choose the best response.

a. When approached to perform an audit for the first time, the CPA (Chartered Professional Accountant) should make inquiries of the predecessor auditor. This is a necessary procedure because the predecessor may be able to provide the successor with information that will assist the successor in determining whether:
   (1) The predecessor's work should be used.
   (2) The company follows the policy of rotating its auditors.
   (3) In the predecessor's opinion, internal control of the company has been satisfactory.
   (4) The engagement should be accepted.

b. A successor would most likely make specific inquiries of the predecessor auditor regarding:
   (1) Specialized accounting principles of the client's industry.
   (2) The competency of the client's internal audit staff.
   (3) The uncertainty inherent in applying sampling procedures.
   (4) Disagreements with management as to auditing procedures.

c. Which of the following circumstances would most likely pose the greatest risk in accepting a new audit engagement?
   (1) Staff will need to be rescheduled to cover this new client.
   (2) There will be a client-imposed scope limitation.
   (3) The firm will have to hire a specialist in one audit area.
   (4) The client's financial reporting system has been in place for 10 years.

6-27 **4** Analytical procedures used in planning an audit should focus on identifying:
   (1) Material weaknesses in internal control.
   (2) The predictability of financial data from individual transactions.
   (3) The various assertions that are embodied in the financial statements.
   (4) Areas that may represent specific risks relevant to the audit.

6-28 **10** A client decides not to record an auditor's proposed adjustments that collectively are not material and wants the auditor to issue the report based on the unadjusted numbers. Which of the following statements is correct regarding the financial statement presentation?
   (1) The financial statements are free from material misstatement, and no disclosure is required in the notes to the financial statements.
   (2) The financial statements do not conform with generally accepted accounting principles (GAAP).
   (3) The financial statements contain unadjusted misstatements that should result in a qualified opinion.
   (4) The financial statements are free from material misstatement, but disclosure of the proposed adjustment is required in the notes to the financial statements.

6-29 **2** For each scenario below, identify the most appropriate client acceptance/continuance risk(s) (A–C).

Client acceptance/continuance risk(s):

A. Independence
B. Scope limitation imposed by client
C. Integrity of management

Scenarios	Risk(s)
The same partner has had this client as part of her portfolio for the past 20 years.	
The managers at one of your clients are experts in their product fields, but struggle with understanding the importance of and the requirements for producing and maintaining financial information.	
One of your client's employees informed you that employees are routinely instructed by one of the directors to alter product quality test results.	
The previous audit manager, who dealt with the audit for the last 15 years, has recently taken a senior finance position at your firm's client.	
Your firm's new partner is the brother of the finance director at one of your firm's clients.	

6-30 **2** For each scenario, identify possible audit engagement acceptance/continuance risk(s) (A–F).

Audit engagement acceptance/continuance risk(s):

A. Firm's ability to audit client (scope limitation)
B. Firm's reputation risk
C. Non-compliance with ethical standards
D. Additional duty of care/increased legal exposure
E. Auditor's lack of sufficient expertise in relation to the industry
F. Integrity of management

Scenarios	Risk(s)
SuperService Inc. offers electronics repair service and is required by its bank to have an audit for the first time. The bank has agreed to provide a loan to SuperService Inc if it adheres to the covenant requirements, which include providing a set of audited financial statements.	
FastMoney Inc. has just fired its current auditor, citing that it was not happy with the services that it was receiving. FastMoney Inc. is a short-term loan company that has grown rapidly. The company would like your firm to conduct a financial statement audit and assist in relation to acquiring a listing on the Toronto Stock Exchange.	
Your firm has been approached to conduct a financial statement audit by Xtreme Inc. The company's previous auditor has resigned. Xtreme Inc. is a fireworks manufacturer. You recently read in the news that Xtreme Inc. had to recall its fireworks as some spontaneously exploded and caused serious injuries to a number of people.	
For a number of years, your firm has been providing internal audit consulting service to Big Joe Burger Inc. Big Joe's management approached you to act as the company's external and internal auditor for the next year. Big Joe's non-active investor asked for audited financial statements.	
Your client is a large international mining company listed on the Toronto Stock Exchange. Your firm has been its group auditor for the last four years. About 90 percent of your client's revenue comes from its foreign mining subsidiaries. During the year, your client purchased a new large mining subsidiary in Brazil. In addition, 50 percent of your client's shares were purchased by Ontario Teachers' Pension Plan.	

6-31 **6** **7** Yummy Pops Ltd. is 100 percent owned by Pops Holding Ltd. The company has been profitable in the past. However, it has incurred a loss in the current year ended December 31, 2018. The parent company has indicated it is considering selling Yummy if it incurs another loss. In response, Yummy is looking into producing private label beverages, which has a higher gross margin than its regular product line, for the supermarket chain, ValueMart Inc. In order to produce ValueMart's private label products, Yummy needs to expand its packaging facility.

To finance its expansion, the company has applied to the Canada Business Bank. The bank has indicated that before it will approve the loan application it requires audited financial statements for 2018. It also wants to ensure the entity has a current ratio of 2:1.

This is the first year your firm, Peters and Peters, has audited Yummy. Graves and Collins, LLP, had been Yummy's auditors for many years; however, due to a disagreement over revenue recognition method, Yummy did not reappoint Graves and Collins.

REQUIRED

a. Based upon the case facts, which benchmark would be most appropriate for overall materiality:
   i.   Current year's assets.
   ii. Current year's net income.
   iii. Previous year's net income.
   iv. Current year's revenue.
   v.   An average of current year's net assets and net income.
b. Provide an explanation for your choice.
c. What benchmark percentage is most appropriate? Use case facts to support your choice.

6-32 **6** **7** Elias Tech (ET) is a private company founded by Sarah House and Rosa Perks. Sara and Rosa each own a 40 percent interest in the company, with the remaining 20 percent owned by a venture capitalist firm that invests in startups. ET develops medical devices and has recently announced that its revolutionary blood-testing device has received government approval and will be available in the coming year. Revenue and net income information for ET's last five years are:

Year Ended September 30	Revenues	Net Income (Loss) Before Income Taxes
2018 (unaudited)	$ 22 000 000	$ (200 000)
2017	24 000 000	(1 200 000)
2016	28 000 000	(900 000)
2015	26 000 000	(1 100 000)
2014	22 000 000	(800 000)

Earlier this calendar year, ET negotiated a $3.5 million term bank loan, which is secured by assets to expand its manufacturing facility. ET is considering going public to help fund the anticipated growth associated with its new blood testing device and, in anticipation of this, has contracted your firm to perform the 2018 audit. A smaller public accounting firm, which does not conduct public company audits, conducted the previous years' audits.

a. Based upon case facts, which benchmark is most appropriate for overall materiality?
   i.   Current year's net income (loss).
   ii. An average of the last five years' net income (loss).
   iii. An average of the last five years' revenue.
   iv. An average of current year's net assets and revenue.
b. Provide an explanation for your choice.
c. What benchmark percentage is most appropriate? Use case facts to support your choice.

6-33 **3** **4** **5** An auditor performs various procedures during audit planning. For each procedure, indicate which of the first four parts of audit planning the procedure primarily relates to: (1) accept the client and perform initial audit planning; (2) understand the client's business and industry; (3) assess the client's business risk; and (4) perform preliminary analytical procedures.

Audit Planning Activities and Procedures
Determine the likely users of the financial statements.
Identify whether any specialists are required for the engagement.
Send an engagement letter to the client.
Tour the client's plant and offices.
Compare key ratios for the company to those for industry competitors.
Review management's risk management controls and procedures.
Review accounting principles unique to the client's industry.
Identify potential related parties that may require disclosure.

Discussion Questions and Problems

⊕ **6-34** ③ ⑤ The minutes of the board of directors of the Tetonic Metals Company for the year ended December 31, 2017, were provided to you.

MEETING OF MARCH 5, 2017

The meeting of the board of directors of Tetonic Metals was called to order by James Cook, the chair of the board, at 8:30 a.m. The following directors were in attendance:

Irene Arnold

Robert Beardsley

Mary Beth Cape

James Cook

Larry Holden

Heather Jackson

Brian McDonald

Tony Williams

The board approved the minutes from the November 22, 2016, meeting.

The board reviewed the financial statements for the most recent fiscal year, which ended December 31, 2016. Due to strong operating results, the board declared an increase in the annual dividend to common shareholders from $0.32 to $0.36 per common share payable on May 10, 2017, to shareholders of record on April 25, 2017.

Tony Williams, CEO, led a discussion of the seven core strategic initiatives in the 2017–19 strategic plan. The most immediate initiative is the expansion of Tetonic operations into Western Canada. The board approved an increased budget for 2017 administrative expenses of $1 million to open offices in the Calgary, Alberta, area.

Williams also led a discussion of a proposed acquisition of one of Tetonic's smaller competitors. The board discussed synergies that might be possible if the operations of the acquired company could be successfully integrated with the operations of Tetonic. The board granted Williams and the management team approval to continue negotiations with the other company's board and management.

The board continued its discussion from prior meetings about the October 2016 environmental protection report regarding dust impact at Tetonic's zinc refineries. Legal counsel for Tetonic updated the board on the status of negotiations with the Ontario Ministry of Environment and Climate Change regarding findings contained in the report. The board asked management to include an update on the status of any resolutions for its next meeting. The board also asked management to schedule a conference call, if necessary, for the board if issues need to be resolved before the next meeting.

Officer bonuses for the year ended December 31, 2016, were approved for payment on April 14, 2017, as follows:

Tony Williams, chief executive officer	$275 000
Mary Beth Cape, chief operating officer	$150 000
Bob Browning, chief financial officer	$125 000

The audit committee and the compensation committee provided an update of issues discussed at each of their respective meetings.

The meeting adjourned at 5:30 p.m.

MEETING OF OCTOBER 21, 2017

The meeting of the board of directors of Tetonic Metals was called to order by James Cook, the chair of the board, at 8:30 a.m. The following directors were in attendance:

Irene Arnold

Robert Beardsley

Mary Beth Cape

James Cook

Larry Holden

Heather Jackson

Brian McDonald

Tony Williams

The board approved the minutes from the March 5, 2017, meeting.

Tony Williams, CEO, provided an overview of financial performance and operating results for the nine months ended September 30, 2017. Given the volatility in the economy, Tetonic sales have fallen by over 8 percent compared to the same period in 2016. To address the drop in revenues, Tetonic has scaled back mining operations by a similar percentage to reduce labour and shipping costs.

Bob Browning, CFO, updated the board on discussions with banks that will be financing the acquisition of the Tetonic competitor. The terms of the $7 million financing include a floating interest rate that is 2 percent above prime over the 10-year life of the loan. Payments will be made quarterly and Tetonic will have to maintain compliance with certain loan covenant restrictions that are tied to financial performance. The board approved the acquisition and related loan transaction and scheduled a closing date for the financing to be November 1, 2017.

To prepare for the proposed acquisition, the board approved an increase in the capital expenditures budget of $1.5 million to cover costs of expanding computer operations, including new servers. The new equipment is needed to successfully integrate IT operations at Tetonic and the acquired company. The equipment will be installed in December 2017. Existing equipment that was purchased in 2015 will no longer be used in the IT operations at Tetonic.

The board discussed the creation of an incentive stock option plan for senior executives as a way to better align management and shareholder incentives. Consultants from a compensation advisory firm and tax attorneys from a national accounting firm led a discussion of the components of the proposed plan, including discussion of the related tax implications. The board asked the consultants to revise the plan based on comments received at the meeting for presentation at the board's next meeting.

Tetonic's external auditor provided an update of its interim work related to tests of the operating effectiveness of internal controls over financial reporting. The audit partner presented a written report that provided information about three deficiencies in internal control considered to be significant by the auditor.

Legal counsel for Tetonic updated the board on final resolution of the Ontario Ministry of Environment and Climate Change report findings. The final settlement requires Tetonic to modify some of the air handling equipment at its zinc refineries that is expected to cost about $400 000. No other penalties were imposed by the provincial ministry.

The audit committee and the compensation committee provided an update of issues discussed at each of their respective meetings.

REQUIRED

a. How do you, as the auditor, know that all minutes have been made available to you?

b. Read the minutes of the meetings of March 5 and October 21. Use the following format to list and explain information that is relevant for the 2017 audit:

Information Relevant to 2017 Audit	Audit Action Required
1.	
2.	

c. Read the minutes of the meeting of March 5, 2017. Did any of that information pertain to the December 31, 2016, audit? Explain what the auditor should have done during the December 31, 2016, audit with respect to 2017 minutes.

6-35 **3** **5** During the audit of Xtra Technology Inc. (XTI), Andrea found the following journal entry occurring at the end of each month:

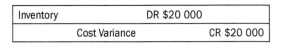

Inventory	DR $20 000	
Cost Variance		CR $20 000

The accounting manager told Andrea that this was a regular entry made every month to account for the deviation from actual cost to standard costing for inventory. Andrea was skeptical of this explanation as it was the same every month, and there were other journal entries that appeared to deal with the cost variances adequately, so she asked for the supporting documents for the entries. The accounting manager told her that there were no supporting documents as this was an automatic entry made every month, authorized by the controller. He had never considered checking it before. When Andrea asked the controller about the entries, she discovered that the company purchased inventory from a company controlled by the same company that owned a controlling interest in XTI. The $20 000 was actually a purchase, but they preferred to record it as a cost variance. The controller told Andrea not to be concerned about it and that the parent company's auditors would take care of all transactions between the two companies in their consolidated accounting.

REQUIRED

Assume that you are a manager with the audit firm and Andrea reports to you. Explain your concerns, if any, over the information that Andrea has learned.

(Extract from AU1 CGA-Canada Examinations developed by the Certified General Accountants Association of Canada © 2011 CGA-Canada. Reproduced with permission. All rights reserved.)

6-36 **3** In your audit of Canyon Outdoor Provision Company's financial statements, the following transactions came to your attention:

1. Canyon Outdoor's operating lease for its main store is with York Properties, which is a real estate investment firm owned by Travis Smedes. Smedes is a member of Canyon Outdoor's board of directors.
2. One of Canyon Outdoor's main suppliers for kayaks is Hessel Boating Company. Canyon Outdoor has purchased kayaks and canoes from Hessel for the last 25 years, under a long-term contract arrangement.
3. Short-term financing lines of credit are provided by Cameron Bank and Trust. Suzanne Strayhorn is the lending officer assigned to the Canyon Outdoor account. Suzanne is the wife of the largest investor of Canyon Outdoor.
4. Hillsborough Travel partners with Canyon Outdoor to provide hiking and rafting adventure vacations. The owner of Hillsborough Travel lives in the same neighbourhood as the CEO of Canyon Outdoor. They are acquaintances, but not close friends.
5. The board of directors consists of several individuals who own stock in Canyon Outdoor. At a recent board meeting, the board approved its annual dividend payable to shareholders effective June 1.

REQUIRED

a. Define what constitutes a "related party."
b. Which of the preceding transactions would most likely be considered to be a related party transaction?
c. What financial statement implications, if any, would each of the above transactions have for Canyon Outdoor?
d. What procedures might auditors consider to help them identify potential related party transactions for clients like Canyon Outdoor?

6-37 **7** **10** Statements of earnings and financial position for Prairie Stores Corporation are shown.

REQUIRED

a. Use professional judgment in determining overall materiality based on revenue, net income before taxes, total assets, and shareholders' equity. Your conclusions should be stated in terms of percentages and dollars.
b. Assume you complete the audit and conclude that financial statement misstatements exceed materiality. What should you do?
c. As discussed in part (b), likely net earnings from continuing operations before income taxes were used as a base for materiality when completing the audit. Discuss why most auditors use before-tax net earnings instead of after-tax net earnings when calculating materiality based on the income statement.

Prairie Stores Corporation
Statement of Earnings

	For the 52 Weeks Ended		
	March 30, 2018	April 1, 2017	April 1, 2016
Revenue			
Net sales	$8 351 149	$6 601 255	$5 959 587
Other income	59 675	43 186	52 418
	8 410 824	6 644 441	6 012 005
Costs and expenses			
Cost of sales	5 197 375	4 005 548	3 675 369
Marketing, general, and administrative expenses	2 590 080	2 119 590	1 828 169
Provision for loss on restructured operations	64 100	–	–
Interest expense	141 62	46 737	38 546
	7 993 217	6 171 875	5 542 084
Earnings from continuing operations before income taxes	417 607	472 566	469 921
Income taxes	196 700	217 200	214 100
Earnings from continuing operations	220 970	255 366	255 821
Provision for loss on discontinued operations, net of income taxes	20 700	–	–
Net earnings	$ 200 207	$ 255 366	$ 255 821

Prairie Stores Corporation
Statement of Financial Position

Assets	March 30, 2018		April 1, 2017	
Current assets				
Cash		$ 39 683		$ 37 566
Temporary investments (at cost, which approximates market)		123 421		271 639
Receivables, less allowances of $16 808 in 2018 and $17 616 in 2017		899 752		759 001
Inventories				
Finished product	680 974		550 407	
Raw materials and supplies	443 175		353 795	
		1 124 149		904 202
Deferred income tax benefits		9 633		10 468
Prepaid expenses		57 468		35 911
Total current assets		2 254 106		2 018 787
Land, buildings, equipment at cost, less accumulated amortization		1 393 902		1 004 455
Investments in affiliated companies and sundry assets		112 938		83 455
Goodwill and other intangible assets		99 791		23 145
Total assets		$3 860 737		$3 129 842
Liabilities and Shareholders' Equity				
Current liabilities				
Notes payable		$ 280 238		$ 113 411
Current portion of long-term debt		64 594		12 336
Accounts and drafts payable		359 511		380 395
Accrued salaries, wages, and vacations		112 200		63 557
Accrued income taxes		76 497		89 151
Other accrued liabilities including goods and services tax		321 871		269 672
Current liabilities		1 214 893		928 522
Long-term debt		730 987		390 687
Other noncurrent liabilities		146 687		80 586
Accrued income tax liability		142 344		119 715
Total liabilities		2 234 911		1 519 510
Shareholders' equity				
Common stock issued, 51 017 shares in 2018 and 50 992 in 2017		200 195		199 576
Retained earnings		1 425 631		1 410 756
Total shareholders' equity		1 625 826		1 610 332
Total liabilities and shareholders' equity		$3 860 737		$3 129 842

Professional Judgment Problems and Cases

6-38 [2] Refer to Auditing in Action 6-1, which contains an excerpt from the audit partner's memo regarding client acceptance/continuance of Enron.

REQUIRED

1. While hindsight provides perfect clarity, what judgment traps do you think may have hindered these partners in making their client-retention decision?
2. What processes does the partner highlight in his memo that address judgment traps?
3. What ethical blind spots do you think may have influenced the partners' decision-making process?

6-39 [4] [5] You are auditing payroll for the Morehead Technologies company for the year ended October 31, 2018. Included next are amounts from the client's trial balance, along with comparative audited information for the prior year.

	Audited Balance	Preliminary Balance (unaudited)
	10/31/2017	10/31/2018
Sales	$51 316 234	$57 474 182
Executive salaries	546 940	615 970
Factory hourly payroll	10 038 877	11 476 319
Factory supervisors' salaries	785 825	810 588
Office salaries	1 990 296	2 055 302
Sales commissions	2 018 149	2 367 962

You have obtained the following information to help you perform preliminary analytical procedures for the payroll account balances.

1. There has been a significant increase in the demand for Morehead's products. The increase in sales was due to both an increase in the average selling price of 4 percent and an increase in units sold that resulted from the increased demand and an increased marketing effort.
2. Even though sales volume increased, there was no addition of executives, factory supervisors, or office personnel.
3. All employees, including executives but excluding commission salespeople, received a 3 percent salary increase starting November 1, 2017. Commission salespeople receive their increased compensation through the increase in sales.
4. The increased number of factory hourly employees was accomplished by recalling employees that had been laid off. They receive the same wage rate as existing employees. Morehead does not permit overtime.
5. Commission salespeople receive a 5 percent commission on all sales on which a commission is given. Approximately 75 percent of sales earn sales commission. The other 25 percent are "call-ins," for which no commission is given. Commissions are paid in the month following the month they are earned.

REQUIRED

a. Use the final balances for the prior year included above and the information in Items 1–5 to develop an expected value for each account, except sales.
b. Calculate the difference between your expectation and the client's recorded amount as a percentage using the following formula:

(Expected value − Recorded amount) / Expected value

c. What are your conclusions from the analytical procedures you performed (do the amounts appear reasonable)? What areas require additional audit work?

6-40 [4] [5] Your comparison of the gross margin percent for Jones Drugs for the years 2015 through 2018 indicates a significant decline. This is shown by the following information:

	2018	2017	2016	2015
Sales (thousands)	$14 211	$12 916	$11 462	$10 351
CGS (thousands)	9 223	8 266	7 313	6 573
Gross margin	$ 4 988	$ 4 650	$ 4 149	$ 3 778
Percent	35.1	36.0	36.2	36.5

A discussion with Nandini Sharma, the controller, brings to light two possible explanations. She informs you that the industry gross profit percent in the retail drug industry declined fairly steadily for three years, which accounts for part of the decline. A second factor was the declining percent of the total volume resulting from the pharmacy part of the business. The pharmacy sales represent the most profitable portion of the business, yet the competition from discount drugstores prevents it from expanding as fast as the nondrug items such as magazines, candy, and many other items sold. Sharma feels strongly that these two factors are the cause of the decline.

The following additional information is obtained from independent sources and the client's records as a means of investigating the controller's explanations:

	Jones Drugs ($ in thousands)				
	Drug Sales	Nondrug Sales	Drug Cost of Goods Sold	Nondrug Cost of Goods Sold	Industry Gross Profit Percent for Retailers of Drugs and Related Products
2018	$5 126	$9 085	$3 045	$6 178	32.7
2017	5 051	7 865	2 919	5 347	32.9
2016	4 821	6 641	2 791	4 522	33.0
2015	4 619	5 732	2 665	3 908	33.2

REQUIRED

a. Evaluate the explanation provided by Sharma. Show calculations to support your conclusions.

b. Which specific aspects of the client's financial statements require intensive investigation in this audit?

6-41 **3** **4** Airship Solutions is an Australian company that provides aerial photography, videography, and advertising, with seven locations around the world. Its blimps, which are filled with nonexploding helium, have Australian Civil Aviation Safety Authority certification, which allows the blimps to be flown where there are large groups of people. There are also many balloon companies that sell blimps of various sizes, starting at $400. Since Airship's product is much more than a balloon, prices start at $3600.

REQUIRED

1. Given that Airship seems to be in two different industries—aerial photography and aerial advertising—how would you decide what would be a reasonable gross margin for Airship Solutions? What sources of information would you use?
2. How vulnerable would Airship be to downturns in the economy? Why?
3. What sources of information would you use to provide yourself with a thorough knowledge of this business?

6-42 **3** **4** You are engaged in the annual audit of the financial statements of Maulack Corp., a medium-sized wholesale company that manufactures light fixtures. The company has 25 shareholders. During your review of the minutes, you observe that the president's salary has been increased substantially over the preceding year by the action of the board of directors. His present salary is much greater than salaries paid to presidents of companies of comparable size and is clearly excessive. You determine that the method of computing the president's salary was changed for the year under audit. In previous years, the president's salary was consistently based on sales. In the latest year, however, his salary was based on net income before income taxes. Maulack Corp. is in a cyclical industry and would have had an extremely profitable year, except that the increase in the president's salary siphoned off much of the income that would have accrued to the shareholders. The president is a minority shareholder of the company.

REQUIRED

a. What is the implication of this condition for the fair presentation of the financial statements?

b. Using the ethical decision making framework from Chapter 3, discuss the auditor's responsibility for disclosing this situation.

c. Discuss the effect, if any, that the situation has on:
  i The fairness of the presentation of the financial statements.
  ii The consistency of the application of accounting principles.

(Adapted from AICPA.)

6-43 **2** Winston Black was an audit partner at Maharajah, Davis, LLP. He was in the process of reviewing the audit files for the audit of a new client, McMullan Resourcing. McMullan was in the business of heavy construction. Winston was conducting his first review after the field work had been substantially completed. Normally, he would have done an initial review during the earlier planning phases as required by his firm's policies; however, he had been overwhelmed by an emergency with his largest and most important client. He rationalized not reviewing the details of the client risk analysis or other audit planning information because (1) the audit was being overseen by Sara Beale, a manager in whom he had confidence, and (2) there were a few days of field work left, when any additional audit work could be completed.

Winston then found that he was confronted with several problems. First, he found that his firm may have accepted McMullan without complying with its new client acceptance procedures. McMullan came to Maharajah, Davis on a recommendation from a friend of Winston's. Winston got "credit" for the new business, which was important to him because it would affect his compensation from the firm. Because Winston was busy, he told Sara to conduct a new client acceptance review and let him know if there were any problems. He never heard from Sara and assumed everything was in order. In reviewing Sara's preplanning documentation, he saw a check mark in the box "contact prior auditors" but found no details indicating if it was done. When he asked Sara about this, she responded, "I called Gardner Smith [the responsible partner with McMullan's prior audit firm] and left a voicemail message for him. He never returned my call. I talked to Ted McMullan about the change of auditors, and he told me that he informed Gardner about the change and that Gardner said, 'Fine, I'll help in any way I can.' Ted said Gardner sent over copies of analyses of property, plant, and equipment, and equity accounts, which Ted gave to me. I asked Ted why they replaced Gardner's firm, and he told me it was over the tax contingency issue and the size of their fee. Other than that, Ted said the relationship was fine."

The tax contingency issue that Sara referred to was a situation in which McMullan had entered into litigation with a bank from which it had received a loan. The result of the litigation was that the bank forgave McMullan several hundred thousand dollars in debt. This was a windfall to McMullan, and they recorded it as a capital gain, taking the position that it was not regular income. The prior auditors disputed this position and insisted that a contingent tax liability be recorded. This upset McMullan, but the company agreed in order to receive an unqualified opinion. Before hiring Maharajah, Davis as their new auditors, McMullan requested that Maharajah, Davis review the situation. Maharajah, Davis believed the contingency was remote and agreed to the elimination of the contingent liability.

The second problem involved a long-term contract with a customer in Montreal. Under IFRS (International Financial Reporting Standards), McMullan was required to recognize income on this contract using the percentage-of-completion method. The contract was partially completed as of the year-end and was material to the financial statements. When Winston went to review the copy of the contract in the audit files, he found three things. First, there was a contract summary prepared by the sales manager that set out its major features. Second, there was a copy of the contract written in French. Third, there was a signed confirmation (in English) confirming the terms and status of the contract. The space on the confirmation requesting information about any contract disputes was left blank, indicating no such problems.

Winston's concern about the contract was that to recognize income in accordance with IFRS, the contract had to be enforceable. Often, contracts contain a cancellation clause that might mitigate enforceability. Because he was not able to read French, Winston could not tell whether the contract contained such a clause. When he asked Sara about this, she responded that she had asked the company's vice-president of sales about the contract and he had told her that it was their standard contract. The company's standard contract did have a cancellation clause in it, but it required mutual agreement and could not be cancelled unilaterally by the buyer.

REQUIRED

a. Evaluate whether Maharajah, Davis, LLP, complied with generally accepted auditing standards in their acceptance of McMullan Resources as a new client. What can they do at this point in the engagement to resolve any deficiencies if they exist?

b. Consider whether sufficient audit work has been done with regard to McMullan's Montreal contract. If not, what more should be done?

c. Evaluate and discuss whether Winston and Sara conducted themselves in accordance with generally accepted auditing standards.

6-44 7 8 9 Chocolates From Heaven Inc. (CFHI) produces small batch artisanal chocolate. It is a private company owned by two equal shareholders, David Chang and Sharjeel Ahmed. They started CHFI in 1996 and have grown a successful business. They intend to sell the business this year (2018) and already have an interested buyer. Collateral for the loan is inventory and accounts receivable. Audited financial statements are a requirement of the loan agreement. Audit Class LLP has been appointed the new auditor this year. The previous auditor was a small local firm (sole-proprietorship) and the owner retired last year.

The following are the *draft* financial statements for the year ended 2018.

Chocolates From Heaven Inc
Extracts from statement of profit and loss
For the year ended December 31, 2018

	2018	2017
	(unaudited)	(audited)
Sales	$2 469 974	$1 481 984
Cost of sales	1 259 687	711 353
Gross margin	1 210 287	770 631
Expenses		
Operating expenses	861 725	565 643
Loss due to fire	53 478	—
	915 203	565 643
Operating income	295 084	204 988
Other expenses (income)		
Interest expenses	8 000	12 000
Net Income before income taxes	287 084	192 988
Income taxes	43 063	28 948
Net Income after taxes	$ 244 021	$ 164 040

Chocolates From Heaven Inc
Extracts from balance sheet
For the year ended December 31, 2018

	2018	2017
	(unaudited)	(audited)
Cash	$ 297	$ 145 768
Receivables, less allowance	411 662	123 499
Inventories	104 974	47 424
Prepaid expenses	55 678	2 500
Property, plant and equipment, net	1 445 260	1 111 739

REQUIRED

You are the audit manager assigned to CFHI and you are performing the materiality assessment.

1. Assess overall materiality.
   a) Who are the users and what economic decision? Conclude on a materiality benchmark.
   b) How sensitive are the users? Conclude on a percentage and calculate the planning materiality.

3. Assess performance materiality.

4. Identify any specific user needs. Recommend a specific materiality.

5. Explain how materiality will impact your audit plan.

6-45 3 The Ontario Securities Commission (OSC) rules require management of public companies to include background information about the business, including discussion and analysis by management about the most recent financial condition and results of operations (referred to as MD&A). While these disclosures are primarily intended for current and future investors, they also provide rich information for auditors, especially during the client acceptance and continuance phase of an audit. Additionally, similar disclosures by a client's competitors in their financial statements may also provide useful industry-specific information that can be helpful during audit planning.

SEDAR is the System for Electronic Document Analysis and Retrieval, the electronic filing system for the disclosure of documents of public companies and investment funds across Canada. All Canadian public companies and investment funds are generally required to file their documents in the SEDAR system.

REQUIRED

1. Visit the SEDAR website (**www.sedar.com**) and locate the most recent MD&A filing for Air Canada (search for, without quotes, company name "Air Canada" and document type "Management's Discussion & Analysis").

2. Review the information contained in the "Overview" section. Describe the nature of information included in this section and discuss how the information might be helpful to auditors in obtaining an understanding of the client's business and industry.

3. Locate the most recent MD&A for WestJet Airlines Ltd. (search for "WestJet"). Review the information contained in the document and describe how WestJet's disclosures might be informative to auditors of Air Canada.

ASSESSING THE RISK OF MATERIAL MISSTATEMENT

So far, we have discussed client acceptance and preliminary planning, including understanding the entity and the environment and preliminary analytical procedures, and the auditors' materiality judgments. This chapter will consider how the evidence which the auditor has gathered through those two processes is used to help the auditor identify significant risks and assess risk of material misstatement, which forms the basis of the audit strategy.

LEARNING OBJECTIVES

After studying this chapter, you should be able to:

1 Define risk in auditing.

2 Distinguish the different types of risk assessment procedures.

3 Identify significant risks that require special audit consideration.

4 Perform a preliminary fraud risk assessment.

5 Describe the fraud triangle and identify conditions for fraud.

6 Develop responses to identify fraud risks.

7 Understand the audit risk model, its components, and its relevance to audit planning.

8 Assess acceptable audit risk.

9 Assess inherent risk.

10 Understand the relationship between risks and audit evidence.

STANDARDS REFERENCED IN THIS CHAPTER

CAS 240 – The auditor's responsibilities relating to fraud in an audit of financial statements

CAS 315 – Identifying and assessing the risks of material misstatement through understanding the entity and its environment

What's the Big Deal About Risk?

With the explosion of the internet over the past decades, new advertising approaches have been launched to market products and services to consumers. A California-based company, WebXU, emerged in 2010 as a performance media company that generated revenues from advertisers interested in finding sales leads from engaged consumers. Advertisers bid in a real-time auction on a cost-per-lead or cost-per-auction basis for access to consumers expressing interest in a particular product.

On December 5, 2011, the Las Vegas–based accounting firm of L.L. Bradford & Company, LLC, was engaged to audit WebXU's financial statements for the year ended December 31, 2011. WebXU filed its 2011 annual financial statements with the Securities and Exchange Commission (SEC) on April 9, 2012, which included L.L. Bradford & Company's opinion that WebXU's financial statements were presented fairly, in all material respects, in accordance with U.S. GAAP. Three short years later, the SEC revoked the registration of the securities of WebXU, an action prompted by WebXU's failure to file any periodic reports with the SEC since it had filed its financial statements for the year ended December 31, 2012.

continued >

continued   The PCAOB alleged that the partner had failed to properly assess the risk of material misstatement with respect to WebXU's 2011 financial statements and had failed to develop an audit plan that included planned risk assessment procedures and responses to the risk of material misstatement. According to the PCAOB, the firm's "risk assessment was performed at a level of aggregation above that permitted by PCAOB standards." For example, the auditor assessed the risk on all assets and all liabilities collectively. "As a result, cash carried the same risk assessment as goodwill." At the time, goodwill recorded in connection with a recent acquisition was the largest item on WebXU's balance sheet and constituted nearly two-thirds of reported assets. Less than nine months later, WebXU wrote off the full value of that goodwill.

Disciplinary proceedings issued by the PCAOB in April 2015 against the engagement partner imposed sanctions that censured and suspended him for one year from the date of the order and also prevented him from being an associated person with a PCAOB-registered firm. In addition to the one-year suspension, the engagement partner was also ordered to not serve as or supervise another person in the role of engagement partner or engagement quality reviewer for one additional year.

Sources: Based on 1. PCAOB Release No. 105-2015-007, April 1, 2015, accessed July 30, 2017, at **pcaobus.org**; 2. SEC Release No. 73869, December 18, 2014, accessed July 30, 2017, at **www.sec.gov**.

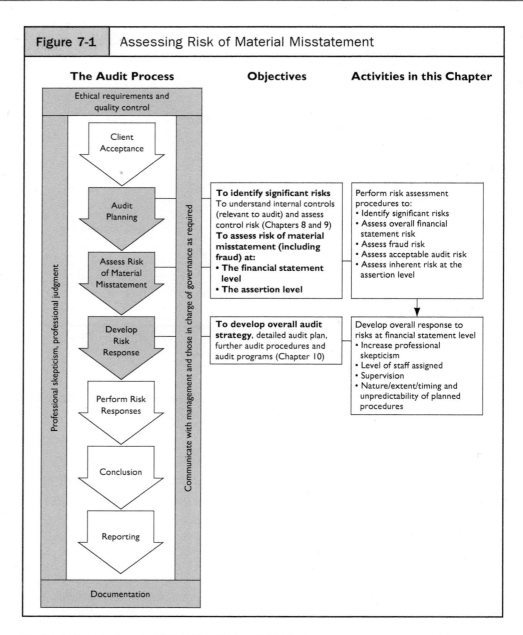

Figure 7-1 | Assessing Risk of Material Misstatement

In this chapter, we cover the auditor's assessment of the risks of material misstatement, including significant risks and inherent risks. When auditors assess risks, they use a considerable amount of the information acquired and documented during client acceptance and audit planning. As illustrated in Figure 7-1, an auditor assesses the risk of material misstatement at the financial statement level and the assertion level in order to develop an appropriate risk response.

As noted in the opening vignette about WebXU's auditor, failure to assess the risk of material misstatement at the appropriate level can be hugely detrimental.

AUDIT RISK

LO **1** Define risk in auditing.

Auditing standards require the auditor to obtain an understanding of the entity and its environment, including its internal controls, to assess the risk of material misstatements in the client's financial statements. Chapter 6 described how the auditor gains an understanding of the client's business and industry to assess client business risk and the risk of material misstatements.

Auditors accept some level of **risk** or uncertainty in performing the audit function. The auditor recognizes, for example, the inherent uncertainty about the appropriateness of evidence, the effectiveness of a client's internal controls, and whether the financial statements are fairly stated when the audit is completed. Because the assessment of risk is a matter of professional judgment, rather than a precise measurement, responding to these risks properly is critical to achieving a high-quality audit.

Risk—the acceptance by auditors that there is some level of uncertainty in performing the audit function.

The risk of material misstatement is a function of the susceptibility of the financial statements as a whole, or of individual accounts and assertions, to misstatement, including the risk that the client's controls may not be effective in preventing or detecting and correcting the misstatements. The risk of material misstatement exists at two levels: at the overall financial statement level *and* at the assertion level for classes of transactions, account balances, and presentation and disclosures.

Assess Risk of Material Misstatement at the Overall Financial Statement Level

The risk of material misstatement at the overall financial statement level refers to risks that relate pervasively to the financial statements as a whole and potentially affect many assertions. It is important for the auditor to consider risks at the overall financial statement level, given that those risks may increase the likelihood of risks of material misstatement across a number of accounts and assertions for those accounts.

A number of overarching factors may increase the risks of material misstatement at the overall financial statement level. For example, deficiencies in management's integrity or competence, as well as weak entity level controls, such as ineffective oversight by the board of directors or inadequate accounting systems and records, increase the likelihood that material misstatements may be present in assertions affecting several classes of transactions, account balances, or financial statement disclosures. Similarly, declining economic conditions or significant changes in the industry may increase the risk of material misstatement at the overall financial statement level.

Assess Risk of Material Misstatement at the Assertion Level

Auditing standards require the auditor to assess the risk of material misstatement at the assertion level for classes of transactions, account balances, and presentation and disclosure in order to determine the nature, timing, and extent of further audit procedures. As discussed in Chapter 5, auditors develop audit objectives for each of the assertions and perform audit procedures to obtain persuasive audit evidence that each of those audit objectives is achieved. As a result, auditors specifically assess the risk related to assertions for classes of transactions, account balances, and presentation and disclosures.

The risk of material misstatement at the assertion level consists of two components: inherent risk and control risk. Inherent risk represents the auditor's assessment of the susceptibility of an assertion to material misstatement, before considering the effectiveness of the client's internal controls. For example, inherent risk may be higher for the valuation assertion related to those accounts that require complex calculations or accounting estimates that involve significant estimation judgment.

Control risk represents the auditor's assessment of the risk that a material misstatement could occur in an assertion and not be prevented or detected on a timely basis by the client's internal controls. For example, control risk may be higher for the valuation assertion of those accounts mentioned if the client's internal control procedures fail to include independent review and verification of the complex calculations or the significant estimates developed. Inherent risk and control risk are the client's risks and they exist independent of the audit of the financial statements. We will discuss both inherent risk and control risk later in this chapter.

Develop an Appropriate Risk Response

As Figure 7-1 illustrates, from the assessment of risk of material misstatement, the auditor develops (1) an overall risk response, which addresses those pervasive risks at the financial statement level, and (2) a risk response at the assertion level, which involves developing tests of controls, if relevant, and substantive audit procedures that will test the specific assertions regarding the relevant classes of transactions, account balances, and disclosures. We have discussed how auditors develop audit procedures to test specific assertions in our chapter on audit evidence (Chapter 5), and in Part 3 of the book, we dig deeper into how to develop an appropriate risk response at the assertion level for the accounts of each cycle.

The overall risk response to risks at the financial statement level represents the overall audit strategy, which we introduced in Chapter 6. As discussed in Chapter 6, possible adjustments to overall audit strategy to address specific risks would be the timing of the audit procedures and types and allocation of resources to be deployed.

Auditing in Action 7-1, regarding the Livent audit also described in the opening vignette of Chapter 4, is an example of how auditors assess risk of material misstatement and develop an overall risk response (audit strategy) to address the identified significant risks. First, the auditors assessed the risk of material misstatement at the financial statement level (pervasive risk factors that could apply to many assertions): management sensitivity to net earnings (Point 1), aggressive accounting policies (Point 3), and high client business risk (Point 4). Included in this risk assessment is also the identification of two significant risks related to the relevant assertions for two accounts: the valuation of preproduction costs (these are costs that were deferred until the shows were in production) (Point 2) and the occurrence of revenue (Point 3). The risk response section of the planning memo summarizes Deloitte's overall risk response (audit strategy)—which included:

- Assign experienced staff to the engagement;
- Instruct staff to use a heightened level of professional skepticism;
- Increase involvement of audit partners and managers; and
- Closer supervision and review.

Although the ICAO (Institute of Chartered Accountants of Ontario, now CPA Ontario) disciplinary committee concluded that three of the four partners involved with the Livent audit failed to meet the standards of professional conduct, the disciplinary committee acknowledged that the audit team had appropriately identified the risks and developed an appropriate overall audit strategy or risk response. The excerpt from the planning memo below illustrates the auditor's risk assessment and risk response.

Risk Assessment

1. The company is a public entity as both an SEC and OSC (Ontario Securities Commission) registrant. The company, its financial reports, and management historically have attracted a high level of scrutiny and public observation. Management is sensitive to reported net earnings levels.
2. The valuation of preproduction costs is subject to management estimation and financial projections. Resultant amortization and/or write-offs of preproduction costs can have significant impact on net earnings.
3. The company has entered into a number of material and unique revenue generating transactions. Management's selection of reporting methods may be aggressive.

4. The company faces both internal and external business and industry risks based on the success of its own theatrical productions and the general health of the live theatrical consumer market.

Risk Response	Comments
Ensure that the assigned audit partners and staff have the requisite experience, skills, and expertise.	The client service team includes senior partners of the firm with the requisite skills.
Increase the professional skepticism of all personnel involved in the audit engagement.	Articulated to audit staff.
Increase involvement of engagement management at all stages of the audit engagement to ensure that the appropriate work is planned and its performance is properly supervised.	The engagement partners and senior audit manager will be involved with all significant audit and financial reporting issues upfront with regard to planning and their audit and resolution.

Source: Based on Institute of Chartered Accountants of Ontario Disciplinary Committee, "In the matter of Douglas Barrington, FCA, Peter Chant, FCA, Anthony Power, FCA, and Claudio Russo, CA, members of the Institute under Rule 206 of Rules of Professional Conduct, Decision and Reasons for Decision, February 11, 2007."

RISK ASSESSMENT PROCEDURES

LO **2** Distinguish the different types of risk assessment procedures.

As discussed in Chapter 6, to obtain an understanding of the entity and its environment, including the entity's internal controls, the auditor performs risk assessment procedures to identify and assess the risk of material misstatement, whether due to fraud or error. Risk assessment procedures include the following:

1. Inquiries of management and others within the entity.
2. Analytical procedures.
3. Observation and inspection.
4. Discussion among engagement team members.
5. Other risk assessment procedures.

Collectively, the performance of risk assessment procedures is designed to help the auditor obtain an understanding of the entity and its environment, including internal controls, for purposes of assessing the risk of material misstatement when planning the audit, as illustrated in Figure 7-2; however, risk assessment procedures do not provide sufficient appropriate (in other words, persuasive) audit evidence to form an audit opinion on the financial statements.

Inquiries of Management and Others Within the Entity

As Figure 7-1 illustrates, ongoing communication with management is necessary for the conduct of the audit. Management and others within the entity may have important information to assist the auditor in identifying the risks of material misstatement. Auditors will frequently interact with members of management and others with

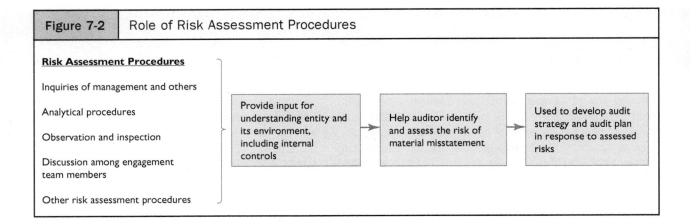

Figure 7-2 Role of Risk Assessment Procedures

Risk Assessment Procedures

Inquiries of management and others

Analytical procedures

Observation and inspection

Discussion among engagement team members

Other risk assessment procedures

Provide input for understanding entity and its environment, including internal controls

Help auditor identify and assess the risk of material misstatement

Used to develop audit strategy and audit plan in response to assessed risks

financial reporting responsibilities to understand the entity and its environment, and to learn about the design and operation of internal controls. In addition to making inquiries of those individuals, auditing standards emphasize the benefits and importance of obtaining information or different perspectives through inquiries of others within the entity and other employees with different levels of authority.

Inquiries of those charged with governance, such as the board of directors or audit committee, may provide information about the overall competitive environment and strategy of the business that may give important insights about overall client business risks. Those charged with governance are often involved in significant strategic and operational decisions, such as the pursuit of acquisitions or new lines of business. As a result, they may have insider knowledge that may help the auditor identify heightened risks of material misstatements. Additionally, inquiries of those charged with governance provide the auditor with important insights about the overall governance oversight provided by the board of directors and others, which is an important aspect of internal control.

Similarly, because internal auditors typically have exposure to all aspects of the client's business and operations, they may have important information about risks at the overall financial statement level or assertion level. Most internal audit functions develop their internal audit scope based on a risk assessment process that considers risks to design their audit strategies. Inquiries of internal audit personnel may provide important information about key risks to the business affecting not only financial reporting, but also operations and compliance with laws and regulations that may increase the likelihood of material misstatements. Because a primary focus of most internal audit functions is evaluating the effectiveness of the entity's internal processes related to financial reporting, operations, and compliance, inquiries of internal audit personnel may provide valuable information about the design and operating effectiveness of internal controls.

Auditors may also benefit from making inquiries of others within the entity who are involved in different roles and who are at different levels within the client's operations. For example, individuals who help manage legal affairs or regulatory compliance for the entity may have knowledge relevant to the auditor's assessment of the risk of material misstatements, especially the impact of noncompliance on financial reporting. Other personnel, such as those involved in marketing or sales or those involved with complex or unusual transactions, may provide insights about risks related to revenue recognition or issues involving valuation of receivables.

Analytical Procedures

As described in Chapter 6, auditors are required to perform preliminary analytical procedures as part of audit planning in every audit to better understand the entity and to assess client business risks. The performance of analytical procedures may help the auditor identify unusual amounts, ratios, or trends that might reveal unusual transactions or events having audit implications. Analytical procedures performed as part of the auditor's risk assessment procedures may include both financial and non-financial information, and they often use data aggregated at a high level. As a result, they may only provide a broad indication about whether a material misstatement exists.

Observation and Inspection

The types of evidence described in Chapter 5 include both observation and inspection. Recall that the evidence obtained through observation generally involves the auditor looking at a process or procedure being performed by others. For example, observation of the entity's operations, such as the manufacturing and shipping of products to customers, and tours of the entity's facilities may increase the auditor's understanding of the entity and its environment. Additionally, the inspection of documents such as the organization's strategic plan, business model, and its organizational structure increases the auditor's understanding of how the business is structured and how it organizes key business functions and leaders in the oversight of day-to-day operations.

In addition to learning about the business and its environment, auditors also observe client personnel performing important processes related to financial reporting to help them understand the design of internal controls related to the financial statements as a whole and to specific audit objectives related to classes of transactions, account balances, and disclosures. Auditors often combine observation of processes with the inspection of documents and records, such as purchase orders, invoices, and receiving reports related to disbursements, that are part of those processes to gain an understanding of the design effectiveness of internal controls related to financial reporting. Together, observation and inspection provide auditors with a basis for understanding internal controls, which is an important input for the assessment of the risk of material misstatement. Understanding internal control is discussed further in Chapter 8.

Discussions Among Engagement Team Members

Auditing standards require the engagement partner and other key engagement team members to discuss the susceptibility of the client's financial statements to material misstatement. Those standards explicitly require that this discussion specifically consider the susceptibility of the client's financial statements to fraud, in addition to their susceptibility to material misstatement due to errors.

Discussion among the engagement partner and other key members of the engagement team provides an opportunity for more experienced team members, including the engagement partner, to share their insights about the entity and its environment, including their understanding of internal controls, with other members of the engagement team. The discussion should include an exchange of ideas or brainstorming among the engagement team members about business risks and how and where the financial statements might be susceptible to material misstatement, whether due to fraud or error.

As highlighted in Chapter 2, one of the key factors underlying audit quality is building the right team and providing the right support. Including key members of the engagement team in discussions with the engagement partner allows all members of the engagement team to become better informed about the potential for material misstatement of the financial statements in the specific areas of the audit assigned to them, and it helps them gain an appreciation for how the results of audit procedures performed by them affect other areas of the audit.

It may not be practical for all members of the engagement team to be included in a single discussion. For example, on large global audit engagements with team members located in multiple cities around the globe, it may not be feasible for all of them to participate in a single discussion. The engagement partner may choose to discuss matters with members of the engagement team who are responsible for audits of components of the financial statement, such as the Asia Pacific region of a multinational company, while delegating discussion with others to other members of the engagement team leadership. Regardless, the engagement partner is responsible for determining which matters should be communicated to engagement team members not involved in the discussion.

Other Risk Assessment Procedures

Other procedures may be performed to assist in the auditor's assessment of the risk of material misstatement. For example, information obtained during the client acceptance or continuance evaluation process, such as discussions with predecessor auditors or insights obtained from background checks for new client engagements, may heighten the auditor's awareness of the risks of material misstatement.

Information obtained from external sources, such as analyst or credit agency reports, trade and economic journals, and regulatory publications, may strengthen the auditor's understanding of the entity and its environment to assess the risk of material misstatement. For example, the auditor may learn about new regulatory requirements that impact the accounting for certain types of transactions within an industry.

CONCEPT CHECK

7-1 At what two levels does the auditor assess risk of material misstatement?

7-2 Describe the types of procedures that constitute risk assessment procedures. Explain why they are not considered persuasive evidence.

LO 3 Identify significant risks that require special audit consideration.

Significant risk—an identified and assessed risk of material misstatement that, in the auditor's professional judgment, requires special audit consideration.

CAS

IDENTIFICATION OF SIGNIFICANT RISKS

As part of the auditor's assessment of the risk of material misstatement, whether due to fraud or error, the auditor is required to determine whether any of the risks identified are, in the auditor's professional judgment, a significant risk. A **significant risk** represents an identified and assessed risk that, in the auditor's professional judgment, requires special audit consideration. If the auditor determines a significant risk exists, he or she is required to obtain an understanding of the controls, including control activities relevant to that risk. We will discuss internal controls in Chapters 8 and 9.

In order to identify significant risks, per CAS 315.28, the auditor is required to consider all of the following:

1. Risk of fraud;
2. Risk related to recent significant economic, accounting, or other developments;
3. Complexity of transactions;
4. Significant transactions with related parties;
5. Degree of subjectivity in the measurement of financial information, especially measurements involving a wide range of measurement uncertainty; and
6. Non-routine transactions—significant transactions that are outside the normal course of business for the entity or that otherwise appear to be unusual.

We will discuss fraud risk in more depth in the next section of this chapter. We have already discussed the consideration of risk factors with regards to recent significant economic, accounting, or other developments, as well as related parties, in Chapter 6.

Complexity of Transactions

Transactions can be complex for a variety of reasons—they may be new to the client, entail the interpretation of complex accounting standards, or involve a complex business arrangement or contract with a customer or supplier. For example, a client may engage in a new type of hedging transaction that management has not done in the past, thereby increasing the potential that the client's lack of experience and expertise in the underlying accounting treatment and estimation process will increase the risks of material misstatement. Similarly, the client may be a contractor that builds large commercial buildings and the contracts are very complex with numerous performance obligations and penalty clauses, making it difficult to determine when to recognize revenue.

Degree of Subjectivity and Estimation Uncertainty

Significant risks also relate to matters that require significant judgment because they include the development of accounting estimates for which significant measurement uncertainty exists. Estimation uncertainty is often related to assumptions about future events, which are difficult to predict. For example, fair value accounting related to unique and material hedging transactions would likely be considered a significant risk.

Nonroutine Transactions and Related Party Transactions

Significant risks often relate to **nonroutine transactions**, which represent transactions that are unusual, either due to size or nature, and that are infrequent in occurrence. For example, a retail client that normally sells its products through company-owned stores across the country may decide to sell to a competitor a large block of inventory located in a distribution centre. The terms of that transaction may be based on significant negotiations that include various buy-back provisions and warranties that increase risks of material misstatement related to revenue recognition and receivables collection.

> **Nonroutine transaction**—a transaction that is unusual, either due to size or nature, and that is infrequent in occurrence.

Nonroutine transactions may increase the risk of material misstatement because they often involve a greater extent of management intervention, including more reliance on manual versus automated data collection and processing, and they can involve complex calculations or unusual accounting principles not subject to effective internal controls due to their infrequent nature. Related party transactions often reflect these characteristics, thereby increasing the likelihood they are considered significant risks.

CONSIDERING FRAUD RISK

> **LO 4** Perform a preliminary fraud risk assessment.

While auditors perform risk assessment procedures to assess the risk of material misstatement due to fraud or error, the risk of not detecting a material misstatement due to fraud is higher than the risk of not detecting a misstatement due to error. As illustrated in Auditing in Action 7-2, fraud often involves complex and sophisticated schemes designed by perpetrators to conceal it. Further, individuals engaged in conducting a fraud often intentionally misrepresent information to the auditor, and they may try to conceal the transaction through collusion with others. As a result, identifying material misstatements due to fraud is difficult.

To assist the auditor in assessing the risk of material misstatement due to fraud, CAS 240 outlines the following procedures the auditor should perform to obtain information that will enable the auditor to assess fraud risk:

1. Discuss with audit team members the risks of material misstatement due to fraud.
2. Make inquiries to management, those in charge of governance, and others regarding processes for identifying and responding to fraud risk.
3. Evaluate unusual and unexpected relationships identified when performing analytical review procedures.
4. Evaluate the risk for revenue fraud and management override, and understand period-end.

The auditor's consideration of the risk of material misstatement due to fraud is made at both the financial statement level and at the assertion level for classes of transactions, account balances, and presentation and disclosures. The auditor's risk assessment should be ongoing throughout the audit, given that the auditor may obtain knowledge and information from the performance of audit procedures that suggest fraud may be present.

Because a number of high-profile instances of fraudulent financial reporting have involved misstatements in revenue recognition, auditing standards require the auditor to presume that risks of fraud exist in revenue recognition. As a result, risks related to audit objectives for revenue transactions and their related account balances and presentation and disclosure are presumed to be significant risks in most audits. We will discuss understanding period end (financial closing) in Chapter 10 and the risk of revenue fraud in Chapter 12.

Discussions Among Audit Team

CAS 240 requires the audit team to conduct discussions to share insights from more experienced audit team members and to brainstorm ideas that address the following:

1. How and where they believe the entity's financial statements might be susceptible to material misstatement due to fraud. This should include consideration of known external and internal factors affecting the entity that might:

- Create an incentive or pressure for management to commit fraud.
- Provide the opportunity for fraud to be perpetrated.
- Indicate a culture or environment that enables management to rationalize fraudulent acts.

2. How management could perpetrate and conceal fraudulent financial reporting.
3. How anyone might misappropriate assets of the entity.
4. How the auditor might respond to the susceptibility of material misstatements due to fraud.

Inquiries of Management, Those in Charge of Governance, and Others

The auditor's inquiries of management should address whether management has knowledge of any fraud or suspected fraud within the company. Auditors should also inquire about management's process of assessing fraud risks and the frequency of these assessments, the nature of fraud risks identified by management, any internal controls implemented to address those risks, and any information about fraud risks and related controls that management has reported to the audit committee.

The audit committee often assumes an active role in overseeing management's fraud risk assessment and response processes. The auditor must inquire of the audit committee or others charged with governance about their views of the risks of fraud and whether they have knowledge of any fraud or suspected fraud. For entities with an internal audit function, the auditor should inquire about internal audit's views of fraud risks and whether they have performed any procedures to identify or detect fraud during the year.

CAS 240 also requires the auditor to make inquiries of others within the entity `CAS` whose duties lie outside the normal financial reporting lines of responsibility. When coming into contact with company personnel, such as the inventory warehouse manager or purchasing agents, the auditor may inquire about the existence or suspicion of fraud. Throughout the audit, inquiries of executives and a wide variety of other employees provide opportunities for the auditor to learn about risks of fraud. When responses are inconsistent, the auditor should obtain additional audit evidence to resolve the inconsistency and to support or refute the original risk assessment.

Evaluate Unusual or Unexpected Relationships Identified

As we discussed in Chapter 5, auditors must perform analytical procedures during the planning and completion phases of the audit to help identify unusual transactions or events that might indicate the presence of material misstatements in the financial statements. When results from analytical procedures differ from the auditor's expectations, the auditor evaluates those results in light of other information obtained about the likelihood of fraud to determine if fraud risk is heightened.

In addition to the ratio analysis performed as part of preliminary analytical procedures described in Chapter 6, the auditor may perform horizontal and vertical analysis of the financial statements. In *horizontal analysis*, the account balance is compared to the previous period, and the percentage change in the account balances for the period is calculated. Figure 7-3 is an example of horizontal analysis applied to the condensed income statement for Hillsburg Hardware. For example, sales increased $11 860 (in 000s) from the prior year, which represents a 9 percent increase ($11 860/$131 226). In *vertical analysis*, the financial statement numbers are converted to percentages. The common-size financial statement in Figure 6-4 (page 181) is an example of vertical analysis applied to the detailed income statement for Hillsburg Hardware, with each income statement amount calculated as a percentage of sales. In vertical analysis of the balance sheet, balances are calculated as a percentage of total assets.

Figure 7-3 | Horizontal Analysis of Income Statement

Hillsburg Hardware Limited
Horizontal Analysis of Income Statement (in thousands)

	Year Ended December 31			
	2018	**2017**	**Change**	**Percentage Change**
Net sales	$143 086	$131 226	$11 860	9.0%
Cost of sales	103 241	94 876	8 365	8.8%
Gross profit	39 845	36 350	3 495	9.6%
Selling, general, and administrative expenses	32 475	29 656	2 819	9.5%
Operating income	7 370	6 694	676	10.1%
Other income and expense				
Interest expense	2 409	2 035	374	18.4%
Gain on sale of assets	(720)	—	(720)	N/A
Total other income/expense (net)	1 689	2 035	(346)	−17.0%
Earnings before income taxes	5 681	4 659	1 022	21.9%
Provision for income taxes	1 747	1 465	282	19.2%
Net income	$ 3 934	$ 3 194	$ 740	23.2%

LO 5 Describe the fraud triangle and identify conditions for fraud.

CAS

Fraud triangle—represents the three conditions for fraud: incentives/pressures, opportunities, and attitudes/rationalization.

CONDITIONS FOR FRAUD

The auditor should pay attention to the three conditions for fraud arising from fraudulent financial reporting and misappropriations of assets as CAS 240.A1. As shown in Figure 7-4, these three conditions of incentives/pressures, opportunities, and attitudes/rationalization are referred to as the **fraud triangle**.

1. *Incentives/pressures.* Management or other employees have incentives or pressures to commit fraud.
2. *Opportunities.* Circumstances provide opportunities for management or employees to commit fraud.

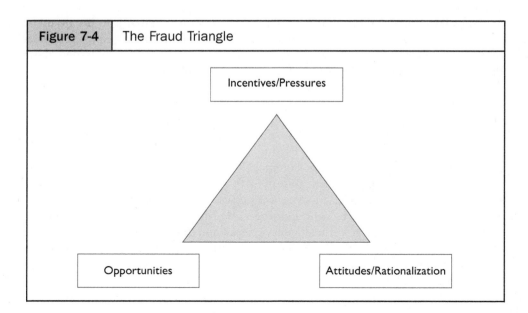

Figure 7-4 | The Fraud Triangle

Incentives/Pressures

Opportunities

Attitudes/Rationalization

3. *Attitudes/rationalization.* An attitude, character, or set of ethical values exists that allows management or employees to intentionally commit a dishonest act, or they are in an environment that imposes pressure sufficient to cause them to rationalize committing a dishonest act.

Risk Factors for Fraudulent Financial Reporting

An essential consideration by the auditor in uncovering fraud is identifying factors that increase the risk of fraud. These are referred to as **fraud risk factors** or red flags of fraud. Table 7-1 below provides examples of fraud risk factors for each of the three conditions of fraud for fraudulent financial reporting.

Fraud risk factors—entity factors that increase the risk of fraud.

Incentives/Pressures A common incentive for companies to manipulate financial statements is a decline in the company's financial prospects. A decline in earnings may threaten the company's ability to obtain financing and continue as a going concern. Companies may also manipulate earnings to meet analysts' forecasts of anticipated earnings for the quarter, to meet debt covenant restrictions, or to artificially maintain or inflate stock prices. In some cases, management may manipulate earnings just to preserve their reputation. Management with significant wealth tied up in stock options may have an incentive to inflate stock prices to increase the profits they earn personally when the options are exercised.

Table 7-1	Examples of Risk Factors for Fraudulent Financial Reporting		
	Three Conditions for Fraud		
	Incentives/Pressures	**Opportunities**	**Attitudes/Rationalization**
	Management or other employees have incentives or pressures to materially misstate financial statements.	Circumstances provide an opportunity for management or employees to misstate financial statements.	An attitude, character, or set of ethical values exists that allows management or employees to intentionally commit a dishonest act, or they are in an environment that imposes pressure sufficient to cause them to rationalize committing a dishonest act.
	Examples of Risk Factors	**Examples of Risk Factors**	**Examples of Risk Factors**
	Financial stability or profitability is threatened by economic, industry, or entity operating conditions. Examples include significant declines in customer demand and increasing business failures in either the industry or overall economy.	Significant accounting estimates involve subjective judgments or uncertainties that are difficult to verify.	Inappropriate or ineffective communication and support of the entity's values.
	Excessive pressure for management to meet the requirements or expectations of third parties, such as the terms of debt covenant requirements.	Ineffective board of directors or audit committee oversight over financial reporting.	Known history of violations of securities laws or other laws and regulations.
	Management or the board of directors' personal net worth is materially threatened by the entity's financial performance.	High turnover or ineffective accounting, internal audit, or information technology staff.	Management's practice of making overly aggressive or unrealistic forecasts to analysts, creditors, and other third parties.

Opportunities The financial statements of all companies are potentially subject to manipulation. However, the risk of fraudulent financial reporting is greater for companies in industries where significant judgments and estimates are involved. For example, valuation of inventories is subject to greater risk of misstatement for companies with diverse inventories in many locations or where the inventory could be obsolete.

Opportunities for misstatement are greater if there is turnover in accounting personnel or other weaknesses in accounting and information processes. In many cases of fraudulent financial reporting, the company had an ineffective audit committee and board of director oversight of financial reporting.

Attitudes/Rationalization The attitude of top management toward financial reporting is a critical risk factor in assessing the likelihood of fraudulent financial statements. This attitude is commonly referred to as the "tone at the top," and it is relevant to fraud risks because a poor tone at the top increases the risk of fraud and results in a poor internal control environment. If the CEO or other top managers display a disregard for the financial reporting process, for example, by consistently issuing overly optimistic forecasts or by being overly concerned about meeting analysts' earnings forecasts, fraudulent financial reporting is more likely. Also, management's character or set of ethical values may make it easier for it to rationalize a fraudulent act.

Risk Factors for Misappropriation of Assets

The same three fraud triangle conditions apply to misappropriation of assets. However, in assessing risk factors, greater emphasis is placed on individual incentives and opportunities for theft. Table 7-2 provides examples of fraud risk factors for each of the three conditions of fraud for misappropriation of assets.

Table 7-2	Examples of Risk Factors for Misappropriation of Assets		
Three Conditions for Fraud			
Incentives/Pressures	**Opportunities**	**Attitudes/Rationalization**	
Management or other employees have incentives or pressures to misappropriate material assets.	Circumstances provide an opportunity for management or employees to misappropriate assets.	An attitude, character, or set of ethical values exists that allows management or employees to intentionally commit a dishonest act, or they are in an environment that imposes pressure sufficient to cause them to rationalize a dishonest act.	
Examples of Risk Factors	**Examples of Risk Factors**	**Examples of Risk Factors**	
Personal financial obligations create pressure for those with access to cash or other assets susceptible to theft to misappropriate those assets.	Presence of large amounts of cash on hand or inventory items that are small, of high value, or are in high demand.	Disregard for the need to monitor or reduce risk of misappropriating assets.	
Adverse relationships between management and employees with access to assets susceptible to theft motivate employees to misappropriate those assets. Examples include the following: • Known or expected employee layoffs. • Promotions, compensation, or other rewards inconsistent with expectations.	Inadequate internal control over assets due to lack of the following: • Appropriate segregation of duties or independent checks. • Appropriate job applicant screening for employees performing key control functions. • Mandatory vacations for employees with access to assets.	Disregard for internal controls by overriding existing controls or failing to correct known internal control deficiencies.	

Incentives/Pressures Financial pressures are a common incentive for employees who misappropriate assets. Employees with excessive financial obligations or with drug abuse or gambling problems may steal to meet their personal financial or other needs. Managers should be alert for signs of these problems in employees with access to assets or accounting records. While a background check should be performed for all potential employees, a credit check may be included for those who will have access to assets. Dissatisfied employees may steal because of a sense of entitlement or as a form of attack against their employers. Companies can reduce fraud risk by dealing fairly with employees and monitoring employee morale.

Opportunities Opportunities for theft exist in all companies. However, opportunities are greater in companies with accessible cash or with inventory or other valuable assets, especially if the assets are small or readily transportable. For example, thefts of laptop computers are fairly common and much more frequent than thefts of desktop systems. Retailers and other organizations that receive revenue in the form of cash are also susceptible to theft. Surveillance methods and inventory coding and tracking systems can reduce the potential for theft. For example, casinos handle extensive amounts of cash with minimal formal records of cash received. As a result, casinos make extensive use of video and human surveillance. On a more basic scale, one Canadian fast-food chain has a small sign attached to its cash registers advising patrons that if they do not receive a receipt, their meal is free. This simple control ensures that the sales are recorded in the cash register. Such a control costs the company nothing to implement, and every patron becomes a watchdog.

Weak internal controls create opportunities for theft. Inadequate separation of duties is practically a licence for employees to steal. Whenever employees have custody or even temporary access to assets and maintain the accounting records for those assets, the potential for theft exists. As an example, if inventory storeroom employees also maintain inventory records, it is relatively easy for them to take inventory items and cover the theft by adjusting the accounting records.

Attitudes/Rationalization Management's attitude toward controls and ethical conduct may allow employees and managers to rationalize the theft of assets. If management cheats customers by overcharging for goods or engaging in high-pressure sales tactics, employees may feel that it is acceptable for them to behave in the same fashion by cheating on expense or time reports.

CONCEPT CHECK

C7-3 Define misappropriation of assets and give two examples.

C7-4 How does brainstorming regarding fraud risk improve auditors' professional judgment? Explain how it helps to mitigate potential judgment traps.

RESPONDING TO RISKS OF MATERIAL MISSTATEMENTS DUE TO FRAUD

LO **6** Develop responses to identified fraud risks.

When the auditor identifies risks of material misstatements due to fraud, CAS 240 requires the auditor to develop responses to those risks at three levels:

- Overall responses,
- Responses at the assertion level, and
- Responses related to management override.

Overall Responses to Fraud Risks

Overall responses to fraud risks relate to adjustments to the overall audit strategy. If the risk of misstatement due to fraud is increased, more experienced personnel may be assigned to the audit. In some cases, a fraud specialist may be assigned to the audit team. Greater emphasis should also be placed on the importance of increased professional skepticism, such as greater sensitivity in the selection and extent of documentation examined in support of transactions and more corroboration of management explanations about unusual matters affecting the financial statements.

Auditors should also consider management's choice of accounting principles. Careful attention should be placed on accounting principles that involve subjective measurements or complex transactions. Because auditors are required to presume fraud risk is present in revenue recognition, they should also evaluate the company's revenue recognition policies.

Fraud perpetrators are often knowledgeable about audit procedures. For this reason, auditing standards require auditors to incorporate unpredictability in the audit strategy. For example, auditors may visit inventory locations or test accounts that were not tested in prior periods. Auditors should also consider tests that address misappropriation of assets, even when the amounts are not typically material.

Responses to Fraud Risk at the Assertion Level

When auditors identify fraud risk at the assertion level, they design appropriate audit procedures to respond to specific fraud risks related to the account being audited and type of fraud risk identified. For example, if concerns are raised about revenue recognition because of cutoff or channel stuffing, the auditor may review the sales journal for unusual activity near the end of the period and review the terms of sales.

The auditor's response to fraud risk at the assertion level may involve changing the nature, timing, and extent of audit procedures. The nature of the procedures may need to be modified to obtain audit evidence that is more reliable and relevant. For example, if the risk of misappropriation of assets has been assessed as high, then the auditor may decide to physically examine certain assets to verify their existence rather than rely on inspection of documentation related to those assets. The timing of procedures may also need to be modified. For example, the auditor may choose to conduct substantive testing at the end of the period rather than performing those procedures based on interim data. The extent of procedures may also be changed to obtain more evidence in response to fraud risk at the assertion level. For example, the auditor may increase sample sizes when testing revenue transactions. We discuss specific fraud procedures relevant to various classes of transactions, account balances, and disclosures for the various cycles in Part 3 of the book.

Responses to Address Management Override of Controls

The risk of management override of controls exists in almost all audits. Because management is in a unique position to perpetrate fraud by overriding controls that are otherwise operating effectively, auditors must perform procedures in every audit to address the risk of management override. CAS 240 requires three procedures to be performed in every audit.

CAS

Examine Journal Entries and Other Adjustments for Evidence of Possible Misstatements Due to Fraud Fraud often results from adjustments to amounts reported in the financial statements, even when effective internal controls exist over the rest of the recording processes. The auditor should first obtain an understanding of the entity's financial reporting process, as well as controls over journal entries and other adjustments, and inquire of employees involved in the financial reporting process about inappropriate or unusual activity in processing journal entries and other adjustments. In some organizations, management uses spreadsheet software to make adjustments to financial information generated by the accounting system. These "top-side adjustments" have been used to manipulate financial statements. CAS 240 requires testing of journal entries and other financial statement adjustments. The extent of testing is affected by the effectiveness of controls and the results of the inquiries.

CAS

Review Accounting Estimates for Biases Fraudulent financial reporting is often accomplished through intentional misstatement of accounting estimates. CAS 240 requires the auditor to consider the potential for management bias when reviewing current-year estimates. The auditor is required to "look back" at significant prior-year estimates to identify any changes in the company's processes or management's judgments and assumptions that might indicate a potential bias. For example, management's estimates may have been clustered at the high end of the range of acceptable amounts in the prior year and at the low end in the current year.

CAS

Evaluate the Business Rationale for Significant Unusual Transactions CAS 240 emphasizes understanding the underlying business rationale for significant unusual transactions that might be outside the normal course of business for the company. The auditor should gain an understanding of the purposes of significant transactions to assess whether transactions have been entered into to engage in fraudulent financial reporting. For example, the company may engage in financing transactions to avoid reporting liabilities on the balance sheet. The auditor should determine whether the accounting treatment for any unusual transaction is appropriate in the circumstances, and whether information about the transaction is adequately disclosed in the financial statements.

CAS

THE AUDIT RISK MODEL

We discussed earlier how the auditor's assessment of the risk of material misstatement at the assertion level consists of two components: inherent risk and control risk. The **audit risk model** is a conceptual tool used by auditors to help develop the audit strategy at the assertion level. It is important to note that it is not a precise formula — it is primarily used for planning purposes. Auditors use the audit risk model to help decide how much and what types of evidence to accumulate for each relevant assertion. It is usually stated as follows:

$$DR = \frac{AAR}{IR \times CR}$$

where

DR = detection risk,

AAR = acceptable audit risk,

IR = inherent risk, and

CR = control risk.

Before we discuss the audit risk model components, review the illustration for a hypothetical company in Table 7-3. The auditor assesses risks at the overall financial statement level and at the assertion level. Table 7-3 illustrates how the auditor might assess the four risks at the transaction (cycle) level for a particular client. The auditor will also assess risk levels across various assertions within an individual class of transactions. For example, risks related to the existence of sales may be greater than risks related to accuracy of sales. Let's walk through the illustration point by point:

- The first row in the table shows the differences among cycles in the frequency and size of expected misstatements (A). Almost no misstatements are expected in payroll, but many are expected in inventory. It is possible that the payroll transactions are routine, while considerable complexities exist in recording and valuing inventory.
- Similarly, internal control effectiveness varies among the five cycles (B). For example, internal controls in payroll are considered highly effective (which leads the auditor to assess control risk as low), whereas those in inventory are considered ineffective (control risk is assessed as high).

Audit risk model—a conceptual model which auditors use as a planning tool to determine how much and what type of evidence to collect for each relevant class of transactions, account balances, and disclosures. The model reflects the relationship among acceptable audit risk (AAR), inherent risk (IR), control risk (CR), and detection risk (DR); $AAR = IR \times CR \times DR$.

Table 7-3	Illustration of Considering Risks in Different Cycles				
	Revenue Cycle	**Acquisition and Payment Cycle**	**Payroll Cycle**	**Inventory Cycle**	**Capital Acquisition and Repayment Cycle**
A Inherent Risk (Assessment of material misstatement before considering controls)	Medium Expect some misstatements	High Expect many misstatements	Low Expect few misstatements	High Expect many misstatements	Low Expect few misstatements
B Control Risk (Assessment of effectiveness of controls)	Medium (Moderate)	Low (High)	Low (High)	High (Ineffective)	Medium (Moderate)
C Acceptable Audit Risk (Willingness to permit material misstatements to exist after completing the audit)	Low Willingness	Low Willingness	Low Willingness	Low Willingness	Low Willingness
D Detection Risk (Extent of substantive testing)	Medium (Medium level)	Medium (Medium level)	High (Low level)	Low (High level)	Medium (Medium level)

- Finally, the auditor has decided on a low willingness for material misstatements to exist (acceptable audit risk) after the audit is complete for all five cycles (C). It is common for auditors to want an equally low likelihood of misstatements for each cycle after the audit is finished to permit the issuance of an unmodified opinion audit report.
- These considerations (A, B, C) affect the auditor's decision about the appropriate nature, timing, and extent of substantive testing to catch material misstatements (D). For example, because the auditor expects few misstatements in payroll (A) and internal controls are effective (B), the auditor plans for less substantive testing in payroll (D) than for the inventory cycle.

Following is a numerical example for discussion. The numbers used are for the inventory cycle in Table 7-3.

$$IR = 100\%$$
$$CR = 100\%$$
$$AAR = 5\%$$

$$DR = \frac{0.05}{1.0 \times 1.0} = 0.05 \text{ or } 5 \text{ percent}$$

Note that the assessments in Table 7-3 are not in numerical form. Most firms perform nonqualitative assessments of risk (such as low, moderate, and high) due to the difficulty in precisely quantifying risk. In this section we briefly discuss all four of the risks to provide an overview of the risks. Acceptable audit risk and inherent risk are discussed in greater detail later in this chapter. Control risk is examined more fully in Chapter 9.

Detection risk—the risk that the audit evidence for an audit assertion will fail to detect misstatements exceeding performance materiality.

Inherent risk—the auditor's assessment of the susceptibility to material misstatement of an assertion about a class of transactions, an account balance, or a disclosure, either individually or in aggregate, before considering the effectiveness of related internal controls.

Detection risk is the risk that the audit procedure for an audit assertion will fail to detect misstatements exceeding performance materiality. There are two key points to know about detection risk: (1) detection risk determines the amount of substantive evidence that the auditor plans to accumulate, and (2) if detection risk is reduced, the auditor needs to accumulate more substantive evidence (conduct more substantive testing) to achieve the reduced planned risk. For example in Table 7-3, detection risk (D) is low for inventory, which causes planned substantive evidence to be high. The opposite is true for payroll.

Inherent risk measures the auditor's assessment of an assertion's susceptibility to material misstatement, before considering the effectiveness of related internal controls. If the auditor concludes that a high likelihood of misstatement exists, the auditor will conclude that inherent risk is high. Internal controls are ignored in setting inherent risk because they are considered separately in the audit risk model as control risk.

In Table 7-3, inherent risk (A) was assessed high for acquisitions and payments and for inventory, and lower for payroll and for capital acquisition and repayment.

Inherent risk is inversely related to planned detection risk and directly related to evidence. Inherent risk for inventory and warehousing in Table 7-3 is high, which results in a lower planned detection risk and more planned evidence than if inherent risk were lower. We'll examine this in greater detail later in the chapter.

In addition to increasing audit evidence for a higher inherent risk in a given audit area, auditors commonly assign more experienced staff to that area and review the completed audit tests more thoroughly. For example, if inherent risk for inventory obsolescence is extremely high, it makes sense for the PA (public accountant) firm to assign an experienced staff person to perform more extensive tests for inventory obsolescence and to more carefully review the audit results.

Control risk measures the auditor's assessment of the risk that a material misstatement could occur in an assertion about a class of transaction, an account balance, or a disclosure, and not be prevented or detected on a timely basis by the client's internal controls.

Control risk is a measure of the auditor's assessment of the likelihood that material misstatements will not be prevented or detected by the client's internal controls. The auditor performs a control risk assessment at the overall financial statement level and at the assertion level. In order to perform this assessment, the auditor must have an understanding of controls at the organization. If the auditor determines controls to be effective, then the auditor may assess control risk as lower. For example, refer to Table 7-3 (C), where control risk for payroll is low because internal controls are highly effective. However, in the case of inventory, the auditor has concluded that control risk is high because internal control is completely ineffective to prevent or detect misstatements.

The audit risk model shows that there is a close relationship between inherent risk and control risk. For example, an inherent risk of 40 percent and a control risk of 60 percent affect planned detection risk and planned substantive evidence in the same way as an inherent risk of 60 percent and a control risk of 40 percent. In both cases, multiplying IR by CR results in a denominator of 24 percent. Recall that the combination of inherent risk and control risk is referred to in auditing standards as the risk of material misstatement. The auditor may make a combined assessment of the risk of material misstatement or the auditor can separately assess inherent risk and control risk. (Remember that inherent risk is the expectation of misstatements *before* considering the effect of internal control.)

As with inherent risk, the relationship between control risk and planned detection risk is inverse, whereas the relationship between control risk and substantive evidence is direct. If the auditor concludes that internal controls are effective, planned detection risk can be increased and substantive evidence therefore decreased. The auditor can increase planned detection risk when controls are effective because effective internal controls reduce the likelihood of misstatements in the financial statements.

Before auditors can set control risk less than 100 percent, they must obtain an understanding of internal control, evaluate how well it should function based on that understanding, and test internal controls for effectiveness. Obtaining an understanding of internal control is required for all audits. The latter two, evaluation and testing, are assessment of control risk steps that are required only when the auditor assesses control risk below maximum (this means "no reliance" will be placed upon controls). If the auditor assesses control risk as low, as in the case of payroll in Table 7-3, then the auditor plans to rely upon internal controls, and therefore plans to perform tests of controls; this allows the auditor to perform less substantive testing.

Auditors are likely to rely upon controls that are effective, especially when day-to-day transaction processing involves highly automated procedures. When controls are likely to be ineffective and inherent risk is high, the use of the audit risk model causes the auditor to decrease planned detection risk and thereby increased planned

Control risk—the auditor's assessment of the risk that a material misstatement could occur in an assertion about a class of transaction, an account balance, or a disclosure, and not be prevented or detected on a timely basis by the client's internal controls.

substantive evidence. We devote Chapters 8 and 9 to understanding internal control, assessing control risk, and evaluating their impact on evidence requirements.

Acceptable audit risk is a measure of how willing the auditor is to accept that the financial statements may be materially misstated after the audit is completed and an unqualified audit opinion has been issued. When auditors decide on a lower acceptable audit risk, they want to be more certain that the financial statements are *not* materially misstated. Zero risk is certainty, and a 100 percent risk is complete uncertainty. Complete assurance (zero risk) of the accuracy of the financial statements is not economically practical. Moreover, as we discussed in Chapter 5, the auditor cannot guarantee the complete absence of material misstatements.

Often, auditors refer to the term **audit assurance** (also called *overall assurance* or *level of assurance*) instead of acceptable audit risk. Audit assurance or any of the equivalent terms is the complement of acceptable audit risk, that is, one minus acceptable audit risk. In other words, acceptable audit risk of 2 percent is the same as audit assurance of 98 percent.

The concept of acceptable audit risk can be more easily understood by thinking in terms of a large number of audits, say, 10 000. What portion of these audits can include material misstatements without having an adverse effect on society? Certainly, the portion is below 10 percent. It is probably much closer to 1 percent or less. If an auditor believes that the appropriate percentage is 1 percent, then acceptable audit risk should be set at 1 percent, or perhaps lower, based on the specific circumstances.

When employing the audit risk model, there is a direct relationship between acceptable audit risk and planned detection risk, and an inverse relationship between acceptable audit risk and planned evidence. If the auditor decides to reduce acceptable audit risk, planned detection risk is thereby reduced, and planned evidence must be increased. For a client with lower acceptable audit risk, auditors also often assign more experienced staff or review the audit files more extensively.

Distinction Among Risks in the Audit Risk Model

There are important distinctions in how the auditor assesses the four risk factors in the audit risk model. For acceptable audit risk, the auditor decides the risk the PA firm is willing to take that the financial statements are misstated after the audit is completed, based on certain client-related factors. An example of a client where the auditor will accept very little risk (low acceptable audit risk) is for an initial public offering. We will discuss factors affecting acceptable audit risk below. Inherent risk and control risk are based on auditors' expectations or predictions of client conditions. An example of a high inherent risk is inventory that has not been sold for two years. An example of a low control risk is adequate separation of duties between asset custody and accounting. The auditor cannot change these client conditions, but can only make a likelihood assessment. Inherent risk factors are discussed later in the chapter and control risk is covered more fully in Chapter 9. Detection risk is dependent completely on the other three risks. It can be determined only after the auditor assesses the other three risks.

ASSESSING ACCEPTABLE AUDIT RISK

To assess acceptable audit risk, the auditor will first consider factors related to **engagement risk**, the risk that the auditor or audit firm will suffer harm after the audit is finished, even if the audit report is correct. Engagement risk is closely related to client business risk, which was discussed in Chapter 6. For example, if a client declares bankruptcy after an audit is complete, the likelihood of a lawsuit against the PA firm is reasonably high, even if quality of the audit is high.

It is worth noting that auditors disagree about whether engagement risk should be considered in planning the audit. Opponents of modifying evidence for engagement risk contend that auditors do not provide audit opinions for different levels of assurance and therefore should not provide more or less assurance because of engagement risk. Proponents contend that it is appropriate for auditors to accumulate additional audit evidence, assign more experienced staff and review the audit more thoroughly on audits where legal exposure is high or other potential adverse actions affecting the audit exist, as long as the assurance level is not decreased below a reasonably high level when low engagement risk exists.

Factors Affecting Acceptable Audit Risk

When auditors modify engagement risk, it is done by control of acceptable audit risk. Research points to several factors affecting engagement risk and, therefore, acceptable audit risk. Only three key factors are discussed here: the degree to which external users rely on the statements, the likelihood that a client will have financial difficulties after the audit report is issued, and the integrity of management.

The Degree to Which External Users Rely on the Statements When external users place heavy reliance on the financial statements, it is appropriate to decrease acceptable audit risk. When the statements are heavily relied on, a great social harm can result if a significant misstatement remains undetected in the financial statements. Auditors can more easily justify the cost of additional evidence when the loss to users from material misstatements is substantial. Several factors are good indicators of the degree to which external users rely on the financial statements:

- *Client's size.* Generally speaking, the larger a client's operations, the more widely the statements are used. The client's size, measured by total assets or total revenues, will have an effect on acceptable audit risk.
- *Distribution of ownership.* The statements of publicly held corporations are normally relied on by many more users than those of closely held corporations. For these companies, the interested parties include the provincial securities commission, the SEC, financial analysts, and the general public.
- *Nature and amount of liabilities.* When statements include a large amount of liabilities, they are more likely to be used extensively by actual and potential creditors than when there are few liabilities.

The Likelihood That a Client Will Have Financial Difficulties After the Audit Report Is Issued In situations where the auditor believes the chance of financial failure or loss to be high and a corresponding increase in engagement risk occurs, acceptable audit risk should be reduced. If a client is forced to file for bankruptcy or suffers a significant loss after completion of the audit, auditors face a greater chance of being required to defend the quality of the audit than if the client were under no financial strain. It is difficult for an auditor to predict financial failure before it occurs, but certain factors are good indicators of significant doubt about the entity's ability to continue as a going concern:

- *Liquidity position.* If a client is constantly short of cash and working capital, it indicates a future problem in paying bills. The auditor must assess the likelihood and significance of a steadily declining liquidity position.
- *Profits (losses) in previous years.* When a company has rapidly declining profits or increasing losses for several years, the auditor should recognize the future solvency problems that the client is likely to encounter.
- *Method of financing growth.* The more a client relies on debt as a means of financing, the greater the risk of financial difficulty if the client's operating success declines. Auditors should evaluate whether fixed assets are being financed with short- or long-term loans, as large amounts of required cash outflows during a short time can force a company into bankruptcy.
- *Nature of the client's operations.* Certain types of businesses are inherently riskier than others. For example, other things being equal, a start-up technology

Table 7-4	Methods Practitioners Use to Assess Acceptable Audit Risk
Factors	**Methods Used to Assess Acceptable Audit Risk**
External users' reliance on financial statements	• Examine the annual report and financial statements, including footnotes. • Read minutes of board of directors meetings to determine future plans. • Read financial analysts' reports for a publicly held company. • Discuss financing plans with management.
Likelihood of financial difficulties	• Analyze the financial statements for financial difficulties using ratios and other analytical procedures. • Examine historical and projected cash flow statements for the nature of cash inflows and outflows.
Management integrity	• Follow the firm's procedures, discussed in Chapter 6, for client acceptance and continuance.

company dependent on one product is much more likely to go bankrupt than a diversified food manufacturer.

- *Competence of management.* Competent management is constantly alert for potential financial difficulties and modifies its operating methods to minimize the effects of short-run problems. Auditors must assess the ability of management as a part of the evaluation of the entity's ability to continue as a going concern.

The Auditor's Evaluation of Management's Integrity As we discussed in Chapter 6, as a part of new client investigation and continuing client evaluation, if a client has questionable integrity, the auditor is likely to assess a lower acceptable audit risk. Companies with low integrity often conduct their business affairs in a manner that results in conflicts with their shareholders, regulators, and customers. A prior criminal conviction of key management personnel is an obvious example of questionable management integrity. Other examples of questionable integrity might include frequent disagreements with previous auditors, the Canada Revenue Agency, and the provincial securities commission. Frequent turnover of key financial and internal audit personnel and ongoing conflicts with labour unions and employees may also indicate integrity problems.

Making the Acceptable Audit Risk Decision

To assess acceptable audit risk, the auditor will first assess each for the factors affecting acceptable audit risk. Table 7-4 illustrates the methods used by auditors to assess each of the three factors already discussed. A typical evaluation of acceptable audit risk is high, medium, or low, where a low acceptable audit risk assessment means a "risky" client requiring more extensive evidence, assignment of more experienced personnel, and/or extensive review of audit documentation. As the engagement progresses, auditors obtain additional information about the client, and acceptable audit risk may be modified.

LO **9** Assess inherent risk.

ASSESSING INHERENT RISK

The inclusion of inherent risk in the audit risk model is one of the most important concepts in auditing. It implies that auditors should attempt to predict where misstatements are most and least likely in the financial statement segments. This information affects the amount of evidence that the auditor needs to accumulate, the assignment of staff, and the review of audit documentation.

Factors Affecting Inherent Risk

The auditor must assess the factors that make up the risk and modify audit evidence to take them into consideration. The auditor should consider several major factors when assessing inherent risk at the assertion level.

Auditors begin their assessment of inherent risk at the planning stage. As highlighted in Figure 7-2, the evidence gathered through risk assessment procedures is a key source of information to aid in the inherent risk assessment (recall that risk of material misstatement is a function of inherent risk and control risk). Below we discuss several factors that auditors would consider when assessing inherent risk.

Nature of the Client's Business Inherent risk for certain accounts and assertions is affected by the nature of the client's business. For example, an electronics manufacturer faces a greater likelihood of obsolete inventory (the valuation assertion) than a steel fabricator does. Further, the level of client business risk specific to the particular organization can have a pervasive effect on the financial statements. Information gained while obtaining understanding of the entity and its environment, as discussed in Chapter 6, is useful for assessing this factor.

Results of Previous Audits Misstatements found in the previous year's audit have a high likelihood of occurring again in the current year's audit, because many types of misstatements are systemic in nature, and organizations are often slow in making changes to eliminate them. For example, if the auditor found significant inventory valuation misstatements in last year's audit, then he or she will likely assess inherent risk as high in the current year's audit, and extensive testing will have to be done as a means of determining whether the deficiency in the client's system has been corrected. If, however, the auditor found no misstatements for the past several years in conducting tests of an audit area, the auditor is justified in reducing inherent risk, provided that no significant changes have occurred.

Related Parties Transactions between parent and subsidiary companies, and those between management and the corporate entity, are examples of related party transactions as defined by accounting standards. Because these transactions do not occur between two independent parties dealing at "arm's length," a greater likelihood exists that they might be misstated or inadequately disclosed. We discussed related party transactions in Chapter 6.

Complex or Nonroutine Transactions Transactions that are unusual for a client, or involve lengthy or complex contracts, are more likely to be incorrectly recorded than routine transactions because the client often lacks experience recording them. Examples include fire losses, major property acquisitions, purchase of complex investments, and restructuring changes resulting from discontinued operations. By knowing the client's business and reviewing minutes of meetings, the auditor can assess the consequences of complex or nonroutine transactions.

Judgment Required to Correctly Record Account Balances and Transactions Many account balances such as certain investments recorded at fair value, allowances for uncollectible accounts receivable, obsolete inventory, asset impairments, and warranty provisions require estimates and a great deal of management judgment related to valuation. Because they require considerable judgment, the likelihood of misstatements increases, and as a result the auditor should increase inherent risk for the relevant assertion.

Makeup of the Population Often, individual items making up the total population also affect the auditor's expectation of material misstatement. For example, the valuation assertion for accounts receivable is higher if most of the accounts are significantly overdue than where most accounts are current. Similarly, if a significant portion of inventory consists of slow-moving items then the inherent risk of valuation assertion would be set as high.

Factors Related to Fraudulent Financial Reporting and Misappropriation of Assets As we discussed earlier, the risk of fraud should be assessed for the overall financial statements as well as the assertion level. For example, a strong incentive for management to meet unduly aggressive earnings expectations would be a pervasive risk factor that affects many accounts and assertions, while the susceptibility of inventory to theft may affect only the inventory account.

It is difficult in concept and practice to separate fraud risk factors into acceptable audit risk, inherent risk, and control risk. For example, management that lacks integrity and is motivated to misstate financial statements is one of the factors in acceptable audit risk, but it may also affect control risk. Similarly, several of the other risk factors influencing management characteristics are a part of the control environment, as will be discussed in Chapter 8. These include the attitude, actions, and policies that reflect the overall attitudes of top management about integrity, ethical values, and commitment to competence.

Management Motivation and Biases Relevant performance measures can lead to biased interpretation of accounting policies and/or development of accounting estimates. For instance, if an organization has a goal to lower income taxes, this potential bias may increase the inherent risk of revenue completeness and expense occurrence.

Initial Versus Repeat Engagement Auditors gain experience and knowledge about the likelihood of misstatements after auditing a client for several years. The lack of previous years' audit results often causes auditors to assess a higher inherent risk for initial audits than for repeat engagements in which no material misstatements were previously found.

Making the Inherent Risk Decision

The auditor must evaluate the information affecting inherent risk to assess the risk of material misstatements at the assertion level. The impact of the factors at the overall financial statement level versus the assertion level depends upon the unique circumstances of each client. As discussed above, many fraud risk factors, such as management integrity, would have a pervasive impact on the financial statements. Similarly,

---

AUDITING IN ACTION 7-3
Potential Judgment Traps in Assessing Risk

While assessing risk requires considerable professional judgment and is meant to help the auditor develop an audit strategy that is unique to the particular circumstances of the client, there is still the possibility that auditors can fall into judgment traps.

For instance, the inherent risk factor of few or no errors in the past can easily lead to the conclusion that inherent risk is low for a particular account. However, when auditors generalize from past experiences with similar businesses, other audit engagements, or even the client (such as few past adjustments), they fall into the judgment trap of the availability bias. This may result in a too low assessment of risk.

Another illustration of this judgment trap is auditing of cash. Cash is typically considered to have a low risk of material misstatement because it is generally not a complex account and most companies tend to have good controls for cash. However, some recent high profile frauds—such as the Italian dairy company, Parmalat—have involved cash. Over a 10-year period,

Parmalat grew its fictitious cash account to almost $5 billion in order to sell public debt and qualify for commercial lines of credit. As one former auditor noted, "What is the one line in an audited balance sheet that no one questions? Answer: the cash and other short-term assets line. And that is precisely where this fraud was directed." An important lesson from this statement is to avoid relying too much on generalizations when performing a risk assessment. Further, the auditor should be diligent and skeptical when assessing risk of material misstatement—particularly when considering the risks associated with management biases and incentives.

Sources: Based on Confirmation.com, *Confirmation Fraud: How Auditors Can Overcome Confirmation Fraud Challenges*, Brentwood, TN: Capital Confirmation, 2012, accessed July 30, 2017, at **http://www.cftc. gov/ucm/groups/public/@newsroom/documents/file/tac072612_ whitepaper.pdf**. "Parma Splat: What are the lessons from the scandal at Europe's largest dairy-products group?" *The Economist*, January 15, 2004.

the fact that it is a new engagement tends to be a pervasive risk factor. In contrast, the impact of many of the other factors will affect only specific accounts and assertions. However, as highlighted in Auditing in Action 7-3, auditors need to be careful of over-generalizing from past experience when making a risk assessment. As revealed by the Parmalat example, it can lead to incorrect risk assessments.

RELATIONSHIP OF RISKS TO EVIDENCE AND FACTORS INFLUENCING RISKS

LO 10 Understand the relationship between risks and audit evidence.

Figure 7-5 summarizes the factors that determine each of the risks in the audit risk model—the effect of the acceptable audit risk, inherent risk, and control risk—on the determination of planned detection risk, and the relationship of all four risks to planned audit evidence. "D" in the figure indicates a direct relationship

Auditors respond to risk primarily by changing the nature and extent of testing and types of audit procedures, including unpredictability in the audit procedures used. In

Figure 7-5	Factors Influencing Risks and Their Relationship to Evidence

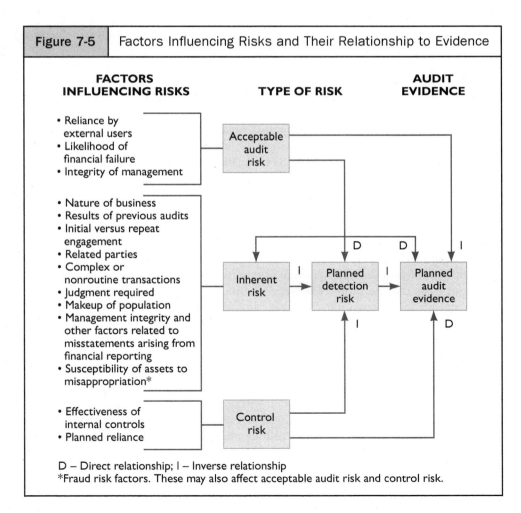

D – Direct relationship; I – Inverse relationship
*Fraud risk factors. These may also affect acceptable audit risk and control risk.

addition to modifying audit evidence, as discussed previously, there are two other ways auditors can change the audit to respond to risks:

1. *The engagement may require more experienced staff.* As highlighted in Auditing in Action 7-1, the Livent audit would be assessed as low acceptable audit risk. Therefore, the emphasis was on appropriate staffing and the importance of professional skepticism. Similarly, if an audit area (such as inventory) has a high inherent risk, it is important to assign that area to someone with experience in auditing it.
2. *The engagement will be reviewed more carefully than usual.* When acceptable audit risk is low, more extensive review is often warranted, including a review by personnel who were not assigned to the engagement (the Livent auditors discussed this as well). If the risk of material misstatements (the combination of inherent risk and control risk) is high for certain assertions for an account, the reviewer will likely spend more time making sure the evidence was appropriate and correctly evaluated.

Audit Risk for Segments

The risk of material misstatements, control risk, and inherent risk are assessed for each assertion in each segment of the audit. The assessments are likely to vary on the same audit from cycle to cycle, account to account, and assertion to assertion. For example, internal controls may be more effective for the existence of cash than for those related to fixed asset accuracy or net realizable value audit objectives. Control risk will therefore be lower for the existence of cash than for fixed asset valuation. Factors affecting inherent risk, such as susceptibility to misappropriation of assets and routineness of the transactions, are also likely to differ from account to account or for the assertions for a single account. For that reason, it is normal to have inherent risk vary for different accounts in the same audit.

Acceptable audit risk is ordinarily assessed by the auditor during planning and held constant for each major cycle and account. Auditors normally use the same acceptable audit risk for each segment because the factors affecting acceptable audit risk are related to the entire audit, not individual accounts. For example, the extent to which external users' decisions rely upon financial statements is usually related to the overall financial statements, not just one or two accounts.

In some cases, however, a *lower* acceptable audit risk may be more appropriate for one account than for others. If an auditor decided to use a medium acceptable audit risk for the audit as a whole, the auditor might decide to reduce acceptable audit risk to low for inventory if inventory is used as collateral for a short-term loan.

Some auditors use the same acceptable audit risk for all segments based on their belief that at the end of the audit, financial statement users should have the same level of assurance for every segment of the financial statements. Other auditors use a different level of assurance for different segments based on their belief that financial statement users may be more concerned about certain account balances relative to other accounts in a given audit. For illustrations in this and subsequent chapters, we use the same acceptable audit risk for all segments in the audit. Note, however, that changing the risk for different segments is also acceptable.

Like control risk and inherent risk, planned detection risk and required audit evidence will vary from cycle to cycle, account to account, or assertion to assertion. This conclusion should not be surprising. As the circumstances of each engagement differ, the extent and nature of evidence needed will depend on the unique circumstances. For example, in a particular engagement, inventory might require extensive testing because of deficient internal controls and the auditor's concerns about obsolescence resulting from technological changes in the industry. On the same engagement, accounts receivable may require little testing because of effective internal controls, fast collection of receivables, excellent relationships between the client and customers, and good audit results in previous years. Similarly, for a given audit of inventory, an auditor may assess a higher inherent risk of a realizable value misstatement because of the higher potential for obsolescence but a low inherent risk of a classification misstatement because there is only purchased inventory.

Measurement Limitations

One major limitation of the application of the audit risk model is the difficulty in measuring the components of the model. Despite the auditors' best efforts, assessments of each of the risk factors are highly subjective. To offset that measurement problem, many auditors use broad and subjective measurement terms such as low, medium, and high. As Table 7-5 shows, auditors use this information to decide on the appropriate amount and types of substantive evidence to accumulate. For example, in Situation 1, the auditor has decided on a high acceptable audit risk for account or assertion. The auditor has concluded that a low risk of misstatement in the financial statements exists and that internal controls are effective. Therefore, a high planned detection risk is appropriate. As a result, a low level of substantive evidence is needed. Situation 3 is at the opposite extreme. If both inherent and control risks are high and the auditor wants a low acceptable audit risk, considerable substantive evidence is required. The other three situations fall between these two extremes.

Using a Decision Aid to Link Risk Assessment to Evidence Planning

Auditors develop various types of decision aids to help link judgments affecting audit evidence with the appropriate evidence to collect. One such worksheet is included in Figure 7-6 for accounts receivable for Hillsburg Hardware Limited (Refer to the Appendix at the end of the book for details on the company and its background.) The five balance-related assertions introduced in Chapter 4 are included in the columns at the top of the worksheet to help the auditor consider the risks related to all the assertions for accounts receivable. Rows 1 and 2 are acceptable audit risk and inherent risk. Below is a discussion of the rationale for the assessment of those two risks.

Table 7-5	Relationships of Audit Risk Model Components to Evidence				
Situation	Acceptable Audit Risk	Inherent Risk	Control Risk	Planned Detection Risk	Amount of Evidence Required
1	High	Low	Low	High	Low
2	Low	Low	Low	Medium	Medium
3	Low	High	High	Low	High
4	Medium	Medium	Medium	Medium	Medium
5	High	Low	Medium	Medium	Medium

	Existence	Rights and Obligations	Completeness	Valuation	Allocation
Audit risk	medium	medium	medium	medium	medium
Inherent risk	medium	low	low	medium	low
Control risk— Sales					
Control risk— Cash receipts					
Control risk— Additional controls					
Analytical procedures					
Planned detection risk for tests of details of balances					
Planned audit evidence for tests of details of balances					

Figure 7-6 Evidence Planning Spreadsheet to Decide Tests of Details of Balances for Hillsburg Hardware Limited—Accounts Receivable

Materiality: $441,000
Performance Materiality: $331,000

Acceptable audit risk was assessed at medium based upon the following factors: Hillsburg is a privately held company, it has a moderate level of debt, it is in good financial condition, and it has high management integrity. No significant issues were noted in the past.

Inherent risk for the accounts receivable is assessed at the assertion level. Inherent risk is medium for the existence assertion due to concerns over revenue recognition. Similarly, it is assessed at medium for valuation because in previous audits, audit adjustments were made to the allowance for doubtful accounts. For the remaining assertions, rights and obligations, completeness, and allocation, inherent risk is assessed at low.

At this point in the audit process, the remaining factors on the evidence-planning worksheet for accounts receivable have not been considered. In the next two chapters we will focus on understanding and assessing control risk as well as the related decision aids auditors use. We will revisit the various risk assessments and audit strategy in Chapter 10 and demonstrate how auditors document those key decisions in the audit process.

SUMMARY

Because the auditor's opinion addresses whether the financial statements are free of material misstatements, audit planning hinges on effective assessments of the risk of material misstatements at both the overall financial statement level and at the assertion level. While auditors accept some level of uncertainty in performing the audit function, the consideration of risk as defined by the audit risk model is necessary for the auditor to effectively address those risks in the most appropriate manner. Using the audit risk model, the auditor determines the audit evidence needed to achieve an acceptable level of audit risk for the financial statements as a whole.

Review Questions

7-1 **1** Why is it important for the auditor to consider risk of material misstatement at the overall financial statement level?

7-2 **1** Provide two examples of factors that might increase the risk of material misstatement at the overall financial statement level.

7-3 **1** Assume that you are concerned that your client has recorded revenues that did not occur. What assertion would you assess as having a high risk of material misstatement?

7-4 **2** Describe the types of procedures auditors perform as part of their risk assessment procedures.

7-5 **2** In addition to inquiring of individuals among management who are involved in financial reporting positions, such as the CFO (chief financial officer) and controller, which additional individuals should you consider making inquiries of as part of your risk assessment procedures? Be sure to describe how those individuals might be helpful to you in assessing risks of material misstatement.

7-6 **2** Auditing standards require that the engagement team members engage in discussion about the risk of material misstatement. Describe the nature of this required discussion and who should be involved.

7-7 **4** **5** **6** Auditing standards require that the engagement team members engage in discussion about the susceptibility of the financial statements to the risk of fraud. How does this discussion relate to the required discussion about the risk of material misstatement?

7-8 **3** **4** Why is it important to distinguish the auditor's assessment of the risk of material misstatement due to fraud from the assessment of the risk of material misstatement due to error?

7-9 **4** How should the auditor consider risks related to revenue recognition when assessing the risk of material misstatement due to fraud?

7-10 **4** **5** **6** What types of inquiries should the auditor make when considering the risk of material misstatement due to fraud?

7-11 **3** What constitutes a significant risk?

7-12 **3** Describe examples of characteristics of transactions and balances that might cause an auditor to determine that a risk of material misstatement is a significant risk.

7-13 **7** Describe which two factors of the audit risk model relate to the risk of material misstatement at the assertion level.

7-14 **7** Explain the causes of an increased or decreased planned detection risk.

7-15 **7** How does engagement risk affect the audit process?

7-16 **9** Explain why inherent risk is estimated for specific accounts rather than for the overall financial statement. What is the effect on the amount of evidence the auditor must accumulate when inherent risk is increased from medium to high for a segment?

7-17 **7** Explain the relationship between audit risk and the legal liability of auditors.

7-18 **8** State the categories of circumstances that affect audit risk, and list the factors that the auditor can use to indicate the degree to which each category exists.

7-19 [7] Explain the effect of extensive misstatements found in the prior year's audit on inherent risk, planned detection risk, and planned audit evidence.

7-20 [4] What is meant by *acceptable audit risk*? What is its relevance to evidence accumulation?

7-21 [10] Auditors have not been successful in measuring the components of the audit risk model. How is it possible to use the model in a meaningful way without a precise way of measuring the risk?

Multiple Choice Questions and Task-Based Simulations

7-22 [1] The following questions concern the assessment of the risk of material misstatements. Choose the best response.

a. Which of the following circumstances most likely would cause the auditor to suspect that there are material misstatements in the entity's financial statements?
(1) The entity's management places no emphasis on meeting publicized earnings projections.
(2) Significant differences between the physical inventory count and the accounting records are not investigated.
(3) Monthly bank reconciliations ordinarily include several large outstanding cheques.
(4) Cash transactions are electronically processed and recorded, leaving no paper audit trail.

b. [1] Which of the following statements describes why a properly designed and executed audit may not detect a material misstatement in the financial statements resulting from fraud?
(1) Audit procedures that are effective for detecting an unintentional misstatement may be ineffective for an intentional misstatement that is concealed through collusion.
(2) An audit is designed to provide reasonable assurance of detecting material errors, but there is no similar responsibility concerning fraud.
(3) The factors considered in assessing control risk indicated an increased risk of intentional misstatements, but only a low risk of unintentional errors in the financial statements.
(4) The auditor did not consider factors influencing audit risk for account balances that have effects pervasive to the financial statements as a whole.

c. [4] Prior to, or in conjunction with, the information-gathering procedures for an audit, audit team members should discuss the potential for material misstatement due to fraud. Which of the following best characterizes the mindset that the audit team should maintain during this discussion?
(1) Presumptive
(2) Judgmental
(3) Criticizing
(4) Questioning

7-23 [7] Some account balances, such as those for pensions and leases, are the result of complex calculations. The susceptibility to material misstatements in these types of accounts is defined as:
(1) Audit risk.
(2) Detection risk.
(3) Inherent risk.
(4) Sampling risk.

7-24 [7] [10] The following questions deal with audit risk and evidence. Choose the best response.

a. Which of the following does not increase the need for sufficient appropriate audit evidence?
(1) A lower acceptable level of detection risk.
(2) An increase in the assessed control risk.
(3) A lower acceptable audit risk.
(4) A decrease in the assessed inherent risk.

b. As lower acceptable levels of both audit risk and materiality are established, the auditor should plan more work on individual accounts to:
(1) Find smaller misstatements.
(2) Find larger misstatements.
(3) Increase the performance materiality in the accounts.
(4) Increase inherent risk in the accounts.

c. Based on evidence gathered and evaluated, an auditor decides to increase the assessed level of control risk from that originally planned. To achieve an overall audit risk level that is substantially the same as the planned audit risk level, the auditor could:

(1) Decrease detection risk.

(2) Increase materiality levels.

(3) Decrease substantive testing.

(4) Increase inherent risk.

7-25 **7** **9** The audit staff have recently completed risk assessment procedures to gain an understanding of Chocolate from Heaven Inc.'s (CFHI) business and to identify risk factors relevant to the risk of material misstatement. (For further background on the company, refer to Question 6-42 on page 205.)

a. For each risk factor below, decide whether each piece of information would fit into your assessment of inherent risk (IR) or control risk (CR), and whether it would increase or decrease the specified risk area.

1	Due to the size of the CFHI's business, only one accounting clerk does most of the accounting.	IR↑ IR↓ CR↑ CR↓
2	In recent years there has been increased competition in the artisanal small batch chocolate business.	IR↑ IR↓ CR↑ CR↓
3	The management bonuses at CFHI are based on net income	IR↑ IR↓ CR↑ CR↓
4	All cheques require the signature of both owners.	IR↑ IR↓ CR↑ CR↓
5	Access to the warehouse at CFHI is restricted to warehouse employees only, who carry their own security cards.	IR↑ IR↓ CR↑ CR↓
6	The chocolate inventory has a one-year shelf life.	IR↑ IR↓ CR↑ CR↓
7	David Chan has developed a personal trusted relationship with each of the cocoa bean farmers in Tanzania, Ecuador, Philippines, and Honduras. He visits each farmer annually. He believes these strong relationships help to ensure farmers send CFHI high-quality beans. High-quality beans are critical to the production of high-quality chocolate.	IR↑ IR↓ CR↑ CR
8	CFHI just switched to an inventory tracking system that was developed by the owner's son as part of a computer programming course. The project received an A grade.	IR↑ IR↓ CR↑ CR↓
9	CFHI customers include major retailers such as Target, Marshalls, and high-end grocery stores. One month before Christmas, a major selling time—representing approximately 30 percent of sales—CFHI's custom-made cocoa butter press broke down. It took two weeks to obtain the necessary part to repair the machine. Orders were shipped to major retailers more than two weeks late and several are refusing to pay for the order, claiming that the delayed delivery resulted in a significant quantity of unsold chocolate.	IR↑ IR↓ CR↑ CR

b. Assuming acceptable audit risk is low, for each situation specific to CFHI listed below, assess Inherent Risk and Control Risk. Determine an appropriate level for Detection Risk and the resulting level of evidence. Use High, Low, and Moderate for your assessments.

Situation 1: Accuracy of recorded sales and valuation of receivables.

CFHI sells goods to the United States and often transacts in US currency. The accounting clerk is inexperienced and not accustomed to recording foreign currency transactions.

Audit risk (AR) =	Inherent risk (IR)	Control risk (CR)	Detection risk (DR)	Level of Evidence
LOW RISK				

Situation 2: Existence of equipment.

All equipment is highly specialized and extremely large. For safety reasons, the equipment is also bolted to the floor in the warehouse. CFHI purchases new equipment once every three to four years. All purchases are authorized by David (the owner). Cheques are signed by both owners after completing a review of the supporting documents.

Audit risk (AR) =	Inherent risk (IR)	Control risk (CR)	Detection risk (DR)	Level of Evidence
LOW RISK				

Situation 3: Existence of finished goods chocolate inventory.

Finished goods (chocolates) are kept in a locked area of the warehouse. Access to finished goods is restricted to warehouse employees only, who carry their own security cards. A video surveillance system monitors the finished goods area. The audit team has verified that the security system is working and has been operational throughout the year. (Refer to Risk Factors 6 and 9 in Part (a) to assist in the assessment of inherent risk.)

Audit risk (AR) =	Inherent risk (IR)	Control risk (CR)	Detection risk (DR)	Level of Evidence
LOW RISK				

Discussion Questions and Problems

7-26 **8** You are the proprietor of a public accounting firm with a growing audit practice. You have accepted the audit of T-Division, one of six separate Canadian divisions of a large, private multinational corporation. Each division operates as a separate entity. The manager of each division receives a salary plus a bonus based on the net profit of the division. In each division, the manager has the authority over all other employees for buying materials, production issues, accounting, and personnel matters.

James has reached the level of manager of T-Division by working very hard and demanding high production levels of his staff. James has advised you that he wants to see all questions you have about accounting issues, and he assures you that he will personally make sure that they are taken care of, without any more effort on your behalf. James explained that he has managed three other divisions in the past for this company, and each one received a "clean audit report," which helped his career. He wants to ensure that T-Division also gets a "clean" audit report and to keep the auditor's work at a minimum.

REQUIRED

a. Determine whether you would set the acceptable audit risk as high, medium, or low for your audit of T-Division. Justify your response.

b. Identify and briefly explain two other items of information about T-Division, besides what you already know, that would be important for you to consider in determining the proper level of acceptable audit risk.

(Extract from AU1 CGA-Canada Examinations developed by the Certified General Accountants Association of Canada © 2009 CGA-Canada. Reproduced with permission. All rights reserved.)

7-27 **1** **2** This problem requires you to access *CPA Canada Assurance Handbook*—CAS 315 *Identifying and Assessing Risks of Material Misstatements Through Understanding the Entity and Its Environment.* Use this standard to answer each of the questions below. For each answer, document the paragraph(s) in CAS 315 supporting your answer.

REQUIRED

a. What types of information does CAS 315 suggest the auditor should consider when obtaining an understanding of the company and its environment?

b. What types of performance measurements might affect the risk of material misstatement?

c. What factors should the auditor consider to determine if a risk is a "significant risk"?

d. What guidance is provided about revising the risk assessment as the audit continues.

7-28 **5** During audit planning, an auditor obtained the following information:

1. Significant operations are located and conducted across international borders in jurisdictions where differing business environments and cultures exist.

2. There are recurring attempts by management to justify marginal or inappropriate accounting on the basis of materiality.

3. The company's controller works very hard, including evenings and weekends, and has not taken a vacation in two years.

4. The company's board of directors includes a majority of directors who are independent of management.

5. Assets and revenues are based on significant estimates that involve subjective judgments and uncertainties that are hard to corroborate.
6. The company is marginally able to meet exchange listing and debt covenant requirements.
7. The company's financial performance is threatened by a high degree of competition and market saturation.
8. New accounting pronouncements have resulted in explanatory paragraphs for consistency for the company and other firms in the industry.
9. The company has experienced low turnover in management and its internal audit function.

REQUIRED

a. Indicate whether the information indicates an increased risk of fraud.
b. If the information indicates an increased risk of fraud, indicate which fraud condition (incentives/pressures, opportunities, or attitudes/rationalization) is indicated.

7-29 **6** This problem requires you to access CPA *Canada Assurance Handbook* and to review CAS 240—*The auditor's responsibilities relating to fraud in an audit of financial statements.*

REQUIRED

a. You have determined that there is a fraud risk related to the existence and accuracy of inventory. Review the guidance in CAS 240 to provide examples of auditor responses involving changes to the nature, timing, and extent of audit procedures related to this assessed fraud risk for inventory.
b. What does CAS 240 say about how the auditor should assess risk related to revenue recognition?
c. What examples of auditor responses to fraud risk related to revenue recognition are provided in CAS 240?

7-30 **7** **8** You are the auditor in charge of the audit of the municipality of Sackville, New Brunswick. The municipality has a budget of about $65 million and has had a balanced budget for the last three years. There are about 10 people in the accounting office and the rest of the employees are operational, dealing with supervision of roadwork, garbage collection, and similar matters. Many services are outsourced, minimizing the need for employees. The municipality has a chief executive officer and a controller and reports to the council of elected representatives.

REQUIRED

For each of the following situations, state a preliminary conclusion for acceptable audit risk, inherent risk, control risk, and detection risk. Justify your conclusions. State any assumptions that are necessary for you to reach your conclusions.

1. This is the first year that you have been auditing Sackville. There has been extensive turnover after the recent election. Costs are out of control, and it looks like it may be necessary to raise realty taxes by as much as 15 percent.
2. For four years now, you have been auditing Sackville. The employees are experienced, and any control recommendations that you have suggested have been discussed and, where feasible, implemented. There is a tiny budget surplus this year, and it looks as if a balanced budget is in sight again for next year.
3. Sackville is being hit by bad press. It seems that one of the purchasing agents set up a fictitious company and was billing the municipality for goods that had not been received. To make it worse, the purchasing agent's wife was the assistant accountant. The office of the provincial auditor general has sent a letter to the controller of Sackville stating that the municipality has been selected for audit by the provincial auditor general's office based on a random sample, and that the provincial auditors will be arriving within two weeks of the completion of your audit.

7-31 **1** Moranda and Sills, LLP, has served for over 10 years as the auditor of the financial statements of Highland Credit Union. The firm is conducting its audit planning for the current fiscal year and is in the process of performing risk assessment procedures. Based on inquiries and other information obtained, the auditors learned that the credit union is finalizing an acquisition of a smaller credit union located in another region of the province. Management anticipates that the transaction will close in the third quarter, and, while there will be some challenges in integrating the IT systems of the acquired credit union with Highland systems, the bank should realize a number of operational cost savings over the long-term.

During the past year, the credit union has expanded its online service options for customers, who can now remotely deposit funds into and withdraw funds from chequing and savings accounts. The system has been well received by customers and the credit union hopes to continue expanding those services. The challenge for Highland is that they are struggling to retain IT personnel given the strong job market for individuals with those skills.

Credit risk management continues to be a challenge for all credit unions, including Highland, and regulators continue to spend a lot of time on credit evaluation issues. The credit union has a dedicated underwriting staff that continually evaluates the collectibility of loans outstanding. Unfortunately, some of the credit review staff recently left the credit union to work for a competitor. Competition in the community banking space is tough, especially given the slow loan demand in the marketplace.

The credit union has expanded its investment portfolio into a number of new types of instruments subject to fair value accounting. Management has engaged an outside valuation expert to ensure that the valuations are properly measured and reported.

Fortunately, the credit union's capital position is strong and it far exceeds regulatory minimums. Capital is available to support growth goals in the credit union's three-year strategic plan.

REQUIRED
a. Describe any risks of material misstatement at the financial statement level.
b. Describe any risks of material misstatement at the assertion level.
c. For each risk factor, indicate whether it is a significant risk.

7-32 〔7〕 Following are six situations that involve the audit risk model as it is used for planning audit evidence requirements in the audit of inventory.

REQUIRED
a. Explain what *low*, *medium*, and *high* mean for each of the four risks and planned evidence.
b. Fill in the blanks for planned detection risk and planned evidence using the terms *low*, *medium*, and *high*.
c. Using your knowledge of the relationships among the foregoing factors, state the effect on planned evidence (increase or decrease) of changing each of the following five factors, while the other three remain constant:
(1) An increase in acceptable audit risk.
(2) An increase in control risk.
(3) An increase in planned detection risk.
(4) An increase in inherent risk.
(5) An increase in inherent risk and a decrease in control risk of the same amount.

	Situation					
Risk	**1**	**2**	**3**	**4**	**5**	**6**
Acceptable audit risk	High	High	Low	Low	High	Medium
Inherent risk	Low	High	High	Low	Medium	Medium
Control risk	Low	Low	High	High	Medium	Medium
Planned detection risk	—	—	—	—	—	—
Planned evidence	—	—	—	—	—	—

7-33 〔7〕 Bohrer, CPA (Chartered Professional Accountant), is considering the following factors in assessing audit risk at the financial statement level in planning the audit of Waste Remediation Services (WRS), Inc.'s financial statements for the year ended December 31, 2018. WRS is a privately held company that contracts with municipal governments to close landfills. Audit risk at the financial statement level is influenced by the risk of material misstatements, which may be indicated by factors related to the entity, management, and the industry environment.
1. This was the first year WRS operated at a profit since 2010 because municipalities received increased federal and provincial funding for environmental purposes.
2. WRS's board of directors is controlled by Tucker, the majority shareholder, who also acts as the chief executive officer.
3. The internal auditor reports to the controller and the controller reports to Tucker.
4. The accounting department has experienced a high rate of turnover of key personnel.

5. WRS's bank has a loan officer who meets regularly with WRS's CEO and controller to monitor WRS's financial performance.

6. WRS's employees are paid biweekly.

7. Bohrer has audited WRS for five years.

8. During 2018, WRS changed its method of preparing its financial statements from the cash basis to generally accepted accounting principles.

9. During 2018, WRS sold one half of its controlling interest in Sanitation Equipment Leasing Co. (SEL). WRS retained a significant interest in SEL.

10. During 2018, litigation filed against WRS in 2005 alleging that WRS discharged pollutants into provincial waterways was dropped by the province. Loss contingency disclosures that WRS included in prior years' financial statements are being removed for the 2017 financial statements.

11. During December 2018, WRS signed a contract to lease disposal equipment from an entity owned by Tucker's parents. This related party transaction is not disclosed in WRS's notes to its 2018 financial statements.

12. During December 2018, WRS increased its casualty insurance coverage on several pieces of sophisticated machinery from historical cost to replacement cost.

13. WRS recorded a substantial increase in revenue in the fourth quarter of 2018. Inquiries indicated that WRS initiated a new policy and guaranteed several municipalities that it would refund provincial and federal funding paid to WRS on behalf of the municipality if it failed a federal or provincial site inspection in 2019.

14. An initial public offering of WRS stock is planned in 2019.

REQUIRED

For each of the 14 factors listed above, indicate whether the item would likely increase audit risk, decrease audit risk, or have no effect on audit risk.*

7-34 🔲7 🔲9 Joanne Whitehead is planning the audit of a newly obtained client, Henderson Energy Corporation, for the year ended December 31, 2018. Henderson Energy is regulated by the provincial utility commission and, because it is a publicly traded company, the audited financial statements must be filed with the Ontario Securities Commission (OSC).

Henderson Energy is considerably more profitable than many of its competitors, largely due to its extensive investment in information technologies used in its energy distribution and other key business processes. Recent growth into rural markets, however, has placed some strain on 2018 operations. Additionally, Henderson Energy expanded its investments into speculative markets and is also making greater use of derivative and hedging transactions to mitigate some of its investment risks. Because of the complexities of the underlying accounting associated with these activities, Henderson Energy added several highly experienced accountants to its financial reporting team. Internal audit, which has direct reporting responsibility to the audit committee, is also actively involved in reviewing key accounting assumptions and estimates on a quarterly basis.

Whitehead's discussions with the predecessor auditor revealed that the client has experienced some difficulty in correctly tracking existing property, plant, and equipment items. This largely involves equipment located at its multiple energy production facilities. During the recent year, Henderson acquired a regional electric company, which expanded the number of energy production facilities.

Whitehead plans to staff the audit engagement with several members of the firm who have experience in auditing energy and public companies. The extent of partner review of key accounts will be extensive.

REQUIRED

Based on the above information, identify factors that affect the risk of material misstatement in the December 31, 2018, financial statements of Henderson Energy. Indicate whether the factor increases or decreases the risk of material misstatement. Also, identify which audit risk model component is affected by the factor. Use the format below:

Factor	Effect on the Risk of Material Misstatement	Audit Risk Model Component
Henderson is a new client	Increases	Inherent risk

*AICPA adapted. Copyright by American Institute of CPAs. All rights reserved. Used with permission.

Professional Judgment Problems and Cases

7-35 〖7〗〖9〗 You are the senior auditor in charge of the December 31, 2018, year-end audit for Cleo Patrick Cosmetics Inc. (CPCI). CPCI is a large, privately held Canadian company that was founded in 1999 by one of Canada's best known hair stylists, Cleo Patrick. Cleo Patrick is a famous celebrity hair stylist who has appeared on a variety of television shows such as *Entertainment Tonight*, and has been the chief stylist for the Oscars and Emmys. The company includes (1) a small chain of 10 upscale salons situated in major cities in Canada and the United States and (2) its well-known signature line of professional hair products that are available at select drug stores and retail chains. The core of its business is its signature hair products line, *Cleo Patrick True Professional*. The *True Professional* line represents 85 percent of the company's total revenue.

During the planning phase of the audit, you performed various planning activities and met with CPCI's management team. You obtained the following information.

1. Your firm has audited CPCI since 2005, when Cleo sold 25 percent of her company to a group of private investors. The investors receive quarterly dividends that are calculated based upon a combination of sales and net income. The investors, all experienced businesspeople, serve as Cleo's board of directors and give her advice on the strategic direction of the company.

2. Your firm has not had any major disputes with CPCI management over accounting issues; however, last year it recommended that CPCI improve the organization of its accounting department—which is understaffed.

3. High-priced mass-market hair products represent a highly competitive supersaturated market. Large multinationals make up about 70 percent of the market, with niche companies such as CPCI making up the remaining 30 percent. Management does not consider multinationals to be a threat: "Unlike our competitors, we are a true salon heritage brand backed by an active celebrity stylist."

4. From your review of the 2017 audited financial statements and the 2018 third quarter unaudited financial statements, you noted the following information:

	Nine Months Ended Sept. 30, 2018 (unaudited) (thousands of dollars)	Year Ended Dec. 31, 2017 (audited) (thousands of dollars)
Sales	$350 000	$ 450 000
Net income	1 000	1 500
Cash	25 000	30 000
Accounts receivable	25 000	25 000
Inventory	45 000	40 000
Property, plant, and equipment	165 000	160 000
Total assets	285 000	280 000
Current liabilities	45 000	40 000

5. Cleo plans to expand into Europe and is negotiating contracts with drug stores in the United Kingdom and Germany. In order to fund this expansion, CPCI's bank has agreed to increase CPCI's operating line of credit. As part of the agreement, CPCI is required to maintain a minimum quick ratio of 1:2 and a positive net income. In addition, CPCI is required to provide the bank with audited financial statements.

6. Your firm has an employee who reads and saves articles about issues that may affect key clients. You read an article that says that two of CPCI's top-selling products recently made "The Dirty Dozen" list. The list, developed by an environmental research foundation, highlights those cosmetic products that have toxic chemicals (some of which are cancer-causing). CPCI claims that all its products are safe and meet the provincial and federal health and safety guidelines. You discuss the issue with CPCI management and find out that it is working on reformulating both products, which should be ready in 2019. CPCI is offering large rebates to retailers in order to encourage sales of its older products. The two "dirty" products currently make up about 20 percent of CPCI's current inventory of $45 million.

7. William Kirk was hired recently as the chief operating officer (COO) to provide closer oversight of the company. Due to all the new products and expansions, Cleo does not have time to spend monitoring the daily operations. Kirk is attempting to bring in a greater emphasis on controls around financial reporting and monitoring (as recommended by your firm in the past). Kirk started in June 2018 and one of the first things he did was to replace the chief financial officer (CFO), who was not very organized and tended to delay handling problems. Kirk also implemented a new bonus plan based upon sales growth and profitability targets. He told you he thinks it is working out really well and sales are growing. However, Kirk has not had a chance to implement all his plans—such as hiring additional accounting staff and performing a formal assessment of the quality of internal controls.

8. In early 2018, CPCI launched two new collections, *Ultimate Moisture* and *Moisture Gloss*. These two products placed an extensive strain on the company's cash flow. CPCI had spent $15 million in product development and $10 million on advertising. However, sales were much lower than predicted. Management had anticipated 2018 sales for the two products to be $9 million to $10 million. However, as of October 2018, actual sales were only $2 million. When you inquired about the low sales, the new CFO explained that the buyer had purchased inappropriate raw materials. This was not discovered during the inspection process when the materials were received. As a result, the finished product did not meet quality standards and was destroyed, and the

new product arrived in stores much later than planned. The CFO stated that the salespeople were working really hard at trying to get product demand back on track by year-end and were offering new contracts, with very favourable terms, to potential customers.

REQUIRED

a. Based on the above information, identify factors that affect the risk of material misstatement in the December 31, 2018, financial statements of CPCI. Indicate whether the factor increases or decreases the risk of material misstatement at the financial statement level or the assertion level.

Risk Factor Identified	Increase/Decrease Risk of Material Misstatement – at Financial Statement level or Assertion Level (Indicate affected account)

b. Make an acceptable audit risk decision for the current year as high, medium, or low, and support your answer.

c. Make a preliminary judgment of overall materiality for the CPCI audit, show your calculations, and provide your rationale for choice of benchmark and percentage.

d. What would you set performance materiality to be? Explain why.

7-36 〔7〕〔9〕 Pamela Albright is the manager of the audit of Stanton Enterprises, a public company that manufactures formed steel subassemblies for other manufacturers. Albright is planning the 2018 audit and is considering an appropriate amount for overall financial statement materiality, what performance materiality should be set, and the appropriate inherent risks at the account/assertion level. Summary financial statement information is shown in Figure 7-7. Additional relevant planning information is summarized next.

1. Stanton has been a client for four years and Albright's firm has always had a good relationship with the company. Management and the accounting people have always been cooperative, honest, and positive about the audit and financial reporting. No material misstatements were found in the prior year's audit. Albright's firm has monitored the relationship carefully, because when the audit was obtained, Leonard Stanton, the CEO, had the reputation of being a "high-flyer" and had been through bankruptcy at an earlier time in his career.

2. Stanton runs the company in an autocratic way, primarily because of a somewhat controlling personality. He

believes that it is his job to make all the tough decisions. He delegates responsibility to others but is not always willing to delegate a commensurate amount of authority.

3. The industry in which Stanton participates has been in a favourable cycle for the past few years, and that trend is continuing in the current year. Industry profits are reasonably favourable, and there are no competitive or other apparent threats on the horizon.

4. Internal controls for Stanton are evaluated as reasonably effective for all cycles but not unusually strong. Although Stanton supports the idea of control, Albright has been disappointed that management has continually rejected Albright's recommendation to improve its internal audit function.

5. Stanton has a contract with its employees that if earnings before taxes, interest expense, and pension cost exceed $7.8 million for the year, an additional contribution must be made to the pension fund equal to 5 percent of the excess.

REQUIRED

a. You are to play the role of Pamela Albright in the December 31, 2018, audit of Stanton Enterprises. Make a preliminary judgment of materiality and determine performance materiality. Prepare an audit schedule showing your calculations. (Instructor option: Prepare the schedule using an electronic spreadsheet.)

b. Make an acceptable audit risk decision for the current year as high, medium, or low, and support your answer.

c. Perform analytical procedures for Stanton Enterprises that will help you identify accounts that may require additional evidence in the current year's audit. Document the analytical procedures you perform and your conclusions. (Instructor option: Use an electronic spreadsheet to calculate analytical procedures.)

d. The evidence planning worksheet to decide tests of details of balances for Stanton's accounts receivable is shown in Figure 7-8. Use the information in the case and your conclusions in Parts (a) through (c) to complete the following rows of the evidence planning worksheet: acceptable audit risk; inherent risk for accounts receivable; and analytical procedures. Also fill in performance materiality for accounts receivable at the bottom of the worksheet. Make any assumptions you believe are reasonable and appropriate and document them.

Figure 7-7 | Stanton Enterprises Summary Financial Statements

Stanton Enterprises Summary Financial Statements

	Balance Sheet	
	Preliminary Dec. 31, 2018	Audited Dec. 31, 2017
Cash	$ 243 689	$ 133 981
Trade accounts receivable	3544 009	2 224 921
Allowance for uncollectible accounts	(120 000)	(215 000)
Inventories	4520 902	3 888 400
Prepaid expenses	29 500	24 700
Total current assets	8 218 100	6 057 002
Property, plant, and equipment:		
At cost	12 945 255	9 922 534
Less accumulated depreciation	(4 382 990)	(3 775 911)
Total prop., plant, and equipment	8 562 265	6 146 623
Goodwill	1 200 000	345 000
Total assets	**$17 980 365**	**$ 12 548 625**
Accounts payable	$ 2 141 552	$ 2 526 789
Bank loan payable	150 000	—
Accrued liabilities	723 600	598 020
Federal income taxes payable	1 200 000	1 759 000
Current portion of long-term debt	240 000	240 000
Total current liabilities	4 455 152	5 123 809
Long-term debt	960 000	1 200 000
Shoulders' equity:		
Common shares	1 250 000	1 000 000
Additional paid-in capital	2 469 921	1 333 801
Retained earnings	8 845 292	3 891 015
Total shareholders' equity	12 565 213	6 224 816
Total liabilities and shareholders' equity	**$17 980 365**	**$12 548 625**

Combined Statement of Income and Retained Earnings

	Preliminary Dec. 31, 2018	Audited Dec. 31, 2017
Sales	$43 994 931	$32 258 015
Cost of goods sold	24 197 212	19 032 229
Gross profit	19 797 719	13 225 786
Selling, general, and administrative expenses	10 592 221	8 900 432
Pension cost	1 117 845	865 030
Interest expense	83 376	104 220
Total operating expenses	11 793 442	9 869 682
Income before taxes	8 004 277	3 356 104
Income tax expense	1 800 000	1 141 000
Net income	6 204 277	2 215 104
Beginning retained earnings	3 891 015	2 675 911
	10 095 292	4 891 015
Dividends declared	(1 250 000)	(1 000 000)
Ending retained earnings	**$ 8 845 292**	**$ 3 891 015**

	Detail tie-in	Existence	Completeness	Accuracy	Classification	Cutoff	Realizable value	Rights
Acceptable audit risk								
Inherent risk								
Control risk—Sales								
Control risk—Cash receipts								
Control risk—Additional controls								
Substantive tests of transactions—Sales								
Substantive tests of transactions—Cash receipts								
Analytical procedures								
Planned detection risk for tests of details of balances								
Planned audit evidence for tests of details of balances								

Figure 7-8 Stanton Enterprises Evidence Planning Worksheet to Decide Tests of Details of Balances for Accounts Receivable

Performance materiality _____

INTERNAL CONTROL AND COSO FRAMEWORK

STANDARDS REFERENCED IN THIS CHAPTER

CAS 315 –Identifying and assessing the risks of material misstatement through understanding the entity and its environment

As highlighted in Chapter 6, part of understanding the entity and the environment is understanding the entity's internal control. In this chapter, we revisit that part of the audit process, planning the audit, and we discuss the components of internal control, based upon the COSO (Committee of Sponsoring Organizations of the Treadway Commission) framework, which will assist the auditor in developing that understanding of the client's internal control.

LEARNING OBJECTIVES

After studying this chapter, you should be able to:

1 Describe the four primary objectives of effective internal control.

2 Contrast management's responsibilities for maintaining controls with the auditor's responsibilities for evaluating and reporting on internal control.

3 Explain the five components of the COSO internal control framework and the 17 principles of effective control.

4 Understand the important risks and controls in small businesses.

Rogue Trader Circumvents Controls Causing $7 Billion in Losses

The size of the trading losses at French bank Société Générale were staggering. Jérôme Kerviel, a junior trader with a modest base salary of around $70 000, had gambled more than the bank's entire net worth in high-risk bets involving unauthorized trades related to European stock index funds.

Kerviel's role was to make trades that bet whether European stock markets would rise or fall. Each bet was supposed to be offset by a trade in the opposite direction to keep risk at a minimum, with the bank making profit or loss based on the difference between the parallel bets. However, within months of joining the trading desk, he began placing his bets all in one direction, rather than hedging the trades as he was expected to do. One bet paid off handsomely after an attack on the London transport system sent European markets into a dive. "Bingo, 500 000 euros," Kerviel said in an interview with investigators. This success led him to make even bolder bets.

Société Générale played up its use of computer systems to ward off risk. The bank's equity-derivatives unit had not experienced a major incident in 15 years. "We didn't think it was possible," said one Société Générale executive discussing the losses. Unfortunately, Kerviel knew how to mask his trades to avoid detection. He disguised his positions with fake trades, creating the illusion that his positions were hedged.

Keeping his trades hidden required constant vigilance. Kerviel needed to continue to delete and re-enter fake trades to avoid detection. As a result, he regularly skipped holidays and rarely took vacation. "It is one of the rules of controls: a trader who doesn't take holidays is a trader who doesn't want his books to be seen by others," Kerviel stated to investigators.

Finally, a fictitious trade made in the name of a German brokerage house triggered an alarm in Société Générale's systems. Under repeated questioning, Kerviel revealed that his bets had over 50 billion euros at risk for the bank. By the time the French bank unwound the bets, it had lost 4.9 billion euros (US$7.4 billion), nearly destroying the 145-year-old bank.

At Kerviel's June 2010 trial, one of the bank's former executives admitted that the bank failed by creating an environment where there was "too much trust." And, his former boss commented, "If you're not looking for anything, you don't find anything."

Sources: Adapted from Nicola Clark and Katrin Behnhold, "A Société Générale trader remains a mystery as his criminal trial ends," *The New York Times*, June 25, 2010. David Gauthier-Villars and Carrick Mollenkamp, "Portrait emerges of rogue trader at French bank," *The Wall Street Journal*, February 2–3, 2008, p. A1.

The vignette involving Société Générale demonstrates how deficiencies in internal control can cause significant losses resulting in material misstatements in financial statements. Financial reporting problems of companies such as Enron and Nortel also exposed serious deficiencies in internal control. To address these concerns, Section 404 of the Sarbanes-Oxley Act in the United States requires auditors of public companies to assess and report on the effectiveness of internal control over financial reporting, in addition to their report on the audit of financial statements. In Canada, although public company management must attest to the quality of the company's internal controls, auditors are not required to provide assurance.

In this chapter and the next, we continue our discussion of planning the audit by focusing on the role of internal controls. As highlighted in Figure 6-3, part of understanding the entity and its environment is an understanding of internal controls. In this chapter we discuss the primary objectives of internal controls and explain management's and the auditors' responsibilities for internal controls. We then discuss an internal control framework (COSO), which management and auditors use to assess the design of internal controls and the effectiveness of those controls. In the next chapter, we will discuss how auditors gather information to obtain an understanding of internal control design and operation, which forms the basis for the preliminary control risk assessment. The auditor then uses this preliminary assessment to plan the audit.

INTERNAL CONTROL OBJECTIVES

LO 1 Describe the four primary objectives of effective internal control.

Internal control—the policies and procedures instituted and maintained by the management of an entity in order to provide reasonable assurance that management's objectives are met.

A system of **internal control** consists of policies and procedures designed and implemented by management to mitigate risk and to provide reasonable assurance that the company can achieve its objectives and goals. These policies and procedures are often called controls, and collectively, they make up the entity's internal control. When thinking about control, one quickly realizes that risk and control are virtually inseparable. Management must first identify and assess the risks and then manage and mitigate those risks by the implementation of a strong system of internal control.

Management designs systems of internal control to accomplish the following four broad objectives:

1. Strategic, high-level goals that support the mission of the entity.
2. Reliability of financial reporting.
3. Efficiency and effectiveness of operations.
4. Compliance with laws and regulations.

While this may sound rather technical, let's think about management of your personal internal control system.

- *Do you review your credit card statements?* If you do, that's an internal control to manage two types of risks—to ensure the accuracy of the transactions as well as to detect fraudulent activities on the account statement.
- *When you came to school today, did you lock the doors to your house?* If you did, that's your "internal control" to safeguard your assets.
- *Do you keep the PIN number for your debit card in place separate from the card?* If you do, that's an internal control to reduce the risk of your funds being stolen.
- *Do you plan the possible shortest route to complete errands?* That is a control to promote efficiency and reduce the risk of wasting an important resource—your time.
- *Do you file your annual personal income tax returns on time?* If you do, you are in compliance with federal tax laws and reducing the risk of incurring fines and penalties or missing a potential tax refund.

LO 2 Contrast management's responsibilities for maintaining controls with the auditor's responsibilities for evaluating and reporting on internal control.

THE RESPONSIBILITIES OF MANAGEMENT AND THE AUDITOR

Management and the auditor have different responsibilities for internal controls. Management, not the auditor, must establish and maintain the entity's internal controls. Also, in the case of public companies, management is required to publicly report on the operating effectiveness of internal controls over financial reporting. In the United States, auditors of large public companies are required to provide an audit opinion on management's report of the effectiveness of internal controls over financial reporting. However, auditors of companies solely listed on Canadian securities exchanges are not required to issue an audit report on the operating effectiveness of internal controls.

Two key concepts underlie management's design and implementation of controls— reasonable assurance and inherent limitations.

Reasonable Assurance

A company should develop internal controls that provide reasonable, but not absolute, assurance that the financial statements are fairly stated. Management develops internal controls after considering both the costs and benefits of the controls. Reasonable assurance is a high level of assurance that allows only a low likelihood that material misstatements will not be prevented or detected on a timely basis by internal control.

Inherent Limitations

Internal controls cannot be regarded as completely effective, regardless of the care followed in their design and implementation. Even if systems personnel could develop, design, and program an ideal system, the effectiveness of the system would also depend on the competence and dependability of the people using it. For example, assume that a procedure for counting inventory is carefully developed and requires two employees to count independently. If neither of the employees understands the instructions or if both are careless in doing the counts, the count of inventory is likely to be incorrect. Even if the count is right, management might override the procedure and instruct an employee to increase the count of quantities in order to improve reported earnings. Similarly, the employees might decide to overstate the counts intentionally to cover up a theft of inventory by one or both of them. This collaborative effort among employees to defraud is called **collusion**.

Collusion—a cooperative effort among employees or management to defraud a business of cash, inventory, or other assets.

Management's Reporting Responsibilities

For public companies in Canada, management is required to publicly report on the operating effectiveness of those controls. The internal control framework used by most public companies is the Committee of Sponsoring Organizations of the Treadway Commission (COSO) *Internal Control—Integrated Framework*. The COSO framework is the internal control equivalent to generally accepted accounting policies (GAAP). In other words, it is the framework that is used to assess the effectiveness of internal control over financial reporting. Management's assessment of internal control over financial reporting consists of two key aspects. First, management must evaluate the design of internal control over financial reporting. Second, management must test the operating effectiveness of those controls.

Auditor's Responsibilities

Auditors are responsible for understanding the entity's internal controls where they are relevant to the audit, in order to achieve the auditors' objective of identifying the risks of material misstatement at the financial statement and assertion level. Obtaining this understanding of internal control applies to all audits, even when an auditor does not intend to place reliance on internal controls.

Relevant Controls Given that management's internal control objectives encompass more than financial reporting, not all controls are relevant to the audit. Typically those controls related to reliability of financial reporting are relevant. Operational controls, such as manufacturing quality control and employee compliance with health and safety guidelines, would not normally be relevant to the audit, except where the information produced is used to develop analytical procedures or the information is required for disclosure in the financial statements. For example, if the auditor is using production statistics as a basis for an analytical procedure, the controls over the accuracy of the data would be relevant (because the auditor is relying upon this information to develop the expectations for the analytical procedure).

Auditors are also concerned with a client's controls over the safeguarding of assets and compliance with applicable laws and regulations if they have a material effect on the financial statements. Controls affecting internal management information, such as budgets and internal performance reports, can also be relevant if the management information is used to develop expectations for analytical procedures.

Entity-Level Controls and Transaction Controls When assessing control risk, auditors are concerned with both entity-level and transaction controls. **Entity-level controls** are those controls that are pervasive in nature and do not address particular transaction cycles but may prevent or detect and correct misstatements in several cycles. As you may recall from Chapter 4, they contribute to "tone at the top" and establish expectations in the control environment. Unlike transactions controls (which we discuss next), they are often less tangible but they form the foundation on which other internal controls are built. Entity-level controls—such as controls over management override, period-end reporting, hiring competent staff, and fraud-risk controls—have an impact on all other control processes. If these entity-level controls are weak or unreliable, the best designed transaction controls will not be effective in preventing key risks such as management override.

Unlike entity-level controls, **transaction controls** are specific controls designed to prevent or detect and correct misstatements in classes of transactions, account balances, or disclosures and their related assertions. The accuracy of the results of the accounting system (the account balances) is heavily dependent upon the accuracy of the inputs and processing (the transactions). For example, if products sold, units shipped, or unit-selling prices are incorrectly billed to customers for sales, both sales

Entity-level controls—controls that are implemented for multiple transaction cycles or for the entire organization.

Transaction controls—controls that are implemented for specific transaction risks and are designed to specifically prevent or detect and correct misstatements in classes of transactions, account balances, or disclosures and their related assertions.

and accounts receivable will be misstated. If controls are adequate to ensure that billings, cash receipts, sales returns and allowances, and charge-offs are correct, the ending balance in accounts receivable is likely to be correct.

When understanding internal control and assessing control risk for a relevant cycle or segment, auditors are primarily focused on risk at the assertion level and are therefore concerned with the **transaction-related audit objectives and assertions**, discussed in Chapter 4. However, the auditor must also gain an understanding of controls over ending balances and presentation and disclosure. For example, transaction-related audit objectives typically have no effect on two balance-related objectives: valuation, and risks and obligations. That is because these assertions are not related to the processing of transactions. Similarly, controls regarding information included in the financial statement notes often do not come directly from the accounting system but rely upon management identification. Relevant controls in those instances could include approval and review by the audit committee or the board.

Transaction-related audit objectives and assertions—five audit objectives that must be met before the auditor can conclude that the total for any given class of transactions is fairly stated; the assertions are occurrence, completeness, accuracy, cutoff, and classification.

LO Explain the five components of the COSO internal control framework and the 17 principles of effective control.

CAS

COSO COMPONENTS OF INTERNAL CONTROL

Internal control as defined by CAS 315 encompasses five components:

1. Control environment.
2. Risk assessment.
3. Control activities.
4. Information and communication.
5. Monitoring.

These components, based upon COSO's *Internal Control—Integrated Framework*, are summarized in Figure 8-1. This framework serves as a useful guide for management in designing its control system and for auditors in developing their understanding of the entity's internal control system and, ultimately, in assessing the effectiveness of controls and determining control risk.

The COSO framework includes 17 broad principles for effective control of components, as well as "points of focus" to provide greater understanding of each principle. We highlight some of those points when discussing the various principles. The COSO principles apply across all types of entities. The five components with the 17 principles are summarized in Table 8-1.

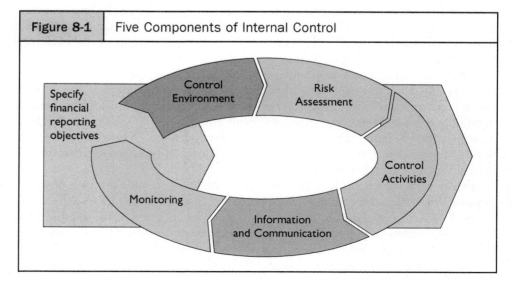

| Figure 8-1 | Five Components of Internal Control |

Table 8-1	COSO Components of Internal Control and Principles for Effective Control

Internal Control

Component	Description of Component	Principles for Effective Control
Control environment	The set of standards, processes, and structures that provide the basis for internal control across the entity. The board of directors and management establish the overall tone regarding internal control and its importance. The control environment has a pervasive impact on the overall system of control.	1. Demonstrate commitment to integrity and ethical values. 2. Board of directors demonstrates independence from management and exercises oversight responsibility. 3. Management, with board oversight, establishes structure, authority, and responsibility. 4. The organization demonstrates commitment to competence. 5. The organization establishes and enforces accountability.
Risk assessment	The process of identification and analysis of risks relevant to the preparation of financial statements in conformity with an applicable financial reporting framework	6. Specifies relevant objectives with sufficient clarity to enable identification of risks. 7. Identifies and assesses risks. 8. Considers the potential for fraud in assessing risk. 9. Identifies and assesses significant changes that could impact internal control.
Control activities	Actions established by policies and procedures to help ensure that management's directives to mitigate risks to achieve its objectives are met. Control activities are performed at all levels of the entity.	10. Selects and develops control activities. 11. Selects and develops general controls over technology. 12. Deploys policies and procedures.
Information and communication	Information is necessary to carry out internal control responsibilities. Communication is the continued, iterative process of providing, sharing, and obtaining necessary information to design, implement, and conduct internal control and to assess its effectiveness.	13. Obtains or generates relevant, quality information. 14. Communicates internally. 15. Communicates externally.
Monitoring	The activities used to ascertain whether the five components of internal control to address the principles are present and functioning.	16. Selects, develops, and performs ongoing and separate evaluations. 17. Evaluates and communicates deficiencies.

Control Environment

The **control environment** is the foundation of effective internal control. It addresses governance and management functions, as well as the attitudes, awareness, and actions of those charged with governance and management concerning internal control and its importance. Controls at this level are generally pervasive in nature. Although they will not directly prevent or detect and correct a material misstatement, they provide the discipline and structure for all other components. If top management believes control is important, others in the organization will sense that and respond by conscientiously observing the policies and procedures established. However, if it is clear to members of the organization that control is not an important concern to top management and is given "lip service" rather than meaningful support, it is almost certain that control objectives will not be effectively achieved. Or, as in the case of Société Générale (in our opening vignette), if management fails in its monitoring role by placing too much trust in the system or the people operating the controls, then the risk for fraud and error is high.

Control environment—the actions, policies, and procedures that reflect the overall attitudes of top management, directors, and owners of an entity about control and its importance to the entity.

CONCEPT CHECK

C8-1 Which of the five categories of COSO internal controls is most important? Justify your response.

C8-2 What are entity-level controls and why are they so important?

In 2014, Penn West Petroleum, one of the largest conventional oil and natural gas producers in Canada, announced the results of an independent internal review conducted by forensic accountants hired by the audit committee, which arose from certain accounting practices that came to the attention of the new CFO (chief financial officer). In determining why the accounting practices were undetected, the audit committee identified the following material weaknesses in the internal control over financial reporting:

- Control environment. Management concluded that the former senior accounting management did not adequately establish and enforce a strong culture of compliance and controls. There was a lack of awareness or unwillingness of some staff with knowledge of improper practices to use the company's whistleblowing hotline or to take other actions that could have brought to light the improper accounting practices much sooner. Management concluded that this material weakness was a factor that contributed to the other weaknesses that were discovered.

- Lack of appropriate review of journal entries. The company had journal entry policies requiring that the person creating an entry be unable to approve the entry and that each entry include appropriate documentation; however, those polices were not followed.

- Management override. Senior accounting management overrode the company's accounting processes and recorded incorrect amounts in the financial statements.

Lynn Turner, former chief accountant of the SEC, in commenting on the weaknesses, noted: "It reflects very poorly on the governance of the company, the integrity of management, and on the ability of the company itself to generate reliable data on which to base investment decisions."

As a result of these material weaknesses, the company had to restate the first quarter of 2014, along with the 2013 and 2012 audited consolidated financial statements. The restatement did not mean "The sky is falling"—the company was onside with all of its debt covenants, its borrowing base had not been affected, and neither had the value of its reserves changed. Further, the senior accounting personnel responsible for the misstatements were no longer with the company and Penn West had taken several remedial actions to rectify the material weaknesses. However, the inappropriate adjustments boosted cash flow and netbacks (a measure of profitability per barrel of oil), two key metrics that influence stock price.

Following the announcement of the restatements, the share price dropped significantly and several class action lawsuits were filed. In the end, Penn West and the investors settled on a $53 million payout.

Sources: Claudia Cattaneo, "Rocked by accounting scandal, Penn West has now turned the corner, CEO says," *Financial Post*, November 2014. Penn West press release, *CNW Newswire*, September 18, 2014, accessed April 6, 2015, at **http://business.financialpost.com/ commodities/energy/rocked-by-accounting-scandal-penn-west-has-now-turned-the-corner-ceo-says**. Daniel Healing, "Settlement revealed to be $53 million in Penn West accounting scandal," *Calgary Herald*, February 17, 2016. David Milstead, "Penn West, WorldCom: The warning signs we may have missed," *The Globe and Mail*, August 8, 2014. Crystal Schlick, "Yedlin: Penn West tries to move forward with release of audit," *Calgary Herald*, September 27, 2014.

Principle 1: Demonstrate Commitment to Integrity and Ethical Values The organization's commitment to integrity and ethical values is demonstrated through the tone set by management and the board of directors. Management and those in charge of governance, through their activities, provide clear signals to employees about what is important. For example, are profit plans and budget data set as "best possible" plans or "most likely" targets? Can management be described as "fat and bureaucratic," "lean and mean," "dominated by one or a few individuals," or "just right"? Does management have a poor attitude toward financial reporting and use aggressive accounting to ensure budgets and goals are met? Understanding these and similar aspects of management's philosophy and operating style give the auditor a sense of its commitment to integrity and ethical values. As highlighted in Auditing in Action 8-1, poor corporate culture or "tone at the top" is often the underlying cause of all other internal control deficiencies.

The organization should have standards that guide its behaviour and a process to communicate those standards of conduct throughout the organization, including external partners and outsourced service providers. If there is a code of ethics, does it establish what is right and wrong? The organization should also have in place a process to evaluate the performance of individuals and teams against those standards of conduct. In addition, the organization should address any deviations in an appropriate and timely manner, and periodically review trends and root causes to determine whether policies should be modified, or if training and controls are necessary.

Principle 2: Board of Directors Exercises Oversight Responsibility An effective board of directors has the appropriate background and expertise, the outside directors are independent of management, and its members are involved in and scrutinize management's activities. To assist the board in its oversight responsibilities for financial reporting and internal control, the board creates an audit committee. The major exchanges (TSX, NYSE, AMEX, and NASDAQ) require that listed companies have an audit committee composed entirely of independent directors who are financially literate, and at least one member of the committee must have financial expertise.

The audit committee considers the potential for management override of internal controls and oversees management's fraud-risk assessment process, as well as antifraud programs and controls. The audit committee is also responsible for maintaining ongoing communication with both external and internal auditors. This allows the auditors and directors to discuss matters that might relate to such things as the integrity or actions of management. In addition to those responsibilities, the audit committee of public companies approves audit and non-audit services done by auditors. The audit committee approval provides a safeguard to potential threats to auditor independence.

The audit committee's independence from management and knowledge of financial reporting issues are important determinants of its ability to effectively evaluate internal controls and financial statements prepared by management. In addition, open lines of communication with the entity's external and internal auditors enhance audit committee effectiveness.

Many privately held companies also create an effective audit committee. For other privately held companies, governance may be provided by owners, partners, trustees, or a committee of management, such as a finance or budget committee. Individuals responsible for overseeing the strategic direction of the entity and the accountability of the entity, including financial reporting and disclosure, are called *those charged with governance* by auditing standards.

Principle 3: Management Establishes Structure, Authority, and Responsibility A well-controlled entity has an organizational structure appropriate for its size and operating activities, and one that clearly defines the lines of responsibilities and authority. Some key questions the auditors should address include the following:

- Are there adequate policies and procedures for authorization and approval of transactions?
- Is there appropriate structure for assigning ownership of data, including who is authorized to initiate and/or change transactions? Is ownership assigned to each application and database?
- Is there appropriate segregation of incompatible activities both physically and through access to IT infrastructure?
- Are outsourced service providers' authority and responsibility limited by the organization's guidelines?
- Are there appropriate policies for accepting new business, conflicts of business, and security practices?

Principle 4: Commitment to Competence The most important aspect of any system of controls is personnel. If employees are competent and trustworthy, other controls can be absent, and reliable financial statements will still result. However, incompetent or dishonest people can have the opposite effect regardless of the number of controls present. Relevant standards for hiring, training, motivating, evaluating, promoting, compensating, transferring, and terminating employment of personnel are key indicators of the effectiveness of this principle. Another important consideration is management's commitment to providing sufficient accounting and financial personnel to keep pace with the growth and/or complexity of the business.

Principle 5: Organization Establishes and Enforces Accountability A well-controlled organization should have a structure and tone at the top that establishes and enforces individual accountability for internal control. Appropriate accountability mechanisms would include performance measures, incentives, and rewards. Some key questions auditors should address include the following:

- Does management set realistic financial targets and expectations for operations personnel?
- Do the board and management act to reduce or remove incentives or temptations that might prompt employees to engage in dishonest, illegal, or unethical acts?

Risk Assessment

Risk assessment—management's identification and analysis of risks relevant to the preparation of financial statements in conformity with an applicable financial reporting framework.

Risk assessment involves a process for identifying and analyzing risks that might prevent the organization from achieving its objectives. There are four underlying principles related to risk assessment: the organization should have clear objectives in order to be able to identify and assess the risks relating to its objectives; it should determine how the risks should be managed; the organization should consider the potential for fraudulent behaviour; and it should monitor changes that could impact internal controls. Specific risks related to information technology (IT) should be considered, as these risks can lead to substantial losses. If IT systems fail, organizations can be paralyzed by the inability to retrieve information or by the use of unreliable information caused by processing errors.

Risk assessment specifically related to financial reporting involves management's identification and analysis of risks relevant to the preparation of financial statements in conformity with an applicable financial reporting framework. For example, if a company frequently sells products at a price below inventory cost because of rapid technology changes, it is essential for the company to incorporate adequate controls to address the risk of overstating inventory. Once management identifies a risk, it estimates the significance of that risk, assesses the likelihood of the risk occurring, and develops specific actions that need to be taken to reduce the risk to an acceptable level.

Management's risk assessment differs from but is closely related to the auditor's risk assessment discussed in Chapter 7. While management assesses risks as a part of designing and operating internal controls to minimize errors and fraud, auditors assess risks to decide the evidence needed in the audit. If management effectively assesses and responds to risks, the auditor will typically choose to accumulate less evidence than when management fails to identify or respond to significant risks.

Principle 6: Organization Specifies Relevant Objectives In order to ensure that the organization meets its objective of reliable external financial reporting, management should consider whether its reporting objectives are consistent with the relevant financial reporting framework and appropriate in the circumstances. Management should also establish a materiality threshold for the purpose of identifying significant accounts; this threshold should take into consideration risks at all locations. The organization's accounting policies, procedures, and processes should ensure that the financial statements reflect the transactions and events that underlie them.

Principle 7: Identifies and Assesses Risks The organization should consider both external and internal risks to the achievement of financial reporting objectives. A risk assessment process would normally address such matters as the following: changes in the operating environment; new or revamped information systems; rapid growth; new business models, products, or activities; corporate restructuring; expanded foreign operations; and new accounting pronouncements. The risk identification process should involve the appropriate levels of management with the necessary expertise. For example, the accounting department should be made aware of changes in the operating environment so that it can consider the impact on accounting policies.

Principle 8: Considers the Potential for Fraud in Assessing Risk As part of the risk assessment process, the organization considers risks related to financial reporting, management override, misappropriation of assets, and corruption. This assessment should include an evaluation of incentives and pressures, opportunities, attitudes, and rationalizations to commit fraud. The results of the fraud-risk assessment should be discussed with the audit committee.

The assessment should consider the various ways that financial reporting fraud could occur. Such factors could include:

- Management bias in selection of accounting policies;
- Degree of estimates and judgments in external reporting;
- Fraud schemes and scenarios common to the industry in which the organization operates;
- Geographic regions;
- Incentives that may motivate fraudulent behaviour;
- Nature of technology and management's ability to manipulate information;
- Unusual or complex transactions subject to significant management influence; and
- Vulnerability to management override and potential schemes to circumvent controls.

Table 8-2 presents some control features and describes how they could reduce fraud risks.

Principle 9: Identifies and Assesses Significant Changes Change creates risk; therefore, management should implement processes that enable it to identify and evaluate changes in the external and internal environment that could significantly impact the system of internal control. When change occurs, such as the introduction of a new business model or even a change in accounting framework (say, from ASPE to IFRS), existing controls may no longer be effective. In addition to changes in business models and accounting frameworks, changes in management can have a significant impact. The auditor should ask, "Does the organization have processes to consider changes in management and their respective attitudes and philosophies?"

Control Activities

Control activities are the actions established by the policies and procedures to help ensure that management directives to mitigate risks are carried out. Control activities are performed at all levels of the entity, at various stages within business processes,

Control activities—policies and procedures that help ensure the necessary actions to address risks in the achievement of the entity's objectives.

Table 8-2	Control Features That Could Reduce Fraud Risks
Control Feature	**How It Could Reduce Fraud Risks**
Management and board promotion of a culture of honesty and high ethics through implementation of programs and controls that are based on core values	Creates an environment that reinforces acceptable behaviour and expectations of each employee
Audit committee oversight of management and internal auditors	Assists in creating an effective "tone at the top" by reinforcing zero tolerance for fraud Serves as a deterrent for management fraud by having a direct reporting relationship with internal and external auditors
Specific management responsibilities for managing risks of fraud	Reduces perceived opportunities to commit and conceal fraud Results in improved Improves internal controls by actively considering risks and implementing controls to mitigate the risks
Articulated and effective fraud-risk management process	Results in clear matching of controls to risks, and keeps risk assessments, controls, and monitoring processes current
Effective general and application control activities that address specific risks of fraud, such as segregation of duties, passwords, and user access rights that limit functions to those needed to complete their jobs, and monitoring of exceptions such as unusual traffic on networks	Prevents unauthorized access to assets, helps to detect potential unauthorized access to assets

and over the technology environment. The three principles applicable to the control activities component are:

1. The organization selects and develops control activities that contribute to the mitigation of risks to the achievement of objectives to acceptable levels.
2. The organization selects and develops general control activities over technology to support the achievement of objectives.
3. The organization deploys control activities through policies that establish what is expected and in procedures that put policies into action.

Control activities may be manual or automated. The effectiveness of **manual controls** depends on both the competence of the people performing the controls and the care they exercise when doing them. For example, when credit department personnel review exception reports that identify credit sales exceeding a customer's authorized credit limit, the auditor may need to evaluate the person's ability to make the assessment and test the accuracy of the exception report. When controls are enacted by computers, they are called **automated controls**. These controls are performed on the data within the IT application and have embedded checks on data validity, accuracy and completeness of processing. Because of the nature of computer processing, automated controls, if properly designed, lead to consistent operation of the controls.

Principle 10: Selects and Develops Control Activities Since an organization develops control activities that are specifically designed to mitigate the risks for that particular organization, control activities will vary among organizations. However, the organization should have in place a process that maps controls to address each risk related to the relevant financial statement assertion. Some key points to consider when determining if all risks are addressed:

- Are all relevant business processes, information technology, and locations where control activities are needed (including outsourced service providers and other business partners) considered?
- Are control activities related to the integrity of information sent to and received from outsourced service providers considered?
- Are the controls performed by outsourced service providers adequate?

Transaction (or Application) Controls Transaction or application controls are control activities implemented to mitigate transaction processing risk for specific business processes, such as the processing of sales or cash receipts. The control activities should be a combination of preventive and detective controls.

Preventive controls are designed to stop errors or fraud from occurring (e.g., supervisor review of journal entry/purchase order or automated input edit controls). **Detective controls** identify errors or irregularities after they have occurred so corrective action can be taken (e.g., reconciliations, validation of results). The controls can be input controls that ensure the completeness, accuracy, and validity of the reference data used in the processing (e.g., master price file), processing controls that prevent and detect errors while transactions are being processed, and output controls that focus on detecting errors after processing (e.g., reconciliations and reviews controls). In general, preventative controls are considered to be more effective than detective controls.

A **business process** is a structured set of activities designed to produce specified output. An individual business process, also called an *application system*, can have different types of control activities. An example of a business process or application system would be a sales system, which processes sales transactions initiated by media such as the internet, telephone, or a purchase order form received in the mail. The sales system should have a range and variety of detective and preventive controls, including manual control activities (such as requiring that large sales be approved by the sales manager), computer-assisted control activities (such as requiring credit manager review of a credit exception report prior to releasing orders for processing), or fully automated control activities (such as having the information system calculate sales taxes due on the sale).

| Figure 8-2 | Control Activities Overseeing Business Processes |

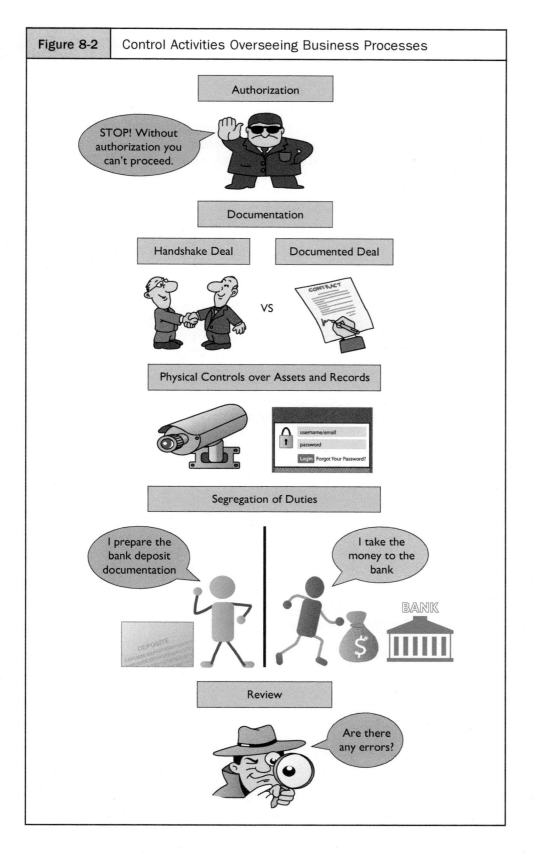

Typical control activities of the business processes, as illustrated in Figure 8-2, would include:

1. Proper authorization of transactions and activities.
2. Adequate documents and records.

3. Physical and logical control over assets and records.
4. Adequate segregation of duties.
5. Independent checks of performance, recorded data, and actual results.

Proper Authorization of Transactions and Activities Every transaction should be properly authorized if controls are to be satisfactory. Authorization encompasses more than transactions; it also includes authorization of new programs and changes to programs, since this affects the way that transactions are processed. Authorization can be either general or specific. Under **general authorization**, management establishes policies, and subordinates are instructed to implement these general authorizations by approving all transactions within the limits set by the policy. General authorization decisions include the issuance of fixed price lists for the sale of products, credit limits for customers, and fixed reorder points for making acquisitions.

Specific authorization applies to individual transactions. For certain transactions, management prefers to authorize each transaction. An example is the authorization of a sales transaction by the sales manager for a used-car company.

The distinction between authorization and approval is also important. Authorization is a policy decision for either a general class of transactions or specific transactions. Approval is the implementation of management's general authorization decisions. An example of a general authorization is management setting a policy authorizing the ordering of inventory when less than a three-week supply is on hand. When a department orders inventory, the clerk responsible for maintaining the perpetual record approves the order to indicate that the authorization policy has been met. In other cases, the computer approves the transactions by comparing quantities of inventory on hand to a master file of reorder points and automatically submits purchase orders to authorized suppliers in the vendor master file. In this case, the computer is performing the approval function using preauthorized information contained in the master files.

Adequate Documents and Records Documents and records are paper or electronic files on which transactions are entered and summarized. They include such diverse items as sales invoices, purchase orders, subsidiary records, sales journals, and employee time cards.

Certain principles dictate the proper design and use of documents and records. Documents should be:

- Prenumbered or automatically numbered consecutively to facilitate control over missing records and to aid in locating records when they are needed at a later date. Prenumbered documents and records are important for the completeness assertion.
- Prepared at the time a transaction takes place, or as soon as possible thereafter, to minimize timing errors (the cutoff assertion).
- Designed for multiple use, when possible, to minimize the number of different forms. For example, a properly designed electronic shipping record can be the basis for releasing goods from storage to the shipping department, informing billing of the quantity of goods to bill to the customer and the appropriate billing date, and updating the perpetual inventory records.
- Constructed in a manner that encourages correct preparation. This can be done by providing internal checks within the form or record. For example, computer screen prompts may force online data entry of critical information before the record is electronically routed for authorizations and approvals. Similarly, screen controls can validate the information entered, such as when an invalid general ledger account number is automatically rejected because the account number does not match the chart of accounts master file.

A control closely related to documents and records is the **chart of accounts**, which classifies transactions into individual balance sheet and income statement accounts.

The chart of accounts is helpful in preventing classification errors if it accurately describes which type of transactions should be in each account.

Physical Control Over Assets and Records If assets are left unprotected, they can be stolen. If records are not adequately protected, they can be duplicated, stolen, damaged, or lost. When a company is highly computerized, its computer equipment, programs, and data files represent the records of the company that must be protected. The most important type of protective measure for safeguarding physical assets and records is the use of physical precautions. An example is the use of storerooms for inventory to guard against theft. Fireproof safes and safety deposit vaults for the protection of assets such as currency and securities are other important physical safeguards.

As with other types of assets, physical controls are used to protect the computer facilities. Examples are locks on doors to the computer room and terminals, adequate storage space for software and data files to protect them from loss, and proper fire-extinguishing systems. Backup and recovery procedures—actions that an organization can take in the event of a loss of equipment, programs, or data—are also important. For example, having a backup copy of programs and critical data files stored in a safe remote location together with information systems recovery procedures is important for maintaining business continuity.

Adequate Segregation of Duties These controls can reduce the opportunities for a person to be in a position to perpetuate and conceal a fraud. Naturally, the extent of **segregation of duties** depends heavily on the size of the organization. In many small companies, it is not practical to segregate the duties to the extent suggested. In these cases, the auditor will likely choose to not rely upon internal controls.

Segregation of duties— segregation of the following activities in an organization: custody of assets, recording/data entry, systems development/ acquisition and maintenance, computer operations, reconciliation, and authorization.

Separation of Custody of Assets From Accounting The reason for not permitting the person who has temporary or permanent custody of an asset to account for that asset is to protect the firm against theft. Indirect access, such as access to cheque signature images, also must be separate. When one person performs both custody and accounting functions, there is an excessive risk of that person's disposing of or using the asset for personal gain and adjusting the records to hide the theft or use. If the cashier, for example, receives cash and is responsible for data entry of cash receipts and sales, it is possible for the cashier to take the cash received from a customer and adjust the customer's account by failing to record a sale or by recording a fictitious credit to the account.

Separation of the Authorization of Transactions from the Custody of Related Assets It is desirable to prevent persons who authorize transactions from having control over the related assets, to reduce the likelihood of embezzlement. For example, the same person should not authorize the payment of a vendor's invoice and also approve the disbursement of funds to pay the bill.

Separation of Operational Responsibility From Record-Keeping Responsibility To ensure unbiased information, record-keeping is typically included in a separate accounting department under the controller. For example, if a department or division oversees the creation of its own records and reports, it might change the results to improve its reported performance. Similarly, in the case of accounting estimates, there should be a segregation of duties between those committing the entity to the underlying transactions and those responsible for making the accounting estimates.

Separation of Reconciliation From Data Entry Reconciliation involves comparing information from two or more sources, or independently verifying the work that has been completed by others. For example, preparation of a bank reconciliation by the accounting manager independent of the accounts receivable or accounts payable personnel would detect unauthorized use or disbursements of cash.

Separation of IT Duties from User Departments As the level of complexity of IT systems increases, the separation of authorization, record keeping, and custody often becomes blurred. For example, sales agents may enter customer orders online. The computer authorizes those sales based on its comparison of customer credit limits to the master file and posts all approved sales in the sales cycle journals. Therefore, the computer plays a significant role in the authorization and record keeping of sales transactions. To compensate for these potential overlaps of duties, it is important for companies to separate major IT-related functions from key user department functions. In this example, responsibility for designing and controlling accounting software programs that contain the sales authorization and posting controls should be under the authority of IT, whereas the ability to update information in the master file of customer credit limits should reside in the company's credit department outside the IT function.

Independent checks—internal control activities designed for the continuous internal verification of other controls.

Independent Checks of Performance, Recorded Data, and Actual Results The need for careful and continuous review of the other controls, often referred to as **independent checks** on performance or internal verification, arises because internal control tends to change over time unless there is a mechanism for frequent review. Computerized accounting systems can be designed so that many internal verification procedures can be automated as part of the system, such as separate addition of subsidiary files for agreement with general ledger totals.

In the case of manual reviews, an essential characteristic of the persons performing internal verification procedures is independence from the individuals originally responsible for preparing the data. The least expensive means of internal verification is the separation of duties in the manner previously discussed. For example, when the bank reconciliation is performed by a person independent of the accounting records and handling of cash, there is an opportunity for verification without incurring significant additional costs.

In addition to reviews that involve verification, controls that involve period performance serve an important means of highlighting unexpected variations that should be investigated and, if necessary, corrected. Effective reviews involve relating different sets of data (operating, financial, internal, and external) to one another. These types of reviews are very helpful in highlighting both potential errors and fraud.

Application controls—controls typically at the business process level that apply to processing transactions, such as the inputting, processing, and outputting of sales or cash receipts.

Input controls—controls designed by an organization to ensure that the information to be processed by the computer is authorized, accurate, and complete.

Software Application Controls In addition to the above-mentioned control activities, **application controls** designed for each software application are intended to help a company satisfy the transaction-related management assertions discussed in previous chapters. Although the objectives for each category are the same, the procedures for meeting the objectives vary considerably. Let's examine each more closely.

Input controls are designed to ensure that the information entered into the computer is authorized, accurate, and complete. They are critical because a large portion of errors in IT systems result from data entry errors and, of course, regardless of the quality of information processing, input errors result in output errors. Typical controls developed for manual systems are still important in IT systems, such as:

- Management's authorization of transactions;
- Adequate preparation of input source documents; and
- Competent personnel.

Controls specific to IT include:

- Adequately designed input screens with preformatted prompts for transaction information.
- Pull-down menu lists of available software options.
- Computer-performed validation tests of input accuracy, such as the validation of customer numbers against customer master files.
- Online-based input controls for e-commerce applications where external parties, such as customers and suppliers, perform the initial part of the transaction inputting.
- Immediate error correction procedures, to provide early detection and correction of input errors.
- Accumulation of errors in an error file for subsequent follow-up by data input personnel.

Table 8-3	Batch Input Controls	
Control	**Definition**	**Examples**
Financial total	Summary total of field amounts for all records in a batch that represent a meaningful total such as dollars or amounts	The total of dollars of all vendor invoices to be paid
Hash total	Summary total of codes from all records in a batch that do not represent a meaningful total	The total of all vendor account numbers for vendor invoices to be paid
Record count	Summary total of physical records in a batch	The total number of vendor invoices to be processed

For IT systems that group similar transactions together into batches, the use of financial batch totals, hash totals, and record count totals helps increase the accuracy and completeness of input. Batch input controls are described in Table 8-3. For example, the comparison of a record count calculated before data entry of the number of vendor invoices to be entered and the number of vendor invoices processed by the system would help determine if any invoices were omitted or entered more than once during data entry.

Processing controls prevent and detect errors while transaction data are processed. General controls, especially controls related to systems development and security, provide essential control for minimizing processing errors. Specific application processing controls are often programmed into software to prevent, detect, and correct processing errors. Examples of processing controls are illustrated in Table 8-4.

Output controls focus on detecting errors after processing is completed, rather than on preventing errors. The most important output control is review of the data for reasonableness by someone knowledgeable about the output. Users can often identify errors because they know the approximate correct amounts. Several common controls for detecting errors in outputs include the following:

- Reconcile computer-produced output to manual control totals.
- Compare the number of units processed to the number of units submitted for processing.

Processing controls—controls designed to ensure that data input into the system are accurately and completely processed

Output controls—controls designed to ensure that computer-generated data are valid, accurate, complete, and distributed only to authorized people.

Table 8-4	Processing Controls	
Type of Processing Control	**Description**	**Example**
Validation test	Ensures that a particular type of transaction is appropriate for processing	Does the transaction code for the processing of a recent purchase match predetermined inventory codes?
Sequence test	Determines that data submitted for processing are in the correct order	Has the file of payroll input transactions been sorted in departmental order before processing?
Arithmetic accuracy test	Checks the accuracy of processed data	Does the sum of net pay plus withholdings equal gross pay for the entire payroll?
Data reasonableness test	Determines whether data exceed prespecified amounts	Does employee's gross pay exceed 60 hours or $1999 for the week?
Completeness test	Determines that every field in a record has been completed	Are employee numbers, names, number of regular hours, number of overtime hours, department numbers, etc., included for each employee?

- Compare a sample of transaction output to input source documents.
- Verify dates and times of processing to identify any out-of-sequence processing.

For sensitive computer output, such as payroll cheques, control can be improved by requiring employees to present employee identification before they receive their cheques or by requiring the use of direct deposit into the employees' pre-approved bank accounts. Also, access to sensitive output stored in electronic files or transmitted across networks, including the internet, is often restricted by requiring passwords, user IDs, and encryption techniques (which we discuss in the next section).

CONCEPT CHECK

C8-3 What are control activities? Explain their role in the financial reporting process.

Principle 11: Selects and Develops General Controls Over Technology Practically all organizations rely upon some sort of information technology to enable reliable financial reporting. For the application (transaction) controls to operate effectively, the organization must have effective general IT controls (normally called **general controls**) over the internal control activities that are pervasive (they operate across applications) and affect multiple classes of transactions or multiple groups of accounts. General computer controls can be manual (such as IT budgets and contracts with service providers) or automated (embedded in the computer programs). Because general controls often apply on an entity-wide basis and affect many different software applications, auditors evaluate general controls for the company as a whole. Application controls are likely to be effective when general controls are effective.

Figure 8-3 illustrates the relationship between general controls and application controls. The oval represents the general controls that provide assurance that all application controls are effective. Effective general controls reduce the risks identified in the boxes outside the general controls oval in Figure 8-3.

General controls—internal controls for automated information systems pertaining to more than one transaction cycle or group of accounts.

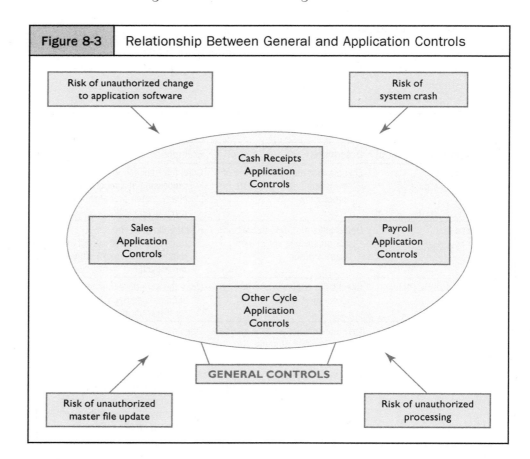

Figure 8-3 Relationship Between General and Application Controls

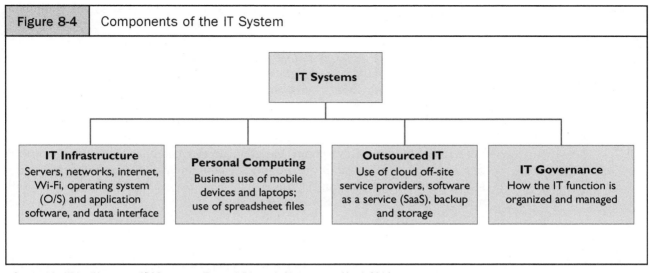

| Figure 8-4 | Components of the IT System |

IT Systems

IT Infrastructure
Servers, networks, internet, Wi-Fi, operating system (O/S) and application software, and data interface

Personal Computing
Business use of mobile devices and laptops; use of spreadsheet files

Outsourced IT
Use of cloud off-site service providers, software as a service (SaaS), backup and storage

IT Governance
How the IT function is organized and managed

Source: John White, "How to use COSO to assess IT controls," *Journal of Accountancy*, May 1, 2014.

Information Technology System The IT system includes the IT infrastructure, personal computing, outsourced IT, and IT governance. Figure 8-4 summarizes the components of the IT system.

The type of IT system will vary based upon factors such as overall size, the functions that are outsourced, and whether the organization has packaged off-the-shelf programs or customized software. Packaged software will have fewer programming errors, and normally cannot be altered, increasing the reliance on accuracy of programming. The nature and organization of the IT infrastructure supporting the organization will affect the types of security controls that should be in place. As Auditing in Action 8-2 illustrates, failure to design an adequate IT system can be quite costly. We briefly discuss a few of the different types of IT systems below.

The use of networks that link equipment such as desktops, midrange computers, mainframes, workstations, servers, and printers is common for most businesses. **Local area networks (LANs)** link equipment within a single or small cluster of buildings and are used only within a company. LANs are often used to transfer data and programs from one computer or workstation using network system software that allows

Local area networks (LANs)— networks that connect computer equipment, data files, software, and peripheral equipment within a local area, such as a single building or a small cluster of buildings, for intracompany use.

AUDITING IN ACTION 8-2
Technology Glitches Bungle Facebook's IPO

The buildup surrounding Facebook, Inc.'s May 18, 2012, initial public offering set expectations high; however, the opening days of trading led quickly to disappointment. Just days before its debut, the company's CFO decided to boost the number of shares to be offered by 25 percent and increased the opening offer price to $38 per share, believing demand would be high. On opening day, massive demand for the social network's initial offering actually led to a 30-minute delay in the start of trading of the stock on the NASDAQ Stock Market. The technology glitch left individual investors puzzled about whether their buy and sell orders had actually been executed, when normally those acknowledgments are instantaneous. When U.S. regulators, including the SEC, initially examined the disruption, they noted that even though the mishap was blamed on a computer malfunction, the underlying cause may have been programmer failure in designing the systems to

be robust enough to handle the volume of orders. In May 2013, NASDAQ agreed to pay a $10 million penalty to the SEC related to the Facebook IPO, and in April 2015, NASDAQ agreed to a settlement of $26.5 million for a class action lawsuit filed by retail investors who suffered damages in the IPO.

Sources: Based on Jacob Blunge, "Regulators Probe Role of 'Glitches' in Market Upheavals," NASDAQ News (June 27, 2012) (HYPERLINK "http://www.nasdaq.com" www.nasdaq.com); John McCrank, "Nasdaq to settle Facebook IPO lawsuit for $26.5 million" (April 23, 2015) (HYPERLINK "http://www.reuters.com" www.reuters.com); John McCrank and Jonathan Spicer, "Facebook Investors Left Guessing after NASDAQ Glitch," Reuters (May 21, 2012) (HYPERLINK "http://www.reuters.com" www.reuters.com); Andrew Tangel, "NASDAQ Offers Brokerages $40 Million for Facebook Glitches," Los Angeles Times (June 6, 2012) (HYPERLINK "http://www.articles.latimes.com" www.articles.latimes.com).

all of the devices to function together. **Wide area networks (WANs)** link equipment in larger geographic regions, including global operations.

In networks, application software and data files used to process transactions are included on several computers that are linked together. Access to the application from desktop computers or workstations is managed by network server software or other interfaces with cloud computing technology. Even small companies can have several computer servers linked together on a network, while larger companies may have hundreds of servers in dozens of locations networked together. It is common for networks to consist of various combinations of equipment and procedures, which may not have standard security options. Lack of equipment compatibility across a network may occur when responsibility for purchasing equipment and software, maintenance, administration, and physical security resides with key user groups rather than with a centralized IT function. Sometimes network security may be compromised when networks consist of equipment with incompatible security features.

Database management systems allow clients to create databases that include information that can be shared across multiple applications. In nondatabase systems, each application has its own data file, whereas in database management systems, many applications share files. Clients implement database management systems to reduce data redundancy, improve control over data, and provide better information for decision making by integrating information throughout functions and departments. For example, customer data, such as the customer's name and address, can be shared in the sales, credit, accounting, marketing, and shipping functions, resulting in consistent information for all users and significant cost reductions. Companies often integrate database management systems within the entire organization using **enterprise resource planning (ERP) systems** that integrate numerous aspects of an organization's activities into one accounting information system. ERP systems share data across accounting and nonaccounting business functions of the organization. For example, customer order data may be used by accounting to record a sale, by production to meet increased production demand, by purchasing to order additional raw materials, and by human resources to arrange labour schedules.

Controls often improve when data are centralized in a database management system by eliminating duplicate data files. However, database management systems also can create internal control risks. Risks increase when multiple users, including individuals outside of accounting, can access and update data files. To counter the risks of unauthorized, inaccurate, and incomplete data files, companies must implement proper database administration and access controls. With the centralization of data in a single system, they must also ensure proper backup of data on a regular basis.

Many clients outsource some or all of their IT needs to an independent organization commonly referred to as a computer **service centre**, including **application service providers (ASPs)** and **cloud computing environments**, rather than maintain an internal IT centre. Cloud computing is a computer resource deployment and procurement model that enables an organization to obtain IT resources and applications from any location via an internet connection. Depending on the arrangement, all or parts of an entity's IT hardware, software, and data might reside in an IT service centre shared with other organizations and managed by a third-party vendor. The name cloud computing comes from the use of a cloud-shaped symbol in systems diagrams to represent complex IT infrastructures.

Smaller companies often outsource their payroll function because payroll is reasonably standard from company to company, and many reliable providers of payroll services are available. Companies also outsource their e-commerce systems to external website service providers, including those that offer cloud computing services as described above. Like all outsourcing decisions, companies decide whether to outsource IT on a cost-benefit basis.

When outsourcing to a computer service centre, the client submits input data, which the service centre processes for a fee; the service centre then returns the agreed-upon output and the original input. For payroll, the company submits data from time records, pay rates, and TD1 tax forms to the service centre. The service centre returns payroll cheques, journals, and input data each week, and T4 tax forms at the end of each year. The service centre is responsible for designing the computer system and providing adequate controls to ensure that the processing is reliable.

Outsourcing can provide challenges from an internal control perspective. Management is responsible for the design and operating effectiveness of internal controls, and this includes controls that are outsourced to a service provider. When selecting a service provider, management needs to consider the ethics and integrity of service providers, as well as the design and functioning of their internal controls; these should also be re-evaluated regularly.

When selecting and designing general controls for the IT system, the focus is on the controls over organization and management, security management, access controls, and program development and changes.

Organization and Management Controls These general controls represent the control activities over the IT control environment. They include:

- IT governance structure;
- How IT risks are identified, mitigated, and managed;
- Segregation of duties; and
- Policies, procedures, and standards affecting areas such as data ownership, data management, software ownership, privacy, the code of conduct with respect to technology, and disaster recovery.

As highlighted in Figure 8-4, IT governance represents a key component of the IT system. **IT governance** is the overall process that enables the organization to provide information resources that meet business needs. It represents the policies, practices, and procedures that help IT resources add value while considering costs and benefits. In addition to adding value, the goal of IT governance is to mitigate risk and prevent disastrous failures, such as information systems implementations that make transaction processing cumbersome. IT governance is a crucial subset of corporate governance. The management information system (MIS) should be viewed as a partner within the business rather than an adversary or servant. The chief information officer (CIO) should be a participant in executive meetings and the board of directors should be involved with IT strategy (many boards have established an IT governance and strategy subcommittee).

To respond to the risk of combining traditional custody, authorization, and record-keeping responsibilities by having the computer perform those tasks, well-controlled organizations separate key duties within IT. Two important areas of segregation of duties related to general controls are:

- *Separation of systems development or acquisition and maintenance from accounting.* Systems development or acquisition comprises activities that create (or purchase) new methods of processing transactions, thus changing the way information is entered, displayed, reported, and posted against files or databases. Maintenance activities involve changes to these processes. These functions should be monitored to ensure that only authorized programs and systems consistent with management objectives are put into place. A programmer who could enter data could enter transactions (e.g., a wage rate increase) and then suppress the logs or other reports showing the transaction. Programmers thus should be allowed to work only with test copies of programs and data so they can only make software changes after proper authorization.
- *Separation of computer operations from programming and accounting.* Separation from authorization, from entry of transactions data, and from the ability to change programs make it harder for personnel to suppress a trail of their activities. Personnel who have physical access to media or the capability to set access rights could steal confidential information or give themselves the right to do

IT governance—the policies, practices, and procedures that help IT resources add value while considering costs and benefits. In addition to adding value, the goal of IT governance is to mitigate risk and prevent disastrous failures.

anything on the system (making such a person a "super-user"). A typical super-user is the individual or team that manages security, passwords, and user access. Such individuals could set up a new user account under an assumed name that gives him or her access to all systems, with the potential to change the super-user's own wage rate or set up fictitious customers or suppliers.

Security Management and Access Control Security management includes control activities regarding security over data, the IT infrastructure, and daily operations. These control activities include controls over program acquisition, implementation, and maintenance. For instance, IT general controls should be in place to ensure that backups of applications, databases, and operating systems are performed at appropriate intervals and periodically tested for recoverability. Other controls include the delivery of information services to users, the management of third-party providers (e.g., Are they required to adhere to the organization's security standards?), and the use of system software, security software, database management, and utility programs.

Security controls include both physical controls and online access controls. Physical controls restrict access to hardware and software, and prevent improper use of programs and data files. Common examples to physically restrict unauthorized use include keypad entrances, badge-entry systems, security cameras, and security personnel. More sophisticated controls only allow physical and online access after employee fingerprints are read or employee retinas are scanned and matched with an approved database. Other physical controls include monitoring of cooling and humidity to ensure that the equipment functions properly and installing fire-extinguishing equipment to reduce fire damage.

Online access controls reduce the likelihood that unauthorized changes are made to software applications and data files. The organization should implement controls regarding issuance/removal and security of user passwords and IDs, internet firewalls and remote-access controls, data encryptions, and access-privilege controls.

Points to consider when assessing the effectiveness of security management include the following:

- The system is able to identify authorized and unauthorized users.
- User profiles only permit access to what the user needs to know.
- The ability to change, modify, or delete data is restricted to those with authority.

Encryption techniques—
computer programs that change a standard message or data file into one that is coded, then decoded using a decryption program

Encryption techniques protect the security of electronic communication when information is transmitted and when it is stored. Computerized encryption changes a standard message or data file into one that is coded (encrypted), requiring the receiver of the electronic message or user of the encrypted data file to use a decryption program to decode the message or data. A public key encryption technique is often used, where one key (the public key) is used for encoding the message and another key (the private key) is used to decode the message. The public key is distributed to all approved users of the e-commerce system. The private key is distributed only to internal users with the authority to decode the message.

Digital signatures—electronic certificates that are used to authenticate the validity of individuals and companies conducting business electronically.

To authenticate the validity of a trading partner conducting business electronically, companies may rely on external certification authorities, who verify the source of the public key by using **digital signatures**. A trusted certification authority issues a digital certificate to individuals and companies engaging in e-commerce. The digital signature contains the holder's name and its public key. It also contains the name of the certification authority and the certificate's expiration date and other specified information. To guarantee integrity and authenticity, each signature is digitally signed by the private key maintained by the certification authority.

The IT system should also ensure that there are controls regarding incident tracking, system logging, and monitoring to identify potential security breaches. As Auditing in Action 8-3 highlights, security breaches can be costly.

The 2017 "WannaCry" cyberattack, which involved 45 000 incidents in 74 countries, demonstrates that the susceptibility to hackers infiltrating client information systems is significant. Hospitals in the UK, a Spanish telecommunication company, European soccer clubs, and Brazil's state-owned oil company are but a few of the organizations affected by the ransomware attack. The attack held the various organizations hostage by freezing computers, encrypting data, and demanding money through online bitcoin payments.

While the "WannaCry" attack had considerable impact, if not for its quick shutdown, it could have been far worse. Consider the effects of the 2014 cyberattack of Sony Pictures. In addition to the cancellation of theatrical release of *The Interview*, thousands of electronic documents were stolen, internal data centres were erased, and 75 percent of the company's servers were destroyed. Among the stolen goods were five movies (that had been widely released), contracts, salary and budget data, medical records, and Social Security numbers.

The cyberattack also affected Sony's financial and accounting applications and caused Sony to miss its stock-market deadline for issuing its third-quarter result. Michael Lynton, CEO of Sony Entertainment, said that Sony was "adequately prepared" but could never have predicted "an attack of this nature." Others claim that Sony's disaster recovery plan was woefully inadequate—it had few backups and no contingency plan to move operations to another place. Further, some computer experts suggest that Sony could have been better prepared by encrypting all sensitive data, by keeping passwords separate from password-protected documents, and by keeping sensitive data separate from other data.

Along with the costs associated with lost productivity and lost revenue, there were considerable costs associated with restoring the IT systems. At the time it announced that its earnings report would be delayed, Sony predicted the hack would cost $15 million "in investigation and remediation costs." However, the figure was subsequently revised to $35 million.

Sources: Warwick Ashford, "Sony admits it was unprepared for November's cyber attack," Computer **Weekly.com**, January 2, 2015, accessed August 2, 2017, at: **http://www.computerweekly.com/news/2240237912/Sony-Pictures-admits-it-was-unprepared-for-Novembers-cyber-attack**. Dan Heilman, "How Sony used old tech to function after hack," *CIO Today*, December 31, 2014, accessed August 2, 2017, at **http://www.cio-today.com/article/index.php?story_id=00100015QE3U**. Tim Hornyak, "Hack to cost Sony $35 million in IT repairs," *IT News*, February 4, 2015, accessed April 6, 2015, at **https://www.networkworld.com/article/2879814/data-center/sony-hack-cost-15-million-but-earnings-unaffected.html**. Adrienne LaFrance, "Global ransomware attack stuns systems in up to 74 countries," *The Atlantic*, May 12, 2017, accessed August 5, 2017 at **https://www.theatlantic.com/technology/archive/2017/05/a-massive-ransomware-attack-on-the-nhs/526524/**. Takashi Mochizuki and Megumi Fujikawa, "Sony hacking attacks delay earnings report," *Wall Street Journal*, January 23, 2015, accessed August 5, 2017, at **http://www.wsj.com/articles/sony-hacking-attacks-delay-earnings-report-1422008085**.

Regarding communications with public networks, the organization should have a firewall. A **firewall** is a system of hardware and software that monitors and controls the flow of e-commerce communications by channelling all network connections through controls that verify external users, grant access to authorized users, deny access to unauthorized users, and direct authorized users to requested programs or data. Firewalls are becoming increasingly sophisticated as the frequency and severity of cyberattacks grow (as highlighted in Auditing in Action 8-3). The firewall should have the following characteristics:

Firewall—a system of hardware and software that monitors and controls the flow of e-commerce communications by channelling all network connections through a control gateway.

- Hides the structure of the network;
- Provides an audit trail of communication with public parties;
- Generates alarms when suspicious activity is suspected; and
- Defends itself and/or the organization's network against attack.

Backup and disaster recovery planning enables the organization to continue operations in the event of failure of part or all of its information systems. Something as simple as a hard drive crash can cause enormous problems if a company has not given careful thought to contingency procedures. Power failures, fire, excessive heat or humidity, water damage, or even sabotage can have serious consequences for businesses using IT. To prevent data loss during power outages, many companies rely on battery backups or on-site generators. For more serious disasters, organizations need detailed backup and contingency plans such as off-site storage of critical software and data files or outsourcing to firms that specialize in secure data storage.

Backup—copies of systems and data that can be used to bring failed system back online.

Disaster recovery plan (DRP)—planning for potential information technology disruptions. The purpose of the DRP is to enable the business to continue operations in event of failure of information systems.

Backup and contingency plans should also identify alternative hardware that can be used to process company data. Companies with small IT systems can purchase replacement computers in an emergency and reprocess their accounting records by using backup copies of software and data files. Larger companies often contract with IT data centres that specialize in providing access to off-site computers and data storage and other IT services for use in the event of an IT disaster.

Program Development and Change An organization needs to select control activities regarding the acquisition and implementation of new applications, systems development and quality assurance, and maintenance of existing applications as well as program changes. For instance, does the organization have a formal systems development methodology that ensures development (or modification) and testing of IT solutions is separated from productions systems?

To ensure that the right software is implemented:

- Involve a team of both IT and non-IT personnel, including key users of the software and internal auditors. This combination increases the likelihood that information needs, as well as software design and implementation concerns, are properly addressed. Involving users also results in better acceptance by key users.
- Test all software to ensure that the new software is compatible with existing hardware and software and to determine whether the hardware and software can handle the needed volume of transactions. Whether software is purchased or developed internally, extensive testing of all software with realistic data is critical. Companies typically use one or a combination of the following two test approaches:
  1. **Pilot testing:** A new system is implemented in one part of the organization while other locations continue to rely on the old system.
  2. **Parallel testing:** The old and new systems operate simultaneously in all locations.
- Proper documentation of the system is required for all new and modified software. After the software has been successfully tested and documented, it is transferred to the librarian in a controlled manner to ensure that only authorized software is ultimately accepted as the authorized version.

Principle 12: Deploys Policies and Procedures The policies and procedures for the control activities should be spelled out in systems documentation (in a manual or on the company intranet) to encourage consistent application. The organization should review its policies periodically to ensure that they are still appropriate or identify if they need to be revised.

> **CONCEPT CHECK**
>
> **C8-4** What are general controls? Explain how they are similar to entity-level controls.

Information and Communication

The purpose of an entity's **accounting information and communication systems** is to initiate, record, process, and report the entity's transactions and to maintain accountability for the related assets. The system includes the entity's business processes as well as the accounting system (accounting software, electronic spreadsheets, and the policies and procedures to prepare periodic financial reports and period-end financial statements).

Figure 8-5 summarizes the inputs, processes, and outputs of the accounting information system.

Pilot testing—a company's computer testing approach that involves implementing a new system in just one part of the organization while maintaining the old system at other locations.

Parallel testing—a company's computer testing approach that involves operating the old and new system simultaneously.

Accounting information and communication systems—entity systems that are used to initiate, record, process, and report the entity's transactions, events, and conditions and to maintain accountability for the related assets.

Figure 8-5	The Accounting Information System

Inputs	• Transactions, events, and conditions
Business Processes	• Initiate, record, process, and report transactions and maintain accountability (safeguard, classify, etc.) for related assets, liabilities, and equity • Resolve incorrect processing of transactions • Process and account for system overrides or bypasses to controls
Accounting Systems	• Transfer information from transaction processing systems to general ledger • Capture information for relevant events/conditions other than transactions (amortization, valuation of inventory, receivables, and other estimates) • Accumulate, record, process, summarize, and appropriately report other information required to be disclosed in the financial statements • Use of standard and other journal entries to record transactions, estimates, and adjustments
Outputs	• Financial statements (including disclosures)

Source: This Auditing, 14Ce includes extracts from the Handbook of International Quality Control, Auditing, Review, Other Assurance, and Related Services Pronouncements, 2016-2017 Edition of the International Auditing and Assurance Standards Board, published by the International Federation of Accountants (IFAC) in December 2016 and is used with the permission of IFAC. All rights reserved. Contact HYPERLINK "mailto:Permissions@ifac.org" Permissions@ifac.org for permission to reproduce, store or transmit, or to make other similar uses of these extracts.

As Figure 8-5 highlights, controls over the accounting systems are distinct from the business processes, and include controls over the following: (1) the transfer of business process information to the general ledger; (2) the capture of relevant events/conditions, such as amortization, valuation of inventory and accounts receivable, and other estimates that are not transaction based; (3) journal entries; and (4) the accumulation and summation of other information that must be disclosed in the financial statements. As mentioned in our earlier discussion of control activities, an important control is the chart of accounts, which lists and classifies transactions into individual balance sheet and income statement accounts.

Principle 13: Obtains or Generates Relevant, Quality Information An organization must have established information requirements to support effective operations of controls within the five components of internal controls. It should ensure that its information systems generate information that is of sufficient quality to support effective operation of control. Controls should be developed and implemented related to:

• Completeness and accuracy of data;
• Capture of data at the necessary frequency;
• Provision of information when needed;
• Protection of sensitive data; and
• Retention of data to comply with relevant business, audit, and regulatory needs.

In addition to internally generated information, the organization should ensure that information from external sources is appropriate, supported by evidence, and of sufficient quality to support effective operation of the control.

Principle 14: Communicates Internally Communication within the organization includes both formal and informal communication, such as policy manuals, newsletters, job descriptions, and training sessions. Some key processes would include training orientation for new employees or employees starting a new position, discussing the nature of the position's responsibilities. The organization's messaging should reinforce the idea that internal control responsibilities must be taken seriously and critical information should be disseminated quickly. There also should be a process for employees to communicate improprieties—often referred to as "whistleblowing." This process should be well communicated, allow for anonymity, and ensure that actions taken by senior management, the board, and the audit committee to address the improprieties are communicated.

Principle 15: Communicates Externally The organization should have in place processes to communicate relevant and timely information to external parties, including shareholders, members, partners, owners, regulators, customers, financial analysts, and any other relevant stakeholder. The communication should be two-way and should involve processes that track communications with customers, vendors, regulators, and other relevant stakeholders. Many organizations have separate communications, such as a whistleblower hotline, to allow direct communication with management and personnel. For instance, some municipalities have implemented fraud and waste hotlines to provide staff and members of the public with a means to report any observed or suspected fraud, waste, or misuse.

CONCEPT CHECK

C8-5 What are the accounting information and communication controls? How are they distinct from business process controls?

Monitoring

Monitoring activities deal with ongoing or periodic assessment of the quality of internal control performance to determine that controls are operating as intended and that they are modified as appropriate for changes in conditions. Monitoring also requires that deficiencies in internal control are reported and appropriate remedial action is taken.

Principle 16: Selects, Develops, and Performs Ongoing and Separate Evaluations Monitoring should include evaluation built into business/financial reporting and performed on a real-time basis (ongoing), as well as separate periodic evaluations. Information for assessment and modification comes from a variety of sources, including studies of existing internal controls, internal auditor reports, exception reporting on control activities, reports by regulators (such as, in the case of financial institutions, the Office of the Superintendent of Financial Institutions), feedback from operating personnel, and complaints from customers about billing charges.

For many companies, especially larger ones, a competent internal audit department is essential for effective monitoring of internal controls, and the department often performs the periodic reviews. For an internal audit function to be effective, it is important that the internal audit staff be independent of both the operating and accounting departments, and that it report directly to a high level of authority within the organization, usually the audit committee of the board of directors.

CONCEPT CHECK

C8-6 How is management's risk assessment relevant to the audit?
C8-7 What is the role of monitoring to support internal controls?

Principle 17: Evaluates and Communicates Deficiencies Internal control deficiencies need to be reported in a timely manner to those responsible for taking corrective action, senior management, and the board of directors (or the audit committee). For instance, results of internal audit activities should be reported to senior management, the audit committee, and the external auditor. Management should take adequate and timely action to address deficiencies reported by the internal audit and other monitoring activities.

UNDERSTANDING CONTROLS OF SMALL BUSINESSES

LO 4 Understand the important risks and controls in small businesses.

Regardless of the size of the organization, the auditor is required to obtain an understanding of internal controls. However, the size of a company does have a significant effect on the nature of internal control activities and the specific monitoring controls. It is often difficult for a small business to establish adequate separation of duties. Further, the entity is unlikely to have in-house expertise in systems and would place more reliance on software and hardware suppliers for system support and maintenance. Passwords may be in use but in simple form (for example, accounting personnel may have a single password that allows access to all systems and functions). Note that this would be a significant control deficiency.

While it is difficult for a small company to formalize all its policies, it is certainly possible for a small company to implement some practical controls, such as a culture that values ethics; competent, trustworthy personnel with clear lines of authority; proper procedures for authorization, execution, and recording of transactions; adequate documents, records, and reports; physical controls over assets and records; and, to a limited degree, checks on performance.

A major control available in a small company is the knowledge and concern of the top operating person, who is frequently an owner–manager. Having knowledge about and a personal interest in the organization and a close relationship with personnel (often called "executive controls"), the owner-manager can carefully evaluate the competence of the employees and the effectiveness of the overall systems. An important owner–manager control is monitoring revenues and expenditures against an established budget and other important performance indicators. Internal control can also be significantly strengthened if the owner conscientiously performs such duties as signing all cheques after carefully reviewing supporting documents, reviewing bank reconciliations, examining accounts receivable statements sent to customers, approving credit, examining all correspondence from customers and vendors, and approving the write-off of bad debts.

CONCEPT CHECK

C8-8 What is the key internal control risk at a small business, and how can a small business owner deal with it?

SUMMARY

This chapter focused on internal controls, including internal controls related to computer-based information systems, and the COSO framework. We use this framework as a basis for discussing the auditor's responsibilities related to internal controls in the next chapter. To rely on a client's internal controls to reduce planned audit evidence for audits of financial statements, the auditor must first obtain an understanding of each of the five components of internal control. Knowledge about the design of the client's control environment, risk assessment, control activities, information and communication, and monitoring activities, and the auditors' evaluation of whether internal control components are effective lays the foundation of the auditor's assessment of control risk at the financial statement level and at the assertion level.

MyLab Accounting
Make the grade with MyLab Accounting: The questions, exercises, and problems marked with a 🌐 can be found on MyLab Accounting. You can practise them as often as you want, and most feature step-by-step guided instructions to help you find the right answer.

Review Questions

8-1 **1** Describe the four broad objectives management has when designing effective internal control.

8-2 **1** Describe which of the four categories of broad objectives for internal controls are considered by the auditor in an audit of both the financial statements and internal controls over financial reporting. Why are these categories considered?

8-3 **2** Compare management's concerns about internal control with those of the auditor.

8-4 **2 3** Frequently, management is more concerned about internal controls that promote operational efficiency than about those that result in reliable financial data. How can the independent auditor persuade management to devote more attention to controls affecting the reliability of accounting information when management has this attitude?

8-5 **3** What are the five components of internal control in the COSO (Committee of Sponsoring Organizations of the Treadway Commission) internal control framework? Provide an example of a control for each component.

8-6 **3** What is the relationship among the five components of internal control?

8-7 **3** What is meant by the "control environment"?

8-8 **3** What is the relationship between the control environment and control systems?

8-9 **3** The separation of operational responsibility from record-keeping is meant to prevent different types of misstatements than the separation of the custody of assets from accounting. Explain the difference in the purposes of these two types of separation of duties.

8-10 **3** Explain what is meant by "independent checks on performance," and give five specific examples.

8-11 **3** Frank James, a highly competent employee of Brinkwater Sales Corporation, had been responsible for accounting-related matters for two decades. His devotion to the firm and his duties had always been exceptional, and over the years, he had been given increased responsibility. Both the president of Brinkwater and the partner of an independent public accounting firm in charge of the audit were shocked and dismayed to discover that James had embezzled more than $500 000 over a 10-year period by not recording billings in the sales journal and subsequently diverting the cash receipts. What major factors permitted the embezzlement to take place?

8-12 **3** Discuss the importance of the control environment, or "setting the tone at the top," in establishing a culture of honesty and integrity in a company.

8-13 **3** For each of the following, give an example of a physical control the client can use to protect the asset or record:
1. Computers
2. Cash received by retail clerks
3. Accounts receivable records
4. Raw material inventory
5. Perishable tools
6. Manufacturing equipment
7. Marketable securities

8-14 **3** Why does the auditor need to assess controls over information systems acquisition, development, and maintenance?

8-15 **3** Describe why auditors generally evaluate entity-level controls before evaluating transaction-level controls.

8-16 **3** Explain how client internal controls can be improved through the proper installation of IT.

8-17 **3** Identify risks for extensive IT-based accounting systems.

8-18 **3** Identify the traditionally segregated duties in IT systems.

8-19 **3** Explain how the effectiveness of general controls impacts the effectiveness of automated application controls.

8-20 **3** Compare the risks associated with network systems and database systems to those associated with centralized IT functions.

8-21 **3** An audit client is creating an online, Web-based sales ordering system for customers to purchase products using personal credit cards for payment. Identify three risks related to an online sales system that management should consider. For each risk, identify an internal control that could be implemented to reduce that risk.

Multiple Choice Questions and Task-Based Simulations

8-22 **1** The following are general questions about internal control. Choose the best response.

a. Which of the following would not be considered an inherent limitation of the potential effectiveness of an entity's internal control structure?
(1) Incompatible duties
(2) Management override
(3) Mistakes in judgment
(4) Collusion among employees

b. Actions, policies, and procedures that reflect the overall attitude of management, directors, and owners of the entity about internal control relate to which of the following internal control components?
(1) Control environment
(2) Information and communication
(3) Risk assessment
(4) Monitoring

c. Vendor account reconciliations are performed by three clerks in the accounts payable department on Friday of each week. The accounts payable supervisor reviews the completed reconciliations the following Monday to ensure they have been completed. The work performed by the supervisor is an example of which COSO (Committee of Sponsoring Organizations of the Treadway Commission) component?
(1) Control activities
(2) Information and communication
(3) Risk assessment
(4) Monitoring

8-23 **3** The following questions concern the characteristics of IT systems and their impact on internal controls. Choose the best response.

a. Which of the following is an advantage of a computer-based system for transaction processing over a manual system? A computer-based system:
(1) Does not require as stringent a set of internal controls.
(2) Will produce a more accurate set of financial statements.
(3) Will be more efficient in generating financial statements.
(4) Eliminates the need to reconcile control accounts and subsidiary ledgers.

b. Which of the following is an example of an application control?
(1) The client uses access security software to limit access to each of the accounting applications.
(2) Employees are assigned a user ID and password that must be changed every quarter.
(3) The sales system automatically computes the total sale amount and posts the total to the sales journal master file.
(4) Systems programmers are restricted from doing applications programming functions.

c. Which of the following is generally *not* considered a category of IT general controls?
(1) Controls that determine whether a vendor number matches the pre-approved vendors in the vendor master file.
(2) Controls that restrict system-wide access to programs and data.
(3) Controls that oversee the acquisition of application software.
(4) Controls that oversee the day-to-day operation of IT applications.

8-24 **3** For each of the following descriptions of internal controls, select which of the five COSO (Committee of Sponsoring Organizations of the Treadway Commission) internal control components (1—Control environment, 2—Risk assessment, 3—Control activities, 4—Information and communication, 5—Monitoring) is best represented by each internal control.

Description of Internal Control	COSO IC Component
The company's computer systems track individual transactions and automatically accumulate transactions to create a trial balance.	
On a monthly basis, department heads review a budget to actual performance report and investigate unusual differences.	

(continued)

Description of Internal Control	COSO IC Component
The company must receive university transcripts documenting all degrees earned before an individual can begin the first day of employment with the company.	
Senior management obtains data about external events that might affect the entity and evaluates the impact of that information on its existing accounting processes.	
Each quarter, department managers are required to perform a self-assessment of the department's compliance with company policies. Reports summarizing the results are to be submitted to the senior executive overseeing that department.	
Before a cash disbursement can be processed, all payee information must be verified by matching the payee to the company's approved vendor listing.	
The system automatically reconciles the detailed accounts receivable subsidiary ledger to the accounts receivable general ledger account on a daily basis.	
The company has developed a comprehensive series of accounting policies and procedures manuals to help provide detailed instructions to employees about how controls are to be performed.	
The company has an organizational chart that establishes the formal lines of reporting and authorization protocols.	
The compensation committee reviews compensation plans for senior executives to determine if those plans create unintended pressures that might lead to distorted financial statements.	

⊕ **8-25** ③ For each of the following internal controls, indicate the type of control activity and the relevant transaction-related assertion (audit objective).

Internal Control	Control Activity	Transaction-related assertion
1. Sales invoices are matched with shipping documents by the computer system and an exception report is generated.		
2. Receiving reports are prenumbered and accounted for on a daily basis.		
3. Sales invoices are independently verified before being sent to customers.		
4. Payments by cheque are received in the mail by the receptionist, who lists the cheques and restrictively endorses them.		
5. Labour hours for payroll are reviewed for reasonableness by the computer system.		
6. Cheques are signed by the company president, who compares the cheques with the underlying supporting documents.		
7. Unmatched shipping documents are accounted for on a daily basis.		
8. The computer system verifies that all payroll payments have a valid employee identification number assigned by the human resources department at the time of hiring.		
9. The accounts receivable master file is reconciled to the general ledger on a monthly basis.		

Discussion Questions and Problems

8-26 **3** The division of the following duties is meant to provide the best possible controls for the Meridian Paint Company, a small wholesale store:

†**1.** Approve credit for customers included in the customer credit master file.

†**2.** Input shipping and billing information to bill customers, record invoices in the sales journal, and update the accounts receivable master file.

†**3.** Open the mail and prepare a prelisting of cash receipts.

†**4.** Enter cash receipts data to prepare the cash receipts journal and update the accounts receivable master file.

†**5.** Prepare daily cash deposits.

†**6.** Deliver daily cash deposits to the bank.

†**7.** Assemble the payroll time cards, input the data to prepare payroll cheques, and update the payroll journal and payroll master files.

†**8.** Sign payroll cheques.

†**9.** Assemble supporting documents for general and payroll cash disbursements.

†**10.** Sign general cash disbursement cheques.

†**11.** Input information to prepare cheques for signature, record cheques in the cash disbursements journal, and update the appropriate master files.

†**12.** Mail cheques to suppliers and deliver cheques to employees.

13. Cancel supporting documents to prevent their reuse.

14. Update the general ledger at the end of each month and review all accounts for unexpected balances.

15. Reconcile the accounts receivable master file with the control account and review accounts outstanding more than 90 days.

16. Prepare monthly statements for customers by printing the accounts receivable master file then mail the statements to customers.

17. Reconcile the monthly statements from vendors with the accounts payable master file.

18. Reconcile the bank account.

REQUIRED

You are to divide the accounting-related duties 1 through 18 among Robert Smith, James Cooper, and Mohini Singh. All of the responsibilities marked with a dagger (†) are assumed to take about the same amount of time and must be divided equally between Smith and Cooper. Both employees are equally competent. Singh, who is president of the company, is not willing to perform any functions designated by a dagger and will perform only a maximum of two of the other functions.*

8-27 **4** Froggledore Realty Limited is a brokerage firm that employs 35 real estate agents. The agents are given an office and basic telephone service (estimated at a $250 value per month) and are paid on a commission basis. The building has wireless computing so that agents can bring in their own computers. Each office has its own lock, and agents are responsible for the contents of their offices. Calls that come into the office are allocated to agents based upon their region in the city, with each agent having a clearly defined region for sales.

Potential purchasers who call in are assigned to the on-call listed agent. The office manager is responsible for accounting and for supplying the office with software and other supplies. She purchased a copy of real estate sales management software (for $750) for the office and has been burning copies, which she sells to new real estate agents for $100; she figures it pays for her time (she usually burns them on her home computer).

The owner of the business, Jim Froggledore, has told her and the accounting staff to bring in any invoices that they have for home computing so that he can use them for the business. Depending upon how well the company does, Jim gives employees a 10–20 percent bonus at the end of the year for the invoices.

Jenny, the receptionist, is a freelance writer and has been writing advertising copy for the business in her spare time. She charges for this as an editing contract from her small business and takes supplies from the office, which she and her husband (who is not employed by Jim) use for their business.

---

*Based on AICPA question paper, American Institute of Certified Public Accountants.

Jim recently had the offices renovated, with new carpeting and wallpaper, by his sister's business. She also painted the recently renovated basement at Jim's home and installed indoor/outdoor carpeting on his patio; all of this was included in the bill to the business. Jim prorated the invoice and charged the real estate agents for the renovations to the office.

REQUIRED

a. Assess the quality of corporate governance at Froggledore Realty Limited.

b. Is the company auditable? Why or why not?

8-28 **4** Recently, you had lunch with some friends at a new restaurant in your neighbourhood. The server entered his password into a computer and punched in your order. The server continued taking orders and you noticed the cook removing a small printout and placing it on the wall in front of him (presumably your order). When the food was ready, it was placed directly below your order. The server looked at the printout, put it in his pocket, and then brought your order to the table.

When you finished eating, the server again entered his password and printed two copies of your bill. One copy was attached to the order slip, and the second was brought to you. You decided to pay by credit card, so two copies of the credit card authorization were brought to the table for signature. You kept one and the signed copy was returned to the server.

REQUIRED

a. What internal controls (manual, computer-assisted, and automated) are present at the restaurant?

b. How could the manager of the restaurant evaluate the effectiveness of the controls?

c. What are the costs and benefits of the restaurant's controls?

8-29 **3** CIBC's Amicus unit, administering 3061 customers of President's Choice Financial, sent incorrect tax information to Canada Revenue Agency (CRA), while sending different (correct) information to the customers. The incorrect information sent to CRA stated that the customers had cashed in some of their 2003 RRSPs, resulting in tax reassessments.

How is it possible that computer systems could send different information to two different parties? The *Toronto Star* reported that the cause was the switch from a manual to a computer-based system. There was either a large-scale programming error or a data-entry error.

In November 2007, Air Canada's reservation systems encountered communications problems with airports so that tickets and tags could not be printed, stranding travellers for over five hours, again affecting thousands of customers. The problem was identified as a computer error of some kind, with no further information provided.

REQUIRED

a. If a client has problems in delivering services, what is the likelihood that there are also information systems processing errors in the accounting systems?

b. What kinds of checks and balances should be in place when an organization implements program changes?

c. How does the quality of information systems affect your understanding of internal control?

Sources: Based on Stuart Laidlaw, "Tax error blamed on systems update," *Toronto Star*, January 27, 2005, p. D3. David Olive, "CIBC is really, really sorry," *Toronto Star*, January 27, 2005, p. D3. Isabel Teotino, "Airline glitch strands travellers," *Toronto Star*, November 17, 2007, p. A10.

8-30 **4** Metro Plastics Limited is a medium-sized manufacturer of rigid plastics. It produces casings for printers, telephones, computer screens, and other types of equipment. It also produces stand-alone plastics, such as baskets and jars. Recently, Metro Plastics was purchased by a large food manufacturing conglomerate. The previous owner of Metro Plastics has agreed to stay on for three years to help provide management transition. He has also been asked to provide a presentation to the board of the conglomerate about the corporate governance and risk management practices of his company. The owner of Metro Plastics has come to you for some guidance about the type of information that he should provide to the board.

REQUIRED

a. What type of information should he provide to the board about corporate governance? List three corporate governance controls that might have been present at the owner-managed company.

b. What type of information should he provide about risk management practices at Metro Plastics? List three risk management practices that might have been present at the owner-managed company.

Professional Judgment Problems and Cases

8-31 [3] You are doing the audit of Phelps College, a private school with approximately 2500 students. With your firm's consultation, they have instituted an IT system that separates the responsibilities of the computer operator, systems analyst, librarian, programmer, and data control group by having a different person do each function. Now, a budget reduction is necessary and one of the five people must be laid off. You are requested to give the college advice as to how the five functions could be done with reduced personnel and minimal negative effects on internal control. The amount of time the functions take is not relevant because all five people also do nonaccounting functions.

REQUIRED

a. Divide the five functions among four people in such a way as to maintain the best possible control system.

b. Assume that economic times become worse for Phelps College and it must terminate employment of another person. Divide the five functions among three people in such a way as to maintain the best possible internal control. Again, the amount of time each function takes should not be a consideration in your decision.

c. Assume that economic times become so severe for Phelps College that only two people can be employed to do IT functions. Divide the five functions between two people in such a way as to maintain the best possible control system.

d. If the five functions were done by one person, will internal controls be so inadequate that an audit cannot be done? Discuss.

8-32 [3] During your audit of Wilcoxon Sports, Inc., a retail chain of stores, you learn that a programmer made an unauthorized change to the sales application program even though no work on that application had been approved by IT management. In order for the sales application program to work, the programmer had to make modifications to the operating software security features. The unauthorized change forced the sales program to calculate an automatic discount for a customer who happens to be the brother-in-law of the programmer. The customer and programmer split the savings from the unauthorized discount. The programmer modified the program and returned it to the librarian, who placed it into the files for live production use. No other information was forwarded to the librarian.

REQUIRED

1. What recommendation do you have for management of Wilcoxon Sports, Inc., to prevent this from recurring?

2. Explain why you believe the suggested internal control improvements will prevent problems in the future.

8-33 [3] Your new audit client, Hardwood Lumber Company, has a computerized accounting system for all financial statement cycles. During planning, you visited with the information systems vice president and learned that personnel in information systems are assigned to one of four departments: systems programming, applications programming, operations, or data control. Job tasks are specific to the individual and no responsibilities overlap with other departments. Hardwood Lumber relies on the operating system software to restrict online access to individuals. The operating system allows an employee with "READ" capabilities to only view the contents of the program or file. "CHANGE" allows the employee to update the contents of the program or file. "RUN" allows the employee to use a program to process data. Programmers, both systems and applications, are restricted to a READ ONLY access to all live application software program files but have READ and CHANGE capabilities for test copies of those software program files. Operators have READ and RUN capabilities for live application programs. Data control clerks have CHANGE access to data files only and no access to software program files. The person in charge of operations maintains access to the operating software security features and is responsible for assigning access rights to individuals. The computer room is locked and requires a card-key to access the room. Only operations staff have a card-key to access the room, and security cameras monitor access. A TV screen is in the information systems vice president's office to allow periodic monitoring of access. The TV presents the live picture and no record is maintained. The librarian, who is in the operations department, is responsible for maintaining the library of program files. The librarian has READ and CHANGE access rights to program files. Backup copies of program files are stored on an external drive, and data files are maintained on a backup server. The external drive and backup server are located in a room adjacent to the computer room.

REQUIRED

a. Identify the strengths of Hardwood Lumber Company's computerized accounting system.

b. What recommendations for change can you suggest to improve Hardwood's information systems function?

8-34 [4] Gaboria Frank is the owner of Frankincents Machining Limited, a custom machining centre with 10 full-time employees and a part-time bookkeeper, Norma, who comes in two days a week. Norma convinced Frank to purchase a small business suite of accounting packages and a desktop computer with a laser printer. Norma has set up the records on the computer, and all accounting work is now handled using the accounting packages (i.e., order entry, accounts receivable, cash disbursements, general ledger, and payroll). It took Norma about three months, and she initially had some difficulty balancing the subsystems, but everything seems to be functioning properly now. Frank did not consult with you, his accountant, prior to implementing the systems.

REQUIRED

a. Identify the risks associated with the current method of handling accounting records at Frankincents Machining Limited.

b. Identify those activities that Frank should handle in sales, accounts receivable, cash disbursements, and payroll. Explain why.

8-35 **3** As discussed in Auditing in Action 8-3, a growing number of organizations have been the target of hacking attacks, or cyberattacks, in recent years. Companies and governments need to consider the risks of a cyberattack, and consider backup plans in the event a cyberattack results in a loss of hardware, software, or data. The Committee of Sponsoring Organizations of the Treadway Commission (COSO) issued a thought paper, *COSO in the Cyber Age*, to help organizations assess and mitigate risks associated with cybersecurity through the existing COSO framework. Visit the COSO Web site (**www.coso.org**) and refer to the "Guidance" tab. Read the thought paper to answer the following questions:

REQUIRED

a. The COSO guidance acknowledges that "cyber risk is not something that can be avoided; instead it must be managed." Why is cyber risk unavoidable? Does this acknowledgement make it more or less difficult to address and mitigate cyber risk?

b. At the control environment level (the first of the five components of internal control), what should organizations do to address cyber risk?

c. The paper identifies five broad categories of cyberattack perpetrators and motivations. Briefly describe each group of perpetrators and their motivation.

d. What types of control activities are recommended to address cyber risks?

ASSESSING CONTROL RISK AND DESIGNING TESTS OF CONTROLS

"Why bother testing internal controls? We can just look at the numbers and the supporting documents, can't we?" Well, no! First of all, audit standards require that the auditor understand internal controls. Second, in a large organization with millions of transactions, ignoring internal controls would lead to a very expensive audit.

LEARNING OBJECTIVES

After studying this chapter, you should be able to:

1 Obtain and document an understanding of internal control.

2 Assess control risk at the financial statement level and at the assertion level.

3 Describe the process of designing and performing tests of controls.

4 Understand and assess controls of outsourced systems.

5 Understand how control risk impacts detection risk and the design of substantive tests.

6 Describe how the complexity of the IT environment impacts control risk assessment and testing.

7 Describe the auditor's responsibilities for reporting significant control risks to those in charge of governance.

8 Explain the difference in the scope of control testing for an audit opinion on the effectiveness of controls over financial reporting versus an audit opinion for financial statements.

STANDARDS REFERENCED IN THIS CHAPTER

CAS 265 – Communicating deficiencies in internal control to those charged with governance and management

CAS 315 – Identifying and assessing the risks of material misstatement through understanding the entity and its environment

CAS 330 – The auditor's responsibilities to assessed risks

CAS 402 – Audit considerations relating to an entity using a service organization

CSAE 3416 – Reporting on controls at a service organization

SECTION 5925 – An audit of internal control over financial reporting that is integrated with an audit of financial statements

Just Because the Computer Did the Work Doesn't Mean It's Right

Aisha Patel's audit client, Excella Coffee, Inc., installed a software program that processed and aged customer accounts receivable. The aging, which indicated how long the customers' accounts were outstanding, was useful to Aisha when evaluating the collectibility of those accounts.

Because Aisha didn't know whether the aging totals were computed correctly, she decided to test Excella's aging by using her own firm's audit software to recalculate the aging, using an electronic copy of Excella's accounts receivable data file. She reasoned that if the aging produced by her audit software was in reasonable agreement with Excella's aging, she would have evidence that Excella's aging was correct.

continued >

continued Aisha was shocked when she found a material difference between her calculated aging and Excella's. Rudy Rose, the manager of Excella's information technology (IT) function, investigated the discrepancy and discovered that programmer errors had resulted in design flaws in Excella's software used to calculate the aging. This outcome caused Aisha to substantially increase the amount of her testing of the year-end balance of the allowance for uncollectible accounts, and it resulted in a significant audit adjustment to Excella's allowance account.

LO **1** Obtain and document an understanding of internal control.

OBTAIN AND DOCUMENT UNDERSTANDING OF INTERNAL CONTROL

In the previous chapter, we discussed the components of the COSO (Committee of Sponsoring Organizations of the Treadway Commission) internal control framework, including how companies integrate technology into their system of internal controls. In this chapter, we return to the audit process and discuss how auditors obtain and document their understanding of internal controls and assess control risk as part of the audit planning process. The opening story about Excella's overreliance on the accuracy of the computer-produced accounts receivable aging illustrates the importance of testing controls and also the efficiency and effectiveness of using audit software. People often assume "the information is correct because the computer produced it." Unfortunately, auditors sometimes depend on the untested accuracy of computer-generated output because they forget that computers perform only as well as they are programmed. Before concluding that information is reliable, auditors must understand and test computer-based controls in the same way they need to understand and test manual controls.

For financial statement audits, auditors need to understand controls that are relevant to the audit in order to identify and assess the risks of material misstatements. Figure 9-1 highlights where assessing control risk and its related activities fit into the audit process.

CAS

CAS 315 requires that auditors obtain and document an understanding of internal controls and evaluate the design effectiveness and implementation. However, the extent of audit work involved in understanding various components of the client's internal control and the evaluation of design effectiveness and implementation varies depending whether the auditor plans to rely upon internal controls for the particular assertion.

Procedures to Obtain an Understanding of Internal Control

Procedures to obtain an understanding—procedures used by the auditor to gather evidence about the design and implementation of specific controls

As part of the auditor's risk assessment procedures, the auditor uses **procedures to obtain an understanding**, which involve gathering evidence about the design of internal controls and whether they have been implemented, and then using that information as a basis for assessing control risk. The auditor generally uses four of the types of evidence described in Chapter 5 to obtain an understanding of the design and implementation of controls: inspection, inquiry of entity personnel, observation of employees performing control processes, and reperformance by tracing one or a few transactions through the accounting system from start to finish.

Methods for Documenting Understanding of Control Activities

Auditors commonly use three types of documents to obtain and document their understanding of the design of internal control: narratives, flowcharts, and internal control questionnaires. These may be used separately or in combination, as discussed

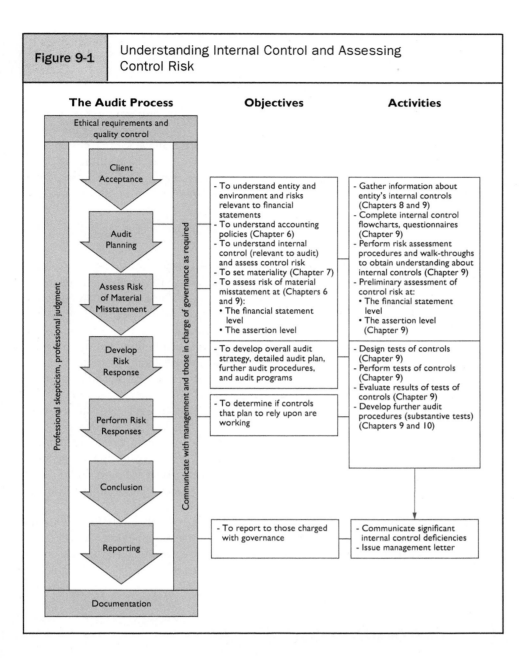

Figure 9-1 Understanding Internal Control and Assessing Control Risk

below. The auditor will use those that are most efficient in the client circumstances; that is, for a simple system a narrative will be enough, whereas for a more complex system flowcharts may be more effective.

Narrative A **narrative** is a written description of a client's internal controls. A proper narrative of an accounting system and related controls includes four characteristics:

1. *The origin of every document and record in the system.* For example, the description should state where customer orders come from and how sales invoices are prepared.
2. *All processing that takes place.* For example, if sales amounts are determined by a computer program that multiplies quantities shipped by stored standard prices, that process should be described.
3. *The disposition of every document and record in the system.* The updating of computer files, method of storing of documents, and transferral to customers or discarding of documents should be described.

Narrative—a written description of a client's internal controls, including the origin, processing, and disposition of documents and records, and the relevant control activities.

4. *An indication of controls relevant to the assessment of control risk.* These typically include separation of duties (e.g., separating recording cash from handling cash), authorization and approvals (e.g., credit approvals), and the nature of internal verification (e.g., comparison of unit selling price to sales contracts).

Flowchart—a diagrammatic representation of the client's documents and records, and the sequence in which they are processed.

Flowchart An internal control **flowchart** is a symbolic, diagrammatic representation of the client's documents and their sequential flow in the organization. An adequate flowchart includes the same four characteristics identified above for narratives.

A well-prepared flowchart aids in identifying inadequacies by facilitating a clear understanding of how the system operates, including segregation of duties. Flowcharts have two advantages over narrative: typically, they are easier both to read and to update. It would be unusual to use both a narrative and a flowchart to describe the same system, since both are intended to describe the flow of documents and records in an accounting system.

Internal control questionnaire—a series of questions about the controls in each audit area used as a means of gaining an understanding of internal control.

Internal Control Questionnaire An **internal control questionnaire** asks a series of questions about the controls in each audit area, including the control environment, as a means of indicating to the auditor aspects of internal control that may be inadequate. In most instances, it is designed to require a "yes" or "no" response, with "no" responses indicating potential internal control deficiencies. Where automated working-paper software is used, the responses can be automatically linked and cross-referenced to supporting documentation and to weakness investigation working papers. The main disadvantages of questionnaires are their inability to provide an overview of the system, their inapplicability to some audits, especially smaller ones, and, as highlighted in Auditing in Action 9-1, poorly designed questionnaires can lead to biased evaluations of the evidence obtained.

The use of questionnaires and flowcharts together is useful for understanding the client's internal control design and identifying internal controls and deficiencies. Flowcharts provide an overview of the system, while questionnaires offer useful checklists to remind the auditor of the many different types of internal controls that should exist.

Figure 9-2 illustrates an excerpt from an internal control questionnaire for the revenue cycle of Hillsburg Hardware Limited. Note that each objective (A through F) is part of a transaction-related objective as it applies to sales transactions (see boxed, shaded portions). The same is true for all other audit areas.

AUDITING IN ACTION 9-1
Knowledge of "Tone at the Top" and Judgment Traps

"Tone at the top" has a pervasive impact on inherent risk and control risk. However, as research has shown, even when an organization has experienced fraud, auditors have a tendency to favour positive evidence, suggesting that auditors' assessments of "tone at the top" may be biased. A recent study conducted by Regan Schmidt provides some insight into how this occurs.

In his study, Schmidt provided auditors with a list of 50 comments from a controller of a hypothetical company related to "tone at the top" (similar to what an auditor would document in a control environment questionnaire). He then asked the auditors to recall either positive or negative evidence from the controllers' list followed by negative or positive evidence. What he found was that the auditors who recalled the positive "tone at the top" evidence prior to the negative evidence had a more favourable mental representation of "tone at the top"

as compared to the auditors who initially recalled negative evidence. This "favourable bias" then transferred to other judgments made later in the audit process—the control environment assessment and the reliability of management's explanations of analytical review results.

So, how can we overcome these judgment traps? Schmidt suggests two remedies—documentation and review. In particular, he recommends that the control environment assessment be formally structured to ensure positive evidence does not suppress negative evidence, and that working paper reviews should incorporate negative evidence of the control environment ineffectiveness.

Source: R.N. Schmidt, "The effects of auditors' accessibility to 'Tone at the Top' knowledge on audit judgments," *Behavioral Research in Accounting*, vol. 26, no. 2, 2014, pp. 73–96.

Figure 9-2 | Partial Internal Control Questionnaire for Revenue

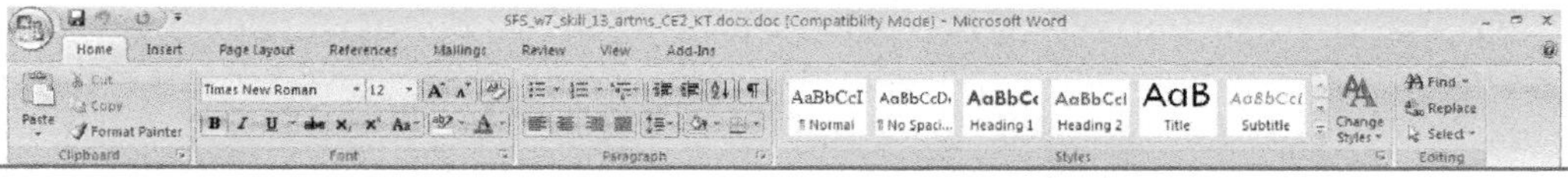

Client __Hillsburg Hardware Limited__ ——— Audit Date _12/31/18_

Auditor _MSW_ Date Completed _9/30/18_   Reviewed by _PR_   Date Completed _10/1/18_

Objective (shaded) and Question	Yes	No	N/A	Remarks
Sales				
A. Recorded sales are for shipments actually made to existing customers.				
1. Is customers' credit approved by a responsible official, and is access to change credit limit master files restricted?	✓			Approved By Chief Financial Officer
2. Is the recording of sales supported by authorized shipping documents and approved customer orders?	✓			Pam Dilley examines underlying documentation.
3. Is there adequate separation of duties between billing, recording sales, and handling cash receipts?	✓			
4. Are sales invoices prenumbered and accounted for?		✓		Prenumbered but not accounted for. Additional substantive testing required.
B. Existing sales transactions are recorded.				
1. Is a record of shipments maintained?	✓			
2. Are shipping documents controlled from the office in a manner that helps ensure that all shipments are billed?	✓			By Pam Dilley
3. Are shipping documents prenumbered and accounted for?	✓			
C. Recorded sales are for the amount of goods shipped and are correctly billed and recorded.				
1. Is there independent comparison of the quantity on the shipping documents to the sales invoices?	✓			
2. Is an authorized price list used, and is access to change the price master file restricted?	✓			
3. Are monthly statements sent to customers?	✓			
D. Sales transactions are properly included in the master files and are correctly summarized.				
1. Does the computer automatically post transactions to the accounts receivable master file and general ledger?	✓			
2. Is the accounts receivable master file reconciled with the general ledger on a monthly basis?	✓			By Erma, the chief accountant
E. Recorded sales transactions are properly classified.				
1. Is there independent comparison of recorded sales to the chart of accounts?			✓	All sales are on account and there is only one sales account.
F. Sales are recorded on the correct dates.				
1. Is there independent comparison of dates on shipping documents to dates recorded?		✓		Unmatched and unrecorded shippers are reviewed weekly.

Methods for Documenting Understanding of Entity-Level Controls and IT General Controls

The methods discussed above are also used to obtain an understanding of entity-level controls and IT general controls. Figure 9-3 is an excerpt of a questionnaire used to evaluate the entity-level controls for Hillsburg Hardware Limited. You will note that the focus is different than in Figure 9-2. Rather than focusing on the control activities, such as segregation of duties, authorization, reconciliations, and so on(which we discussed in Chapter 8), the questionnaire focuses on the other four components of internal control—the control environment, information systems, risk assessment, and monitoring. These components represent the entity-level controls, such as "tone at the top" (see Auditing in Action 9-1), that have a pervasive impact on the financial statements.

In the case of IT general controls, the auditor interviews IT personnel and key users; examines system documentation such as flowcharts, user manuals, program change requests, and system testing results; and reviews detailed questionnaires completed by IT staff. In most cases, auditors should use several of these approaches in understanding general controls because each offers different information. For example, interviews with the chief information officer and systems analysts provide useful information about the operation of the entire IT function, the extent of software development and hardware changes made to accounting application software, and an overview of any planned changes. Reviews of program change requests and system test

| Figure 9-3 | Partial Questionnaire to Assess Design and Implementation of Entity-Level Controls |

Client: _Hillsburg Hardware Limited_

Period End: _12/31/18_

Objective: To document the following components of control:	
Control environment	Financial Reporting (part of information systems)
Risk Assessment	Monitoring

Control Environment	Control Exists?	Describe the Nature of Any Supporting Documentation	What Inquiries/Observations Were Made to Ensure Controls Implemented?	Risk Mitigated?	Initials W/P Reference
Risk: No emphasis on need for integrity and ethical values					
Possible controls: 1. Management continually demonstrates, through words and actions, a commitment to high ethical standards	Y	Management periodically conducts anonymous employee surveys regarding ethical standards and tone at top	Interviewed key management including the CFO and CEO, reviewed survey results	Y	FM
2. Management removes or reduces incentives or temptations that might cause personnel to engage in dishonest or unethical acts	Y	Performance evaluation criteria and compensation packages	Interviewed key management, including the Director of Human Resources, CFO and CEO, and sales staff	Y	FM
3. A code of conduct or equivalent exists that sets out expected standards of ethical behaviour	Y	Code of conduct is posted on company website	Reviewed code of conduct and interviewed employees to determine their understanding of the code	Y	FM
4. Employees clearly understand what behaviour is acceptable and unacceptable and know what to do when they encounter improper behaviour	Y	Employees are required to complete training as well as sign an annual acknowledgement form A third party manages a whistleblower hotline and customer complaints	Reviewed training documentation and acknowledgement forms Reviewed incident reports from third party—no whistleblower reports and customer complaints handled on a timely basis	Y	FM

results are useful to identify program changes in application software. Questionnaires help auditors identify specific internal controls.

Evaluate Internal Control Implementation

In addition to understanding the design of internal controls, the auditor must evaluate whether the controls have been implemented. In practice, the understanding of design and evaluation of implementation are often done simultaneously. This involves:

- Considering whether the controls, when in operation, would achieve this objective;
- Determining whether the controls have been implemented (i.e., the control exists and the company is using it);
- Considering whether appropriately qualified persons are intended to be carrying out the control; and
- Considering the adequacy of information technology (e.g., does it capture relevant information, such as an electronic signature for approval, and does it provide relevant information).

The following methods are commonly used in performing the evaluation.

Update and Evaluate Auditor's Previous Experience With the Entity Most audits of a company are done annually by the same public accounting (PA) firm. Except for initial engagements, the auditor begins the audit with a great deal of information, developed in prior years, about the client's internal controls. It is especially useful to determine whether controls that were not previously operating effectively have been improved.

Make Inquiries of Client Personnel Auditors should ask management, supervisors, and staff to explain their duties. Careful questioning of appropriate personnel helps auditors evaluate whether employees understand their duties and do what is described in the client's control documentation.

Examine Documents and Records The five components of internal control all involve creation of documents and records. By inspecting completed documents, records, and computer files, the auditor can evaluate whether information described in flowcharts and narratives has been implemented.

Observe the Entity's Activities and Operations When auditors observe client personnel carrying out their normal accounting and control activities, including their preparation of document and records, it further improves their understanding and knowledge that controls have been implemented. When the client uses paperless systems, this may require the running of test transactions through the system to verify the understanding, or specialist computer audit assistance.

Perform Walk-Throughs of the Accounting System In a **walk-through**, the auditor selects one or a few documents for a transaction type and traces them from initiation through the entire accounting process. At each stage of processing, the auditor makes inquiries, observes activities, and examines completed documents. Walk-throughs conveniently combine observation, inspection, and inquiry to assure that the controls designed by management have been implemented. However, a walk-through is not sufficient evidence upon which the auditor can conclude that a control is working effectively (that is achieved through tests of controls—which we will discuss later in the chapter).

Walk-through—the tracing of selected transactions through the accounting system.

Aside from being an efficient and effective way of assessing the design and implementation of controls, walk-throughs also provide an opportunity to ask probing questions to assess each person's skills and competence and to determine if he or she has been asked to override controls (and if so, why).

ASSESS CONTROL RISK

LO **2** Assess control risk at the financial statement level and at the assertion level.

The auditor obtains an understanding of the design and implementation of internal controls to make a preliminary assessment of control risk as part of the auditor's overall assessment of the risk of material misstatements. As described in Chapter 7, the auditor uses this preliminary assessment of control risk to plan the audit for each material class of transactions. However, in some instances the auditor may learn that the control deficiencies are significant such that the client's financial statements may not be auditable. For example, if management lacks integrity or the accounting records are deficient, most auditors will not accept the engagement.

In complex IT environments, much of the transaction information is available only in electronic form without generating a visible audit trail of documents and records. In that case, the company is usually still auditable; however, the auditors must assess whether they have the necessary IT skills to perform the audit since it requires gathering electronic evidence or, as mentioned earlier, whether it is necessary to include an IT specialist on the audit team. The IT specialist can:

- Assist in documenting and assessing the IT control environment, including IT general controls and disaster recovery;
- Test general controls;
- Document and assess key automated controls;
- Develop computer assisted audit techniques (CAATs) to test controls and to perform substantive tests; and
- Evaluate weaknesses and develop recommendations on how to improve IT controls.

If the engagement risk is high due to IT risks, an independent systems specialist review may be appropriate as part of engagement quality review at the completion.

Determine Assessed Control Risk Supported by the Understanding Obtained

Assessment of control risk—a measure of the auditor's expectation that internal controls will neither prevent material misstatements from occurring nor detect and correct them if they have occurred.

After obtaining an understanding of internal control, the auditor makes a preliminary **assessment of control risk** as part of the overall assessment of the risk of material misstatement. This assessment is a measure of the auditor's expectation that internal controls will prevent material misstatements from occurring or detect and correct them if they have occurred. The auditor will consider the risk of material misstatement at the overall financial statement level and the assertion level.

At the overall financial statement level, the auditor will focus on those controls which address pervasive risks and for the assertion level, the auditor will consider those controls which address transaction risks. Figure 9-4 illustrates the relationship among the five components of internal control, highlighting which are pervasive in nature and which are specific to particular transaction cycles and application controls. As the figure highlights, information systems controls are both pervasive (general controls) and specific (application controls).

Assess Control Risk at the Financial Statement Level

The starting point for most auditors is the assessment of the entity-level controls—you will note that, in Figure 9-3, in the second last column, the auditor indicates whether the control is effective at mitigating the particular risk. By their nature, entity-level controls (such as many of the elements contained in the control environment, risk assessment, and monitoring components) have an overarching impact on most major types of transactions in each transaction cycle. For example, an ineffective board of directors or management's failure to have any process to identify, assess, or manage key risks has the potential to undermine controls for most of the transaction-related audit objectives (for example, see Auditing in Action 9-2 related to the case of the organization SISO). Thus, auditors generally assess entity-level and general controls before assessing transaction controls (control activities) and IT application controls.

Similarly, auditors should evaluate the effectiveness of IT general controls before evaluating automated application controls or manual controls dependent on IT output. Ineffective general controls create the potential for material misstatements across all systems applications, regardless of the quality of individual application controls.

Figure 9-4 | Pervasive and Specific Controls

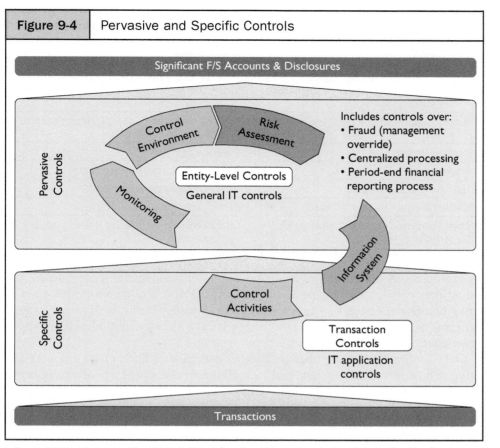

Source: This chart is an extract from *Guide to Using International Standards on Auditing in the Audits of Small and Medium-Sized Entities of the Small and Medium Practices (SMP) Committee,* published by the International Federation of Accountants (IFAC) in 2010, and is used with permission of IFAC.

AUDITING IN ACTION 9-2
Management Privilege and Override at SISO

Settlement and Integration Services Organization (SISO), whose mission was to help immigrants navigate the labyrinth of services available to them, was founded in 1990 by Morteza Jafarpour, an immigrant himself. At its height, SISO was one of southern Ontario's biggest settlement agencies, with an annual budget close to $15 million. Each year, the organization helped more than 8000 immigrants access services, supported 400 government-assisted refugees and employed more than 150 people. But suddenly, in 2010, less than two years after reporting a $2-million surplus, including $1 million in cash and $5 million in assets, the agency collapsed into bankruptcy when the Citizenship and Immigration Canada (CIC) yanked all of its funding commitments after conducting its own audit, in which significant "financial irregularities" were discovered.

In the end, the total fraud amounted to at least $4 million and several SISO executives, including Jafarpour, were found guilty of fraud. Part of the fraud involved making inflated claims to the CIC for payroll, expenses, and purchases, and creating false documents to cover the trail. It also involved cash payments made to various individuals and related party organizations, one a foundation owned by Jafarpour, for which there was no system of internal control.

At one point, Jafarpour ordered an information technology staffer to get rid of all evidence of doctored documents (which, under Jafarpour's and the CFO's direction, the staff member had altered). Although the computer expert did replace the hard drive in Jafarpour's computer, he kept the old one. During the trial, this served as key evidence of the CEO's wrongdoing. The staff member also contacted the chair of the board and another board member about his concerns; however, nothing was done. In another instance, one administrator effectively "wrote cheques to herself" to pay for various personal expenses, such as private schooling for her children and a backyard swimming pool. As the Crown Attorney noted during the fraud trial, "When it came to accessing SISO funds for illegitimate purposes, there were no controls other than the prerequisite of being part of the privileged inner circle."

Sources: Steve Buist, "Ex-SISO staffer pleads guilty to stealing at least $160,000," *Hamilton Spectator,* May 23, 2013, accessed August 15, 2017, at **http://www.thespec.com/news-story/3237410-ex-siso-staffer-pleads-guilty-to-stealing-at-least-160-000/**. Joan Walters, "SISO fraud: The whistleblower," *Hamilton Spectator,* September 7, 2013, accessed on August 15, 2017, at **http://www.thespec.com/news-story/4068435-siso-fraud-the-whistle-blower/**.

Table 9-1	General Guidelines Regarding Effectiveness of Controls

Less Effective	More Effective
Manual control	Automated control
Complex control (involves many steps, multiple calculations, etc.)	Simple control (involves a single step, single calculation, etc.)
Control is performed by a junior, less-experienced person	Control is performed by an experienced person in a position of responsibility
Detective control	Preventive control
Single control	One in a group of overlapping controls
High-level control (analytics)	Detailed, transaction-level control
Control performed on a sample basis	Control performed on each occurrence
Control performed well after the transaction occurs	Control occurs as the transaction takes place or is processed

For example, if the auditor observes that data files are inadequately safeguarded, the auditor may conclude that there is a significant risk of loss of data for every class of transaction that relies on that data to conduct application controls. However, if general controls are effective, the auditor may be able to place greater reliance on application controls whose functionality is dependent on IT.

Once auditors determine that entity-level and general IT controls are designed and placed in operation, they next make a preliminary assessment for each transaction-related audit objective for each major type of transaction in each transaction cycle. For example, in the revenue cycle, the types of transactions usually involve sales, sales returns and allowances, cash receipts, and the provision for and write-off of uncollectible accounts. The auditor also makes the preliminary assessment for controls affecting audit objectives for balance sheet accounts and presentations and disclosures in each cycle. Further, as highlighted in Figure 9-4, the auditor will consider management override controls as well as controls related to centralized processing and the period-end financial reporting process. Although not exhaustive, Table 9-1 provides some general guidelines regarding control effectiveness.

Assess Control Risk at the Assertion Level

Control risk matrix—a methodology used to help the auditor assess control risk by matching key internal controls and internal control weaknesses with transaction-related audit objectives.

Many auditors use a **control risk matrix** to assist in the control-risk assessment process at the assertion level. The purpose is to provide a convenient way of organizing control risk for each assertion and related audit objective. Most controls affect more than one audit objective, and often several different controls affect a given audit objective. The matrix serves as a useful way to identify the multiple relationships.

Figure 9-5 illustrates the use of a control risk matrix for sales transactions of Hillsburg Hardware Limited. We now discuss the process of assessing control risk using the matrix.

Identify Audit Objectives (Assertions) The first step in the assessment is to identify the audit objectives (or assertion) for the classes of transactions, account balances, and presentation and disclosure to which the assessment applies. For instance, this can be done for the class of transactions by identifying the applicable transaction assertion listed below:

- *Occurrence (Validity):* Transactions, including changes to master data, are not fictitious, relate to the business and are authorized.
- *Completeness:* All recorded transactions are accepted by the system (once and only once), and any transactions that are rejected are addressed and fixed.
- *Accuracy:* Key data elements (including master data) for transactions recorded and input to the computer are reasonably correct. Changes to master data are accurately input.

Sales Transaction-Related Audit Objectives

Internal Control	Recorded sales are for shipments actually made to nonfictitious customers (occurrence).	Existing sales transactions are recorded (completeness).	Recorded sales are for the amount of goods shipped and are correctly billed and recorded (accuracy).	Sales transactions are properly included in the accounts receivable master file and are correctly summarized (accuracy).	Sales are recorded on the correct dates (cutoff).	Sales transactions are properly classified (classification).
Controls						
Credit is approved automatically by computer by comparison to authorized credit limits (C1).	C					
Recorded sales are supported by authorized shipping documents and approved customer orders (C2).	C		C			
Separation of duties for billing, recording of sales, and handling of cash receipts (C3).	C	C		C		
Shipping documents are forwarded to billing daily and are billed on the subsequent day (C4).	C				C	
Shipping documents are prenumbered and accounted for weekly (C5).		C			C	
Batch totals of quantities shipped are compared with quantities billed (C6).	C	C	C			
Unit selling prices are obtained from the price list master file of approved prices (C7).			C			
Sales transactions are internally verified (C8).						C
Statements are mailed to customers each month (C9).	C		C	C		
Computer automatically posts transactions to the accounts receivable subsidiary records and to the general ledger (C10).				C		
Accounts receivable master file is reconciled to the general ledger on a monthly basis (C11).				C		
Deficiencies						
There is a lack of internal verification for the possibility of sales invoices being recorded more than once (D1).	D					
There is a lack of control to test for timely recording (D2).					D	
Assessed control risk	Medium	Low	Low	Low	High	Low*

*Because there are no cash sales, classification is not a problem.
C = Control; D = Deficiency.
Note: This matrix was developed using an internal control questionnaire, as well as flowcharts and other documentation of the auditor's understanding of internal control. Weaknesses are carried to an investigation sheet for assessment.

- *Cut-Off*: All recorded transactions are entered and accepted for processing in the proper time period.
- *Classification*: All recorded transactions are allocated to the correct categories (this is closely related to accuracy).

Transaction-related objectives are shown for sales transactions for Hillsburg Hardware at the top of Figure 9-5.

Identify Specific Relevant Controls Next, the auditor uses the information from obtaining and documenting an understanding of internal controls to identify the specific relevant controls that contribute to accomplishing each transaction-related audit objective. The auditor identifies pertinent controls by proceeding through the descriptive information about the client's system. Those policies and procedures that, in his or her judgment, provide control over the transaction involved are identified. In doing this, it is often helpful if the auditor considers the five control activities (segregation of duties, proper authorization, adequate documents and records, physical control, and independent checks) that might exist and asks if they do exist. For example: Is there adequate segregation of duties, and how is it achieved? Are the documents used well designed? Are there controls over inputting to the computer system?

The auditor should identify and include the **key controls**, which are expected to have the greatest impact on meeting the transaction-related audit objectives. The reason for including mainly key controls is that they will be sufficient to achieve the transaction-related audit objectives and should provide audit efficiency. Examples of key controls for Hillsburg Hardware are shown in Figure 9-5.

Associate Controls With Related Audit Objectives (Assertions) Each control satisfies one or more related control objectives. This can be seen in Figure 9-5. For example, the mailing of statements to customers satisfies three control objectives.

CAS

Identify and Evaluate Control Deficiencies, Significant Deficiencies, and Material Weaknesses Auditors must evaluate whether key controls are absent in the design of internal control over financial reporting as part of evaluating control risk and the likelihood of financial statement misstatements. Auditing standards (CAS 265) define three levels of the absence of internal controls:

1. A **control deficiency** exists if the design or operation of controls does not detect and correct misstatements in a timely manner. A design deficiency exists if a necessary control is missing or not properly designed. An operation deficiency exists if a well-designed control does not operate as designed or if the person performing the control is insufficiently qualified or authorized.
2. A **significant deficiency** exists if one or more control deficiencies exist that are less severe than a material weakness (defined below), and, in the auditor's professional judgment, are of sufficient importance to merit the attention of those charged with governance.
3. A **material weakness** exists if a significant deficiency, by itself or in combination with other significant deficiencies, results in a reasonable possibility that internal control will not prevent or detect material financial misstatements on a timely basis.

To determine if a significant internal control deficiency or deficiencies are a material weakness, they must be evaluated along two dimensions: likelihood and significance. The horizontal line in Figure 9-6 depicts the likelihood of misstatement resulting from the significant deficiency, while the vertical line depicts its significance. If there is more than a reasonable possibility (likelihood) that a material

Key controls—controls that are expected to have the greatest impact on meeting the transaction-related audit objectives.

Control deficiency—exists if the design or operation of controls does not detect and correct misstatements in a timely manner.

Significant deficiency—exists if one or more control deficiencies exist that are less severe than a material weakness.

Material weakness—exists if a significant deficiency, by itself or in combination with other significant deficiencies, results in a reasonable possibility that internal control will not prevent or detect material financial misstatements on a timely basis.

Figure 9-6	Evaluating Significant Control Deficiencies

Source: Michael Ramos, "Section 404 Compliance in the Annual Report," Journal of Accountancy, October 2004, pp. 43–48. Copyright by American Institute of CPAs.

misstatement (significance) could result from the significant deficiency or deficiencies, then it could be considered a material weakness.

A five-step approach can be used for identifying significant and/or material internal control weaknesses.

1. *Identify existing controls.* Because weaknesses are the absence of adequate controls, the auditor must first know which controls exist. The methods for identifying existing controls have already been discussed.

2. *Identify the absence of key controls.* Internal control questionnaires, narratives, and flowcharts are useful to identify areas in which key controls are lacking and the likelihood of misstatements is increased. When control risk is assessed as moderate or high, there is usually an absence of controls.

3. *Consider the possibility of compensating (or mitigating) controls.* A **compensating (or mitigating) control** is a control elsewhere in the system that offsets a weakness. Note that any control can be a compensating control. A common example in a smaller company is active involvement of the owner to compensate for lack of segregation of duties. When a compensating control exists, the weakness is no longer a concern because the potential for misstatement has been sufficiently reduced.

4. *Decide whether there is a significant deficiency or material weakness.* The likelihood of misstatements and their materiality are used to evaluate if there are significant deficiencies or material weaknesses.

5. *Determine potential material misstatements that could result.* This step is intended to identify specific errors or fraud and other irregularities that are likely to result from the absence of controls. The importance of a weakness is proportionate to the magnitude of the errors or fraud and other irregularities that are likely to result from it.

Figure 9-7 includes two control deficiencies. Neither deficiency was considered a material weakness; however, the first weakness related to prenumbered sales invoices was considered a significant deficiency.

> **Compensating (or mitigating) control**—a control elsewhere in the system that offsets a weakness.

Figure 9-7	Deficiencies in Internal Control

Client: *Hillsburg Hardware Limited*   Schedule: *P-3*

Deficiencies in Internal Control   Prepared by: *JR*   Date: *10/05/18*

Cycle: *Sales and Collection*   Period: *12/31/18*

Deficiency	Compensating Control	Potential Misstatement	Materiality	Effect on Audit Evidence
1. Prenumbered sales invoices are not accounted for.	None	Duplicate sales recorded	Potentially material	Use audit software to search for duplicate sales invoice numbers. Perform analytical procedures of sales and gross margin.
2. There is no independent comparison of dates on shipping documents to dates recorded.	Unmatched and unrecorded shipments are reviewed weekly.	N/A	N/A	N/A

Associate Control Deficiencies with Related Audit Objective (Assertion) Each control satisfies one or more related audit objectives. This can be seen in Figure 9-5 for sales-transaction-related audit objectives. The body of the matrix is used to show how each control contributes to the accomplishment of one or more transaction-related audit objectives. In this illustration, a C was entered in each cell where a control partially or fully satisfied an objective. A similar control risk matrix would be completed for balance-related and presentation and disclosure-related audit objectives. For example, the mailing of statements to customers satisfies three objectives in the audit of Hillsburg Hardware, which is indicated by the placement of a C on the row in Figure 9-5 describing that control.

Assess Control Risk for Each Related Audit Objective (Assertion) Once controls and weaknesses have been identified and matched to transaction-related audit objectives, there can be an assessment of control risk. This is the critical information in the evaluation of internal control. There are different ways to express this assessment, but most auditors use a subjective expression such as *high, moderate,* or *low.*

The control risk matrix is a useful tool for making the assessment. In Figure 9-5, the auditor assessed control risk for each objective for Hillsburg's sales by reviewing each column for pertinent controls and control deficiencies and asking, "What is the likelihood that a material misstatement would not be prevented or detected, or corrected if it occurred, by these controls, and what is the effect of the deficiencies or weaknesses?" If the likelihood is low, then control risk is low, and so forth. Figure 9-5 for Hillsburg Hardware shows that all objectives are assessed as low except occurrence (which is medium), and timing (which is high).

This assessment is not the final one. Before making the final assessment at the end of the audit, the auditor will test controls and perform substantive tests. These procedures can either support the preliminary assessment or cause the auditor to make changes. In some cases, management can correct deficiencies and material weaknesses before the auditor does significant testing, which may permit a reduction in control risk.

After a preliminary assessment of control risk is made for sales and cash receipts, the auditor can complete the three control-risk rows of the evidence planning worksheet that was introduced in Chapter 7 (Figure 7-6, page 234). If tests of controls do not support the preliminary assessment of control risk, the auditor must modify the worksheet later. Alternatively, the auditor can wait until tests of controls are done to complete the three control-risk rows of the worksheet.

CONCEPT CHECK

C9-1 Describe the activities that the auditor performs to obtain an understanding of internal control and assessing control risk.

C9-2 What is the difference between assessing control risk at the financial statement level and at the assertion level?

C9-3 What is the purpose of a control risk matrix?

LO **3** Describe the process of designing and performing tests of controls.

TESTS OF CONTROLS

Figure 9-8 provides a detailed overview of the decision process that auditors use to understand internal control and assess control risk at the assertion level. So far, we have discussed the first two steps: (1) obtain and document understanding of relevant internal controls and (2) evaluate design effectiveness. We now consider how to (3) assess control risk for each assertion and related audit objective.

Now, we'll address how auditors test controls that are used to support a control risk assessment of moderate or low. For example, in the Control Risk Matrix in Figure 9-5,

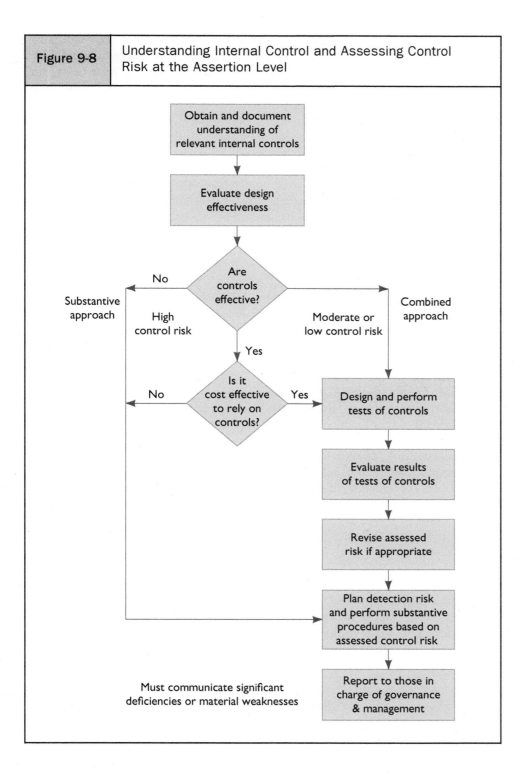

Figure 9-8	Understanding Internal Control and Assessing Control Risk at the Assertion Level

Obtain and document understanding of relevant internal controls

Evaluate design effectiveness

Are controls effective?

No — Substantive approach — High control risk

Moderate or low control risk — Combined approach

Yes

Is it cost effective to rely on controls?

No

Yes — Design and perform tests of controls

Evaluate results of tests of controls

Revise assessed risk if appropriate

Plan detection risk and perform substantive procedures based on assessed control risk

Must communicate significant deficiencies or material weaknesses

Report to those in charge of governance & management

each key control that the auditor intends to rely upon to support a control risk below maximum (either an assessment of medium or low control risk) must be supported by persuasive evidence in the form of tests of controls if the auditor will be relying upon the control.

Purpose of Tests of Controls

Assessing control risk requires the auditor to consider the design, implementation, and operation of controls to evaluate whether they will likely be effective in meeting related audit objectives (in other words, whether they will mitigate the risks associated with the various assertions). During the understanding phase, the auditor will have already gathered some evidence in support of both the design of the controls and their implementation by using procedures to obtain an understanding. In most cases, the auditor *will not* have gathered enough evidence to reduce assessed control risk to a sufficiently low level. The auditor must therefore obtain additional evidence about the operating effectiveness of controls throughout all, or at least most, of the period under audit. The procedures to test effectiveness of controls in support of a reduced assessed control risk are called **tests of controls**.

If the results of tests of controls support the design and operation of controls as expected, the auditor uses the same assessed control risk as the preliminary assessment. If, however, the tests of controls indicate that the controls did not operate effectively, the assessed control risk must be reconsidered. For example, the tests may indicate that the application of a control was curtailed midway through the year or that the person applying it made frequent misstatements. In such situations, the auditor uses a higher assessed control risk, unless compensating controls for the same related audit objectives are identified and found to be effective.

If the auditor has set control risk to be high (either because controls are not reliable or it is not cost effective for the auditor to test controls), the auditor will not perform any control tests. In the case of unreliable controls, based upon what we have learned in earlier chapters—that being that the higher the risk of material misstatement the more evidence is required—this may appear to contradict the logic of sufficient and appropriate evidence. However, if the auditor has already determined that the controls are unreliable, this means that the client's information may not be reliable and therefore the auditor will need to rely upon more persuasive evidence collected primarily through substantive tests. This is what is referred to as the **substantive approach** (as indicated on the left side of Figure 9-8). When auditors decide to rely upon internal controls, this is referred to as a **combined approach**. This approach is called a combined audit approach because the audit evidence to support the relevant assertion consists of both tests of controls *and* substantive tests. We will revisit this in more detail in Chapter 10 when we discuss audit strategy.

Procedures for Tests of Controls

The auditor is likely to use four types of audit procedures to support the operating effectiveness of key internal controls. The four types of procedures are as follows:

Make Inquiries of Appropriate Entity Personnel Although inquiry is not generally a reliable source of evidence about the effective operation of controls, it is still appropriate. For example, to determine that unauthorized personnel are denied access to computer files, the auditor may make inquiries of the person who controls set-up of user identification codes and functional access rights.

Inspect Documents, Records, and Reports Many controls leave a clear trail of documentary evidence (both electronic and paper) that can be used to test controls. Suppose, for example, that when a customer order is received, it is used to create a customer sales order, which is approved for credit. Orders that cause the customer to exceed the credit limit are printed and reviewed by the sales manager. The sales manager initials the listing for those orders that are to be accepted. (See the first and second key controls in Figure 9-5.) The auditor can test the control by examining the credit exception report and ensuring that required signatures or initials are present. Since this is a computer-assisted control (with reliance on an automated exception report), the auditor reviews the general controls file to ensure that general controls are adequate prior to the conduct of this test.

Observe Control-Related Activities Other types of control-related activities do not leave an evidence trail. For example, separation of duties relies on specific persons performing specific tasks, and there is typically no documentation of the separate performance. (See the third key control listed in Figure 9-5.) In order to test controls that leave no documentary evidence, the auditor generally observes them being applied at various points during the year.

Reperform Client Procedures Some control-related activities have related documents and records whose content is insufficient for the auditor's purpose of assessing whether controls are operating effectively. For example, assume prices on sales invoices are automatically retrieved from the computer master file by client personnel and not overridden. (See the seventh key control in Figure 9-5.) There is no documentation of this control, since it relies upon an automated process. In these cases, it is common for the auditor to actually reperform the control activity to see whether the proper results were obtained. For this example, the auditor can reperform the procedure by tracing the sales prices to the authorized price in the master file in effect at the date of the transaction.

Reperformance can also be automated. For example, if the company uses a complex algorithm to calculate its allowance for bad debts based on sales throughout the year, the algorithm could be duplicated and recalculated using **generalized audit software** (general purpose software capable of reading and testing client data using special-purpose modules such as extraction, sampling, and graphing). If no misstatements are found, the auditor can conclude that the procedure is operating as intended.

Generalized audit software— general purpose software capable of reading and testing client data using special-purpose modules such as extraction, sampling, and plotting.

CONCEPT CHECK

C9-4 Explain why the auditor tests controls.

Extent of Procedures

The extent of control testing depends on the preliminary assessed level of control risk. If the auditor wants a lower assessed control risk, more extensive tests of controls are applied, both the number of controls tested and the number of items tested. For example, if the auditor wants to use a low assessed level of control risk, a larger sample size for documentation, observation, and reperformance procedures should be applied.

The extent of testing also depends on the frequency of the operation of the controls, and whether it is manual or automated. For example, some financial reporting controls only operate at the end of the fiscal year, or quarterly, as opposed to operating on a daily basis. The auditor will test year-end controls, but will also test a sample of controls that operate quarterly or monthly.

For manual controls, the auditor will select a sample of transactions and test whether the control is operating effectively. As an example, if the client manually compares a purchase order, receiving report, and vendor's invoice before approving payment to a vendor, an auditor may select a sample of recorded purchases throughout the year and verify that the documents were properly matched and approved for payment. Because manual controls are performed by people, they are always subject to random error or manipulation.

For automated controls, the extent of required testing can vary. As long as the computer is programmed accurately and that program remains unchanged, automated controls will consistently perform as programmed until the software application is changed. Using the purchases example, the matching of the purchase order, receiving report, and vendor's invoice can be automated and the computer can generate a list of exceptions, rather than an employee manually comparing. As a result, when there are effective general controls and an automated application control, the auditor may be able to justify testing only one transaction and may not need to select a sample of transactions to verify. Therefore, the extent of testing will vary. The auditor will use one of several approaches to determine whether the design and implementation of automated controls are appropriate and whether the controls are operating effectively.

These approaches are discussed further later in the chapter when we discuss controls in more complex IT environments.

Reliance on Evidence From Prior Year's Audit When auditors plan to use evidence about operating effectiveness of internal controls obtained in prior audits, CAS 330.14 requires tests of control be performed for each specific control at least once every three years. If auditors determine that a key control has been changed since it was last tested, they should test it in the current year. This applies to both manual and automated controls. When there are a number of controls tested in prior audits that have not been changed, auditing standards require auditors to test some of those controls each year to ensure there is a rotation of controls testing throughout the three-year period.

Testing of Controls Related to Significant Risks As described in Chapter 7, significant risks are those risks that the auditor believes require special audit consideration. When the auditor's risk assessment procedures identify significant risks, the auditor is required to test the operating effectiveness of controls that mitigate these risks in the current year's audit if the auditor plans to rely on those controls to support a control risk assessment below 100 percent (that is, if control risk is assessed at medium or low). The greater the risk, the more audit evidence the auditor should obtain that controls are operating effectively.

Testing Less Than the Entire Audit Period The timing of controls will depend upon the nature of the controls and when the company uses them. For instance, controls dealing with financial statement preparation occur monthly, quarterly, or at year-end and should therefore be tested at those times. For controls that are applied throughout the accounting period, it is usually practical to test them at an interim date. The auditor will then determine whether changes in controls occurred in the period not tested and decide the implication of that change.

Relationship of Tests of Controls to Procedures to Obtain an Understanding

You will notice that there is a significant overlap between tests of controls and procedures to obtain an understanding. Both include inquiry, inspection, and observation. There are two primary differences in the application of these common procedures between phases:

1. In obtaining an understanding of internal control, the procedures are applied to all controls identified during that phase. Tests of controls, however, are applied only when the assessed control risk has not been satisfied by the procedures to obtain an understanding.
2. Procedures to obtain an understanding are performed only on one or two transactions or, in the case of observations, at a single point in time. Tests of controls are performed on larger samples of transactions (perhaps 20 to 100), and often, observations are made at more than one time.

For key controls, tests of controls other than reperformance are essentially an extension of related procedures to obtain an understanding. For that reason, when auditors plan at the outset to obtain a low assessed level of control risk, they may combine both types of procedures and perform them simultaneously. Table 9-2 illustrates this concept in more detail, showing how audit procedures are used differently. Where only the required minimum study of internal control is planned, the auditor will conduct a transaction walk-through. The auditor determines that the audit documentation is complete and accurate, and observes that the control-related activities described are in operation.

The determination of the appropriate sample size for tests of controls is an important audit decision. The topic is covered in Chapter 11.

Table 9-2	Relationship of Planned Assessed Level of Control Risk and Extent of Procedures

	Planned Assessed Level of Control Risk	
Type of Procedure Used	High Control Risk: Obtaining an Understanding Only	Moderate or Low Control Risk: Tests of Controls
Inquiry	Yes—extensive	Yes—some
Inspection	Yes—with transaction walk-through	Yes—using sampling
Observation	Yes—with transaction walk-through	Yes—at multiple times
Reperformance	No	Yes—using sampling

UNDERSTANDING AND ASSESSING CONTROLS OF OUTSOURCED SYSTEMS

LO **4** Understand and assess controls of outsourced systems.

Rather than maintain an internal IT centre, many clients outsource various functions of their operations and some or all of their IT needs to an independent computer service centre that includes application service providers (ASPs) and cloud computing environments. Companies also outsource functions such as call centres, accounting, human resources, pension fund management, internal audit, and payroll. In addition, ecommerce systems are frequently outsourced to external website service providers, including those that offer cloud computing services. As highlighted in our discussion of the various components of internal control, depending upon the function that has been outsourced, it can represent a significant component of the entity's internal controls over financial reporting and would represent relevant controls for the financial statements.

Understanding Internal Controls in Outsourced Systems

When clients use a service centre for processing transactions, such as a payroll service provider or a broker for processing investment transactions, the auditor faces a difficulty when obtaining an understanding of the client's internal controls for these transaction areas. Many of the controls reside at the service centre, and the auditor cannot assume that the controls are adequate simply because it is an independent enterprise.

CAS 402 requires the auditor to consider the need to obtain an understanding and test the service centre's controls if the service centre application involves processing significant financial data. For example, many of the controls for payroll transaction-related audit objectives reside within the software program maintained and supported by the payroll services company, not the audit client.

When obtaining an understanding and testing the service centre's controls, the auditor should use the same criteria that were used in evaluating a client's internal controls. The depth of the auditor's understanding depends on the complexity of the system and the extent to which the control is relied upon to reduce control risk. If the auditor concludes that active involvement at the service centre is the only way to conduct the audit, it may be necessary to obtain an understanding of the internal controls at the service centre and test controls using test data and other tests of controls.

CAS

Reliance on Service Centre Auditors

In recent years, it has become increasingly common for the service centre to engage a PA firm to obtain an understanding, test internal controls of the service centre, and issue a report for use by all customers and their independent auditors. The purpose of this independent assessment is to provide service centre customers with reasonable assurance about the adequacy of the service centre's general and application controls, and to eliminate the need for redundant audits by customers' auditors. If the service centre has many customers and each requires an understanding of the service centre's internal controls by its own independent auditor, the inconvenience and cost to the service centre could be substantial.

CAS

CSAE 3416 provides guidance to auditors who issue reports on the internal control of service organizations (*service auditors*), while CAS 402 provides guidance to auditors of user organizations (*user auditors*) that rely on the service auditor's report. Service auditors may issue two types of reports:

- Report on management's description of a service organization's system and the suitability of the design of controls (referred to as a Type 1 report).
- Report on management's description of a service organization's system and the suitability of the design and operating effectiveness of controls (referred to as a Type 2 report).

A Type 1 report helps auditors obtain an understanding of internal control to plan the audit. However, auditors may also require evidence about the operating effectiveness of controls to assess control risk. This evidence can:

- Be based on the service auditor's Type 2 report that includes tests of the operating effectiveness of controls.
- Come from tests of the user organization's controls over the activities of the service organization.
- Be created when the user auditor does appropriate tests at the service organization.

If the user auditor decides to rely on the service auditors' report, appropriate inquiries should be made about the service auditor's reputation.

CONCEPT CHECK

C9-5 Explain the impact on the audit if the client relies upon outsourced systems that process material transactions.

LO 5 Understand how control risk impacts detection risk and the design of substantive tests.

EVALUATE RESULTS, DECIDE ON PLANNED DETECTION RISK, AND DESIGN SUBSTANTIVE TESTS

As mentioned earlier, where the results of the tests of controls support the design of controls as expected, the auditor uses the same assessed control risk. If, however, the tests of controls indicate that the controls did not operate effectively, the assessed level of control risk must be reconsidered.

The auditor determines planned detection risk and designs substantive tests by linking the control risk assessment to balance-related audit objectives for the accounts affected by the major transaction types and to the four presentation and disclosure objectives. The appropriate level of detection risk for each balance-related audit objective is then decided using the audit risk model. We will discuss this further, along with the design of substantive tests, in Chapter 10.

Cost Effectiveness of Control Tests

Recall from Figure 9-8 that the decision to test controls is based upon the effectiveness of the controls and whether it is cost-effective to perform tests of controls. Performing tests of controls may be more cost efficient than performing substantive procedures in certain situations. For instance, tests of controls generally have smaller sample sizes than substantive tests. If controls are automated, and the general IT controls are effective, a sample size of one item is all that is required. In addition, as mentioned previously, if the control system and personnel have not changed, it is possible to limit testing of internal controls to every three years.

When Tests of Controls Are Required

Although the focus has been on tests of controls when the auditor can choose whether to rely upon controls related to a particular class of transactions and the related assertions, if a client relies upon highly automated systems, such as electronic data interchange and electronic banking, it will be necessary to test the controls regarding the computer programs. That is because the accuracy and completeness of transactions relies upon the computer programs functioning correctly. In this instance, substantive procedures alone (for example, recalculation of interest charges) cannot provide sufficient evidence with respect to those assertions, and the auditor has no choice but to rely upon internal controls. Because the auditor has made the decision to rely upon internal controls, they must be tested.

IMPACT OF IT ENVIRONMENT ON CONTROL RISK ASSESSMENT AND TESTING

LO **6** Describe how the complexity of the IT environment impacts control risk assessment and testing.

The impact of general controls and application controls on audits is likely to vary depending on the level of complexity in the IT environment. Even in a less complex IT environment, the auditor is still responsible for obtaining an understanding of general and application computer controls because such knowledge is useful in identifying risks that may affect the financial statements. However, the extent of testing will depend on the assessment of control risk, as discussed earlier. In this section, we discuss auditing in a more complex IT environment and the opportunities and challenges this provides for auditors (as discussed in Auditing in Action 9-3, this is an area in which auditors have difficulty).

Auditing in More Complex IT Environments

As organizations expand their use of IT, internal controls, only available electronically, are often embedded in applications. When traditional source documents such as invoices, purchase orders, billing records, and accounting records such as sales

---

AUDITING IN ACTION 9-3
Audit Regulators Identify Deficiencies in Control Testing

When auditors fail to properly assess control risk, it will often result in a failure to collect sufficient appropriate audit evidence. Despite the crucial role of internal control in the audit process, as highlighted in its fifth annual survey, the International Forum of Independent Audit Regulators found that internal control testing is consistently an area where audit work is deficient. For instance, in its 2013 summary of practice inspection findings, the PCAOB (Public Company Accounting Oversight Board) found that the most common audit deficiencies include failure to identify and test controls intended to address the risk of material misstatement, improperly assessing management review controls, insufficient testing of controls over system-generated data, and failure to perform appropriate tests when relying on

the work of others. Here in Canada, the CPAB (Canadian Public Accountability Board) also found a common audit deficiency is the improper assessment of management review controls. The CPAB noted that, because auditors often avoid testing controls by "auditing around" the computer system, this may result in an inappropriate reliance on system-generated information that has not been properly tested.

Sources: Canadian Public Accountability Board, *2016 Annual Inspections, Public Report*, 2017. International Forum of Independent Audit Regulators, *Report on 2016 Survey of Inspection Findings*, March 2017. Public Company Accountability Oversight Board, *PCAOB Audit Practice Alert No. 11, Considerations for Audits of Internal Control Over Financial Reporting*, October 24, 2013.

journals, inventory listings, and accounts receivable subsidiary records exist only electronically, auditors must change their approach to auditing. This approach is often called **auditing through the computer**. Auditors use three approaches to test the effectiveness of automated controls when auditing through the computer: test data approach, parallel simulation, and embedded audit module approach.

Test Data Approach In the **test data approach**, auditors process their own test data using the client's computer system and application program to determine whether the automated controls correctly process the test data. Auditors design the test data to include transactions that the client's system should either accept or reject. After the test data are processed on the client's system, auditors compare the actual output to the expected output to assess the effectiveness of the application program's automated controls. Figure 9-9 illustrates the use of the test data approach.

When using the test data approach, auditors have three main considerations:

1. *Test data should include all relevant conditions that the auditor wants tested.* Auditors should design test data to test all key computer-based controls and include realistic data that are likely to be a part of the client's normal processing, including both valid and invalid transactions. For example, assume the client's payroll application contains a limit check that disallows a payroll transaction that exceeds 80 hours per week. To test this control, the auditor can prepare payroll transactions with 79, 80, and 81 hours for each sampled week and process them through the client's system in a manner shown in Figure 9-9. If the limit check control is operating effectively, the client's system should reject the transaction for 81 hours, and the client's error listing should report the 81-hour transaction error.

2. *Application programs tested by auditors' test data must be the same as those the client used throughout the year.* One approach is to run the test data on a surprise

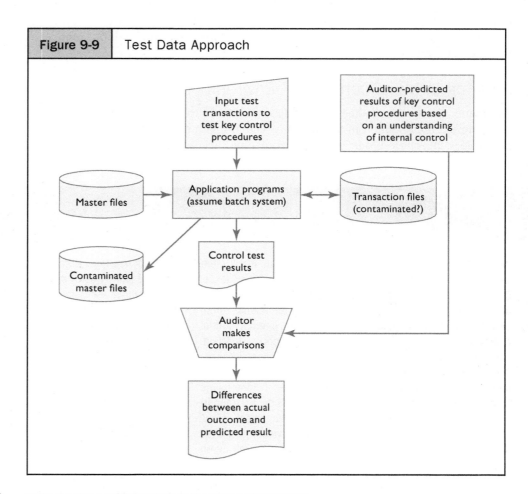

Figure 9-9	Test Data Approach

basis, possibly at random times throughout the year, even though doing so is costly and time consuming. Another method is to rely on the client's general controls in the librarian and systems development functions to ensure that the program tested is the one used in normal processing.

3. *Test data must be eliminated from the client's records.* If auditors process test data while the client is processing its own transactions, auditors must eliminate the test data in the client's master files after the tests are completed to prevent master files and transaction files from being permanently contaminated by the auditor's testing. Auditors can do this by developing and processing data that reverses the effect of the test data.

Because of the complexities of many clients' application software programs, auditors who use the test data approach often obtain assistance from a computer audit specialist. Many larger public accounting firms have staff dedicated to assisting in testing client automated application controls.

Parallel Simulation Auditors often use auditor-controlled software to do the same operations that the client's software does, using the same data files. The purpose is to determine the effectiveness of automated controls and to obtain evidence about electronic account balances. This testing approach is called **parallel simulation testing**. Figure 9-10 shows a typical parallel simulation. Whether testing controls or ending balances, the auditor compares the output from the auditor's software to output from the client's system to test the effectiveness of the client's software and to determine if the client's balance is correct. A variety of software is available to assist auditors.

Auditors commonly do parallel simulation testing using **generalized audit software (GAS)**, which we discussed in Chapter 5. (An example of this approach was provided in the opening vignette of this chapter.)

Parallel simulation testing—an audit testing approach that involves the auditor's use of audit software to replicate some part of a client's application system

Generalized audit software (GAS)—computer programs used by auditors that provide data retrieval, data manipulation, and reporting capabilities specifically oriented to the needs of auditors.

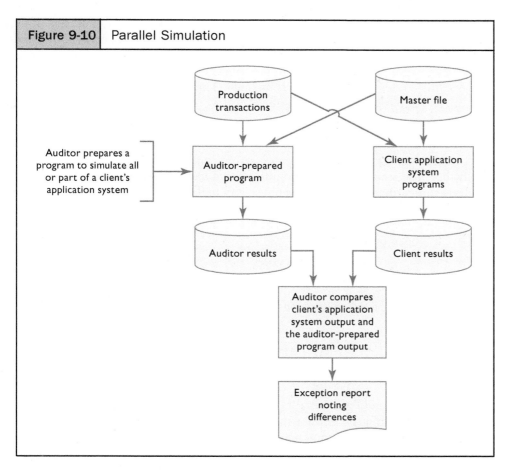

| Figure 9-10 | Parallel Simulation |

Auditor prepares a program to simulate all or part of a client's application system

Production transactions

Master file

Auditor-prepared program

Client application system programs

Auditor results

Client results

Auditor compares client's application system output and the auditor-prepared program output

Exception report noting differences

Embedded Audit Module Approach When using the **embedded audit module approach**, auditors insert an audit module into the client's application system to identify specific types of transactions. For example, auditors might use an embedded module to identify all purchases exceeding $25 000 for follow-up with more detailed examination for the transaction-related audit objectives of occurrence and accuracy. In some cases, auditors later copy the identified transactions to a separate data file and then process those transactions using parallel simulation to duplicate the function done by the client's system. The auditor then compares the client's output with the auditor's output. Discrepancies are printed on an exception report for auditor follow-up.

The embedded audit module approach allows auditors to continuously audit transactions by identifying actual transactions processed by the client, as compared to test data and parallel simulation approaches, which only allow intermittent testing. Internal auditors may also find this technique useful.

Although auditors may use one or any combination of testing approaches, they typically use:

- Test data to do tests of controls and substantive tests of transactions.
- Parallel simulation for substantive testing, such as recalculating transaction amounts and footing master file subsidiary records of account balances.
- Embedded audit modules to identify unusual transactions for substantive testing.

Changes in the IT System

When an organization changes an entire IT system or set of systems, the auditor will need to ensure that the new system's internal controls are documented and evaluated, and an audit of the data conversion is performed. In the case of the data conversion, in order to determine the audit procedures, the auditor will perform a risk assessment. For instance, in order to assess inherent risk, the auditor will take into account the extent of employee training and the rigour of the implementation process. If the implementation process was properly planned, conducted, and supervised, the auditor can rely upon controls. Conversely, if conversion controls are poor or not documented, the auditor will need to conduct substantive tests related to the conversion process; this is referred to as a conversion audit. The emphasis is on the accurate and authorized establishment of new master files, the completeness and existence of data in those files, and cut-off transactions in the appropriate system. The following tests are performed in the **conversion audit**:

- Tests comparing details from the new system with those of the old system to verify that only accurate, authorized information has been established.
- Tests comparing details from the old system to those of the new system to ensure accuracy and that no transactions are omitted.
- Cutoff testing to ensure that transactions are included in the proper system and have not been omitted.

CONCEPT CHECK

C9-6 Explain why the auditor is required to test controls for highly automated systems.

AUDITOR REPORTING ON INTERNAL CONTROL

As part of understanding internal control and assessing control risk, the auditor is required to communicate certain matters to those charged with governance. This information and other recommendations about controls are also communicated to management.

Source: PricewaterhouseCoopers LLP Audit Results Report on the Toronto Transit Commission Consolidated Financial Statements for the Year Ended December 31, 2015.

Communications to Those Charged With Governance and Management Letters

According to CAS 265, the auditor is required to communicate significant control deficiencies in writing to "the audit committee or equivalent." If the client does not have an audit committee, then the communication should go to whoever in the organization has overall responsibility for internal control, such as the board of directors or the owner–manager.

The description of the internal control deficiency and recommendation is usually included in a year-end report, or **internal control letter** to the audit committee. These recommendations are discussed with management to determine the plan of action to resolve any deficiencies noted in the report. Figure 9-11 is an excerpt from the 2015 year-end audit committee report for the Toronto Transit Commission. The report also illustrates the presentation format that auditors use—Control Weakness (what the auditors refer to as Observation), Implication (what can go wrong), and Recommendation. The report also summarizes management's response to the auditor's recommendations. The auditor's analysis along with management's response would be provided to the audit committee.

Internal control letter—a letter or report from the auditor to the audit committee or senior management detailing significant control deficiencies.

Management Letters Auditors often observe less significant internal control-related matters, as well as opportunities for the client to make operational improvements. These types of matters should also be communicated to the client management. The form of communication is often a separate letter for that purpose, called a **management letter**. This letter needs to be clearly identified as a derivative report to indicate that, while the purpose of the engagement was not to determine weaknesses in internal control, such weaknesses were identified as a by-product of the audit.

Management letter—the auditor's written communication to management to point out less significant weaknesses in internal control and possibilities for operational improvements.

LO 8 Explain the difference in the scope of control testing for an audit opinion on the effectiveness of controls over financial reporting versus an audit opinion for financial statements.

REPORTING ON INTERNAL CONTROLS FOR SOME PUBLIC COMPANIES

For some public companies, the auditor reports upon management's assessment of internal control. Such a report is required by Section 404(b) of the Sarbanes-Oxley Act of 2002, affecting Canadian companies that are subsidiaries of American companies or that register securities for sale in the United States. Section 5925 of the *CPA Canada*

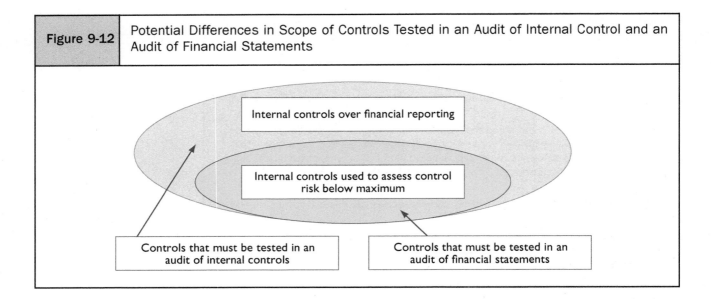

| Figure 9-12 | Potential Differences in Scope of Controls Tested in an Audit of Internal Control and an Audit of Financial Statements |

Internal controls over financial reporting

Internal controls used to assess control risk below maximum

Controls that must be tested in an audit of internal controls

Controls that must be tested in an audit of financial statements

Handbook—"An audit of internal control over financial reporting performed that is integrated with an audit of financial statements"—is substantially equivalent to the U.S. standard. (In Canada, management of public companies must provide a report on the effectiveness of their internal controls; however, no assurance is required.)

The scope of the Section 404(b) internal control assessment is different from the scope of the internal control assessment required for a financial statement audit. Figure 9-12 illustrates the differences in scope. Since the auditor is providing an opinion on the effectiveness of the internal controls that management has assessed, the auditor obtains an understanding of and performs tests of controls for *all* significant account balances, classes of transactions, and disclosures and related assertions in the financial statements. Those controls might or might not be tested in a financial statement audit. Only those controls that the auditor plans to rely upon (control risk is assessed below maximum) are tested. Recall that in the case of the financial statement audit, the auditor is providing assurance over the financial statements not the internal controls.

SUMMARY

MyLab Accounting

Make the grade with MyLab Accounting: The questions, exercises, and problems marked with a ⊕ can be found on MyLab Accounting. You can practise them as often as you want, and most feature step-by-step guided instructions to help you find the right answer.

This chapter focused on the auditor's responsibility for understanding, evaluating, and testing internal controls. To rely on a client's internal controls to reduce planned audit evidence for audits of financial statements, the auditor must first obtain an understanding of each of the five components of internal control. Knowledge about the design of the client's control environment, risk assessment, control activities, information and communication, and monitoring activities and information about whether internal control components have been implemented assist the auditor in assessing control risk for each audit objective.

The chapter also discussed the impact of a more complex information technology environment on control risk assessment and testing. Knowledge about general controls provides a basis for the auditor to rely on automated application controls and may reduce the extent of tests of key automated controls in audits of financial statements and internal controls. Some of the auditor's tests of controls can be done by the computer, often as a way to achieve more effective and efficient audits.

The chapter also included a brief overview of an audit of a public company subject to Section 404(b) of the Sarbanes Oxley Act and PCAOB requirements to report on internal control over financial reporting. For those companies, the auditor is required to provide an opinion on the effectiveness of internal controls. For those auditors who follow Canadian regulations and CAS, it is not required, although auditors may still provide such an opinion.

Review Questions

9-1 **1** What is the auditor's responsibility for obtaining an understanding of internal control?

9-2 **2** What is a walk-through of internal control? What is its purpose?

9-3 **1** **2** Distinguish between obtaining an understanding of internal control and assessing control risk. Also, explain the methodology the auditor uses for each.

9-4 **2** Describe how the nature of evidence used to evaluate the control environment differs from the nature of evidence used to evaluate control activities.

9-5 **1** **2** Jeanne Maier, CPA (Chartered Professional Accountant), believes that it is appropriate to obtain an understanding of internal control about halfway through the audit, after she is familiar with the client's operations and the way the system actually works. She has found through experience that filling out internal control questionnaires and flowcharts early in the engagement is not beneficial because the system rarely functions the way it is supposed to. Later in the engagement, the auditor can prepare flowcharts and questionnaires with relative ease because of the knowledge already obtained on the audit. Evaluate her approach.

9-6 **3** **7** Explain what is meant by "significant deficiencies" as they relate to internal control. What should the auditor do when he or she has discovered significant deficiencies in internal control?

9-7 **3** The auditor's risk assessment procedures identified several risks that the auditor deems to be significant risks. Several internal controls exist that are designed to mitigate the risks identified. Describe the auditor's responsibilities for considering those controls in the current audit.

9-8 **3** Distinguish between a substantive approach and a combined approach in auditing a financial statement assertion.

9-9 **3** During the prior-year audits of McKimmon, Inc., a private company, the auditor did tests of controls for all relevant financial statement assertions. Some of the related controls are manual, while others are automated. To what extent can the auditor rely on tests of controls performed in prior years?

9-10 **4** Your client has outsourced most of the accounting information systems to a third-party data centre. What impact would this have on your audit of the financial statements?

9-11 **5** How does the auditor use information obtained from the control risk assessment and testing of controls to plan audit procedures?

9-12 **5** If the auditor assesses control risk as high for a transaction-related audit objective, what does that imply for detection risk and the level of substantive testing?

9-13 **6** Explain what is meant by auditing through the computer, and describe the challenges and benefits of this approach in an audit of a client that uses IT extensively to process accounting information.

9-14 **6** Explain what is meant by the test data approach. What are the major difficulties with using this approach? Define parallel simulation with audit software and provide an example of how it can be used to test a client's payroll system.

9-15 **8** Explain how control risk assessment differs for an integrated audit versus a financial statement-only audit.

Multiple Choice Questions and Task-Based Simulations

9-16 **2** A material weakness in internal control represents a control deficiency that:

(1) More than remotely adversely affects a company's ability to initiate, authorize, record, process, or report external financial statements reliably.

(2) Results in a reasonable possibility that internal control will not prevent or detect material financial statement misstatements.

(3) Exists because a necessary control is missing or not properly designed.

(4) Reduces the efficiency and effectiveness of the entity's operations.

9-17 〔8〕 An auditor of a large public company that is listed on the SEC (U.S. Securities and Exchange Commission) identifies a material weakness in internal control. The auditor:

(1) Will be unable to issue an unqualified opinion on the financial statements.

(2) Must issue a qualified opinion or disclaimer of opinion on internal control over financial reporting.

(3) May still be able to issue an unqualified opinion on internal control over financial reporting.

(4) Must issue an adverse opinion on internal control over financial reporting.

9-18 〔4〕〔7〕 The auditor's tests of controls revealed that required approvals of cash disbursements were absent for a large number of sample transactions examined. Which of the following is least likely to be the appropriate auditor response?

(1) The auditor will communicate the deficiency to those charged with governance.

(2) The auditor will increase the planned detection risk.

(3) The auditor will not select more sample items to audit.

(4) The auditor will perform more extensive substantive tests surrounding cash disbursements.

9-19 〔3〕 An auditor uses assessed control risk to:

(1) Evaluate the effectiveness of the entity's internal controls.

(2) Identify transactions and account balances where inherent risk is at the maximum.

(3) Indicate whether materiality thresholds for planning and evaluation purposes are sufficiently high.

(4) Determine the acceptable level of detection risk for financial statement assertions.

9-20 〔6〕 As general IT controls weaken, the auditor is most likely to:

(1) Reduce testing of automated application controls done by the computer.

(2) Increase testing of general IT controls to conclude whether they are operating effectively.

(3) Expand testing of automated application controls used to reduce control risk to cover greater portions of the fiscal year under audit.

(4) Ignore obtaining knowledge about the design of general IT controls and whether they have been implemented.

9-21 〔6〕 Before processing, the system validates the sequence of items to identify any breaks in sequence of input documents. This automated control is primarily designed to ensure the:

(1) Accuracy of input.

(2) Authorization of data entry.

(3) Completeness of input.

(4) Restriction of duplicate entries.

9-22 〔6〕 An auditor will use the test data approach to obtain certain assurances with respect to the:

(1) Input data.

(2) Machine capacity.

(3) Procedures contained within the program.

(4) Degree of data entry accuracy.

9-23 〔3〕 Determine whether the provided procedure is appropriate for testing the corresponding control.

Controls	Procedures	Yes/No
Prior to the sales staff processing an order, the customer's credit must be reviewed by a supervisor, who completes and signs a "Customer Credit Review" form.	Select a sample of sales orders and review payment supporting documents (i.e., bank statement) to determine if the customers ended up paying for the order.	
At the end of each month, the accounts receivable (A/R) supervisor prepares the aged A/R list. The list is reviewed by the A/R manager, who must sign off on it.	Enquire of the A/R supervisor how the aged A/R list is used to calculate the allowance for doubtful accounts.	
At the end of each day, warehouse staff submit all unfulfilled customer orders to their supervisor. Only the supervisor is authorized to cancel unfulfilled customer orders in the company's financial system.	Request warehouse staff to log into the financial system and attempt to cancel an unfulfilled customer order.	

Controls	Procedures	Yes/No
Employees responsible for shipping are separate from the employees responsible for accepting and processing the sales orders.	Obtain HR files of employees who work in the shipping department and review whether they ever worked in the sales orders department. Review whether employees working in the sales order department ever worked in the shipping department.	
The quantities on the order delivery note are checked by the warehouse manager against the actual quantities prior to shipment. The manager stamps "Good To Go" on the delivery note for each checked order.	For a sample of orders that were shipped, obtain delivery notes and check if they were stamped.	
All blank cheques are stored and locked in a safe. Only the CFO and the Finance Manager know the code to the safe.	Confirm with the CFO and the Finance Manager that they always keep the safe locked and that the code to the safe contains at least six numbers.	

9-24 **2** Identify the most relevant assertion(s) for each control that is listed below.

Assertions:

A. Existence
B. Completeness
C. Accuracy
D. Valuation
E. Occurrence

Control	Assertion(s)
Customer credit limits are reviewed on a monthly basis and amended in accordance with customer activity.	
Prior to paying for a purchase, supporting documentation (invoices, statements of account) are reviewed for validity.	
Paper timesheets submitted by employees for a given period are reconciled to the corresponding payroll ledger.	
During a full count of all capital assets, all assets are physically labelled with unique identification numbers and their location, description, and quantity are noted.	
The purchasing department, on receipt of the receiving report, matches it to the purchase order to ensure that all ordered goods were received.	
Prior to being entered into the payroll system, all paper timesheets are reviewed by the shift supervisor, who signs off on them.	

9-25 **2** Based upon the case facts, indicate whether the type of control risk—pervasive risk (impacts entire financial statements) or a risk at the assertion level (if so, which account and assertions are affected)—and the impact on control risk (whether the factor increases or decreases control risk).

Scenarios	Type of Control Risk	Impact on Control Risk
There have been a number of discrepancies in the company's cash balance. One of the managers suspects that Dominic (the CFO's cousin) may be removing cash on Friday afternoons. The manager, however, is afraid of "getting in trouble" with the CFO if she confronts Dominic about this issue.		
The company's controller is a very detailed and rules-oriented individual. Last month, she fired an employee from the accounting department who did not complete bank reconciliations on time.		
The new head of purchasing has added six new vendors to the approved vendor list within the first two months of employment. Since the vendors offer products and services at much lower prices compared to other vendors, the CFO did not bother with the usual new vendor verification process.		

(continued)

(Continued)

Scenarios	Type of Control Risk	Impact on Control Risk
A number of warehouse staff called in sick on the day of the annual inventory count. The warehouse manager could have postponed the count to another day, but decided to go ahead with the count and instructed her staff to only check initial count results (they were to double count if they had any time left at the end of the day).		
To complete the financial statements on time, the A/R manager worked all night to estimate the allowance for doubtful accounts. The manager conducted a thorough review of each customer's credit balance. The allowance estimate was thoroughly reviewed by the controller, who noticed and corrected a couple of minor errors.		
Over the past several years, the external auditor of Nicolas Inc., a manufacturer of children's toys, in its management letter expressed concerns about the company's weak internal controls. In response and to address some of the external auditor's concerns, last year Nicolas Inc. established an internal audit department.		

Discussion Questions and Problems

9-26 **1** **2** **7** The following are errors or fraud and other irregularities that have occurred in Fresh Foods Grocery Store Ltd., a wholesale and retail grocery company.
1. The incorrect price was used on sales invoices for billing shipments to customers because the incorrect price was entered into a computer file.
2. A vendor's invoice was paid twice for the same shipment. The second payment arose because the vendor sent a duplicate copy of the original two weeks after the payment was due.
3. Employees in the receiving department stole some sides of beef. When a shipment of meat was received, the receiving department filled out a receiving report and forwarded it to the accounting department for the amount of goods actually received. At that time, two sides of beef were put in an employee's pickup truck rather than in the storage freezer.
4. During the physical count of inventory of the retail grocery, one counter wrote down the wrong description of several products and miscounted the quantity.
5. A salesperson sold several hundred kilograms of lamb at a price below cost because she did not know that the cost of lamb had increased in the past week.
6. On the last day of the year, a truckload of beef was set aside for shipment but was not shipped. Because it was still on hand, it was counted as inventory. The shipping document was dated the last day of the year, so it was also included as a current-year sale.

REQUIRED
a. For each error or fraud and other irregularity, identify one or more types of controls that were absent.
b. For each error or fraud and other irregularity, identify the objectives that have not been met.
c. For each error or fraud and other irregularity, suggest a control to correct the deficiency.

9-27 **1** **2** The following are partial descriptions of internal controls for companies engaged in the manufacturing business:
1. When Mr. Clark orders materials, an electronic copy of the purchase order is sent to the receiving department. During the delivery of materials, Mr. Smith, the receiving clerk, records the receipt of shipment on this purchase order and then sends the purchase order to the accounting department, where it is used to record materials purchased and accounts payable. The materials are transported to the storage area by forklifts. The additional purchased quantities are recorded on storage records.

2. Every day, hundreds of employees clock in using their employee identification cards at Generous Motors Corporation. The data on these time records are used in the preparation of the labour cost distribution records, the payroll journal, and the electronic payments and payroll cheques. The treasurer, Angela Lee, compares the payroll journal with the payroll records, signs the cheques, and returns the payroll notifications and cheques to Charles Strode, the supervisor of the computer department. The payroll cheques and payment notices are distributed to the employees by Strode.

3. The smallest branch of Connor Cosmetics employs Mary Cooper, the branch manager, and her sales assistant, Janet Hendrix. The branch uses a bank account to pay expenses. The account is kept in the name of "Connor Cosmetics—Special Account." To pay expenses, cheques must be signed by Cooper or by the treasurer, John Winters. Cooper receives the cancelled cheques and bank statements. She reconciles the branch account herself and files cancelled cheques and bank statements in her records. She also periodically prepares reports of cash disbursements and sends them to the home office.

REQUIRED

a. List the deficiencies in internal control for each of these situations. To identify the deficiencies, use the methodology that was discussed in this chapter.

b. For each deficiency, state the type(s) of misstatement(s) that is (are) likely to result. Be as specific as possible.

c. How would you improve internal controls for each of the three companies?*

9-28 2 6 Most grocery stores use bar code scanning technologies that interface with cash registers used to process customer purchases. Cashiers use the scanners to read bar code labels attached to each product, which the system then uses to obtain unit prices, calculate transaction totals, including sales taxes, and update perpetual inventory databases. Similarly, cashiers scan bar codes on coupons or member discount cards presented by the customer to process discounts. Along with the scanning technologies, groceries use point-of-sale technologies that allow customers to swipe debit and credit cards for payment, while still maintaining the ability for customers to pay with cash.

REQUIRED

a. Which financial statement accounts are impacted by the use of these technologies in a typical grocery store?

b. Identify risks inherent to this business process in a grocery store that might affect the financial statement accounts identified in Part a. For each risk, describe how these technologies help reduce the inherent risk.

c. How might an auditor use technology to test the operating effectiveness of a bar code scanner–based check-out system?

9-29 2 3 6 Based on a cost-benefit analysis, management at First Community Credit Union decides to contract with Technology Solutions, a local data centre operator, to host all of the credit union's financial reporting applications. To avoid the significant costs of developing and maintaining its own data centre, First Community contracts with Technology Solutions to provide IT server access in a highly secure, environmentally controlled data centre facility owned by Technology Solutions. Similar to First Community, other businesses also contract with Technology Solutions to host applications at the same data center.

The credit union is directly linked through highly secure telecommunication lines to the data centre, which allows bank personnel to transmit data to and from the data centre as if the data centre were owned by First Community. For a monthly fee, Technology Solutions supports the server hardware in an environment with numerous backup controls in the event that power is lost or other hardware failures occur. Credit union personnel are responsible for selecting and maintaining all application software loaded on Technology Solutions servers, and selected bank personnel have access to those servers located at the Technology Solutions data centre. Credit union personnel enter all data, run applications hosted at Technology Solutions, and retrieve reports summarizing the processing of all bank transactions.

REQUIRED

a. What risks might First Community assume with this approach to IT system support?

b. How does the use of Technology Solutions impact First Community's internal controls?

c. What impact, if any, does reliance on Technology Solutions as the data centre provider have on the audit of First Community's financial statements?

*Based on AICPA question paper, American Institute of Certified Public Accountants.

Professional Judgment Problems and Cases

9-30 [2] Hans & Co. LLP is auditing CCC Inc.'s 2018 financial statements. The firm previously audited the company's 2016 and 2017 financial statements. The 2016 audit resulted in a qualified opinion because the auditors were unable to verify the opening inventory for that year, but the 2017 audit resulted in an unqualified opinion. Julia worked on the previous two audits and is familiar with most of the staff at CCC, including the accounting manager, Marcus. Julia was scheduled to meet with Marcus on Monday morning to meet any new staff and have a tour of the office. The accounting manager was unable to meet with Julia on Monday, and instead sent her the following email:

Julia,

I have to take next week off for personal reasons. Therefore, I prepared this email for you. As you are probably aware, CCC Inc. has suffered some loss of sales due to the general economic slowdown experienced by many companies. The office procedures and internal controls are the same as last year. You will have many new staff to meet this year as employee turnover has been high. CCC had to reduce wages for most staff by 20 percent to stay profitable, so several employees complain that they are underpaid, and about 30 percent of the staff actually left for new jobs. As for my own position, accounting manager, my wages were only reduced by 10 percent, because managers are expected to work harder than other staff. The staff generally do not believe that we work harder, but, for example, the controller has refused to take any vacation for the past year and does not want to take her vacation for the next two years. One of the controller's many responsibilities is to approve all payments and purchases from CCC's subsidiary company, CCC-2 Ltd. (As you know from last year's audit, CCC owns 60 percent of the voting shares of CCC-2 and senior executives of both companies own the remaining shares—40 percent.) Being able to purchase goods and materials from CCC-2 at below-market prices is a second reason that CCC has remained profitable, even in the poor economy, so it's very helpful that the controller is never away on vacation. I will be back in the office next week, so we can meet next Monday instead.

Regards, Marcus

REQUIRED

Assess control risk at CCC. Justify your response.

(Extract from AU1 CGA-Canada Examinations developed by the Certified General Accountants Association of Canada © 2011 CGA-Canada. Reproduced with permission. All rights reserved.)

9-31 [2] The following is the description of sales and cash receipts for Ladies' Fashion Fair, a retail store dealing in expensive women's clothing. Sales are for cash or credit, using the store's own billing rather than credit cards.

Each salesclerk has her own sales book with prenumbered, three-copy, multicoloured sales slips attached, but perforated. Only a central cash register is used. It is operated by the store supervisor, who has been employed for 10 years by Alice Olson, the store owner. The cash register is at the store entrance to control theft of clothes.

Salesclerks prepare the sales invoices in triplicate. The original and the second copy are given to the cashier. The third copy is retained by the salesclerk in the sales book. When the sale is for cash, the customer pays the salesclerk, who marks all three copies "paid" and presents the money to the cashier with the invoice copies.

All clothing is put into boxes or packages by the supervisor after comparing the clothing to the description on the invoice and the price on the sales tag. She also rechecks the clerk's calculations. Any corrections are approved by the salesclerk. The clerk changes her sales book at that time.

A credit sale is approved by the supervisor from an approved credit list after the salesclerk prepares the three-part invoice. Next, the supervisor enters the sale in her cash register as a credit or cash sale. The second copy of the invoice, which has been validated by the cash register, is given to the customer.

At the end of the day, the supervisor recaps the sales and cash and compares the totals to the cash register tape. The supervisor deposits the cash at the end of each day in the bank's deposit box. The cashier's copies of the invoices are sent to the accounts receivable clerk along with a summary of the day's receipts. The bank mails the deposit slip directly to the accounts receivable clerk.

Each clerk summarizes her sales each day on a daily summary form, which is used in part to calculate employees' sales commissions. Marge, the accountant, who is prohibited from handling cash, receives the supervisor's summary and the clerk's daily summary form. Daily, she puts all sales invoice information into the firm's computer, which provides a complete printout of all input and summaries. The accounting summary includes sales by salesclerk, cash sales, credit sales, and total sales. Marge compares this output with the supervisor's and salesclerks' summaries and reconciles all differences.

The computer updates accounts receivable, inventory, and general ledger master files. After the update procedure has been run on the computer, Marge's assistant files all sales invoices by customer number. A list of the invoice numbers in numerical sequence is included in the sales printout.

The mail is opened each morning by a secretary in the owner's office. All correspondence and complaints are given to the owner. The secretary prepares a prelist of cash receipts. He totals the list, prepares a deposit slip, and deposits the cash daily. A copy of the prelist, the deposit slip, and all remittances returned with the cash receipts are given to Marge. She uses this list and the remittances to record cash receipts and update accounts receivable, again by computer. She reconciles the total receipts on the prelist to the deposit slip and to her printout. At the same time, she compares the deposit slip received from the bank for cash sales to the cash receipts journal.

A weekly aged trial balance of accounts receivable is automatically generated by the computer. A separate listing of all unpaid bills over 60 days is also automatically prepared. These are given to the store owner, Mrs. Olson, who acts as her own credit collector. She also approves all write-offs of uncollectible items and forwards the list to Marge, who writes them off.

Each month Marge mails statements generated by the computer to customers. Complaints and disagreements from customers are directed to Mrs. Olson, who resolves them and informs Marge in writing of any write-downs or misstatements that require correction.

The computer system also automatically totals the journals and posts the totals to the general ledger. A general ledger trial balance is printed out, from which Marge prepares financial statements. Marge also prepares a monthly bank reconciliation and reconciles the general ledger to the aged accounts receivable trial balance.

Because of the importance of inventory control, Marge prints out the inventory perpetual totals monthly, on the last day of each month. Salesclerks count all inventory after store hours on the last day of each month for comparison with the perpetuals. An inventory shortages report is provided to Mrs. Olson. The perpetuals are adjusted by Marge after Mrs. Olson has approved the adjustments.

REQUIRED

a. For each sales transaction-related audit objective, identify one or more existing controls.
b. For each cash receipts transaction-related audit objective, identify one or more existing controls.
c. Identify deficiencies in internal control for sales and cash receipts.

9-32 **2** **7** Jebrah Manufacturing Limited (JML) is a small company with about 50 employees. It has a local area network, production systems software, timekeeping software, and accounting systems. These are all locally purchased and locally maintained software systems. There are no in-house information systems personnel.

The controller is responsible for setting up new users and changing user capabilities based upon scripts (standard instructions) provided by the network supplier. If she has any problems, she telephones the network supplier, who logs on to the system and makes the changes for her online.

All three accounting personnel and the owner of the company have access to all accounting systems. Manufacturing employees have access to timekeeping and production systems.

The controller prepares the bank reconciliation, but the owner signs payroll cheques and accounts payable cheques (with supporting documentation attached). The controller is responsible for recording all changes in wage rates in the accounting systems and writing off accounts receivable. The receptionist is responsible for printing reports, while there are two staff members who handle both accounts payable and accounts receivable transactions.

REQUIRED

Using the internal control letter format discussed in the chapter (weakness, implication, and recommendation) outline the following:

1. Identify the weaknesses in segregation of duties for each application cycle: payroll, accounts receivable, and accounts payable.
2. State the implication of each weakness (what could go wrong).
3. Make recommendation(s) of some of the practical changes that can be made at this company to improve internal controls.

9-33 **3** As highlighted in Auditing in Action 9-3, the 2016 survey of the International Forum of Independent Audit Regulators found that internal control testing is consistently an area where audit work is deficient, and Canada is no exception. Access the CPAB (Canadian Public Accountability Board) website at **www.cpab-ccrc.ca** and locate the 2013 Public Report (follow the link "news & publications" and then select "reports"). Review "Section Three–2013 Inspections" of the report and locate commentary on "Audit work on internal controls."

REQUIRED

Review the commentary and provide support for your answer to the following questions:

a. Why must control testing cover the entire period in order for the auditor to reach the conclusion that a control is effective?
b. Why are sign-off signature and inquiry considered to be insufficient evidence to demonstrate that controls are effective?
c. What would constitute stronger evidence than sign-off signature and inquiry? Explain why.

DEVELOP RISK RESPONSE: AUDIT STRATEGY AND AUDIT PROGRAM

STANDARDS REFERENCED IN THIS CHAPTER

CAS 240 – The auditor's responsibilities relating to fraud in an audit of financial statements

CAS 300 – Planning an audit of financial statements

CAS 330 – The auditor's responses to assessed risks

CAS 520 – Analytical procedures

There are so many different types of businesses—how can there be a common approach to the financial statement audit? The financial statement auditor must carefully plan his or her strategy, identifying the risks involved with the client and developing an audit approach to complete the engagement.

LEARNING OBJECTIVES

After studying this chapter, you should be able to:

1 Explain and develop an overall audit strategy based upon assessed risks.

2 Use the five types of audit tests to determine whether the financial statements are fairly stated.

3 Select the appropriate types of audit tests.

4 Develop an appropriate evidence mix based upon audit strategy.

5 Design an audit program.

6 Integrate the different components of the audit process.

The Impact of Client Technology on Audit Strategy

Jared and Gabrielle were comparing notes on two of their clients. Jared's client was implementing new enterprise-wide resource software (ERP). ERP, which re-engineers multiple, traditionally separate (cross-functional) processes into a single transactional process connected to a single database, has great potential to improve the efficiency of the financial statement audit. In order to take advantage of these potential improved efficiencies, the auditor must be aware of the increased control and inherent risks that are found in the adoption of an ERP system.

Unfortunately, in the case of Jared's client, the implementation was not managed well. There was a programming error in the new implementation that resulted in work-in-progress work orders being set to zero at the time of the conversion. Although new orders were handled properly, about 3000 jobs were affected. These were noticed about two weeks after the conversion, as billing cycles were concluded and inventory-to-job-cost reconciliations went out of whack. Investigation of data errors and review of account reconciliations after the software conversion at Jared's client meant that the client's year-end financial statement results were delayed by almost two months.

continued >

Jared and his staff spent numerous hours reviewing data conversion plans with the client and helped compare information that was transferred from the old computer systems to the new data. In the end, the client incurred $2 million in additional costs and included a material control weakness in its certification of internal controls report. It was also late filing its reports with the Ontario Securities Commission, which resulted in suspended trading of its shares for a month and threatened delisting of its stock.

In contrast, Gabrielle's client, a clothing manufacturer, had implemented a mass customization process for its individual and retail customers. The client had purchased software and hardware that enabled the linking of orders to the production system and also reduced inventory of work in progress and finished goods by streamlining the link between ordering, production, and shipping. The client found that customer loyalty for customized work was very high.

Gabrielle enthused about her client's new systems: "My client is finally starting to make some money on its line of custom-made skirts and pants. Inventory was individually tracked, and the new information systems were found to be reliable and robust. Because of that, we were able to assess control risk at low and perform fewer substantive tests. In addition, because the change in the system caused a significant reduction in the year-end inventory balance, we had to use only two staff members on the inventory count. Although we now spend more time testing controls than in the past, the overall impact is a 30 percent reduction in the fieldwork on inventory."

Sources: Based on Julie Schlosser, "A handful of companies are finally perfecting made-to-order for the masses. Here's how," *Fortune*, December 13, 2004. R.K. Rainer, Jr., C.G. Cegielski, I. Splettstoesser-Hogeterp, and C. Sanchez-Rodriguez, *Introduction to Information Systems*, John Wiley & Sons Canada, 2011. Marc L. Songini, "Bungled ERP installation whacks Asyst," *Computerworld*, vol. 39, no. 2, 2005.

As the two examples in the opening vignette highlight, changes in the client's technology related to business processes can have a profound impact on audit strategy. Changes in the control environment (such as management turnover), or in business risks (such as unexpected declines in sales), would also impact the type of audit strategy that the auditor develops.

This chapter explains how the auditor integrates all the evidence gathered through audit planning and assessing risk of material misstatement to develop an overall audit strategy, which will result in an effective and efficient audit. It then revisits the audit risk model and examines how the auditor develops a strategy for each transaction cycle. This topic includes discussion of the trade-offs among the types of tests, including the cost of each type. After deciding on the most cost-effective mix of types of tests, the auditor designs a detailed audit program.

Overall audit strategy—the scope, timing, and direction of the audit, which guides the development of the audit plan.

Combined audit strategy—a strategy for auditing financial statement assertions in which the auditor evaluates control risk below maximum and obtains the audit evidence required by using tests of controls and substantive tests.

AUDIT STRATEGY

As introduced in Chapter 6, the auditor develops an **overall audit strategy**, as well as a strategy (or approach) for classes of transactions, balances, presentation and disclosures, and the related assertions. Recall from Chapter 9 that the auditor may use either a **combined audit strategy** (or approach), where the auditor plans to rely upon controls, or a **substantive audit strategy**, when the auditor does not plan to rely upon controls, for testing the assertions for the various accounts and disclosures.

CAS 300 explains that the overall audit strategy guides the development of the audit plan. When developing the overall audit strategy, CAS 300 explains that the auditor should:

- *Identify the characteristics of the engagement that define its scope.* Some audit engagements have specific characteristics that increase the scope of the audit. For example, if the client is a multinational company, the scope would be much wider than for our client, Hillsburg Hardware Limited. Other factors to take into

LO 1 Explain and develop an overall audit strategy based upon assessed risks.

Substantive audit strategy—a strategy for auditing financial statement assertions in which the auditor evaluates control risk at maximum and obtains the audit evidence required by using substantive tests.

consideration (which we discussed in Chapter 6) are whether the auditor can use the work of the internal auditor, or if there is a need to use an IT specialist. You will note that, in the Hillsburg audit strategy memo (Figure 10-1), Leslie has indicated the need for an IT specialist.

- *Determine the reporting requirements.* Reporting requirements will vary from audit to audit. For example, there are particular reporting requirements and deadlines for public companies and, as we have discussed in Chapter 9, if the company is listed on an American stock exchange, such as the New York Stock Exchange, the auditor must report on the effectiveness of internal controls. There may be industry requirements as well. Other communications, such as liaison with subsidiary or parent auditors (depending upon the auditor's role) and communications to management and to those charged with governance, need to be considered as well.

- *Consider the factors that are significant in directing the audit team's efforts.* The strategy must consider issues to do with quality control, such as how resources are managed, directed, and supervised; when team briefing and debriefing meetings are expected to be held; how engagement partner and manager reviews are expected to take place; and the engagement quality control reviews that are needed.

- *Consider the results of preliminary engagement activities.* This refers to the risks identified in the risk assessment stage (including fraud risks and significant events that have occurred since the last audit), and results of previous audits—which includes the evaluation of the operating effectiveness of internal control (including the nature of identified deficiencies and actions taken to address them) and prior misstatements. The auditor's determination of materiality (overall, performance, and specific) is considered as well.

- *Determine the nature, timing, and extent of resources necessary to perform the engagement.* One of the main objectives of developing an audit strategy is to effectively allocate resources to the audit team, such as the use of specialists on particular areas (say, an actuary for the pension valuation), or using a team of highly experienced auditors for a potentially high-risk audit engagement (as we saw in the excerpts from the Livent (Auditing in Action 4-3) and Enron planning memos (Auditing in Action 6-1). If there is a tight deadline, then more resources will be needed to ensure that all the necessary audit work is completed and can be reviewed in time to meet the deadline.

Developing an Overall Audit Strategy at Hillsburg Hardware Limited

In this section, we will use our client, Hillsburg Hardware Limited, to describe how the audit team developed an overall audit strategy. We include excerpts from the *Audit Strategy Memo* (Figure 10-1) as well as two other working papers that provide input for the *Audit Strategy Memo:* Understanding the Entity (Figure 10-2), and *Audit Team Planning Meeting Notes* (Figure 10-3).

You will note that the audit strategy memo provides the "roadmap" for the Hillsburg audit, and it will form the basis for the more detailed audit plan. Much of the information used in developing the overall audit strategy is derived from understanding the entity and its environment and internal control (which we discussed in Chapters 6 and 9). To help better understand how the auditors performed their analysis, refer to the Appendix at the end of the book, which provides a more detailed background on the company and its accounting policies.

As the documentation for Understanding the Entity (Figure 10-2) highlights, the key outcome is to identify the risk of material misstatement at both the financial statement level and the assertion level. As discussed in Chapter 9, in order to assess the risk of material misstatement at the financial statement level, the auditor will consider entity-level controls. For risks at the assertion level, the auditor will identify

| Figure 10-1 | *Audit Strategy Memo—Hillsburg Hardware Limited* |

Client: Hillsburg Hardware Limited
Year-End: December 31, 2018

Characteristics

A private company: majority shareholder is an investment company, and minority (inactive) shareholder is Hillsburg family. Working capital is funded through line of credit. Also has long-term debt.

Timing of Reporting

Year-end is December 31.

Audit fieldwork—see timetable below.

Partner to meet with board in February to discuss results and sign audit report.

Significant Factors

Materiality

Overall materiality. $441 000 (see Figure 6-7)

Performance materiality. $331 000 (see Figure 6-7)

Lower levels of materiality for specific items. $265 000 for accounts receivable and inventory

Internal Control

- No past history of management override of controls. Audit team members will be briefed to remain alert for this risk.
- Management and the board's attitude toward internal control is very positive.
- During the current year, a major change has occurred. The chief accountant left the company and has been replaced by Erma Swanson, who is a qualified CPA with industry experience.
- There has also been some turnover of other accounting personnel. The overall assessment by management is that the accounting personnel are reasonably competent and highly trustworthy.
- Areas where substantive testing will be insufficient and tests of controls are required:
  - Order entry processing
  - Electronic data interchange (EDI) transactions
  - Automated payments
- There are particular controls that we plan to rely on (these are documented in the relevant sections of the audit file).

Results of Previous Audit

No matters were identified during the previous audit to suggest a significant change in audit approach is needed.

Developments in Business

The audit manager held a preliminary meeting with management in June. The purpose of this meeting was to:
  - Discuss the nature, timing, and extent of the audit work
  - Enquire whether there have been any developments in the business since the last audit that may impact the audit in the current period.

There have been no significant changes in the business since the last audit and no changes in the client's staff. This industry is suffering as consumers and businesses cut back on discretionary purchases, but the company has adequate plans of actions and strategies to deal with potentially declining revenue.

Risk Assessment Procedures Performed

A preliminary analytical review of the projected December 31, 2018, accounts was carried out. Hillsburg's sales have increased significantly over the prior period. Costs of goods sold, sales salaries, and commission have also increased but are fairly consistent as a percent of sales. Advertising expense has increased as a percent of sales; however, Hillsburg has developed a new advertising campaign. Repairs and maintenance have also increased. Although there have not been issues in the past, additional work is needed to ensure that there are not any amounts which should be capitalized.

The significant risks are:
  - Valuation of accounts receivable
  - Valuation of inventory

Further details on these risks and other matters giving rise to significant risks and how they are addressed are documented in Figure 10-3.

(continued)

Figure 10-1	(Continued)

Nature, Timing, and Extent of Resources Allocated

Partner: Joe Anthony
Manager: Leslie Nagan
Senior: Fran Moore
Assistants: Mitch Bray and one person to be assigned later.

Note: We will include an information systems audit specialist on the audit team to assist with the documentation and evaluation of general and application controls.

Audit Timetable

Risk Assessment	Amend audit strategy. Update understanding of internal controls. Prepare audit programs.	10-31-18
Risk Response	Perform tests of controls. Confirm accounts receivable. Observe inventory. Perform cut-off tests. Request various other confirmations. Perform analytical procedures. Complete tests of controls and substantive tests.	11-15-18 12-31-18 Balance sheet date 1-7-19 Books closed 3-1-19 to 3-15-19 Perform fieldwork
Completion and Review	Perform procedures to support presentation and disclosure assertions, summarize results, and accumulate final evidence (including analytical procedures). Initiate manager and partner review.	3-15-19 Last day of fieldwork
Reporting	Report audit findings to those in charge of governance. Hold final meeting with board for approval. Sign and audit report.	3-25-19

Prepared by: *Leslie Nagan* (Manager)
Approved by: *Joe Anthony* (Partner)

Figure 10-2	Excerpts From Documentation of Understanding the Entity—Hillsburg Hardware Limited

Client: Hillsburg Hardware Limited
Year End: December 31, 2018

Objective: To obtain an understanding of the entity and its environment sufficient to assess the risks of material misstatement of the financial statements.

Method: Review notes from prior year audit, make enquiries of management (CFO and CEO), review the following: recent industry press, previous year's annual report, and preliminary unaudited financial statements, and calculate key ratios and common-size financial statements.

Information Sources: Permanent file, industry publications and industry data reports, online search of industry and competitors, company website (accessed June 16, 2018).

Nature of Entity
Hillsburg Hardware is a wholesale distributor of hardware equipment to a variety of independent hardware stores in Atlantic Canada. The primary products are power and hand tools, landscaping equipment, electrical equipment, residential and commercial construction equipment, and a wide selection of paint products.

Industry, Regulatory, and External Environment
As a hardware wholesaler, Hillsburg would compete with other wholesalers hardware retailers that offer discounts to commercial purchasers (such as Home Depot and Lowes).

Ownership and Governance
The company is a private company owned by an investment company and the Hillsburg family.

Management is competent and committed to a good control environment. The president, Rick Chulick, has been the chief operating officer for approximately 10 years. He is regarded as a highly competent, honest individual who does a conscientious job.

There is a code of ethics, which employees sign and acknowledge each year. The company has a third party manage the whistleblower hotline and customer complaints.

Hillsburg has an active audit committee and a board that meets regularly. The board conducts a risk assessment (including fraud risk assessment), which is evaluated by the executive management team at a semi-annual day-long retreat. The result of this retreat is incorporated into a risk assessment evaluation and plan that is discussed with the whole board at its quarterly meeting. Each functional area is expected to contribute to the annual strategic plan, which is similarly discussed with the board.

The information systems department participates in the strategic planning exercises to ensure that computing plans address business needs and that technology capabilities are considered during the planning process.

There are no related-party transactions.

Operations and Processes

Organizational structure and financing
The company is a private company, the majority shareholder is an investment company, Wilkshaw Capital, and the minority shareholder is the Hillsburg Family. It also has short-term and long-term debt with a bank.

Accounting Policies
Hillsburg Hardware follows ASPE.

Objectives and Strategies
The operations have remained unchanged for a number of years; it upgraded its IT systems two years ago. The company has plans for actions and strategies to deal with threats from competitors: the company has brought in customer incentives, as well as the ONHAND system, which has been effective at increasing repeat customers.

Measurement and Review of Financial Performance
Management carefully reviews controls and financial results. Key performance indicators include net sales, gross margins, inventory turn-over, and repeat customers.

Impact on Audit—Risks of Material Misstatement

At the Financial Statement Level
No pervasive risks of material misstatement have been identified. The assessment of risk at the financial statement level is low.

At the Assertion Level
Primary areas where judgment is required:
Accounts receivable (valuation)—moderate risk of material misstatement
Inventory (valuation)—moderate risk of material misstatement

Areas Where Errors Were Noted in the Past Audit:
Revenue (cutoff)—moderate risk of material misstatement
Inventory (existence and cutoff)—moderate risk of material misstatement

and assess the relevant controls that mitigate those risks (as illustrated with the control matrix in Chapter 9). Although the analysis presented is not performed at the level of detail necessary to develop tests of controls, the excerpts from the Audit Planning Memo (Figure 10-3) provide an example of the partner evaluating the impact of the controls for vendor rebates and customer refunds, and developing an appropriate risk response for each of these significant risks. Factors that the auditor will consider if the risk is significant are the complexity of the accounting rules (GAAP), the extent of estimation and judgment involved in the valuation of the particular financial statement item, and the introduction of new accounting standards. The audit team planning meeting also considers another significant risk—the risk of fraud (this is one of the fraud risk assessment procedures highlighted in Chapter 7), which is required for all audits. In the case of vendor rebates and customer refunds there is estimation uncertainty as well, as these are both areas that typically have a higher fraud risk for companies such as Hillsburg (a wholesaler).

Figure 10-3	Excerpts From *Audit Team Planning Meeting Notes*— Hillsburg Hardware Limited

Summary of Audit Team Planning Meeting

Client: Hillsburg Hardware Limited
Year-End: December 31, 2018
Date of Meeting: September 14, 2018

Persons in Attendance:
Joe Anthony (Partner)
Leslie Nagan (Manager)
Fran Moore (Senior)
Mitch Bray (Audit assistant)

1. Susceptibility of financial statements to material misstatements due to fraud

a) Team discussion of any known external or internal factors that might result in fraud

Presumed risk of management override of control; risk of revenue recognition fraud (per CAS 240). Risk is considered moderate for customer refunds. (Note that this is a high-risk fraud area in the retail industry, but the good quality controls at Hillsburg lowered fraud risk to moderate.) Low for all other transaction areas except for customer refunds (where it is moderate).

b) Team response to assess risks of material misstatement due to fraud including any additional work required.

Required significant areas of revenue recognition and journal entries to be tested.
Required procedures for management override (per CAS 240)
  • *Testing of journal entries*
  • *Perform retrospective review of estimates*
Tests of controls and tests of details will be performed for customer refunds

2. Susceptibility of financial statements to material misstatement due to error

a) Team discussion of any known external or internal factors that might result in error

Risks of material misstatement for accounts receivable valuation and cutoff, revenue cutoff, and inventory valuation, existence, and accuracy are moderate.
All other areas' risk of material misstatement are low.

b) Team response to assess risks of material misstatement due to error including any additional work required

Will use historical and current data available to assess allowance for doubtful accounts and for inventory valuation. Lower performance materiality for revenue and inventory to address past cut-off and inventory count errors.

3. Overall conclusion on risks of material misstatement at the financial statement level and specific risks of material misstatement and risk

Specific risks of material misstatement and responses are noted above and have been recorded in risk assessment working papers. There is limited risk of material misstatement at the financial statement level as the business is well controlled, and there are no related parties.

Signed by: Joe Anthony (Partner)   Date: September 14, 2018

Audit Strategy, Audit Plan, and Audit Tests

The overall audit strategy, or the general overview of the audit, provides the basis for the audit plan. CAS 300 explains that the audit plan is more detailed than the overall audit strategy in that it includes the nature, timing, and extent of audit procedures to be performed by engagement team members. The audit plan includes the following:

• The nature, timing, and extent of the risk assessment procedures; and
• The nature, timing, and extent of further audit procedures at the assertion level.

So far, in Chapters 6, 7, and 9, we have covered the risk assessment procedures; we now consider the process to design further audit procedures that will address the risks at the assertion level. We will also discuss the type and mix of audit tests that are performed. We first highlight those procedures that are required for all clients, regardless of the entity's specific circumstances.

Financial Closing The period-end financial reporting process includes procedures to:

- Enter transactions totals into the general ledger;
- Select and apply accounting policies;
- Initiate, authorize, record, and process journal entries into the general ledger; and
- Record recurring and nonrecurring adjustments to the financial statements.

Regardless of the audit strategy, per CAS 330, the auditor is required to perform the following procedures related to the financial statement closing process: `CAS`

- Agree or reconcile the financial statements with the underlying accounting records; and
- Examine material journal entries and other adjustments made during the course of preparing the financial statements.

Fraud Risks Although the auditor develops audit tests based upon the risk assessment, `CAS` as we discussed in Chapter 7, CAS 240 requires, as part of the fraud risk assessment, that the auditor presume that the risk of management override is present at all entities and requires the performance of specific procedures (see page 223) to address this presumed risk. In addition, as highlighted in Chapter 7, auditors are expected to perform procedures to address the risk of revenue recognition fraud. Auditing in Action 10-1 provides an excerpt from the auditors' reports for Hilton Food Group plc, a UK-based international retail meat packing company with operations in the UK, Europe, and Australia. PricewaterhouseCoopers explains its responsibilities with regard to these two risks and its risk responses to the two risks.

AUDITING IN ACTION 10-1
Significant Risks at Hilton Food Group plc

In its auditor's report for the year ended December 31, 2013, PricewaterhouseCoopers LLP identified fraud in revenue recognition and management override as two significant risks. Below is PWC's explanation as to why revenue recognition and management override are both significant fraud risks, and PWC's risk response.

Area of Particular Focus	Risk Response
Fraud in revenue recognition ISAs (UK & Ireland)[1] presume that there is a risk of fraud in revenue recognition because of the pressure management may feel to achieve the planned results.	• We focused on the amount and timing of the recognition of revenue, particularly where the contractual customer terms provide for "cost plus" pricing or discounts, which are calculated by management. • We tested revenue by verifying it against supporting documentation, including customer contracts, discounts and incentives, and cash receipts. • We also tested journal entries posted to revenue accounts by identifying and challenging unusual or irregular items.
Management override ISAs (UK & Ireland) require that we consider this.	• We assessed the overall control environment of the Group, including the arrangements for staff to "whistle-blow" inappropriate actions, and interviewed senior management and the Group's internal audit function. • We examined the significant accounting estimates and judgments relevant to the financial statements for evidence of bias by the Directors[2] that may represent a risk of material misstatement due to fraud. In particular, we challenged the estimates in respect to the cost plus revenue adjustments and customer rebates. • We also tested journal entries.

[1] ISAs (UK & Ireland) are those countries' auditing standards. The auditor fraud responsibilities are consistent with CAS 240.

[2] In the UK, the term *Directors* refers to management, not board of directors.

Source: Hilton Food Group plc, *Annual Report and Financial Statements, 2013,* **http://www.hiltonfoodgroupplc.com/financial-reports-2013**.

TYPES OF TESTS

Auditors use five types of tests to determine whether financial statements are fairly stated: (1) risk assessment procedures, (2) tests of controls, (3) substantive tests of transactions, (4) substantive analytical procedures, and (5) substantive tests of balances. Auditors use risk assessment procedures to assess the risk of material misstatement, represented by the combination of inherent risk and control risk as described in Chapters 6, 7, and 9. The other four types of tests represent **further audit procedures** performed in response to the risks identified. Each audit procedure falls into one, and sometimes more than one, of these five categories.

Further audit procedures—the auditor's risk response at the assertion level, which is a combination of tests of controls, substantive tests of transactions, analytical procedures, and substantive tests of balances performed.

Figure 10-4 shows the relationship of the four types of further audit procedures to the audit risk model. As Figure 10-4 illustrates, tests of controls are performed to support the reduced assessment of control risk, while auditors use substantive analytical procedures and substantive tests of balances to satisfy planned detection risk. Substantive tests of transactions affect both control risk and planned detection risk, because they test the effectiveness of controls (if used as part of control testing) and the dollar amount of transactions.

Risk Assessment Procedures

Risk assessment procedures—procedures used to assess the likelihood of material misstatement (inherent risk plus control risk) in the financial statements.

Collectively, the procedures performed to obtain an understanding of the entity and its environment, including fraud risk and internal controls, represent the auditor's **risk assessment procedures**. These procedures are used to assess the likelihood of material misstatement (inherent risk plus control risk) in the financial statements. Chapter 6 discussed how the auditor performs procedures to understand the entity and its environment, and Chapter 7 further described how auditors perform procedures to assess inherent risk and fraud risk, while Chapter 9 illustrated how auditors undertake **procedures to obtain an understanding of internal control** to assess control risk. You will note in Figure 10-2 a brief summary of the risk assessment procedure performed (in the Method section) for Hillsburg Hardware.

Procedures used to obtain an understanding of internal control—procedures used by the auditor to gather evidence about the design and implementation of specific controls.

Tests of Controls

Tests of controls—audit procedures to test the effectiveness of controls in support of a reduced assessed control risk.

The auditor's understanding of internal control is acquired in order to assess control risk for each transaction-related audit objective. When control policies and procedures are believed to be effectively designed and where it is efficient to do so, the auditor will choose to assess control risk at a level (either moderate or low) that reflects that evaluation. To obtain sufficient appropriate evidence to support that assessment, the auditor performs **tests of controls**.

Tests of controls, either manual or automated, may include the following types of procedures: (1) make inquiries of appropriate client personnel, (2) examine

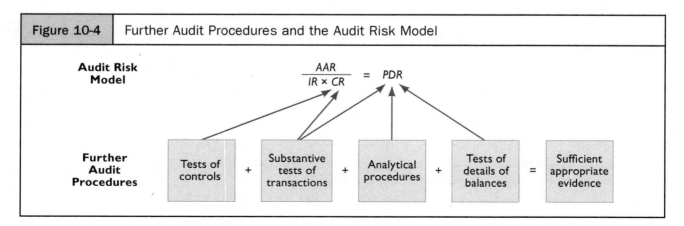

| Figure 10-4 | Further Audit Procedures and the Audit Risk Model |

documents, records, and reports, (3) observe control-related activities, and (4) reperform client procedures.

As discussed in Chapter 9, procedures to obtain an understanding of internal control generally do not provide sufficient evidence that a control is operating effectively. Tests of controls are used to determine whether these controls are effective, and manual controls usually involve testing a sample of transactions. For example, as a test of operating effectiveness of the credit approval process, the audit might examine a sample of 50 sales transactions from throughout the year to determine whether credit was granted before shipment of goods.

For automated controls, the auditor's procedures to determine whether the automated control has been implemented may serve as a test of that control, if the auditor determines that general controls are effective and there is minimal risk that the automated control has changed since the understanding was obtained. Then, no additional tests of control are required.

To illustrate typical tests of controls, it is useful to use the control risk matrix for Hillsburg Hardware Limited in Figure 9-5. For the first 11 controls included in Figure 9-5, tests of controls can be developed. However, for the last two controls, no test of controls will be developed. Since the purpose of tests of controls is to provide evidence that the control is in operation and is effectively addressing the relevant risk, it would make no sense to determine if the absence of a control is being adequately performed.

Substantive Tests

A substantive test is a procedure designed to test for dollar misstatements (due either to errors or to fraud) that directly affect the correctness of financial statement balances. Per CAS 330, substantive procedures consist of:

CAS

- Substantive analytical procedures; and
- Tests of details (which are substantive tests of transactions and substantive tests of balances).

Substantive tests of transactions and balances are often referred to as tests of details since the auditor is obtaining evidence to support the details of an individual transaction (e.g., selecting a sample of sales invoices and agreeing the details with shipping documents) or of an account balance (e.g., selecting a sample of individual account receivable balances and confirming the details with the customers).

Per CAS 330, substantive procedures must be performed for:

- Each material class of transactions, account balance, and disclosure (regardless of the assessed risk of material misstatement); and
- Each significant risk at the assertion level. When the approach to a significant risk consists only of substantive procedures, those procedures shall include tests of details. (Meaning that substantive analytical procedures are not considered sufficient and appropriate evidence.)

As discussed earlier and in Chapter 7, the auditor must assume that revenue recognition is a significant risk; this means that revenue recognition substantive testing (through tests of details) will normally be conducted, regardless of the quality of controls.

Substantive Tests of Transactions Auditors use **substantive tests of transactions** to test the five transaction-related assertions: occurrence, completeness, accuracy, cutoff, and classification. A substantive test of transaction is a test of the accounting system and is normally designed to test for monetary errors. When auditors are confident that all transactions are recorded in the journals and correctly posted, considering all five transaction-related assertions, they are confident that the general ledger totals are correct.

Substantive tests of transactions—audit procedures designed to test for dollar (monetary) misstatements in each class of transactions.

Examples of tests of transactions include the following: (1) select a sample of entries recorded in the cash disbursements journal to determine if valid (the occurrence assertion) by examining supporting documents, or (2) extend the sales prices and units on sales invoices to determine if the amounts are correct (the accuracy assertion). Auditors can perform tests of controls separately from all other tests, but it's more efficient to do them at the same time as substantive tests of transactions. These are referred to as **dual-purpose tests**. For example, auditors can usually apply tests of controls involving inspection and reperformance to the same transactions tested for monetary misstatements. (Reperformance simultaneously provides evidence about both controls and monetary correctness.) In the rest of the book, when the auditor is relying upon controls, we will assume tests of controls and substantive tests of transactions are done at the same time. In the case when the auditor is not relying upon controls, the auditor will perform substantive tests of transactions only (along with substantive tests of balances).

Substantive Analytical Procedures As we discussed in Chapter 5, **analytical procedures** involve comparisons of recorded amounts to expectations developed by the auditor. Auditing standards require that such comparisons be done during the planning and completion of the audit. Although not required, analytical procedures may also be performed to audit an account balance (these are **substantive analytical procedures**). Two of the most important purposes of such substantive analytical procedures in the audit of account balances are to:

1. Indicate possible misstatements; and
2. Provide substantive evidence.

Analytical procedures performed during planning typically differ from those done in the risk response phase. Even if, for example, auditors calculate the gross margin during planning, they probably do it using interim data. Later, during the tests of the ending balances, they will recalculate the ratio using full-year data. If auditors believe that analytical procedures indicate a reasonable possibility of misstatement, they may perform additional analytical procedures or decide to modify tests of details of balances.

When the auditor develops expectations using substantive analytical procedures and concludes that the client's ending balances in certain accounts appear reasonable, certain tests of details of balances may be eliminated or sample sizes reduced. As highlighted in CAS 520, *Analytical procedures*, the extent to which auditors rely on substantive analytical procedures in support of an account balance depends upon several factors, including the quality of internal controls, the precision of the expectation developed by the auditor, performance materiality, and the risk of material misstatement.

Substantive Tests of Balances **Substantive tests of balances** focus on the ending general ledger balances for both balance sheet and income statement accounts, and help to establish monetary correctness. The primary emphasis of most tests of details of balances is on the balance sheet. Examples include confirmation of customers' balances for accounts receivable, physical examination of inventory, and examination of vendors' statements for accounts payable. These tests of ending balances are essential because the evidence is often obtained from a source independent of the client, and such a source is considered to be highly reliable. These tests of details focus on the balance-related assertions. The extent of these tests depends on the results of controls and analytical procedures.

CONCEPT CHECK

C10-1 How is the audit strategy linked to the audit risk assessment processes?
C10-2 Explain the purpose of the five types of audit tests.

Dual-purpose tests—auditing procedures that are both tests of controls and substantive procedures on the same sample of transactions or account balances for efficiency.

Analytical procedures—evaluations of financial information through analysis of plausible relationships among financial and nonfinancial data.

Substantive analytical procedures—an analytical procedure in which the auditor develops an expectation of recorded amounts or ratios to provide evidence supporting an account balance.

CAS

Substantive tests of balances—audit procedures testing for monetary errors or fraud and other irregularities to determine whether the five balance-related audit objectives have been satisfied for each significant account balance.

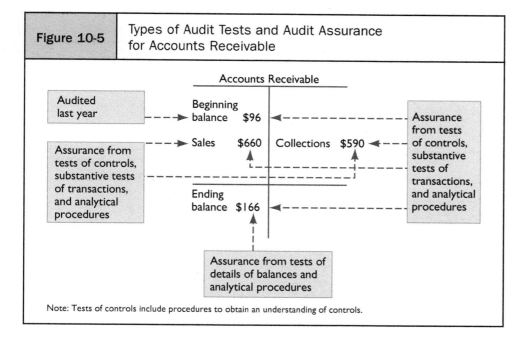

Figure 10-5	Types of Audit Tests and Audit Assurance for Accounts Receivable

Note: Tests of controls include procedures to obtain an understanding of controls.

Summary of Types of Tests

Figure 10-5 illustrates how auditors perform their risk response, using four types of further audit procedures, to obtain assurance over accounts receivable. Tests of controls are used to determine whether the controls over the two classes of transactions—sales and collections—are sufficiently effective to support the reduced assessment of control risk, and thereby allow reduced substantive testing. Substantive tests of transactions are used to verify transactions recorded in the journals and posted in the general ledger. Analytical procedures emphasize the overall reasonableness of transactions and the general ledger balances. Substantive tests of details of balances emphasize the ending balance in the general ledger.

By combining the types of audit tests shown in Figure 10-5, the auditor obtains a higher level for assurance for the accounts receivable balance than the assurance obtained from any one test.

SELECTING WHICH TYPES OF TESTS TO PERFORM

LO 3 Select the appropriate types of audit tests.

Several factors influence the auditor's choice of the types of test to select, including the availability of evidence; relative costs; relationships between tests of controls and substantive tests, and analytical procedures and substantive tests; and the trade-off between tests of controls and substantive tests.

Types of Evidence for Further Audit Procedures

Table 10-1 summarizes the relationship between further audit procedures and type of evidence. We can make several observations about the table:

- More types of evidence are used for tests of details of balances than any other type of test.
- Only substantive tests of details of balances involve physical examination and confirmation.
- Inquiries of the client are made for every type of test.
- Inspection, reperformance, and recalculation are used for every type of test except analytical procedures.

| Table 10-1 | Relationship Between Further Audit Procedures and Evidence |

	Type of Evidence						
Type of Test	**Inspection**	**Observation**	**Inquiries of the Client**	**External Confirmation**	**Recalculation**	**Reperformance**	**Analytical Procedures**
Tests of controls (including procedures to obtain an understanding of internal control)	✓	✓	✓		✓	✓	
Substantive tests of transactions	✓		✓		✓	✓	
Analytical procedures			✓				✓
Substantive tests of balances	✓		✓	✓	✓	✓	

Relative Costs

The following types of tests are listed in order of increasing cost:

- Analytical procedures
- Risk assessment procedures, including procedures to obtain an understanding of internal control
- Tests of controls
- Substantive tests of transactions
- Substantive tests of balances

Analytical procedures are least costly because of the relative ease of making calculations and comparisons. Often, considerable information about potential misstatements can be obtained by simply comparing two or three numbers and looking for unusual relationships. Tests of controls are also low in cost because the auditor is making inquiries and observations, examining such things as initials on documents and outward indications of other control procedures, and conducting reperformances, recalculations, and tracings. Frequently, tests of controls can be done on a large number of items in a few minutes, especially if computer-based work, such as the use of test data, is included. Further, controls that have been tested in previous years can be tested every three years, provided no significant changes have been made. This can further enhance audit efficiency.

Substantive tests of details of balances are almost always considerably more costly than any of the other types of procedures. Given the involvement of the auditor, it is costly to send confirmations and to count assets. Because of the high cost of substantive tests of details of balances, auditors usually try to plan the audit to minimize their use, focusing these tests upon high-risk and material balances. Naturally, the cost of each type of evidence varies in different situations. For example, the cost of an auditor's test counting of inventory (a substantive test of the details of the inventory balance) frequently depends on the nature and dollar value of the inventory, its location, and the number of different items.

Relationship Between Tests of Controls and Substantive Tests

To better understand tests of controls and substantive tests, let's examine how they differ. An exception in a test of control only *indicates* the likelihood of misstatements affecting the dollar value of the financial statements, whereas an exception in a substantive test of transactions or balance is a financial statement misstatement. Exceptions in tests of controls are called *control test deviations*. From Chapter 9, recall that there are three levels of control deficiencies: deficiencies, significant deficiencies, and material weaknesses. Auditors are most likely to believe material dollar misstatements exist in the financial statements when control test deviations are considered to be significant deficiencies or material weaknesses. However, at this point, the auditor cannot quantify the actual misstatement and, therefore, does not know if a material misstatement has actually occurred. This can only be achieved through performing substantive tests of transactions or balances.

Assume that the client's controls require an independent clerk to verify the quantity, price, and extension of each sales invoice, after which the clerk must initial the duplicate invoice to indicate performance. One control test is to inspect a sample of duplicate sales invoices for the initials of the person who verified the information. If a significant number of documents lack initials, the auditor should follow up with substantive tests. This can be done by extending tests of duplicate sales invoices to include verifying prices, extensions, and footings (substantive tests of transactions), or by increasing the sample size for the confirmation of accounts receivable (substantive test of balances). Even though the control is not operating effectively, the invoices may still be correct, especially if the person originally preparing the sales invoices did a conscientious and competent job.

These extra substantive tests are only necessary if the control test determines that the control is ineffective—that is, in this example, if a significant number of documents lack initials. If no documents or only a few of them are missing initials, the control will be considered effective and the auditor can therefore reduce substantive tests of transactions and tests of details of balances. However, some substantive tests of transactions, such as reperformance and recalculation, are still necessary to reassure the auditor that the clerk did not initial documents without actually performing the control procedure or did not perform it carelessly. Because of the need to complete some reperformance and recalculation tests, many auditors perform them as a part of the original tests of controls. These are referred to as dual tests. Others wait until they know the results of the tests of controls and then determine the total sample size needed.

Relationship Between Substantive Analytical Procedures and Other Substantive Tests

Like tests of controls, analytical procedures only *indicate* the likelihood of misstatements affecting the dollar value of the financial statements. Unusual fluctuations in the relationships of an account to other accounts, or to nonfinancial information, may indicate an increased likelihood that material misstatements exist without necessarily providing direct evidence of a material misstatement. When analytical procedures identify unusual fluctuations, auditors should perform substantive tests of transactions or of balances to determine whether dollar misstatements have actually occurred.

If the auditor performs substantive analytical procedures and believes that the likelihood of material misstatement is low, other substantive tests can be reduced. For accounts with small balances and only minimal potential for material misstatements, such as many supplies and prepaid expense accounts, auditors often limit their tests to substantive analytical procedures if they conclude the accounts are reasonably stated.

Trade-Off Between Tests of Controls and Substantive Tests

As explained in Chapter 9, there is a trade-off between tests of controls and substantive tests. The auditor makes a decision while planning the control risk assessment: if control risk is assessed as high, the auditor would follow a substantive approach; if control risk is assessed lower, the auditor could follow a combined approach. Tests of controls must be performed to determine whether the lower assessed control risk is supported. If it is, planned detection risk in the audit risk model is increased and substantive procedures can therefore be reduced. If the control testing reveals that the controls are not functioning, or it is very costly to test internal controls, the auditor may still end up with a substantive approach. Figure 10-6 shows the relationship between substantive

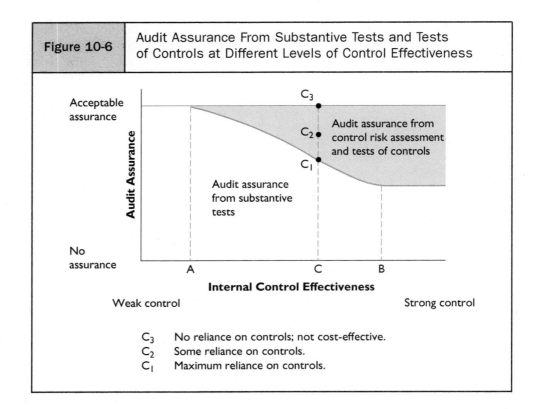

Figure 10-6 Audit Assurance From Substantive Tests and Tests of Controls at Different Levels of Control Effectiveness

C$_3$ No reliance on controls; not cost-effective.
C$_2$ Some reliance on controls.
C$_1$ Maximum reliance on controls.

tests and control risk assessment (including tests of controls) at differing levels of internal control effectiveness.

The shaded area in Figure 10-6 is the maximum assurance obtainable from control risk assessment and tests of controls. For example, at any point to the left of point A, assessed control risk is 1.0 because the auditor evaluates internal control as ineffective. Remember that auditing standards require that the auditor always understand internal controls as part of the audit planning process. At a large organization such as a bank or technology manufacturer, if controls are not reliable, the auditor may not be able to conduct an effective audit. It will be almost impossible to do a substantive audit of an organization that processes hundreds of thousands of transactions (or more) daily.

Any point to the right of point B results in no further reduction of control risk because the public accounting firm has established the minimum assessed control risk that it will permit.

After the auditor determines the effectiveness of the client's internal controls, it is appropriate to select any point within the shaded area (that is, between A and B) of Figure 10-6 consistent with the level of control risk that the auditor determines is appropriate. To illustrate, assume that the auditor contends that internal control effectiveness is at point C. Tests of controls at the C1 level would provide the minimum control risk, given internal control. The auditor could choose to perform no tests of controls (point C$_3$), which would support a control risk of 1.0. Any point between the two, such as C2, would also be appropriate. If C$_2$ is selected, the audit assurance from tests of controls is C$_3$ − C$_2$ and from substantive tests is C − C$_2$. The auditor will likely select C$_1$, C$_2$, or C$_3$ based upon the relative cost of tests of controls and substantive tests.

LO **4** Develop an appropriate evidence mix based upon audit strategy.

EVIDENCE MIX AND AUDIT STRATEGY

Figure 10-7 illustrates the impact of the two different audit strategies, substantive and combined, on the evidence mix. If controls for the particular class of transactions are working as designed (and are cost-effective to test), then the auditor will conduct more

| Figure 10-7 | The Relationship Between Audit Strategy and Evidence Mix |

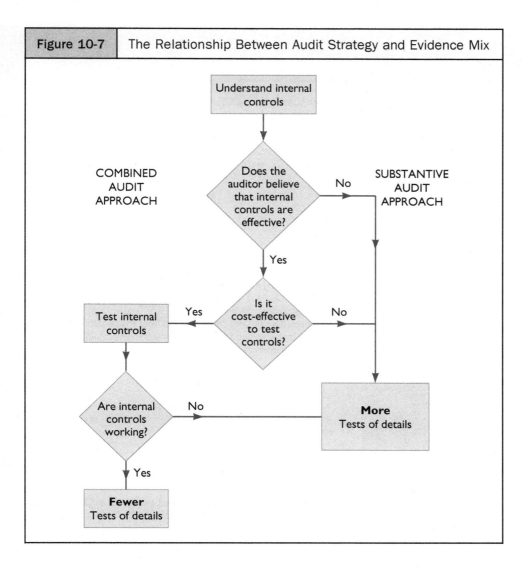

tests of controls and fewer tests of details. If controls for the particular class of transactions are not functioning or are too expensive to test, then the auditor will conduct more tests of details. The audit strategy is a dynamic process—if information arises that alters any of the risk assessments, then the audit strategies and plans are changed to reflect the changes in risks.

For smaller organizations, auditors may make an overall decision to develop a combined (rather than a substantive) approach and apply it to all classes of transactions, balances, and presentation disclosure. However, in many audits, a substantive or combined strategy is applied at the account and assertion level. Let's look at Auditing in Action 10-2, and how the auditor—in this case, KPMG Canada—used a substantive strategy for one group of accounts and a combined strategy for another.

As Auditing in Action 10-2 highlights, these approaches (substantive versus combined) vary in the types of tests that are performed: tests of controls, substantive tests of transactions, analytical procedures, and substantive tests of balances.

There are significant variations in the extent to which the four types of tests can be used in different audits for differing levels of inherent risk and internal control effectiveness. There can also be variations from cycle to cycle within a given audit, from account balance to account balance within a particular cycle, and even between assertions for a particular account balance. This combination of the four types of tests to obtain sufficient appropriate audit evidence for a cycle or account balance is known as **audit evidence mix**. Audit evidence mix is based upon the selected audit strategy.

Audit evidence mix—the combination of the four types of tests to obtain sufficient appropriate audit evidence for a cycle or account balance.

The following is an excerpt from KPMG's Audit Plan, which it presented to the audit committee of the Regional Municipality of York.

KPMG identified 12 significant reporting risks. In the table below, KPMG's audit approaches for two groups of significant accounts that both have a low risk of material misstatement prior to the consideration of internal controls (or inherent risk) are presented:

Identification of Significant Risks

As part of our audit planning, we identify the significant financial reporting risks that, by their nature, require special audit consideration. By focusing on these risks, we establish an overall audit strategy and effectively target our audit procedures.

Accounts	Risk of Material Misstatement Prior to Consideration of Internal Controls	Summary of Planned Audit Approach
Development Charges,* Revenue and Expenses	Low	Substantive approach • Perform substantive tests on development charge collections by vouching to cash receipts and ensure proper classification • Perform interest reasonability test on interest earned relating to development charges • Vouch development charge expenditures to supporting documents and ensure they relate to appropriate programs • Perform analysis on certain over-budgeted projects
Accounts Payable, Accrued Liabilities, and Expenses	Low	Control and substantive approach • Evaluate the design and implementation of controls over payroll expenses • Test the operating effectiveness of the controls • Perform substantive test of details of nonpayroll expenses • Search for unrecorded liabilities • Examine accrued liabilities for accuracy and completeness

*Development charges are charges to developers for water, wastewater, and roads that the region provides to new residential and industrial developments. It represents revenue for the municipality.

Source: Based on KPMG Enterprise, *The Regional Municipality of York, Audit Planning Report for the Year Ended December 31, 2014*, November, 28, 2014, accessed August 3, 2017 at **http://www.york.ca/wps/wcm/connect/yorkpublic/af008954-ebb3-4fe9-8492-63e725da21a4/feb+12+ kpmg.pdf?MOD=AJPERES**.

Comparison of Different Evidence Mixes

Figure 10-8 shows the audit evidence mix for four different audits (note that this is a simplification—as mentioned previously, audit strategy can be varied by cycle or account balance). Audit 1 is of a large company, while Audits 2 through 4 are of medium-sized companies. An analysis of each audit follows. Refer also to Figure 10-7 during this discussion.

Analysis of Audit 1—Sophisticated Internal Controls This client is a large company with sophisticated internal controls, justifying a combined audit approach. The auditor performs extensive tests of controls and relies heavily on the client's internal controls to reduce substantive tests. Extensive analytical procedures are also performed to reduce substantive tests of balances, which are, therefore, minimized. Because of the emphasis on tests of controls and substantive analytical procedures, this audit can be done less expensively than other types of audits.

Analysis of Audit 2—Medium, Some Controls This company is medium-sized, with some controls and some inherent risks. Using a combined audit approach, the auditor has decided to do a medium amount of testing for all types of tests except substantive analytical procedures, which will be done extensively.

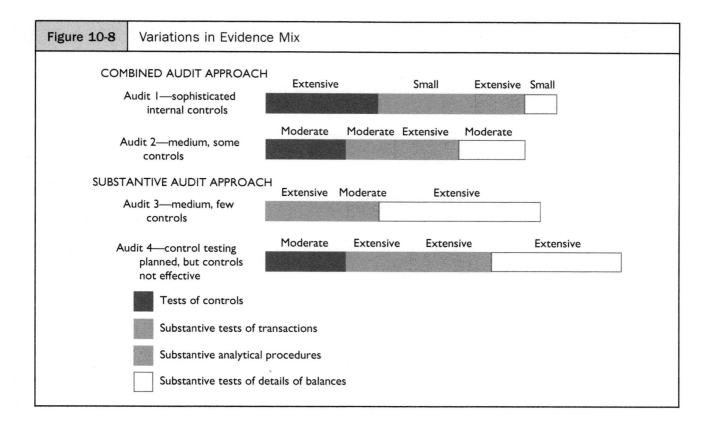

Figure 10-8 | Variations in Evidence Mix

COMBINED AUDIT APPROACH

Audit 1—sophisticated internal controls
Extensive Small Extensive Small

Audit 2—medium, some controls
Moderate Moderate Extensive Moderate

SUBSTANTIVE AUDIT APPROACH

Audit 3—medium, few controls
Extensive Moderate Extensive

Audit 4—control testing planned, but controls not effective
Moderate Extensive Extensive Extensive

■ Tests of controls

▓ Substantive tests of transactions

▒ Substantive analytical procedures

□ Substantive tests of details of balances

Analysis of Audit 3—Medium, Few Controls This company is medium-sized but has few effective controls and significant inherent risks. Management has decided that it is not cost-effective to implement better internal controls. This results in a substantive approach: no tests of controls are done because reliance on internal control is inappropriate when controls are insufficient. The emphasis is on substantive tests of balances, but some substantive analytical procedures are also done; however, limited substantive analytical procedures are performed because the auditor expects misstatements in the account balances. The cost of the audit is likely to be relatively high because of the amount of detailed substantive testing.

Analysis of Audit 4—Medium, Ineffective Controls The original plan on this audit was to follow the approach used in Audit 2 (a combined audit approach). However, the auditor finds extensive control test deviations and significant misstatements using dual-purpose tests and substantive analytical procedures. The auditor therefore concludes that the internal controls are not effective and reverts to a wholly substantive approach. Extensive substantive tests of balances are performed to offset the unacceptable results of the other tests. The costs of this audit are higher because tests of controls and dual-purpose tests are performed but cannot be used to reduce substantive tests of details of balances.

Figure 10-8 shows the relative mix of audit evidence types. It does not reflect total audit cost since the costs associated with the tests will vary, depending on the specific test selected and the extent of computerized support used for conducting the tests.

CONCEPT CHECK

C10-3 Which audit test is the least costly to develop and conduct? Why?

C10-4 If an auditor conducts tests of controls but finds that controls are not functioning effectively, what is the effect upon substantive tests? Why?

DESIGN OF THE AUDIT PROGRAMS

An audit program identifies the audit steps that are the auditor's response to the identified risks. The audit program for most audits is designed in three parts: (1) tests of controls and substantive tests of transactions (if there is no reliance on controls then only substantive tests of transactions); (2) substantive analytical procedures; and (3) substantive tests of balances. There will likely be a separate set of audit programs for each transaction cycle.

Tests of Controls

The tests of controls audit program normally includes a descriptive section documenting the understanding obtained about internal control, linking relevant key controls to risks that the auditor has identified by assertion in the planning meeting. The audit file will also contain the procedures (those necessary to obtain an understanding of internal control and to determine the design effectiveness of those internal controls) performed in order to assess control risk. After assessing control risk, the auditor will assess the significance of the risks and determine the risk of material misstatements at the assertion level.

Then, the auditor will design tests of controls for those tests that are considered cost-effective to address risks at the assertion level. When controls are effective and planned, control risk is low or moderate (i.e., the auditor chooses to rely on internal controls), a combined audit approach will be used and there will be a heavy reliance on tests of controls. Some dual-purpose tests (which are a combined control tests and substantive tests of transactions) would be included. If control risk is assessed at maximum, the auditor will use a substantive audit approach (i.e., only substantive tests will be used), as illustrated in Figure 10-7. For each transaction-related assertion where the auditor determines that reliance will be placed on controls, the auditor will select one or more audit procedures. The audit program will also describe sample size, the items to select, and timing.

Substantive Analytical Procedures

Many auditors perform extensive analytical procedures on all audits because they are relatively inexpensive. Analytical procedures performed during substantive testing, such as for the audit of accounts receivable, are typically more focused and more extensive than those done as part of planning. The auditor is likely to use disaggregated data to increase the precision of the auditor's expectations. During planning, the auditor might calculate the gross margin percentage for total sales, while during substantive testing of accounts receivable, the auditor might calculate gross margin percentage by month or by line of business, or possibly both. Analytical procedures calculated using monthly amounts are typically more effective in detecting misstatements than those calculated using annual amounts, and comparisons by line of business will usually be more effective than companywide comparisons.

If sales and accounts receivable are based on predictable relationships with non-financial data, the auditor often uses that information for analytical procedures. For example, if revenue billings are based on the number of hours professionals charge to clients, such as in law firms and other organizations that provide services, the auditor can estimate total revenue by multiplying hours billed by the average billing rate.

When the auditor plans to use analytical procedures to provide substantive assurance about an account balance, the data used in the calculations must be considered sufficiently reliable. This is true for all data, especially nonfinancial data. For example, if auditors estimate total revenue using hours billed and the average billing rate, they must be confident that both numbers are reasonably reliable.

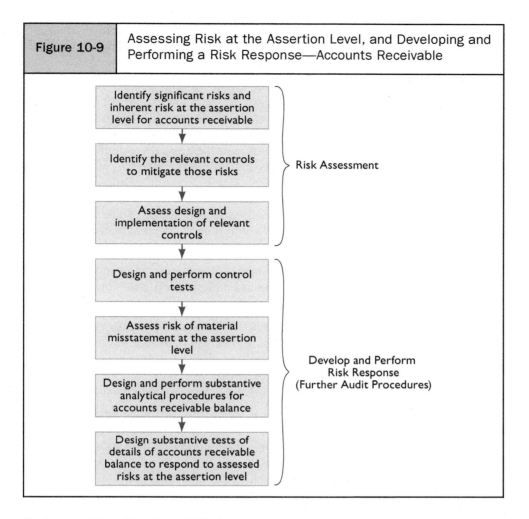

Figure 10-9	Assessing Risk at the Assertion Level, and Developing and Performing a Risk Response—Accounts Receivable

Identify significant risks and inherent risk at the assertion level for accounts receivable

Identify the relevant controls to mitigate those risks

Assess design and implementation of relevant controls

} Risk Assessment

Design and perform control tests

Assess risk of material misstatement at the assertion level

Design and perform substantive analytical procedures for accounts receivable balance

Design substantive tests of details of accounts receivable balance to respond to assessed risks at the assertion level

} Develop and Perform Risk Response (Further Audit Procedures)

Substantive Tests of Balances

In planning substantive tests of balances, which test the balance-related assertions, many auditors follow a process similar to the one shown in Figure 10-9, which uses accounts receivable as the example. Designing such procedures is subjective and requires considerable professional judgment. Let's discuss the key decisions in designing substantive tests of balances.

Identify Significant Risks and Assess Inherent Risk at the Assertion Level As part of gaining an understanding of the client's business and industry, the auditor identifies and evaluates significant client business risks to determine whether they result in a significant risk or increased risk of material misstatement in accounts receivable. If the auditor identifies a significant risk due to either fraud or error, the auditor should identify client controls to mitigate the risk and design substantive procedures to determine whether material misstatements occurred due to the significant risk.

Inherent risk at the assertion level is assessed by considering (1) the nature of the entity and the environment, and (2) the nature of the account itself (e.g., the make-up of the account population estimation uncertainty, the complexity of accounting policies, and management biases and incentives; see Chapter 7 for further guidance). An assertion for which inherent risk has been assessed as high will result in more evidence accumulation than for those assertions with low inherent risk. For example, if there is an economic downturn and the client has customers with high credit limits, the auditor may assess the risk of misstatement, prior to consideration of internal controls, as high. This would likely result in the auditor spending additional time testing the valuation assertion, as the uncollectability of a single large account could have a significant effect.

Identify Relevant Controls to Mitigate Those Risks The auditor would obtain an understanding of controls and identify the controls that would mitigate the identified risks. This process was explained in Chapter 9.

Assess Design and Implementation of Relevant Controls The auditor will use inquiry and walk-throughs to assess the design and implementation of relevant controls and then apply tools like a control risk matrix to help in the control risk assessment. Control risk is discussed in detail in Chapter 9 and in earlier parts of this chapter.

Effective controls will reduce control risk and therefore the extent of evidence required for substantive procedures. Inadequate controls increase the substantive evidence needed. There could be some assertions where substantive testing alone is not enough, due to extensive reliance on automated systems, for example, with automated credit checks. In that case, the auditor may decide that testing of internal controls could be effective, especially where general controls over program changes and information systems access are of high quality.

Design and Perform Tests of Controls The methodology for designing tests of controls and substantive tests of transactions was discussed earlier in this section and will be illustrated in subsequent chapters.

Assess Risk of Material Misstatement (RMM) at the Assertion Level Once control tests have been completed, if performed, the auditor will finalize assessment of risk of material misstatement. If the results of control testing support the original risk assessment, no adjustment to the RMM is necessary. However, if the control tests demonstrate that controls are deficient, then the RMM will need to be updated.

Design and Perform Substantive Analytical Procedures for Accounts Receivable Balance The tests are designed with the expectation that certain results will be obtained. The amount of assurance the auditor would obtain from substantive analytical procedures depends upon the approach (combined or substantive). If control risk is low or moderate (a combined approach), the auditor may use more substantive analytical procedures than substantive tests of details. However, if the control risk is high, the auditor will obtain most of the evidence through substantive tests of details.

Design Substantive Tests of Balances to Respond to Assessed Risks at the Assertion Level To design substantive tests of balances, the auditor determines nature (type of audit procedure), extent (sample size and items to select), and timing. Procedures are designed to test each assertion; however, the extent of testing will vary according to the assessed risks at the assertion level.

One difficulty the auditor faces in designing substantive tests of balances is the need to predict the outcome of the tests of controls and substantive analytical procedures before they are performed. This is necessary because the auditor should design substantive tests of balances during the planning phase, but the appropriate design depends on the outcome of the other tests. If the results of the tests of controls and substantive analytical procedures are not consistent with the predictions, the substantive tests of balances will need to be increased as the audit progresses. This occurs in our example of Audit 4 in Figure 10-8.

Timing of Audit Tests

Audit tests can be conducted throughout the year, or, for a small audit, may be conducted in a concentrated period of time. As highlighted in the Hillsburg audit strategy memo (Figure 10-1), the substantive tests of balances are normally done last. Because the results of tests of controls and substantive tests of transactions are a major determinant of the extent of substantive tests of details of balances, they are often done two or three months before the balance sheet date (as the Hillsburg auditors indicate in their audit timetable). This helps the auditor revise the substantive tests of details of balance audit program for unexpected results in the earlier tests and to complete the audit as soon as possible after the balance sheet date.

For clients with highly sophisticated computerized accounting systems, auditors often perform tests of controls and substantive tests of transactions throughout the year to identify significant or unusual transactions and determine whether any changes have been made to the client's computer system. This approach is often called continuous auditing. When clients want to issue statements soon after the balance sheet date, however, the more time-consuming tests of details of balances will be done at interim audit dates prior to year-end, with additional work being done to **roll forward** the audited interim-date balances to year-end. (A roll forward involves substantive work on journal entries and other activities during this period.) Substantive tests of balances performed before year-end provide less assurance and are not normally done unless internal controls are effective.

Roll forward—substantive work on journal entries and transactions from a date prior to the balance sheet date to the year-end.

Illustrative Audit Program

Table 10-2 shows the substantive tests of details of balances segment of an audit program for accounts receivable. The format used relates the audit procedures to the balance-related audit objectives and presentation and disclosure audit objectives.

Table 10-2	Substantive Tests of Details of Balances Audit Program for Accounts Receivable									
Balance-Related (B) and Presentation and Disclosure (PD)				**Accounts Receivable Audit Objectives**						
Sample Size	**Items to Select**	**Timing***	**Tests of Details of Balances Audit Procedures**	Existence (B, PD)	Rights (B, PD)	Completeness (B, PD)	Accuracy (PD)	Valuation (B, PD)	Allocation (B)	Classification (PD)
Trace 20 items; foot 2 pages and all subtotals	Random	I	1. Obtain an aged list of receivables: trace open items to supporting invoice detail, foot schedule, and trace to general ledger.			x				
All	All	Y	2. Obtain an analysis of the allowance for doubtful accounts and bad debt expense: test accuracy, examine authorization for write-offs, and trace to general ledger.	x		x	x	x		
100	30 largest; 70 random	I	3. Obtain direct confirmation of accounts receivable and perform alternative procedures for nonresponses.	x	x	x	x		x	x
N/A	N/A	Y	4. Review accounts receivable control account for the period. Investigate the nature of, and review support for, any large or unusual entries or any entries not arising from normal journal sources. Also investigate any significant increases or decreases in sales toward year-end.	x	x		x		x	x
All	All	Y	5. Review receivables for any that have been assigned or discounted.			x				
N/A	N/A	Y	6. Investigate collectability of account balances.					x		
All	All	Y	7. Review lists of balances for amounts due from related parties or employees, credit balances, and unusual items, as well as notes receivable due after one year.	x						x
30 transactions for sales and cash receipts; 10 for credit memos	50% before and 50% after year-end	Y	8. Determine that proper cutoff procedures were applied at the balance sheet date to ensure that sales, cash receipts, and credit memos have been recorded in the correct period.						x	

*I—Interim; Y—Year-end; N/A—Not applicable

Note that most procedures satisfy more than one objective. Also, more than one audit procedure is used for each objective.

The audit program in Table 10-2 was developed after consideration of all the factors affecting substantive tests of details of balances. It is based on several assumptions about inherent risk, control risk, and the results of tests of controls and analytical procedures. If those assumptions change, the planned audit program will require revision.

Most large public accounting firms develop their own standard audit programs, organized by industry, and often linked by audit objective to databases, including lists of expected controls and likely audit tests. Smaller firms often purchase similar audit programs from outside organizations. Standard audit programs are normally computerized and can easily be modified to meet the circumstances of individual audit engagements. An example of a standard audit program available for purchase is CPA Canada's *Professional Engagement Guide*.

Standard audit programs, whether developed internally or purchased from an outside organization, can dramatically increase audit efficiency if they are used properly. They should not be used, however, as a substitute for an auditor's professional judgment. As highlighted in Auditing in Action 10-3, if standard audit programs are used incorrectly, auditors may fall prey to judgment traps. Because no two audits are alike, it is usually necessary to add, modify, or delete steps within a standard audit program in order to accumulate sufficient and appropriate audit evidence.

Relationship Between Transaction Assertions to Balance and Presentation and Disclosure Assertions

As we have discussed earlier, substantive tests of details of balances must be designed to test the balance-related assertions for each account, and the extent of these tests can be reduced when tests of controls and substantive tests of transactions are performed (both of which test the transaction-related assertions). It is, therefore, important to understand how each transaction assertion relates to each balance assertion.

With the exception of valuation and rights and obligations, there is a direct relationship between the transaction and balance assertions. For instance, see Figure 10-5,

AUDITING IN ACTION 10-3
Customized Risk-Based Audits Reduce Judgment Traps

Auditors often assume that the audit is mostly unchanged from the prior year, but auditors can fall into the judgment trap of anchoring if they follow the "same as last year" (SALY) mentality. One way to overcome the anchoring judgment trap is to use risk assessment best practices and start with the assumption that some things have changed from the prior year audit. As a result, the first priority of the current year audit is to identify changes and their effect on risk. Auditors should ask questions such as:

- What has *changed* at the entity and its operating environment since the last audit?

- How have inherent risks *changed* as a result of these changes in the entity and operating environment?

- What *changes* in internal control were necessary to address these changes in the environment and inherent risks?

For example, a recessionary economic environment may create a significant inherent risk related to asset valuation for accounts such as inventory, accounts receivable, and other assets. As a result, the company may implement new or revised controls to address these increased risks.

We have highlighted the fact that many firms use standardized audit programs and practice aids provided by external parties. Standardized audit programs may not encourage auditors to apply the appropriate level of skepticism and may encourage what some refer to as a "checklist" mentality. Firms that develop customized, firm-specific audit practice aids that reflect the unique nature of their audit practice and build upon their knowledge are less likely to fall into common judgment traps—which will ultimately lead to more effective and efficient audits.

Source: Adapted from Michael Ramos, "Risk-based audit best practices," *Journal of Accountancy*, December 2009, pp. 32–37. Copyright by American Institute of CPAs. All rights reserved. Used with permission.

which refers to the various tests performed for accounts receivable. You will note that the occurrence of sales transactions increases accounts receivable, and occurrence of collections (or cash receipts) decreases accounts receivable. This means that tests of controls and substantive tests of transactions related to those assertions provide evidence for the balance-related assertions as well. However, few internal controls from either of these classes of transactions are related to the valuation assertion (the credit approval process affects the extent of the tests). The same applies to rights and obligations. In both cases, separate tests of controls, analytical procedures, and tests of details are necessary.

Regarding presentation and disclosure, the first four assertions are similar to the transaction-related and balance-related assertions, and can be audited in the same manner as we have described. The final assertion, understandability, requires the auditor to examine the statements and notes from the perspective of a knowledgeable financial statement user to assess whether information has been clearly presented.

CONCEPT CHECK

C10-5 List the type of information that would be included in an audit program.

C10-6 Describe the type of testing required when the auditor has identified an assertion that has a significant risk of material misstatement.

SUMMARY OF AUDIT PROCESS

LO **6** Integrate the different components of the audit process.

In this chapter, we integrate all the different parts of the audit process, summarized in Figure 10-10, that we have studied up to this point. The shaded boxes highlight the major focus of this chapter: developing a risk response.

Client Acceptance, Audit Planning, and Assess Risk of Material Misstatement

Auditors use information obtained from risk procedures related to client acceptance and audit planning (understanding the entity and its environment) to assess acceptable audit risk and identify significant risks. Auditors use assessment of materiality and risk of material misstatement at the financial statement level to develop an overall audit response (strategy). In order to develop a risk response at the assertion level, auditors consider acceptable audit risk, materiality, and inherent risk and control risk for that particular account/assertion (As illustrated in Figure 10-4, the audit risk model underlies the logic of developing further audit procedures, which represents the risk response at the assertion level.)

Develop Risk Response

In the first part of this chapter, we illustrated how the auditors developed an overall audit strategy for Hillsburg Hardware (Figures 10-1, 10-2, and 10-3). The remainder of the chapter discussed how auditors develop a risk response at the assertion level by creating an evidence mix that matches the appropriate audit approach (strategy) for the relevant account and cycle. At this point of the audit process, the auditors should have a well-defined audit strategy and plan and a specific audit program for each cycle of the entire audit.

Although Figure 10-10 suggests that the audit process is linear, it is important to note that it is an iterative process. This means that as the auditor gathers evidence, original risk assessments may need to be adjusted. For instance, if the results of control tests do not support the original control risk assessment, then the audit strategy would

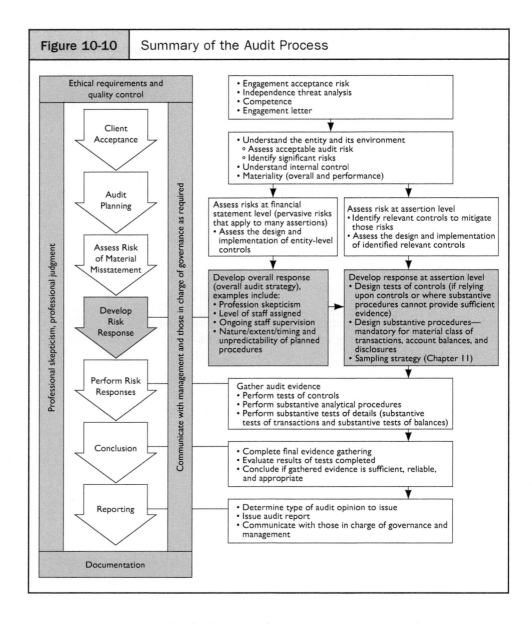

Figure 10-10 | Summary of the Audit Process

Ethical requirements and quality control

Professional skepticism, professional judgment

Communicate with management and those in charge of governance as required

Client Acceptance

Audit Planning

Assess Risk of Material Misstatement

Develop Risk Response

Perform Risk Responses

Conclusion

Reporting

Documentation

- Engagement acceptance risk
- Independence threat analysis
- Competence
- Engagement letter

- Understand the entity and its environment
  ○ Assess acceptable audit risk
  ○ Identify significant risks
- Understand internal control
- Materiality (overall and performance)

Assess risks at financial statement level (pervasive risks that apply to many assertions)
- Assess the design and implementation of entity-level controls

Assess risk at assertion level
- Identify relevant controls to mitigate those risks
- Assess the design and implementation of identified relevant controls

Develop overall response (overall audit strategy), examples include:
- Profession skepticism
- Level of staff assigned
- Ongoing staff supervision
- Nature/extent/timing and unpredictability of planned procedures

Develop response at assertion level
- Design tests of controls (if relying upon controls or where substantive procedures cannot provide sufficient evidence)
- Design substantive procedures—mandatory for material class of transactions, account balances, and disclosures
- Sampling strategy (Chapter 11)

Gather audit evidence
- Perform tests of controls
- Perform substantive analytical procedures
- Perform substantive tests of details (substantive tests of transactions and substantive tests of balances)

- Complete final evidence gathering
- Evaluate results of tests completed
- Conclude if gathered evidence is sufficient, reliable, and appropriate

- Determine type of audit opinion to issue
- Issue audit report
- Communicate with those in charge of governance and management

need to be adjusted. Similarly, if the results of substantive analytical procedures are not as expected, the auditor would need to perform more substantive tests of details. As highlighted in the "develop an overall response" box, in addition to determining the nature and extent of audit procedures, the auditor would also determine the timing of the tests, which we discussed earlier in this chapter.

To further understand how the auditor decides whether the control tests support the risk assessment, in Chapter 11 we will examine more closely sampling strategies (the extent of testing). We will also examine how the auditor evaluates the results of a sample of substantive tests of transactions and balances and concludes whether there is a material misstatement in the class of transactions or the account balances. In Chapters 12 to 17, we examine the cycles more closely and consider how the auditor develops and performs a risk response at the assertion level based upon the risk assessment for each specific cycle.

Conclusion and Reporting

In our earlier chapters, we touched briefly on the last two stages of the audit process. We introduced the audit report and the auditor's reporting responsibilities in Chapter 3, and we discussed the role of analytical procedures in the completions stage of the audit in Chapter 5, as well as the evaluation of misstatements in order to determine whether the financial statements are fairly stated in our discussion of materiality in Chapter 6. We will examine those two stages in more depth in Chapters 18 and 19.

Chapter 18 explains how the auditor concludes whether sufficient appropriate evidence has been gathered. During this phase of the audit process, additional testing is done related to presentation and disclosure-related objectives. Auditors will perform audit procedures related to contingent liabilities and subsequent events and will gather the following evidence for the financial statements as a whole:

- Perform final analytical procedures.
- Evaluate going-concern assumption.
- Obtain client representation letter.

Chapter 18 also summarizes the matters which auditors are required to communicate to those in charge in governance and management upon completion of the audit, if not sooner. We have already discussed the auditor's responsibilities regarding communicating significant internal control deficiencies.

The last component of the audit process is covered in Chapter 19. The type of audit report issued depends upon the evidence accumulated and audit findings. We will also discuss the impending changes to audit report and the introduction of key audit matters for public companies.

SUMMARY

This chapter concludes our discussion of the audit planning process. In earlier chapters, we discussed the risk assessment procedures that the auditor performs to understand the client's business and industry and to assess the risks of material misstatement, including fraud risks and other significant risks. The auditor also gains an understanding of internal control to assess entity-level controls and to assess control risk at the assertion level. The auditor then uses the information obtained from the risk assessment procedures to design further audit procedures, which consist of tests of controls, substantive tests of transactions, substantive analytical procedures, and substantive tests of balances. The evidence mix reflects the emphasis placed on the various types of tests, and depends on the auditor's assessment of risks and the relative costs of each type of test. The auditor's objective in choosing the evidence mix is to obtain sufficient appropriate evidence while minimizing costs. The auditor then selects the specific procedures to be performed, which are combined into the audit program, which contains the detailed instructions for the gathering of audit evidence to support the auditor's opinion.

MyLab Accounting
Make the grade with MyLab Accounting: The questions, exercises, and problems marked with a 🌐 can be found on MyLab Accounting. You can practise them as often as you want, and most feature step-by-step guided instructions to help you find the right answer.

Review Questions

10-1 **1** Explain the difference between overall audit strategy at the financial statement level and audit strategy at the assertion level.

10-2 **2** What are the five types of tests auditors use to determine whether financial statements are fairly stated? Identify which tests are performed to assess control risk and which tests are performed to achieve planned detection risk.

10-3 **2** What is the purpose of risk assessment procedures, and how are they related to or different from the four other types of audit tests?

10-4 **2** Distinguish between a test of controls and a substantive test. Give two examples of each.

10-5 **2** Explain what is meant by "recalculation" and "reperformance." Give an example of each type of audit evidence. Why are recalculation and reperformance often dual-purpose tests?

10-6 [2] [3] An auditor may perform tests of controls and substantive procedures simultaneously as a matter of audit convenience. However, the substantive procedures and sample size are, in part, dependent upon the results of the tests of controls. How can the auditor resolve this apparent inconsistency?

10-7 [2] [3] Explain how the calculation of the gross margin percentage and the ratio of accounts receivable to sales, and their comparison to those of previous years, are related to the confirmation of accounts receivable and other tests of the accuracy of accounts receivable.

10-8 [3] [4] Distinguish between a combined audit approach and a substantive audit approach. Give one example of when each might be appropriate for the acquisition and payment cycle.

10-9 [2] [3] Assume that the client's internal controls over the recording and classifying of capital asset additions are considered weak because the individual responsible for recording new acquisitions has inadequate technical training and limited experience in accounting. How would this situation affect the evidence you should accumulate in auditing permanent assets as compared with another audit in which the controls are excellent? Be as specific as possible.

10-10 [2] For each of the seven types of evidence—inspection, observation, external confirmation, recalculation, reperformance, analytical procedures, and inquiries of the client (discussed in Chapter 5)—identify whether the evidence is applicable to procedures for risk assessment, obtaining an understanding of internal control, tests of controls, analytical procedures, or substantive tests of details.

10-11 [2] [3] The following are three decision factors related to the assessed level of control risk: effectiveness of internal controls, cost-effectiveness of a reduced assessed level of control risk, and results of tests of controls. Identify the combination of conditions for these three factors that is required before a reduction in substantive procedures is permitted.

10-12 [4] Why is it desirable to design tests of details of balances before performing tests of controls? State the assumptions the auditor must make in doing this. What does the auditor do if the assumptions prove to be incorrect?

10-13 [4] [5] Why do auditors frequently consider it desirable to perform audit tests throughout the year rather than wait until year-end? List several examples of evidence that can be accumulated prior to year-end.

10-14 [1] [3] [4] The auditor of Ferguson's, Inc., identified two internal controls in the sales and collection cycle for testing. In the first control, the computer verifies that a planned sale on account will not exceed the customer's credit limit entered in the accounts receivable master file. In the second control, the accounts receivable clerk matches bills of lading, sales invoices, and customer orders before recording in the sales journal. Describe how the presence of general controls over software programs and master file changes affects the extent of audit testing of each of these two internal controls.

10-15 [6] Review the components of the financial statement audit process. List each component that involves risk assessment. State which types of audit procedures would be used during each component that you listed.

Multiple Choice Questions and Task-Based Simulations

10-16 [1] The auditor faces a risk that the audit will not detect material misstatements that occur in the accounting process. To minimize this risk, the auditor relies primarily on:
   (1) Substantive tests.
   (2) Tests of controls.
   (3) Internal control.
   (4) Statistical analysis.

10-17 [1] [3] [4] An auditor's decision either to apply analytical procedures as substantive tests or to perform substantive tests of transactions and account balances usually is determined by the:
   (1) Availability of data aggregated at a high level.
   (2) Relative effectiveness and efficiency of the tests.
   (3) Timing of tests performed after the balance sheet date.
   (4) Auditor's familiarity with industry trends.

10-18 ⬛1⬛ ⬛3⬛ ⬛4⬛ To support the auditor's initial assessment of control risk below maximum, the auditor performs procedures to determine that internal controls are operating effectively. Which of the following audit procedures is the auditor performing?

    (1) Tests of details of balances.

    (2) Substantive tests of transactions.

    (3) Tests of controls.

    (4) Tests of trends and ratios.

10-19 ⬛1⬛ ⬛3⬛ ⬛4⬛ Tests of controls are most likely to be omitted when:

    (1) An account balance reflects many transactions.

    (2) Control risk is assessed at less than the maximum.

    (3) The understanding of the control structure indicates that evaluating the effectiveness of control policies and procedures is likely to be inefficient.

    (4) The auditor wishes to increase the acceptable level of detection risk.

10-20 ⬛2⬛ For the following audit procedures that were taken from an audit program, indicate whether each procedure is:

    (1) A test of control.

    (2) A substantive test of transactions.

    (3) An analytical procedure.

    (4) A test of details of balances.

Audit Procedure	Procedure Type
Foot the accounts payable trial balance and compare the total with the general ledger.	
Confirm accounts payable balances directly with vendors.	
Account for a sequence of cheques in the cash disbursements journal to determine whether any have been omitted.	
Examine vendors' invoices to verify the ending balance in accounts payable.	
Compare the balance in payroll tax expense with previous years. The comparison takes the increase in payroll tax rates into account.	
Examine the internal auditor's initials on monthly bank reconciliations as an indication of whether they have been reviewed.	
Examine vendors' invoices and other documentation in support of recorded transactions in the acquisitions journal.	
Multiply the commission rate by total sales and compare the result with commission expense.	
Examine vendors' invoices and other supporting documents to determine whether large amounts in the repair and maintenance account should be capitalized.	
Discuss the duties of the cash disbursements clerk with him or her and observe whether he or she has responsibility for handling cash or preparing the bank reconciliation.	
Inquire about the accounts payable supervisor's monthly review of a computer-generated exception report of receiving reports and purchase orders that have not been matched with a vendor invoice.	

10-21 Based on the provided procedure, determine the most likely audit strategy (combined or substantive) that an auditor has selected for the specific cycle.

Procedures	Strategy (combined or substantive)
After gaining an understanding of internal controls in the sales cycle, the auditor decided to select a sample of customers and verify that for each customer a credit review form was completed and the form was signed by the manager.	
After gaining an understanding of internal controls in the payroll cycle, the auditor decided to select a sample of reconciliations between timesheets and the payroll ledger. The auditor then reviewed the reconciliations to see if they were done accurately and verified whether they were signed by the payroll supervisor who is responsible for reviewing them.	
After gaining an understanding of internal controls in the purchasing cycle, the auditor decided to select a sample of accounts payable balances and directly confirm these balances with the company's suppliers.	

(continued)

Procedures	Strategy (combined or substantive)
After gaining an understanding of internal controls in the purchasing cycle, the auditor decided to select a sample of inventory receiving reports and verify that all exceptions listed in the reports were resolved and that the reports have been signed by the warehouse manager who is responsible for reviewing the reports on a weekly basis.	
After gaining an understanding of internal controls in the sales cycle, to ensure proper sales cutoff was achieved, the auditor decided to review the dates on all shipping documents one week prior to and one week after the year-end date.	
After gaining an understanding of internal controls in the purchasing cycle, the auditor decided to select a sample of lease agreements and trace all pertinent information from the agreements to the financial accounting system records.	

10-22 **4** **6** Based on facts in each scenario, recommend the most appropriate audit strategy (combined or substantive).

Scenario	Strategy
Big Bank is a multinational bank that operates across the globe. Each day, the bank processes billions of monetary transactions. The bank has a large well-established internal audit department. Last year, internal auditors reported to the board of directors about some control weaknesses that they had identified. These weaknesses are currently being addressed by the bank's senior management.	
In the past year, after starting to work as a controller, Tony has established a strong control environment and tone at the top to ensure employees operate ethically, adhering to stated policies. Tony holds daily management meetings to review operations and financial information. Budget and actual results are also reviewed by Tony, who interprets the results and sets the direction for the next day.	
A year ago, LVSports Inc., a large chain of stores that carry sports equipment, hired a new controller. The controller took it upon herself to conduct a walk-through of each accounting process. The purpose of the walk-throughs was to identify and fix any control gaps. After the gaps were fixed, the controller hired a consultant to review whether the updated controls improved LVSports's control environment. The consultant reported back that, on paper, the updated controls were really good, but that in most cases, staff did not follow them.	
Over the past 12 months, 2Fast Inc., a private consulting company, has lost half of its accounting staff to retirements. For the past six months, the company has relied on temporary staffing agencies to fill the vacant positions. Fraser, the company's new controller, is not happy with the temporary staff provided by the agencies. They are mostly new university graduates with little prior work experience who make a lot of significant mistakes.	
Emilia Inc. provides bridge design engineering services. The company has grown rapidly over the past five years. Last year, the company procured a new financial accounting IT system. After the system was installed, things appeared to be going well until the company realized that it forgot to install required weekly system upgrades. When the upgrades were finally installed, the system crashed several times and a significant amount of financial information was corrupted. Management is in the process of trying to fix the corrupted information.	

Discussion Questions and Problems

🌐 **10-23** **2** The following are audit procedures from different transaction cycles:
1. Examine sales invoices for evidence of internal verification of prices, quantities, and extensions.
2. Select items from the client's perpetual inventory records and examine the items in the company's warehouse.
3. Use audit software to foot and cross-foot the cash disbursements journal and trace the balance to the general ledger.

4. Select a sample of entries in the acquisitions journal and trace each one to a related vendor's invoice to determine whether one exists.
5. Examine documentation for acquisition transactions before and after the balance sheet date to determine whether they are recorded in the proper period.
6. Inquire of the credit manager whether each account receivable on the aged trial balance is collectible.
7. Compute inventory turnover for each major product and compare with that in previous years.
8. Confirm a sample of notes payable balances, interest rates, and collateral with lenders.
9. Use audit software to foot the accounts receivable trial balance and compare the balance with the general ledger.

REQUIRED
a. For each audit procedure, identify the transaction cycle being audited.
b. For each audit procedure, identify the type of evidence.
c. For each audit procedure, identify whether it is a test of control or a substantive test.
d. For each substantive audit procedure, identify whether it is a substantive test of transactions, a test of details of balances, or an analytical procedure.
e. For each test of control or substantive test of transactions procedure, identify the transaction-related assertion being tested.
f. For each analytical procedure or test of details of balances procedure, identify the balance-related assertion being tested.

10-24 ❶ ❸ ❹ Jennifer Schaefer, a public accountant, follows the philosophy of performing interim tests of controls on every December 31 audit as a means of keeping overtime to a minimum. Typically, the interim tests are performed sometime between August and November.

REQUIRED
a. Evaluate her decision to perform interim tests of controls.
b. Under what circumstances is it acceptable for her to perform no additional tests of controls as part of the year-end audit tests?
c. If she decides to perform no additional testing, what is the effect on other tests she performs during the remainder of the engagement?

10-25 ❸ ❹ Kim Bryan, a new staff auditor, is confused by the inconsistency of the three audit partners to whom she has been assigned on her first three audit engagements. On the first engagement, she spent a considerable amount of time in the audit of cash disbursements by examining cancelled cheques and supporting documentation, but almost no time was spent on the verification of capital assets. On the second engagement, a different partner had her do less intensive tests in the cash disbursements area and take smaller sample sizes than in the first audit even though the company was much larger. On her most recent engagement under a third audit partner, there was a thorough test of cash disbursement transactions, far beyond that of the other two audits, and an extensive verification of capital assets. In fact, this partner insisted on a complete physical examination of all capital assets recorded on the books. The total audit time on the most recent audit was longer than that of either of the first two audits despite the smaller size of the company. Bryan's conclusion is that the amount of evidence to accumulate depends on the audit partner in charge of the engagement.

REQUIRED
a. State the differences in risk assessments that could affect the amount of evidence accumulated in each of the three audit engagements as well as the total time spent.
b. What could the audit partners have done to help Bryan understand the differences in the audit emphasis on the three audits?
c. Explain how these three audits are useful in developing Bryan's professional judgment. How could the quality of her judgment have been improved by the audits?

10-26 ❹ ❻ Assume that the client's internal controls over the recording and classifying of fixed asset additions are considered deficient because the individual responsible for recording new acquisitions has inadequate technical training and limited experience in accounting.

REQUIRED
a. What level (high, medium, or low) would you assign to control risk? Why?
b. How will this situation affect the evidence you should accumulate in auditing fixed assets as compared with another audit in which the controls are excellent? Be as specific as possible.

10-27 2 3 The following are independent internal controls commonly found in the acquisition and payment cycle. Each control is to be considered independently.

1. Before a cheque is prepared to pay for acquisitions by the accounts payable department, the related purchase order and receiving report are attached to the vendor's invoice being paid. A clerk compares the quantity on the invoice with the receiving report and purchase order, compares the price with the purchase order, recomputes the extensions, re-adds the total, and examines the account number indicated on the invoice to determine whether it is correctly classified. He indicates his performance of these procedures by initialling the invoice.

2. At the end of each month, an accounting clerk accounts for all prenumbered receiving reports (documents evidencing the receipt of goods) issued during the month and traces each one to the related vendor's invoice and acquisitions journal entry. The clerk's tests do not include testing the quantity or description of the merchandise received.

3. The cash disbursements clerk is prohibited from handling cash. The bank account is reconciled by another person even though the clerk has sufficient expertise and time to do it.

4. Before a cheque is signed by the controller, she examines the supporting documentation accompanying the cheque. At that time, she initials each vendor's invoice to indicate her approval.

5. After the controller signs the cheques, her secretary writes the cheque number and the date the cheque was issued on each of the supporting documents to prevent their reuse.

REQUIRED

a. For each of the internal controls, state the transaction-related audit objective(s) the control is meant to fulfill.

b. For each control, list one test of control the auditor could perform to test the effectiveness of the control.

c. For each control, list one substantive test the auditor could perform to determine whether financial misstatements are actually taking place.

10-28 1 4 The following are three situations, all involving private companies, in which the auditor is required to develop an audit strategy:

1. The client has inventory at approximately 50 locations in a three-province region. The inventory is difficult to count and can be observed only by travelling by automobile. The internal controls over acquisitions, cash disbursements, and perpetual records are considered effective. This is the fifth year that you have done the audit, and audit results in past years have always been excellent. The client is in excellent financial condition.

2. This is the first year of an audit of a medium-sized company that is considering selling its business because of severe underfinancing. A review of the acquisition and payment cycle indicates that controls over cash disbursements are excellent but controls over acquisitions cannot be considered effective. The client lacks receiving reports and a policy as to the proper timing to record acquisitions. When you review the general ledger, you observe that there are many large adjusting entries to correct accounts payable.

3. You are doing the audit of a small loan company with extensive loans receivable from customers. Controls over granting loans, collections, and loans outstanding are considered effective, and there is extensive follow-up of all outstanding loans weekly. You have recommended a new computer system for the past two years, but management believes the cost is too great, given the company's low profitability. Collections are an ongoing problem because many of the customers have severe financial problems. Because of adverse economic conditions, loans receivable have significantly increased and collections are less than normal. In previous years, you have had relatively few adjusting entries.

REQUIRED

a. For Audit 1, recommend an evidence mix for the five types of tests for the audit of inventory and cost of goods sold. Justify your answer. Include in your recommendations both tests of controls and substantive tests.

b. For Audit 2, recommend an evidence mix for the audit of the acquisition and payment cycle, including accounts payable. Justify your answer.

c. For Audit 3, recommend an evidence mix for the audit of outstanding loans. Justify your answer.

Professional Judgment Problems and Cases

10-29 **1** **3** **4** **6** Sidhu, a public accountant, is planning his first audit of Microservices Ltd., a local retailer of computers and related products. Microservices is a new company, and this is the client's first fiscal year of operations. The owner has explained to Sidhu that she wants an audit from the beginning of the fiscal year and for the next several years so that she can build a credible financial track record. She then plans to make a public offering of shares, when market conditions are favourable. Sidhu recommended to the company (which the owner accepted) that the applicable accounting framework to be used should be ASPE.

Because the company is small and has few employees, Sidhu decides to ignore the company's internal controls and rely solely on substantive tests of transactions and balances in this first audit engagement. Sidhu believes that this approach will allow him to perform an audit at minimum cost, and hence charge a minimum audit fee. In later years, as the client's systems become better developed, Sidhu plans to modify his audit approach to incorporate some reliance on the client's internal controls and thereby reduce his level of substantive testing. Before beginning the audit, Sidhu discusses this audit plan with the owner, who fully agrees with Sidhu that this is the most efficient way to proceed, given the circumstances.

REQUIRED

a. Assess Sidhu's actions, using Canadian auditing standards.
b. What judgment traps do you think Sidhu fell into?
c. What recommendations do you make so that Sidhu can improve the quality of his judgments and decisions?

(Reprinted from AU2 CGA-Canada Examinations with permission Chartered Professional Accountants of Canada, Toronto, Canada. Any changes to the original material are the sole responsibility of the author/publisher and have not been reviewed or endorsed by the Chartered Professional Accountants of Canada.)

10-30 **1** **2** **4** Refer to Auditing in Action 10-2.

REQUIRED

a. Based on what you have learned about audit strategy in this chapter, why would KPMG apply a different strategy to two accounts that have the same risk of material misstatement?
b. Below are the audit procedures that KPMG listed for each account. Explain the type of test and which relevant assertion is being tested.

10-31 **1** **3** **4** **6** Gabby Manufacturing Company is a privately owned leading manufacturer and distributor of lockers, locks, and keys for numerous industries. It is best known for its widely used locker system with the plastic orange cap. Gabby sells two types of lockers: postal (used in mail delivery) and nonpostal (i.e., evidence lockers used in law enforcement). Gabby serves a variety of customers in Canada, the United States, Mexico, and Europe. Gabby has had excellent growth and profits in the past decade, primarily as a result of the leadership provided by the owner, Bill Gabby.

Noah Smart, CPA, has been the partner in charge of the audit of Gabby for 15 years. Noah has always enjoyed a close relationship with Bill and prides himself on having made several constructive comments over the years that have aided in the success of the company. Bill always appreciates Noah's management letter points. Several times in the past few years, Noah's firm, Miles and Miles LLP, has considered rotating a different partner onto the engagement, but this has been strongly resisted by both Noah and Bill.

Although there had been problems with internal controls in the early years of the audit, in recent years, internal controls have been strong. There have normally been no audit adjustments, and the audit team has been able to reduce the level of substantive testing. During the past three years, Noah has devoted less time to the audit because of the relative ease of conducting the audit.

In the current year, Gabby acquired RecLocker Inc., a company that produces coin-operated lockers used in amusement parks, water parks, and ski resorts. The acquisition was financed with a new multimillion-dollar, five-year bank loan. Bill was very excited about the acquisition because of the synergies between Gabby and RecLocker. Unfortunately, as a result of the continuing economic recession, the demand for recreational lockers has declined and it appears that it will take several years before Gabby can reap any of the rewards from the acquisition.

Phil Warren is the senior in charge of the audit. He is highly competent, and has a reputation for being able to improve time efficiencies. While planning the audit for the current year, Phil and Noah decided that the previous year's assessment of moderate audit risk and materiality level were appropriate for the current year. (Continued on next page)

Accounts	Audit Procedure	Type of Test	Assertion
Development Charges, Revenue and Expenses	Substantive test development charge collections by vouching to cash receipts and ensure proper classification		
	Perform interest reasonability test		
	Vouch development charge expenditures to supporting documents and ensure they relate to appropriate programs		
	Perform analysis on certain budgeted projects		
Accounts Payable, Accrued Liabilities and Expenses	Evaluate the design and implementation of controls over payroll expenses		
	Test the operating effectiveness of the controls		
	Substantive test of details of nonpayroll expenses		
	Search for unrecorded liabilities		
	Examine accrued liabilities for accuracy and completeness		

They also decided that the prior year's time budget was a reasonable estimate. Although the recent acquisition of RecLocker would probably require additional work, Phil was confident that his efficiency would be able to compensate for it. Noah was glad of this because he had already promised Bill that he would not increase the audit fee this year.

The interim tests of controls took longer than expected. This was partially due to a change in the accounting system to incorporate RecLocker's accounting information as well as a new inventory system. In addition, Gabby experienced significant turnover in its accounting staff. It was also due to the fact that the audit assistants were unfamiliar with the client and that they found more errors than in previous years. Noah and Phil concluded that since all the errors found were immaterial, there was no need to change the initial audit plan. Phil assured Noah that he would make up for the additional time at year-end.

At year-end, in order to save costs, Phil assigned the inventory price tests to Priya Tata, who was competent and extremely fast, but who had not been on the audit before. Despite the increase in the total inventory value, Priya used a smaller sample size than in previous years because few errors had been found in the preceding year. Priya found several items in the sample that were overstated due to costing errors but the total estimated error in the sample was immaterial. Given the numerous errors, Priya consulted with Phil, who concluded that since the total error was immaterial, no further audit work was necessary. Priya completed the tests in 25 percent less time than the preceding year.

While Phil was completing the audit fieldwork, he discovered that the United States Postal Service (USPS) had not renewed its contract with Gabby. Sales to USPS represented approximately 30 percent of total sales and Gabby did not expect to find another postal service interested in the boxes since they were customized for USPS. Phil was glad that this event happened after year-end because it did not affect this year's audit work and he could stay within the originally planned budget. Because it happened after year-end, Phil decided it was not necessary to document the cancellation of the USPS contract.

The entire audit was completed on schedule in slightly less time than the preceding year. As in prior years, Phil concluded that the overall uncorrected misstatements did not have a material effect on the overall financial statements. Given that there were few past problems, Noah performed a limited review of the working papers—he focused on reviewing the draft financial statements and the summary of possible misstatements. In addition, he discussed the results with Phil, who assured him that there were no significant issues or unresolved audit adjustments. Noah was extremely pleased with the results and concluded that sufficient appropriate evidence was collected and that there were no material misstatements.

REQUIRED

a. List the major deficiencies in the audit and state the appropriate actions the auditors should have taken.

b. Based upon the information provided, identify the threats to independence and evaluate the impact of those threats on the auditors' professional judgment and skepticism.

c. For those independence threats that you identified, recommend appropriate safeguards that would have mitigated the threat.

10-32 **1** **6** Ontario Fun Space (OFS) is a privately owned entertainment complex consisting of a theme park, concert venue, and marina in Lion's Head, Ontario. OFS was founded in 1988 by a group of 10 local investors who thought a theme park would be a great way to attract visitors to the area and boost the local economy.

Over the years, OFS has developed a solid reputation as a fun place for families, boating enthusiasts, and concertgoers. However, as its facilities aged, the investors decided it was necessary to seek additional funds. In 2013, the investors sold 80 percent of OFS to FFI, a large American amusement park company. The investors no longer have any active involvement with OFS and receive a dividend based upon net income. FFI is known to have high expectations for return on its investment. To motivate OFS management to run a highly profitable operation, FFI implemented a bonus plan based upon net income. Also, to maintain firm oversight of its investment, FFI required OFS to send it the following monthly operational reports: expenditure to budget, sales, and the list of boats docked in the marina.

In 2013, OFS decided to add a 190-foot observation wheel that would give riders in climate-controlled cars a panoramic view of the beautiful beaches. Because of its potential to attract tourists to the area, OFS was able to obtain a forgivable loan from the Ontario government. One of the conditions of the loan is that OFS must maintain certain levels of employment for 10 years. If OFS does not meet those requirements anytime within that 10-year period, it must repay the entire loan. Per ASPE (Accounting Standards for Private Enterprises) 3800, the loan has been recorded as a credit and is being amortized over the same period of the estimated life of the observation wheel. OFS must supply the Ontario government with an annual employment report as well as audited financial statements.

In 2010, when OFS completed the construction of its concert venue, it signed a 20-year lease agreement with the concert promoter Merek Neal (MN). According to the agreement, MN will promote and operate the OFS's concert venue, and give OFS 20 percent of all box office and concessionary sales revenue.

You are a newly hired senior auditor at Bruce Penn LLP, a mid-size accounting firm located in the Lion's Head area. This is your firm's fourth year performing OFS's financial statements audit. You are in charge of the audit for the year ended March 31, 2018. It is now May 2018.

Here are highlights from the OFS engagement team meeting:

New POS System: Prior to the 2017 theme park season, OFS purchased and implemented a brand new point-of-sale (POS) system. Due to delays with the supplier, OFS was unable to procure the new system until late March 2017. As a result, the POS installation was completed just a day before the theme park's opening day. There was no time to perform any system tests, such as to verify the compatibility between the POS and OFS's accounting system, or to properly train employees. With no time to prepare, OFS cashiers and management were forced to learn the new POS system "on the fly."

There was also no time to install the new system throughout the entertainment complex, and the marina was left without any sales terminals. The old terminals had all been discarded. Thus, marina docking fees could be paid in cash only. Tony is the marina's only employee and has been with OFS since its inception. Although Tony doesn't own a boat, he is an avid sailor who is very much liked and trusted by all marina customers. Each customer must sign a formal agreement, listing the customer's name, the boat's name and dimensions, and the annual docking fee is based on an OFS pricing chart.

Overview of Revenue: In 2018, OFS experienced a considerable drop in revenue, which was attributed to an unusually cool and wet summer and a significant decline in American tourists who usually visit the area. In a typical year, the breakdown of OFS revenues is 80 percent of revenue is generated from the theme park, 20 percent from Merek Neal, and 10 percent from the marina.

Below is a summary of total revenue and net income:

Total Annual Revenue

Year	Revenues	Net Income
2018 (unaudited)	$ 10 000 000	$ 450 000
2017 (audited)	13 000 000	400 000
2016 (audited)	13 800 000	475 000
2015 (audited)	13 600 000	450 000
2014 (audited)	13 700 000	480 000

Annual Marina Revenue

Year	Revenues $
2018 (unaudited)	134 050
2017	152 000
2016	152 500
2015	153 000
2014	152 350

Capital Assets: Below is an excerpt of the capital assets continuity schedule that was provided by OFS accounting clerk.

Restructuring and Potential Sale of OFS: In early August 2017, a rumour leaked to the press that due to problems with its US operations, FFI was no longer interested in operating in Canada. As a result, it was shutting down operations and terminating all staff. At the end of the theme park's season, in late October, FFI publicly announced that it was significantly downsizing and restructuring OFS's operations.

Coinciding with the August rumour, a two-week termination of employment notice was issued to all OFS staff and management, with the exception of Tony, two accounting managers, and two accounting clerks, who were meant to assist with the financial statement audit. The managers and clerks were informed that their employment would end at the audit's completion, expected in June 2018. Both accounting managers are using their vacation days prior to their termination date. They are available to answer questions related to the audit on Tuesdays and Thursdays, the only days they are at work.

OFS management had intended to perform reconciliation on the OFS system's theme-park sales data and bank statements (including monthly credit card reports), but these plans were also put on hold once the termination notices were issued. Also in August 2017, OFS management did not enforce the mandatory reporting and FFI stopped receiving its monthly OFS reporting package.

As part of the management's termination agreement, FFI will pay out 50 percent of net income from OFS's 2018 operations as a severance payment. The amount will be divided and paid to all terminated managers following the audit, at which time FFI intends to bring in its own staff from the United States to temporarily take over OFS operations. FFI plans to finalize its decision about OFS's future over the next six months. Several resort developers are interested in purchasing the property and have approached FFI. FFI is considering two options:

1. Dispose of theme park capital assets individually and sell theme park land to one of the resort developers. OFS would continue operating the observation wheel, marina and concert venue.
2. Sell the entire OFS operation—the theme park, observation wheel, marina and concert venue—to one of the resort developers.

Merek Neal Lawsuit: On February 28, 2018, MN responded to the FFI's decision to shut down park operations by launching a $450K lawsuit against OFS and FFI, accusing the two

Asset Class	Opening Balance March 2017	2018 Capital Asset Additions	2018 Amortization Expense	Ending Balance March 2018	Amortization Rate
Buildings	$ 8 250 000	$ Nil	$ 275 000	$ 7 975 000	40 years
Theme park rides	1 750 000	nil	350 000	1 400 000	20 years
Theme park slides	750 000	nil	150 000	600 000	20 years
Observation wheel	$ 1 275 000	nil	85 000	1 190 000	20 years
Other	200 000	750 000 (Note 1)	52 500	897 500	Various
Total Capital Assets	$ 12 225 000	$ 750 000	$ 912 500	12 062 500	

Note 1: Per management's request, other additions consist of:
- $150K for bird food (amortized over 10 years, the average lifespan of the Canada Goose, which is a big attraction for kids attending the theme park).
- $150K for promotional material with OFS logo (T-shirts, banners, tents, stickers, and pins). Amortized over five years.
- $200K for point of sale system. Amortized over 10 years.
- $250K for "other" capital asset items. Management to provide support and explanation.

parties of breaching the lease agreement and for the loss of potential revenue from concert tickets and concessionary sales. One of the OFS accounting managers believes that MN is just "bluffing" and that once FFI decides about OFS's future, the lawsuit will be withdrawn.

REQUIRED

a. Assess acceptable audit risk for the OFS engagement. Provide support your assessment.

b. Recommend materiality for planning purposes (planning materiality). Be sure to use both quantitative and qualitative analysis as support.

c. Recommend performance materiality for the OFS engagement. Provide support for your recommendation.

d. Identify significant financial reporting risks and explain which key accounts are affected. For each account perform the following:

  i Assess inherent risk (risk of material misstatement prior to consideration of controls). Provide an explanation for your risk assessment and, where applicable, provide support with preliminary analytical review.

  ii Assess control risk and provide an explanation for your risk assessment.

  iii Based upon your assessment of risk of material misstatement, explain the potential misstatement (i.e., over or understatement) for each identified account and what are the relevant assertion(s).

e. Based upon your risk assessment for each account, explain what type of audit strategy would be most appropriate for that account/cycle.

10-33 **1** **6** Auditors develop overall audit plans to ensure that they obtain sufficient appropriate audit evidence. The timing and extent of audit procedures auditors use is a matter of professional judgment, which depends upon a number of factors. Decisions about the mix of audit procedures and the timing of procedures significantly impact the date on which the audit report is issued. Visit the company websites for Scotiabank (**www.scotiabank.com**), BlackBerry (**www.blackberry.com**), and Gildan (**http://www.gildancorp.com/homepage**). Search under "Investor Relations" for the most recent annual report and locate the independent auditor's report.

REQUIRED

a. Identify the year-end for each company. Did any company have a year-end other than December 31? Will the company's year-end have any impact on the audit procedures used and their timing?

b. Based on the number of days between each company's year-end and the date of the audit report and your knowledge of each company's operations, in which audit do you think the auditors placed the greatest reliance on substantive tests of details of balances? Explain.

10-34 **1** **4** **5** **6** Read the Hillsburg Hardware Limited case that appears in the Appendix at the end of the book.

a. Based on the information from the February 26, 2019, meeting between Hillsburg CFO (chief financial officer) Avis Zomer, audit partner Joe Anthony, and audit manager Leslie Nagan, update the audit strategy memo in Figure 10-1 and the Excerpts from Documentation of Understanding the Entity in Figure 10-2. As much as possible, tie your discussion to specific accounts and assertions.

b. Help audit partner Joe Anthony prepare for tomorrow's meeting with the CFO by developing a list of questions that the partner should ask the CFO regarding the potential accounting fraud that was reported through the whistleblower hotline. Think of questions that provide you with information that will help you reassess the inherent and control risks for the Hillsburg audit engagement.

AUDIT SAMPLING CONCEPTS

When we develop our audit strategy, we vary our evidence mix among control testing, substantive analytical procedures, and substantive tests of details. For tests of control and substantive tests of transactions and balances, auditors rely heavily upon sampling. Recall from our discussion of auditors' responsibilities that all audits involve sampling because the auditor cannot examine 100 percent of the transactions. In this chapter, we will see how risk assessment and our planned evidence mix impact many of our sampling decisions. We examine different types of sampling methods, the sampling process, and the important role of professional judgment in the sampling process.

STANDARDS REFERENCED IN THIS CHAPTER

CAS 265 – Communicating deficiencies in internal control to those charged with governance and management

CAS 530 – Audit sampling

LEARNING OBJECTIVES

After studying this chapter, you should be able to:

1 Define audit sampling.

2 Explain the concept of representative sampling and the risks of sampling.

3 Distinguish between statistical and nonstatistical sampling.

4 Select representative samples using nonprobabilistic or probabilistic sample selection methods.

5 Differentiate audit sampling for tests of controls and substantive tests of details.

6 Use attribute sampling for tests of controls.

7 Use nonstatistical sampling for tests of controls.

8 Use nonstatistical sampling for substantive tests of details.

9 Describe statistical sampling for substantive tests of details.

10 Document and apply professional judgment in audit sampling.

Sometimes an Isolated Exception Is the Tip of the Iceberg

David Chen was an experienced assistant on the audit of Sol Systems, a manufacturer of solar panels. While performing tests of controls over sales transactions, he that one of the sales transactions selected for testing was missing shipping information. When asked about the missing documentation, the controller suggested

continued >

this was an isolated clerical mistake. An hour later, he provided David with the shipping document, which appeared to be valid. Since this was the only one in the sample with a problem, David thought that the results of the test would be considered acceptable under the sampling plan his firm had established, even if the transaction was considered an exception. Based upon the controller's explanation, David could even argue that it was an anomaly and conclude that the missing documentation was not an exception at all. Still, the transaction was for a fairly large amount, and David was concerned that the documentation was not initially available.

David consulted with Cindy Hubbard, the experienced senior on the engagement. Her initial reaction was to accept the documentation so David could move on to other testing. After considering it for a few minutes, however, she asked David to look further into the transaction. David discovered that the receivable had not been paid. Instead, a journal entry had been recorded to credit the receivable from the sale. Through a series of journal entries, the receivable ultimately ended up recorded as an asset in a long-term asset account. He examined additional transactions involving this customer and found that they had been handled the same way.

Cindy escalated the findings to the engagement partner, and the firm's forensic auditors discovered that Sol was engaged in a large-scale fraud to overstate sales and earnings. The firm resigned from the engagement and reported the findings to the OSC. David was promoted to audit senior a year earlier than normal.

As demonstrated by the story about David Chen and the audit of Sol Systems, appropriately applying audit sampling is a challenging part of the audit. If David had simply considered the quantitative assessment of his sampling results, he could have concluded that the sample was acceptable and that the control was effective. However, because he evaluated the evidence with professional skepticism, he dug deeper. Remember, as you read the chapter's discussion of how to develop sampling plans for control and substantive tests of details, that it is not simply a mechanical process. Rather, professional judgment and skepticism play a key role in all steps of the sampling process.

LO 1 Define audit sampling.

WHAT IS AUDIT SAMPLING?

Due to the nature of the audit, the auditor does not examine all the available evidence but rather selects evidence from the available population. Sampling is used in testing controls, classes of transactions, and account balances. CAS 530.5(a), *Audit sampling*, defines **audit sampling** as:

CAS

Audit sampling—selective examination of data used when (1) less than 100 percent of the items in the population under examination are being audited, and (2) each item (described as a sampling unit) in the population could be selected as part of the sample.

> The application of audit procedures to less than 100 percent of the items in the population such that all sampling units have a chance of selection in order to provide the auditor with a reasonable basis to make a conclusion on the entire population.

Sampling is appropriate, for example, when the auditor wishes to inspect documents (internal control and substantive testing), reperform calculations (internal control and substantive tests of details of transactions), send out confirmations (substantive tests of details of balances), test fixed asset additions (substantive tests of details of transactions), or perform test counts at an inventory observation (substantive tests of details of balances). Table 11-1 provides a brief summary of what audit sampling is, and what it is not.

LO 2 Explain the concept of representative sampling and the risks of sampling.

REPRESENTATIVE SAMPLING AND ITS RISKS

Sampling represents a key part of the auditor's risk response. A properly planned, performed, and executed sampling process can ensure that the audit tests are both effective (adequately designed to detect control deficiencies or misstatements)

Table 11-1	Audit Sampling: What It Is vs. What It Is Not	
Type of Test	**Audit Sampling**	**Not Audit Sampling**
Control test	Test of attributes on a sample of items for the purpose of concluding on the effectiveness of internal controls through projecting the results to all items	• Test or review of a few transactions to gain an understanding of the nature of the entity's operations or processes • Test of a few transactions to clarify the auditor's understanding of the design of the entity's internal controls
Substantive tests of details	Test of account balance or transaction class details on a sample of items for the purpose of projecting the results to the entire account balance or transaction class to conclude on the fair presentation of the balance or class	• Test of details limited to a specific group of transactions or items within an account balance or transaction class that have a distinct characteristic (i.e., key or unusual items) • 100 percent examination of an account balance or class of transactions

and efficient (the tests do not require excessive effort when no deficiency of misstatement exists).

In this chapter, we will discuss sampling for both tests of controls and substantive tests of details. As summarized in Table 11-1, the objective of sampling when testing controls is to provide the auditor with the evidence necessary to be able to conclude if the controls are effective or ineffective. Recall from Chapters 9 and 10 that if controls are ineffective, then the auditor must adjust the audit strategy (change the nature, timing, and extent of substantive tests). In the case of substantive tests of details, the objective is to estimate the projected misstatement in the class of transactions or account balance. When the projected misstatement exceeds the tolerable misstatement (which is equal to or less than performance materiality), the sample does not provide a reasonable basis to conclude that the class of transactions or account balance is fairly stated.

Although sampling is useful in helping the auditor form conclusions, it is not without its risks. For instance, as illustrated in the control tests examples in Table 11-1, the sample may be too small; or, in the first substantive tests of details example, the sample may not be representative (the auditor is only focusing on items with a distinct characteristic). As a result, the auditor does not have sufficient evidence and could draw an incorrect conclusion.

Whenever an auditor selects a sample from a **population** (the items that make up a class of transactions or an account balance), the objective is to obtain a sample that is representative. A **representative sample** has characteristics of audit interest similar to those in the population as a whole. For example, let us assume that a client's internal controls require a clerk to attach a shipping document to every duplicate sales invoice but that the procedure is *not* followed exactly 3 percent of the time. If the auditor selects a sample of 100 duplicate sales invoices and finds 3 shipping documents missing, the sample is highly representative (of the items and the expected error rate). If two or four such exceptions are found in the sample, the sample is reasonably representative. If many missing items or no missing items are found, the sample is nonrepresentative or the auditor's original understanding of the error rate was incorrect. Similarly, in the case of substantive tests of balances, if the auditor only tests 20 percent of the accounts receivable balance for the existence assertion, it is likely that the sample would not be considered representative of the population (based upon the dollar value of the account balance, the sample size is too small).

In practice, auditors do not know whether a sample is representative, even after all testing is completed (the only way to know if a sample is representative is to

Population—a set of accounts or transactions from which the auditor wishes to draw a conclusion.

Representative sample—a sample with the same characteristics as those of the population.

Sampling risk—the risk of reaching an incorrect conclusion inherent in tests of less than the entire population because the sample is not representative of the population; sampling risk may be reduced by using an increased sample size and an appropriate method of selecting items from the population.

Exception rate—the percentage of items in a population that include exceptions in prescribed controls or monetary correctness.

subsequently audit the entire population). Auditors increase the likelihood of a sample being representative by applying professional judgment, which entails carefully planning the sample, performing appropriate audit tests, and evaluating the sample results. The goal is to avoid an incorrect conclusion due to a sampling error or a nonsampling error. The risks of these two types of errors occurring are called sampling risk and nonsampling risk.

Sampling risk is the risk that the auditor will reach an inappropriate conclusion because the sample is not representative of the population. Sampling risk is an inherent part of sampling that results from testing less than the entire population. For example, assume the auditor decided that a control was not effective if there is a population **exception rate** of 6 percent. Assume the auditor accepts the control as effective based on the tests of the control with a sample of 100 items that had two exceptions. If the population actually had an 8 percent exception rate, the auditor incorrectly accepted the population because the sample was not sufficiently representative.

Auditors have two ways of controlling sampling risk:

1. Adjust sample size.
2. Use an appropriate method of selecting sample items in the population.

Increasing sample size reduces sampling risk and vice versa. At one extreme, a sample of all items of a population has zero sampling risk (which, in reality, is not sampling). At the other extreme, a sample of one or two items has an extremely high sampling risk.

While using the appropriate sample selection method does not eliminate or even reduce sampling risk, it does allow the auditor to measure risk associated with a given sample size if statistical methods of sample selection are used.

Nonsampling risk—the risk of failing to identify existing exceptions in the sampling; nonsampling risk (nonsampling error) is caused by failure to recognize exceptions and by inappropriate or ineffective audit procedures.

Nonsampling risk is the risk that the auditor will draw an incorrect conclusion due to (1) the failure to recognize or interpret exceptions, and/or (2) inappropriate or ineffective audit procedures. Failure to recognize or interpret exceptions may occur because the auditor does not understand what an exception is, or simply because the auditor is bored or tired. Inappropriate or ineffective procedures are those procedures that do not test the relevant transaction or balance-related objective. In our preceding example—the clerk attaches a shipping document to every duplicate sales invoice—an exception would be a missing shipping document or a case where the shipping document's details do not match the sales invoice. An ineffective audit procedure would be to select a sample of shipping documents to determine whether each is attached to a set of duplicate sales invoices. In this case, the auditor would be doing the test in the wrong direction by starting with the shipping document instead of the duplicate sales invoice (because the process is initiated by the sales invoice, not the shipping document). The appropriate procedure would be to examine a sample of duplicate sales invoices to determine if shipping documents were attached. In order to control nonsampling risk, along with proper training, instruction, supervision, and review, audit procedures must be carefully designed to test the relevant assertion(s).

LO **3** Distinguish between statistical and nonstatistical sampling.

STATISTICAL VERSUS NONSTATISTICAL SAMPLING

Audit sampling methods can be divided into two broad categories: statistical sampling and nonstatistical sampling. These categories are similar in that they both involve three phases:

1. *Planning.* Plan the sample and determine sample size.
2. *Performance.* Select the sample and perform the tests.
3. *Evaluation.* Evaluate the results and conclude on the acceptability of the population tested.

Table 11-2	Three Phases of the Sample Process
Phase	**Action**
1. Planning	Decide that a sample size of 100 is needed. Decide which 100 items to select from the population.
2. Performance	Perform the audit procedure for each of the 100 items and determine that three exceptions exist.
3. Evaluation	Reach conclusions about the likely exception rate in the total population when the sample exception rate equals 3 percent.

The purpose of planning the sample is to make sure that the audit tests are performed in a manner that provides the desired sampling risk and minimizes the likelihood of nonsampling error. Selecting the sample involves deciding how to select sample items from the population. Performing the tests involves examining documents and performing other audit tests. Evaluating the results involves both quantitative and qualitative evaluation of the audit tests in order to develop a well supported conclusion.

Assume that an auditor selects a sample of 100 duplicate sales invoices from a population, tests each to determine whether a shipping document is attached, and determines that there are three exceptions. Let's look at those actions step-by-step using Table 11-2.

Statistical sampling differs from nonstatistical sampling in that, by applying mathematical rules, auditors can quantify (measure) sampling risk in planning the sample (Step 1) and evaluating the results (Step 3). (You may remember calculating a statistical result at a 95 percent **confidence level**, which is a statement of probability, in a statistics course. The 95 percent confidence level provides a 5 percent sampling risk.)

In **nonstatistical sampling**, auditors do not quantify sampling risk. Instead, auditors use their professional judgment to select sample items that will provide the most useful information, and to reach their conclusions on the population. For that reason, the selection of nonstatistical samples is often termed **judgmental sampling**. A properly designed nonstatistical sample can be as effective as a properly designed statistical sample.

Probabilistic versus Nonprobabilistic Sample Selection

Both probabilistic and nonprobabilistic sample selection fall under Step 2, performance. When using **probabilistic sample selection**, the auditor randomly selects items such that each population item has a known probability of being included in the sample. This process requires great care and uses one of several methods that we discuss in the next section. In **nonprobabilistic sample selection**, the auditor selects sample items from the population using professional judgment.

SAMPLE SELECTION METHODS

Auditing standards permit auditors to use either statistical or nonstatistical sampling methods. However, it is essential that each method be applied with due care. All steps of the process must be followed carefully. When statistical sampling is used, the sample *must be a probabilistic one*, and appropriate statistical evaluation methods must be used with the sample results to make the sampling risk computations. The most common sample selection methods are summarized in Table 11-3.

Nonprobabilistic Sample Selection

Nonprobabilistic sample selection methods are those that do not meet the technical requirements for probabilistic sample selection. Since these methods are not based on

Statistical sampling—the use of mathematical measurement techniques to calculate formal statistical results and quantify sampling risk.

Confidence level—statement of probability.

Nonstatistical sampling—a sampling procedure that does not permit the numerical measurement of sampling risk.

Judgmental sampling—use of professional judgment rather than statistical methods to select sample items for audit tests.

Probabilistic sample selection—a method of selecting a sample such that each population item has a known probability of being included in the sample; the sample is selected by a random process.

Nonprobabilistic sample selection—a method of sample selection in which the auditor uses professional judgment to select items from the population.

LO **4** Select representative samples using nonprobabilistic or probabilistic sample selection methods.

Table 11-3	Common Sample Selection Methods		
	Nonprobabilistic	**Probabilistic**	**Both Nonprobabilistic and Probabilistic**
	• Directed sample selection	• Simple random sample selection	• Stratified (layers of data) sample selection
	• Block sample selection	• Systematic sample selection	
	• Haphazard sample selection	• Probability proportionate-to-size sample selection	

strict mathematical probabilities, the representativeness of the sample may be difficult to determine. The information content of the sample, including its representativeness, will be based on the knowledge and skill of the auditor in applying his or her judgment in the circumstances.

Directed Sample Selection **Directed sample selection** is a nonprobabilistic method of sample selection in which each item in the sample is selected on the basis of some judgmental criteria (based upon risk) established by the auditor. This is perhaps the most common type of sampling method used in auditing. The auditor does not rely on equal chances of selection, but rather deliberately selects items according to the criteria. Auditors often use generalized audit software (GAS) to list the directed samples or to provide survey summaries that enable the auditor to identify at-risk transactions. The logic underlying this type of sample selection is that if none of the higher-risk items selected contain misstatements, then it is less likely that a material misstatement exists in the population. Table 11-4 shows commonly used criteria.

Block Sample Selection In **block sample selection**, auditors select the first item in a block and the remainder of the block is chosen in sequence. One example of a block sample is the selection of a sequence of 100 sales transactions from the sales journal for the third week of March. A total sample of 100 could also be selected by taking 5 blocks of 20 items each, 10 blocks of 10, or 50 blocks of 2.

It is ordinarily acceptable to use block samples if a reasonable number of blocks are used. If few blocks are used, the probability of obtaining a nonrepresentative sample is too great, considering the possibility of employee turnover, changes in the accounting system, and the seasonal nature of the business. A common use of block testing is testing cutoff. The auditor selects a block of invoices, receiving documents, and shipping documents spanning both sides of the year-end date to ensure that the transactions were recorded in the proper period. GAS is often used to list the transactions that occurred during the period that the auditor is interested in.

Directed sample selection—a nonprobabilistic method of sample selection in which each item in the sample is selected on the basis of some judgmental criteria established by the auditor.

Block sample selection—a nonprobabilistic method of sample selection in which items are selected in measured sequences.

Table 11-4	Commonly Used Directed Sample Selection Methods and Examples	
Commonly Used Directed Sample Selection Method	**Examples**	
Items most likely to contain misstatements	• Receivables outstanding for a long time.	
	• Purchases from and sales to officers or affiliates.	
Items containing selected population characteristics	• Adjustments to sales in the last month of the year.	
	• All transactions from the legal expense account.	
Large dollar coverage	• All sales transactions that equal 75 percent of performance materiality or higher.	
	• Repairs and maintenance expenses that are greater than $10 000 (or 10 percent of materiality).	

When we think of foraging, we usually do not think about financial statement auditing. However, academics argue that when auditors are looking for information or evidence, they often display the same behaviour as animals foraging for food. Simply put, animals will attempt to maximize the amount of food they take within a given period of time. What does this mean for auditing? Basically, auditors will try to minimize their time and effort when gathering evidence to support financial statement assertions, similar to the self-serving bias that we have seen in other auditor decisions. Well, this all sounds fine in theory, but does it really happen?

Several experimental studies, using actual auditors as their subjects, found that auditors are consistently biased when using haphazard sampling—from selecting items on accounts receivable and inventory listings to selecting items on which to perform test counts when observing a client's inventory count. So how can auditors overcome this self-serving bias? A recent study conducted by Benjamin Commerford and his colleagues provides a simple yet effective solution.

In the study, the researchers simulated auditors selecting a sample for control testing—some auditors had a client manager who provided information in a timely manner, while others had a client manager who was slow. This study found that in the situation where the client manager was slow, the auditors decreased sampling from that manager if there had not been any control deviations related to that manager in prior samples. (In other words, the auditors were foraging and ultimately biased in their sample selection.) However, if that slow manager was associated with a control deviation in a prior year's sample, the auditors did not decrease sampling from that manager. (In other words, the auditors exhibited professional skepticism.) That is good news—auditors are appropriately skeptical when there are clear indicators of potential deception. However, the intriguing finding of this study was that, when the auditors were asked to select a sample for another auditor under the same condition of a slow manager with no control deviation, the bias disappeared. In other words, the auditors' foraging instincts did not kick in and they did not select the sample in a self-serving manner. This is a simple yet effective procedure for firms to consider when developing haphazard sampling plans!

Sources: Based on B. Commerford, R. Hatfield, R. Houston, and C. Mullis, "Debiasing auditor judgments from the influence of information foraging behavior," *International Symposium on Audit Research,* 2014, Maastricht, The Netherlands. T. Hall, A. Higson, B.J. Pierce, K. Pierce, and C. Skousen, "Haphazard sampling: Selection biases induced by control listing properties and the estimation consequences of these biases," *Behavioral Research in Accounting*, vol. 24, no. 2, 2012, pp. 101–132.

Haphazard Sample Selection When the auditor goes through a population and selects items for the sample without regard to their size, source, or other distinguishing characteristics, he or she is attempting to select without bias. This is called a **haphazard sample selection**. The most serious shortcoming of haphazard sample selection is the difficulty in remaining completely unbiased in the selection. Because of the auditor's training and unintentional bias, certain population items are more likely than others to be included in the sample. As highlighted in Auditing in Action 11-1, research has demonstrated that auditors are susceptible to this type of bias in various types of sampling situations.

Although haphazard and block sample selection appear to be less logical than directed sample selection, they are often useful as audit tools and should not be ignored. In some situations, the cost of more complex sample selection methods outweighs the benefits obtained from using them. For example, assume that the auditor wants to trace credits from the accounts receivable transaction history files to the duplicate bank deposit slips and other authorized sources as a test for fictitious credits in the data files. A haphazard or block approach is simpler and much less costly than other selection methods in this situation.

> **Haphazard sample selection**—a nonprobabilistic method of sample selection in which items are chosen without regard to their size, source, or other distinguishing characteristics.

CONCEPT CHECK

C11-1 During the audit, a new staff member failed to record a client's 10-cent calculation error as an error. What type of error or risk does this mistake exemplify? Why?

C11-2 Provide two examples of directed sample selection that could be used for the audit of inventory.

Probabilistic Sample Selection

Statistical sampling requires a probabilistic sample to measure sampling risk. For probabilistic samples, the auditor uses no judgment about which sample items are selected, except in choosing which of the four selection methods to use. Generalized audit software (GAS), such as ACL and IDEA, is capable of running all of these sample selection methods. If sample sizes are high and data are accessible, it is more cost-effective for the auditor to use GAS rather than selecting the sample manually.

Simple Random Sample Selection A simple **random sample** is one in which every possible combination of population items has an equal chance of constituting the sample. Simple random sampling is used to sample populations where each item is considered to have the same characteristics for audit purposes. For example, a simple random sample of 60 items contained in the cash disbursements journal throughout the year could be selected. Appropriate auditing procedures would be applied to the 60 items selected, and conclusions would be drawn and applied to all cash disbursement transactions recorded for the year.

Random Number Selection Methods When a simple random sample is obtained, a method must be used to ensure that all items in the population have an equal chance of selection. Suppose that in the above example there were a total of 12 000 cash disbursement transactions for the year. A simple random sample of one transaction would be such that each of the 12 000 transactions would have an equal chance of being selected. This would be done by obtaining a random number between 1 and 12 000. (Random numbers are a series of digits that have equal probabilities of occurring over long runs and that have no discernible pattern.) If the number was 3895, the auditor would select and test the 3895th cash disbursement transaction recorded in the cash disbursements journal.

Replacement versus Nonreplacement Sampling Random numbers may be obtained with replacement or without replacement. In replacement sampling, an element in the population can be included in the sample more than once, whereas in nonreplacement sampling, an element can be included only once. If the random number corresponding to an item is selected more than once in nonreplacement sampling, it is not included in the sample a second time. Although both selection approaches are consistent with sound statistical theory, auditors normally use nonreplacement sampling.

Systematic Sample Selection In **systematic selection** (also known as "systematic sampling"), the auditor calculates an interval and then methodically selects the items for the sample based on the size of the interval. The interval is determined by dividing the population size by the number of sample items desired. For example, if a population of sales invoices ranges from 652 to 3151 and the desired sample size is 125, the interval is 20 [= (3151 − 651)/125]. The auditor must now select a random number between 0 and 19 to determine the starting point for the sample. If the randomly selected number is 9, the first item in the sample is invoice number 661 (= 652 + 9). The remaining 124 items are 681 (= 661 + 20), 701 (= 681 + 20), and so on through item 3141.

The advantage of systematic sampling is its ease of use. For most populations, the systematic sample can be drawn quickly; the approach automatically puts the numbers in sequence, and the appropriate documentation is easy to develop.

A major problem with systematic selection is the possibility of bias. Because of the way systematic selection works, once the first item in the sample is selected, all other items are chosen automatically. This causes no problem if the characteristic of interest (such as a possible control deviation) is distributed randomly throughout the population; however, in some cases, characteristics of interest may not be randomly distributed. For example, if a control deviation occurred at a certain time of the month or with certain types of documents, a systematic sample could have a higher likelihood of failing to be representative than a simple random sample. It is important, therefore, when systematic selection is used, to consider possible patterns in the population data that could cause sample bias.

A variation of systematic sample selection by unit of interest is used by the **probability-proportionate-to-size (PPS) sampling** methods. Here, the individual dollar is considered the unit of interest. The interval is determined based upon a statistical formula, and the transactions associated with that dollar interval are selected. Monetary unit sampling (MUS), which we discuss later in the chapter, uses PPS for its sample selection method.

Stratified Sample Selection When selecting samples, auditors often stratify the sample prior to selecting the sample items. In **stratified sampling**, the sample is split into multiple smaller sets or layers, of which each set has a similar characteristic. Stratification can occur by dollar amount (sales over $50 000; sales under that amount), by location (foreign versus domestic), by customer, by division, or by another criteria, such as noncommission (sales from head office) versus commission-based sales (sales made by sales personnel). It all depends upon how the auditor assesses risk and defines the objective of the audit test.

Auditors often stratify samples. That is because stratification can improve the efficiency of the audit by focusing the audit work on transactions that may be more subject to material error. CAS 530 (Appendix A) explains that the objective of stratification is to reduce variability of items within each stratum and, therefore, allow sample size to be reduced without increasing sampling risk. After data are stratified, the sample will be selected using one of the methods previously discussed (either probabilistic or nonprobabilistic).

As previously mentioned, regardless of whether auditors choose to use nonstatistical or statistical sampling or use probabilistic or nonprobablistic sample selections, they must follow a systematic process. In the next sections, we discuss the audit sampling process and apply it to control tests and substantive tests of balances. Sampling concepts are illustrated for the revenue cycle, but they are equally applicable to other cycles and relevant balances.

> **Probability-proportionate-to-size (PPS) sampling**—a modified form of physical attribute sampling that focuses on the individual dollar (or unit of currency, such as the euro) as the unit of interest, rather than a physical unit. This is also called simply proportionate-to-size sampling, monetary unit sampling, or dollar unit sampling.
>
> **Stratified sampling**—a method of sampling in which all the elements in the total population are divided into two or more subpopulations that are independently tested.
>
>

CONCEPT CHECK

C11–3 List the three features of probabilistic sample selection.

C11–4 List one advantage and one disadvantage associated with systematic sample selection.

THE AUDIT SAMPLING PROCESS FOR TESTS OF CONTROLS AND SUBSTANTIVE TESTS OF DETAILS

> **LO 5** Differentiate audit sampling for tests of controls and substantive tests of details.

Sampling concepts apply to both tests of controls and substantive tests of details. In both cases, an auditor wants to make an inference about the entire population based on a sample. Both sampling and nonsampling risks are therefore important for tests of controls, substantive tests of transactions, and tests of details of balances. The main differences among tests of controls, and substantive tests of details of transactions and of balances are in what the auditor wants to measure, as shown in Table 11-5.

Table 11-5	Differences Among Three Types of Audit Tests
Type of Test	**What It Measures**
Test of controls	The operating effectiveness of controls
Substantive test of details of transactions	The monetary correctness of individual transactions in the accounting system. If performed as part of a dual test, the operating effectiveness of controls.
Substantive test of details of balances	Whether the dollar amounts of account balances are materially misstated

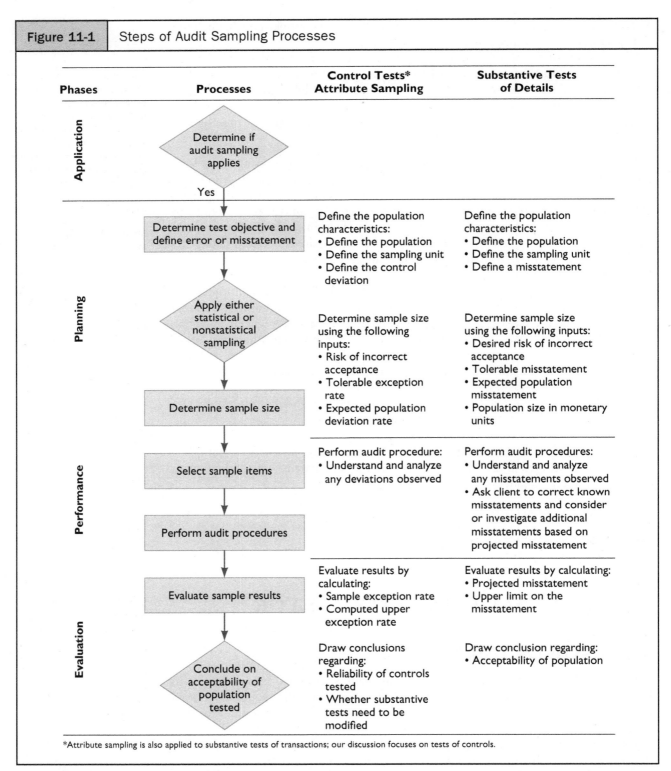

		Control Tests*	**Substantive Tests**
Phases	**Processes**	**Attribute Sampling**	**of Details**

Figure 11-1 | Steps of Audit Sampling Processes

Application

Determine if audit sampling applies

Yes

Planning

Determine test objective and define error or misstatement

Define the population characteristics:
- Define the population
- Define the sampling unit
- Define the control deviation

Define the population characteristics:
- Define the population
- Define the sampling unit
- Define a misstatement

Apply either statistical or nonstatistical sampling

Determine sample size

Determine sample size using the following inputs:
- Risk of incorrect acceptance
- Tolerable exception rate
- Expected population deviation rate

Determine sample size using the following inputs:
- Desired risk of incorrect acceptance
- Tolerable misstatement
- Expected population misstatement
- Population size in monetary units

Performance

Select sample items

Perform audit procedure:
- Understand and analyze any deviations observed

Perform audit procedures:
- Understand and analyze any misstatements observed
- Ask client to correct known misstatements and consider or investigate additional misstatements based on projected misstatement

Perform audit procedures

Evaluation

Evaluate sample results

Evaluate results by calculating:
- Sample exception rate
- Computed upper exception rate

Evaluate results by calculating:
- Projected misstatement
- Upper limit on the misstatement

Conclude on acceptability of population tested

Draw conclusions regarding:
- Reliability of controls tested
- Whether substantive tests need to be modified

Draw conclusion regarding:
- Acceptability of population

*Attribute sampling is also applied to substantive tests of transactions; our discussion focuses on tests of controls.

Source: Republished with permission of American Accounting Association, from R. Elder, A. Akresh, S. Glover, J. Higgs, and J. Liljegren Audit sampling research: A synthesis and implications for future research," 2013. Auditing: A Journal of Practice & Theory 32 (Supplement 1): 99–129, © 2013; permission conveyed through Copyright Clearance Center, Inc.

Figure 11-1 presents the steps in the audit sampling process for attribute sampling (which applies to tests of controls) and substantive tests of details, which are based upon the auditing standards.

The first step in the process is that the auditor must determine if sampling is appropriate. The auditor considers the nature of the population, the account and assertions to be tested, and the assurance needed. The auditor then determines the objectives of the test and defines the deviation (in the case of tests of controls), or misstatement (in the case of substantive tests of details). If sampling applies, the auditor also decides whether to use statistical or nonstatistical sampling and whether the sample will gather evidence on binary characteristics (attribute sampling, which is used in control tests) or on monetary balances (substantive tests).

The auditor then determines sample size, based upon various inputs, and selects the items for testing. As we have already discussed, the items should be representative. The method for obtaining a representative sample can be probabilistic or nonprobabilistic. After performing the audit procedures, the auditor then evaluates the sample results. This part of the process requires considerable professional judgment since the auditor must assess the underlying cause of the deviations or misstatements. This judgment can have a significant impact on the audit strategy. Finally, the auditor will project the sample results over the entire population and make appropriate conclusions. We will now expand upon this process and apply it to the two types of tests to which sampling applies—tests of controls and substantive tests of details.

USING SAMPLING FOR TESTS OF CONTROLS

LO **6** Use attribute sampling for tests of controls.

As we have discussed previously, when the auditor has decided to rely upon controls, the auditor must perform tests of controls focusing on operating effectiveness. The statistical sampling method commonly used for tests of controls is **attribute sampling**, which is designed to answer the question, "What percent of items contain errors?" The **attribute** is a characteristic of the population that is of interest to the auditor. The results of attribute sampling provide a statistical basis for the auditor to conclude whether the control is operating as intended, reflecting a binary (yes/no) proposition (e.g., Is the control operating?). Auditing in Action 11-2 and our opening vignette are both examples of attribute testing.

Attribute sampling—a statistical, probabilistic method of sample evaluation that results in an estimate of the proportion of items in a population containing a characteristic or attribute of interest.

When substantive tests of transactions are being performed in conjunction with control tests, attribute sampling can be also applied to the tests of details with the binary yes/no proposition (e.g., Is the amount correct or incorrect?) to assess effectiveness of controls. In addition, given that substantive tests of details focus on monetary misstatements, the results can be used to project the total misstatement in the particular class of transactions that are being tested.

Attribute—the characteristic being tested for in the population.

AUDITING IN ACTION 11-2
Application of Sampling to Testing Procurement Controls

In 2014, as part of a forensic audit requested by the Ontario Ministry of Education, Ernst & Young (EY) examined the procurement controls for the Toronto District School Board (TDSB). According to their report, the auditors used directed sampling to select the sample items. Based upon specified selection criteria, they selected their sample from the accounts payable transactions for a five-year period. For the selected transactions, EY traced documents to original contracts, invoices, and committee minutes where available. Invoices were analyzed and reviewed for numerical accuracy as well as for appropriate review and approval.

EY found that 45 percent of the 20 samples tested did not use a competitive bid process as required under the policy. Further, almost half of the 45 percent also did not meet the approval requirements. It would appear that the deviation rate was exceptionally high and that the controls were not operating as designed; this is a significant control deficiency. Given that the auditors recommended that all employees involved in the procurement process should be trained, it appears to be an operation deficiency rather than a design deficiency.

Source: Based on Ernst & Young, "Report to the Minister on the Toronto District School Board," December 2, 2013, accessed August 9, 2017, at **http://www.edu.gov.on.ca/eng/new/2013/ErnstYoungReport.pdf**.

Steps in Attribute Sampling

Determine Whether Sampling Applies Sampling does not apply to all tests of controls. For example, in the following incomplete audit program, sampling could only be used for Procedures 3, 4, and 5.

Audit Procedure	Performed by	WP Ref
1. Review sales transactions for large and unusual amounts (analytical procedure or directed sample).		
2. Observe whether the duties of the accounts receivable clerk are separate from the handling of cash (test of control).		
3. Examine a sample of duplicate sales invoices for the following: a. Credit approval by the credit manager (test of control). b. The existence of an attached shipping document (test of control). c. Inclusion of a chart of accounts number (test of control).		
4. Select a sample of shipping documents, and trace each to related duplicate sales invoices for existence (test of control).		
5. Compare the quantity on each duplicate sales invoice with the quantity on related shipping documents (test of control).		

Audit sampling is not appropriate for the first two procedures in this audit program. The first is an analytical procedure. The second is an observation procedure for which no documentation exists to perform audit sampling. Audit sampling generally applies to manual controls. Automated controls can be tested 100 percent using computer-assisted auditing techniques.

Determine the Test Objective The overall objectives of the test must be stated in terms of the risks addressed and the transaction cycle being tested. A typical control test for the sales cycle would be to test the completeness assertion by verifying that goods shipped have been invoiced.

Define Population Characteristics Whenever audit sampling is used, the auditor must carefully define the population characteristics, which consists of three steps: (1) define the attribute and the control deviation, (2) define the population, and (3) define the sampling unit.

Define the Attribute and Control Deviation A clear and precise statement of what constitutes an attribute guides the staff person who performs the audit procedures to properly identify exceptions, thereby reducing nonsampling risk. For example, the attribute of interest is credit approval in the following audit procedure: "Examine a sample of duplicate sales invoices for credit approval by the credit manager." In the case of a manual system, the control deviation (or exception) would be a lack of initials indicating credit approval.

Define the Population The auditor must sample from the entire population as it has been defined. The auditor may generalize only about that population that has been sampled. For example, in performing tests of controls of occurrence for sales, the auditor would define the population as all recorded sales for the year. If the auditor samples from only one month's transactions, it is invalid to draw conclusions about the invoices for the entire year.

It is important that the auditor carefully define the population, which is consistent with the audit objectives and assertions being tested, in advance. For different tests in the audit program of the same cycle, it may be necessary to define more than one population for a given set of audit procedures. For example, if the auditor intends to trace from sales invoices to shipping documents and from shipping documents to duplicate sales invoices, there are two populations (i.e., one population of shipping documents and another of duplicate sales invoices).

An important point to consider is the period of time to be covered by the test. In the case of controls, the relevant time period is the year. However, as discussed in Chapter 9, tests of controls are often performed at interim and may cover 9 to 11 months. If controls are found to be effective at interim, the auditor must take additional steps, through inquiry and some further testing, to assure controls remain effective as of the year-end date.

Define the Sampling Unit The sampling unit is defined by the auditor based on the definition of the population and the objective of the test. It is helpful to think of the sampling unit as the starting point for doing the audit tests. For the revenue cycle, the sampling unit is typically a sales invoice or shipping document number. For example, if the auditor wants to test the occurrence of sales, the appropriate unit is the sales invoices recorded in the sales journal.

Determine Initial Sample Size For attribute sampling, the auditor determines **initial sample size** using the following inputs: (1) tolerable exception rate, (2) acceptable risk of overreliance, and (3) expected population deviation rate. All of these inputs are based upon the auditor's professional judgment.

Initial sample size—sample size determined by statistical tables or by professional judgment (nonstatistical sampling).

Tolerable Exception Rate Establishing the **tolerable exception rate (TER)** for each attribute requires considerable professional judgment. TER represents the highest exception rate that the auditor will permit in the control being tested and still be willing to conclude that the control is operating effectively. For example, assume that the auditor decides that TER for the attribute of sales invoice credit approval is 6 percent. This means that the auditor has decided that even if 6 percent of the sales invoices are not approved for credit, the credit approval control is still effective in terms of the assessed control risk included in the audit plan.

When determining TER, the auditor considers the degree of reliance to be placed on the control and the significance of the control to the audit. If only one internal control is used (meaning it is significant) to support a low control risk assessment for an objective, TER would be lower for the attribute than if multiple controls were used to support a low control risk assessment for the same objective. TER has a significant impact on sample size. A larger sample size is needed for a lower TER than for a higher TER. For example, a larger sample is required for a TER of 4 percent than for a TER of 6 percent.

Tolerable exception rate (TER)—the exception rate that the auditor will permit in the population and still be willing to conclude that the control is operating effectively, and/or the amount of monetary errors or fraud and other irregularities in the transactions that were established as acceptable during planning.

Acceptable Risk of Overreliance **Acceptable risk of overreliance (ARO)** is the auditor's measure of sampling risk. It measures the risk the auditor is willing to take of accepting that a control is effective when the true population exception risk is greater than TER. To illustrate, assume that TER is 6 percent, ARO is 10 percent, and the true population exception rate is 8 percent. The control in this case is not operating (is ineffective) because the true exception rate of 8 percent exceeds TER. The auditor, of course, does not know the true population exception rate. The high ARO of 10 percent means that the auditor is willing to take a fairly substantial risk (10 percent) of concluding that the control is effective after all testing is completed, even when it is ineffective. If the auditor finds the control effective in this illustration, he or she will have overrelied on the system of internal control (used a lower assessed control risk than justified).

In choosing an appropriate ARO for each attribute, auditors must use their best judgment. The main consideration in this decision is the extent to which they plan to reduce assessed control risk. For audits where there is extensive reliance on internal controls, control risk would be assessed at low and, therefore, ARO would also be low (5 percent). Conversely, if the auditor plans to rely on controls only to a limited extent, control risk will be assessed as higher and so will ARO.

The auditor can establish different TER and ARO levels for different attributes of an audit test, depending on the importance of an attribute and related control. For example, auditors typically use higher TER and ARO levels for tests of credit approval than for the occurrence of duplicate sales invoices and bills of lading. This makes sense because exceptions of the latter are more likely to have a direct impact on the financial statements than the former.

Acceptable risk of overreliance (ARO)—the risk that the auditor is willing to take of accepting a control as effective or a rate of monetary errors or fraud and other irregularities as tolerable, when the true population exception rate is greater than the tolerable exception rate.

Estimated Population Exception Rate   Auditors should assess the **estimated population exception rate (EPER)** in advance to plan the appropriate sample size. If EPER is low, a relatively small sample size will satisfy the auditor's tolerable exception rate because a less precise estimate is required. The EPER recognizes that sometimes a control fails or can be bypassed.

Auditors often use the preceding year's audit results to estimate EPER. If prior year results are not available, or if they are considered unreliable, the auditor can take a small preliminary sample of the current year's population to develop an estimate. It is not critical that the estimate be precise, because the current year's **sample exception rate (SER)** is ultimately used to estimate the population characteristics. If a preliminary sample is used, it can be included in the total sample, as long as appropriate sample selection procedures are followed. For example, assume that an auditor takes a preliminary sample of 30 items to estimate the EPER that considers the entire population. Later, if the auditor decides that a total sample size of 100 is needed, only 70 additional items will need to be properly selected and tested.

These three factors—ARO, TER, and EPER—are used to determine the initial sample size. In many cases, the auditor will use GAS (either ACL or IDEA) and will simply input the information into the program. To understand how the program calculates the sample sizes, we will demonstrate using Table 11-6, which gives sample sizes for several combinations of TER and EPER for ARO of 5 percent and 10 percent. As we can see from the completed data sample form (Figure 11-2) for the client, Hillsburg Hardware, this is a fairly straightforward process.

When you refer to Figure 11-2, you will note that the auditor has used an ARO of 10 percent for each of the five controls. Control risk is set higher because there are numerous controls, such as programmed controls and management review for exception rates. Although the auditor is testing five different attributes, she is using the same source documents (in other words, the same population); therefore, the same sampling risk applies for all the tests. However, the TER and EPER for each of the attributes are likely to be different. The EPER for each attribute is very low, in the range of zero to 2 percent. Due to these low exception rates, it is cost-effective to test these controls (note that, in Table 11-6, as TER and EPER increase, so does sample size). To determine sample size, refer to the lower panel (10 percent ARO) and look at the intersection of TER and EPER.

Select the Sample and Perform Audit Procedures

After the auditor has computed the initial sample size for the audit sampling application, she must choose the items in the population to be included in the sample. Although nonprobabilistic methods are acceptable, probabilistic methods are used to choose the sample when using statistical-based attribute sampling. In the case of our sample, as indicated on the attribute sampling data sheet (Figure 11-2), random sampling is used. ACL or IDEA both have random number generators and spreadsheet software, such as Excel, has the same capabilities.

To minimize the possibility of the client altering the sample items, the auditor should not inform the client too far in advance of the sample items selected. The auditor should also control the sample after the client provides the documents. (These are all good examples of applying appropriate professional skepticism in the sampling process.) Several additional sample items may be selected as extras to replace any voided items in the original sample.

The auditor performs the audit procedures by examining each item in the sample to determine whether it is consistent with the definition of the attribute and by recording all exceptions found. CAS 530 requires that if the test cannot be conducted for the item selected, then the auditor must select another transaction. For example, the auditor might select an invoice to conduct a pricing test and find that the item selected was an adjustment invoice, so the pricing test cannot be conducted. In that

CAS

Table 11-6	Determining Sample Size for Attribute Sampling*

5 Percent Risk of Overreliance

Tolerable Exception Rate (in percentage)

Estimated Population Exception Rate (in percentage)	2	3	4	5	6	7	8	9	10	15	20
0.00	149	99	74	59	49	42	36	32	29	19	14
0.25	236	157	117	93	78	66	58	51	46	30	22
0.50	313	157	117	93	78	66	58	51	46	30	22
0.75	386	208	117	93	78	66	58	51	46	30	22
1.00	*	257	156	93	78	66	58	51	46	30	22
1.25	*	303	156	124	78	66	58	51	46	30	22
1.50	*	392	192	124	103	66	58	51	46	30	22
1.75	*	*	227	153	103	88	77	51	46	30	22
2.00	*	*	294	181	127	88	77	68	46	30	22
2.25	*	*	390	208	127	88	77	68	61	30	22
2.50	*	*	*	234	150	109	77	68	61	30	22
2.75	*	*	*	286	173	109	95	68	61	30	22
3.00	*	*	*	361	195	129	95	84	61	30	22
3.25	*	*	*	458	238	148	112	84	61	30	22
3.50	*	*	*	*	280	167	112	84	76	40	22
3.75	*	*	*	*	341	185	129	100	76	40	22
4.00	*	*	*	*	421	221	146	100	89	40	22
5.00	*	*	*	*	*	478	240	158	116	40	30
6.00	*	*	*	*	*	*	*	266	179	50	30
7.00	*	*	*	*	*	*	*	*	298	68	37

10 Percent Risk of Overreliance

	2	3	4	5	6	7	8	9	10	15	20
0.00	114	76	57	45	38	32	28	25	22	15	11
0.25	194	129	96	77	64	55	48	42	38	25	18
0.50	194	129	96	77	64	55	48	42	38	25	18
0.75	265	129	96	77	64	55	48	42	38	25	18
1.00	398	176	96	77	64	55	48	42	38	25	18
1.25	*	221	132	77	64	55	48	42	38	25	18
1.50	*	265	132	105	64	55	48	42	38	25	18
1.75	*	390	166	105	88	55	48	42	38	25	18
2.00	*	*	198	132	88	75	48	42	38	25	18
2.25	*	*	262	132	88	75	65	42	38	25	18
2.50	*	*	353	158	110	75	65	58	38	25	18
2.75	*	*	471	209	132	94	65	58	52	25	18
3.00	*	*	*	258	132	94	65	58	52	25	18
3.25	*	*	*	306	153	113	82	58	52	25	18
3.50	*	*	*	400	194	113	82	73	52	25	18
3.75	*	*	*	*	235	131	98	73	52	25	18
4.00	*	*	*	*	274	149	98	73	65	25	18
5.00	*	*	*	*	*	318	160	115	78	34	18
6.00	*	*	*	*	*	*	349	182	116	43	25
7.00	*	*	*	*	*	*	*	385	199	52	25
8.00	*	*	*	*	*	*	*	*	424	60	25

* = Sample is too large to be cost-effective for most audit applications.

Notes: 1. This table assumes a large population. 2. Tables do not include higher population exception rates, and sample sizes over 500 are not reported. 3. Sample sizes are the same in certain columns even when expected population exception rates differ because of the method of constructing the tables. Sample sizes are calculated for attribute sampling using the expected number of exceptions in the population, but auditors can deal more conveniently with expected population exception rates. For example, in the 15 percent column for tolerable exception rate, at an ARO of 5 percent, initial sample size for most EPERs is 30. One exception, divided by a sample size of 30, is 3.3 percent. Therefore, for all EPERs greater than zero but less than 3.3 percent, the initial sample size is the same.

Source: Data from *AICPA Auditing Sampling Audit Guide*, March 1, 2014, accessed at **www.aicpa.org**.

Figure 11-2	Attribute Sampling Data Sheet

Client Hillsburg Hardware Limited   **Year end** 31/12/18

Audit Area Tests of Controls—Billing Function and Recording of Sales   **Pop. size** 145 853

Define the objective(s) Examine duplicate sales invoices and related documents to determine if the system has functioned as intended and as described in the audit program.

Define the population precisely (including stratification, if any) POS invoices and credit sales invoices for the period 1/1/18 to 31/12/18. First POS number = 140672. Last POS number = 283294. First credit sales invoice number = 3600. Last credit sales invoice number = 6831.

Define the sampling unit, organization of population items, and random selection procedures Sales invoice number, POS invoice numbers, and credit recorded in the sales files sequentially; random sampling.

Description of Attributes	Planned Audit				Actual Results			
	EPER	TER	ARO	Initial sample size	Sample size	Number of exceptions	Sample exception rate	CUER
1. Invoice copy has customer signature.	0	3	10	76				
For Bulk Sales: 2. Bulk order form number is entered on invoice details.	2	8	10	48				
3. Bulk order form details match invoice details.	0	4	10	57				
4. Warehouse copy of bulk order form has customer signature.	1	4	10	96				
5. Customer signature on warehouse copy of bulk order form matches signature on invoice.	0	3	10	76				

Intended use of sampling results:

1. Effect on Audit Plan:

2. Recommendations to Management:

case, the auditor must select an additional item. The audit program should explain in advance how such cases would be handled. For example, the audit program might say that the auditor should choose the next transaction.

When audit procedures have been completed for a sampling application, the auditor will have the required sample size and number of exceptions for each attribute. When exceptions are found, the auditor should follow up and document the cause of the exception (this is very important for the qualitative evaluation of the sample results, which we will discuss in the next section). Going back to our Hillsburg Hardware example, Figure 11-3 is the auditor's documentation of the exceptions found for two of the attributes. In the case of Attribute 1, further follow-up indicated that the exceptions

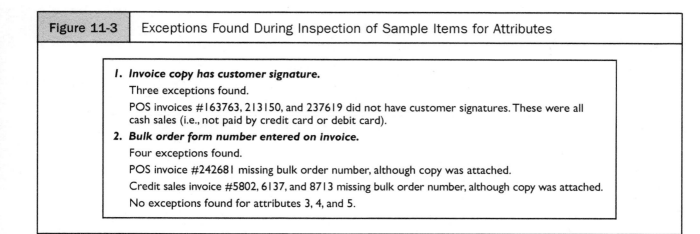

| Figure 11-3 | Exceptions Found During Inspection of Sample Items for Attributes |

> **1. Invoice copy has customer signature.**
>
> Three exceptions found.
>
> POS invoices #163763, 213150, and 237619 did not have customer signatures. These were all cash sales (i.e., not paid by credit card or debit card).
>
> **2. Bulk order form number entered on invoice.**
>
> Four exceptions found.
>
> POS invoice #242681 missing bulk order number, although copy was attached.
>
> Credit sales invoice #5802, 6137, and 8713 missing bulk order number, although copy was attached.
>
> No exceptions found for attributes 3, 4, and 5.

were cash sales and did not require a customer signature (so, in fact, they were not exceptions). As you can see, sampling is an ongoing process that requires diligence in planning, performing, and examination.

Evaluate Sample Results When evaluating the sample results, the auditor's objectives are to understand the cause of the errors and to project the errors observed in the sample to the population, taking into consideration sampling risk. In order to do this, the results need be analyzed quantitatively and qualitatively.

Quantitative Assessment In order to evaluate the sample results, if the auditor is using GAS, the program calculates the **computed upper exception rate (CUER)**, which represents the *most* the exception rate is likely to be. In the Hillsburg example case, the auditor refers to Table 11-7, and compares it to TER. The auditor will consider CUER in the context of specific audit assertions If CUER is in excess of TER, then the auditors would conclude that the population is unacceptable.

> **Computed upper exception rate (CUER)**—the upper limit of the probable population exception rate; the highest exception rate in the population at the given ARO.

Refer to Figure 11-4, the completed attribute sampling data sheet, where the auditor has added the exceptions found, the calculated sample exception rate, and CUER. (To determine CUER, refer to the lower panel of Table 11-7 — 10 percent ARO. CUER is the intersection of sample size and number of deviations found. In the case of Attributes 1 and 5, an average based upon 70 and 80 sample size is used.)

Qualitative Assessment Before concluding on whether or not the control is operating effectively, in addition to the quantitative assessment, the auditor will follow up on deviations to determine the underlying cause and also determine if there are any compensating controls. Exceptions could be caused by carelessness of employees, misunderstood instructions, intentional failure to perform procedures, or many other factors. The auditor should approach intentional errors (or, in the case of David in our opening vignette, errors that appear to be suspicious) with heightened professional skepticism since they might indicate fraud. It is important that any such misstatements be discussed with management and potentially included in the management letter.

Table 11-8 is the auditor's analysis of the exceptions found in our Hillsburg Hardware example. As the auditor's analysis highlights, the causes of exceptions can vary. As we discussed previously, in the case of Attribute 1, the missing signatures were not exceptions. In the case of Attribute 2, the auditor documented management's rationale for the exception and concluded that since there was no financial impact, no further audit work was necessary.

The nature of an exception and its cause can have a significant effect on the evaluation of control risk by assertion. For instance, in two situations provided in

	Evaluating Sample Results Using Attribute Sampling:										
Table 11-7	Tables for Determining Computed Upper or Lower Exception Rate										

	Actual Number of Deviations Found										
Sample Size	**0**	**1**	**2**	**3**	**4**	**5**	**6**	**7**	**8**	**9**	**10**
5 Percent Risk of Overreliance (ARO)											
25	11.3	17.6	*	*	*	*	*	*	*	*	*
30	9.5	14.9	19.5	*	*	*	*	*	*	*	*
35	8.2	12.9	16.9	*	*	*	*	*	*	*	*
40	7.2	11.3	14.9	18.3	*	*	*	*	*	*	*
45	6.4	10.1	13.3	16.3	19.2	*	*	*	*	*	*
50	5.8	9.1	12.1	14.8	17.4	19.9	*	*	*	*	*
55	5.3	8.3	11.0	13.5	15.9	18.1	*	*	*	*	*
60	4.9	7.7	10.1	12.4	14.6	16.7	18.8	*	*	*	*
65	4.5	7.1	9.4	11.5	13.5	15.5	17.4	19.3	*	*	*
70	4.2	6.6	8.7	10.7	12.6	14.4	16.2	18.0	19.7	*	*
75	3.9	6.2	8.2	10.0	11.8	13.5	15.2	16.9	18.4	20.0	*
80	3.7	5.8	7.7	9.4	11.1	12.7	14.3	15.8	17.3	18.8	*
90	3.3	5.2	6.8	8.4	9.9	11.3	12.7	14.1	15.5	16.8	18.1
100	3.0	4.7	6.2	7.6	8.9	10.2	11.5	12.7	14.0	15.2	16.4
125	2.4	3.7	4.9	6.1	7.2	8.2	9.3	10.3	11.3	12.2	13.2
150	2.0	3.1	4.1	5.1	6.0	6.9	7.7	8.6	9.4	10.2	11.0
200	1.5	2.3	3.1	3.8	4.5	5.2	5.8	6.5	7.1	7.7	8.3
10 Percent Risk of Overreliance (ARO)											
20	10.9	18.1	*	*	*	*	*	*	*	*	*
25	8.8	14.7	19.9	*	*	*	*	*	*	*	*
30	7.4	12.4	16.8	*	*	*	*	*	*	*	*
35	6.4	10.7	14.5	18.1	*	*	*	*	*	*	*
40	5.6	9.4	12.8	15.9	19.0	*	*	*	*	*	*
45	5.0	8.4	11.4	14.2	17.0	19.6	*	*	*	*	*
50	4.5	7.6	10.3	12.9	15.4	17.8	*	*	*	*	*
55	4.1	6.9	9.4	11.7	14.0	16.2	18.4	*	*	*	*
60	3.8	6.3	8.6	10.8	12.9	14.9	16.9	18.8	*	*	*
70	3.2	5.4	7.4	9.3	11.1	12.8	14.6	16.2	17.9	19.5	*
80	2.8	4.8	6.5	8.3	9.7	11.3	12.8	14.3	15.7	17.2	18.6
90	2.5	4.3	5.8	7.3	8.7	10.1	11.4	12.7	14.0	15.3	16.6
100	2.3	3.8	5.2	6.6	7.8	9.1	10.3	11.5	12.7	13.8	15.0
120	1.9	3.2	4.4	5.5	6.6	7.6	8.6	9.6	10.6	11.6	12.5
160	1.4	2.4	3.3	4.1	4.9	5.7	6.5	7.2	8.0	8.7	9.5
200	1.1	1.9	2.6	3.3	4.0	4.6	5.2	5.8	6.4	7.0	7.6

* = Over 20 percent

Note: This table presents computed upper deviation rates as percentages and assumes a large population.

Source: Data from *AICPA Auditing Sampling Audit Guide*, March 1, 2014, accessed at **www.aicpa.org**.

Table 11-9, both are related to a manual control—credit authorization approvals and, in both situations, the auditor found the number of exceptions. Both examples highlight that the process may stay the same but the people factor, change in personnel or being busy, can result in a control deficiency. You will note also that the auditor's risk response is quite different due to the underlying cause.

Figure 11-4	Attribute Sampling Data Sheet, Completed

Client Hillsburg Hardware Limited

Year End 31/12/18

Audit Area Tests of Controls—Billing Function and Recording of Sales

Pop. Size 145 853

Define the objective(s) Examine duplicate sales invoices and related documents to determine if the system has functioned as intended and as described in the audit program.

Define the population precisely (including stratification, if any) POS invoices and credit sales invoices for the period 1/1/18 to 31/12/18. First POS number = 140672. Last POS number = 283294. First credit sales invoice number = 3600. Last credit sales invoice number = 6831.

Define the sampling unit, organization of population items, and random selection procedures Sales invoice number, POS invoice numbers, and credit recorded in the sales files sequentially; random sampling.

Description of Attributes	Planned Audit				Actual Results			
	EPER	TER	ARO	Initial sample size	Sample size	Number of exceptions	Sample exception rate	CUER
1. Invoice copy has customer signature.	0	3	10	76	75	0	0	3
For Bulk Sales: 2. Bulk order form number is entered on invoice details.	2	8	10	48	50	4	8	15.4
3. Bulk order form details match invoice details.	0	4	10	57	50	0	0	4.5
4. Warehouse copy of bulk order form has customer signature.	1	4	10	96	100	0	0	2.3
5. Customer signature on warehouse copy of bulk order form matches signature on invoice.	0	3	10	76	75	0	0	3

Intended use of sampling results:

1. Effect on Audit Plan: Controls tested using attributes #1, 3–5 can be relied upon. Policies and procedures to remedy #2 should be discussed with management. No additional audit procedures required, since no financial impact.

In Situation 1, given the CFO's explanation, that she was too busy to make the approvals, the auditor concluded that the approval control was unreliable. Unless there is a compensating control, which in this case there was not, the auditor would conclude that the risk of misstatement for the valuation assertion was high. As a result, the auditor would expand year-end substantive testing related to the evaluation of the allowance of doubtful accounts.

In contrast, in Situation 2 the auditor found that all the exceptions in the tests of internal verification of credit authorization occurred while the person normally

Table 11-8	Analysis of Exceptions

CLIENT: Hillsburg Hardware
ANALYSIS OF EXCEPTIONS
YEAR- END: December 31, 2018.

Prepared by _____
Date:

Attribute	Number of Exceptions	Nature of Exceptions	Effect on the Audit and Other Comments
1, sales	3	Three POS invoices paid by cash did not have customer signatures. Each invoice was for less than $50.	No expansion on tests of controls or substantive tests. Hillsburg policy has been clarified that cash purchase invoices do not require customer signature.
2, sales	4	One POS invoice and three credit sales invoices did not have the bulk order number on the face of the invoice, although the invoice copy was attached.	These omissions would show on the bulk order form exception report showing missing bulk order numbers. Management indicated that, unfortunately, new employees often forget to record this number, resulting in an excessive number of items on the exception report. This usually eases off. Since this does not have a financial effect on the audit (there were no errors in goods shipped), no expansion on tests of control or substantive testing is required.

Anomaly—an exception or misstatement that is nonrepresentative of the population as a whole.

CAS

responsible for performing the approvals was on vacation. In order to determine if the exception is isolated to a particular period, the auditor would first want to corroborate that indeed the credit manager was on vacation. The auditor has set control risk as high for that particular period and plans to review all the transactions that occurred in that period (if there are a large number of transactions, this could easily be performed through the use of a CAAT). This type of exception is called an **anomaly** (often referred to as an isolated error), because it is an exception that is nonrepresentative of the population as a whole. CAS 530 requires that auditors investigate such anomalies, conducting additional audit procedures, with the goal of verifying that the anomaly really is different and not representative of the population for the rest of the year. According to CAS 530, if the auditor concludes that the anomaly is rare, then the exceptions can be excluded from the determination of the sample exception rate. In order to ensure that the auditor can rely upon internal controls for the period not covered by the temporary employee, the auditor may consider expanding the sample; if CUER is less than TER, then the auditor could conclude that the control is effective.

Table 11-9	Developing an Appropriate Risk Response Based Upon Nature of Exceptions

Situation	Attribute	Number of Exceptions	Quantitative Analysis	Nature of Exception	Risk Response
1	Credit is approved	5	CUER exceeds TER	Credit was not approved. Four of these were new customers. Discussed with CFO, who stated that her busy schedule did not permit approving sales.	Expand the year-end procedures extensively in evaluating allowance for uncollectible accounts.
2	Credit is approved	6	CUER exceeds TER	Credit was not approved. Discussed with CFO: six of the errors occurred in same time period, which was when the credit manager was on vacation.	Recheck the invoices processed during the period when the individual was on vacation to determine the actual error rate during that period and report the control deficiency to audit committee.

Conclude on Acceptability of the Population

Recall that the results of the control testing determine whether or not the auditor should adjust the audit strategy. What determines whether or not the audit strategy needs to be adjusted is the auditor's conclusion on the reliability of controls. When the sample results suggest that the control is ineffective, auditors have the following choices:

- Expand testing.
- Test compensating controls.
- Conclude that the control is ineffective, evaluate the severity of the control failure, and revise audit strategy (the nature, timing and/or extent of substantive testing) as illustrated in Situation 1 in Table 11-9.

In practice, as highlighted in Auditing in Action 11-3, if no compensating control exists, most auditors increase substantive testing (meaning that they adjust the audit strategy) rather than increase the sample size for control testing. In our Hillsburg Hardware example, Figure 11-4, at the bottom of the attribute sample sheet, the auditor has concluded that the controls can be relied upon and no adjustment to audit strategy is necessary. The auditor also notes that the procedures to remedy the problem with Attribute 2 should be discussed with management. In Table 11-9, we see in Situation 1 that the auditor concludes that the specific control is unreliable and adjusts the audit strategy accordingly. In Situation 2, once the auditor verifies that the 6 exceptions are anomalies, it is not necessary to include them in the determination of the sample exception rate, which effectively changes CUER. If TER is less than CUER, the auditor can conclude that the control is effective and no adjustment to the audit strategy (meaning the nature, timing, and extent of substantive tests) is necessary.

Communication With the Audit Committee or Management

When the auditor concludes that internal controls are not operating effectively, management must be informed. This is required regardless of the actions management takes to correct the control deficiencies. As highlighted in our Hillsburg Hardware example, the auditor will verbally discuss weaknesses with management. The auditor will also issue a management letter, in which the exception is described, the

AUDITING IN ACTION 11-3
Differences in Sampling Policies for Control Tests

A recent survey of sampling experts at the six largest audit firms provides interesting insights into the sampling policies of these firms. Half of the firms use a statistical sampling approach when sampling for tests of controls, and the other half use a non-statistical approach. Consistent with auditing standards, the firms using a nonstatistical approach note that sample sizes in their firm guidance are comparable to those that would be determined with a statistical approach. When it comes to determining a sample size for tests of controls, the majority of the firms surveyed use the tables in the AICPA's *Audit Guide: Audit Sampling*, which we use throughout this chapter, although one firm indicated that it uses its own audit software. In contrast, the firms tend to use audit software to determine sample sizes for substantive tests of details.

In terms of the inputs used when determining sample size for tests of controls, the firms tend to use a high level of confidence of 90–95 percent, consistent with a high level of assurance. The firms typically use zero expected deviations when determining sample sizes for tests of controls. The tolerable exception rate used by the firms is frequently in the range of 6–10 percent; however, two of the largest audit firms indicated that 10 percent is the standard tolerable exception rate. The firms use various responses if a control exception is identified during testing, but typically they identify alternative compensating controls or increase substantive testing, rather than increase the sample size for the test of control. One firm did indicate that if it were deemed effective to expand testing, the sample would be doubled, and if no additional deviations were found in the larger sample, the auditor could conclude that the control was effective. However, this approach is not typical. As another firm noted, "We typically do not expand our sample because it is likely that we will continue to discover deviations in the expanded sample."

Source: Based on B.E. Christensen, R.J. Elder, and S.M. Glover, "Behind the Numbers: Insights into Large Audit Firm Sampling Practices," *Accounting Horizons*, March 2015, pp. 61–81.

Table 11-10	Comparing Sample Results	
Sample and Results	Attribute 1—Existence of the Sales Invoice Number in the Sales Journal	Attribute 2—Amount and Other Data in the Master File Agree with Sales Journal Entry
(1) Sample Size	100	100
(2) Number of Exceptions	0	4
(3) SER (1) (2)	0%	4%
(4) TER	5%	5%
Sampling Error (Risk) (TER–SER)	5%	1%

implications of the exception are explained (the potential error or fraud), and recommendations for improvement are made. The management letter along with management's responses to all the exceptions is provided to those charged with governance (this is usually the audit committee). CAS 265 requires that all significant internal control deficiencies are reported to the audit committee.

CAS

LO 7 Use nonstatistical sampling for tests of controls.

NONSTATISTICAL SAMPLING APPROACH TO TESTING CONTROLS

Although our discussion has focused on statistical sampling, as highlighted in Auditing in Action 11-3, auditors perform both statistical and nonstatistical sampling, which is allowed by audit standards. As mentioned previously, a key drawback of nonstatistical sampling is that the auditor cannot quantify sampling risk. As highlighted in Auditing in Action 11-2, another shortcoming of nonstatistical sampling is auditor bias in sample selection.

A common method to evaluate sampling risk, when using nonstatistical sampling, is to subtract SER from TER in order to calculate the sampling error. The auditor then evaluates if the difference is sufficiently large enough to conclude that the true population exception rate is acceptable. For example, consider the results of testing two attributes summarized in Table 11-10.

Because the sampling error is the same as TER, it is much more likely that the true population rate is less than or equal to TER for Attribute 1 than Attribute 2. Therefore, most auditors would find the population acceptable for Attribute 1 but not for Attribute 2. In the case of Attribute 2, if the qualitative assessment does not reveal any anomalies, then the control tests do not support the original control assessment. Therefore, the auditor would conclude that control risk must be increased and the audit strategy would be adjusted.

So how would the auditor adjust audit strategy? In this case, the auditor might extend the sample size, test an alternative control, or modify related substantive procedures. Most likely, in the case of Attribute 2, additional emphasis would be needed in accounts/assertions effected by the concerns over the master file and additional substantive testing such as confirmations (existence of accounts receivable), cutoff tests (cutoff of accounts receivable and inventory), and price tests (valuation of inventory) would need to be performed.

USING SAMPLING FOR SUBSTANTIVE TESTS OF DETAILS

Most of the sampling concepts for tests of controls apply equally for substantive tests of details. In both cases, an auditor wants to make an inference about the entire population based upon the sample. As in the case of control testing, both sampling and nonsampling risks are important, and auditors can use either nonstatistical or statistical methods. However, the key difference is in what the auditor wants to measure. In the case of controls, the auditor measures whether the controls are effective, whereas in the case of substantive tests of details, the auditor measures whether the dollar amounts of account balances are materially misstated.

In the following discussion, we focus on sampling for substantive tests of details of balances. We first discuss nonstatistical sampling and then provide an overview of monetary unit sampling, a statistical sampling methodology based upon attribute sampling developed specifically for auditing for substantive tests of balances.

NONSTATISTICAL SAMPLING FOR SUBSTANTIVE TESTS OF DETAILS

LO 8 Use nonstatistical sampling for substantive tests of details.

Audit sampling for tests of details of balances is similar to tests of controls and substantive tests of transactions, although the objectives differ. The process illustrated in Figure 11-1 applies.

Determine Whether Audit Sampling Applies

For substantive tests of balances, while it is common to sample in many accounts, there are situations when sampling does not apply. For the population in Table 11-11, the auditor may decide to audit only items over $5000 and ignore all others because the total of the smaller ones is immaterial. In this case, the auditor has not sampled but has conducted a **census** of the strata over $5000, which consists of auditing all of

Census—an audit of the transactions that satisfy a particular criterion.

Table 11-11	Illustrative Accounts Receivable Population		
Population Item	Recorded Amount	Population Item (cont'd)	Recorded Amount (cont'd)
1	$ 1 410	21	$ 4 865
2	9 130	22	770
3	660	23	2 305
4	3 355	24	2 665
5	5 725	25	1 000
6	8 210	26	6 225
7	580	27	3 675
8	44 110	28	6 250
9	825	29	1 890
10	1 155	30	27 705
11	2 270	31	935
12	50	32	5 595
13	5 785	33	930
14	940	34	4 045
15	1 820	35	9 480
16	3 380	36	360
17	530	37	1 145
18	955	38	6 400
19	4 490	39	100
20	17 140	40	8 435
Total			$207 295

the transactions that satisfy a particular criterion. Similarly, if the auditor is verifying capital asset additions and there are many small additions and one extremely large purchase of a building, the auditor may decide to ignore the small items entirely. Again, the auditor has not sampled but has focused on high-value items instead.

Determine the Test Objective

The audit objectives for substantive tests of balances are designed to provide assurance on one or more financial statement balance related assertions (for example, existence of accounts receivable). The population of 40 accounts receivable in Table 11-11 totalling $207 295 illustrates the application of nonstatistical sampling. An auditor will do tests of details of balances to determine whether the balance of $207 295 is materially misstated.

Define Population Characteristics

The auditor defines the following population characteristics—(1) the misstatement conditions, (2) the population, and (3) the sampling unit.

Define Misstatement Conditions Because audit sampling for tests of details of balances measures monetary misstatements, a misstatement exists whenever a sample item is misstated. For example, in auditing accounts receivable, any client misstatement in a customer balance included in the auditor's sample is a misstatement.

Define the Population In substantive tests of balances, the test objective determines the population's definition. For instance, when testing the existence of accounts receivable, the appropriate population would be recorded dollar population in the accounts receivable subledger balance. However, if the auditor is testing completeness of accounts receivable, it would not be appropriate to define the population as the subledger since the auditor would not be able to detect understatements by sampling the recorded items. Prior to selecting the sample, the auditor will need to ensure that the population being used is complete. A common procedure is to foot whatever list the auditor is using and reconcile it to the general ledger. (Note: this is not testing for the completeness assertion; the auditor has not determined if all items that should be recorded have been recorded on the list. Rather the auditor is testing the accuracy of the list.)

CONCEPT CHECK

C11-5 An auditor is counting a sample of inventory items. Provide two examples of potential errors or misstatement that could occur.

C11-6 The auditor has decided to circularize accounts payable confirmations. What is the likely population?

For many populations, auditors may choose to stratify the population and separate the population into two or more subpopulations before applying audit sampling. Stratification enables the auditor to emphasize certain population items and deemphasize others. In most audit sampling situations, including confirming accounts receivable, auditors want to emphasize the larger recorded dollar values, so they define each stratum on the basis of the size of recorded dollar values. For the population in Table 11-11, assume the auditor decided to stratify as shown in Table 11-12.

Define the Sampling Unit For nonstatistical sampling in tests of details, the sampling unit is almost always the items making up the account balance. For example,

Table 11-12	Example of Stratification		
Stratum	**Stratum Criterion**	**No. in Population**	**Dollars in Population**
1	>$15 000	3	$ 88 955
2	$5 000–$15 000	10	71 235
3	<$5 000	27	47 105
Total		40	$207 295

in the case of accounts receivable, the sampling unit could be customer number (depending upon how the client organizes its records). Auditors can use items making up the recorded population as the sampling unit for testing all audit objectives except completeness. In our accounts receivable example, the sampling unit to test completeness could be customers with zero balances (assuming that all customers are on the list).

Determine Initial Sample Size

Whether using statistical or nonstatistical sampling, the auditor determines sample size. When performing nonstatistical sampling for substantive tests of details, all significant items should be tested. Sample sizes between nonstatistical and statistical sampling should be similar. Accordingly, the auditor may determine the sample size using monetary unit sampling, discussed in the next section. Figure 11-5 presents a simple formula for computing sample sizes based on the AICPA *Audit Guide: Audit Sampling*.

Table 11-13 summarizes the main factors that influence sample size when nonstatistical sampling is used for substantive tests of balances.

With stratified sampling, the sample size is allocated among the strata. As mentioned before, the purpose of stratification is to focus on high risk items, therefore auditors will allocate a higher proportion of the sample to high dollar items. Back in Table 11-12, using that logic, the auditor decides to select all three accounts (a census) from Stratum 1, nine from Stratum 2, and seven from Stratum 3.

Tolerable Misstatement **Tolerable misstatement** is the application of performance materiality to a particular sampling procedure. Tolerable misstatement may be the same amount as performance materiality, or it may be lower. For instance, the auditor

Tolerable misstatement—the application of performance materiality to a particular sampling procedure.

Figure 11-5	Formula for Computing Nonstatistical Tests of Details of Balances Sample Size Based on AICPA Audit Sampling Formula

$$\text{Sample size} = \frac{\text{Population recorded amount* } \times \text{ Confidence factor}}{\text{Tolerable misstatement}}$$

Risk of Incorrect Acceptance	Confidence of Sample	Confidence Factor
37%	63%	1
14%	86%	2
5%	95%	3

*High risk items and individual items exceeding tolerable misstatement are often removed from the population and selected for 100 percent examination.

Table 11-13	Factors Influencing Sample Sizes for Substantive Tests of Balances		
Factor	**Conditions Leading to Smaller Sample Size**	**Conditions Leading to Larger Sample Size**
Inherent risk: Affects acceptable risk of incorrect acceptance	Low inherent risk	High inherent risk
Control risk (ARO): Affects acceptable risk of incorrect acceptance	Low control risk	High control risk
Results of other substantive procedures related to the same assertion (including analytical procedures and other relevant substantive tests): Affects acceptable risk of incorrect acceptance	Satisfactory results in other related substantive procedures	Unsatisfactory results in other related substantive procedures
Tolerable misstatement for a specific account	Larger tolerable misstatement	Smaller tolerable misstatement
Expected size and frequency of misstatements: Affects estimated misstatements in the population	Smaller misstatements or lower frequency	Larger misstatements or higher frequency
Dollar amount of population	Smaller account balance	Larger account balance
Number of items in the population	Almost no effect on sample size unless population is very small	Almost no effect on sample size unless population is very small

may have assessed high inherent risk for the particular account being tested or the population from which the sample is selected is smaller than the account balance (for instance, a census is taken of items over $150 000 and the remaining balance is sampled).

Acceptable Risk of Incorrect Acceptance For substantive tests of balances, the **acceptable risk of incorrect acceptance (ARIA)** is the risk that the auditor is willing to take of accepting a balance as correct when the true misstatement in the balance is greater than materiality. ARIA is equivalent to acceptable risk of assessing control risk too low (ARO) for tests of controls. It measures the auditor's desired assurance for an account balance. For greater assurance, the auditor would set ARIA lower. Like ARO, ARIA can be set quantitatively (such as 5 percent or 10 percent) or qualitatively (such as low, medium, or high).

The primary factor affecting the auditor's decision about ARIA is assessed control risk in the audit risk model. If the auditor concludes that internal controls are likely to be effective, preliminary control risk can be reduced. A lower control risk requires a lower ARO in testing the controls, which requires a larger sample size. If controls are found to be effective, control risk can remain low, which permits the auditor to increase ARIA (through the use of the audit risk model), thereby reducing the sample size required for the substantive testing of the related account balance. Figure 11-6 shows the effect of ARO and ARIA on substantive testing when controls are not considered effective and when they are considered effective.

ARIA is also directly affected by acceptable audit risk and inversely by other substantive tests already performed or planned for the account balance. For example if acceptable audit risk is reduced, ARI should also be reduced. If the results of the analytical procedures indicate that the account balance is fairly stated, then ARIA should be increased. This is because analytical procedures are evidence that supports the account balance; therefore, less evidence from detailed testing using sampling is required to achieve acceptable audit risk. The various relationships affecting ARIA are summarized in Table 11-14.

Acceptable risk of incorrect acceptance (ARIA)—the risk that the auditor is willing to take of accepting a balance as correct when the true misstatement in the balance is greater than tolerable misstatement.

Figure 11-6	Effect of ARO and ARIA on Required Evidence

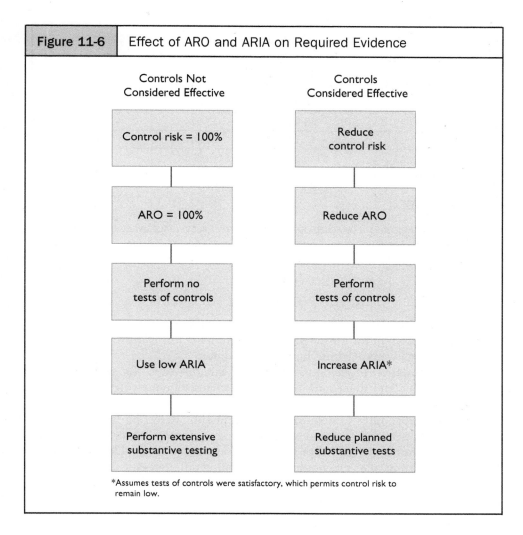

Controls Not Considered Effective

- Control risk = 100%
- ARO = 100%
- Perform no tests of controls
- Use low ARIA
- Perform extensive substantive testing

Controls Considered Effective

- Reduce control risk
- Reduce ARO
- Perform tests of controls
- Increase ARIA*
- Reduce planned substantive tests

*Assumes tests of controls were satisfactory, which permits control risk to remain low.

Estimate Misstatements in Population The auditor typically makes this estimate based on prior experience with the client and by assessing inherent risk, considering the results of tests of controls, substantive tests of transactions, and analytical procedures already performed. The planned sample size increases as the amount of misstatements expected in the population approaches tolerable misstatement.

Table 11-14	Relationship Among Factors Affecting ARIA, Effect on ARIA, and Required Sample Size for Audit Sampling of Substantive Tests of Balances

Factor Affecting ARIA	Example	Effect on ARIA	Effect on Sample Size
Effectiveness of internal controls (control risk)	Internal controls are effective (reduced control risk).	Increase	Decrease
Substantive tests of transactions	No exceptions were found in substantive tests of transactions.	Increase	Decrease
Acceptable audit risk	Likelihood of bankruptcy is low (increased acceptable audit risk).	Increase	Decrease
Analytical procedures	Analytical procedures are performed with no indications of likely misstatements.	Increase	Decrease

Table 11-15	Summarizing Sample Results			
		Dollars Audited		
Stratum	**Sample Size**	**Recorded Value**	**Audited Value**	**Known Misstatement**
1	3	$ 88 955	$ 91 695	$(2 740)
2	9	43 995	43 024	971
3	7	13 105	10 947	2 158
Total	19	$146 055	$145 666	$ 389

CONCEPT CHECK

C11-7 Explain what is meant by *acceptable risk of incorrect acceptance*. What are the major factors affecting ARIA?

C11-8 What is the relationship between ARIA and ARO for tests of controls?

Select Sample and Perform Audit Procedures

The auditor applies appropriate audit procedures to each item in the sample to determine whether it contains a misstatement. If documentation is missing, the auditor must design alternative procedures for the selected item.

In the confirmation of accounts receivable, auditors send the sample of positive confirmations and determine the amount of misstatement in each account confirmed (we discuss this in more depth in Chapter 12). For nonresponses, they use alternative procedures to determine misstatements. Referring to our example in Table 11-15, assume the auditor sends out first and second requests for confirmations and performs alternative procedures. Also assume the auditor reaches the following conclusions after reconciling all the timing differences.

Evaluate the Sample Results

Quantitative Evaluation In order to evaluate the results, the auditor generalizes from the sample to the population by (1) projecting the known misstatements from the sample results to the overall population and (2) considering sampling error and sampling risk (ARIA). The first step is to calculate the **point estimate**. The most common approach is to assume that misstatements in the unaudited population are proportional to the known misstatements in the sample. The calculation is done for each stratum and then totalled, as illustrated in our example in Table 11-16.

The point estimate of the misstatement in the population is $6589, indicating an overstatement. The point estimate, by itself, is not an adequate measure of the population misstatement, however, because of sampling error. In other words, because the estimate is based on a sample, it will be close to the true population misstatement but is unlikely to be exactly the same. Whenever the point estimate ($6589 in the example) is less than tolerable misstatement ($15 000 in the example), the auditor must consider the possibility that the true population misstatement is greater than the

Point estimate—the method of projecting the sample to the population to estimate the population misstatement, commonly assuming that misstatements in the unaudited population are proportional to the misstatements in the sample.

Table 11-16	Evaluating the Sample Results					
Stratum	**Known Misstatement ÷ Recorded Value of the Sample**	×	**Recorded Book Value for the Stratum**	=	**Point Estimate of Misstatement**	
1	$(2 740)/$88 955		$88 955		$(2 740)	
2	$971/$43 995		71 235		1 572	
3	$2 158 /$13 105		47 105		7 757	
Total					$ 6 589	

amount of misstatement that is tolerable in the circumstances. This must be done for both statistical and nonstatistical samples.

An auditor using nonstatistical sampling cannot formally measure sampling error and therefore must subjectively consider the possibility that the true population misstatement exceeds a tolerable amount. Auditors do this by considering:

1. The difference between the point estimate and tolerable misstatement (this is called calculated sampling error).
2. The extent to which items in the population have been audited 100 percent.
3. Whether misstatements tend to be offsetting or in only one direction.
4. The amounts of individual misstatements.
5. The sample size.

In our example, suppose that tolerable misstatement is $40 000. In that case, the auditor may conclude it to be unlikely, given the point estimate of $6589, that the true population misstatement exceeds the tolerable amount (calculated sampling error is $33 411). If, however, the tolerable misstatement is $12 000, which is only $5411 greater than the point estimate, other factors will be considered. In our example, because 100 percent of Stratum 1 (the larger items) was audited, any unidentified misstatements would be restricted to smaller items. If misstatements tend to be offsetting and are relatively small, the auditor may conclude that the true population misstatement is likely to be lower than the tolerable misstatement. Also, the larger the sample size, the more confident the auditor can be that the actual point estimate is closer to the true population misstatement.

Request Client to Correct Known Misstatements It is important to note that, unlike with tests of controls, even if the amount of the likely misstatement is not considered material, the auditor must wait to make the final evaluation when the entire audit is completed. The total estimated misstatement in the sample must be combined with estimates of misstatements in all parts of the audit to evaluate the effect of the misstatements on the financial statements as a whole. However, regardless of whether the sample results support the conclusion that the account is not materially misstated, the auditor should request that the client record an adjustment for known misstatements, unless they are clearly trivial.

Qualitative Assessment Evaluation of the nature and cause of each misstatement found in the tests of details of balances is a critical step in the sampling process. For example, assume that when the auditor confirmed accounts receivable, all misstatements resulted from the client's failure to record returned goods. The auditor will determine why that type of misstatement occurred so often, the implications of the misstatements on the other audit areas, the potential impact on the financial statements, and the effect on company operations.

An important part of this analysis is to decide whether any modification to the audit risk model is needed. In the preceding example, if the auditor concluded that the failure to record the returns was because of a breakdown in internal controls, it might be necessary to reassess control risk. That, in turn, will probably cause the auditor to increase ARIA, which will increase planned sample size.

Conclude on Acceptability of Population

If the error is less than the tolerable misstatement and the auditor is satisfied with the underlying causes of the errors, the population is acceptable. However, if the misstatement in a population is larger than tolerable misstatement after considering sampling error, the population is not considered acceptable. At that point, an auditor has several possible courses of action.

Take No Action Until Tests of Other Audit Areas Are Completed Ultimately, the auditor must evaluate whether the financial statements taken as a whole are materially misstated. If offsetting misstatements are found in other parts of the audit, such as in inventory, the auditor may conclude that the estimated misstatements in accounts receivable are acceptable. Of course, before the audit is finalized, the auditor must evaluate whether a misstatement in one account may make the financial statements misleading even if there are offsetting misstatements.

Perform Expanded Audit Tests in Specific Areas If an analysis of the misstatements indicates that most of the misstatements are of a specific type, it may be desirable to restrict the additional audit effort to the problem area. For example, if an analysis of the misstatements in confirmations indicates that most of the misstatements result from failure to record sales returns, the auditor can make an extended search of returned goods to make sure that they have been recorded. However, care must be taken to evaluate the cause of all misstatements in the sample before a conclusion is reached about the proper emphasis in the expanded tests. Problems may exist in more than one area.

When auditors analyze a problem area and correct it by proposing an adjustment to the client's records, the sample items that led to isolating the problem area can then be shown as "correct." The point estimate can now be recalculated without the misstatements that have been "corrected." (This is only true when the error can be isolated to a specific area.) However, CAS 530.A22 requires that projected misstatement plus the anomalous misstatement must be compared to tolerable misstatement. This means that all errors must be projected to the population being sampled, even if the client adjusts for the error.

Increase the Sample Size When the auditor increases the sample size, sampling error is reduced if the rate of misstatements in the expanded sample, their dollar amounts, and their direction are similar to those in the original sample. Therefore, increasing the sample size may satisfy the auditor's tolerable misstatement requirements.

Increasing the sample size enough to satisfy the auditor's tolerable misstatement standards is often costly, especially when the difference between tolerable misstatement and projected misstatement is small. Moreover, an increased sample size does not guarantee a satisfactory result. If the number, amount, and direction of the misstatements in the extended sample are proportionately greater or more variable than in the original sample, the results are still likely to be unacceptable.

For tests such as accounts receivable confirmation and inventory observation, it is often difficult to increase the sample size because of the practical problem of "reopening" those procedures once the initial work is done. By the time the auditor discovers that the sample was not large enough, several weeks have usually passed.

Despite these difficulties, sometimes the auditor must increase the sample size after the original testing is completed. It is much more common to increase sample size in audit areas other than confirmations and inventory observation, but it is occasionally necessary to do so even for these two areas. When stratified sampling is used, increased samples usually focus on the strata containing larger amounts, unless misstatements appear to be concentrated in other strata.

Adjust the Account Balance When the auditor concludes that an account balance is materially misstated, the client may be willing to adjust the book value based on the sample results. In our example, assume the client is willing to reduce book value by the point estimate ($6589). The auditor's estimate of the misstatement is now zero, but it is still necessary to consider sampling error. Assuming a tolerable misstatement of $12 000, the auditor must now assess whether sampling error exceeds $12 000, not the $5411 originally considered. If the auditor believes sampling error to be $12 000 or less, accounts receivable is acceptable after the adjustment. If the auditor believes it is more than $12 000, adjusting the account balance is not a practical option.

Refuse to Give an Unqualified Opinion If the auditor believes that the recorded amount in an account is not fairly stated, it is necessary to follow at least one of the preceding alternatives or to qualify the audit report. If the auditor believes that there is a reasonable chance that the financial statements are materially misstated, it would be a serious breach of auditing standards to issue an unqualified opinion. Auditors who

A recent study of American audit firm sampling practices found that in the case of substantive tests of account balances, sampling is commonly used when the auditor has decided that solely relying upon specific identification testing is not effective and/or efficient. This usually applies to accounts receivable confirmations, inventory price testing, and inventory test counts. Four of the six firms interviewed emphasized the use of statistical sampling methods in those instances. Not surprisingly, monetary unit sampling (MUS) was the most popular method. When statistical sampling was used, all firms either explicitly required or encouraged that all items greater than tolerable misstatement be selected for specific identification testing. (This is an example of stratification.) This would mean that when selecting the statistical sample, those items greater than tolerable misstatement would be excluded from the population.

As with tests of controls, statistical and nonstatistical approaches were designed to yield similar sample sizes.

However, the difference in planning inputs can result in significant differences in sample sizes. The two methods most commonly used for projection errors were ratio projection (this is the approach used in this chapter—it applies the misstatement ratio observed in the sample to the entire population) and the difference projection (it projects the average misstatement of each item in the sample to all items in the population). However, the respondents noted that auditors often fail to understand how to treat misstatements. As one respondent explained: "teams sometimes fail to project an error because the sample error is relatively small, and they fail to recognize that a projected error coupled with sampling risk might result in a material misstatement."

Source: Based on B.E. Christensen, R.J. Elder, and S.M. Glover, "Behind the Numbers: Insights into Large Audit Firm Sampling Practices," *Accounting Horizons*, March 2015, pp. 61–81.

do not appropriately plan and evaluate sample results can issue an inappropriate audit opinion, which can have serious repercussions. For purposes of reporting on internal control and misstatements to those in charge of governance, the material misstatement should be considered a potential indicator of a material weakness in internal control over financial reporting.

STATISTICAL SAMPLING FOR SUBSTANTIVE TESTS OF DETAILS

LO 9 Describe statistical sampling for substantive tests of details.

Monetary unit sampling (MUS) is a statistical sampling method developed specifically for auditors and, as highlighted in Auditing in Action 11-4, it is the most commonly used statistical method of sampling for tests of details of balances, particularly with regard to accounts receivable confirmation, inventory price tests, and inventory test counts. This is because it has the statistical simplicity of attribute sampling yet provides a statistical result expressed in dollars (or another appropriate currency).

Monetary unit sampling (MUS)—a statistical sampling method that provides misstatement bounds expressed in monetary amounts.

Differences Between MUS and Nonstatistical Sampling

Like nonstatistical sampling, MUS follows the structured process illustrated in Figure 11-1. All the same steps apply and must be performed; however, some of the steps are done differently. We discuss the differences below.

The Definition of the Sampling Unit Is an Individual Dollar In MUS, the sampling unit is an individual dollar in an account balance. For example, in the population in Table 11-11, the sampling unit is one dollar and the population size is 207 295 dollars, not the 40 accounts discussed in nonstatistical sampling. By focusing on the individual dollar as the sampling unit, MUS automatically emphasizes physical units with larger recorded balances. For example, an account with a $5000 balance has a 10 times greater probability of selection than one with a $500 balance, as it contains 10 times as many dollar units. As a result, stratified sampling is unnecessary with MUS. Stratification occurs automatically.

The Population Size Is the Recorded Dollar Population For example, the population of accounts receivable in Table 11-11 consists of 207 295 dollars, which is the

Table 11-17	Accounts Receivable Population	
Population Item (Physical Unit)	Recorded Amount	Cumulative Total (Dollar Unit)
1	$ 357	$ 357
2	1 281	1 638
3	60	1 698
4	573	2 271
5	691	2 962
6	143	3 105
7	2 125	5 230
8	278	5 508
9	242	5 750
10	826	6 576
11	404	6 980
12	396	7 376

population size, not the 40 accounts receivable balances as in the case of the non-statistical sampling.

Because of the method of sample selection in MUS it is not possible to evaluate the likelihood of unrecorded items in the population. Assume, for example, that MUS is used to evaluate whether inventory is fairly stated. MUS cannot be used to evaluate whether certain inventory items exist but have not been counted. If the completeness objective is important in the audit test—and it usually is—that objective must be satisfied separately from the MUS tests.

Sample Selection Is Done Using PPS Monetary unit samples are samples selected with **probability proportional to size sample selection (PPS)**. PPS samples can be obtained by using computer software or systematic sampling techniques. Table 11-17 provides an illustration of an accounts receivable population, including cumulative totals that will be used to demonstrate selecting a sample.

Assume that the auditor wants to select a PPS sample of four accounts from the population in Table 11-17. Because the sampling unit is defined as an individual dollar, the population size is 7376. The auditor would use a computer program to generate four random numbers between 1 and 7376 to generate the sample. In this example, the auditor gets 6586, 1756, 850, and 6599. Referring again to Table 11-17, the items selected are Items 11 (containing dollars 6577 through 6980), 4 (dollars 1699 through 2271), 2 (dollars 358 through 1638), and 11 (dollars 6577 through 6599). These accounts will be audited because the cumulative total associated with these accounts includes the random dollars selected. Item 11 was treated as two sample items because it was randomly selected twice, even though the recorded balance of the account of $404 is much smaller than the sampling interval using systematic selection.

A problem using PPS selection is that population items with a zero recorded balance have no chance of being selected with PPS sample selection, even though they may be misstated. Similarly, small balances that are significantly understated have little chance of being included in the sample. This problem can be overcome by doing specific audit tests for zero- and small-balance items, assuming that they are of concern.

Another problem with PPS is its inability to include negative balances, such as credit balances in accounts receivable, in the PPS (monetary unit) sample. It is possible to ignore negative balances for PPS selection and test those amounts by some other means. An alternative is to treat them as positive balances and add them to the total number of monetary units being tested (which is readily done with audit software by simply using absolute values) and add them to the total monetary units being tested. However, this complicates the evaluation process.

The Auditor Evaluates Sample Results Using MUS Techniques

Regardless of the sampling method selected, the auditor must generalize from the sample to the population by (1) projecting misstatements from the sample results to the population, and (2) determining the related sampling error. The statistical result when MUS is used is called a **misstatement bound**, and is an estimate of the likely maximum overstatement at a given ARIA.

Draw a Conclusion Regarding the Acceptability of the Population Using MUS

The auditor compares the calculated misstatement bound to tolerable misstatement. If the bound exceeds tolerable misstatement, the population is not considered acceptable. The options available to the auditor when the population is rejected are the same ones already discussed for nonstatistical sampling. (Readers interested in more details of computing sample size and evaluating results, with an actual example, may refer to this text's online resources.)

The Pros and Cons of Monetary Unit Sampling

MUS appeals to auditors for at least four reasons:

1. MUS automatically increases the likelihood of selecting high dollar items from the population being audited. Auditors make a practice of concentrating on these items because they generally represent the greatest risk of material misstatements. Stratified sampling can also be used for this purpose, but MUS is often easier to apply.

2. MUS often reduces the cost of doing the audit testing because several sample items are tested at once. For example, if one large item makes up 10 percent of the total recorded dollar value of the population and the sample size is 100, the PPS sample selection method is likely to result in approximately 10 percent of the sample items from that one large population item. Naturally, that item needs to be audited only once, but it counts as a sample of 10. If the item is misstated, it is also counted as 10 misstatements. Larger population items may be eliminated from the sampled population by auditing them 100 percent and evaluating them separately, if the auditor so desires.

3. MUS is easy to apply. Monetary unit samples can be evaluated by the application of simple tables. It is easy to teach and to supervise the use of MUS techniques. Firms that utilize MUS extensively use audit software or other computer programs that streamline sample size determination and evaluation even further than shown in this chapter.

4. MUS provides a statistical conclusion rather than a nonstatistical one. Many auditors believe that statistical sampling aids them in making better and more defensible conclusions.

The main disadvantage of MUS is that the total misstatement bounds resulting when misstatements are found may be too high to be useful to the auditor. This is because these evaluation methods are inherently conservative when misstatements are found and often produce bounds far in excess of materiality. To overcome this problem, large samples may be required. Therefore, auditors commonly use MUS when zero or few misstatements are expected.

ADEQUATE DOCUMENTATION AND PROFESSIONAL JUDGMENT

As highlighted in Chapter 5, it is important that the auditor document the work performed. The auditor needs to retain adequate records of the procedures performed, the methods used to select the sample and perform the tests, the results found in the tests, and the conclusions reached. Documentation is needed for both statistical and nonstatistical sampling to evaluate the combined results of all tests. Throughout our Hillsburg Hardware example, we have seen examples of the types of documentation auditors would use in practice to record the methods used to select the sample and perform the tests, the results found in the tests, and the conclusions drawn.

Not only does documentation serve as a means for the reviewer to assess the auditor's work, in terms of professional judgment, but it helps the auditor to document the process and to ask questions like "Does this address the key risks?" and "Does my assessment or conclusion make sense?" Considering these questions can enhance the auditor's ability to develop representative samples and design tests to address the relevant risks. Further, the auditor will stand back and consider what the results mean within the broader context of the audit engagement.

A criticism occasionally levelled against statistical sampling is that it reduces the auditor's use of professional judgment. A comparison of the audit process discussed in this chapter for nonstatistical and attributes sampling and nonstatistical tests of details and monetary unit sampling shows that this criticism is unwarranted. For proper application, all sampling requires professional judgment in most of the steps. For instance, to select the initial sample size for attribute sampling, auditors depend primarily upon TER and ARO, which require a high level of professional judgment, as well as EPER, which requires a careful estimate. The same applies to MUS. Similarly, the final evaluation of results, which requires both a quantitative and qualitative assessment, depends upon a high-level professional judgment. As Auditing in Action 11-5 illustrates, even with the potential to examine all items through data analytics, professional judgment is still key to deciding when sampling is appropriate and in evaluating the results.

AUDITING IN ACTION 11-5
Data Analytics and Sampling

We have all heard of big data and how it will revolutionize business practices. Not surprisingly, the same predictions are being made about big data's effect on audit practice. One area that some predict will be revolutionized is sampling. It would no longer be necessary to look at a sample of 60; with today's computing power, auditors can now easily test a full population of, say, 50 000 items. However, a recent study conducted by the Institute of Chartered Accountants of England and Wales (ICAEW) suggests that despite the power of big data, it is no replacement for auditors' professional judgment and skepticism, and sampling will continue to be relevant.

For instance, testing the entire population eliminates sampling risk but it can create other problems. Hundreds, and sometimes thousands, of so-called "exceptions" can be produced if care is not taken. Imagine if, upon investigation, the auditor discovers many of these "exceptions" were not exceptions at all; rather, the test was configured improperly or the population was not in fact homogeneous (i.e., it was, in fact, two populations to which different control procedures were applied, for example). These types of risks, what we have referred to as nonsampling risks, exist when testing 100% of the population.

Interestingly, the ICAEW study found that some firms, if faced with thousands of exceptions, would stratify and sample those exceptions to determine which were genuine. Other firms argued that if the test was designed properly in the first place, this situation would not arise. Auditing standards require that all exceptions are followed up. However, given that standards are based upon sampling, the auditors who would "sample" the exceptions argued if they had taken a sample in the first place, they would have found a tiny (if any) number of exceptions and it is not necessary to follow up every tiny exception in detail, provided all exceptions have been considered and an appropriate risk response is developed. As the authors note, "Auditing standards do not prohibit the use of data analytics but nor do they readily facilitate them. 100% testing and the wider effects of straightforward data interrogation are not well addressed." Given that audit standards have not kept up with the advances in data analytics, several standard setters have data analytic projects underway. However, it will not be clear for some time what changes will need to be made to the current auditing standards.

Source: Based on Institute of Chartered Accountants of England and Wales, *Data Analytics for External Auditors: International Auditing Perspectives*, London, 2016.

SUMMARY

In this chapter, we described what audit sampling is, and when and why auditors rely upon audit sampling. We described representative sampling and discussed the difference between statistical and nonstatistical sampling and probabilistic and nonprobabilisitc sample selections. We discussed the process auditors follow for sampling of tests of controls and substantive tests of details. In tests of controls, auditors are concerned with exceptions, or deviations, and use the results to make a conclusion regarding the effectiveness of controls. With regard to substantive tests of details, auditors are concerned about misstatements and generalize the results from the sample to the population to determine whether the class of transactions or account balances are materially misstated. Despite the seemingly objective nature of sampling, it requires a high degree of professional judgment. As highlighted through the various vignettes in this chapter, there is considerable difference among auditors how to determine sample sizes and interpret results.

MyLab Accounting
Make the grade with MyLab Accounting: The questions, exercises, and problems marked with a ⊕ can be found on MyLab Accounting. You can practise them as often as you want, and most feature step-by-step guided instructions to help you find the right answer.

Review Questions

⊕ **11-1** **1** **2** State what is meant by *representative sample*, and explain its importance in sampling audit populations.

⊕ **11-2** **2** Explain the major difference between statistical and nonstatistical sampling. What are the three main parts of statistical and nonstatistical methods?

⊕ **11-3** **3** Explain what is meant by *block sampling*, and describe how an auditor could obtain five blocks of 20 sales invoices from a sales journal.

⊕ **11-4** **2** Distinguish between a sampling error and a nonsampling error. How can each be reduced?

11-5 **2** Define what is meant by *sampling risk*. Does sampling risk apply to nonstatistical sampling, MUS, and attribute sampling? Explain.

11-6 **4** Define *stratified sampling*, and explain its importance in auditing. How could an auditor obtain a stratified sample of 30 items from each of the three strata in the confirmation of accounts receivable?

⊕ **11-7** **3** **4** Explain the difference between replacement sampling and nonreplacement sampling. Which method do auditors usually follow? Why?

⊕ **11-8** **4** What are the two types of simple random sample selection methods? Which of the two methods is used most often by auditors, and why?

⊕ **11-9** **4** Describe systematic sample selection, and explain how an auditor would select 40 numbers from a population of 2800 items using this approach. What are the advantages and disadvantages of systematic sample selection?

11-10 **5** What major difference between tests of controls and tests of details of balances makes attribute sampling inappropriate for tests of details of balances?

11-11 **2** **3** **4** Distinguish between random selection and statistical measurement. State the circumstances under which one can be used without the other.

⊕ **11-12** **5** Describe what is meant by *sampling unit*. Explain why the sampling unit for verifying the existence of recorded sales differs from the sampling unit for testing for the possibility of omitted sales.

⊕ **11-13** **6** Explain the difference between an attribute and an exception condition. State the exception condition for the following audit procedure: the duplicate sales invoice has been initialled, indicating the performance of internal verification.

⊕ **11-14** **8** **9** Distinguish between the point estimate of the total misstatements (likely misstatement) and the true value of the misstatements in the population. How can each be determined?

⊕ **11-15** **6** **7** Identify the factors that an auditor uses to determine the appropriate TER. Compare the sample size for a TER of 7 percent with that of 4 percent, all other factors being equal.

🌐 **11-16** ⑥ ⑦ Identify the factors an auditor uses to determine the appropriate ARO. Compare the sample size for an ARO of 10 percent with that of 5 percent, all other factors being equal.

🌐 **11-17** ⑥ ⑦ ⑧ ⑨ State the relationship between the following:
   A. ARO and sample size.
   B. Population size and sample size.
   C. TER and sample size.
   D. EPER and sample size.

🌐 **11-18** ⑥ When the CUER exceeds the TER, what courses of action are available to the auditor? Under what circumstances should each of these be followed?

🌐 **11-19** ⑥ Assume that the auditor has selected 100 sales invoices from a population of 100 000 to test for an indication of internal verification of pricing and extensions. Determine the CUER at a 10 percent ARO if four exceptions are found in the sample using attributes sampling. Explain the meaning of the statistical results in auditing terms.

🌐 **11-20** ⑥ ⑦ ⑧ ⑨ Explain what is meant by *analysis of exceptions* and discuss its importance.

🌐 **11-21** ⑨ Why is it difficult to determine the appropriate sample size for MUS? How should the auditor determine the proper sample size?

11-22 ⑧ What alternative courses of action are appropriate when a population is rejected using nonstatistical sampling for tests of details of balances? When should each option be followed?

Multiple Choice Questions and Task-Based Simulations

🌐 **11-23** ⑥ ⑦ If all other factors specified in a sampling plan remain constant, changing the TER from 9 percent to 6 percent will cause the required sample size to:
   (1) Increase.
   (2) Remain the same.
   (3) Decrease.
   (4) Become indeterminate.

🌐 **11-24** ⑥ ⑦ ⑩ In addition to evaluating the frequency of deviations in tests of controls, an auditor should also consider certain qualitative aspects of the deviations. The auditor most likely would give additional consideration to the implications of a deviation if it was:
   (1) The only deviation discovered in the sample.
   (2) Identical to a deviation discovered during the prior year's audit.
   (3) Caused by an employee's misunderstanding of instructions.
   (4) Initially concealed by a forged document.

🌐 **11-25** ⑥ The upper precision limit (CUER) in statistical sampling is:
   (1) The percentage of items in a sample that possess a particular attribute.
   (2) The percentage of items in a population that possess a particular attribute.
   (3) A statistical measure, at a specified confidence level, of the maximum rate of occurrence of an attribute.
   (4) The maximum rate of exception that the auditor would be willing to accept in the population without altering the planned reliance on the attribute.

🌐 **11-26** ② Which of the following best illustrates the concept of sampling risk?
   (1) The documents related to the chosen sample may not be available to the auditor for inspection.
   (2) An auditor may fail to recognize errors in the documents from the sample.
   (3) A randomly chosen sample may not be representative of the population as a whole for the characteristic of interest.
   (4) An auditor may select audit procedures that are not appropriate to achieve the specific objective.

11-27 ⑧ Murray decides to use stratified sampling for a test of details of balances. The reason for using stratified sampling rather than unrestricted random sampling is to:
   (1) Reduce as much as possible the degree of variability in the overall population.

(2) Give every element in the population an equal chance of being included in the sample.

(3) Allow the person selecting the sample to use personal judgment in deciding which elements should be included in the sample.

(4) Allow the auditor to emphasize larger items from the population.

11-28 `4` While performing a substantive test of details during an audit, the auditor determined that the sample results supported the conclusion that the recorded account balance was materially misstated. It was, in fact, not materially misstated. This situation illustrates the risk of:

(1) Assessing control risk too high.

(2) Assessing control risk too low.

(3) Incorrect rejection.

(4) Incorrect acceptance.

11-29 `6` `10` Binu is performing tests of controls in the purchases cycle of Oakland Hardware Company. Based on the audit firm guidelines, a sample size of 50 purchases is selected from the cash disbursements file. The following summarizes Binu's results of one of his tests:

	Control (Attribute)	Results and Explanation
1	Upon receipt of goods, the receiver inspects the goods for quality and quantity. The receiving document is initialled by the receiver once the inspection is complete.	All purchases except for two had an associated receiving document that was initialled by the receiver. The two exceptions related to the telephone and electrical bill.
2	Upon the arrival of a supplier invoice, the invoice is matched to the receiving document and the purchase order.	Three purchases did not have a purchase order attached. Further investigation revealed the following:
		One of the purchases related to the monthly telephone bill and one was for the monthly electrical bill. These did not have receiving documents.
		The third exception related to an inventory purchase.
		Upon discussion with the purchasing manager, the purchase order must have been misfiled. The purchasing manager investigated the matter but could not locate the purchase order. The manager noted that the order was valid and related to a raw material purchase.

REQUIRED

a. If the controls that Binu was testing were not effective, what would be the potential misstatement?

b. Complete Table 2 to evaluate Binu's results. Because internal controls were considered effective, Binu used a 10 percent ARO (Acceptable Risk of Overreliance) a zero EPER (Estimated Population Error Rate), and a 5 percent TER (Tolerable Exception Rate) for the attribute. Binu used the information in Table 1 (for a population of 5000 invoices) to evaluate his results results:

Table 1

Sample Size of 50				
Number of Exceptions Found	0	1	2	3
Computed Upper Exception Rate (CUER)	4.5	7.6	10.3	12.9

Table 2

Attribute	Number of Exceptions	Sample Error Rate	CUER	Can the Control Be Relied Upon? (Answer Yes or No)
Existence of receiver approval				
All invoices are attached to the receiving document and purchase order.				

Discussion Questions and Problems

11-30 4 6 7 For the audit of Carbald Supply Company, Farda is conducting a test of sales for the first nine months of the fiscal year ended December 31, 2018. Incorrect revenue recognition has been assessed as a significant risk. Materiality is set at $750 000.

Included in the audit procedures are the following:

1. Foot and cross-foot the sales journal and trace the balance to the general ledger.
2. Review all sales transactions for reasonableness.
3. Select a sample of recorded sales from the sales journal and trace the customer name and amounts to duplicate sales invoices and the related shipping document.
4. Select a sample of shipping document numbers and perform the following tests:
   4.1 Trace the shipping document to the related duplicate sales invoice.
   4.2 Examine the duplicate sales invoice to determine whether copies of the shipping document, shipping order, and customer order are attached.
   4.3 Examine the shipping order for an authorized credit approval.
   4.4 Examine the duplicate sales invoice for an indication of internal verification of quantity, price, extensions, and footings; trace the balance to the accounts receivable master file.
   4.5 Compare the price on the duplicate sales invoice with the sales price in the product master file and the quantity with the shipping document.
   4.6 Trace the total on the duplicate sales invoice to the sales journal and the accounts receivable master file for customer, name, amount, and date.

REQUIRED

a. State the audit objective (or assertion) associated with each of the audit procedures.
b. Identify those audit procedures that are potential controls with respect to revenue recognition. Justify your response.
c. Identify those audit procedures where computer-assisted audit tests (CAATs) can be used for all or part of the audit procedure. State the process that the CAATs can complete.
d. What type of sampling would you use for these audit procedures? Justify your response.
e. State the appropriate sampling unit, define the attribute that you would test, and define exception conditions for each of the audit procedures.
f. Which of the audit procedures are dual-purpose tests? Justify your response.

11-31 8 You are planning to use nonstatistical sampling to evaluate the results of accounts receivable confirmation for the Meridian Company. You have already performed tests of controls for sales, sales returns and allowances, and cash receipts, and they are considered excellent. Because of the quality of the controls, you decide to use an acceptable risk of incorrect acceptance of 10 percent. There are 3000 accounts receivable with a gross value of $6 900 000. The accounts are similar in size and will be treated as a single stratum. An overstatement or understatement of more than $150 000 is considered material.

REQUIRED

a. Calculate the required sample size. Assume your firm uses the following nonstatistical formula to determine sample size:

$$\text{Sample size} = \frac{\text{Population Recorded Amount} \times \text{Confidence Factor}}{\text{Tolerable Misstatement}}$$

A confidence factor of 2 is used for a 10 percent ARIA.

b. Assume that instead of good results, poor results were obtained for tests of controls and substantive tests of transactions for sales, sales returns and allowances, and cash receipts. How will this affect your required sample size? How will you use this information in your sample size determination?
c. Regardless of your answer to Part (a), assume you decide to select a sample of 100 accounts for testing. Indicate how you will select the accounts for testing using systematic selection.
d. Assume a total book value of $230 000 for the 100 accounts selected for testing. You uncover three overstatements totalling $1500 in the sample. Evaluate whether the population is fairly stated.

11-32 ⑨ Lam, a public accountant, is auditing the financial statements of his client, Harvesters Ltd., a company that sells and distributes agricultural equipment across Canada. Lam has performed a preliminary evaluation of the company's internal control over sales transactions and has concluded that the quality of system design is very good. The system was developed for the client and installed by a well-respected consulting firm, and the system relies heavily on automated information systems. Lam decides that performing tests of controls using computer-assisted audit techniques would likely be cost-effective. In addition, after completing his assessment of control risk over revenue transactions, Lam plans to use monetary-unit sampling to verify the client's recorded accounts receivable at year-end. In planning the engagement, Lam has assessed materiality to be $175 000.

REQUIRED

a. Explain the basic principles of sample selection for monetary unit (dollar unit) sampling.

b. Also discuss how computer-assisted audit techniques could be used to assist in sample selection, assuming that the population of year-end accounts receivable is available to Lam as a data file compatible with his software.

c. Assume that the client's recorded accounts receivable total $2 000 000 at year-end and that Lam examines a valid random sample of 50 dollar units, and finds two errors as follows:

	Account Number 26751	Account Number 87523
Recorded amount	$20 000	$10 000
Amount confirmed by customer	10 000	NIL

Both errors were caused by the client's failure to record equipment returned by customers, where the equipment was deemed to be defective. The client agrees with the customer's position in both cases.

What further action is required on the part of the auditor with respect to these errors?

(Extract from AU2 CGA-Canada Examinations developed by the Certified General Accountants Association of Canada © 2010 CGA-Canada. Reproduced with permission. All rights reserved.)

11-33 ③ ⑥ For the examination of the financial statements of Scotia Inc., Rosa, a public accountant, has decided to apply nonstatistical audit sampling in the tests of sales transactions. Based on her knowledge of Scotia's operations in the area of sales, she decides that the estimated population deviation rate is likely to be 3 percent and that she is willing to accept a 5 percent risk that the true population exception rate is not greater than 6 percent. Given this information, Rosa selects a random sample of 150 sales invoices from the 5000 prepared during the year and examines them for exceptions. She notes the following exceptions in her working papers.

Invoice No.	Comment
5028	Sales invoice had incorrect price, but a subsequent credit note was sent out as a correction.
6791	Voided sales invoice examined by auditor.
6810	Shipping document for a sale of merchandise could not be located.
7364	Sales invoice for $2875 has not been collected and is six months past due.
7625	Client unable to locate the printed duplicate copy of the sales invoice.
8431	Invoice was dated three days later than the date of the shipping document.
8528	Customer purchase order is not attached to the duplicate sales invoice.
8566	Billing is for $100 less than it should be due to a pricing error.
8780	Client is unable to locate the printed duplicate copy of the sales invoice.
9169	Credit is not authorized, but the sale was for only $7.65.
9974	Lack of indication of internal verification of price extensions and postings of sales invoice.

a. Which of the invoices in the table should be defined as an exception?
b. Explain why it is inappropriate to set a single acceptable TER and EPER for the combined exceptions.
c. Calculate SER for each attribute tested in the population. (You must decide which attributes should be combined, which should be kept separate, and which exceptions are actual exceptions before you calculate SER.)
d. Calculate TER – SER for each attribute and evaluate whether the calculated allowance for sampling risk is sufficiently large given the 5 percent ARO. Assume TER is 6 percent for each attribute.
e. State the appropriate analysis of exceptions for each of the exceptions in the sample, including additional procedures to be performed.

11-34 **6** You have been asked to do planning for statistical testing in the control testing of the audit of cash receipts. Following is a partial audit program for the audit of cash receipts:

1. Review the cash receipts journal for large and unusual transactions.
2. Trace entries from the prelisting of cash receipts to the cash receipts journal to determine whether each is recorded.
3. Compare customer name, date, and amount on the prelisting with the cash receipts journal.
4. Examine the related remittance advice for entries selected from the prelisting to determine whether cash discounts were approved.
5. Trace entries from the prelisting to the deposit slip to determine whether each has been deposited.

REQUIRED

a. Identify which audit procedures can be tested using attributes sampling. Justify your response.
b. State the appropriate sampling unit for each of the tests in Part (a).
c. Define the attributes that you would test for each of the tests in Part (a). State the audit objective associated with each of the attributes.
d. Define exception conditions for each of the attributes that you described in Part (c).
e. Which of the exceptions would be indicative of potential fraud? Justify your response.
f. Assume an ARO of 5 percent and a TER of 8 percent for tests of controls. The estimated population deviation rate for tests of controls is 2 percent. What is the initial sample size for each attribute?

Professional Judgment Problems and Cases

11-35 **4** **5** **8** Nandini has just completed the accounts receivable confirmation process in the audit of Danforth Paper Company Ltd., a paper supplier to retail shops and commercial users.

Following are the data related to this process:

Accounts receivable recorded balance	$2 760 000
Number of accounts	7 320

A nonstatistical sample was taken as follows:

All accounts over $10 000 (23 accounts)	$465 000
77 accounts under $10 000	$ 81 500
Materiality	$100 000

Inherent and control risk are both high. No relevant substantive analytical procedures were performed. The table below gives the results of the confirmation procedures.

	Recorded Value	Audited Value
Items over $10 000	$465 000	$432 000
Items under $10 000	81 500	77 150
Individual misstatements for items under $10 000:		
Item 12	5 120	4 820
Item 19	485	385
Item 33	1 250	250
Item 35	3 975	3 875
Item 51	1 850	1 825
Item 59	4 200	3 780
Item 74	2 405	0
	19 285	14 935

REQUIRED

a. What type of nonstatistical sampling method would Nandini have used? Justify your response.

b. Explain the advantages and disadvantages of using stratified sampling for the Danforth Paper Company Ltd. sample selection.

c. If statistical sampling were used, which method would be used? Justify your response.

d. Describe the process that would be used to evaluate the results of the nonstatistical sample. Consider both the direct implications of the misstatements found and the effect of using a sample.

11-36 6 7 The following are auditor judgments and audit sampling results for six populations. Assume large population sizes.

	1	2	3	4	5	6
EPER (in percentage)	2	1	1	0	3	8
TER (in percentage)	6	5	20	3	8	15
ARO (in percentage)	5	5	10	5	10	10
Actual sample size	100	100	20	100	60	60
Actual number of exceptions in the sample	2	4	1	0	1	8

REQUIRED

a. For each population, did the auditor select a smaller sample size than is indicated by using attribute sampling tables for determining sample size? Evaluate, selecting either a larger or smaller size than those determined in the tables.

b. Calculate the SER and CUER for each population.

c. For which of the six populations should the sample results be considered unacceptable? What options are available to the auditor?

d. Why is analysis of the exceptions necessary even when the populations are considered acceptable?

e. For the following terms, identify which is an audit decision, a nonstatistical estimate made by the auditor, a sample result, or a statistical conclusion about the population:

1. EPER
2. TER
3. ARO
4. Actual sample size
5. Actual number of exceptions in the sample
6. SER
7. CUER

11-37 2 10 You have just completed control testing for accounts payable. You found three items for which no supporting documentation could be located and noted the exceptions. The explanation for the lack of supporting documentation was that the payments were to a related company and often documentation was lax. You discussed the issue with your senior, who asked you to confirm the details with the related company. The confirmation agreed with the amounts in your client's records, and you concluded that the deviations were anomalous. Your senior agreed with your conclusion and explained, "Since they are not exceptions, we do not have to adjust our audit approach. The partner has been really concerned about the time budget and we do not want to waste time on additional testing just because of poor documentation."

REQUIRED

a. Using the professional judgement framework, explain what is wrong with the alternative procedures performed.

b. What is a possible explanation for the lack of documentation supporting the accounts payable with the related company?

11-38 5 6 Dev is working on the testing of internal controls over price changes in the inventory system. Dev has completed the controls testing to determine whether all price changes were approved by the senior accountant, by reference to master file change forms.

In order to place reliance on this control, his audit supervisor has decided that the estimated population exception rate error rate should be less than 1 percent. When Dev calculated the sample size, he used an ARO of 10 percent and a TER of 4 percent. Based on these decisions, Dev examined 150 inventory price master file change forms.

Based upon Dev's firm sampling guidelines for ARO of 10 percent, the following computed upper exception rate (CUER) for actual number of deviations is:

0 (1.4%), 2 (1.4%), 2 (3.3%), 3 (3.3%), 4 (4.1%), 5 (4.9%)

In his testing, Dev uncovered five deviations. Answer the following questions to explain the impact on the audit.

a. Since the number of deviations represents an actual error rate of 3.3 percent, which is less than TER, Dev concluded that the control is effective. Explain whether or not his conclusion is correct.

b. Assume Dev's quantitative assessment indicates that the control for inventory price changes is ineffective. List two further actions Dev should perform before making his final conclusion. Explain the purpose of each action.

c. What potential misstatement could occur if the controls over price file changes are ineffective? Be sure to identify the affected account(s) and the type of misstatement (over/understated), as well as the relevant assertion(s).

11-39 6 10 Annie Zhao is using attributes sampling in testing controls over sales transactions. She is testing five attributes related to sales invoices using an ARO of 5 percent (confidence level of 95 percent), and zero expected deviations for each attribute based on prior experience with the client. Annie has determined that the tolerable exception rate for each attribute is 5 percent. Using her firm's audit software, she entered the population size (number of invoices), desired confidence level, TER, and EPER, and determined a sample size of 60 invoices. She used the audit software to select a random sample of invoices and performed the control tests. She found zero deviations for four of the five attributes and concluded that the control can be relied upon for each of those attributes. For the remaining attribute, she found one control deviation. In projecting the sample results to the population for the attribute with one control deviation identified, Annie entered the confidence level, sample size, and one deviation into the audit software sampling module and determined that the computed upper exception rate for the attribute is 7.92 percent.

REQUIRED

a. Explain how Annie should interpret the CUER of 7.92 percent.

b. What should Annie conclude about the effectiveness of the control attribute with one identified deviation?

c. What are the alternatives for Annie if she concludes the control cannot be relied upon?

d. Assume Annie discusses the deviation with the controller and learns this deviation occurred while a temporary employee was covering for the regular clerk, who was on vacation. Would this information be relevant in determining which of the alternatives she chooses in Answer c. would be the most appropriate response? What testing and documentation would be needed to conclude this control can be relied upon?

11-40 6 10 Jeff Jacobs is a junior accountant with the public accounting firm of Maxwell and King LLP. Jeff was assigned to do the audit of Astor Electronics Inc. The in-charge auditor informed Jeff that, based upon the procedures performed to obtain the understanding of the controls related to the procurement process, controls are effective and the preliminary assessment of control risk is low. Based upon this assessment, Jeff decided to perform test of controls over procurement transactions using attribute sampling.

Jeff figured that a tolerable exception rate of 9 percent and a 5 percent ARO were appropriate for the tests he planned to perform. He had no idea how many deviations actually might exist in the population so he set the estimated population exception rate at 2 percent to be conservative. Based on the AICPA sampling tables, Jeff selected a sample of 70 items.

Because Jeff believed larger items deserved more attention than smaller items, he selected 50 items with values greater than or equal to $2500 and 20 items with values less than $2500. He thought it would be most appropriate to select transactions near the end of the fiscal year, so he randomly selected items for testing from the last two months.

Jeff was relieved when he found only six deviations from the prescribed controls. One deviation was a missing supplier's invoice. Jeff spoke to the client who informed him that they lost a few invoices during their recent move. Jeff accepted the client's explanation since this was the only supplier invoice missing from the results of his work. Two deviations were missing approval signatures by an authorized manager. The manager explained that he had not approved the supplier invoices because he had been out of the office on the date the invoices were received and entered into the accounts payable system. He reviewed the two supplier invoices in question and told Jeff there were no problems with them. The other three deviations involved dollar errors. Two were errors in the extension of the supplier invoices that had not been detected by the client and the other was a misclassification error between expenses, which did not affect net income. Jeff considered these three dollar errors to be the only three actual control deviations.

Based on the tables, using a 5 percent risk of assessing control risk as low, three deviations found in a sample 70, Jeff determined that the computed upper exception rate was 10.7. Given these results, Jeff concluded that that procurement controls over supplier invoices were effective and accordingly he assessed the control risk at moderate (below maximum).

REQUIRED

Explain the deficiencies you note in Jeff's attribute sampling application.

11-41 1 10 It is hard to believe that standards could differ on something that is as seemingly objective as sampling. However, like many things in auditing, there is often considerable leeway around what is right or wrong (that is why professional judgment is so important). Canadian and PCAOB (Public Company Accounting Oversight Board) standards differ significantly on the treatment of anomalies. Auditors need to obtain evidence if the control deviation or misstatement is an anomaly.

REQUIRED

a. Referring to CAS 530 A19 and PCAOB AU-350.25, explain the differences between the two standards regarding the auditor's responsibility for the consideration of anomalies in projecting the error on the total population.

b. Explain the impact of the two different approaches on audit effectiveness. (*Hint:* Think about which approach would enable an auditor to fail to project errors in order to avoid potential disputes with the client.)

c. Auditing in Action 11-4 discusses large firms' sampling policies with regard to substantive tests of details. Refer to the last comment: "[T]eams sometimes fail to project an error because the sample error is relatively small, and they fail to recognize that a projected error coupled with sampling risk might result in a material misstatement." Is this approach consistent with CAS 530? Explain why or why not.

d. Refer to Auditing in Action 11-5 and read the auditors' explanation regarding stratifying exceptions for follow-up. Is this approach consistent with CAS 530? Explain why or why not.

PART 3

Application of the Audit Process

To understand how auditing is done in practice, it is important to understand how auditing concepts are applied to specific auditing areas. Chapter 11, the first chapter in this part of the book, focuses on the sampling process. In it, we discuss how auditors use various risk judgments to plan and design samples, as well as how the results of the control tests, substantive analytical procedures, and substantive tests of transactions and balances are all interconnected in terms of developing the audit strategy.

Chapters 12 to 16 further demonstrate the application of the risk-based audit process. Specifically, these chapters study the relationships between risks, internal controls, tests of controls, substantive analytical procedures, and substantive tests of details in the audit of the income statement and balance sheet accounts and related disclosures in each cycle. The focus of these chapters is the class of transactions and balances in the following cycles: revenue, acquisition and payment, inventory and distribution, human resources and payroll, and capital acquisition and repayment. Finally, Chapter 17 focuses on the audit of cash balances. This is covered last because cash is affected by the transactions in all other cycles.

AUDIT OF THE REVENUE CYCLE

STANDARDS REFERENCED IN THIS CHAPTER

CAS 240 – The auditor's responsibilities relating to fraud in an audit of financial statements

CAS 505 – External confirmations

CAS 540 – Auditing accounting estimates, including fair value accounting estimates and related disclosures

ASPE 3400 – Revenue

IFRS 15 – Revenue from Contracts with Customers

We have looked at the planning of the audit, including the risk assessment process, and considered how the auditor develops a sampling strategy for tests of controls and substantive tests. We now will apply all of this to developing an audit strategy for a specific cycle. We start with the most significant cycle for most organizations—revenue. We begin by considering the risks associated with revenue and then discuss how we actually design and conduct the testing in response to these risks, which includes designing tests of controls and substantive tests. We finish the chapter by providing actual examples of audit strategies used in the revenue cycle of two very different organizations.

LEARNING OBJECTIVES

After studying this chapter, you should be able to:

1 Identify the accounts and the classes of transactions in the revenue cycle.

2 Describe the business functions, documents, and records of the revenue cycle.

3 Identify significant risks and assess risk of material misstatement in the revenue cycle.

4 Understand key controls for the revenue cycle and assess control risk for the revenue cycle.

5 Use professional judgment to develop an audit approach (strategy) for the revenue cycle.

6 Design and perform tests of control for the revenue cycle.

7 Design and perform substantive analytical procedures for the accounts in the revenue cycle.

8 Design and perform substantive tests of details for revenue accounts and assertions.

9 Design and perform substantive tests of details for accounts receivable and assertions.

10 Obtain and evaluate accounts receivable confirmations.

11 Design and perform fraud procedures for the revenue cycle.

Fictitious Revenue at Poseidon Concepts

On February 6, 2015, after conducting a joint investigation with the SEC, the Alberta Securities Exchange (ASC) released a statement alleging that a once promising oil-field services company, Poseidon Concepts Corp., had issued fraudulent financial statements that overstated revenue by $106 million. Regulators alleged that Joe

continued >

Kostelecky, an executive vice-president based in the United States, had directed junior accounting staff to book revenue without signed contracts and had made false assurances to senior accounting staff that the contracts were valid, existing, and collectible.

Poseidon had two types of arrangements with customers—day-to-day rentals based solely upon actual usage, and take-or-pay contracts that guaranteed access to a set of tanks at a discounted rate for a certain period of time. In the take-or-pay contracts, customers were obligated to pay Poseidon whether or not they took delivery of the tanks or used the tanks. During the first two quarters of 2012, Kostelecky pressured the invoicing clerk to book take-and-pay revenue despite the lack of documentation to support the revenues she was asked to book.

The revenue fraud was uncovered when a new operations controller started to question Kostelecky regarding the collectibility of take-or-pay receivables from US customers, which had grown by over 500 percent in comparison to the previous year. In response to the controller's inquiries for supporting documentation, the invoicing clerk provided him with a list of contracts that she had booked. Only 12 of the 54 contracts were fully executed agreements. The CFO decided to contact customers directly. In an email to the CFO, the controller noted, "Lots of calls being made, lots of blank stairs [sic] and head scratching from our customers' end ... In a lot of cases I have been talking to customers who we have millions of dollars in receivable balances [sic] who have no idea who Poseidon is."

At that point, the company hired EY to perform a forensic review. As a result, the company restated its financial results for the first three quarters of 2012 and informed the public and the securities regulators of the fraud. Share prices plummeted by more than 95 percent and Poseidon subsequently filed for bankruptcy. Kostelecky agreed to pay $75 000 to settle allegations with the SEC. In March 2017, the ASC found Kostelecky guilty of fraud and, in its decision, it stated, "Kostelecky engaged in what we termed ... a campaign of disinformation." Earlier, three other executives reached a settlement with the ASC and agreed to pay a combined total of $375 000 after admitting they filed financial statements that wildly overstated the company's revenue. However, the ASC found Kostelecky to be the "source" and "primary cause" of Poseidon's breach of securities law. At the time of writing, the ASC had not announced Kostelecky's punishment. Kostelecky is also facing criminal charges in the United States. If convicted, he faces a maximum penalty of 20 years in prison on each count and maximum total fines of $6.25 million. Although neither securities regulator charged the auditors (KPMG), class action lawsuits totalling $650 million are still pending.

Sources: Dan Healing, "ASC files new charges against failed Poseidon Concepts," *Calgary Herald*, February 6, 2015. Janet McFarland, "Former Poseidon executive settles with SEC over fraud allegations," *Globe and Mail*, February 6, 2015. Janet McFarland, "Former Poseidon executives reach settlement with ASC over allegations" *Globe and Mail*, June 16, 2016. Amanda Stephenson, "Poseidon Concepts' executive obviously deceitful in breach of securities law: ASC," *Calgary Herald*, March 17, 2017. United States District Court for the District of North Dakota Southwestern Division, *Securities and Exchange Commission Versus Joseph A. Kostelecky*, February 6, 2015.

OVERVIEW OF THE REVENUE CYCLE

LO 1 Identify the accounts and the classes of transactions in the revenue cycle.

The **revenue cycle** involves the decisions and processes necessary for the transfer of the ownership of goods and services to customers after they are made available for sale. It begins with a request by a customer (or a customer selecting and picking up a product) and ends with the conversion of material or service into an account receivable or cash.

A brief summary of the way accounting information flows through the various accounts in the sales and collection cycle is illustrated in Figure 12-1 by the use of T-accounts. This figure shows that there are generally six **classes of transactions in the revenue cycle**, flowing to the general ledger accounts noted below beside the class of transaction (CR = credit, DR = debit):

Revenue cycle—the decisions and processes necessary for the transfer of the ownership of goods and services to customers after they are made available for sale; it begins with a request by a customer and ends with the conversion of material or service into an account receivable, and ultimately into cash.

- Sales (cash and sales on account net of cash discounts taken): CR sales, DR accounts receivable and cash discounts taken.

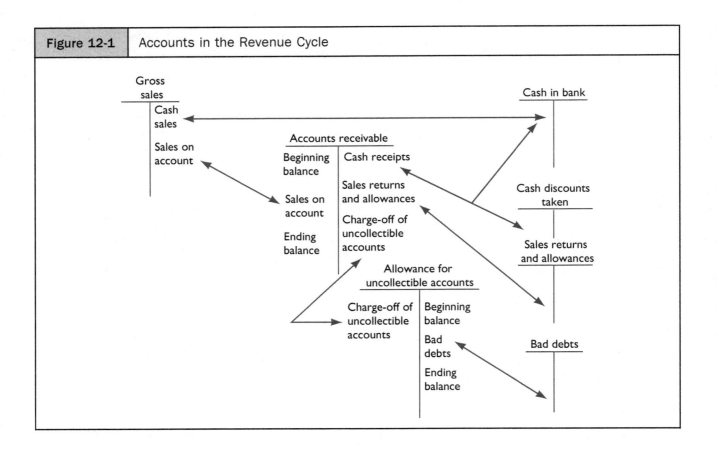

| Figure 12-1 | Accounts in the Revenue Cycle |

- Cash receipts: DR cash in bank, CR accounts receivable.
- Sales returns and allowances: DR sales returns and allowances, CR accounts receivable.
- Charge-off of uncollectible accounts: CR accounts receivable, DR allowance for uncollectible accounts.
- Bad-debt expense: DR bad-debt expense, CR allowance for uncollectible accounts.
- Master file changes: no effect on general ledger accounts; effect is on master files.

BUSINESS FUNCTIONS IN THE CYCLE, AND RELATED DOCUMENTS AND RECORDS

The business functions for a cycle are the key activities that an organization must complete to execute and record business transactions. Table 12-1 lists the common **business functions in the sales and collection cycle**, typical documents and records, and the purposes of those documents or records, which could be in paper or electronic form.

Processing Customer Orders

A customer's request for goods initiates the entire cycle. Legally, a request is an offer to buy goods under specified terms. The receipt of a customer order often results in the immediate creation of a sales order. In a retail environment, the customer order is absent as the customer picks up the product and takes it to a point-of-sale terminal.

Customer Order A customer order is a request for merchandise by a customer. It may be received by telephone, by letter, as a printed form that has been sent to prospective

| Table 12-1 | Classes of Transactions, Business Functions, Related Documents and Records, and Their Purposes for the Revenue Cycle |||

Classes of Transactions	Accounts	Business Functions	Documents and Records
Sales	Sales Accounts receivable	Processing customer orders Granting credit Shipping goods Billing customers and recording sales	Customer order Sales order Customer order or sales order Shipping document Sales invoice Sales transaction file Sales journal or listing Accounts receivable master file Accounts receivable trial balance Monthly statement

Cash receipts	Cash in bank (debits from
	    cash receipts)
	Accounts receivable
		Processing and recording cash
		    receipts
			Remittance advice
			Prelisting of cash receipts
			Cash receipts transaction file
			Cash receipts journal or listing

Sales returns and
    allowances
	Sales returns and allowances
	Accounts receivable
		Processing and recording sales
		    returns and allowances
			Credit memo
			Sales returns and allowances journal

Charge-off of uncollect-
    ible accounts
	Accounts receivable
	Allowance for uncollectible
	    accounts
		Writing off uncollectible accounts
		    receivable
			Uncollectible account authorization form
			General journal

Bad debt expense	Bad debt expense Allowance for uncollectible accounts	Providing for bad debts	General journal

and existing customers, through salespeople, through electronic submission of the customer order through the internet, or through another network linkage between the supplier and the customer.

Sales Order A sales order is a document for communicating the description, quantity, and related information for goods ordered by a customer. This is often used to indicate credit approval and authorization for shipment.

Granting Credit Before goods are shipped, a properly authorized person must *approve credit* to the customer for sales on account. Weak practices in credit approval often result in excessive bad debts and accounts receivable that may be uncollectible. An indication of credit approval on the sales order often serves as the approval to ship the goods. In some companies, the computer automatically approves a credit sale based on preapproved credit limits maintained in a customer master file. The computer allows the sale to proceed only when the proposed sales order total plus the existing customer balance is less than the credit limit in the master file. Once the balance approaches the credit limit, exception reports are produced for the credit manager to review and approve.

Shipping Goods This critical function is the first point in the cycle at which the company gives up assets. Most companies recognize sales when goods are shipped. A shipping document is prepared at the time of shipment, which can be done automatically by a computer, based on sales order information. The shipping document, which is often a multicopy bill of lading, is essential to the proper billing of shipments to customers. Companies that maintain perpetual inventory records also update them based on shipping records.

Shipping Document A shipping document is prepared to initiate shipment of the goods, indicating the description of the merchandise, the quantity shipped, and other relevant data. The company sends the original to the customer and retains one or more copies. The shipping document serves as a signal to bill the customer and may be in electronic or paper form.

One type of shipping document is a bill of lading, which is a written contract between the carrier and the seller of the receipt and shipment of goods. Often, bills of lading include only the number of boxes or pounds shipped, rather than complete details of quantity and description. (For our purposes, however, we will assume that complete details are included on bills of lading.)

The bill of lading is often transmitted electronically—once goods have been shipped—and automatically generates the related sales invoice as well as the entry in the sales journal. Many companies use bar codes and handheld computers to record removal of inventory from the warehouse. This information is used to update the perpetual inventory records.

Billing Customers and Recording Sales

Because billing customers is the means by which the customer is informed of the amount due for the goods, it must be done correctly and on a timely basis. Billing the proper amount is dependent on charging the customer for the quantity shipped at the authorized price, which includes consideration for freight charges, insurance, and terms of payments.

In most systems, billing of the customer includes preparation of an electronic record or a multicopy sales invoice and real-time updating of the sales transactions file, accounts receivable master file, and general ledger master file for sales and accounts receivable. The accounting system uses this information to generate the sales journal and, along with cash receipts and miscellaneous credits, to prepare the accounts receivable trial balance.

Sales Invoice A sales invoice is a document or electronic record indicating the description and quantity of goods sold, the price, freight charges, insurance, terms, and other relevant data. The sales invoice is the method of indicating to the customer the amount of a sale and the payment due date. Companies send the original to the customer, and retain one or more copies. Typically, the computer automatically prepares the sales invoice after the customer number, quantity, destination of goods shipped, and sales terms are entered. The computer calculates the invoice extensions and total sales amount using the information entered, along with prices in the inventory master file.

Sales Transaction File This is a computer-generated file that includes all sales transactions processed by the accounting system for a period, which could be a day, week, or month. It includes all information entered into the system and information for each transaction, such as customer name, date, amount, account classification or classifications, salesperson, and commission rate. The file can also include returns and allowances, or there can be a separate file for those transactions.

The information in the sales transaction file is used for a variety of records, listings, or reports, depending on the company's needs. These may include a sales journal, accounts receivable master file, and transactions for a certain account balance or division.

Sales Journal or Listing This is a listing or report generated from the sales transaction file that typically includes the customer name, date, amount, and account classification or classifications for each transaction, such as division or product line. It also identifies whether the sale was for cash or accounts receivable. The journal or listing is usually for a month but can cover any period of time. Typically, the journal or listing includes totals of every account number for the time period. The same transactions included in the journal or listing are also posted simultaneously to the general ledger and, if they are on account, to the accounts receivable master file. The journal or listing can also include returns and allowances, or there can be a separate journal or listing of those transactions.

Accounts Receivable Master File This is a computer file used to record individual sales, cash receipts, and sales returns and allowances for each customer and to maintain customer account balances. The master file is updated from the sales, sales returns and allowances, and cash receipts computer transaction files. The total of the individual account balances in the master file equals the total balance of accounts receivable in the general ledger. A printout of the accounts receivable master file shows, by customer, the beginning balance in accounts receivable, each sales transaction, sales returns and allowances, cash receipts, and the ending balance.

Accounts Receivable Trial Balance This list or report shows the amount receivable from each customer at a point in time. It is prepared directly from the accounts receivable master file and is usually an *aged trial balance* that includes the total balance outstanding and the number of days the receivable has been outstanding, grouped by category of days (such as less than 30 days, 31 to 60 days, and so on).

Monthly Statement This is a document sent electronically or by mail to each customer, indicating the beginning balance of the account receivable, the amount and date of each sale, cash payments received, credit memos issued, and the ending balance due. It is, in essence, a copy of the customer's portion of the accounts receivable master file.

The four remaining parts of the process involve collecting and recording cash, processing sales returns and allowances, writing off uncollectible accounts, and providing for bad debt expense.

Processing and Recording Cash Receipts

Processing and recording cash receipts includes receiving, depositing, and recording cash. Cash includes both currency and cheques. A potential fraud risk is the possibility of theft. Theft can occur before receipts are entered in the records, referred to as **skimming**. It is the single most common form of cash misappropriation when employees steal incoming funds. The term comes from the fact that the money is taken off the top, the way cream is skimmed from milk. The risk of theft is reduced in the handling of cash receipts when cash handling is separated from deposit and recording in the accounts, and when all cash must be deposited in the bank and recorded on a timely basis.

Skimming—a common form of cash misappropriation in which the employees steal incoming funds prior to their being recorded in the accounting records.

Remittance Advice A remittance advice is a document mailed to the customer and typically returned to the seller with the cash payment. It indicates the customer name, the sales invoice number, and the amount of the invoice. A remittance advice is used as a record of the cash received to permit the immediate deposit of cash and to improve control over the custody of assets. If the customer fails to include the remittance advice with the payment, it is common for the person opening the mail to prepare one at that time.

Prelisting of Cash Receipts This is a list prepared when cash is received by someone who has no responsibility for recording sales, accounts receivable, or cash and who has no access to accounting records. It is used to verify whether cash received was recorded and deposited at the correct amounts and on a timely basis.

Many companies use a bank to process cash receipts from customers. Some companies use a lockbox system in which customers mail payments directly to an address maintained by the bank. The bank is responsible for opening all receipts, maintaining records of all customer payments received at the lockbox address, and depositing receipts into the company's bank account on a timely basis. In other cases, receipts are submitted electronically from a customer's bank account to a company bank account through the use of electronic funds transfer (EFT). When customers purchase goods by credit card, the issuer of the credit card uses EFT to transfer funds into the company's bank account. For both lockbox systems and EFT transactions, the bank provides information to the company to prepare the cash receipt entries in the accounting records.

Cash Receipts Transaction File This is a computer-generated file that includes all cash receipts transactions processed by the accounting system for a period, such as a day, week, or month. It includes the same type of information as the sales transaction file.

Cash Receipts Journal or Listing This listing or report is generated from the cash receipts transaction file and includes all transactions for a time period. The same transactions, including all relevant information, are included in the accounts receivable master file and general ledger.

Processing and Recording Sales Returns and Allowances

When a customer is dissatisfied with the goods, the seller often accepts the return of the goods or grants a reduction in the charges. The company prepares a receiving report for returned goods and returns them to storage. Returns and allowances are recorded in the sales returns and allowances transaction file, as well as the accounts receivable master file. Credit memos are issued for returns and allowances to aid in maintaining control and to facilitate recordkeeping.

Credit Memo A credit memo indicates a reduction in the amount due from a customer because of returned goods or an allowance. It often takes the same general form as a sales invoice, but it supports reductions in accounts receivable rather than increases.

Sales Returns and Allowances Journal This is the journal used to record sales returns and allowances. It performs the same function as the sales journal. Many companies record these transactions in the sales journal rather than in a separate journal.

Writing Off Uncollectible Accounts Receivable

Regardless of the diligence of credit departments, some customers do not pay their bills. After concluding that an amount cannot be collected, the company must write it off. Typically, this occurs after a customer files for bankruptcy or the account is turned over to a collection agency. Controls in this area are very important since it can be used as a way to hide embezzlement of cash.

Uncollectible Account Authorization Form This is a document used internally to indicate authority to write an account receivable off as uncollectible.

Providing for Bad Debts Because companies cannot expect to collect on 100 percent of their sales, accounting principles require them to record bad debt expense for the amount they do not expect to collect. Most companies record this transaction at the end of each month or quarter.

CONCEPT CHECK

C12-1 List the six categories of transactions. For each category, describe how the completeness audit objective would apply to the transaction.

AN OVERVIEW OF THE AUDIT PROCESS FOR THE REVENUE CYCLE

Figure 12-2 provides an overview of the audit process for the revenue cycle. In the remainder of the chapter, we will explain each of the various steps in the process.

Revenue is, for most organizations, one of the largest accounts and an important driver of the organization's results. For that reason, it is usually the most important cycle in the financial statement audit and, as highlighted in Auditing in Action 12-1, it is often an area with which auditors struggle.

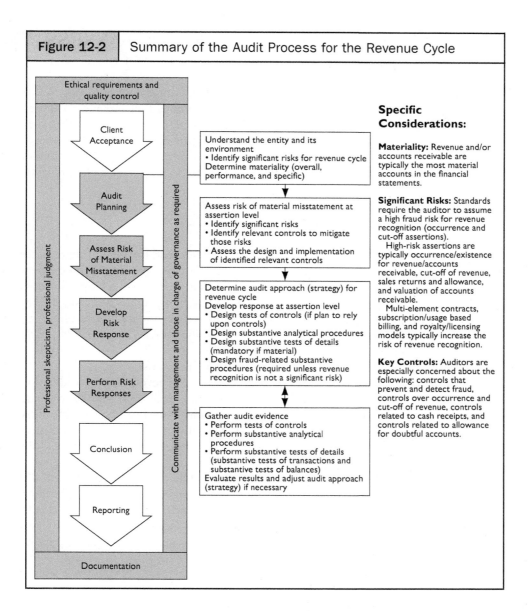

Figure 12-2 | Summary of the Audit Process for the Revenue Cycle

Ethical requirements and quality control

Client Acceptance

Audit Planning

Assess Risk of Material Misstatement

Develop Risk Response

Perform Risk Responses

Conclusion

Reporting

Documentation

Professional skepticism, professional judgment

Communicate with management and those in charge of governance as required

Understand the entity and its environment
• Identify significant risks for revenue cycle
Determine materiality (overall, performance, and specific)

Assess risk of material misstatement at assertion level
• Identify significant risks
• Identify relevant controls to mitigate those risks
• Assess the design and implementation of identified relevant controls

Determine audit approach (strategy) for revenue cycle
Develop response at assertion level
• Design tests of controls (if plan to rely upon controls)
• Design substantive analytical procedures
• Design substantive tests of details (mandatory if material)
• Design fraud-related substantive procedures (required unless revenue recognition is not a significant risk)

Gather audit evidence
• Perform tests of controls
• Perform substantive analytical procedures
• Perform substantive tests of details (substantive tests of transactions and substantive tests of balances)
Evaluate results and adjust audit approach (strategy) if necessary

Specific Considerations:

Materiality: Revenue and/or accounts receivable are typically the most material accounts in the financial statements.

Significant Risks: Standards require the auditor to assume a high fraud risk for revenue recognition (occurrence and cut-off assertions).
   High-risk assertions are typically occurrence/existence for revenue/accounts receivable, cut-off of revenue, sales returns and allowance, and valuation of accounts receivable.
   Multi-element contracts, subscription/usage based billing, and royalty/licensing models typically increase the risk of revenue recognition.

Key Controls: Auditors are especially concerned about the following: controls that prevent and detect fraud, controls over occurrence and cut-off of revenue, controls related to cash receipts, and controls related to allowance for doubtful accounts.

AUDITING IN ACTION 12-1
Auditors Around the World Struggle With Revenue

In a recent report released by the International Forum of Independent Audit Regulators (IFIAR), audit regulators from around the world agree that significant audit deficiencies continue to occur in the audit of revenue. However, auditors often do not sufficiently understand the terms and conditions of complex arrangements, such as in the case of construction-type and production-type contracts. As a result, auditors failed to perform procedures to test the estimated cost to complete and the progress of the contracts. Auditors also do not perform adequate procedures to ensure that revenue is recorded in the correct period. Further, auditors often fail to identify and respond to the presumed fraud risk related to revenue recognition, including not changing the nature of audit procedures.

Some examples of inappropriate procedures highlighted by the Public Company Accounting Oversight Board (PCAOB) in its recent inspections include:

• Insufficient substantive analytical procedures (such as imprecise expectations, failing to test reliability of data, and failing to investigate significant differences and corroborate management's expectations);

• Using too small samples and failing to use representative samples; and

• Inappropriate evaluation of sample results.

Sources: International Forum of Independent Audit Regulators, *Report on 2014 Survey of Inspection Findings,* March 2, 2015. PCAOB, *Staff Practice Alert 12: Matters Related to Auditing Revenue in an Audit of Financial Statements,* September 9, 2014.

IDENTIFY SIGNIFICANT RISKS AND ASSESS RISK OF MATERIAL MISSTATEMENT

As we have highlighted in our discussion of planning and audit strategy in Chapters 6, 7, and 10, the auditor performs risk assessment procedures that provide an understanding of the entity and its environment. These procedures involve inquiry, visiting the client premises, walk-throughs, reviewing minutes and significant contracts, and preliminary analytical review. As part of gaining this understanding, the auditor assesses inherent risk for each assertion for each account in the cycle, such as revenue and accounts receivable.

Identify Significant Risks

As part of the assessment of the risk of material misstatement, the auditor determines whether any of the risks identified are significant. Significant risks represent identified and assessed risks of material misstatement that, in the auditor's professional judgment, requires special audit consideration. Identifying significant risks as part of planning is important, given the audit standards require the auditor to obtain an understanding of the entity's controls relevant to significant risks in order to evaluate the design and implementation of those controls, and the auditor must perform substantive tests related to assertions deemed to have significant risks.

CAS

For most audits, revenue recognition (overstatement of revenue) is considered to be a significant risk because CAS 240 requires the auditor to presume that revenue recognition is a specific fraud risk. When sales are made on account, the double-entry nature of accounting means this presumption typically affects the auditor's assessment of inherent risk for the following assertions and accounts: existence of accounts receivable; revenue cutoff, and sales returns and allowances cutoff. It is also common for clients to unintentionally or fraudulently misstate the allowance for doubtful accounts because of the difficulty in determining the correct balance. That is because the allowance is an estimate that is based upon assumptions regarding future events. Therefore, the auditor may also identify the risk of misstatement related to valuation of accounts receivable as a significant risk. Table 12-2 summarizes a selection of major risks of error or fraud in the revenue cycle.

Preliminary Analytical Review Preliminary analytical procedures, which the auditor performs as part of audit planning, help the auditor identify significant risks. Table 12-3 presents examples of the major types of ratios and comparisons for the revenue cycle that could be used for planning purposes, and potential misstatements that may be indicated by the analytical procedures.

Figure 12-3 is an excerpt from the working paper that documents the preliminary analytical review conducted for Hillsburg Hardware's revenue cycle. You will note that analysis requires not simply making comparisons from year to year, but seeing whether the results make sense in relation to the auditor's knowledge of the business, as well as analyzing the relationships among the various ratios. The auditor also notes that further follow-up is necessary, given the unexpected results.

Analytical procedures are also helpful in highlighting potential warning signals or symptoms of revenue fraud, including the following:

- Gross margins decreasing while sales are increasing could signal a side agreement for a special discount.
- Unusually high returns could be caused by a channel stuffing arrangement or other side agreement permitting reseller returns of unsold goods.
- Unexplained differences in physical inventory counts might indicate that a bill-and-hold fraud is taking place.
- Buildup of aged accounts receivable balances might be caused by backdating agreements, side agreements, or channel stuffing arrangements.

| | Risks of Fraud | |
Risks of Error	Misappropriation of Assets, Other Fraud, or Illegal Acts	Inadequate Disclosure or Incorrect Presentation of Financial Information, Including Fraudulent Financial Reporting
Orders are shipped to a customer with a bad credit rating.		Consignment sales are recorded as revenue.
	Inventory is stolen and the sale is recorded as a fictitious sale (no shipping document).	Fictitious revenue transactions are recorded and reported.
There is incorrect recognition of revenue percentage for long-term contracts or complex revenue arrangements.		There is improper (and intentional) recording of transactions that do not meet revenue recognition criteria (e.g., terms of sale are not completed, unresolved contingencies exist, improperly accelerating the estimated percentage of completion).
	Revenue is recorded when goods have not been delivered.	There is improper (and intentional) recording of bill and hold transactions.
Sales are recorded twice (duplicated) or accidentally omitted.		Subsequent period revenue is deliberately recorded in the current period.
	Channel stuffing: inventory is shipped to customers with favourable terms, such as right of return, so that the client retains risks of ownership.	
Sales are recorded for the incorrect quantity or the incorrect price.		Financing transactions (borrowings) are recorded as revenue. Goods never ordered by the customer are shipped, or defective products are shipped but revenues are recorded at the full amount.
	Long-term service revenue (such as the provision of maintenance) is recorded as current revenue and receivable.	

Table 12-2   Major Risks of Error or Fraud in the Revenue Cycle

- An unusual spike in sales just before the end of the reporting period could indicate that revenue is being recognized prematurely or in the incorrect period.

In some frauds, such as WorldCom, management generated fictitious revenues to make analytical procedures results, such as gross margin, similar to the prior years. In frauds like this, analytical procedures that compare client data with similar

Table 12-3   Analytical Procedures for Planning the Revenue Cycle

Analytical Procedure for Planning	Possible Misstatement
Evaluate the ratio of returns and allowances to sales	Could indicate unusual sales arrangements
Compare bad-debt expense as a percentage of gross sales with that of previous years	Uncollectible accounts receivable that have not been provided for
Compare number of days that accounts receivable are outstanding with that of previous years	Overstatement or understatement of allowance for uncollectible accounts and bad-debt expense
Compare aging categories as a percentage of accounts receivable with those of previous years	Overstatement or understatement of allowance for uncollectible accounts and bad-debt expense
Compare allowance for uncollectible accounts as a percentage of accounts receivable with that of previous years	Overstatement or understatement of allowance for uncollectible accounts
Evaluate cash receipts collected after year-end to cash receipts during the year	If slow, may indicate special sales arrangements

Figure 12-3 | Analytical Review Working Paper

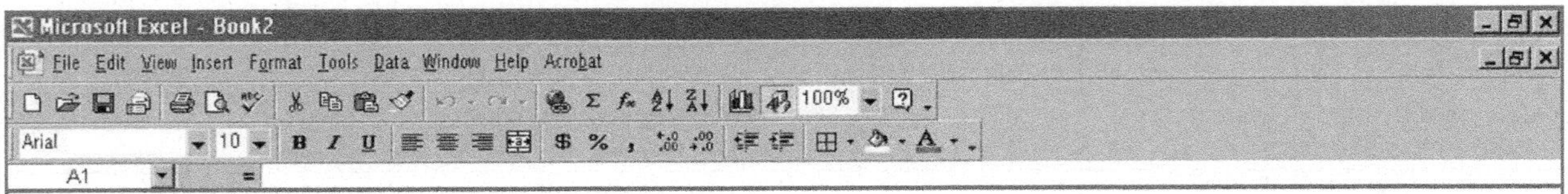

```
Microsoft Excel - Book2                                                    _ 8 X
File  Edit  View  Insert  Format  Tools  Data  Window  Help  Acrobat        _ 8 X
[toolbar icons]  100% ▼ ?
Arial        ▼ 10 ▼  B  I  U  ≡ ≡ ≡ ⊞  $ %  ,  .00 .00  ⊞ ▼ ⊞ ▼ A ▼
A1      ▼       =
```

Hillsburg Hardware Limited
December 31, 2018

Prepared by: F.M.
Approved by: L.N.

	Comparative Information				
	Dollar Amounts (in thousands)				
	31-12-18	**Percentage Change 2017–2018**	**31-12-17**	**Percentage Change 2016–2017**	**31-12-16**
Gross sales	$144 328	9.2%	$132 161	7.1%	$123 438
Sales returns and allowances	1 242	32.8	935	24.2	753
Gross profit	39 845	9.6	36 350	7.0	33 961
Accounts receivable	20 197	15.3	17 521	26.5	13 852
Allowance for Uncollectible accounts	1 240	(5.4)	1 311	2.2	1 283
Bad-debt expense	3 323	33.1	2 496	(10.7)	2 796
Total current assets	51 027	2.3	49 895	1.5	49 157
Net earnings before taxes and extraordinary items	6 401	37.4	4 659	39.0	3 351
Number of accounts receivable	415	7.8	385	3.5	372
Number of accounts receivable with balances over $150 000	19	11.8	17	6.3	16

	31-12-18	**31-12-17**	**31-12-16**
Gross profit/net sales	27.8%	27.7%	27.7%
Sales returns and allowances/gross sales	0.9%	0.7%	0.6%
Bad-debt expense/net sales	2.3%	1.9%	2.3%
Allowance for uncollectible accounts/accounts receivable	6.1%	7.5%	9.3%
Number of days' receivables outstanding	48.1	43.6	39.6
Net accounts receivable/total current assets	37.2%	32.5%	25.6%

Evaluation of Results
Profit margins have remained steady and there do not appear to be any potential misstatements, with the exception of accounts receivable as explained below.

- The allowance as a percentage of accounts receivable has declined from 7.5 percent to 6.1 percent; however, the number of days' receivables outstanding and economic conditions do not justify this change. The potential misstatement is approximately $282 758 ($20 197 000 × [0.075 – 0.061] = Total accounts receivable times the percentage decline).

Conclusion:
Based upon performance materiality of the unexplained difference is not material. However, given the magnitude of the difference, further follow-up is necessary, particularly related to the allowance for doubtful accounts.

prior-period data are typically not useful to signal the fraud. Analytical procedures should also compare client data with industry performance data as well as non-financial data (such as sales per square foot). However, it is important to note that analytical review performed at the planning stage, which is done at a high level of aggregation, is only useful in identifying potential risks of misstatement.

Identify and Assess Fraud Risk

As mentioned previously, auditing standards require auditors to presume revenue recognition is a specific fraud risk. An important part of identifying fraud risk is to understand management's motives and incentives. One obvious example is management compensation (bonuses or stock options) being tied to certain earnings targets. Another example is the role of financial analysts and other market participants, who place increasing emphasis on revenue growth, which pressures management to overstate revenue. Or, there may be considerable pressure to meet earnings forecasts. For example, as described in Auditing in Action 12-2, Nortel management had made growth predictions that would have been very difficult to achieve.

Another important consideration is if the client has transactions that appear to be overly complex with no apparent business rationale. The IAASB (International Auditing and Assurance Standards Board) provides some other examples of indicators that an entity may be engaged in fraudulent financial reporting:[1]

- Management is placing more emphasis on the need for a particular accounting treatment than on understanding the economics of the transaction.
- Transactions that involve nonconsolidated related parties have not been properly reviewed or approved by those in charge of governance.
- The transactions involve previously unidentified related parties that do not have the substance or financial strength to support the transaction without the support of the entity under audit.

Fraud Schemes Revenue is susceptible to manipulation for several reasons. Overstatement of revenues often increases net income by an equal amount because related costs of sales are often not recorded for fictitious or prematurely recognized revenues. Common revenue manipulations are listed below (you will note that the two key assertions are occurrence and cutoff):

- Fictitious revenues or sham sales (occurrence assertion)—As in the case of Poseidon Concepts in the opening vignette, documents supporting fictitious sales could be created; inventory records and shipping documents may also be falsified. (A review of 2014 SEC enforcement cases found that outright fabrication of sales records is a common type of revenue fraud.)[2]
- Premature revenue recognition (occurrence and cutoff assertions)—Sales can be recorded even though the sales involved unresolved contingencies (such as customer acceptance, right of return, etc.).
- Round-tripping or recording loans as sales (occurrence assertion)—Round-tripping involves recording sales by shipping goods to alleged customers and then providing funds to pay back the company.
- Improper cutoff of sales (cutoff assertion)—Subsequent period sales are recorded as current period sales.

---

[1] International Auditing and Assurance Standards Board, *Auditor Considerations Regarding Unusual or Highly Complex Transactions*, New York: IAASB, 2010.

[2] Nicolas Morgan and Shauna Watson, "Revenue recognition changes could spur SEC fraud probes," **CFO.com**, December 12, 2014, accessed August 15, 2017, at **http://ww2.cfo.com/ gaap-ifrs/2014/12/revenue-recognition-changes-spur-sec-fraud-probes/**.

Nortel, once Canada's tech giant and the favourite of investors and analysts, orchestrated several revenue-boosting schemes in order to meet its earnings forecasts. In total, Nortel's revenue boosting schemes overstated its 2000 revenues by approximately $1.4 billion. In 2007, the SEC announced that Nortel paid $35 million to settle financial fraud charges in relation to its revenue fraud schemes.

One example is its use of "vendor financing" whereby Nortel aggressively offered millions of dollars of credit to customers, which some claim were uncreditworthy, so that they could buy Nortel products. As one former employee of Nortel noted, "It allows you to hit your sales objectives. All of this was driven by bonuses and objectives in stock prices." Another way the company boosted its revenue was through the use of bill-and-hold arrangements whereby it recorded undelivered inventory sitting in storage as revenue. This change of accounting policy mainly affected Nortel's optical revenue—a metric watched closely by Wall Street. One project manager, who reported his concerns to the SEC, saw that the company had recorded $900 million in revenue for products that not only had not been built, but had not even been scheduled to be engineered.

The Nortel saga highlights several risk factors that should increase auditors' professional skepticism regarding revenue recognition. One obvious red flag was the change of accounting policy regarding bill-and-holds. Other red flags were the various bonus plans and the pressure to meet earnings forecasts. Coupled with this, at the time of its revenue boosts, Nortel was suffering serious losses due to the widespread economic downturn that impacted the entire telecommunications industry. The auditors had also reported material control weaknesses in their audit report on internal controls over financial reporting—another factor that increases the risk of misstatement. Further, the tone at the top was one that encouraged the manipulation of financial results to meet earnings targets. As one former employee noted, "It becomes part of the culture where numbers become more important than the truth."

Sources: Bruce Livesey, *The Thieves of Bay Street*, Toronto: Vintage Canada, 2013. Theresa Tedesco, "Nortel trial to open old wounds," *Financial Post*, January 12, 2012. Securities and Exchange Commission, "Nortel Networks pays $35 million to settle financial fraud charges," *Litigation Release 2007–2017*, October 15, 2007.

- Improper recording of sales from "bill-and-holds" that do not meet criteria for revenue recognition (occurrence and (possibly) cutoff assertions)—As highlighted in Auditing in Action 12-2, companies may make arrangements with customers for early billing and then hold the goods for shipping. Unless the customer has requested such an arrangement and there appears to be a legitimate business reason, these types of arrangements generally do not meet the revenue recognition criteria.
- Side arrangements that change the original terms of sale (such as a consignment arrangement or generous right of return) or not meeting requirements for recording revenue (occurrence assertion)—Management or sales representatives design "side contracts" with customers that contravene the company's normal business practice and revenue recognition policy.
- Manipulation of adjustments and estimates—Returns and allowances are not recorded or are understated (completeness assertion for returns and allowances, valuation and/or existence for accounts receivable); or bad debts are understated (valuation assertion for accounts receivable).

Lapping of accounts receivable— the postponement of entries for the collection of receivables to conceal an existing cash shortage; a common type of defalcation.

Another common fraud scheme (in the misappropriation of assets category) is **lapping of accounts receivable**, which involves the postponement of entries for the collection of receivables in order to conceal the embezzlement of cash. Lapping is most likely to occur if there is lack of segregation of duties— for example, if the person who handles cash receipts also has access to the accounting records (meaning he or she has the ability to enter the cash receipts into the computer system). He or she takes the cash, defers recording the cash receipts from one customer, and covers the shortages with the receipts of another customer. These receipts, in turn, are covered in the accounting records from the receipts of a third customer a few days later. The employee must continue to cover the shortage through repeated lapping, replace the stolen money, or find another way to conceal the shortage.

Manitoba Telecom Services (MTS) has a variety of revenue streams. It provides wireless, broadband, high-speed internet as well as local and long distance services to residential and business customers in Manitoba. It also provides IP-based communications, data connectivity, and security services to business customers in Canada. In its revenue recognition note, it explains 10 different revenue recognition policies. Here is an excerpt from its revenue recognition policy for three of its revenue streams:

- Revenues from the provision of local voice, wireless, data connectivity, internet, internet protocol television ("IPTV"), security and alarm monitoring services are recognized in the period in which services are provided.

- Monthly network access fees, which are billed in advance, are deferred and recognized on a straight-line basis over the contracted period.

- The company enters into arrangements with customers in which services and products may be sold together. When the components of these multiple element arrangements have stand-alone value to the customer, the components are accounted for separately, based on the relative selling prices.

This complexity increases inherent risk for revenue recognition. For example, given the number of revenue streams and the different points at which revenue is recognized, there is a higher risk of error. Also, for this type of organization, given its size and volume of transactions, the auditors would likely rely on controls. The auditors would therefore need to assess and test the key controls for each separate revenue stream, as well as develop substantive tests for each revenue recognition policy.

Source: Manitoba Telecom Services, consolidated financial statements for the years ended December 31, 2014, and December 31, 2013.

Assess Inherent Risk for Revenue

The basic principle of revenue is that revenue should be recognized when it has been earned or substantially earned. This usually means that revenue is recorded when the control over goods and services is transferred to the customer (when goods are shipped or the services are performed). However, when clients have complex revenue processes (as in the case of Manitoba Telecom, described in Auditing in Action 12-3), the decision as to when to recognize revenue is no longer straightforward.

In order to be able to assess whether the client is recognizing revenue appropriately, the auditor must be knowledgeable about the client's business model, the industry, and the client's different types of sales or service contracts. This includes understanding the client's key products and services that affect revenue, including key contractual arrangements. Although the risk of material misstatement in the revenue cycle is dependent upon the specific circumstances of the client, high revenue risk companies are often companies that use multi-element contracts, subscription/usage-based billings, and royalty/licensing models. These business models increase revenue risk because billings and revenue recognition are managed separately.

For complex revenue transactions, auditors should make inquiries to marketing and sales personnel and/or in-house legal counsel of their knowledge of unusual terms or conditions. Auditors will also need to read sales contracts (for terms and responsibilities of the buyer and seller). If the transactions are complex, it is necessary to ensure that the engagement is staffed with appropriate personnel (for instance, more experienced auditors should be assigned to the revenue stream, as should those with industry specific experience). In some cases, auditors may need to refer to outside specialists or other knowledgeable people within their firm who are not involved in the engagement.

Criteria for Revenue Recognition

In order to assess the client's revenue recognition policies, the auditor must be knowledgeable about the revenue requirements of the relevant accounting framework. The new IFRS standard, IFRS 15, *Revenue from Contracts with Customers*, which is a single comprehensive framework for revenue recognition, is effective for reporting periods beginning on or after January 2018. This standard focuses on the core principle

| Figure 12-4 | IFRS 15—The Five-Step Model of Revenue Recognition |

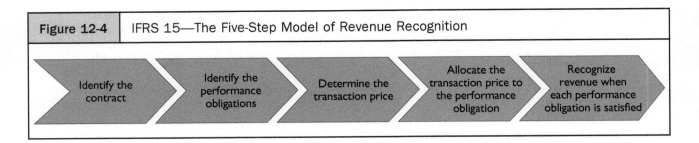

that revenue is recognized when there is a transfer of control. (This is significantly different from the past IFRS standard and ASPE, which is based upon transfer of risks and rewards.) The standard presents a five-step model to determine when to recognize revenue (occurrence), and at what amount (accuracy/valuation).

Figure 12-4 provides a brief overview of the five-step approach.

Identify the Contract and Performance Obligation(s) A contract—which can be written, oral, or implied by the entity's normal business practices—exists if it creates enforceable rights and obligations. A contract must meet the following criteria:

- Collection of the consideration is probable;
- It has a commercial substance;
- Risks to goods or services and payment terms can be identified; and
- It is approved and the parties are committed to their obligations.

Entities that have multi-element contracts must identify each distinct promise to deliver a good or service and account for them separately.

Determine and Allocate Transaction Price The transaction price is the amount of consideration to which the entity expects to be entitled, factoring in the effect of discounts, credits, price concessions, returns, and performance bonuses/penalties. For some entities, if there is uncertainty about future events, this can be quite challenging. In addition, the entity will need to allocate the transaction price to each performance obligation. When there is an observable price from stand-alone sales, this is fairly straightforward; however, if an observable price does not exist, then the entity would attempt to estimate the price customers are willing to pay and forecast expected costs plus gross margins. As you can imagine, this would increase inherent risk since the auditor would face challenges in obtaining evidence and assessing the reasonableness of the estimates.

Recognize Revenue When (or as) the Entity Satisfies Performance Obligation Revenue is recognized either (1) over time, in a manner that depicts the entity's performance, or (2) at a point in time, when control of goods and services is transferred to the customer. The entity recognizes revenue over time when:

1. The customer simultaneously receives and consumes the benefits provided as the entity performs them (e.g., routine or recurring services).
2. The entity's performance creates or enhances an asset that the customer controls (e.g., building an asset on a customer's site).
3. The entity's performance does not create an asset with an alternative use and the entity has an enforcement right of payment for performance completed to date (e.g., building a specialized asset only the customer can use).

If none of those three criteria for recognizing revenue over time is met, the entity recognizes revenue at the point in time when control has passed. Indicators that control has passed include a customer having (1) a present obligation to pay, (2) physical possession, (3) legal title, (4) risks and rewards of ownership, and/or (5) accepted the asset.

In Canada, IFRS is required for publicly accountable entities and optional for private companies. However, those private companies that follow ASPE 3400 may choose to adopt IFRS 15. This change in accounting policy would increase inherent risk. Further, the auditor would need to assess the controls related to accounting change and determine the level of knowledge of the accounting staff. A key issue for those companies who use ASPE is that, when there was no clear guidance, many had referred to US GAAP. In the United States, ASC 606 (which is the equivalent to IFRS 15) will apply to private and public entities. This may mean that some companies will need to reassess their revenue recognition policies to determine if they need to be adjusted.

Assess Inherent Risk for Accounts Receivable

The primary assertions at risk for accounts receivable are existence and valuation. Existence of accounts receivable is directly related to occurrence of sales—if a valid sale did not occur, then a valid receivable does not exist. Similarly, if the company has a high incidence of sales returns (as a result of its return policy or because it has issues with product quality), then it is possible that some receivables are not valid. Valuation is considered high risk mainly because of the judgment involved in evaluating net realizable value (specifically the allowance for doubtful accounts). It would also be high risk if collectibility were questionable. For instance, a client may have adopted liberal credit policies in order to increase sales.

In some circumstances, rights and obligations may also be a concern. Some companies factor their accounts receivable in order to meet cash flow needs. The factor, which is a specialized financial intermediary that purchases accounts receivable at a discount, typically charges interest on the advance plus a commission. The price paid for the receivables is discounted from their face amount to take into account the likelihood of uncollectibility of some of the receivables. If the receivables are sold without recourse, then the factor bears the credit risk; however, if the receivables are sold with recourse, the credit risk remains with the client. As you can imagine, these are important details that financial statement users would want to know.

Some inherent risk factors affecting accounts receivable include the following:

- Long-term receivables are classified as current (i.e., long-term maintenance contracts).
- Receivables are pledged as collateral, assigned to someone else, factored, or sold (restrictions must be disclosed).
- Payment is not required until the purchaser sells to its end customers.
- Collection of the receivable is contingent upon future events (for example, certain royalty arrangements).
- Sales are made to customers with high credit risk.

CONCEPT CHECK

C12-2 Why is occurrence a high-risk assertion for revenue?

C12-3 Why is accounts receivable often an important account to audit?

C12-4 Why is valuation a high-risk assertion for accounts receivable?

IDENTIFY KEY CONTROLS AND ASSESS EFFECTIVENESS OF CONTROLS

LO 4 Understand key controls for the revenue cycle and assess control risk for the revenue cycle.

Figure 12-5 provides an overview of the methodology that an auditor would use to design tests of controls for sales transactions (which is the first type of control test we will discuss). The auditor follows the same process for each class of transactions, balances, and disclosures. The two classes of transactions that we will focus on are sales transactions and cash receipts.

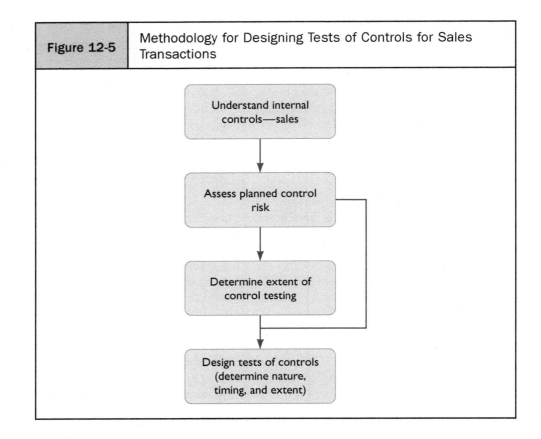

Figure 12-5 Methodology for Designing Tests of Controls for Sales Transactions

Understand internal controls—sales

Assess planned control risk

Determine extent of control testing

Design tests of controls (determine nature, timing, and extent)

Understand Internal Control—Revenue

Recall from Chapter 9, that the auditor needs to understand the entity-level and general controls, those controls that are pervasive and affect multiple transaction cycles, and the control activities for each particular cycle. When assessing control risk for a particular cycle, the auditor will focus on the transaction controls at the account and assertion levels. A typical approach is to conduct interviews, review internal audit working papers, prepare flowcharts (or use the client's flowcharts, if available), prepare internal control questionnaires and control matrixes (see Figures 9-3 and 9-5 for examples related to the revenue cycle), and perform walk-through tests of sales.

Assess Planned Control Risk

The auditor uses the information obtained from understanding of control to assess control risk at the assertion level. In order to do this, the auditor will determine the key controls for revenue and to identify potential weaknesses in internal controls (called "evaluation of design effectiveness"). Knowledge of the following key control activities assists in identifying the key controls and deficiencies:

- *Separation of duties.* Separation of entry of sales data from entry of cash receipts (to prevent theft of cash and then hiding it in the records); separation of credit limit approval from sales (since sales employees may receive bonuses based upon sales and could be motivated to provide higher credit limits to unworthy customers); independent verification of key data, such as credit limits and other master file data, control totals, and journal entries such as bad debt write-offs.
- *Proper authorization.* Authorization by management or independent individuals should be provided and documented for (1) credit prior to a sale, (2) removal of goods for shipment, and (3) sales prices, terms, and charges, to ensure that only authorized goods are shipped at appropriate prices to customers who are good credit risks.

- *Adequate documents and records.* Accurate, complete transactions that cannot be altered should be retained in paper or electronic format that documents the sales-related business events (orders, shipments, sales, returns, credits, adjustments, and master file changes) and can be traced from origin to the general ledger accounts.
- *Sequentially numbered documents.* Automatic sequential numbering that is accounted for and monitored should be present for all transaction types (invoices/credit notes, shipments, adjustments, and master file changes).
- *Mailing of statements.* Whether electronic mailing or through traditional mail, mailing and the entry of sales or cash receipts should be two independent processes (so that customers could report unusual entries in their statements).
- *Independent verification processes.* Whether handled by people or by software, verification can involve checking numerical continuity, matching of orders to shipments to invoices, and production of exception reports for independent follow-up.

After auditors identify key controls and control deficiencies, they assess control risk for the transaction assertions. It is useful to refer to Figure 12-6 to help you understand the relationship between transaction-related and balance-related objectives for the two primary classes of transactions in the revenue cycle (sales and cash receipts), and also between the transaction-related audit objectives and presentation and disclosure audit objectives for sales transactions.

When looking at the relationships, note these key points:

- For sales, the occurrence transaction-related audit objective affects the existence balance-related audit objective, but for cash receipts, the occurrence transaction-related audit objective affects the completeness balance-related audit objective,

Figure 12-6	Relationship Between Transaction-Related, Balance-Related, and Presentation and Disclosure-Related Audit Objectives for the Revenue Cycle												
		Accounts Receivable Balance-Related Audit Objectives					**Accounts Receivable Presentation and Disclosure Audit Objectives**						
Class of Transactions	Transaction-Related Audit Objectives	Existence	Rights and Obligations	Completeness	Valuation	Allocation	Occurrence	Rights and Obligations	Completeness	Accuracy	Valuation	Classification	Understand-ability
Sales	Occurrence	X					X						
	Completeness			X					X				
	Accuracy					X				X			
	Cutoff					X							
	Classification					X						X	
Cash receipts	Occurrence			X									
	Completeness	X											
	Accuracy					X							
	Cutoff												
	Classification												

Assertions where there is no parallel

Allocation is multi-faceted

Existence and completeness complement each other when considering controls in sales and cash use since the recording of a valid cash receipt will help ensure that all accounts receivable are recorded.

- A similar relationship exists for the completeness transaction-related audit objective—an increase in sales increases accounts receivable, and an increase in cash receipts decreases accounts receivable. For example, recording a sale that did not occur violates the occurrence transaction-related audit objective and existence balance-related audit objective (both overstatements). Recording a cash receipt that did not occur violates the occurrence transaction-related audit objective, but it violates the completeness balance-related audit objective for accounts receivable because a receivable that is still outstanding is no longer included in the records if the duplicated or fictitious cash receipt is posted against a valid account receivable.

Two accounts receivable balance-related audit objectives—valuation, and rights and obligations—are not affected by assessed control risk for the sales and cash receipts classes of transactions. Similarly, the three presentation and disclosure audit objectives of rights and obligations, valuation, and understandability are not affected by the assessed control risk for the sales transactions. When the auditor wants to reduce assessed control risk below maximum for these objectives, it is necessary to understand the relevant separate controls in order to develop appropriate control tests (such as those that pertain to the adequacy of the bad debt provision).

Determine Extent of Tests of Controls

The extent of tests of controls is determined by planned reliance on controls. After auditors have identified the key internal controls and weaknesses and assessed risks, but before designing tests of controls, they must decide on the planned reliance on controls. To make this decision, auditors must determine the cost-benefit of testing controls—meaning whether substantive tests will be reduced sufficiently to justify the cost of performing tests of controls. At the same time, auditors will identify assertions where substantive testing is not sufficient and tests of controls are required to reduce risks of material misstatements to a sufficient level. For instance, if the processing of sales transactions were highly automated, it would be necessary to test the relevant controls.

CONCEPT CHECK

C12-5 What are the three types of misstatements that are associated with the occurrence objective for sales?

C12-6 Which balance-related audit objectives are not affected by control risk for classes of transactions? Why?

LO **5** Use professional judgment to develop an audit approach (strategy) for the revenue cycle.

DETERMINE AUDIT APPROACH (STRATEGY) FOR REVENUE CYCLE

Recall from Chapter 10 that the planned reliance on controls determines whether the auditor will use a combined or substantive audit approach (strategy). As we have learned to date, this risk response can vary widely since it depends upon the specific risks and circumstances of the client. In other words, it requires considerable professional judgment.

Let's look at two very different organizations—Vodafone Group Plc, the British telecommunications company, and the City of Toronto, Canada's largest city. As you can see from Table 12-4 (which is based upon the description from the key audit issues in Vodafone's 2014 auditor report and the 2012 City of Toronto Audit Plan), revenue recognition is a significant risk for both organizations; however, the reasons are quite different.

Table 12-4	Comparison of Audit Strategies

Organization	Risk Assessment	Audit Approach
Vodafone Group Plc One of the world's largest telecommunications companies, providing a wide range of services including voice, messaging, data, and fixed broadband	Three areas in relation to revenue recognition and the presumption of fraud risk: • Accounting for new products and tariff plans, including multiple element arrangements • The timing of revenue recognition • The accounting judgments associated with dealer and agency relationships including the presentation of revenue on a net or gross basis and the treatment of discounts, incentives, and commissions	Combined approach (controls testing) and substantive procedures covering: • Audit of the switch to bill process to assess the revenue and cost accruals made at year-end • Testing of the process for capturing and assessing the accounting impact of new tariff plans • Substantive testing of a sample of related transactions • Scrutinizing a sample of dealer and agency contracts and the associated accounting assessments • Testing of the controls around the significant revenue and billing systems by auditors' IT specialists • Assessing that accounting policies are in accordance with IFRS
City of Toronto Canada's largest municipality	Several revenue streams require significant judgment in determining when revenue should be recognized: • Funding transfers from other governments • Revenue from development charges • Taxation from other governments	Combined approach (test revenue controls as well as general controls) and substantive testing. Specific procedures to address key risks: • Using specialists for confirmation of Municipal Land Transfer Tax and Property Assessment Corporation (PAC) for property assessment to test property tax revenue • Assessing competence, objectivity, and results of specialists • Testing controls over management review of deferred revenue and reserve accounts • Performing substantive testing on revenue streams with most pervasive risks • Assessing that accounting policies are in accordance with Canadian GAAP for public sector

Sources: 2014 Audit Report on the Consolidated and Parent Financial Statements for Vodafone Group Plc. PWC, City of Toronto Audit Plan for the Year Ending December 31, 2012.

For Vodafone, the three significant risks with regards to revenue were related to multiple element contracts, the timing of revenue, and significant judgments (the relevant assertions are transaction assertions of occurrence and cutoff, as well as the presentation and disclosure assertion of classification in relation to revenue as gross versus net).

The auditors determined that a combined approach was the most appropriate risk response. Further, given the nature of the control system, an IT specialist was involved in control testing. Some control testing that was highlighted above was related to an area where the client had made a change in its billing process and the processes used to capture and assess the accounting impact of tariff plans. Given the significant risk, substantive testing included scrutinizing a sample of dealer and agency contracts.

For the City of Toronto, the auditors used a combined approach as well. They also highlighted the use of specialists and confirmation of revenue. Note they also noted that they would assess the competence, objectivity, and results of the specialists' work. The property tax revenue test is a substantive analytical procedure—the auditor uses the property assessment provided by a third party (a highly reliable source of data) and then applies the applicable tax rate to calculate the property tax revenue. Because of the predictable relationship between the tax rate and the assessment base, this is a very effective substantive analytical procedure for the occurrence of revenue. The auditors also highlighted testing management review controls for deferred revenue and reserve accounts (these are often a significant risk area in municipal audits).

In both cases, auditors also emphasized that they would ensure that accounting policies were in accordance with the relevant accounting framework (IFRS for Vodafone and Canadian GAAP for the public sector for the City of Toronto). As we have discussed in our risk assessment of revenue, auditors must be knowledgeable of the applicable accounting framework.

We will now take a closer look at how the auditor performs the risk response, including designing and performing tests of controls, substantive analytical procedures, and substantive tests of details.

LO **6** Design and perform tests of control for the revenue cycle.

Design and Perform Tests of Controls for the Revenue Cycle

For each key control that the auditor plans to reduce control risk (in other words, rely upon controls), the auditor must design one or more tests of controls to verify its effectiveness. For example, if the internal control is having the sales system identify orders that cause customers to go over their credit limit and having the orders printed for subsequent approval (occurrence), the test of control would include verifying that the application system is functioning as designed and inspecting the credit exception report for approval.

We start with taking a closer look at designing tests of controls for sales transactions and then discuss another class of transactions—cash receipts. We then discuss how the auditor designs control tests for related accounts as well as other assertions for which control tests for sales transactions or cash receipts would not provide evidence.

Designing Tests of Controls for Sales Transactions Table 12-5 provides an overview of some key sales transaction controls that might be used to mitigate the risk due

Table 12-5	Examples of Key Controls and Tests for Revenue		
Transaction-Related Audit Objective	**Examples of Key Internal Controls**	**How the Control Could Be Tested**	**Implications If Control Is Not Working**
Recorded sales are for shipments actually made to nonfictitious customers (occurrence).	• Shipping records and sales invoices cannot be produced if the customer number is invalid.	• Use test data and observe rejection of invalid customer numbers when entered by client staff into online system.	Revenue is recorded when it has not occurred (either not delivered or in subsequent period), overstating both revenue and accounts receivable.
	• Recording of sales is supported by authorized shipping documents and approved customer purchase orders.	• Inspect copies of sales invoices for supporting bills of lading and customers' purchase orders.	Extend accounts receivable confirmation work.
	• Approval is required to commence selling goods to a new customer, to set up a new customer in the master files, or to change semipermanent billing information.	• Inspect master file change forms for authorization, and compare to master file change reports.	Orders were shipped to a bad credit risk, resulting in uncollectible accounts that are not included in the bad debt allowance.
	• Credit is approved before shipment takes place.	• Examine customer purchase order for credit approval. • Use test data to verify the programmed control that customers exceeding their credit limits will have their orders rejected.	Use GAS to reperform aging and analyze aging and expand confirmation work; conduct audit of bad debt allowance.
		• Examine credit limit exception report for approval.	

Transaction-Related Audit Objective	Examples of Key Internal Controls	How the Control Could Be Tested	Implications If Control Is Not Working
	• Computer automatically generates sequential invoice numbers.	• Use generalized audit software to identify gaps in invoice numbers used.	Gaps in invoice numbers could mean that not all invoices are recorded (completeness). Expand substantive tests of transactions.
	• Monthly statements are sent to customers; complaints receive independent follow-up (also satisfies accuracy).	• Observe whether statements are mailed, and inspect customer correspondence files.	Revenue may be over- or understated. There is possible understatement of allowance for doubtful accounts or returns. Expand accounts receivable confirmations and returns testing (if appropriate).
All existing sales transactions are recorded (completeness).	• Computer checks for gaps in shipping document numbers (i.e., orders shipped but not billed) and prints a report of missing numbers for independent follow-up.	• Account for integrity of numerical sequence of shipping documents using block test. • Inspect report of missing shipping document numbers for evidence of independent follow-up.	Shipments are made that are not billed (or were billed in the subsequent period), understating both revenue and accounts receivable. Conduct tests to ensure that the shipping detail and invoice detail data files are complete.
Recorded sales are for the amount of goods shipped and are correctly billed and recorded (accuracy).	• Invoices are prepared using authorized prices, terms, freight, and discounts established in master files.	• Test access controls. • Take a sample of invoices and trace back to authorized list. • Test for potential override of changes to price list.	Weak controls over price lists can allow misappropriation of assets and potential over/understatement of revenue due to errors or potential fictitious customers. Use GAS to match invoice price to authorized prices, terms, etc. (expand the original test). Confirm sales contract details with customers. Expand accounts receivable confirmation work.
Sales are recorded on the correct dates (cutoff).	• Invoices are prepared using a date equal to the shipping date (or specify the shipping date on the invoice). • System checks reasonableness of date entered. • Management reviews sales and cost of sales analytical reports for reasonableness.	• Compare dates of recorded sales transactions with dates on shipping records. • Inspect shipping records for unbilled shipments and for unrecorded sales. • Verify management walkthrough of analytical reports using inquiry or inspect for evidence of follow-up.	Significant differences in dates indicate a potential cutoff problem (could impact completeness or occurrence of revenue). Perform additional substantive cutoff testing at the year-end date.
Sales transactions are classified to the correct account (classification).	• Adequate chart of accounts is used. • Invoices can be posted only to valid customer accounts. • Posting is done automatically to sales account based upon batch totals or individual transactions. • Management reviews exception reports of unusual customer data.	• Inspect chart of accounts for adequacy. • Inspect customer master file to identify general ledger accounts used for posting. • Conduct manual walk-through of transactions from source to general ledger posting. • Inspect summary reports verifying posting process. • Inquire whether any out-of-balance conditions occurred during the year. • Inspect exception reports for evidence of review.	Expand substantive tests of revenue and accounts receivable. Read contracts to determine all items represent bona fide contracts and not consignment sales, to verify agent/principal, and/or to assess criteria used to allocate components.

to fraud or error related to sales transactions. It also provides some examples of the controls that might be tested—you will note that the tests of controls involve a wide variety of tests—such as selecting samples of invoices, reviewing monitoring controls, observing controls, and using generalized audit software (GAS) and test data. The last column (implications if the control is not working) explains the potential error and/or fraud and the impact on the audit—specifically for the substantive testing.

Tests of controls for separation of duties are usually restricted to the auditor's observations of activities and discussions with personnel. For example, it is possible to observe whether the billing clerk has access to cash when opening incoming mail or depositing cash. It is usually also necessary to ask personnel what their responsibilities are and if there are any circumstances where their responsibilities are different from the normal policy. Allocation of password functionality should also be reviewed to ensure that individuals have not been assigned functions that are incompatible.

Several of the tests of controls in Table 12-5 can be performed using test data. For example, one of the key internal controls to prevent fraudulent or fictitious transactions is the inclusion of procedures to ensure that only approved information was entered into the customer master files. If a nonexistent customer number were entered into the computer, it would be rejected. The auditor can test this control by asking client staff to enter nonexistent customer numbers into the computer after making sure that the computer control is in operation and then observing the rejection of the entry. Other tests use GAS. For example, to test the continuity of sales invoices (which tests the completeness and occurrence assertions), the auditor may conduct a gap test by scanning the entire transaction history file and identifying any gaps in the numeric sequence (and also looking for duplicates).

Designing Tests of Controls for Cash Receipts As we have already discussed, the two main classes of transactions in the revenue cycle are sales and cash receipts. In contrast to sales, the most at-risk assertion for cash receipts is completeness—has all cash been recorded in the accounts and not been stolen?

The same methodology used for designing tests of controls over sales transactions is used for designing tests of controls over cash receipts (per Figure 12-5). Key internal controls and common tests of controls to satisfy each of the internal control objectives for cash receipts are listed in Table 12-6. You will note that the first control tests are more general—these would be supplemented with the substantive tests of transactions (which serve as a dual test). An essential part of the auditor's responsibility in auditing cash receipts is identifying control weaknesses that increase the likelihood of fraud since a key concern in this area is theft of cash.

Designing Other Tests of Controls for the Revenue Cycle As highlighted in our discussion of Figure 12-4, tests of controls related to sales transactions and cash receipts will not provide evidence on the effectiveness of controls related to the two balance-related assertions (rights and obligations, and valuation) or the presentation and disclosure assertions. The key controls for these assertions will vary according to the client's processes and business model; however, the methodology for designing tests of controls is the same as for sales transactions and cash receipts.

Controls Related to Accuracy/Valuation and Rights and Obligations Our earlier discussion of key controls for accuracy/valuation of sales/accounts receivable, such as authorized price lists, is typical for an organization that does not have unusual or complex sales terms. Further, rights and obligations or ownership of revenue is not an issue in organizations that have straightforward sales transactions (such as retail stores). However, for those types of organizations that have more complex sales transactions, the auditor would need to evaluate relevant controls to ensure both accuracy and rights and obligations. For instance, if the company's revenue recognition

Table 12-6	Summary of Transaction-Related Audit Objectives, Key Controls, and Tests of Controls for Cash Receipts			

Transaction-Related Audit Objective	Key Internal Control	General Tests of Controls	Substantive Tests of Transactions (Dual Test)
Recorded cash receipts are for funds actually received by the company (occurrence).	Separation of duties between handling cash and record-keeping or data entry.	Observe separation of duties.	Inspect the cash receipts journal, general ledger, and accounts receivable master file or trial balance for large and unusual amounts.*
	Independent reconciliation or review of bank accounts.	Observe independent reconciliation of bank account.	Trace from cash receipts listing to duplicate deposit slip and bank statements.
All cash received is recorded in the cash receipts journal (completeness).	Separation of duties between handling cash and record-keeping.	Discussion with personnel and observation.	Trace from remittances or prelisting to duplicate bank deposit slip and cash receipts journal.
	Use of remittance advices or a prelisting of cash.	Discussion with personnel and observation.	Inspect reconciliation reports of credit card or electronic funds transfer receipts.
	Immediate endorsement of incoming cheques.	Observe immediate endorsement of incoming cheques.	
	Internal verification of the recording of cash receipts.	Inspect indication of independent internal verification.	
	Regular monthly statements to customers.	Observe whether monthly statements are sent to customers.	
	Authorized use of POS to simultaneously record the sale, cash received, and reduce inventory.	Observe whether use of POS is controlled, such as by means of unique access codes and passwords.	
Cash receipts are deposited and properly recorded at the amount received (accuracy).	Approval of cash discounts.	Inspect remittance advices for proper approval.	Inspect remittance advices and sales invoices to determine whether discounts allowed are consistent with company policy.
	Regular reconciliation of bank accounts.	Inspect monthly bank reconciliations.	
	Comparison of batch totals with duplicate deposit slips and computer summary reports.	Inspect file of batch totals for initials of data control clerk; compare totals with summary reports.	
	Regular monthly statements to customers.	Observe whether statements are mailed.	Foot cash receipts journals, and trace postings to general ledger and accounts receivable master file.
	Comparison of customer master file or aged accounts receivable trial balance totals with general ledger balance.	Inspect documentation verifying that comparison was completed.	
Cash receipts are recorded on correct dates (cutoff).	Procedure requiring recording of cash receipts on a daily basis.	Observe unrecorded cash at any point in time.	Compare dates of deposits with dates in the cash receipts journal.
Cash receipts are properly classified (classification).	Use of adequate chart of accounts or automatic posting to specified accounts.	Review chart of accounts and computer-assigned posting accounts.	Examine documents supporting cash receipts for proper classification.

*This analytical procedure can also apply to other objectives, including completeness, accuracy, and cutoff.

depends upon the terms of the contract, the auditor would assess controls that ensure the capture and analysis of the terms and conditions of contracts, contract changes, and payment terms that affect the timing and amount of revenue to be recognized. Similarly, if the entity has multi-element contracts, the auditor would review controls that ensure timely identification of all elements of the multiple-element arrangement. Common control deficiencies in relation to complex revenue transactions are often related to entity-level and general controls, such as inadequate accounting expertise, supervision, and IT systems.[3] These types of control deficiencies increase the possibility of material misstatements.

In many companies, the sales returns and allowances are immaterial; however, if sales returns and allowances are significant, the auditor will assess control risk for that class of transactions. Control tests designed to test the occurrence assertion can uncover theft of cash from the collection of accounts receivable that was covered up by a fictitious sales return or allowance. However, with regard to financial reporting risk, the completeness assertion is the most relevant assertion since the major risk is that material returns could occur after year-end and the client has not taken this into account. Similarly, the organization may offer sales allowances (also called volume rebates) that customers receive if they achieve a particular sales volume. As highlighted in Auditing in Action 12-4, unrecorded or understated sales returns and allowances can be material and can be used by a company's management to overstate net income.

The realizable value objective (the valuation assertion) for accounts receivable often has high inherent risk because it is an estimate that requires considerable

AUDITING IN ACTION 12-4
Boom and Bust at CV Technologies

In 2006, business for CV Technologies, maker of the popular cold and flu remedy Cold-fX, was booming and the future looked bright. It was one of the fastest-growing small stock companies on the Toronto Stock Exchange, Don Cherry was its spokesperson, and former NHL star Mark Messier had signed on as ambassador for the Edmonton-based firm's much anticipated US launch.

However, the US launch was a bust. American retailers returned millions of dollars' worth of unsold inventory and the company had to restate the financial results for the year ended December 2006 and its first quarter in 2007. Apparently the cause of the restatement was that its revenue recognition policy was not appropriate for the US sales. CV's policy was to recognize revenue upon delivery to retailers based upon the fact that the historical rate of return for its Canadian customers was low. However, before the 2006 financial statements were issued on December 11, 2006, CV's management team was aware that the American sales of Cold-fX were slow, that an order from a US retailer had been cancelled, and that a return by a US retailer of at least $10 million of product (which had been shipped by CV after the September 30 fiscal year-end) was imminent. None of this information was reflected in the year-end financial statements.

As a result of the restatements, previously reported profits turned into losses and three provincial securities regulators issued a cease trading order. The Alberta Securities Commission fined the company $740 000 in penalties and costs. The former CEO paid $125 000 and was barred from being a public company officer for five years. The former CFO was fined $80 000 and three audit committee members were fined as well.

Subsequent to the restatement, CV hired a new auditor and the audit committee was restructured to include a chartered accountant who was a former partner with a Big Four firm. After a three-month trading ban, the shares traded at 40 percent of their previous value and class action suits were filed. In 2009, the company, now renamed Afexa Life Sciences, paid a settlement of $7.1 million.

Sources: David Baines, "Achoo! CV Technologies catches the financial flu," *Canadian Business*, July 11, 2007. Janet McFarland, "Cold-fX maker brings some investor relief," *Globe and Mail*, September 17, 2009. Charles Cullinan and Gail Wright, "CVTechnologies/Cold-fX," *Journal of Accounting Education*, vol. 30, 2012, pp. 194–206. "Cold fX fined by Alberta Securities," *CBC News*, August 7, 2009, accessed August 16, 2017, at **http://www.cbc.ca/news/canada/edmonton/cold-fx-maker-fined-by-alberta-securities-commission-1.849415**.

---

[3] Dana Hermanson, Daniel Ivan, and Susan Iva, "SOX Section 404 Material Weaknesses Related to Revenue Recognition," *CPA Journal*, October 2008, pp. 40–45.

judgment. Ideally, clients establish several controls to reduce the likelihood of uncollectible accounts, such as:

- Credit approval by an appropriate person;
- Preparation of a periodic aged accounts receivable trial balance for review and follow up by the appropriate management personnel; and
- A policy of writing off uncollectible amounts when they are no longer likely to be collected.

With regard to accounts being written off, the auditor's primary concern is that, if controls are weak, then write-offs can be used to conceal the theft of cash. The major control for preventing this type of misstatement is proper authorization of the write-off of uncollectible accounts by a designated level of management only after a thorough investigation of the reason the customer has not paid. A typical control test is the examination of approvals by the appropriate person. For a sample of accounts charged off, the auditor will also verify the uncollectability of the accounts through the following substantive tests:

- Examine correspondence in the client's files to assess reasonableness of write-off.
- Obtain credit reports—such as from Dun & Bradstreet Canada Limited (**www. dnb.ca**) or Equifax (**http://www.consumer.equifax.ca/home/en_ca**) to verify collectability.

CONCEPT CHECK

C12-7   What is the major risk for sales returns?

C12-8   Why is completeness a risk for cash receipts?

C12-9   How are uncollectible accounts related to fraud risks?

C12-10   When deciding upon which controls to test, the auditor considers cost-effectiveness. Which types of controls are likely the least costly to test? Justify your response.

Evaluate Results of Tests of Controls

The results of the tests of controls have a significant effect on the remainder of the audit, especially on the tests of details of balances part of substantive procedures. The parts of the audit most affected by the tests of controls for the revenue cycle are the balances in accounts receivable, cash, bad-debt expense, and allowance for doubtful accounts. Since accounts receivable and cash are significant accounts, the auditor will perform some substantive testing on these balances regardless of the effectiveness of internal controls. However, it is important to note that if the results of the control tests are unsatisfactory, as discussed in Chapter 10, it is necessary to do additional substantive testing for sales, sales returns and allowances, charge-off of uncollectible accounts, and processing of cash receipts.

At the completion of the tests of controls, it is essential to analyze each control test exception to determine its cause and the implication of the exception on assessed control risk, which may affect the supported detection risk and thereby the substantive procedures. Table 12-5 provides examples of the various substantive tests that could be performed.

DESIGN AND PERFORM SUBSTANTIVE ANALYTICAL PROCEDURES

LO 7 Design and perform substantive analytical procedures for the accounts in the revenue cycle.

Earlier in the chapter, we discussed the type of preliminary analytical procedures that the auditor would perform to aid in identifying the risk of material misstatement. In contrast to preliminary analytical procedures, substantive analytical procedures are substantive tests and will likely use disaggregated data, such as sales by month and product based on data for the full year under audit.

If control risk is low, the auditor can rely upon substantive analytical procedures and perform fewer substantive tests of details. Normally, the auditor will perform substantive analytical procedures prior to substantive tests of details. This is to account for the possibility that the substantive analytical procedures indicate potential misstatements. In order for substantive analytical procedures to provide the necessary assurance, the auditor should take into account (1) the nature of the assertion, (2) the plausibility and predictability of the relationship, (3) the availability of reliable data to develop expectations, (4) the precision of the expectation, and (5) the threshold for investigation.

Nature of Assertion

Regarding the assertions, substantive analytical procedures are not effective for all assertions. For example, they tend to be somewhat more effective than tests of details for completeness of revenue and the reasonableness of the allowance for doubtful accounts. They also tend not to be as effective for testing occurrence/existence (although this depends upon the client's revenue model, as illustrated in the City of Toronto Audit Strategy, where the auditor was able to design an effective substantive analytical procedure [see Table 12-4]); nor are substantive analytical procedures always effective for rights and obligations. That is not to say that these procedures are not often performed to test existence/occurrence, but when they are performed, other substantive tests of details will supplement this evidence.

Plausibility and Predictability

The plausibility and predictability of relationships is crucial in developing a properly designed substantive analytical procedure. For example, relationships are less predictable in less stable environments or when amounts are determined from complex processes, subjective judgments, or transactions subject to management discretion. In comparison, relationships are more predictable if they are based upon established relationships such as cash flow based on contract terms (assuming nonpayment risk is low) or verifiable rate–volume determination (for example, a hotel with a fixed number of rooms with a certain room rate).

Availability of Reliable Data

A key concern in assessing the reliability is the source of the data and the conditions upon which it was gathered. In the case of client data, the auditor should either test the design or operating effectiveness of the related controls or perform other procedures to test completeness and accuracy of the data. For example, the client may have performed analysis on an Excel spreadsheet that the auditor is using to develop his or her expectation. In order to assess the reliability of the spreadsheet, the auditor would need to check the accuracy of the formulas and ensure that all the necessary data is included.

Precision of Expectation

Analytical procedures used for planning—those that involve comparisons, ratios, and trend analysis—do not have the precision necessary for the auditor to rely on them alone as a substantive test. A key to developing more precise expectations is to disaggregate the data in order to effectively evaluate the relationship between variables being examined. You will note that, in contrast to the analytical procedures provided in Table 12-3, many of the examples provided in Table 12-7 represent further disaggregation based upon customer or product line. Other potential

Table 12-7	Examples of Substantive Analytical Procedures for Revenue

Substantive Analytical Procedure	Possible Misstatement
Compare gross margin percentage with that of previous years (by product line).	Overstatement or understatement of sales and accounts receivable (fictitious revenue or errors in sales pricing).
Compare sales by month (by product line) over time.	Overstatement or understatement of sales and accounts receivable (cutoff errors).
Compare inventory in a distribution channel with amounts for prior periods.	Indicator of channel stuffing.
Compare discounts to previous periods.	Could indicate unusual sales arrangements.
Examine relationship between sales and cost of sales (for example, using regression analysis).	Understatement or overstatement of sales and accounts receivable (errors in sales or cost pricing).
Compare sales credits, returns, and allowances as a percentage of gross sales with previous years' (by product line).	Understatement or overstatement of sales returns and allowances, and accounts receivable (timing errors).
Compare individual customer balances over a stated amount with that of previous years.	Misstatements in accounts receivable and related income statement accounts (inadequate bad debt allowance or overstated sales).

considerations are by region, store, or whatever is relevant for the particular client. This level of disaggregation is necessary in order for the auditor to further investigate potential misstatements.

Threshold for Investigation

CONCEPT CHECK

C12-11 A company's sales have declined, while the bad-debt expense and accounts receivable have increased. What do these changes tell you?

When substantive analytical procedures uncover unusual fluctuations, the auditor should make additional inquires of management. Management's responses should be critically evaluated to determine whether they adequately explain the unusual fluctuation and whether they are supported by corroborating evidence. As we have discussed before, the threshold for investigation should be based upon performance materiality. Depending upon the risk, auditors may set tolerable misstatement below performance materiality.

Because revenue is considered to be a significant risk, substantive analytical procedures alone are not sufficient; therefore, substantive tests of details are always required in the revenue cycle. We discuss them next.

SUBSTANTIVE TESTS OF DETAILS FOR REVENUE

LO 8 Design and perform substantive tests of details for revenue accounts and assertions.

Figure 12-7 provides an overview of the types of substantive tests of details for revenue that would be performed for an automotive dealership. You will note that the tests primarily involve inspecting client documentation. The tests tend to focus on the occurrence and valuation assertions; however, all assertions are tested.

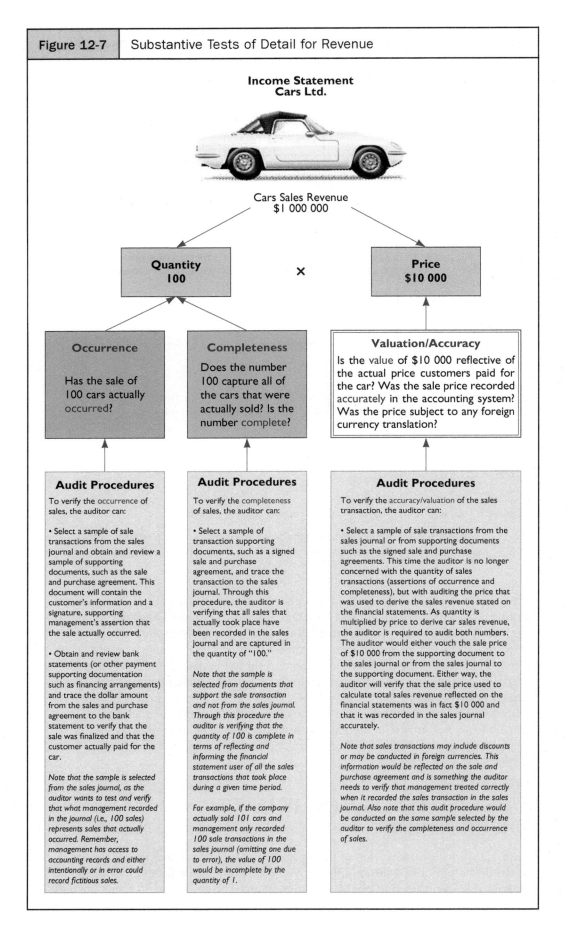

Figure 12-7 | Substantive Tests of Detail for Revenue

Income Statement
Cars Ltd.

Cars Sales Revenue
$1 000 000

Quantity
100

×

Price
$10 000

Occurrence

Has the sale of 100 cars actually occurred?

Completeness

Does the number 100 capture all of the cars that were actually sold? Is the number complete?

Valuation/Accuracy

Is the value of $10 000 reflective of the actual price customers paid for the car? Was the sale price recorded accurately in the accounting system? Was the price subject to any foreign currency translation?

Audit Procedures

To verify the occurrence of sales, the auditor can:

• Select a sample of sale transactions from the sales journal and obtain and review a sample of supporting documents, such as the sale and purchase agreement. This document will contain the customer's information and a signature, supporting management's assertion that the sale actually occurred.

• Obtain and review bank statements (or other payment supporting documentation such as financing arrangements) and trace the dollar amount from the sales and purchase agreement to the bank statement to verify that the sale was finalized and that the customer actually paid for the car.

Note that the sample is selected from the sales journal, as the auditor wants to test and verify that what management recorded in the journal (i.e., 100 sales) represents sales that actually occurred. Remember, management has access to accounting records and either intentionally or in error could record fictitious sales.

Audit Procedures

To verify the completeness of sales, the auditor can:

• Select a sample of transaction supporting documents, such as a signed sale and purchase agreement, and trace the transaction to the sales journal. Through this procedure, the auditor is verifying that all sales that actually took place have been recorded in the sales journal and are captured in the quantity of "100."

Note that the sample is selected from documents that support the sale transaction and not from the sales journal. Through this procedure the auditor is verifying that the quantity of 100 is complete in terms of reflecting and informing the financial statement user of all the sales transactions that took place during a given time period.

For example, if the company actually sold 101 cars and management only recorded 100 sale transactions in the sales journal (omitting one due to error), the value of 100 would be incomplete by the quantity of 1.

Audit Procedures

To verify the accuracy/valuation of the sales transaction, the auditor can:

• Select a sample of sale transactions from the sales journal or from supporting documents such as the signed sale and purchase agreements. This time the auditor is no longer concerned with the quantity of sales transactions (assertions of occurrence and completeness), but with auditing the price that was used to derive the sales revenue stated on the financial statements. As quantity is multiplied by price to derive car sales revenue, the auditor is required to audit both numbers. The auditor would either vouch the sale price of $10 000 from the supporting document to the sales journal or from the sales journal to the supporting document. Either way, the auditor will verify that the sale price used to calculate total sales revenue reflected on the financial statements was in fact $10 000 and that it was recorded in the sales journal accurately.

Note that sales transactions may include discounts or may be conducted in foreign currencies. This information would be reflected on the sale and purchase agreement and is something the auditor needs to verify that management treated correctly when it recorded the sales transaction in the sales journal. Also note that this audit procedure would be conducted on the same sample selected by the auditor to verify the completeness and occurrence of sales.

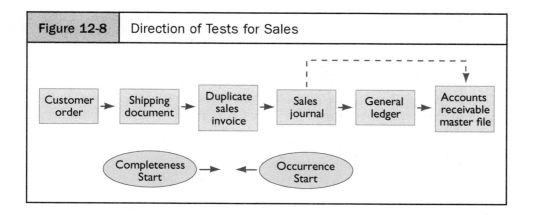

Figure 12-8	Direction of Tests for Sales

Direction of Tests for Completeness and Occurrence

When designing audit procedures for the occurrence and completeness assertions, the starting point for the direction of the tests is essential. Figure 12-8 shows the direction of tests. When tracing from source shipping documents to the journals, the purpose of the test is for *omitted transactions* (completeness). In contrast, when vouching from the journals back to supporting documents, the purpose is to test for *nonexistent transactions* (occurrence). When testing for the other four transaction-related audit objectives, the direction of tests is usually not relevant. For example, the accuracy of sales transactions can be tested by tracing from a duplicate sales invoice to a shipping document, or vice versa.

Revenue: Occurrence Assertion

The tests explained in Figure 12-7 also provide evidence of the existence and valuation of accounts receivable. When designing tests for occurrence, the auditor is concerned about the following potential misstatements:

- Sales being included in journals for which no shipment was made;
- Sales recorded more than once (duplicates); and
- Shipments made to nonexistent customers and recorded as sales (fictitious sales).

The tests rely upon documentation; however, in the case of a paperless system, the auditor would require the assistance of an IT specialist and the use of audit software to perform the substantive tests.

When testing occurrence from complex contractual arrangements, the auditor will need to perform audit procedures to evaluate whether the revenue was recognized appropriately. For instance, in the case of multiple deliverables, the auditor would need to test the value assigned to the separate units. Further, the auditor will often need to test the reasonableness of accounting estimates. CAS 540 requires the **CAS** auditor to obtain an understanding of how management developed the estimate and should use a combination of the following approaches:

- Review and test the process used by management to develop the estimate;
- Develop an independent expectation of the estimate to corroborate the reasonableness of management's estimate; and
- Review subsequent events or transactions to corroborate the reasonableness of the estimate.

Revenue: Completeness Assertion

In many audits, the auditor is not concerned with the completeness assertion on the grounds that overstatement of revenue is a higher risk than understatement. To be able to conduct the tests described in Figure 12-7 the auditor must be confident that all shipping documents are included in the sample population. This can be done by accounting for the numerical sequence of the documents (called a block test).

Revenue: Accuracy Assertion

The accurate recording of sales transactions concerns shipping the correct amount of goods ordered, using the correct price when billing for the amount of goods shipped, and accurately recording the amount billed in the accounting records. The proper inclusion of all sales transactions in the customer master file is essential because the accuracy of these records affects the client's ability to collect outstanding receivables. Similarly, the sales transactions must be correctly totalled and posted to the general ledger if the financial statements are correct.

Where reliance is placed on computer-based systems to perform mathematical calculations, the auditor may use test data to ensure that these calculations are properly performed or use generalized audit software to reperform the calculations.

Revenue: Cutoff Assertion

As highlighted in our discussion of fraud, occurrence and cutoff are the two relevant assertions for revenue. Performing cutoff tests with sales transactions before and after year-end provides assurance of both the completeness and occurrence of sales transactions. Many computer systems require that the shipping date match the invoice date or that the invoice date be within a specified time of the current date, which will reduce the potential for cutoff errors. When the client's internal controls are adequate, the cutoff can usually be verified by obtaining the shipping document number for the last shipment made at the end of the period and comparing this number with current and subsequent period recorded sales, to verify that shipments were invoiced in the correct accounting period.

For many companies, sales returns and allowances are recorded in the accounting period in which they occur, under the assumption of approximately equal, offsetting errors at the beginning and end of each accounting period. This is acceptable as long as the amounts are not significant. Otherwise it is necessary to examine supporting documentation for a sample of sales returns and allowances recorded during several weeks subsequent to the closing date to determine the date of the original sale. If the amounts recorded in the subsequent period are significantly different from unrecorded returns and allowances at the beginning of the period under audit, an adjustment must be considered. If internal controls for recording sales returns and allowances are evaluated as ineffective, a larger sample is needed to verify cutoff.

Auditors may also need to review contracts for terms that may indicate that the recording of the sale should be postponed (for instance, extended periods of right of return), there are additional performance obligations, or collection is based upon a future event. Auditing in Action 12-5 provides an example of an accelerated revenue recognition scheme used at Tesco, a large UK supermarket chain.

Revenue: Classification Assertion

Charging the correct general ledger account is less of a problem in sales than in some other transaction cycles, but it is still important to check. However, as highlighted in the Vodofone example (see Table 12-4) for some sales transactions, it is not always clear whether the company is the seller with a primary obligation to the customer or the company is a seller acting as an agent. The auditor would need to understand the contractual terms of these sales transactions in order to evaluate the presentation of revenue—should it be recorded as the gross amount billed to the customer, or the net amount retained (i.e., the amount billed to a customer less the amount paid to a supplier)? The issue often arises with companies that sell goods or services over the

Determining how much revenue to book and when can be a matter of fine judgment. One recent revenue recognition debacle that highlights this is the announcement made by Tesco, the UK supermarket giant, that it had "accelerated" recognition of £250 million (approximately $465 million Cdn) of commercial income and "delayed accrual of related costs." Commercial income is the payments suppliers make to the supermarkets that meet certain sales targets for their products, run promotions, or place goods in eye-catching places.

In Tesco's May 2014 annual report, the external auditors, PwC, stated in the audit report that commercial income was at "risk of manipulation"; however, the audit committee concluded that Tesco "operates an appropriate control environment which minimizes risks in this area." It appears that the audit committee's conclusion was incorrect. A whistleblower reported the error, which prompted Tesco to launch an investigation. As a result, several senior executives lost their jobs, the chair of the audit committee was replaced, and PwC, who had been Tesco's auditors for 32 years, were replaced.

When Tesco released its second quarter results, it announced the misstatement, which it described as a "timing issue" isolated to the first six months of the financial year (these financial statements would have been unaudited). It was later revealed that the misreporting had been taking place for more than three years, as buyers booked profits into the wrong accounting period.

As a result of the misstatement, several regulatory bodies launched investigations of both Tesco and PwC. On June 2107, the Financial Reporting Council, the UK's audit regulator, closed its investigation of PwC and said there was not "a realistic prospect" of finding PwC guilty of professional misconduct. However, the United Kingdom's Serious Fraud Office investigation resulted in the retailer paying a £129 million fine and funding an £85 million compensation scheme for shareholders. Tesco continues to fight two lawsuits from investors who say they lost hundreds of millions of pounds after relying on Tesco's financial statements.

Sources: "Tesco now faces two City watchdog probes into £250m accounts scandal on top of internal review and threatened grilling by MPs," *Daily Mail*, September 30, 2014. Ian Walker and Costa Paris, "Tesco faces fresh accounting investigation," *Wall Street Journal*, December 22, 2014. Hester Plumridge, "Commercial income: As usual, in Tesco accounting error, there's wiggle room," *Wall Street Journal,* September 22, 2014. Mark Vendevelde, "PwC escapes censure over Tesco accounting scandal," *Financial Times*, June 5, 2017.

internet, but it can also be found in many other business models. For instance, when Amazon and eBay sell merchandise on behalf of others, they are acting as agents. As a result, they only book the fees that they receive as revenue, not the gross amount received from the customer with the amount paid to the merchandiser as an expense. Although both approaches end up with the same net income, given that revenue is an important metric for many financial statement users, reporting the amount as gross can be misleading (and therefore represents a material misstatement—remember that materiality is not simply a quantitative evaluation).

Also, for those companies using more than one sales classification, such as companies issuing segmented earnings statements, proper classification is essential. It is common to test sales for proper classification as part of testing for accuracy. The auditor examines supporting documents to determine the proper classification of a given transaction and compares this with the actual account in which it is recorded.

SUBSTANTIVE TESTS FOR ACCOUNTS RECEIVABLE

LO 9 Design and perform substantive tests of details for accounts receivable assertions.

Figure 12-9 provides an overview of some of the key substantive tests for accounts receivable.

You will note that a key source of information is the **aged accounts receivable trial balance** (a listing of the balances in the accounts receivable customer master file at the balance sheet). An example of the aged trial balance is shown in Figure 12-10.

The aged trial balance is used to:

- Agree the accuracy of the total and agreement between subledger and general ledger, including allocation to correct accounts.
- Select samples for confirmation.

Aged accounts receivable trial balance—a listing of the balances in the accounts receivable master file at a particular date (such as the balance sheet date), broken down according to the amount of time elapsed between the date of sale and the effective date of the report.

Figure 12-9 | Substantive Tests of Details for Accounts Receivable

Balance Sheet
Company XYZ, Inc.

Accounts Receivable $1 000 000

Accounts Receivable Subledger

Customer #1	$ 100 000
Customer #2	250 000
Customer #3	150 000
Customer #4	500 000
A/R balance =	$1 000 000

Existence

The auditor needs to verify that these customers and the balance receivable from each customer actually exist.

The key risk associated with assets is that they are overstated (they don't exist).

Valuation

The auditor needs to verify that the receivable of $1 000 000 is collectible. What if some customers can't or won't pay?

Keep in mind that although a receivable exists, this does not guarantee that the company can collect the full amount. The auditor needs to gain comfort regarding the amount that Company XYZ can reasonably expect to collect.

Audit Procedures

To verify the **existence** of accounts receivable, the auditor can:

• Select a sample of accounts receivable balances from the accounts receivable subledger and mail an accounts receivable balance confirmation to each selected customer.

• Vouch the balance from the confirmation (when it is returned) with the balance according to the accounts receivable subledger.

• Alternatively, review the bank statements subsequent to year-end for proof of payment received from Company XYZ's customers. For example, if Company XYZ received a payment of $250 000 from Customer #2 subsequent to year-end, this payment would be reflected on Company XYZ's bank statement and would give comfort to the auditor that the outstanding A/R balance at year-end of $250 000 existed.

The alternative procedure described above can be used by the auditor in situations where a reply to the A/R confirmation was not received.

Note that under certain circumstances (based on risk assessment) the auditor may also be concerned with the assertion of rights and obligations. For example, Company XYZ could have "factored" (sold) its account receivable. The auditor would verify company's rights to the A/R balance through management inquiry and review of documents such as board of directors' meeting minutes. Keep in mind that just because the A/R balance exists and it's valued correctly, Company XYZ might have factored its A/R and it no longer has the rights to this asset.

Audit Procedures

To verify the **valuation** of accounts receivable the auditor can:

• Obtain an accounts receivable aging schedule. This schedule shows how long A/R balances for specific customers have been outstanding. The longer a balance has been outstanding, the higher is the likelihood that it will not be collected in full or at all. Therefore even though the balance exists, as the likelihood that it will not be collected in full or at all, it should be valued at what the company reasonably can expect to collect.

• Obtain and review documentation that supports how management determined the amount that it deems uncollectible. (Management is required to assess the likelihood of collecting each A/R balance and make a provision for the estimate that it deems uncollectible.) The auditor will assess the reasonableness of the method used and the amount deemed as uncollectible that was recorded by management in the allowance for doubtful accounts.

Note that the risk of the A/R balance being incomplete (completeness assertion) is low, as it is unlikely management would be inclined to understate the A/R balance (an asset). In most situations, the auditor would not be concerned with the "completeness" of the A/R balance.

Hillsburg Hardware Limited
Accounts Receivable
Aged Trial Balance
31/12/18

Schedule
Prepared by Client
Approved by

Date
5/1/19

Account Number	Customer	Balance 31/12/18	Aging, Based on Invoice Date				
			0–30 days	31–60 days	61–90 days	91–120 days	over 120 days
101011	Adams Supply Ltd.	73 290	57 966	15 324			
101044	Argonaut, Inc.	1 542	1 542				
101100	Atwater Brothers	85 518	85 518				
101191	Beekman Bearings Corp.	14 176	12 676	125	1 500		
101270	Brown and Phillips	13 952				13 952	
101301	Christopher Plumbing Ltd.	105 231	104 656		150	200	100
109733	Travellers Equipment Ltd.	29 765	29 765				
109742	Underhill Parts and Maintenance	8 963	8 963				
109810	UJW Co. Ltd.	15 832		9 832	6 000		
109907	Zephyr Plastics Corp.	74 300	60 085	14 215			
		20 196 800	10 334 169	5 598 762	2 598 746	1 589 654	75 469

- Identify unusual transactions using the auditor's criteria. For example, balances that exceed their credit limits, or outstanding transactions over a certain size, or extremely old outstanding transactions could be listed. This can be used to help assess the reasonableness of the allowance for doubtful accounts.
- Evaluate the classification of accounts receivable by reviewing the aged trial balance for material receivables from affiliates, officers, directors, or other related parties.
- Identify credit balances, which if significant should be reclassified as accounts payable.

To identify unusual accounts or related party transactions, the auditor may also run exception tests using GAS against the customer master file at the balance sheet date to determine which accounts should be investigated further.

SUBSTANTIVE TESTS OF DETAILS FOR ACCOUNTS RECEIVABLE: EXTERNAL CONFIRMATIONS

LO 10 Obtain and evaluate accounts receivable confirmations.

One of the most important audit procedures is the external confirmation of accounts receivable. Confirmations, which can be in multiple forms (paper or electronic), are used to satisfy the existence, accuracy, and allocation (cutoff aspect) assertions.

The use of external confirmations is not required. However, if the auditor did not confirm receivables, he or she would gain the required assurance by other means such as review of subsequent payments or examination of documentation supporting the receivable balance. CAS 505 points out that confirmations may be more relevant to certain assertions (such as existence), and leaves the use of confirmations

CAS

up to the auditor. Generally, the auditor will send confirmations unless the following are true:

- Accounts receivable are immaterial. This is common for companies such as retail stores with primarily cash or credit card sales.
- The auditor considers confirmations ineffective evidence because response rates will likely be inadequate or unreliable. In certain industries, such as hospitals, rates of response to confirmations are very low.
- The combined level of inherent risk and control risk is low, and other substantive evidence can be accumulated to provide sufficient evidence. If a client has effective internal controls and low inherent risk for the revenue cycle, the auditor should be able to satisfy the evidence requirements by tests of controls, substantive tests of transactions, and analytical procedures.

Assumptions Underlying Confirmations

An auditor makes two assumptions when accepting an external confirmation from a third party as evidence:

1. *The person returning the confirmation is independent of the company being audited and will provide an unbiased response.* If this assumption is invalid, as would be the case if the confirmation of a fraudulent account receivable were sent to a company owned by an associate of the person committing the fraud, the value of the returned confirmation becomes zero.
2. *The person returning the confirmation has knowledge of the account and the intent of the confirmation* and has carefully checked the balance in his or her records to ensure that the confirmation is in agreement. However, this second assumption may also not always be valid.

Research has shown that some people return confirmations without really checking the balance; such a confirmation would have no value. If the auditor has any doubts about the quality of the confirmation, then the auditor should apply professional skepticism and perform additional audit procedures.

Confirmation Decisions

The auditor must make several decisions about the confirmation that will be sought, including type of confirmation, timing, sample size, and sample selection of the items for testing.

Type of Confirmation Two common types of confirmations are used for confirming accounts receivable: positive and negative. A **positive (accounts receivable) confirmation** is a communication addressed to the debtor requesting him or her to confirm directly with the auditor whether the balance as stated on the confirmation request is correct or incorrect. Figure 12-11 illustrates a positive confirmation in the audit of Island Hardware Ltd.

A variation of the first type of confirmation includes a listing of outstanding invoices making up the balance or a copy of the client customer statement attached by the auditor to the confirmation request. The listing of invoices is useful when the debtor uses a voucher system for accounts payable; attaching the statement makes it easier for the debtor to respond. If the client has unusual or complex sales agreements, the auditor could also request confirmation of terms of sale—such as bill-and-hold transactions, or extended payment terms.

A second type of positive confirmation, often called a **blank confirmation form**, does not state the amount on the confirmation but requests that the recipient fill in the balance or furnish other information. Because blank forms require the recipient to determine the information requested before signing and returning the confirmation, they are considered more reliable than confirmations that include the information.

Positive (accounts receivable) confirmation—a letter, addressed to the debtor, requesting that the recipient indicate directly on the letter whether the stated account balance is correct or incorrect and, if incorrect, by what amount.

Blank confirmation form—a letter, addressed to the debtor, requesting the recipient to fill in the amount of the accounts receivable balance; considered a positive confirmation.

Figure 12-11	Example Positive Confirmation

Cockburn, Pedlar & Co.

Chartered Accountants
Cabot Bldg.
P.O. Box 123
3 King Street North
St. John's, Newfoundland
A1C 3R5

Gamer Hardware
80 Main Street
Corner Brook, Newfoundland
A2H 1C8

August 15, 2018

To Whom It May Concern:

Re: Island Hardware Ltd.

In connection with our audit of the financial statements of the above company, we would appreciate receiving from you confirmation of your account. The company's records show an amount receivable from you of $175.00 on June 30, 2018.

Do you agree with this amount? If you do, please sign this letter in the space below. However, if you do not, please note at the foot of this letter or on the reverse side the details of any differences. Please return this letter directly to us in the envelope enclosed for your convenience.

Sincerely,

Cockburn, Pedlar & Co.

Cockburn, Pedlar & Co.

Per:

Please provide Cockburn, Pedlar & Co. with this information.

J. Doe
_____

J. Doe, Accountant, Island Hardware Ltd.

The above amount, owed by me (us) at the date mentioned.

_____

Research shows, however, that response rates are usually lower for blank confirmation forms. These forms are preferred for accounts payable confirmations when the auditor is searching for understatement of accounts payable.

A **negative confirmation** is also addressed to the debtor but requests a response only when the debtor disagrees with the stated amount. Figure 12-12 illustrates a negative confirmation in the audit of Island Hardware Ltd. It is a gummed label and would be attached to a customer's monthly statement. Often, the client can print the auditor's negative confirmation request directly onto the customer statements.

A positive confirmation is more reliable evidence because the auditor can perform follow-up procedures if a response is not received from the debtor. With a negative confirmation, failure to reply cannot be regarded as a correct response since the debtor may have ignored the confirmation request. This explains why CAS 505 states that negative confirmation should be used only when risks of material misstatement are low and when the following are true:

- The items to be confirmed are homogeneous (i.e., similar in nature) and comprise small account balances.
- No or few exceptions are likely.

Negative confirmation—a letter, addressed to the debtor, requesting a response only if the recipient disagrees with the amount of the stated account balance.

| Figure 12-12 | Example Negative Confirmation |

AUDITOR'S ACCOUNT CONFIRMATION

Please examine this statement carefully. If it does NOT agree with your records, please report any exceptions directly to our auditors

> Cockburn, Pedlar & Co.
> Cabot Bldg.
> P.O. Box 123
> 3 King Street North
> St. John's, Newfoundland
> A1C 3R5

who are making an examination of our financial statements. A stamped, addressed envelope is enclosed for your convenience in replying.

Do not send your remittance to our auditors.

- There is an expectation that the negative confirmations will be read and considered.

Offsetting the reliability disadvantage, negative confirmations are less expensive to send than positive confirmations, and thus more can be distributed for the same total cost. Negative confirmations cost less because there are no second requests and no follow-ups of nonresponses.

Positive confirmations are more effective when the following exist:

- Individual balances of relatively large amounts.
- Few debtors or account balances.
- No suspicions or evidence of fraud or serious error.

Typically, when negative confirmations are used, the auditor puts considerable emphasis on the effectiveness of internal control as evidence of the fairness of accounts receivable. Negative confirmations are often used for audits of municipalities, retail stores, banks, and other industries in which the receivables are due from the general public. In these cases, more weight is placed on tests of controls than on confirmations.

The primary factors affecting the confirmation decision are the materiality of total accounts receivable, the number and size of individual accounts, control risk, inherent risk, the effectiveness of confirmations as audit evidence, and the availability of other audit evidence.

Timing The most reliable evidence from confirmations is obtained when they are sent as close to the balance sheet date as possible, as opposed to confirming the accounts several months before year-end. This permits the auditor to test the accounts receivable balance on the financial statements directly without making any inferences about the transactions taking place between the confirmation date and the balance sheet date. However, as a means of completing the audit on a timely basis, it is frequently convenient to confirm the accounts at an interim date. This works well if internal controls are adequate and can provide reasonable assurance that sales, cash receipts, and other credits are properly recorded between the date of the confirmation and the end of the accounting period.

If the decision is made to confirm accounts receivable prior to year-end, it will be necessary to test the transactions occurring between the confirmation date and the balance sheet date. The nature of testing depends upon the length of time between the confirmation date and the year-end and the quality of internal controls. Testing could include examining such internal documents as duplicate sales invoices, shipping documents, and evidence of cash receipts, in addition to performing internal control testing, or analytical procedures of the intervening period.

Sample Size The main considerations affecting the number of confirmations to send include:

- Performance materiality;
- Inherent risk and risk of material misstatement (relative size of total accounts receivable, number of accounts, prior-year results, and expected misstatements);
- Assessed control risk;
- Achieved detection risk from other substantive tests (extent and results of analytical procedures as substantive tests and other tests of details); and
- Type of confirmation (negatives normally require a larger sample size).

Sample Selection of the Items for Testing Some type of stratification is desirable with most confirmations. A typical approach to stratification is to consider both the size of the outstanding balance and the length of time an account has been outstanding as a basis for selecting the balances for confirmation. In most audits, the emphasis should be on confirming larger and older balances, since these are most likely to include a significant misstatement. However, it is also important to sample some items from every material stratum of the population. In many cases, the auditor selects all accounts above a certain dollar amount and selects a statistical sample (MUS) from the remainder.

Refusal to Permit Confirmation Management may refuse the auditor permission to send certain confirmations, perhaps because there is a dispute about the account. In such cases, CAS 505 requires the auditor to corroborate management's statements and to conduct alternative audit procedures (which would be similar to procedures conducted for nonresponses, discussed below). For example, if an account were under dispute, the auditor would examine correspondence with the client and consider whether the account is still collectible. The auditor needs to consider whether management's reasons for not confirming the account are reasonable and how this fits in to other assessed risks.

CAS

Maintaining Control After the items for confirmation have been selected, the auditor must maintain control of the confirmations until they are returned from the debtor. If the client's assistance is obtained in preparing the confirmations—enclosing them in envelopes or putting stamps on the envelopes—close supervision by the auditor is required. The public accounting firm's return address must be included on all envelopes to make sure that undelivered mail is received by the public accounting firm. Similarly, self-addressed return envelopes accompanying the confirmations must be addressed for delivery to the public accounting firm's office. It is even important to mail the confirmations outside the client's office. All these steps are necessary to ensure independent communication between the auditor and the customer.

Follow-Up on Nonresponses Nonresponses to positive confirmations do not provide audit evidence. Similarly, for negative confirmations, the auditor cannot conclude that the recipient received the confirmation request and verified the information requested. Negative confirmations do, however, provide some evidence of the existence assertion. For example, if the address does not exist, the envelope will be returned to the auditor's offices.

It is common when the auditor does not receive a response to a positive confirmation request to send a second and even a third request for confirmation. Even with these efforts, some debtors will not return the confirmation. The auditor can then (1) perform alternative procedures or (2) treat the nonresponse as an error to be projected from the sample to the population in order to assess its materiality. The objective of the following **alternative procedures** is to determine by a means other than confirmation whether the nonconfirmed account existed and was properly stated at the confirmation date.

Alternative procedures—for confirmations, the follow-up of a positive confirmation not returned by the debtor with the use of documentation evidence to determine whether the recorded receivable exists and is collectible.

Subsequent Cash Receipts Evidence of the receipt of cash subsequent to the confirmation date includes remittance advices, entries in the cash receipts records, or perhaps even subsequent credits in the supporting records. On the one hand, the examination of evidence of subsequent cash receipts is a highly useful alternative procedure because it is reasonable to assume that a customer would not make a payment unless it were for an existing receivable. On the other hand, the fact of payment does not establish whether there was an obligation on the date of the confirmation, since the payment could pertain to sales after the confirmation date. This is why care should be taken to specifically match each unpaid sales transaction with evidence of its payment as a test for disputes or disagreements over individual outstanding invoices, as well as for matching to the correct period.

Duplicate Sales Invoices These are useful in verifying the actual issuance of a sales invoice and the actual date of the billing.

Shipping Documents These are important in establishing whether the shipment was actually made and as a test of cutoff (allocation assertion).

Correspondence With the Client Usually, the auditor does not need to review correspondence as a part of alternative procedures, but correspondence can be used to disclose disputed and questionable receivables not uncovered by other means.

The extent and nature of the alternative procedures depend primarily upon the materiality of the nonresponses, the types of misstatements discovered in the confirmed responses, the subsequent cash receipts from the nonresponses, and the auditor's conclusions about internal control. It is normally desirable to account for all unconfirmed balances with alternative procedures even if the amounts are small, as a means of properly generalizing from the sample to the population.

Analysis of Differences When the confirmation requests are returned by the customer, it is necessary to determine the reason for any reported differences. In many cases, they are caused by a **timing difference** between the client's and the customer's records. It is important to distinguish between these and the exceptions, which represent misstatements of the accounts receivable balance. The most commonly reported types of differences in confirmations follow.

Payment Has Already Been Made Reported differences typically arise when the customer has made a payment prior to the confirmation date, but the client has not received the payment in time for recording before the confirmation date. Such instances should be carefully investigated to determine the possibility of a cash receipts cutoff misstatement, lapping, or a theft of cash.

Goods Have Not Been Received These differences may result because the client records the sale at the date of shipment and the customer records the purchase when the goods are received. The time the goods are in transit is frequently the cause of differences reported on confirmations. These should be investigated to determine the possibility of the customer's not receiving the goods at all or the existence of a cutoff misstatement on the client's records.

Goods Have Been Returned The client's failure to record a credit memo could result from timing differences or the improper recording of sales returns and allowances. Like other differences, these must be investigated.

Timing difference—in an accounts receivable confirmation from a debtor, a reported difference that is determined to be a discrepancy in timing between the client's and debtor's records and therefore not a misstatement.

CONCEPT CHECK

C12-12 ABC Co. has about 300 accounts receivable balances from a variety of businesses, ranging in size from about $500 to $250 000. What types of confirmations would be sent? Justify your response.

Clerical Errors and Disputed Amounts Reported differences in a client's records can occur when the customer states that there is an error in the price charged for the goods, the goods are damaged, the proper quantity of goods was not received, or there are other problems. These differences must be investigated to determine whether the client is in error and what the amount of the error is.

In most instances, the auditor asks the client to reconcile the difference and asks the client to communicate with the customer to resolve any audit disagreements. The auditor must carefully verify the client's conclusions on each significant difference.

Drawing Conclusions When all differences have been resolved, including those discovered in performing alternative procedures, it is important to re-evaluate internal control. Each client misstatement must be analyzed to determine whether it was consistent or inconsistent with the original assessed level of control risk. If there are a significant number of misstatements that are inconsistent with the assessment of control risk, then it is necessary to revise the assessment and consider the effect of the revision on the audit.

As shown in Chapter 11, it is also necessary to generalize from the sample to the entire population of accounts receivable. This conclusion can be reached by using statistical sampling techniques or a nonstatistical basis.

Accounts Receivable: Valuation

Although substantive tests of revenue will provide assurance for the accuracy of accounts receivable, they are not useful in providing assurance as to whether the client will collect the outstanding receivables (net realizable value).

Figure 12-9 provides an overview of the approach to **valuation**, or evaluating the reasonableness of the allowance for doubtful accounts. Since the allowance for doubtful accounts is an estimate of what will not be collected at year-end, there can be considerable uncertainty. The auditor will perform a combination of the following procedures:

Valuation—the amount of the outstanding balances in accounts receivable that will ultimately be collected.

- Inspect the noncurrent accounts on the aged accounts receivable trial balance to determine which have not been paid subsequent to the balance sheet date.
- Compare size and age of unpaid balances with similar information from previous years to evaluate whether the amount of noncurrent receivables is increasing or decreasing over time.
- Examine credit files, discuss with the credit manager, and review customer correspondence files as needed. Consider past history to determine the percentage of current accounts that need to be allowed for.
- Conduct substantive analytical review over time (trend analysis) of bad debts to evaluate quality of accounts receivable.
- Verify accuracy of bad debt expense as a residual, checking validity of charges to the bad debt expense if needed.

Accounts Receivable: Rights and Obligation

For those companies that sell their receivables with or without recourse or have pledged the receivables as collateral, the details need to be disclosed in the notes to the financial statements. Some substantive procedures that would identify these types of transactions include the following:

- Determine whether the receivables have been pledged as collateral, assigned to someone else, factored, or sold at discount by inquiring of management and reviewing minutes of directors' meetings.
- To verify details, send confirmations to banks, and examine correspondence files.

Presentation and Disclosure Assertions: Revenue and Accounts Receivable

Procedures that the auditor may perform to determine that information about the revenue cycle is fairly presented and disclosed in the financial statements include the following:

- Evaluate whether the presentation of revenue on a gross basis (as a principal) versus net (as an agent) is in conformity with the applicable financial reporting framework.
- Evaluate the adequacy and understandability of the presentation of the revenue recognition policy.
- Evaluate the understandability and completeness of the footnotes for accounts receivable: some required footnote disclosure includes information about the pledging, discounting, factoring, assignment of accounts receivable, and amounts due from related parties.
- Determine that trade accounts receivable are segregated from related-party accounts receivable, and that different types of material transactions are clearly listed as separate line items to facilitate the classification and understandability objectives.
- Read management's discussion and analysis (MD&A) to determine whether there are any inconsistencies with the financial statements or other information that the auditor has collected in the course of the audit.

LO 11 Design and perform fraud procedures for the revenue cycle.

DESIGN AND PERFORM FRAUD-RELATED SUBSTANTIVE PROCEDURES

If specific fraud risk factors are present, the auditor will perform fraud-related substantive procedures. Many of the substantive procedures provided in Table 12-4 would address fraud risk for the relevant control weakness. The following are examples of other fraud-related procedures that could be performed:

- Interview client personnel regarding knowledge of unusual sales transactions.
- To test for fictitious customers, GAS can be used to identify post-office box addresses, duplicated addresses, or addresses that are the same as those of employees. (Recall the opening vignette in Chapter 9 regarding the Peregrine fraud—the bank confirmations were sent to a post-office box.)
- To test for unusual or unexpected revenue relationships or transactions, substantive analytical procedures and computer-assisted audit techniques may be useful. Potential analytical procedures include the following: compare credit memo and write-off activity to prior periods; compare the number of weeks of inventory in distribution channels to prior years (if channel stuffing is suspected).
- To test for occurrence of revenue, confirm with customers certain relevant contract terms and the absence of side agreements. Contract terms may include acceptance criteria, delivery and payment terms, the absence of future or continuing vendor obligations, the right to return the product, guaranteed resale amounts, and cancellation or refund provisions.
- If the auditor is concerned about cutoff, he or she should consider being physically present at one or more locations at period-end to observe goods being shipped or being readied for shipment (or returns awaiting processing).
- Review accounting estimates (such as allowance for doubtful accounts or returns allowance) for biases and evaluate whether the bias, if any, represents a risk of material misstatement due to fraud.

Proof of cash receipts—an audit procedure to test whether all recorded cash receipts have been deposited in the bank account by reconciling the total cash receipts recorded in the cash receipts journal for a given period with the actual deposits made to the bank.

If fraud risk is high for theft of cash, a useful audit procedure to test whether all recorded cash receipts have been deposited in the bank account is a **proof of cash receipts**. In this test, the total cash receipts recorded in the cash receipts data files for a given period, such as a month, are reconciled with the actual deposits made to the bank during the same period. There may be a difference in the two due to deposits in transit and other items, but the amounts can be reconciled and compared. The procedure cannot detect cash receipts that have not been recorded in the journals or time lags in making deposits, but it can help uncover recorded cash receipts that have not been deposited, unrecorded deposits, unrecorded loans, bank loans deposited directly into the bank account, and similar errors or misstatements.

SUMMARY

In this chapter, we discussed the audit process for the revenue cycle, which is usually the most significant cycle. In order to understand how to design the audit process, we start with discussing the accounts, classes of transactions and the business functions and documents of the revenue cycle.

To identify significant risks, the auditor will examine various factors such as complexity of the revenue transactions, prior misstatements, client incentives and biases, and client business risk. The auditor will also obtain an understanding of internal controls, which along with the inherent risk assessment will form the preliminary risk of material misstatement. This will form the basis of the audit strategy for the cycle—if the auditor plans to rely upon controls, a combined approach will be used and, if not, a substantive approach will be used.

In the case of the combined approach, if the results of control testing support the initial control risk assessment, the auditor will reduce substantive tests. Because revenue is a significant risk, substantive analytical procedures are not sufficient evidence. The type of substantive tests of details will depend upon the client; however, accounts receivable confirmations are often a key substantive test of detail performed. Performing accounts receivable confirmations is a multi-purpose technique that addresses several audit assertions.

Revenue is unique in that the auditor will assume a high fraud risk for revenue recognition, and audit standards require the auditor to test for revenue recognition fraud. Many procedures designed to test key controls will assist in testing fraud.

Review Questions

🌐 **12-1** **1** Describe the nature of the following documents and records, and explain their use in the sales and collection cycle: bill of lading, sales invoice, credit memo, remittance advice, and monthly statement to customers.

🌐 **12-2** **2** **4** Explain the importance of proper credit approval for sales. What effect do adequate controls in the credit function have on the auditor's evidence accumulation?

🌐 **12-3** **2** Distinguish between the sales journal and the accounts receivable master file. What type of information is recorded in each and how do these accounting records relate?

🌐 **12-4** **2** **3** **4** **BestSellers.com** sells fiction and nonfiction books and ebooks to customers through the company's website. Customers place orders for books by providing their name, address, credit card number, and credit card expiration date. What internal controls could **BestSellers.com** implement to ensure that shipments of books occur only for customers who have the ability to pay for those books? At what point will **BestSellers.com** be able to record the sale as revenue?

🌐 **12-5** **4** **6** List the transaction-related audit objectives for the audit of sales transactions. For each objective, state one internal control that the client can use to reduce the likelihood of misstatements.

🌐 **12-6** **4** **6** State one test of control and one substantive test of transactions that the auditor can use to verify the sales transaction-related audit objective. Recorded sales are stated at the proper amounts.

🌐 **12-7** **4** List the most important duties that should be segregated in the revenue cycle. Explain why it is desirable that each duty be segregated.

12-8 [4] Explain how prenumbered shipping documents and sales invoices can be useful controls for preventing misstatements in sales.

12-9 [4] What three types of authorizations are commonly used as internal controls for sales? For each authorization, state a substantive test that the auditor could use to verify whether the control was effective in preventing misstatements.

12-10 [4] Explain the purpose of footing and cross-footing the sales journal and tracing the totals to the general ledger.

12-11 [8] What is the difference between the auditor's approach in verifying sales returns and allowances and that for sales? Explain the reasons for the difference.

12-12 [3] [11] Explain why auditors usually emphasize the detection of fraud in the audit of cash receipts. Is this consistent or inconsistent with the auditor's responsibility in the audit? Explain.

12-13 [4] List the transaction-related audit objectives for the verification of cash receipts. For each objective, state one internal control that the client can use to reduce the likelihood of misstatements.

12-14 [4] [11] List several audit procedures that the auditor can use to determine whether all cash received was recorded.

12-15 [11] Explain what is meant by a proof of cash receipts and state its purpose.

12-16 [3] [11] Explain what is meant by lapping and discuss how the auditor can uncover it. Under what circumstances should the auditor make a special effort to uncover lapping?

12-17 [3] [10] What audit procedures are most likely to be used to verify accounts receivable written off as uncollectible? State the purpose of each of these procedures.

12-18 [5] [10] State the relationship between the confirmation of accounts receivable and the results of the tests of controls and substantive tests of transactions.

12-19 [10] Which of the five accounts receivable balance-related audit objectives can be partially satisfied by confirmations with customers?

12-20 [8] Explain why you agree or disagree with the following statement: "In most audits, it is more important to test the cutoff for sales than for cash receipts." Describe how you perform each type of test, assuming the existence of prenumbered documents.

12-21 [5] Under what circumstances is it acceptable to perform tests of controls and substantive tests of transactions for sales and cash receipts at an interim date?

12-22 [10] Define what is meant by "alternative procedures," and explain their purpose. Which alternative procedures are the most reliable? Why?

12-23 [5] Diane Smith, CPA (Chartered Professional Accountant), performed tests of controls and substantive tests of transactions for sales for the month of March in an audit of the financial statements for the year ended December 31, 2018. Based on the excellent results of both the tests of controls and the substantive tests of transactions, she decided to significantly reduce her substantive tests of details of balances at year-end. Evaluate this decision.

12-24 [3] [4] ABC is a small manufacturing company that sells all of its products on credit; payment is normally due within 30 days. What are the risks associated with credit sales? What controls can ABC implement to mitigate these risks?

Multiple Choice Questions and Task-Based Simulations

The following questions deal with internal controls in the revenue cycle. Choose the best response.

12-25 [4] The accounting system will not post a sales transaction to the sales journal without a valid bill of lading number. This control is most relevant to which transaction-related objective for sales?

(1) Accuracy
(2) Occurrence
(3) Completeness
(4) Posting and summarization

12-26 [4] Which of the following controls would be most effective in detecting a failure to record cash received from customers paying on their accounts?

(1) A person in accounting reconciles the bank deposit to the cash receipts journal.

(2) Transactions recorded in the cash receipts journal are posted on a real-time basis to the accounts receivable master file.

(3) Monthly statements are sent to customers and any discrepancies are resolved by someone independent of cash handling and accounting.

(4) Deposits of cash received are made daily.

12-27 **4** Which of the following controls most likely will be effective in offsetting the tendency of sales personnel to maximize sales volume at the expense of high bad debt write-offs?

(1) Employees responsible for authorizing sales and bad debt write-offs are denied access to cash.

(2) Employees involved in the credit-granting function are separated from the sales function.

(3) Shipping documents and sales invoices are matched by an employee who does not have the authority to write off bad debts.

(4) Subsidiary accounts receivable records are reconciled to the control account by an employee independent of the authorization of credit.

The following questions deal with audit evidence for the revenue cycle. Choose the best response.

12-28 **8** An auditor is performing substantive tests of transactions for sales. One step is to trace a sample of debit entries from the accounts receivable master file back to the supporting duplicate sales invoices. What will the auditor intend to establish by this step?

(1) Sales invoices represent existing sales.

(2) All sales have been recorded.

(3) All sales invoices have been correctly posted to customer accounts.

(4) Debit entries in the accounts receivable master file are correctly supported by sales invoices.

12-29 **8** Which audit procedure is most effective in testing credit sales for overstatement?

(1) Trace a sample of postings from the sales journal to the sales account in the general ledger.

(2) Vouch a sample of recorded sales from the sales journal to shipping documents.

(3) Prepare an aging of accounts receivable.

(4) Trace a sample of initial sales orders to sales recorded in the sales journal.

12-30 **6** **8** Identify whether each audit procedure listed below is a test of control or a substantive test of transactions.

Audit Procedure	Test of Control or Substantive Test?
Account for a sequence of shipping documents and examine each one to make sure that a duplicate sales invoice is attached.	
Account for a sequence of sales invoices and examine each one to make sure that a duplicate copy of the shipping document is attached.	
Compare the quantity and description of items on shipping documents with the related duplicate sales invoices.	
Trace recorded sales in the sales journal to the related accounts receivable master file and compare the customer name, date, and amount for each one.	
Examine sales returns for approval by an authorized official. Review the prelisting of cash receipts to determine whether cash is prelisted daily.	
Reconcile the recorded cash receipts on the prelisting with the cash receipts journal and the bank statement for a one-month period.	

12-31 **3** For each situation, identify the management assertion(s) most likely affected.

Assertions:

A. Cutoff

B. Accuracy

C. Completeness

D. Existence

E. Valuation

F. Occurrence

Situations	Assertion(s) (A,B,C,D,E,F)
Orders are shipped to a customer with a bad credit rating.	
Consignment sales are recorded as revenue.	
Defective products are shipped to customers. Revenues are recorded at full amount (price).	
Subsequent-period revenue is recorded in the current period.	
Sales are recorded for the incorrect quantity.	
Revenue is recorded when goods have not been delivered.	
Cash sales were accidentally omitted and not recorded.	
Sales are recorded twice (duplicated).	
Goods are shipped that were never ordered by the customer.	

12-32 **4** Identify whether the described control is preventative or detective.

Control	Preventative or Detective?
Management reviews sales and cost of sales analytical reports for reasonableness.	
Invoices can be posted only to valid customer accounts.	
Shipping records and sales invoices cannot be produced if the customer number is invalid.	
Credit is approved before shipment takes place.	
Monthly statements are sent to customers; complaints receive independent follow-up (also satisfies accuracy).	
Approval is required to commence selling goods to a new customer.	
Management reviews exception reports of unusual customer data.	

12-33 **4** Items 1 through 10 below present various internal control strengths or internal control deficiencies. For each, indicate whether the item represents an:
A. Internal control strength for the revenue cycle.
B. Internal control deficiency for the revenue cycle.

Item	Strength/Deficiency
1. Credit is granted by a credit department.	
2. Once shipment occurs and is recorded in the sales journal, all shipping documents are marked "recorded" by the accounting staff.	
3. Sales returns are presented to a sales department clerk who prepares a written, prenumbered receiving report.	
4. Cash receipts received in the mail are received by a secretary with no recordkeeping responsibility.	
5. Cash receipts received in the mail are forwarded unopened with remittance advices to accounting.	
6. The cash receipts journal is prepared by the treasurer's department.	
7. Cash is deposited weekly.	
8. Statements are sent monthly to customers.	
9. Write-offs of accounts receivable are approved by the controller.	
10. The bank reconciliation is prepared by individuals independent of cash receipts recordkeeping.	

Discussion Questions and Problems

12-34 **3** **4** Items 1 through 8 are selected questions of the type generally found in internal control questionnaires used by auditors to obtain an understanding of internal control in the revenue cycle. In using the questionnaire for a particular client, a "yes" response to a question indicates a possible internal control, whereas a "no" indicates a potential weakness.

1. Are sales invoices independently compared with customers' orders for prices, quantities, extensions, and footings?
2. Are sales orders, invoices, and credit memoranda issued and filed in numerical sequence, and are the sequences accounted for periodically?
3. Are the selling function and cash register functions independent of the cash receipts, shipping, delivery, and billing functions?
4. Are all COD, scrap, equipment, and cash sales accounted for in the same manner as charge sales, and is the recordkeeping independent of the collection procedure?
5. Is the collection function independent of, and does it constitute a check on, billing and recording sales?
6. Are customer master files balanced regularly to general ledger control accounts by an employee independent of billing functions?
7. Are cash receipts entered in the accounts receivable system by persons independent of the mail-opening and receipts-listing functions?
8. Are receipts deposited intact on a timely basis?

REQUIRED

a. For each of the Items 1 through 8, state the transaction-related audit objectives being fulfilled if the control is in effect.
b. For each control, list a test of control to test its effectiveness.
c. For each of the items above, identify the nature of the potential financial misstatements.
d. For each of the potential misstatements in Part (c), list an audit procedure to determine whether a material error exists.

12-35 ③ ④ **YourTeam.com** is an online retailer of university, college, and professional sports team memorabilia, such as hats, shirts, pennants, and other sports logo products. Consumers select the university, college, or professional team from a pull-down menu on the company's website. For each listed team, the website provides a product description, picture, and price for all products sold online. Customers click on the product number of the item they wish to purchase. **YourTeam.com** has established the following internal controls for its online sales:

1. Only products shown on the website can be purchased online. Other company products not shown on the website are unavailable for online sale.
2. The online sales system is linked to the perpetual inventory system, which verifies quantities on hand before processing the sale.
3. Before the sale is authorized, **YourTeam.com** obtains credit card authorization codes electronically from the credit card clearing house.
4. Online sales are rejected if the customer's shipping address does not match the credit card's billing address.
5. Before the sale is finalized, the online screen shows the product name, description, unit price, and total sales price for the online transaction. Customers must click on the Accept or Reject sales buttons to indicate approval or rejection of the online sale.
6. Once customers approve the online sale, the online sales system generates a pending sales file, which is an online data file that is used by warehouse personnel to process shipments. Online sales are not recorded in the sales journal until warehouse personnel enter the bill of lading number and date of shipment into the pending sales data file.

REQUIRED

a. For each control, identify the transaction-related audit objective(s) being fulfilled if each control is in effect.
b. For each control, describe potential financial misstatements that could occur if the control were not present.
c. For each control, identify an important general control that would affect the quality of the control.
d. For each control, list a test of control to test its effectiveness.

12-36 ④ ⑥ Jintian Clothing Ltd. manufactures sportswear and sells it to large department stores in Western Canada. The company records sales in a sales journal. When a customer orders merchandise, a sales clerk prepares a sales invoice. The credit manager must approve all sales to new customers, and a record is kept of all approved customers with their credit limit, as established by the credit manager. The company manufactures several styles of sportswear, and each item is listed in a catalogue with the price updated quarterly.

Sales are recorded when goods are shipped. When the goods are shipped, the shipping clerk prepares a bill of lading in triplicate, with one part retained in the shipping department, one part accompanying the shipment, and one part forwarded to accounting. The accounting department matches the bill of lading to the sales invoice, records the sale, and adjusts the inventory records. All documents are sequentially prenumbered.

REQUIRED

Prepare an audit plan to test the internal control objectives of occurrence, completeness, and accuracy at Jintian Clothing Ltd.

(Reprinted from AU1 CGA-Canada Examinations with permission Chartered Professional Accountants of Canada, Toronto, Canada. Any changes to the original material are the sole responsibility of the author/publisher and have not been reviewed or endorsed by the Chartered Professional Accountants of Canada.)

12-37 **3** **9** **10** Charles is an articling public accounting student working on his first financial statement audit engagement. The client is BBB Appliances Inc. One of his duties was to prepare an aging of the company's accounts receivable. His audit supervisor explained that the company's receivables have increased from $650 000 last year to $950 000 this year, which in both cases exceeds performance materiality. These amounts are given as security to the bank for the company's short-term bank loan. Total assets have increased from $4 million to $4.3 million and total sales have increased from $10.3 million to $10.9 million in the year. Charles knows that his firm will be relying on the procedure of positive confirmations to verify valuation, but is wondering why his supervisor has also arranged for a review of the corporate minutes of BBB's board of directors' meetings.

REQUIRED

a. Provide examples of evidence that Charles could obtain related to the accounts receivable and the bank loan from BBB's board of directors' meeting minutes.
b. Using *one* of your examples from Part (a), explain how Charles could use that evidence in inspecting the adequacy of BBB's financial statement notes.
c. Using only the information above for BBB [ignore your answers to Parts (a) and (b)], provide examples of analytical procedures for planning that Charles could use to conduct risk assessment procedures in the audit of BBB's financial statements. Show your calculations.

(Reprinted from AU1 CGA-Canada Examinations with permission Chartered Professional Accountants of Canada, Toronto, Canada. Any changes to the original material are the sole responsibility of the author/publisher and have not been reviewed or endorsed by the Chartered Professional Accountants of Canada.)

12-38 **4** **8** **9** The following misstatements are sometimes found in the revenue account balances:
1. Cash amounts received from collections of accounts receivable in the subsequent period are recorded as current period receipts.
2. The allowance for uncollectible accounts is inadequate due to the client's failure to reflect depressed economic conditions in the allowance.
3. Several accounts receivable are in dispute due to claims of defective merchandise.
4. The pledging of accounts receivable to the bank for a loan is not disclosed in the financial statements.
5. Goods shipped and included in the current period sales were returned in the subsequent period.
6. Long-term interest-bearing notes receivable from affiliated companies are included in accounts receivable.
7. The aged accounts receivable trial balance total does not equal the amount in the general ledger.
8. Several accounts receivable balances in the accounts receivable master file are not included in the aged trial balance report.
9. One accounts receivable customer included in the accounts receivable master file is included in the aged trial balance twice.

REQUIRED

a. For each misstatement, identify the balance-related or presentation and disclosure-related audit objective to which it pertains.
b. For each misstatement, list an internal control that should prevent it.
c. For each misstatement, list one test of details of balances audit procedure that the auditor can use to detect it.

12-39 `11` The following are various potential frauds in the revenue cycle:

1. The company engaged in channel stuffing by shipping goods to customers that had not been ordered.
2. The allowance for doubtful accounts was understated because the company altered the aging of accounts receivable to reduce the number of days outstanding for delinquent receivables.
3. The accounts receivable clerk stole cheques received in the mail and deposited them in an account that he controlled. He issued credit memos to the customers in the amount of the diverted cash receipts.
4. The company asked a major customer to accept a large shipment of goods before year-end. The customer was told that the goods could be returned without penalty if they could not be sold.
5. A cashier stole cash receipts that had been recorded in the cash register.
6. The company recorded "bill-and-hold sales" at year-end. Although the invoices were recorded as sales before year-end, the goods were stored in the warehouse and shipped after year-end.
7. The company did not record credit memos for returns received in the last month of the year. The goods received were counted as part of the company's year-end physical inventory procedures.
8. A cashier stole cash receipts by failing to record the sales in the cash register.
9. The CFO recorded fictitious credit sales at the end of the year without recording the associated cost of sales and reduction in inventory.

REQUIRED

a. Indicate whether the fraud involves misappropriation of assets or fraudulent financial reporting.
b. For those frauds that involve misappropriation of assets, state a control that would be effective in preventing or detecting the misappropriation.
c. For those frauds that involve fraudulent financial reporting, state an audit procedure that would be effective in detecting the fraud.

12-40 `11` The following audit procedures are included in the audit program because of heightened risks of material misstatements due to fraud.

1. Search the accounts receivable master file for account balances with missing or unusual customer numbers (e.g., "99999").
2. Send confirmations to customers for large sales transactions made in the fourth quarter of the year to obtain customer responses about terms related to the transfer of title and ability to return merchandise.
3. Search sales databases for missing bill of lading numbers.
4. Use audit software to search for journal entries posted to the sales revenue account from a nonstandard source (other than the daily sales journal).

REQUIRED

For each audit procedure:
a. Describe the type of fraud risk that is likely associated with the need for this audit procedure.
b. Identify the related accounts likely affected by the potential fraud misstatement.
c. Identify the related audit objective(s) that this procedure addresses.

Professional Judgment Problems and Cases

12-41 `3` `8` Each of the following situations concerns whether and how to recognize revenue.

1. A cell phone provider sells phone hardware and associated voice and data services. The typical contract includes a $200 upfront initial charge and $50 per month for the next two years for voice and data services. The company proposes to recognize 50 percent of revenue immediately, 25 percent at the end of the first year, and 25 percent at the end of second year.

2. Heavy Duty Construction Equipment Builders builds custom machinery for construction companies.

Currently, it is producing machinery for a customer for $25 million. The contracted date to complete the machinery was October, and the company met the contract date. It is now December, and the customer acknowledges the contract and confirms the amount; however, the customer construction company has requested that Heavy Duty Construction hold the machinery, as the construction site where the equipment will be used is not yet under development. Expected start has been delayed and will be some time within the next 6 to 18 months.

3. Bakers Appliances has developed a new line of business where the company will be selling bakeware appliances over the internet. The other lines of business have no return policy, hence no return allowance has ever been set by the company. However, since this is a new line of business, website sales grant each purchaser the right of return for a full refund within one year of date of purchase if the customer is unhappy with the product or finds the product defective.

4. Burer Technologies is a high-growth company that sells custom photographic software, which is a very rapidly changing industry. In order to achieve growth, management has empowered the sales staff to make special deals with clients (discounts and payment terms) to increase sales in the fourth quarter of the year. The sales deals include a price break and an increased salesperson commission.

REQUIRED

For each of Situations 1 through 4:

a. Discuss the key issues to address in determining whether or not revenue should be recognized.

b. Identify additional information required or audit procedures to be performed by the auditor to quantify or otherwise audit the issues identified in Part (a).

c. Use IFRS 15 revenue recognition criteria to explain how the client should recognize revenue.

12-42 **9** Kitchen-Tech is a private large manufacturing firm that is headquartered in Toronto, Ontario. Kitchen-Tech manufactures, distributes, and installs high-tech kitchen equipment and custom made appliances for high-end restaurants. Products are manufactured in Toronto and then transferred to one of five warehouse locations across Canada. The warehouse locations are responsible for final transportation and installation of the equipment at customer premises.

Kitchen-Tech is a profitable company. Since 2010 the company has experienced tremendous growth, especially in the province of Alberta where the economy has been expanding due to the increase in oil prices. However, starting in 2014, oil prices started to collapse and Alberta's economy came to a halt. Local businesses—especially high-end restaurants—continue to be impacted by the economic downturn.

You're an audit senior on the Kitchen-Tech April 30, 2017, year-end audit and are getting started by looking at the accounts receivable balance.

INFORMATION ON KITCHEN-TECH'S RECEIVABLES

The chief accountant has informed you that the days outstanding of accounts receivables have increased from 45 to 60 days over the last year. The chief accountant also informed you that the increase was even greater on outstanding balances from customers located in Alberta. Below is the aging of accounts receivable (all customers):

REQUIRED

a. Assume you plan to use a judgmental sampling method for accounts receivable confirmations. Based upon the aging schedule above, provide four items/categories that you would select to confirm. Explain why.

b. Accounts receivable confirmations provide strong evidence for existence of receivables and completeness of collections, sales discounts, and sales returns, but weak evidence for completeness of the receivable balance. Explain why.

c. What account balance assertion(s) are at most risk for outstanding accounts receivable balances from customers located in Alberta? State the assertion(s) and explain why.

12-43 **9** **10** You are auditing the financial statements of the Reis Company, a small manufacturing firm that has been your client for several years. Because you were busy working on another engagement, you sent a staff accountant to begin the audit, with the suggestion that she start with accounts receivable.

Using the prior year's working papers as a guide, the auditor prepared a trial balance of the accounts, aged them, prepared and mailed positive confirmation requests, examined underlying support for charges and credits, and performed other work she considered necessary to obtain evidence about the validity and collectability of the receivables. At the conclusion of her work, you reviewed the working papers she prepared and found she had carefully followed the prior year's working papers.

Reis Company acquired the assets of another corporation during the year, so the nature and quality of its accounts receivable have changed. It has many more small accounts, as well as three larger international clients involving foreign exchange sales transactions. Sales have gone up substantially, and the accounts receivable balance has doubled. Two of the international accounts are over six months old and involve complex hedging transactions.

REQUIRED

a. What auditing standards have been violated by the personnel in this case? Explain why you feel the standards have been violated.

b. How do the acquisition and the change in the nature of sales and accounts receivable affect control risk and inherent risk of accounts receivable?

c. Describe how you would adjust your audit strategy for the change in sales and accounts receivable. Explain what additional audit procedures would be necessary (be sure to include discussion of the purpose of the procedure).

12-44 **1** **2** **4** Parts for Wheels Inc. has historically sold auto parts directly to consumers through its retail stores. Due to competitive pressure, Parts for Wheels installed an

Range of Balances	Number of Customers	Total Balance	Current	30–60 Days	Over 60 Days
Less than $0	15	$ (87 253)	$ (87 253)	Nil	Nil
$0 to $20 000	197	2 167 762	548 894	$ 643 523	$ 975 345
$20 001 to $50 000	153	5 508 077	2 044 253	2 735 073	728 751
$50 001 or more	23	1 495 498	750 235	672 750	72 513
Total	388	9 084 084	3 256 129	4 051 346	1 776 609

internet-based sales system that allows customers to place orders through the company's website. The company hired an outside website design consultant to create the sales system because the company's IT personnel lack the necessary experience.

Customers use the link to the inventory parts listing on the website to view product descriptions and prices. The inventory parts listing is updated weekly. To get the system online quickly, management decided not to link the order system to the sales and inventory accounting systems. Customers submit orders for products through the online system and provide credit card information for payment. Each day, accounting department clerks print submitted orders from the online system. After credit authorization is verified with the credit card agency, the accounting department enters the sale into the sales system. After that, the accounting department sends a copy of the order to warehouse personnel who process the shipment. The inventory system is updated on the basis of bills of lading information forwarded to accounting after shipment.

Customers may return parts for a full refund within 30 days of submitting the order online. The company agrees to refund shipping costs incurred by the customer for returned goods.

REQUIRED
a. Describe deficiencies in Parts for Wheels' online sales system that may lead to material misstatements in the financial statements. Identify which audit assertion is affected.
b. For each deficiency listed in Part (a), identify changes in manual procedures that could be made to minimize risks, without having to reprogram the current online system.
c. Describe potential customer concerns about doing business online with Parts for Wheels. For each concern, provide one or more controls that could be implemented to address the concerns.

12-45 **5** **9** **10** You are the audit senior for the 2018 year-end audit of Vision Quest (VQ), a publicly traded Canadian company that is one of the largest and fastest online vision care providers in the world. Because of the efficiencies of the internet to bypass middlemen, VQ has a significant competitive advantage in its market. You are responsible for auditing the revenue cycle. Performance materiality for the VQ audit is $100 000. VQ's year-end is October 31, 2018.

Below is a summary of key information regarding the revenue cycle:

Revenue Recognition Policy—Revenue from product sales is recognized when the product has been shipped to the customer. At that point, the amount of sales revenue is determinable, no significant vendor obligations remain, and the collection of the revenue is reasonably assured. A provision is made for product returns. Revenue collected in advance of the product being shipped is deferred.

Audit Strategy for Revenue—The audit strategy relies upon tests of controls (including substantive tests of transactions) and substantive analytical procedures. No accounts receivable confirmations are sent out. Your audit team has tested controls related to revenue transactions and concluded that controls are effective and support the control risk assessment of low for the revenue transaction-related assertions.

Change in Credit Policy—When reviewing the accounts, you noted that a new account, allowance for doubtful accounts, has been set up. Upon investigation, you find that in February 2018, VQ implemented a program where the majority of customers were granted credit. VQ developed this program to attract new customers who might be wary of ordering contact lenses from an online retailer and having to pay for them prior to receiving them. The company's program, named "Invoice Me Later" or "the IML program," allows customers to order from VQ and pay after receiving the product. Management estimates payment should generally be received in less than 15 days.

Estimate for Allowance for Doubtful Accounts—The majority of the balances outstanding are less than $150 and there are a large number of records. Management estimates an allowance based upon the aging of the receivable portfolio. Below is a summary of the aging and management's estimate for the allowance for doubtful accounts.

Aging of Accounts Receivable	2018	2017
Current	$7 714 000	$6 695 000
Aged 60–120 days	88 000	nil
Aged greater than 120 days	66 000	nil
Total receivables	7 868 000	6 695 000
Allowance for doubtful accounts	135 000	nil
Net receivables	$7 733 000	$6 695 000

REQUIRED
a. Explain the impact of the IML program on your audit strategy for the revenue cycle of VQ. (Use the audit risk model and assertions to support your analysis.)
b. Do you agree with the auditors' decision not to send out accounts receivable confirmations? Why or why not?
c. If the auditors planned to send out accounts receivable confirmations, what type of confirmations would you recommend? Explain why.

12-46 **10** Sylvie Beaubien is the engagement manager for the audit of Terra Enterprises. Sylvie is currently planning tests of details of balances for accounts receivable and is considering the use of electronic confirmation requests to improve response rates. The historical response rate to written confirmation requests sent to Terra's customers has been below 50 percent and Sylvie believes they can increase that to over 80 percent using electronic requests. Sylvie is considering two different options. The first option is to use email confirmation requests, with requests emailed directly to customers and the customers emailing responses directly to the audit firm. The second option is to use direct access to customers' electronic records through website links for Terra's largest customers, and then written requests to the remaining customers.

REQUIRED

a. What factors does Sylvie need to consider in deciding whether to use written confirmation requests, email requests, or direct access to electronic records?

b. How will the audit firm ensure the reliability of the responses? For example, how might they verify the email addresses or the reliability of the electronic records? Who should provide the email addresses for the email confirmations, or the website links for direct access to electronic records?

12-47 5 7 You are the audit senior on the audit of Great Eastern Hotel (GEH). This two-star hotel is located in a major coastal city and as such is prone to seasonal fluctuations. The 200-room hotel is open year round with a standard room rate of $90 per night. GEH charges $95 per room in the summer and $85 per room in the winter, the same as the prior year. The hotel includes a bar and restaurant as well as underground parking.

From the audit work performed to date, you are satisfied that GEH has well-established controls. You therefore decide to place reliance on these controls and for the most part use only substantive analytical procedures to test revenue (Summarized below). You are satisfied that this approach will provide you with sufficient assurance on hotel room revenue.

So far, you have obtained a breakdown of room rental revenue by quarter and gathered some statistics on occupancy rates from the local tourist board.

Great Eastern Hotels Statement of Income for the Year Ended December 31

Revenue:	2018	2017 (audited)
Hotel Room Rental	$5 535 617	$5 165 176
Food & Beverage	1 497 612	1 488 619
Parking, Telephone, Other	417 602	396 158
Interest	56 711	58 610
	$7 507 542	$7 108 563
Expenses:		
Direct Costs:		
Hotel Room Rental	3 165 992	3 105 644
Food & Beverage	1 388 691	1 452 107
Other	389 917	365 223
	$4 944 600	$4 922 974
Gross Margin	$2 462 942	$2 185 589
General & Administration	1 617 532	1 574 805
Advertising & Promotion	364 817	349 576
Other	216 911	166 978
	$2 199 260	$2 091 359
Net Income Before Tax	$ 163 682	$ 94 230
Income Tax Expense	26 754	40 519
Net Income	$ 236 928	$ 52 711

2018 Breakdown of Room Revenue by Quarter ($000s)

	Q1	Q2	Q3	Q4
Hotel Room Rental	1 193	1 445	1 471	1 427

2018 Hotel Occupancy Rates

	Q1	Q2	Q3	Q4
	Summer	Fall	Winter	Spring
First Class	77%	75%	86%	71%
Two Star	76%	70%	84%	71%
Third Rate	69%	74%	78%	60%

REQUIRED

a. Comment on the quality of information you have obtained so far, considering its source, audit assertions, and level of detail in your discussion.

b. What additional analytical procedures would you be required to perform in order to ensure the degree of precision necessary to provide adequate assurance for hotel room revenue?

c. Develop an expectation of GEH's rental revenue. Based upon this analysis, provide your conclusion on GEH's 2018 hotel revenue.

d. Based on your analysis and conclusion in Part (b), describe what further inquiries you would make of GEH management and corroborating evidence you would request. Tie your discussion to specific audit assertion(s) you are concerned with.

e. Despite the well-established controls at GEH and your decision to place reliance on them, is it appropriate to use only substantive analytical procedures to gain assurance over revenue accounts? Explain why.

12-48 5 Biomed Products Incorporated (BPI) is a public company, listed on the Toronto Stock Exchange (TSX), that manufactures and markets various types of medical equipment that monitors patients' vital signs (i.e., heart rate, breathing, blood pressure). BPI has been audited by Cooper & Zhang, a large public accounting firm, since its inception 10 years ago. You are the audit senior responsible for the March 2019 year-end audit. Within the next day or two, you will be meeting with the audit manager to go over significant accounting and audit issues regarding the revenue cycle.

Excerpts from the income statement for the first nine months of the current fiscal year and the previous two years are below:

BIOMED PRODUCTS INCORPORATED Income Statement Excerpts (in thousands of dollars)

	9 months ended December 31, 2018 (unaudited)	Year Ended March 31, 2018 (audited)	Year Ended March 31, 2017 (audited)
Equipment sales	$31 250	$47 500	$49 000
Cost of sales	12 500	19 500	19 000
Gross profit	18 750	28 000	30 000
Expenses	10 250	17 250	18 000
Interest	4 200	4 200	4 200
General and administration	3 200	4 500	4 700
Amortization	2 500	3 700	4 200
Warranty provision	2 500	1 500	1 500
Net loss	(3 900)	(3 150)	(2 600)

Over the past week, you have been updating the preliminary planning related to the revenue cycle, visiting BPI's premises, and interviewing the client staff. Your notes are summarized below.

1. The preliminary materiality is based upon revenue and overall materiality is set at $250 000. Performance materiality is $200 000. Due to each hospital contract being unique, inherent risk for revenue recognition is high; however, controls have been effective; therefore, risk of material misstatement is set at moderate.

2. Cooper & Zhang have relied upon internal controls in past audits. The internal control environment is strong. The staff members in the accounting area are competent and there is adequate segregation of duties. Based upon your update and testing of the systems, no changes have occurred in the accounting area. However, your documentation of the processing of revenue reveals that BPI has begun to expand into foreign countries through distributor agreements. This is different from its usual customer base of Canadian hospitals. Your preliminary discussions with the VP sales reveal that initial contacts with the distributors are made through foreign trade shows. He notes that before signing a deal, BPI does background and credit checks on the companies. However, the quality of information received varies by country.

3. Your review of foreign revenue reveals that BPI has entered into a distribution agreement with a Russian distributor for a five-year period commencing June 2019. BPI is quite excited about the agreement since the opportunities in Russia are vast—a significant portion of hospital medical equipment is worn and needs replacement. BPI believes this agreement has phenomenal prospects since the distributor is established and knows which hospitals are refurbishing and have money.

    As part of the agreement, the distributor has paid BPI an up-front and nonrefundable fee of $250 000. BPI has recorded the fee as part of its current revenue. As part of normal Russian business practice, the distributor pays the individual hospital administrator a commission for agreeing to purchase BPI products. Each month, the distributor will submit a list of individuals who have received the commission and BPI will reimburse the distributor the amount. Although no hospital sales have been finalized, the distributor has the promise of three separate administrators and has paid them each a commission of $5000. The distributor has requested that BPI reimburse it the $15 000.

4. In late August, BPI shipped 500 units (at a sale price of $650 per unit and a cost of $400 per unit) to the distributor so that the distributor may have stock on hand. BPI has recorded this shipment as a sale since part of the agreement is that the distributor pays for all goods received. You note that the Russian distributor balance is still outstanding as of December 31, 2018. The VP sales is not concerned since it is normal for BPI customers to pay anywhere between 30 and 60 days after receiving the invoice.

REQUIRED

a. Explain how the expansion of BPI to foreign markets impacts the audit strategy for Biomed Products.

b. The two key accounting issues are the upfront fee and the shipment of the 500 units in November. For each accounting issue perform the following:
   i Analyze the accounting issue.
   ii Identify the accounts and assertions most at risk related to this transaction. Provide your rationale.
   iii Provide one substantive audit procedure that would address the assertions at risk.

c. Explain the audit implications of the upfront commission payable to the Russian hospital administrators.

12-49 **5** **8** **9** It is October 21, 2018, and you, an audit manager at E&N LLP, are in charge of reviewing the audit engagement file of Eye in the Sky Inc., which has a year-end of July 31, 2018. Today you will be reviewing audit work performed by your colleague Peter on Eye's revenue section. Peter has been with E&N LLP for almost two years. He recently passed the CFE and this was his first time working on such a large and complex audit section.

Company Background

Eye is a privately controlled Canadian company that uses specialized drone technology to offer aerial imagery services for surveying and monitoring mining sites. The company also sells high-end specialized drones that customers can buy and use themselves. Most of Eye's customers are located in Africa and South America, where many new mines are currently under development.

Revenue – Significant Risks

Per the draft financial statements, total revenue for the year was $4 500 000. During planning, occurrence and cutoff of revenue and valuation of accounts receivable were identified as significant risks.

Completed Audit Work

1. On July 1, 2018, Big Dig, a mining company operating in Tajikistan, placed an order for 15 specialized drones equipped with infrared monitoring cameras. Each drone sells for about $75 000. The company was planning to use the drones to monitor its mines at night. Eye shipped the drones to Tajikistan on July 14, and they arrived in Dushanbe (capital city of Tajikistan) on July 25. The plan was to deliver the drones the next day to Big Dig's location in the Pamir Mountains. However, due to heavy rains, the road through the mountains flooded and the drones couldn't be delivered until August 4, 2018. Eye recognized revenue related to this sale when the drones landed in Dushanbe.

    As part of verifying cutoff of revenue, Peter wrote an email to Eye's sales manager asking him to confirm the date the drones were delivered to Big Dig. The manager replied that the drones were delivered on August 4. In his reply, the manager also wrote that he is currently away on a three-week vacation in Europe, but that from what he remembers the delivery term in the contract was FOB shipping point.

2. On July 29, Eye transferred an encrypted video file, containing surveillance images of potential mining sites, to one of its customers in Zimbabwe. For this work, Eye billed the customer $150 000. The customer wasn't able to open or use the file because Eye used an encryption key not compatible with the customer's computer system. After the customer reported the problem, Eye reformatted the file and sent it back on August 2, 2018.

As part of verifying the occurrence and cutoff of revenue, Peter obtained the contract related to this transaction and matched contract details such as price and customer information to the invoice. Peter also matched the invoice total of $150 000 to a deposit in Eye's September bank statement, as the customer had already paid for these services.

3. On June 25, Eye completed a mine surveying contract for a client operating in the El Caura region in Venezuela. Eye invoiced the customer $20 000 for the work. Due to strict Venezuelan banking rules enforced by President Maduro's government, payment to foreign companies that conduct work in Venezuela can only be made in local currency, the Venezuelan bolivar. Money transfers in Venezuelan bolivar and conversion of the bolivar into other currencies fall under international anti-money laundering rules governed by the International Monetary Fund (IMF). In the course of their investigations, the IMF places a 90-day freeze on all international currency conversions and transfers of the bolivar, only releasing the funds to the recipient after the 90-day freeze elapses.

Due to an unstable political situation, Venezuela's inflation rate in 2018 is estimated to have reached 1640%. This has had a significant effect on the exchange rate between the Venezuelan bolivar and the Canadian dollar.

As part of verifying the existence and valuation of accounts receivable, Peter sent a confirmation letter to the IMF to confirm the amount of funds subject to the 90-day freeze. The IMF responded back saying that it had 1 500 000 bolivars and that it will approve the conversion and transfer of the funds to Eye on September 23, 2018.

4. In March 2018, a company operating mines in Peru ordered 11 drones from Eye with an upgraded long-lasting battery. The battery can extend flight times between recharges by up to 50%. Eye shipped the drones in April 2018, but unfortunately five of the shipped drones were not equipped with the upgraded battery. In June 2018, the mining company sent the drones on a long-distance flight and the five deficient drones ran out of power and crashed in a remote mountainous region of Peru. The customer immediately informed Eye about the crash. In July 2018, Eye uncovered the shipping mistake through an internal investigation and issued a $95 000 refund to the customer the next month.

As part of verifying the occurrence and cutoff of revenue, Peter obtained Eye's August 2018 bank statement and searched for the refunded amount. He then vouched the amount to the credit note and the original contract.

5. In February 2018, Eye was hired by the King of Swaziland, Mswati III, to conduct drone surveillance of opposition group members. The King feared these members were trying to destabilize the country and overthrow him. A dispute arose when, having shipped too few drones to Swaziland, Eye was not able to carry out the surveillance to the extent that it promised to the King. The King now refuses to pay $300 000 for the work that Eye performed.

Despite the dispute, the King really liked Eye's drones and bought five of them for $375 000. Eye delivered the drones to the King in June 2018 and he paid for them in September 2018.

As part of verifying the existence and valuation of accounts receivable, Peter sent a confirmation letter to the King of Swaziland in early October. After waiting over two weeks for a response, Peter contacted the King's representative. The representative told him that the confirmation has been received; however, everyone is on a one-month holiday celebrating King Mswati III's birthday, and the confirmation won't be processed until late November. Peter couldn't wait that long, so he tested the existence and valuation of accounts receivable through an alternative procedure, looking at payments made by the King subsequent to year end. After finding the $375 000 payment on the September 2018 bank statement, Peter concluded that the entire $675 000 accounts receivable balance was stated correctly at year end.

REQUIRED

a. Review the audit work performed by Peter. For each of the five audit issues, discuss if the evidence he obtained is reliable and if his work related to the stated assertion.

b. Where applicable, suggest more reliable evidence that Peter should obtain and, if his work did not relate to the stated assertion, propose additional audit procedures.

12-50 **3** **5** Refer to Auditing in Action 12-5, which provides a brief overview of the restatement of Tesco's commercial income from its suppliers related to payments for the use of promotional space as well as various discounts and rebates. Go to Tesco's 2014 annual report at **https://www.tescoplc. com/media/264147/annual_report_14.pdf**. Access the 2014 auditor's report via the link provided.

REQUIRED

a. Read the Areas of Particular Audit Focus and explain (1) why commercial income was an area of focus (significant risk), and (2) the audit approach for that risk.

b. Based upon what you have read in the chapter, does the audit approach appear reasonable? Explain why.

c. Why do you think the auditors concluded that the financial statements were not materially misstated?

12-51 **3** **5** The Ontario Securities Commission (OSC) found that Zungui Haixi Corporation, a manufacturer of athletic footwear, apparel, accessories, and casual footwear based in China, had fraudulently overstated its revenue. The OSC also alleged the audit firm, Ernst & Young LLP (EY), failed on the Zungui Haixi audit for its role in the accounting violations. The OSC and EY subsequently reached a settlement agreement.

REQUIRED

a. Access the Statement of Allegations against EY at **https://www.osc.gov.on.ca/en/Proceedings_soa_20111107_zungui.htm**. Read the statement and briefly summarize the alleged revenue fraud.

b. Summarize the fraud risks identified by EY and the type of fraud procedures performed by EY in response to those risks.

c. Explain why the OSC alleged that EY failed to obtain sufficient and appropriate audit evidence regarding the CBI Reports for distributors and suppliers.

d. Explain why the OSC alleged that EY failed to exercise appropriate professional skepticism in its examination of accounts receivable confirmations.

e. Explain why an Initial Public Offering (IPO) audit is a higher risk audit and why the OSC alleged that EY did not adequately adjust its overall audit strategy for this higher risk.

AUDIT OF THE ACQUISITION AND PAYMENT CYCLE

STANDARDS REFERENCED IN THIS CHAPTER

Section 3061 – Property, plant, and equipment

IAS 16 – Property, plant, and equipment

IAS 37 – Provisions, contingent liabilities, and contingent assets

Organizations pay their bills in many different ways. Auditors need to be concerned, first of all, that only appropriate bills are recorded in the financial statements and none are omitted. In this chapter, we will look at these two basic questions in more detail.

LEARNING OBJECTIVES

After studying this chapter, you should be able to:

1. Identify the accounts and the classes of transactions in the acquisition and payment cycle.

2. Describe the major business functions, documents, and records in the acquisition and payment cycle.

3. Identify significant risks, and assess risk of material misstatement for the acquisition and payment cycle.

4. Understand key controls, and assess planned control risk for the acquisition and payment cycle.

5. Use professional judgment to develop an audit approach (strategy) for the acquisition and payment cycle.

6. Design and perform tests of control for the acquisition and payment cycle.

7. Design and perform substantive analytical procedures for accounts payable and accrued liabilities.

8. Design and perform substantive tests of details for accounts payable and accrued liabilities.

9. Determine the reliability of audit evidence for accounts payable.

10. Design and perform substantive tests (substantive analytical review and tests of details) for related-party transactions and selected accounts related to the acquisition and payment cycle.

False Purchases Camouflage Overstated Profits

Comptronix Corporation announced that senior members of its management team had overstated profits, and there would be material adjustments to the prior years' audited financial statements. Central to the fraud was the use of

continued >

fictitious purchases of large equipment items to overstate property, plant, and equipment and to hide fictitious sales.

The senior executives circumvented Comptronix's existing internal controls by bypassing the purchasing and receiving departments so that no one at Comptronix could discover the scheme. Comptronix employees usually created a fairly extensive paper trail for equipment purchases. Company internal controls over acquisition and cash disbursement transactions typically required a purchase order, receiving report, and vendor invoice before payment could be authorized by the chief operating officer or the controller/treasurer, but they were both participants in the fraud. As a result, the executives were able to bypass controls over cash disbursements and authorize payment for nonexistent purchases without creating any documents for the fictitious transactions.

The company also created fictitious sales and related receivables. The company issued cheques to pay for the false purchase transactions, which were then redeposited into the company's bank account and recorded as collections on the fictitious receivables. As a result, it appeared that the fictitious sales were collected, and that payments were made to support the false fixed asset purchases.

The fraud scheme grossly exaggerated the company's performance by reporting profits when the company was actually incurring losses. On the day that the public announcement of the fraud was made, Comptronix's common stock price declined abruptly by 72 percent! The SEC ultimately charged the executives with violating the antifraud provisions of the Securities Act of 1933 and the Securities Exchange Act of 1934. The SEC permanently barred the executives from serving as officers or directors of any public company, ordered them to repay bonuses and trading losses avoided, and imposed civil monetary penalties against them.

Source: Based on *Accounting and Auditing Enforcement Release No. 543*, Chicago: Commerce Clearing House, Inc.

We'll now discuss the acquisition and payment cycle. The acquisition of goods and services includes the acquisition of such things as raw materials, equipment, supplies, utilities, repairs and maintenance, and research and development. In the first part of the chapter, we'll discuss the significant risks in the cycle—particularly those related to accounts payable, the account through which acquisition and payment transactions typically flow. We will then consider assessing control risk and designing tests of controls and substantive tests of transactions for the classes of transactions in the acquisition and payment cycle. Then we'll cover performing substantive tests for accounts payable and accrued liabilities followed by related party transactions and selected accounts typically associated with transactions in the acquisition and payment cycle

AN OVERVIEW OF THE ACQUISITION AND PAYMENT CYCLE

LO 1 Identify the accounts and the classes of transactions in the acquisition and payment cycle.

Acquisition and payment cycle—the transaction cycle that includes the acquisition of and payment for goods and services from suppliers outside the organization.

The **acquisition and payment cycle** involves the decisions and processes necessary for obtaining the goods and services for operating a business. The cycle typically begins with the initiation of a purchase requisition by an authorized employee who needs the goods or services and ends with payment for the benefits received. Although the topics that follow deal with a small manufacturing company that makes tangible products for sale to third parties, the same principles apply to a service company, a government unit, or any other type of organization. An overview of the acquisition and payment cycle is presented in Table 13-1.

Table 13-1	Classes of Transactions, Accounts, Business Functions, and Related Documents and Records for the Acquisition and Payment Cycle		
Classes of Transactions	**Accounts**	**Business Functions**	**Documents and Records**
Acquisitions	Inventory	Processing purchase orders	Purchase requisition
	Property, plant, and equipment; Purchase orders; Prepaid expenses; Leasehold improvements	Receiving goods and services	Receiving report
	Accounts payable	Recognizing the liability	Vendor's invoice
	Manufacturing expenses		Debit memo
	Selling expenses; Administrative expenses		Voucher; Acquisitions transaction file; Acquisitions journal or listing; Accounts payable master file; Accounts payable trial balance; Vendor's statement
Cash disbursements	Cash in bank (from cash disbursements)	Processing and recording cash disbursements	Cheque or electronic payment
	Accounts payable		Cash disbursements transaction file
	Purchase discounts		Cash disbursements journal or listing

THE FOUR BUSINESS FUNCTIONS AND THEIR DOCUMENTS AND RECORDS

Next, we examine in more detail each of the four business functions, paying particular attention to the typical documents and records used. These are listed in the fourth column of Table 13-1.

Processing Purchase Orders

The request for goods or services by the client's personnel is the starting point for the cycle. The exact form of the request and the required approval depend on the nature of the goods and services and company policy. Common documents include the purchase requisition and purchase order.

Purchase Requisition A purchase requisition is used to request goods and services by an authorized employee. This may take the form of a request for such acquisitions as materials by production staff or the storeroom supervisor, outside repairs by office or plant personnel, or insurance by the vice president in charge of property and equipment. Companies often rely on prespecified reorder points used by the computer to initiate inventory purchase requisitions automatically.

Purchase Order A purchase order is a document used to order goods and services from vendors. It includes the description, quantity, and related information for goods and services the company intends to purchase, and is often used to indicate authorization of the acquisition. Companies often submit purchase orders electronically to vendors who have made arrangements for electronic data interchange (EDI).

Receiving Goods and Services

The receipt by the company of goods or services from the vendor is a critical point in the cycle because it is when most companies first recognize the acquisition and related liability on their records. When goods are received, adequate control requires examination for description, quantity, timely arrival, and condition. A receiving report is a paper or electronic document prepared at the time goods are received. It includes a description of the goods, the quantity received, the date received, and other relevant data.

Recognizing the Liability

The proper recognition of the liability for the receipt of goods and services requires *prompt and accurate* recording. The initial recording affects the financial statements and the actual cash disbursement; therefore, companies must take care to include all acquisition transactions, only acquisitions that occurred, and at the correct amounts. Common documents and records include the vendor's invoice, the debit memo, the voucher, the acquisitions transaction file, the acquisitions journal or listing, the accounts payable master file, the accounts payable trial balance, and the vendor's statement.

Vendor's Invoice A vendor's invoice is a document received from the vendor that shows the amount owed for an acquisition. It indicates the description and quantity of goods and services received, price (including freight), cash discount terms, date of the billing, and total amount. The vendor's invoice is important because it indicates the amount recorded in the acquisition transaction file. For companies using EDI, the vendor's invoice is transmitted electronically, which affects how the auditor evaluates evidence.

Debit Memo A debit memo is also a document received from the vendor and indicates a reduction in the amount owed to the vendor because of returned goods or an allowance granted. It often takes the same form as a vendor's invoice, but it supports reductions in accounts payable rather than increases.

Voucher A voucher is commonly used by organizations to establish a formal means of recording and controlling acquisitions, primarily by enabling each acquisition transaction to be sequentially numbered. Vouchers include a cover sheet or folder for containing documents and a package of relevant documents such as the purchase order, a copy of the packing slip, the receiving report, and the vendor's invoice. After payment, a copy of the cheque or electronic funds transfer is added to the voucher package.

Acquisitions Transaction File This is a computer-generated file that includes all acquisition transactions processed by the accounting system for a period, such as a day, week, or month. It contains all information entered into the system and includes information for each transaction, such as vendor name, date, amount, account classification or classifications, and description and quantity of goods and services purchased. The file can also include purchase returns and allowances or there can be a separate file for those transactions. Depending on the company's needs, the information in the acquisitions transaction file is used for a variety of records, listings, or reports, such as an acquisitions journal, accounts payable master file, and transactions for a certain account balance or division.

Acquisitions Journal or Listing The acquisitions journal or listing, often referred to as the purchases journal, is generated from the acquisitions transaction file and typically includes the vendor name, date, amount, and account classification or classifications for each transaction, such as repair and maintenance, inventory, or utilities. It also identifies whether the acquisition was for cash or accounts payable. The journal or listing can cover any time period, typically a month. The journal or listing includes totals of every account number included for the time period. The same transactions included in the journal or listing are also posted simultaneously to the general ledger and, if they are on account, to the accounts payable master file.

Accounts Payable Master File An accounts payable master file records acquisitions, cash disbursements, and acquisition returns and allowances transactions for each vendor. The master file is updated from the acquisition, returns and allowances, and cash disbursement computer transaction files. The total of the individual account balances in the master file equals the total balance of accounts payable in the general ledger. A printout of the accounts payable master file shows, by vendor, the beginning balance in accounts payable; each acquisition, acquisition return, acquisition allowance, and cash disbursement; and the ending balance. Many companies do not maintain an accounts payable master file by vendor. These companies pay on the basis of individual vendors' invoices. Therefore, the total of unpaid vendors' invoices in the master file equals total accounts payable.

Accounts Payable Trial Balance An accounts payable trial balance listing includes the amount owed to each vendor or for each invoice or voucher at a point in time. It is prepared directly from the accounts payable master file.

Vendor's Statement A vendor's statement is a document prepared monthly by the vendor and indicates the beginning balance, acquisitions, returns and allowances, payments to the vendor, and ending balance. These balances and activities are the vendor's representations of the transactions for the period, not the client's. Except for disputed amounts and timing differences, the client's accounts payable master file should be the same as the vendor's statement.

Processing and Recording Cash Disbursements

The payment for goods and services represents a significant activity for all entities. This activity directly reduces balances in liability accounts, particularly accounts payable. Documents associated with the disbursement process that auditors examine include the cheque, the cash disbursements transaction file, and the cash disbursements journal or listing.

Cheque This document is commonly used to pay for the acquisition when payment is due. Most companies use computer-prepared cheques based on information included in the acquisition transactions file at the time goods and services are received. Cheques are typically prepared in a multi-copy format, with the original going to the payee, one copy filed with the vendor's invoice and other supporting documents, and another filed numerically. In most cases, individual cheques are recorded in a cash disbursements transaction file.

After a cheque is signed by an authorized person, it is an asset. Therefore, signed cheques should be mailed by the signer or a person under the signer's control. When cashed by the vendor and cleared by the client's bank, the cheque is called a *cancelled cheque*. At this point it is no longer an asset, but is now a document. In many EDI arrangements, the company submits payments to the vendor electronically through an electronic funds transfer (EFT) between the company's bank and the vendor's bank.

Cash Disbursements Transaction File This is a computer-generated file that includes all cash disbursements transactions processed by the accounting system for a period, such as a day, week, or month. It includes the same type of information discussed for the acquisitions transaction file.

Cash Disbursements Journal or Listing This is a listing or report generated from the cash disbursements transaction file that includes all transactions for any time period. The same transactions, including all relevant information, are included in the accounts payable master file and general ledger.

An Overview of the Audit Process for the Acquisition and Payment Cycle

Figure 13-1 provides an overview of the audit process of the acquisition and payment cycle.

As highlighted in Table 13-1, several classes of transactions related to the acquisition and payment cycle represent major expenses incurred by the organization, and thus constitute a major component in determining net income. The transactions also relate to the acquisition of major classes of assets such as inventory and property, plant, and equipment.

Figure 13-1	Summary of the Audit Process for the Acquisition and Payment Cycle

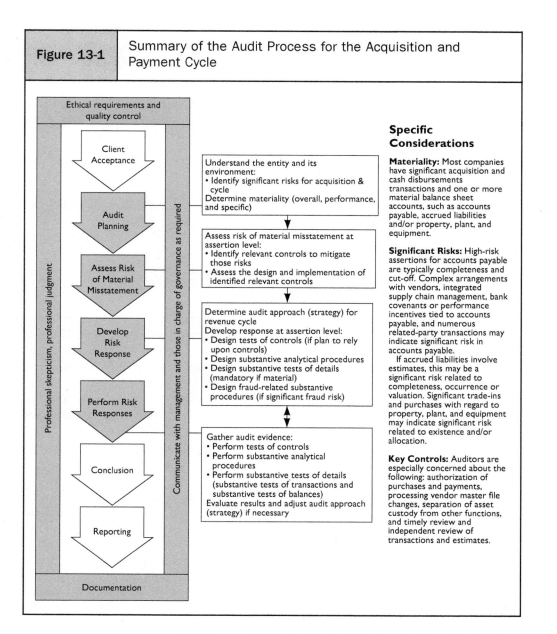

Specific Considerations

Materiality: Most companies have significant acquisition and cash disbursements transactions and one or more material balance sheet accounts, such as accounts payable, accrued liabilities and/or property, plant, and equipment.

Significant Risks: High-risk assertions for accounts payable are typically completeness and cut-off. Complex arrangements with vendors, integrated supply chain management, bank covenants or performance incentives tied to accounts payable, and numerous related-party transactions may indicate significant risk in accounts payable.

If accrued liabilities involve estimates, this may be a significant risk related to completeness, occurrence or valuation. Significant trade-ins and purchases with regard to property, plant, and equipment may indicate significant risk related to existence and/or allocation.

Key Controls: Auditors are especially concerned about the following: authorization of purchases and payments, processing vendor master file changes, separation of asset custody from other functions, and timely review and independent review of transactions and estimates.

IDENTIFY SIGNIFICANT RISKS AND ASSESS RISK OF MATERIAL MISSTATEMENT

When performing risk assessment procedures, the auditor gathers information that helps to assess significant risk at the financial statement level, as well as the account and assertion level. Once these risks have been identified, the auditor can determine the appropriate risk response. With regard to accounts payable and accrued liabilities, auditors are especially concerned about the completeness and cutoff balance-related audit objectives because of the potential for understatements in the account balance.

Identify Significant Risks

In identifying significant risks, the auditor should consider pervasive risk factors that could motivate management to misstate expenditures (which affect the completeness assertion for both payables and expenses). Examples of such pervasive risk factors include the following situations:

- The client's bank covenants or performance incentives are tied to accounts payable and/or related accounts (e.g., current ratio and/or net income).
- The client is facing ongoing liquidity problems or going concern doubts that may pressure management to understate payables in order to maintain a higher working capital.

These pervasive factors mainly pertain to the completeness assertion. The significant risks in accounts payable and related accounts will vary from organization to organization. Below are other potential significant risk factors related to accounts payable and accrued liabilities:

- The client has complex arrangements with vendors (such as chargebacks and allowances): this affects many assertions.
- The client has integrated supply chain management: this affects many assertions.
- A high volume of transactions affects many assertions.
- The client has numerous related-party transactions: this affects occurrence and valuation assertions.

Identify and Assess Fraud Risk

As in other cycles, a client could make data entry errors, such as recording amounts in the wrong periods or to wrong subledger accounts (wrong vendors). Table 13-2 lists examples of major risks of error or fraud in this cycle. Cases of fraudulent financial reporting involving accounts payable are relatively common, although less frequent than frauds involving inventory or accounts receivable. As Table 13-2 points out, the bias in recording accounts payable is often understatement (assuming profit maximization). This can be accomplished by not recording accounts payable until the subsequent period (cutoff and completeness assertions) or by recording fictitious reductions to accounts payable (completeness). When the relevant assertion is completeness, it is more difficult for the auditor because there is no audit trail (remember that the auditor is auditing for what is not there).

Companies often have complex arrangements with suppliers, which result in reductions to accounts payable for advertising credits and other allowances. These arrangements may not be as well documented as acquisition transactions. Some companies have used fictitious reductions to accounts payable to overstate net income. Auditors should read agreements with suppliers when amounts are material and make sure the financial statements reflect the substance of the agreements.

Many frauds in the acquisitions area are misappropriation of assets. A common fraud is for the perpetrator to issue payments to fictitious vendors and deposit the

Table 13-2	Examples of Major Risks of Error or Fraud in the Acquisition and Payment Cycle	
Risks of Error	**Risks of Misappropriation of Assets, Other Fraud, or Illegal Acts**	**Risks of Inadequate Disclosure or Incorrect Presentation of Financial Information, Including Fraudulent Financial Reporting**
	Deliberately recording accounts payable in the next period.	
Amounts posted to accounts payable are for goods in transit where shipping terms indicate that the risks and rewards of ownership have not yet passed to the entity.		Omitting disclosure of a related-party transaction.
	Use fictitious vendor allowances to reduce accounts payable.	
Provisions are understated because a provision has not been recorded.		Understating provision, which can understate net income Omitting disclosure of a contingent liability
	Issue payments to fictitious vendors and steal the funds.	
Payments are posted to the wrong vendor account.		Incorrect disclosures relating to various components of plant, property, and equipment.
	Theft of property, plant, and equipment, such as portable computing equipment.	
Incorrect rates used to amortize plant, property, and equipment.		Incorrect and confusing information disclosed about vendor allowances.

cheques in a fictitious account. These frauds can be prevented by allowing payments to be made only to approved vendors and by having authorized personnel carefully scrutinize documentation supporting the acquisitions before payments are made. However, some are able to work around this type of control by issuing payments that are below approval amounts. Auditors can use GAS (generalized audit software) to devise tests that identify patterns for such transactions (a search by employee and amount).

In other misappropriation cases, the accounts payable clerk or another employee steals a cheque to a legitimate vendor. The purchases information is then resubmitted for payment to the vendor. Such fraud can be prevented by cancelling supporting documents to prevent their being used to support multiple payments. Other frauds involve corruption, such as the bid-rigging and kickback schemes described in Auditing in Action 13-1. The success of such schemes is based upon collusion between the employee and the vendor, which is much more difficult to detect.

Property, plant, and equipment, also called fixed assets, represents a large balance sheet account for many companies and are often based on subjectively determined valuations. As a result, property, plant, and equipment may be a target for financial statement manipulation, especially for companies without material receivables or inventories. For example, companies may capitalize repairs or other operating expenses as property, plant, and equipment. Such frauds could be detected if the auditor examines evidence supporting additions to property, plant, and equipment. Because of their value and saleability, property, plant, and equipment are also targets for theft. This is especially true for items that are readily portable, such as laptop computers. To reduce the potential for theft, such fixed assets should be physically protected whenever possible, engraved or otherwise permanently labelled, and periodically inventoried.

Table 13-2 summarizes a selection of major risks of error and fraud in the acquisition and payment cycle.

An Apple Computer manager, Paul Shin Devine, was sentenced to one year in prison and required to pay restitution of $4.2 million for receiving $2.4 million in kickbacks from Asian suppliers of iPhone and iPod accessories. The manager transmitted confidential information to the suppliers, which allowed them to negotiate favourable contracts with Apple.

The contact within the supplier, who was related to Devine by marriage, was charged in Singapore for "corruptly giving gratifications" to Devine. Apple found cached files on Devine's laptop related to emails. According to the court documents, he and his contact kept a detailed spreadsheet of their payments, and that spreadsheet was among the files found in the email cache.

The kickback scheme involved a chain of U.S. and foreign bank accounts, as well as a front company to receive payments.

The manager reportedly opened bank accounts in several countries in Asia to receive the kickbacks, and also received payments directly when travelling to Asia. The payments were referred to by code words such as "sample" to avoid detection by co-workers.

Sources: Pete Carey, "Apple manager indicted in kickback scheme," *San Jose Mercury News*, August 13, 2010. Bryan Chaffin, "Email cache alerted Apple, provided details of kickback scheme," *The Mac Observer*, August 17, 2010, accessed September 12, 2017, at **https://www.macobserver.com/tmo/article/e-mail_cache_alerted_apple_provided_details_of_kickback_scheme**. Brandon Lowrey, "Ex Apple exec gets 1 year, pays $4.5 million in kickback scheme," *Law 360*, December 4, 2014, accessed September 12, 2017, at **https://www.law360.com/articles/601818/ex-apple-exec-gets-1-year-pays-4-5m-in-kickback-scheme**.

Assess Inherent Risk for Accounts Payable and Accrued Liabilities

In order to be able to assess inherent risk for accounts payable and accrued liabilities, the auditor must be knowledgeable about the client's supply chain and contractual arrangements with its suppliers and vendors. The recent focus by many companies on improving their supply chain management activities has led to numerous changes in the design of systems used to initiate and record acquisition and payment activities. Efforts to streamline the purchasing of goods and services—including greater emphasis on just-in-time inventory purchasing, increased sharing of information with suppliers, and the use of technology and ecommerce to transact business—are changing all aspects of the acquisition and payment cycle for many companies. These arrangements and systems can be complex.

Significant client business risks may arise from these changes. For example, suppliers may have greater access to accounts payable records, allowing them to continually monitor the status of payable balances and to perform detailed reconciliations of transactions. Access by external parties (such as suppliers) to accounting records threatens the likelihood of misstatement if that access is not properly controlled. Also, increased focus on improving the logistics of physically moving inventory throughout a company's distribution chain may increase the difficulty of establishing effective cutoff of accounts payable balances at year-end. The auditor needs to understand the nature of changes to these systems to identify whether client business risks and related management controls affect the likelihood of material misstatements in accounts payable.

Assess Inherent Risk for Other Accounts Related to the Cycle

Other significant accounts in the cycle that we will discuss in this chapter are accruals and/or provisions, and property, plant, and equipment. Factors that increase inherent risk for those accounts include the following:

- Provisions require considerable judgment: this affects valuation and completeness;
- A high volume of disposals and additions to property, plant and equipment affects classification and valuation assertions; and
- There is considerable judgment regarding whether a cost should be capitalized or expensed, which affects the classification assertion.

Recognition and Measurement of Payables, Accruals, and Provisions Accounts payable are unpaid obligations (liabilities) for goods and services received in the ordinary course of business. It is sometimes difficult to distinguish between accounts payable and accrued liabilities for classification on the financial statements. The account payable is a liability if the total amount of the obligation is known and owed at the balance sheet date. The accounts payable account then includes obligations for the acquisition of raw materials, equipment, utilities, repairs, and many other types of goods and services that were received before the end of the year and will be paid in the next fiscal year.

IFRS and ASPE measure and recognize accruals and provisions somewhat differently. Under both GAAPs, an obligation is an accrued liability if a reliable estimate of the amount due can be made. Under ASPE, an obligation is recognized if there is a "likely" probability that a payment will be required. Under IAS 37, an obligation is recognized if there is a "more than likely" probability and there is either a legal or "constructive" obligation (which represents valid expectation). However, IFRS makes a distinction between the classification of accruals and provisions. Obligations that have a high degree of certainty would be recognized and reported as payables and accruals. This would include legal obligations such as trade payables, and constructive obligations such as unpaid holiday bonuses, which were promised but not yet paid. However, obligations with a lower degree of certainty, but that are still more than likely, would be recognized and reported as provisions. This could include legal obligations such as a contested lawsuit or constructive obligations such as warranties.

UNDERSTAND INTERNAL CONTROL AND ASSESS CONTROL RISK

LO 4 Understand key controls, and assess planned control risk for the acquisition and payment cycle.

The same process that was introduced in Chapter 12 (see Figure 12-5), for understanding controls and assessing planned control risk in relation to the revenue cycle also applies to the acquisition and payment cycle. The auditor gains an understanding of internal control for the acquisition and payment cycle as part of performing risk assessment procedures by studying clients' flowcharts, reviewing internal control questionnaires, and performing walk-through tests for acquisitions and cash payment transactions. The auditor will use that documentation to assess the effectiveness of controls. The auditor will also take into account whether it is cost-effective to test controls. When control risk is assessed to be less than high, tests of controls will be included in the audit strategy (this is referred to as a combined strategy).

The key controls for each of the business functions that we discussed in the overview of the cycle are examined below.

Authorization of Purchases

Proper authorization for acquisitions and changes to the vendor master file (such as adding a new vendor) is an essential part of this function because it ensures that the goods and services acquired are for authorized company purposes, and it avoids the acquisition of excessive and unnecessary items. Most companies permit general authorization for the acquisition of regular operating needs, such as inventory at one level and acquisitions of capital assets or similar items at another. For example, acquisitions of capital assets in excess of a specified dollar limit may require board of directors' action. Items acquired relatively infrequently, such as insurance policies and long-term service contracts, are approved by certain officers. As illustrated in Auditing in Action 13-2, employee expense reimbursements require specific authorization and monitoring.

Supplies and services costing less than a designated amount are approved by supervisors and department heads, and some types of raw materials and supplies are reordered automatically whenever they fall to a predetermined level, often by direct communication with vendors' computers. Where automatic purchase orders are generated, care must be taken to ensure that reorder points are monitored so that only those goods still required by the company are purchased. For good internal control, the purchasing department should not be responsible for authorizing the acquisition or receiving the goods.

In addition to these controls, it is important to have a monthly reconciliation of vendors' statements with recorded liabilities and of the outstanding unpaid invoice transaction file with the vendor master file and the general ledger. This should be done by an independent person or using computer software.

Processing Vendor Master File Changes

New suppliers should undergo a credit check while other suppliers should be subject to periodic review for quality of service, product, delivery times, and other criteria approved by management. Then, after approval, new suppliers can be added to the supplier master file. The master file change forms should be independently approved (i.e., not by someone who approves payments, to prevent establishment of fictitious companies) and the data entry independently verified.

Timely Recording and Independent Review of Transactions

The accounts payable department should have processes in place to ensure liabilities are recorded on a timely basis. The department should be also responsible for verifying the appropriateness of the transactions. Either an individual or the computer should match documents and verify invoice accuracy. An important control is to require that the persons who make acquisitions do not have access to cash, marketable securities, and other assets.

Authorization of Payments

The most important controls in the cash disbursements function include the following:

- The signing of cheques (or authorization of payment release) by an individual with proper authority;
- Separation of responsibilities for approving the payments and performing the accounts payable function;

- Careful examination of the supporting documents by the cheque signer at the time the cheque is signed; and
- Use of a password (preferably two different passwords by two people) before electronic payments are released.

The cheques should be prenumbered and printed on special paper that makes it difficult to alter the payee or amount. Care should be taken to provide physical control over blank, voided, and signed cheques. It is also important to have a method of cancelling the supporting documents to prevent their reuse as support for another cheque at a later time. A common method is to mark the documents as "entered" when recorded in the computer system and to write the cheque number or electronic payment number on the supporting documents when payments are made.

DETERMINE AUDIT APPROACH (STRATEGY) FOR ACQUISITION AND PAYMENT CYCLE

LO **5** Use professional judgment to develop an audit approach (strategy) for the acquisition and payment cycle.

The audit strategy depends upon the significant risks and the extent to which the auditor relies upon internal controls. Auditing in Action 13-3 highlights why accounts payables and accruals are often a significant risk for not-for-profit organizations and

AUDITING IN ACTION 13-3
Accounts Payable and Accruals—Significant Risks in Not-For-Profit Organizations

The financial statement users of not-for-profit organizations and municipalities often pay particular attention to the reported surplus. For example, consider a not-for-profit organization that is heavily dependent upon provincial government funding. If the organization is under budget, management may be biased to understate the surplus and overstate expenses for fear that the following year's funding will be reduced. However, others, such as Frimley Health NHS Foundation Trust, a hospital and health

services provider in London, England, may be motivated to overstate the surplus in order to demonstrate fiscal responsibility to the government's Department of Health (the main source of its funds).

The excerpt below, derived from Frimley Health's auditor's report for the year ended March 31, 2016, summarizes PWC's assessment of significant risks related to accounts payable and accruals, as well as its audit approach to those risks.

Assessment of Significant Risks—Accounts Payable and Accruals	
We have judged there to be a significant audit risk that expenditure may be understated to improve the reported surplus. We considered the risk of misstatement in expenditure recognition and judged this to be more prevalent at the year-end, when attempts to fraudulently manipulate the financial statements may be made on the basis of the Trust's expected financial position. The transactions posted in the final month of the year are also routinely subject to greater levels of estimate, particularly accruals and provisions, where third-party supporting documentation such as supplier invoices may not be available.	
Key Areas of Audit Focus	**Audit Approach**
Management estimates (expenditure accruals and provisions)	We evaluated the accounting estimates for accruals and provisions and the basis of their calculation by assessing the amounts recognized against relevant information available from third parties, including agreements with suppliers and subsequent purchase invoices.
Timing of expenditure other than salaries, depreciation, and interest, whereby costs related to 2015–2016 could be inappropriately deferred to 2016–2017	We tested a sample of expenditure transactions recognized either side of the year-end to check that the amounts recognized in 2015–2016 are accurate. In order to determine the accounting periods that each sampled transaction related to, we traced (where applicable) to: • Expenditure contracts • Purchase invoices • Goods receipts documentation
Manipulation of journal postings to reduce reported expenditure	We used data analysis techniques to identify the journals impacting revenue and expenditure recognition that we judged had higher risk characteristics and tested them to supporting information. No evidence of incorrect recognition of revenue or of misstatements of expenditure were identified from the journals tested.

Source: Frimley Health NHS Foundation Trust, *Annual Reports and Accounts 2015–2016.*

provides an example of the audit approach for Frimley Health NHS Foundation Trust, a large not-for-profit organization that provides hospital and health care services in London, England.

In the case discussed in Auditing in Action 13-3, the auditors concluded that the two high-risk assertions were completeness and cutoff. In the first area of focus, accruals and provisions, the auditors considered the existence assertion to be high risk due to greater estimation uncertainty given the lack of availability of some third-party documentation. In the second area, the auditors describe the extensive substantive tests of details to test the cutoff assertion as well as accuracy. The third area highlights the auditors' use of data analytics to identify unusual journal entries.

LO 6 Design and perform tests of control for the acquisition and payment cycle.

DESIGN AND PERFORM TESTS OF CONTROLS FOR ACQUISITION AND PAYMENT CYCLE

In a typical audit, the most time-consuming accounts to verify by tests of details of balances are accounts receivable, inventory, capital assets, accounts payable, and expense accounts. Of these five, all but accounts receivable are directly related to the acquisition and payment cycle. The audit time saved can be dramatic if the auditor can reduce tests of details by using tests of controls to verify the effectiveness of internal controls for acquisitions and cash disbursements.

Tests of controls for the acquisition and payment cycle are divided into two broad areas: tests of acquisitions and tests of payments. Acquisition tests concern four of the five functions discussed earlier in the chapter: processing purchase orders, vendor master file changes, receiving goods and services, and recognizing the liability. Tests of payments concern the fifth function, processing and recording cash disbursements.

The five transaction-related audit objectives (assertions) are used as the frame of reference for designing tests of controls for acquisition and cash disbursement transactions. For each objective, the auditor must go through the same logical process that has been discussed in previous chapters. First, the auditor must understand the general controls applicable to the cycle and the cycle's internal controls to determine which controls exist and assess their design effectiveness. Then, an initial assessment of control risk and risk of material misstatement can be made for each objective. The auditor must decide which controls to test to satisfy the initial assessment of control risk. After the auditor has developed the audit procedures for each objective, the procedures can be combined into an audit program that can be efficiently performed. Four of the audit objectives for acquisitions deserve special attention, and a discussion of each of these objectives follows:

- *Recorded acquisitions are for goods and services received, consistent with the best interests of the client (occurrence).* If the auditor is satisfied that the controls are adequate for this objective, substantive tests for improper and nonexistent transactions can be greatly reduced. In some instances, improper transactions can be readily identified, such as the acquisition of unauthorized personal items by employees or the actual embezzlement of cash by recording a duplicate purchase in the purchases journal. Others are more difficult to evaluate, such as the payment of officers' memberships in country clubs, expense-paid vacations to foreign countries for members of management and their families, and management-approved illegal payments to officials of foreign countries. If the controls over improper and nonexistent transactions are inadequate, extensive examination of supporting documentation is necessary.
- *Existing acquisitions are recorded (completeness).* Failure to record the acquisition of goods and services received directly affects the balance in accounts payable and may result in an overstatement of net income and owners' equity. Because of this, auditors are usually very concerned about the completeness objective.

- *Acquisitions are accurately recorded (accuracy).* The controls over the acquisitions included in the perpetual records are normally tested as part of the tests of controls for acquisitions, and the controls over this objective play a key role in the audit. The inclusion of both quantity and unit costs in the inventory perpetual records permits a reduction in the tests of the physical count and the unit costs of inventory if the controls are operating effectively. As another example, if the auditor has found that controls over the accuracy of capital assets are good, it is acceptable to test fewer current period acquisitions.
- *Acquisitions are correctly classified (classification).* Since performing documentation tests of current-period capital asset acquisitions and expense accounts for accuracy are relatively time-consuming audit procedures, if reliance on controls is possible, the saving in audit time can be significant.

CONCEPT CHECK

C13-3 How do high-quality perpetual records affect the auditor's tests of controls of inventory acquisitions?

C13-4 Provide examples of two controls that improve completeness over recording of acquisitions transactions.

Once the auditor has decided on audit procedures, the acquisitions and cash disbursements tests are typically performed concurrently. For example, for a transaction selected for examination from the acquisitions journal, the vendor's invoice and the receiving report are examined at the same time as the related cancelled cheque or direct deposit payment record. Table 13-3 summarizes transaction-related audit objectives, key controls, and tests of controls and substantive tests of transactions for acquisitions.

Table 13-3	Summary of Transaction-Related Audit Objectives, Key Controls, and Tests of Controls and Substantive Tests of Transactions for Acquisitions		
Transaction-Related Audit Objective	**Key Internal Control**	**Common Tests of Controls**	**Common Substantive Tests of Transactions**
Recorded acquisitions are for goods and services received, consistent with the best interests of the client (occurrence).	Existence of purchase requisition, purchase order, receiving report, and vendor's invoice attached to the voucher.[†] Approval of acquisitions at the proper level. Cancellation of documents to prevent their reuse.	Inspect supporting documents for existence and match details (e.g., quantity, description, and amount). Inspect invoice for indication of approval. Inspect invoice for indication of cancellation.	Review the acquisitions journal, general ledger, and transaction files for large or unusual amounts.[*] Inspect underlying documents for reasonableness and authenticity (vendors' invoices, receiving reports, purchase orders, and requisitions). Trace inventory purchase details to inventory files.
	Independent verification of vendors' invoices, receiving reports, purchase orders, and purchase requisitions.[†] New vendors and changes to vendor file approved. Vendor master file independently examined periodically.	Inspect invoice for indication of independent verification.[‡] Inspect master file change forms for approval; trace details to vendor master file. Discuss review and approval process with management.	Physically inspect capital assets acquired. Inspect vendor master file for unusual credit terms, prices, or post office box addresses.[‡]
Existing acquisition transactions are recorded (completeness).	Purchase orders are prenumbered and accounted for. Receiving reports are prenumbered and accounted for.[†]	Account for a sequence of purchase orders.[‡] Account for a sequence of receiving reports.[‡]	Trace from a file of vendors' invoices to the acquisitions journal. Trace from a file of receiving reports to the acquisitions journal.[†]

(continued)

Transaction-Related Audit Objective	Key Internal Control	Common Tests of Controls	Common Substantive Tests of Transactions
Recorded acquisition transactions are correct (accuracy).	Batch totals are compared with computer summary reports.	Examine file of batch totals for initials of data control clerk; compare totals to summary reports.‡	Compare recorded transactions in the acquisitions journal with the vendor's invoice, receiving report, and other supporting documentation.†‡
	Approval of acquisitions for prices and discounts.	Inspect for indication of approval.	Recompute the clerical accuracy on the vendors' invoices, including discounts and freight.‡
	Independent verification of calculations and amounts.	Inspect for indication of internal verification.‡	Test clerical accuracy by footing the journals and tracing postings to general ledger and accounts payable and inventory master files.‡
	Comparison of accounts payable master file or trial balance totals with general ledger balance.	Inspect initials on general ledger summary reports indicating comparison.	
Acquisition transactions are recorded on the correct dates (cutoff).	Procedures require that transactions be recorded as soon as possible after the goods and services have been received.	Inspect procedures manual; observe whether unrecorded vendors' invoices exist.	Compare dates of receiving reports and vendors' invoices with dates in the acquisitions journal.†
	Transaction date must be system date (today's date) or a reasonable date.	Observe data entry process and dates used.	
Acquisition transactions are properly classified (classification).	Adequate chart of accounts. Automatic updates of and posting to general ledger accounts.	Inspect procedures manual and chart of accounts. Enter test transactions or observe entry; trace to correct file.	Compare classification with chart of accounts by reference to vendors' invoices.

* This analytical procedure can also apply to other objectives, including completeness, valuation, and cutoff.

† Receiving reports are used only for tangible goods and are therefore not available for services, such as utilities or repairs and maintenance. Frequently, vendors' invoices are the only documentation available.

‡ This control would be tested on many audits by using a computer.

Because of the importance of tests of controls for acquisitions and cash disbursements, the use of attribute sampling is common in this audit area. Many of the types of errors or fraud and other irregularities that may be found in this cycle represent a misstatement of earnings and are of significant concern to the auditor. For example, there may be inventory cutoff misstatements or an incorrect recording of an expense amount. Because of this, the tolerable exception rate selected by the auditor in tests of many of the attributes in this cycle is relatively low. Since the dollar amounts of individual transactions in the cycle cover a wide range, it is also common to segregate very large and unusual items and to test them on a 100 percent basis.

LO **7** Design and perform substantive analytical procedures for accounts payable and accrued liabilities.

DESIGN AND PERFORM SUBSTANTIVE ANALYTICAL PROCEDURES FOR ACCOUNTS PAYABLE AND RELATED ACCOUNTS

The use of analytical procedures is as important in the acquisition and payment cycle as it is in every other cycle. Table 13-4 illustrates several substantive analytical procedures for the balance sheet and income statement accounts in the acquisition and

Table 13-4	Substantive Analytical Procedures for the Acquisition and Payment Cycle

Substantive Analytical Procedure	Possible Misstatement
Compare acquisition-related expense account balances with prior years.	Misstatement of accounts payable and expenses.
Compare the ratio of expense account balances to sales in current and prior years.	An unusually low expense account may indicate an unrecorded liability.
Calculate ratios such as purchases divided by accounts payable, and accounts payable divided by current liabilities.	Unrecorded or nonexistent accounts payable, or misstatements.
Inspect list of accounts payable for unusual, nonvendor, and interest-bearing payables.	Classification misstatement for nontrade liabilities.
Compare individual accounts payable with previous years.	Unrecorded or nonexistent accounts payable, or misstatements.

payment cycle that are useful for uncovering areas in which additional investigation is desirable.

Important analytical procedures for uncovering misstatements of accounts payable include comparing current-year expense totals with those of prior years and comparing the ratio of expense account balances to sales in current and prior years. For example, by comparing current utilities expenses with that of prior years, the auditor may determine that the last utilities bill for the year was not recorded. Comparing expenses with those of prior years is an effective analytical procedure for accounts payable if income is relatively stable. It is also very effective for relatively stable expense accounts, such as rent, utilities, and other expenses billed on a regular basis.

DESIGN AND PERFORM TESTS OF DETAILS OF ACCOUNTS PAYABLE AND ACCRUED LIABILITIES

LO 8 Design and perform substantive tests of details for accounts payable and accrued liabilities.

The overall objective in the audit of accounts payable is to determine if the accounts payable balance is fairly stated and properly disclosed. Figure 13-2 provides an overview of the most common substantive tests of details for accounts payable. The actual audit procedures will vary considerably depending on the nature of the entity, the materiality of accounts payable, the nature and effectiveness of internal controls, and inherent risk.

When reviewing the substantive tests of details for accounts payable compared to those for accounts receivable, you will note that the emphasis is on understatement or omitted liabilities, whereas for accounts receivable it is overstatement that is emphasized. The difference in emphasis in auditing assets and liabilities is based upon the assumption that management is motivated to overstate net income. This means that when auditing liabilities, the auditor looks primarily for understatements, which usually have the effect of understating liabilities and overstating income. In our discussion, we will focus on the two most common high-risk assertions for accounts payable and accrued liabilities: completeness and cutoff.

Payables and Accrued Liabilities: The Completeness Assertion

As highlighted in Figure 13-2, the emphasis in liability accounts is on understatements. Tests to uncover unrecorded accounts payable, frequently referred to as "the search for unrecorded accounts payable," are important. The extent of testing depends

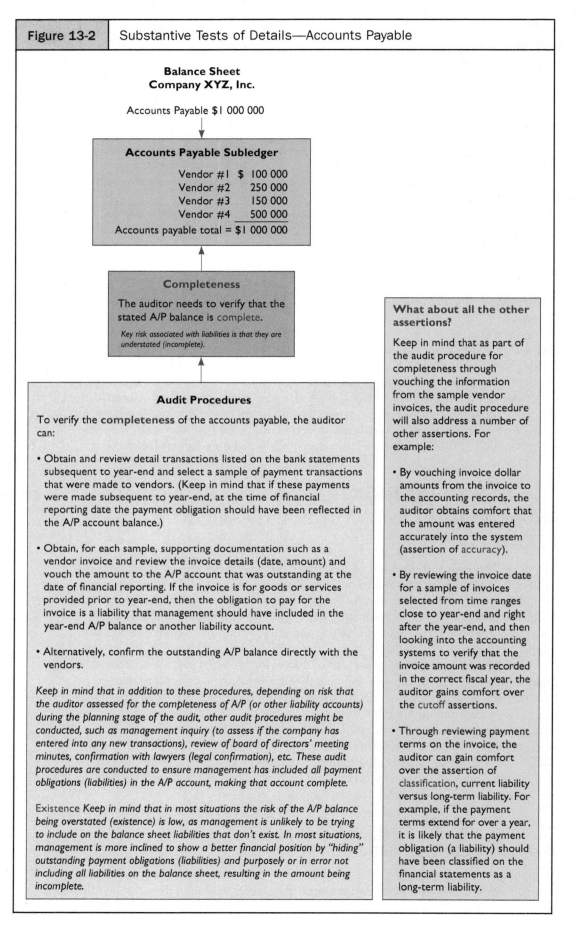

Figure 13-2 | Substantive Tests of Details—Accounts Payable

Balance Sheet
Company XYZ, Inc.

Accounts Payable $1 000 000

Accounts Payable Subledger

Vendor #1 $ 100 000
Vendor #2 250 000
Vendor #3 150 000
Vendor #4 500 000

Accounts payable total = $1 000 000

Completeness

The auditor needs to verify that the stated A/P balance is complete.

Key risk associated with liabilities is that they are understated (incomplete).

Audit Procedures

To verify the **completeness** of the accounts payable, the auditor can:

• Obtain and review detail transactions listed on the bank statements subsequent to year-end and select a sample of payment transactions that were made to vendors. (Keep in mind that if these payments were made subsequent to year-end, at the time of financial reporting date the payment obligation should have been reflected in the A/P account balance.)

• Obtain, for each sample, supporting documentation such as a vendor invoice and review the invoice details (date, amount) and vouch the amount to the A/P account that was outstanding at the date of financial reporting. If the invoice is for goods or services provided prior to year-end, then the obligation to pay for the invoice is a liability that management should have included in the year-end A/P balance or another liability account.

• Alternatively, confirm the outstanding A/P balance directly with the vendors.

Keep in mind that in addition to these procedures, depending on risk that the auditor assessed for the completeness of A/P (or other liability accounts) during the planning stage of the audit, other audit procedures might be conducted, such as management inquiry (to assess if the company has entered into any new transactions), review of board of directors' meeting minutes, confirmation with lawyers (legal confirmation), etc. These audit procedures are conducted to ensure management has included all payment obligations (liabilities) in the A/P account, making that account complete.

Existence Keep in mind that in most situations the risk of the A/P balance being overstated (existence) is low, as management is unlikely to be trying to include on the balance sheet liabilities that don't exist. In most situations, management is more inclined to show a better financial position by "hiding" outstanding payment obligations (liabilities) and purposely or in error not including all liabilities on the balance sheet, resulting in the amount being incomplete.

What about all the other assertions?

Keep in mind that as part of the audit procedure for completeness through vouching the information from the sample vendor invoices, the audit procedure will also address a number of other assertions. For example:

• By vouching invoice dollar amounts from the invoice to the accounting records, the auditor obtains comfort that the amount was entered accurately into the system (assertion of accuracy).

• By reviewing the invoice date for a sample of invoices selected from time ranges close to year-end and right after the year-end, and then looking into the accounting systems to verify that the invoice amount was recorded in the correct fiscal year, the auditor gains comfort over the cutoff assertions.

• Through reviewing payment terms on the invoice, the auditor can gain comfort over the assertion of classification, current liability versus long-term liability. For example, if the payment terms extend for over a year, it is likely that the payment obligation (a liability) should have been classified on the financial statements as a long-term liability.

heavily on assessed control risk and the materiality of the potential balance in the account. We briefly discuss some typical audit procedures and their purpose:

- *Inspect underlying documentation for subsequent cash disbursements.* The purpose of this audit procedure is to uncover payments made in the subsequent accounting period that represent liabilities at the balance sheet date. If it is a current-period obligation, the auditor should trace the transaction to the accounts payable trial balance to ensure it is included. The receiving report is a useful document since it indicates the date the purchase was received. Vendor invoices also indicate date. Frequently, documentation for payments made in the subsequent period is examined for several weeks, especially when the client does not pay its bills on a timely basis.

- *Inspect underlying documentation for bills not paid several weeks after the year-end.* This procedure is carried out in the same manner as the preceding one and serves the same purpose. The only difference is that it is done for unpaid obligations near the end of the examination rather than for obligations that have already been paid. For example, in an audit with a March 31 year-end, if the auditor examines the supporting documentation for cheques paid until June 28, bills that are still unpaid at that date should be examined to determine whether they are obligations of the year ended March 31.

- *Trace receiving reports issued before year-end to related vendors' invoices.* All merchandise received before the year-end of the accounting period, indicated by the issuance of a receiving report, should be included as accounts payable. By tracing receiving reports issued at and before year-end to vendors' invoices and making sure they are included in accounts payable, the auditor is testing for unrecorded obligations.

- *Trace vendors' statements that show a balance due to the accounts payable trial balance.* If the client maintains a file of vendors' statements, any statement indicating a balance due can be traced to the accounts payable listing to make sure it is included as an account payable.

- *Send confirmations to client's vendors.* Although the use of confirmations for accounts payable is less common than that for accounts receivable, it is common testing for vendors omitted from the accounts payable list, potential omitted transactions, and misstated account balances. Sending confirmations to active vendors for which a balance has not been included in the accounts payable list is a useful means of searching for omitted amounts. This type of confirmation is commonly referred to as "zero balance confirmation." See Figure 13-3 for an example.

Payables and Accrued Liabilities: Cutoff Assertion

Cutoff tests for accounts payable are intended to determine whether transactions recorded a few days before and after the balance sheet date are included in the correct period. The audit procedures discussed in the preceding section are directly related to cutoff for acquisitions, but they emphasize understatements. To test for overstatement cutoff amounts, the auditor should trace receiving reports issued after year-end to related invoices to make sure they are not recorded as accounts payable (unless they are inventory in transit, which will be discussed shortly). Invoices for services would be examined to determine the date the service was performed.

Two aspects are expanded upon here: the examination of receiving reports and the determination of the amount of inventory in transit.

Relationship of Cutoff to Physical Observation of Inventory In determining that the accounts payable cutoff is correct, it is essential that the cutoff tests be coordinated with the physical observation of inventory. For example, assume that an inventory acquisition for $40 000 is received late in the afternoon of December 31, after the physical inventory is completed. If the acquisition is included in accounts payable and purchases but excluded from inventory, the result is an understatement of net earnings of $40 000. Conversely, if the acquisition is excluded from both inventory

Figure 13-3	Accounts Payable Confirmation Request

Roger Mead Ltd.
1600 Westmount Ave. N.
Kenora, Ontario
P9N 1X7

January 15, 2019

Szabo Sales Co. Ltd.
2116 King Street
Kenora, Ontario
P9N 1G3

To Whom It May Concern:

Our auditors, Adams and Lelik, LLP, are conducting an audit of our financial statements. For this purpose, please furnish directly to them, at their address noted below, the following information as of December 31, 2018.

(1) Itemized statements of our accounts payable to you showing all unpaid items.
(2) A complete list of any notes and acceptances payable to you (including any which have been discounted) showing the original date, dates due, original amount, unpaid balance, collateral, and endorsers.
(3) An itemized list of your merchandise consigned to us.

Your prompt attention to this request will be appreciated. A stamped, addressed envelope is enclosed for your reply.

Yours truly,

Sally Palm

Adams and Lelik, LLP
215 Tecumseh Crescent
Kenora, Ontario
P9N 2K5

Roger Mead Ltd.
per Sally Palm

and accounts payable, there are understatements in the balance sheet, but the income statement is correct. The only way the auditor will know which type of misstatement has occurred is to coordinate cutoff tests with the observation of inventory.

The cutoff information for purchases should be obtained during the physical observation of the inventory. At this time, the auditor should review the procedures in the receiving department to determine that all inventory received was counted, and the auditor should record in the working papers the last inventory receiving report number. During the year-end fieldwork, the auditor should then test the accounting records for cutoff. The auditor should trace receiving report numbers to the accounts payable records to verify that they are correctly included or excluded.

Inventory in Transit When inspecting accounts payable vendor invoices, the auditor needs to check for the method of shipping. With **FOB destination** shipping, goods are free on board (FOB) destination and title passes to the buyer when they are received for inventory. Therefore, goods received prior to the balance sheet date should be included in inventory and accounts payable at year-end. When an acquisition is on an **FOB origin** basis, title passes to the buyer when goods are shipped, so the inventory and related accounts payable must be recorded in the current period if shipment by the vendor occurred before the balance sheet date.

While we do not discuss the remaining assertions in depth, Auditing in Action 13-4 provides an example of substantive tests of transactions that focus on classification. It is a useful illustration of the type of problems auditors can encounter if the client selects the sample.

FOB destination—shipping contract in which title to the goods passes to the buyer when the goods are received.

FOB origin—shipping contract in which title to the goods passes to the buyer at the time that the goods are shipped.

TV Communications Network (TVCN), a Denver, Colorado–based wireless cable television company, materially understated losses in its financial statements by improperly recording $2.5 million of expenses as a direct decrease in stockholders' equity. The misstatement took the company from an actual net loss of $4.7 million to a reported loss of only $2.2 million.

According to the investigation by the SEC, the expenses charged to equity were from disbursements for the development and distribution of brochures promoting the company's business prospects. The payments should have been expensed and reflected in the income statement as advertising expenses.

The internal controls associated with the advertising expenses were clearly inadequate. TVCN typically did not have invoices or other documentation available when payments were made by the company's president, who controlled the bank account. Because of the lack of adequate documentation, when the financial statements were prepared, TVCN employees responsible for recording the expenses did not have sufficient information to properly classify the disbursements. The SEC found that even when documentation was available, the accounts where the transactions were recorded conflicted with the supporting documentation.

Unfortunately, TVCN's auditor relied on inquiry of the company president as the primary evidence about the nature of the advertising payments. In his substantive testing of transactions exceeding $10 000, the auditor relied on the company controller to identify all transactions meeting the criteria for review. Needless to say, the controller did not present all transactions meeting the $10 000 scope. As you might expect, the SEC brought charges against the auditor for failing to comply with auditing standards.

Source: Based on *Accounting and Auditing Enforcement Release No. 534*, Chicago: Commerce Clearing House, Inc.

RELIABILITY OF AUDIT EVIDENCE

LO **9** Determine the reliability of audit evidence for accounts payable.

In determining the appropriate evidence to accumulate for verifying accounts payable, it is essential that the auditor understand the relative reliability of the three primary types of evidence typically used: vendors' invoices, vendors' statements, and confirmations.

Evidence Quality Distinction Between Vendors' Invoices and Vendors' Statements

In verifying the amount due to a vendor, the auditor should make a major distinction between vendors' invoices and vendors' statements. In examining vendors' invoices and related supporting documents, such as receiving reports and purchase orders, the auditor gets highly reliable evidence about individual transactions. A vendor's statement is not as desirable as invoices for verifying individual transactions because a statement includes only the total amount of the transaction. The units acquired, price, freight, and other data are not included. However, a statement has the advantage of including the ending balance according to the vendor's records.

- *Which of these two documents is better for verifying the correct balance in accounts payable?* The vendor's statement is superior for verifying accounts payable because it includes the ending balance. The auditor could compare existing vendors' invoices with the client's list and still not uncover missing ones, which is the primary concern in accounts payable.
- *Which of these two documents is better for testing acquisitions in tests of control?* The vendor's invoice is superior for verifying transactions because the auditor is verifying individual transactions and the invoice shows the details of the acquisitions.

Evidence Quality Difference Between Vendors' Statements and Confirmations

The most important distinction between a vendor's statement and a confirmation of accounts payable is the source of the information. A vendor's statement has been prepared by an independent third party, but it is in the hands of the client at the time the auditor examines it. This provides the client with an opportunity to alter a vendor's statement or to make particular statements unavailable to the auditor. A confirmation of accounts payable, which normally is a request for an itemized statement to be sent directly to the public accountant's office, provides the same information but can be regarded as more reliable. In addition, confirmations of accounts payable frequently include a request for information about notes and acceptances payable, as well as consigned inventory that is owned by the vendor but stored on the client's premises. An illustration of a typical accounts payable confirmation request is given in Figure 13-3.

The confirmation of accounts payable is less common than confirmation of accounts receivable. If the client has adequate internal controls and vendors' statements are available for examination, then confirmations are normally not sent. However, when the client's internal controls are weak, when statements are not available, or when the auditor questions the client's integrity, then it is desirable to send confirmation requests to vendors. Because of the emphasis on understatements of liability accounts, the accounts confirmed should include large accounts, active accounts, accounts with a zero balance, and a representative sample of all others.

When vendors' statements are examined or confirmations are received, there must be a reconciliation of the statement or confirmation with the accounts payable list. Frequently, differences are caused by inventory in transit, cheques mailed by the client but not received by the vendor at the statement date, and delays in processing the accounting records. The documents typically used to reconcile the balances on the accounts payable list with the confirmation or vendor's statement include receiving reports, vendors' invoices, and cancelled cheques.

CONCEPT CHECK

C13-5 Why is an organization more likely to have poor internal controls over accounts payable than over accounts receivable?

C13-6 Provide two examples of analytical procedures that could indicate a possible misstatement in accounts payable.

LO 10 Design and perform substantive tests (substantive analytical review and tests of details) for related-party transactions and selected accounts related to the acquisition and payment cycle.

EXAMINING OTHER ACCOUNTS AND RELATED-PARTY TRANSACTIONS

An important characteristic of the acquisition and payment cycle is the large number of accounts involved. These include accounts payable, professional fees, a variety of asset accounts, a variety of expense accounts, taxes payable, and others. Table 13-5 highlights many of the typical accounts associated with transactions in the acquisition and payment cycle transactions.

Here, we will focus on (1) audit or related-party transactions, (2) the audit of accrued liabilities and provisions, and (3) the audit of property, plant, and equipment.

Table 13-5	Accounts Typically Associated with Acquisition and Payment Cycle Transactions	
Assets	**Expenses**	**Liabilities**
Cash	Cost of goods sold	Accounts payable
Inventory	Rent expense	Rent payable
Supplies	Property taxes	Accrued professional fees
Property, plant, and equipment	Income tax expense	Accrued property taxes
Patents, trademarks, and copyrights	Insurance expense	Other accrued expenses
Prepaids (such as rent, property taxes, and insurance)	Professional fees	Income taxes payable
	Retirement benefits	
	Utilities	

Related-Party Transactions

Related-party transactions may represent a significant class of transactions and account balances for some organizations. If that is the case, they can increase inherent risk for the acquisition and payment cycle. During the risk assessment process, the auditor must consider risks of material misstatement or fraud that could be associated with related-party transactions. The auditor will also consider the controls and procedures that management has in place for the identification and disclosure of such transactions. In particular, if the client does not disclose related-party transactions to the auditor and the auditor discovers these, the auditor would need to carefully reassess why such transactions were not detected by the client's regular processes.

A general approach to auditing related-party transactions includes the following steps:

- Obtain a list of related parties and develop a list of all transactions with those entities during the year;
- Carefully examine all unusual transactions (especially around period closing); and
- Determine appropriateness of disclosure.

When a client deals with related parties, the *CPA Canada Handbook* requires that the nature of the relationship, the nature and extent of transactions, and amounts due to and from the related parties, including contractual obligations and contingencies, be properly disclosed for the financial statements to be in conformity with GAAS. Services and inventory acquired from related parties must be properly valued, and other exchange transactions must be carefully evaluated for propriety and reasonableness. Therefore, related-party transactions must be audited more extensively than those with third parties.

Audit of Accrued Liabilities and Provisions

Accrued liabilities and/or provisions are estimated unpaid obligations for services or benefits that have been received prior to the balance sheet date. Recall from our discussion of ASPE versus IFRS that recognition and measurement for these liabilities are slightly different under these two GAAPs.

> **Accrued liabilities and/or other provisions**—estimated unpaid obligations for services or benefits that have been received prior to the balance sheet date; include accrued commissions, accrued income taxes, accrued payroll, and accrued rent.

Throughout our discussion of accounts payable, we also referred to accrued liabilities, because many of the substantive tests are designed to uncover unrecorded accruals for regular as-yet-unpaid services that result from the passage of time but are not payable at the balance sheet date. For example, the benefits of property rental accrue throughout the year; therefore, at the balance sheet date, a certain portion of the total rent cost that has not been paid should be accrued. Other examples are accrued wages, payroll taxes, bonuses, accrued pension costs, and accrued professional fees. However, as highlighted in our discussion of recognition and measurement of payables, some accruals or provisions, such as warranty expense and retirement benefits, must be estimated. Therefore, as illustrated in the discussion of the Frimley Health NHS Foundation Trust (see Auditing in Action 13-3), the auditor must evaluate management's estimates and underlying assumptions.

The key risks for these liabilities are completeness (that they are all included), accuracy (that they are calculated correctly), and allocation or cutoff (that they are allocated correctly among prior, current, and future fiscal periods). In the case of accruals or provisions that require judgment in determining the future obligation, the auditor would also be concerned with valuation (that it represents the future obligation and that the client is using the appropriate recognition criteria—"likely" in the case of ASPE and "more than likely" in the case of IFRS).

For both accruals and provisions, the auditor will inquire of management to determine which accruals exist, determine the policy for establishing the accrual, inspect the related documentation (such as subsequent payroll journals for accrued wages, payroll taxes, and bonuses), recalculate the accrual, and assess the reasonableness of assumptions (if applicable). With regard to assessing assumptions, the auditor can perform several substantive procedures to assess the reasonableness of the estimate, such as considering the outcome of prior years and comparing the estimate to corroborating evidence prepared by experts.

Audit of Property Plant and Equipment

Property, plant, and equipment are assets with expected lives of more than one year, are used in the business, and are not acquired for resale. The intent is to use the assets as part of the operation of the client's business, and their expected lives of more than one year are significant characteristics that distinguish them from other assets such as inventory.

Often property, plant, and equipment are material accounts and, as highlighted in Auditing in Action 13-5, may have significant risks. Misallocations between the asset and repairs and maintenance (classification or allocation objectives) could be highly material. Errors in the class or in the amortization rate could affect income (accuracy or allocation), while errors or deliberate manipulation of the estimates of remaining life of the asset could be used to smooth or alter income (accuracy, allocation). These risks are unique to assets that are amortized, with the nature of the accounting framework selected having a large impact, since IFRS is more complex than ASPE with respect to the accounting methods used to record asset values and depreciation/amortization.

Because the audits of property, plant, and equipment accounts are similar, one example, equipment is used to illustrate the approach to auditing to these three types of accounts.

Overview of Equipment-Related Accounts

The accounts commonly used for manufacturing equipment are illustrated in Figure 13-4. Since the source of debits in the asset account is the acquisitions journal, the accounting system has already been tested for recording the current period's additions to manufacturing equipment as part of the test of the acquisition and payment cycle.

AUDITING IN ACTION 13-5
Capitalization versus Expense

Considerable judgment is often involved in determining whether to capitalize or expense certain costs. For instance, British American Tobacco plc has been undergoing restructuring and rolling out a single IT system (called SAP) at its subsidiaries. Below is an excerpt from the auditors' report describing the risks associated with auditing restructuring and integration costs. You will note that it follows a process similar to that described for the audit of manufacturing equipment. The auditors focus on accuracy and classification. The first risk response involved assessing the reasonableness of the accounting policy (do the costs have future benefit?) and the timing of amortization. The second risk response is an example of typical substantive test of details with regard to verifying additions.

Risk of Material Misstatement	Risk Response
Accounting judgment is required regarding whether costs incurred meet the criteria to be capitalized as part of the global SAP system (the IT system used) within intangible assets, or whether they should be expensed immediately.	We challenged the appropriateness of the Group's policies in respect of project costs, including the nature of costs to be capitalized, and the timing of commencing amortization. We did this by confirming that the project costs eligible for capitalization set out within the policies were directly attributable to the development of the software assets, including the global single instance of SAP, associated with the Group's new operating model.
	We tested a sample of costs incurred during the period in order to test the appropriateness of £115 million costs capitalized versus £176 million that were expensed.

Source: PricewaterhouseCoopers, *Independent Auditors' Report*, February 25, 2015, in British American Tobacco plc, *Annual Report: Financial Statements, 2014*, London, 2015.

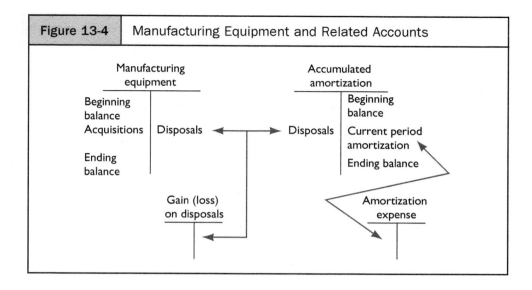

Figure 13-4 | Manufacturing Equipment and Related Accounts

The primary accounting record for manufacturing equipment and other capital asset accounts is generally a property or **capital asset master file** with supporting purchase, disposal, and amortization transactions. The contents of the data files must be understood for a meaningful study of the audit of manufacturing equipment. The files will be composed of a set of records, one for each piece of equipment and other types of property owned. In turn, each record will include descriptive information, date of acquisition, original cost, current-year amortization, and accumulated amortization for the property. The files will also contain information about property acquired and disposed of during the year. Proceeds, gains, and losses will be included for disposals. If IFRS is the financial reporting framework and the client is reporting assets at fair market value, then the capital asset master file will also need to track fair market value changes and the resulting effects on residual values and amortization according to IAS 16. Note that the *CPA Canada Handbook* Section 3061 for ASPE uses the term *amortization* rather than *depreciation*. We will be using these two terms interchangeably. Totals of the master file should agree to totals in the general ledger.

> **Capital asset master file**—a computer file containing records for each piece of equipment and other types of property owned; the primary accounting record for manufacturing equipment and other capital asset accounts.

Equipment is normally audited differently from current asset accounts for three reasons: (1) there are usually fewer current-period acquisitions of manufacturing equipment, (2) the amount of any given acquisition is often material, and (3) the equipment is likely to be kept and maintained in the accounting records for several years.

Because of these differences, the emphasis in auditing equipment is on the verification of current-period acquisitions and on changes to carrying values and useful life estimates rather than on the balance in the account carried forward from the preceding year. In addition, the expected life of assets over one year requires amortization and accumulated amortization accounts, which are verified as part of the audit of the assets. Additions should be traced to the capital cost allowance section of the tax working papers.

Although the approach to verifying equipment differs from that used for current assets, several other asset accounts, such as patents and copyrights, are verified in the same manner. In the audit of equipment and related accounts, it is helpful to separate the tests into the following categories:

- Perform substantive analytical procedures.
- Verify current-year acquisitions.
- Verify current-year disposals.
- Verify ending balance in the asset account.
- Verify amortization expense.
- Verify the ending balance in accumulated amortization.

Table 13-6	Analytical Procedures for Planning for Manufacturing Equipment

Analytical Procedure	Possible Misstatement
Compare amortization expense divided by gross manufacturing equipment cost with that of previous years.	Misstatement in amortization expense and accumulated amortization.
Compare accumulated amortization divided by gross manufacturing equipment cost with that of previous years.	Misstatement in accumulated amortization.
Compare monthly or annual repairs and maintenance, supplies expense, small tools expense, and similar accounts with those of previous years.	Expensing amounts that should be capital items.
Compare gross manufacturing cost divided by some measure of production with those of previous years.	Idle equipment or equipment that has been disposed of but not written off.

Perform Substantive Analytical Procedures

As in all audit areas, the nature of the analytical procedures depends on the nature of the client's operations. Table 13-6 provides examples of analytical procedures for planning for manufacturing equipment.

Verify Current-Year Acquisitions

The proper recording of current-year additions is important because of the long-term effect the assets have on the financial statements. The failure to capitalize a capital asset, or the recording of an acquisition at the improper amount, affects the balance sheet until the firm disposes of the asset. The income statement is affected until the asset is fully amortized. Accuracy and classification are usually the major objectives for this part of the audit, although physical inspection would cover the existence objective.

Prior to the audit, the auditor requests from the client a schedule that provides relevant details by asset: the date of the acquisition, vendor, description, notation whether new or used, life of the asset for amortization purposes, amortization method, cost and revaluations (and salvage value, if any), and any relevant income tax information such as capital cost allowance rates and the investment tax credit if applicable. The information in this schedule is the focus of the audit. The audit steps conducted for current-year acquisitions are as follows:

- *Inspect supporting documentation for asset costs.* Vendors, invoices, and receiving reports are examined to verify the nature of the asset, its cost, and the date acquired to determine that it has been recorded in compliance with the client's capitalization policies in the correct account. Costs should include foreign exchange, installation, and shipping. The sample would be at-risk transactions (large amounts, certain dates, or certain asset classes), as well as a sample of the remainder. The size of the sample for substantive testing depends upon the assessed inherent and control risks.
- *Inspect grant documents.* Reading of grant documents provides information used to determine that the grant has been properly recorded, tax effects determined correctly, and its terms disclosed in the financial statements.
- *Inspect large repair and maintenance documentation.* Similar to the first point above, verify details of the invoice to determine whether the transaction is in fact for repairs and maintenance or should be capitalized or allocated to other accounts. While looking at asset acquisitions, the auditor would also determine whether any of the capitalized amounts inspected should be expensed. The auditor would consider both the client's policies as well as tax regulations during this assessment.
- *Search for trade-ins.* See the discussion below under asset disposal.
- *Physically inspect the asset or repair.* Tour the physical location or ask for a photo of the asset to verify that it matches the supporting documentation.

- *Reassess risks based upon findings.* If there are errors in classification of assets to particular accounts or in accuracy of recording, the auditor may need to reassess risks or expand the extent of testing.

Verify Current-Year Disposals

The next step is to audit current-year disposals. Recording disposals relies more on internal controls than does the recording of acquisitions, since assets may be removed without receiving any funds (i.e., retired). Controls need to be in place to inform management and capital asset recordkeeping of the authorized sale, trade-in, abandonment, or theft of recorded machinery and equipment. Once documented and notified, there should be independent verification of these changes to prevent unauthorized changes and ensure accuracy. The primary assertions for the following audit tests are occurrence and accuracy:

- *Inquire about the nature of the disposals.* Inquire of management with respect to the quantity and nature of the disposals. For example, determine whether assets were replaced or simply retired and how they were disposed of to identify the type of documentation that would be present for the disposal.
- *Inspect documentation of the disposal.* Inspect documentation to determine that the amounts were accurately recorded and allocated to the correct asset in the capital asset master files.
- *Recalculate gains and losses.* Recalculate the amounts and determine whether gains and losses were accurately recorded to the correct accounts (e.g., to miscellaneous income or expense).
- *Assess income tax effects.* Determine whether an asset class has been fully disposed of and whether recapture of capital cost allowance has occurred and is properly calculated.
- *Trace postings to the correct accounts.* As noted above, disposals should be removed from the asset master file (relieving both cost and accumulated amortization or depreciation) and gains and losses recorded to the correct income or expense account.
- *Physically inspect the plant location.* Tour the physical location (or obtain a photo) to determine that the asset is no longer on the premises.
- *Inspect related accounts for potential unrecorded disposals.* Inspect postings to related accounts such as miscellaneous income or expense, goods and services or sales taxes, or details of insurance coverage for sold or removed assets.
- *While inspecting asset acquisition, search for trade-ins.* A common error on the part of the client is to record a new acquisition with a trade-in at the net amount (i.e., new cost less trade-in amount). By searching for trade-ins, the auditor can verify that the new asset has been recorded at full cost and that the disposed-of asset is properly removed from the accounts.

Verify Opening and Closing Balances

Once assets and disposals have been verified, the auditor decides on the extent of testing needed for opening and closing balances. Since the focus is on auditing additions and disposals, if the auditor audited the opening balance, and the client has a capital asset master file that agrees with the opening balance, the auditor would normally only check that the opening balance agrees to the ending balance of the prior year's audit for each fixed asset account. For the closing balance, two tests of accuracy (allocation) would need to be completed:

- *Reconcile opening to closing balance.* Opening balance plus additions minus disposals should agree to the ending balance.
- *Agree subsidiary totals to closing balance.* Add the capital asset master file and agree the total to the ending balance.

Additional tests of ending balances include the following:

- *Valuation objective.* Assets may need to be written down if their net realizable value has dropped due to changing technology or the presence of nonoperating equipment. The auditor will need to be aware of the client's business environment, the cost of recent additions, and the replacement cost of comparable equipment. Nonoperating equipment disclosures would need to be reviewed for completeness and understandability. Assets recorded at market value would require documentation, such as an independent appraisal to document the value used. The auditor would need to evaluate the competence and quality of the appraisal, and, if there is uncertainty regarding the quality of the appraisal, may need to have another independent appraisal conducted.
- *Completeness of disclosure.* Property, plant, and equipment are often used as collateral for loans or may be purchased using debt. The auditor would read the legal agreements that pertain to this debt to assess adequacy and thoroughness of disclosure in the financial statements.
- *Accuracy and understandability of disclosure.* Details of property, plant, and equipment need to be adequately and clearly shown in the financial statements, distinguishing between owned and leased assets, and identifying commitments for payments under leases and debt.

Verify Amortization Expense

Allocation—the division of certain expenses, such as amortization and manufacturing overhead, among several expense accounts.

Amortization expense is one of the few expense accounts that are not verified as a part of tests of controls since the recorded amounts are determined by internal **allocation** to particular expense accounts rather than by exchange transactions with outside parties. When amortization expense is material, more tests of details of amortization expense are required than for an account that has already been verified through tests of controls.

The most important objectives for amortization expense are valuation and accuracy. These involve determining whether the client is following a consistent amortization policy from period to period and whether the client's calculations are accurate.

When assessing amortization policy, there are four considerations: the remaining useful life of assets, the method of amortization, the estimated salvage/residual value, and the policy of amortizing assets in the year of acquisition and disposition. The client's policies can be determined by having discussions with the client and comparing the responses with the information in the auditor's permanent files.

In deciding on the reasonableness of the useful lives assigned to assets, the auditor must consider a number of factors: any changes in value to the recorded assets, the actual physical life of the asset, the expected useful life (taking into account obsolescence and the company's normal policy of upgrading equipment), and established company policies on trading-in equipment. The effect of these on amortization must be carefully evaluated. The auditor needs to consider management bias toward higher or lower income and the overall risk of material misstatement when examining such accounting policies.

CONCEPT CHECK

C13-7 What possible misstatements could occur with manufacturing equipment?

C13-8 Why does the auditor need to ask if any equipment purchases are from a related party?

A useful method of testing amortization is to make a calculation of its overall reasonableness using analytical review as a substantive test. The calculation is made by multiplying the unamortized capital assets by the amortization rate for the year. In making these calculations, the auditor must make adjustments for current-year additions and disposals, assets with different lengths of life, and assets with different methods of amortization. The calculations can be made fairly easily if the public accounting firm includes in the permanent file a breakdown of the capital assets by method of amortization and length of life. If the overall calculations are reasonably close to the client's totals and if assessed control risk for amortization expense is low, tests of details for amortization can be minimized.

Checking the accuracy of amortization calculations is done by recomputing amortization expense for selected assets to determine whether the client is following a proper and consistent amortization policy. To be relevant, the detailed calculations should be tied into the total amortization calculations by footing the amortization expense in the capital asset master file and reconciling the total with the general ledger.

Verify Accumulated Amortization

Two objectives are usually emphasized in the audit of accumulated amortization (the ending balance):

- Accumulated amortization as stated in the asset master file agrees with the general ledger. This objective can be satisfied by test footing the accumulated amortization on the asset master file and tracing the total to the general ledger.
- Accumulated amortization in the master file is properly valued.

In some cases, the life of manufacturing equipment may be significantly reduced because of such changes as reductions in customer demands for products, unexpected physical deterioration, or a modification in operations. Because of these possibilities and if the decline in asset value is permanent, it may be appropriate to write the asset down to net realizable value, which could result in a change to the accumulated amortization.

SUMMARY

Given the nature of its transactions, the acquisition and payment cycle represents a significant cycle. To adequately audit the numerous accounts associated with the acquisition and payment cycle, auditors need an understanding of key accounts, classes of transactions, business functions, documents, and records related to the cycle's transactions. The auditor needs to be able to identify significant risks and have an understanding of the controls in order to develop an appropriate audit strategy that is appropriate for the various accounts and class of transactions. Many of these accounts—accounts payable, accrual and provisions, and property, plant, and equipment—have unique characteristics that affect how the auditor gathers sufficient evidence about related account balances. The interrelationships between different audit tests in the acquisition and payment cycle can provide a basis for the auditor's verification of many financial statement accounts.

MyLab Accounting
Make the grade with MyLab Accounting: The questions, exercises, and problems marked with a ⊕ can be found on MyLab Accounting. You can practise them as often as you want, and most feature step-by-step guided instructions to help you find the right answer.

Review Questions

⊕ **13-1** **1** **4** What is the importance of cash discounts to the client, and how can the auditor verify whether they are being used in accordance with company policy?

⊕ **13-2** **1** **2** **4** Explain why most auditors consider the receipt of goods and services the most important point in the acquisition and payment cycle.

13-3 **4** List one possible internal control for each of the five transaction-related audit objectives for cash disbursements. For each control, list a test of controls to test its effectiveness.

13-4 **4** List one possible control for each of the five transaction-related audit objectives for acquisitions. For each control, list a test of controls to test its effectiveness.

⊕ **13-5** **9** Distinguish between a vendor's invoice and a vendor's statement. Which document should ideally be used as evidence in auditing acquisition transactions and which for directly verifying accounts payable balances? Why?

13-6 **7** The Chartered Professional Accountant examines all unrecorded invoices on hand as of February 28, 2019, the last day of the audit. Which of the following misstatements is most likely to be uncovered by this procedure? Explain.
a. Accounts payable are overstated at December 31, 2018.
b. Accounts payable are understated at December 31, 2018.

c. Operating expenses are overstated for the 12 months ended December 31, 2018.

d. Operating expenses are overstated for the two months ended February 28, 2019.

(AICPA adapted. Copyright by American Institute of CPAs. All rights reserved. Used with permission.)

13-7 `7` What are the similarities and differences in the objectives of the following two procedures?

a. Select a random sample of receiving reports and trace them to related vendors' invoices and acquisitions journal entries, comparing the vendor's name, type of material and quantity acquired, and total amount of the acquisition.

b. Select a random sample of acquisitions journal entries, and trace them to related vendors' invoices and receiving reports, comparing the vendor's name, type of material and quantity acquired, and total amount of the acquisition.

13-8 `5` `7` Explain the relationship between tests of the acquisition and payment cycle and tests of inventory. Give specific examples of how these two types of tests affect each other.

13-9 `5` `6` Evaluate the following statement by an auditor concerning tests of acquisitions and cash disbursements: "In selecting the acquisitions and cash disbursements sample for testing, the best approach is to select a random month and test every transaction for the period. Using this approach enables me to thoroughly understand internal control because I have examined everything that happened during the period. As a part of the monthly test, I also test the beginning and ending bank reconciliations and prepare a proof of cash for the month. At the completion of these tests I feel I can evaluate the effectiveness of internal control."

13-10 `1` `5` `10` Explain the relationship between tests of controls for the acquisition and payment cycle and tests of details of balances for the verification of capital assets. Which aspects of capital assets are directly affected by the tests of controls, and which are not?

13-11 Explain why it is common for auditors to send confirmation requests to vendors with "zero balances" on the client's accounts payable listing but uncommon to follow the same approach in verifying accounts receivable.

13-12 `5` In testing the cutoff of accounts payable at the balance sheet date, explain why it is important that auditors coordinate their tests with the physical observation of inventory. What can the auditor do during the physical inventory to enhance the likelihood of an accurate cutoff?

13-13 `10` Explain why the emphasis in auditing capital assets is on the current-period acquisitions and disposals rather than on the balances in the account carried forward from the preceding year. Under what circumstances would the emphasis be on the balances carried forward?

13-14 `10` What is the relationship between the audit of fixed asset accounts and the audit of repair and maintenance accounts? Explain how the auditor organizes the audit to take this relationship into consideration.

13-15 `10` List and briefly state the purpose of all audit procedures that might reasonably be applied by an auditor to determine that all capital asset retirements have been recorded on the books.

13-16 `10` In auditing amortization expense, what assertions should the auditor keep in mind? Explain how each can be verified.

13-17 `5` `7` List the factors that should affect the auditor's decision whether or not to analyze a particular account balance. Considering these factors, list four expense accounts that would be important to verify in audit engagements.

13-18 `10` Why does the auditor examine transaction details for subsidiaries, affiliates, officers, and directors?

Multiple Choice Questions and Task-Based Simulations

The following question concerns internal controls in the acquisition and payment cycle. Choose the best response.

13-19 `3` Budd, the purchasing agent of Lake Hardware Wholesalers, has a relative who owns a retail hardware store. Budd arranged for hardware to be delivered by manufacturers to the relative's retail store on a COD basis, thereby enabling his relative to buy at Lake's wholesale prices. Budd was probably able to accomplish this because of Lake's poor internal control over:

(1) Purchase requisitions.

(2) Purchase orders.

(3) Cash receipts.

(4) Perpetual inventory records.

The following question concerns accumulating evidence in the acquisition and payment cycle. Choose the best response.

⊕ **13-20** 〔4〕 In auditing accounts payable, an auditor's procedures will most likely focus primarily on management's assertion of:
(1) Existence.
(2) Realizable value.
(3) Completeness.
(4) Valuation and allocation.

The following question concerns the audit of accounts payable. Choose the best response.

⊕ **13-21** 〔4〕 For effective internal control, the accounts payable department generally should:
(1) Stamp, perforate, or otherwise cancel supporting documentation after payment is mailed.
(2) Ascertain that each requisition is approved as to price, quantity, and quality by an authorized employee.
(3) Omit information about the quantity ordered on the copy of the purchase order forwarded to the receiving department prior to receipt of goods.
(4) Establish the agreement of the vendor's invoice with the receiving report and purchase order.

The following question concerns internal controls in the acquisition and payment cycle. Choose the best response for each.

⊕ **13-22** 〔10〕 Equipment acquisitions that are misclassified as maintenance expense most likely would be detected by an internal control that provides for:
(1) Segregation of duties of employees in the accounts payable department.
(2) Authorization by the board of directors of significant equipment acquisitions.
(3) Investigations of variances within a formal budgeting system.
(4) Independent verification of invoices for disbursements recorded as equipment acquisitions.

The following questions concern analytical procedures in the acquisition and payment cycle. Choose the best response for each.

⊕ **13-23** 〔10〕 Which of the following analytical procedures might suggest that certain repairs and maintenance expenses have been inappropriately capitalized?
(1) The ratio of additions to equipment divided by the beginning balance in the equipment account is significantly lower than the same ratio from the prior three years.
(2) The balance in the repairs and maintenance expense account is noticeably lower than amounts recorded in the past several years.
(3) The balance in the gross equipment account has decreased this year compared to the prior year.
(4) The ratio of amortization expense divided by gross equipment is higher in the current year compared to prior years.

13-24 〔8〕 From the list, select the type of audit evidence used for each of the procedures in the table. Note that a selection may be used not at all or more than once.
(1) Inspection
(2) Recalculation
(3) Analytical procedures
(4) Reperformance

Procedure	Type of Audit Evidence
Vouch the transaction to the voucher package that includes the matched receiving report, purchase order, and vendor invoice.	
Verify that the purchase order was approved by an authorized purchasing agent.	
Verify that the initials of the accounts payable clerk are present, indicating that the documents have been appropriately matched and that amounts on the vendor invoice were verified.	
Recalculate the invoice amount and compare the dollar amounts per the invoice to the amount recorded in the acquisitions journal.	
Examine whether the transaction was recorded to the correct vendor in the accounts payable master file.	
Determine if the transaction was recorded in the correct month, based on when the goods were received and the terms of the transaction.	
Review the chart of accounts to determine if the transaction was charged to the appropriate general ledger account.	

13-25 [8] For each procedure, identify which balance-related audit objective(s) (assertions) were satisfied.

AUDIT PROCEDURE	Assertions					
	Existence	Completeness	Accuracy	Classification	Cutoff	Obligations
Obtain a list of accounts payable. Re-add and compare with the general ledger.						
Trace from the general ledger trial balance and supporting documentation to determine whether accounts payable, related parties, and other related assets and liabilities are properly included on the financial statements.						
For liabilities that are payable in a foreign currency, determine the exchange rate and check calculations.						
Discuss with the bookkeeper whether any amounts included on the accounts payable list are due to related parties, debit balances, or notes payable.						
Obtain vendors' statements from the controller and reconcile them to the listing of accounts payable.						
Obtain vendors' statements directly from vendors and reconcile them to the listing of accounts payable.						
Examine supporting documents for cash disbursements several days before and after year-end.						
Examine the acquisitions and cash disbursements journals for the last few days of the current period and first few days of the succeeding period, looking for large or unusual transactions.						

Discussion Questions and Problems

13-26 [3] [4] Each year near the balance sheet date, when the president of Bargon Construction, Inc., takes a three-week vacation to Mexico, she signs several cheques to pay major bills during the period she is absent. Jack Morgan, head bookkeeper for the company, uses this practice to his advantage. Morgan makes out a cheque to himself for the amount of a large vendor's invoice, and because there is no acquisitions journal, he records the amount in the cash disbursements journal as an acquisition from the supplier listed on the invoice. He holds the cheque until several weeks into the subsequent period to make sure that the auditors do not get an opportunity to examine the cancelled cheque. Shortly after the first of the year when the president returns, Morgan resubmits the invoice for payment and again records the cheque in the cash disbursements journal. At that point, he marks the invoice "paid" and files it with all other paid invoices. Morgan has been following this practice successfully for several years and feels confident that he has developed a foolproof method.

REQUIRED
a. What is the auditor's responsibility for discovering this type of embezzlement?
b. What weaknesses exist in the client's internal control?
c. What evidence could the auditor use to uncover the fraud?

(AICPA adapted. Copyright by American Institute of CPAs. All rights reserved. Used with permission.)

13-27 [5] [8] As part of the audit of different audit areas, it is important to be alert to the possibility of unrecorded liabilities.

REQUIRED
For each of the following audit areas or accounts, describe a liability that could be uncovered and the audit procedures that could uncover it.
a. Minutes of the board of directors' meetings.
b. Land and buildings.

c. Rent expense.
d. Interest expense.
e. Cash surrender value of life insurance.
f. Cash in the bank.
g. Officers' travel and entertainment expense.

13-28 **5** **8** Because of the small size of the company and the limited number of accounting personnel, Dry Goods Wholesale Company Ltd. initially records all acquisitions of goods and services at the time that cash disbursements are made. At the end of each quarter when financial statements for internal purposes are prepared, accounts payable are recorded by adjusting journal entries. The entries are reversed at the beginning of the subsequent period. Except for the lack of a purchasing system, the controls over acquisitions are excellent for a small company. (There are adequate prenumbered documents for all receipt of goods, proper approvals, and adequate internal verification wherever possible.)

Before the auditor arrives for the year-end audit, the bookkeeper prepares adjusting entries to record the accounts payable as of the balance sheet date. The aged trial balance is listed as of the year-end, and a manual schedule is prepared adding the amounts that were entered in the following month. Thus, the accounts payable balance equals the aged trial balance plus the following month's journal entry for invoices received after the year-end. All vendors' invoices supporting the journal entry are retained in a separate file for the auditor's use.

In the current year, the accounts payable balance has increased dramatically because of a severe cash shortage. (The cash shortage apparently arose from expansion of inventory and facilities rather than lack of sales.) Many accounts have remained unpaid for several months, and the client is getting pressure from several vendors to pay the bills. Since the company had a relatively profitable year, management is anxious to complete the audit as early as possible so that the audited statements can be used to obtain a larger bank loan.

REQUIRED
a. Explain how the lack of a complete aged accounts payable trial balance will affect the auditor's tests of controls for acquisitions and cash disbursements.
b. What should the auditor use as a sampling unit in performing tests of acquisitions?
c. Assume that no misstatements are discovered in the auditor's tests of controls for acquisitions and cash disbursements. How will that assumption affect the verification of accounts payable?
d. Discuss the reasonableness of the client's request for an early completion of the audit and the implications of the request from the auditor's point of view.
e. List the audit procedures that should be performed in the year-end audit of accounts payable to meet the cutoff objective.
f. State your opinion as to whether it is possible to conduct an adequate audit in these circumstances.

13-29 **5** **8** You were in the final stages of your examination of the financial statements of Ozine Corporation for the year ended December 31, 2018, when the corporation's president came to talk to you. He believed that there was no point to your examining the 2019 acquisitions data files and testing data in support of 2019 entries. He stated that (1) bills pertaining to 2018 that were received too late to be included in the December acquisitions data files were recorded by the corporation as of the year-end by journal entry, (2) the internal auditor made tests after the year-end, and (3) he would furnish you with a letter confirming that there were no unrecorded liabilities.

REQUIRED
a. Should a public accountant's test for unrecorded liabilities be affected by the fact that the client made a journal entry to record 2018 bills that were received late? Explain.
b. Should a public accountant's test for unrecorded liabilities be affected by the fact that a letter is obtained in which a responsible management official confirms that, to the best of his knowledge, all liabilities have been recorded? Explain.
c. Should a public accountant's test for unrecorded liabilities be eliminated or reduced because of the internal audit tests? Explain.
d. Assume that the corporation, which handled some government contracts, had no internal auditor but that an auditor from the auditor general's office spent three weeks auditing the records and was just completing her work at this time. How would the public accountant's unrecorded liability test be affected by the work of the auditor from the auditor general's office?
e. What sources in addition to the 2019 acquisitions data files should the public accountant consider to locate possible unrecorded liabilities?

13-30 **7** **10** You are the manager in the audit of Vernal Manufacturing Company and are turning your attention to the income statement accounts. The in-charge auditor assessed control risk for all cycles as low, supported by tests of controls. There are no major inherent risks affecting income and expense accounts. Accordingly, you decide that the major emphasis in auditing the income statement accounts will be to use analytical procedures. The client prepared a schedule of the key income statement accounts that compares the prior-year totals with the current-year totals. The in-charge auditor completed the last column of the audit schedule, which includes explanations of variances obtained from discussions with client personnel. The audit schedule is included below.

Vernal Manufacturing Co.
Income Statement Accounts
12/31/18

Account	Per G/L 12/31/17	Per G/L 12/31/18	Change Amount	Change Percent	Explanations by Client
Sales	$8 467 312	$9 845 231	$1 377 919	16.3	Sales increase due to two new customers who
Sales returns and allowances	(64 895)	(243 561)	(178 666)	275.3	account for 20% of volume. Larger returns
Gain on sale of assets	43 222	(143 200)	(186 422)	−431.3	due to need to cement relations with these
Interest income	243	223	(20)	−8.2	customers.
Miscellaneous income	6 365	25 478	19 113	300.3	Trade-in of several sales cars that needed
	8 452 247	9 484 171	1 031 924	12.2	replacement.
Cost of goods sold:					
Beginning inventory	1 487 666	1 389 034	(98 632)	−6.6	
Purchases	2 564 451	3 430 865	866 414	33.8	Increase in these accounts due to increased
Freight in	45 332	65 782	20 450	45.1	volume with new customers as indicated above.
Purchase returns	(76 310)	(57 643)	18 667	−24.5	
Factory wages	986 755	1 145 467	158 712	16.1	
Factory benefits	197 652	201 343	3 691	1.9	
Factory overhead	478 659	490 765	12 106	2.5	
Factory depreciation	344 112	314 553	(29 559)	−8.6	
Ending inventory	(1 389 034)	(2 156 003)	(766 969)	55.2	Inventory being held for new customers.
	4 639 283	4 824 163	184 880	4.0	
Selling, general, and administrative:					
Executive salaries	167 459	174 562	7 103	4.2	Normal salary increases.
Executive benefits	32 321	34 488	2 167	6.7	
Office salaries	95 675	98 540	2 865	3.0	
Office benefits	19 888	21 778	1 890	9.5	
Travel and entertainment	56 845	75 583	18 738	33.0	Sales and promotional expenses increased in
Advertising	130 878	156 680	25 802	19.7	an attempt to obtain new major customers.
Other sales expense	34 880	42 334	7 454	21.4	Two obtained and program will continue.
Stationery and supplies	38 221	21 554	(16 667)	−43.6	Probably a misclassification; will investigate.
Postage	14 657	18 756	4 099	28.0	Normal increase.
Telephone	36 551	67 822	31 271	85.6	Normal increase.
Dues and memberships	3 644	4 522	878	24.1	Normal increase.
Rent	15 607	15 607	0	0.0	
Legal fees	14 154	35 460	21 306	150.5	Timing of billing for fees.
Accounting fees	16 700	18 650	1 950	11.7	Normal increase.
Amortization, SG&A	73 450	69 500	(3 950)	−5.4	Normal change.
Bad debt expense	166 454	143 871	(22 583)	−13.6	Haven't reviewed yet for the current year.
Insurance	44 321	45 702	1 381	3.1	Normal change.
Interest expense	120 432	137 922	17 490	14.5	Normal change.
Other expense	5 455	28 762	23 307	427.3	Amount not material.
	1 087 592	1 212 093	124 501	11.4	
	5 726 875	6 036 256	309 381	5.4	
Income before taxes	2 725 372	3 447 915	722 543	26.5	
Income taxes	926 626	1 020 600	93 974	10.1	Increase due to increased income before tax.
Net income	$1 798 746	$2 427 315	$ 628 569	34.9	

a. Examine the schedule prepared by the client and your staff and write a memorandum to the in-charge that includes criticisms and concerns about the audit procedures performed and questions for the in-charge auditor to resolve.

b. Evaluate the explanations for variances provided by client personnel. List any alternative explanation to those given.

c. Indicate which variances are of special significance to the audit and how you believe they should be responded to in terms of additional audit procedures.

Professional Judgment Problems and Cases

13-31 **4** Donnen Designs, Inc., is a small manufacturer of women's casual-wear jewellery, including bracelets, necklaces, earrings, and other moderately priced accessory items. Most of its products are made of silver, various low-cost stones, beads, and other decorative jewellery pieces. Donnen Designs is not involved in the manufacturing of high-end jewellery items such as those made of gold and semiprecious or precious stones.

Personnel responsible for purchasing raw material jewellery pieces for Donnen Designs would like to place orders directly with suppliers who offer their products for sale through websites. Most suppliers provide pictures of all jewellery components on their websites, along with pricing and other sales-term information. Customers that have valid business licences are able to purchase the products at wholesale, rather than retail, prices. Customers can place orders online and pay for those goods immediately by using a valid credit card. The suppliers ship purchases made by credit card once the credit approval is received from the credit card agency, which usually occurs the same day. Customers can also place orders online with payment being made later by cheque. However, in that event, purchases are not shipped until the cheque is received and cashed by the supplier. Some of the suppliers have a 30-day full-payment refund policy, whereas other suppliers accept returns but only grant credit toward future purchases from that supplier.

REQUIRED

a. Identify advantages for Donnen Designs if management allows purchasing personnel to order goods online through supplier websites.

b. Identify potential risks associated with Donnen Designs' purchase of jewellery pieces through supplier websites.

c. Describe advantages of allowing purchasing agents to purchase products online using a Donnen Designs credit card.

d. Describe advantages of allowing purchasing agents to purchase products online with payment made only by cheque.

e. What internal controls could be implemented to ensure the following?

(1) Donnen allows purchasing agents to purchase jewellery items using Donnen credit cards, and purchasing agents do not use those credit cards to purchase nonjewellery items for their own purposes.

(2) Purchasing agents do not order jewellery items from the suppliers and ship those items to addresses other than Donnen addresses.

(3) Donnen does not end up with unused credits with jewellery suppliers as a result of returning unacceptable jewellery items to suppliers that only grant credit toward future purchases.

13-32 **5** **10** PawLow Inc. is a private manufacturer of specialized lubricants for the space industry. Its lubricants are used to cover moving mechanical parts inside rocket ships, the Space Station, and the Mars Rover. Its year-end was February 28, 2018, and the unaudited net income before tax is $4 million. You are an audit manager who is responsible for reviewing PawLow's year-end audit file. The audit file contains the following information:

- In 2019, PawLow will be expanding its business and establishing operations in Russia and China. These two countries have their own space programs and PawLow sees great opportunities there. To fund the expansion, in November 2017 the company obtained a loan from a bank. As part of the loan agreement, the bank requires PawLow to provide audited financial statements and to maintain a specific debt ratio (Debt Ratio = Total Debt/Total Assets) loan covenant.

- In 2017, management undertook an extensive review of PawLow's non-current asset valuations and as a result decided to update the carrying value of all property, plant, and equipment. The VP of finance, Thomas Wolanski, contacted his brother, Joseph who is a valuer, and requested that Joseph's firm undertake the valuation, which took place in September 2017.

AUDIT WORK PERFORMED

- Enquired Thomas Wolanski about the competence and capability of the valuer, Joseph Wolanski.
- Verbally confirmed with Thomas that Joseph has proper qualification as a valuer and that Joseph is a member of a professional body and has experience in valuing the type of assets that are at PawLow.
- Obtained a schedule of all PPE revalued during the year. Reviewed the formulas used in the Excel calculation sheet and manually recalculated all the totals.
- To confirm completeness and accuracy of the revaluation adjustment traced all totals from the schedule to the trial balance and financial statements.

PawLow's main customer, the National Aeronautics and Space Administration (NASA), has had its space exploration budget significantly reduced. As a result NASA has been late paying PawLow for some of its largest orders. This had a significant impact on PawLow's cashflow and the company had to miss its January and February 2018 monthly bank loan repayments.

- Obtained PawLow's cash flow forecast and reviewed the cash in and out flows. Assessed the assumptions for reasonableness and discussed the findings with management to determine whether the company will have sufficient cash flows to meet liabilities as they fall due.
- Discussed with management the current bank agreement and inquired whether any key ratios or covenants have been breached with regard to the bank loan.

QUESTIONS

1. Review the audit procedures and discuss the method and reliability of the gathered audit evidence in relation to the risks discussed in the case.

2. What other procedures could the auditor have used to gather evidence?

3. What more reliable evidence would you suggest the auditor gather in order to adequately address the risks?

13-33 **10** You are doing the audit of the UTE Corporation for the year ended December 31, 2018. The following schedule for the property, plant, and equipment and related allowance for amortization accounts has been prepared by the client. You have compared the opening balances with your prior year's audit documentation.

UTE Corporation Analysis of Property, Plant, and Equipment and Related Allowance for Amortization Accounts				
Year Ended December 31, 2018				
Description	Final 12/31/17	Additions	Retirements	Per Books 12/31/18
Assets				
Land	$225 000	$50 000		$275 000
Buildings	1 200 000	175 000		1 375 000
Machinery and equipment	3 850 000	404 000	260 000	3 994 000
	$5 275 000	$629 000	$260 000	$5 644 000
Allowance for Amortization				
Building	$600 000	$51 500		$651 500
Machinery and equipment	1 732 500	392 200		2 124 700
	$2 332 500	$443 700		$2 776 200

The following information is found during your audit:

1. All equipment is amortized on the straight-line basis (no salvage value taken into consideration) based on the following estimated lives: buildings, 25 years; all other items, 10 years. The corporation's policy is to take one-half year's amortization on all asset acquisitions and disposals during the year.

2. On April 1, the corporation entered into a 10-year lease contract for a die-casting machine with annual rentals of $50 000, payable in advance every April 1. The lease is cancellable by either party (60 days' written notice is required), and there is no option to renew the lease or buy the equipment at the end of the lease. The estimated useful life of the machine is 10 years with no salvage value. The corporation recorded the die-casting machine in the machinery and equipment account at $404 000, the present value at the date of the lease, and $20 200, applicable to the machine, has been included in amortization expense for the year.

3. The corporation completed the construction of a wing on the plant building on June 30. The useful life of the building was not extended by this addition. The lowest construction bid received was $175 000, the amount recorded in the buildings account. Company personnel were used to construct the addition at a cost of $160 000 (materials, $75 000; labour, $55 000; and overhead, $30 000).

4. On August 18, $50 000 was paid for paving and fencing a portion of land owned by the corporation and used as a parking lot for employees. The expenditure was charged to the land account.

5. The amount shown in the machinery and equipment asset retirement column represents cash received on September 5, upon disposal of a machine acquired in July 2014 for $480 000. The bookkeeper recorded amortization expense of $35 000 on this machine in 2018.

6. Crux City donated land and a building appraised at $100 000 and $400 000, respectively, to the UTE Corporation for a plant. On September 1, the corporation began operating the plant. Because no costs were involved, the bookkeeper made no entry for the foregoing transaction.

REQUIRED

a. In addition to inquiry of the client, explain how you would have found each of these six items during the audit.

13-34 [3] Read Auditing in Action 13-1, "Apple Manager Sentenced to One Year for Receiving Kickbacks Related to iPhone and iPod."

REQUIRED

a. Explain why it would be difficult to detect kickbacks.
b. What types of procedures could an auditor perform to detect kickbacks?

13-35 [3] [4] [5] [8] Read Auditing in Action 13-4, "Incorrect Classifications Hide a Greater Net Loss," regarding fraudulent reporting at TV Communications Network (TVCN).

REQUIRED

a. Explain why the auditor's substantive testing was deficient.
b. How might the availability tendency have affected the auditor's evaluation of the evidence?
c. How might the confirmation bias have affected the auditor's evaluation of the evidence?

13-36 [3] [7] Data analytics is a powerful tool in fraud detection and is often used to search for signs of fraud in the purchasing function. To learn more about data analytics as a fraud detection tool in purchasing, visit *Fraud Magazine*'s website (**www.fraud-magazine.com**) and search for the January 2013 article "Devil in the Details: Anti-fraud Data Analytics," by Robert Tie.

a. The article discusses purchasing fraud that occurred in a state government agency. What was the nature of the internal controls over the purchasing function in the agency that provided the opportunity for fraud to occur? What were the incentives of the purchasing department to commit fraud?
b. How can data analytics tools be used to detect fraud in the purchasing function?
c. Describe three analyses a fraud examiner could perform to detect fraud related to a particular vendor (e.g., calculate year-to-year percentage changes in total purchases from each vendor).

AUDIT OF THE INVENTORY AND DISTRIBUTION CYCLE

STANDARDS REFERENCED IN THIS CHAPTER

CAS 240 – The auditor's responsibilities relating to fraud in an audit of financial statements

CAS 620 – Using the work of an auditor's expert

CAS 501 – Audit evidence: specific considerations for selected items

IAS 2 – Inventories

For many companies, next to revenue, inventory processes are the most critical factors to their continued success. For example, Apple, well known for its supply chain management, can quickly scale up operations to meet customer demand. In cooperation with its supply chain partners, it has developed several patented manufacturing processes, all of which contribute to its product quality and its ability to effectively manage its supply chain. In this chapter, we will learn more about these critical processes and how the auditor develops a risk-based audit strategy for the inventory cycle.

LEARNING OBJECTIVES

After studying this chapter, you should be able to:

1 Identify the accounts and the classes of transactions in the inventory cycle.

2 Describe the business functions, documents, and records of the inventory cycle.

3 Identify significant risks and assess risk of material misstatement in the inventory cycle.

4 Understand key controls for the inventory cycle and assess control risk for inventory.

5 Use professional judgment to develop an audit approach (strategy) for inventory.

6 Design and perform tests of controls for the inventory cycle.

7 Design and perform substantive analytical procedures for the inventory cycle.

8 Design and perform substantive tests of details for the inventory cycle.

9 Design and perform fraud procedures for the inventory cycle.

Phantom Inventory

Mickey Monus was the local hero in Youngstown, Ohio. He acquired a local drugstore and within 10 years, added 299 more stores to form the national deep-discount retail chain Phar-Mor Inc. The company was viewed as the rising star by some retail experts and was considered to be the next Wal-Mart. Even Sam Walton announced that the only company he feared in the expansion of Wal-Mart was Phar-Mor.

Phar-Mor sold a variety of household products and prescription drugs at substantially lower prices than other discount stores. Monus described the company's strategy as "power buying," whereby

continued >

Phar-Mor loaded up on products when suppliers were selling at rock-bottom prices and passed those savings to cost-conscious customers through deeply discounted prices.

Actually, Phar-Mor's prices were so low that the company was selling goods for less than their cost, causing the company to lose money. However, Monus continued to argue internally that through Phar-Mor's power buying, it would get so large that it could sell its way out of trouble. Unwilling to allow these shortfalls to damage Phar-Mor's appearance of success, Monus and his team began to engage in creative accounting so that Phar-Mor never reported these losses in its financial statements.

Management dumped the losses into "bucket accounts," only to reallocate those amounts to the company's hundreds of stores in the form of phantom increases in inventory costs. Monus's team issued fake invoices for merchandise purchases, made fraudulent journal entries to increase inventory and decrease cost of goods sold, and overcounted and double-counted inventory items.

Unfortunately, the auditors never uncovered the fraud. They allegedly observed inventory in only four stores out of 300, and they informed Phar-Mor management months in advance about the stores they would visit. Phar-Mor executives fully stocked the four selected stores but allocated the false inventory increases to the other 296 stores.

The fraud was ultimately uncovered when a travel agent received a Phar-Mor cheque signed by Monus paying for expenses that were unrelated to Phar-Mor. The agent showed the cheque to her landlord, who happened to be a Phar-Mor investor, and he contacted David Shapiro, Phar-Mor's CEO. Subsequent investigation of the invalid expenditure led to the discovery of the inventory fraud.

Monus was eventually convicted and went to jail for five years. The CFO, who did not profit personally, was sentenced to 33 months in prison. The audit failure cost the audit firm over $300 million in civil judgments.

Sources: Mark Beasley, Frank Buckless, Steven Glover, and Douglas Prawitt, *Auditing Cases: An Interactive Learning Approach*, 5th edition, Prentice-Hall, 2012, pp. 119–131; Joseph T. Wells, "Ghost Goods: How to Spot Phantom Inventory," *Journal of Accountancy*, June 2001, pp. 33–36.

As the opening vignette demonstrates, finding misstatements in inventory can be challenging. To add to this challenge, the inventory and distribution cycle is closely interconnected with the other transaction cycles. For a manufacturing company, raw material enters the inventory and distribution cycle from the acquisition and payment cycle, while direct labour enters from the payroll cycle. The inventory and distribution cycle ends with the sale of goods in the revenue cycle and returns. For the auditor, that means being able to make the connections among the various cycles and classes of transactions.

OVERVIEW OF THE INVENTORY AND DISTRIBUTION CYCLE

LO 1 Identify the accounts and the classes of transactions in the inventory cycle.

Inventory takes many different forms, depending on the nature of the business. For retail or wholesale businesses, the most important inventory is merchandise on hand that is available for sale. A manufacturing company has raw materials, goods in process, and finished goods available for sale. For an organization to have the optimum quantity and quality of inventory, it has to have a well-organized supply chain.

Figure 14-1 shows the physical flow of goods and the flow of costs in the **inventory and distribution cycle** for a manufacturing company. The linkage between the inventory and distribution cycle and the acquisition and payment cycle, and between the inventory and distribution cycle and the human resources and payroll cycle, can be seen by examining the debits to the raw materials, direct labour, and manufacturing overhead T-accounts. The linkage to the revenue cycle occurs at the point where finished goods are relieved (credited) and a charge is made to cost of goods sold.

Inventory and distribution cycle—the transaction cycle that involves the physical flow of goods through the organization, as well as related costs.

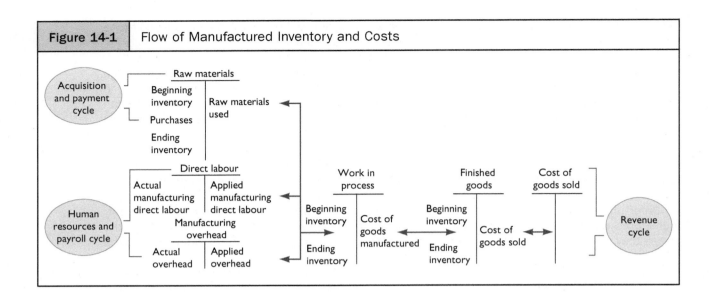

Figure 14-1 | Flow of Manufactured Inventory and Costs

LO **2** Describe the business functions, documents, and records of the inventory cycle.

INVENTORY CYCLE BUSINESS FUNCTIONS, DOCUMENTS, AND RECORDS

The inventory and distribution cycle can be thought of as comprising two separate but closely related systems, with one involving the actual *physical flow* of goods and the other the *related costs*. Figure 14-2 shows some of the business functions and reports of the cycle as a flow diagram, while Table 14-1 provides business functions analysis and sample documents and records of the cycle for a manufacturing organization. This is only one example, however; manufacturing organizations vary widely in the type of inventory and how they manage it.

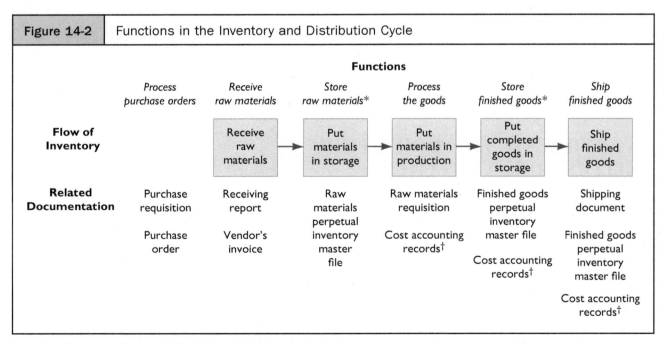

Figure 14-2 | Functions in the Inventory and Distribution Cycle

Functions

	Process purchase orders	Receive raw materials	Store raw materials*	Process the goods	Store finished goods*	Ship finished goods
Flow of Inventory		Receive raw materials	Put materials in storage	Put materials in production	Put completed goods in storage	Ship finished goods
Related Documentation	Purchase requisition	Receiving report	Raw materials perpetual inventory master file	Raw materials requisition	Finished goods perpetual inventory master file	Shipping document
	Purchase order	Vendor's invoice		Cost accounting records†	Cost accounting records†	Finished goods perpetual inventory master file
						Cost accounting records†

*Inventory counts are taken with perpetual and book amounts at any stage of the cycle. The auditor compares the documentation related to the receipt, payment, and sale of inventory with the physical location of the items to ensure proper cutoff and classification of inventory as raw material, work-in-process, or finished goods. The count must ordinarily be taken once a year. If the perpetual inventory system is operating well, this can be done on a cycle basis throughout the year.

†Includes cost information for materials, direct labour, and overhead.

Table 14-1	Business Functions Analysis: Inventory and Distribution Cycle	

Business Function (and Cycle Where Tested)	Examples of Documents and Records (and Purpose of Document or Record)	Sample Control Associated With the Documents or Records (and Assertion)
Acquire and record raw materials, overhead (acquisition and payment cycle), and labour (human resources and payroll cycle).	Purchase requisition and purchase order (order materials or components).	Purchase requisitions and purchase orders should be approved (existence). Account for numerical sequence of purchase orders (completeness).
	Receiving report, vendor invoice, and cash disbursement (receive materials or components and pay for them).	Independent matching of details of receiving report to vendor invoice (existence, completeness, accuracy). Inspect goods received for quality and quantity (accuracy).
	Time records, payroll journal, and payroll cost allocation report (allocate labour and other costs to inventory).	
Internal storage, production, and transfer of inventory and costs (inventory and distribution).	Raw material, work in progress, and finished goods transaction files* (track activities associated with individual inventory items).	Independent verification of data entered or use of scanning devices to record transactions (accuracy). Automatic posting of transaction dollar totals to the general ledger (completeness, existence).
	Materials requisition (move materials internally).	Use of authorized materials requisition form for internal transfers (existence).
	Inventory master file* (provide status of inventory).	Totals of inventory master file should agree with the inventory general ledger account (allocation).
	Cost accounting records (describe inventory costs).	Changes to inventory costing methods should be independently verified (accuracy).
	Production forecasts and reports (plan production and describe production).	Production forecasts and actual production plans should be approved (existence).
Ship goods and record revenue and cost of goods sold (sales and collections).	Shipping documents and customer invoice (ship goods to and bill customers).	Credit check should be done on all new customers (existence).
Physically count inventory (inventory and distribution).	Count sheets or records (document inventory on hand).	Teams of two people should be used to count inventory (existence, accuracy).
	Inventory adjustment records (adjust records to agree with counted inventory).	Adjustments to inventory should be approved and independently verified (existence, accuracy).
	Obsolete or damaged goods report.	Obsolete or damaged goods adjustments approved by someone independent of custody of inventory (existence, valuation).
Price and compile inventory values (inventory and distribution).	Inventory price adjustments (correct or update inventory prices).	Inventory price adjustments verified for clerical accuracy (accuracy).
	Inventory count reports (document inventory quantities and costs at a point in time).	Inventory count reports agreed to the general ledger inventory account (allocation).

*These documents and records are used for multiple business functions.

Distributing organizations, such as Hillsburg Hardware, would have many business functions similar to those described in Table 14-1. For example, Hillsburg needs to make sure that only authorized inventory is acquired that can be sold, that the inventory is priced correctly, and that costs of goods sold are recorded accurately when goods are sold.

An Overview of the Audit Process for Inventory

The overall objective in the audit of the inventory and distribution cycle is to determine that raw materials, work in process, finished goods inventory, and cost

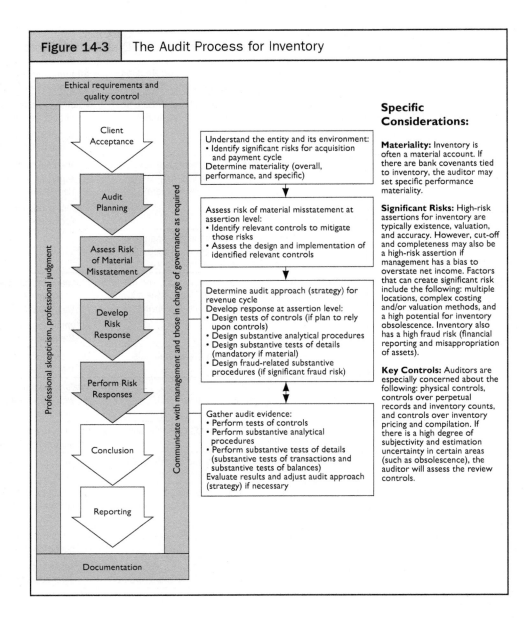

Figure 14-3 The Audit Process for Inventory

Ethical requirements and quality control

Client Acceptance

Audit Planning

Assess Risk of Material Misstatement

Develop Risk Response

Perform Risk Responses

Conclusion

Reporting

Documentation

Professional skepticism, professional judgment

Communicate with management and those in charge of governance as required

Understand the entity and its environment:
• Identify significant risks for acquisition and payment cycle
Determine materiality (overall, performance, and specific)

Assess risk of material misstatement at assertion level:
• Identify relevant controls to mitigate those risks
• Assess the design and implementation of identified relevant controls

Determine audit approach (strategy) for revenue cycle
Develop response at assertion level:
• Design tests of controls (if plan to rely upon controls)
• Design substantive analytical procedures
• Design substantive tests of details (mandatory if material)
• Design fraud-related substantive procedures (if significant fraud risk)

Gather audit evidence:
• Perform tests of controls
• Perform substantive analytical procedures
• Perform substantive tests of details (substantive tests of transactions and substantive tests of balances)
Evaluate results and adjust audit approach (strategy) if necessary

Specific Considerations:

Materiality: Inventory is often a material account. If there are bank covenants tied to inventory, the auditor may set specific performance materiality.

Significant Risks: High-risk assertions for inventory are typically existence, valuation, and accuracy. However, cut-off and completeness may also be a high-risk assertion if management has a bias to overstate net income. Factors that can create significant risk include the following: multiple locations, complex costing and/or valuation methods, and a high potential for inventory obsolescence. Inventory also has a high fraud risk (financial reporting and misappropriation of assets).

Key Controls: Auditors are especially concerned about the following: physical controls, controls over perpetual records and inventory counts, and controls over inventory pricing and compilation. If there is a high degree of subjectivity and estimation uncertainty in certain areas (such as obsolescence), the auditor will assess the review controls.

of goods sold are fairly stated on the financial statements. Figure 14-3 provides an overview of the audit process.

Inventory is generally a major item on the balance sheet, and it is often the largest item making up the accounts included in working capital, making it a high-risk audit area requiring substantial audit effort. As illustrated in this chapter's opening vignette, it is a balance sheet account that can be particularly problematic for auditors.

LO 3 Identify significant risks and assess risk of material misstatement in the inventory cycle.

IDENTIFY SIGNIFICANT RISKS

Significant risks are likely to vary depending upon the client industry, the type of product and business processes. Examples of potentially significant risks include the following:

- The company has or is attempting to obtain financing secured by inventory.
- The inventory is difficult to count or value.
- The company is a manufacturer or has a complex system to determine the value of inventory.
- The company is involved in technology or another volatile or rapidly changing industry.

Table 14-2	Major Risks of Error or Fraud in the Inventory and Distribution Cycle

Risks of Error	Risks of Misappropriation of Assets, Other Fraud, or Illegal Acts	Risks of Inadequate Disclosure or Incorrect Presentation of Financial Information, Including Fraudulent Financial Reporting
	Intentional overstatement (or understatement) of inventory on consignment or on hand.	
Incorrect calculation used to determine inventory cost.		Intentional inclusion of inventory held on consignment as owned inventory.
	Intentional cutoff errors (e.g., excluding returns from inventory or including shipments already sold).	
Valuation of obsolete inventory at full price.		Omission of disclosure that inventory is being used as collateral for debt.
	Employee theft of inventory.	
Incorrect valuation method used to determine cost of inventory.		Misallocation of inventory between raw material and finished goods.
	Unauthorized journal entries used to overstate inventory, so subsidiary records do not agree to the general ledger.	
Inventory counts done poorly, resulting in incorrect quantity on hand being recorded.		Accounting policy used for calculating inventory values is described in a confusing way.

Some common sources of business risk for inventory include short product cycles, potential obsolescence, use of just-in-time inventory and other potential vulnerabilities created with suppliers' practices, reliance on a few key suppliers, and use of sophisticated inventory management technology.

Auditors often have a greater concern for misstatements when inventory is stored in multiple locations, the costing method is complex, and the potential for inventory obsolescence is great. Inventory also has high fraud risk—if management is going to engage in fraud, inventory is often an account that is involved.

Table 14-2 summarizes the major risks of fraud or error in the inventory or distribution cycle. In addition to these risks, significant adjusting journal entries that have increased inventory or material reversing entries after the close of an accounting period may be indicators of fraud or error as well.

CONCEPT CHECK

C14-1 Provide two reasons why there could be a material error in inventory.

C14-2 Describe the two separate subsystems used to assess controls in the inventory and distribution cycle, and provide an example of a business function for each subsystem.

Identify and Assess Fraud Risk

As highlighted in Auditing in Action 14-1, fictitious inventory has been at the centre of several major cases of fraudulent financial reporting. Many large companies have varied and extensive inventory in multiple locations, making it relatively easy for the company to add fictitious inventory to the accounting records. Further, a lack of third-party evidence means that it is often easier to overstate inventory than other assets such as cash or trade receivables.

There are many potential warning signs or symptoms that point to inventory fraud. Analytical procedures, especially gross margin percentage and inventory turnover, often help uncover inventory fraud. Fictitious inventory understates cost of goods sold and overstates the gross margin percentage. Auditing in Action 14-1 provides some examples of fraud indicators that can be uncovered through the preliminary analytical review.

Assess Inherent Risk for Inventory

As Table 14-2 points out, the bias in recording inventory is often toward overstatement (assuming profit maximization or asset inflation), accomplished by valuing inventory too high (the accuracy and valuation assertions) or including inventory that does not exist (existence). However, there are also many common errors and frauds that relate to excluding inventory that has been returned or used in cost of goods sold (completeness and cutoff assertions) when the client has poor controls over cutoff or when the bias is to overstate net income. Some inherent risk factors affecting inventory include the following:

- Inventory is often stored in different locations, which makes physical control and counting difficult.
- Inventory is easily transportable, is easy to steal, and may be hard to access.
- Inventory that consists of items such as jewels, chemicals, and electronic parts is often difficult for the auditor to observe and value. In these circumstances, the auditor may need specialist assistance for both counting and valuation.
- The industry is categorized by rapid and significant technological innovation, which increases the risk of obsolescence.
- Customer returns are frequent, which causes accuracy, timing, and cutoff issues with recording of the physical return and the corresponding credit in sales. Poor quality client return processes will result in the need for increased audit tests.
- There are several acceptable inventory valuation methods under ASPE and IFRS, which the auditor must determine have been applied consistently from year to year.

LO **4** Understand key controls for the inventory cycle and assess control risk for inventory.

UNDERSTANDING AND ASSESSING CONTROL RISK

Internal controls vary widely from company to company. Inventory controls may be quite complex depending upon the type of inventory system. In addition to transaction controls, the auditor is concerned about control related to inventory observation.

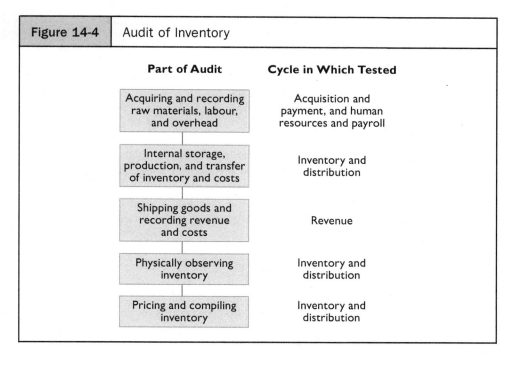

Figure 14-4 | Audit of Inventory

Part of Audit	Cycle in Which Tested
Acquiring and recording raw materials, labour, and overhead	Acquisition and payment, and human resources and payroll
Internal storage, production, and transfer of inventory and costs	Inventory and distribution
Shipping goods and recording revenue and costs	Revenue
Physically observing inventory	Inventory and distribution
Pricing and compiling inventory	Inventory and distribution

Before we discuss the controls specific to inventory, it is important to understand how the audit of inventory is connected with the audit of various other cycles, in particular, acquisition and payment, payroll, and revenue. The audit of the inventory cycle can be divided into five distinct activities:

- Acquiring and recording raw materials, labour, and overhead.
- Internal storage, production, and transfer of inventory and costs.
- Shipping goods and recording revenue and costs.
- Physically observing inventory.
- Pricing and compiling inventory.

Figure 14-4 identifies in which cycle each of these activities is tested. We provide a brief discussion of each activity.

Acquiring and Recording Raw Materials, Labour, and Overhead

This part of the inventory and distribution cycle includes the first three functions in Figure 14-2: processing of purchase orders, receipt of raw materials, and storage of raw materials. However, as Figure 14-4 demonstrates, the internal controls over these three functions are first studied, then tested, as part of performing tests of controls in the acquisition and payment cycle and the human resources and payroll cycle. At the completion of the acquisition and payment cycle, the auditor is likely to be satisfied that acquisitions of raw materials and manufacturing costs are correctly stated. Samples should be designed to ensure that these systems are adequately tested. Similarly, when labour is a significant part of inventory, the human resources and payroll cycle tests should verify the proper accounting for these costs.

Internal Storage, Production, and Transfer of Inventory and Costs

Internal transfers include the fourth and fifth functions in Figure 14-2: processing the goods and storing finished goods. The accounting records concerned with these functions of manufacture, processing, and storage are referred to as the **cost accounting records**.

Cost accounting records—the accounting records concerned with the manufacture and processing of the goods and storing finished goods.

Shipping Goods and Recording Revenue and Costs

The recording of shipments and related costs, the last function in Figure 14-2, is part of the sales and collection cycle. The internal controls over this function are studied and tested as part of auditing the revenue cycle, including procedures to verify the accuracy of the perpetual inventory master files.

Physically Observing Inventory

Observing the client taking a physical inventory count is necessary to determine whether recorded inventory actually exists at the balance sheet date and is properly counted by the client. The procedures related to observing the client's inventory count are both tests of controls and substantive tests (we discuss this in more detail later in the chapter). The vignette at the beginning of the chapter describing the Phar-Mor inventory fraud demonstrates the importance of observing inventory.

Pricing and Compiling Inventory

Costs used to value the physical inventory must be tested to determine whether the client has correctly followed an inventory method that is in accordance with generally accepted accounting principles and is consistent with the method of previous years. Audit procedures to verify these costs are called price tests. In addition, the auditor must perform inventory compilation tests, which verify whether physical counts were correctly summarized, quantities and prices were correctly extended, and extended inventory was correctly footed to equal the general ledger account.

KEY CONTROLS

When assessing control risk, the auditor is primarily concerned about (1) physical controls and internal controls over (2) perpetual records, (3) inventory counts, and (4) inventory compilation and pricing.

Physical Controls

Physical controls over assets prevent loss from misuse and theft. The use of physically segregated, limited-access storage areas for raw materials, work in process, and finished goods is one major control for protecting assets. In some instances, the assignment of custody of inventory to specific responsible individuals may be necessary to protect the assets. Approved prenumbered documents for authorizing movement of inventory also protects the assets from improper use. Copies of these documents should be sent directly to accounting by the persons issuing them, bypassing people with custodial responsibilities. An example of an effective document of this type is an approved materials requisition for obtaining raw materials from the storeroom.

Perpetual Records

Perpetual inventory data files maintained by persons who do not have custody of or access to assets are another important cost accounting control. Perpetual inventory data files provide a record of items on hand, which is used to initiate production or purchase of additional materials or goods; they provide a record of the use of raw materials and the sale of finished goods, which can be reviewed for obsolete or slow-moving items; and they provide a record that can be used to pinpoint responsibility for custody as part of the investigation of differences between physical counts and the amounts shown on the records.

Inventory Counts

Regardless of the inventory recordkeeping method, the client must make a periodic physical count of inventory, but not necessarily every year. The physical count may be performed at or near the balance sheet date, at an interim date, or on a cycle basis throughout the year. The latter two approaches are appropriate only if there are adequate controls over the perpetual inventory master files.

Adequate controls over the physical count of inventory include proper instructions for the physical count, supervision by responsible company personnel, independent internal verification of the counts by other client personnel, independent reconciliations of the physical counts with perpetual inventory master files, and adequate control over count sheets or tags used to record inventory counts.

Inventory Compilation and Pricing

Adequate internal controls surrounding the tracking of unit costs that are integrated with production and other accounting records provides assurance that clients use reasonable costs for valuing ending inventory. Below are some key controls:

- Standard cost records that indicate variances in material, labour, and overhead costs to help evaluate the reasonableness of production records;
- A review of the reasonableness of costs conducted by someone independent of the department responsible for determining the costs;
- A formal review, conducted by a knowledgeable employee, of obsolete, slow-moving, damaged, and overstated inventory items (Auditing in Action 14-2 describes how Blackberry Limited performs its inventory obsolescence review);
- Inventory compilation internal controls to ensure that the physical counts are correctly summarized, priced at the same amount as the unit records, correctly

---

AUDITING IN ACTION 14-2
BlackBerry's Inventory Obsolescence Woes

Managing inventory obsolescence is a key business risk of the smartphone industry—it depends upon product development, predicting demand, and managing the supply chain. Consider Blackberry's experience in 2014 with its poorly performing BlackBerry 10 phones. Prior to year-end (March 1), BlackBerry decided to reduce its handset inventory by offering incentives on sales, especially on devices built on its latest platform, BlackBerry 10. This price cut had a large impact on sales. For instance, in India, prices were slashed by 60 percent and BlackBerry ran out of stock in a few days.

In the end, BlackBerry was forced to take a nearly $1.6 billion inventory write-down. Here is how BlackBerry describes its inventory obsolescence evaluation process in its 2014 annual financial statements:

> The Company performs an assessment of inventory during each reporting period, which includes a review of, among other factors, demand requirements, component part purchase commitments of the Company and certain key suppliers, product life cycle and development plans, component cost trends, product pricing, and quality issues.

If customer demand subsequently differs from the Company's forecasts, requirements for inventory write-offs that differ from the Company's estimates could become necessary. If management believes that demand no longer allows the Company to sell inventories above cost or at all, such inventory is written down to net realizable value or excess inventory is written off.

Commenting on the write-down in a conference call to investors, the new CEO, John Chen, said BlackBerry planned to focus its attention on its traditional business of serving businesses and governments, particularly groups that require high levels of security.

Sources: Ian Austen, "Blackberry staggers to a deeper $4.4 billion loss," *New York Times*, December 2013. BlackBerry Limited, Annual information return (Form 40-F) for fiscal year ended March 31, 2014. "BlackBerry Z10 goes out of stock in India after price cut," *The Times of India*, March 4, 2014, accessed September 5, 2017, at **http://timesofindia.indiatimes.com/tech/tech-news/BlackBerry-Z10-goes-out-of-stock-in-India-after-price-cut/articleshow/31414229.cms**.

extended and totalled, and included in the perpetual inventory master file and related general ledger inventory accounts at the proper amount; and

- Adequate controls over the programs that perform calculations, with internal verification or review of entry of prices and of output reports by a competent, independent person.

LO **5** Use professional judgment to develop an audit approach (strategy) for inventory.

DEVELOP AN AUDIT APPROACH (STRATEGY) FOR INVENTORY

So far, we have discussed the factors that impact risk of material misstatement in the inventory cycle. As we have learned to date, the risk response can vary widely since it depends upon the specific risks and circumstances of the client. In other words, it requires considerable professional judgment.

Let's look at the significant risk factors identified by the auditors for two very different companies—Burberry Group plc, the British luxury goods manufacturer, and Lonmin Mines, a British mining company. As you can see from Table 14-3 (which is based upon the description from the key audit issues in the 2014 auditor reports), the significant risks with regard to inventory are quite different.

For Burberry, the high risk (or relevant) assertion is valuation, whereas for Lonmin, it is existence, completeness, and accuracy. As a result, the risk responses developed by the auditors are very different. The auditors of Burberry focus on the methodology for calculating the obsolescence provision, whereas the auditors of Lonmin focus on the inventory count and the client's experts (who play a key role in determining the inventory quantity). You will note that the auditors would consider the competence of the client's independent experts. This demonstrates skepticism in questioning the reliability of the evidence (recall that evidence from third parties is reliable if the source is competent and objective) and meets the requirement of CAS 620, *Using the Work of an Auditor's Expert*.

CAS

Note that the auditors would have tested the other assertions as well; however, these are significant risks (or key audit matters) that the auditors included in their audit report. For instance, the Burberry auditors would have also observed the

Table 14-3	Comparison of Two Audit Strategies		
Company	**Key (Relevant) Assertion**	**Risk Assessment**	**Risk Response**
Burberry Group plc British luxury fashion house known for its iconic tartan pattern. It manufactures and distributes outerwear, fashion accessories, fragrances, sunglasses, and cosmetics.	Net realizable value (valuation)	• Judgment is required to assess the appropriate provision for items which may ultimately be sold below cost. • Luxury goods are subject to changing consumer demands and fashion trends, increasing the level of judgment involved in estimating provisions.	• Tested the methodology for calculating the provisions; challenged the appropriateness and consistency of assumptions; and considered the suitability of historic data used in estimating the provisions. • Considered the aging profile of inventory, the process for identifying problem inventory, and historic loss rates to assess reasonableness of provisions.
Lonmin plc British mining company with operations in South Africa. It refines and markets platinum group metals.	Physical quantities of inventory (existence and accuracy)	• Physical quantities of metal inventory are determined by sampling, and assays are taken to determine the metal content. • The accuracy of these samples and assays can vary quite significantly and requires significant estimation and management judgment.	• Attended the physical count at year-end. • Assessed the competence of the client's independent metallurgists and results of their report. • Corroborated reasons for unusual movements in inventory quantities between the accounting records and the results of the sampling and assays. • Compared results to historical client data and industry.

inventory counts. However, the key (relevant) assertions would take considerable time, and more experienced auditors would be assigned to the tasks. Neither audit report described the type of control testing performed for inventory; however, given the size of the organizations, extensive tests of controls would have been performed.

DESIGN AND PERFORM TESTS OF CONTROLS

LO **6** Design and perform tests of controls for the inventory cycle.

Physical Controls Over Inventory

The auditor's tests of physical controls over raw materials, work in process, and finished goods are usually limited to observation and inquiry. For example, the auditor can examine the raw materials storage area to determine whether the inventory is protected from theft and misuse by the existence of a locked storeroom. The existence of an adequate storeroom with a competent custodian in charge also results in the orderly storage of inventory. If the auditor concludes that the physical controls are so inadequate that the inventory will be difficult to count, the auditor should expand his or her observation of physical inventory tests to ensure that an adequate count is carried out.

Documents and Records for Transferring Inventory

The auditor's primary concerns in verifying the transfer of inventory from one location to another are that recorded transfers exist, all actual transfers are recorded, and the quantity, description, and date of all recorded transfers are accurate. Products labelled with standardized bar codes that can be scanned by laser bar-code readers and other technologies make it easier for clients to track the movement of goods through production.

After auditors understand the internal controls, they can easily perform tests of controls or substantive tests of transactions by examining documents and records to test the occurrence and accuracy objectives for the transfer of goods from the raw material storeroom to manufacturing. Some of that testing may be done electronically when the related controls are automated. Similarly, the auditor may compare completed production records with perpetual inventory master files to be sure that all manufactured goods were physically delivered to the finished goods storeroom.

Perpetual Inventory Master and Transaction Files

The reliability of perpetual inventory master files affects the *timing* and *extent* of the auditor's physical examination of inventory. When perpetual inventory master files are accurate, auditors can test the physical inventory before the balance sheet date. An interim physical inventory or use of cycle counts throughout the year can result in significant cost savings for both the client and the auditor, and it enables the audit to be completed earlier. The auditor may also reduce tests of physical inventory counts when the client has reliable perpetual inventory records and when assessed control risk related to physical observation of inventory is low.

Auditors test perpetual inventory master files by examining documentation that supports changes to inventory amounts in the master files. Usually, it is relatively easy to test the accuracy of the perpetual inventory master files after the auditor determines the adequacy of the design and implementation of inventory internal controls and the related level of assessed control risk. Auditors test the perpetual records for acquisitions of raw materials in the acquisition and payment cycle, while reductions in finished goods for sale are tested in the sales and collection cycle.

For many companies, traditional documents exist only in electronic form and the perpetual inventory system is integrated with other accounting cycles. As a result, the auditor can test computer controls to support a reduction in control risk, which reduces substantive testing and can result in audit efficiencies.

Unit Cost Records

Obtaining accurate cost data for raw materials, direct labour, and manufacturing overhead is an essential part of cost accounting. Adequate cost accounting records must be integrated with production and other accounting records in order to produce accurate costs of all products. The valuation of ending inventory depends on the proper design and use of these records. Because internal controls over cost accounting records vary significantly among companies, specific tests of controls are not discussed here. Auditors should design appropriate tests based on their understanding of the cost accounting records and the extent to which they will be relied on to reduce substantive tests.

LO 7 Design and perform substantive analytical procedures for the inventory cycle.

PERFORM SUBSTANTIVE ANALYTICAL PROCEDURES

Substantive analytical procedures are as important in auditing inventory and distribution as in any other cycle. Table 14-4 includes several common substantive analytical procedures and possible misstatements that may be indicated when fluctuations exist. Note that, for the auditor to derive the adequate assurance from these substantive analytical procedures, the tests must have an adequate level of precision, and many of the tests would be performed at a more disaggregated level of detail (say by product line, location, or market).

In addition to examining the relationship between the inventory account and other financial accounts, auditors often use nonfinancial information to assess the reasonableness of inventory. For example, auditors may need knowledge about the size and weight of inventory products, their methods of storage (stacks, tanks, etc.), and the capacity of storage facilities (available square footage) to determine whether recorded inventory is consistent with available storage.

Table 14-4	Substantive Analytical Procedures for the Inventory and Distribution Cycle
Substantive Analytical Procedure	**Possible Misstatement**
Compare gross margin percentage with that of previous years.	Overstatement or understatement of inventory and cost of goods sold.
Compare inventory turnover (costs of goods sold divided by average inventory) with that of previous years.	Overstatement or understatement of inventory and cost of goods sold (obsolete inventory).
Compare unit costs of inventory with those of previous years.	Overstatement or understatement of inventory.
Compare extended inventory value with that of previous years.	Misstatements in compilation, unit costs, or extensions that affect inventory and cost of goods sold.
Compare current-year manufacturing costs with costs of previous years (variable costs should be adjusted for changes in volume).	Misstatements of unit costs of inventory, especially direct labour and manufacturing overhead, which affect inventory and cost of goods sold.

SUBSTANTIVE TESTS OF DETAILS FOR INVENTORY BALANCES

LO **8** Design and perform substantive tests of details for the inventory cycle.

The focus of most substantive tests of details for inventory are (1) physical observation and (2) pricing and compilation.

Physical Observation of Inventory

Prior to the late 1930s, audit evidence for inventory quantities was usually restricted to obtaining a certificate from management stating that the recorded amount was correct. However, a financial reporting fraud involving a U.S. company, McKesson & Robbins, led to questioning the auditors' responsibilities regarding inventory. In brief, the financial statements for McKesson & Robbins at December 31, 1937, which had been "certified" by a major accounting firm, reported total consolidated assets of $87 million. Of this amount, approximately $19 million were fictitious ($10 million in inventory and $9 million in receivables). The auditing firm was not held directly at fault in the inventory area because it had followed GAAS that were in effect at that time. However, the judge noted that if certain procedures, such as observation of the physical inventory, had been carried out, the fraud would probably have been detected.

Per CAS 501, *Audit evidence: specific considerations for selected items*, when inventory is material, the auditor should attend the client's physical inventory count unless it is impractical to do so. The purpose of attendance is to observe that the inventory actually exists and to assess its condition (this provides some evidence for the valuation objective). The CAS provides specific instructions for audit procedures that the auditor should perform in evaluation of the processes used during the count, including methods to record count results and tracking count results to their final recording into financial records.

CAS

If for some reason the auditor cannot attend the physical count, the auditor may consider other procedures; however, the decision not to attend the count must be justified. For instance, despite the inconvenience of driving 100 kilometres to a remote location, the auditor would be required to attend the inventory count. In contrast, it would be impractical to count inventory if the auditor was appointed after a company's year-end. The alternative procedures would need to be of high quality and developed based upon management biases and assessed risks of material misstatement.

Controls An important aspect of the auditor's understanding of the client's physical inventory controls is having a thorough understanding of the controls before the inventory-taking begins. This is necessary to evaluate the effectiveness of the client's procedures, but it also enables the auditor to make constructive suggestions beforehand. If the inventory instructions do not provide adequate controls, the auditor must spend more time ensuring that the physical count is accurate.

Timing The auditor decides whether the physical count can be taken prior to year-end primarily on the basis of the accuracy of the perpetual inventory files. When an interim physical count is performed, the auditor observes it then and also tests the accuracy of the perpetuals for transactions from the date of the count to year-end. When the perpetuals are accurate, it may be unnecessary for the client to count the entire inventory every year. Instead, the auditor can compare the perpetuals with the actual inventory on a sample basis at a convenient time. When there are no perpetuals and the inventory is material, a complete physical inventory must be taken by the client near the end of the accounting period and tested by the auditor at the same time.

Figure 14-5 summarizes the assertions for the inventory balance of diamonds and the various substantive tests of details normally performed.

In most instances, the issues regarding quantity of inventory are the same regardless of the type of inventory (although as we will see in our later discussion of the mining

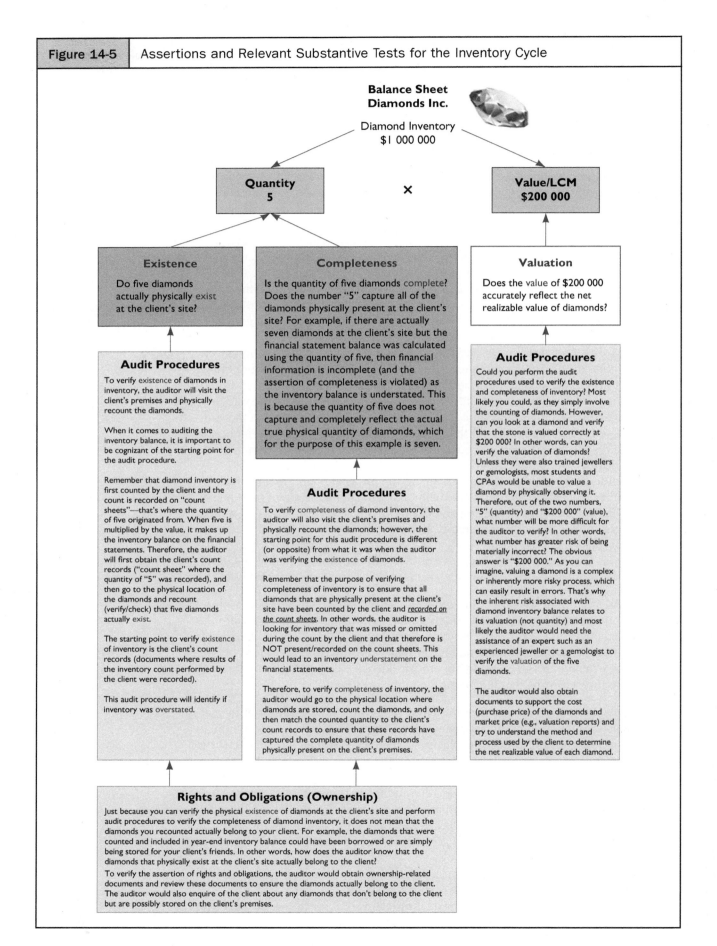

Figure 14-5 Assertions and Relevant Substantive Tests for the Inventory Cycle

Balance Sheet Diamonds Inc.

Diamond Inventory $1 000 000

Quantity 5 × **Value/LCM $200 000**

Existence

Do five diamonds actually physically exist at the client's site?

Completeness

Is the quantity of five diamonds complete? Does the number "5" capture all of the diamonds physically present at the client's site? For example, if there are actually seven diamonds at the client's site but the financial statement balance was calculated using the quantity of five, then financial information is incomplete (and the assertion of completeness is violated) as the inventory balance is understated. This is because the quantity of five does not capture and completely reflect the actual true physical quantity of diamonds, which for the purpose of this example is seven.

Valuation

Does the value of $200 000 accurately reflect the net realizable value of diamonds?

Audit Procedures

To verify existence of diamonds in inventory, the auditor will visit the client's premises and physically recount the diamonds.

When it comes to auditing the inventory balance, it is important to be cognizant of the starting point for the audit procedure.

Remember that diamond inventory is first counted by the client and the count is recorded on "count sheets"—that's where the quantity of five originated from. When five is multiplied by the value, it makes up the inventory balance on the financial statements. Therefore, the auditor will first obtain the client's count records ("count sheet" where the quantity of "5" was recorded), and then go to the physical location of the diamonds and recount (verify/check) that five diamonds actually exist.

The starting point to verify existence of inventory is the client's count records (documents where results of the inventory count performed by the client were recorded).

This audit procedure will identify if inventory was overstated.

Audit Procedures

To verify completeness of diamond inventory, the auditor will also visit the client's premises and physically recount the diamonds; however, the starting point for this audit procedure is different (or opposite) from what it was when the auditor was verifying the existence of diamonds.

Remember that the purpose of verifying completeness of inventory is to ensure that all diamonds that are physically present at the client's site have been counted by the client and _recorded on the count sheets_. In other words, the auditor is looking for inventory that was missed or omitted during the count by the client and that therefore is NOT present/recorded on the count sheets. This would lead to an inventory understatement on the financial statements.

Therefore, to verify completeness of inventory, the auditor would go to the physical location where diamonds are stored, count the diamonds, and only then match the counted quantity to the client's count records to ensure that these records have captured the complete quantity of diamonds physically present on the client's premises.

Audit Procedures

Could you perform the audit procedures used to verify the existence and completeness of inventory? Most likely you could, as they simply involve the counting of diamonds. However, can you look at a diamond and verify that the stone is valued correctly at $200 000? In other words, can you verify the valuation of diamonds? Unless they were also trained jewellers or gemologists, most students and CPAs would be unable to value a diamond by physically observing it. Therefore, out of the two numbers, "5" (quantity) and "$200 000" (value), what number will be more difficult for the auditor to verify? In other words, what number has greater risk of being materially incorrect? The obvious answer is "$200 000." As you can imagine, valuing a diamond is a complex or inherently more risky process, which can easily result in errors. That's why the inherent risk associated with diamond inventory balance relates to its valuation (not quantity) and most likely the auditor would need the assistance of an expert such as an experienced jeweller or a gemologist to verify the valuation of the five diamonds.

The auditor would also obtain documents to support the cost (purchase price) of the diamonds and market price (e.g., valuation reports) and try to understand the method and process used by the client to determine the net realizable value of each diamond.

Rights and Obligations (Ownership)

Just because you can verify the physical existence of diamonds at the client's site and perform audit procedures to verify the completeness of diamond inventory, it does not mean that the diamonds you recounted actually belong to your client. For example, the diamonds that were counted and included in year-end inventory balance could have been borrowed or are simply being stored for your client's friends. In other words, how does the auditor know that the diamonds that physically exist at the client's site actually belong to the client?

To verify the assertion of rights and obligations, the auditor would obtain ownership-related documents and review these documents to ensure the diamonds actually belong to the client. The auditor would also enquire of the client about any diamonds that don't belong to the client but are possibly stored on the client's premises.

company Lomnin, sometimes verifying quantity may involve specialists). As you can imagine, verifying the quantity (existence and completeness) of five diamonds or five cellphones would involve the same type of audit procedures. After all, the quantity of any inventory is verified through the process of recounting. Therefore, whether the auditor is recounting diamonds to verify their existence or is recounting cellphones to verify the completeness of the inventory balance presented on financial statements, the process is the same. What is important, as explained in Figure 14-5, is the starting point for the recount as, depending on where the auditor starts the count, either the assertion of existence or the assertion of completeness is being addressed through the audit procedure.

Completeness and Cutoff In addition to the test counts mentioned in Figure 14-5, the auditor performs cutoff tests of receipts and shipments of inventory at year-end to ensure that all items are recorded in the correct period. At the count, if the client continues shipping and receiving, the auditor will usually ensure that the client has appropriate procedures in place to account for inventory movement. If client has inventory held at third-party locations, the auditor would obtain confirmation from those third parties, thus negating the need to attend counts at those locations.

Selection of Items Care should be taken to observe the counting of all of the most significant items and a representative sample of typical inventory items. The auditor also inquires about items that are likely to be obsolete or damaged, and discusses with management the reasons for excluding any material items.

Physical Observation Tests

The auditor should be present while the physical count is taking place. When the client's employees are not following the inventory instructions, the auditor must either contact the supervisor to correct the problem or modify the auditor's physical observation procedures. For example, if the procedures require one team to count the inventory and a second team to recount it as a test of accuracy, the auditor should inform management if both teams are observed counting together.

CONCEPT CHECK

C14-5 Why does observing inventory only provide limited evidence on the valuation objective?

C14-6 Although attending the client's count is important for substantive testing, it is perhaps more important to assess internal controls over the count. Explain why.

In addition to procedures highlighted in Figure 14-5 and our discussion, the auditor should walk through all areas where inventory is warehoused to make sure that all inventory has been counted and properly tagged. When inventory is in boxes or other containers, these should be opened on a sample basis during test counts. A reasonableness test that is usually performed is a comparison of the high-dollar-value inventory with counts in the previous year and inventory master files as a test of reasonableness. These two procedures should be done after the client has completed the physical counts.

Pricing and Compilation Substantive Tests

The purpose of pricing and compilation substantive tests is to make certain the physical counts were properly priced and compiled. Pricing substantive tests includes the tests of the client's unit prices to determine whether they are correct. Compilation substantive tests includes testing the summarization of the physical counts, extending price times quantity, footing the inventory summary, and tracing the totals to the general ledger.

The client's inventory listing—which includes the item description, quantity, unit price, and extended value—is the basis for these tests. In performing pricing (valuation) tests, three things about the client's method of pricing are extremely important: the method must be in accordance with an acceptable financial accounting framework, the application of the method must be consistent from year to year, and cost versus market value (replacement cost or net realizable value) must be considered.

As discussed in Figure 14-5, verifying the valuation of diamonds in inventory is something more challenging and complex, and would most likely require the auditor to involve an expert to assist in this process. However, what about verifying the valuation or cost of cellphones? Assume your client's inventory balance consists of five phones at $100 each. Recall that inventory must be stated at the lower of cost and net realizable value. As discussed earlier, the auditor would assess management's review process (to assess the controls effectiveness). For substantive tests, the auditor would focus on verifying both the product cost and the net realizable value of the cellular phone inventory. The objective is to determine which value is lower and then to ensure that the $100 used to value the inventory is the lower amount.

Substantive Tests of Product Costs To verify the cost of cellular phone inventory, the auditor may use statistical sampling (as we discussed in Chapter 11) to select the items and then obtain and review supporting purchase documents, such as invoices, to determine what amount the client paid for the cellular phones.

In selecting specific inventory items for pricing, emphasis should be on those items that have the greatest risk of material misstatement—larger dollar amounts, products that are known to have wide price fluctuations, and slow moving inventory. However, the auditor should ensure that there is a representative sample of all types of inventory and all departments should be included. It is important that a sufficient number of invoices be examined to account for the entire quantity of inventory for the particular item being tested, especially for the FIFO (first-in, first-out) valuation method. If specific items or projects have different cost structures, the auditor should also be careful that the invoice relates to the specific item being tested (IAS 2.23), perhaps by checking serial numbers or locations.

In the case of manufactured goods, the auditor reviews direct labour rates and compares to authorized wage rates, test computation of overhead rates, and examine analyses of purchasing and manufacturing variances. The proper manufacturing overhead is dependent on the approach being used by the client. The auditor evaluates the method being used for consistency and reasonableness, as well as recomputing to determine whether overhead is correct.

Substantive Tests for Replacement Cost and Net Realizable Value Inventory is reduced, when appropriate, to net realizable value or replacement cost. For purchased finished goods and raw materials, the most recent vendor's invoice of the subsequent period is a useful and straightforward means of testing for replacement cost. However, testing inventory obsolescence requires considerable professional judgement because the client may be overly optimistic about the saleability of the goods, and replacement cost and net realizable value are estimates of future events. In the case of our cellular phones, the auditor would perform some research to find out what price (less costs to facilitate the sale) the cellular phones can be sold for. This often involves speaking to company employees in a variety of areas outside of accounting, and it requires a considerable amount of professional judgment. To verify this information, the auditor could review documents supporting the most recent sales made by the client, such as payments made by customers (remember, inquiry gives low-quality evidence).

CONCEPT CHECK

C14-7 The inventory balance is highly material. Does the auditor have a choice with respect to observation of inventory? Why or why not?

C14-8 Why is the audit technique of observation important during the physical inventory count?

DESIGNING FRAUD SUBSTANTIVE PROCEDURES FOR INVENTORY

LO **9** Design and perform fraud procedures for the inventory cycle.

Unlike with revenue, the auditor is not required to presume the risk of fraud for inventory, although next to revenue it is the area where financial reporting fraud would most likely occur. However, if the auditor has determined that there is a heightened fraud risk, CAS 240 suggests that he or she should consider performing fraud procedures such as those listed below:

- Perform surprise visits and counts to inventory locations.
- Perform additional procedures at the count—for example, more rigorously examine contents of boxed items, how goods are stacked or labelled, and the quality of liquid substances such as perfumes and specialty chemicals. Using an expert may be required to perform an appropriate assessment.
- Use computer-assisted audit techniques to further test compilation of inventory counts to check for possible omissions or duplications.

Other procedures to consider include the following:

- Ensure that the audit plan is confidential and not discussed with the client, particularly regarding the locations, times, and sampling amounts of the physical inventory counts.
- Perform nonfinancial analytics to determine unusual relationships (e.g., calculating volume required for holding reported inventory and comparing that to the actual space in the existing warehouse to discover an overstatement or double counting).
- Inquire of personnel in the shipping department about recent shipments between inventory warehouse locations close to the physical inventory count date.[1]

---

[1] This list is from W. Stephen Albrecht, Chad O. Albrecht, Conan C. Albrecht, and Mark F. Zimbelman, *Fraud Examination*, South Western–Cengage Learning, 2012.

SUMMARY

In this chapter, we discussed the audit of the inventory and distribution cycle. Because of the difficulties with establishing the existence and valuation of inventories, this cycle is often the most time-consuming and complex part of the audit. The cycle is also unique because many of the tests of the inputs to the cycle are tested as parts of the audit of other cycles. Substantive tests of details focus on the physical observation of the inventory (which the standards require unless it is impractical), tests of the pricing, and compilation of ending inventory and the cost records.

MyLab Accounting
Make the grade with MyLab Accounting: The questions, exercises, and problems marked with a 🌐 can be found on MyLab Accounting. You can practise them as often as you want, and most feature step-by-step guided instructions to help you find the right answer.

Review Questions

🌐 **14-1** **3** **4** Give the reasons why inventory is often the most difficult and time-consuming part of many audit engagements.

🌐 **14-2** **1** **3** Explain the relationship between the acquisition and payment cycle and the inventory and distribution cycle in the audit of a manufacturing company. List several audit procedures in the acquisition and payment cycle that support your explanation.

🌐 **14-3** **2** What is meant by *cost accounting records*, and what is their importance in the conduct of an audit?

14-4 **[4]** Many auditors assert that certain audit tests can be significantly reduced for clients with adequate perpetual records that include both unit and cost data. What are the most important tests of the perpetual records that the auditor must make before he or she can reduce the assessed level of control risk? Assuming the perpetuals are determined to be accurate, which tests can be reduced?

14-5 **[4] [8]** In obtaining an understanding of inventory procedures for a small manufacturing company, the auditor obtains a copy of the client's inventory instructions and reviews them with the controller before the physical examination. Two deficiencies are identified: (1) shipping operations will not be completely halted during the physical examination, and (2) there will be no independent verification of the original inventory count by a second counting team. Evaluate the importance of each of these deficiencies, and state their effects on the auditor's observation of inventory.

14-6 **[8]** At the completion of an inventory observation, the controller requested a copy of all recorded test counts from the auditor to facilitate the correction of all discrepancies between the client's and the auditor's counts. Should the auditor comply with the request? Why or why not?

14-7 **[8]** What major audit procedures are involved in testing for the ownership of inventory during the observation of the physical counts and as part of subsequent valuation tests?

14-8 **[3] [8]** In the verification of the amount of the inventory, the auditor should identify slow-moving and obsolete items. List the auditing procedures that could be employed to determine whether slow-moving or obsolete items have been included in inventory.

14-9 **[8]** During the taking of physical inventory, the controller intentionally withheld several inventory tags from the employees responsible for the physical count. After the auditor left the client's premises at the completion of the inventory observation, the controller recorded nonexistent inventory on the tags and thereby significantly overstated earnings. How could the auditor have uncovered the misstatement, assuming there are no perpetual records?

14-10 **[8]** Explain why a proper cutoff of purchases and sales is heavily dependent on the physical inventory observation. What information should be obtained during the physical count to make sure cutoff is accurate?

14-11 **[8]** Define what is meant by *compilation tests*. List several examples of audit procedures to verify compilation.

14-12 **[8]** Included in the December 31, 2018, inventory of Kupitz Supply Ltd. are 2600 deluxe ring binders in the amount of $5902. An examination of the most recent purchases of binders showed the following costs: January 26, 2019, 2300 at $2.42 each; December 6, 2018, 1900 at $2.28 each; and November 26, 2018, 2400 at $2.07 each. What is the misstatement in valuation of the December 31, 2018, inventory for deluxe ring binders assuming FIFO inventory valuation? What would your answer be if the January 26, 2019, purchase were for 2300 binders at $2.12 each?

14-13 **[7]** Ruswell Manufacturing Ltd. applied manufacturing overhead to inventory at December 31, 2018, on the basis of $3.47 per direct labour hour. Explain how you would evaluate the reasonableness of total direct labour hours and manufacturing overhead in the ending inventory of finished goods.

14-14 **[8]** Assuming that the auditor properly documents receiving report numbers as part of the physical inventory observation procedures, explain how he or she should verify the proper cutoff of purchases, including tests for the possibility of raw materials in transit, later in the audit.

Multiple Choice Questions and Task-Based Simulations

The following question concerns internal controls in the inventory and warehousing cycle. Choose the best response.

14-15 **[3] [9]** Which of the following procedures will best detect the theft of valuable items from an inventory that consists of hundreds of different items selling for $1 to $10 and a few items selling for hundreds of dollars?

(1) Maintain a perpetual inventory master file of only the more valuable items with frequent periodic verification of the validity of the perpetuals.

(2) Have an independent CPA (Chartered Professional Accountant) firm prepare an internal control report on the effectiveness of the administrative and accounting controls over inventory.

(3) Have separate warehouse space for the more valuable items with sequentially numbered tags.

(4) Require an authorized officer's signature on all requisitions for the more valuable items.

The following questions concern testing the client's internal controls for inventory and distribution. Choose the best response.

14-16 〔4〕 Which of the following internal control procedures most likely would be used to maintain accurate inventory records?

(1) Perpetual inventory records are periodically compared with the current cost of individual inventory items.

(2) A just-in-time inventory ordering system keeps inventory levels to a desired minimum.

(3) Requisitions, receiving reports, and purchase orders are independently matched before payment is approved.

(4) Periodic inventory counts are used to adjust the perpetual inventory records.

14-17 〔4〕 Which of the following sets of duties related to inventory and distribution causes the greatest concern about inadequate segregation of duties?

(1) Individuals in charge of approving disbursements related to inventory purchases have "read-only" ability to view the list of vendors in the preapproved vendor master file.

(2) Purchasing agents who arrange for shipment of raw materials from vendors are responsible for verifying actual receipt of the inventory items at the receiving dock.

(3) The receiving department has access to copies of the purchase orders that exclude information about quantities ordered.

(4) Accounts payable personnel have access to receiving reports and purchase orders in addition to vendor invoices for inventory purchases.

14-18 〔5〕〔8〕 On December 31, 2018, Best Cement Inc., a cement wholesaler, conducted its annual year-end inventory count. Best Cement stores all of its cement in large storage silos (very tall cylinder-shaped metal bins). Best Cement's staff member Aston Matthews was assigned to help with the year-end cement inventory count. The weight of the cement (in kilograms) is estimated using a mathematical formula and the dimensions of the silo and the space taken up by cement inside the silo. To figure out the space taken up by cement inside the silos, Aston was supposed to climb on top of each silo and use a long measuring stick to find out the depth of cement inside each silo. Since it was cold and windy, Aston didn't feel like climbing on top of the silos. He simply guessed the depth of cement and gave his numbers to the company's controller, who used them and the mathematical formula to derive the weight of cement inventory on hand at year-end.

REQUIRED

a. Based on the facts depicted in the case, identify the *relevant* management assertion(s) at most risk of being incorrect:

1) Valuation	4) Rights and Obligations
2) Cutoff	5) Completeness
3) Existence	6) Classification

b. Propose a control that Best Cement Inc. could implement to ensure the cement inventory count is done correctly.

c. How should an auditor deal with the inventory count issues discussed in Part a?

14-19 〔5〕〔8〕 Big Tasty Bird Inc. (BTB) is a turkey farm. BTB year-end is September 30, 2018. It takes about four to six months to raise a turkey from the time the chicks hatch from their eggs. A full-grown and healthy turkey that is ready for sale can weigh anywhere between 16 and 24 lbs. Such turkeys usually sell for about $4 per lb. Turkeys are susceptible to different diseases, including turkey pox. Turkeys that get this disease stop growing, and it costs more to look after them. At full maturity, turkeys that have turkey pox end up weighing just 5 to 6 lbs. In prior years, BTB would vaccinate all of its turkeys against turkey pox. However, in 2018, due to financial pressures, management decided to "risk it" and did not vaccinate any of the birds. The decision was paying off, until in the summer of 2018, when about half of the turkeys at BTB got turkey pox.

REQUIRED

a. Based on facts depicted in the case, identify the *relevant* management assertion that is at most risk of being misstated:

1) Valuation	4) Rights and Obligations
2) Cutoff	5) Completeness
3) Existence	6) Classification

b. Propose an audit procedure to test the assertion you chose in Part a.

⊕ **14-20** `4` `7` `8` For each audit procedure commonly performed in the inventory and distribution cycle for a manufacturing company, identify whether each of the procedures is primarily a test of controls or a substantive test.

Procedure	Test of Controls/Substantive Test
Read the client's physical inventory instructions and observe whether they are being followed by those responsible for counting the inventory.	
Account for a sequence of inventory tags and trace each tag to the physical inventory to make sure it actually exists.	
Compare the client's count of physical inventory at an interim date with the perpetual inventory master file.	
Trace the auditor's test counts recorded in the audit files to the final inventory compilation and compare the tag number, description, and quantity.	
Compare the unit price on the final inventory summary with vendors' invoices.	
Account for a sequence of raw material requisitions and examine each requisition for an authorized approval.	
Trace the recorded additions on the finished goods perpetual inventory master file to the records for completed production.	

Discussion Questions and Problems

⊕ **14-21** `8` In connection with her examination of the financial statements of Knutson Products Co. Ltd., an assembler of home appliances, for the year ended May 31, 2018, Raymonde Mathieu, public accountant, is reviewing with Knutson's controller the plans for a physical inventory at the company warehouse on May 31, 2018.

Finished appliances, unassembled parts, and supplies are stored in the warehouse, which is attached to Knutson's assembly plant. The plant will operate during the count. On May 30, the warehouse will deliver to the plant the estimated quantities of unassembled parts and supplies required for May 31 production, but there may be emergency requisitions on May 31. During the count, the warehouse will continue to receive parts and supplies and will ship finished appliances. However, appliances completed on May 31 will be held in the plant until after the physical inventory.

REQUIRED

What procedures should the company establish to ensure that the inventory count includes all items that should be included and that nothing is counted twice?

⊕ **14-22** `4` Items 1 through 8 are selected questions typically found in questionnaires used by auditors to obtain an understanding of internal controls in the inventory and distribution cycle. In using the questionnaire for a particular client, a "yes" response to a question indicates a possible internal control, whereas a "no" indicates a potential weakness.
1. Does the receiving department prepare prenumbered receiving reports and account for the numbers periodically for all inventory received, showing the description and quantity of materials?
2. Is all inventory stored under the control of a custodian in areas where access is limited?
3. Are all shipments to customers authorized by prenumbered shipping documents?
4. Is a detailed perpetual inventory master file maintained for raw materials inventory?
5. Are physical inventory counts made by someone other than storekeepers and those responsible for maintaining the perpetual inventory master file?
6. Are standard cost records used for raw materials, direct labour, and manufacturing overhead?
7. Is there a stated policy with specific criteria for writing off obsolete or slow-moving goods?
8. Is the clerical accuracy of the final inventory compilation checked by a person independent of those responsible for preparing it?

a. For each of the preceding questions, state the purpose of the internal control.

b. For each internal control, list a test of controls to test its effectiveness.

c. For each of the preceding questions, identify the nature of the potential financial misstatement(s) if the control is not in effect.

d. For each of the potential misstatements in Part (c), list a substantive audit procedure to determine whether a material misstatement exists.

14-23 3 5 8 Below are four independent client scenarios:

1. Colburn Pharmacy Inc. has 77 stores located in Eastern Canada. Approximately 60 percent of the inventory recorded on the balance sheet for the consolidated company is located at one of two distribution warehouses, which are in Montreal, QC, and Moncton, NB. The remainder of inventory is spread across the 77 stores. The high-dollar-value items in the inventory consist of prescription drugs that are stored in secure areas both in the distribution centres and at the individual stores.

2. Zenith Inc. manufactures high-end motorcycles in production facilities located in Windsor and St. Thomas, ON. During 2018, the company also opened major production facilities in India and Brazil. Each production facility receives raw materials that are then assembled into motorcycles. Manufactured motorcycles are stored at the production facilities until orders are received from dealers.

3. Texide Electronics manufactures component parts that are used in customers' computers and other electronics products. Given that customer products differ, each of Texide's products is designed uniquely for each customer's production process. Individual parts are quite small, and the interior components are not visible to the human eye. All inventory items are stored in Texide's only manufacturing plant.

4. Food Giant is a regional grocery store chain located in Western Canada. Rather than operate a company-owned distribution centre, Food Giant uses five different independent storage warehouse companies across the region to store most of its grocery inventory before shipping to the individual stores. Typically, about 75 percent of the inventory is located at the storage warehouses with the remaining inventory located at one of Food Giant's 42 stores.

REQUIRED

a. For each independent client scenario, describe issues the auditor should consider when determining which locations to visit to physically observe the client's inventory count.

b. How would you determine which locations to visit?

c. For each scenario, how does the type of inventory create potential risks of material misstatements in the inventory balances?

d. How might the auditor address the risks noted in Part (c)?

14-24 3 5 7 Your client, Ridgewood Heating and Cooling, specializes in residential air conditioning and heating installations. The company maintains an inventory of air conditioning units, furnaces, and air handling ductwork. The client has provided the following selected financial statement information for the year ending December 31, 2018:

	12/31/2018	12/31/2017	12/31/2016
Total sales	$55 443 900	$52 700 440	$50 384 300
Cost of goods sold	47 771 880	46 810 900	44 670 400
Ending inventory	9 582 960	8 100 220	7 730 660

Following is a breakdown of the ending inventory account as of December 31, 2018:

Inventory Description	Quantity	Ending Balance
AC unit – Model 635	1 240 units	$ 806 000
AC unit – Model 770	1 733 units	1 940 960
Furnace – Model 223	1 992 furnaces	2 589 600
Furnace – Model 225	2 008 furnaces	2 761 000
Air handling ducts	11 883 boxes	1 485 400
Total		$9 582 960

Ridgewood stores inventory in a 100 000-square-foot warehouse facility at a location different from its corporate office. A single air conditioning unit is stored on a 4-foot-by-4-foot pallet.

Warehouse storage shelves allow the company to store one pallet on the floor while two additional pallets are placed on shelves above the first pallet. Furnaces are also stored on similar sized pallets. Due to the height of the furnaces, only one unit can be stored on a shelf above another pallet that rests on the floor. Air handling ducts are stored in boxes that are 5 feet by 5 feet at the base and 7 feet tall. Three boxes can be stacked on top of the box that sits on the floor.

REQUIRED

a. Design analytical procedures to evaluate the reasonableness of the ending inventory account.

b. What concerns, if any, do you have about the ending inventory at Ridgewood Heating and Cooling?

14-25 **8** You encountered the following situations during the December 31, 2018, physical inventory of Latner Shoe Distributing Corp.

a. Latner maintains a large portion of its shoe merchandise in 10 warehouses throughout eastern and central Canada. This ensures swift delivery service for its chain of stores. You were assigned alone to the Halifax warehouse to observe the physical inventory process. During the inventory count, several express trucks pulled in for loading. Although infrequent, express shipments must be attended to immediately. As a result, the employees who were counting the inventory stopped to assist in loading the express trucks. What should you do?

b. (1) In one storeroom of 10 000 items, you test counted about 200 items of high value and a few items of low value. You found no misstatements. You also noted that the employees were diligently following the inventory instructions. Do you think you have tested enough items? Explain.

(2) What would you do if you counted 150 items and found a substantial number of counting errors?

c. In observing an inventory of liquid shoe polish, you noted that a particular lot was five years old. From inspection of some bottles in an open box, you found that the material had solidified in most of the bottles. What action should you take?

d. During your observation of the inventory count in the main warehouse, you found that most of the prenumbered tags that had been incorrectly filled out were being destroyed and thrown away. What is the significance of this procedure, and what action should you take?

Professional Judgment Problems and Cases

14-26 **3** **5** Read Auditing in Action 14-1, which describes BlackBerry's inventory obsolescence review process.

REQUIRED

a. What types of procedures do you think an auditor would use to assess the reasonableness of the writedown?

b. Explain how the change in business direction, as announced by the chief executive officer, would impact the inherent risk of inventory.

14-27 **3** **4** **5** You are the in-charge accountant on the audit of Dezine Inc. (DI). It is March 25, 2018, and your firm is partway through the audit for the year ended January 31, 2018. You are currently assigned to work on various sections within the accounts payable and inventory section of the audit file. Inventory at year-end is $5.2 million. Materiality is set at $225 000.

COMPANY BACKGROUND

DI is a small manufacturer of women's jewellery (including bracelets, necklaces, and earrings). Most of its products are made of silver, 14 Kt gold, and various semiprecious stones.

DI has its financial statements audited due to a $15 million loan with RBC Business Financing Group. The terms of the loan require meeting certain financial covenants—a minimum inventory value of $5 million carried at "lower of cost and market" and a current ratio of 2:1. DI is also required to submit, within 90 days of its year-end, audited financial statements to RBC.

INFORMATION ON INVENTORY CYCLE

Most of the inventory consists of raw materials and finished goods. DI uses a periodic inventory system to track the physical quantity of goods on hand. The count is performed annually on January 31 of each year. Below are some details on the inventory and accounts payable cycle:

Raw Materials Inventory

- DI uses the average costing method to price its raw materials (metals, stones, supplies, and packaging).
- The semiprecious stones and metals are purchased from suppliers in India and Mexico. Goods are shipped FOB shipping point ("free on board shipping point" means that ownership passes to the purchaser when goods leave the premises in India or Mexico).
- Goods take on average three weeks to arrive once the supplier has shipped them. The supplier notifies DI that the goods were shipped by emailing the freight and shipping documents.

- The party responsible (DI or the vendor) for insuring the goods during shipment is agreed to before shipment.
- All purchase orders are sent to the accounting department once issued.
- Shipping documents and freight/carrier invoices are emailed directly to the warehouse, after being reviewed (daily) by the purchasing manager and operations manager.
- All documents and freight/carrier invoices are sent to the accounting department.
- The accounting department matches the purchase orders and freight documents and then accrues the purchase.

Work-in-Process and Finished Goods Inventory

- DI uses a job order costing system. Costs are applied to the finished goods as they pass through casting, polishing, stone setting, and packaging.
- A manual job ticket is attached to each production batch with quantity of metals, stones, packaging, and number of labour hours (the value is applied at standard labour hour rates).

REQUIRED

a. Identify and explain the inherent risks that are present in the inventory cycle at DI. Tie each risk to the key assertion(s). Specifically tie your risks to case facts (not the inventory cycle in general). You can use the format of the table below to structure your answer.

Risk	Explanation	Key Assertion(s)

b. Identify and explain control risk factors that are present in the inventory cycle at DI that could impact existence, cutoff, and valuation of inventory at DI. For each control risk, provide an internal control that would prevent that risk from occurring. You can use the format of the table below to structure your answer:

Control Risk Factor	Explanation and Relevant Assertion(s)	Internal Control That Would Prevent That Risk From Occurring

14-28 🟦8 PawLow Inc. is a private manufacturer of specialized lubricants for the space industry. Its lubricants are used to cover moving mechanical parts inside rocket ships, the Space Station, and the Mars Rover. Its year end was February 28, 2018, and the unaudited net income before tax is $4 million.

In 2019, PawLow will be expanding its business and establishing operations in Russia and China. These two countries have their own space programs and PawLow sees great opportunities there. To fund the expansion, in November 2017 the company obtained a loan from a bank. As part of the loan agreement, the bank requires PawLow to provide audited financial statements as well maintain a specific debt ratio (Debt Ratio = Total Debt/Total Assets) loan covenant.

You are an audit manager who is responsible for reviewing PawLow's year-end audit file and you are currently reviewing the inventory section. Below is an excerpt from the audit working papers:

During the year-end inventory count, the count supervisor noted that a special order of lubricant for the Space X rocket, with a value of $1 920 000, had an odd viscosity [viscosity is thickness or consistency of the lubricant] and colour. This was most likely caused by a defect in compounding, in that the chemical mix or proportions were incorrect. The VP of finance, Thomas Wolanski, believes that the lubricant can still be sold at a discounted price of about $500 000 to one of the large car manufacturers that use similar types of lubricants inside the engines of the vehicles that they manufacture.

AUDIT WORK PERFORMED

- For the defective special order, discuss with management the plans for disposing of the lubricant and why management believes it can be sold for $500 000.
- Agree the cost of $1 920 000 for the special order to management's calculations to confirm the raw material cost, labour cost, and any overheads attributed to the cost have been added and allocated correctly.

REQUIRED

a. Review the audit procedures and discuss the method and reliability of the gathered audit evidence in relation to the risks discussed in the case.

b. What other methods could the auditor have used to gather evidence?

c. What more reliable evidence do you suggest the auditor gather?

14-29 🟦3 🟦5 Today is August 21, 2018, and you are an audit manager working on an audit plan for the inventory section of Jolanta's Inc. (Jola) July 31, 2018, year-end financial statement audit. Jola's year-end inventory balance is $22 000 000.

Your notes and the audit file contain the following information:

Jola is an independent Canadian distributor of Nikola batteries used for electrifying homes. Nikola batteries can power an average four-bedroom home for a full day. The batteries can be recharged with green energy sources such as solar power. This allows homeowners to reduce their carbon footprint and offers them, over the long term, potential savings, since they can become self-reliant and disconnect from the main central electricity grid.

Over the past four years, Jola experienced significant growth in sales of the Nikola batteries. This growth was mainly spurred by the British Columbia (BC) and Ontario provincial governments' new incentives designed to promote green energy. One such incentive, introduced in 2012, offers homeowners a 50 percent rebate on the price of a Nikola battery. The rebate is significant as each battery costs about $17 000. Since this rebate program was introduced, the demand for Nikola batteries in BC and Ontario has grown exponentially.

On April 1, 2017, the federal government introduced new "green" fines. The federal government decided to impose fines on companies that rely on carbon-emitting transportation (diesel-fuelled rail, truck, airplane, or cargo ships) to transport their raw materials or products. Jola was not aware of the new fines and in late July 2017, hired an Indonesian cargo shipping company to transport Nikola batteries from China (where they are manufactured) to Canada. The shipping company operates diesel-fuelled cargo ships. When the batteries arrived in Canada, the Canada Border Services Agency

(CBSA) fined Jola $1 200 000 for shipping its product on diesel-fuelled cargo ships. The amount was calculated based on a set fine rate of 15 percent of the value of transported batteries. Jola paid the amount but is in the process of appealing the fine. As a result, the amount wasn't recognized in its financial records. In addition, Jola received an invoice for 2.5 billion Indonesian Rupiah from the shipping company; this amount was expensed.

After being fined, Jola stopped shipping its batteries on diesel-fuelled cargo vessels and instead switched to companies that operate ships powered by green energy. These ships take twice as long to transport the batteries to Canada, sometimes as long as three months. As a result, on June 15, 2018, the Chinese battery manufacturer changed its shipping terms from FOB Destination to FOB Shipping Point, meaning that Jola takes delivery of the batteries once they leave the Chinese supplier's shipping dock.

During shipment, the batteries must be stored in specially sealed cargo containers. This is to prevent moist air coming into contact with the batteries. Moist air that's close to the ocean water carries small particles of salt. If the chemicals inside the batteries come into contact with salt, the battery becomes damaged and in some instances the damage can cause the battery to overheat or even catch fire.

On June 29, 2018, a large shipment of batteries left China. On its way to Canada, the cargo ship ran into a severe storm that caused its cargo to become loose and shift. The shipping company informed Jola that this caused damage to a significant number of the sealed containers that housed the batteries. The batteries are not expected to arrive in Canada until September 2018.

During the summer of 2018, there were three news reports in B about Nikola batteries overheating to the point that the outer shell of the battery melted. The three batteries were recently installed in homes located on Victoria Island. The Island is surrounded by waters from the Pacific Ocean. Residents of Victoria Island are very environmentally conscious, and the demand for Nikola batteries on the Island is very high. To save on shipping costs, in early 2018 Jola decided to lease a warehouse on the Island to store about 25 percent of its battery inventory destined for the BC market. Jola's management believed that the salt content in the air on the Island is not high enough to damage the batteries.

In Ontario, on May 3, 2018, a newly elected government cancelled all green energy government incentives, including the 50 percent Nikola battery rebate program. As a result, demand for Nikola batteries dropped by 97 percent. In response to this, in early July 2018, Jola slashed its battery prices by 50 percent. Although this forces Jola to sell batteries below their cost, this price reduction is only temporary, as Jola believes that over the next three to six months it can lobby the new government to bring back the 50 percent Nikola battery rebate program.

To reduce labour costs, Jola's management decided not to undertake a year-end inventory count, but instead last year started to carry out monthly continuous (perpetual) inventory counts and adjust any errors identified in the accounting system for that month. In June and July 2018, the monthly counts were not done as many of Jola's employees were on vacation.

REQUIRED

a. Audit standards require the auditor to consider inherent risk at the account level. Set the level of inherent risk for inventory. Ensure that you fully justify and support your risk level assessment.

b. Identify and explain which case facts (risks) would impact your assessment of the inherent risk for the inventory account at assertion level.

c. Explain which specific assertions would most likely be impacted by the risks you identified in Part (b).

14-30 **3** **4** **5** iBee is a private corporation located in Punkeydoodles Corners, Ontario, that owns and maintains a large honeybee colony. Tom Doodles established the company as a small hobby business in 1967. Over time, Tom's great-tasting and high-quality honey grew into a large business. In 2002, Tom incorporated iBee and split the company's share ownership with his two children, Emilia and Mark. Following incorporation, Emilia and Mark each held 33.33 percent of iBee shares. Tom was always the sole decision maker at iBee, overseeing all production and administrative matters. He taught Emilia and Mark everything he knows about good beekeeping practices and honey production.

During a family vacation to Iceland in 2010, Tom noticed the potential market that the country presented for his honey. The following year, Tom signed a contract with an Icelandic honey distributor named Hnit. The opening of the Icelandic market caused an increased demand for iBee's honey. Icelanders strongly prefer iBee's honey over other brands and will pay a premium price for it because iBee's honey always comes in a liquid form and it has a high nutritional value. When honey is stored at low temperatures for long enough, it will crystallize (change from a liquid to a solid). Crystallized honey can be changed back to its liquid form by heating it at a high temperature, but this process significantly reduces its nutritional value. As a result, honey processed by this method is priced at 50–60 percent less than untreated liquid honey.

In response to this increased demand, Tom contemplated a plan to expand the company by acquiring three nearby, private beekeeping operations. In anticipation of financing these acquisitions, Tom approached your accounting firm, Accounting-iS-fuN LLP, in early 2017, requesting an audit of iBee's financial statements. The audit was performed and an unqualified opinion was issued.

It is now November 25, 2018, and you are the senior auditor at Accounting-iS-fuN LLP, in charge of the iBee financial statement audit for the November 30, 2018, year-end. Following are the highlights from the iBee engagement team meeting and audit notes from the prior year.

Change in Management—In the fall of 2018, Tom was injured in a car accident. His recovery was very slow, which forced him to transfer iBee's day-to-day operations to his children in early 2018. Emilia, who recently completed her MBA, took over all accounting and administrative matters. Mark had always shown a passion for beekeeping so he became head beekeeper, managing the bees and the production, storage, and distribution of honey. Tom, meanwhile, focused on his recovery and became an inactive owner.

In early 2018, Emilia pursued her father's plans to purchase the three private beekeeping companies, but her application for a bank loan was denied due to the economic downturn. As a result, Emilia explored alternative financing options. That summer, she struck a deal with a private financing company to securitize (also known as factoring or selling) 80 percent of the outstanding balance of iBee's accounts receivable, based on the audited financial statements as of November 30, 2018.

During the transitional period in early 2018, Emilia did not review several monthly bank reconciliations that were prepared by iBee accounting department employee Lidia Gdansk. She also did not perform two quarterly budgeted versus actual sales and expense reviews.

Emilia did not realize her omissions until they were brought to her attention by Lidia in early July 2018. Lidia said that Emilia, as she took over Tom's responsibilities, should also have reviewed and established credit limits for new customers. Following her discussion with Lidia, Emilia began performing these tasks. However, Emilia remains unsure if credit limits for all new customers were reviewed and assessed prior to year-end. She also did not get a chance to catch up with the review of all the bank reconciliations prior to year-end.

Previously, Tom would adjust the allowance for doubtful accounts prior to year-end after reviewing and assessing the collectability of each outstanding account. This year, Emilia delegated this task to Lidia, who simply applied the same percentage as last year because she did not think that demand for honey changed materially year-over-year.

Renewal of Hnit Contract—Iceland's sudden and severe economic downturn and associated banking crisis did not adversely impact demand for iBee's honey. However, on August 1, 2018, iBee's Icelandic distributor, Hnit, refused to renew its distribution contract unless it included the following clause: "Hnit reserves the right to return to iBee all honey inventory that has crystallized during transportation or storage within six months of receipt. Hnit is not responsible for any shipping or storage costs of honey that has crystallized on its premises."

After some discussion, Emilia and Mark agreed to include the clause in iBee's agreement with Hnit, which was signed and went into effect on August 15, 2018.

Emilia instructed Lidia to journalize (process an accounting entry) all honey sales to Iceland at the time customers placed their preorders at the beginning of the year. As iBee always prioritized the Icelandic orders, and all honey sales were shipped and delivered prior to year-end, Emilia believed this method would not impact the financial statements and could be used as a tool to forecast honey demand for the year.

Shipment Accident—Due to a phenomenon called hygroscopy, honey will absorb moisture directly from the air, including any pollutants and odours contained in it. Thus, honey must be carefully packaged to protect it from dust, vehicle exhaust fumes, strong food odours, and other pollutants. Polluted honey is usually unfit for consumption and should be discarded.

On July 1, 2018, due to a shortage of proper transport containers, Mark resorted to transporting a large quantity of honey from the beehives to the storage warehouse in unsealed, inadequate containers. A highway accident caused a delay and the truck carrying the shipment was forced to idle for an extended period. Upon testing at iBee's processing facility, it was determined that the honey had indeed absorbed a large quantity of exhaust fumes and was polluted.

Mark could not discard the polluted honey because 2018 was already a low production year and doing so could delay or even cancel the fulfillment of Icelandic orders. To overcome this challenge, Mark wants to gamble and ship the polluted honey mixed in with a shipment of "clean" honey with the hope that it will not be tested by the Icelandic Food Safety Agency (IFSA). Mark plans to include the polluted honey with the last shipment to Iceland scheduled for December 29, 2018. The IFSA has very strict inspection protocols for all food imports, testing on a sample basis 5–10 percent of all shipments entering the country. IFSA inspection protocols require testing honey for pollutants and ensuring that its actual nutritional value matches the facts indicated on the label.

REQUIRED

a. Audit standards require the auditor to consider audit risk at the account level. Set the level of audit risk for accounts receivable and inventory. Make sure to fully justify and support your risk level assessment.

b. Identify and explain which case facts (risks) would impact your assessment of the inherent risk and fraud risk for the financial statements as a whole and at the account and assertion level.

c. Explain at what level you would set the inherent risk and fraud risk for the financial statements as a whole.

d. Explain which specific assertions would most likely be impacted by the risks you identified in Part (b).

e. Identify and explain which case facts (risks) would impact your assessment of control risk.

14-31 ▣5 Auditors are required to understand the client's industry and business but may not be experts in identifying the quantity and value of certain inventory items. For example, with regards to the audit strategy of Lonmin Mines (see Table 14-3, the auditor relied upon the work of a specialist to determine the existence of inventory. Auditing standards provide guidance on whether and how an auditor can rely on a specialist. Refer to CAS 620, *Using the Work of an Auditor's Expert*, to answer the following questions.

a. List three examples of inventory items for which an auditor may need to use a specialist for testing existence and valuation, or both. How would an auditor use a specialist in each example?

b. What characteristics should the auditor consider to ensure the specialist is qualified?

c. Does the specialist need to be independent of the client and the auditor?

AUDIT OF THE HUMAN RESOURCES AND PAYROLL CYCLE

STANDARDS REFERENCED IN THIS CHAPTER

CAS 402 – Auditor considerations relating to an entity using a service organization

CSAE 3416 – Reporting on controls at a service organization

IAS 24 – Related-party disclosures

For many types of businesses, service organizations, and manufacturers, payroll can be the largest expense. It is an important consideration in the valuation of inventory in manufacturing, construction, and other industries.

LEARNING OBJECTIVES

After studying this chapter, you should be able to:

1 Identify the accounts and transactions in the human resources and payroll cycle.

2 Describe the business functions and related documents and records in the human resources and payroll cycle.

3 Identify significant risks, and assess risk of material misstatement for the payroll cycle.

4 Understand internal control, and assess control risk for the human resources and payroll cycle.

5 Use professional judgment to develop an audit approach (strategy) for the human resources and payroll cycle.

6 Design and perform tests of control for the human resources and payroll cycle.

7 Design and perform substantive analytical procedures for the human resources and payroll cycle.

8 Design and perform substantive tests of details for the human resources and payroll cycle.

9 Design and perform fraud procedures for the human resources and payroll cycle.

Payroll Headaches for Nova Scotia Nurses

After the Victorian Order of Nurses (VON) in Nova Scotia implemented its new payroll system, hundreds of nurses and home support workers employed by VON missed paycheques or received inaccurate paycheques that did not reflect overtime or mileage. Others were overpaid. A union representative for the nurses noted, "It used to be, 'Thank God it's Friday.' Now, 'Oh my God it's Friday.' We [the union] dread Fridays because the calls will come in from nurses who have issues with the payroll."

A union representative for the 400 home care workers observed, "We haven't gone through a pay cycle yet where there hasn't been a problem." One home care worker actually quit over money owed with regard to mileage and overtime.

Consultant Jarret Pazahanick commented on the system implementation, saying "The payroll software is solid technology, but tricky to implement given all the variables with worker pay, as well as the job of mapping over details from the legacy system." He further explained that many of these system conversion failures can be attributed to "junior consultants and weak testing."

continued >

In order to rectify the problem, VON brought in an independent auditor and had each nurse's pay record checked—which took about eight hours for each nurse. While VON's problems have been quite costly, they are nothing compared to the issues with the custom payroll system developed for New York City, which incurred costs of more than US $600 million and led to a criminal investigation.

Sources: CBC News, "VON nurses overpaid due to payroll problems," January 13, 2012, accessed October 18, 2017, at **http://www.cbc.ca/news/canada/nova-scotia/von-nurses-overpaid-due-to-payroll-problems-1.1265562**. CBC News, "VON nurses getting shorted on pay," July 5, 2011, accessed October 18, 2017, at **http://www.cbc.ca/news/canada/nova-scotia/von-nurses-getting-shorted-on-pay-1.1052429**. Chris Kanaracus, "SAP–IBM system woes foul up nurses' pay," *PC World*, July 14, 2011, accessed October 18, 2017, at **http://www.pcworld.com/article/235738/article.html**.

As the opening vignette highlights, payroll problems cause big headaches. For an organization like VON—Canada's largest, national, not-for-profit, charitable home and community care organization—payroll is the biggest expense. The situation is similar for many other not-for-profits. We start the chapter by considering the components of the human resources cycle.

AN OVERVIEW OF THE HUMAN RESOURCES AND PAYROLL CYCLE

LO **1** Identify the accounts and transactions in the human resources and payroll cycle.

Although the human resources and payroll cycle is closely related to the acquisition and payment cycle, due to its unique nature, organizations often have separate processes. The **human resources and payroll cycle** begins with the hiring of personnel. It includes obtaining and accounting for services from the employees. It ends with payment to the employees for the services performed and to the government and other institutions for withheld and accrued employee benefits. It involves the employment and payment of all employees, regardless of classification or method of determining compensation.

There are several important differences between the human resources and payroll cycle and other cycles in a typical audit:

Human resources and payroll cycle—the transaction cycle that begins with the hiring of personnel, includes obtaining and accounting for services from the employees, and ends with payment to the employees for the services performed and to the government and other institutions for withheld and accrued employee benefits.

- There is only one class of transactions for payroll. Most cycles include at least two classes of transactions. For example, the revenue cycle includes both sales and cash receipts transactions and often sales returns and charge-off of uncollectibles. Payroll has only one class because the receipt of services from employees and the payment for those services through payroll occur within a short period.
- Transactions are far more significant than related balance sheet accounts. Balances in payroll-related accounts such as accrued payroll and withheld taxes are usually small compared with the total amount of transactions for the year.
- Internal controls over payroll are effective for almost all companies, even small ones. The reasons for effective controls are harsh federal and provincial penalties for errors in withholding and paying payroll taxes, and employee morale problems if employees are not paid or are underpaid.

Because of these three characteristics, auditors typically emphasize tests of controls, substantive tests of transactions, and analytical procedures in the audit of payroll. Tests of balances often take relatively little audit time for most payroll accounts. Before we discuss the tests in the cycle, let's review the transactions and account balances, as well as the documents and records used in the human resources and payroll cycle in a typical company.

FUNCTIONS IN THE CYCLE, AND RELATED DOCUMENTS AND RECORDS

The human resources and payroll cycle begins with the hiring of personnel and ends with payment to the employees for the services performed. Payment is made to the government and other institutions for employee withholdings (i.e., income tax, Canada [or Quebec] Pension Plan, Employment Insurance), and employee benefits (i.e., required contributions by the employer for the Canada [or Quebec] Pension Plan, Employment Insurance, workplace safety insurance, hospital insurance plans, provincial health and education taxes; and voluntary or negotiated employer contributions to company pension, medical, or dental plans). In between, the cycle involves obtaining services from the employees consistent with the objectives of the company and accounting for the services in a proper manner. Table 15-1 summarizes the key documents and records in the human resources and payroll cycle.

Human Resources and Employment

The human resources department provides an independent source for interviewing and hiring of qualified personnel. Reference checks and a police check of new

Table 15-1	Business Functions, Related Documents and Records, and Their Purposes for the Human Resources and Payroll Cycle	
Business Function	**Documents and Records**	**Purpose of Document or Record**
Human resources and employment	Payroll and employment records	Tracks the employee's semi-permanent information, including wages, tax codes, and job responsibilities.
	Deduction authorization form	Documents employee approval of discretionary deductions and status of mandatory deductions, such as income tax deduction codes.
	Initial wage-rate authorization form	Documents employee status and wage rate.
Master file change	Employee change form	Documents and approves changes in employee semi-permanent information, such as address, deduction code.
	Wage-rate change form	Documents changes in wage rate and job responsibilities.
Access rights management	Access rights approval form	Describes the information systems functions (e.g., menu items) the person may have access to, including capabilities (e.g., read-only or update).
	Access rights change form	Documents and approves changes to access rights based upon employee promotions, transfers, or terminations.
	Code of conduct statement	Signed by each employee, identifies responsibilities associated with information systems and organizational assets, including privacy, confidentiality, and ownership.
Timekeeping and payroll preparation	Time record	A document or electronic record tracking start time, end time, and total hours worked.
	Job time record	A record that allocates hours worked against a manufacturing or service job, allocating the work to a job order reference or client reference.
	Summary payroll report	Lists total wage costs by account number, department, job number, or other useful allocation.
	Payroll journal	Lists the details of current pay, such as gross pay, hours worked, statutory withholdings, and net pay.
	Payroll master file	Electronic record of the current status of an employee (e.g., payments and deductions to date, name, address, employee number, social insurance number).
	Payroll transaction and history files	Electronic record of all payments and adjustments made to the employee master file.
Payment of payroll	Payroll cheque or direct bank deposit	Payment method of amounts due to employees.
	Employee remittance advice	Documentation of the details of employee payroll, such as gross pay, deductions, and net pay.
Preparation of employee withholdings and benefit remittance forms and their payment	T4 form	Provides totals of wage and benefit payments to and deductions from each employee for the calendar year.
	Employee withholdings and benefit remittance forms	Reporting and payment forms sent to federal and provincial authorities for the payment of withholdings and employee benefits and deductions.
	Other reporting forms	Other reporting forms may be required, such as group insurance forms, and workplace safety and health reports.

employees can identify past criminal activity and help prevent fraud. The HR department is also an independent source of records for the internal verification of wage information and for confirming segregation of duties by means of access rights.

Personnel Records **Personnel records** are used to keep track of semi-permanent information for employees. Here, documentation is kept of discretionary deductions (such as health care benefits or registered pension plans), rates that should be used for calculating income taxes (by means of tax deduction codes), as well as the category of job the person is employed in and wage rates. Written or electronic documentation should be present for all changes, including changes to address, marital status, or wages.

Personnel records—records that include such data as the date of employment, personnel investigations, rates of pay or changes to them, authorized deductions, performance evaluations, and termination of employment.

THE AUDIT PROCESS FOR HUMAN RESOURCE AND PAYROLL CYCLE

Figure 15-1 summarizes the audit process for the human resource and payroll cycle. The process is the same as that followed in Chapter 12 for the revenue cycle.

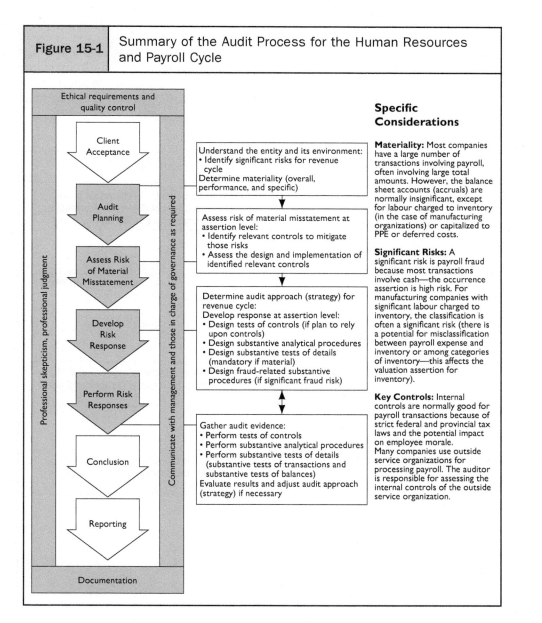

| Figure 15-1 | Summary of the Audit Process for the Human Resources and Payroll Cycle |

IDENTIFY SIGNIFICANT RISKS AND ASSESS RISK OF MATERIAL MISSTATEMENT

Significant business risks affecting payroll are unlikely for most companies. However, there may be complex compensation arrangements, including bonus and stock option plans and other deferred compensation arrangements. Examples of other risks include events such as renegotiation of union contracts and employee lawsuits.

The payroll cycle is different from most cycles because there are many repeated transactions (such as an employee weekly salary). As highlighted in the opening vignette, if there are errors in a wage rate, such errors can rapidly escalate into material amounts. This cycle's major risks of fraud or error fall into three categories, as shown in Table 15-2.

Assess Inherent Risk

Three high-risk areas in human resources and payroll are payroll withholdings and remittances, the potential for misstatement of inventory of payroll, including fraud, and the potential for nonexistent (fictitious) employees. Risks of error or fraud are higher (1) when payroll significantly affects the valuation of inventory and (2) when the auditor is concerned about the possibility of material fraudulent payroll transactions.

Payroll Withholdings and Benefits Remittance Forms and Payments This area is high risk since the amounts are often material and because the potential liability for failure to file forms in a timely manner can be severe. The withholdings of concern in these tests are such items as those for income taxes, Canada (or Quebec) Pension Plan, Employment Insurance, union dues, and life insurance.

Table 15-2	Major Risks of Error or Fraud in the Human Resources and Payroll Cycle		
Risks of Error	**Risks of Misappropriation of Assets, Other Fraud, or Illegal Acts**	**Risks of Inadequate Disclosure or Incorrect Presentation of Financial Information, Including Fraudulent Financial Reporting**
	Unauthorized wage-rate increases, payment of overtime, overstated hours, or overstated commissions or bonuses	
Undetected data-entry errors (e.g., wage rates, hours worked, deduction codes, or others); employees paid twice, or other payment errors		Overstated net income and inventory by recording excess labour costs in inventory
	Setup of and payment to fictitious employees	
Late or incorrect provincial or federal payroll remittances		Overstated net income by capitalizing excess labour costs as part of constructed fixed assets
	Wages of terminated employees continue to be paid or are paid to unauthorized persons	
Incorrect functional allocation of access rights, allowing employees to have unauthorized access to assets		Understatement of pension obligations or pension costs (understating expenses or liabilities)
	Unauthorized access to confidential or private data leading to loss of cash (etheft)	
Inappropriate response to phishing emails revealing access codes that lead to unauthorized access to assets and theft of assets		Inadequate disclosure of related-party transactions

Indications of high risk of errors in the forms include the past payment of penalties and interest for improper payments, new personnel in the payroll department who are responsible for the preparation of the remittance forms, the lack of independent verification of the information, and the existence of serious liquidity problems for the client.

Payroll and Inventory Valuation For audits where payroll is a significant portion of inventory (common for manufacturing and construction companies), the improper account classification of payroll can significantly affect asset valuation for accounts such as work in process, finished goods, or construction in process. For example, the overhead charged to inventory at the balance sheet date can be overstated if the salaries of administrative personnel are charged to indirect manufacturing overhead. Similarly, the valuation of particular jobs is affected if the direct labour cost of individual employees is improperly charged to the wrong job or process. When some jobs are billed on a cost-plus basis, revenue and the valuation of particular jobs are both affected by charging labour to incorrect jobs.

Fraudulent Payroll Transactions There are several ways employees can significantly defraud a company in the payroll area. For example, an employee could make unauthorized changes to HR or payroll records for his or her own benefit, fictitious or "ghost" employees could be created, or salaries could be paid to unverified bank accounts.

UNDERSTANDING INTERNAL CONTROL AND ASSESSING CONTROL RISK

LO **4** Understand internal control, and assess control risk for the human resources and payroll cycle.

Internal control for payment of payroll is normally highly structured and well controlled in order to control cash disbursements and to minimize employee complaints and dissatisfaction. It is common to use information technology to prepare all journals and payroll payments, either in-house systems or outside service-centre systems, such as those of banks and financial institutions, are used. Thus, general controls such as control over program changes and program updates and over access to data files must be evaluated, particularly over payroll calculations, since consistent errors could escalate into material amounts rapidly.

An important consideration when obtaining an understanding of controls is whether or not the organization uses a service centre. As discussed in Auditing in Action 15-1, payroll is a commonly outsourced system, and the auditor will need to consider whether or not the controls at the service centre will need to be assessed (CAS 402), as discussed in Chapter 9. If that is the case, the auditor may be able to obtain the service auditors' CSAE 3416 report.

CAS

It is usually easy to establish good control over payments in the human resources and payroll cycle. For factory and office employees, there is usually a large number of relatively homogeneous, small-amount transactions. There are fewer executive payroll transactions, but they are consistent in timing, content, and amount. High-quality computer software packages are available, resulting in good controls over program changes. Although auditors seldom expect to find exceptions in testing payroll transactions, as our opening vignette illustrates that does not mean it does not happen (particularly when new systems are implemented). Most monetary errors are corrected by internal verification controls or in response to employee complaints.

Where auditors tend to find problems is with management of access controls. Small- to medium-sized businesses may have inadequate controls over access to information systems, resulting in the need to rely solely on substantive tests. Larger organizations with more formal systems tend to have better controls over the initial set-up of employees but may have weaknesses in access-control change management. Next we discuss some key controls for the cycle.

Payroll is picky. The amounts have to be exact, many deductions have to be taken, and several remittances and forms must be submitted to regulatory agencies. Fines are heavy if you remit too little or if you remit late. A small business owner could spend several hours per week doing payroll or checking the work of an employee who prepares the payroll, thus losing productive time.

NEBS Payweb.ca is an example of a payroll system that works for both small and large businesses. It is web-based so hours and wage rates can be entered from any location that has internet access. Then the payroll payment is deposited directly into the employee bank account or to a debit card activated by the employer. NEBS Payweb.ca also takes care of providing remittances (such as federal taxes), by withdrawing the funds from the company bank account and remitting to the regulatory agency with the appropriate reports. Transaction reports can be viewed online or printed.

While this type of outsourcing allows the organization to be more effective, it is not without its risks. Unauthorized access to the corporate account could be obtained by a hacker, who could set himself or herself up as an employee, and get paid repeatedly, withdrawing corporate funds. Hackers could also get in and make unauthorized changes to existing data.

With regard to the audit, if the auditor is relying upon the internal controls at NEBS Payweb.ca, then the service auditor's report can provide the auditor with evidence about the controls in place at NEBS Payweb.ca. For NEBS Payweb.ca, this would reduce the costs associated with many auditors contacting them and asking them about controls. A disadvantage for NEBS Payweb.ca is that such a report can be costly to obtain, and may not cover the period under audit for many of its clients.

Source: Danny Bradbury, "Payroll work makes for a heavy load," *National Post*, February 11, 2008, p. FP4. NEBS Payweb.ca, accessed August 25, 2017, at **www.payweb.ca**.

Proper Authorization

The most important control is clear, properly approved documentation of the employee's job responsibilities and wages by the appropriate level of authority. This could be a supervisor together with a controller, a manager together with human resources, or the board of directors. Note that in each case, at least two people should be involved in this approval process to prevent setup of fictitious employees.

Adequate Segregation of Duties

Segregation of duties is extremely important; it helps prevent unauthorized changes to wage rates, deductions, or other payroll data. No individual with access to time recording, payroll records, or cheques should also be permitted access to personnel records. A second important control is the adequate investigation of the competence and trustworthiness of new employees, which helps prevent error (due to lack of competence) or fraud.

Master File Change

Master file change—the process used to change semi-permanent information in an employee record, such as deduction codes, addresses, or wage rates.

Master file data is the semi-permanent data in an employee's file. Any **master file change** needs to be adequately supported. For example, a change of marital status would be supported by a copy of a marriage certificate, and then the employee would be able to justify a reduction of income tax deductions by completing a change form that would be approved by a manager. In order to prevent unauthorized changes in wage rates or deduction codes, all forms should be approved by at least two people.

Access Rights Management

Access rights management—the process used to identify and manage access to physical and logical assets (including information technology and user identification management).

This process includes identifying which information systems and which functions within a particular information system the employee is to have access to. When employees change jobs within the company (perhaps due to promotion), or leave the company, these access rights need to be updated. **Access rights management** is important because it is the organization's method of enforcing segregation of duties. Incorrect or weak access controls can provide unauthorized access to data or programs, leading to the ability to issue payroll cheques or make unauthorized changes to wages or deductions.

Timekeeping and Payroll Preparation Controls

Timekeeping and payroll preparation involves adequate control over the time in the time records and includes the use of a time clock and magnetic swipe card or other method of making certain that employees are paid for the number of hours they work. There should also be controls to prevent anyone from checking in for several employees or submitting a fraudulent time record. Advanced information technology includes the use of biometric data (e.g., a fingerprint) to record and track time. For example, the website **www.paypunch.com** illustrates the PayPunch time and attendance system. Employees clock in using an employee number and a handprint or fingerprint. Instead of an employee number, for greater security, employees could use a PIN (personal identification number).

The summarization and calculation of the payroll can be controlled by well-defined policies for the payroll department, separation of duties to provide automatic cross-checks, reconciliation of payroll hours with independent production records, and independent internal verification of all important data. For example, payroll policies should require a competent, independent person to review actual hours worked for the proper approval of all overtime, and examine time records for deletions and alterations or for unusually long hours. These controls prevent unauthorized changes to the data and addition of unauthorized persons to the payroll (as well as preventing payment to terminated employees). Periodically, a printout of wage and withholding rates included in the computer files can be obtained and compared with authorized rates in the personnel files. Where the data volumes are large, such testing would be completed using audit software.

When manufacturing labour affects inventory valuation, a knowledgeable manager should approve wage allocations to make sure labour is distributed to the proper accounts. Independent comparison of the approved amounts to the actual data entered helps prevent error.

Payroll Payment Controls

Controls over cheques or direct deposit authorization should include limiting the authorization to a responsible employee who does not have access to timekeeping or the preparation of the payroll, to prevent unauthorized changes. Payroll software should permit only one payment for each employee per pay period. Where physical cheques are used, the distribution of payroll should be by someone who is not involved in the other payroll functions to detect unauthorized payments or fictitious employees. Any unclaimed cheques should be immediately returned for redeposit. If a cheque-signing machine is used to replace a manual signature, the same controls are required; in addition, the cheque-signing machine must be carefully controlled.

To enable tracking, cheques, bank deposit transactions, and employee remittance advices should be sequentially numbered and accounted for.

Most companies use an **imprest payroll account** to prevent the payment of unauthorized payroll transactions. An imprest payroll account is a separate payroll account in which a small balance is maintained. A cheque for the exact amount of each net payroll is transferred from the general account to the imprest account immediately before the distribution of the payroll. The advantages of an imprest account are that it limits the client's exposure to payroll fraud (manual or electronic), allows the delegation of payroll cheque-signing duties, separates routine payroll expenditures from irregular expenditures, and facilitates cash management. It also simplifies the reconciliation of the payroll bank account if it is done at the low point in the payment cycle—for example, if the reconciliation is done a week after the last payroll and there is no payroll due in the current week.

Where employee payments are made directly into employees' bank accounts, reports produced by the bank or payroll service provider should be independently approved before the bank is given authority to transfer the funds.

Timekeeping and payroll preparation—processes used to record employee hours worked, allocate payroll costs to account, make payments to employees, and regulatory authorities.

Imprest payroll account—a bank account to which the exact amount of payroll for the pay period is transferred by cheque from the employer's general cash account.

Employee Withholdings and Benefits Remittance Controls

As a part of understanding the internal control structure, the auditor should review the preparation of at least one of each type of employee withholding and benefits remittance form that the client is responsible for filing.

The timely preparation and mailing of T4 slips and employee withholdings and benefits remittance forms is required by federal and provincial laws. Late payments result in heavy fines. The most important control in the preparation of these returns is a well-defined set of policies that carefully indicate when each form must be filed. Most automated payroll systems include the preparation of payroll tax returns using the information in the payroll transaction and master files. The independent verification of the output by a competent individual is an important control to prevent misstatements and potential liability for taxes and penalties.

CONCEPT CHECK

C15-1 Why is it important for the auditor to audit the payroll cycle?

C15-2 Why is it likely that the auditor will focus on the audit of payroll transactions rather than payroll balances?

C15-3 How does the audit of access rights management in the payroll cycle affect the audit of other transaction cycles?

LO 5 Use professional judgment to develop an audit approach (strategy) for the human resources and payroll cycle.

DEVELOP AN AUDIT APPROACH FOR HUMAN RESOURCES AND PAYROLL

Auditors often use a combined audit approach for the human resources and payroll cycle. As we have discussed, controls tend to be good in this area. In most audits, the risk of material misstatement for the related balance sheet accounts is low. That is because the amounts are small. These accounts can easily be verified if the auditor is confident that payroll transactions are correctly recorded and that withholding and benefit remittance forms are properly prepared.

Although the accruals and expenses related to the human resources and payroll cycle tend not to be a significant risk, in situations where the organization is capitalizing costs (either as part of inventory or some other type of asset, classification may be a relevant assertion. See Table 15-3 below, which is excerpted from the audit report of

Table 15-3	Example of an Audit Approach When Capitalization of Payroll Costs Is a Significant Risk

Significant Risk	Audit Approach
Identification of Risk—Cutoff between development and production phase of mining for Styldrift I project; management has concluded Styldrift I is currently in the development phase. **Rationale**—We focused on this area as the cutoff between development and production phase of mining is becoming more significant as the company gets closer to reaching commercial levels of production. Thus, more judgment is involved in assessing whether the criteria for capitalization have been met, per the requirements of IAS 16 (*Property, plant, and equipment*). The cutoff could have a significant impact on the financial statements, due to the materiality of costs capitalized.	We tested the costs capitalized to property, plant, and equipment in order to determine whether these are directly attributable to bringing the asset to the condition necessary for it to be capable of operating in the manner intended by management. This was done by comparing such costs to supporting documentation, such as invoices. We also inspected payroll records to ensure that payroll costs were related to employees who are involved in the Styldrift I project.

Source: Royal Bafokeng Mining Integrated Annual Report, 2015, accessed August 26, 2017, at **http://www.bafokengplatinum.co.za/reports/integrated-report-2015/afs-iarep.php**.

Royal Bafokeng Platinum, a mining company located in South Africa, regarding the auditor's risk response to classification of payroll costs. You will note that the auditors refer to cutoff, which is closely related to classification, since the auditors are attempting to determine at which point in time the mining project, Styldrift I, moves from the development stage to the production stage. The auditor is using substantive testing to assess the classification/cutoff of costs. Given the size of the organization, the auditor would have tested the controls in the payroll cycle.

DESIGN AND PERFORM TESTS OF CONTROLS

LO 6 Design and perform tests of control for the human resources and payroll cycle.

Tests of control procedures are the most important means of verifying account balances in the human resources and payroll cycle. The emphasis on tests of controls is due to the lack of independent third-party evidence, such as confirmation for verifying accrued wages, withholdings, accrued benefits payable, and other balance sheet accounts. Table 15-4 summarizes key controls and common tests of controls.

Table 15-4	Summary of Transaction-Related Audit Objectives, Key Controls, and Tests of Controls for Payroll	
Transaction-Related Audit Objectives	**Key Internal Controls**	**Common Tests of Controls**
Recorded payroll payments are for work actually performed by existing employees (occurrence).	• Time records are approved by supervisors. • Time clock is used to record time. • Methods are in place to uniquely identify employees upon clocking in or out. • Personnel files are adequately documented. • Separation of duties between personnel, timekeeping, and payroll disbursements is supported by authorized access rights. • Setup and changes to payroll master files are adequately documented and approved. • Independent authorization is needed to issue cheques or initiate direct deposit payments.	• Examine time records for indication of approvals. • Review personnel policies. • Review organization chart, discuss with employees, and observe duties being performed. • Compare authorized duties with duties permitted on access rights forms. • Examine printouts of transactions rejected by the computer as having nonexistent employee numbers, or determine whether invalid entries are accepted at point of entry.[†] • Examine personnel records for evidence of approval; compare wage rate to payroll master file or payroll journal. • Review the payroll journal, general ledger, and payroll earnings records for large or unusual amounts.[*†] • Compare cancelled cheques or direct deposit amounts with payroll journal for name, amount, and date. • Examine cancelled cheques for proper endorsement.
Existing payroll transactions are recorded (completeness).	• Payroll cheques are prenumbered and accounted for. • Bank reconciliation is prepared independently.	• Account for a sequence of payroll cheques or direct deposits, or conduct gap testing.[†] • Discuss payroll bank account reconciliation process with employees and observe reconciliation. • Reconcile the disbursements in the payroll journal with the disbursements on the payroll bank statement. • Prove the bank reconciliation.
Recorded payroll transactions are for the amount of time actually worked and at the proper pay rate; withholdings are properly calculated (accuracy).	• Calculations and amounts are verified independently. • Batch totals are compared with computer summary reports. • There is authorization of wage rate, salary, or commission rate. • There is authorization of withholdings, including amounts for insurance and registered retirement plans.	• Examine indication of independent internal verification. • Examine file of batch totals for initials of approval; compare totals with summary reports.[†] • Examine personnel records for indication of independent approval. • Recompute hours worked from time records.[†] • Compare pay rates with union contract, approval by board of directors, or other sources. • Recompute gross pay and net pay.[†] • Check withholdings by reference to appropriate tables[†] and authorization forms in personnel file. • Compare cancelled cheque or direct deposit with payroll journal for amount.

(continued)

Table 15-4	Summary of Transaction-Related Audit Objectives, Key Controls, and Tests of Controls for Payroll (*Continued*)	

Transaction-Related Audit Objectives	Key Internal Controls	Common Tests of Controls
Payroll transactions are properly classified (classification).	• The chart of accounts is adequate. • There is internal independent verification of classification.	• Review chart of accounts. • Examine indication of internal verification; determine that software posts to correct accounts.[†] • Compare classification with chart of accounts or procedures manual. • Review time records for employee department and job records for job assignment, and trace through to labour distribution.
Payroll transactions are recorded on the correct dates (cutoff).	• Procedures require recording payroll transactions on a regular payment, immediately after payment. • There is independent internal verification.	• Examine the procedures manually and observe when recording takes place. • Examine indication of internal verification. • Compare date of recorded cheques or direct deposits to the payroll journal dates and time records. • Compare date on cheque with date the cheque was cleared by the bank.
Payroll transactions are properly included in the payroll master file and transaction files; they are properly summarized (accuracy—posting and summarization).	• There is periodic independent comparison of payroll master file contents to personnel records. • There is automatic posting of payroll transaction amounts to general ledger accounts.	• Examine initialled summary total reports indicating comparisons have been made. • Test clerical accuracy by footing the payroll journal and tracing postings to general ledger and the payroll master file.[†]

*This analytical procedure also applies to other objectives, including completeness, valuation, and cutoff.

[†]This control would be tested on many audits by using a computer, possibly with generalized audit software.

In addition to the control tests highlighted in Table 15-4, if labour is a material factor in inventory or deferred costs valuation, there should be special emphasis on testing controls over proper classification of payroll transactions. Another control the auditor would want to test is that payroll withholdings and benefits are paid in a timely manner. The auditor must first determine the client's requirements for submitting the payments. The requirements are determined by reference to such sources as tax laws, Canada Pension Plan rules, Employment Insurance rules, union contracts, and agreements with employees. Then, check whether the client has paid the proper amount on time by comparing the subsequent payment with the payroll records.

CONCEPT CHECK

C15-4 Why might auditors limit the number of transactions tested in the payroll cycle?

C15-5 Provide two examples of payroll tests that could be used to verify the accuracy of payroll costs included in inventory.

LO **7** Design and perform substantive analytical procedures for the human resources and payroll cycle.

DESIGN AND PERFORM SUBSTANTIVE ANALYTICAL PROCEDURES

The use of analytical procedures is as important in the human resources and payroll cycle as it is in every other cycle. Table 15-5 illustrates substantive analytical procedures for the balance sheet and income statement accounts in the human resources and payroll cycle. Most of the relationships included in Table 15-5 are highly predictable and are useful for uncovering areas in which additional audit work may be needed. The auditor should consider any changes in business policies or business practices when conducting the analytical procedures to help explain variations.

Table 15-5	Analytical Procedures for the Human Resources and Payroll Cycle

Analytical Procedure	Possible Misstatement Detected in
Compare payroll expense account balance with previous years (adjusted for pay-rate increases and increases in volume).	Payroll expense accounts
Compare direct labour as a percentage of sales with that of previous years.	Direct labour
Compare commission expense as a percentage of sales with that of previous years.	Commission expense
Compare payroll benefits expense as a percentage of salaries and wages with that of previous years (adjusted for changes in the benefits rates).	Payroll benefits expense and payroll benefits liability
Compare accrued payroll benefits accounts with that of previous years.	Accrued payroll benefits and payroll benefits expense

DESIGN AND PERFORM SUBSTANTIVE TESTS

LO **8** Design and perform substantive tests of details for the human resources and payroll cycle.

Substantive tests of details of the human resources and payroll accounts will be conducted if the amounts are significant or if the auditor considers that there is a risk of material misstatement. The auditor also considers the cost-effectiveness of testing.

Substantive Tests of Detail: Payroll Liability and Expense Accounts

The verification of the liability accounts associated with payroll, often termed **accrued payroll liability/expenses,** is straightforward if internal controls are operating effectively. When the auditor is satisfied that payroll transactions are being properly recorded in the payroll journal and the related employee withholding and benefits remittance forms are being accurately prepared and promptly paid, the tests of details of balances can be completed rapidly.

Accrued payroll liability/ expenses—the liability accounts associated with payroll, including accounts for accrued salaries and wages, accrued commissions, accrued bonuses, and accrued employee benefits.

The objectives in testing payroll-related liabilities are to determine whether accruals in the trial balance are stated at correct amounts (accuracy) for all payroll accounts (completeness) and whether transactions in the human resources and payroll cycle are recorded in the proper period (cutoff). The primary concern in both objectives is to make sure there are no understated or omitted accruals. Table 15-6 illustrates examples of tests of details of balances for payroll liability and expense accounts.

Most of the tests listed in Table 15-6 can be conducted efficiently, except for the recalculation of total commissions, payroll, and benefits, which can be complex since most benefits do not apply to all of a person's pay. For example, there are ceilings on pension and Employment Insurance benefits. This means that most auditors will conduct the tests listed for the liability accounts and for officers' compensation. The other tests will be conducted only if control risk is very high or the auditor suspects fraud or other material misstatements. We examine a few of those tests more closely below.

Payroll Withholdings and Benefits The auditor may request that the client prepare a detailed reconciliation of the information on the remittance forms and the payroll records if the auditor believes that there is a reasonable chance the remittance forms may be improperly prepared.

Allocation of Payroll Costs to Inventory or Capital Assets When labour is a material factor in inventory valuation or asset capitalization, the auditor will be concerned

Table 15-6	Examples of Tests of Details of Balances for Payroll Liability and Expense Accounts

Account Description	Tests of Detail and Balance-Related Audit Assertion
Liability Accounts	
Amounts withheld from employees' pay: • Income taxes • Canada (or Quebec) Pension Plan • Employment Insurance • Other (e.g., union dues, bonds, insurance)	Compare balance with payroll journal (completeness). Compare balance with subsequent period cash disbursements (allocation).
Accrued salaries and wages	Determine whether policy for accruing wages is consistent with prior year. Evaluate reasonableness of the method (valuation). Recalculate the accrual (allocation, completeness, existence).
Accrued commissions	Determine nature of commission agreements or policies with employees; evaluate consistency with prior year (allocation, valuation). Verify that the commission agreements or policies have been correctly applied to appropriate employees (allocation). Confirm amounts due with employees or compare balance with subsequent cash disbursements (allocation).
Accrued bonuses	Compare to amount authorized in the minutes of the board of directors' meetings (or by owner of the company) (allocation, completeness).
Accrued statutory benefits, vacation pay, sick pay, and other benefits	Determine policy for accrual; evaluate consistency with prior years (valuation). Recalculate the accruals; examine remittance forms and recalculate amounts (allocation, completeness). Agree payments to subsequent payments (existence, allocation).
Expense Accounts	
Officers' compensation	Compare authorized salary to the amount in the minutes of the board of directors' meetings (existence, allocation). Compare authorized salary to amounts paid (allocation).
Commissions expense	See Accrued commissions (above). In addition: Recalculate total commissions using stated policies or formulae, in total (for analytical review) or in detail (for particular employees or using generalized audit software) (allocation, completeness).
Employee benefit expense	Reconcile annual payroll paid to total payroll stated on annual remittance forms; multiply total payroll times benefit rate (allocation, completeness).
Total payroll	Reconcile total payroll paid to the annual T4 summary submitted to the Canada Revenue Agency (allocation, completeness).

about the classification assertion (see Table 15-3, for an example of a significant risk related to Royal Bafokeng Mining). Substantive tests of transactions that can be performed include tracing job records or other evidence that an employee has worked on a particular job or process to the accounting records that affect inventory valuation. In the case of asset capitalization, it is similar. As illustrated in Table 15-3, the auditor would also want to ensure that appropriate cutoff has occurred and that costs are only allocated to the asset up to the point in time that the asset goes into production.

Substantive Tests of Details: Presentation and Disclosure

The auditor would also need to consider the correctness, completeness, and adequacy of disclosure of management remuneration in the financial statements, as required by accounting standards. For example, disclosure of the salaries and other compensation of the top five officers is required by certain provincial securities commissions. IAS 24, *Related-party disclosures*, requires that key management personnel be disclosed, showing separately salary and share-based payments, as well as different categories of benefits. The auditor of a private company converting to IFRS would need to look carefully at the quality of related-party transactions, since

IAS 24 requires more disclosures (for example, key management compensation) that have in the past only been required for public companies.

As highlighted in Auditing in Action 15-2, public companies often have specific regulatory disclosure requirements with regard to executive compensation. Recall from our discussion of materiality in Chapter 6 that, in order to avoid misstatements and to ensure that the information is complete, auditors will perform a 100 percent audit on these items. (The auditors have concluded that users are concerned about these numbers and won't tolerate any errors; therefore, specific materiality is zero.)

CONCEPT CHECK

C15-6 Describe three assertions that are important when testing payroll-related liabilities, and provide an example of an audit test for each assertion.

C15-7 When would the auditor conduct tests of details of balances for payroll expense accounts?

Design and Perform Fraud Procedures

LO 9 Design and perform fraud procedures for the human resources and payroll cycle.

This discussion is limited to fraud procedures for the two most common types of payroll fraud—nonexistent employees and fraudulent hours.

Nonexistent Employees The issuance of payroll payments to individuals who do not work for the company (nonexistent employees) frequently results from continuing to pay an employee after his or her employment has been terminated. Usually, the person committing this type of defalcation is a payroll clerk, supervisor, fellow employee, or perhaps former employee. Certain procedures can be performed on cancelled cheques as a means of detecting defalcation. A procedure used on payroll audits is comparing the names on cancelled cheques with time cards and other records for authorized signatures and reasonableness of the endorsements. It is also common to scan endorsements on cancelled cheques for unusual or recurring second endorsements as an indication of a possible fraudulent cheque. The examination of cheques that are recorded as voided is also desirable to make sure they have not been fraudulently used. Where employees are paid automatically by bank deposits to the employees' accounts, the auditor can look for duplicated bank account numbers, post office boxes, or common employee addresses using audit software.

One test for nonexistent employees traces selected transactions recorded in the payroll journal to the human resources department to determine whether the employees were actually employed during the payroll period. The endorsement on the cancelled cheque written out to an employee is compared with the authorized signature on the employee's withholding authorization forms.

One procedure that tests for proper handling of terminated employees selects several files from the personnel records for employees who were terminated in the current year to determine whether each received termination pay and severance. Continuing payments to terminated employees are tested by examining the payroll records in the subsequent period to verify that the employee is no longer being paid. This procedure is effective only if the personnel department is informed of terminations.

Fraudulent Hours Fraudulent hours exist when an employee reports more time than was actually worked. Because of the lack of available evidence, it is usually difficult for an auditor to determine whether an employee records more time in his or her time record than was actually worked. One procedure is reconciling the total hours paid according to the payroll records with an independent record of the hours worked, such as those often maintained by production control.

SUMMARY

This chapter described the audit of the human resources and payroll cycle. A combined approach is often the approach used by auditors because of the significance of transactions and the high quality of internal controls in most organizations. Tests of details of balances are normally limited to substantive analytical procedures and verification of accrued liabilities related to payroll. However, if allocation of payroll costs to either inventory or capital assets is a significant risk, then auditors will focus on classification of those costs as well as cutoff (in the case of capital assets).

Review Questions

⊕ **15-1** **1** **2** Explain the relationship between the human resources and payroll cycle and inventory valuation.

15-2 **2** **3** List three risks of error that could occur in the human resources and payroll cycle. For each risk of error, identify a control that would prevent or mitigate the error.

15-3 **2** **3** List three risks of misappropriation of assets or fraud that could occur in the human resources and payroll cycle. For each risk of misappropriation or fraud, identify a control that would prevent or mitigate the error.

15-4 **2** **3** List three risks of inadequate disclosure or fraudulent financial reporting in the human resources and payroll cycle. For each risk of inappropriate disclosure, identify a control that would prevent or detect it.

⊕ **15-5** **3** Explain why the percentage of total audit time in the cycle devoted to performing tests of controls may be less for the human resources and payroll cycle than for the sales and collection cycle.

⊕ **15-6** **1** **2** Explain what an *imprest payroll account* is. What is its purpose as a control over payroll?

⊕ **15-7** **1** **2** Distinguish among a payroll master file, a TD-1 form, and a T4 payroll summary return. Explain the purpose of each.

⊕ **15-8** **1** **2** **4** List the types of authorizations in the human resources and payroll cycle, and state the type of misstatement that is increased when each authorization is lacking.

15-9 🔲4 What is the purpose of testing both employee access rights setup and employee access rights changes? What would be the impact upon the audit if either or both of these processes had control weaknesses?

15-10 🔲3 The company you are auditing has a local area network with office automation software, accounting software, and point of sale equipment. Provide examples of five different categories of access rights, and state the control purpose of each access right category.

15-11 🔲4 🔲5 Evaluate the following comment by an auditor: "My job is to determine whether the payroll records are fairly stated in accordance with generally accepted accounting principles, not to find out whether the client is following proper hiring and termination procedures. When I conduct an audit of payroll, I keep out of the personnel department and stick to the time cards, journals, and payroll cheques. I don't care who the client hires or who it fires, as long as it properly pays the employees it has."

15-12 🔲7 Distinguish between the following payroll audit procedures, and state the purpose of each: (1) Trace a random sample of sequentially numbered time records to the related payroll cheques in the payroll register, and compare the hours worked with the hours paid, and (2) trace a random sample of payroll cheques from the payroll register to the related time records, and compare the hours worked with the hours paid. Which of these two procedures is typically more important in the audit of payroll? Why?

15-13 🔲6 🔲7 List several audit procedures that the auditor can use to determine whether payroll transactions are recorded at the proper amount.

15-14 🔲4 DrinkOh Limited uses an application service provider to process its payroll. Its employees enter their hours using their smartphones. The payroll clerk collects the smartphone data and transmits it to the application service provider for payroll processing. Describe three controls that should be present over payroll processing at DrinkOh Limited. For each control, describe the risk of error or fraud that is mitigated or prevented by the control.

15-15 🔲2 🔲4 In auditing payroll withholding and payroll benefits expense, explain why emphasis should normally be on evaluating the adequacy of the preparation procedures for employee withholding and benefits remittance forms rather than on the employee withholding and benefits liability. Explain the effect that inadequate preparation procedures will have on the remainder of the audit.

15-16 🔲7 List several analytical procedures for the human resources and payroll cycle, and explain the type of error that might be indicated when there is a significant difference in the comparison of the current year's and previous years' results for each of the tests.

15-17 🔲8 Explain why it is common to verify total officers' compensation even when the tests of controls results in payroll are excellent. What audit procedures can be used to verify officers' compensation?

Multiple Choice Questions and Task-Based Simulations

The following questions concern internal controls in the payroll and personnel cycle. Choose the best response.

15-18 🔲2 🔲4 A factory foreman at Steblecki Corporation discharged an hourly worker but did not notify the human resources department. The foreman then forged the worker's signature on time cards and work tickets and, when giving out the cheques, diverted the payroll cheques drawn for the discharged worker to his own use. The most effective procedure for preventing this activity is to:
(1) Require written authorization for all employees added to or removed from the payroll.
(2) Have a paymaster who has no other payroll responsibility than to distribute the payroll cheques.
(3) Have someone other than persons who prepare or distribute the payroll obtain custody of unclaimed payroll cheques.
(4) From time to time, rotate persons distributing the payroll.

15-19 🔲2 🔲4 An auditor found that employee time records in one department are not properly approved by the supervisor. Which of the following could result?
(1) Duplicate paycheques might be issued.
(2) The wrong hourly rate could be used to calculate gross pay.

(3) Employees might be paid for hours they did not work.

(4) Payroll cheques might not be distributed to the appropriate employees.

🌐 **15-20** [4] [8] A common audit procedure in the audit of payroll transactions involves tracing selected items from the payroll journal to employee time cards that have been approved by supervisory personnel. This procedure is designed to provide evidence in support of the audit proposition that:

(1) Only proper employees worked and their pay was correctly computed.

(2) Jobs on which employees worked were charged with the appropriate labour cost.

(3) Internal controls over payroll disbursements are operating effectively.

(4) All employees worked the number of hours for which their pay was computed.

🌐 **15-21** [3] [4] [8] An auditor reviews the reconciliation of payroll tax forms that a client is responsible for filing to:

(1) Verify that payroll taxes are deducted from employees' gross pay.

(2) Determine whether internal control activities are operating effectively.

(3) Uncover fictitious employees who are receiving payroll cheques.

(4) Identify potential liabilities for unpaid payroll taxes.

🌐 **15-22** [4] [8] Following are some of the tests of controls and substantive tests of transactions procedures often performed in the payroll and personnel cycle. (Each procedure is to be done on a sample basis or using audit software.)

Identify whether each of the procedures is primarily a test of control or a substantive test of transactions.

Procedures	Test of Control or Substantive Test?
Reconcile the monthly payroll total for direct manufacturing labour with the labour cost distribution.	
Examine the time card for the approval of a foreman.	
Recompute hours on the time card and compare the total with the total hours for which the employee has been paid.	
Perform a surprise payroll payoff and observe employees picking up and signing for their cheques.	
Compare the employee name, date, cheque number, and amounts on cancelled cheques with the payroll journal.	
Trace the hours from the employee time cards to job tickets to make sure that the total reconciles, and trace each job ticket to the job-cost record.	
Use audit software to account for the sequence of payroll cheques in the payroll journal.	

Discussion Questions and Problems

🌐 **15-23** [2] [4] Items 1 through 9 are selected questions typically found in questionnaires used by auditors to obtain an understanding of internal control in the human resources and payroll cycle. In using the questionnaire for a client, a "yes" response to a question indicates a possible internal control, whereas a "no" indicates a potential deficiency.

1. Does an appropriate official authorize initial rates of pay and any subsequent changes in rates?

2. Are written notices documenting reasons for termination required?

3. Are formal records such as time records used for keeping time?

4. Is approval by a department head or foreperson required for all time records before they are submitted for payment?

5. Does anyone verify pay rates, overtime hours, and computations of gross payroll before direct deposits are made?

6. Do adequate means exist for identifying jobs or products, such as work orders, job numbers, or some similar identification provided to employees to ensure proper coding of time records?
7. Are payroll direct deposits authorized by persons independent of timekeeping?
8. Are employees required to show identification when requesting changes to their address or other personal information in company files?
9. Are authorized master file change forms used to document and implement changes in functional access rights?

REQUIRED

a. For each of the questions, identify the nature of the potential financial misstatement(s) if the control is not in effect.
b. For each of the questions, state the transaction-related audit objective(s) being fulfilled if the control is in effect.
c. For each control, list a test of control to test its effectiveness.
d. For each of the potential misstatements in Part (c), list a substantive audit procedure for determining whether a material misstatement exists.

15-24 〔4〕〔5〕 Ling is responsible for planning the audit over inventory and payroll cycles for a new client. Her supervisor gave her an internal control questionnaire for payroll, on which the supervisor had written the client's answers to several questions about internal controls. After reviewing the internal control questionnaire, Ling felt that the questions asked were very thorough. Since the answers were all positive, indicating good internal controls, she recommended the internal control risk for payroll be assessed as low.

Ling proceeded to design substantive procedures for payroll transactions. She also tested the controls over the client's payroll processing and inventory count procedures at year-end, just prior to the inventory count. Ling felt that she could not assess the control risks for the inventory count until she reviewed those procedures.

REQUIRED

State whether you agree with Ling's assessment of control risk and her plan of action. Justify your response.

(Reprinted from AU1 CGA-Canada Examinations, with permission Chartered Professional Accountants of Canada, Toronto, Canada. Any changes to the original material are the sole responsibility of the author/publisher and have not been reviewed or endorsed by the Chartered Professional Accountants of Canada)

15-25 〔4〕〔6〕〔8〕 The following misstatements are included in the accounting records of Lathen Manufacturing Company:
1. Joe Block and Frank Demery take turns "punching in" for each other every few days. The absent employee comes in at noon and tells his foreman that he had car trouble or some other problem. The foreman does not know that the employee is getting paid for the time.
2. The foreman submits a fraudulent time card for a former employee each week and delivers the related payroll cheque to the employee's house on the way home from work. They split the amount of the paycheque.
3. Employees often overlook recording their hours worked on job-cost tickets as required by the system. Many of the client's contracts are on a cost-plus basis.
4. Direct labour was unintentionally charged to Job 620 instead of Job 602 by the payroll clerk when he key-entered the labour distribution sheets. Job 602 was completed and the costs were expensed in the current year, whereas Job 620 was included in work-in-process.
5. The payroll clerk prepares a cheque for the same nonexistent person every week when he enters payroll transactions in the computer system, which also records the amount in the payroll journal. He submits it along with all other payroll cheques for signature. When the cheques are returned to him for distribution, he takes the cheque and deposits it in a special bank account bearing that person's name.
6. In withholding payroll taxes from employees, the computer operator deducts $0.50 extra federal income taxes from several employees each week and credits the amount to his own employee earnings record.
7. The payroll clerk manually prepares payroll cheques but often forgets to record one or two cheques in the computer-prepared payroll journal.

a. For each misstatement, state a control that should have prevented it from occurring on a continuing basis.
b. For each misstatement, state a substantive audit procedure that could uncover it.

15-26 **4** **5** **8** During the first-year audit of Omato Wholesale Stationery Ltd., you observe that commissions amount to almost 25 percent of total sales, which is somewhat higher than in previous years. Further investigation reveals that the industry typically has larger sales commissions than Omato and that there is significant variation in rates depending on the product sold.

At the time a sale is made, the salesperson records his or her commission rate and the total amount of the commissions on the office copy of the sales invoice. When sales are entered into the information system for the recording of sales, the debit to sales commission expense and credit to accrued sales commission are also recorded. As part of recording the sales and sales commission expense, the accounts receivable clerk verifies the prices, quantities, commission rates, and all calculations on the sales invoices. Both the customer master file and the salesperson's commission master files are updated when the sale and sales commission are recorded. On the fifteenth day after the end of the month, the salesperson is paid for the preceding month's sales commissions.

REQUIRED

a. What additional information do you require to complete the audit of sales commissions?
b. Develop an audit program, by assertion, to verify sales commission expense assuming that no audit tests have been conducted in any audit area to this point.
c. Develop an audit program, by assertion, to verify accrued sales commissions at the end of the year, assuming that the tests you designed in Part (a) resulted in no significant misstatements.

15-27 **3** **4** **6** Janbec Limited is a distributor of health care products. It has about $450 000 in accounts receivable and about $600 000 in inventory. It has been a tough winter, with many people sick with the flu or falling on ice, breaking legs or dislocating shoulders so that they could not come in to work.

As a result, people have been helping out in various departments. For example, the accounts receivable clerk has been helping with payroll data entry and in receiving and shipping, making sure that forms and documents are filled in properly. The accounting manager has been helping the purchasing desk when placing needed orders for inventory replenishment, and the warehouse supervisor has also been helping out with purchasing, making sure that quantities are ordered that will fit on the shelves.

A new clerk in the accounts receivable department is all thumbs at the computer and is painfully slow at data entry. However, she is bright and cheerful and seems to be catching up on the filing backlog. Her excellent telephone manner seems to also have sped up some of the late payments from customers, resulting in an excellent collection ratio in accounts receivable.

Janbec uses an application service provider (ASP) for its computing needs. Users log in via the internet, enter data, and request reports. The ASP is a local computer store a few blocks away, while the physical server is located downtown. Janbec prints all of the reports on premises after retrieving them from the ASP. If there are any problems with the software, they are dealt with by telephone.

REQUIRED

a. Explain control problems that could have arisen due to the employees "filling in" and how these potential problems could be mitigated by Janbec management.
b. How does the use of the ASP affect the audit engagement?
c. What risks are present for Janbec with respect to the ASP?

15-28 **7** **8** In comparing total employee benefits expense with that of the preceding year, Marilyn Brendin, public accountant, observed a significant increase, even though the total number of employees had only increased from 175 to 195. To investigate the difference, she selected a large sample of payroll disbursement transactions and carefully tested the withholdings for each employee in the sample by referring to Canada Pension Plan, Employment Insurance, and other benefits withholding tables. In her test, she found no exceptions; therefore, she concluded that employee benefits expense was fairly stated.

REQUIRED

a. Evaluate Brendin's approach to testing employee benefits expense.
b. Discuss a more suitable approach for determining whether employee benefits expense was properly stated in the current year.

Professional Judgment Problems and Cases

15-29 **4** **9** Cilly Stress, a fourth-year honours computer science student at a highly regarded university, was working as part-time cleaning staff at the Classy Manufacturing Company (CMC) when she was expelled from school for misuse of the university's computer resources.

Cilly was able to improve her employment status to full-time cleaning staff. She enjoyed working the night shift, where she found lots of time and opportunity to snoop around the company's office and computing centre. She learned from documentation in the recycling bins that CMC was in the process of updating its extensive policy and procedures documentation and placing it online.

Through continued efforts in searching waste bins and documents left on desktops and in unlocked cabinets, as well as some careful observation of password entry by people who were working late, Cilly soon learned enough to log in to the company's information systems and ultimately to print out lists of user identification codes and passwords using a Trojan horse program. She was able to obtain all the passwords she needed to set herself up as a supplier, customer, and systems support technician.

As a customer, she was able to order enough goods so that the inventory procurement system would automatically trigger a need for purchase of products. Then, as a supplier, she was ready to deliver the goods at the specified price (by returning the goods that she had "purchased"). As a supervisor, she was able to write off the uncollected accounts receivable from her customer accounts while being paid as a supplier. On average, she was able to embezzle about $125 000 per month.

Cilly's fraud was detected by a suspicious delivery person, who wondered why he was delivering goods to an empty building lot.

REQUIRED

a. Describe weaknesses in human resources and access policies at CMC. For each weakness, indicate the impact and provide a recommendation for improvement.

b. Identify routine audit procedures that might have produced evidence that, with further investigation, could have revealed the fraud. Describe the evidence in the test results that would have triggered the investigation.

15-30 **7** **8** Archer Uniforms Inc. is a distributor of professional uniforms to retail stores that sell work clothing to professionals such as doctors, nurses, and security guards. Traditionally, most of the sales are to retail stores throughout Canada and the United States. Most shipments are processed in bulk for direct delivery to retail stores or to the corporate warehouse distribution facilities for retail store chains. In early 2018, Archer Uniforms began offering the sale of uniforms directly to professionals through its company website. Professionals can access information about uniform styles, sizes, and prices. Purchases are charged to the customer's personal credit card. Management made this decision based on its conclusion that the online sales would tap a new market of professionals who do not have easy access to retail stores. Thus, the volume of shipments to retail stores is expected to remain consistent.

Given that Archer's IT staff lacked the experience necessary to create and support the online sales system, management engaged an IT consulting firm to design and maintain the online sales system.

REQUIRED

a. Before performing analytical procedures related to the human resources and payroll cycle accounts, develop expectations of how these recent events at Archer Uniforms Inc. will affect payroll expense for the following departments during 2018 compared with prior years' payroll expense. Indicate the degree (extensive, moderate, little) to which you expect the payroll expense account balance to increase or decrease during 2018, with reasons supported by the facts of the case.
1. Warehouse and shipping department
2. IT department
3. Accounts receivable department
4. Accounts payable department
5. Receiving department
6. Executive management
7. Marketing

b. Provide additional audit procedures (by assertion) that might be required.

15-31 **3** **4** You are assessing internal control in the audit of the human resources and payroll cycle for the Kowal Manufacturing Company, a company specializing in assembling computer systems from purchased parts. Kowal employs approximately 200 hourly and 30 salaried employees in three locations. Each location has one foreman who is responsible for overseeing operations. The owner of the company lives in Victoria, British Columbia, and is not actively involved in the business. The two key executives are the vice president of sales and the controller, both of whom have been employed by the company for more than 15 years.

Whenever there is a job opening at a location, the factory foreman interviews applicants and, on the basis of the interview, either hires or rejects them. When applicants are hired, they prepare a TD1 (employee's withholding exemption certificate) and give it to the foreman. The foreman writes the hourly rate of pay for the new employee in the corner of the TD1 form and then gives the form to the location's office manager as notice that the worker has been employed. The foreman verbally advises the office manager when there are wage-rate adjustments.

Since each hourly employee works independently, Kowal has a highly flexible work schedule policy, as long as employees start after 7:00 a.m. and are finished by 6:00 p.m. Employees are issued magnetic stripe cards with a PIN (personal identification number) that they use to scan in and out. Every Friday at 6:00 p.m., the office manager retrieves the time records and prints the time records with hours worked. The foreman reviews the list, and signs and dates it indicating his approval. Once the time records are approved, the office manager transmits the time records to head office in Mississauga, Ontario. Employees without a time record do not receive pay.

In Mississauga, the accounting supervisor retrieves the file for transfer into the payroll system, which is used to calculate the pay amounts and create a payroll journal. The payroll journal for the three locations is printed and reviewed by the controller. The payroll package then generates a direct deposit file, which is sent to the bank by the accounting supervisor every Monday afternoon.

Except for the foremen and office managers, all salaried employees work at the Mississauga location. The vice president of sales or the controller hires all salaried employees, depending on their responsibilities, and determines their salaries and salary adjustments. The owner determines the salary of the vice president of sales and the controller. The accounting supervisor processes the payroll transactions for salaried employees using the same payroll software that is used for hourly employees. The monthly payroll journal is approved by the controller before the office manager transmits the salaried payroll direct deposit file to the bank.

The payroll software package has access controls that are set up by the controller. She is the only person who has access to the salary and wage rate module of the software. She updates the software for new wage rates and salaries and makes changes to existing ones. The accounting supervisor has access to all other payroll modules. The controller's assistant has been taught to reconcile bank accounts and does the monthly payroll bank reconciliation.

REQUIRED

a. List the risks of error or fraud that are present at Kowal Manufacturing. For each risk, state the type of misstatement that could occur.

b. State whether the fraud risk could lead to misappropriation of assets or fraudulent financial reporting. Explain how these frauds could take place.

c. For each risk of error or fraud, provide both preventive and detective controls to prevent or detect the fraud.

(© 2015, AICPA. All rights reserved. Reprinted by permission.)

15-32 3 4 9 Read "The Payroll Payoff," by Edward Nagel, *CA Magazine*, May 2004, at **http://nagel-forensics. com/wp-content/uploads/2010/07/CAmagazine-May-2004-The-payroll-payoff.pdf**, and then answer the following questions.

REQUIRED

a. For each of the three cases described in the article, identify and discuss the pressure, opportunity, and rationalization the employee used to commit payroll-related fraud.

b. What combination of fraud detecting and/or preventative steps (see end of article) would prevent and/or detect fraud in each of the three situations?

AUDIT OF THE CAPITAL ACQUISITION AND REPAYMENT CYCLE

The final transaction cycle we discuss is the capital acquisition and repayment cycle, which concerns the acquisition of capital resources such as interest-bearing debt and owners' equity, as well as the repayment of capital. Owners' equity may be considered a residual account for corporations—this is where the result of current operations is posted. However, other large transactions, such as dividend payments, effects of revaluation of property, plant, and equipment, and the equity portion of financial instruments, also flow through this account.

STANDARDS REFERENCED IN THIS CHAPTER

IAS 32 – Financial instruments: Presentation

LEARNING OBJECTIVES

After studying this chapter, you should be able to:

1 Identify the accounts and unique characteristics of the capital acquisition and repayment cycle.

2 Identify the accounts and transactions for notes payable.

3 Identify significant risks, and assess risk of material misstatement for notes payable and related accounts.

4 Understand key controls, and assess control risk for notes payable and related accounts.

5 Use professional judgment to develop an audit approach (strategy) for notes payable and related accounts.

6 Design and perform tests of controls for notes payable and related accounts.

7 Design and perform analytical procedures for notes payable and related accounts.

8 Design and perform substantive tests of details for notes payable and related accounts.

9 Identify the key risks in the audit of owners' equity transactions.

10 Design and perform tests of controls and substantive tests for share capital and retained earnings.

Audit Staff Continuity Supports Client Discontinuity

Flanagan Holdings was a growing consolidator of companies in the Canadian real estate industry. During the four years since its initial public offering, Flanagan experienced significant staff turnover, including at senior executive levels. Geoff, the new chief financial officer (CFO) of Flanagan, was responsible for completing

continued >

continued the unaudited interim financial statements for the quarter ended June 30, 2012. He had reviewed the company's working papers and loan agreements and had come to the conclusion that Flanagan was in breach of a bank loan with Big Blue Bank due to the devaluation of some of Flanagan's investment papers.

Geoff contacted the loan manager at his Big Blue branch (who was also new, having been assigned to his company's account for only six months), and they both agreed that it seemed that Flanagan had been in violation of the loan agreement since the inception of the loan two years ago. Feeling concerned, Geoff contacted the partner assigned to Flanagan's audit to find out what the financial statement disclosure issues were. The partner stated that if Flanagan was in breach of the loan agreement, the debt would be classified as a current liability and additional note disclosures explaining the breach would be required, unless the bank issued a waiver for the offending clause. However, the partner referred Geoff to Lana, the audit manager who had been working with Flanagan since its inception four years ago.

Lana reviewed the 2010 audit files—the year the lending agreement was executed. She remembered having analyzed the loan agreements carefully due to their magnitude. Lana found in the firm's permanent file her analysis of the loans and also a reference to a legal interpretation that the audit firm had obtained. The legal interpretation clarified the terms of the loan agreement and confirmed that Flanagan was not in violation of the loan. Lana provided a copy of the legal interpretation to Geoff and to Big Blue's loan manager.

Flanagan's story illustrates the importance of maintaining well-documented and organized audit files in respect of client issues. The audit firm was able to support both the auditor's report and a client on an important issue. By understanding the impact to the financial statements and having legal support for a highly technical issue, the firm was able to provide continuity where both the client and the bank had employee turnover.

Source: Contributed by a qualified accountant in public practice.

Loan agreements and methods of borrowing and investing funds are not stable—new types of instruments are regularly created. Some are stable, while others turn out to be problematic, such as the mortgage-backed papers that crashed in 2008 and 2009 and continue to have marketability problems. Specialists on the audit team help to assess risks and provide audit support for short-term and long-term financial instruments during the engagement. In this chapter, we start with an overview of the capital acquisition and payment cycle and then focus on (1) notes payable and (2) certain owners' equity transactions to illustrate the audit of the capital acquisition cycle.

LO ❶ Identify the accounts and unique characteristics of the capital acquisition and repayment cycle.

Capital acquisition and repayment cycle—the transaction cycle involving the acquisition of capital resources in the form of interest-bearing debt and owners' equity, and the repayment of the capital.

AN OVERVIEW OF THE CAPITAL ACQUISITION AND REPAYMENT CYCLE

The accounts in a **capital acquisition and repayment cycle** depend upon the type of business the company operates and how its operations are financed. As with other cycles, cash is an important account in the cycle because both the acquisition and repayment of capital affect the cash account.

Four unique characteristics of the capital acquisition and repayment cycle significantly influence the audit of these accounts:

1. *Relatively few transactions affect the account balances, but each transaction is often highly material in amount.* For example, bonds are infrequently issued by most companies, but the amount of a bond issue is normally large. Due to the large size of most bond issues, it is common to verify each transaction taking place in the cycle for the entire year as part of verifying the balance sheet

accounts. Audit working papers include the beginning balance of every account in the capital acquisition and repayment cycle and document every transaction that occurred during the year.

2. *The exclusion of a single transaction could be material in itself.* Considering the effect of understatements of liabilities and owners' equity, which was discussed in Chapter 13, omission (completeness assertion) is a major audit concern.

3. *There is a legal relationship between the client entity and the holder of the stock, bond, or similar ownership document.* As the opening vignette illustrates, the auditor must determine whether the client has met the requirements of debt or equity agreements. In the audit of the transactions and amounts in the cycle, the auditor must ensure that the significant legal requirements affecting the financial statements have been properly fulfilled and adequately and clearly disclosed in the statements. As a result, the presentation and disclosure-related audit objectives are emphasized in the capital acquisition and repayment cycle.

4. *There is a direct relationship between the interest and dividend accounts and debt and equity.* In the audit of interest-bearing debt, it is desirable to simultaneously verify the related interest expense and interest payable. This holds true for owners' equity, dividends declared, and dividends payable.

The audit process for the capital acquisition accounts is the same as that followed for all other accounts. To best understand the audit procedures for many of the accounts in the capital acquisition and repayment cycle, representative accounts that are significant parts of the cycle for a typical business are included in this chapter. In the following sections, we focus on (1) the audit of notes payable and related interest expenses to illustrate interest-bearing capital and (2) the audit of share capital.

NOTES PAYABLE

A **note payable** is a legal obligation to a creditor, which may be unsecured or secured by assets. Typically, a note is issued for a period of somewhere between one month and one year, but there are also long-term notes of over a year. Notes are issued for many different purposes, and the pledged property includes a wide variety of assets such as securities, inventory, and capital assets. The principal and interest payments on the notes must be made in accordance with the terms of the loan agreement. For short-term loans, a principal and interest payment is usually required only when the loan becomes due, but for loans over 90 days, the note usually calls for monthly or quarterly interest payments.

Note payable—a legal obligation to a creditor, which may be unsecured or secured by assets.

Overview of Accounts for Notes Payable

The accounts used for notes payable and related interest are shown in Figure 16-1. Auditors commonly include tests of principal and interest payments as a part of the audit of the acquisition and payment cycle, because the payments are recorded in the cash disbursements journal. But in many cases, because of their relative infrequency, no capital transactions are included in the auditor's sample for tests of controls and transactions.

The methodology for notes payable is shown in Figure 16-2.

LO 2 Identify the accounts and transactions for notes payable.

Identify Significant Risk and Assess Risk of Material Misstatement for Notes Payable and Related Accounts

Auditors often learn about capital acquisition transactions while gaining an understanding of the client's business and industry, and as illustrated in Auditing in Action 16-1, by reading various agreements as part of the auditor's risk assessment procedures. Also,

LO 3 Identify significant risks, and assess risk of material misstatement for notes payable and related accounts.

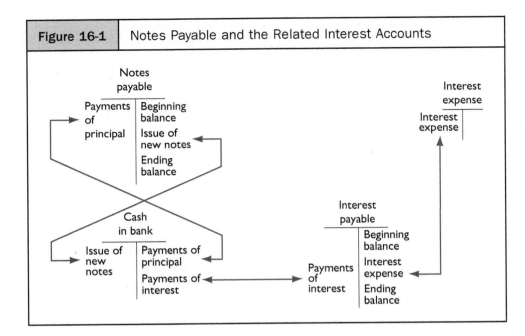

Figure 16-1 | Notes Payable and the Related Interest Accounts

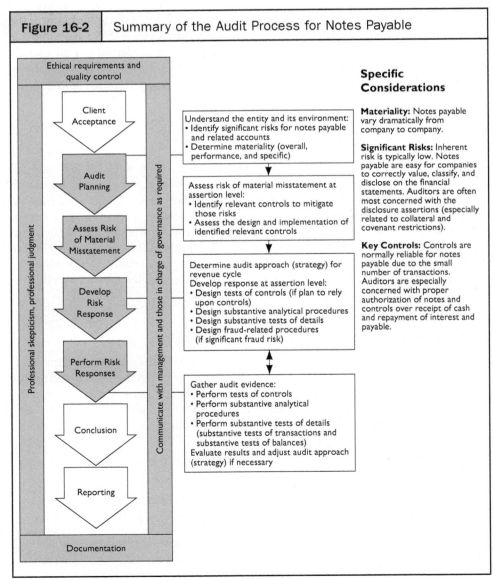

Figure 16-2 | Summary of the Audit Process for Notes Payable

when public companies issue additional debt and equity securities during the year, securities regulators require auditor consideration of financial information in the new securities offering prospectus.

Assess Inherent Risk and Fraud Risk

Inherent risks are primarily concerned with the authorization of notes payable, receipt of funds, recording of transactions, and compliance with the debt covenants. One particular factor that can increase inherent risk and fraud risk is the presence of related-party transactions.

The most important balance-related assertions in notes payable are completeness and accuracy because misstatement could be material if even one note is omitted or incorrect. The presentation and disclosure assertions of completeness and understandability are important because generally accepted accounting principles require that the footnotes adequately describe the terms of notes payable outstanding and the assets pledged as collateral for the loans. If significant restrictions on the activities of the company are required by the loans, such as compensating balance provisions or restrictions on the payment of dividends, these must also be disclosed in the footnotes.

The following are risks of fraud and error for notes payable:

- Errors in calculating interest payments, posting such amounts to the wrong period, or omitting them.
- Misclassifying debt as equity or vice versa, or misclassifications between current and long-term.
- Recording debt transactions in the wrong period.
- Incorrect or inaccurate disclosure of terms or amounts.
- Deliberate misclassification of debt as revenue or other fraudulent manipulations.

UNDERSTANDING INTERNAL CONTROL AND ASSESSING CONTROL RISK

LO 4 Understand key controls, and assess control risk for notes payable and related accounts.

There are four important controls over notes payable:

1. *Proper authorization for the issue of new notes (existence).* Renewals or new notes should be approved by the board of directors (as evidenced in the minutes) or by senior management with two signatures, depending upon the size of the note. The amount of the loan, the interest rate, the repayment terms, and the particular assets pledged are all part of the approved agreement.

2. *Adequate controls over the repayment of principal and interest (accuracy/allocation and completeness).* Due dates for interest and principal payments of notes should clearly be communicated to those responsible for cash disbursements, with payments appropriately approved.

3. *Proper documents and records (existence and completeness).* These include the maintenance of subsidiary records and control over blank and paid notes by a responsible person. Paid notes should be cancelled and retained under the custody of an authorized official.

4. *Periodic, independent verification (accuracy/allocation and completeness).* Authorized employees should perform independent recalculation of interest and reconciliation of the notes payable balance to the general ledger.

LO 5 Use professional judgment to develop an audit approach (strategy) for notes payable and related accounts.

DEVELOP AUDIT APPROACH (STRATEGY) FOR NOTES PAYABLE AND RELATED ACCOUNTS

Because there are usually few transactions in these accounts, it is often not cost-effective to test controls. Therefore, a substantive approach is often the most effective approach in this area of the audit.

LO 6 Design and perform tests of controls for notes payable and related accounts.

Design and Perform Tests of Controls

Although tests of controls are not normally performed, the audit tests are part of tests of controls for cash receipts for receipt of principal (Chapter 12) and cash disbursements for payment of interest and principal (Chapter 13).

In certain instances, additional tests of controls may be performed as part of tests of details of balances due to the materiality of individual transactions. Tests of controls for notes payable and related interest should emphasize testing the four important internal controls discussed above.

LO 7 Design and perform analytical procedures for notes payable and related accounts.

Design and Perform Substantive Analytical Procedures

Analytical procedures are essential for notes payable because tests of details for interest expense and accrued interest can frequently be eliminated when results are favourable. Table 16-1 illustrates typical analytical procedures for notes payable and related interest accounts.

The auditor's independent estimate of interest expense, using average notes payable outstanding and average interest rates, tests the reasonableness of interest expense but also tests for omitted notes payable. If actual interest expense is materially larger than the auditor's estimate, one possible cause could be interest payments on unrecorded notes payable.

Table 16-1	Analytical Procedures for Notes Payable
Analytical Procedure	**Possible Misstatement**
Analytical procedures for planning	
Compare total balance in notes payable, interest expense, and accrued interest with prior years.	Misstatement of notes payable, interest expense, or accrued interest.
Analytical procedures as substantive tests	
Recalculate approximate interest expense on the basis of average interest rates and overall monthly notes payable.	Misstatement of interest expense or accrued interest, or omission of an outstanding note payable.
Compare individual notes outstanding with the prior years.	Omission or misstatement of a note payable.

Design and Perform Substantive Tests of Details

The normal starting point for the audit of notes payable is a schedule of notes payable and accrued interest obtained from the client. A typical schedule is shown in Figure 16-3. The usual schedule includes detailed information for all transactions that took place during the entire year for principal and interest, the beginning and ending balances for notes and interest payable, and descriptive information about the notes, such as the due date, the interest rate, and the assets pledged as collateral. Such a schedule is also used to ensure adequate disclosure in the financial statements. Tests for presentation and disclosure are included in the last row of Table 16-2.

LO 8 Design and perform substantive tests of details for notes payable and related accounts.

| Figure 16-3 | Schedule of Notes Payable and Accrued Interest |

Favron Corp.
Notes Payable
12/31/18

Schedule AA-4
Prepared by Client/DB 1/12/19
Approved by JL 1/16/19

Payee	Date Made	Date Due	Face Amount of Note	SECURITY Description	SECURITY Valuation	Balance at Beginning of Period
First Canadian Bank	9/30/17	9/30/18	10 000	Investments	15 000	10 000
Second City Bank	9/30/18	9/30/19	10 000	Investments	16 000	
Third Regional Bank	10/31/18	10/31/19	10 000	Fixed Assets	22 000	
			30 000		53 000	10 000 ⑦

continued

NOTES Additions	Payments	Balance at End of Period	INTEREST Rate	Paid to	Accrued at Beginning of Period	Expense	Paid	Accrued at End of Period
	10 000 ③	-0- ④	9½% ④	Maturity	238	712 ⑥	950 ③	-0-
10 000 ②		10 000 ④	10% ④	Maturity		250 ⑥		250 ⑥
10 000 ②		10 000 ④	10% ④	Maturity		167 ⑥		167 ⑥
20 000	10 000	20 000 ⑤			238 ⑦	1129 ⑤	950	417 ⑤

① — Traced to prior year audit schedule.
② — Obtained copy of note included in permanent file.
③ — Examined cancelled note and/or cheque.
④ — Agreed to confirmation received from bank.
⑤ — Traced to general ledger.
⑥ — Recomputed expense and accrued interest; no differences noted.
Λ — Footed.
χ — Cross-footed.

| | Table 16-2 | Objectives and Tests of Details for Notes Payable and Interest |

Balance-Related Audit Objectives	Common Tests of Details of Balances Procedures	Comments
Notes payable listed in the client's note payable schedule exist (existence).	Confirm notes payable. Examine duplicate copy of notes for authorization. Examine corporate minutes for loan approval.	The existence objective is generally not as important as completeness or accuracy.
The company has an obligation to pay the notes payable (rights and obligations).	Examine notes to determine whether the company has obligations for payment.	
Existing notes payable are included in the notes payable schedule and in the general ledger (completeness).	Examine notes paid after year-end to determine whether they were liabilities at the balance sheet date. Obtain a standard bank confirmation that includes specific reference to the existence of notes payable from all financial institutions with which the client does business. (Bank confirmations are discussed more fully in Chapter 17.) Review the bank reconciliation for new notes credited directly to the bank account by the bank. (Bank reconciliations are also discussed more fully in Chapter 17.) Obtain confirmations from creditors who have held notes from the client in the past and are not currently included in the notes payable schedule. This is the same concept as a "zero balance" confirmation in accounts payable. Analyze interest expense to uncover a payment to a creditor who is not included in the notes payable schedule. Examine paid notes for cancellation to make sure they are not still outstanding. Review the minutes of the board of directors for authorized but unrecorded notes. Foot the notes payable list for notes payable and accrued interest. Trace the totals to the general ledger. Trace the individual notes payable to the master file.	This objective is important for uncovering both errors and fraud, and other irregularities. The first three of these procedures are done on most audits. The next three are frequently done only when internal controls are weak. Frequently, confirmations are done on a 100 percent basis because of the small population size. Interest expense is also normally analyzed on a 100 percent basis because of the small population size. In some cases, it may be necessary to calculate, using present-value techniques, the imputed interest rates, or the principal amount of the note. An example is when equipment is acquired for a note. Notes should be included as current-period liabilities when dated on or before the balance sheet date.
Notes payable and accrued interest on the schedule are accurate and included in the correct period (accuracy and cutoff).	Examine duplicate copies of notes for principal and interest rates. Confirm notes payable, interest rates, and last date for which interest has been paid with holders of notes. Recalculate accrued interest. Examine duplicate copies of notes to determine whether notes were dated on or before the balance sheet date.	
Notes payable in the schedule are properly classified, and fully and clearly disclosed (classification, completeness, and understandability).	Examine due dates on duplicate copies of notes to determine whether all or part of the notes are a noncurrent liability. Review notes to determine whether any are related-party notes or accounts payable.	Note that these are presentation and disclosure audit objectives, rather than balance-related audit objectives.

The objectives and common audit procedures are summarized in Table 16-2. The amount of testing depends heavily on materiality of notes payable and the effectiveness of internal controls.

CONCEPT CHECK

C16-1 What audit assertion is at most risk for the audit of capital?

C16-2 Who should be responsible for the approval of new debt such as notes payable? Why?

When PC manufacturing giant Dell, Inc. closed its $25 billion leveraged buyout in October 2013, it represented the largest company in terms of revenue to move from being a public company to one that is now privately held. Facing unmet expectations of investors and fending off a number of hostile takeover attempts, Michael Dell, CEO, orchestrated a buyout that allowed him to assume a 75 percent stake in the company he had founded in a dorm room.

The decision to take the company private meant the company was no longer subject to the regulations required for public companies, allowing Michael Dell and his management team the freedom to make decisions faster—and with less public scrutiny and oversight.

Pursuing the leveraged buyout was a huge, risk-taking venture for Dell, given that the company had to take on $17.5 billion in new debt. While it no longer has to focus on investor demands, it now has to think about the expectations of debtholders. Attention has moved to metrics related to cash-flow management rather than earnings per share.

Sources: David McCann, "A year later: A new Dell emerges?" *CFO.com*, November, 4, 2014. Connie Guglielmo, "Dell officially goes private: Inside the nastiest tech buyout ever," *Forbes*, November 2013.

AUDIT OF OWNERS' EQUITY

LO 9 Identify the key risks in the audit of owners' equity transactions.

Auditing in Action 16-2 discusses Dell, Inc.'s transformation from a public company to a private company (which some refer to as "going dark"). As the vignette illustrates, public companies face much greater regulatory requirements than their private counterparts.

Public companies are permitted by their articles of incorporation to issue shares to the public whereas **closely held corporations** tend to be private companies with restricted share ownership. In most closely held corporations, there are few, if any, transactions during the year for share capital accounts, and there are typically only a few shareholders. The only transactions entered in the owners' equity section are likely to be the change in owners' equity for the annual earnings or loss and the declaration of dividends, if any. The amount of time spent verifying owners' equity is frequently minimal for closely held corporations even though the auditor must test the existing corporate records.

For **publicly held corporations**, the verification of owners' equity is more complex due to the larger numbers of shareholders and frequent changes in the individuals holding the shares, and there may be more complex **equity instruments**. In this section, the appropriate tests for verifying the major accounts—share capital, retained earnings, and the related dividends—in a publicly held corporation are discussed. The other accounts in owners' equity are verified in much the same way as these.

Closely held corporations— corporations whose shares are not publicly traded; typically, there are only a few shareholders and few, if any, share capital account transactions during the year; such companies are also known as private corporations.

Publicly held corporations— corporations whose shares are publicly traded; typically, there are many shareholders and frequent changes in the ownership of the shares.

Equity instruments—contracts that have the characteristics of equity (i.e., there are residual interests in the assets of an entity, usually after deduction of a liability portion in the contract (IAS 32.11)).

Audit Objectives

The objectives of the auditor's examination of owners' equity is to determine whether:

- The internal controls over share capital and related dividends are adequate.
- Owners' equity transactions are recorded properly as defined by the transaction-related audit objectives.
- Owners' equity balances are properly presented and disclosed as defined by the balance-related and presentation and disclosure-related audit objectives for owners' equity accounts. (Rights and obligations and valuation are not applicable.)

CAS

Key Internal Controls

Several important internal controls are of concern to the independent auditor in owners' equity:

- *Proper authorization of transactions.* Type, nature, timing, and terms (if any) should be approved by the board of directors as evidenced in the minutes of meetings.

LO 10 Design and perform tests of controls and substantive tests for share capital and retained earnings.

- *Proper recordkeeping and adequate segregation of duties between maintaining owners' equity records and handling cash and stock certificates:* In addition, there should be (1) well-defined policies for preparing share certificates and recording share transactions and (2) independent verification of both transaction details and amounts. One of the objectives of the controls is to maintain current share capital records, which will be used to pay dividends or repurchase shares (part of the acquisitions and payments cycle) and to record issues of shares.
- *The use of an independent registrar and share transfer agent.* The **independent registrar** issues shares in accordance with the provisions in the articles of incorporation and as authorized by the board of directors. The **share transfer agent** maintains shareholder records (including changes in ownership), adding independence to this process. The share transfer agent may also disburse dividends. A company may use one or two organizations for these processes.

Audit of Share Capital

The inherent risks for owners' equity varies from organization to organization. The following are risks of fraud and error for owners' equity and its related accounts:

- Misclassifying equity as debt, or misclassifications between current and long-term equity.
- Recording equity transactions in the wrong period.
- Incorrect or inaccurate disclosure of terms or amounts.
- Equity issues or dividends that violate debt covenants.
- Backdating stock options.
- Paying dividends to wrong parties or at incorrect amounts.
- Deliberately misclassifying equity as revenue or other fraudulent manipulations.

There are four main concerns in auditing share capital:

1. *Existing share capital transactions are recorded (completeness).* If a registrar or transfer agent is used, the auditor confirms balances and transactions with them. The auditor may also review minutes of board of directors' meetings and examine client-held share records.
2. *Recorded share capital transactions exist and are accurately recorded (occurrence and accuracy).* All share capital transactions are verified (e.g., due to mergers, issuance, or repurchase) by looking for authorizations in the minutes of board of directors' meetings and agreement with share transfer agent records (using confirmations or physical inspection at their offices). Changes due to mergers and acquisitions will require inspection of relevant legal documents and may require auditor specialist assistance on the audit team.
3. *Share capital is accurately recorded (accuracy).* Confirmation with the share transfer agent will provide balances and details. If the auditor inspects share records, then the auditor would verify mechanical accuracy of the records, check that certificates (if used) are properly cancelled, and determine that complex types of capital (such as convertible securities) have been properly figured into the calculations.
4. *Share capital is fully presented and clearly disclosed (completeness and understandability).* Based upon review of the prior audit working paper file, articles of incorporation and minutes of directors' meetings, the auditor evaluates the completeness and quality of disclosure. Items to consider are type of capital, terms, amounts, dividend declaration dates, and similar matters.

Audit of Dividends The emphasis in the audit of dividends is on the transactions rather than the ending balance. The exception is when there are dividends payable.

Dividends are usually audited or confirmed with outside agents on a 100 percent basis and cause few problems. The following are the most important objectives, including those concerning dividends payable:

- Recorded dividends occurred (occurrence).
- Existing dividends are recorded (completeness).
- Dividends are accurately recorded (accuracy).
- Dividends that exist are paid to shareholders (existence).
- Dividends payable are recorded (completeness).
- Dividends payable are accurately recorded (accuracy).

Existence of recorded dividends can be checked by examining the minutes of board of directors' meetings for the amount of the dividend per share and the dividend date. When the auditor examines the board of directors' minutes for dividends declared, the auditor should be alert to the possibility of unrecorded dividends declared, particularly shortly before the balance sheet date. A closely related audit procedure is to review the permanent audit working-paper file to determine whether there are restrictions on the payment of dividends in bond indenture agreements or preferred share provisions.

The accuracy of a dividend declaration can be audited by recomputing the amount on the basis of the dividend per share and the number of shares outstanding. If the client uses a transfer agent to disburse dividends, the total can be traced to a cash disbursement entry to the agent and also confirmed.

When a client keeps its own dividend records and pays the dividend itself, the auditor can verify the total amount of the dividend by recalculation and reference to cash disbursed. In addition, it is necessary to verify whether the payment was made to the shareholders who owned the stock at the dividend record date. The auditor can test this by selecting a sample of recorded dividend payments and tracing the payee's name on the cancelled cheque to the dividend records to ensure the payee was entitled to the dividend. At the same time, the amount and the authenticity of the dividend cheque can be verified.

Tests of dividends payable should be done in conjunction with declared dividends. Any unpaid dividend should be included as a liability.

Audit of Retained Earnings

For most companies, the only transactions involving retained earnings are net earnings for the year and dividends declared. But there may also be corrections of prior-period earnings, prior-period adjustments charged or credited directly to retained earnings, and the setting up or elimination of appropriations of retained earnings.

The starting point for the audit of retained earnings is an analysis of retained earnings for the entire year. The audit schedule showing the analysis, which is usually part of the permanent file, includes a description of every transaction affecting the account. The audit of the credit to retained earnings for net income for the year (or the debit for a loss) is accomplished by tracing the entry in retained earnings to the net earnings figure on the income statement.

Once the auditor is satisfied that the recorded transactions are appropriately classified as retained earnings transactions, the next step is to decide whether they are accurately recorded. The audit evidence necessary to determine accuracy depends on the nature of the transactions. If there is a requirement for an appropriation of retained earnings for a bond sinking fund, the correct amount of the appropriation can be determined by examining the bond indenture agreement.

Another important consideration in the audit of retained earnings is evaluating whether there are any transactions that should have been included but were not. If a stock dividend was declared, for instance, the market value of the securities issued should be capitalized by a debit to retained earnings and a credit to share capital. Similarly, if the financial statements include appropriations of retained earnings, the auditor should evaluate whether it is still necessary to have the appropriation as of the balance sheet date. As an example, an appropriation of retained earnings for a bond sinking fund should be eliminated by crediting retained earnings after the bond has been paid off.

CONCEPT CHECK

C16-3 Provide examples of outsourcing as applied to management of share records.

C16-4 List examples of complex transactions that could affect retained earnings.

Of primary concern in determining whether retained earnings are correctly disclosed on the balance sheet is the existence of any restrictions on the payment of dividends. Frequently, agreements with bankers, shareholders, and other creditors prohibit or limit the amount of dividends the client can pay. These restrictions must be disclosed in the footnotes to the financial statements.

SUMMARY

MyLab Accounting

Make the grade with MyLab Accounting: The questions, exercises, and problems marked with a 🌐 can be found on MyLab Accounting. You can practise them as often as you want, and most feature step-by-step guided instructions to help you find the right answer.

This chapter discussed the audit of the capital acquisition and repayment cycle, which includes the primary sources of financing for most businesses. The cycle generally involves few transactions, but the individual transactions are often material, which influences the design and performance of tests in the cycle. The approach to auditing this cycle was illustrated for notes payable, for related interest expense and accrued interest, and for owners' equity and related accounts.

Review Questions

🌐 **16-1** **1** List four examples of interest-bearing liability accounts commonly found in balance sheets. What characteristics do liabilities have in common? How do they differ?

🌐 **16-2** **1** **2** Why are liability accounts that are included in the capital acquisition and repayment cycle audited differently from accounts payable?

🌐 **16-3** **3** **5** It is common practice to audit the balance in notes payable in conjunction with the audit of interest expense and interest payable. Explain the advantages of this approach.

🌐 **16-4** **4** With which internal controls should the auditor be most concerned in the audit of notes payable? Explain the importance of each.

🌐 **16-5** **7** Which analytical procedures are most important in verifying notes payable? Which types of misstatements can the auditor uncover by the use of these tests?

🌐 **16-6** **3** **8** Why is it more important to search for unrecorded notes payable than for unrecorded notes receivable? List several audit procedures the auditor can use to uncover unrecorded notes payable.

🌐 **16-7** **3** **8** What is the primary purpose of analyzing interest expense? Given this purpose, what primary considerations should the auditor keep in mind when doing the analysis?

🌐 **16-8** **6** **8** Distinguish between the tests of controls and tests of details of balances for liability accounts in the capital acquisition and repayment cycle.

🌐 **16-9** **2** List four types of restrictions that long-term creditors often put on companies when granting them a loan. How can the auditor find out about each restriction?

🌐 **16-10** **9** What are the primary objectives in the audit of owners' equity accounts?

16-11 [9] Evaluate the following statements: "The corporate charter and the bylaws of a company are legal documents; therefore, they should not be examined by the auditors. If the auditor wants information about these documents, a lawyer should be consulted."

16-12 [9] What are the major internal controls over owners' equity?

16-13 [9] Describe the duties of a share registrar and a transfer agent. How does the use of their services affect the client's internal controls?

16-14 [9] What kinds of information can be confirmed with a transfer agent?

16-15 [9] Evaluate the following statement: "The most important audit procedure to verify dividends for the year is a comparison of a random sample of cancelled dividend cheques with a dividend list that has been prepared by management as of the dividend record date."

16-16 [10] Explain how the audit of dividends declared and paid is affected if a transfer agent disburses dividends for a client. What audit procedures are necessary to verify dividends paid when a transfer agent is used?

16-17 [9] What should be the major emphasis in auditing the retained earnings account? Explain your answer.

16-18 [9] Explain the relationship between the audit of owners' equity and the calculations of earnings per share. What are the main auditing considerations in verifying the earnings-per-share figure?

Multiple Choice Questions and Task-Based Simulations

The following question concerns interest-bearing liabilities. Choose the best response.

16-19 [4] Which of the following controls will most likely justify a reduced assessed level of control risk for the completeness assertion for notes payable?
   (1) The accounting staff reviews board of directors' meeting minutes for any indication of any transactions involving outstanding debt to make sure all borrowings are included in the general ledger.
   (2) All borrowings that exceed $500 000 require approval from the board of directors before loan contracts can be finalized.
   (3) Before approving disbursement of principal payments on notes payable, the treasurer reviews terms in the note.
   (4) Accounting maintains a detailed schedule of outstanding notes payable that is reconciled monthly to the general ledger.

The following questions concern the audit of accounts in the capital acquisition and repayment cycle. Choose the best response.

16-20 [8] [10] During an audit of a publicly held company, the auditor should obtain written confirmation regarding debenture transactions from the:
   (1) Debenture holders.
   (2) Client's lawyer.
   (3) Internal auditors.
   (4) Trustee.

16-21 [9] [10] An auditor usually obtains evidence of shareholders' equity transactions by reviewing the entity's:
   (1) Minutes of board of directors' meetings.
   (2) Transfer agent's records.
   (3) Cancelled stock certificates.
   (4) Treasury stock certificates book.

16-22 [10] Which of the following audit procedures would be most relevant when examining the completeness transaction-related audit objective for share capital?
   (1) The auditor examines minutes of the board of directors' meetings to identify any actions involving the issuance of share capital.
   (2) The auditor vouches entries in the client's share capital records to board minutes.
   (3) Confirmations of new stock issuances are sent to the client's stock transfer agent.
   (4) The auditor traces entries of new stock issuances to the cash receipts journal.

16-23 **[8]** From the list below, identify the presentation and disclosure-related audit objective(s) for each of the following audit procedures that were performed to address presentation and disclosure-related audit objectives related to notes payable. (Items from the list below can be used more than once.)

(1) Completeness
(2) Classification and understandability
(3) Occurrence and rights and obligations
(4) Accuracy and valuation

Audit Procedure	Presentation and Disclosure-Related Objective
The schedule of notes payable in the footnotes includes all notes outstanding.	
The footnote identifies which notes are due to related parties.	
The total of notes payable in the footnotes agrees with the total of notes payable on the balance sheet.	
The footnote listing of notes payable includes only those obligations that are the responsibility of the company.	
The footnote clearly describes the assets that are collateral for the note obligations.	

Discussion Questions and Problems

16-24 **[8]** The following are frequently performed audit procedures for the verification of bonds payable issued in previous years:

1. Obtain a copy of the bond indenture agreement and review its important provisions.
2. Determine that each of the bond indenture provisions has been met.
3. Analyze the general ledger account for bonds payable, interest expense, and unamortized bond discount or premium.
4. Reperform the client's calculations of interest expense, unamortized bond discount or premium, accrued interest, and bonds payable.
5. Obtain a confirmation from the bondholder.

REQUIRED

a. State the purpose of each of the five audit procedures listed.
b. List the provisions for which the auditor should be alert in examining the bond indenture agreement.
c. For each provision listed in Part (b), explain how the auditor can determine whether its terms have been met.
d. Explain how the auditor should verify the unamortized bond discount or premium.
e. List the information that should be requested in the confirmation of bonds payable with the bondholder.

16-25 **[5]** **[8]** Evangeline Ltd. took out a 20-year mortgage for $2 600 000 on June 15, 2018, and pledged its only manufacturing building and the land on which the building stands as collateral. Each month, a payment of $20 000 is made to the mortgagor. You are in charge of the current-year audit for Evangeline, which has a balance sheet date of December 31, 2018. The client has been audited previously by your public accounting firm, but this is the first time Evangeline Ltd. has had a mortgage.

REQUIRED

a. Explain why it is desirable to prepare a working paper for the permanent file for the mortgage. What type of information should be included in the working paper?
b. Explain why the audits of mortgage payable, interest expense, and interest payable should all be done together.

c. List the audit procedures that should ordinarily be performed to verify the issue of the mortgage, the balance in the mortgage and interest payable accounts at December 31, 2018, and the balance in interest expense for the year 2018.

16-26 **3 5 8** The Fox Company is a medium-sized industrial client that has been audited by your public accounting firm for several years. The only interest-bearing debt owed by Fox Company is $200 000 in long-term notes payable held by the bank. The notes were issued three years previously and will mature in six more years. Fox Company is highly profitable, has no pressing needs for additional financing, and has excellent internal controls over the recording of loan transactions and related interest costs.

REQUIRED

a. Describe the auditing procedures that you think will be necessary for notes payable and related interest accounts in these circumstances.

b. How would your answer differ if Fox Company were unprofitable, had a need for additional financing, and had weak internal controls?

16-27 **9 10** Bee Corporation's partial balance sheet includes the following information:

	2018	2017
Long-term investments		
Shares and negotiable securities	$ 400 000	$ 40 000
Shareholders' equity		
Common shares		
10 000 000 issued		
8 000 000 outstanding—		$16 000 000
December 31, 2017	$12 000 000	
6 000 000 outstanding—	$ 1 000 000	$ 6 000 000
December 31, 2018		
Contributed capital		

REQUIRED

a. Design two audit procedures to test existence related to the above investments for Bee's 2018 financial statements.

b. Design two audit procedures to test authorization related to the above investments for Bee's 2018 financial statements.

c. Assuming the company's share transactions are handled by a transfer agent, explain two important facts that the auditor would need to confirm or verify with the transfer agent for the 2018 audit.

(Extract from AU1 CGA-Canada Examinations developed by the Certified General Accountants Association of Canada © 2011 CGA-Canada. Reproduced with permission. All rights reserved.)

16-28 **9 10** The following audit procedures are commonly performed by auditors in the verification of owners' equity:

1. Review the articles of incorporation and bylaws for provisions about owners' equity.

2. Review the minutes of the board of directors' meetings for the year for approvals related to owners' equity.

3. Analyze all owners' equity accounts for the year and document the nature of any recorded change in each account.

4. Account for all certificate numbers in the share capital listing for all shares outstanding.

5. Examine the share certificate listing for any shares that were cancelled.

6. Recompute earnings per share.

7. Review debt provisions and senior securities with respect to liquidation preferences, dividends in arrears, and restrictions on the payment of dividends or the issue of shares.

REQUIRED

a. State the purpose of each of these seven audit procedures, including the audit assertion(s).

b. List the types of misstatements the auditors could uncover by the use of each audit procedure.

16-29 **10** The Bergonzi Corporation is a medium-sized wholesaler of grocery products with 4000 shares of stock outstanding to approximately 25 shareholders. Because of the age of several retired shareholders and the success of the company, management has decided to pay dividends six times a year. The amount of the bimonthly dividend per share varies depending on the profits, but it is ordinarily between $5 and $7 per share. The chief accountant, who is also a shareholder, prepares the dividend cheques, records the cheques in the dividend journal, and reconciles the bank account. Important controls include manual cheque signing by the president and the use of an imprest dividend bank account.

The auditor verifies the dividends by maintaining a schedule of the total shares issued and outstanding in the permanent working papers. The total amount of shares outstanding is multiplied by the dividends per share authorized in the minutes to arrive at the current total dividend. This total is compared with the deposit that has been made to the imprest dividend account. Since the transfer of shares is infrequent, it is possible to verify dividends paid for the entire year in a comparatively short time.

REQUIRED

a. Evaluate the usefulness of the approach followed by the auditor in verifying dividends in this situation. Include both the strengths and the weaknesses of the approach.

b. List other audit procedures that should be performed in verifying dividends in this situation. Explain the purpose of each procedure.

Professional Judgment Problems and Cases

16-30 **7** **8** **10** E-Antiques Inc. is an internet-based market for buyers and sellers of antique furniture and jewellery. The company allows sellers of antique items to list descriptions of those items on the E-Antiques website. Interested buyers review the website for antique items and then enter into negotiations directly with the seller for purchase. E-Antiques receives a commission for each transaction.

The company, founded in 2000, initially obtained capital through equity funding provided by the founders and through loan proceeds from financial institutions. In early 2018, E-Antiques became a publicly held company when it began selling shares on a national stock exchange. Although the company had never generated profits, the stock offering generated huge proceeds based on favourable expectations for the company, and the share price quickly increased to above $100 per share.

Management used the proceeds to pay off loans to financial institutions and to reacquire shares issued to the company founders. Proceeds were also used to fund purchases of hardware and software to support the online market. The balance of unused proceeds is currently held in the company's bank accounts.

REQUIRED

a. Before performing analytical procedures related to the capital acquisition and repayment cycle accounts, consider how the process of becoming publicly held would affect accounts at E-Antiques Inc. Describe whether each of the following balances would increase, decrease, or experience no change between 2017 and 2018 because of the public offering:

(1) Cash
(2) Accounts receivable
(3) Property, plant, and equipment
(4) Accounts payable
(5) Long-term debt

(6) Common shares
(7) Retained earnings
(8) Dividends
(9) Revenues

b. During 2018, the share price for E-Antiques plummeted to around $19 per share. No new shares were issued during 2018. Describe the impact of this drop in share price on the following accounts for the year ended December 31, 2018:

(1) Common shares
(2) Retained earnings

c. How does the decline in share price affect your assessment of client business risk and acceptable audit risk?

16-31 **3** **8** The ending general ledger balance of $186 000 in notes payable for Sisam Manufacturing Inc. is made up of 20 notes to 8 different payees. The notes vary in duration anywhere from 30 days to 2 years and in amount from $1 000 to $10 000. In some cases, the notes were issued for cash loans; in other cases, the notes were issued directly to vendors for the purchase of inventory or equipment. The use of relatively short-term financing is necessary because all existing properties are pledged for mortgages. Nevertheless, there is still a serious cash shortage.

Recordkeeping procedures for notes payable are not good, considering the large number of loan transactions. There is neither a notes payable master file nor an independent verification of ending balances; however, the notes payable records are maintained by a secretary who does not have access to cash.

The audit has been done by the same public accounting firm for several years. In the current year, the following procedures were performed to verify notes payable:

1. Obtain a list of notes payable from the client, foot the notes payable balances on the list, and trace the total to the general ledger.

2. Examine duplicate copies of notes for all outstanding notes included on the listing. Compare the name of the lender, amount, and due date on the duplicate copy with the list.
3. Obtain a confirmation from lenders for all listed notes payable. The confirmation should include the due date of the loan, the amount, and interest payable at the balance sheet date.
4. Recompute accrued interest on the list for all notes. The information for determining the correct accrued interest is to be obtained from the duplicate copy of the note. Foot the accrued interest amounts and trace the balance to the general ledger.

REQUIRED

a. What should be the emphasis in the audit of notes payable in this situation? Explain.
b. State the purpose of each of the four audit procedures listed.
c. Evaluate whether each of the four audit procedures was necessary. Evaluate the sample size for each procedure.

d. List other audit procedures that should be performed in the audit of notes payable in these circumstances.

16-32 **9** Before a company can begin trading on an exchange, it must meet certain initial requirements. In order to be listed on the Toronto Stock Exchange, companies must meet minimum requirements. Review the listing requirements for the TSX per the TSX Company Manual at **https://www.tsx.com/ listings/listing-with-us/listing-guides** to answer the following questions.

REQUIRED

a. Referring to Section 302, what are the basic eligibility requirements to be listed on the TSX?
b. What are the three categories that the TSX uses for companies (ignore SPACs [special purpose acquisition corporations]), and what are the listing requirements for each category?
c. Refer to Section 311, Management, and explain the requirements for management and the board of directors.

CHAPTER

17

STANDARDS REFERENCED
IN THIS CHAPTER

Section 1540 – Cash flow
statement

IAS 7 – Statement of cash
flows

AUDIT OF CASH BALANCES

Cash is the way that companies acquire assets and discharge debts, so it has a pivotal role in the accounting process, being one side of many different types of transactions. Here, we will look at different types of cash accounts and how they are audited.

LEARNING OBJECTIVES

After studying this chapter, you should be able to:

1 Identify the major types of cash accounts maintained by business entities.

2 Understand the relationship of cash in the bank to the various transaction cycles.

3 Identify significant risks and assess risk of material misstatement for cash balances.

4 Understand and assess control risk, and design tests of controls for cash.

5 Design and perform substantive procedures for cash.

6 Design and perform fraud procedures for cash.

Fake Bank Confirmation Hides Massive Fraud

Calisto Tanzi formed Parmalat in 1961 at the age of 22 after inheriting a small family-run pasteurization plant in the Italian town of Parma. In 1990, the company went public on the Milan stock exchange. By the end of that decade, Parmalat employed more than 30 000 people in 30 countries, was Italy's eighth largest company, and was a global consumer brand that sought to be the "Coca-Cola of milk."

Parmalat began engaging in fraudulent transactions involving fictitious sales as early as 1993, and investigators indicate that without the fraud, Parmalat would have reported losses every year from 1990 until the fraud was revealed in 2003. During the period, the company took on increasing levels of debt to finance international acquisitions. To raise money and increase sales, Parmalat established three Caribbean shell companies. The shell companies pretended to sell Parmalat products, and Parmalat used credit notes from the shell companies to raise money from banks.

In 1999 the activities of the shell companies were transferred to the Cayman Islands. Two outside auditors allegedly came up with the audacious creation of a bogus milk producer in Singapore that provided 300 000 tons of milk powder to a Cuban importer through the company's Cayman Islands subsidiary. Parmalat claimed that the Cayman Islands subsidiary held €3.95 billion in cash in a New York bank, but the account did not exist. A forged bank confirmation was sent to the subsidiary's auditors to support the fraudulent cash balance.

continued >

Parmalat's losses totalled €12 billion, and in 2008, Tanzi was sentenced to 10 years in prison for his role in the fraud. The company restructured and in 2005 was relisted on the Milan stock exchange.

Source: Peter Gumbel, "How it all went so sour," *Time*, November 21, 2004, accessed September 15, 2017, at **http://content.time.com/time/magazine/article/0,9171,785318,00.html**.

Cash is the only account included in every cycle except inventory and distribution. It makes sense to study this audit area last because the evidence accumulated for cash balances depends heavily on the results of the tests in other cycles. For example, if the auditors' understanding of internal control and tests of controls and substantive tests of transactions in the acquisition and payment cycle cause them to believe that it is appropriate to reduce assessed control risk to low, they can reduce detailed tests of the ending balance in cash. If, however, auditors conclude that assessed control risk should be higher, extensive year-end testing may be necessary.

Cash is important because of its susceptibility to theft, and cash can also be significantly misstated as illustrated in the case of Parmalat. This chapter highlights the linkage of cash in the bank to transaction cycles and describes the audit process for the cash balance (in particular, the general cash account).

TYPES OF CASH ACCOUNTS

LO 1 Identify the major types of cash accounts maintained by business entities.

We begin by discussing the types of cash accounts commonly used by most companies, because the auditing approach to each varies. Auditors are likely to learn about the various types of cash and financial instruments balances when they obtain an understanding of the client's business. The following are the major types of accounts.

It is important to understand the different types of cash accounts because the auditing approach to each varies. Table 17-1 describes the major types of cash accounts or balances. Although cash management is not really a cycle (since its transactions come from other cycles), we refer to it here as a cycle for convenience.

Table 17-1	Major Types of Cash Accounts or Balances and Their Purposes
Type of Cash Account or Balance	**Purpose of Cash Account**
General cash account—the primary bank account for most organizations; virtually all cash receipts and disbursements flow through this account at some time.	• Used to make payments (for expenses and capital assets) and to record cash received from operations (such as cash sales and accounts receivable). • Small companies who have only one account have this type of account.
Imprest payroll account—a bank account to which the exact amount of payroll for the pay period is transferred from the general cash account. A fixed balance, such as $1 000, may also be kept in the account.	• Used to pay employees, and may also be used to pay employee remittances to Canada Revenue Agency. • Helps improve control over cash and reduce time to reconcile bank accounts.
Branch bank account—a separate bank account maintained at a local bank by a branch of a company. Can be either a general cash account or an imprest type account. Usage depends upon what is authorized by head office.	• Provides more rapid deposits and/or payments at the local level. • Builds business relationships with local banks.
Imprest petty cash fund—a fund of cash maintained within the company for small cash payments; its fixed balance is comparatively small, and it is periodically reimbursed.	• Used for small cash purchases that can be paid more conveniently and quickly by cash than by cheque (e.g., office supplies).
Cash equivalents—short-term, highly liquid investments (such as term deposits) that have a known value and an insignificant risk of change in value (Section 1540.06, IAS 7). Where bank overdrafts are in normal use (i.e., a fluctuating bank balance), the bank overdraft would also be considered a cash equivalent, even though it is a liability rather than an asset.	• Used to manage fluctuating cash balances so that cash is available for short-term operating needs.

All cash either originates from or is deposited into general cash. This chapter focuses on the general cash account. The general cash account is considered significant in almost all audits, even when the ending balance is immaterial. The amount of cash flowing into and out of the cash account is frequently larger than for any other account in the financial statements. Furthermore, the susceptibility of cash to defalcation is greater than for other types of assets because most other assets must be converted to cash to make them usable.

LO **2** Understand the relationship of cash in the bank to the various transaction cycles.

THE RELATIONSHIP BETWEEN CASH IN THE BANK AND TRANSACTION CYCLES

In the audit of cash, an important distinction should be made between verifying the client's reconciliation of the balance on the bank statement to the balance in the general ledger and verifying whether recorded cash in the general ledger correctly reflects all cash transactions that took place during the year. It is relatively easy to verify the client's reconciliation of the balance in the bank account to the general ledger, which is the primary subject of this chapter, but a significant part of the total audit of a company involves verifying whether cash transactions are properly recorded by considering cash transactions in each cycle. For example, each of the examples of errors or fraud in Table 17-2 are improper payments or failures to cash, but none will normally be discovered as a part of the audit of the bank reconciliation.

> ## CONCEPT CHECK
>
> **C17-1** Describe the difference between a general cash account and an imprest bank account.
> **C17-2** For each of the following transaction cycles, provide an example of an error in cash that would affect the cycle: sales and accounts receivable, acquisition and payment, human resources and payroll.

The discovery of these misstatements would have been the result of tests of controls or substantive tests of transactions in those cycles. Entirely different types of misstatements, such as the following, are normally discovered as part of the tests of a bank reconciliation:

- Failure to include on the outstanding cheque list a cheque that has not cleared the bank, even though it has been recorded in the cash disbursements journal.
- Cash received by the client subsequent to the balance sheet date but recorded as cash receipts in the current year.

Table 17-2	Examples of Errors and Fraud in Transaction Cycles Affecting Cash
Transaction Cycle	**Examples of Errors or Fraudulent Transactions**
Revenue	Failure to bill a customer
	Billing a customer at a lower price than called for by company policy
	A defalcation of cash by interception of collections from customers before they are recorded
	Charging the account receivable off as a bad debt
	Fictitious refunds, whereby the employee takes the refund
Acquisition and payment	Duplicate payment of a vendor's invoice
	Improper payments of officers' personal expenditures
	Payment for raw materials that were not received
Human resources and payroll	Payment to an employee for more hours than he or she worked
	Payment to fictitious employees
Capital acquisition and repayment	Payment of interest to a related party for an amount in excess of the going rate

- Deposits recorded as cash receipts near the end of the year, deposited in the bank, and included in the bank reconciliation as a deposit in transit.
- Payments on notes payable that were debited directly to the bank balance by the bank but were not entered in the client's records.

An Overview of the Audit Process for the General Cash Account

The audit process for auditing year-end cash is essentially the same as for all other balance sheet accounts. Figure 17-1 provides an overview of the audit process for cash in bank.

IDENTIFY SIGNIFICANT RISKS AND ASSESS RISK OF MATERIAL MISSTATEMENT IN CASH

LO **3** Identify significant risks, and assess risk of material misstatement for cash balances.

The cash balance is often immaterial on many audits, but the cash transactions affecting the balance are almost always extremely material. There is, therefore, often potential for material misstatement of cash. Inappropriate cash management policies or inappropriate use of restricted cash may signal a significant risk in cash. If a business has plenty of cash but there never seem to be any customers about

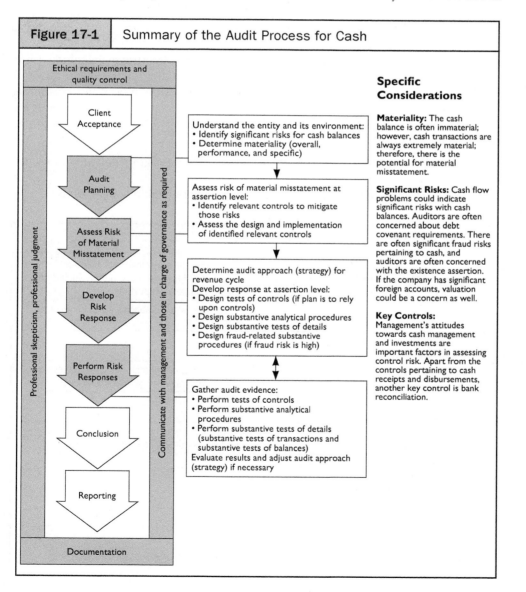

Figure 17-1 | Summary of the Audit Process for Cash

(such as at a restaurant), then this may be a fraud risk indicator that the business could be engaging in money laundering. If, as in the case of Fairfield Sentry (see Auditing in Action 7-2), an investment company invests in questionable or even non-existent marketable securities, then the company will be in a cash squeeze, as it can no longer liquidate its investments.

Cash is an inherently risky asset, and errors in processing cash or cash fraud could affect any cycle. When assessing risk of material misstatement, the auditor should consider whether the client has any cash flow problems in meeting its current obligations on a timely basis, or whether there are any particular debt covenants (or regulatory requirements) pertaining to the cash balance. Cycle-based indicators that could indicate cash liquidity problems include gradually aging accounts receivable, obsolete inventory or poorly managed inventory, an inability to take advantage of cash discounts in accounts payable, and difficulty meeting payroll or income tax obligations.

Because cash is more susceptible to theft than other assets (since it is highly liquid), there is high inherent risk for the existence objective. If there is a high volume of activity, there is also a higher chance of manipulation.

Table 17-3 shows examples of the major types of error or fraud that could occur. Since cash impacts every cycle, many different types of error or fraud exist.

LO **4** Understand and assess control risk, and design tests of controls for cash.

UNDERSTAND INTERNAL CONTROL AND ASSESS CONTROL RISK

Management attitudes toward cash and the nature of the treasury management function are important factors in assessing control risk. By asking management about its policies with respect to cash management and cash investment, as well as gathering information from the different cycles, the auditor will obtain information about the likelihood of cash misstatements. Some important points to keep in mind regarding understanding internal control include the following:

- Internal control effectiveness over cash balances varies significantly for different companies.
- The most important internal control is independent bank reconciliations.

Table 17-3	Examples of Major Risks of Error or Fraud in the Cash Cycle	
Risks of Error	**Risks of Misappropriation of Assets, Other Fraud, or Illegal Acts**	**Risks of Inadequate Disclosure or Incorrect Presentation of Financial Information, Including Fraudulent Financial Reporting**
Cash received could be posted in the incorrect period.		Funds received as debt financing could be recorded as revenue.
	Payments in cash (rather than by cheque) could be stolen rather than recorded.	
Cash received could be recorded at the wrong amount.		Cash received from related parties could be recorded as cash received from general operations.
	Payments could be made to a fictitious supplier for goods not received.	
Suppliers could be paid twice for their invoices.		Payments to associated companies or companies controlled by the company are not disclosed.
	Management steals cash by authorizing personal payments (e.g., home renovations) as business expenses.	
Employees could be paid using the wrong wage rate.		Cash equivalents are incorrectly classified as marketable securities.
	Blank cheques are stolen and signatures forged to steal funds, or bank accounts are hacked into and cash stolen.	

- Internal controls over cash receipts and disbursements are important for assessing control risk.
- Individuals who are super users or have incompatible functions granted to them using computer systems (e.g., ability to steal cash and alter the accounting records) could result in control risk being assessed as high.

Electronic Cash Transactions Many organizations use **electronic data interchange (EDI)** (the electronic transfer of business documents, such as invoices or purchase orders) and **electronic funds transfer (EFT)** (the electronic transfer of funds, either as payment or receipt, among banks, collecting from customers, paying employees, and paying vendors. Under these systems, cash is transferred instantly. These systems have the potential to improve internal controls, since there is no cash handling by employees. However, as illustrated in Auditing in Action 17-1, the risk of incorrect transfers or theft by unauthorized transfers still exists.

When assessing internal controls, the auditor needs to evaluate and document controls in all software involved (data communications, data transfer, specialized EDI programs, and access). With electronic payments, year-end balances of accounts receivable, accounts payable, or inventory may be reduced since funds are received closer to the date of the transaction. Where funds are transferred electronically, there is an increased need for the enhanced security features of encryption, access control, and authentication (verifying the identity of the parties to a transaction).

> **Electronic data interchange (EDI)**—the electronic transfer of business documents, such as invoices and purchase orders.
>
> **Electronic funds transfer (EFT)**—the electronic transfer of funds, either as payment or receipt (e.g., using a debit card).

Key Controls

Internal controls over the year-end cash balances in the general account can be divided into two categories: (1) controls over the transaction cycles affecting the recording of cash receipts and disbursements; and (2) independent bank reconciliations.

Controls affecting the recording of cash transactions are discussed in chapters pertaining to those cycles. For example, in the acquisition and payment cycle, major controls include the adequate segregation of duties between the cheque signing and the accounts payable functions; the signing of cheques by only a properly authorized

---

AUDITING IN ACTION 17-1
Masquerading for Cash

While businesses have always been concerned about someone entering their premises to steal cash on hand, they now have to focus on another type of security threat in which criminals can be in another part of the world but still confiscate an organization's cash. In this new type of fraud, known as "masquerading," fraudsters hack into an organization's email or other communications system and pose as a senior executive, such as the CEO, CFO, or controller, and direct a lower-level employee to urgently execute a financial transaction that involves the disbursement of funds. Money is then wired or transmitted through the banking system to an account controlled by the criminal. In some cases, the fraudsters are so bold that they even pick up the telephone to make the request. While wire transfers can sometimes be cancelled before the transaction is executed, in most cases it is hard to get the money back.

Financial institutions are working hard to raise awareness of masquerading as a fraud technique. Bank of the West offers the following tips:

- Confirm that the request to initiate the wire is from an authorized source within the company.

- Double- and triple-check email addresses.
- Establish a multi-person approval process for transactions above a certain dollar threshold.
- Slow down and be aware that fraud may be present any time wire transfers include tight deadlines.
- Be suspicious of confidentiality of the transaction.
- Require all wire transfers to be linked to a valid approved purchase or service.

Source: David McCann, "Criminals posing as CFOs to commit wire fraud," *CFO.com*, August 13, 2014, accessed September 15, 2017, at **http://ww2.cfo.com/fraud/2014/08/criminals-posing-cfos-commit-wire-fraud/**.

person; the use of prenumbered cheques that are printed on special paper; adequate control of blank and voided cheques; careful review of supporting documentation by the cheque signer before cheques are signed; and adequate internal verification. If the controls affecting cash-related transactions are adequate, it is possible to reduce the audit tests of the year-end bank reconciliation.

An essential control over the cash balance is a monthly **bank reconciliation** of the differences between the cash balance recorded in the general ledger and in the general bank account, performed on a timely basis by someone independent of the handling or recording of cash receipts and disbursements. The reconciliation is important to ensure that the books reflect the same cash balance as the actual amount of cash in the bank after consideration of reconciling items, but even more important, the independent reconciliation provides a unique opportunity for an independent internal verification of cash receipts and disbursements transactions. If the bank statements are received unopened by the reconciler and physical control is maintained over the statements until the reconciliations are complete, the cancelled cheques, deposit information, and other documents included in the statement can be examined without concern for the possibility of alteration, deletions, or additions. A careful bank reconciliation by competent client personnel includes the following:

- Compare cancelled cheques with the cash disbursements journal for date, payee, and amount.
- Examine cancelled cheques for signature, endorsements, and cancellation.
- Compare deposits in the bank with recorded cash receipts for date, customer, and amount.
- Account for the numerical sequence of cheques, and investigate missing ones.
- Reconcile all items causing a difference between the book and the bank balance, and verify their propriety.
- Reconcile total debits on the bank statement with the totals in the cash disbursements journal.
- Reconcile total credits on the bank statement with the totals in the cash receipts journal.
- Review month-end interbank transfers for propriety and proper recording.
- Follow up on outstanding cheques and stop-payment notices.

Because of the importance of the monthly reconciliation of bank accounts, another common control for many companies is having a responsible employee review the monthly reconciliation as soon as possible after its completion.

Design and Perform Control Tests

Because the cash balance is affected by all other cycles except inventory and distribution, an extremely large number of transactions affect cash. In several earlier chapters, we discussed in detail the appropriate tests of controls for each cycle. For example, controls over cash receipts were studied in Chapter 12, and controls over cash disbursements were studied in Chapter 13. Cash transactions are audited through these transaction cycle tests.

LO 5 Design and perform substantive procedures for cash.

DESIGN AND PERFORM SUBSTANTIVE TESTS FOR CASH

Substantive Analytical Procedures

In many audits, the year-end bank reconciliation is extensively audited. Using substantive analytical procedures to test the reasonableness of the cash balance is therefore less important than it is for most other audit areas.

Auditors commonly compare the ending balance on the bank reconciliation, deposits in transit, outstanding cheques, and other reconciling items with the prior-year

---

Bank reconciliation—the monthly reconciliation, usually prepared by client personnel, of the differences between the cash balance recorded in the general ledger and the amount in the bank account.

reconciliation. Similarly, auditors normally compare the ending balance in cash with previous months' balances. These substantive analytical procedures may uncover misstatements in cash.

Substantive Tests of Details for Cash Balances

Figure 17-2 summarizes the majority of key tests for the balance-related assertions of cash balances.

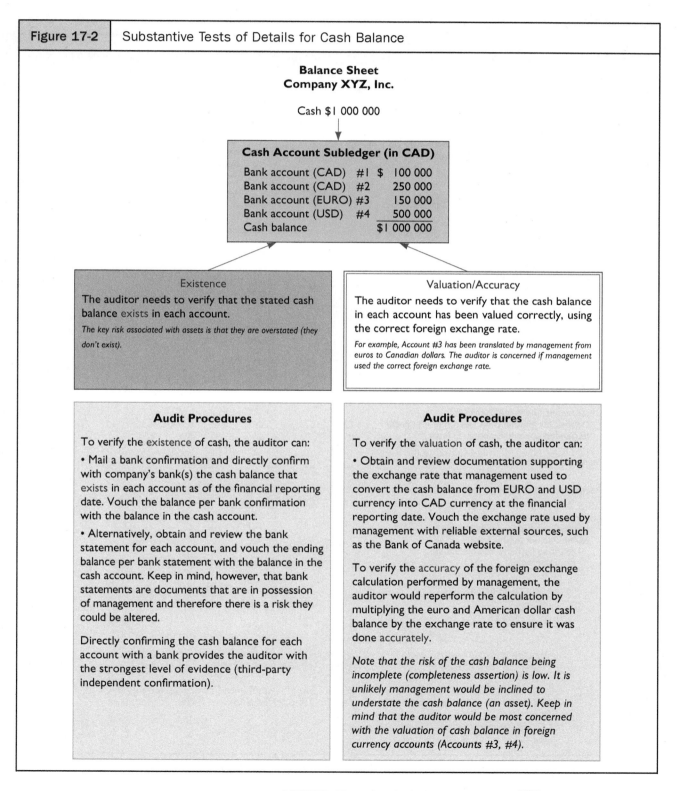

| Figure 17-2 | Substantive Tests of Details for Cash Balance |

Balance Sheet
Company XYZ, Inc.

Cash $1 000 000

Cash Account Subledger (in CAD)

Bank account (CAD)	#1	$	100 000
Bank account (CAD)	#2		250 000
Bank account (EURO)	#3		150 000
Bank account (USD)	#4		500 000
Cash balance			$1 000 000

Existence

The auditor needs to verify that the stated cash balance exists in each account.

The key risk associated with assets is that they are overstated (they don't exist).

Valuation/Accuracy

The auditor needs to verify that the cash balance in each account has been valued correctly, using the correct foreign exchange rate.

For example, Account #3 has been translated by management from euros to Canadian dollars. The auditor is concerned if management used the correct foreign exchange rate.

Audit Procedures

To verify the existence of cash, the auditor can:

• Mail a bank confirmation and directly confirm with company's bank(s) the cash balance that exists in each account as of the financial reporting date. Vouch the balance per bank confirmation with the balance in the cash account.

• Alternatively, obtain and review the bank statement for each account, and vouch the ending balance per bank statement with the balance in the cash account. Keep in mind, however, that bank statements are documents that are in possession of management and therefore there is a risk they could be altered.

Directly confirming the cash balance for each account with a bank provides the auditor with the strongest level of evidence (third-party independent confirmation).

Audit Procedures

To verify the valuation of cash, the auditor can:

• Obtain and review documentation supporting the exchange rate that management used to convert the cash balance from EURO and USD currency into CAD currency at the financial reporting date. Vouch the exchange rate used by management with reliable external sources, such as the Bank of Canada website.

To verify the accuracy of the foreign exchange calculation performed by management, the auditor would reperform the calculation by multiplying the euro and American dollar cash balance by the exchange rate to ensure it was done accurately.

Note that the risk of the cash balance being incomplete (completeness assertion) is low. It is unlikely management would be inclined to understate the cash balance (an asset). Keep in mind that the auditor would be most concerned with the valuation of cash balance in foreign currency accounts (Accounts #3, #4).

The starting point for the verification of the balance in the general bank account is obtaining a bank reconciliation (such as the one shown in Figure 17-3) from the client for inclusion in the auditor's working papers. Note that the last number in the working paper is the adjusted balance in the general ledger. Although the bank reconciliation is normally prepared manually or using a spreadsheet, many accounting systems allow the client to use computerized systems to prepare the list of outstanding cheques.

Figure 17-3	Working Paper for a Bank Reconciliation

Microsoft Excel - Book2

File Edit View Insert Format Tools Data Window Help Acrobat

Arial 10 B I U $ % 100%

A1 =

Clawson Industries
Bank Reconciliation
12/31/18

Schedule	A-2	Date
Prepared by	Client / DED	1/10/19
Approved by	SW	1/18/19

Acct. 101 – General account, First Canadian Bank

Balance per Bank			109 713	X A-2/1
Add:				
Deposits in transit				
12/30		10 017 ✓		
12/31		11 100 ✓	21 117	
Deduct				
Outstanding cheques				
# 7993	12/16	3 068 X		
8007	12/16	9 763 X		
8012	12/23	11 916 X		
8013	12/23	14 717 X		
8029	12/28	A-7 37 998 X		
8038	12/30	A-7 10 000 X	<87 462>	
Other reconciling items: Bank error				
Deposit for another bank customer credited				
to general account by bank, in error			<15 200>	A-3
Balance per bank, adjusted			28 168	T/B
			W	
Balance per general ledger before adjustments			32 584	A-1
Adjustments:				
Unrecorded bank service charge		216		A-3
Non-sufficient funds cheque				
returned by bank, not collectible				
from customer		4 200	<4 416>	C-3/1
Balance per general ledger, adjusted			28 168	A-1
			W	

X Traced and agreed to bank confirmation.

✓ Traced deposit to the December 2018 cash receipts records and to the January 2019 bank cut-off statement, noting its proper classification as a deposit in transit at 12/31/18

X Traced cheque to December 2018 cash disbursements records and to the January 2019 bank cut-off statement, noting its proper classification as an outstanding cheque at 12/31/18

T/B Traced to 12/31/18 adjusted trial balance

W Footed

Receipt of a Bank Confirmation The direct receipt at the auditor's location of a confirmation from every bank or other financial institution with which the client does business is necessary for every audit, except when there are an unusually large number of inactive accounts. If the bank does not respond to a confirmation request, the auditor must send a second request or ask the client to telephone the bank. As a convenience to accountants as well as to bankers, the bank responds to the **standard bank confirmation form**.

Standard bank confirmation form—a form approved by CPA Canada and the Canadian Bankers Association; the bank uses the form to respond to the auditor's request for information about the client's bank balances, loan information, and contingent liabilities.

The importance of bank confirmations in the audit extends beyond the verification of the actual cash balance. It is typical for the bank to confirm loan information and bank balances on the same form. Information on liabilities to the bank for notes, mortgages, or other debt typically includes the amount of the loan, the date of the loan, its due date, interest rate, and the presence of collateral.

After the bank confirmation has been received by the auditor, the balance in the bank account confirmed by the bank should be traced to the amount stated on the bank reconciliation. All other information on the bank reconciliation should be traced to the relevant audit working papers. If the information is not in agreement with client records, an investigation must be made of the difference. While the bank should exercise due care in completing the confirmation, errors can occur. The auditor may wish to communicate with the bank if there is any information on the returned confirmation about which he or she is doubtful or if any information that was expected is not reported.

Many auditors prove the subsequent-period bank statement if a **cutoff bank statement** is not received directly from the bank. The purpose of this proof is to test whether the client's employees have omitted, added, or altered any of the documents accompanying the bank statement. It is a test for intentional misstatements. The auditor performs the proof in the month subsequent to the balance sheet date by (1) footing all the cancelled cheques, electronic payments, debit memos, deposits, and credit memos; (2) checking to see that the bank statement balances when the footed totals are used; and (3) reviewing the items included in the footings to make sure they were cancelled by the bank in the proper period and do not include any alterations.

Cutoff bank statement—a partial-period bank statement and the related cancelled cheques, duplicate deposit slips, and other documents included in bank statements, mailed by the bank directly to the auditor. The auditor uses it to verify reconciling items in the client's year-end bank reconciliation.

Tests of the Bank Reconciliation The reason for testing the bank reconciliation is to verify whether the client's recorded bank balance is the same amount as the actual cash in the bank except for deposits in transit, outstanding cheques, and other reconciling items. In testing the reconciliation, the cutoff bank statement provides the information for conducting the tests. Several major procedures are involved:

- Verify that the client's bank reconciliation is mathematically accurate.
- Trace the balance on the cutoff statement to the balance per bank on the bank reconciliation. A reconciliation is incomplete until these two are the same.
- Trace cheques included with the cutoff bank statement to the list of outstanding cheques on the bank reconciliation and to the cash disbursements journal.
- Investigate all significant cheques or payments included on the outstanding cheque list that have not cleared the bank on the cutoff statement. The reason for the cheque not being cashed should be discussed with the client, and if the auditor is concerned about the possibility of fraud (such as deliberate holding of cheques), the vendor's accounts payable balance should be confirmed.
- Trace deposits in transit to the subsequent bank statement. All cash receipts not deposited in the bank at the end of the year should be traced to the cutoff bank statement to ensure they were deposited shortly after the beginning of the next fiscal year.
- Account for other reconciling items on the bank statement and bank reconciliation. These include such items as bank service charges, bank errors and corrections, and unrecorded note transactions debited or credited directly to the bank account by the bank. These reconciling items should be carefully investigated to ensure they have been treated properly by the client.

The extent of audit work conducted on the bank reconciliation depends on the assessed quality of internal controls. There are usually fewer outstanding bank transactions for electronic transactions than for paper transactions sent via mail, since the timing difference between invoice and receipt is minimal. When client personnel prepare the bank reconciliation, electronic payments should be verified against an authorized schedule of such payments by date, payee account number, and amount. The auditor would review the authorized schedule of payments and controls over its preparation. Similarly, deposits would be traced to the client's POS (point-of-sale) system records.

Although most debit card transactions are processed accurately, a very small percentage of transactions are not. Most organizations keep track of payment methods automatically using their POS systems. Thus, the daily sales are broken down by cash, debit card, credit card, cheque, and accounts receivable. When performing the bank reconciliation, the debit card total should agree with the amounts automatically deposited into the bank. This reconciliation should be handled by a person independent of the POS function. These receipts should be tested as part of the sales and receivables transaction cycle.

> **CONCEPT CHECK**
>
> C17-3 Why do the risks of every transaction cycle affect cash?
> C17-4 What is the purpose of a bank reconciliation?

LO 6 Design and perform fraud procedures for cash.

FRAUD-ORIENTED PROCEDURES

Despite the banks' efforts to combat it (as illustrated in Auditing in Action 17-1 and 17-2), a major consideration in the audit of the general cash account is the possibility of fraud. The auditors must extend their year-end audit procedures to test more extensively for the possibility of material fraud when there are inadequate controls, especially the improper segregation of duties between handling cash and the recording of cash or the lack of an independently prepared bank reconciliation. Also, as the Parmalat, Cinar, and Satyam frauds and several others we have discussed throughout the textbook highlight, the possibility of management override increases the risk of fraud in cash.

AUDITING IN ACTION 17-2
Positive Pay Reduces Cheque Fraud

Positive pay is an automated fraud detection tool offered by most banks. An organization using positive pay sends a file of issued cheques to the bank each day that cheques are written. The file sent to the bank includes the cheque number, account number, issue date, and dollar amount. The positive pay service matches the account number, cheque number, and dollar amount of each cheque presented for payment against the list of cheques provided by the organization. All three components of the cheque must match exactly for the cheque to be paid. When a cheque is presented that does not match, it is reported as an exception and an image of the cheque is sent to the organization so that it can make a pay/no pay decision and can instruct the bank either to pay or to return the cheque.

These are good controls that assist the client in preventing cheque fraud. Auditors who have clients with this capability would need to consider controls over the issuing of the cheque details to the bank, as well as controls over who has the ability to instruct the bank to either pay or return the cheque, in addition to the positive pay features provided by the bank.

Sources: Canadian Imperial Bank of Commerce, "CIBC positive pay," *CIBC.com*, **www.cibc.com/ca/commercial/business-solutions/cash-management/positive-pay.html**, accessed September 12, 2017. Royal Bank, "RBC Express positive pay," **http://www.rbcroyalbank.com/commercial/cashmanagement/rx-positive.html**, accessed September 12, 2017.

In designing procedures for uncovering fraud, auditors should carefully consider the nature of the deficiencies in internal control, the type of fraud that is likely to result from the deficiencies, the potential materiality of the fraud, and the audit procedures that are most effective in uncovering the fraud.

When auditors are specifically testing for fraud, they should keep in mind that audit procedures other than tests of details of cash balances can also be useful. Procedures that may uncover fraud in the cash receipts area include:

- Confirmation of accounts receivable.
- Tests performed to detect lapping.
- Review of the general ledger entries in the cash account for unusual items.
- Comparison of customer orders to sales and subsequent cash receipts.
- Examination of approvals and supporting documentation for bad debts and sales returns and allowances.

Similar tests can be used for testing for the possibility of fraudulent cash disbursements.

Even with reasonably elaborate fraud-oriented procedures, it is extremely difficult to detect thefts of cash, as well as fraudulent financial reporting involving cash, especially omitted transactions and account balances. If, for example, a company has illegal offshore cash accounts and makes deposits to those accounts from unrecorded sales, it is unlikely that an auditor will uncover the fraud. Nevertheless, auditors are responsible for making a reasonable effort to detect fraud when they have reason to believe it may exist. The following procedures for uncovering fraud are directly related to year-end cash balances: extended tests of the bank reconciliation, proofs of cash, and tests of interbank transfers.

Extended Tests of the Bank Reconciliation

When the auditor believes that the year-end bank reconciliation may be intentionally misstated, it is appropriate to perform extended tests. The purpose of the extended tests is to verify whether all transactions included in the journals for the last month of the year were correctly included in or excluded from the bank reconciliation and to verify whether all items in the bank reconciliation were correctly included.

Assume that there are material internal control weaknesses and the client's year-end is December 31. A common approach is to start with the bank reconciliation for November and compare all reconciling items with cancelled cheques and other documents in the December bank statement. All remaining cancelled cheques and deposit slips in the December bank statement should be compared with the December cash disbursements and receipts journals. All uncleared items in the November bank reconciliation and the December cash disbursements and receipts journals should be included in the client's December 31 bank reconciliation. Similarly, all reconciling items in the December 31 bank reconciliation should be items from the November bank reconciliation and December's journals that have not yet cleared the bank.

Proof of Cash

Auditors sometimes prepare a proof of cash when the client has material internal control weaknesses in cash. A **proof of cash** is a four-column working paper used to reconcile the bank's records of the client's beginning balance, cash deposits, cleared cheques, and ending balance for the period with the client's records. It includes the following:

- A reconciliation of the balance on the bank statement with the general ledger balance at the beginning of the proof-of-cash period.
- A reconciliation of cash receipts deposited with the cash receipts journal for a given period.

Proof of cash—a four-column working paper prepared by the auditor to reconcile the bank's records of the client's beginning balance, cash deposits, cleared cheques, and ending balance for the period with the client's records.

- A reconciliation of cancelled cheques or electronic payments clearing the bank with the cash disbursements journal for a given period.
- A reconciliation of the balance on the bank statement with the general ledger balance at the end of the proof-of-cash period.

A proof of cash can be performed for one or more interim months, the entire year, or the last month of the year. The auditor uses a proof of cash to determine whether the following occurred:

- All recorded cash receipts were deposited.
- All deposits in the bank were recorded in the accounting records.
- All recorded cash disbursements were paid by the bank.
- All amounts that were paid by the bank were recorded.

The concern in an interim-month proof of cash is not with adjusting account balances, but rather with reconciling the amounts per accounting records and the bank.

The proof of cash is an excellent method of comparing recorded cash receipts and disbursements with the bank account and with the bank reconciliation. However, the auditor must recognize that the proof of cash disbursements is not for discovering cheques written for an improper amount, fraudulent cheques, or other misstatements in which the dollar amount appearing on the cash disbursements records is incorrect. Similarly, the proof of cash receipts is not useful for uncovering the theft of cash receipts or the recording and deposit of an improper amount of cash.

Tests of Interbank Transfers (Kiting)

Kiting—the transfer of money from one bank account to another and improperly recording the transfer so that the amount is recorded as an asset in both accounts; used by embezzlers to cover a defalcation of cash.

Embezzlers occasionally cover a defalcation of cash by a practice known as **kiting**: transferring money from one bank to another and improperly recording the transaction, which overstates cash. The day before the balance sheet date, a cheque is drawn on one bank account and immediately deposited in a second account for credit before the end of the accounting period. In making this transfer, the embezzler is careful to make sure that the cheque is deposited at a late enough date that it does not clear the first bank until after the end of the period. Assuming that the bank transfer is not recorded until after the balance sheet date, the amount of the transfer is recorded as an asset in both banks. Although there are other ways of perpetrating this fraud, each involves the basic device of increasing the bank balance to cover a shortage by the use of bank transfers.

To test for kiting, as well as for unintentional errors in recording bank transfers, auditors can list all bank transfers made a few days before and after the balance sheet date and tracing each to the accounting records for proper recording. Similarly, transfers deposited in the bank near the end of the year or included in deposits not yet credited can be traced to the cash receipts or payments journal to ensure they have been recorded in the journal in the appropriate period.

CONCEPT CHECK

C17-5 When could kiting occur and what does it do? How would it be accomplished?
C17-6 How can the auditor test for kiting?

Even though audit tests of bank transfers are usually fraud-oriented, they are often performed on audits in which there are numerous bank transfers, regardless of the internal controls. When there are numerous intercompany transfers, it is difficult to be sure that each is correctly handled unless a schedule of transfers near the end of the year is prepared and each transfer is traced to the accounting records and bank statements. In addition to the possibility of kiting, inaccurate handling of transfers could result in a misclassification between cash and accounts payable. Due to the materiality of transfers and the relative ease of performing the tests, many auditors believe that the tests should always be performed.

SUMMARY

In this chapter, we have seen that transactions in most cycles affect the cash account. Because of the relationship between transactions in several cycles and the ending cash account balance, the auditor typically waits to audit the ending cash balance until the results of tests of controls for all cycles are completed and analyzed. Tests of the cash balance normally include tests of the bank reconciliations of key cash accounts, such as the general cash account, imprest payroll account, and imprest petty cash fund. If auditors assess a high likelihood of fraud in cash, they may perform additional tests such as extended bank reconciliation procedures, a proof of cash, or tests of inter-bank transfers.

MyLab Accounting

Make the grade with MyLab Accounting: The questions, exercises, and problems marked with a ⊕ can be found on MyLab Accounting. You can practise them as often as you want, and most feature step-by-step guided instructions to help you find the right answer.

Review Questions

17-1 **1** What is an imprest bank account for a branch operation? Explain the purpose of using this type of bank account.

17-2 **1** **2** Explain the relationships among the initial assessed level of control risk, tests of controls for cash disbursements, and tests of details of cash balances. Give one example in which the conclusion reached about internal controls in cash disbursements would affect the tests of cash balances.

17-3 **1** **2** **3** Assume that a client with excellent internal controls uses an imprest payroll bank account. Explain why the verification of the payroll bank reconciliation ordinarily takes less time than the tests of the general bank account, even if the number of cheques exceeds those written on the general account.

17-4 **3** **4** Why is there a greater emphasis on the detection of fraud in tests of details of cash balances than for other balance sheet accounts? Give two specific examples that demonstrate how this emphasis affects the auditor's evidence accumulation in auditing year-end cash.

17-5 **2** Why is the monthly reconciliation of bank accounts by an independent person an important internal control over cash balances? Which individuals would generally not be considered independent for this responsibility?

17-6 **2** **5** Evaluate the effectiveness and state the shortcomings of the preparation of a bank reconciliation by the accountant in the manner described in the following statement: "When I reconcile the bank account, the first thing I do is to sort the cheques in numerical order and find which numbers are missing. Next I determine the amount of the uncleared cheques by referring to the cash disbursements journal. If the bank account reconciles at that point, I am all finished with the reconciliation. If it does not, I search for deposits in transit, cheques from the beginning of the outstanding cheque list that still have not cleared, other reconciling items, and bank errors until it reconciles. In most instances, I can do the reconciliation in 20 minutes."

17-7 **5** How do bank confirmations differ from positive confirmations of accounts receivable? Distinguish between them in terms of the nature of the information confirmed, the sample size, and the appropriate action when the confirmation is not returned after the second request. Explain the rationale for the differences between these two types of confirmations.

17-8 **5** Evaluate the necessity for following this practice described by an auditor: "In confirming bank accounts, I insist upon a response from every bank the client has done business with in the past two years, even though the account may be closed at the balance sheet date."

17-9 **5** Describe a cutoff bank statement and state its purpose.

17-10 **3** **5** Why are auditors usually less concerned about the client's cash receipts cutoff than the cutoff for sales? Explain the procedure involved in testing for the cutoff for cash receipts.

17-11 **5** How would a company's bank reconciliation reflect an electronic deposit of cash received by the bank—from credit card agencies that make payments on behalf of customers purchasing products from the company's website—but not recorded in the company's records?

17-12 [5] When the auditor fails to obtain a cutoff bank statement, it is common to "prove" the entire statement for the month subsequent to the balance sheet date. How is this done and what is its purpose?

17-13 [6] Distinguish between lapping and kiting. Describe audit procedures that can be used to uncover each.

17-14 [4] [5] Explain why, in verifying bank reconciliations, most auditors emphasize the possibility of a nonexistent deposit in transit being included in the reconciliation and an outstanding cheque being omitted, rather than the omission of a deposit in transit and the inclusion of a nonexistent outstanding cheque.

Multiple Choice Questions and Task-Based Simulations

The following question deals with auditing year-end cash and financial instruments. Choose the best response.

17-15 [3] [5] The auditor should ordinarily send confirmation requests to all banks with which the client has conducted any business during the year, regardless of the year-end balance, because:
  (1) This procedure will detect kiting activities that would otherwise not be detected.
  (2) The confirmation form also seeks information about indebtedness to the bank.
  (3) The sending of confirmation requests to all such banks is required by auditing standards.
  (4) This procedure relieves the auditor of any responsibility with respect to nondetection of forged cheques.

17-16 [5] [6] A CPA obtains a January 10 cutoff bank statement for a client directly from the bank. Very few of the outstanding cheques listed on the client's December 31 bank reconciliation cleared during the cutoff period. A probable cause for this is that the client:
  (1) Is engaged in kiting.
  (2) Is engaged in lapping.
  (3) Has overstated its year-end bank balance.
  (4) Transmitted the cheques to the payees after year-end.

The following questions deal with discovering fraud in auditing year-end cash. Choose the best response.

17-17 [5] The auditor should control and verify all liquid assets simultaneously to prevent:
  (1) Unrecorded disbursements.
  (2) Conversion of assets to conceal a shortage.
  (3) Unauthorized disbursements.
  (4) Embezzlement.

17-18 [5] Which of the following is one of the better auditing techniques to detect kiting?
  (1) Review composition of authenticated deposit slips.
  (2) Review subsequent bank statements and cancelled cheques received directly from the banks.
  (3) Prepare year-end bank reconciliations.
  (4) Prepare a schedule of bank transfers from the client's books.

17-19 [5] Will the audit procedures concerned with tests of details of general cash address the assertion listed?

Audit Procedure	Assertion	Yes/No?
Obtain a standard bank confirmation from each bank with which the client does business.	Completeness	
Compare the balance on the bank reconciliation obtained from the client with the bank confirmation.	Accuracy	
Inquire of management whether all bank accounts have been disclosed and presented in the financial statements.	Existence	
Verify that balances in foreign currency bank accounts have been translated using correct exchange rates at year-end.	Cutoff	

Discussion Questions and Problems

17-20 [3] You are auditing general cash for Trail Supply Corp. for the fiscal year ended July 31. The client has not prepared the July 31 bank reconciliation. After a brief discussion with the owner, you agree to prepare the reconciliation with assistance from one of Trail Supply's clerks. You obtain the following information:

	General Ledger	Bank Statement
Beginning balance	$ 4 611	$ 5 753
Deposits		25 056
Cash receipts journal	25 456	
Cheques cleared		(23 615)
Cash disbursements journal	(21 811)	
July bank service charge		(87)
Note paid directly		(6 100)
NSF cheque		(311)
Ending balance	$ 8 256	$ 696

June 30 Bank Reconciliation: Information in General Ledger and Bank Statement	
Balance per bank	$5 753
Deposits in transit	600
Outstanding cheques	1 742
Balance per books	4 611

In addition, the following information is obtained:
1. The total of outstanding cheques on June 30 was $1692.
2. The total for cheques that were recorded in the July disbursements journal was $20 467.
3. A cheque for $1060 cleared the bank but had not been recorded in the cash disbursements journal. It was for an acquisition of inventory. Trail Supply uses the periodic inventory method.
4. A cheque for $396 was charged to Trail Supply but had been written on an associated company's bank account.
5. Deposits included $600 from June and $24 456 for July.
6. The bank withdrew from Trail Supply's account a nonsufficient funds (NSF) customer cheque totalling $311. The credit manager concluded that the customer intentionally closed its account and that the owner had left the city. The account was turned over to a collection agency.
7. The bank deducted $5800 plus interest from Trail Supply's account for a loan made by the bank under an agreement signed four months ago. The note payable was recorded at $5800 on Trail Supply's books.

REQUIRED
a. Prepare a bank reconciliation that shows both the unadjusted and adjusted balances per the general ledger.
b. Identify the nature of adjustments required.
c. What audit procedures would you use to verify each item in the bank reconciliation?

17-21 [4] [5] [6] The following are fraud and other irregularities that might be found in the client's year-end cash balance. (Assume the balance sheet date is June 30.)
1. A cheque was omitted from the outstanding cheque list on the June 30 bank reconciliation. It cleared the bank July 7.
2. A cheque was omitted from the outstanding cheque list on the bank reconciliation. It cleared the bank September 6.
3. Cash receipts collected on accounts receivable from July 2 to July 5 were included as June 29 and June 30 cash receipts.
4. A loan from the bank on June 26 was credited directly to the client's bank account. The loan was not entered in the books as of June 30.

5. A cheque that was dated June 26 and disbursed in June was not recorded in the cash disbursements journal, but it was included as an outstanding cheque on June 30.
6. A bank transfer recorded in the accounting records on July 2 was included as a deposit in transit on June 30.
7. The outstanding cheques on the June 30 bank reconciliation were underfooted by $2000.

REQUIRED

a. Assuming that each of these misstatements was intentional, state the most likely motivation of the person responsible.
b. What control could be instituted for each intentional misstatement to reduce the likelihood of occurrence?
c. List an audit procedure that could be used to discover each misstatement.

17-22 3 5 Below are seven potential misstatements due to errors or fraud, preceded by a list of auditing procedures (a through h) the auditor could consider performing to gather evidence to determine whether an error or fraud is present.

LIST OF AUDITING PROCEDURES

a. Send a standard bank confirmation confirming the balance in the bank at year-end.
b. Compare the details of the cash receipts journal entries with the details of the corresponding daily deposit slips.
c. Count the balance in petty cash at year-end.
d. Agree gross amount on payroll cheques to approved hours and pay rates.
e. Obtain the cutoff bank statement and compare the cleared cheques to the year-end reconciliation.
f. Examine invoices, receipts, and other documentation supporting reimbursement of petty cash.
g. Examine payroll cheques clearing after year-end with the payroll journal.
h. Prepare a bank transfer schedule.

REQUIRED

For each possible misstatement below, identify one audit procedure that would be most effective in providing evidence regarding the potential misstatement. Listed auditing procedures may be used once, more than once, or not at all.

Possible Misstatements Due to Errors or Fraud	Audit Procedure to Provide Evidence (a to h)
1. The auditor suspects that a lapping scheme exists because an accounting department employee who has access to cash receipts also maintains the accounts receivable ledger and refuses to take any vacation or sick days.	
2. The auditor suspects that the entity is inappropriately increasing the cash reported on its balance sheet by drawing a cheque on one account and not recording it as an outstanding cheque on that account, while simultaneously recording it as a deposit in a second account.	
3. The entity's cash receipts of the first few days of the subsequent year were properly deposited in its general operating account after the year-end. However, the auditor suspects that the entity recorded the cash receipts in its books during the last week of the year under audit.	
4. The auditor noticed a significant increase in the number of times that petty cash was reimbursed during the year and suspects that the custodian is stealing from the petty cash fund.	
5. The auditor suspects that a kiting scheme exists because an accounting department employee who can issue and record cheques seems to be leading an unusually luxurious lifestyle.	
6. During tests of the reconciliation of the payroll bank account, the auditor notices that a cheque to an employee is significantly larger than other payroll cheques.	
7. The auditor suspects that the controller wrote several cheques and recorded the cash disbursements just before year-end but did not mail the cheques until after the first week of the subsequent year.	

17-23 3 4 5 Santasgiftworld.com is an online retailer of children's toys. The chief executive officer has noticed that margins have been deteriorating over those of previous years due to an increase in cost of goods sold coupled with a much faster increase in freight out and bad-debt expenses. He has also heard through the grapevine that some customers have complained of unauthorized charges on their credit cards. Other customers have complained of placing orders and never having received them, necessitating replacement shipments. Still more complaints of unauthorized charges have been received from individuals claiming never to have ordered products at all. You have been contacted to help Santasgiftworld.com improve its operations and prevent possible litigation arising from continuing problems of this type.

Santasgiftworld.com employs 100 individuals. Its customer base consists mainly of individuals but also smaller toy stores, day-care centres, and schools, all of which order through the company's website. The website has pages where customers can view all of its products and prices. A virtual shopping cart is available for each customer once he or she has set up an account. A customer choosing to make a purchase simply clicks on the direct link to the shopping cart from the desired product and proceeds to the checkout. There, the customer is prompted to choose a major credit card payment method and enter a shipping address. Once this information has been entered, the customer chooses a shipping method: Canada Post, UPS, or Federal Express. The customer is then informed of the total price and the date to expect shipment.

Every two hours, the orders placed on the website are reviewed and then entered into the company's main database for fulfillment. Once an order is shipped, credit card information is extracted and transmitted for settlement in Santasgiftworld.com's favour.

Orders have been placed with the company, but the customers in question honestly deny ever submitting those orders. It turns out that many of those orders had been placed by the children of the customers, without the customers' knowledge. The children were able to gain access to their parents' accounts after the web ordering system recognized cookies on the hard drives. When the children went to the website, the page recognized them as the users of the account and gave them authorized access to make purchases.

REQUIRED

Identify control weaknesses at Santasgiftworld.com. For each control weakness:
a. State the exposure created.
b. Provide a recommendation to prevent or detect the exposure.
c. Provide an audit test of detail that could be used in assessing the impact on the financial statements.
d. Identify the audit objective(s) addressed by the audit tests.

Professional Judgment Problems and Cases

17-24 **4** **6** Yip-Chuk Inc. had weak internal control over its cash transactions. Facts about its cash position at November 30 were as follows.

The cash account showed a balance of $18 901.62, which included undeposited receipts. A credit of $100 on the bank's records did not appear on the records of the company. The balance per bank statement was $15 550. Outstanding cheques

were #62 for $116.25, #183 for $150.00, #284 for $253.25, #8621 for $190.71, #8623 for $206.80, and #8632 for $145.28.

The cashier, Khalid Nasser, embezzled all undeposited receipts in excess of $3794.41 and prepared the reconciliations shown in the table.

Balance, per general ledger, November 30		$18 901.62
Add: Outstanding cheques		
#8621	$ 190.71	
#8623	206.80	
#8632	145.28	
		442.79
		19 344.41
Less: Undeposited receipts		3 794.41
Balance per bank, November 30		15 550.00
Deduct: Unrecorded credit		100.00
True cash balance, November 30		$15 450.00

REQUIRED

a. Prepare a supporting schedule showing how much Khalid embezzled.

b. How did he attempt to conceal his theft?

c. Using only the information given, name two specific features of internal control that were apparently missing.

(© 2015, AICPA. All rights reserved. Reused by permission.)

17-25 [4] Three years ago, Peng started a business providing translation and document services to businesses that source goods from China for the Canadian retail market. At first, Peng did all of the work himself, marketing his services to potential customers, receiving orders, translating documents, suggesting improvements for wording, billing accounts, preparing the bank deposits, and maintaining the account information in a simple accounting system. The business has now grown to include preparing various advertising materials for foreign companies that sell goods in China.

Peng has hired you as the accounting manager and two other clerical staff, Xiaoli and Weihua, to handle the new accounting system and the accounting needs of the organization. Peng has suggested that the accounting duties include the following responsibilities:

REQUIRED

a. Review the listed duties that are numbered (1) through (6). Indicate whether the duty should be reassigned and why.

b. Prepare a revised table of duties that takes into consideration the reasons that you mentioned in Part (a).

(©2009, in Adapted from AU2 CGA-Canada Examinations developed by the certified Accountants Association of Canada.)

17-26 [3] In an attempt to save costs, routine tasks such as audit work related to bank reconciliations are being offshored to cheaper locations such as India. For instance, the Big 4 Firms in Canada, the United States, and the United Kingdom all have offshore centres in India. Read "Analysis: As More U.S. Audit Work Moves to India, Concerns Arise," by Dena Aubin and Sumeet Chatterjee, at **https://www.reuters.com/article/us-usa-audit-india/analysis-as-more-u-s-audit-work-moves-to-india-concerns-arise-idUSBRE89F1GC20121016**.

REQUIRED

Provide a supported discussion on your views about "offshoring" of audit work. Include in your analysis a discussion about both the pros and cons of this approach considering the potential impact on the Canadian CPA profession and audit quality.

Xiaoli	Weihua	Peng	Accounting Manager
• Receives inquiries from new customers and arranges for Peng to contact them (1)	• Prepares the bank deposit	• Provides service quotes for new customers	• Authorizes a vendor invoice for payment (5)
• Receives vendor invoices	• Keeps custody of payments received and takes the deposit to the bank (3)	• Determines what prices to charge for services	• Records vendor invoices in the accounts payable system (6)
• Records the sales and receivables (2)	• Prepares the bank reconciliation (4)	• Authorizes the quoted price	

Completing the Audit, Reporting, and Other Assurance Engagements

Part 4 includes two chapters on the final two phases of the audit process. Chapter 18 focuses on the conclusion phase of the audit. If the planning phases and the other risk response phases are performed well, the completion phase is typically relatively easy. However, even when auditors perform the other phases well, if they do a poor job of carrying out the completion and review phase, the quality of the audit will be low. Chapter 19 addresses the audit reporting component of the final phase of the financial statement audit. In this chapter, we look at the audit reporting decision. We examine the standard audit report, detail alternatives to the standard audit report, discuss the role of professional judgment, and consider the value of the audit report.

The last chapter, Chapter 20, expands upon Chapter 1's discussion of the different types of assurance engagements performed by public accountants. In this chapter, we explore the other Canadian standards. We start with compilation and review engagements of historical financial information, then consider other types of assurance engagements, as well as two types of engagements that fall within other related services: specified procedures and reports of supplemental information. We conclude by considering the future of assurance services offered by the public accounting profession.

COMPLETING THE AUDIT

High quality audits depend upon the audit team continually reviewing the work performed. This ongoing review process ensures that the necessary audit steps have been completed and that the originally planned risks were appropriate (and if not, that the audit strategy has been adjusted accordingly). In addition to this ongoing review, auditors must perform additional review activities and non-cycle-specific audit tests at the completion stage. Then the auditor can decide whether sufficient appropriate evidence has been collected to provide an audit opinion. In addition, as the auditor completes the audit, there are several communications with management and those charged with governance.

LEARNING OBJECTIVES

After studying this chapter, you should be able to:

1. Design and perform audit tests related to presentation and disclosure audit objectives.
2. Review and assess contingent liabilities, commitments, and contingent assets.
3. Review and assess confirmations from the client's external and/or in-house legal counsel (legal letters).
4. Conduct a post-balance-sheet review for subsequent events.
5. Design and perform procedures to accumulate final evidence to complete the audit.
6. Integrate the audit evidence gathered and evaluate the overall audit results.
7. Evaluate other information included in the annual report.
8. Communicate effectively with the audit committee and management.

Good Review Requires More Than Looking at Working Papers

Larry Bedard, an audit senior at Messier, Nixon, & Royce, was assigned to staff assistant Clawson Lum for the audit of accounts payable of Westside Industries Ltd., a large equipment manufacturer. Accounts payable is a major liability account for a manufacturing company, and testing accounts payable cutoff is an important audit area. Testing primarily involves reviewing the liability recorded by the client by examining subsequent payments to suppliers and other creditors to assure that they were properly recorded in the correct period.

Larry observed that Clawson was spending a lot of time on the phone, apparently on personal matters. Shortly before the audit was completed, Clawson announced that he was leaving the firm. In spite of Clawson's distractions due to his personal affairs, he completed the audit work he was assigned within the budgeted time.

Because of Larry's concern about Clawson's work habits, he decided to review the working papers with extreme care. Every schedule he reviewed was properly prepared, with tick marks entered and explained by Clawson, indicating that he had made an extensive examination of underlying data and documents and had found the client's balance to be adequate as stated. Specifically, there were no payments subsequent to year-end for inventory purchases received during the audit period that had not been accrued by Westside.

When Larry finished the audit, he turned the working papers over to Kelsey Mayburn, an audit manager on the engagement, for review. She had considerable knowledge about equipment manufacturers and about Westside Industries. Kelsey reviewed all the working papers, including the analytical procedures performed during the audit. After performing additional analytical procedures during her review, she contacted Larry to inform him that accounts payable did not seem reasonable to her. She asked him to do some additional checking. Larry went back and looked at all the documents that Clawson had indicated in the working papers that he had inspected. It was quickly apparent that Clawson either had not looked at the documents or did not know what he was doing when he inspected them. Almost $1 million of documents applicable to the December 31, 2015, audit had not been included as liabilities. Since the misstatement was material, Kelsey's review likely saved Messier, Nixon, & Royce significant embarrassment as well as potentially worse consequences.

This case illustrates the importance of reviews that should be performed throughout the engagement as well as when the audit programs are complete. As the Westside case demonstrates, a high-quality review requires a careful and thoughtful review by an experienced and knowledgeable person. Kelsey's actions ensured that Messier, Nixon, & Royce did not issue an inappropriate audit opinion.

In this chapter, we focus on the activities involved in completing the audit, shown in Figure 18-1, which assist the auditor in making an overall conclusion that sufficient appropriate evidence has been collected and that the financial statements are fairly stated. The auditor will then determine what type of audit opinion to issue, which we will cover in depth in the next chapter.

Although the review of working papers is an important part of the completion stage, as you read this chapter, you will learn that critical aspects of this final risk response phase of the financial statement audit process include final evidence gathering, evaluating the results (including drafting the audit report), and communication with those in charge of governance and management.

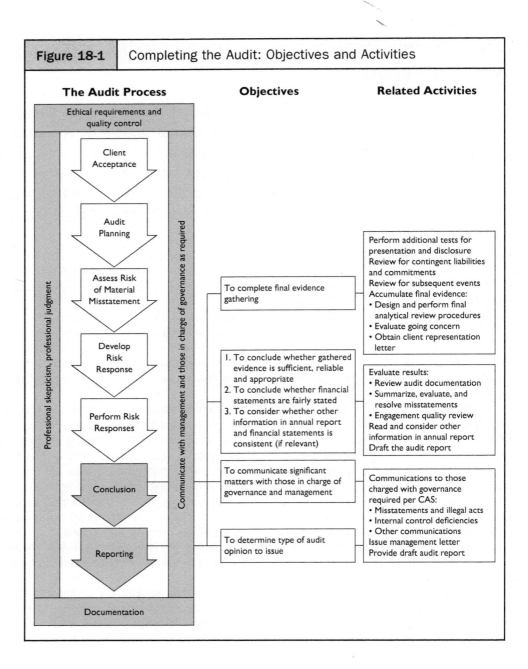

Figure 18-1 | Completing the Audit: Objectives and Activities

The Audit Process

Ethical requirements and quality control

Professional skepticism, professional judgment

Client Acceptance

Audit Planning

Assess Risk of Material Misstatement

Develop Risk Response

Perform Risk Responses

Conclusion

Reporting

Communicate with management and those in charge of governance as required

Documentation

Objectives

To complete final evidence gathering

1. To conclude whether gathered evidence is sufficient, reliable and appropriate
2. To conclude whether financial statements are fairly stated
3. To consider whether other information in annual report and financial statements is consistent (if relevant)

To communicate significant matters with those in charge of governance and management

To determine type of audit opinion to issue

Related Activities

Perform additional tests for presentation and disclosure
Review for contingent liabilities and commitments
Review for subsequent events
Accumulate final evidence:
• Design and perform final analytical review procedures
• Evaluate going concern
• Obtain client representation letter

Evaluate results:
• Review audit documentation
• Summarize, evaluate, and resolve misstatements
• Engagement quality review
Read and consider other information in annual report
Draft the audit report

Communications to those charged with governance required per CAS:
• Misstatements and illegal acts
• Internal control deficiencies
• Other communications
Issue management letter
Provide draft audit report

COMPLETE FINAL EVIDENCE GATHERING

In this section, we discuss the first objective: to gather final evidence. This stage includes the performance of additional procedures for presentation and disclosure objectives, review for contingent liabilities (or assets), and review for subsequent events.

LO 1 Design and perform audit tests related to presentation and disclosure audit objectives.

Perform Additional Tests for Presentation and Disclosure

Auditors perform procedures to satisfy the three categories of audit objectives: transaction-related audit objectives, balance-related audit objectives, and presentation and disclosure-related audit objectives. Auditors test presentation and disclosure assertions in a manner consistent with the other two types of assertions related to a particular cycle or account:

• Perform procedures to obtain an understanding of controls related to presentation and disclosure assertions as part of risk assessment procedures.

Table 18-1 | Presentation and Disclosure Audit Objectives

Assertions: Audit Objectives	Examples of Substantive Procedures
Occurrence and rights and obligations—Disclosed events and transactions have occurred and pertain to the entity.	Review debt contracts to determine that accounts receivable are pledged as collateral.
Completeness—All disclosures that should have been included in the financial statements have been included.	Use a disclosure checklist to determine whether the financial statements include all disclosures required by accounting standards.
Classification and understandability—Financial information is appropriately presented and described, and disclosures are clear and understandable to users.	Review financial statements to determine if assets are properly classified between current and noncurrent categories. Read the notes for clarity.
Accuracy and valuation—Financial and other information are disclosed accurately and at appropriate amounts.	Reconcile amounts included in the long-term debt notes to information examined and supported in the auditor's long-term debt audit working papers.

- Conduct tests of controls related to disclosures if planned control risk is below maximum.
- Perform substantive procedures to test all assertions related to the information and amounts presented and disclosed in the financial statements.

Table 18-1 lists the presentation and disclosure assertions and the related audit objectives along with examples of substantive procedures related to the presentation and disclosure objectives.

Often, procedures for presentation and disclosure-related objectives are integrated with the auditor's tests for transaction-related and balance-related objectives. For example, as part of the audit of accounts receivable, auditors evaluate the need to separate notes receivable and amounts due from affiliates and trade accounts due from customers. They must also determine that current and noncurrent receivables are classified separately and any factoring or discounting of notes receivable is disclosed.

While much of the information presented and disclosed in the financial statements is audited as part of the auditors' testing of the particular accounts and cycles, at this point in the audit process, auditors will evaluate evidence obtained during the earlier phases of the audit to assess whether additional evidence is needed for the presentation and disclosure objectives. Auditors will also evaluate whether the overall presentation of the financial statements and related footnotes complies with the relevant accounting framework. This includes an evaluation of whether individual financial statements reflect the appropriate classification and description of accounts consistent with requirements and whether the information is presented in proper form and with the proper terminology required by the accounting framework.

One of the auditor's primary concerns in relation to presentation and disclosure-related objectives is determining whether management has disclosed all required information (completeness objective for presentation and disclosure). To assess risks that the completeness objective for presentation and disclosure is not satisfied, auditors consider information obtained during the first phases of audit testing to determine if they are aware of facts and circumstances that should be disclosed.

As part of the final review for financial statement disclosure, many public accounting firms require the completion of a **financial statement disclosure checklist** for every engagement. An illustration of a partial financial disclosure checklist for property, plant, and equipment is shown in Figure 18-2. This questionnaire is designed to remind auditors of common disclosure problems encountered on audits and to facilitate the final review of the entire audit by an engagement quality control reviewer. Naturally, a checklist is not sufficient to replace an auditor's professional judgment regarding the application of accounting standards for circumstances of the particular audit.

Financial statement disclosure checklist—a questionnaire that reminds the auditor of disclosure problems commonly encountered in audits and that facilitates the final review of the entire audit by an independent partner.

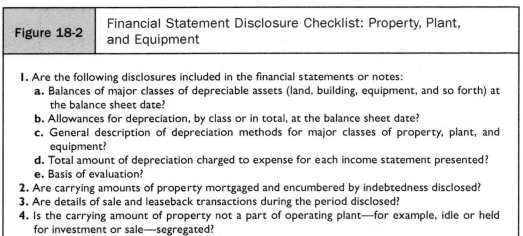

| Figure 18-2 | Financial Statement Disclosure Checklist: Property, Plant, and Equipment |

1. Are the following disclosures included in the financial statements or notes:
 a. Balances of major classes of depreciable assets (land, building, equipment, and so forth) at the balance sheet date?
 b. Allowances for depreciation, by class or in total, at the balance sheet date?
 c. General description of depreciation methods for major classes of property, plant, and equipment?
 d. Total amount of depreciation charged to expense for each income statement presented?
 e. Basis of evaluation?
2. Are carrying amounts of property mortgaged and encumbered by indebtedness disclosed?
3. Are details of sale and leaseback transactions during the period disclosed?
4. Is the carrying amount of property not a part of operating plant—for example, idle or held for investment or sale—segregated?
5. Has consideration been given to disclosure of fully amortized capital assets still in use and capital assets not presently in use?

Due to the unique nature of the disclosures related to contingent liabilities and subsequent events, auditors often assess the completeness and valuation (since the amounts for contingent liabilities are based upon estimates) as high-risk assertions. Given that audit tests performed earlier in the audit often do not provide sufficient appropriate evidence about contingent liabilities and subsequent events, auditors design and perform procedures in every audit for contingent liabilities and subsequent events. These procedures are discussed next.

Review for Contingent Liabilities and Commitments

A **contingent liability** is a potential future obligation to an outside party for an unknown amount resulting from activities that have already taken place. Three conditions are required for a contingent liability to exist:

1. There is a potential future payment to an outside party or the impairment of an asset that resulted from an existing condition;
2. There is uncertainty about the amount of the future payment or impairment; and
3. The outcome will be resolved by some future event or events.

For example, a lawsuit that has been filed but not yet resolved meets all three conditions. It is important to note that the terminology for APSE and IFRS differs, reflecting the difference in accounting treatments. ASPE uses the terminology of *liabilities* and *contingencies*, whereas IFRS uses the terms *liabilities*, *provisions*, and *contingent liabilities*. Under both ASPE and IFRS, an obligation is recognized depending on the likelihood of the outflow of resources to settle the obligation and on the ability to reasonably determine the amount of the outflow; however, the ASPE recognition threshold of "likely" is higher than the IFRS threshold of "probable." You will note that ASPE allows the recognition of a "reasonable" estimate whereas IFRS is more stringent in its requirement of a "best" estimate.

Table 18-2 compares the ASPE and IFRS financial statement treatment of contingencies. The decision as to the appropriate treatment requires considerable professional judgment. ASPE and IFRS agree that a contingent gain (or a contingent asset) should never be accrued, but rather, if its future confirmation is very likely, it should be disclosed in the notes.

When the proper disclosure in the financial statements of material contingencies is through notes to the financial statements, the note should describe the nature of the contingency to the extent it is known, an estimate of the amount, or a statement that the amount cannot be estimated. Since ASPE allows for a reasonable estimate, any exposure in excess of the amount accrued is disclosed.

Table 18-2	Likelihood of Occurrence of Contingencies and Financial Statement Treatment			
Likelihood of Occurrence		**Financial Statement Treatment**		
ASPE Section 3290	**IFRS IAS 37**	**Recognition**	**Note Disclosure**	
Unlikely to occur	Likelihood is remote	No	No	
Not determinable	Possible	No	Yes	
Likely to occur (this is a higher recognition threshold than probable).	Probable (more likely than not—50% chance).	Amount accrued if a reliable estimate can be made (ASPE's *reasonable* estimate vs. IFRS's *best* estimate).*	If amount cannot be reasonably estimated, then note disclosure is necessary. Under ASPE, any exposure in excess of the amount accrued would be disclosed.	

*Under IFRS, if the amount is recognized, it is referred to as a provision. ASPE does not make that distinction and refers to it as a contingent liability.

Auditors are especially concerned about certain contingent liabilities:

- Pending litigation for patent infringement, product liability, or other actions.
- Income tax disputes.
- Product warranties.
- Notes receivable discounted.
- Guarantees of obligations of others.
- Unused balances in outstanding letters of credit.

Auditing standards make it clear that management, not the auditor, is responsible for identifying and deciding the appropriate accounting treatment for contingent liabilities. In many audits, it is impractical for auditors to uncover contingencies without management's cooperation. Further, as highlighted in Auditing in Action 18-1, without management's cooperation, auditors would not be able to adequately assess the completeness of the disclosure.

The auditor's objectives in verifying contingent liabilities are:

- Evaluate the accounting treatment of known contingent liabilities to determine whether management has properly classified the contingency (classification);
- Evaluate the reasonableness of management's estimate of the contingent liability (valuation); and
- Identify, to the extent practical, any contingencies not already identified by management (completeness).

AUDITING IN ACTION 18-1
Corruption and Contingent Liabilities at SNC-Lavalin

In 2012, Canada's SNC-Lavalin Inc., considered to be the world's largest and most respected engineering and construction firm, was facing a wide variety of investigations around the world pertaining to charges of bribery and corruption. In its 2013 financial statements contingent liabilities note, the company disclosed several ongoing investigations—one conducted by the Royal Canadian Mounted Police (RCMP) and another by the Autorité des marchés financiers (the AMF), Quebec's securities regulator. It also disclosed a settlement with the World Bank related to bribery charges connected with projects in Bangladesh and Cambodia. Although the settlement did not involve a financial penalty, SNC-Lavalin was barred from bidding on World Bank Group funded projects for 10 years.

In order to ensure that the financial statement notes were accurate and complete, the external auditors, Deloitte & Touche, worked closely with SNC-Lavalin management and the law firm Stikeman Elliott, LLP. Interestingly, SNC-Lavalin had to go to court in order to be able to provide Deloitte & Touche with access to the details of the AMF investigation. Apparently, the AMF feared risk of collusion if the auditors were provided details. However, SNC-Lavalin successfully argued that Deloitte & Touche would likely not approve the financial statements without access to the details of the investigation. It is safe to assume that without access to the documentation, Deloitte & Touche would be unable to conclude that the financial statements were free of material error.

Sources: Based on Tamsin McMahon, "Boardroom blunders at SNC-Lavalin," *Macleans*, December 7, 2012, accessed September 14, 2017, at **http://www.macleans.ca/economy/business/boardroom-blunders/**. Ross Marowits, "Supreme Court confirms SNC-Lavalin's victory over Quebec regulator," *Financial Post*, September 5, 2013, accessed September 14, 2017, at **http://business.financialpost.com/2013/09/05/supreme-court-confirms-snc-lavalins-legal-victory-over-quebec-regulator/**.

Audit Procedures for Finding Contingencies (Completeness Assertion) Many of these potential obligations are ordinarily verified as an integral part of various segments of the engagement rather than as a separate activity near the end of the audit. For example, guarantees of obligations of others may be tested as part of confirming bank balances and loans from banks. Similarly, income tax disputes can be checked as part of analyzing income tax expense, reviewing the general correspondence file, and examining Canada Revenue Agency reports and statements. Even if the contingencies are verified separately, it is common to perform the tests well before the last few days of completing the engagement to ensure their proper verification. The tests of contingent liabilities near the end of the engagement are more a review than an initial search.

The first step in the audit of contingencies is to *determine whether any contingencies exist* (occurrence, presentation, and disclosure objective). As you know from studying other audit areas, it is more difficult to discover unrecorded transactions or events than to verify recorded information. Once the auditor knows that contingencies exist, their materiality and the footnote disclosures can ordinarily be satisfactorily evaluated.

The following are some audit procedures commonly used to search for contingent liabilities. The list is not all-inclusive, and each procedure is not necessarily performed on every audit.

- Inquire of management (orally and in writing) regarding the possibility of unrecorded contingencies. In these inquiries, the auditor must be specific in describing the different kinds of contingencies that may require disclosure. Naturally, inquiries of management are not useful in uncovering the intentional failure to disclose existing contingencies, but if management has overlooked a particular type of contingency or does not fully comprehend accounting disclosure requirements, the inquiry can be fruitful. At the completion of the audit, management is typically asked to make a written statement as part of the letter of representation that it is unaware of any undisclosed contingent liabilities.
- Review current and previous years' Canada Revenue Agency notices of assessment. The reports may indicate areas in which disagreement over unsettled years is likely to arise. If an audit by the Canada Revenue Agency has been in progress for a long time, there is an increased likelihood of an existing tax dispute.
- Review the minutes of directors' and shareholders' meetings for indications of lawsuits or other contingencies.
- Analyze legal expense for the period under audit, and review invoices and statements from the client's law firms for indications of contingent liabilities, especially lawsuits and pending tax assessments.
- Obtain a confirmation from all major law firms performing legal services for the client as to the status of pending litigation or other contingent liabilities. This procedure is discussed in more depth shortly.
- Review existing working papers for any information that may indicate a potential contingency. For example, bank confirmations may indicate notes receivable discounted or guarantees of loans.
- Obtain letters of credit in force as of the balance sheet date, and obtain a confirmation of the used and unused balances.
- Read contracts, agreements, and related correspondence and documents.

Evaluation of Known Contingent Liabilities (Valuation, Classification, and Completeness Assertions) If the auditor concludes that there are contingent liabilities, he or she must evaluate the significance of the potential liability and the nature of the disclosure that is necessary in the financial statements. The potential liability is sufficiently well known in some instances to be included in the statements as an actual liability under the probability threshold (see Table 18-2). In other instances, disclosure may be unnecessary if the contingency is highly remote or immaterial. Auditors often obtain a separate evaluation of a potential liability from its own legal counsel, especially highly material ones, rather than relying upon management or the external

| Figure 18-3 | Example of Risk Assessment and Risk Response for Contingent Liabilities and Provisions from Legal Claims, Proceedings, and Investigations |

Risk Assessment	**Risk Response**
The company and certain of its group companies and former group companies are involved as a party in legal proceedings, including regulatory and other governmental proceedings, as well as investigations by authorities, such as for example the patent infringement lawsuit of Masimo Corporation, several CRT antitrust litigations and a civil matter with the US Department of Justice relating to the external defibrillator business in the US.	Our audit procedures included: • Testing the effectiveness of the Company's internal controls around the identification and evaluation of claims, proceedings, and investigations at different levels of the group, and the recording and continuous re-assessment of the related (contingent) liabilities and provisions and disclosures
The area is significant to our audit since the accounting and disclosure for (contingent) legal liabilities is complex and judgmental (due to the difficulty of predicting the outcome of the matter and estimating the potential impact if the outcome is unfavourable), and the amounts involved are, or can be, material to the financial statements as a whole.	• We inquired with both legal and financial staff in respect of ongoing investigations or claims, proceedings, and investigations, inspected relevant correspondence, inspected the minutes of the meetings of the Audit Committee, Supervisory Board, and Executive Committee, requested a confirmation letter from the group's in-house legal counsel and obtained external legal confirmation letters form a selection of external legal counsels. • For claims settled during the year, such as Medsage and Masimo, we vouched the cash payments, as appropriate and read the related settlement agreements in order to verify whether the settlements were properly accounted for. • We assessed the adequacy of Company's disclosure regarding contingent liabilities from legal proceedings and investigations as contained in note 19, *Provisions* and note 25.

Source: Ernst & Young, "Report on the Audit of the Financial Statements, 2016," February 21, 2017, in Royal Philips, *Annual Report, 2016: A Focused Leader in Health Technology,* Amsterdam: Koninklijke Philips N.V., 2017.

and/or in-house legal counsel. That is because they are advocates for the client and may be biased in their assessment of the likelihood of losing a case or the amount of the potential judgment.

Figure 18-3 is an excerpt from the Auditors' Report for Philips, the global company headquartered in Amsterdam and known for its health technology and lighting products, explaining the auditors' risk assessment and response with regard to legal and regulatory provisions. The auditors explained that contingent liabilities were a significant risk because they are material and complex, and have high estimation uncertainty. You will note that the auditors' risk response included both testing controls and many substantive procedures (inquiries, inspection, confirmations) highlighted in our earlier discussion. We will discuss the importance of legal confirmation letters in the next section.

Review for Commitments

Closely related to contingent liabilities are **commitments** (agreements that the entity will hold to a fixed set of conditions), such as to purchase raw materials or to lease facilities at a certain price, agreements to sell merchandise at a fixed price, bonus plans, profit-sharing and pension plans, royalty agreements, and similar items. For a commitment, the most important characteristic is the agreement to commit the firm to a set of fixed conditions in the future, regardless of what happens to profits or the economy as a whole. Commitments are ordinarily either described together in a separate note or combined in a note related to contingencies.

Commitments—agreements that the entity will hold to a fixed set of conditions, such as the purchase or sale of merchandise at a stated price, at a future date, regardless of what happens to profits or to the economy as a whole.

Audit Procedures for Finding Commitments The search for unknown commitments is usually performed as part of each audit area. For example, in verifying sales transactions, the auditor should be alert to sales commitments. Similarly, commitments for raw materials or equipment can be identified as a part of the audit of each of these accounts. The auditor should be aware of the possibility of commitments when reading minutes, contracts, and correspondence files.

Obtain Confirmations From Client's External and/or In-house Legal Counsel

A major procedure on which auditors rely for evaluating known litigation or other claims against the client and identifying additional ones is sending a **legal inquiry letter**. The letter is addressed to either the client's external legal counsel or the in-house legal counsel. A recent update, effective December 2016, of the "Joint Policy Statement Concerning Communications with Law Firms Regarding Claims and Possible Claims in Connection with the Preparation and Audit of Financial Statements" (referred to as JPS), an Appendix to CAS 501, *Audit evidence – specific consideration for selected items*, has expanded the definition of law firm to include in-house legal counsel who is representing or advising the entity with respect to claims and possible claims. This change reflects the evolution of the in-house legal counsel role since 1978, the last the time the JPS was revised. Often, organizations will use in-house legal counsel in addition to or in place of external legal counsel. You will note, as indicated in Figure 18-3, that this is the case with Philips: the auditors sent inquiry letters to both legal and in-house counsel.

There are two categories of lawsuits an **outstanding claim** (or *asserted claim*) exists when a suit has been brought or when the client has been notified that a suit will be brought; an **unasserted claim** (or *possible claim*) exists when no suit has been filed but is possible. In Figure 18-3, one asserted claim to which the Philips auditors refer is a patent infringement case.

The auditor relies on the lawyer's expertise and knowledge of the client's legal affairs to provide a professional opinion about the expected outcome of existing lawsuits and the likely amount of the liability, including court costs. The lawyer is also likely to know of pending litigation and claims that management may have overlooked.

Many public accounting firms analyze legal expense for the entire year and have the client send a standard lawyer's letter to every law firm with which it has been involved in the current or preceding year, plus any law firm that it occasionally engages. In some cases, this involves a large number of law firms, including some dealing in aspects of law that are far removed from potential lawsuits.

The standard legal inquiry letter to the client's law firm and/or in-house legal counsel, which should be prepared on the client's letterhead and signed by one of the company's officials, should include the following:

- A list, prepared by management and/or in-house legal counsel, of outstanding and possible claims with which the lawyer has had significant involvement.
- A description of the nature and the current status of each claim and possible claim.
- An indication of management's evaluation of the amount and likelihood of loss or gain for each listed claim and possible claim.
- A request that the lawyer reply to the client, with a signed copy going to the public accounting firm, advising whether management's descriptions and evaluations of the outstanding and possible claims are reasonable.

Lawyers are not required to mention any omission of possible claims in their response to the inquiry letter and thus do not directly notify the auditor of them. Instead, lawyers discuss these possible claims with the client separately and inform management of its responsibility to inform the auditor. Whether management does so or not is its decision; CAS 501.12 requires the auditor to obtain a letter of representation from management that it has disclosed all known outstanding and possible claims. In short, unless management discloses the existence of possible claims to the auditor, the auditor has no means of discovering whether or not any such claims exist.

Any differences between management's identification and assessment of outstanding and possible claims and the law firm's would be resolved, if possible, in a meeting of the law firm, the auditor, and management. Failure to resolve the differences would force the auditor to consider a reservation of opinion (discussed in Chapter 19) on the auditor's report.

An example of a standard inquiry letter sent to a lawyer's office is shown in Figure 18-4. The letter should be sent toward the end of the audit so that the lawyer is communicating about contingencies up to approximately the date of the auditor's report.

Figure 18-4	Typical Legal Inquiry Letter

Peppertree Produce Inc.
293 rue Crecy
Montreal, Quebec

January 25, 2019

Amerski and Iacobelli, Lawyers, LLP
412 Cote des Neiges
Montreal, Quebec
H3C 1J7

Dear Sir/Madam:

We write this letter to you at the request of our auditors pursuant to the Joint Policy Statement of April 2016 between the Canadian Bar Association and the Auditing and Assurance Standards Board.

In connection with the preparation and audit of our financial statements for the fiscal period ended December 31, 2018, we seek your confirmation with respect to our evaluation of claims and possible claims on which your firm has represented or advised Peppertree Produce Inc.

Please provide us, and our auditors, with your acknowledgement of receipt of this inquiry letter.

Based on an examination of your records, we seek your confirmation, as of February 18, 2019, of the following:
a) The claims and possible claims listed are appropriately described;
b) Our evaluations are reasonable; and
c) All outstanding claims are included in this inquiry letter (other than the exclusions described below).

If there are outstanding claims omitted from this inquiry letter (other than the exclusions described below), we ask that you indicate in your response letter the names of the parties and the amounts claimed.

If there are possible claims omitted from this inquiry letter (other than any exclusions described below), we ask that you contact us to discuss such items and the application of the Joint Policy Statement to those possible claims.

Description	Evaluation
Calvert Growers vs. Peppertree Inc., non-payment of debt in the amount of $16 000, trial date not set.	Peppertree Produce Inc. disputes this billing on the grounds that the produce was spoiled and expects to successfully defend this action.
Desjardins, Inc. vs. Peppertree Inc., damages for breach of contract in the amount of $40 000, trial date not set.	It is probable that this action will be successfully defended.
Foodex Ltd. has a possible claim in connection with apples sold to them by Peppertree Produce Inc. The apples apparently had not been properly washed by the growers to remove pesticides, and a number of Foodex Ltd.'s customers became ill after eating said apples.	No claim has yet been made, and we are unable to estimate possible ultimate loss.

We would appreciate receiving your response by February 23, 2019.

We understand that you will normally require five business days after the effective date of response to prepare your letter. If you are unable to meet this response date, please advise us and our auditors as soon as practicable. Please address your reply, marked "Privileged and Confidential" to this entity, and send a signed copy of the reply directly to our auditors: Jeannerette & Cie, Comptables Agrees, 1133 rue Sherbrooke, Montreal, Quebec, H3C 1M8.

We have authorized our auditors to request, if they deem necessary, an updated response letter with a new effective date of response.

Yours truly,

Charles D. Peppertree, President.

c.c. Jeannerette & Cie

Limited or Nonresponses From Law Firms Law firms in recent years have become reluctant to provide certain information to auditors because of their own exposure to legal liability for providing incorrect or confidential information. The nature of the refusal of law firms to provide auditors with complete information about contingent liabilities falls into two categories: the refusal to respond due to a lack of knowledge about matters involving contingent liabilities, and the refusal to disclose information that the lawyer regards as confidential. As an example of the latter, the lawyer might be aware of a violation of a patent agreement that could result in a significant loss to the client if the violation were public knowledge (possible claim). The inclusion of the information in a note could actually cause the lawsuit and therefore be damaging to the client. When the nature of the lawyer's legal practice does not involve contingent liabilities, the lawyer's refusal to respond causes no audit problems.

A serious audit problem does arise, however, when a lawyer refuses to provide information that is within the lawyer's jurisdiction and may directly affect the fair presentation of financial statements. If a lawyer refuses to provide the auditor with information about material existing lawsuits (outstanding claims) or possible claims, the auditor's opinion would be qualified due to the lack of available evidence. The JPS was developed to ensure that lawyers do not violate client privilege, thus encouraging lawyers to cooperate with auditors in obtaining information about contingencies.

Review for Subsequent Events

LO 4 Conduct a post-balance-sheet review for subsequent events.

CAS

Subsequent events—transactions and other pertinent events that occurred after the balance sheet date and that affect the fair presentation or disclosure of the statements being audited.

Review for subsequent events—the auditing procedures performed by auditors to identify and evaluate subsequent events.

Subsequent events are transactions and events occurring after the balance sheet date (see CAS 560). The auditor must conduct a **review for subsequent events** to determine whether anything occurred that might affect the fair presentation or disclosure of the statements being audited.

The auditor's responsibility for reviewing for subsequent events is normally limited to the period beginning with the balance sheet date and ending with the date of the auditor's report. The date of the auditor's report corresponds with the approval of the financial statements by the board of directors or other executive management. The subsequent events review should be completed near the end of the engagement and may require returning to the client premises if approval of the financial statements is delayed. Figure 18-5 shows the period covered by a subsequent events review and the timing of that review.

Types of Subsequent Events

Two types of subsequent events require consideration by management and evaluation by the auditor: (1) those that have a direct effect on the financial statements and

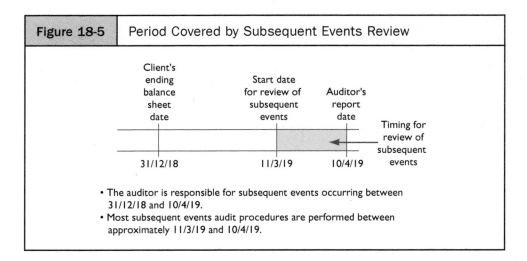

Figure 18-5	Period Covered by Subsequent Events Review

- The auditor is responsible for subsequent events occurring between 31/12/18 and 10/4/19.
- Most subsequent events audit procedures are performed between approximately 11/3/19 and 10/4/19.

require adjustment, and (2) those that have no direct effect on the financial statements but for which disclosure is required.

Direct Effect on Financial Statements; Require Adjustment These events or transactions provide additional information to management in determining the valuation of account balances as of the balance sheet date and to auditors in verifying the balances. For example, if the auditor is having difficulty determining the correct valuation of inventory because of obsolescence, the sale of raw material inventory as scrap in the subsequent period should be used as a means of determining the correct valuation of the inventory as of the balance sheet date.

Subsequent period events, such as the following, require adjustment of account balances in the current year's financial statements if the amount is material:

- Declaration of bankruptcy by a customer with an outstanding accounts receivable balance because of the customer's deteriorating financial condition;
- Settlement of litigation at an amount different from the amount recorded on the books; or
- Disposal of equipment not being used in operations at a price below the current book value.

When subsequent events are used to evaluate the amounts included in the statements, the auditor must distinguish between conditions that existed at the balance sheet date and those that came into being after the end of the year. The subsequent information should not be incorporated directly into the statements if the conditions causing the change in valuation did not take place until after year-end. For example, assume one type of a client's inventory suddenly became obsolete because of a technology change after the balance sheet date. The sale of obsolete inventory at a loss in the subsequent period is not relevant to the valuation of the inventory.

No Direct Effect on Financial Statements; Disclosure Is Advisable Subsequent events of this type provide evidence of conditions that did not exist at the date of the balance sheet being reported on, but are so significant that they require disclosure even though they do not require adjustment. Ordinarily, these events can be adequately disclosed by the use of notes, but occasionally one event may be so significant as to require supplementing the historical statements with statements that include the effect of the event as if it had occurred on the balance sheet date (i.e., pro forma statements). An example would be an extremely material merger.

Examples of events or transactions occurring in the subsequent period that may require disclosure rather than an adjustment in the financial statements include decline in the market value of securities held for temporary investment, issuance of bonds or shares, uninsured loss of inventories as a result of fire, or the purchase of a business or trademark.

Audit Procedures for Subsequent Events There are two categories of audit procedures for subsequent events review:

- Procedures normally integrated as part of the verification of year-end account balances; and
- Procedures performed specifically for the purpose of discovering events or transactions that must be recognized as subsequent events.

The first category includes cutoff and valuation tests that are done as part of the tests of details of balances. For example, subsequent-period sales and acquisition transactions are examined to determine whether the cutoff is accurate. Similarly, many valuation tests involving subsequent events are performed as part of the verification of account balances. As an example, it is common to test the collectability of accounts receivable by reviewing subsequent-period cash receipts.

The second category of tests is performed specifically for the purpose of obtaining information that must be incorporated into the current year's account balances or notes. These tests include inquiry of management and in-house legal counsel, correspondence with law firms, review of internal financial statements prepared subsequent to the balance sheet date, review of records prepared subsequent to the balance sheet date, examination of minutes prepared subsequent to the balance sheet date, and acquisition of a letter of representation.

Inquiry of Management Inquiries vary from client to client but normally are about the existence of potential contingent liabilities or commitments, significant changes in the assets or capital structure of the company, the current status of items that were not completely resolved at the balance sheet date, and the existence of unusual adjustments made subsequent to the balance sheet date. Inquiries of management about subsequent events must be held with the proper client personnel to obtain meaningful answers. For example, discussing tax or union matters with the accounts receivable supervisor would not be appropriate. Most inquiries should be made of the controller, in-house legal counsel, the vice-presidents, or the president, depending on the information desired.

CONCEPT CHECK

C18-1 Why are contingent liabilities difficult to identify?

C18-2 When reviewing legal expenses, which transactions should the auditor examine, and why?

C18-3 List three audit techniques that could be used to identify relevant subsequent events.

Correspondence With Law Firms Correspondence with law firms, which was previously discussed, takes place as part of the search for contingent liabilities. In obtaining confirmation letters from law firms and/or in-house legal counsel, the auditor will ask the lawyer to confirm up to effective date, which is the expected approval date for the financial statements, and ask the lawyer to respond within five days of that date.

Review of Internal Financial Statements Prepared Subsequent to the Balance Sheet Date The emphasis in the review should be on (1) changes in the business relative to results for the same period in the year under audit, and (2) changes after year-end. The auditor should pay particular attention to major changes in the business or environment in which the client is operating. The statements should be discussed with management to determine whether they are prepared on the same basis as the current-period statements, and there should be inquiries about significant changes in operating results.

Review of Records Prepared Subsequent to the Balance Sheet Date Journals, data files, and ledgers should be reviewed to determine the existence and nature of any transaction related to the current year. If the journals are not kept up to date, the documents relating to the journals should be reviewed.

Examination of Minutes Prepared Subsequent to the Balance Sheet Date The minutes of shareholders' and directors' meetings subsequent to the balance sheet date (including draft minutes) must be examined for important subsequent events affecting the current-period financial statements.

Acquisition of Letter of Representation The letter of representation written by the client to the auditor formalizes statements the client has made about different matters throughout the audit, including discussions about subsequent events. We will discuss the representation letter in more depth later in the chapter.

LO 5 Design and perform procedures to accumulate final evidence to complete the audit.

ACCUMULATE FINAL EVIDENCE

The auditor has a few final accumulation responsibilities that apply to all cycles besides the search for contingent liabilities and the review for subsequent events. We discuss three types of evidence accumulation here: design and perform final analytical review procedures (refer to CAS 520), evaluate the going concern assumption and obtain a client representation letter.

CAS

Design and Perform Final Analytical Procedures

Analytical procedures are normally used as part of planning the audit, during the performance of detailed tests in each cycle as part of substantive procedures, and at the completion of the audit, where they are useful as a final review for material misstatements or financial problems not noted during other testing to help the auditor take a final objective look at the financial statements. It is common for a partner to do the analytical procedures during the final review of audit documentation and financial statements. Typically, a partner has a good understanding of the client and its business because of ongoing relationships. This knowledge, combined with effective analytical procedures, helps the partner identify possible oversights in an audit.

When performing analytical procedures during the final review stage, the partner generally reads the financial statements, including footnotes, and considers the adequacy of evidence gathered about unusual or unexpected account balances or relationships identified during planning or while conducting the audit. The partner also considers unusual or unexpected account balances or relationships that were not previously identified.

As the Westside Industries case (our opening vignette) illustrates, results from final analytical procedures may indicate possible oversights in the audit and that additional audit evidence is necessary. Kelsey's careful analysis identified a previously unrecognized risk of misstatement of unrecorded liabilities.

Evaluate the Going Concern Assumption

In preparing the financial statements, management is responsible for assessing the organization's ability to continue as a going concern in the foreseeable future (usually one year). If management has significant doubt, then additional disclosure of the matters related to going concern is required. The financial statements use the going concern basis of accounting, unless management intends to liquidate or has no realistic alternatives but to liquidate. CAS 570 requires the auditor to obtain sufficient appropriate evidence in order to conclude that management's use of the going concern assumption is appropriate. Although both management's and the auditor's responsibilities have been clearly stated in the accounting and auditing standards, the recent revision of the audit report now explicitly state these responsibilities.

CAS

Auditors make the initial evaluation of going concern as a part of planning but may revise it after obtaining new information. For example, an initial assessment may need revision if the auditor discovers during the audit that the company has defaulted on a loan, lost its primary customer, or decided to dispose of substantial assets to pay off loans. If the auditor concludes that there is material uncertainty related to events or conditions that may cast substantial doubt of a going concern, then the auditor must inquire of management and consider actions that it is taking, such as specific plans for refinancing, that would enable the entity to continue its operations. However, inquiry is not sufficient evidence; the auditor must independently test management's plans to deal with the issue(s) causing doubt for the entity to continue as a going concern.

A key part of the auditor's analysis is assessing and corroborating management's assumptions. For instance, if management's plans rest upon actions of a third party (such as a potential investor or creditor), then the auditor should confirm the details. Auditors will also use analytical procedures and their knowledge of the client's business and industry to assess management's plans. In some cases, it may be necessary to involve other experts, such as legal, insolvency, and/or valuation specialists, in the going concern evaluation.

In the United States, as a result of the economic recession, the percentage of audit opinions containing going concern explanatory paragraphs reached a high of 21 percent for publicly traded companies in 2008, and continued at high rates in 2009 and 2010. The most frequently cited concerns raised by auditors in their justification for including a going concern explanatory paragraph related to operating losses, development stage enterprises, and working capital deficiencies. Even with these high rates, many companies still filed for bankruptcy despite receiving an audit opinion without an explanatory paragraph. Given the significant level of judgment required in this part of the audit process, this is not altogether surprising.

Surprisingly, although Canada appeared to suffer less from the global meltdown than the United States, the percentage of going concern explanatory paragraphs by Canadian SEC filers was comparable to their US counterparts. This can be attributed to the fact that a high proportion of Canadian public companies are in the mining and resource industry, and thus highly dependent upon commodity prices and the ability to get financing for further exploration. As one audit industry expert explained, "There are simply too many unknowns in this business, too many risks. You start out by digging a hole but have no idea what you will find and how much of it. This makes auditors nervous."

Sources: Based on Mark Chaffers, Don Whalen, and Ryan Siècles, "Going concern overview," *Audit Analytics*, July 2011. PCAOB Standing Advisory Group Meeting, "Going concern," May 17, 2012, accessed September 20, 2017, at **http://pcaobus.org/News/Events/Documents/ 05172012_SAGMeeting/Going_Concern.pdf**. Gundi Jeffrey, "Drop in going concerns reflects slow recovery: Report," *The Bottom Line*, December 2013, accessed September 20, 2017, at **http://www.audi- tanalytics.com/doc/BottomLine_GC_Article_Dec_2013.pdf**.

CAS As previously mentioned, accounting standards require that when management is aware of material uncertainties that can cast significant doubt on the entity's ability to continue as a going concern, those uncertainties must be disclosed (this is referred to as the going concern note). As with all disclosures, the auditor is required to review the disclosure for accuracy, completeness, and understandability. However, unlike most other disclosures, CAS 570 requires that the auditor's report should include a separate paragraph, *Material Uncertainty Related to Going Concern*, following the opinion paragraph to draw the readers' attention to the relevant note in the financial statements (See Auditing in Action 18-2). The auditor also explains that the opinion has not been modified. However, in cases where the disclosure is inadequate, the auditor is required to issue a qualified opinion. If management does not disclose the uncertainties that cast significant doubt on the entity's ability to continue as a going concern, then the auditor will issue an adverse opinion. These reporting decisions are discussed further in Chapter 19.

The auditor's professional judgment plays a key role in making the assessment of the going concern assumption. This is an area where management may be unduly optimistic and therefore biased in its assessment. Management may also resist the required disclosure and audit report modification on the basis that it may cause investors, creditors, and customers to question the viability of the business, therefore causing the company to fail. For the same reason, auditors may be reluctant to include the explanatory paragraph that highlights the going concern issue. The auditor's integrity, objectivity, relevant knowledge, and experience, as well as awareness of threats to judgment, are particularly important when making a going concern assessment.

Obtain a Client Representation Letter

CAS CAS 580, *Written representations*, requires that the auditor obtain a written management representation letter from management to confirm information that has been provided to the auditor during the audit engagement. The auditor may obtain written representations for any audit area. However, auditing standards require written representations from management of the following:

1. (Non)compliance with laws and regulations (CAS 250).
2. Related-party transactions and their disclosure (CAS 550).

3. Confirmation of any verbal representations and a statement that subsequent events have been adjusted or disclosed (CAS 560).
4. If there is a material uncertainty regarding going concern, a description of future plans and the feasibility of those plans (CAS 570).
5. That outstanding and possible legal claims have been disclosed (CAS 501).

CAS 580 explains that a **written representation** is a written statement by management that documents management's representations or other audit evidence (normally oral information) that has been provided during the audit. The client representation letter is prepared on the client's letterhead, addressed to the public accounting firm, and signed by high-level corporate officials, usually the president and chief financial officer.

The written representation (also called a management representation letter or client representation letter) has two purposes:

- To impress upon management its responsibility for the assertions in the financial statements: For example, if the letter of representation includes a reference to pledged assets and contingent liabilities, honest management may be reminded of its unintentional failure to disclose the information adequately. To fulfill this objective, the written representation should be sufficiently detailed as to be a reminder to management.
- To document the responses from management to inquiries about various aspects of the audit: This provides written documentation of client representations in the event of disagreement or a lawsuit between the auditor and the client.

The letter should be dated subsequent to the date of completion of field work and prior to the date of the audit report. To prevent surprises, the auditor should discuss the types of representations with the client during the planning of the audit and as needed throughout the engagement. The representation letter implies that it has originated with the client, but it is common practice for the auditor to prepare the letter and request the client to type it on the company's letterhead and sign it if management is in agreement. Refusal by a client to prepare and sign the letter should probably cause the auditor to consider a qualified opinion or disclaimer of opinion of the auditor's report, as described further in Chapter 19.

In addition to the required representations, many other matters should be included, such as:

- Management's acknowledgment of its responsibility for the fair presentation of the financial statements in conformity with Canadian generally accepted accounting principles or [an appropriately disclosed] basis of accounting;
- Availability of all financial records and related data;
- Completeness and availability of all minutes of meetings of shareholders, directors, and committees of directors;
- Plans or intentions that may affect the carrying value or classification of assets or liabilities; and
- Disclosure of compensating balances or other arrangements involving restrictions on cash balances and disclosure of lines of credit or similar arrangements.

A client-written representation is a written statement from a nonindependent source and therefore cannot be regarded as reliable evidence. Accordingly, where possible, the auditor should seek evidence to substantiate management's assertions. The letter does provide minimal evidence that management has been asked certain questions, but its primary purposes are to have a psychological effect on management and to protect the auditor from potential claims by management that it was unaware of its responsibilities. There are occasions, though, when written representations may be the only source of audit evidence (for example, evidence of management's intent to launch a new product line).

CAS

Written representation—a written statement by management that documents management's representations or other audit evidence (normally oral information) that has been provided during the audit.

CONCEPT CHECK

C18-4 Why is partner examination of final analytical review important?

C18-5 Describe management's and the auditor's responsibilities with respect to the going concern assumption.

LO 6 Integrate the audit evidence gathered and evaluate the overall audit results.

EVALUATE RESULTS

Ultimately, the auditor must decide whether sufficient appropriate audit evidence has been accumulated providing one integrated conclusion that the financial statements are stated in accordance with generally accepted accounting principles. The evidence gathered in each part of the audit process (as depicted in Figure 18-1) must be reviewed in the evaluation of results. The emphasis is on satisfactory mitigation of risks identified in the planning stage of the audit. The reviewer will also review the conclusions reached through tests of controls, substantive analytical procedures, and substantive tests of details for each of the functional transaction cycles audited.

Sufficiency of Evidence

A major step in this process is to review the audit programs to make sure that all parts have been accurately completed and documented, and that risks by audit objectives (assertions) have been addressed. The reviewer evaluates whether the audit program is adequate considering the problem areas that were discovered as the audit progressed. For example, if misstatements were discovered as part of the tests of sales, the initial plans for the tests of details of accounts receivable balances may have been insufficient.

Completing the engagement checklist—a reminder to the auditor of aspects of the audit that may have been overlooked.

As an aid in drawing final conclusions about the adequacy of the audit evidence, auditors frequently use **completing the engagement checklist**, which is a reminder of what may have been overlooked. Figure 18-6 illustrates part of the engagement checklist.

If auditors conclude that sufficient evidence has *not* been obtained to decide whether the financial statements are fairly presented, they have two choices: (1) accumulate additional evidence, or (2) issue a qualified audit opinion or disclaimer of opinion (this is explained further in Chapter 19).

Summarize, Evaluate, and Resolve Misstatements

Auditors are required to accumulate all unadjusted misstatements assessed as not "clearly trivial" and to request that management correct the financial statements

Figure 18-6	Completing the Audit Checklist

	YES	NO
1. Examination of prior year's audit documentation		
a. Were last year's audit files examined for areas of emphasis in the current year audit?	——	——
b. Was the permanent file reviewed for items that affect the current year?	——	——
2. Internal control		
a. Has internal control been adequately understood?	——	——
b. Is the scope of the audit adequate in light of the assessed control risk?	——	——
c. Have all significant deficiencies and material weaknesses been reported in writing to those charged with governance?	——	——
3. General documents		
a. Were all current year minutes and resolutions reviewed, abstracted, and followed up?	——	——
b. Has the permanent file been updated?	——	——
c. Have all major contracts and agreements been reviewed and abstracted, copied, or downloaded to ascertain that the client complies with all existing legal requirements?	——	——

Table 18-3	Levels of Misstatements
Factual misstatements	These are misstatements about which there is no doubt and which are clearly an error (for example, posting a sales invoice in the wrong period).
Judgmental misstatements	These are differences that arise from management's judgment concerning accounting estimates, or the selection or application of accounting policies that the auditor considers inappropriate. These may be difficult to reconcile since they may be a matter of professional judgment.
Projected misstatements	This is the auditor's best estimate of misstatements in populations, involving projection of misstatements identified in audit samples (see Chapter 11 for further discussion).

Factual misstatements—misstatements about which there is no doubt and which are clearly an error.

Judgmental misstatements—differences that arise from management's judgment concerning accounting estimates, or the selection or application of accounting policies that the auditor considers inappropriate.

Projected misstatements—the auditor's best estimate of misstatements in populations, involving projection of misstatements identified in audit samples.

(per CAS 450). Therefore, an essential part of evaluating whether the financial statements are fairly stated involves summarizing, evaluating, and resolving the misstatements uncovered in the audit. It may be difficult to determine the appropriate amount of adjustment because the exact amount of the misstatement may be unknown if it involves an estimate or includes sampling errors. Nevertheless, the auditor must decide on the required adjustment(s). Table 18-3 summarizes the different levels of misstatements discussed in CAS 450.

Many auditors use a **summary of identified misstatements worksheet** or *summary of possible adjustments* to track known and potential misstatements. An example of a summary of identified misstatements worksheet is shown in Figure 18-7. Auditors are also required to consider carry forward misstatements from the previous year that were not corrected.

The schedule in Figure 18-7 includes both factual misstatements that the client has decided not to adjust and projected misstatements, including sampling errors, and total possible misstatements for several financial statement categories. At the end of the audit schedule, the auditor considers whether it is necessary to revise materiality as a result of the misstatements (for instance, if the auditor used the unaudited net income as the basis of materiality) and any additional work due to the misstatements. The auditor also documents the discussion with management and requests that management post the proposed adjustments. A summary of this audit schedule would be presented to the audit committee and should be included with management's representation letter reporting that the uncorrected misstatements are immaterial.

When evaluating materiality of a misstatement, a high level of professional judgment is involved. It is not simply a quantitative analysis of the dollar magnitude of the misstatement. In some cases, the dollar amount of some misstatements cannot be accurately measured. For example, if a mining client omits in its disclosure that a significant decline in the demand for a metal led to an impairment loss, this could be a material misstatement despite the impairment loss being recorded appropriately. The materiality question the auditor must evaluate in such situations is the effect on statement users of the failure to make the disclosure. This type of omission is likely material since it could affect users' economic decisions, such as to buy or hold investments in the company or to provide financing.

As highlighted in Chapter 6, when auditors consider whether a misstatement or omission is material, it is important to also consider the nature of the item and its qualitative features. The following are some features that may cause a quantitatively small misstatement to be material:

1. The item is illegal or fraudulent.
2. The item may materially affect some future period, even though it is immaterial when only the current period is considered.

Summary of identified misstatement worksheet—a summary of misstatements used to help the auditor assess whether the combined amount is material; also known as a summary of possible adjustments.

Figure 18-7 | Summary of Identified Misstatements Worksheet

Peppertree produce Inc.
Summary of Identified Misstatements
31/12/18

Schedule   A-3   Date
Prepared by   LF   3/15/19
Approved by   JA   3/15/19

Description	Circumstances of Occurrence	Assets	Liabilities	Pre-tax Income	Equity	Financial Statement Disclosures	Corrected? Yes/No	W/P Ref
Understated allowance for uncollectible accounts	Judgmental—based upon review of aging and subsequent payments	95 000		95 000	95 000		Yes	B-4
Accounts receivable/Sales cutoff misstatements	Factual—cutoff error	(60 000)		(60 000)	(60 000)		Yes	C-8
Difference between physical inventory and book figures	Factual—Resulting from oversight	(120 000)		(120 000)	(120 000)		Yes	D-2
Unrecorded liabilities	Projection from representative sample	(185 000)	(285 000)	100 000	100 000		No	H-7/2
Repairs expense that should have been capitalized	Judgmental—Error in applying accounting policy	(90 000)		(90 000)	(90 000)		Yes	V-10
Total identified misstatements during audit		(360 000)	(285 000)	(75 000)	(75 000)			
Misstatements corrected by management		175 000		175 000	175 000			
Total uncorrected misstatements		(185 000)	(285 000)	100 000	100 000			
Effect of uncorrected misstatements on income taxes					(25 000)			
Effected of uncorrected misstatements from prior periods								
Uncorrected misstatements to be carried forward					75 000			

Amount of over (under) misstatement in the financial statements

Evaluation of Misstatements	W/P Ref	Yes/No	Responses and any difficulties required
1. Revise the overall/performance materiality for any new information obtained.		N/A	Overall materiality (based upon income before taxes) $441 000 performance materiality $331 000 No changes from preliminary.
2. Describe any additional work required as a result of misstatements.		N/A	
3. Identify and discuss with management.		Yes	Misstatements went both ways (over and under), so no pattern of possible bias identified.
4. Ask management to correct all identified misstatements		Yes	Management was not prepared to post the projected misstatement. As the amount is less than performance materiality and the remaining misstatements have been corrected, there is no impact on the audit opinion. TCWG agreed with management's position on the projected misstatement.

CONCLUSION
In my opinion, the identified and uncorrected misstatements (if any) are not material or in aggregate to the financial statements.

Leslie Nagan 3/15/19.

Basis for Conclusion
All misstatements identified, with the exception of the projected misstatement from the accounts payable confirmations.

3. The item has a "psychic" effect (for example, the item changes a small loss to a small profit, maintains a trend of increasing earnings, or allows earnings to exceed analysts' expectations).
4. The item may be important in terms of possible consequences arising from contractual obligations (for example, the effect of failure to comply with a debt restriction may result in a material loan being called).
5. The item has an effect of increasing management's compensation—for instance, being able to meet bonus plan requirements or other types of incentive plans.

If the auditor believes that there is sufficient evidence but that the financial statements are materially misstated, the auditor again has two choices: (1) the statements must be revised to the auditor's satisfaction, or (2) a modified audit opinion must be issued. To assist with this decision, the auditor will recalculate materiality if there are misstatements that affect the base that was used to calculate materiality (for example, net income). (This is because materiality calculated at the planning stage was based upon the client's preliminary financial statements, which the auditor has subsequently concluded are materially misstated.)

As highlighted in Auditing in Action 18-3, management incentives are an important consideration when evaluating misstatements. These incentives may bias management's willingness to correct detected misstatements, and management may pressure the auditor to "waive" the adjustment. In these situations, an audit firm culture that maintains the appropriate balance between commercialism and professionalism plays an important role. Auditors may also be unconsciously swayed by management's arguments and, as a result, not exercise the appropriate level of professional skepticism when assessing the evidence. As highlighted in Chapter 2 and in the next section, reviews and consultation with others in the firm serve an important role in counteracting these pressures and potential auditor biases.

Working Paper Review

As the audit process diagram (see Figure 18-1) highlights, quality control is an ongoing process—regular planning meetings, consultation, and the use of specialists are part of the audit process for most large audit engagements. Records of these planning meetings and their results would be included in the working paper file. Ongoing **working paper review** consists primarily of documenting ongoing

Working paper review—a review of the completed audit working papers by another member of the audit firm to ensure quality and to counteract bias.

AUDITING IN ACTION 18-3
Cookie Jars, Materiality, and Nortel's Bonus Plan

On January 14, 2013, in the Superior Court of Justice, Associate Chief Justice Frank Marrocco acquitted three former executives of Nortel Networks Inc. of charges that they had fraudulently manipulated the booking and release of accrued liabilities in order to create false financial statements. This practice is commonly referred to as using "cookie jar" reserves to manage earnings. The logic behind this type of earnings management is that management builds up reserves and, when needed, pulls them out of the "cookie jar." In this case, the supposed motivation for the manipulation was to trigger bonuses.

A key issue in the trial was the concept of materiality. In his decision, Judge Marrocco referred to a memo prepared by the external auditors, Deloitte & Touche, which analyzed whether or not the release of $80 million in accrued liabilities was material

to Nortel's financial statements. The memo concluded that Nortel achieved positive earnings with or without the $80 million. Therefore, the two bonuses, Return to Profitability Bonus and Success Plan Bonus, would have been achieved whether the $80 million was released into the profit and loss statement or not. In its consideration of materiality, Deloitte focused on the qualitative factors, the nature of the item, and management's intentions, which led to the conclusion that the $80 million did not have a material effect on the financial statements.

Source: Based on Janet McFarland and Richard Blackwell, "Three former Nortel executives found not guilty of fraud," *The Globe and Mail*, January 14, 2013, accessed September 15, 2017, at **http://www. theglobeandmail.com/report-on-business/industry-news/the-law-page/three-former-nortel-executives-found-not-guilty-of-fraud/ article7319241/**.

supervision that has taken place during the conduct of the engagement by means of independent examination of the working papers by another member of the audit firm. There are three main reasons why it is essential that the working papers be thoroughly reviewed by another member of the audit firm at the completion of the audit:

1. To evaluate the performance of inexperienced personnel;
2. To make sure that the audit meets the public accounting firm's standard of performance; and
3. To counteract the bias that frequently enters into the auditor's judgment.

Except for a pre-issuance review, which is discussed shortly, someone who is knowledgeable about the client and the unique circumstances in the audit should conduct the review of the working papers. Therefore, the auditor's immediate supervisor normally does the initial review of the working papers prepared by any given auditor. For example, the least experienced auditor's work is ordinarily reviewed by the audit senior; the senior's immediate supervisor, who is normally a supervisor or manager, reviews the senior's work and also reviews less thoroughly the papers of the inexperienced auditor.

When several staff members are working together at an engagement, team review by means of interview is used. The senior meets with staff on a daily basis, discusses the nature of findings, and ensures that these are appropriately recorded in the electronic working papers before the actual client documents are returned to the client. Finally, the partner assigned to the audit must review all working papers, but the partner reviews those prepared by the supervisor or manager more thoroughly than the others. Most of the working paper review is done as each segment of the audit is completed.

Engagement Quality Control Review

CAS

Engagement quality control review (EQCR)—an objective evaluation of the significant judgments made by the engagement team and the conclusions reached in formulating the audit report. An EQCR is required for all listed entity audits and for certain other engagements.

Both CSQC 1 and CAS 220 require that an **engagement quality control review (EQCR)** be performed on all audits of listed entities. In the case of nonlisted entities, CSQC requires that the public accounting firms develop criteria to determine when an EQCR is needed. Essentially, these criteria should identify high-risk engagements. The engagement partner will determine whether an EQCR is needed at the planning stage; however, CAS 220 emphasizes that the engagement partner must remain alert throughout the engagement to situations that may require an EQCR.

An EQCR, often referred to as second-partner review, is an objective evaluation performed by the engagement quality partner. In order to maintain the objectivity, CSQC 1.A49 advises that the engagement quality partner (1) not be selected by the engagement partner, (2) not participate in the engagement during the review, and (3) not make decisions for the audit team.

The EQCR is a risk-based review, with the reviewer paying particular attention to significant judgments made by the engagement team and the conclusions reached in formulating the report. The extent of the EQCR depends upon the complexity of the engagement and requires considerable professional judgment; however, some common procedures that should be performed include:

- Evaluating procedures performed by the engagement team to verify team and firm independence;
- Evaluating the engagement team's assessment of and responses to significant risks, including fraud risks;
- Evaluating the rigour applied to determining materiality and whether adjusted and unadjusted misstatements (including uncorrected disclosures) have been treated appropriately;
- Evaluating whether significant matters noted in the engagement were satisfactorily resolved;

- Evaluating whether audit documentation supports conclusions reached by the audit team;
- Reviewing financial statements and cross-checking for completeness of significant issues;
- Assessing whether appropriate matters have been communicated to those charged with governance; and
- Reviewing the proposed audit report and evaluating whether it aligns with engagement outcomes.

In addition to the EQCR, some firms require a pre-issuance technical review of the financial statements conducted by a technical expert who has not participated in the engagement and who is independent of the engagement team and the engagement quality partner. Although this type of review is not required by the audit standards, the CPAB recently recommended that these technical reviews should be mandatory for high-risk engagements or where accounting issues have been noted in past internal or external inspections.

CONCEPT CHECK

C18-6 What method does the auditor use to determine whether sufficient appropriate audit evidence has been collected?

C18-7 What is the purpose of the engagement quality control review?

C18-8 What are some procedures used for the engagement quality control review?

Draft the Audit Report

The auditor should wait to decide the appropriate audit report to issue until all evidence has been accumulated and evaluated, including all the steps for completing the audit so far. Because the audit report is the only thing that most users see in the audit process, and the consequences of issuing an inappropriate audit opinion can be severe, it is critical that the report be correct. In the case of public companies, per CAS 701, auditors may also choose to report key audit matters, which in the auditors' professional judgment, were matters of most significance to the audit and required significant auditor attention and resources. For instance, in Figure 18-3, in the excerpt from the audit report, the auditors explain why contingent liabilities represent a key audit matter for the Philips' 2016 audit. (Note: Although the new audit report is effective for year-ends of December 15, 2018, or later, the requirement that key audit matters be mentioned remains within the auditor's discretion, unless there is a regulatory requirement.)

When a public accountant decides that the standard unmodified report is inappropriate, there will almost certainly be extensive discussions among technical partners in the audit firm and often with client personnel. As Auditing in Action 18-4, highlights, in the case of the Ontario government, the discussions were particularly extensive, with several stakeholders involved. We will revisit the different types of audit opinions in Chapter 19, when we discuss the audit reporting decision process.

Evaluate Other Information in the Annual Report

As with the financial statements, management is responsible for the preparation of the **other information** that is published with the financial statements, which typically is the **annual report** of a company. In addition to the financial statements, the annual report usually includes information about the entity's developments, its future outlook, and any risks and uncertainties, as well as information regarding corporate governance. While the auditor's opinion for the financial statements does not include other information (OI), CAS 720 outlines the auditor's specific responsibilities for OI.

Other information—financial and non-financial information that is not a part of published financial statements but is published with them for which the auditor is responsible

Annual report—a document, or combination of documents, prepared on an annual basis by management or those charged with governance in accordance with law, regulation, or custom, the purpose of which is to provide owners (or similar stakeholders) with information on the entity's operations and the entity's financial results and financial position as set out in the financial statements.

LO **7** Evaluate other information included in the annual report.

AUDITING IN ACTION 18-4
Balanced Budget: An Election Promise That Makes Assets Reappear

The audited consolidated financial statements of the Ontario government are supposed to be tabled 180 days after the end of the fiscal year. In 2016, however, the September 27 deadline was missed because of a dispute between Auditor General of Ontario Bonnie Lysyk and the government.

The dispute related to the government's choice to account for pension plans that it co-sponsors by recognizing them as an asset on its balance sheet. The Auditor General didn't agree with the asset recognition and refused to issue an unqualified opinion. The dollar impact of this dispute was $10.7 billion that would have to be added to the net provincial debt and accumulated deficit, and an increase in the 2015–16 annual deficit of $1.5 billion.

With the provincial election scheduled to be held on or before June 7, 2018, and the Ontario Liberal government promising to balance the budget, there was pressure on the government to eliminate the deficit.

On October 3, 2016, without an audit opinion and nearly a week past the legal deadline, the Ontario government released its consolidated financial statements for the 2015–16 fiscal year. The same day, Ontario's Minister of Finance, Charles Sousa, came out publicly and said that the government had only learned of Ms. Lysyk's problem with the government's accounting methods on September 13. He also insinuated that the Auditor General's office had leaked information to the Opposition party about the dispute, and that any discussions between the Opposition and the Auditor's office would be unacceptable.

The Auditor General responded to Mr. Sousa saying that she had been meeting with the government to discuss the pension issue as recently as October 3, and the Liberals gave her no indication that they were about to release the unaudited financial statements. Lysyk added that her office had first told the government of its concerns over the pension accounting in June, and further that she had not told the Opposition anything about the matter.

The next day, the government agreed to change its accounting for pension plans, and on October 5, the Auditor General issued an opinion. The opinion was still qualified, however, as the government refused to restate its prior year comparative period consolidated financial statements, which constitutes a departure from public sector accounting standards.

The public dispute between the Auditor General and the government continued, as the next day the government formed an expert panel to deliver advice and recommendations as to the application of public sector accounting standards to Ontario's pension assets. On February 13, 2017, the panel came back with a report that sided with the government's initial accounting for the pension plans it co-sponsors, recognizing them as an asset on its balance sheet. The government accepted the panel's recommendation and claimed that "Ontario remains on track to balance the budget by 2017–18 and remain balanced in 2018–19."

Sources: Ontario, Ontario Releases 2015–16 Public Accounts, news release, October 6, 2016, accessed October 20, 2017, at **https// news.ontario.ca/tbs/en/2016/10/ontario-releases-2015-16-public-accounts.html**. Ontario, Release of Ontario's 2015–16 Financial Statements, news release, October 3, 2016, accessed October 20, 2017, at **https://news.ontario.ca/tbs/en/2016/10/release-of-ontarios-2015-16-financial-statements.html**. David Reevely, "Ontario Liberals shoot themselves in the foot during needless feud with Auditor General," National Post, October 5, 2016, accessed October 20, 2017, at **http://news.nationalpost.com/full-comment/david-reevely-ontario-liberals-shoot-themselves-in-the-foot-during-needless-feud-with-auditor-general**. "Liberals in spat with AG: Ontario says province's deficit is $3.5B, but auditor general says it's $1.5B more," National Post, October 3, 2016, accessed October 20, 2017, at **http://news.nationalpost.com/news/canada/canadian-politics/liberals-in-spat-with-ag-ontarontario-says-provinces-deficit-is-3-5b-but-auditor-general-says-its-1-5b-more**. Ontario, Pension Asset Expert Advisory Panel Submits Report, news release, February 13, 2017, accessed October 20, 2017, at **https://news.ontario.ca/tbs/en/2017/02/pension-asset-expert-advisory-panel-submits-report.html**. Adrian Morrow, "Liberals and provincial Auditor-General clash over deficit disparity," The Globe and Mail, October 3, 2016, accessed October 20, 2017, at **https://www.theglobeandmail.com/news/national/ontario-liberals-fighting-with-ag-over-deficit-discrepancy/article32211594/**. Robert Benzie, "Ontario Liberals unveil balanced budget that features free youth pharmacare plan," Toronto Star, April 27, 2017, accessed October 20, 2017, at **https://www.thestar.com/news/canada/2017/04/27/ontario-liberals-unveil-balanced-budget-that-features-free-youth-pharmacare-plan.html**. Ontario, Consolidated Financial Statements, 2015–2016, accessed October 31, 2017, at **https://files.ontario.ca/web_2015-2016_annual_report_eng.pdf#page=55**. Antonella Artuso, "Liberals paid panel 'ridiculous' $435G to resolve dispute with AG: OPSEU," Toronto Sun, February 17, 2017, accessed October 21, 2017, at **http://www.torontosun.com/2017/02/15/panels-435000-package-ridiculous-opseu**.

The auditor is required to determine, through discussion with management, which document(s) are expected to be issued that meet the definition of "other information." For many clients, this is fairly straightforward since the documents that make up the annual report are defined by certain laws, regulations, or customs. However, there are instances where this may not be clear. In Canada, documents or reports that auditors typically encounter that would be considered OI include:

- Management Discussion and Analysis (referred to as the MD&A—the general purpose is to describe the company's performance and the risks within which it operates);

- Management Report of Fund Performance issued by investment funds under the provisions of Canadian securities legislation;
- Financial Statement Discussions and Analysis or equivalent documents issued by public sector entities; and
- Form 10-K for U.S. Securities and Exchange Commission filers (these companies are often cross-listed).

Reading and Considering Other Information At this point in the audit process, client management will usually have a "close to final" version of the annual report that the auditor will review. The auditor is required to evaluate the consistency of OI with the financial statements by selecting amounts or other items and comparing to the financial statements. For example, assume that the president's letter in the annual report refers to an increase in earnings per share from $2.60 to $2.93. The auditor is required to compare that information with what is in the financial statements to make sure that it corresponds. Selecting the amounts or other items to compare is a matter of professional judgment. Some factors to consider include (1) the significance of the item to the users (e.g., a key ratio or amount); (2) the relative size of the amount compared with accounts or items in the financial statements or the other information; and/or (3) the sensitivity of the particular amount or other item in the other information (e.g., share-based payments for senior management).

Per CAS 720, the auditor's primary objectives when reviewing other information are:

CAS

- To consider whether there is a material inconsistency between the other information and the financial statements;
- To consider whether there is a material inconsistency between the other information and the auditor's understanding of the entity;
- To respond appropriately to identified material inconsistencies or material misstatements in other information; and
- To report other information appropriately in the audit report (we will discuss this further in the next chapter).

Responding to Material Inconsistencies If the auditor believes that a material inconsistency appears to exist or that a **misstatement of other information** is material, the auditor is required to discuss with management and, if necessary, perform procedures. If, after discussion and performing procedures, the auditor concludes that a material inconsistency exists in OI, then the auditor shall request that management correct the misstatement in the annual report. If management refuses to make the correction to OI, then the auditor will inform those in charge of governance and may need to consider the implications for the audit (for instance, it may raise concerns over management integrity) and the audit report (which we will discuss in Chapter 19). In situations where the auditor has concerns over management integrity, a disclaimer of the audit opinion or withdrawal from the engagement may be the best response. If the financial statements have already been released, then the auditor may be able to bring the matter to the attention of the financial statement users at the annual general meeting. In some cases, the auditor may be required by law, regulation, or other professional standards to communicate the matter to a regulator or relevant professional body.

In addition to considering whether OI is misstated, while reading the OI, the auditor may become aware of new information that could have implications for the financial statements as well as the audit itself, which are summarized in Table 18-4.

If an error exists in the financial statements and the statements have not been issued yet, the auditor will request that management correct the error. If the financial statements have been issued, the auditor should treat the error as a subsequent discovery of a misstatement (CAS 560), notify management, and modify the audit report. We will discuss the auditor's reporting responsibilities for these situations, as

CAS

> **Misstatement of other information**—a misstatement of other information exists when the other information is incorrectly stated or otherwise misleading (including because it omits or obscures information necessary for a proper understanding of a matter disclosed in the other information).

Table 18-4	Potential Implications of Material Inconsistencies in OI for Financial Statements, the Audit, and the Auditor's Responsibilities

Possible Impact	Auditors' Responsibilities
Financial statements may be materially misstated.	The auditor must evaluate the effect of identified and uncorrected misstatements on the audit.
The auditor's understanding of entity and environment may be incorrect.	The auditor will need to consider whether risk assessments need to be adjusted.
There may be potential subsequent events.	See the earlier discussion of auditor's responsibilities related to subsequent events.

well as when management refuses to adjust the financial statements, in more depth in Chapter 19.

LO 8 Communicate effectively with the audit committee and management.

COMMUNICATE WITH THE AUDIT COMMITTEE AND MANAGEMENT

As highlighted in the Audit Process diagram in Figure 18-1, ongoing discussion with those in charge of governance and management is essential in each part of the audit. As part of the planning process, the auditor would have communicated the planned scope and timing of the audit with those charged with the governance of the entity. CAS 260 requires that the auditor examine the organizational structure of the entity to determine that reporting is being done to the appropriate person or group. In most large organizations, this will be the audit committee but will also include one or more individuals in executive management. Many of the examples used throughout this book are excerpts from audit plans presented to various organizations' audit committees.

Communicate Misstatements and Illegal Acts

CAS 260.12 requires that the auditor ensure that the appropriate level of management is informed of material weaknesses in the design, implementation, or operating effectiveness of internal control. CAS 450 requires that the auditor communicate all except clearly trivial misstatements and ask management to correct them. In addition, the auditor must ensure that the audit committee or similarly designated group (e.g., the board of directors or board of trustees) is informed of all significant misstatements, whether or not they are adjusted. This includes intentional (fraud or other irregularities) and unintentional (errors) misstatements. Either the auditor or management can inform the audit committee, and this should be done on a timely basis.

If those in charge of governance decide to direct management not to correct any of the identified misstatements, CAS 450.14 requires auditors to obtain a representation from those charged with governance explaining why the misstatements have not been corrected. Generally, there are two reasons for this—either they believe the misstatement to be immaterial or they do not agree with the auditors over a judgmental misstatement.

Illegal acts are violations of laws or government regulations. CAS 250 requires the auditor to understand the regulatory environment in which the entity operates so that any observed illegal or possibly illegal acts, such as noncompliance with waste disposal regulations, can be communicated to the audit committee or equivalent group on a timely basis. The audit committee may also expect the auditor to communicate such matters as unusual actions that increase the risk of loss to the company; actions that could cause serious embarrassment to the entity, such as breaches of the company's code of conduct; significant transactions that appear to be inconsistent with the ordinary course of business; and other matters. The audit committee's wishes should be discussed and clarified with the audit committee before the auditor starts the audit fieldwork.

Communicate Internal Control Deficiencies

Per CAS 260, misstatements that indicate significant deficiencies in the design or operation of internal control must be reported to the audit committee. Although the auditor has no duty to report to the client less significant internal control weaknesses identified during the audit, he or she commonly does so as a client service. In addition, some auditors provide suggestions for improvements in internal control (called a "management letter"). In larger companies, communication of both reportable internal control conditions and other improvements are made to the audit committee, and in smaller companies, to the owners or senior management.

Other Communication With Audit Committee

Like all communications with the audit committee (or alternative individuals responsible for the governance of the entity), the purpose of the following *other communication* is to encourage two-way communication and to keep the committee informed of auditing issues and findings. There are five principal purposes of this required communication:

1. *To communicate auditor responsibilities in the audit of financial statements.* This communication includes discussion of the auditor's responsibilities under generally accepted auditing standards, including responsibility for understanding and evaluating internal control and the concept of reasonable rather than absolute assurance.
2. *To provide an overview of the scope and timing of the audit.* The purpose of this required communication is to provide a high-level overview of the auditor's approach to addressing significant risks and consideration of internal control, as well as timing of the audit. This would include areas of perceived high risk, materiality and risk levels selected, and planned reliance on other auditors (including the internal audit department).
3. *To confirm the auditor's independence.* This will include a breakdown (billed between audit and other services) of the fees, and a disclosure of any relationships between the auditor and the client (or its related entities or directors, officers, or employees).
4. *To provide those charged with governance with significant findings arising during the audit.* These communications include discussion of material misstatements detected during the audit that were corrected by the client and uncorrected misstatements that were accumulated by the auditor. The auditor's view of qualitative aspects of significant accounting principles and policies and estimates should be presented, as well as significant difficulties encountered during the audit, including disagreements with management, lack of availability of client personnel, failure to obtain necessary information, and an unreasonable timetable in which to complete the audit.
5. *To obtain from those charged with governance information relevant to the audit.* The audit committee or others charged with governance, such as the full board of directors, may share strategic decisions that may affect the nature and timing of the auditor's procedures.

Communication with the audit committee normally takes place more than once during each audit and can be oral, written, or both, although certain communications, such as the independence letter and possible material misstatements, must be in writing. For example, issues dealing with the auditor's responsibilities and significant accounting policies are usually discussed early in the audit, preferably during

| Figure 18-8 | Excerpt of Auditor Communications with the Audit Committee of the City of Ottawa |

The first two are required per CAS 260; the management letter is optional.

Planned written communications to:
- Management and the Audit Committee describing significant deficiencies identified during our audit, if any
- The Audit Committee noting any independence matters in accordance with Canadian professional standards

Issue a letter to management including recommendations for improvements in controls and procedures, if necessary.

The auditor has concluded that there are no material misstatements.

Status of Audit

The 2015 audit is progressing as planned; after completing our remaining procedures, as outlined in "Open items" below, we expect to issue an unqualified opinion on the consolidated financial statements.

The auditor was not required to modify the audit plan.

Scope

Our audit scope is consistent with the plan communicated in November 2015; we continually reassess our planned audit approach to address risk and areas of emphasis throughout the audit.

The auditor is highlighting that there are no significant differences with management and has advised the audit committee of any significant misstatements.

Results
- The City's analysis of significant accounting matters is reasonable;
- Consistent methodology and reasonable judgments have been used by management to account for sensitive accounting estimates; any significant differences identified as part of our audit procedures are described in this report;
- Corrected and uncorrected misstatements were identified as a result of the audit; any significant differences identified as part of our audit procedures are described in this report;
- We were able to rely on certain information technology (IT) general controls as well as certain controls over accounts payable, expenditures, and payroll for purposes of our audit; and
- Ongoing cooperation and communication between the City and EY supported an effective audit process.

Accumulate Final Evidence: Note that the auditor indicates that the subsequent event review and legal confirmations are as of the date the financial statements are to be approved.

Open Items
- Obtain a letter of representation from management as of the date that the consolidated financial statements are approved by Council (anticipated approval to be June 2016);
- Perform final procedures relating to our review of the City's consolidated financial statements and the annual report;
- Complete subsequent events review procedures up until June 2016, the anticipated date of approval of the City's consolidated financial statements;
- Obtain legal letters from internal and external counsel, up until June 2016, the anticipated date of approval of the City's consolidated financial statements; and
- Assess any fraud or subsequent events information provided by members of the Audit Committee upon review of this document.

Based on Ernst & Young, *The City of Ottawa 2015 Audit Results*, May 26, 2016.

the planning phase. Disagreements with management and difficulties encountered in performing the audit would be communicated after the audit is completed or earlier if the problems hinder the auditor's ability to complete the audit. The most important matters are communicated in writing to minimize misunderstanding and to provide documentation in the event of subsequent disagreement.

Figure 18-8 is an excerpt of the information that Ernst & Young (EY) reported to the City of Ottawa's audit committee. You will note that EY discusses many of the items highlighted in this chapter. The auditors also mention that they will issue a management letter, which we will discuss next.

Management Letters

The purpose of a management letter is to inform the client of the public accountant's recommendations for improving the client's business. Many of the recommendations focus on suggestions for more efficient operations. The combination of the auditor's experience in various businesses and a thorough understanding gained in conducting the audit place the auditor in a unique position to provide management with assistance.

A management letter is different from the required communication of material weaknesses in internal control mandated by CAS 260. The latter is required whenever there are significant internal control weaknesses. A management letter is optional and is intended to help the client operate its business more effectively. Auditors write management letters for two reasons: (1) to encourage a better relationship between the public accounting firm and management, and (2) to suggest additional tax and management advisory services that the public accounting firm can provide.

`CAS`

There is no standard format or approach for writing management letters. Each letter should be developed to meet the style of the auditor and the needs of the client, consistent with the public accounting firm's concept of management letters. It should be noted that many auditors combine the management letter with the required communication on internal control-related matters.

CONCEPT CHECK

C18-9 List two examples of information that must be communicated by the auditor to the audit committee.

C18-10 Why would an auditor submit a management letter to the client?

SUMMARY

This chapter discussed the completion stage of the audit, which is critical to ensuring a quality audit. At this point of the audit, auditors perform additional tests for presentation and disclosure, including reviewing contingencies and subsequent events. Auditors also review the sufficiency of the audit evidence and the decisions reached to determine whether they support the audit opinion. Auditors then communicate with the audit committee and management about the important audit findings and other matters.

MyLab Accounting
Make the grade with MyLab Accounting: The questions, exercises, and problems marked with a ⊕ can be found on MyLab Accounting. You can practise them as often as you want, and most feature step-by-step guided instructions to help you find the right answer.

Review Questions

⊕ **18-1** **1** Identify and describe the four presentation and disclosure audit objectives.

⊕ **18-2** **1** Describe the purpose of a financial statement disclosure checklist and explain how it helps the auditor determine whether there is sufficient appropriate evidence for each of the presentation and disclosure objectives.

18-3 [2] Distinguish between a contingent liability and an actual liability, and give three examples of each.

18-4 [2] In the audit of James Mobley Ltd., you are concerned about the possibility of contingent liabilities resulting from income tax disputes. Discuss the procedures you could use for an extensive investigation in this area.

18-5 [3] Explain why the analysis of legal expense is an essential part of every audit engagement.

18-6 [3] During the audit of the Merrill Manufacturing Company, Ralph Pyson, PA, has become aware of four lawsuits against the client through discussions with the client, reading corporate minutes, and reviewing correspondence files. How should Pyson determine the materiality of the lawsuits and the proper disclosure in the financial statements?

18-7 [3] Describe the action that an auditor should take if a law firm refuses to provide information that is within its jurisdiction and may directly affect the fair presentation of the financial statements.

18-8 [4] Distinguish between subsequent events requiring adjustment and those requiring disclosure. Give two examples of each type.

18-9 [3] [4] Explain why an auditor would be interested in a client's future commitments to purchase raw materials at a fixed price.

18-10 [4] What major considerations should the auditor take into account in determining how extensive the review of subsequent events should be?

18-11 [1] [6] Compare and contrast the accumulation of audit evidence and the evaluation of the adequacy of the disclosures in the financial statements. Give two examples in which adequate disclosure could depend heavily on the accumulation of evidence, and two others in which audit evidence does not normally significantly affect the adequacy of the disclosure.

18-12 [5] Explain the meaning of the following statement: "The auditor should actively evaluate whether there is substantial doubt about the client's ability to continue as a going concern."

18-13 [5] Distinguish between a management representation letter and a management letter, and state the primary purpose of each. List some items that might be included in each letter.

18-14 [6] Distinguish between regular working paper review and engagement quality control review, and state the purpose of each. Give two examples of important potential findings in each of these two types of review.

18-15 [8] Describe matters that the auditor must communicate to audit committees of public companies.

Multiple Choice Questions

18-16 [2] [4] When a contingency is resolved subsequent to the issuance of audited financial statements and it is correctly disclosed in the footnotes based on information available at the date of issuance, the auditor should:
(1) Take no action regarding the event.
(2) Insist that the client issue revised financial statements.
(3) Inform the audit committee that the report cannot be relied on.
(4) Inform the appropriate authorities that the report cannot be relied on.

18-17 [3] Which of the following would be least likely to be included in a standard inquiry to the client's lawyer?
(1) A list provided by the client of pending litigation or asserted or unasserted claims with which the lawyer has had some involvement.
(2) A request for the lawyer to opine on the correct accounting treatment associated with an outstanding claim or pending lawsuit outcome.
(3) A request that the lawyer provide information about the status of pending litigation.
(4) A request for the lawyer to identify any pending litigation or threatened legal action not identified on a list provided by the client.

18-18 [8] Which of the following is not a required item to be communicated by the auditor to the audit committee or others charged with governance?
(1) Information about the auditor's responsibility in an audit of financial statements.
(2) Information about the overall scope and timing of the audit.

(3) Recommendations for improving the client's business.

(4) Significant findings arising from the audit.

18-19 ⑤ Written management representations obtained by the auditor in connection with a financial statement audit should include a:

(1) Summary of all corrected misstatements.

(2) Statement of management's belief that any uncorrected misstatements are in fact not misstatements.

(3) Statement of management's belief that the effects of uncorrected misstatements are not material.

(4) Summary of all uncorrected misstatements.

18-20 ④ ⑥ The following questions concern subsequent events. Read the background information related to company and the description of each event, and answer the related questions.

BACKGROUND INFORMATION

Silo Inc. manufactures industrial chemicals. It has a chemical plant in Sarnia, Ontario, and four offsite storage locations for finished goods. Silo's year-end was October 31, 2018. It is now November 25: the audit has been completed, and the auditors plan to have the closing meeting with the audit committee for approval of the financial statements next week.

Planning materiality is $280 000 and performance materiality is $170 000. Net income before taxes is $5 600 000. The total of uncorrected misstatements is $50 000 overstatement of net income.

The following two events have occurred subsequent to the year-end. At this point, no adjustments or additional disclosures have been made in the financial statements with regards to the two events.

Subsequent Event 1

Silo undertakes extensive quality control checks prior to delivering its chemicals. Based upon testing performed on November 3, 2018, quality control concluded that a batch of chemicals produced in October was defective. The cost of this batch was $350 000. Management does not have any other options except to sell the chemicals for scrap (at a value of $100 000).

a. Before concluding on the appropriate financial statement treatment, provide two audit procedures that the auditor could perform to assess the impact of the event.

b. Choose the best response. Assuming that the auditor has performed additional audit procedures to corroborate the details of the event, the auditor should:

(1) Advise client management to adjust the financial statements for the $300 000 write-down of inventory and disclose the details of the event.

(2) Advise client management to include a note explaining the details of the event with no adjustment to the financial statements.

(3) Post the adjustment to the summary of identified misstatements, with no further action required.

(4) Revise planning materiality.

Subsequent Event 2

An explosion occurred at the smallest of the four offsite storage locations on November 20, 2018. This resulted in some damage to inventory and property, plant, and equipment. Based upon its internal investigation, Silo management determined the cause was lack of safety training. As a result, it does not think that insurance will cover the losses or repair costs. Management has decided to close the storage facility and move the chemicals to another facility. The estimated value of damaged inventory and property, plant, and equipment was $900 000, with no scrap value.

c. Before concluding on the appropriate financial statement treatment, provide two audit procedures that the auditor could perform to assess the impact of the event.

d. Choose the best response. Assuming that the auditor has performed additional audit procedures to corroborate the details of the event, the auditor should:

(1) Advise client management to adjust the financial statements, write off the $900 000 value of the assets, and disclose the details of the event.

(2) Advise client management to include a note explaining the details of the event and describing the value of the assets affected, with no adjustment to the financial statements.

(3) Post the adjustment to the summary of identified misstatements, with no further action required.

(4) Revise planning materiality.

Discussion Questions and Problems

18-21 **2** Kathy Choi, a public accountant, has completed the audit of notes payable and other liabilities for Valley River Electrical Services Ltd. and now plans to audit contingent liabilities and commitments.

REQUIRED

a. Distinguish between contingent liabilities and commitments, and explain why both are important in an audit.

b. Describe how Kathy's testing of notes payable earlier in the audit process might help her obtain evidence about the presentation and disclosure audit objectives.

c. Identify three useful audit procedures for uncovering contingent liabilities that Kathy would likely perform in the normal conduct of the audit, even if she had no responsibility for uncovering contingencies.

d. Identify three other procedures Kathy would likely perform specifically for the purpose of identifying undisclosed contingencies.

18-22 **2** **4** In an examination of Marco Corporation as of December 31, 2018, the following situations exist. No related entries have been made in the accounting records.

1. Marco Corporation has guaranteed the payment of interest on the 10-year, first-mortgage bonds of Chen Corp., an affiliate. Outstanding bonds of Chen Corp. amount to $5 500 000 with interest payable at 5 percent per annum, due June 1 and December 1 each year. Chen issued the bonds on December 31, 2016, and that company has met all interest payments, with the exception of the payment due December 1, 2018. Marco Corporation states that it will pay the defaulted interest to the bondholders on January 15, 2019.

2. During 2018, Marco Corporation was named as a defendant in a suit by Dalton Inc. for damages for breach of contract. A decision adverse to Marco Corporation was rendered, and Dalton Inc. was awarded $4 000 000 in damages. At the time of the audit, the case was under appeal to a higher court.

3. On December 23, 2018, Marco Corporation declared a common share dividend of 1000 shares with a stated value of $1 000 000, payable February 2, 2019, to the common shareholders of record on December 30, 2018.

REQUIRED

a. Describe the audit procedures that you would use to learn about each of the above situations.

b. Describe the nature of the adjusting entries or disclosure, if any, that you would require for each of these situations.

(Adapted from AICPA.)

18-23 **3** In analyzing legal expense for Boastman Bottle Company, Bart Little, a public accountant, observes that the company has paid legal fees to three different law firms during the current year. In accordance with his accounting firm's normal operating practice, Bart requests standard confirmation letters as of the balance sheet date from each of the three law firms.

On the last day of fieldwork, Bart notes that one of the confirmations has not yet been received. The confirmation from the second law firm contains a statement to the effect that the law firm deals exclusively in registering patents and refuses to comment on any lawsuits or other legal affairs of the client. The confirmation letter from the third law firm states that there is an outstanding unpaid bill due from the client and recognizes the existence of a potentially material lawsuit against the client, but refuses to comment further to protect the legal rights of the client.

REQUIRED

a. Evaluate Bart's approach to requesting the confirmations and his follow-up on the responses.

b. What should Bart do about each of the confirmations?

18-24 **3** The controller of Kim Engineering Ltd. (KEL) sent a legal confirmation letter to KEL's law firm at the request of the company's auditors. The controller told the auditors that there are no lawsuits presently ongoing. The lawyers replied to the letter, agreeing that there were no outstanding or possible claims of which they have knowledge, or for which their advice has been sought.

However, the controller was not aware that the board of directors had sought legal advice from a second law firm regarding a harassment lawsuit. Due to the nature of the matter, the board of directors did not want anyone to know about the possible claim. There are no records outside of the president's office, but the auditor noticed it when reviewing the minutes of the board of directors' meetings. The auditor therefore requested that a letter be sent to the second law firm as well.

REQUIRED

a. Indicate what the effect would be on the audit if the auditor received no response from the second law firm.

b. If the second law firm replies and provides information to the auditor, indicate how the auditor should treat this information for financial statement purposes.

(Extract from AU1 CGA-Canada Examinations developed by the Certified General Accountants Association of Canada © 2011 CGA-Canada. Reproduced with permission. All rights reserved.)

18-25 **5** Callie Peters is completing the audit of **MakingNewFriends.com** for the year ended December 31, 2018. Callie has been the audit manager on this engagement for the past three years. **MakingNewFriends.com** issued shares two years ago, but has had difficulty establishing a loyal client base and generating advertising revenues. In reviewing results for the current year, Callie noted the client has had operating losses for the past three years, and its working capital ratio has declined from 1.2 in 2017 to 0.9 in 2018. Callie discussed plans for the future with the management of **MakingNewFriends.com**, which indicated that it is planning to obtain debt financing in 2018; however, management has not yet secured the financing with a bank. Management also indicated that it was aggressively pursuing new advertising contracts and plans to increase advertising revenues by 20 percent in 2019.

REQUIRED

a. Refer to CAS 570 and explain the auditor's obligation to consider whether the client can continue as a going concern.

b. Over what time period is the auditor required to consider the client's ability to continue as a going concern?

c. What factors discussed above are relevant for a going-concern assessment for **MakingNewFriends.com**? What additional information might the auditor consider in the going concern assessment?

d. What responsibility does the auditor have to evaluate whether management's plans will be effective?

18-26 **6** The following items were discovered during the December 31, 2018, audit of the financial statements of Westmoreland Corporation.

1. The company's financial statements did not include an accrual for bonuses earned by senior management in 2018 but payable in March 2019. The aggregate bonus amount was $125 000.

2. Equipment originally costing $725 000 was fully amortized with a remaining residual value of $60 000. This equipment was sold for $85 000 on December 29, 2018. The purchaser agreed to pay for the equipment by January 15, 2019.

3. Based on close examination of the client's aged accounts receivable trial balance and correspondence files with customers, the auditor determined that management's allowance for bad debts is overstated by $44 000.

4. Expenses totalling $52 000 associated with the maintenance of equipment were inappropriately debited to the equipment account.

5. Marketing expenses of $43 000 were incorrectly classified as cost of goods sold.

6. The company received new computer equipment on January 3, 2019, that was ordered and shipped FOB shipping point to Westmoreland on December 27, 2018. No entry has been recorded for this purchase that was financed by a long-term note payable due in full June 30, 2020.

REQUIRED

a. Prepare a Summary of Identified Misstatements Audit Schedule using the following format (see Figure 18-7 as an example):

Description of Possible Misstatement	Circumstances of Occurrence	Amount of Over (Under) Misstatement in the Financial Statements			
		Assets	Liabilities	Pre-Tax Income	Equity

b. Planning materiality for the audit of Westmoreland financial statements is $100 000 and performance materiality is $75 000. Assuming that Westmoreland management does not want to post any of the identified misstatements to the adjustments, what is your conclusion about the financial statements?

18-27 6 Access CPA Canada's CAS 450, *Evaluation of misstatements identified during the audit*, to answer the following questions:

a. What are the three types of misstatements that can be identified by an auditor? What factors might suggest that the misstatement is not an isolated occurrence?

b. Refer to Auditing in Action 18-4. What type of misstatement is described in this vignette?

c. What factors should the auditor consider in determining whether uncorrected misstatements are material, either individually or in aggregate?

d. What documentation is required by CAS 450 in the auditors' consideration of a misstatement?

e. Refer to Auditing in Action 18-4. What factors do you think the Auditor General was taking into consideration when determining that the misstatement was material?

18-28 5 Ruben Chavez, a public accountant, has prepared a management representation letter for the president and controller to sign. It contains references to the following items:

1. Inventory is fairly stated at the lower of cost and net realizable value, and includes no obsolete items.

2. All actual and contingent liabilities are properly included in the statements.

3. All subsequent events of relevance to the financial statements have been disclosed.

REQUIRED

a. Why is it desirable to have a letter of representation from the client concerning the above matters, when the audit evidence accumulated during the course of the engagement is meant to verify the same information?

b. To what extent is the letter of representation useful as audit evidence? Explain.

c. List several other types of information commonly included in a letter of representation.

18-29 7 Access CPA Canada's CAS 720, *Auditors' responsibilities relating to other information*, to answer the following questions:

a. What is the definition of "other information"?

b. List some examples of other information provided in CAS 720.

c. What are some procedures CAS 720 describes that the auditor could perform to assess whether there is a material inconsistency or misstatement in other information?

d. Do you think it would be appropriate to request a junior auditor to perform these procedures? Explain why or why not.

e. If, in reading the president's report included in the annual report, the auditor found several items that were not consistent with the financial statements, what are the auditor's responsibilities in that instance?

18-30 5 Melania Tsipras is a public accountant in a medium-sized public accounting firm who takes an active part in the conduct of every audit she supervises. She follows the practice of reviewing all working papers of subordinates as soon as it is convenient, rather than waiting until the end of the audit.

When the audit is nearly finished, Melania reviews the working papers again to make sure she has not missed anything significant. Since she makes most of the major decisions on the audit, there is rarely anything that requires further investigation. When she completes the review, she prepares draft financial statements, gets them approved by management, and has them assembled in her firm's office. No other public accountant reviews the working papers because Melania is responsible for signing the auditor's reports.

REQUIRED

a. What are the pros and cons of the practice of reviewing the working papers of subordinates on a continuing basis rather than when the audit is completed?

b. Is it acceptable for Melania to prepare the financial statements rather than have the client assume that responsibility?

c. Evaluate the practice of not having a review of the working papers by another public accountant in the firm.

d. Assume Melania is an engagement quality control reviewer and she follows the same practice of reviewing while the engagement is in process. What are the pros and cons of this approach in the context of the EQCR?

18-31 8 In a letter to the audit committee of Cline Wholesale Company, Jerry Schwartz, a public accountant, informed the committee of weaknesses in the control of inventory. In a separate letter to senior management, he elaborated on how the weaknesses could result in a significant misstatement of inventory caused by the failure to recognize the existence of obsolete items. In addition,

Jerry made specific recommendations in the management letter on how to improve internal control and save clerical time by installing a computer system for the company's perpetual records.

Management accepted the recommendations and installed the system under Jerry's direction. For several months, the system worked beautifully, but unforeseen problems developed when a master file was erased. The cost of reproducing and processing the inventory records to correct the error was significant, and management decided to scrap the entire project. The company sued Jerry for failure to use adequate professional judgment in making the recommendations.

REQUIRED

a. What is Jerry's legal and professional responsibility in the issuance of management letters?

b. Discuss the major considerations that will determine whether he is liable in this situation.

c. Did Jerry abide by the Professional Rules of Conduct? Explain your reasoning.

Professional Judgment Problems and Cases

18-32 **6** You are a public accountant in the public accounting firm of Lind and Hemming. One of your larger clients is Yukon Corp., a company incorporated under the Canada Business Corporations Act. Yukon Corp. has a December 31 year-end. The entity's 2017 audit was completed in January 2018; the auditor's report was dated January 28, 2018.

It is now August 2018 and professional staff from your office are working at Yukon doing interim work on the December 31, 2018, audit. Yesterday, the senior in charge of the audit gave you a memo dated August 4, 2018, revealing that the staff have discovered that several large blocks of inventory were materially overpriced at December 31, 2017, and have since been written down to reflect their true value.

You have just finished reviewing again the 2017 working papers and have determined that the error was a sampling error; your firm does not appear to have been negligent.

REQUIRED

Using the ethical decision making framework from Chapter 4, explain what action you would take and why. Support your answer.

18-33 **6** In your audit of Aviary Industries for calendar year 2018, you found a number of matters that you believe represent possible adjustments to the company's books. These matters are described below. Management's attitude is that "once the books are closed, they're closed," and management does not want to make any adjustments. Planning materiality for the audit was $100 000, determined by computing 5 percent of expected income before taxes. Actual income before taxes on the financial statements prior to any adjustments is $1 652 867.

Possible adjustments:

1. Several credit memos that were processed and recorded after year-end relate to sales and accounts receivable for 2018. These total $26 451.

2. Inventory cutoff tests indicate that $25 673 of inventory received on December 30, 2018, was recorded as purchases and accounts payable in 2019. These items were included in the inventory count at year-end and therefore were included in ending inventory.

3. Inventory cutoff tests indicate several sales invoices recorded in 2018 for goods that were shipped in early 2019. The goods were included in inventory even

though they were set aside in a separate area. The total amount of these shipments was $41 814.

4. The company wrote several cheques at the end of 2018 for accounts payable that were held and not mailed until January 15, 2019. These totalled $43 671. Recorded cash and accounts payable at December 31, 2018, are $2 356 553 and $2 666 290, respectively.

5. The company has not established a reserve for obsolescence of inventories. Your tests indicate that such a reserve is appropriate in an amount somewhere between $15 000 and $30 000.

6. Your review of the allowance for uncollectible accounts indicates that it may be understated by between $35 000 and $55 000.

REQUIRED

a. Determine the adjustments that you believe must be made for Aviary's financial statements to be fairly presented. Include the amounts and accounts affected by each adjustment.

b. Why may Aviary Industries' management resist making these adjustments?

c. Explain what you consider the most positive way of approaching management personnel to convince them to make your proposed changes.

d. Describe your responsibilities related to unadjusted misstatements that management has determined are immaterial individually and in the aggregate.

18-34 **2** **4** **6** **8** You are the audit senior who has recently been assigned to the year-end audit of Ontario Agra Corporation (OAC). After the end of the audit fieldwork, the senior on the engagement resigned suddenly to care for his ill child. Most of the audit has been completed, and you have been given the responsibility to review the working paper files and ensure that all outstanding issues are dealt with, and to assist in finalizing the audit.

COMPANY BACKGROUND

OAC owns and operates over 400 acres of greenhouse gardens in southern Ontario, and produces several types of vegetables for most of the year. OAC started operations in 2005 with 50 acres under production, and has been growing steadily ever since by acquiring adjacent land and expanding its greenhouse buildings.

OAC was founded by two entrepreneurs, Holly Green and Poppy Oakes. Each owns 25 percent of the company. The remaining 50 percent is held by a group of 10 investors who are not active in the company's operations. In the past few years, Holly has become very active with the Ontario Greenhouse Association and its Grow Local Campaign and she has had little time to devote to the day-to-day operations of OAC. As a result, in 2014, Holly, Poppy, and the 10 investors agreed that Poppy will be responsible for OAC's day-to-day operations, Holly and the 10 investors must approve and agree to all major financial decisions that Poppy proposes, and audited financial statements must be provided to all shareholders. Because of her added duties, Poppy receives a 5 percent bonus on net income in excess of $100 000.

In 2014, OAC engaged your firm to perform the audit. Holly, Poppy, and the 10 investors meet semi-annually to approve the operating plan, major capital expenditures for the upcoming year, the financial statements, and Poppy's bonus, and to review the auditor's internal control report.

YOUR REVIEW OF WORKING PAPERS

Based on your review of previous years' audit working papers and OAC's draft March 31, 2018, annual financial statements, you learned that OAC's production is sold primarily to large grocery store chains and produce wholesalers in Canada and the United States. One customer, Wholesome Foods, accounts for about 40 percent of OAC's total 2018 revenues, and its nine next largest customers account for about 30 percent of 2018 revenues. Products are delivered by third-party carriers or are picked up by customer trucks at OAC's packaging plant.

The growing season for sweet peppers and tomatoes is March through November. Cucumbers can be produced all year long. The main raw material used in production is water. Other materials required are mainly growing medium, plant nutrient mixtures, and packaging materials. The greenhouse growing process is labour intensive.

In 2017, OAC made a major overhaul of its operations and invested heavily in equipment to clean, sort, and package the vegetables so that they are attractive and appetizing once they reach the store shelves. The Government of Ontario provided financing for the equipment. A requirement of the financing is that OAC must provide audited financial statements.

OAC's net income from the greenhouse business has been increasing steadily over the past four years, with profits rising as the production and sales volumes have increased significantly, while labour costs have been reduced by the investment the company made in 2013 for new processing equipment.

Materiality for the 2018 audit was set at $20 000. Information for the past four years' revenue and net income follows:

	2018 (unaudited)	2017 (audited)	2016 (audited)	2015 (audited)
Revenues	$3 800 000	$3 200 000	$2 600 000	$2 000 000
Net income (loss)	450 000	400 000	(200 000)	(500 000)

Based upon your review of the current year's working papers and discussions with the audit team, you concluded that three issues were outstanding:

1. While inspecting the company's equipment, the audit staff noted a large processing machine that appeared to be idle. The greenhouse manager told the staff that the machine had been purchased in 2016 for processing eggplants; however, several attempts to grow eggplants had failed due to insufficient sunlight in this part of Ontario. The manager has been trying to sell the equipment to greenhouse operations farther south, but it seems unlikely that it can be sold at a price that would cover the costs of moving it a great distance. The equipment's carrying amount in the 2018 financial statements is $900 000.

2. The audit team was unable to reconcile the difference between the Wholesome Foods accounts receivable confirmation and OAC's records. Wholesome Foods claims that OAC owes it $175 000 in promotional fees for prominent display and promotion of OAC products at its stores and has deducted this amount from its last payment to OAC. The controller was unable to locate a current contract between OAC and Wholesome Foods. Poppy stated that she had negotiated a special deal with a buyer who is no longer with Wholesome Foods and that there is no money owing. She has instructed the controller not to book any adjustment.

3. In examining the April 2018 bank records, the audit staff noted that a payment of $1 500 000 was received on April 15. According to OAC's controller, this amount is the total amount paid by a real estate development company, owned by Poppy's husband, for its interest in a joint venture with OAC to develop five acres of OAC's land. The audit team also noted that Poppy's husband was paid $50 000 for consulting services over the year. The audit team had requested copies of the purchase agreement and the consulting contract. The controller provided a copy of the purchase agreement and noted that Holly and the investors had authorized the joint venture. However, there was no evidence of a consulting contract or authorization. The controller advised the audit team that the fee did not meet the criteria of a major financial decision and no authorization was required.

The partner has asked you to prepare a memo outlining all outstanding issues so he can advise Holly and Poppy when the audit should be complete so that they can arrange a meeting of the investor group.

REQUIRED

a. Prepare a memo to the partner explaining the risk of material misstatement for each outstanding issue and what audit procedures are required in order to resolve each issue.

b. Prepare a separate memo outlining the issues that should be reported to those in charge of governance (the 10 investors, Holly, and Poppy).

18-35 **6** On May 20, 2014, the U.S. Securities Exchange Commission (SEC) issued an accounting and auditing enforcement release against two Canadian CPAs, Bryce Walker and Spence Walker, in relation to their performance of the 2007 to 2010 audits of Subaye Inc. Bryce and Spence were partners in DNTW Chartered Accountants LLP, an association of four local firms. The SEC's case against the pair came after Subaye Inc., a purported cloud-computing provider in China, collapsed amidst questions about its business.

The SEC concluded that Bryce Walker, the engagement partner, failed to properly supervise assistants, obtain sufficient competent evidence, properly perform the confirmation process, and act with due care. Regarding Spence Walker, the engagement quality control review partner, the SEC concluded that he failed to act with due care because he should have been aware of the shortcoming of the audit in obtaining sufficient competent evidence and he did not appropriately evaluate numerous significant risks.

REQUIRED

Access Accounting and Auditing Enforcement Release No. 3555 at **http://www.sec.gov/litigation/admin/2014/ 34-72199.pdf** and answer the following:

a. Summarize and explain how Bryce Walker failed to properly supervise assistants. What actions could Bryce had taken to ensure adequate supervision?

b. One area where there was significant shortcoming in the audit was the confirmation of accounts receivable. What "red flags" were documented in the file that should have increased Spence's skepticism?

c. Assume you were performing the engagement quality review; provide a list of questions you would have asked regarding the accounts receivable confirmations.

d. Given that Bryce and Spence were the only two partners in their office, do you think it was appropriate for Spence to perform the engagement quality control review? Explain.

AUDIT REPORTS ON FINANCIAL STATEMENTS

Once the audit is completed, the auditor usually issues an audit report that includes the auditor's opinion. Chapter 2 provided a brief introduction to the audit report. In this chapter, we revisit this key outcome of the audit process and examine the decision process that underlies the appropriate audit report for any given audit situation. The chapter will highlight the professional standards and principles that guide the auditor's decision process and will explain why materiality is such an important factor in the reporting decision process. It will also consider how the audit report adds value for financial statement users.

LEARNING OBJECTIVES

After studying this chapter, you should be able to:

1 Explain the auditor's reporting responsibilities.

2 Specify the conditions required to issue the unmodified audit opinion.

3 Describe the elements of the auditor's report with an unmodified audit opinion.

4 Explain the auditor's reporting responsibilities in relation to going concern.

5 Identify key audit matters that are required to be disclosed in an audit report.

6 Understand the issues that may arise during the course of an audit that could require an Emphasis of Matter or Other Matter paragraph to be included in the audit report.

7 Apply professional judgment to determine if the audit opinion must be modified.

8 Describe financial statement audits where the auditor decides that a qualified audit opinion is necessary and explain the required modifications.

9 Describe financial statement audits where the auditor decides that an adverse opinion is necessary and explain the required modifications.

10 Describe financial statement audits where the auditor decides that a disclaimer of opinion is necessary.

11 Discuss how the audit report adds value for the financial statement users.

The Revised Auditor's Report: A Step Towards Narrowing the Expectations Gap

In April 2017, the Canadian Auditing and Assurance Standards Board (AASB) approved the new and revised audit reporting standards. For periods ending on or after December 15, 2018, Canadian auditors will issue audit reports following these reporting standards. This is a change many claim has been long overdue.

Over the years, there has been considerable debate over how to make the audit report more informative to users. According to most research, investors considered the former standard unqualified audit report, which had remained virtually unchanged since the 1940s, to be of limited value. After the 2008 financial crisis, standard setters around the world began to explore how to improve the audit report so that it would add value to financial reports. In January 2015, the International Auditing and Assurance Standards Board (IAASB) revised ISA 700, *Forming an opinion and reporting on financial statements*, along with several other standards, and introduced a new audit reporting standard, ISA 701, *Communicating key audit matters in the independent auditor's report*. To date, more than 110 countries have adopted the standards.

While the elements and format of the audit report have been significantly revised, the introduction of key audit matters (KAM) is the most revolutionary change. This new standard was developed in response to users' desire to learn about audit strategy and key auditor judgments. In the UK, where the expanded reporting model has been in effect since 2012, auditors, audit committees, and investors all agree that the expanded audit report is much more insightful and useful. Sir David Tweedie, a past chair of the International Accounting Standards Board, concluded, "This has been development in respect to both stewardship and increasing stakeholders' understanding of what an audit can and cannot do, therefore potentially narrowing the expectations gap, and we hope increasing the confidence in the audit."

As a follow up to the April 2017 release of the new standards, the chair of the AASB explained that the final CASs issued in June 2017 did not contain the IAS mandatory key audit matter reporting for listed entities in Canada. Unless required by law or regulation, it is at the auditor's discretion to include key audit matters in the audit report. The rationale for this modification was to avoid having significant differences in the requirements for key audit matter reporting for cross-listed entities, which could create confusion and affect comparability of information across North American markets. After release of the CASs, the U.S. Public Company Accounting Oversight Board (PCAOB) announced that it will be phasing in mandatory critical audit matters (its term for KAM) effective June 30, 2019, for large filers and December 15, 2020, for smaller filers. Now it is clear that there are not significant differences between the American and Canadian approach to key (critical) audit matter reporting, the AASB is considering whether to make KAM mandatory for the December 31, 2019, year-end or to defer it to 2020.

Sources: IFAC, *The New Auditor's Report: Greater Transparency Into the Financial Statement Audit*, 2015. Eric Turner, "'New auditor reporting is creating value,' say UK panelists at PCAOB public meeting," *Conversations About Audit Quality*, May 22, 2014, accessed September 30, 2017, at **https://www.cpacanada.ca/en/connecting-and-news/blogs/audit-quality-blog/2014/may/new-auditor-reporting-is-creating-value-say-uk-panelists-at-pcaob-public-meeting**. Auditing and Assurance Standards Board, *Message from the Chair: New auditor reporting and other standards issued*. May 2017, accessed July 15, 2017, at **http://www.frascanada.ca/auditing-and-assurance-standards-board/item84397.pdf**. Eric Turner, "New U.S. auditor reporting standard and implications for Canada," *Conversations about Audit Quality,* September 7, 2017, accessed November 1, 2017, at **https://www.cpacanada.ca/en/connecting-and-news/blogs/audit-quality-blog/2017/september/canadian-implications-of-us-reporting-standard**.

The opening vignette highlights recent significant changes in the audit reporting standards. As you will learn throughout the chapter, decisions pertaining to what to include in the audit report and when to modify the audit opinion involve considerable professional judgment.

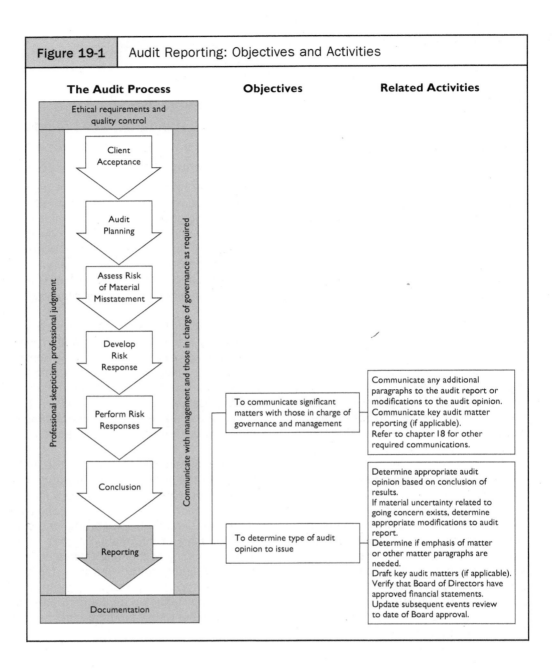

Figure 19-1 | Audit Reporting: Objectives and Activities

The Audit Process	Objectives	Related Activities

Ethical requirements and quality control

Client Acceptance

Audit Planning

Assess Risk of Material Misstatement

Develop Risk Response

Perform Risk Responses

Conclusion

Reporting

Documentation

Professional skepticism, professional judgment

Communicate with management and those in charge of governance as required

To communicate significant matters with those in charge of governance and management

Communicate any additional paragraphs to the audit report or modifications to the audit opinion. Communicate key audit matter reporting (if applicable). Refer to chapter 18 for other required communications.

To determine type of audit opinion to issue

Determine appropriate audit opinion based on conclusion of results.
If material uncertainty related to going concern exists, determine appropriate modifications to audit report.
Determine if emphasis of matter or other matter paragraphs are needed.
Draft key audit matters (if applicable).
Verify that Board of Directors have approved financial statements.
Update subsequent events review to date of Board approval.

LO 1 Explain the auditor's reporting responsibilities.

CAS

THE AUDIT OPINION AND THE AUDITORS' REPORTING RESPONSIBILITIES

As highlighted in Figure 19-1, the final outcome of the audit is the auditors' report. When auditors perform the financial statement audit, they have the responsibility to (1) form an opinion on the financial statements, and (2) issue the opinion in a written report that describes the basis of the conclusion.

The standards that serve as the foundation of the auditor's reporting decision are summarized in Figure 19-2. As highlighted in the introduction of CAS 700, *Forming an opinion and reporting on financial statements*, the reporting standards aim to address an appropriate balance between the need for consistency and comparability in auditor reporting globally and the need to provide the most relevant information to users.

In order to form an opinion, auditors evaluate whether the financial statements are free of material error and are fairly stated, and whether sufficient and appropriate evidence has been collected to make that evaluation. In Chapter 2, an auditor report

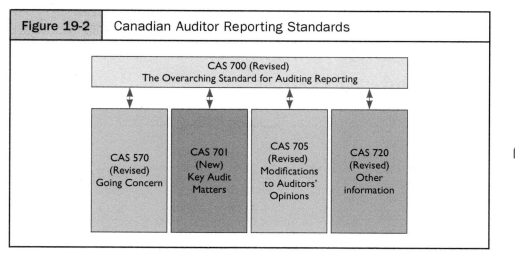

Figure 19-2 | Canadian Auditor Reporting Standards

CAS 700 (Revised)
The Overarching Standard for Auditing Reporting

CAS 570 (Revised) Going Concern

CAS 701 (New) Key Audit Matters

CAS 705 (Revised) Modifications to Auditors' Opinions

CAS 720 (Revised) Other information

CAS

with an unmodified audit opinion for a private company, Hillsburg Hardware Limited, was presented. The unmodified audit opinion (also referred to as an *unqualified* or "clean" audit opinion) for all types of entities follows the same format. However, if the auditors disagree with management about the financial statements or were unable to carry out all the work they feel is necessary (in other words, are limited in their scope), the auditors will modify their opinion—a qualified opinion, or an adverse opinion, or issue a disclaimer of an opinion. So what does all that mean? Essentially, auditors are expected to issue an unmodified opinion or explain why that is not possible.

THE UNMODIFIED AUDIT OPINION

An independent auditor's report that provides an **unmodified audit opinion** is the most common type of audit report. It is the most common report because most organizations will typically make the required adjustments to the financial statements and disclosures rather than receive a modified opinion. In the case of public companies, except in rare occasions, securities legislation requires an unmodified audit opinion.

When issuing an unmodified audit opinion, the auditor concludes that the financial statements are fairly stated in accordance with the applicable financial reporting framework and all material misstatements have been corrected. In order for the auditor to issue an unmodified opinion, the following conditions must be met:

1. An audit engagement has been undertaken to express an opinion on financial statements.
2. The auditor followed generally accepted auditing standards (GAAS).
3. The auditor is independent and complies with the relevant ethical standards.
4. The auditor was able to obtain sufficient appropriate evidence to conclude that the financial statements as a whole are free from material misstatement.
5. The financial statements, which include the balance sheet, the income statement, the statement of retained earnings, the cash flow statement, and the notes to the financial statements, are fairly presented in accordance with an appropriate applicable financial reporting framework.

When these conditions are met, an unmodified audit opinion, which we introduced in Chapter 2 (see Figure 2-2), is issued.

ELEMENTS OF THE AUDITOR'S REPORT

The auditor's report includes several distinct elements. Figure 19-3 provides an audit report for a consolidated listed entity and highlights the key elements of the audit report. If you compare it to the audit report presented in Figure 2-2, you will note

LO 2 Specify the conditions required to issue the unmodified audit opinion.

Unmodified audit opinion—the opinion (also referred to as an "unqualified" or "clean" opinion) a public accountant issues when all auditing conditions have been met, no significant misstatements have been discovered and left uncorrected, and the auditor believes that the financial statements are fairly stated in accordance with the applicable financial reporting framework.

LO 3 Describe the elements of the auditor's report with an unmodified opinion.

Figure 19-3	Elements of the Unmodified Auditor's Report for a Consolidated Listed Entity

<table>
<tr><td>Report Title</td><td>INDEPENDENT AUDITORS' REPORT</td></tr>
<tr><td>The report is addressed to the members or shareholders of the organization.</td><td>To the Shareholders of The Great Canadian Outdoors Incorporated.</td></tr>
</table>

This section identifies the applicable reporting period, name of company, and what was audited and for what period.

Opinion

We have audited the consolidated financial statements of The Great Canadian Outdoors Incorporated (the Entity), which comprise the consolidated financial position as at December 31, 2018 and December 31, 2017, and the consolidated statements of comprehensive income, changes in equity and cash flows for the years then ended, and notes to the consolidated financial statements, including a summary of significant accounting policies.

The auditor sets out its overall finding in an opinion and the applicable accounting framework (IFRS). This is an example of an unmodified or "clean" audit opinion.

In our opinion, the accompanying consolidated financial statements present fairly, in all material respects, the consolidated financial position of The Great Canadian Outdoors Incorporated as at December 31, 2018 and December 31, 2017, and its consolidated financial performance and its consolidated cash flows for the year ended in accordance with International Financial Reporting Standards (IFRS).

The auditor explains the basis of conclusion: the auditor conducted the audit in accordance with Canadian GAAS and obtained sufficient and appropriate audit evidence to provide basis for the opinion. The report also informs readers that the auditor is independent and in compliance with ethical requirements.

Basis for opinion

We conducted our audit in accordance with Canadian generally accepted auditing standards. Our responsibilities under those standards are further described in the *Auditor's Responsibilities for the Audit of the Financial Statements* section of our report. We are independent of the Entity in accordance with the ethical requirements that are relevant to our audit of the financial statements in Canada, and we have fulfilled our other ethical responsibilities in accordance with these requirements. We believe that the audit evidence we have obtained is sufficient and appropriate to provide a basis for our opinion.

Key audit matters (KAM) are matters that posed significant challenges and required significant audit attention in the current period.

Key Audit Matters

Key audit matters are those matters that, in our professional judgment, were of most significance in our audit of the financial statements of the current period. These matters were addressed in the context of our audit of the financial statements as a whole, and in forming our opinion thereon, and we do not provide a separate opinion on these matters.

[Description of each key audit matter in accordance with CAS 701 – see Figure 19-5 for an example.]

This separate section is required when the entity prepares other information, such as an annual report. It explains management's and the auditor's responsibilities.

Other information

Management is responsible for the other information. The other information comprises the information included in the annual report, but does not include the financial statements and our auditor's report thereon.

Our opinion on the financial statements does not cover the other information and we do not express any form of assurance conclusion thereon.

In connection with our audit of the financial statements, our responsibility is to read the other information and, in doing so, to consider whether the other information is materially inconsistent with the financial statements or our knowledge obtained in the audit, or otherwise appears to be materially misstated. If, based on the work we have performed, we conclude that there is a material misstatement of this other information, we are required to report that fact. We have nothing to report in this regard.

Responsibilities of Management and Those Charged with Governance for the Financial Statements

Management is responsible for the preparation and fair presentation of these financial statements in accordance with International Financial Reporting Standards, and for such internal control as management determines is necessary to enable the preparation of financial statements that are free from material misstatements, whether due to fraud or error.

In preparing the financial statements, management is responsible for assessing the Entity's ability to continue as a going concern, disclosing, as applicable, matters related to going concern using the going concern basis of accounting unless management either intends to liquidate the Entity or to cease operations, or has no realistic alternative but to do so.

Those charged with governance are responsible for overseeing the Entity's financial reporting process.

> Management is responsible for preparing the financial statements according to applicable accounting framework (in this case IFRS), for internal controls in the company, and assessing the going concern assumption.

> TCWG are responsible for oversight

Responsibilities for the Audit of Financial Statements

Our objectives are to obtain reasonable assurance about whether the financial statements as a whole are free from material misstatement, whether due to fraud or error, and to issue the auditor's report that includes our opinion. Reasonable assurance is a high level of assurance, but not a guarantee that an audit conducted in accordance with Canadian generally accepted auditing standards will always detect a material misstatement when it exists. Misstatements can arise from fraud or error, and are considered material if, individually or in aggregate, they could reasonably be expected to influence the economic decisions of users taken on the basis of these financial statements.

As part of an audit in accordance with Canadian generally accepted audit standards, we exercise professional judgment and maintain professional skepticism throughout the audit. We also:

- Identify and assess the risks of material misstatement of the financial statements, whether due to fraud or error, design and perform audit procedures responsive to those risks, and obtain audit evidence that is sufficient and appropriate to provide a basis for our opinion. The risk of not detecting a material misstatement resulting from fraud is higher than one resulting from error, as fraud may involve collusion, forgery, intentional omissions, misrepresentations, or the override of internal control.
- Obtain an understanding of internal control relevant to the audit in order to design audit procedures that are appropriate in the circumstances, but not for the purpose of expressing an opinion on the effectiveness of the Company's internal control.
- Evaluate the appropriateness of accounting policies used and the reasonableness of accounting estimates and related disclosures made by management.
- Conclude on the appropriateness of management's use of the going concern basis of accounting and, based on the audit evidence obtained, whether a material uncertainty exists related to events and conditions that may cast significant doubt on the Entity's ability to continue as a going concern. If we conclude that a material uncertainty exists, we are required to draw attention in our auditor's report to the related disclosures in the financial statements, or if such disclosures are inadequate, to modify our opinion. Our conclusions are based on the audit evidence obtained up to the date of our auditor's report. However, future events or conditions may cause the Entity to cease to continue as a going concern.

> This section provides an overview of the objective of the audit, explains the concepts of reasonable assurance and materiality, and provides details of the auditor's responsibilities.

> Because the auditor is reporting on consolidated financial statements, it also includes the responsibilities of the group auditor.

(continued)

Figure 19-3 | *(Continued)*

Name of engagement partner required for listed entities

- Evaluate the overall presentation, structure, and content of the financial statements, including the disclosures, and whether the financial statements represent the underlying transaction and events in a manner that achieves fair presentations.
- Obtain sufficient appropriate audit evidence regarding the financial information of the entities or business activities with the Group to express an opinion on the financial statements. We are responsible for the direction, supervision, and performance of the group audit. We remain solely responsible for our audit opinion.

This section also explains the details of the audit which are communicated with TCWG.

The reporting of compliance with ethical requirements and independence is required for listed entities.

The last section explains the auditor's responsibilities for KAMs.

We communicate with those charged with governance regarding, among other matters, the planned scope and timing of the audit and significant audit findings, including any deficiencies in internal control that we identify during the audit.

We also provide those charged with governance with a statement that we have complied with relevant ethical requirements regarding independence, and to communicate with them all relationships and other matters that may reasonably be thought to bear on our independence, and where applicable, related safeguards.

For those matters communicated with those charged with governance, we determine those matters that were of most significance to the audit of the financial statements of the current period and therefore the key audit matters. We describe these matters in our auditor's report unless law or regulation precludes public disclosure about the matter or when, in extremely rare circumstances, we determine that a matter should not be communicated in our report because the adverse consequences of doing so would reasonably be expected to outweigh the public interest benefits of the communication.

Report on Other Legal and Regulatory Matters

[The form and content of this section of the auditor's report would vary depending on the nature of the auditor's other reporting responsibilities prescribed by local law, regulation, or auditing standards. See Figure 19-7 for an example.]

The engagement partner on the audit resulting in this independent auditor's report is [name]

[Signature in the name of the audit firm, the personal name of the auditor, or both, as appropriate for the particular jurisdiction]

Boritz, Kao, Kadous & Co., Ltd.

March 1, 2019

Halifax, Nova Scotia

several differences. Throughout our discussion, we will highlight the reporting differences between listed and non-listed entities. On the left-hand side of the figure, we explain the purpose of those elements of the report. We discuss each section below.

Opinion Paragraph

The first paragraph does two things. First, it makes the simple statement that the public accounting firm has done an audit. Second, it lists the financial statements that were audited, including the statement of financial position (or balance sheet) date and the period for the (comprehensive) income statement, the statement of changes in equity (retained earnings), and the statement of cash flows, and other explanatory information, which would include the notes to the financial statements.

The opinion paragraph states the auditor's conclusions based on the results of the audit. The opinion paragraph is stated as an opinion, rather than as a statement of absolute fact or as a guarantee. The intent is to indicate that the conclusions are based on professional judgment. The phrase "in our opinion" indicates that there may be some information risk associated with the financial statements, even though the statements have been audited.

The opinion paragraph is directly related to the generally accepted auditing reporting standards. The auditor is required to state an opinion about the financial statements taken as a whole, including a conclusion about whether the company followed an appropriate applicable financial reporting framework, such as ASPE or IFRS. The audit report presented in Chapter 2 (see Figure 2-2) was for Hillsburg Hardware Limited, a private company that followed ASPE. The ASPE financial reporting framework normally requires the auditor to report only on the current year's financial statements, called the **corresponding figures approach**. The example in Figure 19-3 illustrates a publicly listed organization, which uses IFRS. You will note that audit report refers to both periods under audit, called the **comparative financial statements approach**.

Corresponding figures approach—the auditor reports only on the current year's financial statements.

Comparative financial statements approach—both periods under audit (current and prior) are reported on.

Basis for Opinion

Following the opinion paragraph is a brief overview of the basis for the conclusion — that the auditors believe they have obtained sufficient and appropriate evidence. The auditors also indicate that they can fulfill their performance responsibilities by following Canadian GAAS, being independent, and fulfilling their ethical responsibilities.

Key Audit Matters

The introductory paragraph explains what **key audit matters** are (those matters that were of the most significance in the audit for the current period, even when the auditor provides an opinion on comparative financial statements), that the matters were addressed within the context of the audit, and that the auditor does not provide a separate opinion.

Key audit matters (KAM)—those audit matters that, in the auditor's professional judgment, are of most significance to the audit in the current period.

How key audit matters are described in the audit report is open to professional judgment, which means there will be considerable variation among audit reports. However, CAS 701 indicates that descriptions will always include the following: (1) why the matter was considered of most significance to the audit, (2) how the matter was addressed in the audit (e.g., an overview of procedures), and (3) reference to key disclosure(s) in the financial statements, if any.

CAS

As discussed in the opening vignette, the audit reporting standards issued in June 2017 did not adopt the IAS 701 mandatory requirement of key audit matter reporting for listed entities. Instead CAS 701 indicates that, unless required by law or regulation, key audit matter reporting is at the discretion of the auditor. Given that the PCAOB has announced it will be phasing in mandated key audit matter reporting starting June 30, 2019, CAS 701 will be revised to include mandatory key matter reporting for listed entities. The effective date, which has not been confirmed as of the date of this writing, will be either December 31, 2019, or December 31, 2020. The AASB also announced it is considering the possibility of expanding KAM reporting to other types of entities.

Other Information

The auditor's responsibilities for other information was first discussed in Chapter 18 as part of completing the audit. *Other information* refers to information, whether financial or non-financial (other than the financial statements and the auditors' report), included in the entity's annual report. Publicly listed entities, as in the fictitious company in the example audit report in Figure 19-3, commonly issue annual reports; however, CAS 720, *The auditor's responsibilities relating to other information*, is applicable to all audits where other information is issued. For example, many not-for-profit organizations and cooperative organizations issue annual reports.

CAS

In this section of the audit report, it is explained clearly that the auditor does not express any form of assurance conclusion on the other information. However, the auditor has the responsibility to read the information and consider whether the other information is materially consistent with the financial statements or the auditor's knowledge obtained in the audit.

In this example, the auditor has obtained all the other information prior to the date of the auditor's report and has not identified a material misstatement of the other information. In the case of listed entities (such as our example in Figure 19-3), if the auditor expects to obtain either some or all the other information after the report date, the auditor's report is required to include a description of the other information that is expected to be obtained after the date of the auditor's report. However, in the case of non-listed entities, there are no reporting requirements. In both instances, the auditor still has the responsibilities under CAS 720 to perform necessary procedures on the other information. (Refer to Chapter 18 for further discussion.)

Paragraphs on the Responsibilities of Management and Those in Charge of Governance

The first paragraph explains that management is responsible for developing financial statements using a fair presentation reporting framework. The paragraph also highlights management's responsibility for the internal controls: this includes designing and implementing controls; selecting and applying appropriate accounting policies; making reasonable accounting estimates; and preventing material misstatements due to fraud or error. The second paragraph clearly explains management's responsibility for assessing the entity's ability to continue as a going concern. The last paragraph explains that those charged with governance are responsible for overseeing the financial reporting process.

Paragraphs on the Auditor's Responsibility

The first paragraph affirms that the auditor followed generally accepted auditing standards and explains the purpose of the audit—to obtain reasonable assurance that the statements are free of material misstatement. It explains that "reasonable assurance" is not a guarantee and that an audit cannot be expected to completely eliminate the possibility that a material error or fraud or other irregularity will exist. It also explains what "material" is, and the fact that auditors search for significant misstatements, not minor errors that do not affect users' economic decisions.

The next paragraph and related bullet points briefly describe what an audit does and does not include. The section starts by explaining that the auditor exercises professional judgment and maintains professional skepticism throughout the audit. The first bullet point states that the auditor designs and performs audit procedures that respond to the identified risks. It explains that the risk assessment includes assessing internal controls over financial reporting systems but does not include providing an opinion over those controls. The next three bullet points explain how the auditor evaluates management's responsibilities as they are described in the report. The auditor evaluates the appropriateness of the accounting policies, the reasonableness of estimates, management's use of the going concern basis of accounting, and the overall presentation of the financial statements. The auditor cannot simply accept management's representations about appropriateness. The final bullet point refers to the quality of the evidence collected: sufficient and appropriate. This means that the auditor obtained enough high-quality evidence to provide an opinion on the financial statements. Note that, because the auditor is providing an opinion on the consolidated financial statements, the report explains the auditor's responsibility for the group audit.

The next three paragraphs highlight the auditor's reporting responsibilities to those charged with governance (TCWG), many of which apply to the completion of the audit, which was discussed in Chapter 18. The third paragraph applies to all audits, while the fourth paragraph is required for listed entities. The last paragraph highlights the reporting responsibilities to TCWG when the auditor includes key audit matters in the audit report.

This section of the audit report, which is considerably longer than the previous CAS 701 version of the audit report, can be located in an Appendix to the audit report (per CAS 700.41(b)), rather than in the main body of the audit report.

Report on Other Legal and Regulatory Matters

If the auditor addresses other reporting responsibilities in the auditor's report in addition to those responsibilities under CASs, the audit report will include them in this section. The form and content of this section will vary depending upon the nature of the auditor's reporting responsibilities.

Name of Engagement Partner and Auditor's Signature

In the case of listed entities, the name of the engagement partner is included in the audit report (per CAS 700.45).

The signature identifies the public accounting firm or sole practitioner who has performed the audit. CAS 700.A64 states that the auditor's signature is either the name of the audit firm, the personal name of the auditor, or both. The audit report also includes the location of the auditor.

Date of the Auditor's Report

The audit report can be dated only when the board of directors (or, in the case of smaller organizations, the primary shareholder) has approved the financial statements. This date is important to users because it indicates the last day that the auditor is responsible for the review of significant events that occurred after the date of the financial statements. For example, if the balance sheet is dated December 31, 2018, and the audit report is dated March 1, 2019, then the auditor must have searched for material, unrecorded transactions, and events that occurred up to March 1, 2019.

Double Dating the Auditor's Report

CAS 560, *Subsequent events*, discusses, among other things, double dating the auditor's report. Double dating is done when a material event occurs after the date of the auditor's report and before the date the report is issued. The preference is for the auditor to do additional fieldwork based upon the revised, reapproved financial statements so that the audit report applies to the whole set of financial statements (CAS 560.11). However, if it is possible for the auditor to conduct work separately for the material event, the auditor may double date the report as follows:

March 1, 2019, except for Note 17, which is as of April 2, 2019.

If the effect of the event was so material as to change the 2018 financial statements significantly, the auditor would probably extend the audit for the financial statements as a whole and date the report with the revised date as approved by the board. In the example provided, the new date of the auditor's report would be April 2, 2019.

CONCEPT CHECK

C19-1 What criteria does the auditor use to assess the client's financial statements?
C19-2 What are the auditor's responsibilities that are included in the independent auditor's report?
C19-3 What is the appropriate date for the auditor's report?
C19-4 Describe the difference between the corresponding figures and the comparative financial statements approach.

LO **4** Explain the auditor's reporting responsibilities in relation to going concern.

CAS

REPORTING MATERIAL UNCERTAINTY FOR GOING CONCERN

Per CAS 570, *Going concern*, if adequate disclosure is made in the financial statements about material events or uncertainties that would cause doubt about the entity's ability to continue as a going concern, then the auditor shall issue an unmodified audit opinion and include a section in the audit report titled "Material Uncertainty Related to Going Concern." The section should (1) draw the users' attention to the note in the financial statements, and (2) state the events or conditions that indicate a material uncertainty. The section immediately follows the basis of opinion paragraph and is before the key matters section (if applicable).

If management does not have adequate disclosure about the material uncertainty, then the auditor will either express a qualified or adverse audit opinion. If the use of the going concern basis of accounting is not appropriate, then the auditor will issue an adverse opinion. We will discuss modifications to the audit opinion in more depth later in this chapter.

LO **5** Identify key audit matters that are required to be disclosed in an audit report.

CAS

IDENTIFY AND DISCLOSE KEY AUDIT MATTERS

As highlighted in the opening account of the new and revised audit reporting standards, the most significant change is the introduction of key audit matters. Although it is anticipated that the new standard, CAS 701, *Communicating key audit matters in the independent auditor's report*, will be revised, key audit matters (KAM) reporting for listed entities is not mandatory (as it is for ISA 701). At the time the standard was issued, unless required by regulation or legislation, key audit matters are included at the discretion of the auditor.

Throughout this textbook, we have provided numerous examples of key audit matters from audit reports to illustrate how the auditor addressed various high-risk areas. Key audit matters are essentially those areas that the auditor considered to be of most significance in the current audit. Significant matters are those that often involve difficult and complex auditor judgments. Key audit matters include (1) areas of higher assessed risk of material misstatement and items that require significant judgment (such as estimates); (2) items for which the auditor encountered significant difficulty (such as in obtaining sufficient evidence); and (3) modifications to the planned approach due to control deficiencies.

KAM are selected from matters communicated to TCWG. As the audit report highlights, the auditor has various reporting responsibilities to the TCWG, including the audit plan, significant audit findings, and significant internal control deficiencies. Figure 19-4 outlines the framework used to decide what key audit matters to include in the audit report.

In our discussion of the elements of the audit report, we highlighted the reporting requirements in the introductory paragraph to KAM, as well as the three required components of the description. The description is intended to be a succinct and balanced explanation. While CAS 701 provides some flexibility to enable auditors to include entity-specific information, KAM is not a substitute for expressing a modified opinion. Figure 19-5 provides an example of one key audit matter from Royal Philips 2015 Audit Report. You will note that the auditors did not refer to the financial statement notes since the audit matter was directly related to the overall audit strategy rather than a specific financial statement item.

Key Audit Matters and Going Concern

As we have learned earlier, the auditor addresses going concern at the beginning of the audit, and if the auditor has doubt over the going concern, then the audit

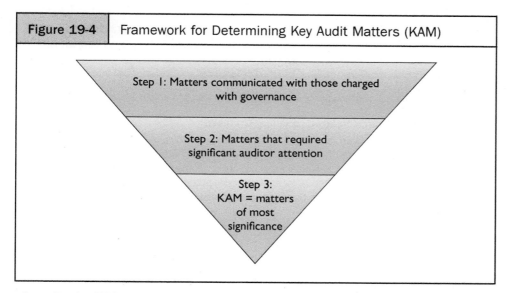

| Figure 19-4 | Framework for Determining Key Audit Matters (KAM) |

Step 1: Matters communicated with those charged with governance

Step 2: Matters that required significant auditor attention

Step 3: KAM = matters of most significance

Source: Based on CPA Canada, *Audit and Assurance Alert: CAS 701—Key Audit Matters*, May 2017.

strategy will be adjusted accordingly. Therefore, by their very nature, issues related to going concern are key audit matters. Where the auditor has identified conditions that cast doubt over going concern, but audit evidence confirms that no material uncertainty exists, this is what is referred to as a "close call" that can be disclosed as a KAM as defined by CAS 701. This is because, while the auditor may conclude that no material uncertainty exists, the auditor's assessment of the various matters related to this conclusion are key audit matters (recall the definition refers to items that are high risk of material misstatement or that require significant auditor judgement). For example, while assessing management's plans, the auditor may need to assess the impact of substantial operating losses, available borrowing facilities and possible debt refinancing, or non-compliance with loan agreements and related mitigating factors.

CAS

| Figure 19-5 | Example of a Key Audit Matter (KAM): First-Year Audit |

Key audit matter

Financial year 2015 is the first year that KPMG Accountants NV audited the financial statements of ASMI. As a result, our audit involved considerations not associated with recurring audits. Additional planning activities and considerations were necessary to establish an appropriate audit strategy and audit plan.

Our response

Our audit procedures included, among other things, meeting with the Board of Management and Audit Committee in the final meeting with the predecessor auditor. We have had several meetings at the Company's headquarters and shared services centre to gain an initial understanding of the Company and its business, including its control environment and information systems, sufficient to make audit risk assessments and develop the audit strategy and audit plan. We also have inquired with the predecessor auditor and performed a file review to obtain sufficient appropriate audit evidence in respect of the opening balance per January 1, 2015, including evidence with respect to the appropriate selection and application of accounting principles. During the performance of our procedures, we were provided with sufficient information to gain an understanding to base our audit strategy and detailed audit plan on.

Source: Based on Royal Philips, *Annual Report, 2015: Creating Two Companies With a Bright Future*, Amsterdam: Koninklijke Philips N.V., 2016.

<table>
<tr><td rowspan="1">**Figure 19-6**</td><td>Excerpts from Independent Auditor's Report: Unmodified Opinion When Material Uncertainty Exists and Key Audit Matters Are Reported</td></tr>
</table>

There are no modifications to opinion and the basis of opinion paragraphs of the audit report.

Material Uncertainty Related to Going Concern

We draw attention to Note 6 in the financial statements, which indicates that the Company incurred a net loss of $125 000 during the year ended December 31, 2018, and, as of that date, the Company's current liabilities exceeded its total assets by $105 000. As stated in Note 6, these events or conditions, along with other matters as set forth in Note 6, indicate a material uncertainty to continue as a going concern. Our opinion is not modified in respect to this matter.

Key Audit Matters

Key audit matters are those matters that, in our professional judgment, were of most significance in our audit of the financial statements of the current period. These matters were addressed in the context of our audit of the financial statements as a whole, and in forming our opinion thereon, we do not provide a separate opinion on these matters. In addition to the matter described in the Material Uncertainty Related to Going Concern section, we have determined the matters described below to be the key audit matters to be communicated in our report.

Description of key audit matters in accordance with CAS 701.

The remaining paragraphs (Other Information, Responsibilities of Management and Those Charged with Governance, and Auditor Responsibilities) are not modified.

Source: The New Auditor's Report, retrieved from http://www.accaglobal.com/ie/en/student/exam-support-resources/fundamentals-exams-study-resources/f8/technical-articles/auditor-report.html

In summary, if a confirmed material uncertainty exists, it must be disclosed in accordance with CAS 570 (as discussed earlier) and where there is a "close call" over going concern that has been determined by the auditor to be a KAM, it will be disclosed as outlined in CAS 701. (Note: This only applies if the auditor is required to report KAM due to regulation or legislation, or the auditor has decided to report KAM.)

Figure 19-6 provides an example of an audit report with an unmodified opinion and includes KAM reporting when a material uncertainty related to going concern exists and adequate disclosure is made in the financial statements.

LO 6 Understand the issues that may arise during the course of an audit that could require an Emphasis of Matter or Other Matter paragraph to be included in the audit report.

DETERMINE WHETHER EMPHASIS OF MATTER OR OTHER MATTER PARAGRAPHS ARE NECESSARY

As highlighted in CAS 706, there are some circumstances in which the auditor issues an unmodified opinion but decides it is necessary to communicate certain matters in the audit report either in an *emphasis of matter* or *other matter* explanatory paragraph.

Emphasis of Matter(s) Paragraph

The emphasis of matter paragraph does not affect the audit opinion; however, there may be certain matters that, even if they are clearly disclosed in the financial statement, are such that the auditor considers it necessary to draw the user's attention to them. In those instances, the auditor includes the paragraph immediately after the basis of opinion section and uses the heading "Emphasis of Matter" with reference to the relevant note disclosure. When, as in our example in Figure 19-3, a key audit matters section is presented in the auditor's report, an Emphasis of Matter paragraph may be presented either directly before or after the key audit matters. Per CAS 706.A16, it is based on the auditor's professional judgment of the significance of the issue.

CAS

Examples of circumstances in which an emphasis of matter paragraph may be necessary include the following:

- Significant uncertainty regarding the future outcome of exceptional litigation or regulatory action (such as income taxes that may be collectible or payable).
- Early application of a new accounting standard that has a pervasive effect on the financial statements.
- A major catastrophe that has had or continues to have an impact on the entity.
- Threats of expropriation of assets.
- Significant transactions with related parties.
- Unusually important subsequent events.

Other Matter(s) Paragraph

The auditor may consider it necessary to use the audit report to communicate to users relevant information not in the financial statements. CAS 706, A5–A9, highlights possible circumstances in which the auditor may consider other matter(s) paragraph(s) necessary:

CAS

- Law, regulations, or a common practice requires or permits the auditor to elaborate on certain matters.
- The auditor has other reporting responsibilities that are in addition to the financial statements.
- The entity has prepared more than one set of financial statements; for example, one in accordance with a national framework and one in accordance with IFRS.
- The financial statements were prepared for a special purpose and the auditor considers it necessary to highlight that the distribution of the report is restricted to certain intended users.

In those instances, the auditor provides this information in an *other matter(s)* paragraph in the auditor's report. CAS 710, *Comparative information*, requires that if a predecessor auditor had provided an opinion on the comparative information, the following information must be disclosed in the other matter(s) paragraph:

CAS

1. That the financial statements of the prior period were audited by the predecessor auditor;
2. The type of opinion expressed by the predecessor auditor and, if the opinion was modified, the reasons therefore; and
3. The date of that report.

The other matter(s) paragraph can appear in various places. If there is a key audit matters section in the report, the auditor may place other matter(s) after the KAM section, and may consider adding further context to the heading, such as "Other Matter—Scope of the Audit" to help users differentiate the other matter from the individual matters described in the KAM section. Figure 19-7 is an illustration of an independent auditor's report that includes a key audit matters section, an emphasis of matter paragraph, and an other matter paragraph.

If the other matter(s) paragraph is included to draw the user's attention to a matter related to the auditor's other reporting responsibilities, the paragraph may be included in the Report on Other Legal and Regulatory Requirements.

Key Audit Matters Versus Emphasis of Matter and Other Matter Paragraphs

As we have already learned, a key audit matter is one that is fundamental to the understanding of the financial statements, the audit, the audit responsibilities, or

Figure 19-7	Excerpt on Independent Auditor's Report that Includes a Key Audit Matters Section, an Emphasis of Matter Paragraph, and an Other Matter Paragraph B

There are no modifications to opinion and the basis of opinion paragraphs of the audit report.

Emphasis of Matter

We draw your attention to Note 24 of the financial statements, which describes the effects of a fire in the Company's production facilities. Our opinion is not modified in respect to this matter.

Key Audit Matters

Explanation paragraph (see Figure 19-3) and description of each key audit matter in accordance with CAS 701.

Other Matter

The financial statements of XYZ Company for the year ended December 31, 2017, were audited by another auditor who expressed an unmodified opinion on those statements on March 31, 2018.

The remaining paragraphs (Other Information, Responsibilities of Management and Those Charged with Governance, and Auditor Responsibilities) are not modified.

Source: CPA Canada, CAS 706, Appendix 3, *CPA Canada Handbook—Assurance*, Toronto: CPA Canada, 2017.

the audit reports. As such, it would meet the definition of what is included in the emphasis of matter or other matter paragraphs. However, it is important to note that the emphasis of matter and other matter paragraphs are not substitutes for KAM.

There may be instances when a matter is not a KAM (because it did not require significant auditor attention), but is fundamental to users' understanding of the financial statements, the audit, the auditor's responsibilities, or the auditor's report (such as a subsequent event). If it is considered necessary to draw users' attention to such a matter, the matter is included in an emphasis of matter or other matter paragraph as appropriate.

CONCEPT CHECK

C19-5 Explain the difference between key audit matters and emphasis of matter and other matter paragraphs.

C19-6 Explain the difference between an emphasis of matter paragraph and an other matter paragraph.

LO 7 Apply professional judgment to determine if the audit opinion must be modified.

DECIDE WHETHER MODIFICATIONS TO THE AUDIT OPINION ARE NECESSARY

Whenever the auditor faces either a GAAP departure or a scope limitation, and it is material, a report other than an unmodified audit opinion must be issued. By modifying the opinion, the auditor brings to the readers' attention any concerns auditors have about the quality of the financial statements. The four main types of modified auditor's reports issued under these two conditions are (1) qualified opinion—GAAP departure; (2) qualified opinion—scope limitation; (3) adverse opinion; and (4) disclaimer of opinion. Table 19-1 summarizes the conditions under which a modification would be necessary and the appropriate type of modified report.

Table 19-1	Conditions and Types of Modified Reports	
Condition	**Auditor's Judgment About Pervasiveness of Effect or Possible Effects on the Financial Statements**	
	Material but Not Pervasive	**Material and Pervasive**
Financial statements are materially misstated (GAAP departure).	Qualified (except for) opinion	Adverse opinion
Inability to obtain sufficient appropriate audit evidence (scope limitation).	Qualified (except for) opinion	Disclaimer of opinion

Source: Based on CPA Canada, CAS 705, "*Modifications to the opinion in the independent auditor's report,*" *CPA Canada Handbook—Assurance,* Toronto: CPA Canada, 2017.

As Table 19-1 highlights, the type of modification depends upon the condition, the materiality of the condition, and the auditor's judgment regarding the pervasiveness of the effects or possible effects of the condition on the financial statements. An item is material if it could influence the economic decisions of users. A condition that is considered material but not pervasive has a limited and isolated effect on the financial statements. In contrast, a material and pervasive condition is such that its effect(s) cannot be isolated to specific accounts or items, meaning that it has an extensive effect on the financial statements and it impacts many assertions. Or, if the effect can be isolated, it represents a substantial portion of the financial statements. In the case of disclosures, pervasive disclosures are those considered fundamental to the users' understanding of the financial statements. As discussed earlier, going concern disclosure could represent a pervasive disclosure.

Figure 19-8 summarizes the various steps in the decision process that the auditor uses to decide on what type of audit report to issue. Given that the auditor has specific reporting obligations regarding going concern, this is singled out from other misstatements. The key factors that are taken into consideration are the materiality and pervasiveness of the condition(s), and in the case of scope limitation, whether or not the auditor was able to obtain sufficient appropriate evidence through alternative procedures.

Communication With Those Charged With Governance

As highlighted in Figure 19-1, an important consideration in all audit reporting decisions is informing those charged with governance. Whenever the auditor believes that additional paragraphs, such as going concern, emphasis of matter, or other matters, are necessary, and regardless of whether the opinion remains unqualified, the auditor is required to communicate this fact to those charged with governance as soon as possible (CAS 705.28). (Recall that in Figure 18-8 on page 590, Ernst & Young, the auditor of the City of Ottawa, informed the audit committee when presenting its audit results that it planned to issue an unqualified audit opinion.) Most likely this would not be surprising, since the auditor advises those charged with governance of any disputes with client management, client-imposed scope restrictions, and any other scope restrictions.

CAS

With regards to key audit matters, it is likely that the auditor will have a preliminary list developed at the planning stage of the audit of those matters that are likely to be KAM and will communicate those to TCWG as part of the audit plan. However, this might change over the course of the audit; therefore, the auditor will likely have further communication about KAM when communicating audit findings.

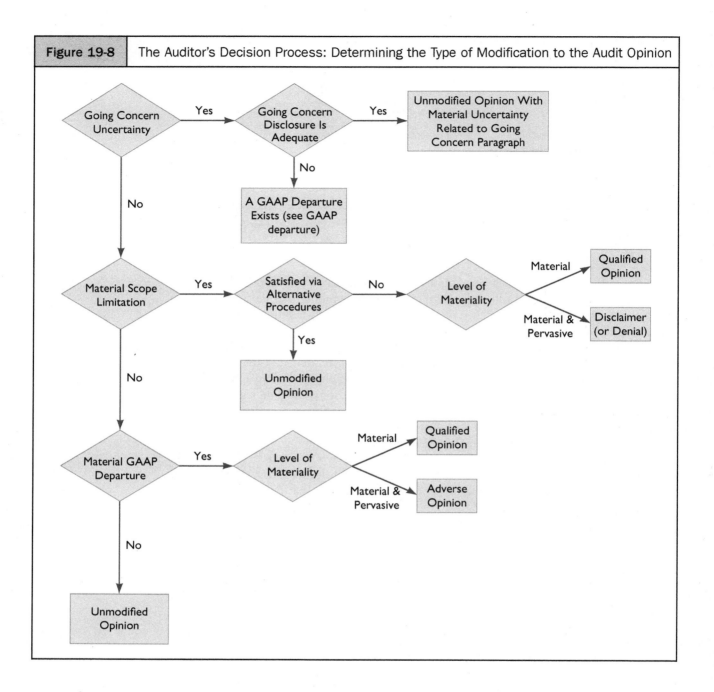

| Figure 19-8 | The Auditor's Decision Process: Determining the Type of Modification to the Audit Opinion |

QUALIFIED AUDIT OPINIONS

Whenever an auditor issues a **qualified opinion**, he or she must use the term *except for* or, less frequently, *except that* or *except as* in the opinion paragraph. This implies that the auditor is satisfied that the overall financial statements are fairly stated "except for" a particular part. Details of the exception are provided in a separate section, "Basis for Qualified Opinion," which follows the qualified opinion section. Although the qualified opinion highlighted in Figure 19-10 is fairly common in the not-for-profit sector, for most for-profit organizations, a qualified opinion is a rare occasion. The provincial securities commissions will not accept qualified statements from a public company except in unusual situations. Similarly, lenders or creditors generally do not accept qualified audit opinions from private companies.

Qualified Audit Opinion: Financial Statements Are Materially Misstated but Not Pervasive

CAS 705.A3, highlights the causes of financial misstatements:

1. An inappropriate accounting treatment (for example, expensing capital assets);
2. An inappropriate or unreasonable estimate (for example, failure to provide an adequate allowance for doubtful accounts); and
3. A failure to disclose essential information in an informative manner (for example, failure to adequately disclose a going concern problem or a material contingency).

When the auditor knows that the financial statements may be misleading because of material misstatements due to inappropriate accounting treatment or valuation of an item, the auditor should issue a qualified or **adverse opinion**, depending upon the pervasiveness of its effects. The opinion must clearly state the nature and the amount of the misstatement, if it is known. Figure 19-9 shows an example of a qualified opinion when a client did not apply the appropriate value to inventory as required by IFRS. As shown, the opinion paragraph is titled "Qualified Opinion." The introductory paragraph of the opinion section is not modified; however, the opinion paragraph is modified to include the following statement: "except for the effects of the matter described in the Basis for Qualified Opinion section of our report." In the basis of opinion section, it is modified with the addition of the first paragraph, which explains the effects of the matter. The last sentence of the second paragraph is modified to refer to the qualified opinion.

In the case of inadequate disclosure, as shown in Figure 19-6, if management refuses to make the appropriate disclosure(s), the auditor should issue a qualified or

---

Qualified opinion—the audit opinion issued when the auditor believes that financial statements are fairly stated but that either there was (1) a failure to follow the accounting principles of the applicable financial reporting framework that resulted in a material, but not pervasive, misstatement in the financial statements, or (2) a material, but not pervasive, limitation in the scope of the audit.

CAS

Adverse opinion—a report issued when the auditor believes the financial statements are materially misstated or misleading as a whole such that they do not present fairly the entity's financial position or the results of its operations and cash flows in conformity with the applicable financial reporting framework, or there is a known material error.

Figure 19-9	Qualified Opinion Due to Material Misstatement of Financial Statements

Qualified Opinion

The opening paragraph is not modified.

In our opinion, except for the effects of the matter described in the Basis for Qualified Opinion section of our report, the accompanying financial statements present fairly, in all material respects, the financial position of the Company as at December 31, 2018, and its financial performance and its cash flows for the year ended in accordance with International Financial Reporting Standards (IFRSs).

Basis for Qualified Opinion

The Company's inventories are carried in the statement of financial position at $2 000 000. Management has not stated the inventories at the lower of cost and net realizable value but has stated solely at cost, which constitutes a departure from IFRSs. The Company's records indicate that, had management stated the inventories at the lower of cost and net realizable value, an amount of $500 000 would have been required to write the inventories down to their net realizable value. Accordingly, cost of sales would have been increased by $500 000 and income tax, net income, and shareholders' equity would have been reduced by $100 000, $400 000, and $400 000 respectively.

We conducted our audit in accordance with Canadian generally accepted auditing standards. Our responsibilities under those standards are further described in the *Auditor's Responsibilities for the Audit of the Financial Statements* section of our report. We are independent of the Entity in accordance with the ethical requirements that are relevant to our audit of the financial statements in Canada, and we have fulfilled our other ethical responsibilities in accordance with these requirements. We believe that the audit evidence we have obtained is sufficient and appropriate to provide a basis for our qualified opinion.

Source: CPA Canada, CAS 705, Appendix, Illustration 1, *CPA Canada Handbook—Assurance*, Toronto: CPA Canada, 2017.

adverse opinion, depending upon the pervasiveness of the omitted or uninformative disclosures. As in the case of misstatements, the auditor should explain how these disclosures are misstated in a basis paragraph and provide the omitted information in the audit report.

Qualified Audit Opinion: Scope Limitation That Is Material but Not Pervasive

A scope restriction refers to the auditor's inability to obtain sufficient appropriate evidence. These restrictions may occur due to conditions beyond the client's control, or circumstances related to the timing and nature of the auditor's work, or may be imposed by client management.

Examples of conditions beyond the client's control are often related to the accounting records. For instance, the records may be lost, destroyed, or seized indefinitely by government authorities. A common situation, related to the timing and nature of the auditor's work occurs when the auditor is appointed after the client's balance sheet date. Due to the timing of the fieldwork, the auditor may not be able to collect sufficient appropriate evidence concerning opening inventory because certain cutoff procedures, physical examination of inventory, or other important procedures may not be possible. However, if the auditor is able to perform alternative procedures, then the scope limitation no longer exists and an unqualified opinion is possible.

Clients occasionally impose restrictions related to the observation of physical inventory count(s) and the confirmations of accounts receivable, but other restrictions may also occur. The reasons for client-imposed scope restrictions may be to save audit fees or, as in the case of receivable confirmations, to prevent possible conflicts between the client and customer when amounts differ. Unfortunately, scope restrictions have also been used to hide fraud, so a client-imposed scope restriction can be a huge warning sign with respect to potential fraud or financial statement manipulation.

CAS Given the heightened risk associated with a client-imposed scope restriction, CAS 705, par. 11-13 provides an escalating set of actions that the auditor should take. First, the auditor should request that the scope restriction be removed. If that is not done, then the auditor is required to communicate with those charged with governance (such as the board of directors) to ensure that they are aware of the scope restriction and to describe the impact on the audit. If the scope limitation is both material and pervasive, the first choice is for the auditor to resign from the engagement. If the auditor cannot resign or this is considered impractical, only then would the auditor issue a **disclaimer of opinion** in the audit report.

Disclaimer of opinion—a report issued when the auditor has not been satisfied that the overall financial statements are fairly presented.

Figure 19-10 presents an opinion that is qualified because of the auditors' inability to obtain evidence on the completeness of revenues from donations and fundraising activities for a not-for-profit organization.

Reliance on Another Auditor or a Specialist

When other auditors perform part of the audit, the group (parent company) auditor is required to make reference to the other (component) auditors. However, the group auditor takes responsibility for the audit opinion, and only the name of the group CAS auditor appears on the auditor's report. CAS 600 and CAS 620 highlight that during the audit engagement the auditor is responsible for ensuring that the other auditors or any specialist hired are competent, conduct high-quality fieldwork, and maintain confidentiality. (Per Auditing in Action 19-1, not all stakeholders agree on non-disclosure of other auditors and specialists.)

As we learned in Chapter 5, as part of an auditor's responsibilities, if the component operation is significant—in terms of either size or risk—the group auditor may need to visit the component auditors, review their work, and obtain extracts of working papers that are necessary to support the consolidated audit opinion. If the quality

Figure 19-10 | Qualified Opinion Due to Scope Limitation

Qualified Opinion

The opening paragraph is not modified.

In our opinion, except for the possible effects of the matter described in the Basis for Qualified Opinion section of our report, the accompanying financial statements present fairly, in all material respects, the financial position of the Canadian Not-for-Profit Organization as at March 31, 2018, and its financial performance and its cash flows for the year ended in accordance with Canadian accounting standards for not-for-profit organizations.

Basis for Qualified Opinion

In common with many not-for-profit organizations, Canadian Not-For-Profit Organization derives revenues from donations and fund-raising activities, the completeness of which is not susceptible to satisfactory audit verification. Accordingly, verification of these revenues was limited to the amounts recorded in the Organization. Therefore, we were not able to determine whether any adjustments might be necessary to donations and fund-raising revenue, deficiency of revenue over expenses, and cash flows from operations for the year ended.

We conducted our audit in accordance with Canadian generally accepted auditing standards. Our responsibilities under those standards are further described in the *Auditor's Responsibilities for the Audit of the Financial Statements* section of our report. We are independent of the Entity in accordance with the ethical requirements that are relevant to our audit of the financial statements in Canada, and we have fulfilled our other ethical responsibilities in accordance with these requirements. We believe that the audit evidence we have obtained is sufficient and appropriate to provide a basis for our qualified opinion.

AUDITING IN ACTION 19-1
Is It Important to Disclose Involvement of Other Auditors?
CPAB Says It Is

In 2014, the International Accounting and Assurance Standards Board (IAASB) asked stakeholders to provide feedback on its proposed changes to the audit reporting model. In its comments on the proposed standard, the Canadian Public Accountability Board (CPAB) stated it was "disappointed that the IAASB has chosen not to pursue a requirement to disclose the extent of involvement of other auditors in the audit . . . and such disclosure would provide greater transparency to users."

So why is CPAB concerned about this? What type of useful information does disclosing the involvement of other auditors convey?

CPAB noted in its 2012 and 2013 inspection reports that it was concerned over the degree to which group auditors rely upon work performed by foreign auditors without the appropriate involvement of the group auditor in the work of the foreign auditor. The American Public Company Accountability Oversight Board (PCAOB) has similar concerns. Both CPAB and the PCAOB had argued that disclosure of the involvement of other auditors would provide users with transparency around who is doing the audit. The current requirement that only the group auditor

need sign the audit report gives the impression that the group auditor solely performed the audit. The PCAOB argued that this disclosure would allow users to research publicly available information about the other auditors and specialists to understand where they are headquartered and potential issues around quality. However, the IAASB argued that, rather than being more transparent, such disclosure will only confuse users about the quality of the audit. After all, the current standards require the group auditor to have significant involvement in the planning and review of the work of other auditors, as well as of specialists.

Source: Based on Canadian Public Accountability Board, *CBAB 2013 Public Report,* Toronto: CPAB, 2014. Public Company Accountability and Oversight Board (PCAOB), *Improving the Transparency of Audits: Proposed Amendments to PCAOB Auditing Standards to Provide Disclosure in the Auditor's Report of Certain Participants in the Audit,* PCAOB Release No. 2013-009, December 4, 2013. Eric Turner, "Taking responsibility: IAASB and PCAOB disagree on auditor's report disclosures," *Conversations About Audit Quality,* March 13, 2014, accessed May 12, 2015, at **https://www.cpacanada.ca/en/connecting-and-news/blogs/audit-quality-blog/2014/march/taking-responsibility-iaasb-and-pcaob-disagree-on-auditors-report-disclosures**.

of work of the component auditor is poor, then the group auditor must try to remedy the matter, perhaps by sending staff to the remote or foreign location.

If the group auditor is unable to remedy the quality of the component's auditors' work, and the group auditor decides that he or she is unable to rely upon the work of the component auditors, a qualified opinion or disclaimer of opinion is the most appropriate course of action. In the explanation of the qualification or in the basis for disclaimer paragraph, the auditor could mention the name of the component auditor in explaining the reason for the qualification (scope limitation).

In the case of reliance on a specialist, such as an actuary, the auditor would normally not mention the specialist or reliance on the specialist, since if the quality of work of the specialist is poor, the auditor could hire another specialist. However, if the auditor believes that a qualified opinion or disclaimer of opinion is appropriate and the qualification arises because of an inability to rely on the work of the specialist, the explanation of the qualification in the basis paragraph would mention the name of the specialist in explaining the reason for the qualification (scope limitation).

CONCEPT CHECK

C19-7 What type of audit opinion is issued when the only errors found during the audit are immaterial? Why?

C19-8 What is the difference between material, and material and pervasive?

C19-9 Under what conditions does the auditor issue a qualified opinion?

LO **9** Describe financial statement audits where the auditor decides that an adverse opinion is necessary and explain the required modifications.

ADVERSE AUDIT OPINION

Adverse audit opinions are rare and should cause concern for users of the financial statements. An adverse opinion is used only when the auditor concludes that the financial statements contain material and pervasive misstatement(s); this also includes lack of important disclosures that are pervasive. This means that the auditor has concluded that the financial statements, taken as a whole, are materially misstated or misleading. For example, if the financial statements have been prepared on a going

---

AUDITING IN ACTION 19-2
These Statements Aren't Reliable: Auditor General of Saskatchewan Issues First Ever Adverse Opinion

Although adverse opinions are rare, they do occur. The Auditor General of Saskatchewan had issued a qualified opinion of the province's General Revenue Fund (GRF) financial statements for several years; however, during the fiscal 2012–13 audit, the auditor found additional errors and decided an adverse opinion was necessary. According to the acting Auditor General, Judy Ferguson, "Because of the nature of those errors and the other errors we just felt that moved it from being a qualified to adverse opinion. We felt that a normal, average public person would not be able to readily make the adjustments to figure out what the statements were actually saying."

Judy Ferguson's comments highlight the fact that deciding whether errors are material versus material and pervasive, which is what differentiates a qualified opinion from an adverse opinion, involves considerable professional judgment. Her comments also show that, in order to determine

materiality, it is necessary to focus on the users. In this case, an important user is the "average public person" who is interested in knowing where the government is spending its money. Although adverse opinions can raise alarm and potentially impact the entity's cost of borrowing, all users are not equal. In this case, some argue that more sophisticated users—such as bond raters, whose job is to study the financial statements— know where to get the information they require. As Nola Buhr, past chair of Canada's Public Sector Accounting Board (PSAB) and of the Province of Saskatchewan's audit committee, noted, "The adverse opinion against the GRF shouldn't affect their ability to interpret information and should not affect Saskatchewan's bond rating."

Source: Based on Jeffrey Buckstein, "Adverse opinion sparks backlash in Saskatchewan," *The Bottom Line*, February 2014.

Figure 19-11	Example of Adverse Opinion due to a Material Misstatement of Consolidated Financial Statements

Adverse Opinion

The opening paragraph is not modified.

In our opinion, because of the significance of the matter discussed in the Basis for Adverse Opinion section of our report, the accompanying consolidated financial statements do not present fairly, in all material respects, the financial position of the Company as at December 31, 2018, and its financial performance and its cash flows for the year ended in accordance with International Financial Reporting Standards (IFRSs).

Basis for Adverse Opinion

As explained in Note 10, the Group has not consolidated subsidiary XYZ Company that the Group acquired during 2018 because it has not yet been able to determine the fair values of certain of the subsidiary's material assets and liabilities at the acquisition date. This investment is therefore accounted for on the cost basis. Under IFRSs, the Company should have consolidated this subsidiary and accounted for the acquisition based on provisional amounts. Had XYZ Company been consolidated, many elements in the accompanying consolidated financial statements would have been materially affected. The effects on the consolidated financial statements of the failure to consolidate have not been determined.

We conducted our audit in accordance with Canadian generally accepted auditing standards. Our responsibilities under those standards are further described in the *Auditor's Responsibilities for the Audit of the Financial Statements* section of our report. We are independent of the Group in accordance with the ethical requirements that are relevant to our audit of the financial statements in Canada, and we have fulfilled our other ethical responsibilities in accordance with these requirements. We believe that the audit evidence we have obtained is sufficient and appropriate to provide a basis for our adverse opinion.

Source: CPA Canada, CAS 705, Appendix, Illustration 2, *CPA Canada Handbook—Assurance*, Toronto: CPA Canada, 2017.

concern basis but, after evaluating management's plans for future action, the auditor concludes that the going concern basis is not appropriate, the auditor should issue an adverse opinion.

When the amounts are so material and pervasive that an adverse opinion is required, the title of the opinion section is Adverse Opinion, and the opening paragraph is not modified; however, the second paragraph explains that because of the significance of the matter discussed in the Adverse Opinion section, the financial statements do not present fairly the financial position of the entity. The Basis for Adverse opinion provides the explanation. Figure 19-11 is an example of materially misstated consolidated financial statements due to non-consolidation of a subsidiary. In comparison to the qualified opinion for material misstatement, the explanation refers to the pervasive effect of the non-consolidation. Note the use of the phrases "many elements" and "the effects are not determined."

DISCLAIMER OF OPINION

LO 10 Describe financial statement audits where the auditor decides that a disclaimer of opinion is necessary.

A disclaimer of opinion is issued whenever the auditor has been unable to satisfy him- or herself that the overall financial statements are fairly presented. The necessity for denying ("disclaiming") happens because of a severe limitation on the scope of the audit examination, which would prevent the auditor from expressing an opinion on the financial statements as a whole.

Like the adverse opinion, a disclaimer (or denial) of an opinion is a rare event. This is especially true since in most circumstances, when the auditor is faced with a disclaimer of opinion, the auditor withdraws from the engagement. Disclaimers are often considered to be a signal of financial distress or fraud. In contrast to the

| Figure 19-12 | Disclaimer of Opinion Due to Scope Restriction |

Disclaimer of Opinion

We were engaged to audit the consolidated financial statements of ABC Company and its subsidiaries (the Group), which comprises the consolidated statement of financial position as at December 31, 2018, and the consolidated statement of comprehensive income, consolidated statement of changes in equity and consolidated statement of cash flows for the year then ended, and notes to the consolidated financial statements, including a summary of significant accounting policies.

We do not express an opinion on the accompanying consolidated financial statements of the Group. Because of the significance of the matter described in the Basis for Disclaimer of Opinion section of our report, we have not been able to obtain sufficient appropriate evidence to provide a basis for an audit opinion on these consolidated financial statements.

Basis for Disclaimer of Opinion

The Group's investment in its joint venture XYZ Company is carried at $1 000 000 on the Group's consolidated statement of financial position, which represents over 90 percent of the Group's net assets as at December 31, 2018. We were not allowed access to the management and the auditors of XYZ Company, including XYZ auditors' audit documentation. As a result, we were unable to determine whether any adjustments were necessary in respect to the Group's proportional share of XYZ Company's assets that it controls jointly, its proportional share of XYZ Company's liabilities for which it is jointly responsible, its proportional share for XYZ's income and expenses for the year, and the elements making up the consolidated statement of changes in equity and the consolidated cash flow statement.

(i) Auditor's Responsibilities for the Audit of the Consolidated Financial Statements Our responsibility is to conduct an audit of the Group's consolidated financial statements in accordance with Canadian generally accepted accounting standards and to issue an auditor's report. However, because of the matter described in the Basis for Disclaimer of Opinion section of our report, we were not able to obtain sufficient appropriate audit evidence to provide a basis for an audit opinion on these consolidated financial statements.

We are independent of the Group in accordance with the ethical requirements that are relevant to our audit of the consolidated financial statements in Canada, and we have fulfilled our other ethical responsibilities in accordance with these requirements.

Source: CPA Canada, CAS 705, Appendix, Illustration 3, *CPA Canada Handbook—Assurance*, Toronto: CPA Canada, 2017.

adverse opinion, the disclaimer occurs due to the auditor's lack of knowledge. In order to issue an adverse opinion, the auditor must know that the financial statements are not fairly stated. When an auditor decides to disclaim an opinion, the auditor has concluded that the extent to which he or she is unable to obtain sufficient appropriate audit evidence is so severe that it is not possible to form an opinion on the financial statements.

When a disclaimer of opinion is required, the introductory paragraph is modified to indicate that the auditors were engaged to audit (rather than that they conducted the audit). The second paragraph indicates that the auditors do not express an opinion. The basis of disclaimer section provides the necessary explanation. The auditor's responsibility section is severely truncated, reflecting the fact that an audit could not be conducted, as shown in Figure 19-12.

CONCEPT CHECK

C19-10 Under what conditions does the auditor issue an adverse opinion?

C19-11 Why is a report that contains a disclaimer of opinion normally shorter than other reports?

HOW THE AUDIT REPORT ADDS VALUE

LO **11** Discuss how the audit report adds value for the financial statement users.

Recall that the audit opinion is not a guarantee, but rather a statement of professional judgment. It does not provide absolute assurance that the financial statements are free of fraud or error, nor does it guarantee the future stability of the company. Yet, because users place a high degree of trust in auditors, they do value the audit report. Qualified opinions, adverse opinions, and disclaimer of opinions can lead to lower credit ratings, lower share price, and/or higher interest rates charged by lenders. In the case of public companies, the securities commission can issue a "cease trading" order and the company can be potentially delisted.

Table 19-2 summarizes the recent significant changes that have been made to the reporting standards.

As we review this list, perhaps the most significant change is the placement of the audit opinion and the various changes regarding going concern. Many claim that these changes will help reduce the confusion over management's and the auditor's responsibilities with regards to going concern.

As we highlighted in our discussion of key audit matters, the current standards have not mandated the KAM reporting for listed entities. While most consider this new standard to be a welcome improvement, some wonder whether the lack of uniformity and comparability will cause confusion, and others are concerned that auditors will adopt a "boilerplate" approach to reporting. The IAASB states that these changes increase the transparency and informational value of the audit report and have the benefits of enhanced communications between auditors and investors as well as between auditors and those in charge of governance.

Table 19-2	Summary of Significant Changes to Reporting Standards
Mandatory for All Audits	
Auditor's Opinion	Opinion moved from the end of the report to the beginning.
Auditor's Independence and Ethics	An explicit statement of the auditor's independence in accordance with relevant ethical requirements and the auditor's fulfillment of other ethical responsibilities.
Going Concern	When a material uncertainty exists and is adequately disclosed in the financial statements, a separate section titled *Material Uncertainty Related to Going Concern* is included in the auditor's report (previously this was included as an emphasis of matter paragraph).
Other Information	A separate section explaining the auditor's and management's responsibilities.
Roles and Responsibilities	Enhanced descriptions of management's responsibilities (going concern) and inclusion of those charged with governance (TCWG).
	Enhanced description of auditor's responsibilities (going concern, group audits, and communication with TCWG).
Mandatory for All Audits of Listed Entities	
Roles and Responsibilities	New description of auditor's responsibilities to provide to TCWG a statement that the auditor has complied with his or her ethical responsibilities.
Engagement Partner	New disclosure of name of engagement partner.
Applied at the Discretion of the Auditor (unless required by legislation or regulation)	
Key Audit Matters	New reporting standard. This section discloses those audit areas that the auditor considered to be of most significance in the current audit. There is no standard format for presentation of key audit matters.

SUMMARY

In this chapter, we discussed the final phase of the audit process—the audit report. When auditors perform the financial statement audit, they have the responsibility to: (1) form an opinion on the financial statements, and (2) issue the opinion in a written report that describes the basis of the conclusion. Essentially, auditors are expected to issue an unmodified opinion or explain why that is not possible. Because users place a high degree of trust in auditors, they do value the current audit report. Modified opinions, which include qualified opinions, adverse opinions, and disclaimers of opinion, can lead to severe consequences, such as lower credit ratings, lower share price, higher interest rates charged by lenders, and potential delisting from a stock exchange. Recently, standard setters have made significant changes to the audit reporting standards, including introducing key audit matter (KAM) reporting. While the current CAS 701 does not mandate KAM for listed companies, it is expected that the standard will be revised to be consistent with the U.S. and those jurisdictions that have implemented the international auditing standards.

Review Questions

⊕ **19-1** **1** Explain why auditors' reports are important to users of financial statements.

⊕ **19-2** **1** **2** What five circumstances are required for an unqualified opinion?

19-3 **1** **2** **3** List the elements of the auditor's report with an unmodified opinion and explain the meaning of each part.

⊕ **19-4** **3** What are the purposes of the opinion paragraph in the auditor's report? Identify the most important information included in the opinion paragraph.

19-5 **3** What are the purposes of the basis of opinion paragraph in the auditor's report? Identify the most important information included in the basis of opinion paragraph.

19-6 **3** **5** What is the purpose of key audit matters in the auditor's report? Why do the international standards only mandate key audit matters for listed entities?

19-7 **4** Explain what is meant by a "close call" in evaluating the going concern. If, in assessing a "close call," the auditor concludes that the client does not need to disclose a material uncertainty related to going concern, why is it likely to be considered a key audit matter?

19-8 **2** **3** What are the purposes of the management responsibility paragraph in the auditor's report? Identify the most important information included in the paragraph.

19-9 **2** **3** What are the purposes of the auditor responsibility section in the auditor's report? Identify the most important information included in the section.

⊕ **19-10** **2** **3** On February 17, 2019, a public accountant completed the examination of the financial statements for Buckheizer Corporation for the year ended December 31, 2018. The audit is satisfactory in all respects. On February 26, the auditor completed the tax return and the pencil draft of the financial statements. Management approved these financial statements on March 1, 2019. The final auditor's report was completed, attached to the financial statements, and delivered to the client on March 7, 2019. What is the appropriate date on the auditor's report?

⊕ **19-11** **2** **3** Explain what is meant by "contingencies." Give an example of a contingency, and discuss its appropriate disclosure in the financial statements.

⊕ **19-12** **6** Why would an auditor use an emphasis of matter or an other matters paragraph with an unqualified audit report?

⊕ **19-13** **7** **8** List the conditions requiring modification to the audit opinion, and give one specific example of each of those conditions.

⊕ **19-14** **7** **8** **9** **10** Distinguish among a qualified opinion, an adverse opinion, and a disclaimer of opinion, and explain the circumstances under which each is appropriate.

⊕ **19-15** **7** Define "materiality" as it is used in audit reporting. What conditions will affect the auditor's determination of materiality?

⊕ **19-16** **7** Distinguish between the levels of materiality and pervasiveness an auditor considers when assessing how to deal with an inappropriate use of an accounting principle or known material error in the financial statements.

19-17 **[7] [8]** How does an auditor's opinion differ between scope limitations caused by client restrictions and limitations resulting from conditions beyond the client's control? What is the effect of each on the auditor's work?

19-18 **[7]** Munroe Corp. had a bad year financially and the president, Jan de Boer, instructed the controller not to amortize the capital assets so that the company would show a small profit. The controller argued that ASPE required Munroe to amortize the capital assets on a regular basis and a qualified auditor's report would likely result. Jan told the controller to disclose the failure to record amortization in the notes to the financial statements. You are the auditor in charge on the Munroe audit. Write a memo to Jan in response to the controller's comments.

19-19 **[7] [8]** At times, for a variety of reasons, an auditor must rely on another firm of auditors to perform part of an audit. What reference does the primary (group) auditor make to the secondary (component) auditor in the auditor's report? Refer to the appropriate CASs.

Multiple Choice Questions

19-20 **[2]** Which of the following is not a required element of an unqualified audit report for a private company issued in accordance with CAS?
(1) A title that emphasizes the report is from an independent auditor.
(2) The name of the engagement partner.
(3) The city and province or territory of the audit firm issuing the report.
(4) A statement explaining management's responsibilities for the financial statements.

19-21 **[2] [3]** An entity changed from the straight-line method to the declining-balance method of amortization for all newly acquired assets. This change has no material effect on the current year's financial statements but is reasonably certain to have a substantial effect in later years. If the change is disclosed in the notes to the financial statements, the auditor should issue a report with a(n):
(1) Unmodified opinion.
(2) Unmodified opinion with explanatory paragraph.
(3) Either (1) or (2).
(4) Qualified opinion regarding consistency.

19-22 **[2] [3]** When the financial statements are fairly stated but the auditor concludes there is substantial doubt whether the client can continue in existence, the auditor should issue a(n):
(1) Adverse opinion.
(2) Qualified opinion only.
(3) Unmodified opinion.
(4) Unmodified opinion with a significant uncertainty regarding going concern paragraph.

The following questions concern audit reports other than unmodified audit reports with standard wording. Choose the best response.

19-23 **[7] [8] [9] [10]** The annual audit of Midwestern Manufacturing revealed that sales were accidentally being recorded as revenue when the goods were ordered, instead of when they were shipped. Assuming the amount in question is material and the client is unwilling to correct the error, the CPA should issue:
(1) An unmodified opinion or adverse opinion.
(2) A qualified "except for" opinion or disclaimer of opinion.
(3) A qualified "except for" opinion or adverse opinion.
(4) An unmodified opinion with an emphasis of matter paragraph

19-24 **[7] [10]** Under which of the following circumstances would a disclaimer of opinion not be appropriate?
(1) The auditor is unable to determine the amounts associated with an employee fraud scheme.
(2) Management does not provide reasonable justification for a change in accounting principles.
(3) The client refuses the auditor permission to confirm certain accounts receivable or apply alternative procedures to verify their balances.
(4) The chief executive officer is unwilling to sign the management representation letter.

Discussion Questions and Problems

19-25 **1** **2** **3** Roscoe, a public accountant, has completed the examination of the financial statements of Excelsior Corporation as of and for the year ended December 31, 2018. Roscoe also examined and reported on the Excelsior financial statements for the prior year.

REQUIRED:

Review the following facts and explain the impact on the auditor's report.
- Excelsior is presenting comparative financial statements.
- Excelsior prepares an annual report for its investors.
- Excelsior does not wish to present a cash flow statement for either year.
- During 2018, Excelsior changed its method of accounting for long-term construction contracts, properly reflected the effect of the change in the current year's financial statements, and restated the prior year's statements. Roscoe is satisfied with Excelsior's justification for making the change. The change is discussed in footnote 12.
- Roscoe was unable to perform normal accounts receivable confirmation procedures, but alternative procedures were used to satisfy Roscoe as to the existence of the receivables.
- Excelsior Corporation is the defendant in a lawsuit, the outcome of which is highly uncertain. If the case is settled in favour of the plaintiff, Excelsior will be required to pay a substantial amount of cash, which might require the sale of certain capital assets. The litigation and the possible effects have been properly disclosed in footnote 11.
- Excelsior issued debentures on January 31, 2018, in the amount of $10 000 000. The funds obtained from the issuance were used to finance the expansion of plant facilities. The debenture agreement restricts the payment of future cash dividends to earnings after December 31, 2019. Excelsior declined to disclose these essential data in the footnotes to the financial statements.

(Adapted from AICPA.)

19-26 **4** **7** **8** **9** **10** For the following independent situations, assume you are the audit partner on the engagement. For each situation, using the framework for reporting decisions, decide what type of audit opinion should be issued and provide your rationale. If your decision depends on additional information, state the alternative opinions you are considering and the additional information you need to make the decision.

1. During your examination of Debold Batteries Ltd., you conclude there is a possibility that inventory is materially overstated. The client refuses to allow you to expand the scope of your examination sufficiently to verify whether the balance is actually misstated.
2. You are auditing Woodcolt Linen Services Inc. for the first time. Woodcolt has been in business for several years but has never had an audit before. After the audit is completed, you conclude that the current year balance sheet is stated correctly in accordance with ASPE. The client did not authorize you to do test work for any of the previous years.
3. You were engaged to examine Cutter Steel Corp.'s financial statements after the close of the corporation's fiscal year. Because you were not engaged until after the balance sheet date, you were not able to physically observe inventory, which is very material. On the completion of your audit, you are satisfied that Cutter's financial statements are presented fairly, including inventory, about which you were able to satisfy yourself by the use of alternative audit procedures.
4. Four weeks after the year-end date, a major customer of Prince Construction Ltd. declared bankruptcy. Because the customer had confirmed the balance due to Prince at the balance sheet date, management refuses to write off the account or otherwise disclose the information. The receivable represents approximately 10 percent of accounts receivable and 20 percent of net earnings before taxes.
5. You complete the audit of Johnson Department Store Ltd., and, in your opinion, the financial statements are fairly presented. On the last day of the examination, you discover that one of your supervisors assigned to the audit had a material investment in Johnson.
6. Auto Delivery Company Ltd. has a fleet of several delivery trucks. In the past, Auto Delivery had followed the policy of purchasing all equipment. In the current year, it decided to lease the trucks. This change in policy is fully disclosed in footnotes.

7. One of your audit clients has a material investment in a privately held biosciences company. Your audit firm engaged a business valuation specialist to assist in evaluating the client's estimation of the investment's fair value. You conclude that the valuation specialist's work provides sufficient appropriate audit evidence.

8. As part of your completion, you request that the chief financial officer sign the management representation letter. However, she refuses to sign the letter.

19-27 `4` `7` `8` `9` `10` For the following independent situations, assume you are the audit partner on the engagement. For each situation, using the framework for reporting decisions, identify the appropriate audit report from the list below and briefly explain a rationale for selecting the report.

(1) Unmodified opinion
(2) Unmodified opinion with material uncertainty related to going concern paragraph
(3) Unmodified opinion with emphasis of matter or other matter paragraph
(4) Qualified opinion—inappropriate accounting policy or material misstatement
(5) Qualified opinion—scope limitation
(6) Disclaimer
(7) Adverse opinion

1. Kieko Corporation has prepared financial statements but has decided to exclude the cash flow statement. Management explains to you that the users of its financial statements find that particular statement confusing and prefer not to have it included.

2. HardwareFromHome.com is an internet-based start-up company created to sell home hardware supplies online. Although the company had a promising start, a downturn in ecommerce retailing has negatively affected the company. The company's sales and cash position have deteriorated significantly, and you have reservations about the ability of the company to continue in operation for the next year.

3. A different public accounting firm, which you had selected, performed approximately 20 percent of the audit for Furtney Farms Inc. You have reviewed its working papers and believe it did an excellent job on its portion of the audit. Nevertheless, you are unwilling to take complete responsibility for its work.

4. The controller of Fair City Hotels Co. Ltd. will not allow you to confirm the receivable balance from two of its major customers. The amount of the receivable is material in relation to Fair City's financial statements. You are unable to satisfy yourself as to the receivable balance by alternative procedures.

5. In the last three months of the current year, Oil Refining Corp. decided to change direction and go significantly into the oil-drilling business. Management recognizes that this business is exceptionally risky and could jeopardize the success of its existing refining business but feels that there are significant potential rewards. During the short period of operation in drilling, the company has had three dry wells and no successes. The facts are adequately disclosed in footnotes.

19-28 `4` `7` `8` `9` `10` The following are independent situations for which you will recommend an appropriate auditor's report. For each situation, using the framework for reporting decisions, identify the appropriate audit report from the list below and briefly explain a rationale for selecting the report.

(1) Unmodified opinion
(2) Unmodified opinion with material uncertainty related to going concern paragraph
(3) Unmodified opinion with emphasis of matter or other matter paragraph
(4) Qualified opinion—inappropriate accounting policy or material misstatement
(5) Qualified opinion—scope limitation
(6) Disclaimer
(7) Adverse opinion

1. Subsequent to the date of the financial statements, as part of the post-balance sheet date audit procedures, a public accountant learned of heavy damage to one of a client's two plants due to a recent fire; the loss will not be reimbursed by insurance. The newspapers described the event in detail. The financial statements and appended notes as prepared by the client do not disclose the loss caused by the fire.

2. A public accountant is engaged in the examination of the financial statements of a large manufacturing company with branch offices in many widely separate cities. The public accountant was not able to count the substantial undeposited cash receipts at the close

of business on the last day of the fiscal year at all branch offices. As an alternative to this auditing procedure used to verify the accurate cutoff of cash receipts, the public accountant observed that deposits in transit as shown on the year-end bank reconciliation appeared as credits on the bank statement on the first business day of the new year. The public accountant was satisfied as to the cutoff of cash receipts by the use of the alternative procedure.

3. On January 2, 2019, the Retail Auto Parts Company Limited received a notice from its primary supplier that effective immediately all wholesale prices would be increased by 10 percent. On the basis of the notice, Retail Auto Parts revalued its December 31, 2018, inventory to reflect the higher costs. The inventory constituted a material proportion of total assets; however, the effect of the revaluation was material to current assets but not to total assets or net income. The increase in valuation is adequately disclosed in the footnotes.

4. E-lotions.com Inc. is an online retailer of body lotions and other bath and body supplies. The company records revenues at the time customer orders are placed on the website, rather than when the goods are shipped, which is usually two days after the order is placed. The auditor determined that the amount of orders placed but not shipped as of the balance sheet date is not material.

5. During the course of the examination of the financial statements of a corporation for the purpose of expressing an opinion on the statements, a public accountant is refused permission to inspect the minute books. The corporate secretary instead offers to give the public accountant a certified copy of all resolutions and actions relating to accounting matters.

6. For the past five years, a Chartered Professional Accountant (CPA) has audited the financial statements of a manufacturing company. The company applies the ASPE framework to its financial statements. During this period, the audit scope was limited by the client as to the observation of the annual physical inventory. Because the CPA considered the inventories to be material and he was not able to satisfy himself by other auditing procedures, he was unable to express an unqualified opinion on the financial statements in each of the five years. The CPA was allowed to observe physical inventories for the current year ended December 31, 2018, because the client's banker would no longer accept the audit reports. However, to minimize audit fees, the client requested that the CPA not extend his audit procedures to the inventory as of the beginning of the year, January 1, 2019.

(Adapted from AICPA.)

Professional Judgment Problems and Cases

19-29 **2** **3** **4** **7** You are in charge of the audit of Saskatoon Building Products Limited (SBP), a company listed on the Vancouver Stock Exchange. In the course of your audit, you discover that SBP's working capital ratio is below 2:1 and that, therefore, the company is in default on a substantial loan from Prairie Bank. Management announces to you its intention to sell a large block of provincial bonds, which were included in long-term investments, and some land that had been purchased for expansion, which was included in capital assets. Management proposes including the bonds and land as current assets pending disposition. Such inclusion would increase the current ratio to 2.2:1.

Prairie Bank and your client have not enjoyed cordial relations of late, and you have been advised by Avril Chui, the manager of Prairie Bank's Saskatoon branch, that the bank is "looking forward to receiving the audited statements because we are concerned that SBP has been having problems."

REQUIRED
a. Draft the memo to your partner outlining the problem.
b. Draft the auditor's report.

19-30 **6** Materia Blues Inc. is a company that manufactures and distributes books internationally. The company has proposed that the following comments be included in the company's 2018 annual report to the shareholders:

"The integrity of the financial information reported by Materia Blues Inc. is the responsibility of the company's management. Fulfilling this responsibility requires the preparation of financial statements in accordance with International Financial Reporting Standards."

"Materia Blues Inc. has established an excellent system of accounting and internal controls, used to gather and process financial data. Management believes that the role of the internal audit department is sufficient to ensure the high quality of the business practices and monitoring activities that are used to keep operations functioning smoothly at the company."

"Our public accounting firm is engaged to provide an independent opinion on our financial statements. Together with our audit committee, they provide high-quality oversight over the financial accounting processes at Materia Blues Inc. The audit committee has checked the audit report prepared by the auditors and believes that it is sound. The external auditors have had free and clear access to the audit committee and to management and employees of the company during the conduct of their audit engagement."

REQUIRED

Describe the incorrect assumptions that are implicit in the above comments. For each incorrect assumption, provide an example of more appropriate wording that might be included in the annual report to more accurately reflect healthy business practices.

19-31 **2** **7** Lesley, a public accountant, is auditing the financial statements of a jewellery store specializing in the sale of fine diamonds. Because of the difficulties in authenticating gemstones, Lesley reviews a report from a gemologist retained by the client who assisted in valuing the inventory. However, upon inquiry of various sources, Lesley is not satisfied that the gemologist is qualified to do the work. Accordingly, she selects a large sample of stones from those included on the client's inventory listing to ensure that they indeed exist and appear to be genuine. She does not notice anything unusual, and therefore issues an unmodified opinion on the client's financial statements.

REQUIRED

Using the professional judgment framework from Chapter 4, assess Lesley's actions.

(Extract from AU2 CGA-Canada Examinations developed by the Certified General Accountants Association of Canada © 2010 CGA-Canada. Reproduced with permission. All rights reserved.)

19-32 **4** **5** **7** You are the in-charge accountant on the audit of Amazing Inc. (AI). It is March 25, 2019, and your firm is part way through the 2018 audit. You are currently assigned to work on various sections within the accounts payable and inventory section of the audit file. Inventory at year-end is $5.2 million. Materiality is set at $225 000.

COMPANY BACKGROUND

AI is a small manufacturer of women's jewellery (including bracelets, necklaces, and earrings). Most of its products are made of silver, 14 Kt gold, and various semiprecious stones.

AI has its financial statements audited due to a $15 million loan with RBC Business Financing Group. The terms of the loan require meeting certain financial covenants—a minimum inventory value of $5 million carried at "lower of cost and market" and a current ratio of 2:1. AI is also required to submit, within 90 days of its year-end, audited financial statements to RBC.

VENDOR DISPUTE

In your review of legal expense, you came across a bill related to a vendor dispute. Upon inquiry with management you found that on January 10, 2019, a ship carrying AI's merchandise sank off the coast of India. Unfortunately, AI's insurers are denying AI's claim for the value of the goods on board. The insurer argued that it is not responsible since the carrier has had numerous past safety violations and the accident is due to the carrier's neglect. AI has not paid the vendor and does not consider this a valid purchase. The vendor is suing AI and the insurer for recovery of the cost of goods on board. Based on the purchase order, the goods on board cost $1 340 000.

AI's management has decided not to accrue, or disclose in the notes to the financial statements, any liability to the vendor. They have concluded it is unlikely that they will be required to pay the vendor, since the goods sank only kilometres away from the shipping dock.

The legal letter indicates that the vendor's claim is outstanding but the lawyer is unable to provide an opinion on the likelihood of payment. When you discuss the matter with in-house legal counsel, you find there are questions surrounding the transfer of ownership and whose responsibility it was to insure the goods (the vendor or AI). If the amount is accrued, AI will not meet its required current ratio per the bank covenant.

REQUIRED

a. Based upon the case facts, evaluate the impact of the shipping accident claim on the financial statements and provide a recommendation on the appropriate accounting treatment(s).

b. Assume the auditor plans to include key audit matters in the audit report, would this matter qualify as a key audit matter? Why or why not?

c. Using the professional judgment framework from Chapter 4, discuss the appropriate actions the auditor should take if management does not accrue or disclose the vendor's lawsuit related to the shipping accident.

19-33 **4** **5** **7** You are the audit partner for Yogis Inc., a privately owned company that specializes in unique and fashionable yogawear. Over the years, the company has been quite successful; however, recently it has run into problems with supplier quality and, as a result, demand has declined. After reviewing all the evidence and management's future plans and its assessment of Yogis' ability to continue as a going concern, you are not comfortable with the company not including a going concern note in the financial statements. While management is quite confident that the company will realize its forecasted sales, you conclude that there is too much uncertainty regarding the predictions.

You have just met the CEO (chief executive officer) and CFO (chief financial officer) to discuss the issue. You have never had any disputes with the client in the past regarding adjustments and are somewhat taken aback by their response. Both are strongly opposed to any disclosure. The CEO stated, "You might as well shut us down now. Who is going to lend us money and how are we going to maintain credit with our suppliers if we are saying there is substantial doubt about our ability to continue as a going concern?"

After leaving the meeting, you reflect on the CEO's concerns and you conclude his arguments have merit. However, it does not help resolve your problem regarding the disclosure over going concern.

a. Explain management's responsibilities regarding the going concern assumption.

b. Explain the auditor's responsibilities regarding auditing the going concern assumption.

c. Based upon your understanding of the case facts, what are the partner's choices regarding the type of audit report?

d. If the partner has decided to report key audit matters, how will that impact the partner's reporting decision?

e. Using the ethical decision framework from Chapter 4, develop your recommendation on how the partner should resolve his dilemma.

19-34 **1** **7** **9** **11** Refer to Auditing in Action 19-2.

REQUIRED

a. How does an auditor determine who are the key users of the financial statements?

b. Why do you think the auditor general emphasized the average public person over the sophisticated user?

19-35 **1** **5** **11** Access Rolls-Royce's 2016 annual report at **https://www.rolls-royce.com/investors/annual-report-2016.aspx#priorities-for-2017**. Refer to the Auditor's Report.

REQUIRED

a. If you were a shareholder of the company, what information in the auditor's report would you consider to be really useful in helping you assess the quality of Rolls-Royce's financial statements?

b. Under U.K. auditing standards, public company audit reports also include materiality. Do you think users benefit from this information? Why or why not?

OTHER ASSURANCE AND NONASSURANCE SERVICES

In Chapter 1, we noted that public accounting firms offer a wide variety of assurance and nonassurance services. However, up until this chapter, the book has primarily focused on audits of historical financial statements prepared in accordance with the Canadian Auditing Standards (CAS). In this chapter, we will examine types of assurance and nonassurance services, such as reviews of historical financial statements, compilation engagements, and assurance engagements of nonfinancial information. The chapter will demonstrate that regardless of the type of information for which the public accountants are providing assurance, they are required to perform the engagement with due care and integrity, and (usually) to be independent.

LEARNING OBJECTIVES

After studying this chapter, you should be able to:

1 Distinguish between Other Canadian Standards (OCS) and Canadian Audit Standards and know the types of engagements to which they apply.

2 Understand the level of assurance and evidence requirements for review and compilation services, and recommend appropriate assurance engagements.

3 Understand the requirements for review engagements and discuss relevant professional standards.

4 Understand the requirements for compilation engagements and discuss relevant professional standards.

5 Explain review engagements of interim financial statements.

6 Explain the umbrella assurance standards for nonfinancial information.

7 Apply professional judgment to the issues related to conducting assurance engagements for nonfinancial information.

8 Describe engagements to report compliance with agreements.

9 Describe specified procedures engagements.

10 Describe reports on supplemental matters engagements.

11 Discuss the future of assurance engagements.

chapter 20

STANDARDS REFERENCED IN THIS CHAPTER

CSOA 5000 – Use of Practitioner's Communication or Name

CSRE 2400 – Engagements to review historical financial statements

OCS 7060 – Auditor review of interim financial statements

CSAE 3000 – Attestation engagements other than audits or reviews of historical financial information

CSAE 3001 - Direct Engagements

CSAE 3410 – Assurance engagements on greenhouse gas statements

CSAE 3416 – Reporting on controls at a service organization

OCS 5800 – Special reports: Introduction

OCS 5815 – Special reports: Audit reports on compliance with agreements, statutes, and regulations

OCS 5925 – An audit of internal control over financial reporting that is integrated with an audit of financial statements

CSRS 4460 – Reporting on supplementary matters arising from an audit or review engagement

OCS 9100 – Reports on the results of applying specified auditing procedures to financial information other than financial statements

OCS 9110 – Agreed upon procedures regarding internal control over financial reporting

OCS 9200 – Compilation engagements

Professional Skepticism Is Not Just for Financial Statement Audits

Menard Construction Ltd. was a contractor specializing in apartment complexes in Alberta. The owner of the construction company, Tony Menard, reached an agreement with a promoter named Alice Mayberry to serve as contractor on three projects that Alice was marketing. One problem with the agreement was that Tony would not receive final payment for the construction work until all partnership units in the complexes were sold.

The first partnership offering was completely sold and Tony was paid. Unfortunately, the next two partnerships were not completely sold. To solve this problem, Tony loaned money to relatives and key employees who bought the necessary interests for the partnerships to close so that Tony would receive the final payment.

Renée Fortin, a public accountant and sole practitioner, was engaged to conduct of review of Menard's financial statements. She noticed that the accounting records showed loans receivable from a number of employees and individuals with the last name Menard. She also observed that the loans were made just before the second and third partnerships closed, and they were for amounts that were multiples of $15 000, the amount of a partnership unit. Renée asked Tony to explain what happened. Tony told her, "When I received the money from the first partnership escrow, I wanted to do something nice for relatives and employees who had been loyal to me over the years. This is just my way of sharing my good fortune with the ones I love. The equality of the amounts is just a coincidence."

When Renée considered the reasonableness of this scenario, she found it hard to believe. First, the timing was odd. Second, the identical amounts were an unusual coincidence. Third, if Tony really had wanted to do something special for these folks, why didn't he give them something, rather than loaning them money? Renée asked that the promoter, Alice, to send her detailed information on the subscriptions to each partnership. Alice refused, stating that she was under legal obligation to keep all information confidential. When Renée pressed Tony, he also refused further cooperation, although he did say he would "represent" to her that the loans had nothing to do with closing the partnerships so he could get his money. At this point, Renée withdrew from the engagement and would not issue the accountant's report.

As the title of the opening vignette illustrates, professional skepticism is a key factor which ensures public accountants carry out high quality assurance engagements, regardless of the level of assurance or the type of information for which they are providing assurance. As discussed in Chapters 1 and 2, it is because public accountants perform assurance engagements with a high level of due care that the public trusts public accountants' reports to assure the integrity of information. We start the chapter with a brief overview of the Other Canadian Standards that apply to assurance engagements other than audits of financial statements. We then move on to discuss two other common services that PAs provide in relation to financial statements—reviews (moderate or limited assurance) and compilations—followed by the variety of other types of engagements that PAs perform.

LO 1 Distinguish between Other Canadian Standards (OCS) and Canadian Audit Standards and know the types of engagements to which they apply.

Other Canadian Standards (OSC)—standards issued by CPA Canada for engagements other than audits of historical financial statements.

OVERVIEW OF OTHER CANADIAN STANDARDS

The primary focus of the book has until now been on the financial statement audit. In Chapter 1, we touched upon other types of assurance and nonassurance engagements that PAs perform, such as assurance over greenhouse gas emissions and sustainability reporting. In Chapter 9, we discussed two assurance engagements related to nonfinancial information, specifically internal controls—OSC 5925 and CSAE 3416. You will note that the applicable standards for both engagements are not the Canadian Auditing Standards (CASs), which apply to audits of financial statements, but **Other Canadian Standards (OCS)** of the *CPA Canada Handbook—Assurance*.

Figure 20-1 summarizes the types of assurance, information, and related services to which the various OCSs apply. The left side of the diagram refers to assurance engagements, either audits or reviews (limited assurance), for other information, which is nonfinancial. The centre column refers to review engagements related to financial statements and other historical financial information. The right side refers to related services—meaning the PA has not been engaged to perform an assurance engagement (either an audit or a review) of the relevant information. Although these are not assurance engagements, PAs are often asked to perform these types of engagements and, therefore, standards have been developed to help guide them in doing so.

REVIEWS AND COMPILATIONS OF FINANCIAL STATEMENTS

LO **2** Understand the level of assurance and evidence requirements for review and compilation services, and recommend appropriate assurance engagements.

The first types of engagements that we will discuss are reviews and compilations of financial statements. Although Figure 20-1 makes a distinction between reviews performed for financial statements and other historical financial information versus those performed for other information, the general principles related to the level of assurance and the relationship between the level of assurance and evidence applies to all reviews, regardless of the type of information. We will discuss the other types of review engagements later in the chapter.

Level of Assurance and Users' Needs

Many nonpublic companies have their financial statements reviewed or compiled by a public accountant. The opening vignette about Menard Construction is an

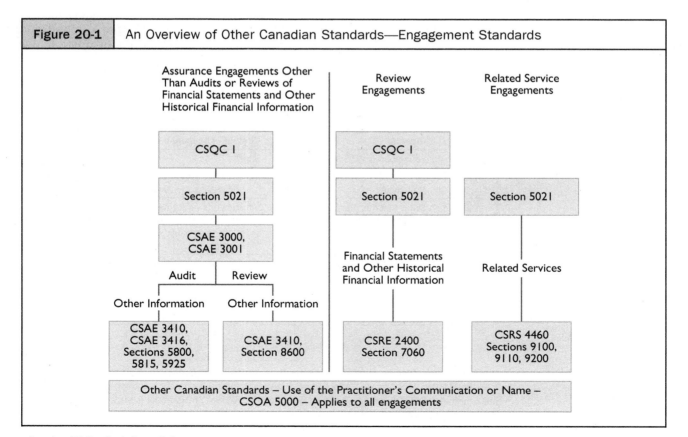

| Figure 20-1 | An Overview of Other Canadian Standards—Engagement Standards |

Based on CPA Handbook, Appendix 4

example of a review engagement. A company's management may believe an audit to be unnecessary because no bank or regulatory agency requires audited financial statements. Instead, the company's management may engage a public accountant to perform either a review or a compilation engagement. For instance, an organization may apply for a loan from a bank to be secured by its inventory and receivables. As a condition of the loan, the bank may request monthly information and limited assurance on the annual financial statements. Recall that in Chapter 1, we discussed information risk; the bank is minimizing information risk through the monthly statements, and because of the size of the loan, limited assurance is considered sufficient. A review provides limited assurance on the financial statements, whereas a compilation provides no assurance. In the case of small loans, lenders often put little weight on the financial statements and minimize the risk of default through specific collateral. As Table 20-1 highlights, the type of assurance that the PA provides depends upon the users' needs.

CAS

The standards for review engagements and compilations of financial statements are covered in the Other Canadian Standards (OSC) part of the *CPA Canada Handbook*. The relevant standard is CSRE 2400, *Engagements to review historical financial statements*. This standard is based upon the International Standard, ISRE 2400, with some modifications to reflect the needs of Canadian practitioners. For compilations, the relevant standard is OCS 9200.[1] Because they are not performing audits, the OCSs refer to those PAs performing review or compilation services as practitioners or accountants, not auditors.[2]

Because the assurance provided by reviews and compilations is considerably below that of audits, less evidence is required for these services and they can be provided at a lower fee than an audit. While cost is one of the factors that contributes to the demand for reviews and compilations, as highlighted in Table 20-1, users' needs and regulatory requirements are what determines the appropriate level of assurance. Figure 20-2 illustrates the difference in evidence accumulation and level of assurance needed for each engagement. As Figure 20-2 highlights, reasonable assurance provides a high level of assurance, limited assurance is moderate, and a compilation provides no assurance. In the case of all three engagements, the amount of assurance and evidence needed is not specifically defined by the profession and, therefore, it

Table 20-1	Matching the Engagement With the Users' Assurance Needs
Financial Statement Users	**Suitable Engagement**
Stakeholders of a publicly accountable entity	Audit
A private company that has outside investors or external financing	An audit, review, or compilation depending upon the assurance needs of the stakeholders
A private company that has plans to grow and attract new stakeholders and financing	An audit or a review, depending upon the assurance needs of the stakeholders. If the company has plans to go public, then an audit would be advisable.
Family members and a few close friends of a private company	A review or a compilation, depending upon how involved the users are with the company operations
Management and for the tax returns	A review or a compilation

[1] At the time of writing, the AASB has issued a consultation paper, "Compilation Engagements: Exploring Options for Change" and has held several roundtables to consider the scope of such engagements. The new standard will take into consideration International Standard on Related Services (ISRS) 4400, *Compilation engagements*.

[2] CSRE 2400, *Engagements to review historical financial statements*, uses the term "practitioner" whereas OSC 9200 uses the term "accountant."

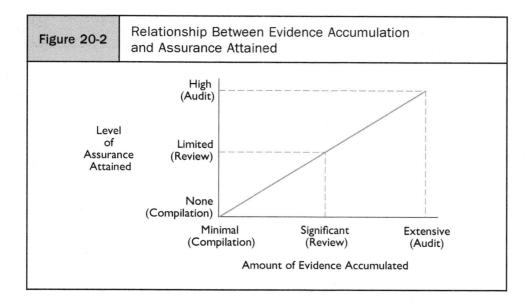

| Figure 20-2 | Relationship Between Evidence Accumulation and Assurance Attained |

depends upon the public accountant's professional judgment. Table 20-2 compares audits, reviews, and compilations.

As mentioned in Chapter 3, a common type of client litigation is related to misunderstanding over the types of services being provided. Because review and compilation services provide considerably less assurance than audits, and misunderstandings can occur around the type of service being provided, the accountant should establish an understanding with the client about the services provided through a written engagement letter. The understanding should include a description of the objectives of the engagement, management's responsibilities, the accountant's responsibilities, the type and limitations of the service to be provided, and a description of the compilation or review report that will be issued. In the following discussion, the requirements for review and compilation services are discussed in greater detail.

Limited assurance—the level of assurance obtained where engagement risk is reduced to a level that is acceptable in the circumstances of the engagement, but where the risk is greater than for a reasonable assurance engagement; also referred to as moderate assurance. It is expressed in the form of negative assurance as to the PA's awareness of any information indicating that the assertions are not presented in conformity with the applicable criteria.

THE REVIEW ENGAGEMENT PROCESS

A **review engagement** allows the accountant to express **limited assurance** that the financial statements are in accordance with the applicable accounting standards. This is a key difference from the objective of the audit, which is to obtain reasonable assurance to support a positive opinion on whether the financial statements are fairly presented. The review engagement report is limited to a conclusion whether the accountant became aware of any matter that may cause the financial statements to be materially misstated.

As Figure 20-2 highlights, reviews involve a level of assurance somewhere between that of an audit and the absence of assurance provided by a compilation.

LO 3 Understand the requirements for review engagements and discuss relevant professional standards.

Review engagement—nonaudit engagement that consists primarily of inquiry, analytical procedures, and discussion. The practitioner's conclusion is based upon the practitioner obtaining limited assurance.

Table 20-2	Comparison of Audit, Review, and Compilations of Historical Financial Statements			
Engagement	**Standards**	**Assurance**	**Work Effort**	**Form of Conclusion**
Audit	CASs	Reasonable	Risk assessment and procedures that respond to risks identified	Positive opinion
Review	CSRS 2400	Limited	Primarily inquiry and analysis	Conclusion on what came to the PA's attention
Compilation	OCS 9200	None	Assisting management prepare financial statements	Report stating no assurance is provided

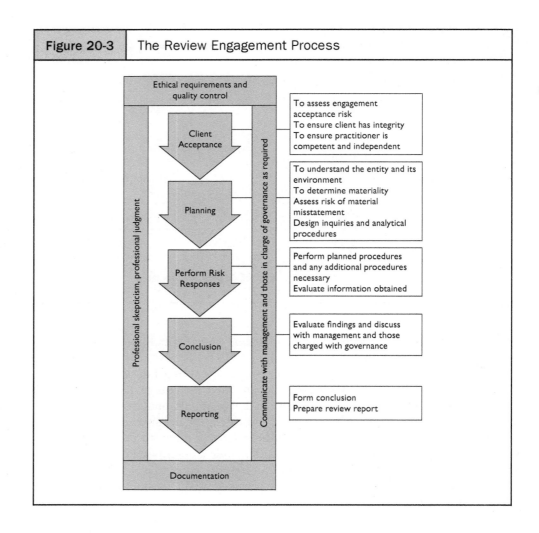

Figure 20-3 | The Review Engagement Process

In the review engagement, the practitioner assesses the plausibility of the information using appropriate criteria. Due to the level of assurance, the accountant would mainly rely upon inquiry, analytical procedures, and discussion during the engagement. A review generally does not involve substantive tests such as independent confirmation, nor does it involve tests of controls. However, if inquiry and analytical procedures do not provide adequate assurance, then the practitioner will need to perform further procedures.

The limited level of assurance of the review engagement does not exempt the practitioner from applying an appropriate level of professional skepticism. As highlighted in the opening case, Renée's professional skepticism caused her to question the rationale behind Tony's decision and alerted her to the possibility that the financial statements were materially misstated. Her attempt to obtain outside confirmation (the request for a listing) from the promoter did not dispel her earlier suspicion; if anything, it reinforced her earlier suspicions, and led her to conclude that she should resign from the engagement.

Figure 20-3 summarizes the review engagement process. You will note that, with the exception of the types of procedures (inquiries and analytical), it is quite similar to the audit process.

Perform Acceptance and Continuance Procedures

As in the case of an audit of financial statements, the public accountant will perform acceptance and continuance procedures. The procedures, which are similar to an audit engagement, include determining the purpose of the review engagement, that the practitioner has access to all information and permission to speak to the appropriate people, and that the deadlines are realistic. At this stage, the practitioner will take into consideration the integrity of management and, in the case of continuing engagements, any past disputes with management. The practitioner should only accept a review engagement if the accountant has the necessary competence and is independent of the client.

Determine Materiality

In the case of review engagements, the practitioner determines materiality based upon the financial statements as a whole and applies that materiality in designing procedures and evaluating results. As in the case of the audit, materiality is based upon the extent to which misstatements would affect the economic decisions of an informed group of users. However, because a review engagement is based upon inquiry and analytical review, there is no need to determine performance materiality (which is used to determine the extent of testing for classes of transactions, balances, and disclosures).

Obtain an Understanding of the Entity

In order to obtain an understanding of the entity, the practitioner should consider:

- The nature of the client's organization (including "tone at the top" and the control environment through which the entity addresses risks related to financial reporting) and business transactions;
- Its accounting records and employees;
- The basis, form, and content of the financial statements; and
- Accounting matters peculiar to the client's business and industry.

Note that the practitioner does not have a responsibility to evaluate the design of controls, to determine whether they have been implemented, or to evaluate their operating effectiveness. Therefore, the understanding is based upon inquiry (and is much less comprehensive than an audit).

Without adequate understanding of the entity, the practitioner would not be able to adequately assess the risk of misstatement or make informed inquiries. For instance, it would be difficult to assess the plausibility of manufactured inventory if the practitioner did not have an understanding of the company's products and manufacturing processes. Similarly, if the practitioner discovers that the system for tracking revenue does not work well, then this knowledge will assist the practitioner in designing specific inquiries and analytical procedures, as well as additional procedures.

Design Inquiries and Analytical Procedures

Since the review engagement provides limited assurance, the PA develops procedures that address all material financial statement areas and any likely misstatements. Procedures are normally limited to inquiry, analytical procedures, and discussion. It is not necessary to design substantive tests or tests of controls.

Perform Planned Procedures and Any Additional Procedures Necessary

The two key types of procedures are inquiry and analytical procedures. The objective of inquiries is to seek information from management and other people in the entity in order to determine whether the financial statements are fairly presented. Part of the purpose of performing inquiries is to evaluate responses provided by management and others.

Analytical procedures involve the analysis of financial information through evaluation of relationships among financial and nonfinancial information. Analytical procedures are used to identify areas where material misstatements may exist based upon the practitioner's initial inquiries. They also identify inconsistencies or variances from expected trends, values, or norms in the financial statements, and they provide corroborative evidence in relation to other inquiries and analytical procedures already performed.

When the practitioner becomes aware of a matter that suggests the financial statements may be materially misstated, the practitioner must conduct more extensive procedures. These additional procedures may be warranted because the plausibility of the evidence is questionable. For instance, in our opening vignette, Renée's request for a listing from an outside third party, the promoter, represents an audit procedure. In the case of Renée, the explanations appeared suspicious and not reliable; therefore, she had to perform more extensive procedures. Additional procedures may also be warranted in areas that the practitioner has identified as being at high risk of material misstatement due to inadequate controls.

Evaluate the Information Obtained

In order to determine the sufficiency and appropriateness of evidence, the practitioner would ask whether the procedures performed provided the anticipated evidence. If not, additional procedures are required. As with the completion of the audit, the practitioner evaluates the results of the procedures performed and considers whether any key matters could cause the financial statements to be materially misstated.

Evaluate Findings and Discuss With Management or Those Charged With Governance

As in the case of an audit, the practitioner will accumulate and evaluate uncorrected misstatements. Although it is not required for the practitioner to request that management adjust the misstatements, it is considered best practice. The practitioner will also discuss with those in charge of governance significant matters such as use and application of accounting policies; the calculation and reasonableness of estimates; material uncertainties that cast significant doubt regarding going concern; any disagreements with management and how they were resolved; whether or not misstatements were corrected; the wording of the practitioner's conclusion in the review report; and any other relevant matters.

Form a Conclusion and Issue a Review Engagement Report

In order to form a conclusion about the financial statements, the practitioner takes into consideration identified misstatements and omissions, along with the implications of any uncorrected misstatements. The conclusion, whether modified or unmodified, is expressed in a prescribed review engagement report. Figure 20-4 provides an example of a review engagement report issued under CSRE 2400 and explains its components. You will note that the report clearly makes a distinction that it is less extensive than an audit and that the conclusion states, "nothing has come to our attention," which provides considerably less assurance than an audit opinion.

Modifications to Review Engagement Report Like audits, modifications may be required to the review engagement report under certain circumstances. As in the case of an audit, the practitioner will modify his or her conclusion when the practitioner determines the financial statements are materially misstated or when the practitioner is unable to obtain sufficient appropriate evidence. Depending upon the circumstances, the practitioner will use the heading "qualified conclusion," "adverse conclusion," or "disclaimer of a conclusion" and a separate paragraph describing the matter giving rise to the modification.

Figure 20-4	The Standard Review Engagement Report Explained

INDEPENDENT PRACTITIONERS' REVIEW ENGAGEMENT REPORT

The report is addressed to the members or shareholders of the organization. In this case it is the owner.	To R. Fortin
This section sets out the basic details of the engagement: the applicable reporting period, name of company, and what was audited.	We have reviewed the accompanying financial statements of Leger Inc. that comprise the balance sheet as at December 31, 2018, and the statement of income, retained earnings, and cash flows for the year then ended, and a summary of significant accounting policies and other explanatory.
Management is responsible for preparing the financial statements according to applicable accounting framework (in this case ASPE) and for internal controls in the company.	*Management's Responsibility for the Financial Statements* Management is responsible for the preparation and fair presentation of these financial statements in accordance with Canadian accounting standards for private enterprises, and for such internal control as management determines is necessary to enable the preparation of financial statements that are free from material misstatements, whether due to fraud or error.
The practitioner is expressing a conclusion, not an opinion as in the case of an audit on the financial statements. This section also provides a brief description of a review engagement and clearly indicates that it is substantially less work than an audit.	*Practitioners' Responsibility* Our responsibility is to express a conclusion on these financial statements. We conducted our review in accordance with Canadian Standard on Review Engagements (CSRE) 2400, Engagements to Review Historical Financial Statements. CSRE requires us to conclude whether anything has come to our attention that causes us to believe that the financial statements, taken as a whole, are not prepared in all material aspects in accordance with the applicable financial reporting framework. This standard also requires us to comply with relevant ethical requirements. A review of financial statements in accordance with CSRE 2400 is a limited assurance engagement. The practitioner performs procedures, primarily consisting of making inquiries to management and others within the entity, as appropriate, and applying analytical procedures, and evaluates the evidence obtained. The procedures performed in a review are substantially less in extent than, and vary in nature from, those performed in an audit conducted in accordance with Canadian Auditing Standards. Accordingly, we do not express an audit opinion on these financial statements.
The practitioner states his or her conclusion. It is in the form of a negative: "nothing has come to our attention." This is an example of an unmodified conclusion.	*Conclusion* Based on our review, nothing has come to our attention that causes us to believe that these financial statements do not present fairly, in all material respects, the financial position of Leger Inc. as at December 31, 2018, and the results of its operations and its cash flows for the year then ended in accordance with Canadian accounting standards for private enterprises. Montreal Quebec [signature of] March 1, 2019 Chartered Professional Accountants

If the financial statements include a going concern note and the disclosure is adequate, CSRE 2400 requires the addition of an emphasis of matter paragraph. The following is an example of the suggested wording:

Emphasis of Matter

Without qualifying our conclusion, we draw attention to Note W in the financial statements, which indicates that the Company incurred a net loss of ZZZ during the year ended December 31, 20XX, and, as of that date, the Company's current liabilities exceeded its total assets by YYY. These conditions, along with other matters as set forth in Note W, indicate the existence of a material uncertainty that may cast significant doubt about the Company's ability to continue as a going concern.

CSRE 2400 also highlights other circumstances when another matter paragraph is required to be included: when another practitioner reported on the prior period's financial statements, and when the prior period financial statements had not been subjected to a review or audit engagement.

COMPILATION ENGAGEMENTS

LO **4** Understand the requirements for compilation engagements and discuss relevant professional standards.

Compilation engagement—non-audit engagement in which the public accountant provides assistance in compiling financial statements but is not expected to provide assurance about the statements.

CAS

The objective of a **compilation engagement** is to compile unaudited financial information into financial statement format based upon the information provided by the client. This is a common service provided by smaller public accounting firms, which mainly provide bookkeeping services, monthly or quarterly financial statements, and tax services for smaller clients. A compilation engagement is often suitable for small businesses or businesses owned by one person or family members, and usually when there are not any lenders or insurers who rely upon the statements. Sometimes, as we will discuss in interim financial information, a compilation is requested to supplement an annual audit or a review engagement.

The applicable standard for compilations of financial statements is OCS 9200. (At the time of writing, the AASB was in the process of consulting with various stakeholders; an exposure draft is anticipated in the second half of 2018). Refer back to Figure 20-1 and you will note that this section falls into the category of Other Related Services—those for which the PA does not provide any assurance. As explained in OCS 9200, the public accountant provides assistance in compiling financial statements but is not required to provide any assurance about the statements. Therefore, the engagement is not an assurance engagement. The statements may be complete (i.e., they include a balance sheet, income statement, statement of retained earnings, and cash flow statement); they may be part of a complete set of financial statements; or they may be for the whole enterprise or for a part of the enterprise.

In a compilation engagement, the accountant assembles the information supplied by the client and ensures that it is arithmetically correct. It is the most basic service that a PA can offer and it usually involves assistance with bookkeeping, posting adjusting entries, and preparing the annual tax return. Unlike an audit or a review, in a compilation engagement, the accountant does not provide any assurance as to the accuracy or completeness of the information or whether the financial statements comply with an acceptable financial reporting framework. However, the PA must still comply with professional standards and abide by basic accounting principles. This means that despite providing no level of assurance on the financial statements, the PA must apply professional judgment and consider the reasonability of the information provided by the client. As explained in CSOA 5000, Use of the Practitioner's Communication or Name (which applies to all engagements), the accountant cannot knowingly be associated with false or misleading financial statements.

As one can imagine that, due to the accountant's limited involvement, determining whether the statements are false or misleading can be difficult. Despite the difficulty, this does not absolve the accountant from any responsibility. OCS 9200.12 sets out the criteria for accepting a compilation engagement: the accountant must have

Not-for-profit organizations (NPOs) do not have shareholders, but they do have boards of directors. These directors are elected by members, rather than shareholders, so the accountant needs to find out how membership is determined. Although the independence standard allows an accountant who is a member of a not-for-profit organization (such as a golf and country club) to perform a review engagement, some may view this as a conflict of interest. In order to safeguard against this perceived threat, the accountant may request a bylaw stating that the accountant cannot vote for board members. This is particularly relevant, since the accountant must report a number of issues to the audit committee (a subcommittee of the board).

Important issues for NPOs include the following:

- *Awareness of fraud risks.* Is leadership organized, rather than chaotic, and aware of the risks of fraud? Are random supervision and volunteer/staff rotation used to encourage early detection? Does the environment make it easy to report suspicious behaviour?

- *Completeness of revenues.* Are numbered receipts issued? How is fundraising handled? What is the mix between government grants and fundraising?

- *Valuation of donated assets or services.* How are donated services or donated assets valued? Are charitable donation receipts given for these items and services? Are valued amounts defensible for tax purposes? Is volunteer time recorded at nil?

- *Existence of donated assets.* Are these items added to a capital assets ledger, even if they were donated and have been recorded at a nil value?

- *Compliance with regulations.* Are funds disbursed in accordance with their intended purpose? Is an accounting system in place that properly tracks and distributes restricted funds? How does the NPO ensure that directors do not receive any funds or benefits?

---

no reason to believe that the statements are false or misleading, and the client must clearly understand the nature and scope of the engagement, including its limitations. In particular, OCS 9200.12 states that the PA should be clear that the client understands that the statements may not be appropriate for general use and uniformed readers may be misled unless they are aware of the possible limitations of the statements and the PA's limited involvement.

Performance Standards

The compilation services should be performed and the report prepared by individuals who have adequate technical training and proficiency in accounting, and who complete their work with due care. Like other types of engagements, planning and proper conduct of the work is required. Any assistants should be properly supervised. Unlike assurance engagements, the accountant is not required to be independent. However, an independence threat analysis is still required and if the conclusion is that an independence threat remains, it should be disclosed.

If something comes to the attention of the public accountant indicating that the financial statements may be false or misleading, additional information must be obtained and the statements amended, or the accountant should resign from the engagement.

Form of Report

The communication from the public accountant in a compilation engagement is entitled "Notice to Reader." Each page of the statements should include either the "Notice to Reader" heading itself or the statement "Unaudited—See Notice to Reader." Figure 20-5 is an example of a Notice to Reader. The report states that the accountant has not audited or otherwise checked the information that was provided by management. Because the statements might not be in accordance with an acceptable financial reporting framework, the report also includes a warning with respect to the use of the financial statements. Departures from an acceptable financial reporting framework should not be referred to in the report, as this may suggest that the public accountant has a responsibility to detect and report all such departures. However,

Figure 20-5	Example of a Compilation Report With an Independence Threat

NOTICE TO READER

On the basis of information provided by management, I have compiled the balance sheet of New B Ltd. as at March 31, 2018, and the statements of income, retained earnings, and cash flows for the year then ended.

I have not performed an audit or a review engagement in respect of these financial statements and, accordingly, I express no assurance thereon.

Readers are cautioned that these statements may not be appropriate for their purposes.

A partner in this accounting firm owns 37 percent of the Class A shares and 15 percent of Class B of New B Ltd.

Halifax, N.S.
June 12, 2018

R. Fundy

Chartered Accountant

if the public accountant is aware that such departures are misleading to the users, then the PA should consider whether it is necessary to withdraw from the engagement.

As mentioned earlier, since a compilation engagement is not an assurance engagement, the PA is not required to be independent. However, in the interest of transparency, the Independence Standard in the Rules of Professional Conduct requires that the independence threat must be disclosed in the notice to reader. This means that the accountant must perform (and document) an independence threat analysis. The example in Figure 20-5 includes disclosure when there is a threat to independence that is not adequately safeguarded.

LO 5 Explain review engagements of interim financial statements.

REVIEW OF INTERIM FINANCIAL STATEMENTS

Interim financial statements may be audited, reviewed, or compiled by a public accountant. The decision depends on how much assurance is desired from the accountant's involvement and how timely the information must be. Estimates normally have to be made in order to prepare the information on a timely basis. Therefore, the information may not be as reliable as annual financial information. Since the objective of producing interim financial information is to provide up-to-date information to users of the statements, such information is usually not audited.

OCS 7060, *Auditor review of interim financial statements*, provides guidance for review of a public company's financial statements for a financial reporting period that is shorter than the fiscal year. (The 7000 series of the Other Canadian Standards of the *CPA Canada Handbook* refers to special reporting engagements specific to securities legislation.) Unlike companies listed on the American stock exchanges, companies listed on Canadian exchanges are not required to engage the auditor to perform a review of interim financial statements. Despite this, many Canadian companies do have the auditor perform the interim review. However, the review report is not public and is provided to the audit committee.[3] Since the purpose of

---

[3] Although the review engagement report is not public, the companies are required to disclose whether or not the external auditor conducted a review of the interim financial statements.

this type of engagement is to provide assistance to the audit committee, as indicated in the standard, the distribution of the report is restricted. The auditor can provide written consent to include the interim review report in a prospectus only if it is required by securities legislation.

The key objective of this type of review is for the auditor to obtain a basis for reporting to the audit committee as to whether the auditor is aware of any material modification that should be made to the interim financial statements for those statements to be in accordance with the applicable financial reporting framework. The auditor also reads the interim management discussion and analysis (MD&A) to ensure that the information is not materially inconsistent with the interim financial statements.

CONCEPT CHECK

C20-1 What is an important difference between a compilation engagement and a review engagement?

C20-2 Evaluate the following statement: "For a compilation engagement, the accountant does not check the financial statements, so they are very likely to contain material misstatements."

C20-3 If reviews provide less assurance than audits, and compilations provide no assurance, why is there a demand for these types of services?

C20-4 What is the difference between the review reports for a private company under CSRE 2400 and the interim financial statements for a public company?

ASSURANCE ENGAGEMENTS FOR NONFINANCIAL INFORMATION

LO **6** Explain the umbrella assurance standards for nonfinancial information.

CAS

Assurance Engagement—An engagement in which the practitioner obtains sufficient appropriate evidence in order to express a conclusion designed to enhance the degree of confidence of the intended users other than the responsible party about the outcome of the measurement or evaluation of an underlying subject matter against criteria.

As we learned in Chapter 1, there are many more types of nonfinancial information for which public accountants can provide assurance, such as human rights, health and safety, carbon emissions, and even the ballot process of the Academy Awards. The standards to which practitioners would refer to for this type of information are CSAE 3000, *Attestation engagements other than audits or reviews of historical financial information*, and CSAE 3001, *Direct engagements*. These two standards are what are referred to as the "umbrella standards" and are meant to cover a broad range of **assurance engagements** on a wide variety of underlying subject matter. Table 20-3 highlights the variety of potential subject matter that public accountants could potentially provide assurance.

Table 20-3	Types of Information and Assurance Engagements	
Type of Information	**Examples**	**Applicable Standards**
Financial performance or conditions	Historical financial statements	CASs, CAS 800, 805, CSAE 2400
	Nonhistorical (pro-forma) statements	
Nonfinancial performance or conditions	Environmental performance or corporate social responsibility reports	CSAE 3000, 3001, CSAE 3416
	Key performance indicators which show efficiency of particular area	
Physical characteristics	Existence of mineral reserves or production capacity of machinery	CSAE 3000, CSAE 3001
Systems and processes	Internal controls	CSAE 3410, CSAE 5925
	Outsourced activities (payroll, IT, etc.)	
Behaviour	Corporate governance, human resource practices, compliance with laws, regulations, policies, labour practices	CSAE 3000, 3001, OSC 5815

Source: The information and examples are extracted from: Institute of Chartered Accountants of England and Wales, 2007. Assurance: Engaging Practitioners.

It is important to note that the concepts in the assurance framework of CSAE 3000 and 3001 are not new—they have always been present in the financial statement audit. However, given the nature of the different types of subject matter, criteria, and the associated challenges related to providing assurance, standards have been developed to provide practitioners with the necessary guidance. These engagements are carried out in the same manner as any audit or review of historical financial statements. As in the case of other assurance engagements, the auditor must be independent, be competent, and comply with the ethical requirements. Below are the three performance standards:

- The work should be adequately planned, and there should be proper supervision.
- The practitioner should consider both significance (similar to materiality) and engagement risk (similar to audit risk) when planning and performing the engagement.
- Sufficient evidence should be gathered to support the conclusion the practitioner expresses in his or her report.

The umbrella standards encompass both high and moderate assurance engagements, as well as attestation and direct reporting engagements. As in the case of historical financial statements, determining the appropriate level of assurance is based upon the users' assurance needs (which may be defined by regulatory requirement); however, due to the nature of the particular subject matter, it may not be possible to provide reasonable assurance. As you can well imagine, this decision requires considerable professional judgment. We will discuss this in more depth shortly.

Recall from Chapter 1 that an **attestation engagement** involves the auditor evaluating the information, using suitable criteria, assessing the preparer's (usually management) assertions, and issuing a report that attests to the reliability of the information. With the exception of compilations, all the engagements we have discussed up to this point, including the historical financial statement audit, have been attestation engagements.

In the case of a **direct engagement** (or *direct reporting engagement*), the auditee does not make a public assertion or prepare a report such as a set of financial statements. In these types of engagements, the assertion is implied. The auditor directly measures or evaluates the underlying subject matter against the criteria, and issues a report that includes the subject matter information and a conclusion as to whether the subject matter conforms to the applicable criteria. The best examples of comprehensive direct reporting engagements based upon CSAE 3001 are the special examinations performed by the various auditors general, including the Auditor General of Canada.[4] Table 20-4 below illustrates the key differences between a CSAE 3000 attestation engagement and a CSAE 3001 direct engagement, using the example of a performance (or value-for-money) audit of a hospital's emergency room.

Apply Professional Judgment to Assurance of Nonfinancial Information

These types of engagements require the practitioner to exercise considerable professional judgment. When faced with a request to provide assurance regarding nonfinancial information, the public accountant first needs to consider whether assurance can actually be provided. We next provide an overview of some key factors that the auditor considers in order to determine (1) whether an assurance engagement can be conducted, (2) what level of assurance can be provided, and (3) which type of engagement to perform.

Attestation engagement—a special form of assurance engagement, such as a financial statement audit, in which the auditor evaluates the information provided by one party, using suitable criteria, and issues a report about the reliability of this information to another party.

Direct engagement—a special form of assurance engagement, such as the Report of the Auditor General of Canada, in which the auditor directly measures and evaluates the underlying subject matter against the criteria, and issues a report that includes the subject matter information and a conclusion as to whether the subject matter conforms to the applicable criteria.

LO 7 Apply professional judgment to the issues related to conducting assurance engagements for nonfinancial information.

---

[4] For more details, refer to Auditor General of Canada, *Direct Engagement Manual*, April 2017, accessed October 15, 2017, at **http://www.oag-bvg.gc.ca/internet/methodology/performance-audit/manual/index.shtm**.

Table 20-4	Comparison of Attestation and Direct Engagements	
	CSAE 3000 – Attestation Engagement	**CSAE 3001 – Direct Engagement**
Measurer/Evaluator	Hospital Management	Practitioner
Underlying Subject Matter	Activities of an emergency department in hospital	
Suitable Criteria	Selected or developed based upon regulations and best practices	
Subject Matter information	Measurement/evaluation by management of emergency department against suitable criteria	Measurement/evaluation by practitioner of emergency department against suitable criteria
Assurance Conclusion	Whether management's assessment of value for money is appropriate	Whether emergency department provides value for money or not

Accountability Relationship A simple question that the auditor can ask to help assess whether there is a three-way accountability relationship is: "Who will benefit from the assurance?" As mentioned in Chapter 1, an assurance engagement involves three separate parties: a practitioner, an accountable party (usually management), and the intended users of the report. If a three-way accountability relationship does not exist, then the practitioner may recommend a non-assurance engagement such as a consulting engagement (discussed in Chapter 1).

As we have highlighted in the audit of the financial statements, the accountable party (management) must acknowledge its responsibility for the subject matter to ensure that a proper relationship exists between the practitioner and the accountable party. Further, the practitioner must be able to identify the intended users so as to be able to determine the appropriate criteria to assess the subject matter and to determine materiality.

Appropriate Subject Matter The practitioner needs to determine whether there exists an appropriate underlying subject matter—one that is capable of consistent measurement or evaluation against identifiable criteria—as well as whether evidence is available to support the practitioner's conclusion.

Suitable Criteria It can also be quite difficult to determine suitable criteria since the underlying subject matter is often qualitative in nature, rather than quantitative, and involves complex systems and processes. For instance, what criteria would a practitioner use when asked to provide assurance of the sustainability activity of an oil and gas company? Criteria are the benchmarks against which the subject matter is evaluated. For example, in the case of the audit or review of the historical financial statements, the criteria are the relevant accounting framework (e.g., ASPE or IFRS). In the case of effectiveness of internal controls, the criterion is COSO. The umbrella standards recommend that the criteria be:

- relevant (to the users' decision making);
- reliable (allows consistent evaluation);
- neutral (free of bias);
- understandable (by the users); and
- complete (including benchmarks for presentation and disclosure).

In the case of the hospital emergency room the practitioner may have to use some combination of relevant regulatory standards and the company's own policies and practices to evaluate the subject matter. However, it would still be difficult for the practitioner to determine the appropriate criteria—particularly if the subject matter were outside his or her area of expertise. It may also be difficult to identify suitable criteria when the practitioner is carrying out a new type of assurance engagement for which criteria have not been established; while the practitioner may determine criteria relevant to the engagement, there may be other criteria that could assess the subject matter as well. Therefore, in order to avoid misunderstandings, it is important that the practitioner clearly communicate the criteria to the users.

Ability to Obtain Sufficient and Appropriate Evidence When considering whether the practitioner has the ability to obtain sufficient and appropriate evidence, he or she considers the nature of the subject matter and the criteria, as well as the practitioner's ability to evaluate the evidence. It is thus not surprising that, in many of these engagements, it is necessary to have a multidisciplinary team in order to perform the engagement. As in the case of audits and reviews of historical financial information, the nature and extent of the audit evidence is a matter of professional judgment based upon the practitioner's assessment of materiality, risk of misstatement, and the quality and quantity of the available evidence.

Level of Assurance When determining the appropriate level of assurance on financial statements, the practitioner focuses on the users' assurance needs. However, when providing assurance for information that does not have such well-defined or established standards and/or is not so easily quantifiable, it is also necessary to take into consideration the criteria and the subject matter. Not surprisingly, many of these assurance engagements are reviews (limited assurance) rather than audits (reasonable assurance). Auditing in Action 20-2, provides some insight into the challenges associated with providing assurance over information, in this case integrated reports (the subject matter), that have vague standards (the criteria).

Materiality and Significance Another decision that requires considerable judgment is determining the appropriate level of significance (the term used in CSAE 3001) or materiality (CSAE 3000). Like the financial statement audit, materiality is based upon common information needs of the intended users as a group. However, unlike the financial statement audit, the quantitative thresholds have not been firmly established (or may not even be relevant) and for many of these engagements, the users and their needs are not easily defined. Therefore, defining an appropriate materiality is much more difficult.

It also requires considerable professional judgment to determine whether a misstatement is material or whether a deviation is significant. Per CSAE 3000, since management measures and assesses the subject matter, the objective of an attestation engagement is to obtain reasonable assurance or limited assurance about whether the subject matter information is free from material misstatement. A misstatement is defined as a difference between the subject matter information and

AUDITING IN ACTION 20-2
Assurance on Integrated Reporting: A Work in Progress

While many claim that integrated reporting is the next major evolution of corporate reporting, it still remains very much a work in progress. For instance, although South African listed companies have been required to issue integrated reports since 2010, those companies are still trying to figure out what to include in those reports, how they are going to collect the relevant data, and what stakeholders actually want.

Since there is a general consensus that integrated reporting adds value, it is logical that users would want assurance over these reports. However, a recent study of assurance providers in South Africa shows that several technical challenges must be overcome before being able to provide assurance over the entire report. The current practice is to express an opinion on the financial statements and to provide limited or reasonable assurance on specific elements of the integrated report. The downside of these types of engagements is that they are limited in scope, focusing on the more factual subject matter while excluding the forward-looking information and subjective management assessments that investors find to be the most useful.

Several reasons explain why these engagements are limited in scope. Some of the assurance providers interviewed for the study felt that the current IIRC framework (the criteria by which the subject matter is evaluated) was too vague, thus making it difficult to provide assurance. Others noted that the degree of judgment exercised by management in deciding what to include in the report makes it impossible to assess the completeness assertion. To overcome those challenges, some interviewees suggested an "integrated assurance model" may be needed to overcome these challenges. As this point in time, it is difficult to predict if the standard setters will consider this sort of model.

Source: Based on William Maroun and Jill Atkins, *The Challenges of Assuring Integrated Reports: Views from the South African Auditing Community*, London: Association of Chartered Certified Accountants, 2015.

appropriate measurement or evaluation in accordance with criteria. The objective of a CSAE 3001 engagement is to obtain either reasonable or limited assurance about whether the underlying subject matter conforms, in a material respect, to the applicable criteria. Instead of a material misstatement, this standard uses the term *significant deviation*.

Regardless of the terminology, determining a material misstatement or significant deviation requires considerable professional judgment. For instance, referring back to our performance audit for a hospital's emergency room (Table 20-4), let's assume that the criteria include the speed of the services provided, the quality of the services, the number of patients treated during a shift, and the cost of the services, measured against other similar hospitals. If the first three criteria are satisfied but the last one is not satisfied by a small margin, is that a material misstatement or a significant deviation? Needless to say, professional judgment is needed to conclude whether the hospital's emergency department represents value for money as a whole.

In the case of sustainability reporting, several organizations are attempting to provide guidance on how to determine materiality. For instance, the Sustainability Accounting Standards Board proposes that a highly material issue would be one that is important to stakeholders (defined as what "a reasonable investor" would be concerned about), and that has the potential of a significant financial impact (i.e., profits [revenue and/or costs], assets and liabilities, and/or cost of capital). However, several commentators have suggested that this type of definition is too narrow since it only focuses on the users' economic decisions.

Type of Engagement and Report The final outcome of the assurance engagement is the assurance report. As discussed earlier, whether the engagement is an attestation versus a direct engagement is dependent upon who measures and evaluates the subject matter against a certain criteria. The attestation report prepared in Figure 20-6 issued by the Auditor General of British Columbia with regard to the Vancouver Community College's Statement of Full-time Equivalent (FTE) Enrollment, illustrates the basic components of a CSAE 3000 attestation report with a reasonable [CAS] assurance opinion.

Direct engagement reports are tailored to the specific characteristics of the engagement and can be quite lengthy. Figure 20-7 provides a brief extract of a reasonable assurance direct report, prepared by the Auditor General of Canada, regarding the systems and practices for corporate and operations management of the Canadian Museum of Nature. The report itself was 31 pages and, as illustrated in Figure 20-7, the auditor used a wide variety of criteria in order to assess the subject matter and come to the conclusion.

As highlighted in Figure 20-1, there are several standards that fall under the umbrella standards, which have been specifically developed for particular subject matters. CSAE 3410, *Assurance engagements on greenhouse gas statements* (men- [CAS] tioned in Chapter 1), states that the practitioner may provide reasonable or limited assurance for this particular subject matter (in the UPS example in Chapter 1, the auditors provided limited assurance). The other two standards, CSAE 3416, *Reporting on controls at a service organization*, and OCS 5925, *An audit of internal control over financial reporting that is integrated with an audit of financial statements*, are both reasonable assurance standards that we discussed in Chapter 9 in connection with assessing the effectiveness of internal controls. Both the reports issued under these standards are attestation reports that follow the format of CSAE 3000. In addition to those three types of information, there is compliance with agreements (to which OSC 5800, 5815, and 8600 apply), which we discuss next.

CONCEPT CHECK

C20-5 Why is it so difficult to determine materiality for assurance engagements involving nonfinancial information?

Figure 20-6	Example of Attestation Engagement Report (CSAE 3000)

INDEPENDENT AUDITOR'S REPORT

To the Board of Governors of Vancouver Community College

I have audited the accompanying FTE Enrolment Statement of Vancouver Community College, for the year ended March 31, 2016, and accompanying notes.

Management's Responsibility for the FTE Enrolment Statement
Vancouver Community College's management is responsible for the preparation of the FTE Enrolment Statement and supporting schedules in accordance with the requirements of the Ministry of Advanced Education as set out in its Student FTE Enrolment Reporting Manual, and for such internal control as management determines is necessary to enable the preparation of the report that is free from material misstatement, whether due to fraud or error.

Auditor's Responsibility
It is my responsibility to express an opinion about the FTE Enrolment Statement and supporting schedules based on my audit. I conducted my audit in accordance with Canadian Standards on Assurance Engagements (CSAE 3000). Those standards require that we comply with ethical requirements and plan and perform the audit to obtain reasonable assurance about whether the enrolment report is free from material misstatement.

The Office of the Auditor General of British Columbia applies the Canadian Standards on Quality Control CSQC 1 and, accordingly, maintains a comprehensive system of quality control, including documented policies and procedures regarding compliance with ethical requirements, professional standards and applicable legal and regulatory requirements. In this respect, I have complied with the independence and other ethical requirements of the code of professional conduct of the Chartered Professional Accountants of BC, which are founded on fundamental principles of professional behaviour, integrity and due care, professional competence, confidentiality, and objectivity.

My audit involved performing procedures to obtain audit evidence about the amounts and disclosures in the FTE Enrolment Statement. I selected procedures based on my judgement including an assessment of the risks of material misstatement of the FTE Enrolment Statement, whether due to fraud or error. In making those risk assessments, I considered internal control relevant to the entity's preparation of the FTE Enrolment Statement in order to design audit procedures that are appropriate in the circumstances, but not for the purpose of expressing an opinion on the effectiveness of the entity's internal control. My audit also included evaluating the appropriateness of reporting policies used and the reasonableness of estimates made by management, as well as evaluating the overall presentation of the FTE Enrolment Statement.

In my view, the audit evidence I have obtained is sufficient and appropriate to provide a basis for my audit opinion.

Opinion
In my opinion, the FTE Enrolment Statement for the year ended March 31, 2016 is presented, in all material respects, in accordance with the requirements of the Ministry of Advanced Education as set out in its Student FTE Enrolment Reporting Manual.

Restriction on Distribution and Use
The FTE Enrolment Statement is prepared for the purpose of compliance with the Student FTE Enrolment Reporting Manual, and therefore may not be suitable for another purpose.

Other Matters
The FTE Enrolment Statement of Vancouver Community College for the year ended March 31, 2015, were audited by another professional accounting firm who expressed an unmodified opinion on those statements on May 27, 2015.

Russ Jones

Victoria, British Columbia
June 10, 2016

Russ Jones, FCPA, FCA
Deputy Auditor General

Figure 20-7	Extracts from the Direct Engagement Report—Canadian Museum of Nature (CSAE 3001)

Subject Matter

The objective of this audit was to determine whether the systems and practices we selected for examination of the Canadian Museum of Nature were providing it with reasonable assurance that its assets were safeguarded and controlled, its resources were economically managed and efficiently and its operations were carried out effectively as required by section 138 of the Financial Administration Act.

Criteria used to assess systems and processes

- Corporate Governance – Six different guidelines (i.e., OECD Guidelines on Corporate Governance of State-owned Enterprises)
- Strategic and operational planning, risk management, and performance and reporting – Six different guidelines (i.e., *20 Questions Directors Should Ask About Risk*, CPA Canada, 2006)
- Information Technology – Several IT control guidelines (e.g., COBIT 5 Framework)
- Research, Collections, and Public Offer Activities – Museum Act, Museum of Nature Corporate Plan

Conclusion

In our opinion, based on the criteria established, there were no significant deficiencies in the Canadian Museum of Nature's systems and practices that we examined for corporate management and operations management. We concluded that the Corporation has maintained these systems and practices during the period covered by the audit in a manner that provided the reasonable assurance required under section 138 of the Financial Administration Act.

Source: Based on Office of Auditor General of Canada, Report of Auditor General of Canada to the Board of Trustees of the Canadian Museum of Nature – Special Examination – 2017. Available at: oag.bvg.gc.ca.

ASSURANCE OVER COMPLIANCE WITH AGREEMENTS AND REGULATIONS

LO 8 Describe engagements to report compliance with agreements.

Recall from Chapter 1 that the compliance audit is a common type of audit performed by public accountants. In these types of engagements, the public accountant provides assurance on an entity's compliance with a particular statute, regulation, and/or agreement. It could include compliance with a funding agreement, leasing agreements, bank covenants, or performance requirements under legislation, such as hospital wait times.

The relevant standards for these types of audits, OCS 5800 and OCS 5815, are referred to as the Special Report Standards. In the case that a moderate level of assurance is more appropriate, the relevant standard is OCS 8600. At the time of writing, the AASB had re-exposed its original exposure draft and proposed to issue two new standards: CSAE 3530, *Special Considerations—Attestation Engagements to Report on Compliance*, and CSAE 3531, *Special Considerations—Direct Engagements to Report on Compliance*, which will link to CSAE 3000 and 3001 respectively.

The proposed two standards will replace OSC 5800, 5815, and 8600, and will apply to both reasonable and limited assurance engagements. The original exposure draft had proposed one standard; however, stakeholders were concerned about unnecessary confusion with regard to making a distinction between who has performed the measurement and assessment. Subject to feedback from stakeholders, the new standards will be effective for practitioner reports dated on or after April 1, 2019.

In these assurance engagements, auditors first need to clarify whether the users want assurance with regard to management's statement that it is in compliance with the particular agreement or the historical financial information or any other type of information included with management's statement that it is in compliance. If the users wish assurance on management's assertion that it is compliant with an agreement, the auditors identify the relevant provisions of the agreement or regulations (the criteria) with which the assessment of compliance applies. The auditor would need to determine how the client monitors its compliance with the provisions, and consider whether the provisions have been consistently applied. As with CSAE 3000 and 3001, the practitioner will perform a risk assessment and determine materiality or significance; given the nature of the subject matter, this can be difficult and requires considerable professional judgment. For instance, if the entity has complied with nine provisions of a relevant agreement or regulation, it will require considerable professional judgment to conclude whether the entity complied with the agreement as a whole. As in the case of all assurance engagements, the practitioner is expected to take into consideration the common information needs of the users as a group and consider the importance of the provision with which the entity did not comply.

RELATED SERVICE ENGAGEMENTS

We now turn to the left-hand side of Figure 20-1: related service engagements. In addition to compilation engagements (which we have already discussed earlier in the chapter), related services engagements include specified procedures engagements (OSC 9100 and 9110), reports on supplemental matters arising from an audit or a review engagement (CSRS 4460), and various 7000 standards related to public offerings (we discussed Section 7060 earlier; the remaining sections are beyond the scope of our textbook). In this section we will discuss two types of related services that public accountants typically perform: specified procedures engagements and reports on supplemental matters.

SPECIFIED PROCEDURES ENGAGEMENTS

LO 9 Describe specified procedures engagements.

Specified procedures engagements—engagements in which the procedures are agreed upon by the PA, the responsible party making the assertions, and the intended users of the report; there is no opinion or conclusion provided by the PA.

Specified procedures engagements are at the other end of the assurance spectrum, as they involve audit procedures but provide no assurance through an opinion or conclusion. However, unlike compilations, the practitioner must be independent in order to be able to provide the service. In these types of engagements, the auditor and management or a third-party user agrees that the engagement will be limited to certain specified procedures. The procedures should be specific and not subjective (otherwise the practitioner will have flexibility in determining the procedures). For instance, a procedure such as "perform cutoff procedures on revenue" is very much open to interpretation. As we have learned throughout the textbook, procedures should provide specific details of how, what, and why. A much better procedure would provide specific details of what to select (invoices), where to select them (from the sales journal), how many, what to examine (dates), and what to report (if the sales occurred between January 1 and December 31).

CAS

The auditor does not perform an audit or provide an opinion on the subject matter or the assertion related to the subject matter. The *CPA Canada Handbook* has two standards that address specified procedures engagements: OCS 9100, *Reports on the results of applying specified auditing procedures to financial information other than financial statements*, and OCS 9110, *Agreed upon procedures regarding internal control over financial reporting*. In this section we will only discuss OSC 9100.

CAS

This type of engagement appeals to public accountants because management or the third-party user specifies the procedures to be performed and the public accountant's report simply describes the factual results of the procedures applied, including any errors found. Imagine the difficulty a public accounting firm faces if it is asked to issue an opinion to the Real Estate Council of British Columbia that a real estate broker has complied with the Real Estate Services Act using the special report standards (OCS 5800 and OCS 5815). Instead, the BC Real Estate Council specifies the audit procedures that the public accountant must do to satisfy the Council.

If the accountant does not review or audit the financial statements of the broker, OCS 9100 would apply. (However, as we will discuss later, if the accountant was engaged to perform a review or audit of the broker, then CSR 4460 applies.) An engagement based on OCS 9100 or CSR 4460 is much easier to manage than the CSAE 3000 and/or 3001 standards. In both instances, because the accountant is not performing an assurance engagement, there is no need to determine materiality or assess internal controls.

Like all other engagements, a specified procedures engagement must be adequately planned and carried out with due care. Figure 20-8 shows an example of a report on specified procedures for accounts payable.

You will note that in order to avoid confusion over the objective of the engagement, the engagement report specifies the procedures actually performed and the

---

| **Figure 20-8** | Example of Report on Specified Auditing Procedures |

REPORT ON SPECIFIED AUDITING PROCEDURES

To: The Audit Committee, Fictional Limited

As specifically agreed with you, we have performed the following specified auditing procedures enumerated below with respect to the accounts payable of Fictional Limited as at October 31, 2018, as set forth in the accompanying schedules. Our engagement was performed in accordance with Canadian generally accepted standards for specified auditing procedures engagements. The procedures were performed to solely to assist you in evaluating the validity of the accounts payable and are summarized, along with the findings, as follows:

Specified Auditing Procedures Performed	Factual Findings	Errors or exceptions identified
1. We obtained and recalculated the mathematical accuracy of accounts payable trial balance as at October 31, 2018 prepared by Fictional Limited, and we compared the total to the balance in the related general ledger account.	We found the addition to be correct and the total amount to be in agreement.	None
2. We compared the attached list of major suppliers and the amounts owing at October 31, 2018 to each of the related names and amounts in the trial balance.	We found the amounts compared to be in agreement.	None.
3. For 25 suppliers randomly selected from the attached list we obtained suppliers' statements or requested suppliers to confirm balances owing at December 31, 2018.	We found there were suppliers' statements for all such suppliers.	None.
4. We compared statements or confirmations to the amounts referred to in 2. For amounts which did not agree, we obtained reconciliations from Fictional Limited. For reconciliations obtained, we identified and listed outstanding invoices, credit notes and outstanding cheques, each of which was greater than $1,000. We located and examined such invoices and credit notes subsequently received and cheques subsequently paid and determined that they should have in fact been listed as outstanding on the reconciliations.	We found that the amounts agreed, or with respect to amounts that did not agree, we found that Fictional Limited had prepared reconciliations and that the credit notes, invoices and outstanding cheques over $1,000 were appropriately listed as reconciling items with the following exceptions:	[Detail the exceptions]

Because the above procedures do not constitute an audit or review of the accompany schedules, we do not express any assurance on accounts payable as of October 31, 2018.

This report is solely for the purpose set forth in the first paragraph of this report and used for your information and is not to be used for any other purpose or to be distributed to any other parties without our prior written consent.

[signature of]

Boritz, Kao, Kadous & Co., LLP
December 18, 2018
Halifax, Nova Scotia

---

findings. It is only with this knowledge that a reader of the report can determine how much assurance he or she should derive from it. The report also highlights the purpose of the report, that it is not an audit or a review, and that the report should not be distributed or used by parties other than those users who agreed to the specified procedures.

LO 10 Describe reports on supplemental matters engagements.

REPORTS ON SUPPLEMENTAL MATTERS ARISING FROM AN AUDIT OR REVIEW ENGAGEMENT

Often regulators, funders, and other users want to know about specific matters regarding the entity—such as, does it maintain adequate books and records? Many would argue that the best source of information for these types of requests for supplemental information is the public accountant. However, often this information is beyond what is reported in the financial statements—that is why it is considered to be supplemental in nature.

CAS

CSR 4460 addresses circumstances when a practitioner has been asked to accept another reporting responsibility having all of the following attributes:

- The practitioner is already engaged to perform an audit or review of the financial statements.
- The practitioner has received a request from a third party, or is required by law, regulation, or agreement to provide a written report on supplemental material.
- The practitioner has not been engaged to perform an audit or a review engagement on the supplemental matter.
- No other standards are applicable to the requested report.

Like other engagements, the practitioner must adequately plan the engagement and ensure assistants are adequately supervised. The practitioner must ensure that the engagement team performing the related audit or review is aware of the other reporting responsibility. The practitioner must perform procedures necessary to form a basis for the report. The practitioner should identify the relevant criteria to assess the supplemental matter and determine if the supplemental matter complies with the criteria.

> **CONCEPT CHECK**
>
> **C20-6** If the PA does not issue an opinion or conclusion based upon the audit findings, why would a user request a specified audit procedures engagement?
>
> **C20-7** How does an engagement to report on supplemental matters differ from a specified audit procedures engagement?

CAS

Until the introduction of CSR 4460, there was no consistency among PAs when asked to report on this information: some PAs would sign a report provided by the regulator or the funder, but others would issue a Section 9100 report. However, PAs will now issue reports following the new standard. It is important to note that what distinguishes CSR 4460 engagements from OCS 9100 engagements is that, in the case of 4460 engagements, the practitioner is also engaged to perform an audit or review engagement on financial statements or other information.

LO 11 Discuss the future of assurance engagements.

THE FUTURE OF ASSURANCE SERVICES

As highlighted in Chapter 1 and in this chapter, the nature of assurance is changing: organizations are producing new kinds of reports and stakeholders want assurance on this information. For instance, many companies are now producing what integrated reports, which some claim that this is the next major evolution in corporate reporting, following financial reporting and then sustainability reporting. While most observers predict that the historical financial statement audit will remain the cornerstone of the public accounting profession, many also say that the profession will continue to evolve as it redefines its services for new forms of both financial and nonfinancial information. For instance, as highlighted in Auditing in Action 20-2, many public accounting firms are providing assurance on the integrated reports. Although the public accounting profession does not represent the only assurance provider of nonfinancial information, because of its rigorous training and standards, its members are often the preferred service providers.

On the standards front, as we have seen in this chapter and Chapter 19, assurance standards continue to evolve and change as users' needs change. This could involve reaching out to new disciplines and forming partnerships with other specialties. Even the financial statement audit world is predicted to change, to include "programmers, gamers—the 'Flash Boys' type, investigators and detectives, great communicators, scientists who understand the algorithms, and exceptional auditors and the deepest accountants."[5] Given the predicted changes, an audit career may take you in directions you never planned.

CONCEPT CHECK

C20-8 Why do assurance providers often perform limited assurance engagements for integrated reports?

---

[5] Alan MacGibbon, corporate director and former CEO of Deloitte, quoted in CPAB, *Audit Quality Symposium—Changing Expectations*, November 2014.

SUMMARY

In this chapter we focused on the various engagements that will fall under the Other Canadian Standards of the CPA Canada Assurance Handbook. We started by covering the two remaining engagements related to historical financial statements—reviews and compilations. We learned that review engagements are similar to audits; however, the level of assurance is significantly lower. The review engagement meets the users' need for assurance while being less costly than an audit engagement. Further, although compilation engagements do not provide any assurance, because the engagement is performed by a public accountant, users place value on the information compiled by the PA.

The chapter highlighted the various types of assurance engagements that public accountants can provide for nonfinancial information and the relevant standards. As in the case of a financial statement audit, practitioners must have adequate proficiency to perform the engagement, having knowledge of the business or subject matter, and the engagement must be completed with due care and an objective state of mind. However, due to the nature of the subject matter, it may be difficult to determine what is "material" or significant.

We also discussed the standards for two related services that PAs provide: specified procedures and reports on supplemental matters. Although neither engagement provides assurance, the practitioner is required to be independent and follow due care. As such, there is a demand for these types of services since they enhance the credibility of the underlying information.

We concluded with a brief discussion of the future of assurance services. Although most predict that the audit of the financial statements will remain the cornerstone of the public accounting profession, as the demand for assurance over different types of reports and information grows, it is anticipated that the public accounting profession will provide a wider range of assurance services than it does currently.

Review Questions

🌐 **20-1** **1** Explain the difference between Other Canadian Standards (OSCs) and Canadian Audit Standards (CASs).

🌐 **20-2** **2** What is meant by "level of assurance"? How does the level of assurance differ for the audit of historical financial statements, a review, and a compilation engagement?

20-3 **2** **3** What is negative assurance? Why is it used in a review engagement report?

20-4 **2** You have a new client that is a private company planning to go public in the near future. The predecessor public accountant prepared a review engagement report and the accounting framework was ASPE. What type of engagement and accounting framework would you recommend for the client? Explain why.

20-5 **2** **3** Explain how the review engagement for a nonprofit organization differs from the review engagement for a profit-oriented entity.

🌐 **20-6** **5** What is the difference between the review report for a private company under CSAE 2400 and for the interim financial statements of a public company?

🌐 **20-7** **4** Discuss the standards for compilation engagements, and explain why they differ from those for review engagements and audits.

20-8 **4** The financial statements prepared for a compilation engagement may not be complete according to an acceptable financial reporting framework. Why is this exception permitted? Provide examples of information that might be excluded.

20-9 **9** Why do public accountants prepare reports on the results of applying specified auditing procedures to financial information other than financial statements?

20-10 **9** Why do the reporting standards for specified auditing procedures state that the distribution of the report be limited to the specific users?

🌐 **20-11** **6** You have been asked to provide assurance on information contained in New Dominion's Corporate Sustainability Report. What standards would you use to perform this engagement?

🌐 **20-12** **6** Distinguish between an "attestation engagement" and a "direct reporting engagement."

20-13 **6** Explain why criteria are so important with respect to assurance engagements that fall under the umbrella assurance standards.

20-14 **6** Identify the three parties to an accountability relationship for the assurance engagement, and explain the roles of each.

Multiple Choice Questions

🌐 **20-15** **2** **3** A CPA is performing review services for a small, closely held manufacturing company. As a part of the follow-up of a significant decrease in the gross margin for the current year, the accountant discovers that there are no supporting documents for $40 000 of disbursements. The chief financial officer assures her that the disbursements are proper. What should the CPA do?

(1) Include the unsupported disbursements without further work in the statements on the grounds that she is not doing an audit.

(2) Modify the review opinion or withdraw from the engagement unless the unsupported disbursements are satisfactorily explained.

(3) Exclude the unsupported disbursements from the statements.

(4) Obtain a written representation from the chief financial officer that the disbursements are proper and should be included in the current financial statements.

20-16 **2** **4** Which of the following best describes the responsibility of the CPA in performing compilation services for a company?

(1) The CPA has to satisfy only him- or herself that the financial statements were prepared in conformity with accounting standards.

(2) The CPA must understand the client's business and accounting methods, and read the financial statements for reasonableness.

(3) The CPA should obtain an understanding of internal control and perform tests of controls.

(4) The CPA is relieved of any responsibility to third parties.

20-17 **7** **8** Ward is performing an attestation engagement regarding an entity's compliance with the requirements of a major assistance program offered by the provincial government. Ward detected noncompliance with the regulations governing the program, which he concluded were material. Ward's report on compliance should express:

(1) No assurance on the compliance with the relevant agreement.

(2) A reasonable assurance opinion on compliance with the relevant agreement.

(3) A qualified or adverse opinion.

(4) An adverse opinion or a disclaimer of an opinion.

Discussion Questions and Problems

20-18 **2** **3** Joseph, a public accountant, has been keeping the books for his father's business, JoPar Tech Ltd., in the evenings, while working with other clients during the day. Yesterday, Joseph's father proudly announced that he had negotiated a loan with the Federal Business Development Bank at favourable rates so that he could purchase $120 000 in new machinery and equipment. Upon reviewing the loan agreement, Joseph discovered that one of the requirements of the loan agreement is that JoPar Tech Ltd. submit financial statements that have been reviewed by a public accountant within 90 days of the fiscal year-end.

REQUIRED

a. Can Joseph complete a review engagement report for JoPar Tech Ltd.? Why or why not?

b. What type of engagement can Joseph complete with respect to the financial statements of JoPar Tech Ltd.?

c. What would you advise Joseph to do? Why?

20-19 **2** **3** You are doing a review engagement and the related tax work for Regency Tools Inc., a tool-and-die company with $2 000 000 in sales. Inventory is recorded at $125 000. Prior-year unaudited statements, prepared by the company without assistance from a public accounting firm, disclose that the inventory is based on "historical cost estimated by management." You obtain the following facts:

1. The company has been growing steadily for the past five years.

2. The unit cost of typical material used by Regency Tools has increased dramatically for several years.

3. The inventory cost has been approximately $125 000 for five years.

4. Management intends to use a value of $125 000 again for the current year-end financial statements.

When you discuss with management the need to get a physical count and an accurate inventory, the response is negative. Management is concerned about the effects on income taxes of a more realistic inventory. The company has never been audited and has always estimated the historical cost of inventory. You are convinced, based upon inquiry and ratio analysis, that a conservative evaluation would be $500 000 at historical cost.

REQUIRED

a. What are the generally accepted accounting requirements for valuation and disclosure of inventory for unaudited financial statements with a review report?

b. Identify the potential legal and professional problems that you face in this situation.

c. What procedures would you normally follow for a review engagement when the inventory is a material amount? Be as specific as possible.

d. How should you resolve the problem in this situation? Identify alternatives, and evaluate the costs and benefits of each.

20-20 [2] [3] [4] The following items represent a series of unrelated procedures that an accountant may consider performing in an engagement to review or compile the financial statements of a nonpublic entity. Procedures may apply to only one type of engagement, both, or neither.

1. The accountant should establish an understanding with the entity regarding the nature and limitations of the services to be performed.
2. The accountant should make inquiries concerning actions taken at the board of directors' meetings.
3. The accountant should obtain a level of knowledge of the accounting principles and practices of the entity's industry.
4. The accountant should obtain an understanding of the entity's internal control.
5. The accountant should perform analytical procedures designed to identify relationships that appear to be unusual.
6. The accountant should send a letter of inquiry to the entity's lawyer to corroborate the information furnished by management concerning litigation.
7. The accountant should obtain a management representation letter from the entity.
8. The accountant should make inquiries about events subsequent to the date of the financial statements that would have a material effect on the financial statements.
9. The accountant should perform a physical examination of inventory.

REQUIRED

a. Indicate which procedures are required to be performed on a review engagement.
b. Indicate which procedures are required to be performed on a compilation engagement.

20-21 [2] [3] Chow, a PA, is assisting his client, Western Resources Inc., a closely held company that is seeking to secure a new line of credit from a local bank. Chow has performed a review of the company's financial statements for several years and always issued a review engagement report without modification or reservation. However, the bank is not satisfied with the reviewed financial statements and is particularly concerned about the value of the client's accounts receivable, which will be pledged as collateral for the new line of credit.

The chief executive officer of Western Resources has asked Chow to perform his normal review of the financial statements this year, as well as to confirm a large sample (to be jointly selected by the CEO and Chow) of the company's accounts receivable at year-end directly with debtors. He then wants Chow to write a special report to the bank describing his findings with respect to the confirmation of receivables. Chow agrees to perform both of these services for the client for a fixed fee of $15 000, which is about 50 percent more than the usual fee for performing a review.

REQUIRED

Discuss reporting issues with respect to the new engagement.

(Reprinted from AU2 CGA-Canada Examinations with permission Chartered Professional Accountants of Canada, Toronto, Canada. Any changes to the original material are the sole responsibility of the author/publisher and have not been reviewed or endorsed by the Chartered Professional Accountants of Canada.)

Professional Judgment Problems and Cases

20-22 [2] [3] [4] You are performing a review engagement and related tax services for Murphy Construction Company. You have made extensive inquiries of management about the financial statements and have concluded that management has an excellent understanding of its business and is honest, but lacking in knowledge of technical accounting issues. In doing the review, you determine the following:

1. Repairs and maintenance expense has increased significantly compared to the preceding year. The president states that this seems to have been a year with a lot of repairs, in part because the equipment is getting older.

2. Property tax expense is the same as last year even though Murphy purchased a new building, including the land. The president states that there are no real estate taxes on the new building and land until next year.

3. Based on your knowledge of the construction industry you know that the pipes Murphy uses in construction have had a decrease in selling price to construction companies near the end of the current year. The president states that even though they have a large pipe inventory it will all be used in the next year or two, so the current price doesn't matter because they won't need to buy any new pipes.

4. Accounts receivable has increased almost 25 percent compared to the previous year, but the allowance for uncollectible accounts has stayed the same. The president states that even though receivables have increased, they still expect uncollectible accounts to be less than the stated allowance.

5. In discussions with the president, you determine that there is a material uninsured lawsuit against the company from a former customer. The president believes it is a frivolous lawsuit and will not permit a footnote about it for fear that it will result in similar lawsuits from other customers.

REQUIRED

a. Beyond inquiries and analytical procedures, what are the accountant's responsibilities in performing review service engagements?

b. Describe what you should do in each of the preceding situations, assuming each one is material.

20-23 [2] [3] [4] Stephanie Biggs, Chartered Professional Accountant, has compiled the financial statements for her sister's pharmacy business since it started four years ago. The financial statements are attached to the pharmacy's corporate tax return, and are also provided to the company's banker to support the company's operating credit line. The banker has been satisfied with receiving tax-based financial statements compiled by Stephanie.

REQUIRED

a. What modifications, if any, must Stephanie make to her compilation report?

b. Assume that, in the fifth year, Stephanie's sister decides to increase her bank credit line to renovate the pharmacy store and stock an expanded product line. To approve the higher credit line, the banker now requires financial statements prepared in accordance with GAAP. What actions must Stephanie take under these new circumstances? How would these requirements differ if Stephanie was not related to the pharmacy's owner?

20-24 [2] [3] Ballantine Church has been located on a central downtown street in Toronto for over 120 years. Originally, the church was in the middle of farmland, but is now surrounded by high-rise apartments and condominiums. The church has an active parish community that engages in fundraising in the neighbourhood, assisting the homeless and providing drop-in housing during the winter. Francine, the parish priest, and the church board have decided it is time to have a review engagement completed for the church finances. You, a public accountant, are a member of the church and Francine has approached you to perform the review engagement. In the past, another PA had performed a compilation engagement.

The church organizes its finances based on five funds: operating, endowment, youth, homeless, and music scholarship. Any transfers from the endowment fund to the operating fund must be approved by the board. The church has about $1.2 million in cash and marketable securities in the bank. The church is valued at zero on the balance sheet.

The church also owns a large house. Francine lives in a section of the house and the rest of the property is used to provide storage, office space for three permanent church staff, and meeting space.

REQUIRED

a. What should you do before you accept the review engagement?

b. Outline the process for conducting the review engagement and describe any analytical review procedures that you would conduct specific to the church. What type of questions would you ask that are specific to the church to address plausibility of financial information?

20-25 [2] [3] [4] You are a senior with Tick and Bop, Public Accountants. Stupendous Soups is one of your clients, and your firm prepares a compilation report for the company for income tax purposes.

Stupendous Soups was started by two stay-at-home moms, Polly Star and Tomiko Moon. Polly and Tomiko prepare and deliver homemade soup for office workers in the downtown core. The demand for their soup has been overwhelming and, as a result, the two owners have decided to expand and are seeking financing from their local bank. They gave the bank manager the last two years' financial statements and the accompanying compilation reports. However, the bank manager told Polly that he would need some sort of assurance on the financial statements if the company wants the loan.

You receive a voicemail message from Polly Star, who wants to know what the bank manager means by "assurance" and whether you can provide assurance on the past two years' financial statements. You have taken out the Stupendous Soups file to familiarize yourself with it again. Below are some notes you have made:

1. Stupendous Soups' kitchen is located in rented space at a local strip mall.
2. The balance sheet consists of a small cash balance, some fixed assets (kitchen equipment, office equipment, and a delivery van), and shareholder loans. Food inventory is negligible.
3. The major items on the income statement are soup sales, cost of sales, rent, utilities, and salaries.
4. Polly and Tomiko purchase all the inventory supplies and do all the food preparation.
5. Polly is in charge of administration (she prepares the invoices, does all the bookkeeping, and makes the bank deposits), and Tomiko is in charge of marketing and promotion.
6. They have one part-time employee who helps out with deliveries.

REQUIRED

a. Explain what type of assurance engagement best meets Polly and Tomiko's needs? Provide support for your answer.

b. Provide an overview of the type of engagement you are recommending, the types of procedures you would perform, and the nature of your report.

c. Based upon the financial statement items, are there any concerns about whether or not you can provide assurance on Stupendous Soups' financial statements for the past two years?

20-26 [2] [4] You are an audit senior and have recently moved from a large public accounting firm to a smaller firm. At the large accounting firm, you were only exposed to audits of large corporations. You are excited to be involved with smaller entrepreneurial organizations. You have been assigned your first review engagement, Excel Coffee Inc.

The founders and sole shareholders of Excel are two engineers, Bob Christie and Anoop Patel, who are actively involved with all aspects of the business. Bob and Anoop were inspired to create a brewing technique that would overcome the complaints with the traditional French press: removing grit, stopping extraction once pressed, and maintaining heat. Its signature product, the Excel press, has received rave reviews in a variety of business and home magazines. With its range of innovative products designed to achieve consistently great results, Excel Coffee Inc. is carving an important niche among coffee and tea aficionados.

In the past, Bob and Anoop had used the crowd-funding platform Kickstarter to fund its product development. Through Kickstarter, individuals pledge from $50 to $400 to the particular product development project. Upon completion, the individuals receive a certain number of products based upon the size of their pledge. If the project is not successful, their funds are returned. While Bob and Anoop found this was a quick and effective way of obtaining funds, it is hard to obtain large sums of money this way. Therefore, in order to fund its current expansion plans, Excel has recently received $1 million from East Capital, a commercial lender that specializes in small to medium-sized businesses.

REQUIRED

a. What does it mean that a review engagement provides limited assurance?

b. Explain why a review engagement is appropriate for a company such as Excel?

c. As part of the analytical procedures, you developed a current ratio expectation for Excel Coffee of 0.6. The actual current ratio at year-end is 0.9.
  i Do you think this change in current ratio is significant? Explain.
  ii Assuming you have concluded that the change is significant, provide an inquiry you would ask of management.

d. As part of your analytical review, you noted a significant increase in legal expense. Further inquiry revealed that expenses were related to a patent infringement suit that Excel has launched against SurePress, a Seattle-based company. What further inquiries would you make regarding the lawsuit?

20-27 **6** **7** **10** You are an audit manager employed by Deslauriers and Gupta LLP. You have just been on the phone with one of your partners, whose audit client, RockOn (a local radio station located in Winnipeg), has asked if your firm can provide an audit opinion on a listener survey that was prepared by a media and marketing firm, Pollus Inc. Pollus Inc. is a well-known national media and marketing research firm whose core business is measuring network and local-market radio audiences. The goal of the survey is to provide RockOn with demographics and information on radio-listening habits of Winnipeg area residents. RockOn provides a copy of the survey to its advertisers to help them decide what time slots and shows are most appropriate for advertising their businesses. RockOn's management wants to attach your firm's audit report to the survey report in order to add credibility to the survey report when it is used to sell advertising and set advertising rates.

The key information included in the survey report prepared by Pollus is as follows:

AQH share[1]

Format share[2]

Station audience share

Weekday listening by station by time of day (includes proportion away from home and proportion listening at home)

Weekend listening by station by time of day (includes proportion away from home and proportion listening at home)

Time spent listening to station by demographics (gender, age, education level, and household income)

Education level of listeners by station

Education level of listeners by format

Household income of listeners by station

Household income of listeners by format

Notes:
1. AQH is the average number of persons listening to a particular station for at least 5 minutes during a 15-minute period. Share is the percentage of those listening to radio in the Winnipeg area who are listening to a particular radio station.
2. Format share is the percentage of those listening to radio in the Winnipeg area who are listening to a particular radio format.

REQUIRED

a. The first step in the professional judgment framework is to frame the issue. Would you consider RockOn to be the accountable party in the three-way accountability relationship required for an assurance engagement? If not, how do you resolve this issue in order to provide the requested assurance?

b. Assuming that there is an accountability relationship, you have researched the standards and concluded that the applicable standards are CSR 4460, OCS 9100, Specified Procedures, or CSAE 3000 or 3001. Which type of engagement would you recommend?

c. If OCS 9100 applies to the engagement, do you think it is appropriate to include the accountant's report with the survey data?

d. What issues do you anticipate in performing this engagement?

e. What are some audit procedures you could perform?

20-28 **9** In October 2014, the province of Nova Scotia announced that it would provide Nova Star Cruises Limited, the new operator of the ferry between Yarmouth, NS, and Bangor, Maine, with $5 million in addition to its original subsidy of $21 million. As part of the new funding agreement, Nova Star is to provide the province with weekly reports and projections of its cash flows, and twice-weekly reports on its bookings and other business information. The province contracted KPMG to perform certain specified procedures to assist it in validating the operating costs reported by Nova Star. Michel Samson, Nova Scotia's Minister of Economic and Rural Development and Tourism, explained, "We're helping Nova Star cover these costs, with more reporting required by the company and more monitoring to protect taxpayers."

Access the KPMG Report at **https://novascotia.ca/tran/ yarmouthferry/StartupCosts011815.pdf** to answer the following questions.

a. One of your friends, who is a reporter for a local newspaper, has asked you to help make sense of the report and its findings. Provide the explanation requested by your friend. In your discussion, explain the purpose of this type of engagement, why the Government of Nova Scotia would request this type of engagement, the purpose of the procedures, and the significance of the findings.

b. Several newspapers in Canada and the United States have referred to the KPMG engagement as an audit. Others have referred to the engagement as a review. Is either of these descriptions correct? Explain.

20-29 **6** **7** **11** With greater frequency, organizations are issuing corporate social responsibility (CSR) reports that describe how they are engaging in socially responsible activities. Read the report many believe that users will increasingly want assurances from PAs about the reliability of the information presented by management in these reports. Access the Loblaw Companies Limited 2016 corporate social responsibility report at **http://www.loblaw.ca/en/responsibility.html**.

Read the letter contained in the report from the executive chairman and president of Loblaw, Galen Weston, and then answer the following questions.

REQUIRED

a. What kinds of assertions are being made by management about its progress toward socially responsible goals?

b. To what extent might users of the report demand more assurance about the information contained in the report?

c. What challenges would PAs face in providing assurance about information contained in this report?

Boritz, Kao, Kadous & Co., LLP (BKK) is a Canadian accounting firm with offices located in each of the major cities across Canada. BKK, for the second year in a row, has been selected as the auditor for Hillsburg Hardware Limited, a privately owned company located in Halifax, Nova Scotia. Hillsburg's year end is December 31, 2018. The audit team assigned to the client includes Partner Joe Anthony, Audit Manager Leslie Nagan, Audit Senior Fran Moor, and Assistants Mitch Bray and you.

HILLSBURG HARDWARE LIMITED COMPANY HISTORY

Hillsburg Stores Ltd. began operations in 1980 in Halifax, Nova Scotia, as a family-owned retail hardware store chain. On September 25, 1986, Hillsburg merged with Handy Hardware and Lumber Company, which established the concept of selling high-quality hardware through wholesale distribution outlets in 1981, to form Handy-Hillsburg Inc. On June 5, 1990, after spinning off all of its lumber-related assets to Handy Cooperation, the company changed its name to Hillsburg Hardware Limited. In 2002, the Hillsburg family sold a controlling interest in the company to Wilkshaw Capital, an investment group. Although the Hillsburg family is no longer actively involved in the company operations, it maintains a minority interest in the company and receives annual dividends.

OVERVIEW

Hillsburg Hardware Limited is a wholesale distributor of hardware equipment to a variety of independent, high-quality hardware stores in Atlantic Canada. The primary products are power and hand tools, landscaping equipment, electrical equipment, residential and commercial construction equipment, and a wide selection of paint products. More than 90 percent of the company's products are purchased from manufacturers and shipped either directly to customers or to the main warehouse in Halifax, Nova Scotia, where shipments are combined to minimize costs of freight and handling.

Now more than ever, independent hardware retailers find it advantageous to purchase from Hillsburg rather than directly from manufacturers. Hillsburg makes it possible for smaller, independent retailers to purchase on an as-needed basis, rather than in bulk, and offers its customers a range of high-quality products that are sometimes hard to locate. Hillsburg also offers far more post-sale services to its customers than are offered by manufacturers and other national distributors. For instance, it provides detailed product information to retailers. It converts the manufacturer's information, which is often aimed at professional renovators and contractors, into easy-to-understand language for the do-it-yourself purchaser. Hillsburg simplifies the purchasing process by assigning each of its customers a permanent salesperson. Each salesperson becomes involved in the sales process and also acts as a liaison between the customer and post-sales service areas. For example, when customers experience technical problems with recently purchased hardware, their salesperson coordinates both exchanges and warranty repairs with the manufacturer. This process adds value for customers and makes post-sales service more efficient and less problematic. Low turnover and extensive sales training of Hillsburg's salespeople enhance this service.

To further encourage customer loyalty, each customer is given access to Hillsburg's internal database system, ONHAND (Online Niche-Hardware Availability Notification Database). The ONHAND system lets customers check the availability of hard-to-find products instantly over the internet. Moreover, the system includes data such as expected restock dates for items that are currently sold out and expected availability dates for items that will soon be introduced to market.

Because of the permanent salesperson for each customer and customer access to ONHAND, Hillsburg has managed to maintain a repeat-customer base. Nearly 75 percent of all first-time customers make an additional purchase within one year of their first purchase from Hillsburg.

Recently, there has been major consolidation in the wholesale and retail hardware industry. More and more independent hardware stores are either participating in buying groups or are becoming part of large dealer networks like Home Hardware. Hillsburg believes this consolidation trend is advantageous to its operations as a distributor of hard-to-find, high-quality hardware equipment. The recent consolidation of Builder's Plus Hardware Inc., one of the top-ten largest national hardware store chains, is a case in point. One month after consolidation, Builder's Plus decided not to carry high-end construction and landscaping equipment in order to focus on what is called the "typical hardware customer."

PRODUCTS

To more effectively manage inventory, Hillsburg carefully monitors the composition of net sales by category of items sold. The breakdown of revenues (in thousands) from different products is listed in the chart below:

SEGMENTED REPORTING		
	2018	**2017**
Power Tools	$ 35 519	$ 30 663
Hand Tools	21 463	19 684
Landscaping Equipment	14 309	15 645
Electrical Equipment	17 170	15 849
Residential Construction Merchandise	18 372	15 949
Commercial Construction Merchandise	10 498	9 815
Paint Products	25 755	23 621
	$143 086	$131 226

CUSTOMERS

The majority of Hillsburg's customers are located in Nova Scotia, Prince Edward Island, New Brunswick, and Newfoundland and Labrador. Its current customer base consists of approximately 300 independently owned hardware stores. Approximately 25 percent of Hillsburg's customers make up more than 80 percent of total sales revenue. To promote long-standing relationships with customers, Hillsburg offers an array of incentive and customer appreciation programs. In addition, in order to ensure that customers maintain proper inventory levels, it invests heavily in its distribution infrastructure and technology.

EMPLOYEES AND MANAGEMENT

Hillsburg has 108 full-time employees (a sales force of 12 people, a distribution centre staff of 35, and 61 working in head office). The senior management team consists of Rick Chulick, the President and Chief Executive Officer; Avis Zomer, the Chief Financial Officer; Brandon Mack, VP Sales and Marketing; Mary Moses, VP Merchandising; Vanessa Namie, VP Operations; and Joseph Akuroi, VP Quality Assurance.

PROPERTIES

Hillsburg owns and operates its main distribution centre and an administrative office. The distribution centre and administrative office are in the same 475 000 square-foot building. Hillsburg also rents a second distribution centre located in Sydney, Nova Scotia, for $312 000 annually.

CONTROL ENVIRONMENT

The overall control environment is good. There is no past history of management override of controls, and management's and the board's attitude toward internal controls is very positive. Duties are segregated as much as is practical. Information systems support personnel do not have access to accounting data.

All information systems have current anti-virus software, and firewalls are in place for the group of internet-accesible machines. Company offices are now open from 7:00 a.m. to 6:00 p.m. All systems are left up and running 24 hours a day. There is a comprehensive backup and disaster recovery plan, and maintenance plans for all purchased hardware and software.

Hillsburg, however, has no agreement with an external cyber-security vendor for IT experts to be on standby in case the company needs help to deal with a sophisticated cyber attack.

FINANCIAL INFORMATION

During 2018, Hillsburg experienced another year of noticeable improvements. From 2017 to 2018, net sales increased by $11 860 000, or 9 percent. This increase was partly due to the overall growth in the home renovation market. However, it was largely attributed to an aggressive product rebranding strategy that the company launched in the second half of 2017. The growth in sales resulted in gross profit increasing by $3 495 000, or 9.6 percent, from 2017. This growth allowed senior management to reach the year-end gross profit growth bonus target of 9.1 percent.

During 2018, the company's working capital requirements were primarily financed through a line of credit, under which Hillsburg is permitted to borrow up to the lesser of $7 000 000 or 75 percent of accounts receivable outstanding less than 30 days. In 2018, interest expense increased by $374 000, or approximately 18.4 percent, compared to 2017. This increase was due to an overall interest rate increase due to the restructuring of debt covenants that Hillsburg was close to breaching.

Hillsburg's unaudited 2018 financial statements, with audited 2017 comparative results, are shown below.

HILLSBURG HARDWARE LIMITED
Balance Sheet
December 31, 2018 (in thousands)

ASSETS	2018 (unaudited)	2017 (audited)
Non-current assets		
Land	3 456	3 456
Buildings	32 500	32 500
Equipment, furniture, and fixtures	6 304	8 160
Less: Accumulated amortisation	(31 920)	(33 220)
Total property, plant and equipment	$10 340	$10 896
Total non-current assets	**10 340**	**10 896**
Current assets		
Inventories	29 865	31 600
Trade receivables (net of allowances of $1 240 and $1 311)	18 957	16 210
Other receivables	945	915
Prepaid expenses	432	427
Cash and bank balances	828	743
Total current assets	51 027	49 895
Total assets	**$61 367**	**$60 791**
EQUITY AND LIABILITIES		
Capital		
Issued capital	$8 500	$8 500
Retained earnings	13 963	11 929
Total equity	22 463	20 429
Non-current liabilities		
Notes payable	24 120	26 520
Deferred income tax liability	738	722
Other long-term payables	830	770
Total non-current liabilities	25 688	28 012
Current liabilities		
Trade accounts payable	4 720	4 432
Notes payable	4 180	4 589
Accrued payroll	1 350	715
Accrued payroll taxes	120	116
Accrued interest and dividends payable	2 050	1 975
Accrued income tax	796	523
Total current liabilities	**13 216**	**12 350**
Total liabilities	**38 904**	**40 362**
Total equity and liabilities	**$61 367**	**$60 791**

Notes: Accounts Receivable

During 2018, Hillsburg's working capital requirements were primarily financed with the line of credit, under which Hillsburg is permitted to borrow up to 75 percent of its accounts receivable outstanding less than 30 days. Net trade receivables turned over approximately 7.6 times in 2018 and 2017. Days to collect accounts receivable were 48.1 and 48.0 in 2018 and 2017, respectively. Hillsburg's market consists of smaller, independent hardware stores that need more favourable receivable terms.

<table>
<tr><td colspan="3" align="center">HILLSBURG HARDWARE LIMITED
Statement of Comprehensive Income
For the Year Ended December 31, 2018 (in thousands)</td></tr>
</table>

	2018 (unaudited)	2017 (audited)
Revenue	$143 086	$131 226
Cost of sales	103 241	94 876
Gross profit	39 845	36 350
Selling, general, and administrative expenses	(32 475)	(29 656)
Interest expense	(2 409)	(2 035)
Gain on sale of assets	720	—
Profit before tax	5 681	4 659
Income tax expense	(1 747)	(1 465)
Total comprehensive income for the year	$3 934	$3 194
Earnings per share	$0.79	$0.64

HILLSBURG HARDWARE LIMITED

Statement of Changes in Equity
For the Year Ended December 31, 2018 (in thousands)

	Common Stock		Contributed Surplus	Retained Earnings	Total Shareholders Equity
	Shares	Value			
Balance as at December 31, 2017	5 000	$5 000	$3 500	$10 635	$19 135
Net Income				3 194	3 194
Dividends paid				(1 900)	(1 900)
Balance as at December 31, 2018	5 000	$5 000	3 500	11 929	20 429
Net Income				3 934	3 934
Dividends paid				(1 900)	(1 900)
Balance as at December 31, 2018	5 000	$5 000	$3 500	$13 963	$22 463

HILLSBURG HARDWARE LIMITED

Statement of Cash Flows
For the Year Ended December 31, 2018 (in thousands)

	2018 (unaudited)	2017 (audited)
Cash flows from operating activities		
Cash flows provided by (used in) operating activities		
Net income	$ 3 934	$ 3 194
Amortisation	1 452	1 443
Loss on sale of assets	(720)	–
Deferred income taxe liability increase (decrease)	16	(8)
Changes in non-cash working capital		
Trade and other receivables	(2 777)	(393)
Inventories	1 735	(295)
Prepaid expenses	(5)	(27)
Accounts payable	288	132
Accrued liabilities	714	77
Income taxes payable	273	23
Net cash provided by operating activities	4 910	4 146
Cash flows from investing activities		
Capital expenditures	(10 500)	(1 800)
Sale of equipment	10 324	–
Net cash used in investing activities	(176)	(1 800)
Cash flows from financing activities		
Dividend payment	(1 900)	(1 900)
Proceeds (repayments) from borrowings (net)	(2 749)	(423)
Net cash used in financial activities	(4 649)	(2 323)
Net increase in cash	85	23
Cash at the beginning of year	743	720
Cash at the end of year	$ 828	$ 743

TRANSCRIPT OF MEETING

On April 29, 2019, Hillsburg's CFO, Avis Zomer, met with BKK audit partner Joe Anthony and BKK audit manager Leslie Nagan in Hillsburg's administrative office.

Joe Anthony (JA): Thanks for seeing us, Avis.

Avis Zomer (AZ): You're welcome, Joe. What can I do for you?

JA: I need to ask you some questions about the changes that happened over the past year at Hillsburg. With the impressive growth in sales, it looks like the company is back on track.

AZ: Yes, indeed we are. In 2018, we made a significant investment in a new advertising campaign to promote our new brand of specialized hardware equipment. Operating as a wholesaler, we realized that the end costumer is not aware of the "Hillsburg" name. We wanted to change that, and associate "Hillsburg" with quality and specialized hardware equipment. So in late 2017, in partnership with one of our key suppliers, we launched the Hillsburg brand of specialized hardware equipment. To promote the brand, various radio, newspaper, magazine, and television advertisements were purchased at the local and regional levels using Hillsburg's new catchphrase, "Quality Hardware Equipment for Hard Workers." The new jingle with the catchphrase has been partially responsible for the fiscal 2018 increase in sales of 9 percent.

JA: Oh, yes, the new jingle! I recently had to replace my lawnmower and went to my local independent hardware store where I saw the Hillsburg name and the catchphrase painted on the side of the store. It was an impressive, large, and colourful advertisement. I bet advertising like that is expensive.

AZ: You're right. It is expensive, but we found a way to get around that. We also found this form of advertising to be very effective, so we tried to find ways to paint Hillsburg's name and the catchphrase on as many independently owned hardware stores as possible. Last year, we entered into an agreement with about 200 stores. As we are the largest wholesale distributor of paint in Nova Scotia, the major paint manufacturers, in exchange for having their name included on the advertisement, agreed to give us free paint for the ads.

JA: Oh yes, I remember seeing the name Dureux Paints on the ad that I saw.

AZ: It is Dureux! You auditors have a great memory. Our salespersons looked for store locations where the ads could be painted. In exchange for faster product delivery and extended payment terms, they negotiated with the owners for space to paint the ads. Some owners were hesitant at first to give us "free" space. For those owners, we offered an extended product return or exchange terms. Now they have an extra 120 days to return or exchange any unsold products. At the end of the day, the painted ads haven't yet cost us a cent. That was really important to Hillsburg, since with all the fuss the banks caused last year with us getting close to breaching the loan covenants, it's critical that we manage our cash flow well.

Lesley Nagan (LN): I'm glad that we discussed this new advertising arrangement.

JA: Talking about my lawnmower again, I don't think that when, in a few years, I need to replace it again, my local independent hardware store will be in existence. It seems that the mega Fortune 500 American companies like Lowe's and Home Depot will eventually dominate the market.

AZ: You're right! Although Lowe's and Home Depot do not currently operate in Atlantic Canada, some speculate that through various consolidations they will eventually enter that market. However, our primary concern is when independents either join a dealer network, such as Home Hardware, or are purchased by one of the dominant players, such as Kenny's or TIMBR. Each time that happens, we run the risk of losing a potential customer since Home Hardware is essentially a wholesaler for its dealers and Kenny's has its own suppliers. For instance, Kenny's recently purchased the Allied Hardware Chain, which was one of our biggest customers. We were really worried whether Allied would continue to purchase from us.

We are also concerned about the increasing number of large American distributors entering the Canadian market by opening distribution centres. For instance, Orvill, a large New England-based distributor, recently opened a distribution centre in New Brunswick, which it plans to use to service the Quebec and Atlantic Canada markets.

LN: How is this affecting Hillsburg's operations?

AZ: Our approach is to ask, "What are the opportunities?" We used our relationship with Allied to get into the door with Kenny's with the goal of Hillsburg becoming its main hardware supplier for hard-to-find, high-quality hardware equipment. We saw this as a great opportunity; however, Kenny's had been in the process of negotiating a deal with Orvill. In order to convince Kenny's to consider us, we offered deep discounts on some of the equipment, selling it below our cost. Now that we established a relationship with Kenny's, in the long run, we will recover these losses on other merchandise that we sell to them.

LN: Are you still selling some equipment to Kenny's below cost?

AZ: Yes we are; however, those initial agreements will expire soon. And as part of negotiating the next round of agreements, we plan to increase our prices on those items.

JA: It seems like 2018 is the year for global cyber attacks. Has your ONHAND system that your customers can use to check the availability of hard-to-find products over the internet been affected?

AZ: Unfortunately, the ONHAND system was hit by the WannaCry cyber attack, and we did not have an external cyber security vendor on stand-by, so it took some time to find IT specialists who could help us. We eventually found experts and were able to recover, but not before WannaCry damaged some of our system's software. We are still trying to recover some of the inventory data that was damaged by the WannaCry attack.

LN: Was a lot of data lost?

AZ: Initially we thought that the damage was minimal, but later, the external IT specialists discovered that the damage was significant. Anyhow, they've told me that it will take some time, but all of the data can be recovered. You will need to speak to them directly to find out how far they have progressed with fixing this thing.

LN: How are things since the Chief Accountant left Hillsburg in early 2018?

AZ: The transition has been good. The accounting personnel seem to like working for Erma Swanson. Erma is a qualified CPA with industry experience. She stood out when I did the interviews for the Chief Accountant position. I think Erma has been doing a terrific job since she came to Hillsburg. I am more concerned with a couple of calls that we received to our whistleblower hotline. As you know, our hotline is run by a third party and the caller's identity remains confidential. I only receive a report from them stating what the caller said during the call. Since the previous Chief Accountant left, there were a couple of calls to the whistleblower hotline that concerned me. However, due to the sensitive nature of this matter, I would prefer to discuss these alone with Joe. I'm sorry. I hope you understand and are fine with this.

LN: Sure.

AZ: Joe, can we schedule a meeting tomorrow for you and me to discuss this alone?

JA: Sure, how about 10:00 a.m.? Will that work?

AZ: How about 9:00 a.m.? I was planning on taking a vacation day tomorrow. This way, at least I can take the afternoon off.

JA: Ok, I will put it in my calendar and send you an Outlook meeting invitation.

AZ: Hold on. Actually, can you include in that meeting invitation Nicolas Alexandre, our legal counsel? Now that I think about it, since this relates to potential fraud, I think it would be a good idea for Nicolas to be in that meeting as well.

JA: Sure, I will invite Nicolas.

AZ: Great. Do my auditors have any other questions for me, or are we done and I get to catch a round of golf this afternoon?

LN: Actually, there is one more thing I wanted to ask you.

AZ: Sure.

LN: In 2017, you mentioned that you were planning to procure some analytics software that would review Hillsburg's purchasing and sales data to identify how these could be optimized so Hillsburg could take advantage of more vendor rebates. Did that project go ahead?

AZ: I'm glad you asked! Yes it did! As you know, in the past we purchased hardware and other products from more than 300 manufacturers. No single vendor accounted for more than 5 percent of our purchases, but our 25 largest vendors used to account for about 35 percent. We didn't really have many long-term vendor agreements. I think that's why we weren't taking advantage of vendor rebates. The analytics software allowed us to identify opportunities to consolidate our purchases. This allowed us to start buying larger quantities of merchandise from fewer vendors and take advantage of vendor rebates. We entered into six new long-term purchasing agreements with vendors that offered us the largest rebates. The amount of the rebate is tied to a minimum quantity of merchandise that we must purchase during the year. As long as, before year end, we buy enough from these six vendors to hit these targets, we qualify for significant rebates. I think in 2018 we qualified for rebates from four out of the six vendors. To make sure our inventory turnover ratio stays reasonable, in early 2017, Hillsburg established its own rebate program. It only makes sense to pass some of the saving to our major customers. In fact, the rebate program that we offered to our customers was really successful. Our merchandise inventory turnover increased from 3.0 in 2017 to 3.4 in 2018. Right before year end, our customers placed so many orders to meet their minimum purchase targets that we had to bring in temporary staff to help out with shipping in the Halifax warehouse.

LN: I'm glad that I asked that last question. Is there anything that you would like to discuss?

AZ: No, I think this is it. Tomorrow I will chat with Joe about the possible accounting fraud we discovered through the whistleblower hotline. So I think this meeting covers everything.

LN: That's great! Next week we will be starting our fieldwork at Hillsburg, so I will see you then.

AZ: For sure.

JA: See you tomorrow at 9:00.

AZ: Yes. Just make sure you're not late.

JA: I promise I won't be. I have a scheduled round of golf for tomorrow afternoon as well.

AZ: That's great. We should play together sometime.

JA: Sure.

AZ: We will chat about it tomorrow. Bye.

Index

Note: Page numbers followed by *f*, *t*, or *n* represent figures, tables, or notes, respectively.

biases, 97. *See also* judgment traps/tendencies
  confirmation, 98
  management, 230
  overconfidence, 98
  reviewing accounting estimates for, 223
biases/motives, of providers, 7
"Big Four" international firms, 25, 26*t*
billings, 59
bill of lading, 393, 394
Black, Carson, 68
BlackBerry, 489
Blackwell, Richard, 583*n*
blank confirmation form, 424–425
block sample selection, 352, 353
bookkeeping services, 18
Bradbury, Danny, 512*t*
Bre-X Minerals Ltd., 183
Buckless, Frank, 481*n*
budgets
  balanced, 586
  client data compared with, 143
  defined, 143
Building Sustainable Audit Quality (CPAB), 39
business failure, 67–68
business functions, 392
  acquisition and payment cycle, 446–449
  billing customers, 394–395
  cash receipts, 395–396
  customer orders processing, 392–394
  granting credit, 393
  in human resources and payroll cycle,
    508–509, 508*t*
  in inventory and distribution cycle, 482, 482*f*,
    483, 483*t*
  in revenue cycle, 393*t*
  sales recording, 394–395
  sales returns and allowances, 396
  shipment of goods, 393
  uncollectible accounts, 396
business process
  control activities, 256–258, 257*f*
  defined, 256
business risk
  for customer, 7
  factors responsible for, 168

C

CAAT. *See* computer-assisted audit tests (CAAT)
Calgary Herald, 391*n*
Canada Business Corporations Act, 15
Canada Pension Plan, 508
Canada Revenue Agency (CRA), 5, 8, 10, 12, 570
Canadian Auditing Standards (CAS), 29, 33–34, 33*t*
Canadian Business, 414*n*
Canadian Public Accountability Board (CPAB), 25, 29–30
  annual inspections, 42
  annual report, 42

Audit Quality Symposiums, 30
Building Sustainable Audit Quality, 39
  mission, 29
  practice inspection program, 29–30
  priorities, 29
  report of 2103, 144
  research and consultation, 42–43
Canadian Standards on Quality Control (CSQC), 40
capital acquisition and repayment cycle
  defined, 528
  note payable. *See* note payable
  overview of, 528–529
capital asset master file, 467
capitalization *vs.* expense, 466
Career Incubator, 28
CAS. *See* Canadian Auditing Standards (CAS)
cash
  auditing of, 544–556
  in bank, and transaction cycles, 546–547, 546*t*
  control tests for, 550
  masquerading for, 549
  proof of, 555–556
  substantive tests of details for, 550–554, 551*f*
cash accounts. *See also* general cash account
  proof of, 555–556
  types of, 545, 545*t*
cash receipts
  processing/recording of, 395–396
  proof of, 430
  tests of controls for, 412, 413*t*
cash transactions
  assessment of risk of material misstatement in, 547–548
  errors and fraud in, 546–547, 546*t*
  significant risks identification in, 547–548
Castor Holdings Limited, 71
CBC News, 507*n*
census, 369
CEO. *See* chief executive officer (CEO)
Certified Fraud Examiner (CFE), 13
Certified in Financial Forensics (CFF), 13
Certified Internal Auditor (CIA), 11
CFE. *See* Certified Fraud Examiner (CFE)
CFF. *See* Certified in Financial Forensics (CFF)
CFO. *See* chief financial officer (CFO)
Chaffers, Mark, 578*n*
Charest, Micheline, 91
Chartered Professional Accountants Canada (CPA Canada),
    13, 28–29. *See also* Canadian Institute of Chartered
    Accountants (CICA)
  AASB, 29
  Audit Quality Blog, 43
  provincial organizations, 29
  research and consultation process, 42–43
chart of accounts, 258–259
chief executive officer (CEO), 87
chief financial officer (CFO), 87, 527
Chisholm, Yvonne, 68
Christensen, B.E., 367*n*, 377*n*